Freedom

The findings of *Freedom in the World 2003* include events from January 1, 2002 through December 31, 2002.

Freedom in the World
The Annual Survey of Political Rights & Civil Liberties
2003

Edited by Adrian Karatnycky, Aili Piano, and Arch Puddington

Freedom House • New York, NY and Washington, DC
Rowman & Littlefield Publishers, Inc. • Lanham, Boulder,
New York, Toronto, Oxford

ROWMAN & LITTLEFIELD PUBLISHERS, INC.

Published in the United States of America
by Rowman & Littlefield Publishers, Inc.
A wholly owned subsidiary of The Rowman & Littlefield Publishing Group, Inc.
4501 Forbes Boulevard, Suite 200, Lanham, Maryland 20706
www.rowmanlittlefield.com

P.O. Box 317, Oxford OX2 9RU, United Kingdom

British Library Cataloguing in Publication Information Available

Library of Congress Cataloging-in-Publication Data

Freedom in the world / —1978–
New York : Freedom House, 1978–
v. : map; 25 cm.—(Freedom House Book)
Annual.
ISSN 0732-6610=Freedom in the World.
1. Civil rights—Periodicals. I. R. Adrian Karatnycky, et al. I. Series.
JC571 .F66 323.4'05—dc 19 82-642048
AACR 2   MARC-S
Library of Congress [84101]

ISBN 0-7425-2869-3 (alk. paper)—ISBN 0-7425-2870-7 (pbk. : alk. paper)
ISSN 0732-6610

Printed in the United States of America

The paper used in this publication meets the minimum requirements of American
National Standard for Information Sciences—Permanence of Paper for Printed Library
Materials, ANSI/NISO Z39.48-1992.

Contents

Foreword

Freedom in the World is an institutional effort by Freedom House to monitor the progress and decline of political rights and civil liberties in 192 nations and 18 related and disputed territories. These year-end reviews of freedom began in 1955, when they were called the *Balance Sheet of Freedom* and, later, the *Annual Survey of the Progress of Freedom*. This program was expanded in the early 1970s, and has appeared in a more developed context as a yearbook since 1978.

Since 1989, the survey project has been a year-long effort produced by our regional experts, consultants, and human rights specialists. The survey derives its information from a wide range of sources, including the many human rights activists, journalists, and political figures around the world who keep us informed of the human rights situation in their respective countries. The survey team also consults a vast array of published materials, ranging from the reports of other human rights organizations to regional newspapers and journals.

Throughout the year, Freedom House personnel conduct fact-finding missions to gain more in-depth knowledge of the vast political transformations affecting our world. During these investigations, we make every effort to meet a cross-section of political parties and associations, human rights monitors, religious figures, representatives of both the private sector and trade union movements, academics, and journalists.

The survey team is grateful to the input of our *Freedom in the World* academic advisory board, consisting of David Becker, Kenneth Bollen, Daniel Brumberg, Larry Diamond, Charles Gati, Jeane J. Kirkpatrick, Thomas Lansner, Peter Lewis, Andrew Moravcsik, Alexander Motyl, Joshua Muravchik, Daniel Pipes, Jack Snyder, Arturo Valenzuela, Ashutosh Varshney, and Bridget Welsh.

Among those responsible for the production of *Freedom in the World* are Linda Stern, copy editor; Mark Wolkenfeld, production coordinator; and Trish Fox, proofreader.

Principal support for *Freedom in the World* has been generously provided by the Lynde and Harry Bradley Foundation and the Smith Richardson Foundation.

The Survey Team

Martin Edwin "Mick" Andersen is an investigative reporter for *Insight* magazine. He has worked as a special correspondent for *Newsweek* and *The Washington Post* in Argentina, a staff member of the Senate Foreign Relations Committee, and senior adviser for policy planning with the criminal division of the U.S. Justice Department. He serves as the Latin America analyst for *Freedom in the World*.

Gordon N. Bardos is assistant director of the Harriman Institute at Columbia University. His research interests focus on problems of nationalism and ethnic conflict, and he is a frequent commentator on the Balkans in the U.S. and European press. He serves as the Balkans analyst for *Freedom in the World*.

Peter Doran is a research assistant at Freedom House. Previously, he worked as a program assistant at the Jamestown Foundation in Washington, DC. He serves as an East-Central Europe analyst for *Freedom in the World*.

Gary C. Gambill is editor of the *Middle East Intelligence Bulletin* and a research associate at the Middle East Forum. He has written extensively on Lebanese and Syrian politics, authoritarianism in the Arab World, and American foreign policy in the region. He serves as a Middle East-North Africa analyst for *Freedom in the World*.

Michael Gold-Biss is a consultant in business strategy and security based in Washington, D.C. He is the author of *The Discourse on Terrorism: Political Violence and the Subcommittee on Security and Terrorism, 1981-1986* and co-editor with Richard L. Millett of *Beyond Praetorianism: The Latin American Military in Transition*. He holds a doctorate in international relations from American University. He serves as the Central America and Caribbean analyst for *Freedom in the World*.

Michael Goldfarb is senior press officer at Freedom House. He has worked as a reporter in Israel for United Press International and as a writer for Time.com, the Website of *Time* magazine. He serves as a Middle East-North Africa analyst for *Freedom in the World*.

Michael Gordon is the Middle East, Africa, and Europe editor for the Economist Intelligence Unit's *Country Commerce* and *Country Finance* publications and is a contributor to *The Middle East*. He is also adjunct lecturer at New York University, where he teaches courses on political Islam and the Persian Gulf. He serves as the South Europe analyst for *Freedom in the World*.

Charles Graybow is a former managing editor of both *Nations in Transit*, a survey of political and economic conditions in the post-Communist world, and *Freedom in the World*. He has participated in human rights missions to several Asian and West African countries. He serves as the East and Southeast Asia analyst for *Freedom in the World*.

Kelli Henry is a former Europe editor at the Economist Intelligence Unit. She holds a Ph.D. in sociology from New York University. She has lived and worked in both Western and Eastern Europe, including the United Nations in Geneva, Switzerland, and served as an international election observer in Romania. She serves as the West Europe analyst for freedom in the world.

Adrian Karatnycky is senior scholar and counselor at Freedom House, advising the organization on programs, policy, and research. He is also a co-editor of both *Freedom in the World* and *Nations in Transit*. From 1996 until 2003, he served as president of Freedom House. He is co-author of three books on East European politics and editor or co-editor of 16 volumes of studies on global political rights, civil liberties, and political transitions.

Karin Deutsch Karlekar is a senior researcher at Freedom House and editor of Freedom House's annual *Freedom of the Press* survey. She holds a PhD in Indian history from Cambridge University and previously worked as a consultant for Human Rights Watch. She serves as the South and Southeast Asia analyst for *Freedom in the World*.

Edward R. McMahon is dean's professor of applied politics and the director of the Center on Democratic Performance at Binghamton University (SUNY). Previously, he served as regional director for West, East, and Central Africa at the National Democratic Institute for International Affairs and as a diplomat with the U.S. Department of State. He currently is a contributing editor for the *Political Handbook of the World*. He serves as an Africa analyst for *Freedom in the World*.

Aili Piano is a senior researcher at Freedom House and a co-editor of *Freedom in the World*. She has written for Freedom House's *Nations in Transit*, a survey of political and economic conditions in the post-Communist world, since its inception in 1994, and served as the managing editor of the 1999-2000 edition. Previously, she worked as a diplomatic attache at the Estonian Mission to the United Nations. She serves as the Eurasia analyst for *Freedom in the World*.

Arch Puddington is director of research at Freedom House and a co-editor of *Freedom in the World*. He has written widely on American foreign policy, race relations, organized labor, and the history of the Cold War. He is the author of *Broadcasting Freedom: The Cold War Triumph of Radio Free Europe and Radio Liberty* and is currently writing a biography of the late trade union leader, Lane Kirkland. He serves as the United States and Canada analyst for *Freedom in the World*.

Amanda Schnetzer is a senior fellow at Freedom House and a co-editor of *Nations in Transit*, a survey of political and economic conditions in the post-Communist world. Previously, she was a foreign policy researcher at the American Enterprise Institute (AEI) and the program director of AEI's New Atlantic Initiative. She serves as an East-Central Europe analyst for *Freedom in the World*.

Cindy Shiner is a freelance journalist who has spent much of her time in Africa. She has written for *The Washington Post*, done broadcasts for National Public Radio, and worked as a consultant on Africa issues for Human Rights Watch. She serves as an Africa analyst for *Freedom in the World*.

ACADEMIC ADVISERS

David Becker is associate professor in the department of government, Dartmouth College.

Kenneth Bollen is Immerwahr distinguished professor in sociology and director of the Odum Institute for Research in Social Science, University of North Carolina, Chapel Hill.

Daniel Brumberg is associate professor in the department of government, Georgetown University, and a visiting scholar at the Carnegie Endowment for International Peace.

Larry Diamond is senior fellow at the Hoover Institution and co-editor of the *Journal of Democracy*.

Charles Gati is senior adjunct professor in European studies and fellow at the Foreign Policy Institute, School for Advanced International Studies, Johns Hopkins University.

Jeane J. Kirkpatrick, former U.S. ambassador to the United Nations, is senior fellow and director of foreign and defense policy studies, American Enterprise Institute.

Thomas Lansner is adjunct assistant professor of international affairs, School of International and Public Affairs, Columbia University.

Peter M. Lewis is associate professor in the School of International Service, American University.

Alexander J. Motyl is professor in the department of political science and deputy director of the Center for Global Change and Governance, Rutgers University-Newark.

Andrew Moravcsik is professor of government and director of the European Union Program, Harvard University.

Joshua Muravchik is resident scholar, American Enterprise Institute.

Daniel Pipes is director of the Middle East Forum and a columnist for the *New York Post* and *The Jerusalem Post*.

Jack Snyder is Robert and Renée Belfer professor of international relations in the department of political science, Columbia University.

Arturo Valenzuela is professor of government and director of the Center for Latin American Studies, Georgetown University.

Ashutosh Varshney is professor of political science and director of the Center for South Asian Studies, University of Michigan, Ann Arbor

Bridget Welsh is assistant professor of Southeast Asian Studies at the School for Advanced International Studies, Johns Hopkins University.

Trish Fox, proofreader
Linda Stern, copy editor
Mark Wolkenfeld, production coordinator

Liberty's Expansion in a Turbulent World:

Thirty Years of the Survey of Freedom

Adrian Karatnycky

THE YEAR'S TRENDS

In 2002, there were significant gains for freedom around the world. Brazil, Lesotho, and Senegal entered the ranks of Free countries after holding free and fair national elections. Yugoslavia, too, joined the roster of Free countries as a result of the dynamic expansion of independent civic life and the growth of free media in the aftermath of the 2000 electoral defeat of Slobodan Milosevic. Significant progress for freedom was also registered in Bahrain, which saw contested elections for a parliament with limited powers, and Kenya, which saw increased space for opposition political movements. Kenya and Bahrain saw their status improve from Not Free to Partly Free. By contrast, Cote D'Ivoire fell from Partly Free to Not Free, after a military revolt plunged the country into violent civil war, and Togo also dropped from Partly Free to Not Free as a result of legislative elections that were neither free nor fair.

As a result of these developments, at the end of 2002 there were 89 Free countries in which there is broad scope for open political competition, a climate of respect for civil liberties, significant independent civic life, and independent media. The number of Free countries increased by four in the last year, meaning that both the number of Free countries and their proportion (46 percent) are the highest in the history of the survey. This represents 2.718 billion people and 43.85 percent of the global population. There were 55 Partly Free countries in which there is limited respect for political rights and civil liberties, a decrease of four. These states also suffer from an environment of corruption, weak rule of law, ethnic and religious strife, and often a setting in which a single political party enjoys dominance despite the façade of limited pluralism. Approximately 20.87 percent of the world's population, 1.293 billion persons, lived in such Partly Free societies. There were 2.186 billion people (35.28 percent of the global population) living in 48 Not Free countries, where basic political rights are absent and basic civil liberties were widely and systematically denied, the same as the previous year.

ADVANCES FOR FREEDOM OUTPACE REVERSALS BY A MARGIN OF THREE TO ONE

Additionally, this year 22 countries registered significant improvements in the expansion of political rights and/or civil liberties without changing categories, while only 9 countries saw an erosion of political rights and/or civil liberties. Taken together, category changes and numerical changes registered in the survey yielded upward momentum for 28 countries and regression away from freedom for 11 countries—a margin of nearly three to one. Minor adjustments to the survey

Freedom in the World—2003

The population of the world as estimated in mid-2002 is 6,197.0 million persons, who reside in 192 sovereign states. The level of political rights and civil liberties as shown comparatively by the Freedom House Survey is:

Free: 2,717.6 million (43.85 percent of the world's population) live in 89 of the states.

Partly Free: 1,293.1 million (20.87 percent of the world's population) live in 55 of the states.

Not Free: 2,186.3 million (35.28 percent of the world's population) live in 48 of the states.

A Record of the Survey
(population in millions)

SURVEY DATE	FREE	PARTLY FREE	NOT FREE	WORLD POPULATION
1973	1,324.5 (35.05%)	666.9 (17.65%)	1,787.6 (47.30%)	3,779.0
1983	1,665.1 (36.32%)	918.8 (20.04%)	2,000.2 (43.64%)	4,584.1
1993	1,352.2 (24.83%)	2,403.3 (44.11%)	1,690.4 (31.06%)	5,446.0
1994	1,046.2 (19.00%)	2,224.4 (40.41%)	2,234.6 (40.59%)	5,505.2
1995	1,119.7 (19.97%)	2,243.4 (40.01%)	2,243.9 (40.02%)	5,607.0
1996	1,114.5 (19.55%)	2,365.8 (41.49%)	2,221.2 (38.96%)	5,701.5
1997	1,250.3 (21.67%)	2,260.1 (39.16%)	2,260.6 (39.17%)	5,771.0
1998	1,266.0 (21.71%)	2,281.9 (39.12%)	2,284.6 (39.17%)	5,832.5
1999	2,354.0 (39.84%)	1,570.6 (26.59%)	1,984.1 (33.58%)	5,908.7
2000	2,324.9 (38.90%)	1,529.0 (25.58%)	2,122.4 (35.51%)	5,976.3
2001	2,465.2 (40.69%)	1,435.8 (23.70%)	2,157.5 (35.61%)	6,058.5
2002	2,500.7 (40.79%)	1,462.9 (23.86%)	2,167.1 (35.35%)	6,130.7
2003	2,717.6 (43.85%)	1,293.1 (20.87%)	2,186.3 (35.28%)	6,197.0

methodology led to upward trends in 14 additional countries and to downward trends in 3.

At the same time, the number of electoral democracies held steady at 121 of the world's 192 governments (63 percent)—again matching the highest number and proportion in the thirty-year record of the survey of freedom. While some electoral democracies had poor human rights records and weak democratic institutions, such states afforded considerable space for political opposition movements, provided opposition parties and viewpoints access to the media, and met the minimum standard of a fair vote count in conditions of ballot secrecy and relatively open election campaigning.

The year's trends toward greater freedom were registered amid the prosecution of a global war on terrorism and signs of an increase in the number of coordinated terrorist acts carried out by extremist political movements. On the surface, the year's positive trends might seem contrary to the expectation that widespread transnational terrorism carried out by international networks and the responses to interdict such political violence would result in a significant erosion of freedoms. According to the current Freedom House survey results for the year 2002, fears that such a trend might emerge were not justified.

However, it is important to note that most of the significant upward momentum for freedom has occurred preponderantly in countries in which the impact of ideological terrorism has thus far been marginal or absent. Additionally, many of the countries confronting transnational terrorism are established democracies with a strong rule of law and have successfully preserved a wide array of personal, political, and civil freedoms that have allowed a high degree of freedom, although a number of counter-terrorism measures have raised civil liberties concerns that bear continued close monitoring.

At the same time, while the Middle East, North Africa, and Central Asia continue to lag behind global trends towards freedom, the survey has registered progress this year in a number of countries with majority Muslim populations, defying some who argue that Islamic beliefs are somehow contrary to democratic development. Of the six countries that saw improvements in their freedom rating, two—Bahrain and Senegal—are majority Muslim. Among the 22 countries with significant gains for freedom, five—Afghanistan, Albania, Comoros, Tajikistan, and Turkey—have Islamic majorities.

The Global Trend

	Free	Partly Free	Not Free
1973	43	38	69
1983	54	47	64
1993	75	73	38
2003	89	55	48

Tracking Democracy

Number of Electoral Democracies

1993	99
1998	117
2003	121

THIRTY-YEAR TRENDS

This is the 30th anniversary of *Freedom in the World*, a comparative survey of political rights and civil liberties. The survey initiated its comprehensive analysis of global trends in political rights and civil liberties in 1972, just before the start of the third wave of democratization, which is dated by many scholars to the collapse of the Portuguese dictatorship in 1975.

The evidence of the ebb and flow of democracy during this thirty-year period indicates dramatic changes in the global political landscape in the expansion of freedom. One important trend over this period is the expansion of sovereign states, which has grown from 150 in 1972 to 192 in 2002. As a result of the collapse of the USSR and Yugoslavia, the bifurcation of states such as Czechoslovakia, and the independence from colonial rule of others, the roster of the world's countries has expanded at the rate of just under one-and-a-half per year.

There has been dramatic progress in the expansion of freedom and democratic governance over the life of the survey. In 1972, there were 43 Free countries, while 38 were Partly Free and 69 were rated Not Free. Today, there are 89 states rated Free by the survey, 55 rated Partly Free and 48 rated Not Free. This means that over the last thirty years, the number of Free countries has more than doubled; the number of Partly Free states has grown by 17; while the number of the most repressive Not Free states has declined by 21. This represents a landmark change in the political landscape of the world.

The trends in broad political status are also reflected in more nuanced trends represented through numerical ratings. Freedom House provides a numerical expression of the state of political rights and civil liberties on a 1 to 7 scale for each, with 1 representing a high degree of compliance with these rights and standards and 7 representing their complete absence, negation, or suppression. According to this numerical scale, the average political rights rating of the survey has progressed from 4.5 on political rights in 1972 to 3.4 in 2002, and there has been a significant improvement in the average civil liberties rating, which has gone from an average of 4.2 in 1972 to 3.4 in 2002.

The gains in terms of the global population, however, have proved to be somewhat more modest. In 1972, 1,325 million people (35 percent of the world's population) lived in Free countries with democratic governments and broad compliance with human rights. Today the number of people who live in Free countries has grown to 2,718 million people, almost 44 percent of the global population. At the same time, the number of people living in Not Free countries has risen from 1,788 million people to 2,186 million people. This represents a decline in the proportion of people living under Not Free systems from 47 percent in 1972 to 35 percent of the global population today. It is important to note that of the 2.153 billion people living in Not Free countries, almost 60 percent, or 1.27 billion, live in the People's Republic of China, whose rating over thirty years has edged up from a 7 rating for civil liberties in 1972, the lowest possible rating, to a 6, as a result of the expansion of personal freedoms and free private discussion and the emergence of some significant space for private sector economic activity.

The 9 Worst Rated Countries

Burma
Cuba
Iraq
North Korea
Libya
Saudi Arabia
Sudan
Syria
Turkmenistan

The 2 Worst Rated Disputed Territories

Chechnya (Russia)
Tibet (China)

The scale of political progress is particularly dramatic in Latin America, the Asia-Pacific region, and Central and Eastern Europe, where the impact of the third wave of democratization has been acutely felt. Modest though significant progress toward greater political freedom also has been registered in Africa over the life of the survey. At the same time, despite some ferment and several important instances of democratic opening, countries in the Middle East, North Africa, and the former Soviet Union have been far more resistant to democratization, and progress toward improved human rights has stagnated. Indeed, the Middle East has seen virtual stagnation in terms of its overall levels of freedom over the last three decades.

In 1972, the Americas and the Caribbean region had 13 Free countries, 9 that were Partly Free, and 4 that were Not Free. The region has experienced a dramatic political change in the last 30 years. Today, there are 23 Free Countries, 10 are Partly Free, and 2 (Haiti and Cuba) are Not Free.

In 1972, Western Europe had 18 Free states, while 4 countries were Partly Free, and 3 were Not Free (Portugal, Spain, and Greece). Today, 24 of the European states are rated Free, and only Turkey, which is included in the roster of European states, is rated as Partly Free.

In the Asia-Pacific region, important progress also has been registered. In 1972, less than a third of the region's states, 8, were rated Free, while there were 13 Partly Free countries and 11 Not Free states. Today, there are 18 Free countries, more than double the number thirty years before, while the numbers of Partly Free and Not Free states are 10 and 11, respectively. This political progress has also been accompanied by impressive rates of economic progress over the last decade in such countries as the Philippines, South Korea, and Thailand, each of which has seen an expansion of political freedoms and civil liberties. This trend has discredited the idea of "Asian values" as representing a specific regional path of authoritarian political and economic development.

In Central and Eastern Europe and the former Soviet Union, all nine of the Communist states were Not Free in 1972. With the collapse of the USSR and Yugoslavia, the bifurcation of Czechoslovakia, and the reunification of Germany, today there are 12 Free countries, 9 that are Partly Free, and 6 Not Free. However, it is important to note that dramatic progress in terms of rights has been registered primarily in the Central and East European states, where there are 12 Free countries and 3 Partly Free states. By contrast, in the non-Baltic states that emerged from the breakup of the Soviet Union, there are no Free countries, while 6 states are Partly Free and 6 are Not Free. As important, the post-Communist countries that have progressed most significantly in terms of democratization have seen political reforms matched by economic reform and impressive economic growth rates. The significant progress made by these states has been confirmed by their rapid integration into the security and economic structures of Europe and the Euro-Atlantic community.

In 1972, there were 2 Free countries in sub-Saharan Africa, while 9 were Partly Free, and 28 were Not Free. Today, 11 countries are Free, 21 are Partly Free, and 16 are Not Free. Africa has seen progress in terms of the decline in the number of Not Free countries, although there has been less progress in the number of new entrants into the Free category. The region has seen enormous political dynamism and significant instability, with steps forward in some countries often followed by reversals. Nevertheless, the general trend for freedom in sub-Saharan Africa has been positive over the last thirty years.

Among the countries of the Middle East and North Africa, there has been virtually no significant progress toward democratization in the three decades of the survey. In 1972, the survey rated only 2 countries—Israel and Lebanon—as Free, while 3 states were Partly Free, and 14 were rated Not Free. Today, Israel remains the region's sole democracy and Free country. There are 4 Partly Free and 13 Not Free states, virtually the same distribution as in 1972.

RELIGION AND POLITICAL CHANGE

In past years the survey has examined the correlations between religion—by tradition and belief—and democratic reform. The survey has found that as a pattern, waves of democratic expansion appear to have moved through cultures and civilizations linked by religious adherence. Social scientists who looked at the political map of the world in the early 1970s were struck by a high degree of correlation between democracy, freedom and majority-Protestant Christian countries. The third wave of democratization—by contrast—showed a high degree of democratic momentum in the majority-Catholic world from the mid-1970s to the late 1980s. Thus, as this author has argued in past reviews of trends in freedom in these pages, there is no inherent relationship between adherence to a major religious belief system and one's predisposition or antipathy to democratic values.

That said, the survey analysis does indicate some correlation between majority Muslim countries and political change. Here the thirty-year record of the survey indicates that the states with majority Muslim populations, as a rule, have not experienced movement toward democracy. Indeed, among countries with Muslim majorities, the last 30 years have seen a trend diametrically opposite to the global trend toward political liberalization. In 1972, there were 2 Free countries with a majority Muslim population, 11 Partly Free states, and 23 Not Free states. Today, there are again two Free countries, Mali and Senegal. There are 18 Partly Free majority Muslim countries—an increase of 7—and 27 Not Free countries, up from 23 in 1972. This contrasts dramatically with trends in the non-Islamic world, where the number of Free countries has expanded from 41 to 87, the number of Partly Free states has increased from 27 to 37, while the number of Not Free states has declined from 46 to 21.

All this, however, should not suggest some kind of inexorable link between Islam and tyranny. In fact, today, when one takes into account the fact that the largest populations of Muslims are found in such states as India, Bangladesh, Indonesia, Turkey, and Nigeria, as well as the Muslim minorities that participate in the democratic life of Western Europe and North America, the majority of the world's 1.2 billion Muslims live under democratically elected governments. At the same time, there is evidence in this year's survey of a transition to freedom in majority-Muslim Senegal and of democratic ferment or democratization in several of the Gulf kingdoms—notably, Bahrain, where there has been movement toward constitutional monarchy and the devolution of some power toward a democratically accountable government. Qatar, too, has seen its emir proclaim his intention to move in the direction of constitutional monarchy, and a new draft constitution is being prepared, although its provisions are not yet public and the process has not been conducted openly and transparently.

The lack of progress on democratic reform in large swaths of the world populated by Muslim majorities can be attributed to many factors, none of them directly related to religious beliefs as such. One crucial factor is the persistent influence of regimes and political movements that came into power through military coups. Another key factor influencing political life in the Islamic world has been the persistence of monarchies that have resisted the devolution of power to democratically accountable governments, and in some cases have resorted to repression and censorship in their bid to stem democratic civic activism. A further factor is the phenomenon of personal authoritarianism—in which individual leaders have maintained a monopoly over economic and political power—which is the dominate political system in the North African and Middle Eastern region. Moreover, much of the Islamic world suffers from the influence of two extremist ideologies. One—Ba'athism—is secular in orientation; the second—revolutionary or jihadist Islamism—claims religious justification for acts of violence and repression. Both ideologies were shaped by founders who developed their political ideas and models of activism in the 1930s, when totalitarian movements dominated the European landscape. Both ideologies base their activism on the creation of vanguard parties or movements that seek to foment revolutionary change

Over the last several decades, Ba'athism and revolutionary Islamism have given birth to several tyrannical regimes and violent political movements that have contributed to the destabilization of the region and produced a great deal of internecine conflict. In many cases, these ideologies have been used as the bases of tyrannical regimes. The threat posed by these movements has also been manipulated by the military-dominated dictatorships and authoritarian monarchies as a justification for the absence of political reforms or as cover for the repression of peaceful and democratic political forces. Ba'athist and revolutionary Islamist movements have themselves targeted moderate, democratic voices with violence and repression. These factors have converged to suppress and preempt the emergence of a vibrant democratic alternative in large swaths of the Arabic and Islamic worlds.

The political map of the world at the end of 2002 showed 121 electoral democracies among the world's 192 states (63 percent). The 1987-88 survey found just 66 of 167 countries (40 percent) were electoral democracies. In short, the number of new democratically elected governments has increased by 55 over the space of 15 years, an average of nearly four per year. This gradual, sustained expansion of electoral democracy has helped to create a framework for improvements in basic human rights. At the same time, the survey finds that only 89 of these electoral democracies have an environment in which there is broad respect for human rights and a stable rule of law. This means that 32 electoral democracies fail to provide systematic protection for basic civil liberties. The reasons for this are numerous. Some electoral democracies (Ukraine) are riddled by widespread corruption. Others (Nigeria and Macedonia) are marred by unresolved inter-religious and inter-ethnic tensions. Still others (Colombia and Sri Lanka) confront civil wars, terrorism, and insurgencies. Some states (Indonesia) are just emerging from protracted periods of tyranny and have not yet established the broad array of effective rule of law structures that would allow for the wide-ranging implementation of human rights standards. In others (Russia), there are powerful oligarchic interests and wide discrepancies in income that have an impact on the rule of law and equal political participation.

In addition, a cohort of electoral democracies has stagnated and failed to deepen their progress on civil liberties, and to build effective democratic institutions. Among the electoral democracies that have remained Partly Free and have not significantly improved their development over a period of more than a decade are Georgia, Guatemala, Moldova, Mozambique, Paraguay, Russia, Sri Lanka, and Ukraine.

For policymakers, there is a key challenge on how to work to generate reform momentum in these rather diverse, semi-democratic countries.

While it is true that some authoritarian regimes are demagogically using the global war on terrorism as a justification for internal crackdowns on political opponents, violent and peaceful, the year's survey findings do not suggest that the world has seen a serious erosion of human rights since the global efforts to combat terrorism were launched in the wake of September 11, 2001.

RATING FREEDOM IN A VIOLENT WORLD

Each year the survey team grapples with ratings in settings characterized by mass terrorism, insurgency, and civil war. Rating polities that confront these often destabilizing threats poses substantial challenges for a ratings system that attempts to provide a unified score for the performance of an entire country.

In the end, the analysts base their ratings on the on-the-ground reality, taking into account the extent of the violent threat and the scope of its disruption of civic and political life.

In a world in which terrorism and insurgencies are widespread, this places significant burdens on the ratings process. When insurgencies are longstanding, are based on internationally recognized territorial divisions, or have evidence of stable de facto autonomous governance, we treat such regions as distinct territories and rate them separately from the country as a whole. This is the case with both Palestine (Israeli Occupied) and the Palestinian Authority, India- and Pakistan-controlled Kashmir, and Chechnya.

Thus Israel's categorization as an electoral democracy and its Free rating reflects the treatment it accords its citizens within its internationally recognized borders, not the far more troubling picture for human rights in the Palestinian populated areas, which are assessed separately.

In the case of Colombia, Sri Lanka, and Nepal, where there is no international recognition of areas controlled by insurgents or where insurgents do not control stable contiguous areas but operate over shifting territories, the ratings process attempts to provide an overall assessment of the state of political rights and civil liberties that incorporates the zones controlled both by the state and by violent insurgent movements.

Another problem faced by the survey team is how to deal with the efforts to interdict terrorism in open democracies like the U.S., Britain, France, and Germany. The effects of counter-terrorism measures and the de facto restrictions on freedom that result from the operation of terrorist groups are factored in through the ratings process. Moreover, the survey team seeks to be attuned to the dangers of civil liberties restrictions as a result of counter-terrorism measures and understands that these bear systematic monitoring. Nevertheless, survey data reflect that despite some missteps and some overreaching by democratic governments in 2002 (which may yet have implications in the future), states with strong traditions of freedom and the rule of law have generally not seen a significant decline in their overall levels of political rights and civil liberties as measured by the survey. At the same time, because the Survey measures the on the ground state of freedom, more assertive counter-terrorism measures are at times offset in the ratings by improvements in personal safety and in the elimination of threats of mass violence, which also are factors that inhibit freedom.

COUNTRY TRENDS IN 2002

The year registered an improvement in category status for six countries. Senegal and Brazil advanced from Partly Free to Free, in large measure as a result of free and fair elections that led to a rotation of power through the victory of an opposition party. Lesotho entered the ranks of Free countries as it saw its ratings improve after free and fair parliamentary elections. Yugoslavia also entered the ranks of Free countries as a result of the vibrance of civic life, improvements in free media, and gains in the rule of law. Bahrain made political progress and moved from the ranks of Not Free to Partly Free states as a consequence of an election that led to the partial devolution of power to a new democratically accountable legislature. Kenya's status improved from Not Free to Partly Free, due to increased political and civic pluralism, the effects of a constitutional review commission, and a national election campaign.

Only two countries—Cote d'Ivoire and Togo—saw their category status decline, in this case from Partly Free to Not Free. Cote d'Ivoire's status declined amid widening violence and the takeover of approximately one-half of the country by rebellious military forces, while that of Togo declined following legislative elections that were neither free nor fair

In the disputed territory of Indian-administered Kashmir, a relatively fair election with a high degree of voter participation amid intimidation of voters by militant Islamic groups led to an improvement in political rights and a consequent status change from Not Free to Partly Free. By contrast, substantial restrictions on political rights in Pakistan-administered Kashmir meant that the contested region was rated as Not Free.

In addition to four entrants into the ranks of Free countries and two countries that progressed from Not Free to Partly Free, 22 countries experienced significant gains. A further 14 countries experience a modest upgrade in their ratings on account of minor changes in the ratings methodology linked to a question on the effects of corruption that was added to the political rights assessment and a question on academic freedom that was added to the civil liberties criteria.

MOVEMENT TOWARD GREATER FREEDOM

Afghanistan registered modest progress as a consequence of stabilization, and the expansion of limited representational rights through a process of selection of the Loya Jirga, which in turn selected the new government. But while the Taliban's totalitarian repression was dismantled, schools reopened, culture was partly liberalized, and while some rights for women and girls were restored, the country's capital, Kabul, registered more dramatic improvement than outlying provinces and remote rural areas. The country's overall rating remained Not Free as a consequence of severe lawlessness, insecurity, and the inordinate influence of warlords, who controlled large swaths of the country.

Albania's civil liberties improved as a result of the continuing normalization after the civil unrest and violence of 1997.

Angola, which remains Not Free, saw civil liberties register modest gains after of the death of UNITA guerrilla movement leader Jonas Savimbi. His death resulted in a cease-fire that has ended hostilities and provided for the return of many civilians to their former homes.

In Bhutan, gains were registered due to greater accountability of the monarchy to the people.

Bosnia-Herzegovina's political rights strengthened after indigenous Bosnian institutions successfully organized general elections for the first time since the country's brutal civil war.

Bulgaria's civil liberties improved amid consistent attempts to bring the county's political, economic, and social environment in line with European standards, improved tolerance towards ethnic minorities, and more openness towards non-traditional religious groups.

Chile's civil liberties rating improved due to President Ricardo Lagos' adroit handling of the country's thorny civil-military relationship.

Comoros' political rights rating improved after a largely successful free and fair presidential election on the archipelago's three islands.

East Timor improved due to direct elections that led it to join the ranks of electoral democracies. Still, the absence of a strong parliamentary opposition, weak media and undeveloped civil society prevented the country from improving its status to Free.

Greece's civil liberties rating improved after the relaxation of laws relating to the now-defunct November 17 urban guerrilla group.

Macedonia's political rights and civil liberties ratings improved amid increased stability in the country and the gradual implementation of the 2001 Ohrid Agreement that led to an end of hostilities between the Macedonian government and ethnic Albanian insurgents.

In Mexico, a deepening of reforms in the justice system that reinforced the rule of law contributed to an upward trend.

Mongolia's civil liberties rating improved as a result of the strengthening of the rule of law, including an improvement of conditions in the country's prisons.

Slovenia's civil liberties improved as a result of legislation satisfying European Union membership requirements. These include an employment bill banning any form of discrimination, and legislation giving increased rights to foreigners with permanent resident status.

The Solomon Islands' political rights and civil liberties ratings improved as a result of an improvement in the country's security situation.

Tajikistan's civil liberties rating improved as a result of a gradual strengthening of the rule of law and the renewal of civic life in the aftermath of a civil war that ended in 1997.

Turkey registered forward progress as a result of the loosening of restrictions on Kurdish culture. Legislators made progress on an improved human rights framework, the product of Turkey's effort to integrate into European structures. At the same time, political rights were enhanced as the country's military showed restraint in the aftermath of a free and fair election that saw the sweeping victory of a moderate Islamist opposition party.

Despite significant political tensions, Venezuela's civil liberties rating improved as a result of the dynamism and resilience of civic organizations and independent media in the face of intense pressures from the government of Hugo Chavez.

The ratings of 14 countries improved as a result of minor adjustments in the survey methodology: Belgium, Brunei, Burundi, France, Germany, Italy, Nauru, Spain, Tanzania, Uganda, the United Kingdom, Vanuatu, Yemen, and Zambia.

DECLINES IN FREEDOM

While Cote d'Ivoire and Togo fell into the ranks of Not Free countries, nine other countries registered setbacks in their freedoms without changing categories and three others declined as a result of modest changes in the Survey's methodology:

Bolivia saw a decline in its political rights standing amid significant evidence of increased political corruption and the influence of campaign funding linked to drug interests.

The Congo (Brazzaville) rating declined as a result of presidential and legislative elections that were not fair.

Equatorial Guinea regressed as earlier moves that had created hopes for a political opening proved cosmetic. The government also moved to speed up elections to reduce the ability of opposition groups to mount a campaign and establish effective election monitoring mechanisms.

Guatemala's political rights rating declined due to the continuing decay of political institutions, impunity, increased violence, rampant corruption, and the reappearance of death squads.

Jordan's political rights rating declined as a result of the monarchy's postponement of elections and the adoption by decree of numerous temporary laws.

Madagascar's political rights rating declined from 2 to 3 due to controversy that erupted over the country's presidential elections.

Malawi's civil liberties ratings were set back as a result of increased political violence, including the arrest of opposition leaders.

Nepal suffered a setback in political rights as the king dissolved parliament and postponed elections amid a violent insurgency led by Marxist-Leninist guerrillas.

Peru's political rights rating declined from 1 to 2 due to slippage on government pledges to openness and transparency.

In addition, three countries—Bangladesh, Moldova, and Taiwan—registered a decline in their numerical ratings—though no status change—as a result of minor changes in the survey methodology.

WORST OF THE WORST

There are 48 states that are rated as Not Free and in which a broad range of freedoms are systematically denied. Of these, 25 have majority Islamic populations. Among the Not Free countries, 9 states have been given the survey's lowest rating of 7 for political rights and 7 for civil liberties. The 9 worst rated countries represent a narrow range of systems and cultures. Two—Cuba and North Korea—are one-party Marxist-Leninist regimes. Six are majority Islamic countries (Iraq, Libya, Saudi Arabia, Sudan, Syria, and Turkmenistan). The remaining worst rated state is Burma, a tightly controlled military dictatorship.

There are two worst rated territories: Tibet (under Chinese jurisdiction) and Chechnya, where an indigenous Islamic population is engaged in a brutal guerrilla war for independence from Russia.

CONCLUSION

The largely positive trends indicated by the survey are reinforced by the growing technological and economic dominance of open societies. With the People's Republic of China the one glaring and important exception, basic statistical evidence suggests that Free countries have, as a rule, expanded their economic output more rapidly than closed societies. In 2002, for example, the GDP of Free countries stood at $27.8 trillion, (representing 86 percent of the global economy) while the GDP of Not Free countries was $1.8 trillion.

This means that today open societies command a vast advantage in terms of military, technological, economic, and cultural resources. There are also important signs that the world's democracies are looking for new mechanisms through which to improve the governance and accountability of international institutions and to advance democratic change through aid and development programs. All this augurs well for the hope that the trends of the last thirty years will continue and that human freedom will make further significant progress in the new millennium.

Adrian Karatnycky is senior scholar and counselor at Freedom House.

Freedom Under Challenge

The following two essays deal with two serious challenges to freedom. One challenge is the problem of regions of sovereign states that are seeking independence or autonomy and have taken up arms or embraced terrorism to achieve their goals. These territorial conflicts pose a real impediment to freedom in countries where democracy is new and fragile: Sri Lanka, Russia, Georgia, and Indonesia. They have also plagued stable democracies, such as Spain and the United Kingdom. Our author, Sumantra Bose, looks at several of these territorial conflicts and assesses the best and worst strategies to resolve territorial disputes.

The second essay takes up the question of democracy's future in Latin America. The transformation of politics in that part of the world has been regarded as one of freedom's signal gains over the past quarter-century. Indeed, the transition of Latin America from a region dominated by *juntas* and *caudillos* to one where democratically elected governments are the rule actually predated the fall of the Berlin Wall and the collapse of communism. Yet even though democratic systems continue to hold sway throughout the region, several worrisome trends have emerged that raise questions about South American political stability. These include a serious, near region wide economic downturn, the inability of the authorities to stem a wave of violent crime, racial and ethnic tensions, and the rise of populist demagogues as political forces in a number of Andean countries. Michael Shifter, a veteran observer of Latin American political developments, assesses how the region is coping with its multiple burdens.

The Implications of Ethno-National Conflict

Sumantra Bose

What are the implications of internal ethno-national conflict—particularly "secessionist" or "separatist" claims—for democratic states? First, why do such conflicts arise at all in democracies? Second, especially when such conflicts assume a violent form, what are the likely consequences for the health of democracy in the country in question? Third, how should democracies respond to such conflicts, and what strategies and institutional options might usefully address the claims of ethno-national movements confronting the state?

THE CAUSES AND CONSEQUENCES OF ETHNO-NATIONAL MOVEMENTS

Ethno-national movements are born and radicalized primarily because of the real failure of states, including liberal-democratic and partially democratic regimes, to treat all communities in the state fairly. States, however, are typically unwilling or unable to come to terms with the reality that the primary impetus to secessionist rebellion lies in their own policies. Instead of pursuing reforms to democratize the state, political elites tend to respond by stigmatizing ethno-national separatism as "terrorist" and as an intolerable threat to territorial integrity that must be crushed. This is especially true if the internal conflict has an external, transnational dimension that involves neighboring countries in the activities of the secessionist movement. The protracted armed conflicts that result can have several possible outcomes, including a military stalemate and, in some cases, even a military victory for the state. However, such violent conflicts between the state and separatists typically damage the democratic credentials of established liberal democracies and undermine prospects for democratic development in partially democratic systems. The costs for democracy may not remain restricted to abuses of human and civil rights in the war zones of the country, but spill over to undermine democratic standards and processes in the rest of the country.

If established democracies wish to preserve their credentials, and partially democratic states wish to continue to progress towards democracy, they should rise above a narrowly defined "security"-obsessed mind-set and respond with reformist policies that address the grievances of the secessionist population. The international community, including multilateral organizations and states with global and/or regional influence, should encourage them to do so. Democracies have a built-in institutional capacity to devise substantive answers to problems of this nature. Although strategies of accommodation and compromise will normally be resisted by both government hard-liners and secessionist radicals and will thus have their limits, they offer the best hope of preserving or advancing democracy, and of ensuring longer-term peace and stability. Four current situations illustrate these arguments: the conflict in and over Kashmir, the ethnic war (and peace process to end that war) in Sri Lanka, the Kurdish question in Turkey, and the interesting example of the Basque region in Spain.

THE CONFLICT IN KASHMIR

The Kashmir conflict is one of the gravest menaces to South Asian and global peace and security, and during 2002 it threatened to spark war between India and Pakistan, both nuclear-weapons-capable states with huge conventional capabilities. The current stance of Indian officials reduces the Kashmir conflict to a problem of "cross-border terrorism" fomented by and from within Pakistan. It is true that the Pakistani military and its intelligence agencies have been deeply involved in materially supporting armed insurgency in Indian-controlled Kashmir since the late 1980s, and that radical Islamist groups based in Pakistan have become active in waging guerrilla warfare in Indian-controlled Kashmir since the mid-1990s. However, the armed rebellion, and to some extent the popularly backed insurrection, that have raged in Indian-controlled Kashmir since 1990 have their roots in a four-decade long history—from the early 1950s to 1990—of repressive, antidemocratic, and authoritarian policies pursued by successive Indian governments vis-à-vis Indian-controlled Kashmir. Motivated by fear of Pakistani designs and suspicion of the loyalty of large sections of the majority Muslim population of Indian-controlled Kashmir, Indian political elites ruling Indian-controlled Kashmir, frequently in collusion with local client elites, have used strategies antithetical to India's professed principles of liberal democracy and institutional federalism. As a result, civil liberties were severely curtailed in Indian-controlled Kashmir, competitive elections were reduced to a doctored, stage-managed farce by intervention and manipulation from New Delhi, and Indian-controlled Kashmir's autonomous regime within the Indian Union was effectively revoked and destroyed. This subversion of democratic rights, processes, and institutions turned Indian-controlled Kashmir into a glaringly anomalous enclave of police state-like repression and authoritarian central control in a country whose political system is otherwise based on robust multiparty politics and a quasi-federal structure of government.[1]

Eventually, this led to an uprising against Indian rule, originally led by groups that believe in the ideology of an independent state of Kashmir separate from both India and Pakistan. Since 1993, however, the armed struggle has been dominated by pro-Pakistan groups present in Indian-controlled Kashmir and, since the mid-1990s, has been increasingly infiltrated by radical Islamist groups based in Pakistan. The outbreak of intense violence between Indian military, police, and other state-security forces on the one hand and guerrilla groups on the other fostered a human rights crisis in Indian-controlled Kashmir through the 1990s and beyond, which contributed to further radicalization of the conflict.[2]

The path to peace in Kashmir lies in a peace process with interconnected, mutually reinforcing, international and domestic dimensions. The major elements of such a process would be:

· An overarching framework of intergovernmental cooperation between India and Pakistan on the Kashmir dispute;

· The negotiation of a self-rule framework between New Delhi and the spectrum of groups advocating self-determination in Indian-controlled Kashmir—one that is also approved by political groups in Indian-controlled Kashmir that are pro-India;

· The establishment of a framework of devolution and multi-tiered autonomy within Indian-controlled Kashmir, a socially and politically heterogeneous territory, to take account of the wishes of its various regions, ethnicities, and religions;

· The establishment of institutional linkages of cross-border contact and cooperation between Indian-controlled Kashmir and the smaller, less populous areas of Pakistani-controlled Kashmir that lie beyond the Line of Control (LOC)—in other words, the transformation of the LOC from a heavily militarized iron curtain and flashpoint of armed hostilities into a linen curtain between self-governing Indian and Pakistani regions of Kashmir and their democratically constituted, inclusive governments.[3]

India's framework of multiparty pluralism and its quasi-federal structure of government have endured, indeed deepened, over more than 50 years, and this is a significant achievement given the country's context of poverty and massive social and ethnic diversity. However, a hard-line stance on the Kashmir conflict is not just unsustainable in both ethical and practical terms, but also rife with deeply negative domestic and international implications. Within India, a hard-line Kashmir policy—ironically, historically devised and implemented for the most part by ostensibly liberal, "secular" governments—and the increasingly bellicose rhetoric against Pakistan that underpins that policy are closely linked to the rise and political prospects of India's fundamentally illiberal "Hindu nationalist" movement and its venomous stance towards India's large Muslim minority population of 150 million. In other words, the festering of the Kashmir conflict has important adverse implications for India's own political stability. Internationally, the festering of the Kashmir conflict as a flash point of military confrontation between India and Pakistan constitutes a severe peril for peace and security in the entire subcontinent.

ETHNIC WAR, AND PEACE, IN SRI LANKA

The current peace process in Sri Lanka, ongoing since early 2002, provides a glimmer of hope that even protracted and bloody ethno-national conflicts can be amenable to peace-making and compromise. The Sri Lankan peace process also provides important pointers on how such a peace process can be built in concrete terms, by combining confidence-building measures and postwar normalization and reconstruction with a longer-term, substantive strategy of recognizing majority and minority communities as cultural equals and institutionalizing political autonomy for the aggrieved minority.

Sri Lanka, an idyllic island country of 20 million off the southern tip of the South Asian subcontinent, is among a relative handful of postcolonial states that embarked upon and sustained a liberal-democratic path of political development after independence from Britain in 1948. It seems puzzling, therefore, that the country would become the theater of a brutal civil war between its Sinhalese majority and its Tamil minority (who are concentrated in northern and, to a lesser degree, eastern Sri Lanka) for two decades, from the early 1980s to the end of 2001. The seeds of conflict were sown during the 1950s, when the Westminster-style democracy bequeathed to Sri Lanka by the British was deformed into an instrument of dominance by a majority defined in ethno-national terms—the Buddhist Sinhalese, who make up 70 percent of the population. The unitary and centralized structure of the state, also a British institutional legacy, facilitated the takeover of the Sri Lankan state by the ethnic majority and the enactment of a host of discriminatory policies directed at the Sri Lankan Tamil 13 percent minority. The Tamils were severely disadvantaged by the declaration of Sinhalese as the sole official and national language of the country in 1956, which not only marginalized their language and culture in a symbolic sense but also had negative consequences for their access to educational and employment opportunities. At least 10 percent of deputies elected to the Sri Lankan parliament in regular elections were Sri Lankan Tamils elected from Tamil-dominant districts in the north and east of the country, but they were relegated to being a powerless, bypassed opposition caucus. These Tamil representatives called for language rights and for a federalist reconstitution of the Sri Lankan state to enable self-government for predominantly Tamil areas in the north and east, but autonomy pacts negotiated in 1958 and 1965 between the Sinhalese-Buddhist and Tamil political elites were not implemented.

In 1972, a new constitution was passed formally enshrining the supremacy of the ethno-national majority, and more discriminatory measures were adopted to deny young Tamils access to university education and professional employment. When Tamils protested, members of the community living in predominantly Sinhalese parts of the country were subjected to pogrom-like violence in a series of ethnic riots that began in 1977 and culminated in a massacre of 2,000 to 3,000 Tamils in 1983. Sinhalese political parties, the police, and the predominately all-Sinhalese Sri Lankan military were deeply complicit in organizing and perpetrating this violence. A small Tamil guerrilla movement, which emerged in the north among radicalized youth in the late 1970s, spread and expanded rapidly in response to the pogroms in the Sinhalese-majority south and to the police and military repression in the Tamil-majority north. By 1984, Sri Lanka was in the grip of escalating civil war. The activities of the armed Tamil rebels were greatly facilitated by the support of India, the region's geo-political power. Tamil guerrilla groups received training and weapons from India's armed forces and intelligence agencies, and territory populated by ethnic Tamils in southern India became a base, sanctuary, and launching post for guerrilla war in northern and eastern Sri Lanka. Hysterical Sinhalese complaints about Indian support for armed insurgency against a neighboring state were well-founded, but like Indian condemnations of Pakistani support for insurgency in Kashmir, neglected the vital fact that the roots of war lay squarely in internal factors, namely the deformation of Sri Lankan democracy by the ethnic majority.[4]

What motivated the Sri Lankan belligerents to enter into the current peace process, after almost two decades of progressively escalating civil war? On the Tamil side, a strategic shift by the hegemonic military and political movement, the Liberation Tigers of Tamil Eelam (LTTE), appears to have been caused by an assessment that the establishment of a separate, sovereign Tamil state covering northern and eastern Sri Lanka was unattainable, for two reasons. First, while the Tigers are an impressive fighting force, not just on land but also at sea, they have failed to come anywhere close to a conclusive victory in the civil war. Second, there is no hope of international support and recognition for Tamil secession. India, the patron of the early phase of the insurgency, had a bitter estrangement with the Tigers in the late 1980s, and during the 1990s the Tigers earned a well-deserved international reputation for brutality. On the Sinhalese side, a new, pragmatic government that had assumed office on a peace platform in 2001 realized that the economic costs of interminable civil war were unsustainable for the Sri Lankan state and that the Tigers could not be defeated militarily. The leaders of this government committed themselves to dealing with the Tigers as equals and to negotiating a substantive settlement that goes some way towards meeting Tamil aspirations to self-determination.

The peace process has massive support among the Tamil population, who are exhausted by two decades of war. Among the Sinhalese, support is also widespread, although some jingoistic opposition to compromise with the Tamils exists. Most ordinary Sinhalese are, however, as weary of the war and its costs as Tamils are. Not only has the war physically and economically ruined the Tamil-majority north and east, but it has also held the Sinhalese south's economic prospects for ransom for years, a plight exacerbated by occasional but well-timed and deadly Tiger terror attacks in the south. Thousands of Sinhalese families have lost sons, brothers, and husbands in an unwinnable war in the north and east. Although Sri Lanka has precariously maintained its institutions of multiparty politics and competitive elections through the war years, the war has severely compromised human rights and civil liberties not just in the north but in the south as well. At the end of the 1980s, for example, intra-Sinhalese disagreements over how to deal with the Tamil problem precipitated a vicious civil war among the Sinhalese, in which tens of thousands were killed.

The peace process is just a year old, and even given an optimistic prognosis, several more years will be needed to negotiate and institutionalize a complete resolution of the issues. However, the basic contours of that settlement have already emerged. Following the most recent round of peace talks in Thailand in December 2002, the LTTE announced that it had reached agreement with the government of Sri Lanka to pursue "internal self-determination" for the Tamil people based on "regional self-government" and "a system of self-rule" for Tamil-majority northeastern Sri Lanka "within a federal structure" for the country, with appropriate guarantees and safeguards for non-Tamils, especially Muslims, who live in the north and east. Officials from Norway's government and Foreign Ministry have played key roles in facilitating the peace process and in mediating problems and differences between the parties. However, the Norwegian role has, in turn, been enabled by the willingness of the parties to engage in a substantive peace process in the first place. Outsiders can play constructive roles in peace processes, but the lesson from Sri Lanka is that the basic impulse and impetus has to come from the belligerents themselves.

THE KURDS IN TURKEY

Unlike India and Sri Lanka, which both qualify as liberal-democratic polities under Robert Dahl's criteria,[5] Turkey can be classified as a hybrid regime that combines democratic institutions and processes with deeply authoritarian characteristics. Turkey's deeply embedded authoritarian traits have their origins in the Turkish republic's formation as a praetorian state under the leadership of Mustafa Kemal.[6] The most overt manifestation of the Turkish state's hybrid nature is the Turkish armed forces' (specifically its officer corps) autonomy and extensive powers of intervention and control vis-à-vis the civilian polity and society.[7] Three military coups between 1960 and 1980 stunted Turkey's potential to develop in a liberal-democratic direction. The constitution introduced by the military regime in 1982 imposes severe curbs on many elementary rights to free expression and association that are fundamental to any liberal democracy. Such antidemocratic features coexist uneasily with a restricted institutional pluralism of multiple parties and competitive elections subject to the regulatory authority of the armed forces' leadership—whose role is institutionalized in the National Security Council—and its allies.

One of the hallmarks of Kemalism has been the exaltation of a monolithic ideal of Turkish identity and Turkish nationalism.[8] This statist-authoritarian ideal, with its emphasis on homogeneity and conformity, is in varying forms and to varying degrees uncomfortable with and intolerant of the social and political differentiation of Turkish society—be it Islamist politics in tension with the shallow official dogma of "secularism," the presence of Alevis as a distinct heterodox confessional minority alongside the majority Sunnis, or the presence of an ethnic Kurdish minority population of perhaps 20 percent alongside the Turkish majority.

Elements of the Kurdish population rose in revolt against the oppressively centralizing and coercively assimilationist policies of the new Turkish state as early as the 1920s and 1930s, and were subjected to severe repression as well as the full blast of various "civilizing" and "nation-building" projects. The existence of a Kurdish identity was formally denied—effectively criminalized—and Kurds dominant in large regions of eastern and southeastern Turkey were infamously referred to as "mountain Turks."[9] Kurdish-identity politics reemerged cautiously in the relatively liberal atmosphere of the 1960s and became an important part of left-wing activism in Turkey. Following the last and most repressive military coup of 1980, however, the voice of pluralism was almost entirely stifled, and with that, prospects of accommodating Kurdish social and political identity in a democratized Turkey evaporated.

The emergence of a Kurdish guerrilla movement, the Workers' Party of Kurdistan (PKK), in eastern and southeastern Turkey in 1984 signaled the beginning of a 15-year war between the Turkish state and Kurdish nationalist rebels. To the Turkish establishment, particularly the military elite, the PKK-led rebellion (separatist terrorism) represented the most intolerable form of political dissidence, since it threatened the Turkish state's territorial control in extensive areas of the country and directly challenged the monolithic Kemalist conception of national identity and statehood. The most authoritarian and militarist aspects of the Turkish state were unleashed in the fight against the Kurdish insurgency. Extraordinary human rights abuses were perpetrated, including the systematic destruction of several thousand Kurdish villages in the conflict zones and the forced displacement of their populations in order to deny the guerrilla "fish" their natural habitat. Through the 1990s, Turkish land and air forces also carried out repeated incursions into northern Iraq to chase or trap PKK fighters and destroy their bases, and in 1998 the Turkish military command openly threatened another neighbor, Syria, with war unless its government took steps to end PKK activities on its soil. By the end of the decade, the Turkish army, air force, and auxiliary forces had won a military victory over the PKK, a success sealed in 1999 by the capture of PKK leader Abdullah Ocalan. In the process, large tracts of the eleven eastern and southeastern provinces subject to "emergency rule" had been turned into either desolate wastelands or heavily policed prison camp for a repressed population.

The effects of the Kurdish war did not remain limited to eastern and southeastern Turkey. Draconian laws and regulations were deployed to muzzle and punish various enemies of the state in the rest of Turkey, including critical intellectuals, human rights activists, moderate Kurdish politicians and groups, and leftist dissenters. Death-squad murders and torture, commonplace in the war zones, occurred on a lesser scale in other parts of Turkey as well. The main Kurdish political party was continually prosecuted and closed down during the 1990s (a form of harassment also endured by the country's main Islamist party), and several deputies elected from Kurdish districts to Turkey's parliament were tried for treason and sentenced to long terms of imprisonment. The result was twofold: reinforcement of the most antidemocratic, authoritarian, and repressive aspects of the Turkish state, and severe damage to Turkey's international reputation, especially—and of critical importance—in Europe.

Current prospects of democratization of Turkey's hybrid regime are closely tied to progress in democratically tackling the Kurdish question. That question is not limited to eastern and southeastern Turkey, since several million Turkish Kurds now live outside that region (for example, in Istanbul), because of voluntary migration as well as forced displacement. The civilian government led by moderate and modernist Islamists that assumed office in late 2002 could conceivably make significant progress in addressing the Kurdish question. However, the implementation of a policy that can substantively address Kurdish grievances faces formidable obstacles in the rigidly hidebound nature of the Turkish state, whose hegemonic ideology is resistant to reform and change, and in the continued power of the Turkish military's hierarchy in alliance with right-wing political forces.

During 2002, some steps were taken to decriminalize the private use of the Kurdish language and the private expression of Kurdish culture, and martial law was formally ended in the former war zones. However, these moves proved insufficient to decisively advance Turkey's bid for membership in the European Union (EU), a cherished dream for decades. Despite heavy pressure on the EU to "welcome Turkey" exerted by the United States, the mentor and backer of the Turkish state and military throughout the Cold War era and during the war against the Kurdish revolt, the otherwise-enlarging EU adopted the Franco-German preference for once again putting Turkey's bid on hold until it makes further progress toward meeting minimal EU norms for democratization. It is not clear what can or will be done in the near term in Turkey about recognizing and respecting Kurdish identity and rights. What is clear are the domestic and international costs of a conflict that may be militarily settled but remains politically unresolved.[10]

THE BASQUE REGION OF SPAIN

The Basque issue in Spain is a legacy of the country's authoritarian past. Much as the Turkish state has throughout its existence, the authoritarian regime of Francisco Franco that ruled Spain from 1939 to 1975 suffered from a fear of ethno-national diversity in its territory. Following the Nationalist victory in the 1936–1939 Spanish civil war, minority regional identities in the Basque region and Catalonia were brutally suppressed, and even their most innocuous cultural manifestations criminalized. The political autonomy granted to both regions under the Spanish Second Republic (1931–1936) was eradicated and replaced by an ultracentralized state based on a national-unitarian ideology of Spanish identity and nationhood.

In the late 1960s, an armed Basque nationalist group known by its Basque acronym, ETA (Basque Homeland and Freedom), emerged from the growing working-class, student, and clerical movements against the Franco regime in the Basque region. During the first half of the 1970s, the regime responded to ETA's emergence with a policy of severe repression in the Basque region. As Spain became democratized in the second half of the 1970s, the Basque region continued to be the site of ETA assassinations, bombings, and kidnappings—which in fact escalated—and the police-state apparatus of the old regime continued to operate with impunity in the troubled region. In the late 1970s, it became evident that surging violence in the Basque region posed a serious threat not just to Spain's cohesion as a state but to the prospects of its uncertain transition to democracy, then still in danger from an unreconstructed authoritarian right wing with a sizeable presence in both the armed forces and the formerly Francoist national police.

The turning point, for the better, was reached after 1980, when the Madrid government and the leading Basque nationalist party—nationalist but nonviolent, founded during the formative phase of Basque nationalism in the late nineteenth century—negotiated an autonomous status for the Basque region, coupled with the restoration of cultural rights (such as use of the Basque language in school and the media) denied for decades. The establishment of institutions of self-rule in the Basque region sharply strengthened the credibility of the new Spanish democracy in the region, helped persuade a slight majority of the region's populace of the compatibility of Spanish and Basque identities, and convinced one faction of the ETA movement to lay down arms and enter the democratic political space of labor unionism and multiparty competition in regional (as well as national) elections.[11] This in turn helped stabilize Spain's transition to democracy and pave the way for the country's accession to the EU in 1986. The decentralization of power from Madrid was originally intended to assuage culturally and historically based movements for autonomy in the Basque region and Catalonia, but devolution was then extended to the rest of Spain. As a result Spain became a moderately decentralized state consisting of 17 regional communities.[12]

However, one stream of the ETA movement rejected the recognition and institutionalizing of cultural specificity and the right to political autonomy of the Basque people in a democratized Spain—including establishment of a Basque parliament, president, police force, educational system, and Basque-language media—as unworthy trivializations of the collective destiny and right to self-determination in an independent homeland of the Basque nation. This strand of Basque nationalism rejects inclusion in and accommodation with any Spanish state and remains tied to a romantic vision of a Basque nation-state comprising the three provinces that constitute the autonomous Basque region of Spain—one adjacent province claimed on historical grounds as "Basque," and three Basque provinces located across the border in France. The violent actions of this radical wing of Basque nationalism enjoy the political support of a highly mobilized minority of up to 15 percent of the Basque region's population. This is sufficient to keep the Basque question alive, especially since the idea of a Basque nation-state enjoys the tacit sympathy of a substantially larger proportion—almost one-half—of the Basque region's population. A strongly entrenched popular culture linked to Basque nationalist radicalism continues to recruit young adherents to the cause. Politics in the Basque region remain polarized between *abertzales* (Basque "patriots") and *espanolistas* (Spain-oriented people, mostly among the large proportion of Basque-region residents who are immigrants from other parts of Spain). A further complication is the linkage-cum-cleavage between moderates (who reluctantly work within the Spanish framework) and maximalists (who demand nation-state status) within the Basque nationalist camp. Tensions within the Basque region and between Basque nationalists and the Spanish central government were exacerbated in 2002 by a controversial decision by the right-of-center government in Madrid to ban ETA's front and affiliate organizations from political activity.

The Basque case in Spain[13] demonstrates the efficacy as well as the limits of democratic approaches to the ethno-national questions of contemporary states. The democratization and decentralization of the Spanish state indisputably mitigated the salience of the Basque problem, but has not eliminated the conflict. Nevertheless, the recognition and validation of cultural diversity and the establishment and operation of institutions of political autonomy within states, complemented by the progressive dilution of rigid interstate borders through the creation of blocs of cooperation between neighboring states, provide the best general road map for democracy and stability in such circumstances.[14] This is the type of approach—adapted of course to the particular context and needs of each situation—that could produce great dividends in Sri Lanka, Kashmir, and Turkey.

Sumantra Bose is associate professor of Comparative Politics at the London School of Economics and Political Science (LSE). His most recent books are Kashmir: Roots of Conflict, Paths to Peace *(Harvard University Press, August 2003), and* Bosnia after Dayton: Nationalist Partition and International Intervention *(Oxford University Press, 2002).*

NOTES

1. On this history, see Sumantra Bose, *Kashmir: Roots of Conflict, Paths to Peace* (Cambridge, MA and London: Harvard University Press, 2003), especially Chapter 2.

2. On the guerrilla war in Indian-controlled Kashmir and the Indian state's response between early 1990 and early 2003 see Bose, *Kashmir*, Chapter 3.

3. See Bose, *Kashmir*, Chapter 5.

4. On Sri Lanka, see Sumantra Bose, *States, Nations, Sovereignty: Sri Lanka, India, and the Tamil Eelam Movement* (New Delhi, Thousand Oaks and London: Sage Publications, 1994).

5. Robert A. Dahl, *Polyarchy: Participation and Opposition* (New Haven: Yale University Press, 1971).

6. Erik Zurcher, *Turkey: A Modern History* (London: IB Tauris, 2000); Metin Heper, *The State Tradition in Turkey* (Beverley: Eothen Press, 1985).

7. William Hale, *Turkish Politics and the Military* (London: Routledge, 1994); Umit Cizre

Sakallioglu, "The Anatomy of the Turkish Military's Political Autonomy," *Comparative Politics* (January 1997), pp. 151-166.

8. Hugh Poulton, *Top Hat, Grey Wolf and Crescent: Turkish Nationalism and the Turkish Republic* (London: Hurst, 1997).

9. David McDowall, *A Modern History of the Kurds* (London: IB Tauris, 2000); Martin van Bruinessen, *Agha, Shaikh and State: The Social and Political Structures of Kurdistan* (London: Zed Books, 1992).

10. For recent research, see Kemal Kirisci and Gareth Winrow, *The Kurdish Question and Turkey* (London: Frank Cass, 1997); Henri Barkey and Graham Fuller, *Turkey's Kurdish Question* (Lanham, MD: Rowman and Littlefield, 1998); and Umit Cizre Sakalloiglu, "Historicizing the Present and Problematizing the Future of the Kurdish Problem," *New Perspectives on Turkey* (Spring 1996), pp. 1-22.

11. Paul Preston, *The Triumph of Democracy in Spain* (London: Routledge, 1990); Goldie Shabad, "After Autonomy," in Stanley Payne (ed.), *The Politics of Democratic Spain* (Chicago: Chicago Council on Foreign Relations, 1986); and Juan Linz and Alfred Stepan, "Political Identities and Electoral Sequences: Spain, the Soviet Union, and Yugoslavia," *Daedalus* (Fall 1992), pp. 121-139.

12. Antoni Monreal, "The New Spanish State Structure," in Michael Burgess (ed.), *Federalism and Federation in Western Europe* (London: Croom Helm, 1986); Audrey Brasloff, "Spain: The State of the Autonomies," in Murray Forsyth (ed.), *Federalism and Nationalism* (Leicester: Leicester University Press, 1989).

13. See Marianne Heiberg, *The Making of the Basque Nation* (Cambridge: Cambridge University Press, 1989); Joseba Zulaika, *Basque Violence: Metaphor and Sacrament* (Reno: University of Nevada Press, 1988); and Goldie Shabad and Francisco Jose Llera Ramo, "Political Violence in a Democratic State: Basque Terrorism in Spain," in Martha Crenshaw (ed.), *Terrorism in Context* (University Park: Pennsylvania State University Press, 1995).

14. For an argument on these lines, see Strobe Talbott, "Self-Determination in an Interdependent World," *Foreign Policy* (Spring 2000), pp. 152-163.

The Future of Democracy in Latin America

Michael Shifter

In Latin America, perhaps more so than in other regions, there remains an acute, gnawing sense of a missed opportunity. After all, the fall of the Berlin Wall coincided not only with the culmination of a vigorous process toward democratic, constitutional government, but also with a growing support for deepening economic ties throughout the Americas. It was during the administration of George Herbert Walker Bush (1988–1992) that the Western Hemisphere experienced a cluster of such promising developments, generating enthusiasm from Santiago, Chile, to Washington, DC. Even Canada, long reluctant to join a divisive hemispheric community steeped in Cold War politics, decided to become a member of the Organization of American States, hoping to ride the region's optimistic wave.

Just over a decade later, those days seem like an entirely different era. President George W. Bush is dealing with a Latin America that differs markedly from the region his father found attractive enough to engage both politically and economically. Every serious survey, study, and journalistic account points to a gloomy, sour mood, a perceptible drop in confidence in political institutions and leaders, and widespread pessimism about Latin America's future. There are, to be sure, sharp variations from country to country, and especially among different subregions. However, there is little question that the specter of political divisiveness once again threatens to overtake and poison a Latin America that not too long ago appeared bound on an inexorable path toward stronger democratic institutions and social peace.

For the most part, the region's political leaders have failed to undertake fundamental reforms of often fossilized governmental institutions needed to address mounting citizen demands and multiple problems. These problems include crime, increasingly drug related, along with rising unemployment, in a general environment of economic decline and social disintegration. The performance of Latin American political parties has been especially disappointing. The lack of any tangible economic and social results derives from the weakness and incapacity of such critical democratic institutions to carry out their most elemental functions.

Of course, viewed in a broader historical perspective—and compared with other regions in the world—Latin America's condition is not altogether gloomy. Expectations of a decade ago may have been unrealistic. In addition, every piece of evidence suggests that the norm of civilian, constitutional government is in fact generally held throughout the region. By many measures, given the enormous strains and pressures the region has been subjected to in recent years, the persistence of democratic rule is quite remarkable and, indeed, something to celebrate. With the note-worthy exception of Cuba, all Latin American governments are democratically elected. However ineffective, discredited, and precarious such governments may be, at least they have legality on their side.

VENEZUELA: MOST EXTREME CASE

Few countries more dramatically illustrate Latin America's sharp decline than Venezuela under the government of President Hugo Chavez. Chavez, freely elected in 1998 and again in 2000, is the product and beneficiary of a traditional political system that was regarded by most Venezuelans as corrupt and unresponsive. Though the Venezuelan president's policies have been erratic and unpredictable, he has been consistent in at least one crucial regard: Chavez, a former paratrooper who attempted a failed military coup in 1992, explicitly rejects "representative democracy" and instead favors something he calls "participatory democracy." Michael Coppedge, a noted political scientist and Venezuela specialist, invokes the term "popular sovereignty." He argues that such a notion is mainly based on and inspired by majoritarian principles, and that it prizes broad social support more than checks and balances or the rule of law. In various hemispheric forums since assuming office in early 1999, Chavez has made his case against the dominant, consensual idea—representative democracy—that particularly marked Latin America in the early 1990s.

To date, the Chavez phenomenon has brought little more than heightened polarization, mistrust, and bitterness to Venezuelan society. Chavez's authoritarian tendencies and relentless assaults on key sectors of civil society—including the media and the church—have further corroded institutions, undermined the government's legitimacy, and raised questions about its capacity to sustain itself. Some of the critical elements that in fact gave rise to the Chavez phenomenon can be found in other Latin American societies as well, and should help warn observers about the real possibility of further democratic regression in the region. Again, the underlying problem is that democratic, constitutional governments—political parties particularly—have failed to deliver results and satisfy mounting citizen demands.

INEQUALITY OF WEALTH: LATIN AMERICA'S ACHILLES' HEEL

The principal problem—an old, familiar issue that is in some respects Latin America's Achilles' heel—is that of poverty and inequality. The data offer little to cheer about. In 2002, Latin America, which according to the World Bank stands out as the most inequitable region in the world, experienced its worst economic performance in two decades. Given a drop in the overall growth rate of more than 1 percent, it should not be surprising that poverty and, particularly, inequality, worsened in most countries as well. Venezuela and Argentina led the way with stunning negative growth rates of 10 and 15 percent, respectively, which helped account for the dramatic political meltdowns in both countries. Unemployment and underemployment rates have grown to reach alarming levels in country after country. Predictably, as fundamental economic and social conditions become more acute, the levels of public disenchantment with constitutional governments increase correspondingly.

In the context of globalization, the problem is substantially compounded. With greater access to information and a growing awareness of the widening gulf that separates the rich from the poor throughout the region, the most excluded and disadvantaged sectors have higher expectations and have exerted increased pressure for what they regard as their rightful share of the national wealth. In addition, the middle class in such countries as Argentina has shrunk considerably. Many formerly in the middle class have joined the ranks of the marginal, and have put pressure on governments to restore their previous economic status. The democratic strains accompanying an old problem—poverty—become exacerbated in a relatively new environment marked by rapid technological changes and spreading information, resulting in what noted political scientist Stanley Hoffman has referred to as "people power."

The growing discontent in Latin America is directed chiefly towards the region's political institutions and political leaders, who command scant public confidence and support. In many, though certainly not all, countries, political parties, charged with representing and aggregating public concerns, are in disarray and are broadly discredited. Marta Lagos, who coordinates the Latinobarometro, an annual public opinion survey that covers 17 Latin American countries, has suggested that the low efficacy of many democratic, constitutional governments in producing satisfactory economic results has begun to effect and weaken their legitimacy. Though democracy continues to be favored over any other political system, the tendency of bad performance, if unabated, could further erode Latin Americans' commitment to representative democracy.

RAMPANT CRIME, ELUSIVE JUSTICE

Added to the long-standing problems of poverty and insecurity is the more recent and increasingly serious issue of common crime throughout much of Latin America. Although politically motivated violence has declined and can now be found only in Colombia and, to a lesser extent, Peru and Mexico, street crime, chiefly in urban centers and much of it fueled by drugs, has increased dramatically over the last decade, according to available data from the Inter-American Development Bank. Spreading criminal activity and insecurity in Argentina—since the return of democracy in the early 1980s, the model country for safety and security in Latin America—has been especially noteworthy and disturbing. The country's violent crime rate has more than doubled in the last six years. Public opinion surveys throughout Latin America consistently point to growing dissatisfaction with governments that have been unable to deal effectively with the problem. Indeed, along with unemployment, crime ranks as a top concern of most of the region's citizens. Rising levels of personal insecurity can, moreover, be directly related to progressively declining levels of interpersonal trust, as revealed in recent polling by the Latinobarometro. Such problems hardly provide fertile ground for the development of democratic political institutions.

High crime levels help underline a major deficiency in many Latin American democracies: weak administration of justice systems. Despite a broad commitment to the rule of law and public consensus that meaningful judicial reform is essential for democratic progress and economic development, there is little evidence of any major advance in this critical area. To be sure, multilateral developmental organizations such as the World Bank and Inter-American Development Bank have undertaken judicial reform efforts in many countries, and some judiciaries are clearly more efficient as a result. In addition, ombudsman offices, built on the European model, have been set up over the last decade in a dozen Latin American countries to monitor adherence to the rule of law.

However, many reliable accounts assert that judiciaries in most countries generally remain unresponsive, corrupt, and in some cases quite politicized. For democratic governments that not long ago appeared on the verge of consolidation, impunity continues to be unacceptably high. Indeed, in a region that has seen the gradual fading of sharp, ideological schisms, profound defects in the administration of justice constitute Latin America's most serious human rights challenge.

Once again, the case of Venezuela is instructive. It is precisely there where decayed political institutions have been particularly unable to deal with the multiple problems of economic decline, social disintegration, and a deepening lack of security, which have come together in most dramatic fashion. As a measure of the country's stunning deterioration, it is useful to recall that as late as 1979 Venezuela's per capita income was at the same level as Spain's. In 2002, Venezuela's was less than half that of Spain's. It is difficult to imagine that under such dire conditions, Venezuela's democratic development—quite impressive by historical and Latin American standards—could be even remotely robust.

ECUADOR: RISK OF MILITARY IN POLITICS

While Venezuela may be an extreme situation, other countries, particularly in the Andean region, exhibit some comparable features. Like Chavez, Lucio Gutierrez, Ecuador's democratically elected president, is a former military officer who, in January 2000, helped lead a coup against a constitutional government. (In this case, Gutierrez succeeded, although the coup was short lived.) Gutierrez, too, is an outsider who expresses the thoroughgoing rejection of Ecuador's traditional political order that has, for many years, failed to deliver any tangible results to most of the country's citizens. Unemployment has gone up, and crime has worsened. The country's justice system is widely regarded as corrupt and lacking in accountability.

Most strikingly in the case of Ecuador is the country's fragmented political party system, arguably the most fragmented in all of Latin America. This feature, together with notoriously sharp geographic and ethnic divisions, makes effective governing exceedingly difficult. As evidence, Ecuador's politics have been unusually unsettled: Gutierrez is the country's fifth president in six years. If Gutierrez does not succeed, there is a risk of even further divisiveness, which could have wider implications in an already uncertain region. In addition, the fact that he is an untested political leader—with scant support in congress—means that forging alliances to pursue a wide-ranging reform agenda will be tougher than usual.

Gutierrez is not only a political neophyte, but a former military official as well. Indeed, both the Venezuela and Ecuador cases raise the crucial question, central to the wider vision and goal of democratic consolidation in Latin America, of the military's role in politics. Given the vacuum left by political parties and other institutions that are breaking apart and the urgent problems that require immediate attention, there is a temptation to assign to the military those roles that previously, and properly, were assumed by civilians. In the case of Venezuela there are troubling signs of such a shift, or at least of Chavez's intention to have the military supplant political institutions. To what extent this will take place in Ecuador remains to be seen. Thus, while it is possible to celebrate the declining political influence of the military in some Central American countries, and others (like Argentina and Brazil) in South America, in parts of the Andean region the trend is considerably less positive.

PERU: OPPORTUNITY FOR REFORM?

Peru also illustrates many of the complex issues related to the challenge of building enduring democracies in Latin America. As a forerunner to what was later to take place in Venezuela, Peru's traditional political parties, unable to address the country's deep problems of political violence and economic disorder, practically imploded in the late 1980s. The result was the stunning election of the political novice Alberto Fujimori, who governed Peru for a decade. Particularly following his April 1992 "self-coup," Fujimori installed an authoritarian regime in Peru, relying on the country's military and intelligence services as key pillars of support. He also controlled and manipulated the media, the judiciary, and electoral bodies. Fujimori, the ultimate expression in Latin America of "anti-politics," presided over unprecedented levels of corruption, reportedly linked to his national security chief, Vladimiro Montesinos.

With the collapse of the Fujimori regime in November 2000, Peru embarked on the difficult and complicated course of democratic transition. After a highly successful and productive caretaker government, Peruvians turned to another political novice and outsider, Alejandro Toledo, to lead their country. Although the Toledo government has made considerable progress in pursuing the corruption that dominated the Fujimori period, and in reviving democratic institutions, some of the fundamental problems that brought Fujimori to power in 1990 remain unresolved. Peru's political parties—including Toledo's, Peru Possible—are weak and lack a solid organization and coherent programmatic agenda. Chief concerns for many Peruvians are acute social conditions, especially the lack of jobs. A relatively sound macroeconomic picture is not enough. Protests will continue, even increase, unless critical social needs are addressed. Toledo's precipitous drop in public support in his first year in office, from nearly 70 to less than 20 percent, reflected unfulfilled promises and lack of political leadership.

Moreover, although Peru has a free press and greater checks and balances than existed under the Fujimori regime, the country's administration of justice continues to have serious problems. Poverty is widespread and social divisions are deep, which tends to leave the vast bulk of citizens without access to a viable justice system. The end of authoritarian rule and the turn to constitutional, democratic government may be a precondition for building an effective judicial system, but formidable obstacles remain.

COLOMBIA: CAN URIBE TURN THE TIDE?

As the only Latin American country in the midst of a civil conflict, Colombia has the most critical human rights situation in the hemisphere. The data are alarming: more than half of the world's kidnappings, roughly 3,000, take place in Colombia. More than 3,500 Colombians are killed each year as a result of the civil conflict. The country has the third-largest internally displaced population in the world—some figures are as high as two million—after Sudan and Angola. A historically weak government, without substantial control of large swaths of territory, has struggled to contend with heavily armed and well-financed actors. The three main groups—the leftist FARC (Revolutionary Armed Forces of Colombia), the ELN (National Liberation

Army), and the paramilitary umbrella organization AUC (United Self-Defense Forces of Colombia)—rely substantially on criminal activities, including the drug trade, extortion, and kidnapping, to sustain their operations. The spreading drug problem, which dates from the 1980s, has contributed substantially to the pervasive corruption of Colombia's institutions, both public and private. This has led to a sharp drop in public confidence in the country's political parties and leaders, thereby undermining democratic prospects.

At the same time, however, Colombia is a paradox. Despite being a human rights and humanitarian disaster, Colombia blends both negative, troubling features with some noteworthy democratic assets. The country can, after all, point to an impressive democratic tradition, as shown by having had just four years of military rule in the twentieth century. In addition, elections in Colombia are prized, and regularly practiced, despite remarkable levels of violence and great risks. Moreover, the country has political experience in responding to severe crises, forging agreements among contending forces, and reaching a consensus on a shared agenda for the future.

There are some signs that the government led by Alvaro Uribe, which began in August 2002, is undertaking a series of measures to help restore legitimate authority and bring a greater degree of democratic governance to Colombia. Uribe appears committed to serious reforms of the country's governmental institutions. His focus on "democratic security" aims to improve the capacity of the security forces to better protect Colombian citizens, and to do so in accordance with human rights norms and the rule of law. To be sure, some of the Uribe government's measures are highly risky and controversial, and raise important concerns about the possible erosion of civil liberties in Colombia. However, in the absence of government action and more forceful measures, the security situation was gradually deteriorating, making democratic safeguards very problematic. All available options carry substantial risks. If President Uribe, who enjoys widespread support in Colombia, can turn around the country's conditions of lawlessness—and do so without sacrificing human rights— he might be able to lay the foundation for a more genuine, high-quality democracy. That goal will call for thoroughgoing social reform, a more responsive and effective judicial system, and the renovation of an array of political institutions, including parties.

OPENINGS AND NEW VOICES IN LATIN AMERICA'S POLITICS

Indeed, the Colombian case, as well as the situation in a number of other Latin American countries, suggests evidence of progress in extending democracy and the potential for accomplishing considerably more. A number of Latin American countries have adopted new constitutions that seek to include representation of ethnic minorities and women. (Colombia's 1991 constitution, for example, designated one Chamber and two Senate seats for representatives of indigenous communities and two Chamber seats for Afro-Colombians.) Indeed, the trend of Latin American constitutions and legislation has recently been positive in extending rights to, and providing for greater political participation on the part of, previously excluded groups. In Guatemala and Bolivia, the indigenous groups have notably raised their profile and visibility and expanded their participation in the political process. The highly mobilized and politically powerful indigenous confederation called CONAI was originally one of the main pillars that backed the Gutierrez government in Ecuador. There are, moreover, encouraging indications that African-Latin Americans, who make up a sizable share—nearly 30 percent—of the region's population and who generally lack a voice in their country's democratic politics, are beginning to organize more actively to claim their rights. In addition, through quota laws, a variety of other legislative measures, and more sustained political work, women are also occupying more important political positions in many countries, which adds substantially to the quality of representation and to democracy generally.

To be sure, progress in improving political representation and opening up the political system has been slow, uneven, and often enormously difficult. Considerable resistance by traditional political sectors remains, and in some places there has been a backlash against the gains that have been made. Fragile political institutions, moreover, are under great stress and typically struggle to handle and respond to the increased demands and ever-higher expectations of newly mobilized groups. However, overall, the trend in this fundamental respect appears unmistakable, and irreversible.

Democracy has been extended not only to new groups and sectors of society, but also from the national to the state and local levels. In such countries as Colombia, Peru, Venezuela, and Bolivia, reforms over the past 10 to 15 years have led to greater decentralization of political authority and the direct election (previously they were appointed) of local officials. The multilateral banks have also largely supported this trend. In fact, democracy at the local level often appears more vibrant and promising than at the national level. At the same time, however, there is a tradeoff involved in pursuing such reforms. Decentralization can, under some conditions, contribute further to the fragmentation of political parties, since it tends to encourage independents and candidates from smaller parties. Moreover, as in the case of Colombia and to some extent Argentina, devolving control can add to fiscal imbalances, which can in turn produce serious strains and pressures on the national budget and finances.

BRAZIL AND MEXICO: PROMISE OF DEMOCRATIC RENEWAL

Yet, in considering Latin America's highly variegated and often sobering political landscape, it is instructive to examine the region's two major countries: Brazil and Mexico. Though both present formidable challenges and disturbing problems, they are—particularly when viewed with a longer-term historical perspective—moving in a positive direction, toward greater democracy.

In Brazil, Fernando Henrique Cardoso presided over eight years of democratic stability and a general respect for political institutions—surely, no mean achievement in light of the country's politically troubled history. The government of Luiz Inacio Lula da Silva promises to extend this stretch and bring greater continuity on the democratic front. Lula's principal challenge is to attempt to advance Brazil's social agenda, especially to reduce the country's glaring disparities in wealth. This has long been Brazil's most intractable problem and a significant obstacle to further democratic progress. In addition, Brazil continues to experience high levels of social violence and crime, much of it fueled by the drug trade and concentrated in major urban centers such as Sao Paulo and Rio de Janeiro. The judicial system is highly deficient and seldom offers meaningful human rights protections to marginalized groups. Full adherence to the rule of law remains a major challenge for future Brazilian governments.

Yet, Lula differs from many of the other leaders who have recently emerged on Latin America's political stage. His democratic credentials are impeccable, and initial signs point to a commitment to real reform. What particularly sets him apart is his long-standing dedication to building the Workers' Party (PT), widely regarded not only as the most solid and coherent political party in Brazil, but as among the most effective parties in Latin America. Lula's two-decade project, born under a Brazilian dictatorship that began in the 1960s and came to an end only in 1985, is especially noteworthy in a region where political parties are in deep crisis, broadly discredited, and perceived as ossified and corrupt.

Although the PT has yet to be tested at the national level, it has had ample, and for the most part successful, governing experience at the state and especially municipal levels in Brazil. The PT is a far cry from the amorphous movements and inchoate groupings that often pose as political parties in other Latin American countries.

Mexico, too, represents a sea change in terms of its democratic politics. The country that the Peruvian novelist Mario Vargas Llosa not long ago characterized as the "perfect dictatorship" has evolved from more than seven decades of single-party authoritarian rule into a more competitive, open system since Vicente Fox became president in December 2000. Mexico's political life, reflected in its vigorous press, which features spirited debates, is unusually dynamic. Fox has escaped the many serious charges of corruption that have been leveled against the previous Institutional Revolutionary Party (PRI) administrations. Still, questions have been raised about Fox's political skills, especially his ability to deal with a PRI-dominated congress and to instill in the government the necessary discipline to achieve his main policy aims. Moreover, endemic problems of social injustice, exacerbated by considerable drug-fueled violence, continue to plague Mexico and pose important obstacles to democratic progress.

CONCLUSION: THE NEED FOR EFFECTIVE LEADERSHIP

The urgent need for new political leadership in Latin America that is both effective and honest can be seen clearly in the case of Argentina. The country suffered a financial and political meltdown in December 2001 that resulted in the collapse of the government of Fernando de la Rua. There is an unprecedented problem of wholesale rejection of traditional political parties and leaders, reflected in plummeting levels of confidence in survey after survey. Yet, it is reassuring that despite such a severe crisis and widespread questioning of political institutions, no one has seriously called for a return to military rule. Argentines still recall the nightmarish period of the late 1970s and early 1980s. They, like most Latin Americans, are committed to playing the democratic game, and they resist alternative political systems. They just want better results.

Such political learning and evolution is similarly evident at the regional level where, despite so many unexpectedly great problems and such general disappointment, there is an appreciable shift in norms and attitudes. Democratic practices and institutions, however flawed, are now expected to be part of all Latin American societies. In fact, in September 2001, in Lima, Peru, all of the relevant declarations and resolutions in the Organization of American States along these lines were codified in an Inter-American Democratic Charter, signed by all member governments.

Ironically, the democratic government that expressed most reservations about the charter was its first beneficiary. Once again, the Venezuela case illustrates a critical point. The coup mounted against the Chavez government in April 2002 activated the charter for the first time, which called for a hemispheric response to a potential escalation of violence. As a result, the Organization of American States, together with the Carter Center and the United Nations Development Program, set up a tripartite instrument to seek a resolution of the impasse between the Venezuelan government and opposition. In January 2003, a "Group of Friends" vehicle was also formed, reflecting broader concern about the continued political deterioration and social polarization in Venezuela. The key question is whether the external actors involved are prepared to translate the positive normative change at the regional level into sufficient effort, imagination, and backbone, and apply pressure on both parties to reach a reasonable compromise and thus help avoid an escalation of violence.

There is a real risk that the continued degeneration of the Venezuelan crisis could make the region's politics even more divisive. In country after country, as Latin Americans grope for solutions to worsening problems, there is an insistent public demand for honest political leaders who are prepared to seriously tackle their countries' reform agendas, deal more effectively with multiple pressures, and deliver concrete results. In the current context, Brazil's Lula and Colombia's Uribe offer some promise. They appear particularly committed to reforming key institutions and making them better-equipped to address their societies' fundamental concerns. It is important that such leaders succeed in their efforts. If not, Latin America could well experience greater setbacks, which would be particularly regrettable in view of the many impressive strides that have recently been made in the region—and the sanguine outlook for democratic progress a mere decade ago.

Michael Shifter is vice president for policy at the Inter-American Dialogue, a forum on Western Hemisphere affairs. He is also adjunct professor of Latin American Studies at Georgetown University's School of Foreign Service.

Introduction to Country and Related Territory Reports

The *Freedom in the World 2003* survey contains reports on 192 countries and 18 related and disputed territories. Each country report begins with a section containing basic political, economic, and social data arranged in the following categories: **polity, economy, population, purchasing power parities (PPP), life expectancy, religious groups, ethnic groups, capital, political rights** [numerical rating], **civil liberties** [numerical rating], and **status** [Free, Partly Free, or Not Free]. Each territory report begins with a section containing the same data, except for PPP and life expectancy figures.

The **polity** category contains an encapsulated description of the dominant centers of freely chosen or unelected political power in each country or territory. The following polity descriptions were used in this year's survey: *presidential*—the president enjoys predominant power beyond ceremonial functions, while the legislature, if there is one, enjoys limited or no independence from the executive; *parliamentary*—the government (i.e., prime minister, cabinet) is approved by the legislature, and the head of state, if there is one, enjoys a largely ceremonial role; *presidential-parliamentary*—the president enjoys predominant power beyond ceremonial functions, and the government is approved by the legislature; *traditional chiefs*—traditional chiefs wield significant political power; *traditional monarchy*—the country's monarch enjoys predominant power through hereditary rule (as opposed to a constitutional monarchy); *principality*—the country's monarch is a prince who may enjoy either predominant power or a largely ceremonial role (constitutional monarchy); *dominant party*—the ruling mass-based party or front dominates the government, while allowing other parties to organize and compete short of taking control of the government; *one party*—absolute rule is enjoyed by the one legal party in the country; *military*—the military enjoys predominant power, despite the possible existence of a head of state or legislature; *international protectorate* – an international governing body, such as the United Nations, administers the country. In addition, the term "democracy" may be added to those polities in which the most recent national elections met minimum standards for free and fair elections as judged by international observers.

Polities may be modified by one or more of the following descriptions: insurgency, military-dominated, military-influenced, clergy-dominated, dominant party, federal, transitional, post-conflict. While the preceding list of polities may be applied to most countries, exceptions do occur. In those rare cases where the polities listed above do not adequately reflect the current situation in a particular country, other polity descriptions have been used.

The reports contain a brief description of the **economy** of each country or territory. Non-industrial economies are called *traditional* or *pre-industrial*. Developed market economies and developing countries with a modern market sector have the designation *capitalist*. *Mixed capitalist* countries combine predominantly private enterprise with substantial governmental involvement in the economy for social welfare purposes. *Capitalist-statist* economies have both large market sectors and government-owned productive enterprises. *Mixed capitalist-statist* economies have the characteristics of capitalist-statist economies, as well as major social welfare programs. *Statist* economies place virtually the entire economy under direct or indirect governmental control. *Mixed statist* economies are primarily government-controlled, but also have some private enterprise. Economies in transition between statist and capitalist forms may have the word "transitional" included in their economy description.

The **population** and **life expectancy** figures were obtained from the *2002 World Population Data Sheet* of the Population Reference Bureau. Population figures for territories were obtained from sources including *The World Almanac and Book of Facts 2003*, the CIA *World Factbook 2002*, the World Gazetteer, and the Unrepresented Nations and Peoples Organization (UNPO).

The **purchasing power parities (PPP)** show per capita gross domestic product (GDP) in terms of international dollars in order to account for real buying power. These figures were obtained from the *2002 United Nations Development Program Human Development Report*. For some countries, especially tiny island nations, this information was not available.

Data on **religious groups** was obtained primarily from the 2002 U.S. State Department International Religious Freedom Reports, *The World Almanac and Book of Facts 2003*, and the CIA *World Factbook 2002*.

Information about the **ethnic groups** in a country or territory is provided in order to assist with the understanding of certain issues, including minority rights, addressed by the survey. The primary sources used to obtain this information were *The World Almanac and Book of Facts 2003* and the CIA *World Factbook 2002*.

The **political rights** and **civil liberties** categories contain numerical ratings between 1 and 7 for each country or territory rated, with 1 representing the most free and 7 the least free. The **status** designation of Free, Partly Free, or Not Free, which is determined by the combination of the political rights and civil liberties ratings, indicates the general state of freedom in a country or territory. The ratings of countries or territories which have improved or declined since the previous survey are indicated by asterisks next to the ratings. Positive or negative trends which do not warrant a ratings change since the previous year may be indicated by upward or downward trend arrows, which are located next to the name of the country or territory. A brief explanation of ratings changes or trend arrows is provided for each country or territory as required. For a full description of the methods used to determine the survey's ratings, please see the chapter on the survey's methodology.

Following the section on political, economic, and social data, each country report is divided into two parts: an **overview** and an analysis of **political rights and civil liberties**. The overview provides a brief historical background and a description of major recent events. The political rights and civil liberties section summarizes each country or territory's degree of respect for the rights and liberties which Freedom House uses to evaluate freedom in the world.

The related and disputed territory reports follow the country reports. In most cases, they are comparatively more brief than the country essays.

Afghanistan

Polity: Transitional   **Political Rights:** 6*
Economy: Mixed statist   **Civil Liberties:** 6*
Population: 27,800,000   **Status:** Not Free
PPP: na
Life Expectancy: 45
Religious Groups: Sunni Muslim (84 percent),
Shi'a Muslim (15 percent), other (1 percent)
Ethnic Groups: Pashtun (44 percent), Tajik (25 percent),
Hazara (10 percent), Uzbek (8 percent), other (13 percent)
Capital: Kabul
Ratings Change: Afghanistan's political rights rating improved from 7 to 6 due to
the holding of the Loya Jirga and the establishment of the Transitional Authority in
June. Its civil liberties rating improved from 7 to 6 due to increased personal free-
doms in some areas of the country.

Ten-Year Ratings Timeline (Political Rights, Civil Liberties, Status)

1993	1994	1995	1996	1997	1998	1999	2000	2001	2002	2003
6,6NF	7,7NF	7,7NF	7,7NF	7,7NF	7,7NF	7,7NF	7,7NF	7,7NF	7,7NF	6,6NF

Overview: After decades of violence, Afghanistan faced its first real
hope for peace following the military defeat of the ultraconservative Taliban movement and the installation of an in-
terim government in December 2001. Although Afghanistan's prospects continued
to improve in 2002, the war-ravaged country remained wracked by severe food shortages, drought, and some armed conflict. President Hamid Karzai's Transitional Authority struggled to improve security outside of the capital and to curb the power of
the regional warlords, while the slow disbursement of foreign aid hampered reconstruction efforts. Improvements in human rights, particularly in the areas of media
freedom and personal autonomy, were tempered by reports of continuing violations
of women's rights, violence against ethnic minorities, and serious security problems.

Located at the crossroads of the Middle East, Central Asia, and the Indian subcontinent, Afghanistan has for centuries been caught in the middle of great power
and regional rivalries. After besting Russia in a contest for influence in Afghanistan, Britain recognized the country as an independent monarchy in 1921. King Zahir
Shah ruled from 1933 until he was deposed in a 1973 coup. Afghanistan has been in
continuous civil conflict since 1978, when a Communist coup set out to transform
this highly traditional society. The Soviet Union invaded in 1979, but faced fierce
resistance from U.S.-backed *mujahideen* (guerrilla fighters) until troops finally withdrew in 1989.

The mujahideen factions overthrew the Communist government in 1992 and then
battled each other for control of Kabul, killing more than 25,000 civilians in the capital by 1995. Consisting largely of students in Islamic schools, the Taliban militia
entered the fray and seized control of Kabul in 1996. Defeating or buying off
mujahideen commanders, the Taliban soon controlled most of the country except
for parts of northern and central Afghanistan, which remained in the hands of the

Tajik-dominated Northern Alliance coalition. Pakistan and Saudi Arabia were the Taliban's main supporters, while Iran, Russia, India, and Central Asian states backed the Northern Alliance.

Following the terrorist attacks of September 11, 2001, the United States launched a military campaign in October 2001 aimed at toppling the Taliban regime and eliminating Saudi militant Osama bin Laden's terrorist network, al-Qaeda. Simultaneously, Northern Alliance forces engaged the Taliban from the areas under their control. The Taliban crumbled quickly throughout the country, losing Kabul to Northern Alliance forces in November and surrendering the southern city of Kandahar, the movement's spiritual headquarters, in December.

As a result of the Bonn Agreement of December 2001, a broad-based, interim administration, which enjoyed the nominal support of Afghanistan's provincial governors, took office. It was led by Pashtun tribal leader Hamid Karzai. The UN-brokered deal that put Karzai in office sought to balance demands for power by victorious Tajik, Uzbek, and Hazara military commanders with the reality that many Pashtuns, who are Afghanistan's largest ethnic group, would not trust a government headed by ethnic minorities. Karzai named 18 Northern Alliance officials to his 30-member cabinet, including military leader Mohammad Fahim as defense minister. The International Security Assistance Force (ISAF) began patrolling Kabul in December 2001, but security outside the capital remained tenuous in 2002. Throughout the rugged countryside, military commanders, tribal leaders, rogue warlords, and petty bandits continued to hold sway. Bolstered by arms, money, and political support from the United States and neighboring governments, many warlords maintained private armies and refused to obey the writ of the central administration. Cities were affected by a number of bombings, rocket attacks, and other sporadic violence by suspected Taliban sympathizers throughout the year. Two government ministers were assassinated, and Karzai himself survived an attempt on his life in September.

In June 2002, the formerly exiled King Zahir Shah convened a *loya jirga*, or traditional council of tribal elders and other notables, which appointed a Transitional Authority to rule Afghanistan for a further 18 to 24 months. Karzai won more than 80 percent of the delegates' votes to become president, decisively defeating two other candidates, including one woman. The Tajik-dominated Northern Alliance filled half of the cabinet positions, while the remainder were given to Pashtuns and representatives of other ethnic groups. In an attempt to curb the power of the regional warlords, President Karzai signed a decree in December banning political leaders from taking part in military activity.

Political Rights and Civil Liberties: With the fall of the Taliban, residents of Kabul and most other cities were able to go about their daily lives with fewer social and religious restrictions, and were less likely to be subject to harassment from the authorities. However, the political rights and civil liberties of all Afghans remained severely circumscribed in 2002.

The interim administration appointed in December 2001 functioned as a central government, but its authority over areas outside Kabul remained limited. The loya jirga convened in June was charged with choosing a head of state and key ministers for the Transitional Authority, which was mandated to rule for up to 24 months while a new constitution was drawn up and elections scheduled for 2004 were organized. The majority of the delegates to the loya jirga were selected through a two-stage electoral process, but places were also reserved for women and refugees. While the United Nations declared that the delegates represented every region, ethnic group, educational level, and occupation, human rights groups charged that the delegate selection process was characterized by "widespread and systematic" manipulation and intimidation from local military commanders.

The loya jirga itself was marred by complaints of behind-the-scenes deals involving warlords, the United States, and the UN, which were said to have subverted the voting process. In addition, many delegates complained of threats by warlords and Islamic fundamentalists during the convening of the loya jirga, and about 70 walked out of the gathering to protest their lack of a free vote. While the vote on Karzai's presidency was held by secret ballot, later votes on the arrangement of the government and its key personnel were "highly irregular," according to a statement issued by Human Rights Watch.

Conditions for Afghanistan's media improved markedly in 2002. A new Press Law, adopted in February, guaranteed the right to press freedom. Authorities have granted more than 100 licenses to independent publications, although some regional warlords have refused to allow independent media in the areas under their control. Journalists in Kabul reported several instances of threats and harassment at the hands of authorities, according to the *Index on Censorship*. Many practice self-censorship or avoid writing about sensitive issues such as Islam, national unity, or crimes committed by the warlords. Television broadcasts were restored in January after a total ban under the Taliban. However, in August, officials in Kabul banned the airing of Indian films on TV and ruled that radio must not broadcast women singing.

For Muslim Afghans, the end of Taliban rule meant that they were no longer forced to adopt the movement's ultraconservative Islamic practices. Taliban militants required men to maintain beards of sufficient length, cover their heads, and pray five times daily, while women were subject to rigid strictures regarding appropriate dress and appearance in public. The minority Shia population has traditionally faced discrimination from the Sunni majority. While the new administration attempted to pursue a policy of greater religious tolerance, it remained subject to pressure from Islamic fundamentalist groups.

The Taliban's downfall meant that Afghans were generally able to speak more freely and openly in many areas of the country. They also were able to enjoy routine leisure activities banned by the Taliban, including listening to music, watching movies and television, and flying kites. Rights to assembly, association, and free speech were formally restored, but were applied erratically in different regions. For example, a Human Rights Watch report issued in November detailed numerous violations of these rights in the province of Herat. In November, after protests at Kabul University over poor living conditions, police forces fired on a peaceful student march, killing three students and wounding more than 20. According to Human Rights Watch, police also beat students at the university dormitory and threatened injured students at the hospital.

Throughout Afghanistan, new rulers faced the question of whether to bring to justice, take revenge on, or simply to ignore perpetrators of past abuses. During their rule, the Taliban detained and tortured thousands of Tajiks, Hazaras, and members of other ethnic minorities, some of whom were killed or disappeared. In October, mass graves, thought to contain the remains of ethnic Hazaras killed by the Taliban, were uncovered in northern Afghanistan. Meanwhile, Northern Alliance commanders were criticized for the deaths of up to 1,000 Taliban soldiers captured during fighting in the fall of 2001.

Dealing with past abuses as well as protecting basic rights is particularly difficult in a country where courts are rudimentary and judges are easily pressured by those who enter the courtroom with guns. The Karzai administration intends to create an independent judiciary that would uphold *Sharia* (Islamic law), but progress on legal reform and training for judges remained slow. The Bonn Agreement established a national Human Rights Commission to monitor and investigate human rights conditions, but it does not yet have sufficient resources to effectively carry out its mandate. In some provinces, local warlords sanctioned widespread abuses by the police, military, and intelligence forces under their command, including politically motivated arrests, torture, and extortion.

Although the Bonn Agreement recognized the need to create a national army and a professional police force, little progress was made on unifying Afghanistan's various armed factions in 2002. Training programs for soldiers and police have thus far been limited to Kabul, and no credible demobilization or disarmament efforts were undertaken. Continuing rivalries between various warlords resulted in localized fighting that has killed dozens of civilians and displaced thousands from their homes. In northern Afghanistan, aid workers as well as ethnic Pashtuns were targets of the violence. The reluctance of the international community to expand the International Security Assistance Force (ISAF) has meant that the security situation in much of the country remains extremely poor.

The end of Taliban rule freed women in Kabul and most other cities from harsh restrictions and punishments that had kept them veiled, isolated, and, in many cases, impoverished. Women's formal rights to education and employment were restored, and they were once again able to participate in public life. In a move long on symbolism, Karzai named two women to his interim cabinet in December 2001. Nearly 200 women participated in the loya jirga in June, and Sima Samar was elected as its deputy chairman, although she and other female delegates were subjected to threats from other participants. As a result of continued lawlessness and inter-ethnic clashes, women continued to be subject to sexual violence. The *Christian Science Monitor* reported in August that since the Taliban's fall, dozens of women had attempted self-immolation to escape family problems or unwanted marriages. In certain areas, ruling warlords continued to impose Taliban-style behavioral restrictions on women. A report issued in December by Human Rights Watch detailed the increasing strictures imposed on women by Ismail Khan's administration in Herat, which include mandatory usage of the *burqa*, or head-to-toe covering; a ban on traveling with unrelated men; and gynecological examinations for women suspected of immodest behavior. While many children returned to school in 2002, a number of girls' schools were subject to arson and rocket attacks from Islamic fundamentalists during the year.

Hundreds of thousands of Afghan refugees returned to their homes during 2002, but at year's end as many as one million civilians remained displaced within the country, including up to 120,000 Pashtuns who had fled violence and ethnic discrimination in the north. By November, an estimated 1.7 million refugees had returned to Afghanistan from Pakistan, Iran and other countries, according to the UN High Commissioner for Refugees (UNHCR). However, well over one million refugees remain in both Pakistan and Iran. Humanitarian agencies and Afghan authorities were ill-equipped to deal with the unexpected scale of the repatriation, while the poor security situation meant that many refugees were unable to return to their homes and instead congregated in and around major urban centers. In June, the UNHCR suspended returning refugees to parts of northern Afghanistan because of the continued fighting between different ethnic factions.

Albania

Polity: Presidential-parliamentary democracy
Economy: Capitalist-statist
Population: 3,100,000
PPP: $3,506
Life Expectancy: 74
Religious Groups: Muslim (70 percent), Albanian Orthodox (20 percent), Roman Catholic (10 percent)
Ethnic Groups: Albanian (95 percent), Greek (3 percent), other (2 percent)
Capital: Tirana

Political Rights: 3
Civil Liberties: 3*
Status: Partly Free

Ratings Change: Albania's civil liberties rating improved from 4 to 3 due to continuing normalization after the civil unrest and violence of 1997.

Ten-Year Ratings Timeline (Political Rights, Civil Liberties, Status)

1993	1994	1995	1996	1997	1998	1999	2000	2001	2002	2003
4,3PF	2,4PF	3,4PF	3,4PF	4,4PF	4,4PF	4,5PF	4,5PF	4,5PF	3,4PF	3,3PF

Overview:

Albania experienced some political turmoil in 2002, going through three prime ministers during the course of the year, as well as switching presidents. On the more positive side, in June the Union for Victory parliamentary coalition, led by former president Dr. Sali Berisha's Democratic Party (DP), ended its boycott of parliament, bringing the legislature to its full complement, and Albanian political leaders were finally able to agree on a compromise candidate to become the country's new president.

From World War II until 1990, former dictator Enver Hoxha's xenophobic Communist regime turned Albania into the most isolated country in Europe. In 1990, however, the Communist regime collapsed, and in March 1992, multiparty elections brought the DP, led by Dr. Berisha, to power. Continuing poverty and corruption, however, weakened Berisha's government, and in 1997 the collapse of several pyramid investment schemes caused much of Albania's population to lose their life savings and nearly resulted in civil war.

In the years since the unrest of 1997, during which Albania has been ruled by the Socialist Party (SP), the central government in Tirana has been unable to reimpose meaningful control over much of Berisha's stronghold in northern Albania. Although a number of small parties run in elections, the most important political organizations are the DP and the SP. The differences between them, however, are more a matter of the personalities leading the parties than of serious programmatic or ideological approaches.

Albania's first parliamentary elections since 1997 were held over four rounds between June and August 2001. Although international monitoring groups admitted that there were "serious flaws" in the election process, the polls were nevertheless deemed valid. Socialists now hold 73 out of 140 seats in parliament, as against 46 by the opposition, the DP-led Union for Victory coalition. Berisha's DP announced a boycott of parliament in protest against electoral irregularities, and did not return to parliament until January 2002.

Albania's political scene remains turbulent, which was shown by the considerable political reshufflings that took place during the course of 2002. Prime Minister Ilir Meta was forced to resign in January and was replaced by former prime minister Pandeli Majko. In July, however, Majko himself was replaced by the leader of the SP, Fatos Nano. In June, a potential political crisis looming over the country since September 2001 was finally resolved when the DP and the SP agreed on a new president for the country, retired general Alfred Moisiu.

The country's dismal economic situation showed little improvement in 2002, with official unemployment figures averaging 14.4 percent and an estimated one out of every three Albanians living below the poverty line. Although Albania was invited to open negotiations with the EU on a Stabilization and Association Agreement in October, realistic analyses of the country's situation suggested that it has far to go join European integration efforts.

Political Rights and Civil Liberties:

The Albanian constitution guarantees citizens freedom of association, freedom of movement, freedom of the press, and freedom of expression. On the whole these rights are respected, but significant problems remain. Several political parties exist and compete for power, and the country likewise has several active trade unions and independent nongovernmental organizations (NGOs). There were no significant reports of governmental harassment of either foreign or domestic NGOs in 2002. Academic freedom, however, is considered limited. There are no reported political prisoners in the country.

The Albanian constitution provides for an independent judiciary. Overall, however, the judiciary (along with law enforcement agencies) remains inefficient and prone to corruption, and judges are often inexperienced and untrained. The combination of a weak economy and the growth of powerful organized crime syndicates makes judges susceptible to bribery and intimidation. In June, the government drafted what observers hailed as an important piece of legislation to combat official corruption—a new bill setting up an oversight committee in parliament to investigate the property holdings of some 5000 mid- and high-level government officials. A recent survey by United States Agency for International Development (USAID) found Albania to be the most corrupt country of any in the region, and a World Bank study released in 2002 claimed that Albania provided "a startling picture of systemic corruption . . . [that] is deeply institutionalized."

The Albanian constitution provides for freedom of religion and religious practice, and on the whole Albania has not been the victim of the interreligious tensions typical of its neighbors. Albanian Orthodox Church officials complained about provocations and vandalism of church property directed towards their congregations in 2002, but they attributed the incidents to weak state authority more than to religious persecution. There have also been reports of a rise in interreligious tensions (involving Roman Catholics and Muslims) in northern Albania. Albania's small Greek Orthodox minority (approximately 3 percent of the population, concentrated in southern Albania) has intermittently been subjected to various forms of discrimination. The restitution of church properties confiscated during the Communist period remains unresolved.

Freedom of the press has shown marked improvement since the fall of communism, but considerable harassment of journalists persists. A report issued in 2002 stated that journalists in Albania risk harassment, physical assault, and criminal charges for defamation if they report critically on public officials or the police.

The Albanian constitution places no legal impediments to women's role in politics and society, although women are vastly underrepresented in most governmental institutions. The Albanian labor code mandates that women are entitled to equal pay for equal work, but data are lacking on whether this is respected in practice. Traditional patriarchal social mores, moreover, pose significant problems for the position of women in Albania. Many segments of Albanian society, particularly in northern Albania, still abide by a medieval moral code according to which women are considered chattel property and may be treated as such.

The trafficking of women and girls remains a significant problem; according to some estimates, up to 30,000 Albanian women (a figure representing almost one percent of the population) are working as prostitutes in Western Europe. Nevertheless, in June the U.S. State Department promoted Albania to "tier-two" status, implying that the country had made sufficient efforts to combat trafficking in humans to bring itself into compliance with international standards, although the U.S. government has threatened to impose sanctions on Albania if trafficking persists at current levels.

Widespread lawlessness plagues large parts of Albania, especially its mountainous north. Weak state institutions have increased the power of international criminal syndicates, and international law enforcement officials claim that Albania has become an increasingly important transshipment point for drug smugglers moving opiates, hashish, and cannabis from southwest Asia to Western Europe and the United States. The weakness of state institutions in northern Albania has also resulted in the resurgence of traditional tribal law in these areas, most importantly the tradition of blood feuds between different families and clans. Up to 2,000 children belonging to rival families engaged in blood feuds are being kept inside their homes for fear of them becoming targets of revenge killings.

Algeria

Polity: Dominant party **Political Rights:** 6
(military-influenced) **Civil Liberties:** 5
Economy: Statist **Status:** Not Free
Population: 31,400,000
PPP: $5,308
Life Expectancy: 70
Religious Groups: Sunni Muslim (99 percent), Christian
and Jewish (1 percent)
Ethnic Groups: Arab-Berber (99 percent), other (1 percent)
Capital: Algiers

Ten-Year Ratings Timeline (Political Rights, Civil Liberties, Status)

1993	1994	1995	1996	1997	1998	1999	2000	2001	2002	2003
7,6NF	7,6NF	7,7NF	6,6NF	6,6NF	6,6NF	6,5NF	6,5NF	6,5NF	6,5NF	6,5NF

Overview: Although Algeria's Islamist insurgency continued to wane
in its tenth year, brutal terror attacks by small bands of Islamic militants claimed the lives of more than 1,100 civilians
and undermined public confidence in the government. The Berber uprising that began
last year continues to smolder, and a Berber boycott of parliamentary elections in
May resulted in the lowest overall turnout in Algerian history. On the whole, however, civil liberties improved slightly.

Following 130 years of French colonial rule, Algeria won its independence in
1962. The National Liberation Front (FLN) ruled as a virtual one-party regime for
more than a quarter-century. Following the collapse of world oil prices in the mid-
1980s, housing shortages, unemployment, and other severe economic problems
rapidly fueled antigovernment sentiments, which culminated in the "hunger" riots
of October 1988 in Algiers and other major cities that left more than 500 people dead.
In response, President Chadli Benjedid introduced a new constitution that permitted the formation of independent political parties and presided over the country's
first multiparty elections. In January 1992, however, the army canceled a second round
of legislative elections in order to forestall a victory by the radical Islamic Salvation
Front (FIS), banned the group, and arrested its leadership.

The coup set off a bloody civil war that has claimed 100,000 to 150,000 lives,
mostly civilians. Although radical Islamists have been responsible for most of the
massacres, government-backed militias have also been accused of committing mass
killings. Human rights groups have charged Algerian security forces with responsibility for thousands of "disappearances." The country remains under martial law.

In 1997, the government reached a truce with the Islamic Salvation Army (AIS),
the outlawed military wing of the FIS. After President Abdelaziz Bouteflika took office in 1999, the government introduced a "civil harmony" law that granted amnesty
or leniency to Islamist rebels who renounced violence. Up to 6,000 Islamist rebels
took advantage of the amnesty, and the AIS was formally disbanded. However, two
AIS offshoots, the Armed Islamic Group (GIA) and the Salafist Group for Preaching
and Combat (GSCP), rejected the amnesty and have continued their violent struggle.

Around 2,500 Algerians are believed to have died in 2000 as a result of the fighting; nearly 2,000 died in 2001.

The April 2001 death of a Berber teenager in the custody of the gendarmerie sparked massive riots in the northeastern Kabylie region and demonstrations erupted throughout the country against abuses by the security forces, government corruption, housing shortages, unemployment, and political stagnation. Riots resulted in the deaths of some 80 protestors during the year.

Although a commission set up to investigate the violence concluded that the gendarmes used excessive force in suppressing the uprising, it did not attribute responsibility to any high-level officials. The government also refused to meet any of the core demands made by the association of local village councils that led the uprising, the CADC (Coordination des aarouch, dairas et communes). Although the gendarmes vacated some positions in the heart of Tizi Ouzou, the regional capital, the authorities refused to completely withdraw the gendarmes from Kabylie. In March 2002, President Bouteflika announced that Tamazight, the native Berber language, would be recognized as a "national language." His proposal fell short of Berber demands that Tamazight have official status on par with Arabic. These limited concessions were overshadowed by the arrests of scores of CADC leaders and hundreds of their supporters in 2002.

The government's paralysis in dealing with the Berber uprising and growing public disaffection is widely attributed to the continuing grip on power of senior military officers, who have obstructed economic reforms needed to improve social conditions and combat corruption. The generals control much of Algeria's oil and gas wealth, as well as many private sector monopolies. As a result, despite a relatively sound macroeconomic situation and $22 billion in oil and gas revenues in 2001, more than half of the population lives on less than $1 per day and unemployment remains around 30 percent. The corrupt legal system, which perpetuates this imbalance of prosperity, has also made the country unattractive to foreign investors outside the hydrocarbon sector.

Algerians frequently complain that unlike military dictatorships elsewhere in the world, the generals who hold real power in Algiers cannot even provide the security they have long awaited. Despite the killing of GIA head Antar Zouabri, in February, violence by Islamic extremists continued in 2002. An upsurge in Islamist violence in the month preceding the May 30 parliamentary elections left 390 dead.

Political Rights and Civil Liberties: The right of Algerians to choose their government freely is heavily restricted. Although the president and lower house of parliament are elected by popular vote, and two-thirds of the upper house is chosen by elected municipal and provincial councils, all of these institutions are subservient to a clique of military and intelligence officers, commonly known as the *decideurs* or the *pouvoir*, who wield real power. Moreover, the electoral process is flawed. On the eve of the 1999 presidential election, all other candidates except Abdelaziz Bouteflika withdrew from the race, alleging fraud.

Although the last two rounds of parliamentary elections were free of systemic fraud and vote-rigging, the government's refusal to license FIS and other radical Islamist groups limited the choices of voters to a panoply of regime-approved parties. Turnout for parliamentary elections in May 2002 hit an all-time low as a result of electoral boycotts by the two leading pro-Berber parties, the Socialist Forces Front (FFS) and the Rally for Culture and Democracy (RCD), and a grassroots campaign by the CADC to obstruct access to the polls in Kabylie, where turnout was a mere 3 percent.

The main result of the elections was a transfer of seats from one political vehicle of the regime to another. The National Democratic Rally (NDR), established by military circles prior to the 1997 elections, saw its 155-seat bloc reduced to 48, while the FLN, which is close to Bouteflika and other civilian political elites, tripled its number of seats, from 64 to 199. While the results may have bolstered Bouteflika's position vis-a-vis the pouvoir, they did not produce a substantial parliamentary opposition. The FLN consolidated its political resurrection during municipal elections in October, winning a majority of the seats in 43 out of 48 provincial assemblies and 668 out of 1,541 local assemblies.

A variety of legislation passed under the state of emergency imposed in 1992 restricts the right of detainees to due process. Although extrajudicial execution, torture, and the arbitrary arrest and detention without trial of suspects by security forces and pro-government militias have continued to decline, abuses continue, particularly in Kabylie. The government's failure to bring any high-ranking gendarmerie commanders to trial in connection with the 2001 massacres in Kabylie highlights the continuing impunity enjoyed by the security services in Algeria. The number of political prisoners is estimated to be several thousand, mainly suspected members of radical Islamic groups and their sympathizers.

The judiciary in Algeria is not independent. Since judges are appointed to ten-year terms by the Ministry of Justice and can be removed at will, in practice the judiciary is squarely dependent on the executive branch. In August 2000, President Bouteflika replaced 80 percent of lower court judges and all but three higher court judges, a move that both "reformed" the judiciary by removing corrupt judges and demonstrated the president's power over this branch of government. Civilians arrested for security-related offenses are often tried in military courts, where due process rights are frequently ignored. Some lawyers refuse to represent individuals accused of security offenses, particularly Islamists, out of fear of retribution from the security forces.

Press freedom is limited by government control of the broadcast media, laws that ban vaguely defined defamation of state officials, and the overall lack of security. At least 70 journalists have been murdered since the early 1990s. A June 2001 amendment to the penal code increased the penalties for defamation of any "authority of public order" and facilitates their prosecution. Nevertheless, the print media remain among the most vibrant in the Arab world. While many journalists were interrogated by the authorities in 2002, and a handful were charged with press offenses, the few who were convicted did not received prison sentences. Nevertheless, journalists continue to be harassed, beaten, and sometimes killed under mysterious circumstances. In March 2002, a journalist in Tizi-Ouzou was severely injured by a tear gas grenade fired by police (he was not in the vicinity of any public disturbances). In July, a journalist in the northern town of Tebessa, Abdelhai Beliardouh, was kidnapped and beaten by the head of the local chamber of commerce and his henchmen as police looked on (Beliardouh committed suicide in November). Also in July, the body of a television correspondent was found bound and gagged in his

Algiers apartment. In August, a caricaturist for the daily *El Youm* went into hiding after being threatened by employees of a state-owned television station. In December, two papers complained that the state-owned Algiers Printing Company (SIA) had repeatedly delayed printing their issues, a method that they say is used by the government to impose extrajudicial financial penalties on opposition print media.

Emergency legislation restricts freedom of assembly and association. The Interior Ministry has refused to license some political parties, mostly on the grounds that they are linked to the FIS. Workers have the right to establish trade unions and to strike, though the government can deny or revoke licenses to unions if their objectives are deemed contrary to public order or morals.

The country's vibrant human rights movement operates openly, and most demonstrations are tolerated unless they turn violent. However, investigation of abuses by the security forces, particularly the fate of an estimated 4,000 Algerians who disappeared since 1993 following their arrests by security forces and government-backed militias, is clearly off-limits. Organizations that focus exclusively on this issue, such as the Association of Families of the Disappeared of the Province of Constantine, have been denied legal registration. Human rights groups that investigate this issue continue to be jailed on defamation charges. In February 2002, the president of the Relizane branch of the Algerian League for the Defense of Human Rights (LADDH) was sentenced to a year in prison. Abderrahmane Khelil, a leading official of SOS Disparus, which represents families of the disappeared, was arrested three different times in 2002 and received a six-month suspended sentence in May. Demonstrations by families of the disappeared were violently dispersed by police on several occasions during the year.

Islam is the state religion, though small Christian and Jewish communities are allowed to practice without governmental interference. The government exerts considerable control over mosques. All Muslim preachers must be approved by the government and can be imprisoned on charges of delivering sermons that are "contrary to the noble nature of the mosque" or that undermine "the cohesion of society."

Berbers do not face official discrimination, but their cultural identity and language are not fully recognized under the law. Those who openly celebrate Berber culture have been targeted by Islamic radicals, while security forces have used excessive force in dispersing Berber demonstrations. Government spending for housing and other services in Kabylie is not on par with that for other regions.

The family code, based on *Sharia* (Islamic law), discriminates against women in matters of marriage, divorce, inheritance, and child custody. Women have also been attacked by radical Islamists for such activities as working outside the home or going to beauty salons. Bouteflika appointed the country's first female provincial governor in 1999 and has improved the representation of women in other areas of government, though the proportion of men to women remains unbalanced.

Andorra

Polity: Parliamentary
democracy
Economy: Capitalist
Population: 100,000
PPP: na
Life Expectancy: na

Political Rights: 1
Civil Liberties: 1
Status: Free

Religious Groups: Roman Catholic (predominant)
Ethnic Groups: Spanish (43 percent), Andorran (33 percent),
Portuguese (11 percent), French (7 percent), other (6 percent)
Capital: Andorra la Vella

Ten-Year Ratings Timeline (Political Rights, Civil Liberties, Status)

1993	1994	1995	1996	1997	1998	1999	2000	2001	2002	2003
--	2,1F	1,1F	1,1F	1,1F	1,1F	1,1F	1,1F	1,1F	1,1F	1,1F

Overview:

The standoff between the Andorran government and the Organization for Economic Co-operation and Development (OECD) continued in 2002, with Andorra remaining on the OECD's blacklist of tax havens with 'prejudicial' tax practices. Negotiations with the European Union (EU) over the issue of Andorra's taxation policy also remained unresolved.

For more than 700 years, Andorra was ruled jointly by the French state and the Spanish bishops of Seo de Urgel, until it acquired independence and adopted its first written constitution in 1993. The constitution defines Andorra as a "parliamentary co-principality" in which the president of France and the bishop of Seo de Urgel serve as co-princes, heads of state with limited and largely symbolic power. Sovereignty rests with Andorra's citizens. In March 2001, Andorra held general elections, in which Marc Forne of the Liberal Party of Andorra (PLA) was reelected as the head of government. The PLA acquired 15 of the 28 Consell General (parliament) seats; the Social Democratic Party (PSD), 6; the Democratic Party, 5; and the Unio Laurediana Party, 2.

Andorra has no national currency, but circulates Spanish *pesetas* and French *francs*. By virtue of its association with Spain and France, it has also adopted the euro despite not being a member of the European Monetary Union. In 1991, Andorra established a customs union with the European Union (EU) that permits free movement of industrial goods. Andorra became a member of the United Nations in 1993 and a member of the Council of Europe in 1994. A Trilateral Treaty on free movement of labor between Andorra, France and Spain is due to go into effect in early 2003.

With the creation of the EU internal market, Andorra has lost its privileged duty-free status. Tourism, the mainstay of Andorra's economy, accounts for about 90 percent of gross domestic product. Because of banking secrecy laws and Andorra's tax haven status, the financial services sector is of growing importance to the economy. However, the threat of economic sanctions arising from being blacklisted by the OECD could reduce Andorra's attractiveness as a site for foreign investment.

Political Rights and Civil Liberties: Andorrans can change their government democratically. The March 2001 elections, in which 81.6 percent of eligible voters took part, chose members of the Consell General, which selects the head of government. Popular elections to the 28-member Consell are held every four years, with 14 members chosen by the national constituency and 14 chosen to represent the seven parishes, or administrative divisions.

The judiciary, based on the French and Spanish civil codes, is independent and efficient, and citizens enjoy full due process rights. The national police force is under civilian control, and generally respect the rights of citizens.

Freedoms of speech and the press are guaranteed in law and in practice. The domestic press consists of two daily and several weekly newspapers. Andorra has two radio stations, one state-owned and one privately owned, and six television stations. Most French and Spanish stations can be received in Andorra.

There are no limitations on domestic or foreign travel, emigration, or repatriation. Andorra does not expel persons with valid claims to refugee status, and cooperates with the UN High Commissioner for Refugees and other humanitarian organizations in assisting refugees.

Freedom of religion is respected. Catholicism is the predominant religion and the Constitution acknowledges a special relationship with the Roman Catholic Church; however, the Church no longer receives subsidies from the government. According to the U.S. Department of State's 2002 report on International Religious Freedom, foreign missionaries are able to "operate without restriction."

The constitution recognizes the right of all workers to form unions, but the legislation required to implement this provision does not yet exist. Nevertheless, a number of associations have registered with the government. Some immigrant workers complained that despite legal protections, they were not given the same labor rights and security as citizens.

Women enjoy the same legal, political, social, and professional rights as men, although they are underrepresented in government. Of the 28 members of the Consell General, only 4 are women. Violence against women remains a problem, as does discrimination against women in the workplace. The Association of Andorran Women actively promotes women's issues through education and outreach programs.

Angola

Polity: Presidential-parliamentary (insurgency)
Economy: Statist
Population: 12,700,000
PPP: $2,187
Life Expectancy: 45

Political Rights: 6
Civil Liberties: 5*
Status: Not Free

Religious Groups: Religious Groups: Indigenous beliefs (47 percent), Roman Catholic (38 percent), Protestant (15 percent)
Ethnic Groups: Ovimbundu (37 percent), Kimbundu (25 percent), Bakongo (13 percent), mestico (2 percent), European (1 percent), other (22 percent)
Capital: Luanda
Ratings Change: Angola's civil liberties rating improved from 6 to 5 due to a ceasefire that ended hostilities and provided for the return of civilians to their homes.

Ten-Year Ratings Timeline (Political Rights, Civil Liberties, Status)

1993	1994	1995	1996	1997	1998	1999	2000	2001	2002	2003
6,6NF	7,7NF	7,7NF	6,6NF	6,6NF	6,6NF	6,6NF	6,6NF	6,6NF	6,6NF	6,5NF

Overview:

Angola's best chance for peace after nearly three decades of civil war emerged in February 2002, when the man who came to symbolize the struggle against the ruling Popular Movement for the Liberation of Angola (MPLA) was shot and killed. The bullet-ridden body of Jonas Savimbi, leader of the National Union for the Total Independence of Angola (UNITA), was displayed on national television. Two months later, the remaining UNITA leadership signed a ceasefire with the government of President Jose Eduardo dos Santos. The two factions of the former rebel group—UNITA and UNITA-Renovada—joined together to become one political party.

Angola has been at war since shortly after independence from Portugal in 1975. During the Cold War, the United States and South Africa backed UNITA while the former Soviet Union and Cuba supported the Marxist Dos Santos government. A peace accord that led to presidential and legislative elections in 1992 disintegrated when Savimbi lost his bid for the presidency and went back to war. A subsequent peace agreement in 1994 also fell apart. The UN Security Council voted in February 1999 to end the UN peacekeeping mission in Angola following the collapse of the peace process and the shooting down of two UN planes.

Although the United Nations is playing a leading humanitarian role in the rehabilitation of Angola, it did not send peacekeepers as it had in the past. UNITA appears committed to ending hostilities for good; about 80,000 former UNITA soldiers and more than 300,000 of their family members are camped in transition centers around the country. Fighters have disarmed, and about 5,000 of them have been integrated into the armed forces and the police.

Angola faces major obstacles if it is to establish lasting peace. The MPLA and UNITA so far disagree about how rapidly political and economic reforms can occur, and both sides will need to demonstrate a commitment to rebuilding the country rather than to simply divide up Angola's economic pie. The peace process is likely to have a better chance if it includes the broad-based civil society movement that has been pressing for an end to the war for the past several years.

The conflict has claimed at least half a million lives. There are more than 4 million Angolans who are internally displaced and another 470,000 Angolan refugees in other countries. More than 1.5 million people require food aid, and about 500,000 of them became accessible to humanitarian agencies for the first time in 2002. An estimated 7 million land mines are spread across the country, and at least 70,000 people have lost limbs to them. Roads, bridges, and the communication infrastructure have been severely damaged. The health and educational systems are barely functioning. More than 50 percent of rural children do not attend school. Only 3 out of 10 rural women older than 15 years of age can read and write.

Angola is Africa's second-largest oil producer. Petroleum accounts for 90 percent of government revenues, but corruption and the war have prevented the average Angolan from benefiting from the wealth. An estimated $1 billion in oil revenue goes missing every year. The government has used its oil revenues to procure weapons, while UNITA has used diamonds to fund its arms purchases. In December 2002, the UN Security Council lifted a diamonds, fuel, and arms embargo against UNITA. A travel ban imposed on UNITA leaders was also lifted.

Political Rights and Civil Liberties: Angolans freely elected their own representatives for the only time in the September 1992 UN-supervised presidential and legislative elections. The vote was described by international observers as generally free and fair despite many irregularities. However, Savimbi rejected his defeat to Dos Santos in the first round of presidential voting and resumed the guerrilla war.

The MPLA dominates the 220-member National Assembly, although 70 UNITA members continue to occupy seats. More than 100 political parties exist in Angola, and so far they have shown no real movement towards cohesion. Although the National Assembly has little real power, it is not a rubber stamp. Members engage in heated debates, and legislation proposed by the opposition is considered and sometimes passed. A parliamentary peace commission is based on a bill put forward by a UNITA deputy. Dos Santos has said he would not stand for reelection. Polls that were originally being considered for 2002 are not expected to take place until 2004.

Local courts rule on civil matters and petty crime in some areas, but an overall lack of training and infrastructure inhibit judicial proceedings, which are also heavily influenced by the government. Many prisoners are detained for long periods in life-threatening conditions while awaiting trial.

Serious human rights abuses, including torture, abduction, rape, sexual slavery, and extrajudicial execution, were perpetrated during the war by both government and UNITA security forces. Although such violations subsided in 2002, New York-based Human Rights Watch warned that the United Nations and the Angolan government were not doing enough to ensure the safety of displaced Angolans returning to their homes. The rights group said Angolans faced harassment and restriction of movement, and were being forced to relocate where they might risk political persecution and human rights abuses. A separatist rebellion in the enclave of

Cabinda, marked by low-scale guerrilla activity and sporadic hostage-taking of foreign nationals, continued in 2002.

Despite constitutional guarantees of freedom of expression, the media are subject to severe and sometimes violent measures by both the government and UNITA. There are several independent weeklies and at least five independent radio stations. Defamation of the president or his representatives is a criminal offense and is punishable with imprisonment or fines. There is no truth defense to defamation charges. Press repression eased in 2002 following the renewal of the peace process.

Religious freedom is generally respected. Despite legal protections, de facto societal discrimination against women remains strong, particularly in rural areas. There is a high incidence of spousal abuse. The war has contributed to violence against women, forced servitude, and sexual slavery. Women are most likely to become victims of land mines because they are usually the ones who forage for food and firewood. Women, however, do occupy cabinet positions and numerous National Assembly seats.

Labor rights are guaranteed by the constitution, but only a few independent unions are functioning, and those exist in the cities. The government dominates the labor movement and restricts worker rights to strike and bargain collectively. The vast majority of rural agricultural workers remain outside the modern economic sector.

Antigua and Barbuda

Polity: Dominant party
Economy: Capitalist-statist
Population: 100,000
PPP: $10,541
Life Expectancy: 71
Religious Groups: Anglican (predominant)
Ethnic Groups: Black, British, Portuguese, Lebanese, Syrian
Capital: St. John's

Political Rights: 4
Civil Liberties: 2
Status: Partly Free

Ten-Year Ratings Timeline (Political Rights, Civil Liberties, Status)

1993	1994	1995	1996	1997	1998	1999	2000	2001	2002	2003
3,3PF	4,3PF	4,3PF	4,3PF	4,3PF	4,3PF	4,3PF	4,3PF	4,2PF	4,2PF	4,2PF

Overview:

In 2002 the embattled administration of Prime Minister Lester Bird survived popular street protests staged by the opposition United Progressive Party (UPP) in an effort to force the resignation of the government. In a further indication of the endemic corruption of state institutions, a Royal Commission of Inquiry concluded that there were serious instances of fraud in the medical-benefits program. The prime minister's brother, Vere Bird, continued to serve as minister of agriculture despite an arms-trafficking inquiry that concluded he should be barred from government service. In October the government promised to introduce new anticorruption legislation to Parliament.

Top officials, including the prime minister, were cleared by a commission of inquiry after being accused by a female minor of drug and sex offenses.

Antigua and Barbuda, a member of the Commonwealth, gained independence in 1981. The 1981 constitution establishes a parliamentary democracy: a bicameral legislature is composed of the 17-member House of Representatives (16 seats go to Antigua, 1 to Barbuda) in which members serve 5-year terms, and an appointed senate. Eleven senators are appointed by the prime minister, 4 by the parliamentary opposition leader, 1 by the Barbuda Council, and 1 by the governor-general.

In 1994, Vere Bird stepped down as prime minister in favor of his son Lester. In the run-up to the 1994 election, three opposition parties united to form the UPP, which campaigned on a social-democratic platform emphasizing rule of law and good governance. Parliamentary seats held by the Antigua Labour Party (ALP) fell from 15 in 1989 to 11, while the number of the UPP rose from 1 to 5. After assuming office, Lester Bird promised a less corrupt, more efficient government. Yet the government continued to be dogged by scandals and in 1995, the prime minister's brother, Ivor, received only a fine after having been convicted of cocaine smuggling. In the March 1999 elections, the ALP won 12 parliamentary seats and the UPP 4, providing Bird with a strong vote of confidence for policies that have made the nation one of the region's most prosperous.

Political Rights and Civil Liberties: The constitution provides for democratic changes in government. Political parties, labor unions, and civic organizations can organize freely. However, the ruling party's monopoly on patronage makes it difficult for opposition parties to attract membership and financial support. The government has been planning to reform the electoral system by establishing an Independent Electoral Commission to review electoral law and redraw constituency boundaries, create a new voter registry, and introduce voter identification cards; however, the relevant legislation has not yet been introduced.

The government introduced anticorruption and integrity legislation in parliament in October 2002. If the bills are approved, public officials would be required to make an annual declaration of assets, with failure to comply becoming a punishable offence. The Integrity in Public Life Act 2002 and the Prevention of Corruption Act 2002, which are being submitted as part of Organization of American States and United Nations anticorruption treaties signed by the country, will help establish provisions for regulating and guaranteeing good governance. The administration and enforcement of the acts would fall to an independent commission. The legislation also aims to define corruption.

The country's legal system is based on English common law. The ruling party has manipulated the nominally independent judicial system, which has been powerless to address corruption in the executive branch. The islands' security forces are composed of the police and the small Antigua and Barbuda Defense Forces. The police generally respect human rights; basic police-reporting statistics, however, are confidential. The country's prison is in primitive condition and has been criticized for the abuse of inmates, though visits are permitted by independent human rights groups.

The ALP government and the Bird family continue to control television, cable, and radio outlets. The prime minister filed a $3 million lawsuit against the Observer media group and opposition leader Baldwin Spencer for "libelous fabrications" in conjunction with the drug and sex offense accusations made against him and members of the government. Opposition parties complain of receiving limited coverage from, and having little opportunity to present their views on, the government-controlled electronic media. The Declaration of Chapultepec on press freedoms was signed in September 2002. Freedom of religion is respected.

Social discrimination and violence against women are problems. The governmental Directorate of Women's Affairs has sought to increase awareness of women's legal rights. Child abuse is also a problem, and despite numerous statements, the government has done little to protect children's rights in practice.

A resolution to ratify the International Labour Organization Convention Concerning Equal Remuneration for Men and Women Workers for Work of Equal Value was presented to Parliament in late 2002. The Industrial Court mediates labor disputes, but public sector unions tend to be under the sway of the ruling party. Demonstrators are occasionally subject to police harassment.

⬇ Argentina

Polity: Presidential-
parliamentary democracy
(federal)
Economy: Capitalist
Population: 36,500,000
PPP: $12,377
Life Expectancy: 74

Political Rights: 3
Civil Liberties: 3
Status: Partly Free

Religious Groups: Roman Catholic (92 percent),
Protestant (2 percent), Jewish (2 percent), other (4 percent)
Ethnic Groups: White [mostly Spanish and Italian] (97 percent), other, including mestizo, Indian (3 percent)
Capital: Buenos Aires
Trend Arrow: Argentina received a downward trend arrow due to the absence of an elected president and generalized corruption pervading all three branches of government.

Ten-Year Ratings Timeline (Political Rights, Civil Liberties, Status)

1993	1994	1995	1996	1997	1998	1999	2000	2001	2002	2003
2,3F	2,3F	2,3F	2,3F	2,3F	2,3F	3,3F	2,3F	1,2F	3,3FP	3,3PF

Overview:

The steep devaluation of the peso and a debilitating default on its foreign debt left Argentina teetering on the brink of political and economic collapse throughout 2002, as newly appointed President Eduardo Duhalde took time out from his long-running feud with former chief executive Carlos Menem to try, without much success, to run the country. An attempt by the Argentine congress to impeach a highly politicized supreme court loyal to Menem was dropped, after international financial institutions said the move would endanger the country's access to foreign credit, and the legislature itself was the target of persistent and apparently well-founded accusations of bribery. Unemployment soared to levels unheard of since the founding of the republic, and violent crime spiraled out of control, with several of the country's police forces roundly criticized both for not being able to stop the crime wave, and for contributing to it through deep-seated corruption and frequent use of excessive force.

Menem's own hopes for succeeding Duhalde in presidential elections slated for March 2003 dimmed after the *New York Times* tied him to the cover-up of a 1994 bombing of a Jewish community center, in which 85 people died. Reeling from the charges, which had already been published by the Argentine newspaper, *Clarin*, Menem, while denying any link to the bombing, subsequently admitted he owned a secret Swiss bank account. Menem's claims for special status with the United States also appeared to be jeopardized by his selection of the governor of a poor, cocaine-ridden province as a running mate. Documents declassified by the U.S. State Department in July provided yet another direct link between former U.S. secretary of state Henry Kissinger and the military-led "dirty war" of the 1970s and 1980s.

The Argentine Republic was established after independence from Spain in 1816. Democratic rule was often interrupted by military coups. The end of Juan Peron's authoritarian regime in 1955 led to a series of right-wing military dictatorships as well as left-wing and nationalist violence. Argentina returned to elected civilian rule in 1983, after seven years of vicious and mostly clandestine repression of leftist guerrillas and other dissidents.

As amended in 1994, the 1853 constitution provides for a president elected for four years with the option of reelection to one term. Presidential candidates must win 45 percent of the vote to avoid a runoff. The legislature consists of the 257-member Chamber of Deputies elected for six years, with half the seats renewable every three years, and the 72-member Senate nominated by elected provincial legislatures for nine-year terms, with one-third of the seats renewable every three years. Two senators are directly elected in the autonomous Buenos Aires federal district.

As a provincial governor, Menem, running an orthodox Peronist platform of nationalism and state intervention in the economy, won a six-year presidential term in 1989, amidst hyperinflation and food riots. As president, he implemented, mostly by decree, an economic liberalization program. He also won praise for firmly allying the country with U.S. foreign policy, particularly during the Gulf War with Iraq.

In the October 1997 elections, voter concerns about rampant corruption and unemployment resulted in the first nationwide defeat of Menem's Peronists, whose macroeconomic stabilization plan collapsed due to the "tequila effect" resulting from serious economic problems in Mexico, as well as the Asian financial crisis and a dramatic devaluation of the currency in neighboring Brazil. Buenos Aires mayor and Radical Party leader Fernando de la Rua was chosen as the nominee of the center-left Alliance for presidential elections to be held October 24, 1999. Menem's feud with the hapless Duhalde, the Peronist Party presidential nominee and governor of Buenos Aires province, sealed the latter's fate. Duhalde was defeated by De la Rua 48.5 percent to 38 percent. Weak, indecisive and facing an opposition-controlled

Congress, De la Rua sought to cut spending, raise taxes, and push forward with unpopular labor reforms. He also issued sweeping rules and regulations designed to rein in public corruption. In April 2000, De la Rua dismissed a nine-member military tribunal after it claimed military rather than civilian courts had jurisdiction over cases in which military personnel had been accused of kidnapping, and in some cases killing, hundreds of babies born to detainees during the 1970s and early 1980s. In October, Vice President Carlos Alvarez stepped down after De la Rua stonewalled calls for a serious investigation of the reported buying of congressional votes, in order to pass the labor legislation. In December, a judge who himself was under investigation for "illegal enrichment," dropped the charges against the 11 senators named in the scandal.

Unable to halt the economic crisis, De la Rua called upon Menem's former economy minister to restore credibility to the government's economic program and to stave off default on Argentina's $128 billion in public sector debt. Record unemployment, reduced and delayed wages to federal and provincial workers, and the closing of public schools created the kind of social mobilization and protest unseen for nearly a generation. A congressional report on rampant money laundering during Menem's rule raised questions about senior officials of De la Rua's government. In the October 2001 congressional by-elections, the opposition Peronist Party bested the ruling Alliance coalition. However, citizen anger resulted in an unprecedented 21 percent of the votes being spoiled or nullified. Public outrage was also in full throttle after the Supreme Court, dominated by Menem loyalists, set aside prosecution of the former president, under house arrest on international arms trafficking and other charges.

In December 2001, government efforts to stop a run on Argentina's banking system sparked widespread protests. Massive demonstrations by middle class housewives—the bulwark of the government coalition's base—combined with riots and looting of supermarkets in poorer districts, some of which, at least, appeared to have been organized by rivals within the opposition Peronists and by disaffected serving or former members of the Argentina's intelligence services. As the death toll reached 27, De la Rua resigned. He was replaced by an interim president, who himself was forced to quit less than a week later. On December 31, 2001, Duhalde, De la Rua's former rival in the 1999 presidential contest, was selected as the new president. Few had many hopes for Duhalde, who critics charged had a penchant for rampant nepotism, who had left the province with its biggest debt in history, and whose past friendships with drug traffickers and crime figures went hand-in-hand with presiding over one of the most violent, corrupt police forces in the region. On a positive note, a decade-old law prohibiting the use of the military for internal security, a sizable reduction in military strength carried out by the Menem government, and continuing civilian revulsion of the still-conflictive legacy of the "dirty war," all helped keep the military from intervening in politics during the weeks-long transition.

Throughout 2002 the contractionary fiscal policies urged by the IMF and pursued by the government were not matched by increases in foreign investment, which exacerbated Argentina's high debt load—$141 billion—and deepened the economic depression. According to official government statistics, between October 2001 and May 2002, about 5.2 million people belonging to the middle class sank below the poverty line. At the same time, public opinion polls showed broad rejection of the country's traditional political figures and parties. The top justice official in populous Buenos Aires province admitted that overflow from crowded jails made police stations "almost concentration camps;" human rights groups say that torture by police of detainees was endemic countrywide. At the same time, concerns over personal security in much of the country skyrocketed. In 2002 Argentina slipped from 57th to 70th out of 102 countries ranked on Transparency International's Corruption Perceptions Index.

Political Rights and Civil Liberties:

Citizens can change their government through elections, although Eduardo Duhalde's interim presidency is due entirely to an agreement reached by the country's political establishment. Constitutional guarantees regarding freedom of religion and the right to organize political parties, civic organizations, and labor unions are generally respected.

Former president Carlos Menem's authoritarian ways and manipulation of the judiciary resulted in the complete undermining of the country's separation of powers and the rule of law. The judicial system remains politicized, inefficient, and riddled with the corruption endemic to all branches of government. The tenure of scores of incompetent and—it is widely believed—corrupt judges remains a grave problem.

The press, which was frequently under attack during Menem's presidency, enjoys broad credibility and influence, the latter in part due to the discredit of public institutions and the major political parties. However, more than 150 journalists reportedly receive monthly payments from the state intelligence service (SIDE).

Labor is dominated by Peronist unions. Union influence, however, has diminished dramatically because of corruption scandals, internal divisions, and restrictions on public sector strikes decreed by Menem to pave the way for his privatization program.

Public safety is a primary concern for Argentines. Within a decade, crime in Argentina has doubled, and in Buenos Aires, tripled. In May 2002, the Argentine penal code was changed; the penalty for being convicted of killing of a police officer became a life sentence without possibility of parole. Police misconduct includes growing numbers of allegedly extrajudicial executions by law enforcement officers. The Buenos Aires provincial police have been heavily involved in drug trafficking, extortion, and vice. Arbitrary arrests and ill-treatment by police are rarely punished in civil courts owing to intimidation of witnesses and judges, particularly in Buenos Aires province. The torture of detainees in police custody in the province is widespread. In 2002, the armed forces—quietly encouraged by the Pentagon—pressed ahead with a plan to be once again permitted to participate in internal security, a role prohibited by two model laws passed in the 1980s and 1990s as a result of the military's legacy of dictatorship and "political" policing.

Prison conditions are generally substandard throughout the country.

Military impunity continued its slow decline when, in September 2002, a judge indicted former military dictator Gen. Leopoldo Galtieri and 24 other alleged military rights violators for the disappearance of 20 former guerrillas captured in 1980.

The investigation of the 1994 car bombing of a Jewish community organization has languished because of sloppy police work at the crime scene and the alleged complicity by members of the security forces with the terrorists. On September 24, 2001, seven years after the outrage, the trial of several suspects—most of them policemen—began in Buenos Aires, but a senior U.S. law enforcement official called the effort "a joke," and suggested that complicity in the attack went high into Menem's inner circle. The 250,000-strong Jewish community is a frequent target of anti-Semitic vandalism. Neo-Nazi organizations and other anti-Semitic groups, frequently tied to remnants of the old-line security services, some of whom retain their posts, remain active. The Roman Catholic majority enjoys freedom of religious expression.

Argentina's estimated 700,000 to 1.5 million indigenous people are largely neglected. Approximately 70 percent of the country's rural indigenous communities lack title to their lands. In 2002, the total budget for the National Institute of Indigenous Affairs was less than $2 million.

Women actively participate in politics in Argentina. However, domestic abuse remains a serious problem, and child prostitution is reported to be on the rise. On a positive note, in 2002 the city of Buenos Aires significantly expanded the legal rights of gay and lesbian couples.

Armenia

Polity: Presidential-parliamentary democracy
Economy: Capitalist-statist
Population: 3,800,000
PPP: $2,559
Life Expectancy: 72
Religious Groups: Armenian Apostolic (94 percent), other Christian (4 percent), Yezidi (2 percent)
Ethnic Groups: Armenian (93 percent), Azeri (3 percent), Russian (2 percent), Kurd and others (2 percent)
Capital: Yerevan

Political Rights: 4
Civil Liberties: 4
Status: Partly Free

Ten-Year Ratings Timeline (Political Rights, Civil Liberties, Status)

1993	1994	1995	1996	1997	1998	1999	2000	2001	2002	2003
4,3PF	3,4PF	3,4PF	4,4PF	5,4PF	5,4PF	4,4PF	4,4PF	4,4PF	4,4PF	4,4PF

Overview: Local elections in October 2002 resulted in an expected victory for the ruling Republican Party. At the same time, the fractured political opposition attempted to unite in a bid to unseat President Robert Kocharian from power in the upcoming February 2003 presidential poll. The third anniversary of the attacks on parliament, in which five gunmen killed the prime minister and other senior officials, was marked by continuing speculation about who may have been behind the shootings.

Following a brief period of independence from 1918 to 1920, part of the predominantly Christian Transcaucasus republic of Armenia became a Soviet republic in

1922, while the western portion was ceded to Turkey. Armenia declared its independence from the Soviet Union in September 1991.

The banning of nine political parties prior to the 1995 parliamentary elections ensured the dominance of President Levon Ter Petrosian's ruling Armenian National Movement's (ANM) coalition. In February 1998, Petrosian stepped down following the resignation of key officials in protest over his gradualist approach to solving the conflict over Nagorno-Karabakh, the disputed Armenian enclave in Azerbaijan. Prime Minister Robert Kocharian, the former president of Nagorno-Karabakh, was elected president in March with the support of the previously banned Armenian Revolutionary Federation-Dashnaktsutiun.

Parliamentary elections in May 1999 resulted in an overwhelming victory for the Unity bloc, a new alliance of Defense Minister Vazgen Sarkisian's Republican Party and former Soviet Armenian leader Karen Demirchian's People's Party, which campaigned on a populist platform of greater state involvement in the economy and increased social spending. In June, Sarkisian was named prime minister while Demirchian became speaker of parliament. The relationship between Sarkisian and Demirchian on the one hand, and Kocharian on the other, was marked by power struggles and policy differences.

The country was plunged into a political crisis on October 27, when five gunmen stormed the parliament building and assassinated Sarkisian, Demirchian, and several other senior government officials. The leader of the gunmen, Nairi Hunanian, maintained that he and the other assailants had acted alone in an attempt to incite a popular revolt against the government. Meanwhile, allegations that Kocharian or members of his inner circle had orchestrated the shootings prompted opposition calls for the president to resign. However, because of an apparent lack of evidence, prosecutors did not to press charges against Kocharian, who gradually consolidated his power over the following year. In May 2000, Kocharian named Republican Party leader Andranik Markarian as prime minister, replacing Vazgen Sarkisian's younger brother, Aram, who had served in the position for only five months following the parliamentary shootings.

The trial of the five gunmen, plus eight others charged with complicity in the parliamentary shootings, began in February 2001. A final verdict in the trial had not been reached by the end of 2002. Three years after the massacre, many in the country maintain that the gunmen were acting on orders from others and continue to speculate about who may have masterminded the attacks.

In the October 20, 2002, local elections, the ruling Republican Party won a widely anticipated landslide victory across the country. International observers, including the Council of Europe, concluded that the elections were conducted according to international standards despite reported violations, including the stuffing of ballot boxes, the buying of votes, and inflated voter turnout figures.

During the second half of 2002, politicians began positioning themselves for the February 2003 presidential vote. In August, 16 opposition parties announced their intention to field a joint candidate in the hopes of defeating Kocharian in his reelection bid. However, widespread doubts about the ability of the perennially divided opposition to form a united front appeared to be justified when, by the end of the year, several of the parties had declared their intentions to nominate their own candidates.

In a controversial privatization deal, the government sold 80.1 percent of the revenue-losing Armenian Electricity Network (AET) in August to an obscure British offshore firm, Midland Resources Holding. Western donors, including the World Bank and European Bank for Reconstruction and Development (EBRD), criticized the selection of Midland for its reported lack of experience in the energy sector. The EBRD announced that it would overturn its earlier decision to buy the remaining 19.9 percent stake in AET once a foreign investor was found. In November, Armenia and Russia signed an agreement under which Armenia would transfer ownership to Russia of five state-owned enterprises in exchange for the canceling of $98 million in debts.

Despite continued internationally led meetings between the Armenian and Azerbaijani leadership, little progress was made during the year on reaching a breakthrough on the long-standing Nagorno-Karabakh conflict. With the presidents of both countries seeking reelection in 2003, neither is likely to risk the domestic political consequences of making major public concessions over the disputed territory before then.

Political Rights and Civil Liberties:

Armenians can change their government democratically, although the 1995 and 1999 parliamentary and 1996 presidential elections were characterized by serious irregularities. International observers reported some improvements regarding the 1999 parliamentary vote over previous elections, including the adoption of a new electoral code in February containing some recommendations by the international community, more balanced media coverage, and the return to the political arena of previously banned parties. However, they also cited serious problems with significant inaccuracies of voter lists, the presence of unauthorized persons in polling stations, and the lack of effective and impartial electoral commissions. In July 2002, parliament adopted amendments to the election law that increased from 37 to 56 the number of parliamentary seats based on single-mandate constituencies, and that decreased from 94 to 75 the number elected on a proportional party-list basis. Opposition deputies charge that the purpose of these changes is to increase the chances of victory for the ruling party in the May 2003 parliamentary elections. President Kocharian signed the amendments into law in August.

The 1995 constitution provides for a weak legislature and a strong, directly elected president who appoints the prime minister. Most parties in Armenia are dominated by specific government officials or other powerful figures, suffer from significant internal dissent and division, or are otherwise weak and ineffective.

Self-censorship among journalists is common, particularly in reporting on Nagorno-Karabakh, national security, or corruption issues. While most newspapers are privately owned, the majority operate with limited resources and consequently are dependent on economic and political interest groups for their survival. There are a number of private television stations, and most radio stations are privately owned.

On April 3, 2002, the independent television station A1+ lost its license after the national television and radio broadcasting commission granted a tender for its broadcasting frequency to an entertainment channel. Journalists and opposition politicians criticized the closure of A1+, which had a reputation for objective reporting, as a politically motivated decision to control media coverage in the run-up to the 2003 presidential and parliamentary elections. Following the decision, thousands of people demonstrated in a number of weekly protests over the station's closure and to demand President Kocharian's resignation. A1+ lost its final appeal in June regarding the loss of its broadcasting frequency and remained closed at the end of the year, The founder and the executive director of Abovian television were beaten in August by a group of men believed to have been hired by the mayor of Abovian in retaliation for critical reports aired by the station. On October 22, journalist Mark Grigorian was seriously injured in a grenade attack in Yerevan; at the time, he was preparing an investigative report on the October 1999 parliamentary attacks.

Freedom of religion is somewhat respected in this overwhelmingly Christian country. The Armenian Apostolic Church, to which over 90 percent of Armenians formally belong, has been granted official status as the national church and is not subject to certain restrictions imposed on other religious groups, including having to register with the State Council on Religious Affairs. In August, authorities announced the formation of a new religious council to advise the government on religious matters. The council will include representatives of the Armenian Apostolic, Catholic, and Protestant churches, but not of the country's various nontraditional denominations. In September 2002, the Ministry of Education ordered the compulsory display of the Armenian flag and portraits of President Kocharian and the head of the Armenian Apostolic Church in secondary schools. The history of the Apostolic Church is already a required school subject.

The government generally respects freedom of assembly and association, although the registration requirements are cumbersome and time consuming. While the constitution enshrines the right to form and join trade unions, in practice, labor organizations are weak and relatively inactive. The judiciary, which is subject to political pressure from the executive branch, is characterized by widespread violations of due process. Police frequently make arbitrary arrests without warrants, beat detainees during arrest and interrogation, and use torture to extract confessions.

While citizens have the right to own private property and establish businesses, an inefficient and often corrupt court system and unfair business competition hinder operations. Key industries remain in the hands of oligarchs and influential clans who received preferential treatment in the early stages of privatization. Domestic violence and the trafficking in women and girls for the purpose of prostitution are believed to be serious problems.

Australia

Polity: Parliamentary democracy (federal)
Economy: Capitalist
Population: 19,700,000
PPP: $25,693
Life Expectancy: 80

Political Rights: 1
Civil Liberties: 1
Status: Free

Religious Groups: Anglican (26 percent), Roman Catholic (26 percent), other Christian (24.3 percent), non-Christian (11 percent), other (12.7 percent)
Ethnic Groups: White (92 percent), Asian (7 percent), other, including Aboriginal (1 percent)
Capital: Canberra

Ten-Year Ratings Timeline (Political Rights, Civil Liberties, Status)

1993	1994	1995	1996	1997	1998	1999	2000	2001	2002	2003
1,1F	1,1F	1,1F	1,1F	1,1F	1,1F	1,1F	1,1F	1,1F	1,1F	1,1F

Overview:

An October terrorist bombing in Indonesia that killed scores of Australian vacationers underscored Australia's vulnerability to Islamic militancy. Coming as the government mulled how many troops to contribute to a potential U.S.-led war against Iraq, the attack on the resort island of Bali left some Australians questioning the human costs of being a staunch U.S. ally in the campaign against terrorism. The economy, meanwhile, rode out the global downturn in 2002 despite a crop-killing drought that gripped much of the country.

Claimed by the British in 1770, and settled in good part by convicts, Australia gained independence in 1901 as a commonwealth of six states. The sparsely populated Northern Territory and Canberra, the capital, were adopted in 1911 as territorial units. Since World War II, political power in this parliamentary democracy has alternated between the center-left Labor Party and the conservative coalition of the Liberal Party and the smaller, rural-based National Party. Under Bob Hawke and then Paul Keating, Labor governments in the 1980s and early 1990s won five straight elections as they worked to sharpen the competitiveness of what had been a protected, commodities-dependent economy. They slashed tariffs, privatized many firms, and deregulated financial markets.

The Liberal and National parties capitalized on discontent with high unemployment and an economic recession to oust Labor in the 1996 elections. Since then, their coalition government has been reelected twice. Led by John Howard, 63, the conservative coalition has introduced a goods-and-services tax, championed small- and medium-sized business interests, and tried to restrict trade union power.

Aside from labor relations, the Howard government has most visibly shifted Australian politics to the right on the cultural issues of Aboriginal rights and immigration. In its first term, the government amended legislation to limit Aboriginal land claims at the behest of farmers and miners.

Howard has also angered mainstream Aboriginal leaders by rejecting their long-standing demands for an official apology and some form of reparation for past abuses against Aborigines. These abuses include the forced removal of some 100,000 Aboriginal children from their parents under an official assimilation policy between 1910 and the early 1970s. At the same time, however, Howard ordered the Northern Territory, which is under federal control, to exempt juveniles from a 1997 mandatory sentencing law that critics said disproportionately affected Aborigines.

The Liberal-National coalition's third straight election victory, in November 2001, came after Howard deftly turned illegal immigration and the September terrorist attacks in the United States into pressing national security issues. With the election up for grabs, support for the coalition surged after the government sent a small contingent of troops to assist U.S. forces in Afghanistan; pushed through parliament tough new laws against illegal immigrants, most of whom are Muslims; and ordered the navy to send boats carrying immigrants and asylum seekers to Nauru and Papua New Guinea for refugee processing. The Liberal Party won 68 seats and the National Party took 13, while Labor managed only 65. Minor-party candidates and independents took the remaining 4 seats in the 150-seat lower house.

The Bali bombing may come to be seen as yet another coming-of-age moment for a country that has borne heavy costs for its engagement abroad ever since the ill-fated Gallipoli landing during World War I. Attributed to Islamic militants, the Bali attack killed some 90 Australians, and around 190 people overall.

Australia's economy continued to be one of the most buoyant among first world countries, growing at a 3.7 percent annual rate in the third quarter compared with a year earlier. However, a drought that some called the worst in a century could knock off up to one percentage point from Australia's economic growth in 2003, analysts said late in the year.

Political Rights and Civil Liberties:

Australians can change their government through elections, and they enjoy a full range of basic rights. The 1900 constitution created the directly elected parliament, which currently consists of the 76-member Senate and the 150-member House of Representatives. In a 1999 referendum, voters rejected a proposal to replace the Queen of England as head of state with a president elected by parliament. Polls showed a majority of Australians favoring a republic, but with a directly elected president.

Australia's primary human rights concern involves alleged discrimination and other abuses against its 399,000 Aborigines and Torres Strait Islanders, who make up roughly 2 percent of the population. Despite government initiatives, Aborigines face "inferior access to medical and educational institutions, greatly reduced life expectancy rates, elevated levels of unemployment, and general discrimination," according to the U.S. State Department's global human rights report for 2001, released in March 2002. Aborigines say that they are also routinely mistreated and discriminated against by police and prison officials.

Moreover, Aborigines were jailed nationwide at a rate 14 times higher than that of whites in 1999, according to a 2001 report by the Australian Institute of Criminology. The UN Committee on the Elimination of Racial Discrimination (CERD) says that a mandatory sentencing law in the state of Western Australia seems to target petty offenses that are disproportionately committed by Aborigines.

Aboriginal leaders link Aboriginal crime, as well as high rates of domestic violence among Aborigines, to poverty, high unemployment, alleged discrimination, and inferior job and schooling opportunities. Recent governments have generally been responsive to these concerns and have introduced numerous health care and educational programs for Aborigines.

Meanwhile, Aboriginal leaders said that a December High Court ruling in a land claim case created a strict standard of evidence that would make it harder for Aborigines to gain title to ancestral lands. The court upheld a lower court rejection of an Aboriginal land claim on the grounds that the applicants failed to meet their burden, under Australia's Native Title Act, of proving a continuous link to the land before white settlers kicked them off.

Australia's immigration policies have also come under international scrutiny. Domestic and international human rights groups have criticized the government's practices of redirecting emigrants intercepted at sea to Pacific island-states for processing and of detaining nearly all illegal immigrants, including political asylum seekers, pending resolution of their claims. Most asylum cases are decided within weeks, but a small number of asylum seekers are detained for years while their cases are on appeal. Detainees in camps at Curtin and Woomera rioted and staged hunger strikes in 2002.

Domestic violence affects up to one Australian family in three or four, according to social analysts. Various studies put women's earnings at anywhere from 66 to 85 percent, on average, of their male counterparts' wages.

Australian trade unions are independent and vigorous. A recent law, however, has contributed to a decline in union rolls and power by promoting enterprise-level or even individual employment contracts that are subject to relatively few governmental regulations. By contrast, the federal and state governments traditionally have handed down minimum wage awards that were supplemented by industry or company-level bargaining. The law, the 1996 Workplace Relations Act, also banned closed shops, tightened restrictions on secondary boycotts, and limited redress and compensation for unfair dismissal. Union membership has slumped to about 25 percent of the workforce in 2001 from 40 percent in 1990.

Austria

Polity: Parliamentary
democracy (federal)
Economy: Mixed
capitalist
Population: 8,100,000
PPP: $26,765
Life Expectancy: 78

Political Rights: 1
Civil Liberties: 1
Status: Free

Religious Groups: Roman Catholic (78 percent), Protestant
(5 percent), Muslim and other (17 percent)
Ethnic Groups: German (98 percent), other, including Slovenian, Croatian,
and Hungarian (2 percent)
Capital: Vienna

Ten-Year Ratings Timeline (Political Rights, Civil Liberties, Status)

1993	1994	1995	1996	1997	1998	1999	2000	2001	2002	2003
1,1F	1,1F	1,1F	1,1F	1,1F	1,1F	1,1F	1,1F	1,1F	1,1F	1,1F

Overview:

The collapse of the right-of-center coalition government composed of the center-right People's Party and the far-right Freedom Party lead to an early general election on November 24, which returned the People's Party to power, but without an absolute majority. Press freedom groups expressed concern over media controls that serve as obstacles to freedom of expression. The government introduced anti-immigration measures and a stricter asylum policy that could dislocate hundreds of asylum seekers. Austria also passed legislation prohibiting minors from direct participation in armed conflict.

The Republic of Austria was established in 1918, after the collapse of the Austro-Hungarian Empire, and was reborn in 1945, seven years after its annexation by Nazi Germany. Occupation by the Western Allies and the Soviet Union ended in 1955 under the Austrian State Treaty, which guaranteed Austrian neutrality and restored national sovereignty.

In October 2001, the government proposed an "integration package" requiring German-language courses for residents from outside the European Economic Area (EEA). Anyone refusing the course would not be granted a visa extension and would be deported.

Austria currently bars some asylum seekers from government-run shelters while their asylum requests are being processed. The new regulation, put into effect on October 1 2002, could lead to the eviction of hundreds of people.

The collapse of the right-of-center coalition government on September 9, following internal divisions in the Freedom Party, led Austrians to make the People's Party the largest party in parliament in the early vote on November 24, 2002. The chancellor is Wolfgang Schussel. Mathias Reichhold was elected the new Freedom Party leader on September 21, after Jörg Haider decided not to run for reelection. Mr. Haider stirred controversy by openly espousing an anti-Semitic, populist, xenophobic, and pro-Nazi platform in successful national elections in 1999. The party saw its level of support decline sharply in local elections in Burgenland on October 6, 2002.

Political Rights and Civil Liberties: Austrians can change their government democratically. The country's provinces possess considerable latitude in local administration and can check federal power by electing members of the upper house of parliament. Voting is compulsory in some provinces. The independent judiciary is headed by the Supreme Court and includes both constitutional and administrative courts.

Austrian media are considered free, but ownership of television and press outlets remains highly concentrated. On January 1, 2002, a law ended Europe's last state monopoly of TV and radio, the state-run ORF; the law authorized private TV stations and created a new audiovisual regulatory body, Komm-Austria. Nevertheless, two press groups own most of the newspapers and magazines in a market of six million. By 2002, most news magazines were under the control of one group, News, and close ties exist between News and the two groups controlling the written daily press. These ties seriously undermine media diversity in Austria, according to Reporters Sans Frontieres (RSF).

A broadcasting law protects the media from political interference. However, journalists and media outlets suffered harassment and lawsuits by Freedom Party leaders in 2001, as reported by RSF. Most of these cases were dropped in 2002.

A 1955 treaty prohibits Nazis from exercising freedom of assembly and association. Nazi organizations are illegal, but Nazis are welcomed in the Freedom Party. In 1992, public denial of the Holocaust and justification of approval of Nazi crimes against humanity were outlawed. In general, Austrian police enforce these anti-Nazi statutes more enthusiastically when extremists attract international attention. Nevertheless, Austria was made to pay $36 million in August 2001 to those who were Austrian-based, Nazi-era slaves and forced laborers during World War II.

As of October 1, 2002, asylum seekers from countries negotiating entry into the European Union are barred from government-run accommodations. Nationals of Russia, Turkey, Georgia, Armenia, Azerbaijan, Nigeria, Yugoslavia, and the former Yugoslav Republic of Macedonia can access government-run shelters only while their initial application for asylum is being considered. On October 3, Austria returned Kosovan asylum seekers to Pristina. Human rights groups Amnesty International and the UN refugee agency (UNHCR) have criticized the policy, which is expected to evict hundreds of people, saying it breaches European Union guidelines and denies asylum seekers the right to a fair hearing.

In July 2002, parliament struck down the law prohibiting women from night work, bringing Austrian law into line with that of the EU. Women are allowed to serve in the military. The ruling Social Democratic Party, which is likely to be a partner in any coalition the People's Party forms, has pledged to begin to address gender biases by ensuring that women occupy 40 percent of all party and government posts by 2003.

The Optional Protocol to the Convention on the Rights of the Child regarding the involvement of children in armed conflict went into effect on February 12, 2002. The protocol raises the minimum age for direct participation in hostilities and for military conscription from the customary 15 to 18. In Austria, voluntary enlistment is allowed at 17.

Trade unions retain an important independent voice in Austria's political, social, and economic life. The 14 national unions are reorganizing into three main groups, all of which will continue to belong to the Austrian Trade Union Federation and which are managed by supporters of the country's traditional political parties. The right to strike is protected.

Azerbaijan

Polity: Presidential (dominant party)
Economy: Capitalist-statist
Population: 8,200,000
PPP: $2,936
Life Expectancy: 72
Religious Groups: Muslim (93 percent), Russian Orthodox (3 percent), Armenian Orthodox (2 percent), other (2 percent)
Ethnic Groups: Azeri (90 percent), Dagestani (3 percent), Russian (3 percent), Armenian (2 percent), other (2 percent)
Capital: Baku

Political Rights: 6
Civil Liberties: 5
Status: Partly Free

Ten-Year Ratings Timeline (Political Rights, Civil Liberties, Status)

1993	1994	1995	1996	1997	1998	1999	2000	2001	2002	2003
5,5PF	6,6NF	6,6NF	6,6NF	6,5NF	6,4PF	6,4PF	6,4PF	6,5PF	6,5PF	6,5PF

Overview:

A controversial August 2002 national referendum led to the adoption of a series of constitutional amendments, some of which critics charged would further strengthen the ruling party's grip on power. Throughout the year, a number of demonstrations were held to demand various political and economic changes, including the resignation of the country's authoritarian president, Heydar Aliev. In June, an unarmed protestor was shot and killed by police in the town of Nardaran, the first time that such a tragedy had occurred since Azerbaijan's independence more than ten years ago.

After having been controlled by the Ottoman Empire since the seventeenth century, Azerbaijan entered the Soviet Union in 1922 as part of the Transcaucasian Soviet Federal Republic, becoming a separate Soviet republic in 1936. Following a referendum in 1991, Azerbaijan declared independence from the disintegrating Soviet Union.

In June 1992, Abulfaz Elchibey, leader of the nationalist opposition Azerbaijan Popular Front, was elected president in a generally free and fair vote. A military coup one year later ousted him from power and installed the former first secretary of the Azerbaijan Communist Party, Heydar Aliev, in his place. In the October 1993 presidential elections, President Aliev reportedly received almost 99 percent of the vote. Azerbaijan's first post-Soviet parliamentary elections, held in November 1995, saw five leading opposition parties and some 600 independent candidates barred from the vote in which Aliev's Yeni Azerbaijan Party won the most seats. In October

1998, Aliev was chosen president with more than 70 percent of the vote in an election characterized by serious irregularities.

In a widely expected outcome, the ruling Yeni Azerbaijan Party captured the majority of seats in the November 2000 parliamentary election. The Azerbaijan Popular Front and the Communist Party came in a distant second and third, respectively. International monitors from the Organization for Security and Cooperation in Europe and the Council of Europe cited mass electoral fraud, including the intimidation of those gathering signatures for candidates' registration before the poll, the stuffing of ballot boxes, and a strong pro-government bias in state-run media. Despite widespread criticism of the elections, the Council of Europe approved Azerbaijan's application for membership just days after the vote, a decision widely criticized by international human rights groups.

Vocal opposition to Aliev's heavy-handed rule was evidenced throughout 2002. In the capital city of Baku and elsewhere in the country, thousands of protestors organized by opposition political groups participated in a number of rallies to demand the president's resignation. Police forcibly dispersed unsanctioned demonstrations, injuring and detaining dozens of participants. In the town of Nardaran, public protests during the first half of the year over various political, economic, and social issues culminated in one person being shot to death during a rally on June 3. The incident represented the first time that police had killed an unarmed civilian at a demonstration since the country's independence in 1991. A series of meetings between government representatives and Nardaran village elders failed to defuse the situation, and protests continued in Nardaran and other parts of the country throughout the year.

Despite international criticism and opposition calls for a postponement or boycott, a controversial national referendum on 39 amendments to Azerbaijan's constitution was held on August 24. Certain provisions—such as the creation of a civilian service as an alternative to conscription and a guarantee that citizens could appeal to the constitutional court—were praised as enhancing the protection of civil liberties in keeping with Council of Europe standards. However, other key amendments were seen as moves toward the greater concentration of power in the hands of the president and his ruling party. In particular, critics cited a provision replacing the proportional-representation system, under which one-fifth of the members of parliament were elected, with single-mandate constituency races, under which the remaining four-fifths of parliament were already chosen. Opposition parties argued that the proportional system was the only way for them to participate in elections, since most lack nationwide organizations. Another contentious amendment would alter the presidential succession process so that the prime minister would become president if the head of state resigns or becomes incapacitated. Critics charged that President Aliev would appoint his son, Ilham, prime minister and then engineer a transfer of power.

According to official results, each of the amendments was approved by more than 96 percent of voters. However, opposition groups and the OSCE charged that the referendum was marred by fraud, including ballot-box stuffing, the pressuring of voters, intimidation of election monitors and officials, and inflated voter-turnout figures of nearly 90 percent. The vote was followed by further public protests demanding an annulment of the referendum and President Aliev's resignation.

In return for Azerbaijan's cooperation in the U.S.-led antiterrorism campaign, President George W. Bush lifted Amendment 907 to the Freedom Support Act banning certain U.S. assistance to Azerbaijan. In December 2001, the U.S. Congress had authorized President Bush to waive, on an annual basis, the controversial nine-year-old sanctions, which were enacted during the war with Armenia over the disputed territory of Nagorno-Karabakh.

The long-awaited start of construction on the first major Caspian oil export route bypassing Russian territory was marked by a ceremony near Baku on September 18. The U.S.-backed Baku-Ceyhan oil pipeline, which will run from Azerbaijan through Georgia to the Turkish port of Ceyhan, is scheduled to be completed in 2004, with the first oil due to flow in 2005.

The most recent internationally-led peace talks over Nagorno-Karabakh failed to achieve a lasting settlement at year's end. Although Aliev remains publicly committed to negotiations, many Azerbaijanis support the idea of military action to recapture the territory from Armenia. Neither Armenia's president, Robert Kocharian, nor Aliev is likely to risk the domestic political consequences of making major public concessions over the disputed enclave ahead of presidential elections scheduled in both countries for 2003.

Political Rights and Civil Liberties: Citizens of Azerbaijan cannot change their government democratically. The 1995 constitution gives the president control over the government, legislature, and judiciary. The 1993 and 1998 presidential and 1995 and 2000 parliamentary elections were considered neither free nor fair by international observers. Opposition political party members face frequent harassment and arrest by the authorities. On October 1, 2002, two secretaries of the Democratic Party of Azerbaijan (DPA) and six members of the Musavat Party were arrested in two separate incidents. Spokesmen for the parties said they believed that the arrests were linked to plans to convene an opposition demonstration in Baku on October 5.

Although the constitution guarantees freedoms of speech and the press, journalists who publish articles critical of the president or other prominent state officials are routinely prosecuted, and self-censorship is common. Many newspapers struggle financially in the face of low circulation, low advertising revenues, and heavy fines or imprisonment of their staff. According to the Azerbaijan Council of Editors, 31 court cases were brought against media outlets between January and November 2002. Mubariz Djafarli of the opposition *Yeni Musavat* newspaper was attacked and beaten in June by two men who made reference to his having insulted President Heydar Aliev's son, Ilham, in a recent article. In December, the paper was found guilty of insulting the honor and dignity of a local government official in an article published in October, fined $615,000, and ordered to publish a retraction of the article. On July 29, publisher and editor in chief Elmar Huseynov and reporter Eynulla Fetullayev of the independent magazine *Monitor* were found guilty of defamation, fined $10,200, and ordered to print a retraction of an article critical of the military. A 2002 presidential decree on state secrets requires journalists to ask a government commission whether sensitive material is a state secret before publishing it; journalists could also be required to reveal their sources. Following widespread criticism of the new rules, the length of the commission's review period was shortened from 7 days to 48 hours, and the protection of journalists' sources was guaranteed.

The government restricts some religious activities of foreigners and Azerbaijanis who are members of "nontraditional" religious groups through burdensome registration requirements and interference in the dissemination of printed materials. Islam, Russian Orthodoxy, and Judaism are considered "traditional" religions and their members can worship freely.

The government frequently restricts freedom of assembly and association, particularly for political parties critical of the government. Following international and domestic protests, President Aliev refused to sign controversial amendments to the law on grants that had been adopted by parliament in March. The amendments would have required that only officially registered groups could receive grants from foreign governments and nongovernmental organizations, sources of funding on which most unregistered groups depend. Most trade unions belong to the state-run Azerbaijani Labor Federation, and there is no effective collective bargaining system.

The judiciary, which does not function independently of the executive branch, is inefficient and corrupt. Detainees are often held for long periods before trials, and their access to evidence and lawyers is restricted. Police abuse of suspects during arrest and interrogation reportedly remains commonplace, with torture often used to extract confessions. According to the Council of Europe and opposition and human rights groups, several hundred political prisoners are held in detention throughout the country. The more than 750,000 refugees who fled the war in Nagorno-Karabakh remain in Azerbaijan, often living in appalling conditions. Most are unable or unwilling to return to their homes because they fear for their safety and have concerns over dismal economic prospects in the breakaway territory.

Significant parts of the economy are in the hands of a corrupt nomenklatura, which severely limits equality of opportunity. Most women work in the low-paying public sector, and traditional norms perpetuate discrimination and violence against women. Muslim women wearing head scarves have been prevented by some universities from attending classes.

Bahamas

Polity: Parliamentary democracy
Economy: Capitalist-statist
Population: 300,000
PPP: $17,012
Life Expectancy: 72

Political Rights: 1
Civil Liberties: 1
Status: Free

Religious Groups: Baptist (32 percent), Anglican (20 percent), Roman Catholic (19 percent), other Protestant (18 percent), other (11 percent)
Ethnic Groups: Black (85 percent), white (12 percent), Asian and Hispanic (3 percent)
Capital: Nassau

Ten-Year Ratings Timeline (Political Rights, Civil Liberties, Status)

1993	1994	1995	1996	1997	1998	1999	2000	2001	2002	2003
1,2F	1,2F	1,2F	1,2F	1,2F	1,2F	1,2F	1,1F	1,1F	1,1F	1,1F

Overview:

In the May 2002 elections, the Free National Movement (FNM) party, which had ruled for the previous ten years, was defeated by the Progressive Liberal Party (PLP). Prime Minister Hubert Ingraham retired from politics, fulfilling a promise he had made prior to the elections. He was replaced by Perry Christie, leader of the PLP. Out of the 40 seats in the House of Assembly, the PLP won 29 seats, while the FNM received only 8. Christie and Ingraham are close personal friends and business partners, which may indicate that the new prime minister's economic and political policies are not likely to diverge much from those of his predecessor. Ingraham is credited with having improved the country's international reputation with policies that reduced money laundering and by improving counternarcotics cooperation with the United States. The Bahamas has promoted tourism and allowed the banking industry to grow; as a result the country has become one of the Caribbean's most affluent.

The Bahamas is a 700-island archipelago in the Caribbean. It gained independence in 1973 and is part of the Commonwealth. The 1973 constitution established a 49-member House of Assembly, directly elected for five years, and a 16-member appointed Senate. The prime minister appoints 9 members, the leader of the parliament opposition 4, and the governor-general 3. The assembly has been reduced in size to 40, in keeping with a campaign promise by the FNM.

Lynden Pindling served as first prime minister and head of the PLP for 25 years. After years of allegations of corruption and involvement by high officials in narcotics trafficking, Pindling was defeated by the FNM in 1992. Prime Minister Ingraham promised honesty, efficiency, and accountability in government. The FNM won 32 seats in the House of Assembly, to the PLP's 17.

In the 1997 election, Ingraham took credit for revitalizing the economy by attracting foreign investment, and his FNM received 34 seats to the PLP's 6. In April 1997, Pindling resigned as opposition leader and was replaced by Perry Christie, who had served in the PLP cabinet until he denounced government corruption in the wake of a drug probe.

Rising crime rates in the late 1990s, which undermined the early accomplishments of the Ingraham government, were linked to illegal trafficking in narcotics and gunrunning. The Ingraham administration set up a new antidrug intelligence unit and announced plans to bring the financial sector into full compliance with international standards and practices by strengthening requirements to report suspicious and unusual transactions.

Political Rights and Civil Liberties: Constitutional guarantees are generally respected, including the right to organize political parties, civic organizations, and labor unions, as is the free exercise of religion. Human rights organizations have broad access to institutions and individuals. The judicial system is headed by the Supreme Court and a court of appeals, with the right of appeal under certain circumstances to the Privy Council in London. Significant progress has been reported in reducing both the length of court cases and the backlog of criminal appeals.

Violent crime is a continuing concern and was a focus of the Ingraham government. Nongovernmental organizations have documented the occasional abuse of prisoners, arbitrary arrests, and lengthy pretrial detentions. The Royal Bahamas Police Force has made progress in reducing corruption in the force, including introducing new procedures to limit unethical or illegal conduct. While the police have been recognized for their key role in regional efforts to stem the drug trade, coordination with the Royal Bahamas Defence Force (RBDF) has presented more difficulties that reflect general ambivalence about the RBDF's role in law enforcement. Violence against women is a serious and widespread problem, and child abuse and neglect remain serious.

The Ingraham administration made important efforts to relieve overcrowding of prisoners. There are persistent reports of overcrowding, and poor medical facilities are still the norm. Children continue to be housed with adults, and there have been reports of sexual abuse. The Bahamas is an accessible transit area for illegal aliens seeking entrance to the United States. The Bahamian government forcibly repatriates most asylum seekers, including Haitians and Cubans.

Daily and weekly newspapers, all privately owned, express a variety of views on public issues, as do the government-run radio station and four privately owned radio broadcasters. Opposition politicians claim that the state-run television system, the Broadcasting Corporation of the Bahamas, gives preferential coverage to the ruling party. Full freedom of expression is constrained by strict libel laws. Media laws were amended to allow for private ownership of broadcasting outlets.

Labor, business, and professional organizations are generally free from governmental interference. Unions have the right to strike, and collective bargaining is prevalent.

Discrimination against the disabled and persons of Haitian descent persists. Between 25,000 and 40,000 Haitians reside illegally in the Bahamas. Strict citizenship requirement and a stringent work permit system leave Haitians with few rights. The influx has created social tension because of the strain on government services.

Bahrain

Polity: Traditional monarchy
Economy: Capitalist-statist
Population: 700,000
PPP: $15,084
Life Expectancy: 74
Religious Groups: Shi'a Muslim (70 percent), Sunni Muslim (30 percent)
Ethnic Groups: Bahraini (63 percent), Asian (19 percent), other Arab (10 percent), Iranian (8 percent)
Capital: Manama

Political Rights: 5*
Civil Liberties: 5
Status: Partly Free

Ratings Change: Bahrain's political rights rating improved from 6 to 5, and its status from Not Free to Partly Free, due to relatively free and fair parliamentary elections.

Ten-Year Ratings Timeline (Political Rights, Civil Liberties, Status)

1993	1994	1995	1996	1997	1998	1999	2000	2001	2002	2003
6,5PF	6,6NF	6,6NF	6,6NF	7,6NF	7,6NF	7,6NF	7,6NF	7,6NF	6,5NF	5,5PF

Overview:

Bahrain held parliamentary elections in 2002 for the first time in 30 years. It also became the first Gulf Cooperation Council (GCC) country to allow the participation of women in national elections, both at the polls and on the ballot, and the second GCC country to allow the establishment of independent labor unions.

Bahrain, an archipelago with a population of just 700,000, has been ruled by the al-Khalifa family since 1782. After 110 years as a British protectorate, Bahrain became independent in 1971 under the leadership of Emir Isa ibn Salman al-Khalifa. Although the country's 1973 constitution provided for a partially elected national assembly, the emir dissolved the body in 1975 and ruled with few checks on his power for the next quarter century.

Although Bahrain's 70 percent Shi'a majority has long resented the Sunni ruling elite, tensions were kept in check by prosperity during the 1970s oil boom. However, the 1979 revolution in predominantly Shi'a Iran brought to power an Islamic fundamentalist regime committed to spreading its creed to Shi'a minorities throughout the Arab world. During the decline of oil revenues in the 1980s, challenges to the emir's authority by Shi'a and leftist opposition activity steadily intensified.

The emir established a consultative council of appointed business and religious leaders in 1993, but the creation of an advisory body with no legislative power did little to stem increasingly strident calls for political liberalization. The following year, a Shi'a cleric and several Sunni former members of parliament were arrested after petitioning for the reinstatement of democratic institutions. The arrests sparked a period of violent unrest that left more than 40 people dead, thousands arrested, hundreds imprisoned, and more than 500 exiled. While the government blamed Iran for inciting the unrest, most informed observers pointed to the government's failure to resolve widespread social and economic problems, particularly unemployment, that disproportionately affect the Shi'a population.

Following the death of Bahrain's aging emir in 1999 and the ascension of his son, Hamad, the country witnessed a sustained process of economic and political liberalization. On the economic front, measures were introduced to reduce the country's reliance on dwindling oil reserves by strengthening industries such as banking, tourism, petrochemicals, aluminum smelting, and ship repair. Restrictions on foreign investment were eased and the distribution of social services improved in hopes of alleviating the economic disparities that fuel Shi'a disaffection.

On the political front, Hamad released political prisoners and allowed exiles to return, abolished emergency laws and courts, and eased restrictions on freedom of expression and association. In late 2000, the emir unveiled the National Charter, which calls for the country's transformation into a constitutional monarchy with an elected parliament, an independent judiciary, and political rights for women. The charter was overwhelmingly approved in a February 2001 referendum.

However, constitutional amendments introduced to enact the charter, as well as a succession of royal decrees, imposed limits on the political reform process. A February 2002 decree conferred equal legislative power on an appointed upper house of parliament (the Consultative Council), giving the king a de facto veto over the elected body. Measures to limit the electoral power of Shi'a's included decrees granting residents from other, predominantly Sunni GCC states the right to vote in municipal elections and to obtain Bahraini citizenship. Also, an August 2002 electoral law gerrymandered parliamentary district boundaries to dilute Shi'a votes. Other measures included a law prohibiting associations from "participating in any electoral campaign," a controversial press law, and royal decrees that granted immunity to government officials, as well as military and police officers, for all previous criminal acts and prohibited the incoming legislature from questioning them about matters predating its first session in December.

Vocal opposition to these measures prompted the king to suspend enforcement of the ban on political campaigning, but four main Shi'a and leftist groups nevertheless boycotted the October 2002 parliamentary elections. Despite the fact that the government allowed opposition groups favoring a boycott to hold mass rallies just days before the vote, 53 per cent of registered voters went to the polls. The results, as widely expected, were a victory for opposition candidates, especially Islamists. Many were surprised that the new cabinet unveiled in November included the former head of the London-based Bahrain Freedom Movement, Majed Alawi, as labor and social affairs minister.

Much like the introduction of reforms elsewhere in the Arab world, the political liberalization process in Bahrain has been intended to preserve the regime's grip on power. However, unlike most of its counterparts in the region, the Bahraini government appears increasingly committed to acquiring the consent of the governed and nurturing a truly democratic political culture.

Political Rights and Civil Liberties:

Bahrainis have only a limited capacity to change their government democratically. The king appoints the cabinet and controls appointments to the Consultative Council, the upper house of parliament, which can effectively veto decisions by the elected lower house. Municipal and legislative elections held in 2002 were considered free and fair. Although political parties remain illegal, opposition groups operate openly in the country and even those that boycotted the elections have been allowed to stage rallies of up to 30,000 people.

Bahrainis enjoy protection from arbitary arrest and detention. The government has the authority to monitor telephone calls and other private correspondence.

The judiciary in Bahrain is not independent, as the king appoints all judges, in consultation with the Supreme Judicial Council. Although courts have been subject to government pressure concerning verdicts and sentencing in the past, defendants receive due process protections and trials are open and reasonably fair.

Freedom of expression is limited, but growing. The broadcast media are state-owned and reflect official views, but privately owned newspapers and other print media criticize government policies on most issues and reflect a diverse range of opinions. Overt criticism of the royal family remains rare, but unflattering coverage is becoming more tolerated. In November 2001, journalist Hafez al-Shaikh Saleh was charged with undermining national unity after he criticized Hamad for visiting the United States. He was acquitted, however. The government barred the Qatar-based satellite channel Al-Jazeera from covering municipal elections in May. A November 2002 press law limited the state's capacity to close down publications arbitrarily, but vaguely worded provisions of the new law prohibiting activities such as the "propagation of immoral behavior" leave the door open for state pressure on the media.

Restrictive laws requiring governmental permission to form associations and the ban on political parties remain in place, but in practice the king has allowed the establishment of dozens of advocacy associations, including an independent human rights organization. The government allows access to the country by international human rights groups, including Amnesty International.

In September 2002, King Hamad issued a landmark law allowing the establishment of independent labor unions without government permission. However, a vaguely worded statute stipulating that strikes can be held "only to achieve the workers' social and economic demands" appears intended to depoliticize unions, and strikes are prohibited entirely in areas such as telecommunications and electricity and water supply, as well as in hospitals, airports, and ports. Foreign laborers are frequently mistreated and enjoy little protection under Bahraini law.

Women enjoy most of the same rights as men, but face legal discrimination in divorce and inheritance cases and are underrepresented in the workplace and government. There are a large number of women's rights groups active in Bahrain.

Islam is the state religion, and the government controls all official religious institutions. Small non-Muslim minorities, including Jews, Christians, Hindus, and Baha'is, are free to practice, maintain places of worship, and display religious symbols. Sunni Muslims enjoy favored status, while Shi'a's generally receive inferior educational, social, and municipal services. In 1999, Shiites were permitted to work in the defense forces and the Interior Ministry for the first time, but only in subordinate positions.

Bangladesh

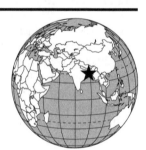

Polity: Parliamentary democracy
Economy: Capitalist-statist
Population: 133,600,000
PPP: $1,602
Life Expectancy: 59

Political Rights: 4*
Civil Liberties: 4
Status: Partly Free

Religious Groups: Muslim (83 percent), Hindu (16 percent), other (1 percent)
Ethnic Groups: Bengali (98 percent), other, including Bihari (2 percent)
Capital: Dhaka
Ratings Change: Bangladesh's political rights rating declined from 3 to 4 due to changes in the survey methodology.

Ten-Year Ratings Timeline (Political Rights, Civil Liberties, Status)

1993	1994	1995	1996	1997	1998	1999	2000	2001	2002	2003
2,3F	2,4PF	2,4PF	3,4PF	2,4PF	2,4PF	2,4PF	3,4PF	3,4PF	3,4PF	4,4PF

Overview:
While the ruling Bangladesh Nationalist Party (BNP) made some progress on economic reform after winning elections in October 2001, Bangladesh remained plagued by lawlessness, rampant corruption, and violent political polarization during 2002. The opposition Awami League used a parliamentary boycott and national strikes to impede

the functioning of the BNP-led coalition. For its part, the government initiated a sweeping anticrime drive in October and appeared to grow increasingly intolerant of criticism as the year progressed. Leaders of the political opposition, foreign and domestic journalists, and human rights advocates were detained under national security legislation and some were subjected to torture and criminal charges.

With the partition of British India in 1947, what is now Bangladesh became the eastern part of the newly formed state of Pakistan. Bangladesh won independence in December 1971 after Indian troops helped defeat West Pakistani forces stationed in Bangladesh in a nine-month war. The 1975 assassination of Prime Minister Sheikh Mujibur Rahman by soldiers precipitated 15 years of military rule and continues to polarize Bangladeshi politics. The country's democratic transition began with the resignation in 1990 of the last military ruler, General H. M. Ershad, after weeks of pro-democracy demonstrations. Elections in 1991 brought the BNP to power under Khaleda Zia.

The political strikes and parliamentary boycotts began in 1994, when Sheikh Hasina Wajed's center-left Awami League began boycotting parliament to protest alleged corruption in Zia's BNP government. The Awami League and the BNP differ relatively little on domestic policy. Many disputes reflect the personal animosity between Hasina, the daughter of independence leader Sheikh Mujibur Rahman, and Zia, the widow of a former military ruler allegedly complicit in Mujibur's assassination. The Awami League boycotted the February 1996 elections, which the BNP won, but forced Zia's resignation in March. At the June 1996 elections, the Awami League won 146 of 300 parliamentary seats while the BNP won 113. Under Hasina, the government signed an accord ending a low-grade insurgency in the Chittagong Hill Tracts. An October 2000 World Bank report praised Bangladesh's economic growth, but noted that each one-day nationwide strike costs the economy $60 million. However, Hasina's government exacerbated political tensions in January 2000 by passing a controversial public order law. The opposition said the law could be used against its members and to break general strikes.

Political gridlock continued in 2001, as the opposition BNP boycotted parliament and organized several nationwide strikes. Ignoring the opposition's demand for early elections, Sheikh Hasina Wajed became the first prime minister to complete a full five-year term in office in June 2001. However, in October, the Awami League was voted out of office in elections marred by political violence and intimidation. A new four-party coalition, dominated by the BNP and also including two hard-line Muslim parties, the Jamaat-e-Islami and the Islami Oikyo Jote, was sworn into power with a convincing majority of 214 of the 300 seats in parliament. Zia announced soon after taking office that her top priority would be to free Bangladesh from lawlessness and corruption.

The Awami League refused to accept the election results and boycotted parliament from October 2001 through June 2002. Reneging on a pledge she made during the election campaign, Hasina also organized several nationwide strikes during the year. Unexplained bomb blasts in crowded cinemas in September and December killed dozens and injured hundreds of people. Meanwhile, the government deployed nearly 40,000 army personnel in "Operation Clean Heart" in October as part of an anticrime drive during which thousands were arrested.

Political Rights and Civil Liberties: Bangladeshis can change their government through elections. A referendum held in 1991 transformed the powerful presidency into a largely ceremonial head-of-state position in a parliamentary system. Lower-house elections are held in single-member districts under a simple-plurality rule. The June 1996 vote was the first under a constitutional amendment requiring a caretaker government to conduct elections; it was Bangladesh's freest election despite some violence and irregularities. The October 2001 elections, which were monitored by more than 300,000 observers, were described as generally free and fair despite concerns over intimidation and violence. More than 140 people were killed throughout the campaign period in what was Bangladesh's most violent election to date.

Both major parties have undermined the legislative process through lengthy parliamentary boycotts while in opposition. In recent years, political violence during demonstrations and general strikes has killed hundreds of people in major cities and injured thousands, and police often use excessive force against opposition protesters. Student wings of political parties continue to be embroiled in violent campus conflicts. During the year, four municipal officials in Dhaka were murdered, allegedly because of their criminal links. Aid donors blame corruption, a weak rule of law, limited bureaucratic transparency, and political polarization for undermining government accountability and economic development. In August, Transparency International listed Bangladesh at the bottom of a 102-country list on its 2002 Corruption Perceptions Index.

Conditions for the press worsened in 2002. Although the print media are diverse, journalists face considerable pressure from organized-crime groups, political parties, the government, and Islamic fundamentalists, and they practice some self-censorship. A report published by Reporters Sans Frontieres in June alleged that Bangladesh had the highest incidence worldwide of violence against members of the press. A reporter was murdered in March, and journalists are frequently the targets of death threats and violent attacks. During the year, a number of journalists were detained by security forces after they reported on topics such as corruption, the rise of Islamic fundamentalism, and human rights abuses. Political considerations influence the distribution of government advertising revenue and subsidized newsprint, upon which most publications are dependent. The state owns most broadcast media, whose coverage favors the ruling party. Ekushey Television, the country's only independent broadcaster, was forced to close in August after the Supreme Court upheld the withdrawal of its license.

Islam is the official religion. Hindus, Christians, and other minorities worship freely but face societal discrimination and remain underrepresented in government employment. Violence against Bangladesh's Hindu minority flared up after the October 2001 elections, when BNP supporters reportedly attacked Hindus because of their perceived support for the rival Awami League. Atrocities, including murder, rape, destruction of property, and kidnapping, forced hundreds of Hindus from their homes, some across the border into India. There are also occasional reports of violence against members of the Ahmadiya religious minority.

The constitution provides for freedom of assembly, but the government frequently limits this right in practice. According to the U.S. State Department human rights report for 2001, nongovernmental human rights organizations say they face some harassment by government intelligence agents, ruling party activists, and Muslim religious leaders. In March, two staff members of Proshika were arrested and detained, allegedly because they were in possession of documents relating to attacks against Hindus following the 2001 elections. Several universities were closed during the year following student protests and clashes between students and security forces.

Union formation is hampered by a 30 percent employee approval requirement and restrictions on organizing by unregistered unions. Employers can legally fire or transfer workers suspected of union activities. The law prohibits many civil servants from joining unions; these workers can form associations but are prohibited from bargaining collectively. The U.S. Agency for International Development has reported that almost half of children aged 10 to 14 are working in Bangladesh, mostly as domestic servants, farm workers, or rickshaw pullers.

The Supreme Court is independent, but according to the U.S. State Department's report, lower-level courts are "reluctant to challenge government decisions." Lower courts are also rife with corruption and are severely backlogged, and pretrial detention is lengthy. Many defendants lack counsel, and poor people have limited recourse through the courts. Prisoners are routinely subject to physical abuse and demands for bribes from corrupt law-enforcement officials. The Economist Intelligence Unit reported that of 480,097 people arrested between July 2001 and August 2002, 206,643 were not charged with any crime, which left the police considerable scope to abuse their powers. Amnesty International's 2002 annual report noted that authorities "appeared to ignore torture allegations" despite dozens of custodial deaths during the year. Police also routinely rape suspects and prisoners. The majority of police abuses go unpunished, which results in a climate of impunity. However, in June, 13 policemen were sentenced to life imprisonment for the torture and murder of a student in their custody in 1998. Prison conditions are extremely poor, and severe overcrowding is increasingly common.

Authorities continued to arbitrarily detain political opponents and ordinary citizens under the 1974 Special Powers Act and other national security legislation, and used serial detentions to prevent the release of political activists. Several hundred opposition activists were rounded up without arrest warrants in August, and some were reportedly subject to torture. According to a UNDP report on the criminal law system released in September, almost 90 percent of "preventative detention" cases that reach the courts are judged to be unlawful. Under Section 54 of the Criminal Procedure Code, individuals may be detained for suspicion of criminal activity without a warrant. As part of the government's anticrime drive launched in October, the army detained nearly 3,500 people, including members of both political parties. In a December press release, Amnesty International highlighted a pattern of politically motivated detentions throughout 2002, noting that senior opposition politicians, academics, journalists, and human rights activists critical of government policies were particularly at risk of prolonged detention and ill-treatment in custody. Amnesty International also raised concern about the deaths of at least 32 people in army custody between October and December.

Tribal minorities have little control over land issues affecting them, and minority rights groups say that Bengalis have cheated many tribal people out of their land. A 1997 accord between the government and the Chittagong Hill Tracts (CHT)

People's Solidarity Association ended a 24-year insurgency in the CHT that sought autonomy for indigenous tribes and killed 8,500 soldiers, rebels, and civilians. However, Amnesty International's annual report for 2001 noted that violent clashes between tribal inhabitants and Bengali settlers continued to be reported in the CHT.

Roughly 260,000 Rohingyas fleeing forced labor, discrimination, and other abuses in Burma entered Bangladesh in 1991 and 1992; some 20,000 Rohingya refugees and 100,000 other Rohingyas not documented as refugees remain in the country. Bangladesh also hosts some 300,000 Urdu-speaking Biharis, who were rendered stateless at independence in 1971 and seek repatriation to Pakistan.

Rape, dowry-related assaults, acid throwing, and other violence against women occur frequently. According to the Acid Survivors Foundation, several hundred acid attacks are registered each year; the majority are carried out against women fleeing arranged marriages. A September 2000 UN report said that 47 percent of all Bangladeshi women are subjected to domestic violence. A law requiring rape victims to file police reports and obtain medical certificates within 24 hours of the crime in order to press charges prevents most rape cases from reaching the courts. Police also accept bribes not to register rape cases and rarely enforce existing laws protecting women. In rural areas religious leaders occasionally issue *fatwas* (religious edicts) that impose floggings and other punishments on women accused of violating strict moral codes. Women also face discrimination in health care, education, and employment, and are underrepresented in politics and government. As a result of parliamentary deadlocks, a provision that granted women 30 reserved seats in parliament was allowed to lapse in 2001. However, in December, an initial group of 20 women were commissioned as officers in Bangladesh's army.

Human rights activists estimate that organized groups traffick nearly 25,000 Bangladeshi women and children each year into Middle Eastern and other South Asian countries for the purposes of prostitution and low-paid labor. Law enforcement officials rarely investigate trafficking, and rights groups allege the police are often engaged in these and other crimes.

Barbados

Polity: Parliamentary democracy
Economy: Capitalist
Population: 300,000
PPP: $15,494
Life Expectancy: 73

Political Rights: 1
Civil Liberties: 1
Status: Free

Religious Groups: Protestant (67 percent), Roman Catholic (4 percent), none (17 percent), other (12 percent)
Ethnic Groups: Black (80 percent), white (4 percent), other (16 percent)
Capital: Bridgetown

Ten-Year Ratings Timeline (Political Rights, Civil Liberties, Status)

1993	1994	1995	1996	1997	1998	1999	2000	2001	2002	2003
1,1F	1,1F	1,1F	1,1F	1,1F	1,1F	1,1F	1,1F	1,1F	1,1F	1,1F

Overview:

Barbados has not escaped the increase in crime experienced by much of the Caribbean region. In October 2002 Attorney General Mia Mottley announced that a National Commission on Law and Order would be set up to reduce lawlessness. In dealing with issues that have threatened the island's vital tourism industry, the commission will address legislative reform, law enforcement, the administration of justice, and penal reform. As part of an effort to reduce the backlog of several thousand legal cases, four judges and two magistrates will also be appointed. Mottley also strongly voiced reservations about the Inter-American Convention on Corruption, claiming that it did not sufficiently regulate private sector corruption. Prime Minister Owen Arthur appointed Mottley, who at 35 is the youngest person, as well as the first woman, to hold the post, in 2001. The economy is under continued pressure from the dual onslaught of a fall in tourism following the terrorist attacks of September 2001 and the reduced demand of its traditional export of sugar due to the downturn of the global economy.

Barbados became independent in 1966 and is a member of the Commonwealth. The government is a parliamentary democracy with a bicameral legislature and a party system with universal suffrage. The 28-member House of Assembly is elected for a five-year term. The 21-member Senate is appointed by the governor-general: 12 on the advice of the prime minister, 2 on the advice of the leader of the opposition, and the remaining 7 at the discretion of the governor-general. The prime minister is the leader of the political party with a majority in the House. Power has alternated between two centrist parties—the Democratic Labour Party (DLP) and the Barbados Labour Party (BLP).

By 1994, after a recession, the economy appeared to be improving, but unemployment was still at nearly 25 percent. Prime Minister Erskine Sandiford's popularity suffered, and he was increasingly criticized for his authoritarian style of government. He lost a no-confidence vote in parliament when nine BLP legislators were joined by four DLP backbenchers and one independent legislator who had quit the DLP. David Thompson, the young finance minister, replaced Sandiford.

In the 1994 elections the BLP won 19 seats; the DLP, 8; and the New Democratic Party (NDP), a splinter of the DLP established in 1989, 1 seat. Owen Arthur, an economist elected in 1993 to head the BLP, promised to build "a modern, technologically dynamic economy," create jobs, and restore investor confidence. The BLP retained power in 1999 by winning 26 of 28 parliamentary seats, leaving Arthur firmly in control of his country.

The Arthur government made efforts to reduce dependence on tourism and sugar through diversification into the financial and computer services industries. The September 11 terrorist attacks in the United States badly hurt the vital tourism sector. Joint patrols of the Royal Barbados Police Force (RBPF) and the all-volunteer Barbados Defence Force have been initiated to patrol the island as violent crimes, many linked to narcotics trafficking, increased.

Political Rights and Civil Liberties: The government can be changed through democratic elections. The January 1999 elections were free and fair. The constitution guarantees freedom of religion, and the right to organize political parties, labor unions, and civic organizations is respected. Apart from the parties holding parliamentary seats, there are other political organizations, including the small, left-wing Workers' Party of Barbados.

The judicial system is independent, and the Supreme Court includes a high court and a court of appeals. Lower-court officials are appointed on the advice of the Judicial and Legal Service Commission. The prison system is overcrowded and outdated, with more than 800 inmates held in a building built for 350. The government allows private groups to visit prisons. The high crime rate, fueled by an increase in drug abuse and narcotics trafficking, has given rise to human rights concerns. A constitutional change allows convicts to be hanged as soon as possible after their appeals are exhausted. There are occasional reports of extrajudicial killings as well as complaints of excessive force used by the RBPF to extract confessions, along with reports that police do not always seek warrants before searching homes.

Freedom of expression is fully respected. Public opinion expressed through the news media, which are free of censorship and government control, has a powerful influence on policy. Newspapers are privately owned, and there are two major dailies. Private and government radio stations operate. The single television station, operated by the government-owned Caribbean Broadcasting Corporation, presents a wide range of political viewpoints.

There are two major labor unions, and various smaller ones are active. Women make up roughly half of the workforce. A domestic violence law was passed in 1992 to give police and judges greater power to protect women. Violence and abuse of women and children continue to be major social problems.

Belarus

Polity: Presidential
Economy: Statist
Population: 9,900,000
PPP: $7,544
Life Expectancy: 69
Religious Groups: Eastern Orthodox (80 percent), other (20 percent)
Ethnic Groups: Belarusian (81.2 percent), Russian (11.4 percent), Polish, Ukrainian, and other (7.4 percent)
Capital: Minsk

Political Rights: 6
Civil Liberties: 6
Status: Not Free

Ten-Year Ratings Timeline (Political Rights, Civil Liberties, Status)

1993	1994	1995	1996	1997	1998	1999	2000	2001	2002	2003
4,3PF	5,4PF	4,4PF	5,5PF	6,6NF	6,6NF	6,6NF	6,6NF	6,6NF	6,6NF	6,6NF

Overview:

Belarusian president Alyaksandr Lukashenka has declared, "Our people live quietly and live well"; however, his statement is deceiving. On the whole, Belarusian citizens indeed live quietly, but they do so in fear of a regime that systematically disregards the most basic political rights and civil liberties. In certain respects, it also appears that Belarusians live well. Official unemployment hovers around 2 percent, and spending on health and education as a percentage of gross domestic product (GDP) is approximately 7 percent. Yet the economy of Belarus today remains largely indistinguishable from its economy under the former Soviet command system. According to the European Bank for Reconstruction and Development, the country's private sector share of GDP, at 20 percent, is the lowest of all the post-Communist countries. World Bank data also show that more than a quarter of the population lives below the national poverty line.

The year 2002 saw no positive change in this situation. Rather, the year was marked by retaliation against individuals and institutions that opposed the president's reelection the year before. Lukashenka also signed into law two pieces of legislation that further threaten civil liberties. The first, consisting of amendments to the Law on Religion, bans unregistered religious activity and places severe limits on the work of minority faiths. The second, the Law on the Fight Against Terrorism, threatens freedom of expression by allowing government authorities to take control of the media during so-called counter-terrorism operations. According to the U.K.-based group Article 19, which monitors censorship around the world, the new law "[goes] beyond what is necessary to combat terrorism."

In response to Lukashenka's postelection behavior and reports that since September 11, 2001, Belarus has been a regular supplier of military equipment and technicians to rogue states like Sudan and Iraq, Western leaders have grown more assertive in expressing their disapproval of Europe's last dictatorship. The Czech government, for example, refused to grant Lukashenka a visa so that he could attend a historic summit in Prague on NATO enlargement. Days later, 14 members of the EU imposed a complete travel ban on the president in response to the country's poor human rights record. Only Portugal abstained from the ban, which came just prior to an OSCE meeting in Lisbon that Belarus was expected to attend. Even Russian president Vladimir Putin, who is generally supportive of Lukashenka's regime, angered the Belarusian leader when he proposed absorbing Belarus into the Russian Federation as an alternative to their existing union treaty.

When Belarus declared independence in 1991, it ended centuries of foreign ascendancy by Lithuania, Poland, Russia, and ultimately the Soviet Union. Stanislaw Shushkevich, a reform-minded leader, served as head of state from 1991 to 1994. That year voters made Alyaksandr Lukashenka the country's first post-Soviet president. He has pursued a close union with Russia, subordinated the government and courts to his political whims, denied citizens basic rights and liberties, and ruled by decree ever since his election.

In a 1996 referendum, Belarusian citizens favored constitutional amendments that extended Lukashenka's term through 2001, broadened presidential powers, and created a new bicameral parliament. When the president ignored a court ruling that the referendum was nonbinding, Prime Minister Mikhail Chyhir resigned in protest. Since July 1999, when the president's original mandate expired, most Western nations have refused to recognize him as the legitimate head of state. Instead, they recognize the pre-1996 Supreme Soviet as the legitimate legislative body.

The year 2001 marked Belarus's tenth anniversary of post-Soviet independence, but the country had little to show for it. That year, despite accusations that the president was directing a government-sponsored death squad aimed at silencing his opponents, Lukashenka proved victorious in a controversial bid for reelection. Western nations declared the vote unfree and unfair, while domestic supporters of opposition candidate Vladimir Goncharik accused the government of falsifying the results. If one could glean anything positive from the election, it was the role played by opposition parties and civil society. Although the opposition parties backing Vladimir Goncharik represented a broad political spectrum, they agreed on one thing: defeating Lukashenka. Their decision to rally around a single candidate represented an important step in their development.

In 2002, anyone who had opposed Lukashanka during the campaign became a potential target of the president's revenge. In June, for example, a Belarusian court sentenced Mikola Markevich and Paval Mazheika of the independent newspaper *Pahonya* to two-and-a-half and two years of hard labor, respectively, for libeling Lukashenka during the campaign. That same month, journalist Viktar Ivashkevich, the editor-in-chief of the independent paper *Rabochy*, was charged with defaming Lukashenka in an article that accused the president and his administration of corruption. Ivashkevich was convicted in September and sentenced to 2 years of hard labor. Also, in November, Anatoly Lebedko, the chairman of the opposition United Civic Party, was detained by Belarusian KGB agents after visiting the U.S. embassy in Minsk. Democratic activists found this incident particularly disturbing because Belarusian authorities threatened to charge Lebedko with treason for simply meeting with foreign diplomatic officials. The move, some said, harked back to the Soviet period.

Political Rights and Civil Liberties: Despite a constitutional guarantee of universal, equal, and direct suffrage, citizens of Belarus cannot change their government democratically. Although Belarusian citizens had three candidates from whom to choose on September 9, 2001, the outcome of the country's presidential election was never in doubt. During the campaign, the government and its supporters harassed would-be candidates and independent media outlets. They also sought votes in exchange for promises of better wages. On election day, incumbent Alyaksandr Lukashenka declared himself the victor with 78 percent of the vote over candidates Vladimir Goncharik (12 percent) and Sergei Gaidukevich (2 percent). However, opposition parties claimed that Lukashenka received only 47 percent of the vote and Goncharik 41 percent—an outcome that by law would have forced a second round.

In October 2000, Belarus held elections to the Chamber of Representatives, parliament's lower house. State media coverage of the campaign was limited and biased, and approximately half of all opposition candidates were denied registration. Nongovernmental organizations reported irregularities such as ballot-box stuffing and tampering with voter registration lists. Seven opposition parties boycotted the elections when the government failed to ensure a fair campaign and to give parliament more substantial duties. Some opposition candidates participated in the election, but only three received a mandate.

The year 2001 marked the five-year anniversary of Belarus's union treaty with Russia. However, Russian enthusiasm for the union appears to have waned, and progress has slowed in implementing the treaty's provisions. In 2002, Putin angered Lukashenka when he put forth two new proposals on future ties. Lukashenka categorically rejected Putin's ideas, particularly on the creation of a union state that folds Belarus into the Russian Federation.

The Lukashenka regime systematically curtails press freedoms. State media are subordinated to the president, and harassment and censorship of independent media are routine. Libel is both a civil and a criminal offense. The State Press Committee can issue warnings to publishers for unauthorized activities such as changing a publication's title or distributing copies abroad. It also can arbitrarily shut down publications without court orders.

In 2002, Lukashenka oversaw a systematic crackdown on journalists and media outlets that criticized or opposed him during the 2001 presidential election. A popular method of harassment was the use of libel and defamation laws to try to cripple the finances of media outlets and silence reporters. Also during the year, according to Radio Free Europe/Radio Liberty, the state replaced the editors of four state-supported journals with individuals loyal to Lukashenka and issued a list of "undesirable" writers and poets. RFE/RL itself, a chief source of independent reporting in the country, came under increased harassment by the regime as well.

Despite constitutional guarantees that "all religions and faiths shall be equal before the law," Belarusian government decrees and registration requirements have increasingly restricted the life and work of religious groups in Belarus. In 2002 alone, uniformed troops bulldozed a new Autocephalous Orthodox Church on its day of consecration; police fined Hindus for meditating in a public park; and authorities took members of the Baptist Church to court for singing hymns in public. President Lukashenka also signed into law amendments to the Law on Religions that provide for government censorship of religious publications and prevent foreign citizens from leading religious groups. The amendments also place strict limitations on religious groups that have been active in Belarus for less than 20 years.

The Lukashenka government rigorously limits freedom of assembly and association. Protests and rallies require authorization from local authorities, who can arbitrarily withhold or revoke permission. When public demonstrations do occur, police typically break them up and arrest participants.

Although the country's constitution calls for judicial independence, courts are subject to weighty government influence. Opposition members, independent journalists, and other persons who oppose government policies experience arbitrary arrest and imprisonment. The right to a fair trial is not always respected.

The constitution outlines a range of personal liberties and freedoms, but the government honors them selectively. Wiretapping by state security agencies limits the right to privacy; arbitrary search and seizure compromises the inviolability of the home; and the internal passport system controls freedom of movement and choice of residence. The country's command economy also severely limits economic freedom.

Belgium

Polity: Parliamentary democracy (federal)
Economy: Capitalist
Population: 10,300,000
PPP: $27,178
Life Expectancy: 78
Religious Groups: Roman Catholic (75 percent), Protestant or other (25 percent)
Ethnic Groups: Fleming (58 percent), Walloon (31 percent), other (11 percent)
Capital: Brussels

Political Rights: 1
Civil Liberties: 1*
Status: Free

Ratings Change: Belgium's civil liberties rating improved from 2 to 1 due to changes in the survey methodology.

Ten-Year Ratings Timeline (Political Rights, Civil Liberties, Status)

1993	1994	1995	1996	1997	1998	1999	2000	2001	2002	2003
1,1F	1,1F	1,1F	1,1F	1,2F	1,2F	1,2F	1,2F	1,2F	1,2F	1,1F

Overview:

The Convention on the Future of Europe, established under the Belgian EU presidency, commenced work in 2002.

Tensions between the two dominant ethnic groups, the Walloons and the Flemings, continued as the Lambermont devolution reforms took effect. Human rights groups criticized the treatment of resident minorities, asylum seekers, and journalists. Belgium sold arms to Nepal, and Belgium's law of universal jurisdiction suffered setbacks. Belgium apologized for having deported Jews to Nazi Germany. Minors were barred from participation in armed conflict.

Modern Belgium dates from 1830, when the territory broke away from the Netherlands and formed a constitutional monarchy. Today, the monarchy is largely ceremonial. Ethnic and linguistic antagonism during the 1960s prompted a series of constitutional amendments, during 1970–1971 and in 1993, which devolved power to regional councils at the central government's expense. A 1993 amendment made the country a federation of Dutch-speaking Flanders, French-speaking Wallonia, and bilingual Brussels (located in Flanders, with a Francophone population), with the German-speaking area accorded cultural autonomy. Another 1993 amendment established three directly elected regional assemblies with primary responsibilities for housing, transportation, public works, education, culture, and the environment. The weak central government continues to oversee foreign policy, defense, justice, monetary policy, taxation, and the management of the budget deficit.

A Green-Liberal-Socialist coalition has ruled Belgium since July 1999. Municipal voting in 2000 gave the right-wing, anti-immigrant Vlaams Blok, which seeks an independent Flanders, substantial electoral gains.

Ethnic and linguistic tensions between Walloons and Flemings intensified, partly owing to Flemings' resentment of the Lambermont accords, effective January 2002, which allow for subsidy transfers—ostensibly from Flemish tax revenues—to Wallonia, where unemployment is higher and gross domestic product lower. In September, the Council of Europe rebuked Belgium for violating Walloons' rights. The federal government, but not regional and national parliaments, signed the council's minority-protection convention.

Through the Convention on the Future of Europe, which started work in February, Belgium is pursuing a common EU citizenship, immigration and asylum policy, and increased rights for subnational regions.

In February, the International Court of Justice ruled that Belgium cannot prosecute the Congolese foreign minister, Yerodia Ndombasi, for the 1998 killings of ethnic Tutsis because he is entitled to diplomatic immunity. In July, a Belgian appeals court ruled that Israeli Prime Minister Ariel Sharon cannot be tried for war crimes in absentia. Sharon, then defense minister, was charged for his role in the killings of civilians at the Sabra and Chatila refugee camps in 1982.

The health minister, a member of the Flemish Green party, Agalev, resigned in August to protest the sale of 5,500 automatic rifles from a Walloon-based factory to Nepal to help quell a Maoist rebellion.

Political Rights and Civil Liberties:

Belgians can change their government democratically. Non-voters are subject to fines. Political parties generally organize themselves along ethnic lines. Constitutional disputes arise when a member of an ethnic group elected to office in the territory of a different ethnic group refuses to take a competency test in that territory's dominant language.

Freedom of speech and the press is guaranteed. Belgian law prohibits some pornography and incitements to violence. Libel laws have minor restraining effects on the press. Restrictions on civil servants' rights to criticize the government reduces the right of civil speech. Autonomous public boards govern the state television and radio networks and ensure linguistically pluralistic public broadcasting.

The daily newspapers have a combined circulation of two million. Sixteen are French; ten, Flemish; one, German; and one has both Flemish and French editions. The three state-run television and radio services serve each of the three language groups. In May, a Brussels court fined two reporters for the Belgian daily *De Morgen* for not revealing their sources in an article saying Belgian State Railways had over-shot its budget to build a new high-speed train station in Liège.

Belgians enjoy freedom of religion and association. Christian, Jewish, and Mus-lim institutions are state subsidized in this overwhelmingly Roman Catholic coun-try, and other faiths are not restricted. Immigrants and linguistic minorities argue that linguistic zoning limits opportunity. Human rights groups voiced concern in May about increased anti-Semitism because synagogues, Jewish-owned stores, and the chief rabbi of Brussels were attacked. In October, Belgium apologized for the deportation of Jews to Nazi Germany. Jewish Holocaust survivors and Belgian banks agreed to US$54 million in compensation for cash left in accounts whose owners were killed.

A 1993 law allows Belgian courts to try alleged war criminals. The law was ex-panded in 1999 to allow courts to hear cases of genocide, and other crimes against humanity, committed anywhere, and involving non-Belgian defendants.

The European Court of Human Rights ordered the Belgian government in Octo-ber to pay compensation to a Roma family that had accused Belgium of human rights violations during the 1999 deportation of dozens of asylum-seeking Slovak Roma.

Also in October, the European Committee for the Prevention of Torture and In-human or Degrading Treatment or Punishment (CPT), noted that Belgium had im-proved its deportation practices. Human rights groups had criticized Belgium's pro-cedures, citing the death of Nigerian asylum seeker Semira Adamu in 1998 during expulsion.

In October 2002, Belgium's Senate's Justice Commission voted to allow same-sex marriages. If the bill passes parliament, Belgium will be the second country, after the Netherlands, to legalize gay marriages.

Labor unions have the right to strike.

As of February, the Optional Protocol to the Convention on the Rights of the Child on the involvement of children in armed conflict raised the minimum age for direct participation in hostilities, and for compulsory government recruitment, to 18. Voluntary recruitment is allowed at 16.

The "Smet-tobback" law introduced a rule in 1994 that at least one-third of all people elected at all levels of government should be women. In 1975 a collective agreement was signed for equal pay; nevertheless, women still earn only 79.6 per-cent of what men earn, according to the European Industrial Relations Observatory.

Belize

Polity: Parliamentary democracy
Economy: Capitalist
Population: 300,000
PPP: $5,606
Life Expectancy: 72

Political Rights: 1
Civil Liberties: 2
Status: Free

Religious Groups: Roman Catholic (49.6 percent), Protestant (27 percent), other (23.4 percent)
Ethnic Groups: Mestizo (48.7 percent), Creole (24.9 percent), Maya (10.6 percent), Garifuna (6.1 percent), other (9.7 percent)
Capital: Belmopan

Ten-Year Ratings Timeline (Political Rights, Civil Liberties, Status)

1993	1994	1995	1996	1997	1998	1999	2000	2001	2002	2003
1,1F	1,1F	1,1F	1,1F	1,1F	1,1F	1,1F	1,1F	1,1F	1,2F	1,2F

Overview:

The long-running border dispute between Belize and Guatemala appeared to near a peaceful resolution after the August 2002 announcement that both governments would submit to popular vote the decision rendered by mediators of the Organization of American States. In September 2002 the government of Prime Minister Said Musa proposed a constitutional amendment to end appeals to the Judicial Committee of the Privy Council, located in the United Kingdom. The Belize Court of Appeals would be established as the final court of appeals for cases carrying a mandatory death sentence. There has been a moratorium on executions since 1985, but there is concern that a change in the law could lead to a resumption of capital punishment. In recent years Belize has experienced increases in the rates of violent crime, drug trafficking, and money laundering. Corruption and fraud continue to haunt the Immigration and Nationality Department over nationality applications and passport processing.

Belize achieved independence in 1981 and is a member of the Commonwealth. Formerly British Honduras, the name was changed in 1973. The government has changed hands three times, alternating between the center-right United Democratic Party (UDP) and the center-left People's United Party (PUP). In 1993, the UDP and the National Alliance for Belizean Rights (NABR) formed a coalition, winning 16 of the 29 seats in the House of Representatives. The August 1998 elections proved to be a referendum on Prime Minister Manuel Esquivel's largely unfulfilled pledge that his UDP would create jobs. The PUP won 26 out of 29 seats in parliament. Said Musa, a former attorney general, promised adherence to international treaties on indigenous and women's rights. His government later blocked efforts by Indian groups to make claims on their land rights before the Inter-American Commission on Human Rights.

Political Rights and Civil Liberties:

Democratic government change takes place with free and fair elections. The 29-seat House of Representatives is elected for a five-year term. Members of the Senate are appointed: 5 by the governor-general on the advice of the prime minister; 2 by the leader of the parliamentary opposition; and 1 by the Belize Advisory Council. There are no restrictions on the right to organize political parties, and there are mestizo, Creole, Maya, and Garifuna parties in parliament. A large number of nongovernmental organizations are active in social, economic, and environmental areas.

The judiciary is independent and nondiscriminatory, and the rule of law is generally respected. Judges and the director of public prosecutions negotiate the renewal of their employment contracts which makes them vulnerable to political influence. There are lengthy backlogs of trials, in part due to the high turnover of judges, the result of their low pay. Cases often go on for years while defendants are free on bail. Reports of police misconduct are investigated by the department's internal affairs office or by an ombudsman's office. Extrajudicial killing and use of excessive force are the country's primary rights concerns. Reports of abuses have nearly doubled in recent years. Prisons do not meet minimum standards. Drug trafficking and gang conflict have contributed to an increase in crime. An antinarcotics agreement was signed with the United States in September of 2002. Projects aimed at suppressing the cultivation, processing, and trafficking of drugs, curbing violent crime, and eliminating money laundering will be funded.

The Belize Human Rights Commission is independent and effective. Human rights concerns include the conditions of migrant workers and refugees from neighboring countries, and charges of labor abuses by Belizean employers. Most of the estimated 40,000 Spanish speakers who have immigrated to the largely English-speaking country since the 1980s do not have legal status.

There are judicial restrictions on freedom of the press, including prison terms for those who question the validity of financial disclosure statements submitted by public officials. Belize has six privately owned newspapers, three of which are subsidized by major political parties. The mostly English-language press is free to publish a variety of political viewpoints, including those critical of the government, and there are Spanish-language media. Belize has a literacy rate of more than 90 percent. Fourteen private television stations operate, including four cable systems. There is an independent board to oversee operations of the government-owned outlets.

There is freedom of religion, and the government actively discourages racial and ethnic discrimination. Although the Maya claim to be the original inhabitants of Belize, they have no secure title to their ancestral lands, which include some 700,000 acres of rain forest. Labor unions are independent and well organized and have the right to strike, but the percentage of the workforce that is organized has declined. Unionized workers can earn two to three times as much as their neighbors. Disputes are adjudicated by official boards of inquiry, and businesses are penalized for failing to abide by the labor code. Violence against women and children is a serious problem.

Benin

Polity: Presidential-
parliamentary democracy
Economy: Mixed statist
Population: 6,600,000
PPP: $990
Life Expectancy: 54
Religious Groups: Indigenous beliefs (50 percent),
Christian (30 percent), Muslim (20 percent)
Ethnic Groups: African [42 ethnic groups, including
Fon, Adja, Bariba, Yoruba] (99 percent), other (1 percent)
Capital: Porto-Novo

Political Rights: 3
Civil Liberties: 2
Status: Free

Ten-Year Ratings Timeline (Political Rights, Civil Liberties, Status)

1993	1994	1995	1996	1997	1998	1999	2000	2001	2002	2003
2,3F	2,3F	2,3F	2,2F	2,2F	2,2F	2,2F	2,3F	2,2F	3,2F	3,2F

Overview:

Benin was preparing for municipal and regional elections at the end of 2002 and had appointed new members to the Autonomous National Electoral Commission to oversee the voting. The government of President Mathieu Kerekou was involved in regional efforts to bring peace to nearby Cote d'Ivoire in September after rebellious Ivorian troops seized much of the northern area of that country. Benin maintained a good human rights record in 2002 and made efforts to curb the practice of child trafficking. The International Court of Justice helped resolve a dispute between Benin and Niger over their common border.

Benin was once the center of the ancient kingdom of Dahomey, the name by which the country was known until 1975, when Kerekou renamed it. Six decades of French colonial rule ended in 1960, and Kerekou took power 12 years later, ending successive coups and countercoups. He imposed a one-party state under the Benin People's Revolutionary Party and pursued Marxist-Leninist policies. However, by 1990, economic hardships and rising internal unrest had forced Kerekou to agree to a national conference that ushered in democracy. The transition culminated in his defeat by Nicephore Soglo in the March 1991 presidential elections. The country's human rights record subsequently improved. Kerekou made a comeback in the 1996 elections and won again in 2001.

Historically, Benin has been divided between northern and southern ethnic groups, which are the main roots of current political parties. The south has enjoyed more advanced development. Northern ethnic groups enlisted during Kerekou's early years in power still dominate the military, although efforts have been made in recent years to rectify this situation.

Benin is a poor country whose economy is based largely on subsistence agriculture. The International Monetary Fund in 2002 commended Benin for its economic progress, although poverty indicators have not improved significantly.

Political Rights and Civil Liberties: Benin held its first genuine multiparty elections in 1991 and now has more than 100 political parties. Presidential elections in 2001 were marred by technical and administrative problems, as well as by a boycott by the second- and third-place finishers in the second round of voting. The boycott gave incumbent President Mathieu Kerekou a solid victory with 84 percent of the vote. Former President Nicephore Soglo and Adrien Houngbedji claimed fraud after they had won 29 percent and 14 percent, respectively, in the first round of voting, compared with Kerekou's 47 percent. Kerekou ended up running against an obscure fourth-place candidate in the second round.

Several members of the Autonomous National Electoral Commission had stepped down in protest before the second round of voting, citing a lack of transparency and poor administration of the election. In the 1999 elections for the unicameral National Assembly, opposition parties won 42 parliamentary seats against 41 by candidates backed by President Kerekou.

The judiciary is generally considered to be independent, but it is inefficient and susceptible to corruption at some levels. The executive retains important powers. The Constitutional Court has demonstrated independence, but was accused of bias in favor of the president during the 2001 presidential elections. Lawmakers in 2001 replaced the colonial criminal code.

Freedom of assembly is respected in Benin, and requirements for permits and registration are often ignored. Human rights are largely respected, although concern has been raised about the operation of anticrime vigilante groups and the failure of the police to curb vigilantism. Prison conditions are harsh, marked by poor diet and inadequate medical care. Numerous nongovernmental organizations and human rights groups operate without hindrance.

Harsh libel laws have been used against journalists, but constitutional guarantees of freedom of expression are largely respected in practice. An independent and pluralistic press publishes articles highly critical of both government and opposition leaders and policies. Benin has more than a dozen daily newspapers, 40 magazines, about a dozen private radio stations, and two television stations.

Religious freedom is respected. Although the constitution provides for equality for women, they enjoy fewer educational and employment opportunities than men, particularly in rural areas. In family matters, in which traditional practices prevail, their legal rights are often ignored. Women's rights groups have been effective in drafting a family code that would improve the status of women and children under the law. Female genital mutilation is not illegal. The government has cooperated with efforts by nongovernmental organizations to raise awareness about the health dangers of the practice.

Smuggling children into neighboring countries for domestic service and meager compensation is reportedly widespread. Many, especially young girls, suffer abuse. Efforts are under way in Benin to fight child abuse and child trafficking through media campaigns and education.

The right to organize and join unions is constitutionally guaranteed and respected in practice. Strikes are legal, and collective bargaining is common.

Bhutan

Polity: Traditional monarchy
Economy: Pre-industrial
Population: 900,000
PPP: $1,412
Life Expectancy: 66
Religious Groups: Mahayana Buddhist (75 percent), Hindu (25 percent)
Ethnic Groups: Bhote (50 percent), Nepalese (35 percent), indigenous or migrant tribes (15 percent)
Capital: Thimphu

Political Rights: 6*
Civil Liberties: 5*
Status: Not Free

Ratings Change: Bhutan's political rights rating improved from 7 to 6 due to increased accountability of the monarchy to the people. It civil liberties rating improved from 6 to 5 due to changes in the survey methodology.

Ten-Year Ratings Timeline (Political Rights, Civil Liberties, Status)

1993	1994	1995	1996	1997	1998	1999	2000	2001	2002	2003
7,6NF	7,7NF	7,7NF	7,7NF	7,7NF	7,7NF	7,6NF	7,6NF	7,6NF	7,6NF	6,5NF

Overview:

The 39-member drafting committee established by the government held a series of discussions throughout 2002 on the structure of a new constitution. In December, the committee presented a draft constitution for deliberation and debate by the National Assembly as well as grassroots administrative bodies. The constitution is expected to lead to Bhutan's emergence as a constitutional monarchy with some form of parliamentary democracy.

Britain began guiding this Himalayan land's affairs in 1865, and in 1907 installed the still-ruling Wangchuk monarchy. However, a 1949 treaty gave India control over Bhutan's foreign affairs. In 1972, the current monarch, Jigme Singye Wangchuk, succeeded his father to the throne.

Reversing a long-standing policy of tolerating cultural diversity in the kingdom, the government in the late 1980s began requiring all Bhutanese to adopt the dress of the ruling Ngalong Drukpa ethnic group. Authorities said they feared for the survival of Drukpa culture because of the large number of Nepali speakers, also known as Southern Bhutanese, in the south. The situation worsened in 1988, when the government began using a strict 1985 citizenship law to arbitrarily strip thousands of Nepali speakers of their citizenship. The move came after a census showed Southern Bhutanese to be in the majority in five southern districts.

Led by the newly formed Bhutanese People's Party (BPP), Southern Bhutanese held demonstrations in September 1990 against the new measures. Accompanying arson and violence led authorities to crack down on the BPP. As conditions worsened, tens of thousands of Southern Bhutanese fled to Nepal in the early 1990s, many of them forcibly expelled by Bhutanese forces. Credible accounts suggest that soldiers raped and beat many Nepali-speaking villagers and detained thousands as "anti-nationals."

In early 2001, a ten-person, bilateral team began certifying citizenship documents and interviewing family heads of the estimated 100,000 Bhutanese refugees currently in Nepal. However, the process stalled after the completion of the verification procedure in the first of seven camps in December 2001. A European Union delegation, which visited the camps in July, expressed concern at the situation and urged both governments to speed up the verification process.

Relations with India continue to be strained by the presence in Bhutan of a number of Indian separatist militant groups. After holding talks with the Bhutanese government, the United Liberation Front of Assam (ULFA) agreed in June 2001 to reduce its presence within the country. However, there is little evidence that it has honored this commitment. In July 2002, the National Assembly recommended holding a final meeting with ULFA, after which it said that military action might become inevitable. Other Indian guerrilla groups continue to operate from Bhutanese soil despite mounting diplomatic pressure from New Delhi.

Political Rights and Civil Liberties: Bhutanese cannot change their government through elections and enjoy few basic rights. King Wangchuk and a small group of elites make key decisions and wield absolute power, although the king did take several steps in 1998 to increase the influence of the National Assembly. He removed himself as chairman of Bhutan's Council of Ministers; in addition, he gave the National Assembly the power to remove the king from the throne and to elect cabinet members from among candidates nominated by the king. The proposed constitution is expected to formalize the separation of powers and to address the king's status.

The government discourages the formation of political parties, and none exist legally. The 150-member National Assembly has little independent power, although some analysts note that debate within the assembly has become more lively and critical in recent years. Every three years village headmen choose 105 National Assembly members, while the king appoints 35 seats and religious groups choose 10 seats. For the 105 district-based seats, each village nominates one candidate for its district, though it must do so by consensus. Votes are cast by family heads rather than by individuals. Human rights activists say that in reality, authorities suggest a candidate to the headman in each village and the headman asks families to approve the candidate.

Bhutanese authorities sharply restrict freedoms of expression, assembly, and association. The government prohibits criticism of King Wangchuk and Bhutan's political system. Bhutan's only regular publication, the weekly *Kuensel*, reports news that puts the kingdom in a favorable light. The only exception is occasional coverage of criticism by National Assembly members of government policies during assembly meetings. Similarly, state-run broadcast media do not carry opposition positions and statements. Cable television service, which carries foreign programming, thrives in some areas but is hampered by a high sales tax and the absence of a broadcasting law.

While Bhutanese of all faiths generally can worship freely, government policy favors the Drukpa Kagyupa school of Mahayana Buddhism, which is the official religion. The government subsidizes Drukpa monasteries and shrines and helps fund the construction of Drukpa Kagyupa and Ningmapa temples and shrines, according to the U.S. State Department's 2002 Report on International Religious Freedom. Drukpa monks also wield political influence. Some members of the country's small Christian minority are reportedly subject to harassment by local authorities.

Citizens may only participate in a peaceful protest if the government approves of its purpose. The government does not allow nongovernmental groups to work on human rights or other overtly political issues. In recent years, security forces have arrested Bhutanese for taking part in peaceful pro-democracy demonstrations in eastern Bhutan. They have also arrested and deported Bhutanese refugees living in Nepal who entered and demonstrated inside Bhutan for the right to return home. The government prohibits independent trade unions and strikes. In any case, some 85 percent of the workforce is engaged in subsistence agriculture. Draft labor legislation under preparation would prohibit forced labor, discrimination, sexual harassment, and child employment in the private sector.

Bhutan's judiciary is not independent of the king, and legal protections are incomplete as a result of the lack of a fully developed criminal procedure code and deficiencies in police training. Arbitrary arrest, detention, and torture remain areas of concern. According to Amnesty International, 15 political prisoners arrested during demonstrations in 1997, in addition to an estimated 50 prisoners arrested in southern Bhutan around 1990, continue to serve lengthy prison sentences. However, the government's human rights record has improved since the early 1990s, when soldiers and police committed grave human rights abuses against Nepali-speaking Bhutanese. These abuses included arbitrary arrests, beatings, rapes, robberies, and the destruction of homes.

Conditions for Nepali speakers living in Bhutan have somewhat improved, but several major problems remain. A September 2002 Amnesty International report noted that ethnic Nepalese are still required to obtain official "security clearance certificates" to enter schools, take government jobs, or travel abroad. Many primary schools in the Nepali-speaking areas of southern Bhutan shut by the government in 1990 remain closed. At the same time, the government has in recent years eased some cultural restrictions that specifically targeted Southern Bhutanese. Although a 1989 royal decree forced all Bhutanese to adopt the national dress and customs of the ruling Drukpas, recent enforcement has been sporadic.

The government's expulsion of tens of thousands of Nepali-speaking Bhutanese in the early 1990s, and recent bilateral efforts to repatriate them, have underscored the tentative nature of citizenship in the kingdom. Prior to the expulsions, the government stripped thousands of Southern Bhutanese of their citizenship under a 1985 law that tightened citizenship requirements. The new law required both parents to be Bhutanese citizens in order for citizenship to be conferred on a child. In addition, Bhutanese seeking to verify citizenship had to prove that they or both their parents resided in Bhutan in 1958. That meant presenting land-tax receipts or other documents from 1958, nearly 30 years earlier.

The UN High Commissioner for Refugees says that the overwhelming majority of Bhutanese refugees who entered camps in Nepal since screening began in 1993 have documentary proof of Bhutanese nationality. However, the Bhutanese government continues to maintain that many of the refugees either left Bhutan voluntarily or were illegal immigrants. A bilateral verification process begun in 2001 has stalled amid disputes over how the refugees should be classified. Meanwhile, the government in 1998 began resettling Bhutanese from other parts of the country on land in southern Bhutan vacated by those who fled to Nepal. A report published by Habitat International Coalition in January documented specific cases of the appropriation of houses and land and noted that this policy will considerably complicate the refugee repatriation process.

Women make up only 23 percent of civil servants and are underrepresented in the National Assembly, although they increasingly are becoming senior officials as well as private sector entrepreneurs. Female school enrollment has risen in response to government policies.

Bolivia

Polity: Presidential-parliamentary democracy
Economy: Capitalist
Population: 8,800,000
PPP: $2,424
Life Expectancy: 63
Religious Groups: Roman Catholic (95 percent), Protestant [Evangelical Methodist]
Ethnic Groups: Quechua (30 percent), mestizo [mixed white and Amerindian ancestry] (30 percent), Aymara (25 percent), European (15 percent)
Capital: La Paz (administrative), Sucre (judicial)

Political Rights: 2*
Civil Liberties: 3
Status: Free

Ratings Change: Bolivia's political rights rating declined from 1 to 2 due to the increased influence of drug money in politics and burgeoning political corruption.

Ten-Year Ratings Timeline (Political Rights, Civil Liberties, Status)

1993	1994	1995	1996	1997	1998	1999	2000	2001	2002	2003
2,3F	2,3F	2,3F	2,4F	2,3F	1,3F	1,3F	1,3F	1,3F	1,3F	2,3f

Overview:
In the midst of growing social unrest and a continuing economic downturn, in 2002 the Bolivian congress elected former President Gonzalo Sanchez de Losada, a 72-year-old U.S.-educated millionaire, after he had barely beat Evo Morales, a radical Indian leader of the country's coca growers, in the popular vote. Sanchez de Losada's selection after his two-point popular vote victory over Morales dissipated, for now, fears that the poor Andean nation would be converted into a narco-socialist state.

The new president, who ruled a corruption-plagued though somewhat reformist administration from 1993 to 1997, promised that Bolivians would "work with austerity," while he pushed ahead with five major public works projects. Since 1998, Bolivia has eradicated more than 90,000 acres of coca cultivation and taken more than 230 tons of cocaine out of the illegal global market. However, Morales's showing in the polls was evidence of how unpopular these policies are among the country's majority Indian population, who have been shut out from the benefits of U.S.-backed economic reforms.

After achieving independence from Spain in 1825, the Republic of Bolivia endured recurrent instability and military rule. However, the armed forces, responsible for more than 180 coups in 157 years, have stayed in their barracks since 1982.

As a result of recent reforms, presidential terms run five years and congress consists of a 130-member House of Representatives and a 27-member Senate. The principal traditional parties are the conservative National Democratic Action (ADN); its governing coalition partner, the social-democratic Movement of the Revolutionary Left (MIR); and Sanchez de Losada's center-right Revolutionary Nationalist Movement (MNR). In 2002, the Socialist Movement (MAS) and the Pachacutti Indian Movement (MIP) gained significant electoral support as well.

In 1985, former dictator Gen. Hugo Banzer Suarez came in first in the popular vote, but a parliamentary coalition instead selected the octogenarian former president, Victor Paz Estenssoro, the founder of the MNR. In 1989 the MIR's Jaime Paz Zamora, who had run third in the polls, became president through an alliance with the ADN.

In 1993, the MIR-ADN candidate was Banzer, who came in second to the MNR's Sanchez de Losada, a planning minister in Paz Estenssoro's 1985-1989 administration. Sanchez de Losada oversaw the massive privatization of Bolivia's state-owned enterprises and, under U.S. pressure, stepped up coca eradication. A series of labor strikes and mass protests in early 1995 was followed by the imposition by Sanchez de Losada of a six-month state of siege.

Throughout 1996, the government privatization program brought regular street protests. As Sanchez de Losada's term ended, initiatives such as improved access to the courts, efforts to reform a corrupt, inefficient judiciary, and broad decentralization were overshadowed by increasingly bitter labor disputes. In nationwide municipal elections held in December 1999, conducted using the electoral code and political party legislation recently approved by congress, the ruling coalition made a strong showing, although the opposition MNR won the largest number of council seats and votes as a single party.

Banzer succeeded Sanchez de Losada for the presidency in 1998 and embarked on an ambitious program to eradicate the country's illegal coca production, taking 85 percent of the acreage out of cultivation. In doing so, Bolivia became America's most successful state crusader against the production of narcotics. Banzer also promoted efforts to reform the constitution in order to decentralize and broaden political participation, overcome social exclusion, and establish a social pact to strengthen the country's democratic institutions. In the months before the terminally ill Banzer's August 6, 2001, resignation, the dictator-turned-democrat tried to convene a "national dialogue" on Bolivia's mounting problems as a means of creating a policy consensus among the government, the opposition, and nongovernmental organizations.

Vice President Jorge Quiroga, known for his firm anticorruption stance, succeeded Banzer. By law, he could fill out the one year remaining of Banzer's term, but could not seek election in 2002. Quiroga pledged to continue Banzer's fight against governmental and judicial corruption and for more foreign investment as a means to stimulate economic growth and reduce poverty. At the end of 2001, a serious police corruption scandal added significantly to challenges Quiroga faced.

An anti-coca expeditionary task force paid for by the U.S. Embassy and made up of 1,500 former Bolivian soldiers in 2002 was the subject of frequent charges of the use of excessive force and human rights violations ranging from torture to murder. Critics say that the creation of a military force paid for by foreign funds violates both the Bolivian constitution and military regulations. Defenders of the force point out that the coca growers work closely with narcotics traffickers and claim that the traffickers include snipers and experts in booby traps.

According to the UN Development Fund, Bolivia remains a hemisphere leader in unequal distribution of wealth, with the richest 20 percent of the population accounting for 61 percent of the nation's income, and 38 times the income of the poorest 20 percent. Crime in La Paz and other major cities is increasing steadily. In September 2002, a breakdown in talks between the government and Indian farmers demanding land reform resulted in a partial paralysis of the country and left at least ten peasants and four soldiers dead.

Political Rights and Civil Liberties: Citizens can change their government through elections. The 2002 elections were generally free and fair, although U.S. government officials say they had evidence that Colombian drug lords financed some of Morales's political organization.

The judiciary, headed by the Supreme Court, remains the weakest branch of government and is corrupt, inefficient, and the object of intimidation by drug traffickers, as are Bolivia's mayoral, customs, and revenue offices. The Banzer government made serious efforts to improve the administration of justice, including making it more accessible. In his previous administration, the current president, Sanchez de Losada, did the same. The broad immunity from prosecution enjoyed by legislators is a serious stumbling block in the fight against official corruption.

Government-sponsored as well as independent human rights organizations exist, and they frequently report on security force brutality. The congressional Human Rights Commission is active and frequently criticizes the government. However, rights activists and their families are subject to intimidation. Prison conditions are harsh, with some 5,500 prisoners held in facilities designed to hold half that number, and nearly three-quarters of prisoners are held without formal sentences.

Evidence abounds that drug money has been used to finance political campaigns and buy the favor of government officials, including that of police and military personnel. Critics say that Law 1008, the Law to Regulate Coca and Controlled Substances, passed in 1988, is excessively harsh, restricts suspects' constitutional rights, and violates international norms and standards of due process.

The constitution guarantees free expression, freedom of religion, and the right to organize political parties, civic groups, and labor unions. However, freedom of speech is subject to some limitations. Unions have the right to strike.

The languages of the indigenous population are officially recognized, but the 40 percent Spanish-speaking minority still dominates the political process. More than 520 indigenous communities have been granted legal recognition under the 1994 Popular Participation Law, which guarantees respect for the integrity of native peoples. Indian territories are often neither legally defined nor protected, and coca growers and timber thieves exploit Indian lands illegally. Some Indians are kept as virtual slaves by rural employers through the use of debt peonage, with employers charging workers more for room and board than they earn. The observance of customary law by indigenous peoples is common in rural areas; in the remotest areas, the death penalty, forbidden by the constitution, is reportedly sometimes used against those who violate traditional laws or rules. In the 2002 campaign, Indian advocates demanded that the Bolivian constitution be amended to explicitly grant them greater participation in government and clearer land rights.

The press, radio, and television are mostly private. Journalists covering corruption stories are occasionally subject to verbal intimidation by government officials, arbitrary detention by police, and violent attacks. Violence against women is pervasive.

Bosnia-Herzegovina

Polity: International protectorate
Economy: Mixed statist
Population: 3,400,000
PPP: na
Life Expectancy: 68
Religious Groups: Muslim (40 percent), Orthodox (31 percent), Roman Catholic (15 percent), Protestant (4 percent), other (10 percent)
Ethnic Groups: Bosniac (44 percent), Serb (31 percent), Croat (17 percent), other (8 percent)
Capital: Sarajevo

Political Rights: 4*
Civil Liberties: 4
Status: Partly Free

Ratings Change: Bosnia-Herzegovina's political rights rating improved from 5 to 4 after indigenous Bosnian institutions successfully organized general elections for the first time since the country's brutal civil war.

Ten-Year Ratings Timeline (Political Rights, Civil Liberties, Status)

1993	1994	1995	1996	1997	1998	1999	2000	2001	2002	2003
6,6NF	6,6NF	6,6NF	6,6NF	5,5PF	5,5PF	5,5PF	5,5PF	5,4PF	5,4PF	4,4PF

Overview:

Bosnia-Herzegovina's seventh full year of peace provided little evidence that the political deadlock in the country's postwar evolution was being surmounted. Elections held in October returned to power the same nationalist parties that had led Bosniacs, Croats, and Serbs through 43 months of war. Immediately upon being recognized as an independent state in April 1992, Bosnia-Herzegovina plunged into civil war. In November 1995, the Dayton Accords brought an end to 43 months of civil war by creating a loosely knit state composed of the Bosniac-Croat "Federation of Bosnia-Herzegovina" and the Republika Srpska (RS). The Dayton Accords also gave the international community a decisive role in running post-Dayton Bosnia-Herzegovina, manifested in the significant powers and authorities granted to international civilian agencies such as the Office of the High Representative (OHR). Peace and security in post-Dayton Bosnia is provided by the NATO-led Stabilization Force, numbering some 20,000-strong. Despite these considerable efforts by the international community, however, most aspects of political, social, and economic life in postwar Bosnia-Herzegovina remain divided along ethnic lines.

Bosnia-Herzegovina (hereafter Bosnia) made little progress toward viable statehood in 2002. Bosnia's much-heralded "non-nationalist" ten-party ruling coalition, the Alliance for Change, largely cobbled together by international officials, formally fell apart in June after achieving little in its two years in power. Despite being publicized as a non-nationalist government, the Alliance for Change was rent by infighting between the different ethnically based parties that made up the coalition. In general elections held on October 5, the major nationalist parties again emerged as the strongest political movements in the country. One very important positive note from the elections, however, was that these elections were the first held in Bosnia's postwar history which were organized and supervised by Bosnians themselves, marking an important development in the country's post-1995 political evolution. In addition, the fact that they were held without any major glitches was an important indicator of the competence of local officials.

Political Rights and Civil Liberties: In general, voters are allowed to freely elect their representatives and are allowed to form political parties insofar as their programs are compatible with the Dayton Accords. The High Representative, however, has the authority to remove publicly elected officials from office if they are deemed to be obstructing the peace process. The High Representative also has the right to impose laws and regulations on the country when local officials are unable to agree on important matters. Indicative of the limited sovereignty of the country, however, is that the High Representative has no popular mandate; all four of the high representatives in the postwar period have been appointed by the international community, and the peoples of Bosnia have had no role whatsoever in choosing the most powerful political official in their country. Another extension of the High Representative's powers was announced in October. Henceforth, the High Representative will vet cabinet-level appointees in various levels of government.

Citizens enjoy the right to freedom of assembly, and demonstrations, strikes, and other forms of public protest and discussion are commonplace. Free trade unions exist and are very active.

Corruption in the judiciary, police forces, and the civil service provides a considerable obstacle to establishing the rule of law in Bosnia. Bosnia has four times as many judges per capita as Germany (which has the highest number in Europe), but handle only 25 percent as many cases per year. International officials claim that there is an "imbalance between the components of the rule of law." Local police and corrections personnel are believed to have reached a baseline of professional competence and democratic policing, but the judicial system—courts, judges, prosecutors, legal codes, rules of evidence and criminal procedures, and the witness protection program—are believed to still require radical reform and restructuring. Many indicted war criminals remain at large.

A plethora of independent electronic and print media organizations operate in Bosnia, but they are hampered by their dependence on foreign donations for survival, low levels of journalistic professionalism, their appeal to narrow ethnic constituencies, and occasional harassment by official institutions.

Individuals enjoy freedom of religious belief and practice in areas dominated by members of their own ethnic group, but the same does not hold true for individuals who are members of a local ethnic minority. In this sense, religious intolerance is often a reflection of the prevailing atmosphere of intolerance for ethnic minorities in various parts of the country, rather than religious persecution per se. All three major religious organizations in the country—Islamic, Roman Catholic, and Orthodox—have claims against the government for property confiscated during the Communist period.

International officials continued to cite encouraging statistics about the return of refugees and internally displaced persons (IDPs) to and within Bosnia in 2002, but whether the statistics tell the real story is debatable. Refugee and IDP returns to areas in which they are members of a local ethnic minority showed an increase of 40 percent over the same period in 2001. Anecdotal evidence, however, suggests many people are returning to their prewar homes only to sell their property and move back to areas in which they are members of the local ethnic majority.

Legally, women are entitled to full equality with men, but in practice they are significantly underrepresented in politics and government, and are frequently discriminated against in the workplace in favor of demobilized soldiers. To compensate for the absence of women in public life, political parties have to list three women among the top ten names on their lists of candidates.

A significant problem in postwar Bosnia has become its emergence as a destination country for trafficked women. UN reports claim that a substantial part of the market for trafficked women working in brothels in Bosnia is due to the large international civil and military presence in the country. Efforts led by the UN mission to Bosnia have strengthened border controls and led to a significant decrease in the number of individuals able to enter Bosnia illegally.

Botswana

Polity: Parliamentary democracy and traditional chiefs
Political Rights: 2
Civil Liberties: 2
Status: Free
Economy: Capitalist
Population: 1,600,000
PPP: $7,184
Life Expectancy: 39
Religious Groups: Indigenous beliefs (85 percent), Christian (15 percent)
Ethnic Groups: Tswana (79 percent), Kalanga (11 percent), Basarwa (3 percent), other (7 percent)
Capital: Gaborone

Ten-Year Ratings Timeline (Political Rights, Civil Liberties, Status)

1993	1994	1995	1996	1997	1998	1999	2000	2001	2002	2003
1,2F	2,3F	2,3F	2,2F	2,2F	2,2F	2,2F	2,2F	2,2F	2,2F	2,2F

Overview:

The government of President Festus Mogae in 2002 was defending its policy toward the country's indigenous Basarwa, or San (red people). Authorities early in the year cut off remaining services, such as health care, to the 600 to 700 Basarwa who were still living on traditional lands in the Central Kalahari Game Reserve, saying the cost was prohibitive. Opponents to the relocation scheme, however, contend that the government wants to protect diamond reserves in the region from potential claims by the Basarwa. The government denies this. The Basarwa lost their court bid against their removal from the game reserve in April 2002 on a technicality. They have the right to appeal.

Botswana is Africa's longest continuous multiparty democracy; elected governments have ruled the country since it gained independence from Britain in 1966. In 1999 Botswana held its seventh general elections since independence. President Mogae, a former central bank chief, succeeded Ketumile Masire as president in 1998, and Mogae was confirmed as the country's leader in 1999. A referendum on whether the president should be directly elected was withdrawn shortly before a scheduled vote in late 1997.

Economic progress in Botswana has been built on sound fiscal management and low rates of corruption. Privatization is progressing slowly. Efforts are underway to diversify an economy where diamonds account for 75 percent of all export earnings. AIDS has taken a toll on the country's economy and has torn its social fabric. More than one-third of the country's population is infected with HIV.

Political Rights and Civil Liberties: Botswana's National Assembly, elected for five years, chooses the president to serve a concurrent five-year term. The assembly's choice is confirmed by the courts when the winning party receives more than half the seats in the parliament. The Independent Election Commission created in 1996 has helped consolidate Botswana's reputation for fairness in voting.

Botswana uses a constituency system in which the candidate who polls the highest number of votes in a constituency wins the parliamentary seat. The ruling Botswana Democratic Party (BDP), which has held power since independence, won by a wide majority in legislative and local elections in October 1999, soundly defeating a fractured opposition. In the October 1999 election the BDP swept 33 of 40 National Assembly seats. The opposition had gone into the election holding 13 seats.

The House of Chiefs represents the country's major tribes and some smaller ones, and mainly serves an advisory role to the National Assembly and the government. Critics say it favors majority tribes.

Botswana's courts are generally considered to be fair and free of direct political interference. Trials are usually public, and those accused of the most serious violent crimes are provided public defenders. Prisons are overcrowded, but new facilities were under construction in 2002.

Botswana has an excellent record in Africa for human rights although there are occasional reports of police misconduct and poor treatment of the indigenous San. Almost 50,000 San have been resettled from the Central Kalahari Game Reserve to villages or as laborers on farms. The Botswana Center for Human Rights, Ditshwanelo, said the government's move in 2002 to cut off basic services to the remaining San on the reserve was "wrongful and unlawful."

There is a free and vigorous press in cities and towns, and political debate is open and lively. Several independent newspapers and magazines are published in the capital. The opposition and government critics, however, receive little access to the government-controlled broadcast media. Botswana easily receives broadcasts from neighboring South Africa. The private Gaborone Broadcasting Corporation television system has a limited reach. There are two private radio stations. Journalists in 2001 protested a draft bill to set up a press council that could impose fines and jail terms against journalists and publishers.

Freedom of religion is guaranteed, although all religious organizations must register with the government. Progress in improving the rights of women has been slow, but analysts say the election of more women to parliament in 1999 and the appointment of more women to the cabinet were important steps. Domestic violence is reportedly rampant, but security forces rarely intervene in domestic affairs, especially in rural areas.

Concentration of economic power has hindered labor organization. While independent unions are permitted, workers' rights to strike and to bargain for wages are restricted.

Brazil

Polity: Presidential-
parliamentary democracy
(federal)
Economy: Capitalist-
statist
Population: 173,800,000
PPP: $7,625
Life Expectancy: 69

Political Rights: 2*
Civil Liberties: 3
Status: Free

Religious Groups: Roman Catholic (80 percent), other (20 percent)
Ethnic Groups: White (55 percent), mixed (38 percent), black (6 percent),
other (1 percent)
Capital: Brasilia
Ratings Change: Brazil's political rights rating improved from 3 to 2, and its status from Partly Free to Free, due to the holding of free and fair elections in which an opposition presidential candidate of a markedly different ideology from the ruling coalition was elected.

Ten-Year Ratings Timeline (Political Rights, Civil Liberties, Status)

1993	1994	1995	1996	1997	1998	1999	2000	2001	2002	2003
2,3F	3,4PF	2,4PF	2,4PF	2,4PF	3,4PF	3,4PF	3,4PF	3,3PF	3,3PF	2,3F

Overview: In October 2002, former leftist anti-dictatorial firebrand and political prisoner Luiz Inácio "Lula" da Silva, "the Lech Walesa of Brazil," overwhelmingly won the Brazilian presidency on his fourth try, as his country leaned leftward in a search for economic security and a respite from crime, including rampant political corruption. The victory of the one-time leader of the metalworkers union marked a sea change in the political landscape of Latin America's largest economy and the world's fourth most populous democracy, as well as in the economically troubled South American region. Da Silva's election broke a historic monopoly on power by a small southern elite, military rulers, and local political bosses in a country with one of the worse income distributions in the world and 50 million people living in poverty. Although da Silva's win transcended regional and class distinctions, his mandate for change was nonetheless conditioned on his coalition's lack of a parliamentary majority; on winning acceptance from Wall Street; and on a $30 billion loan from the International Monetary Fund that set stringent conditions on future spending.

After gaining independence from Portugal in 1822, Brazil retained a monarchial system until a republic was established in 1889. Democratic rule has been interrupted by long periods of authoritarian rule, most recently under military regimes from 1964 to 1985, when elected civilian rule was reestablished. A new constitution, which went into effect in 1988, provides for a president to be elected for four years and a bicameral congress consisting of an 81-member Senate elected for eight years and a 503-member Chamber of Deputies elected for four years.

Civilian rule has been marked by corruption scandals. The scandal with the greatest political impact eventually led to the impeachment, by congress, of President Fernando Collor de Mello, in office from 1989 to 1992. Collor resigned and was replaced by a weak, ineffectual government led by his vice president, Itamar Franco.

In early 1994, Fernando Henrique Cardoso, a former Marxist who was Franco's finance minister and is a market-oriented centrist, forged a three-party, center-right coalition around Cardoso's Brazilian Social Democratic Party (PSDB). Cardoso's "Plan Real" stabilized Brazil's currency and gave Brazilian wage earners greater purchasing power. In October 1994 Cardoso won the presidency with 54 percent of the vote, against 27 percent for da Silva, the leader of the leftist Workers' Party (PT) and an early front-runner. However, Cardoso's coalition did not have a majority in either house of congress.

Cardoso embarked upon an ambitious plan of free market reforms, including deep cuts in the public sector and mass privatizations of state enterprises. He also ushered in a new era of dialogue with international human rights organizations and good-government groups. At the same time, a radicalized group representing landless peasants continued to occupy mostly fallow land in rural areas to pressure the government to settle rural families. The activism contributed to scores of violent conflicts between peasants on the one hand and, on the other hand, the military, the police, and private security forces, which act with virtual impunity.

In 1998, Cardoso's first-ballot victory (nearly 52 percent of the votes cast) over da Silva, his nearest rival, was tempered somewhat by a less convincing win at the congressional and gubernatorial levels. His win was also overshadowed by published accounts of corruption among senior government officials. The revelation in 1999 of a vast criminal conspiracy centered in the jungle state of Acre highlighted the lawlessness of Brazil's remote areas and moved Cardoso to take firm measures to combat organized crime.

In September 2000, a congressional committee probing organized crime and drug trafficking released an explosive report implicating nearly 200 officials in 17 of Brazil's 27 states. In 2001 the ruling PSDB's legacy of reform was badly tarnished by an energy crisis and a growing number of accusations of corruption at senior levels. The energy crisis, in particular, seemed to drive a wedge between the PSDB and its fractious coalition partners, although causes of the crisis went beyond an alleged lack of government foresight and managerial talent.

Faced with rampant street crime, urban sprawl, rural lawlessness, and the devastation of the Amazon basin, Brazilians also increasingly voiced concerns that political corruption severely limited the government's ability to address difficult problems. Long a transshipment country for cocaine produced in the Andean region, Brazil had, by the turn of the century, become the world's second-largest consumer of the illegal drug, after the United States. Violence in several major Brazilian cities, most notably Rio de Janeiro, involving rival drug gangs and the sometimes outgunned police was fueled by the volume of cocaine and its cheaper derivates consumed locally.

During the 2002 campaign, as the economy staggered under the weight of some $260 billion in foreign debt, unemployment soared and the country's currency lost more than 40 percent of its value against the U.S. dollar. Da Silva, 57, campaigned by attacking both the government's economic record and the effects of globalization while abandoning his party's previous anti-free market stands and its willingness to default on its foreign debt. After far outdistancing his rivals in a first-round ballot on October 6, in the runoff election held three weeks later da Silva received 52.5 million votes, besting Jose Serra, a center-left former PSDB health minister and Princeton University alumnus, 61 to 39 percent.

At the end of 2002, da Silva appeared to reach out to parties outside his coalition for support and met with Cardoso to ensure a smooth transition. His apparent moderation reflected some stark political realities. Economic hardship limited the new president's ability to use financial incentives to attract potential political partners. The Workers' Party won fewer than 20 percent of the seats in both houses of the Brazilian congress, while all important governorships in the 5 largest of Brazil's 27 states were won by other parties. Meanwhile, congress was poised to grant full autonomy to the Central Bank, which would limit da Silva's control over economic policy. Also, it had approved legislation that severely restricts da Silva's powers to issue decrees in the face of congressional opposition, as Cardoso frequently had.

Political Rights and Civil Liberties: Citizens can change their government through elections. The 2002 elections, in which the entire 513-seat congress and two-thirds of the 81-seat Senate were renewed, were free, fair, and the cleanest ever, as a result of a new electronic voting system. The constitution guarantees freedom of religion, freedom of expression, and the right to organize political and civic organizations.

Brazil has the highest rate of homicides caused by firearms of any country not at war—more than 70 percent. Police say that most violent crime—perhaps as much as 70 to 80 percent—in the country is related, directly or indirectly, to the illegal drug trade, including most of the 37,000 annual murders. An estimated 200,000 Brazilians are employed in the narcotics business, with at least 5,000 heavily armed gang members working for different drug-trafficking groups in Rio de Janeiro alone. A UN-sponsored study conduced in 2002 showed that 6,000 children or adolescents between 10 and 18 were armed as "soldiers" in the war between Rio's drug traffickers—with nearly 4,000 of these killed during a 13-year period.

Since 1994, the federal government has deployed the army to quell police strikes and bring order to Rio de Janeiro's 400 slums, most of which are ruled by gangs in league, or in competition, with corrupt police and local politicians. In June 2002, the Brazilian justice minister charged that organized crime had created "a parallel state" throughout the country. During each of the October elections, thousands of federal troops were deployed in Rio de Janeiro state after drug lords threatened to disrupt the polls. That same month, police uncovered a plot by organized crime to blow up the Sao Paulo Stock Exchange with a car bomb.

The climate of lawlessness is reinforced by a weak judiciary, which is overtaxed, plagued by chronic corruption, and virtually powerless in the face of organized crime, although recently some improvements have been made. Public distrust of the judiciary has resulted in poor citizens taking the law into their own hands, with hundreds of reported lynchings and mob executions.

Brazil's police are among the world's most violent and corrupt, and they systematically resort to torture to extract confessions from prisoners. Extrajudicial killings are usually disguised as shootouts with dangerous criminals. In many cities "death squads," often composed of off-duty state police, terrorize shantytown dwellers and intimidate human rights activists attempting to investigate abuses. Police are often grossly underpaid in the lower ranks, and in most states, salaries start at the minimum wage level of $72 a month. Working conditions are poor. There are some 1.3 million private security guards in Brazil, more than twice the number of police serving the country's 27 states.

The prison system in Brazil is anarchic, overcrowded, and largely unfit for human habitation, and human rights groups charge that torture and other inhumane treatment common to most of the country's detention centers turns petty thieves into hardened criminals. Some 200,000 people are incarcerated in Brazil, nearly half of them in Sao Paulo.

The press is privately owned. There are dozens of daily newspapers and numerous other publications throughout the country. The print media have played a central role in exposing official corruption. In recent years TV Globo's near monopoly on the broadcast media has been challenged by its rival, Sistema Brasiliero de Televisao (STB). On June 2, 2002, Tim Lopes, a TV Globo reporter who was investigating allegations of drug trafficking and sexual exploitation in a Rio slum, was tortured and dismembered by area drug dealers.

Large landowners control nearly 60 percent of arable land, while the poorest 30 percent share less than 2 percent. In rural areas, violence linked to land disputes is declining, but courts have increasingly supported the eviction of landless farmers. Thousands of workers are forced by ranchers in rural areas to work against their will and have no recourse to police or the courts.

Brazil is a source country for victims of both domestic and international trafficking of human beings, the majority of whom are women and girls trafficked for the purpose of sexual exploitation to Europe, Japan, Israel, and the United States. Occasionally, women are employed as domestic servants in conditions tantamount to slavery.

In August 2001, the Brazilian congress approved a legal code that for the first time in the country's history makes women equal to men under the law. However, violence against women and children is a common problem. Protective laws are rarely enforced. Forced prostitution of children is widespread. Child labor is prevalent, and laws against it are rarely enforced. In June 2001, a decree granted same-sex partners in Brazil the same rights as married couples with respect to pensions, social security benefits and taxation.

Violence against Brazil's 250,000 Indians mirrors generalized rural lawlessness. A decree issued by Cardoso opened Indian land to greater pressure from predatory miners and loggers. In some remote areas, Colombian drug traffickers have been using Indians to transport narcotics.

Industrial labor unions are well organized and politically connected; many are corrupt. The right to strike is recognized, and there are special labor courts. Hundreds of strikes have taken place in recent years against attempts to privatize state industries.

Brunei

Polity: Traditional monarchy **Political Rights:** 6*
Economy: Capitalist-statist **Civil Liberties:** 5
Population: 400,000 **Status:** Not Free
PPP: $16,779
Life Expectancy: 74
Religious Groups: Shafeite (67 percent), Buddhist
(13 percent), Christian (10 percent), Indigenous beliefs
and other (10 percent)
Ethnic Groups: Malay (67 percent), Chinese (15 percent), other (18 percent)
Capital: Bandar Seri Begawan
Ratings Change: Brunei's political rights rating improved from 7 to 6 due to changes
in the survey methodology.
Ten-Year Ratings Timeline (Political Rights, Civil Liberties, Status)

1993	1994	1995	1996	1997	1998	1999	2000	2001	2002	2003
7,6NF	7,6NF	7,6NF	7,5NF	7,5NF	7,5NF	7,5NF	7,5NF	7,5NF	7,5NF	6,5NF

Overview: Consisting of two enclaves on the northern coast of Borneo in Southeast Asia, Brunei has been under the absolute rule of Sultan Haji Hassanal Bolkiah Mu'izzaddin Waddaulah since 1967, when the country was still a British protectorate. Since 1970, the sultan has ruled mainly by decree under constitutionally granted emergency powers. Those powers have been in effect since 1962, when British troops crushed a left-wing separatist rebellion. The British granted full independence in 1984.

The 1959 constitution provided for five advisory councils, although only two still meet: the Council of Ministers, stacked with the sultan's relatives, and the appointed Legislative Council. The only legal political party is the Brunei National Solidarity Party, an offshoot of a party that the sultan banned in 1988. Led by Haji Mohamed Attah, the party has pledged to support the government and does little more than hold periodic meetings.

Oil exports have given Brunei a per capita income rivaling that of many Western societies. Reserves are dwindling, however. In response, the fifty-six-year-old sultan, himself one of the world's richest men, has taken recent steps to diversify the economy and to trim government spending in order to reduce a chronic budget deficit. In a scandal that fueled public anger over the opulent lifestyles of royal family members, the sultan's brother, Prince Jefri, was accused of misappropriating nearly $15 billion of Brunei's foreign reserves following the 1998 collapse of the Amedeo Development Corporation, a large holding company that the prince headed. A case against Prince Jefri settled out of court in 2000.

The specter of Islamic extremism cast a pall over Brunei in 2002. While there was no public indication of specific threats, reports emerged that an Islamic group, Jemaah Islamiyah, seeks to destabilize Brunei and other Southeast Asian nations through terrorist attacks. Jemaah Islamiyah was implicated in the deadly October bombing on the Indonesian island of Bali.

Political Rights and Civil Liberties: Citizens of Brunei cannot change their government through elections. The sultan wields broad powers under a state of emergency that has been in effect since 1962, and legislative elections have not been held since 1965. One of the few formal channels for citizens to convey concerns to their leaders is a traditional system under which elected village chiefs meet periodically with senior government officials.

The sultan promotes local culture and the primacy of the monarchy as the defender of Islam through an ideology called "Malay Muslim Monarchy." Critics say that the ideology is in part a ruse to ward off calls for democratization.

The government occasionally detains suspects under the tough Internal Security Act. Recent detainees included seven Christians, for alleged subversion; a leader of the 1962 rebellion after he returned from exile in Malaysia; and several citizens who distributed allegedly defamatory letters about the royal family and senior government officials regarding the collapse of the Amedeo company. All were released by the end of 2001.

Courts in Brunei generally "appear to act independently," according to the U.S. State Department's global human rights report for 2001, released in March 2002. *Sharia* (Islamic law) supercedes civil law in some areas, such as divorce, inheritance, and some sexual crimes. It does not apply to non-Muslims. In civil cases, there is a right of final appeal to the Privy Council in London.

The government further restricted press freedom in 2001 with legislation that allows officials to shut down newspapers without showing cause and to fine and jail journalists who write or publish articles considered "false and malicious." The country's largest daily, the *Borneo Bulletin*, practices self-censorship, the U.S. State Department report said, but often publishes letters criticizing government policies. Another daily, the *News Express*, also carries some critical letters to the editor.

The Shafeite sect of Islam is the official religion in this predominantly Muslim country. The government restricts religious freedom for non-Muslims by prohibiting proselytizing, banning the import of religious teaching materials or scriptures such as bibles, and ignoring requests to expand or build new temples, churches, and shrines, the U.S. State Department report said. The government has voiced concern over Islamic fundamentalism, and one Islamist group, Al-Arqam, is banned.

In this highly traditional society, women have recently made gains in education and now make up nearly two-thirds of Brunei University's entering classes. Women who do not hold university degrees, however, can work for the government only on a month-to-month basis. This restriction does not apply to men and results in fewer benefits for women. Moreover, Islamic law governing family matters favors men in divorce, inheritance, custody, and several other areas. The *tudong*, a traditional head covering, is mandatory for female students in state schools, though it is worn, in any case, by most women.

Employers at times beat their mostly foreign female domestic servants, make them work long hours without rest days, withhold pay, or forbid them to leave home on their days off, the U.S. State Department report said. Officials generally investigate individual cases and punish offenders when complaints are brought, the report added.

Brunei's few trade unions are independent but not very active. The three registered unions are all in the oil sector, and their membership makes up less than 5 percent of that industry's work force. Strikes are illegal, although foreign workers in garment factories have carried out work stoppages to protest poor working and living conditions and forced payroll deductions for employment agents or sponsors. For local workers, however, wages and benefits tend to be generous. Moreover, education is free, medical care is heavily subsidized, and there is virtually no poverty except for small pockets in tiny villages in remote areas.

Bulgaria

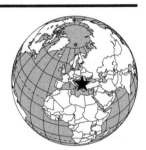

Polity: Parliamentary democracy
Economy: Mixed capitalist
Population: 7,800,000
PPP: $5,710
Life Expectancy: 72

Political Rights: 1
Civil Liberties: 2*
Status: Free

Religious Groups: Bulgarian Orthodox (83.8 percent), Muslim (12.1 percent), other (4.1 percent)
Ethnic Groups: Bulgarian (83.6 percent), Turk (9.5 percent), Roma [Gypsy] (4.6 percent), other (2.3 percent)
Capital: Sofia
Ratings Change: Bulgaria's civil liberties rating improved from 3 to 2 due to continued efforts to bring the country's political, economic, and social environment in line with European standards, improved tolerance towards ethnic minorities, and more openness towards nontraditional religious groups.

Ten-Year Ratings Timeline (Political Rights, Civil Liberties, Status)

1993	1994	1995	1996	1997	1998	1999	2000	2001	2002	2003
2,3F	2,2F	2,2F	2,2F	2,2F	2,2F	2,2F	2,2F	2,2F	1,3F	1,2F

Overview:

In 2002, Bulgaria continued to make slow progress towards its main foreign policy goal of joining European political, economic, and security structures, while debate over proposed amendments to the constitution dominated public discourse in the latter half of the year.

Throughout the Cold War, Bulgaria was regarded as the Soviet Union's most loyal satellite. After the Red Army swept through Bulgaria in 1944, a Communist-led government was established, and from 1954 to 1989 Communist Party leader Todor Zhivkov ruled the country. Zhivkov was forced to resign in 1989 in the wake of a mass pro-democracy rally in Sofia inspired by the broader political changes then sweeping across Eastern Europe.

Throughout the post-Communist period, the Bulgarian political spectrum has revolved around two main political groupings: the Union of Democratic Forces (UDF), and the Bulgarian Socialist Party (BSP). With the exception of a short-lived, UDF-led government elected in 1991, the BSP dominated Bulgaria's parliament from 1989 to 1997.

In November 1996, a deepening economic crisis and growing crime and corruption rates sparked a week of mass street demonstrations and succeeded in forcing the BSP to agree to early parliamentary elections the following year. In the April 1997 vote for the National Assembly, the UDF and its allied factions won 52 percent of the vote and 137 of the 240 seats. UDF leader Ivan Kostov was named prime minister.

Despite various economic and political problems, the UDF's tenure in office from 1997 to 2001 represented the first government in Bulgaria's post-Communist history to serve a full four-year term in office. It was credited with success in privatizing and restructuring most of the state economy as well as winning an invitation for EU membership talks.

In 2001, a new factor entered the Bulgarian political scene in the form of the country's former king, Simeon II, who returned from his European exile and formed the National Movement for Simeon II (NDSV). Promising quicker integration into Europe, Simeon attracted a large segment of Bulgaria's electorate, and in the 2001 parliamentary elections, the NDSV won 120 of the 240 seats; the UDF, 51; the Coalition for Bulgaria (which includes the BSP), 48; and the Turkish Movement for Rights and Freedoms (MRF), 21. The NDSV formed a coalition with the MRF after failing to gain an outright majority. In November 2001, Georgi Parvanov of the BSP was elected president of Bulgaria, winning 53 percent and defeating the incumbent, Petar Stoyanov.

In July 2002, two different proposals for improving the constitutional and governmental system in order to increase the country's chances for joining the European Union were put forth, one by the opposition and one by the government. The proposals ranged from reforming parliament and the judiciary to strengthening the presidency and local and regional governments. Given the complexity of the proposed constitutional changes, little action had been taken by the end of the year. Bulgaria is making slow progress towards further integration into European political, economic, and security structures. In June, Bulgarian officials announced that they had "closed" talks on 20 of the 30 chapters of legislation needed to join the European Union (and by October, 2 more were reported closed), although EU officials claimed much of the work reportedly accomplished was superficial. NATO invited Bulgaria to join the organization in November 2002.

Political Rights and Civil Liberties: Bulgarians can change their government democratically. The president is elected for a five-year term, and the unicameral National Assembly, composed of 240 members, is elected every four years. The 1999 local and the 2001 parliamentary and presidential elections were regarded as free and fair by the OSCE.

The constitution guarantees freedom of the press. A controversy, however, has emerged regarding amendments to Bulgaria's Media Law; specifically, appointments to the Electronic Media Council (EMC), which monitors compliance with the Media Law. Under the new amendments, the president and parliament can recall and elect members to the EMC, which critics claim is a limitation on freedom of the press. Despite such complaints, in March the Bulgarian Constitutional Court rejected a petition by 50 members of parliament to repeal the amendments.

The constitution permits the formation of trade unions, and the 1992 Labor Code recognizes the right to strike and bargain collectively. Bulgaria's two largest unions are the Confederation of Independent Trade Unions, a successor to the Communist-era union, and Podkrepa, an independent federation established in 1989. The constitution does, however, forbid the formation of political parties along religious, ethnic, or racial lines.

Freedom of religion is on the whole respected in Bulgaria, although the government has in recent years made it difficult for "non-traditional" religious groups to obtain registration permits allowing them to be active. (Those groups considered "traditional" in Bulgaria are the Orthodox, Roman Catholic, Islamic, and Jewish communities.) In May 2002, Pope John Paul II visited Bulgaria. His was the first-ever papal visit to the country, and was considered a watershed event in Orthodox-Catholic relations in Bulgaria

The judiciary is legally guaranteed independence and equal status with the executive and legislative branches of government. However, corruption, inadequate staffing, and low salaries continue to hamper the system. An example of the extent to which corruption afflicts official institutions was the August arrest of six leading members of the Barrets, a security unit charged with protecting the president, cabinet ministers, and foreign dignitaries. The six were implicated in a drug-smuggling operation.

Excessive physical force and discrimination by law enforcement officials towards the Roma (Gypsy) population continue to remain serious problems. Nevertheless, there are indications that Bulgarian officials are becoming more sensitive to the need to improve the country's treatment of ethnic minorities. The involvement of the ethnic Turkish MRF in the ruling coalition indicates that many Bulgarians have accepted a multiethnic government, a positive development considering the problems between these two ethnic communities in the 1980s and 1990s. Similarly, government officials, including Prime Minister Georgi Parvanov, have declared that the country must do more to improve the situation of the Roma minority in the country, especially in improving educational opportunities for Roma children.

Women now hold 63 of the 240 seats in parliament, having doubled their membership since the last general elections. Trafficking of women for prostitution remains a serious problem.

↑ Burkina Faso

Polity: Presidential-
parliamentary
(dominant party)
Economy: Mixed statist
Population: 12,600,000
PPP: $976
Life Expectancy: 47

Political Rights: 4
Civil Liberties: 4
Status: Partly Free

Religious Groups: Indigenous beliefs (40 percent),
Muslim (50 percent), Christian (10 percent)
Ethnic Groups: Mossi, Gurunsi, Senufo, Lobi, Bobo,
Mande, Fulani
Capital: Ouagadougou
Trend Arrow: Burkina Faso received an upward trend arrow due to the holding of legislative elections that were more free and fair than in previous years.

Ten-Year Ratings Timeline (Political Rights, Civil Liberties, Status)

1993	1994	1995	1996	1997	1998	1999	2000	2001	2002	2003
5,5PF	5,4PF	5,4PF	5,4PF	5,4PF	5,4PF	5,4PF	4,4PF	4,4PF	4,4PF	4,4PF

Overview:

Burkina Faso in 2002 was bracing for the possible influx of up to two million Burkinabe who have been working in neighboring Cote d'Ivoire. Burkinabe, Muslims, and members of northern Ivorian ethnic groups were among those being targeted after Cote d'Ivoire accused Burkina Faso of supporting mutinous Ivorian soldiers. The rebellious troops had seized much of the northern region of Cote d'Ivoire following a failed coup attempt in September 2002. Burkina Faso denied that it had supported the rebellion. A sudden repatriation of Burkinabe would have a devastating effect on Burkina Faso's economy, straining limited resources and cutting off remittances used to support families. In May 2002, the country held legislative elections that were considered more free and fair than previous polls. Opposition parties made significant gains.

After gaining independence from France in 1960 as Upper Volta, Burkina Faso suffered a succession of army coups. In 1983, Blaise Compaore installed himself as president in a violent coup against members of a junta that had seized power four years earlier and had pursued a watered-down Marxist-Leninist ideology. The populist, charismatic President Thomas Sankara and 13 of his closest associates were murdered. More Sankara supporters were executed two years later.

Burkina Faso is one of the world's poorest countries, although gains have been made in life expectancy, literacy, and school attendance. More than 80 percent of the population relies on subsistence agriculture.

**Political Rights
and Civil Liberties:**

Burkina Faso's 1991 constitution guarantees its people the right to elect their government freely through periodic multiparty elections. In practice, this right has not been fully realized. Presidential polls in December 1991 were marred by widespread violence and an opposition boycott. President Blaise Compaore was returned to office for a second seven-year term in November 1998 with nearly 88 percent of the vote. The election was marked by heavy use of state patronage, resources, and media by the ruling party.

The 2002 National Assembly elections were overseen by the reconstituted Independent National Electoral Commission and were considered among the most free and fair polls in Burkina Faso to date. The commission includes representatives from the government, civil society, and the opposition. The 2002 polls marked the first time that a simple ballot was used in voting, which was a measure that opposition parties had urged for several years. The ruling Congress for Democracy and Progress party won 57 of the 111 National Assembly seats, compared with 101 during the 1997 polls. Opposition parties in 2002 fared better than they had any time previously.

The Burkinabe judiciary is subject to executive interference in political cases, but is more independent in civil and criminal cases. National security laws permit surveillance and arrest without warrants. Police routinely ignore prescribed limits on detention, search, and seizure. Security forces commit abuses with impunity, including torture and occasional extrajudicial killing. Prison conditions are harsh, with overcrowding, poor diets, and minimal medical attention.

Many nongovernmental organizations, including human rights groups, which have reported detailed accounts of abuses by security forces, operate openly and freely. The London-based human rights group Amnesty International, in February 2002, called for an investigation into allegations that more than 100 people had been killed extrajudicially in a crackdown on suspected criminals. Authorities acknowledged there had been killings but said the deaths occurred during shoot-outs.

Burkina Faso has a vibrant free press, and freedom of speech is protected by the constitution and generally respected in practice. There is some self-censorship. At least 50 private radio stations, a private television station, and numerous independent newspapers and magazines function with little governmental interference. The media, which are often highly critical of the government, play an important role in public debate.

There has been less press repression since demands began for an investigation into the 1998 murder of prominent journalist Norbert Zongo. His death galvanized civil society to fight against the abuses committed by the country's security forces. A former presidential guard in 2001 was charged with Zongo's murder. Zongo was killed while investigating the torture death of a driver who had worked for President Compaore's brother. Three presidential guards, including the one charged in Zongo's killing, were sentenced to between 10 and 20 years of imprisonment for the driver's killing.

Burkina Faso is a secular state, and religious freedom is respected. Freedom of assembly is constitutionally protected and generally respected, with required permits usually issued routinely. However, demonstrations are sometimes violently suppressed or banned altogether.

Constitutional and legal protections for women's rights are nonexistent or poorly enforced. Customary law sanctions discrimination against women. Female genital mutilation is still widely practiced, even though it is illegal, and a government campaign has been mounted against it. Burkina Faso is used as a transit point for the trafficking of women and children for purposes of forced labor and prostitution, but the government has made an effort to stop this criminal activity.

Labor unions and their rights are provided for in the constitution. Unions are a strong force in society and routinely stage strikes about wages, human rights abuses, and the impunity of security forces.

✦ Burma (Myanmar)

Polity: Military
Economy: Statist
Population: 49,000,000
PPP: $1,027
Life Expectancy: 56
Religious Groups: Buddhist (89 percent), Christian (4 percent), other (7 percent)
Ethnic Groups: Burman (68 percent), Shan (9 percent), Karen (7 percent), Rakhine (4 percent), Chinese (3 percent), Mon (2 percent), Indian (2 percent), other (5 percent)
Capital: Rangoon

Political Rights: 7
Civil Liberties: 7
Status: Not Free

Trend Arrow: Burma received an upward trend arrow due to the release of Aung Sang Suu Kyi from house arrest and the increased latitude granted to the NLD opposition party.

Ten-Year Ratings Timeline (Political Rights, Civil Liberties, Status)

1993	1994	1995	1996	1997	1998	1999	2000	2001	2002	2003
7,7NF	7,7NF	7,7NF	7,7NF	7,7NF	7,7NF	7,7NF	7,7NF	7,7NF	7,7NF	7,7NF

Overview:

A quiet dialogue begun in October 2000 between the military junta and pro-democracy leader Aung San Suu Kyi bore fruit this year, when the Nobel laureate was released from house arrest in May. Several hundred political prisoners were freed throughout 2002, and Suu Kyi's National League for Democracy (NLD) was permitted to re-open a number of party offices. However, since Suu Kyi's release, there have been no further discussions regarding a possible return to constitutional government, and the ruling junta continues to wield a tight grip over all aspects of Burmese life.

After being occupied by the Japanese during World War II, Burma achieved independence from Great Britain in 1948. The military has ruled since 1962, when the army overthrew an elected government buffeted by an economic crisis and a raft of ethnic-based insurgencies. During the next 26 years, General Ne Win's military rule helped impoverish what had been one of Southeast Asia's wealthiest countries.

The present junta, currently led by General Than Shwe, has been in power since the summer of 1988, when the army opened fire on peaceful, student-led pro-democracy protesters, killing an estimated 3,000 people. In the aftermath, a younger generation of army commanders who succeeded Ne Win created the State Law and Order Restoration Council (SLORC) to rule the country. The SLORC refused to cede power after holding elections in 1990 that were won in a landslide by the NLD. The junta jailed dozens of members of the NLD, which won 392 of the 485 parliamentary seats in Burma's first free elections in three decades.

Than Shwe and several other generals who headed the junta refashioned the SLORC as the State Peace and Development Council (SPDC) in 1997. The generals appeared to be trying to improve the junta's international image, attract foreign investment, and encourage an end to U.S.-led sanctions linked to the regime's grim human rights record. Yet the junta took few concrete steps to gain international support. It continued to sentence peaceful pro-democracy activists to lengthy jail terms, force NLD members to quit the party, and periodically detain dozens of NLD activists.

However, in late 2000, encouraged by the efforts of UN special envoy Razali Ismail, the regime began holding talks with Suu Kyi, which led to an easing of restrictions on the NLD by mid-2002. Suu Kyi was released "unconditionally" from house arrest on May 6 and has been allowed to make several political trips outside the capital, while the NLD has been permitted to re-open some 45 offices in greater Rangoon. Nevertheless, analysts note that further talks have not taken place, and remain doubtful whether these signs of progress noted will evolve into a more meaningful dialogue over the future restoration of democracy.

The junta continued to face low-grade insurgencies in border areas waged by the Karen National Union (KNU) and at least five smaller ethnic-based rebel armies, although a number of other rebel groups have reached ceasefire deals with the junta since 1989. A serious dispute with neighboring Thailand erupted in late May, when the junta accused the Thai government of aiding rebel ethnic-minority forces along the border. For its part, Thailand criticized the Burmese government for its support to the United Wa State Army, which is involved in the production and trafficking of millions of methamphetamine tablets to Thailand each year. A series of military clashes led to the deaths of dozens of fighters, the closure of the border, and an escalation of nationalist rhetoric on both sides.

Political Rights and Civil Liberties:

Burma continues to be ruled by one of the world's most repressive regimes. The junta rules by decree, controls the judiciary, suppresses nearly all basic rights, and commits human rights abuses with impunity. Military officers hold most cabinet positions, and active or retired officers hold most top posts in all ministries. Official corruption is reportedly rampant.

Since rejecting the results of the 1990 elections, the junta all but paralyzed the victorious National League for Democracy (NLD). Authorities jailed many NLD leaders, pressured thousands of party members and officials to resign, closed party offices, and periodically detained hundreds of NLD members at a time to block planned party meetings. Although the NLD has been allowed somewhat greater freedom following the resumption of talks between the junta and party leader Aung San Suu Kyi, it continues to face restrictions on its activities. Besides the NLD, there are more than 20 ethnic political parties that remain suppressed by the junta.

Although several hundred political prisoners were released at intervals throughout 2002, more than 1,400 remain incarcerated, according to an Amnesty International report released in July. Most political prisoners are held under broadly drawn laws that criminalize a range of peaceful activities. These include distributing pro-democracy pamphlets and distributing, viewing, or smuggling out of Burma videotapes of Suu Kyi's public addresses. The frequently used Decree 5/96 of 1996 authorizes jail terms of 5 to 25 years for aiding activities "which adversely affect the national interest." The few nongovernmental groups in Burma generally work in health care and other nominally nonpolitical fields.

The junta sharply restricts press freedom, owning or tightly controlling all daily newspapers and radio and television stations and jailing dissident journalists. It also subjects most private periodicals to prepublication censorship. In October, dozens of dissidents were arrested and detained for possession of banned newspapers, and a number of journalists remained in jail throughout 2002.

Authorities continued to arbitrarily search homes, intercept mail, and monitor telephone conversations. The regime's high-tech information warfare center in Rangoon reportedly can intercept private telephone, fax, e-mail, and radio communications. Laws and decrees criminalize possession and use of unregistered telephones, fax machines, computers and modems, and software.

Since the 1988 student pro-democracy demonstrations, the junta has sporadically closed universities, limiting higher educational opportunities for a generation of young Burmese. Moreover, since reopening universities in 2000 after a four-year hiatus, authorities have lowered standards and shortened the academic term at many schools, made students pledge loyalty to the regime, barred political activity on campuses, and relocated some schools to relatively remote areas. In August, 15 university students were arrested and two were sentenced to prison terms for distributing pro-democracy pamphlets.

Ordinary Burmese generally can worship freely. The junta, however, has tried to control the Buddhist clergy by placing monastic orders under a state-run committee, monitoring monasteries, and subjecting clergy to special restrictions on speech and association. A number of monks remain imprisoned for their pro-democracy and human rights work. Burma was once again designated a "country of particular concern" by the U.S. Commission on International Religious Freedom, which noted systematic official discrimination against members of minority religious groups. A Human Rights Watch report published in June alleged that the government had failed to protect Muslims from a significant increase in anti-Muslim violence throughout 2001, and that it had imposed restrictions on Muslim religious activities and travel.

Independent trade unions, collective bargaining, and strikes are illegal. Several labor activists continued to serve long prison terms for their political and labor activities. Child labor has become increasingly prevalent, according to the U.S. State Department report.

The regime continued to use forced labor despite formally banning the practice in October 2000, just days prior to an unprecedented call by the International Labor Organization (ILO) for its members and UN agencies to "review" their relations with Burma. Many interpreted the resolution as a call to tighten sanctions against the regime. The ILO, the U.S. State Department, and other sources say that soldiers routinely force civilians to work without pay under harsh conditions. Soldiers make civilians construct roads, clear minefields, porter for the army, or work on military-backed commercial ventures. Forced labor appears to be most widespread in states dominated by ethnic minorities. A report published in October by the International Confederation of Free Trade Unions (ICFTU) alleged that the use of forced labor was on the rise and pointed to the complicity of multinational corporations in condoning the practice. However, the ILO was permitted to set up a liaison office in Rangoon in June.

Burmese courts respect some basic due process rights in ordinary criminal cases but not in political cases, according to the U.S. State Department report. Corruption, the misuse of overly broad laws, and the manipulation of the courts for political ends continue to deprive citizens of their legal rights. Prisons and labor camps are overcrowded, and inmates lack adequate food and health care. Amnesty International's 2001 report noted that at least 64 political prisoners have died in custody since 1988. However, conditions in some facilities have reportedly improved somewhat since the junta began allowing the International Committee of the Red Cross access to prisons in 1999.

The UN Commission on Human Rights in Geneva condemns the regime each year for committing grave human rights abuses; this year's resolution, passed in April, accused Rangoon of "a continuing pattern of gross and systematic violations of human rights," including extrajudicial, summary, or arbitrary executions; enforced disappearances; rape, torture, inhuman treatment, and forced labor, including the use of children; forced relocation and the denial of freedom of assembly, association, expression, religion, and movement; the lack of an independent judiciary; and delaying the process of national reconciliation and democratization.

Some of the worst human rights abuses take place in Burma's seven ethnic-minority-dominated states. In these border states, the *tatmadaw*, or Burmese armed forces, often kill, beat, rape, and arbitrarily detain civilians with impunity, according to the United Nations, the U.S. State Department, and other sources. A report issued in May by the Shan Human Rights Foundation and the Shan Women's Action Network accused the tatmadaw of systematically raping more than 600 women in Shan state between 1996 and 2001. Soldiers also routinely seize livestock, cash, property, food, and other goods from villagers, as well as destroying property.

Tens of thousands of ethnic minorities in Shan, Karenni, Karen, and Mon states and Tenasserim Division remain in squalid and ill-equipped relocation centers set up by the army. The army forcibly moved the villagers to the sites in the 1990s as part of its counterinsurgency operations. Press reports suggested that the army continued to forcibly uproot villagers in Karen, Shan, and other states, and that an estimated two million people have been internally displaced by such tactics. Thailand continues to host some 120,000 Karen and Karenni refugees in camps near the Burmese border and some 100,000 Shan refugees who are not permitted by Thai authorities to enter the camps.

The junta denies citizenship to, and has committed serious abuses against, the Muslim Rohingya minority in northern Arakan state. Lacking citizenship, the Rohingyas face restrictions on their movement and right to own land and are barred from secondary education and most civil service jobs. The government denies citizenship to most Rohingyas on the grounds that their ancestors allegedly did not reside in Burma in 1824, as required under the 1982 citizenship law. More than 100,000 Rohingya refugees remain in Bangladesh, where they fled in the 1990s to escape extrajudicial execution, rape, forced labor, and other abuses, according to reports by Human Rights Watch and other sources. The refugees include some of the 250,000 Rohingyas who fled to Bangladesh in the early 1990s but then largely returned to Burma, as well as newer arrivals.

While army abuses are the most widespread, some rebel groups forcibly conscript civilians, commit extrajudicial killing and rape, and use women and children as porters, according to the U.S. State Department. A report issued in October by Human Rights Watch documented the widespread use of child-soldiers by insurgent groups as well as by the Burmese army.

Criminal gangs have in recent years trafficked thousands of Burmese women and girls, many from ethnic minority groups, to Thailand and other destinations for prostitution, according to reports by Human Rights Watch and other groups. Although Burmese women have traditionally enjoyed high social and economic status, they are underrepresented in the government and civil service.

Burundi

Polity: Civilian-military (transitional)
Economy: Mixed statist
Population: 6,700,000
PPP: $591
Life Expectancy: 41
Religious Groups: Christian (67 percent), indigenous beliefs (23 percent), Muslim (10 percent)
Ethnic Groups: Hutu [Bantu] (85 percent), Tutsi (14 percent), Twa [Pygmy] (1 percent)
Capital: Bujumbura

Political Rights: 6
Civil Liberties: 5*
Status: Not Free

Ratings Change: Burundi's civil liberties rating improved from 6 to 5 due to changes in the survey methodology.

Ten-Year Ratings Timeline (Political Rights, Civil Liberties, Status)

1993	1994	1995	1996	1997	1998	1999	2000	2001	2002	2003
6,5PF	7,7NF	6,7NF	6,7NF	7,7NF	7,7NF	7,6NF	6,6NF	6,6NF	6,6NF	6,5NF

Overview:

Amidst ongoing violence, Burundi continued to make excruciatingly slow progress in resolving the multifaceted crisis that has wracked the country since 1993. For the first time, South African-mediated negotiations in Tanzania brought together all the combatant groups, and by the end of 2002 all factions had agreed to end the violence except for the Hutu-dominated National Liberation Front (FNL). Continued instability within the Great Lakes region further complicated efforts at reconciliation.

With the exception of a brief period following democratic elections in 1993, the minority Tutsi ethnic group has largely governed the country since independence in 1962. The military, judiciary, educational system, business sector, and news media have also been dominated by the Tutsi. Violence between the country's two main ethnic groups has occurred repeatedly since independence, but the assassination of the newly elected Hutu president, Melchoir Ndadaye, in 1993, has resulted in sustained and widespread violence. Since 1993 an estimated 200,000 Burundi citizens, out of a population of 5.5 million, have lost their lives.

Ndadaye's murder fatally weakened the hold on power of the Hutu-backed political party, the Front for Democracy in Burundi, (FRODEBU). Negotiations on power-sharing took place over the succeeding months, as ethnically backed violence continued to wrack the country. Ndadaye's successor was killed, along with Rwandan President Juvenal Habyarimana, in 1994 when their plane was apparently shot down while approaching Kigali airport in Rwanda. This event triggered the Rwandan genocide and intensified killings in Burundi.

Under a 1994 power-sharing arrangement between the main political parties, Hutu politician Sylvestre Ntibantunganya served as Burundi's new president until his ouster in a 1996 military coup led by Pierre Buyoya, who had formerly been president. Buyoya claimed to have carried out the coup to prevent further human rights violations and violence. Peace and political stability within the country continued to be elusive, as armed insurgents sporadically staged attacks and the government security forces pursued an often ruthless campaign of intimidation. The search for peace eventually led to an agreement to allow a measure of political space for the parliament, which has a FRODEBU majority, and the beginning of negotiations in Arusha in 1998.

In 2001 Burundi made an important, but tentative, step towards a peaceful settlement. The Arusha negotiations, mediated by former South African President Nelson Mandela, resulted in an agreement in principle by most parties on a future democratic political solution to the conflict. Nineteen organized groups from across the political spectrum agreed to recommendations from committees on the nature of the conflict, reforms in the nation's governing institutions, security issues, and economic restructuring and development. The form of the political institutions through which power would be shared and the reform of the military proved to be especially sensitive and difficult issues. A transitional government was installed on November 1, with President Buyoya temporarily remaining chief of state and Domitien Ndayizeye, the secretary-general of FRODEBU, the Hutu-dominated opposition party, vice president. A potentially fatal weakness of the agreement, however, was the failure of key elements of the FDD and FNL to sign on, resulting in continued negotiations and violence.

Political Rights and Civil Liberties:

Political and civil liberties within Burundi continue to be circumscribed, although parties and civic organizations do function. President Pierre Buyoya is an unelected chief of state, although he is due to leave office in April 2003. The constitution was suspended when he took power, as was the legitimately elected parliament. In June 1998 a transitional constitution was put into place; it reinstituted and enlarged the parliament through the appointment of additional members and created two vice presidents. The parliament's powers remain limited in practice, although it provides an outlet for political expression and remains an important player in determining the nation's future.

The negotiated political agreement, which entered into force in November 2001, allows Buyoya to remain president until April 2003 and then for the presidency to be occupied by Domitien Ndayizeye for a subsequent 18 months until presidential and parliamentary elections are held in November 2004. As part of the agreement, the parliament's legitimacy was heightened by the nominations of key political figures.

Jean Minani, a leading member of FRODEBU who returned from exile, was chosen by the National Assembly to be speaker.

There are more than a dozen active political parties, ranging from those that champion radical Tutsi positions to those that hold extremist Hutu positions. Most are small in terms of membership. FRODEBU and the Tutsi-dominated Unity for National Progress (UPRONA) party remain the leading political parties.

Burundians continue to be subject to arbitrary violence, whether from the government or from guerilla groups. Although detailed, specific figures on the number of dead or injured are difficult to obtain, widespread violence continued in parts of Burundi in 2002. This has been documented by respected independent organizations inside and outside Burundi, including Amnesty International, Human Rights Watch, and the ITEKA Human Rights League. Amnesty International issued several appeals during the year, for example, for investigations into human rights abuses allegedly conducted by both guerilla and government forces. In addition to operations of the government security forces, there has been intense activity in parts of the country by armed opposition groups.

Reprisals by the armed forces have often been brutal and indiscriminate, and have resulted in hundreds of extrajudicial executions, mainly of members of the Hutu ethnic group. For example, the Burundian army admitted killing 173 civilians in the central province of Gitega in September. An army spokesman claimed, however, that Forces for the Defense of Democracy (FDD) fighters were "fully responsible for all the civilian deaths," and claimed that the rebels had taken the civilians as "hostages" and "accomplices."

According to Human Rights Watch, Burundian army soldiers forced more than 30,000 civilians from their homes in Ruyigi province in eastern Burundi in late April and early May, and authorities refused to allow humanitarian aid groups to provide assistance to the displaced persons, who are suffering from malnutrition and disease. Much of the military's violence has been committed in zones where the local civilian and military authorities ordered the civilian population to leave the area because of counterinsurgency operations. The continued impunity of the armed forces and the weakness of the Burundian judicial system are important contributing factors to the violence.

Some different viewpoints are expressed in the media, although media outlets operate under significant self-censorship and the opposition press functions only sporadically. The government-operated radio station allows a measure of diversity. The European Union has funded a radio station. The Hutu extremist radio broadcasts sporadically and has a limited listening range.

Constitutional protections for unionization are in place, and the right to strike is protected by the labor code. The Organization of Free Unions of Burundi is the sole labor confederation and has been independent since the rise of the multiparty system in 1992. Most union members are civil servants and have bargained collectively with the government. Freedom of religion is generally observed.

Women have limited opportunities for advancement in the economic and political spheres, especially in the rural areas. Only 5 percent of females, for example, are enrolled in secondary school. Burundi's mainly subsistence economy (its gross domestic product) is estimated to have contracted by 25 percent over the last five years. The five-year conflict and two years of economic sanctions imposed by neighboring states have crippled the economy and worsened social indicators. Over the five years of conflict and economic sanctions, poverty has increased by 80 percent in rural areas and more than doubled in urban areas. Child malnutrition is estimated to be 38 percent, and reported cases of major endemic diseases have increased by more than 200 percent since 1993. Access to basic social and health services has been severely diminished.

Cambodia

Polity: Dominant party (military-influenced)
Economy: Statist
Population: 12,300,000
PPP: $1,446
Life Expectancy: 56
Religious Groups: Theravada Buddhist (95 percent), other (5 percent)
Ethnic Groups: Khmer (90 percent), Vietnamese (5 percent), Chinese (1 percent), other (4 percent)
Capital: Phnom Penh

Political Rights: 6
Civil Liberties: 5
Status: Not Free

Ten-Year Ratings Timeline (Political Rights, Civil Liberties, Status)

1993	1994	1995	1996	1997	1998	1999	2000	2001	2002	2003
6,6NF	4,5PF	4,5PF	6,6NF	6,6NF	7,6NF	6,6NF	6,6NF	6,6NF	6,5NF	6,5NF

Overview:

The ruling party's landslide victory in Cambodia's February 2002 local polls strengthened autocratic Prime Minister Hun Sen's hand in advance of national elections due in 2003. The vote followed a violent campaign that included several election-related killings, threats, vandalism, and other acts of intimidation against the opposition. The elections continued the political dominance of Hun Sen, 50, and his Cambodian People's Party (CPP) by keeping control of local security forces and resources in the hands of trusted officials.

After winning independence from France in 1953, Cambodia was ruled in succession by King Norodom Sihanouk, the U.S.-backed Lon Nol regime in the early 1970s, and the Chinese-supported Khmer Rouge between 1975 and 1979. Under the Maoist Khmer Rouge, at least 1.7 million of Cambodia's 7 million people died by execution, disease, overwork, or starvation. Vietnam invaded in December 1978 and installed a Communist government in January 1979 under the Khmer People's Revolutionary Party (KPRP).

During the 1980s, the KPRP government fought the allied armies of Sihanouk, the Khmer Rouge, and a former premier, Son Sann. An internationally brokered peace deal signed in 1991 formally ended the war and put the impoverished Southeast Asian country on the path to multiparty elections, although the Khmer Rouge continued to wage a low-grade insurgency from the jungle.

In Cambodia's first free parliamentary elections, in 1993, the royalist United Front for an Independent, Neutral, and Free Cambodia (FUNCINPEC), headed by Prince Norodom Ranariddh, a Sihanouk son, defeated the CPP, the successor to the KPRP. Following the vote, CPP leader Hun Sen, a onetime Khmer Rouge cadre, used his control over the army to force FUNCINPEC to include the CPP in a coalition government.

Backed by Cambodia's security forces, Hun Sen harassed and intimidated FUNCINPEC members, opposition groups, and the press in the mid-1990s before ousting Ranariddh in a bloody coup in 1997. The Khmer Rouge, meanwhile, largely disintegrated within a year of the coup following the death of its leader, Pol Pot, and the defections of top commanders.

Since the coup, Hun Sen has faced few real threats to his power, while the end of the Khmer Rouge insurgency has brought peace to Cambodia for the first time since the 1960s. The CPP, which continues to have close ties to the military, won a flawed election in 1998 that appeared to be held primarily to convince donors to resume aid they had suspended after the coup. The CPP won 64 seats; FUNCINPEC, 43; and the Sam Rainsy Party (SRP), led by Cambodia's leading dissident, 15. Turnout was officially more than 90 percent. Hun Sen brought FUNCINPEC into a coalition government as a junior partner, with Prince Ranariddh serving as president of the National Assembly.

International donors resumed aid to Cambodia in 1999, and their grants and soft loans now make up more than half of the government's annual budget. Many donors viewed the February 3, 2002, local elections—the country's first local vote since the 1960s—as a test of the government's commitment to political reform. Between January 2001 and January 2002, however, 15 opposition party members and candidates were killed, according to the New York-based Human Rights Watch. Using a slightly different time frame, the United Nations reported that 12 opposition figures were killed under suspicious circumstances in 2001. The CPP won around 1,600 of Cambodia's 1,621 communes, or local bodies.

Meanwhile, the UN in February pulled out of negotiations over a tribunal to try former Khmer Rouge leaders accused of crimes against humanity and other grave human rights abuses. The world body said that a Cambodian law on the tribunal did not include sufficient safeguards to ensure independent and impartial trials.

In another development, courts in 2001 and 2002 convicted more than 90 men for their roles in a November 2000 attack on government buildings in Phnom Penh that killed at least eight people. Amnesty International and other human rights groups criticized the investigation and trial procedures leading to the convictions. A California-based antigovernment group, the Cambodian Freedom Fighters, claimed responsibility for the attack.

Political Rights and Civil Liberties: Cambodia's most recent parliamentary elections, in 1998, were neither free nor fair because of violence, restrictions on press coverage and campaign opportunities, and an eleventh-hour manipulation of the rules for allocating parliamentary seats among parties. At least 21 politically motivated killings, mainly of FUNCINPEC supporters, took place between late May and the June 26, 1998, election, UN observers reported. In any case, although the National Assembly is becoming a forum for debate, it "does not provide a significant check to executive power," according to the U.S. State Department's global human rights report for 2001, released in March 2002.

Local officials reportedly harass FUNCINPEC and SRP members through threats of death or loss of citizenship papers and by withholding routine services, the U.S. State Department report said. Courts recently have convicted some suspects in political killings, but judges, the government, and police investigators tend to downplay or ignore possible political motives in these cases.

Cambodia's judiciary "is not independent" because of interference from Hun Sen's administration and the National Assembly, according to the U.S. State Department report, which also stated that the court system suffers from chronic corruption, limited resources, poorly trained and underpaid judges, and a severe shortage of lawyers. The report added that investigators sometimes beat or threaten suspects to extract confessions from them, defendants often lack adequate legal counsel and must bribe judges for favorable verdicts, and at the same time, corruption or delays allow many suspects to escape prosecution.

Human rights groups say that police, soldiers, and local officials at times illegally detain suspects or hold them well beyond the legal limits without bringing any charges. Suspects who are charged, meanwhile, generally spend long periods in detention before their trials. Despite recent reforms, Cambodian prisons remain dangerously overcrowded, and inmates often lack sufficient food, water, and health care, the U.S. State Department report said.

Dozens of alleged criminals have been killed by vengeance-seeking mobs in recent years. Observers say that these vigilante killings reflect popular frustration with the poor state of Cambodian law enforcement.

Cambodia's private press routinely criticizes governmental policies and senior officials, including Prime Minister Hun Sen. Officials, however, have recently used a strict 1995 press law to suspend several newspapers for 30-day periods for criticizing the government or monarchy. The law provides journalists with some rights, but also permits the Information Ministry to suspend newspapers, subjects journalists to criminal statutes, and broadly prohibits publishing articles that affect national security or political stability.

Television and radio programming are consistently biased towards the ruling CPP, according to Human Rights Watch. Unlike their print counterparts, broadcast journalists reportedly practice self-censorship, the U.S. State Department report said. The Information Ministry has denied repeated requests from opposition leader Sam Rainsy for a license to operate a radio station.

Women enjoy equal access with men to education, but they play relatively limited roles in government, politics, and private sector management. They also hold an outsized share of the low-paying agricultural, industrial, and service sector jobs.

Nongovernmental groups say that rape and domestic violence are common. They also allege that trafficking of women and girls within the country continues to be widespread despite some recent prosecutions of traffickers and sporadic crackdowns on Phnom Penh brothel owners. Many of Cambodia's estimated 80,000 to 100,000 prostitutes, one-third of whom are under the age of 18, are trafficking victims. Prostitutes frequently are abused and held in conditions of bonded servitude by brothel owners, the U.S. State Department report said.

Buddhism is Cambodia's state religion, and more than 95 percent of the population is Buddhist. Cham Muslims and other religious minorities can worship freely. The estimated 200,000 to 500,000 ethnic Vietnamese in Cambodia face harassment and discrimination both by officials and within mainstream society, according to the U.S. State Department report.

Workers, teachers, students, and others held numerous protests throughout the year with little interference, although police or government-organized groups broke up some demonstrations. Cambodia's 40-odd nongovernmental human rights groups face some intimidation by local officials but, for the most part, freely investigate abuses and carry out training programs and other activities.

Cambodia's few independent trade unions are active, but they are small, have limited resources, and generally have little clout in negotiating with management. Workers frequently staged strikes and held demonstrations in Phnom Penh to protest against low wages, forced overtime, poor and dangerous working conditions, and dismissal of pro-union staff. In a country where some 80 percent of workers are subsistence farmers, union membership is estimated at less than one percent of the workforce.

With Cambodian courts largely unable to enforce property rights, and the land registration system a shambles, military and civilian officials have in recent years forcibly evicted several thousand families from their land, according to Cambodian human rights groups such as LICADHO. Observers say that the dispute resolution procedures used by local committees set up to settle land disputes are plagued by inconsistency, a lack of transparency, and conflicts of interest among committee members.

Government officials, soldiers, and police often tolerate, and reportedly at times take part in, gunrunning, drug trafficking, and money laundering schemes as well as prostitution rings run by mainland Chinese. Businessmen, aid workers, and diplomats say that corruption is widespread in government offices and private banks, with many bribes going to fund CPP and FUNCINPEC outreach programs and election campaigns, the Hong Kong-based *Far Eastern Economic Review* reported in March. Cambodia's long-term economic growth prospects, meanwhile, are clouded by poor infrastructure and a mounting foreign debt nearly equaling the size of the economy.

↑Cameroon

Polity: Presidential (dominant party)
Economy: Capitalist
Population: 16,200,000
PPP: $1,703
Life Expectancy: 55

Political Rights: 6
Civil Liberties: 6
Status: Not Free

Religious Groups: Indigenous beliefs (40 percent), Christian (40 percent), Muslim (20 percent)
Ethnic Groups: Cameroon Highlander (31 percent), Equatorial Bantu (19 percent), Kirdi (11 percent), Fulani (10 percent), Northwestern Bantu (8 percent), Eastern Nigritic (7 percent), other African and non-African (14 percent)
Capital: Yaounde
Trend Arrow: Cameroon received an upward trend arrow due to an easing of repression of the media.

Ten-Year Ratings Timeline (Political Rights, Civil Liberties, Status)

1993	1994	1995	1996	1997	1998	1999	2000	2001	2002	2003
6,5NF	6,5NF	6,5NF	7,5NF	7,5NF	7,5NF	7,5NF	7,6NF	7,6NF	6,6NF	6,6NF

Overview: The ruling Cameroon People's Democratic Movement (CPDM) dominated legislative and municipal elections in 2002 that were no more free and fair than previous polls, despite the creation of the National Observatory of Elections. Although there were fewer incidents of harassment of the press in 2002, Cameroon's overall record for human rights failed to improve substantially and members of the security forces continued to commit abuses with impunity, according to local and international human rights groups.

Cameroon was seized during World War I, in 1916, and divided between Britain and France after having been a German colony from 1884. Distinct Anglophone and Francophone areas were reunited as an independent country in 1961. Approximately one-fourth of Cameroonians are Anglophone. The administration of President Paul Biya remains largely Francophone, and the country's main opposition is from Anglophone Cameroonians. The linguistic distinction constitutes the country's most potent political division. Cameroon's population comprises nearly 200 ethnic groups. For three decades after independence, Cameroon was ruled under a repressive one-party system. As prime minister, Biya succeeded President Ahmadou Ahidjou in 1982.

The International Court of Justice at The Hague in October 2002 ruled in favor of Cameroon in its long-running dispute with Nigeria over ownership of the oil-rich Bakassi Peninsula. Nigeria said that the ruling would have no effect on its claim to oil and natural gas reserves there. Cameroon and Nigeria have occasionally clashed militarily over the region. Most Bakassi residents consider themselves Nigerian. Privatization and economic growth in Cameroon have progressed, but graft and the absence of independent courts inhibit business development.

Political Rights and Civil Liberties: Although Cameroon's constitution provides for a multiparty republic, citizens have not been allowed to choose their government or local leaders by democratic means. Presidential elections have been devalued by rampant intimidation, manipulation, and fraud. In 1996, the constitution extended the presidential term to seven years and allowed President Paul Biya to run for a fourth term. His reelection in 1997, with 93 percent of the vote, was marred by serious procedural flaws, and a boycott by the three major opposition parties.

Legislative elections have also been fraudulent. In the June 2002 elections, the ruling CPDM increased the number of its seats in the 180-member National Assembly from 116 to 149. The main opposition, the Social Democratic Front, won 22 seats, down from 43 it had held previously. Smaller parties won the remainder. Municipal elections, which had been postponed from January 2001, were also dominated by the CPDM.

Cameroon's courts remain highly subject to political influence and corruption. The executive controls the judiciary and appoints provincial and local administrators. Military tribunals may exercise jurisdiction over civilians in cases involving civil unrest or organized armed violence. In the north, powerful traditional chiefs known as *lamibee* run their own private militias, courts, and prisons, which are used against the regime's political opponents. Torture and ill-treatment of prisoners and detainees are routine. Indefinite pretrial detention under extremely harsh conditions is permitted either after a warrant is issued or in order to "combat banditry." Inmates routinely die in prison.

The London-based human rights group Amnesty International called for an investigation into reports that dozens of extrajudicial executions were carried out in 2002 as part of an anti-crime campaign. A military court in July 2002 acquitted six of eight gendarmes accused of killing nine young men who disappeared in January 2001 after being detained by an anticrime squad called the Operational Command. Two other gendarmes were given suspended sentences.

Numerous nongovernmental organizations generally operate without hindrance. Various intelligence agencies operate with impunity, and opposition activists are often held without charges or disappear while in custody. Security forces routinely impede domestic travel, repress demonstrations, and disrupt meetings. Steps have been taken in Belgium by political and civil society groups to institute legal proceedings against Biya for crimes against humanity.

The constitution provides for freedom of the press, but criminal libel law has often been used to silence regime critics. There are at least 20 private newspapers that publish regularly. Eleven years after the National Assembly passed a bill liberalizing the audio and visual media, Biya signed the legislation into force in 2001. A handful of private radio stations were already operating without a license, but they only broadcast religious or music programs locally. Repression of the press eased somewhat in 2002. Fewer arrests and convictions were reported.

Freedom of religion is generally respected. Slavery reportedly persists in parts of the north, and discrimination exists against indigenous Pygmies and other ethnic minorities while the Beti and Bula dominate the civil service and state-run businesses. Violence against women is reportedly widespread. Women are often denied inheritance and landownership rights, even when these are codified, and many other laws contain unequal gender-based provisions and penalties. Cameroon is a transit center and market for child labor and traffickers.

Trade union formation is permitted, but is subject to numerous restrictions. Workers have the right to strike but only after arbitration, the final decisions of which the government can overturn.

Canada

Polity: Parliamentary democracy (federal)
Economy: Capitalist
Population: 31,300,000
PPP: $27,840
Life Expectancy: 79
Religious Groups: Roman Catholic (46 percent),
Protestant (36 percent), other (18 percent)
Ethnic Groups: British Isles origin (28 percent),
French (23 percent), other European (15 percent), other (34 percent)
Capital: Ottawa

Political Rights: 1
Civil Liberties: 1
Status: Free

Ten-Year Ratings Timeline (Political Rights, Civil Liberties, Status)

1993	1994	1995	1996	1997	1998	1999	2000	2001	2002	2003
1,1F	1,1F	1,1F	1,1F	1,1F	1,1F	1,1F	1,1F	1,1F	1,1F	1,1F

Overview:

Canada continued to be concerned about policies to curb terrorism and involved in a growing debate over the impact of antiterrorism measures on the country's civil liberties. Canadians were also faced with the announcement and possible implementation of major changes in the leadership of the country's three main political parties.

Colonized by French and British settlers in the seventeenth and eighteenth centuries, Canada came under the control of the British Crown under the terms of the Treaty of Paris in 1763. After granting home rule in 1867, Britain retained a theoretical right to overrule the Canadian parliament until 1982, when Canadians established complete control over their own constitution. The country is governed by a prime minister, a cabinet, and parliament. Parliament consists of the elected, 301-member House of Commons and the appointed, 104-member Senate. The British monarch, represented by a ceremonial governor-general appointed by the prime minister, remains nominal head of state.

The war against terrorism has been a leading item on Canada's agenda since the attacks of September 11, 2001 on the United States. Shortly after those attacks, Canada joined other members of the Group of 8, a forum of industrialized countries, in devising measures to combat international terrorism, including stopping funds for foreign terrorist groups. In December 2001, Canada and the United States undertook a comprehensive bilateral agreement on improving cross-border security.

Concern about terrorism was reinforced in 2002 when leaders of al-Qaeda issued statements suggesting that the country might be targeted for violent acts.

Canada has adopted several measures in the name of curbing terrorist organizations. Several have drawn criticism on civil liberties grounds. Two measures in an omnibus antiterror bill drew particular concern. One allows police to make preventive arrests of those suspected of planning a terrorist act. Another requires suspects to testify before a judge, even if they have not been formally accused of a crime. Concern about terrorism was behind passage, in 2002, of the Public Safety Act, which was introduced in October. The law's sections on data sharing drew criticism from civil liberties groups and from the country privacy commissioner, who expressed concern over the possible retention of data on private citizens for long periods of time and the possibility that information could be used for purposes other than terrorism investigations.

In August, Prime Minister Jean Chretien announced his intention to resign in February 2004. Chretien's Liberal Party won a sweeping electoral victory in 2000, but was plagued by charges of scandal in 2002. The Canadian Alliance, the chief opposition party, elected Stephen Harper as its new leader in March. Alexa McDonough, the leader of the country's third-largest party, the New Democratic Party, announced her intention to step down in January 2003.

Political Rights and Civil Liberties:

Canadians can change their government democratically, and as a result of government canvassing Canada has nearly 100 percent effective voter registration. Prisoners have the right to vote in federal elections, as do citizens who have lived abroad for fewer than five years.

The judiciary is independent. Limitations on freedom of expression range from unevenly enforced "hate laws" and restrictions on pornography to rules on reporting. Recently, there have been complaints that the judiciary has become overly activist and has issued decisions that have the effect of usurping the powers of the legislature.

The media are generally free.

Civil liberties have been protected since 1982 by the federal Charter of Rights and Freedoms, but have been limited by the constitutional "notwithstanding" clause, which permits provincial governments to exempt themselves by applying individual provisions within their jurisdictions. Quebec has used the clause to retain its provincial language law, which restricts the use of languages other than French on signs. The provincial governments exercise significant autonomy. However, Canada's criminal law, which is based on British common law, is uniform throughout the country. Civil law is also based on the British system, except in Quebec, where it is based on the French civil code.

The status of Quebec has become a less contentious issue in the past several years. Demands for the establishment of an independent Quebec have diminished since a 1995 referendum, in which voters in the province narrowly rejected a separatist course.

In 1996, parliament amended the constitution to outlaw discrimination based on "sexual orientation" by adding this term to the 1977 Human Rights Act list that includes age, sex, race, religion, and disability. Canada has also taken important steps to protect the rights of native groups, although some contend that indigenous peoples remain subject to discrimination.

Canada boasts a generous welfare system that supplements the largely open, competitive economy. Trade unions and business associations enjoy high levels of membership and are free and well organized.

Religious expression is free and diverse. A recent controversy has broken out over the policy of some provinces to single out for support the school systems run by certain denominations. In 2000, a major scandal was triggered by a series of legal actions taken by members of native groups who had been subjected to physical and sexual abuse while being educated in schools operated by religious denominations under federal charter. In November, officials of the Anglican Church reached an agreement with the government to establish a fund to compensate the aboriginal victims of abuse.

Canada maintains relatively liberal immigration policies. However, concern has mounted over the possible entry into Canada of individuals who have been involved in terrorist missions. In 2002, the Immigration and Refugee Protection Act was passed. It seeks to continue Canada's tradition of liberal immigration and refugee policies while making it more difficult for potential terrorists to enter the country.

Cape Verde

Polity: Presidential-par-
liamentary democracy
Economy: Mixed statist
Population: 500,000
PPP: $4,863
Life Expectancy: 69

Political Rights: 1
Civil Liberties: 2
Status: Free

Religious Groups: Roman Catholic, Protestant
Ethnic Groups: Creole [mulatto] (71 percent), African (28 percent), European (1 percent)
Capital: Praia

Ten-Year Ratings Timeline (Political Rights, Civil Liberties, Status)

1993	1994	1995	1996	1997	1998	1999	2000	2001	2002	2003
1,2F	1,2F	1,2F	1,2F	1,2F	1,2F	1,2F	1,2F	1,2F	1,2F	1,2F

Overview:

Faced with a growing hunger problem, Cape Verde in 2002 made its first request for emergency food aid in more than 20 years. International humanitarian organizations said 30,000 of the country's 500,000 people were threatened by hunger in 2002. The island nation has few exploitable natural resources and traditionally relies heavily on imported food; moreover, food production dropped by 23 percent in 2001 because of drought. The food crisis appeared to have no adverse effect on the new government of President Pedro Verona Rodrigues Pires.

After achieving independence from Portugal in 1975, Cape Verde was governed for 16 years under Marxist, one-party rule by the African Party for the Independence of Guinea and Cape Verde, which is now the African Party for the Independence of Cape Verde (PAICV). The Movement for Democracy (MPD) won a landslide 1991 victory in the first democratic elections when Cape Verde became the first former Portuguese colony in Africa to abandon Marxist political and economic systems. In 1995, the MPD was returned to power with 59 percent of the vote. Antonio Mascarenhas Monteiro's mandate ended in 2001 after he had served two terms as president.

The country's stagnant economy has been bolstered somewhat by increased exports and tourism, but infrastructure improvements are still needed to assist in private sector development. Cape Verde is one of Africa's smallest and poorest lands. Foreign aid and remittances by Cape Verdean expatriates provide a large portion of national income.

Political Rights and Civil Liberties: The president and members of the National People's Assembly are elected through universal suffrage in free and fair elections. Since the country's 1991 transition to multiparty democracy, Cape Verdeans have changed their government three times by democratic means.

Cape Verde had a spectacularly close presidential election in 2001. In the second round of voting, opposition candidate Pedro Verona Rodrigues Pires defeated ruling party contender Carlos Alberto Wahnon de Carvalho Veiga, by only 12 votes, in an election that overturned a decade of rule by the Movement for Democracy (MPD). Both presidential candidates have served as prime ministers. It was a test for Cape Verde's democracy that despite the closeness of the election, trust remained in the country's institutions and the results were accepted. The PAICV also defeated the MPD in the 2001 legislative polls. The change in voting appeared to be a reflection of the popular attitude that the MPD had grown complacent. The PAICV won 40 seats compared with 30 for the MPD and 2 for the Democratic Alliance for Change. Disagreements within the MPD in 2000 resulted in a split and the formation of a new party, the Democratic Renewal Party, which won no assembly seats.

Reforms to strengthen an overburdened judiciary were implemented in 1998. The judiciary is independent, although cases are frequently delayed. Free legal counsel is provided to indigents. Judges must bring charges within 24 hours of arrest. Human rights groups, including the National Commission on the Rights of Man and the Ze Moniz Association, operate freely. Prison conditions are poor and are characterized by overcrowding. Freedom of peaceful assembly and association is guaranteed and respected. The constitution requires the separation of church and state, and religious rights are respected in practice. The vast majority of Cape Verdeans belong to the Roman Catholic Church.

Freedom of expression and of the press is guaranteed and generally respected in practice. No authorization is needed to publish newspapers and other publications. Broadcasts are largely state controlled, but there is a growing independent press. There are six independent radio broadcasters and one state-run radio broadcaster, in addition to one state-run television station and two foreign-owned stations. Criticism of the government by state-run media is limited by self-censorship resulting from citizens' fear of demotion or dismissal.

Discrimination against women persists despite legal prohibitions against gender discrimination, as well as provisions for social and economic equality. Many women do not know their rights or do not possess the means to seek redress, especially in rural areas. They are also subject to allegedly common, but seldom reported, domestic violence. Serious concerns about child abuse and the prevalence of child labor persist. Domestic nongovernmental organizations have undertaken campaigns to promote the rights of women and children.

The constitution protects the right to unionize, and workers may form and join unions without restriction. Two confederations, the Council of Free Labor Unions and the National Union of Cape Verde Workers, include 25 unions with approximately 30,000 members. Collective bargaining is permitted, but it occurs rarely.

Central African Republic

Polity: Presidential-parliamentary
Economy: Capitalist-statist
Population: 3,600,000
PPP: $1,172
Life Expectancy: 44

Political Rights: 5
Civil Liberties: 5
Status: Partly Free

Religious Groups: Indigenous beliefs (35 percent), Protestant (25 percent), Roman Catholic (25 percent), Muslim (15 percent)
Ethnic Groups: Baya (33 percent), Banda (27 percent), Mandjia (13 percent), Sara (10 percent), Mboum (7 percent), other (10 percent)
Capital: Bangui

Ten-Year Ratings Timeline (Political Rights, Civil Liberties, Status)

1993	1994	1995	1996	1997	1998	1999	2000	2001	2002	2003
6,5PF	3,4PF	3,4PF	3,4PF	3,5PF	3,5PF	3,4PF	3,4PF	1,3,4PF	5,5PF	5,5PF

Overview:

Fighting erupted in Bangui, the capital of the Central African Republic (CAR), in October 2002 between rebels and government forces backed by Libyan jets and troops. The attack appeared to have been launched by renegade troops led by the CAR's former head of the armed forces, General Francois Bozize. He had fled to neighboring Chad in November 2001, after forces loyal to President Ange-Felix Patasse attempted to arrest him for his alleged involvement in a May 2001 coup attempt. That 2001 uprising was apparently led not by Bozize, but by former military ruler Andre Kolingba, who then sought exile in Uganda. In 2002, a court in the CAR sentenced Kolingba, along with at least 20 others, to death in absentia.

The CAR, a sparsely populated country, gained independence from France in 1960 after a period of particularly brutal colonial exploitation. Colonel Jean-Bedel Bokassa seized power in 1967 and, as self-declared emperor, imposed an increasingly bizarre personal dictatorship on the CAR, which he renamed Central African Empire. After Bokassa began to murder schoolchildren, French forces finally ousted him in 1979. A French-installed successor was deposed by General Kolingba in 1981. Kolingba accepted a transition to a multiparty system that led to democratic elections in 1993 and 1999, both of which Patasse won, defeating Kolingba. Until the elections, members of Kolingba's Yakoma ethnic group occupied a disproportional number of positions in the government, security forces, and state-owned businesses. The May 2001 coup attempt left at least 250 people dead in the capital, Bangui, and forced 50,000 others to flee their homes. Human rights abuses were rampant during the ten days of fighting, and the Yakoma were singled out for persecution. Relations between Chad and the CAR have deteriorated since Bozize and his followers sought refuge in Chad. In December 2002, leaders from the Central African region sent 350 troops from Cameroon, Gabon, Equatorial Guinea, Mali, and the Republic of Congo to monitor the border region and to patrol Bangui.

Restructuring of the security forces has been slow following military uprisings in 1996 and 1997. Kolingba played a part in both of those. UN peacekeepers withdrew in February 2000 following democratic elections and were replaced by a peace-building office.

Most of the CAR's people are subsistence farmers. Diamonds and forestry are the government's main source of foreign exchange. The UN Security Council has welcomed the government's efforts to stamp out corruption and establish good governance. At least a dozen senior government officials were arrested in 2002 on charges of embezzlement.

Political Rights and Civil Liberties: Presidential and legislative elections were held in 1993 in line with the 1986 constitution, giving the CAR's people their first opportunity to choose their leaders in an open and democratic manner. President Ange-Felix Patasse, leader of the Movement for the Liberation of the Central African People, was reelected in 1999 for another six-year term, defeating Andre Kolingba. The incumbent narrowly won the first round, eliminating the need for a runoff. UN peacekeepers watched over the voting, and international observers judged the vote to be free, although there were reports of irregularities such as ballot shortages in some areas with a strong opposition following. Kolingba and other candidates claimed fraud.

President Patasse's triumph was not matched by his party in the 1998 National Assembly elections, which produced a nearly even split between his supporters and his opponents. Opposition parties held one more seat than the ruling party, but one of their members defected, giving the ruling party a majority.

The Independent Electoral Commission was established in 1999, but it was largely controlled by administrators loyal to the president. A decree later subordinated it to the state Organ of Control to oversee the election process.

Corruption, political interference, and lack of training hinder the efficiency and impartiality of judicial institutions. However, some human rights leaders hailed what they called the independent decision of a court in 2001 to acquit a former defense minister who had been implicated in the May 2001 coup attempt. Limitations on searches and detention are often ignored. Conditions for prisoners, including many long-term pretrial detainees, are extremely difficult and sometimes life threatening. Juveniles are not separated from adults. Police brutality is also a serious problem, and security forces act with impunity. However, several human rights and other nongovernmental organizations operate unhindered.

Broadcast media are dominated by the state and offer little coverage of opposition activities. There are several independent newspapers. The only licensed private radio stations are music- or religion-oriented, although some carry programming on human rights and peace-building issues. Legislation enacted in 1998 rescinded the government's authority to censor the press, but authorities have occasionally been restrictive and have used draconian criminal libel laws to prosecute journalists. Several journalists fled the country following the May 2001 coup attempt. Some journalists were tortured.

Religious freedom is generally respected, but the government occasionally infringes on these rights. Open public discussion is permitted, but constitutionally guaranteed freedom of assembly is not always honored by authorities. Discrimination against indigenous Pygmies exists. Societal discrimination in many areas relegates women to second-class citizenship, especially in rural areas, and constitutional guarantees for women's rights are generally not enforced. However, women have made some gains in the political sphere. Female genital mutilation is still practiced, but it was made illegal in 1996 and is reportedly diminishing. Human rights groups said more than 100 women were raped during the October 2002 military uprising.

The CAR's largest single employer is the government, and government employee trade unions are especially active. Worker rights to form or join unions are legally protected. The law does not provide for collective bargaining specifically, but workers are protected from employer interference.

Chad

Polity: Presidential-
parliamentary
(military-dominated)
Economy: Capitalist
Population: 9,000,000
PPP: $871
Life Expectancy: 51

Political Rights: 6
Civil Liberties: 5
Status: Not Free

Religious Groups: Muslim (51 percent), Christian (35 percent),
other (14 percent)
Ethnic Groups: Sara (28 percent), Arab (12 percent), many others (60 percent)
Capital: N'Djamena

Ten-Year Ratings Timeline (Political Rights, Civil Liberties, Status)

1993	1994	1995	1996	1997	1998	1999	2000	2001	2002	2003
6,6NF	6,5NF	6,5NF	6,5NF	6,5NF	6,5NF	6,4NF	6,5NF	6,5NF	6,5NF	6,5NF

Overview:
In 2002, President Idriss Deby continued to dominate Chad's political landscape as a result of his government's control of Chad's political and electoral processes. Deby's Patriotic Salvation Movement (MPS) increased its dominance of the parliament in elections held in May. The elections were boycotted by several opposition parties that claimed the electoral process lacked transparency. The government was buoyed by progress on a financially lucrative ($3 billion) but controversial oil pipeline project.

Serious questions remain about the government's ability to manage these revenues in a transparent and accountable fashion. In northern Chad intermittent fighting continued as part of a long-standing conflict between government forces and Libyan-supported rebels, whose leader, former Defense Minister Youssouf Togoimi, died in 2001 from wounds received in a land-mine explosion.

Chad has been in a state of almost constant war since achieving its independence from France in 1960. President Deby gained power by overthrowing Hissein Habre in 1990. Turmoil resulting from ethnic and religious differences is exacerbated by clan rivalries and external interference. The country is divided between Nilotic and Bantu Christian farmers who inhabit the country's south, and Arab and Saharan peoples who occupy arid deserts in the north.

Chad was a militarily dominated one-party state until Deby lifted the ban on political parties in 1993. A national conference that included a broad array of civic and political groups then created a transitional parliament, which was controlled by the MPS. Scores of political parties are registered.

Chad's army and political life are largely in the hands of members of the small Zaghawa and Bideyat groups from President Deby's northeastern region. This is a source of ongoing resentment among the more than 200 other ethnic groups in the country. The formal exercise of deeply flawed elections and democratic processes has produced some opening of Chadian society, but real power remains with President Deby.

France, which remains highly influential in Chad, maintains a 1,000-member garrison in the country and, despite a sometimes rocky bilateral relationship, serves as Deby's main political and commercial supporter. Brutality by Chadian soldiers and rebels alike marked insurgencies in the vast countryside, but the large-scale abuses of the past have abated somewhat.

Tensions rose with the Central African Republic (CAR) in 2002, and several skirmishes were reported. The former CAR army commander, General Francois Bozize, was granted asylum in Chad in November 2001, having fled his country following his alleged involvement in a failed coup d'etat. Adding to the tension was the concurrent raiding of southern Chad by Chadian rebels based in CAR territory.

In September 2002, the World Bank reaffirmed its support of the Chad-Cameroon pipeline project despite earlier concerns expressed by bank personnel that the project could harm the environment and fail to meet other goals.

Political Rights and Civil Liberties: In theory Chadians have the right to choose their political leaders. In practice, this right is severely restricted. In a referendum held in March 1996, voters approved a new constitution based on the French model and providing for a unified and presidential state. An ostensibly independent election commission law was passed in 2000, despite significant opposition. The law gives the predominance of seats to government representatives and those of parties in the ruling coalition.

Chad has never experienced a peaceful, fair, and orderly transfer of political power. Recent legislative and presidential elections have been marred by serious irregularities and indications of outright fraud. In May 2001, Idriss Deby was reelected president of Chad with more than 67 percent of the vote. The six opposition presidential candidates alleged that the election was marred by fraud and called for the result to be annulled. They undertook a civil disobedience campaign and were briefly arrested. The government subsequently banned gatherings of more than 20 people, although political protests continued. The European Union "regretted" the many shortcomings in the organization of the poll and the resultant irregularities, and expressed concern about the restriction of liberties observed during the electoral period.

The legislature is unicameral. The sole chamber, the National Assembly, has 155 members, directly elected for a four-year term. In April the ruling MPS won a sweeping majority in parliament, capturing 110 of the 155 parliamentary seats. Its parliamentary ally, the Rally for Democracy and Progress, won 12 seats, with the opposition Action Federation for the Republic obtaining 9 seats. Two opposition parties—the Union for Democracy and the Republic and the Party for Liberty and Development—boycotted the election, saying the authorities had not provided sufficient guarantees that the vote would be free and fair. They had held 7 seats between them in the outgoing 125-seat parliament.

Independent human rights groups have credibly charged Chadian security forces and rebel groups with killing and torturing with impunity, although such claims diminished in 2002. A comprehensive peace agreement with northern rebels was signed in Libya in January 2002, but factions of the Movement for Democracy and Justice in Chad (MDJT) resumed fighting in May 2002. In recent years tens of thousands of Chadians have fled their country to escape politically inspired violence. Several of the 20 or more other armed factions have reached peace pacts, but many of these agreements have failed. Chad's long and porous borders are virtually unpoliced. Trade in weapons among nomadic Sahelian peoples is rife, and banditry adds to the pervasive insecurity.

The rule of law and the judicial system remain weak, with courts heavily influenced by the executive. Security forces routinely ignore constitutional protections regarding search, seizure, and detention. Overcrowding, disease, and malnutrition make prison conditions life threatening, and many inmates spend years in prison without charges.

Newspapers critical of the government circulate freely in N'Djamena, but have little impact among the largely rural and illiterate population. According to the BBC, radio is the medium of mass communication, but state control of broadcast media allows few dissenting views. Radiodiffusion Nationale Tchadienne, the national broadcaster, operates a network of national and regional radio stations. Despite high licensing fees for commercial radio stations, a number of private stations are on the air, some operated by nonprofit groups including human rights groups and the Roman Catholic Church. These broadcasters are subject to close official scrutiny and were banned from airing political material in the run-ups to recent parliamentary and presidential elections. The only television station, Teletchad, is state owned and its coverage favors the government.

Despite harassment and occasional physical intimidation, the Chadian Human Rights League, Chad Nonviolence, and several other human rights groups operate openly and publish findings critical of the government. Although religion is a source of division in society, Chad is a secular state and freedom of religion is generally respected. Women's rights are protected by neither traditional law nor the penal code, and few educational opportunities are available. Female genital mutilation is commonplace. Workers' right to organize and to strike is generally respected, but the formal economy is small. Union membership is low. Most Chadians are subsistence farmers.

Chile

Polity: Presidential-
parliamentary democracy
Economy: Capitalist
Population: 15,600,000
PPP: $9,417
Life Expectancy: 77
Religious Groups: Roman Catholic (89 percent),
Protestant (11 percent)
Ethnic Groups: White and mestizo (95 percent),
 Indian (3 percent), other (2 percent)
Capital: Santiago

Political Rights: 2
Civil Liberties: 1*
Status: Free

Ratings Change: Chile's civil liberties rating improved from 2 to 1 due to President Ricardo Lagos's adroit handling of Chile's still thorny civil-military relationship.

Ten-Year Ratings Timeline (Political Rights, Civil Liberties, Status)

1993	1994	1995	1996	1997	1998	1999	2000	2001	2002	2003
2,2F	2,2F	2,2F	2,2F	2,2F	1,2,2F	3,2F	2,2F	1,2,2F	2,2F	2,1F

Overview:

Despite a slowing economy and opposition from within Chile's powerful business class, Chilean President Ricardo Lagos maintained high public approval ratings throughout 2002, as a result, in part, of his firmness in dealing with thorny issues ranging from strikes by bus drivers to civilian control of the military. Adroit maneuvering by Lagos resulted in the resignation of the head of the air force after the service's senior officer was accused of hiding details about human rights abuses during the dictatorship of Capt. Gen. Augusto Pinochet Ugarte. The affair allowed Lagos to reopen contentious constitutional issues concerning civilian primacy over the armed forces and came amidst a series of court actions against military human rights offenders. In July, however, the Chilean Supreme Court effectively ended efforts to hold Pinochet accountable for human rights abuses by ruling that he was mentally unfit to stand trial.

The Republic of Chile was founded after independence from Spain in 1818. Democratic rule predominated in the twentieth century until the 1973 overthrow of Salvador Allende by the military under Pinochet. An estimated 3,000 people were killed or "disappeared" during his regime. The 1980 constitution provided for a plebiscite in which voters could reject another presidential term for Pinochet. In the 1988 vote, 55 percent of voters said no to eight more years of military rule, and competitive presidential and legislative elections were scheduled for 1989.

In 1989, Christian Democrat Patricio Aylwin, the candidate of the center-left Concertacion for Democracy, was elected president and the Concertacion won a majority in the Chamber of Deputies. However, with eight senators appointed by the outgoing military government, the coalition fell short of a senate majority. Aylwin's government was unsuccessful in its efforts to reform the constitution, and was stymied by a right-wing Senate bloc in its efforts to prevent Pinochet and other military chiefs from remaining at their posts until 1997.

Eduardo Frei, a businessman and the son of a former president, carried his Concertacion candidacy to an easy victory in December 1993 elections, defeating right-wing candidate Arturo Alessandri. Frei promised to establish full civilian control over the military, but he found he lacked the votes in congress, as the 48-seat Senate included a senator-for-life position for Pinochet and 9 designated senators mandated by the 1980 constitution. Frei also was forced to retreat on his call for full accountability for rights violations that occurred under military rule.

In October 1997 Frei selected the army chief of staff as Pinochet's replacement from a list of names Pinochet submitted. In December, the ruling coalition won a convincing victory in an election in which all 120 lower house and 20 of 49 senate seats were open. However, the binomial electoral system resulted in pro-Pinochet forces retaining their veto on constitutional reforms.

The detention of Pinochet in London in October 1998, the result of an extradition order from Spain, where he was wanted for alleged rights crimes against Spanish citizens living in Chile, at first produced a strong political polarization in Chile. His continued imprisonment, however, was viewed as a reaffirmation of the rule of law, albeit due to foreign intervention.

On December 12, 1999, Lagos, a moderate Concertacion socialist, faced right-wing Alliance for Chile candidate Joaquin Lavin, the mayor of a Santiago suburb and a former advisor to Pinochet, winning 47.96 percent to Lavin's 47.52 percent. Both candidates, however, fell short of the 50 percent majority needed to win outright in a first round.

Lagos won the January 16, 2000, runoff election, taking a 2.6 percent lead over Lavin. Although the Concertacion coalition had 70 seats to the opposition's 50 in the lower house, it held just 20 seats in the senate to 18 held by the opposition. A bloc of 11 others were either senators-for-life, or had been designated under Pinochet's rules. Lagos's strong early performance appeared, by late 2000, to be threatened by soaring unemployment, price increases, and charges of government corruption. In October 2000 municipal elections, Lavin won 61 percent of the votes in the contest for the Santiago mayoralty. Although the ruling coalition won 51.2 percent of the votes nationwide, the opposition raised the number of its mayoral seats to 163 from 126, out of a total of 341, and garnered 40.9 percent of the vote.

In December 2000, a judge indicted Pinochet on homicide and kidnapping charges, in a year that saw the judiciary rule that allegations of crimes against humanity, including torture, kidnapping, and genocide, fell within its purview and were not subject to amnesty decrees. In July 2001, an appeals court in Santiago dropped the charges against Pinochet after it found that he suffered from dementia. In 2001, a much-touted report by the military about the fate of the "disappeared"—meant to show its desire to be part of a reconciliation with Chilean society—proved to be misleading at best.

In 2001 the Chilean right was locked in internecine warfare; it was revealed that contending factions had engaged in a "dirty war" in which one group had employed former secret police personnel to blackmail a senior political figure into renouncing a bid for the Senate in elections held December 16, 2001. In that contest, Chileans voted for a completely new lower house and half of the 38 Senate seats were decided by popular vote. Pinochet supporters made big gains in the legislative elections, although they failed to win control of congress from the governing center-left coalition.

In September 2002, the family of a constitutionalist Chilean military commander murdered in a botched 1971 kidnap attempt sued former U.S. Secretary of State Henry Kissinger and former CIA Director Richard Helms of orchestrating the covert activities that led to his death. Helms died of natural causes the next month.

Political Rights and Civil Liberties: Citizens can change their government democratically. The 2001, 2000, and 1999 elections were considered free and fair, although low registration rates among young voters are a cause for concern.

In 1990, the Truth and Reconciliation Commission was formed to investigate rights violations committed under military rule. Its report implicated the military and secret police leadership in the death or forcible disappearance of 2,279 people between September 1973 and March 1990. Since the return of democracy, hundreds of cases of human rights violations have been brought to civilian courts, and there were an increasing number of convictions. In August 2002, in a positive development, 12 people who served as officers under Pinochet, including four generals, were sentenced to prison terms for the 1982 killing of a prominent labor leader. In October, a judge indicted six current and retired army officers, including two generals, for the 1993 slaying in Uruguay of a chemist and assassin who worked for Pinochet's intelligence service.

Chilean media generally operate without constraint, although some Pinochet-era laws remain in effect and some self-censorship continues. Nevertheless, on October 30, 2002, the Senate approved a bill that will eliminate censorship of films in Chile.

Chile has two national police forces—a uniformed force, the Carabineros, one of Latin America's best law enforcement institutions with a history of popular support and respect; and a smaller, plainclothes investigations force. In recent years, the Carabineros have been the subject of complaints about the inadequate number of uniformed police patrolling the streets and allegations of increasing narcotics-related corruption. Police brutality and the lack of due process rights for detainees are also alleged. Prisons in Chile are overcrowded and antiquated, with facilities nationally running at about 163 percent of capacity.

Workers may form unions without prior authorization as well as join existing unions. Approximately 12 percent of Chile's 5.7 million workers belong to unions. Native American groups in the country's southern region are increasingly vocal about their rights to ancestral lands that the government and private industry seek to develop. Chile has some 1.2 million indigenous people, more than 10 percent of the country's total population, two-thirds of them Mapuches. Upon taking office, President Ricardo Lagos began to make good on a campaign promise that the "Indian question" would receive priority attention. In May 2000, he announced the creation of a "historical truth and new deal commission" to consider the needs of Mapuche communities. He also announced that the Mapuche will be given 370,000 acres of government-owned land.

In 2000, Lagos appointed five women to his 16-person cabinet. The Chilean defense minister, Michelle Bachelet Jeria, is the daughter of a Chilean general tortured to death for his opposition to the 1973 coup. Violence and discrimination against women and violence against children remain problems.

China

Polity: One party
Economy: Mixed statist
Population: 1,280,700,000
PPP: $3,976
Life Expectancy: 71
Religious Groups: Daoist (Taoist), Buddhist, other
Ethnic Groups: Han Chinese (92 percent), other, including Tibetan, Mongol, Korean, Manchu, and Uighur (8 percent)
Capital: Beijing

Political Rights: 7
Civil Liberties: 6
Status: Not Free

Ten-Year Ratings Timeline (Political Rights, Civil Liberties, Status)

1993	1994	1995	1996	1997	1998	1999	2000	2001	2002	2003
7,7NF	7,7NF	7,7NF	7,7NF	7,7NF	7,7NF	7,6NF	7,6NF	7,6NF	7,6NF	7,6NF

Overview:

The ruling party's carefully scripted leadership changes, aimed at giving the impression of a smooth transition to a younger generation of leaders, ended up creating some uncertainty over who actually wields decisive power in the world's most populous country. Hu Jintao, the sixty-year-old state vice president and an engineer by training, formally took the reigns of the all-powerful Chinese Communist Party (CCP) from veteran party boss Jiang Zemin, 76, at a November party congress. Jiang, however, held on to a key military post, leading to speculation that he intends to be a power broker behind the scenes. Regardless of who really is on top, the party is expected to continue its overarching policy of gradually freeing up the economy while crushing political dissent as it faces rising unemployment, widespread labor protests, and growing income inequalities.

The CCP took power in 1949 under Mao Zedong after defeating the Koumintang, or Nationalists, in a civil war that began in the 1920s. Aiming to tighten the party's grip on power, Mao led several brutal, mass mobilization campaigns that resulted in millions of deaths and politicized nearly every aspect of public life. Following Mao's death in 1976, Deng Xiaoping emerged as China's paramount leader. While maintaining the CCP's absolute rule, Deng scaled back the party's role in everyday life and launched China's gradual transition from central planning to a market economy. The party showed its intent to hold on to power at all costs with the June 1989 massacre of hundreds, if not thousands, of student protesters in and around Beijing's Tiananmen Square. The Beijing demonstrations, along with similar student rallies in cities across China, protested official corruption and demanded democratic reforms. Following the crackdown, the CCP tapped Jiang, then the Shanghai mayor and party boss, to replace the relatively moderate Zhao Ziyang as party secretary-general. Jiang became state president in 1993 and was widely recognized as China's new paramount leader following Deng's death in 1997.

Against opposition from die-hard Marxists within the party, Jiang continued Deng's policies of selling off state firms, encouraging private enterprise, and rolling back China's "iron rice bowl" welfare system. He also oversaw China's emergence from its pariah status following the Tiananmen Square massacre to become a more engaged player in world affairs, even as the government continuously faced foreign criticism over its appalling human rights record.

CCP leaders appear now to have reached a consensus that continued economic reforms are needed in order to boost living standards and stave off broad calls for political reform. They fear, however, that freeing up the economy too fast—thereby giving people ever more freedom in their day-to-day lives—will create social unrest.

While the student activism of the late 1980s has largely died down, factory workers and farmers have in recent years held thousands of street protests over hardships associated with economic restructuring. Tens of thousands of workers demonstrated over mass layoffs, poor severance pay, low or unpaid wages or pensions, and other labor grievances in spring 2002 in the northeastern cities of Liaoyang and Daqing and in the eastern mining town of Fushun. These hardships are expected to increase as the government slashes tariffs and takes other measures to open up China's economy to trade and foreign investment in line with its commitments as a World Trade Organization (WTO) member.

Already, the privatization of thousands of small- and medium-sized state-owned enterprises has thrown tens of millions out of work in a country that lacks a viable system of unemployment benefits, health insurance, and pensions. The government also faces the difficult choice of either cleaning up China's ailing state banks, which would involve yet more painful job cuts at state firms, or allowing the billions of dollars in bad loans held by these banks to continue choking off lending to private firms and risking a financial crisis. Analysts suggest that, at least in the near term, China's leadership will continue stoking the economy with massive public spending rather than take tough measures to clean up state banks or reform money-losing large state firms.

Meanwhile, in the countryside, home to 70 percent of the population—or roughly 900 million Chinese—thousands of riots and demonstrations by farmers in recent years have protested against high and often arbitrary local government fees and taxes. Rural China also has too many workers chasing too few farm and factory jobs. This has contributed to a "floating population" of some 80 million to 130 million people, by official count, who have left their rural homes in search of work in cities, where the migrants increasingly compete with locals for jobs. China's WTO membership could make matters worse for many peasants if cheaper agricultural imports chip away at their incomes. Already, China has wide income gaps between the dynamic, export-oriented coastal and southern areas and the ailing rural and rust-belt interior.

Corruption, meanwhile, has flourished in a country that has a rapidly expanding economy but lacks independent courts, regulators, investigative agencies, and a free press. Corruption consumes 13 to 17 percent of economic output annually, according to official figures. Chinese authorities have responded recently by executing hundreds, possibly thousands, of people for corruption.

Against this backdrop, the CCP's sixteenth party congress in November—an event held only once every five years—was carefully stage-managed to project an image of an orderly transfer of power. Hu was named secretary-general of the CCP, reportedly having been tapped by Deng a decade ago as Jiang's successor. Jiang is expected to also give up the state presidency to Hu when his term expires in March. Jiang continues, however, to head the Central Military Commission, a post that effectively keeps him in charge of China's 2.5 million-strong armed forces. By virtue of this position, Jiang, not Hu, is officially listed as the head of the new party leadership.

Analysts say, moreover, that five or six of the cadres on the powerful, nine-member Politburo Standing Committee, which Hu heads, are Jiang proteges. The Jiang allies include Zeng Qinghong, 63, described by some observers as a potential political rival to Hu. In addition to formally endorsing the new leadership lineup, the congress also approved Jiang's controversial decision to allow private entrepreneurs to join the CCP.

Chinese authorities, meanwhile, continue to stifle any organized calls for political reform. Since 1998, courts have sentenced more than 30 leaders of a would-be opposition party, the China Democracy Party, to prison terms of up to 13 years on subversion or other charges. The government has also jailed thousands of followers of the Falun Gong spiritual movement, which in 1999 organized the biggest protest in the capital since 1989, to demand official recognition.

Wary of separatism, the government has also tried to crush pro-independence movements among the seven million ethnic Uighurs and other, smaller Turkic-speaking Muslim groups in China's northwestern Xinjiang province. Since the early 1990s, officials have detained "tens of thousands" of Uighurs and other Muslims in Xinjiang, executing several for alleged separatist activities, the human rights group Amnesty International said in a March report. Most Uighur independence activities appear to be peaceful. Beijing, however, has used allegations that Uighur militants carried out several bombings and assassinations in the 1990s—and, more recently, the post-September 11 campaign against pan-Islamic terrorism—to brand all Uighur dissidents as terrorists.

Political Rights and Civil Liberties: China is one of the most authoritarian states in the world. Opposition parties are illegal, the CCP controls the judiciary, and ordinary Chinese enjoy few basic rights.

The CCP Politburo's Standing Committee makes nearly all key political decisions and sets governmental policy. Party cadres hold nearly all top national and local governmental, police, and military posts. China's legislature, the National People's Congress, is constitutionally the most powerful state body. Its handpicked delegates now routinely register protest votes over the government's handling of crime and other issues. For the most part, though, the congress merely rubberstamps the Politburo's decisions.

China's only real experiment with democracy has been at the local level, mainly with elections for so-called village committees. These bodies, however, cannot levy taxes, and hold few executive powers. Moreover, "In general the CCP dominates the local electoral process, and roughly 60 percent of the members elected to the village committees are CCP members," according to the U.S. State Department's global human rights report for 2001, released in March 2002. More recently, however, tens of thousands of villages have held elections for the more powerful position of local party secretary, a party researcher told the Hong Kong-based *Far Eastern Economic Review*.

The government controls the judiciary, with the CCP directing verdicts and sentences in sensitive cases, according to the U.S. State Department report. Recent reforms aimed at making ordinary trials fairer "have not brought the country's criminal procedures into compliance with international standards," and officials often subject prisoners to "severe psychological pressure" to confess using legal loopholes to prevent suspects from obtaining counsel, according to the report. Trials are generally little more than sentencing hearings. Moreover, corruption and inefficiency in the judicial system are "endemic," the report added.

Officials bypass the courts entirely in jailing, without trial, hundreds of thousands of Chinese each year under two types of administrative detention. "Re-education through labor" camps held some 310,000 Chinese as of early 2001, and the number has very likely grown since then, Amnesty International said in an October report. Meanwhile, a system called "custody and repatriation" is used to detain one million Chinese each year, many of them homeless people and other "undesirable" city dwellers, the report said.

By most accounts, Chinese prisons, re-education camps, and detention centers hold thousands of political prisoners, although the exact number is not known. Even after they are released, many former political prisoners face unrelenting police harassment that prevents them from holding jobs or otherwise leading normal lives.

China executes thousands of people each year, more than all other countries combined, according to Amnesty International. Many are executed immediately after summary trials, and often for nonviolent crimes. As part of Beijing's national "Strike Hard" campaign against crime that began in 2001, many Chinese have been executed for nonviolent offenses such as corruption, pimping, hooliganism, or the theft of farm animals or rice.

Law enforcement officials routinely torture suspects to extract confessions, Amnesty International said in a September report. Courts have recently sentenced some officials convicted of torture to heavy prison sentences, although most perpetrators go unpunished. Deaths of criminal suspects in custody continue to be a concern, according to the U.S. State Department report, which did not provide figures on the number of such cases each year.

Conditions in Chinese prisons and labor camps for both political prisoners and ordinary criminals are "harsh and frequently degrading," the U.S. State Department report said. Prisoners are kept in overcrowded jails with poor sanitation and often receive inadequate food and medical care. Forced labor in prisons is "common," the report added.

The regime sharply restricts press freedom. It bars the media from promoting political reform, covering internal party politics or the inner workings of government, criticizing Beijing's domestic and international policies, or reporting financial data that the government has not released. At the same time, officials often allow the media to report on certain problems that the CCP itself seeks to alleviate. These include corruption, arbitrary decision making, and other abuses by local officials. Newspapers, however, cannot report on corruption without government and party approval.

Chinese jails held 36 journalists as of December 2002, 14 of whom were serving time for publishing or distributing information online, according to the New York-based Committee to Protect Journalists. Other journalists have been harassed, detained, threatened, or dismissed from their jobs over their reporting. Officials also recently have suspended or shut down some liberal magazines, newspapers, and publishing houses. While China's press is both public and private, the government owns and operates all radio and television stations.

The government promotes use of the Internet, which it believes to be critical to economic development, but regulates access, monitors use, and restricts and regulates content. Amnesty International, in a December report on state control of the Internet in China, said that it knows of 33 Chinese who have been detained or jailed for offenses related to their use of the Internet. Some 45 million Chinese regularly log on to the Internet, a government-funded industry group reported in mid-2002, and the number is growing rapidly.

China has hundreds of thousands of nongovernmental organizations (NGOs). They all work in areas that, at least on the surface, do not challenge the government's authority, such as the environment and the provision of social services. Officials use a complex vetting process to deny licenses to human rights or other politically oriented groups. Once registered, NGOs must report regularly to specific government departments.

Workers, farmers, and others have held thousands of public protests in recent years over labor and economic issues and corruption by local officials. Security forces, however, have forcibly broken up many demonstrations, particularly those with overt political and social messages or where protesters became unruly. Police, for example, broke up a May protest in the town of Yaowan over a lack of adequate compensation for the more than one million villagers who will be displaced by the controversial Three Gorges Dam, the London-based *The Economist* magazine reported.

Beijing sharply restricts religious freedom by placing religious groups under the tight control of state-sponsored bodies and cracking down on religious leaders and ordinary worshippers who reject this authority. For each of the five religions recognized by the government, the respective "patriotic association" appoints clergy; monitors religious membership, funding, and activities; and controls publication and distribution of religious books and other materials. Beijing does not allow the Roman Catholic patriotic association and its member churches to be openly loyal to the Vatican. The five recognized religions are Buddhism, Taoism, Islam, Protestantism, and Catholicism. Buddhism claims the most adherents.

The extent to which congregations must actually submit to these regulations varies by region. In many areas, unregistered Protestant and Catholic congregations worship freely. Elsewhere, however, zealous local officials sometimes break up underground services. They also harass and at times fine, detain, beat, and torture church leaders or ordinary worshippers, and raid, close, or demolish underground churches, mosques, temples, and seminaries, according to the U.S. State Department report and other sources.

In Xinjiang, officials sharply restrict the building of new mosques, limit Islamic publications and education, ban religious practice by those under 18, and control the leadership of mosques and religious schools. Officials recently have also shut down many mosques in Xinjiang, Amnesty International says.

Tens of thousands of Falun Gong practitioners continue to be detained in China, with the vast majority apparently held without trial in "reeducation through labor" camps, Amnesty International said in a September report. At least 200 Falun Gong adherents reportedly have died in detention since 1999, according to the U.S. State Department Human Rights report. Chinese authorities generally show leniency toward ordinary practitioners who recant, while severely punishing those who refuse, as well as core leaders. "Anti-cult" laws developed to crush the Falun Gong, which combines *qiqong* (a traditional martial art) with meditation, have also been used to sentence members of at least 16 other religious groups to long prison terms, the New York–based Human Rights Watch reported in February.

China's one-child family planning policy is applied fairly strictly in the cities and less so in the countryside. While urban couples seldom receive permission to have a second child, rural couples generally may have a second child if their first is a girl. Couples failing to comply face demotion or loss of jobs, fines of up to three times their annual salary, or loss of benefits or access to social services. Local officials have at times demolished or confiscated homes and personal property to punish couples for unpaid fines. Some officials have also forced women to undergo abortions or to be sterilized in order to meet government birth targets, the U.S. State Department report said. The government, however, appears to be relaxing the family planning policy somewhat in the cities, the report added.

Chinese women face considerable unofficial discrimination in employment and other areas and are far likelier than men to be laid off when state firms are slimmed down or privatized, according to the U.S. State Department report. Violence occurs in about 30 percent of Chinese families, with 80 percent of cases involving husbands abusing their wives, according to a 2000 survey by the official All-China Women's Federation. Trafficking in women and children, and the kidnapping and sale of women and girls for prostitution or marriage are serious problems, although the number of victims each year is not known, the State Department report said.

Muslims and other minorities face unofficial discrimination in access to jobs and other areas, and minorities credibly claim that the majority Han Chinese have reaped an outsized share of benefits from government programs and economic growth, according to the U.S. State Department report. China's 55 ethnic minorities make up just under 9 percent of the population, according to 1995 government figures.

In the absence of vigorous unions or strong enforcement of labor laws, private factories often pay workers below-minimum wages, force them to work overtime, sometimes without extra pay, and arbitrarily dismiss employees. Although the law does not guarantee the right to strike, officials frequently allow workers to strike or demonstrate against layoffs, dangerous conditions, or unpaid wages, benefits, or unemployment stipends. The government prohibits independent trade unions, requires all unions to belong to the state-run All China Federation of Trade Unions, and has detained or jailed several independent labor activists.

The economic reforms launched in the late 1970s have freed millions of Chinese from party control of their day-to-day lives. Many now work for private firms, which account for around 30 percent of China's economic output. In urban areas, however, many state workers still must belong to company-based, government-linked work units, which control many aspects of everyday life including housing, health care, permission to have children, and approval to apply for passports. All government offices, public schools, and state firms still have party committees that handle budgets, political education, and personnel decisions. The economic reforms have also lifted hundreds of millions of Chinese out of absolute poverty, although some 200 million still live on less than $1 per day, according to the World Bank.

Colombia

Polity: Presidential-parliamentary democracy (insurgencies)
Economy: Capitalist-statist
Population: 43,800,000
PPP: $6,248
Life Expectancy: 71

Political Rights: 4
Civil Liberties: 4
Status: Partly Free

Religious Groups: Roman Catholic (90 percent), other (10 percent)
Ethnic Groups: Mestizo (58 percent), white (20 percent), mulatto (14 percent), black (4 percent), other, including Indian (4 percent)
Capital: Bogota

Ten-Year Ratings Timeline (Political Rights, Civil Liberties, Status)

1993	1994	1995	1996	1997	1998	1999	2000	2001	2002	2003
2,4PF	2,4PF	3,4PF	4,4PF	4,4PF	4,4PF	3,4PF	4,4PF	4,4PF	4,4PF	4,4PF

Overview:

In May 2002, war-weary Colombians gave Alvaro Uribe Velez, a hard-line former provincial governor who ran independently of the country's two dominant political parties, an unprecedented first-round victory that was a referendum on how best to end Colombia's decades-long civil strife. The victim of an assassination attempt by leftist guerrillas just a month before the vote, Uribe quickly moved to redeem his promise of a stepped-up military campaign against leftist guerrillas who still control a large swath of national territory. With some analysts predicting that the election would usher in a much closer relationship with the United States, Uribe moved to double defense spending, to give the generals a freer hand in the spiraling, drug-financed warfare, and to create a million-member defense force. At the same time, critics charged that Uribe's support from paramilitary death squads and his own hard-line stance promised to stoke the violence and made a ceasefire less likely.

Following independence from Spain in 1819, and after a long period of federal government which oversaw what are now Venezuela, Ecuador, and Panama, the Republic of Colombia was established in 1886. Modern Colombia has been marked by the corrupt machine politics of the Liberals and Conservatives, whose leadership has largely been drawn from the traditional elite; left-wing guerrilla insurgencies; right-wing paramilitary violence; the emergence of vicious drug cartels; and gross human rights violations committed by all sides. In the 1994 legislative elections, the Liberals retained a majority in both houses of congress. Ernesto Samper, a former economic development minister, won the Liberal presidential nomination. The Conservative candidate was Andres Pastrana, a former mayor of Bogota and the son of a former Colombian president. Both candidates pledged to continue Gaviria's free-market reforms.

Samper won in a June 1994 runoff election and, with strong U.S. encouragement, presided over the dismantling of the Cali drug cartel, most of whose leaders were captured in 1995. The arrests, however, netted persuasive evidence that the cartel had given $6 million to the president's campaign, with Samper's approval.

In the June 21, 1998, election, Pastrana won the presidency of Latin America's third most populous country in an impressive victory over the Liberal Party candidate, Interior Minister Horacio Serpa. In an effort to consolidate the peace process, in November Pastrana oversaw the regrouping by Revolutionary Armed Forces of Colombia (FARC) guerrillas within, and the withdrawal by a dispirited military from, a so-called demilitarized zone of five southern districts. The move, strongly resisted by the military, gave the guerrillas de facto control over a territory the size of Switzerland.

The bold gamble, however, sputtered and then failed, although Pastrana did at the same time achieve some success in severing ties between the armed forces and the United Self-Defense Forces of Colombia (AUC), right-wing paramilitary death squads. Colombia's most notorious death squad leader admitted what has long been an open secret—not only do the paramilitary groups make big money from the drug trade (as do the guerrillas), but they are also financed by local and foreign private enterprise. In a two-year period, 1998 to 2000, the paramilitary forces nearly doubled their numbers. Meanwhile, Colombia's neighbors continued to be alarmed at the spillover effects—assassinations, armed incursions and a flood of refugees—of the worsening civil war.

In 2001, it became clear that the FARC's "demilitarized zone" was actually a "state within a state" that the guerrillas used as a sanctuary for coordinating military operations, a rest area for battle-weary insurgents, and a base for criminal activities such as drug trafficking and hostage warehousing. Rather than being contained or defeated on the battlefield, the FARC grew in size and threat, although a smaller guerrilla organization, the National Liberation Army (ELN), suffered a series of devastating military defeats at the hands of right-wing paramilitary forces. On September 10, 2001, U.S. secretary of state Colin Powell announced that the AUC would finally join the FARC and the ELN in their classification as international terrorist organizations.

Uribe emerged from a six-candidate field with 52 percent of the vote, compared with his nearest competitor, Serpa, running again as the Liberal candidate, who received 32 percent. Uribe's inauguration in August was marred by guerrilla attacks that left 19 people dead. In response Uribe decreed a state of emergency, stepped up anti-guerrilla efforts in urban areas, and created "special combat zones" in 27 municipalities in which the U.S.-backed military was allowed to restrict civilian movement and conduct warrantless searches. He also established a "war tax" to finance thousands of additional troops and tightened restrictions on the foreign press. By late 2002, three months of intensive aerial spraying in the coca-rich province of Putumayo, part of a $1.3 billion U.S. antidrug aid effort, resulted in the almost complete destruction of the cocaine-producing crop. However, in November, the former head of the notorious Cali drug cartel once responsible for trafficking 80 percent of the cocaine reaching the United States, Gilberto Rodriguez Orejuela, was released from prison by a court, over Uribe's strong objections.

Political Rights and Civil Liberties: Citizens can change their government through elections. Although in 2002 Colombians were largely able to express their preferences by voting, electoral participation was inhibited because of threats of death squads operating with impunity as well as guerrilla violence, particularly in rural areas where the latter engaged in an explicit campaign of intimidation. The abstention rate was 54 percent, higher than during the previous presidential contest, and more than 200,000 soldiers, police, and security agents were deployed during the voting in a largely successful attempt to keep the peace.

Public corruption remains one of the most serious problems facing Colombia, affects virtually all aspects of public life, and extends far beyond the narcotics trade. For example, foreign businessmen with contracts with the military complain that the armed forces sometimes do not honor their contracts and that they are subject to intimidation if they protest. Anticorruption activists say that the annual cost of systemic problems exceeds $2.2 billion, and that corruption, rather than the internal war, may be a greater threat to the country's institutional survival.

The justice system remains slow and compromised by corruption and extortion. The civilian-led Ministry of Defense is responsible for internal security and oversees both the armed forces and the national police; civilian management of the armed forces, however, is limited. In 2000 the FARC began to routinely execute policemen it captured after attacking police outposts; human rights monitors point out that many officers are not involved in the government's anti-guerrilla operations. In 2002, the Colombian national police got a new chief after a corruption scandal involving 71 cops—including the head of antinarcotics operations—were accused of stealing more than $2 million in U.S. aid. Previously the 85,000-strong force was seen as a bulwark against corruption.

Colombia's 165 prisons, which were built for 32,000 people but hold more than 47,000, are frequent sites of murders and riots. A penal code approved by congress in June 2001 is designed to relieve the strain on Colombia's prisons and allows convicts to be released after serving 60 percent of their sentences, rather than the 80 percent previously required.

Constitutional rights regarding free expression and the freedom to organize political parties, civic groups, and labor unions are severely restricted by politically motivated and drug-related violence and the government's inability to guarantee the security of its citizens. Colombia is one of the most violent countries in the world. More than 3,000 people are kidnapped each year in Colombia, and there is a greater risk of being kidnapped there than in any other country in the world.

Political violence in Colombia continues to take more lives than in any other country in the Western Hemisphere, and civilians are prime victims. In the past decade an estimated 40,000 have died and more than 1.5 million have been displaced from their homes. More than 90 percent of violent crimes go unsolved. Human rights violations have soared to unprecedented highs, with atrocities being committed by all sides in the conflict. Human rights workers in Colombia are frequently murdered by a military often lacking in personal and tactical discipline, and by rightist paramilitary forces. In November 2002, Human Rights Watch issued a scathing report in which it accused Attorney General Luis Camilo Osorio of interfering with military and paramilitary human rights abuses. It charged that Osorio had failed to support, and had even fired, prosecutors investigating the cases.

Left-wing guerrillas, some of whom also protect narcotics-production facilities and drug traffickers, also systematically violate human rights, with victims including Sunday churchgoers and airline passengers. The FARC guerrillas also regularly extort payments from hundreds of businessmen throughout the country.

Journalists are frequently the victims of political and revenge violence, and the Committee for the Protection of Journalists ranks Colombia as the second most dangerous country in the world for the media, after Algeria. More than 120 journalists were murdered in the past decade, and many were killed for reporting on drug trafficking and corruption. Nevertheless, in 2002, two former soldiers were convicted of the assassination of two TV cameramen and each sentenced to 19 years in prison.

Another problem concerns "social cleansing"—the elimination of drug addicts, street children, and other marginal citizens by vigilante groups often linked to police.

There are approximately 80 distinct ethnic groups among Colombia's 800,000-plus indigenous inhabitants, who live on more than 50 million acres of land granted to them by the government, often located in resource-rich, strategic regions fought over by the warring outside armed groups. These Native Americans are frequently the targets of forced recruitment by the guerrillas and selective assassination by the paramilitary forces despite their seeking to remain neutral in the armed conflict. In a three-year period, human rights groups say, more than 1,500 Indians have been press-ganged into service with the guerrillas. In 1999, FARC guerrillas kidnapped three U.S. Native American rights activists and killed them. Indian claims to land and resources are under challenge from government ministries and multinational corporations. In 2002, paramilitary groups kidnapped and killed several prominent Indian leaders.

The murder of trade union activists increased significantly, and Colombia remained the most dangerous country in the world for organized labor, a significant reason for the fact that only about 6 percent of the country's work force is unionized, one of the lowest percentages in Latin America. More than 2,500 trade union activists and leaders have been killed in little more than a decade. Labor leaders are targets of attacks by paramilitary groups, guerrillas, narcotics traffickers, and other union rivals.

According to the United Nations, some 948,000 Colombian children under the age of 14 work in "unacceptable" conditions. An estimated 60 percent of FARC fighters are believed to be under the age of 15, and female child-soldiers are reported to be subjected to sexual abuse. Child-soldiers attempting to leave without permission are executed by firing squad.

Although women are active in politics and community organizations, domestic violence is a problem in Colombia.

Comoros

Polity: Presidential (military-dominated)
Economy: Capitalist
Population: 600,000
PPP: $1,588
Life Expectancy: 56
Religious Groups: Sunni Muslim (98 percent), Roman Catholic (2 percent)
Ethnic Groups: Antalote, Cafre, Makoa, Oimatsaha, Sakalava
Capital: Moroni

Political Rights: 5*
Civil Liberties: 4
Status: Partly Free

Ratings Change: Comoros' political rights rating improved from 6 to 5 due to the holding of largely free and fair presidential elections on each of the archipelago's three islands.

Ten-Year Ratings Timeline (Political Rights, Civil Liberties, Status)

1993	1994	1995	1996	1997	1998	1999	2000	2001	2002	2003
4,2PF	4,4PF	4,4PF	4,4PF	4,4PF	5,4PF	5,4PF	6,4PF	6,4PF	6,4PF	5,4PF

Overview:

Comoros made a few steps toward restoring democracy in 2002 and took one step back as well. Although elections for the president of each of the three islands that make up the new federation appeared to have been largely free and fair, the poll for the executive leader of the federation was not. Former Colonel Azali Assoumani, who had seized power in 1999 on the main island, Grande Comore, won the executive presidency with 75 percent of the vote. However, he was the only candidate. His two opponents had claimed fraud and dropped out of the race.

Two mercenary invasions and at least 18 other coups and attempted coups have shaken the Indian Ocean archipelago of Comoros since independence in 1975. In 1990, in the country's first contested elections, Supreme Court Justice Said Mohamed Djohara won a six-year term as president. French soldiers reversed a 1995 attempted coup by elements of the Comoros security forces, who were aided by foreign mercenaries. An interim government ruled for five months until President Mohamed Taki Abdoulkarim was elected in 1996 in internationally monitored elections that were considered free and fair. Tadjidine Ben Said Massonde became the interim ruler when Taki died suddenly in November 1998.

Comoros comprises three islands: Grande Comore, Anjouan, and Moheli. Anjouan voted for self-determination in a 1997 referendum, repulsed an attempted invasion by the government, and then dissolved into violence as rival separatist groups took up arms against each other. Separatists on Moheli also declared independence. Mayotte Island, the fourth island of the Comorian archipelago, voted to remain a French overseas territory in a 1974 referendum and today enjoys a far higher, French-subsidized standard of living than the other islands do.

Efforts to end the separatist crisis began with the 1999 Antananarivo agreement. Anjouan's refusal to sign the agreement led to violence on Grande Comore and Assoumani's subsequent coup. A reconciliation deal, known as the Fomboni Declaration, was signed in 2000 between the Assoumani government and Anjouan separatists. A national referendum was approved in December 2001 for a new constitution that gave greater autonomy to the three islands of the Comoros within the framework of a confederation, and provided for a rotating executive presidency among the islands every four years.

The country's electoral commission said the 2002 vote for the executive presidency was not fair, but then the commission was dissolved and a body of five magistrates ruled that the election would stand. Since the elections, a power struggle has emerged between Assoumani and Abdou Soule Elbak, who was elected president of Grande Comore after defeating an Assoumani-backed candidate. The core of the struggle between the two leaders appears to be over economic control of the island. At one point, Assoumani dispatched the military to surround some key ministries.

Comorians are among the world's poorest people. The country relies heavily on foreign aid and earns a small amount through exports of vanilla, ylang-ylang, and cloves. The International Monetary Fund said in July 2002 that it was unlikely that development assistance would be forthcoming until administrative control issues were clarified on Grande Comore.

Political Rights and Civil Liberties:

Comorians have the constitutional right to change their government democratically, although this right has only partially been realized. Presidential elections held in 2002 for each of the archipelago's three islands were considered to be largely fair, while the vote for the executive presidency turned into a one-horse race whose outcome was contested. Comorians exercised their constitutional right to change their government democratically in open elections for the first time in the 1996 parliamentary and presidential elections. Mohamed Taki Abdoulkarim won the presidency in a runoff election with more than 60 percent of the vote. The conservative Islamic main opposition party held several seats in the National Assembly. New parliamentary elections are scheduled for December 2002.

The Comorian legal system is based both on *Sharia* (Islamic law) and on remnants of the French legal code and is subject to influence by the executive and other elites. Most minor disputes are settled by village elders or a civilian court of first instance. Harsh prison conditions are marked by severe overcrowding and the lack of adequate sanitation facilities, medical attention, and proper diet.

Freedoms of expression and association are guaranteed and are generally respected. The semiofficial weekly *Al-Watwan* and several private newspapers sharply critical of the government are published in the capital, but they appear only sporadically because of limited resources. All are believed to exercise extensive self-censorship. Two state-run radio stations broadcast, and up to ten independent radio stations operate without overt governmental interference.

Islam is the official state religion. Non-Muslims are legally permitted to practice, but there were reports of restrictions, detentions and harassment. Detainees are sometimes subjected to attempts to convert them to Islam. Christians are not allowed to proselytize.

Women possess constitutional protections despite the influence of Islamic law. In practice, however, they enjoy little political or economic power and have far fewer opportunities for education or salaried employment than men do. Economic hardship has forced more and more young girls, known as *mpambe,* into domestic servitude. They receive room and board, but little or no pay.

Unions have the right to bargain and strike, but collective bargaining is rare in the country's small formal (business) sector.

Congo, Republic of (Brazzaville)

Polity: Military (transitional)
Economy: Mixed statist
Population: 3,200,000
PPP: $825
Life Expectancy: 51
Religious Groups: Christian (50 percent), animist (48 percent), Muslim (2 percent)
Ethnic Groups: Kongo (48 percent), Sangha (20 percent), Teke (17 percent), M'Bochi (12 percent), other (3 percent)
Capital: Brazzaville

Political Rights: 6*
Civil Liberties: 4
Status: Partly Free

Ratings Change: Congo's (Brazzaville's) political rights rating declined from 5 to 6 due to the resumption of fighting in March and presidential and legislative elections that were not fair.

Ten-Year Ratings Timeline (Political Rights, Civil Liberties, Status)

1993	1994	1995	1996	1997	1998	1999	2000	2001	2002	2003
3,3PF	4,4PF	4,4PF	4,4PF	4,4PF	7,5NF	7,5NF	6,5NF	6,4PF	5,4PF	6,4PF

Overview:

Congo was getting back on its feet after years of sporadic warfare, but fighting erupted again in March 2002, exposing weaknesses in a peace agreement that was signed at the end of 1999. The peace process was controlled by President Denis Sassou-Nguesso and excluded key members of Congo's political class. Presidential and legislative elections held in 2002 were not deemed fair, in part because of irregularities and the absence of an independent electoral commission.

A decade after Congo's independence from France, a 1970 coup established a Marxist state in the country. In 1979, General Sassou-Nguesso seized power and maintained one-party rule as head of the Congolese Workers' Party. Domestic and international pressure forced his acceptance of a national conference leading to open, multiparty elections in 1992. Pascal Lissouba won a clear victory over former Prime Minister Bernard Kolelas in a second-round presidential runoff that excluded Sassou-Nguesso, who had run third in the first round.

Disputes over the 1993 legislative polls led to armed conflict. The fighting subsided but flared once again among ethnic-based militias in 1997. Sassou-Nguesso, who has had military support from Angola and political backing from France, built a private army in his native northern Congo and forcibly retook the presidency in October 1997. Peace agreements signed in late 1999 included an amnesty for combatants who voluntarily disarmed. A new constitution was adopted by referendum in January 2002, providing for a multiparty system and establishing wide-ranging powers for the president, who would be directly elected for a seven-year term.

The renewed outbreak of hostilities in combination with contraction of the oil sector hurt Congo's growth in 2002. Congo is the fourth largest producer of oil in Sub-Saharan Africa.

Political Rights and Civil Liberties: Since the outbreak of civil war in 1997, Congolese have been only partly able to exercise their constitutional right to change their leaders through democratic elections. Competitive multiparty elections were held for the first time in 1992 and 1993. Presidential elections held in March 2002 were marred by irregularities and there was no independent electoral commission, but international observers hailed the peaceful nature of the vote. Denis Sassou-Nguesso was virtually assured a victory when his main challenger, former Prime Minister Andre Milongo, dropped out of the race just before the election, claiming irregularities. Sassou-Nguesso won the election with 89 percent of the vote.

Elections for the 137-member National Assembly in May and June 2002 were dominated by Sassou-Nguesso's Congolese Workers' Party and other parties affiliated with it.

Scarce resources and understaffing have created a backlog of court cases and long periods of pretrial detention. The judiciary is subject to corruption and political influence. The court system was generally considered to be politically independent until the civil war. In rural areas, traditional courts retain broad jurisdiction, especially in civil matters.

Atrocities against civilians committed mainly by militia members increased in 2002. Fighting broke out in March in the southern Pool region after members of the Ninja militia responded to reports that security forces were attempting to arrest their leader. At least 60,000 people were displaced. There were also reports of arbitrary detentions, beatings, and other abuses committed by security forces. Local and international human rights groups have petitioned the government to explain the disappearance of more than 350 Congolese refugees who returned from exile in the Democratic Republic of Congo (Kinshana) in 1999. The UN Development Program, in conjunction with the Congolese government, was engaged in human rights training for hundreds of local authorities, police officers, and members of civil society in 2002 to help promote peace.

Prison conditions are life threatening, with reports of beatings, overcrowding, and other ill-treatment. Women and men, as well as juveniles and adults, are incarcerated together. Human rights groups and the International Committee of the Red Cross have been allowed access. Nongovernmental organizations (NGOs) generally operate freely.

Freedom of assembly and association is constitutionally guaranteed, and this right is generally respected in practice, although public demonstrations are rare. The government generally respects press freedom, but continues to monopolize the broadcast media. The government, in 2000, abolished censorship and sharply reduced penalties for defamation. About ten private newspapers appear weekly in Brazzaville, and they often publish articles and editorials that are critical of the government.

Religious freedom is guaranteed and respected. Ethnic discrimination persists. Pygmy groups suffer discrimination, and many are effectively held in lifetime servitude through customary ties to Bantu "patrons." Members of virtually all ethnic groups practice discrimination in hiring practices.

There is extensive legal and societal discrimination against women despite constitutional protections. Access to education and employment opportunities, especially in the countryside, are limited, and civil codes regarding family and marriage formalize women's inferior status. Violence against women is reportedly widespread. After declining in 2000 and 2001, incidents of rape increased in 2002 with the renewed outbreak of hostilities. NGOs have drawn attention to the issue and provided counseling and assistance to victims.

Workers' rights to join trade unions and to strike are legally protected. Collective bargaining is practiced freely. Most workers in the formal (business) sector are union members, and unions have made efforts to organize informal sectors such as those of agriculture and retail trade.

↑ Congo, Democratic Republic of (Kinshasa)

Polity: Presidential (military-**Political Rights:** 6
dominated)(insurgencies)   **Civil Liberties:** 6
Economy: Capitalist-statist   **Status:** Not Free
Population: 55,200,000
PPP: $765
Life Expectancy: 49
Religious Groups: Roman Catholic (50 percent), Protestant (20 percent), Kimbanguist (10 percent), Muslim (10 percent), other (10 percent)
Ethnic Groups: More than 200 tribes, mostly Bantu
Capital: Kinshasa
Trend Arrow: Congo Kinshasa received an upward trend arrow for signing a peace deal with the government of Rwanda that led to a withdrawl of Rwandan troops.

Ten-Year Ratings Timeline (Political Rights, Civil Liberties, Status)

1993	1994	1995	1996	1997	1998	1999	2000	2001	2002	2003
6,5NF	7,6NF	7,6NF	7,6NF	7,6NF	7,6NF	7,6NF	7,6NF	7,6NF	6,6NF	6,6NF

Overview: The signing of a peace agreement in July 2002 between the Democratic Republic of Congo (DRC) and its main external adversary, Rwanda, raised hopes that real progess could be made in ending the four-year war. The agreement requires President Joseph Kabila's government to disarm the Rwandan Hutu militia, the Interahamwe, which was responsible for the massacre of about 800,000 Tutsis and moderate Hutus in Rwanda in 1994. The agreement also obliges Rwanda, which entered the DRC ostensibly to pursue Interahamwe, to withdraw its troops. The Rwandan government said nearly all of its 20,000 forces had withdrawn by November. Uganda, Zimbabwe,

Angola, and Namibia were near completion of withdrawal of their troops. However, the United Nations said in a report in October 2002 that the initial motivations for the war have been replaced largely by economic interests. The armies of Uganda, Zimbabwe, and Rwanda have, the UN report said, established permanent paramilitary and criminal proxies in the DRC to control that country's trade in diamonds, gold, and other natural resources. Unless there is large-scale disarmament, the withdrawal of foreign troops could lead to more instability as rival militias and factions battle for control.

As the Belgian Congo, the vast area of Central Africa that is today the DRC was exploited with a brutality that was notable even by colonial standards. The country was a center for Cold War rivalries from Belgium's withdrawal in 1960 until well after Colonel Joseph Mobutu came to power with CIA backing in 1964. The pro-Western Mobutu was forgiven by Western governments for severe repression and financial excesses that made him one of the world's richest men and his countrymen among the world's poorest people. Domestic agitation for democratization forced Mobutu to open up the political process in 1990. In 1992, his Popular Revolutionary Movement, the sole legal party after 1965, and the Sacred Union of the Radical Opposition and Allied Civil Society, a coalition of 200 groups, joined scores of others in a national conference to establish the High Council of the Republic to oversee a democratic transition. Mobutu manipulated and delayed the transition.

Despite widespread domestic opposition to his rule, it was the 1994 genocide in neighboring Rwanda that triggered Mobutu's demise, after he allowed Hutu Interahamwe fighters to base themselves in his country, which was then known as Zaire. Rwanda and Uganda easily tapped into popular hatred for Mobutu in their seven-month advance on Kinshasa. They installed Laurent Kabila, who at the time was a semi-retired guerrilla fighter, as the head of their rebellion and toppled the Mobutu regime in May 1997. Mobutu fled to Morocco and died of cancer a few months later. The new war erupted in late 1998 after Kabila fell out with those who had put him in power. Kabila was assassinated in January 2001. His son, Joseph, revived the 1999 Lusaka peace accord and furthered the consolidation of a ceasefire.

The war at some point has drawn forces from at least eight countries into the fighting—Zimbabwe, Angola, Namibia, Chad, and Sudan on the side of Kabila; and Uganda, Rwanda, and Burundi on the part of the rebels. More than 4,000 UN troops are in the country to help monitor the ceasefire and troop withdrawals, but they have faced repeated obstacles in deploying in the east. UN Secretary-General Kofi Annan in 2002 recommended increasing the number of troops to 8,700. A voluntary disarmament program is to follow the deployment.

In December 2002, the Goma faction of the Congolese Rally for Democracy (RCD), the Ugandan-backed Movement for the Liberation of Congo (MLC), various militia leaders, civil society representatives, and unarmed political opposition parties signed the first all-inclusive agreement to establish a government of national unity. Under the deal, Kabila will remain in office for the next two years until elections are held. Kabila would be assisted by four vice presidents, including representatives from the RCD, the MLC, the DRC government, and the unarmed opposition.

The conflict in the DRC has directly and indirectly claimed an estimated 2.5 million lives in the past four years, and more than 2 million people have been uprooted. Fighting in the northeast in December 2002 forced more than 130,000 people from their homes. Human rights abuses remained rampant across the country in 2002. Opposition supporters, journalists, and human rights workers are routinely arrested and harassed, and public demonstrations are suppressed. Rapes, unfair trials, and extrajudicial executions are also reported.

The October UN report said that peace agreements signed in Zambia, Angola, and South Africa were unlikely to lead to peace, in the short term, in the DRC. The report recommended imposing a financial and travel ban on 83 individuals and companies, including foreign businessmen; senior Congolese, Rwandan, Ugandan, and Zimbabwean military officers; and multinational firms from Africa, Europe, and the former Soviet Union. The report said that 85 multinational firms are in violation of guidelines established by the Organization of Economic Cooperation and Development governing corporate conduct in conflict zones.

The black market in the DRC has largely replaced the formal (business) economy. Most people live marginal lives as subsistence farmers despite the country's vast resources. Agreements with the World Bank and International Monetary Fund have led to the pledge of more than $1.7 billion in assistance, which was expected to begin flowing to the government at the end of 2002. Economic reforms are under way, and growth is expected in 2002. Inflation has dropped dramatically.

Political Rights and Civil Liberties:

The people of the DRC have never been able to choose or change their government through democratic and peaceful means. There are no elected representatives in the entire country. Mobutu Sese Seko's successive unopposed presidential victories and legislative polls were little more than political theater. Infrastructure and institutions to support a free and fair election are almost entirely absent.

At least 400 political parties registered after their 1990 legalization, but they were later banned under Laurent Kabila. Restrictions on political parties were eased in May 2001, but opposition members are routinely harassed and prevented from holding press conferences.

Despite guarantees of independence, in practice the judiciary is subject to corruption and manipulation. The civil judiciary is largely dysfunctional. Military courts, such as the Court of Military Order, deliver harsh sentences to civilians for questionable security and political convictions. President Joseph Kabila has promised to limit the powers of the Court of Military Order, which is to try 135 people accused of involvement in the assasination of his father, Laurent Kabila. Many of the suspects are likely to face the death penalty. Defendants have no automatic right of appeal to a higher court; many lack counsel, are held incommunicado, and can be subjected to torture. Long periods of pretrial detention are common in prisons in which poor diet and medical care can be life threatening.

Serious human rights abuses by Kabila's armed forces and rebel soldiers continued in 2002, although most abuses were reported in rebel-held areas of the east. Violations included extrajudicial execution, torture, rape, beating, and arbitrary detention. Ethnically-based killings by both government and rebel forces have been reported.

Numerous nongovernmental organizations, including human rights groups, operate despite intimidation and arrest. New York-based Human Rights Watch protested the detention of N'sii Luanda Shandwe, of the Committee for the Observance of Human Rights, who had been detained for more than four months by September 2002, apparently for hosting a former political detainee at his home. He was charged with treason and for sheltering criminals and faces trial before the Court of Military Order. If found guilty, he could be sentenced to death.

Freedom of expression and freedom of assembly are sharply limited by decree. Statutes provide for freedom of the press, but the government continued to sharply restrict the work of journalists. Church radio networks, as well as several local and community-based broadcasters (many are affiliated with political groups or military factions), are growing, but the state-controlled broadcasting network reaches the largest numbers of citizens. The UN broadcaster, Radio Okapi, has expanded its coverage of the country to include several local languages. At least 30 independent newspapers are published regularly in Kinshasa, but they are not widely circulated beyond the city. Independent journalists are frequently threatened, arrested, or attacked. Common accusations include "relaying intelligence to the enemy," "discouraging the population of soldiers," and "divulging state secrets or defense secrets."

The New York–based Committee to Protect Journalists (CPJ) in September 2002 protested the imprisonment and sentencing of two Kinshasa-based journalists, Raymond Kabala and Delly Bonsange, of the independent newspaper *Alerte Plus*. Kabala said he was tortured in jail. CPJ said the journalists were detained in July and later convicted of "harmful accusation" and "falsification of a public document" after an article appeared that said the minister of public order and security, Mwenze Kongolo, had allegedly been poisoned. The newspaper printed a correction the next day. Kabala and Bonsange were each sentenced to between 6 to 12 months in jail and fined between $100,000 and $200,000. Several other journalists were detained across the country in 2002 and held in life-threatening conditions.

Freedom of religion is respected in practice, although religious groups must register with the government to be recognized. Members of the Roman Catholic Church in rebel-held areas face intimidation. Ethnic tension is rife in the east. Fighting in northeast Ituri province in 2002 left hundreds of civilians dead and thousands displaced. A senior UN official warned of ethnic hatred in the east and said the country could face "a massacre of horrific proportions" if the problem is not adequately addressed. Ethnic societal discrimination is practiced widely among the country's 200 ethnic groups.

Despite constitutional protections, women face de facto discrimination, especially in rural areas. They also enjoy fewer employment and educational opportunities than men and often do not receive equal pay for equal work. Violence against women, including rape and forced sexual slavery, has soared since the onset of armed conflict in 1996. Children faced forced conscription by all sides in the conflict, although the government appeared to be scaling back this practice.

More than 100 new independent unions registered after the end of one-party rule in 1990. Previously, all unions had to affiliate themselves with a confederation that was part of the ruling party. Some unions are affiliated with political parties, and labor leaders and activists have faced harassment. There is little union activity, owing to the breakdown of the country's formal (business) economy.

Costa Rica

Polity: Presidential-
parliamentary democracy
Economy: Capitalist-statist
Population: 3,900,000
PPP: $8,650
Life Expectancy: 77
Religious Groups: Roman Catholic (76.3 percent),
Evangelical (13.7 percent), other (10 percent)
Ethnic Groups: White and mestizo (94 percent),
black (3 percent), Indian (1 percent), other (2 percent)
Capital: San José

Political Rights: 1
Civil Liberties: 2
Status: Free

Ten-Year Ratings Timeline (Political Rights, Civil Liberties, Status)

1993	1994	1995	1996	1997	1998	1999	2000	2001	2002	2003
1,1F	1,2F	1,2F	1,2F	1,2F	1,2F	1,2F	1,2F	1,2F	1,2F	1,2F

Overview:

The 2002 elections were unusual in leading to a four-way draw. After increasing voter dissatisfaction with the two traditional parties—the Social Christian Party (PUSC) and the National Liberation Party (PLN)—two smaller upstarts, the Citizens Action Party (PAC) and the Libertarian Movement (ML), received significant support. Only 69 percent of the population cast votes. Abel Pacheco of the PUSC won the runoff election. By 1998, economic diversification had succeeded in earning the country more from high technology than from the traditional reliance on coffee, bananas, and tourism. The global economic downturn that began in 2001 severely affected Costa Rica, as it included the burst of the technology bubble and a drop in tourism revenue following the terrorist attacks in the United States.

Costa Rica achieved independence from Spain in 1821 and became a republic in 1848. The 1949 constitution bans the formation of a national army. In the 1994 elections Jose Maria Figueres, son of the legendary President Jose "Pepe" Figueres, defeated Miguel Angel Rodriguez of the PUSC. The outgoing president, Rafael A. Calderon, Jr., of the PUSC had promoted neoliberal economic policies, and Figueres campaigned against them. Despite his campaign pledges, Figueres's last two years in office saw the passing of free-market policies championed by his opponent in the presidential elections. In the 1998 elections Rodriguez bested Jose Miguel Corrales of the PLN.

Simmering tensions with the country's northern neighbor, Nicaragua, were exacerbated in 2001 when the Costa Rican government began to build a seven-foot-high fence along the Penas Blancas border crossing on the Pan-American Highway along the Pacific Coast. Claims that the wall was to control heavy-goods traffic in a region that has become a favored route for drug smuggling were dismissed in Nicaragua. For many years there has been a consistent flow of Nicaraguans searching for employment in Costa Rica. There are more than 400,000 Nicaraguans in Costa Rica, many of whom work without papers on farms where they are paid subsistence wages. In 1998, Costa Rica declared a temporary amnesty for these and other illegal Central American immigrants, and some 160,000 Nicaraguans legalized their status.

Political Rights and Civil Liberties: Democratic government changes take place with free and fair elections. There are guarantees for the freedom of religion and the right to organize political parties and civic organizations. In response to allegations of drug money financing the elections, new campaign laws have been passed to make party funding more transparent. The president and the 57-member Legislative Assembly are elected for a four-year term and are banned from seeking a second term.

The judicial branch is independent, with members elected by the legislature. There is a supreme court, courts of appeals, and district courts. The Supreme Court can rule on the constitutionality of laws and chooses an independent national election commission. There are long delays in the justice system partly as a result of budget cuts. Prisons are notoriously overcrowded. A 1994 police code was designed to depoliticize and professionalize the police in order to create a permanent career path within the institution. Independent rights monitors report increases in allegations of arbitrary arrest and brutality. Human rights complaints are investigated by an ombudsman who has the authority to issue recommendations for rectification, including sanctions against government bodies, for failure to respect rights. Corruption is not considered to be a serious problem in the public security forces and, when discovered, is usually dealt with in a decisive manner.

Illegal narcotics trafficking and money laundering have increased in Costa Rica. The country is a regional leader in the enactment of progressive antidrug statutes, including the use of wiretaps, controlled deliveries, and undercover agents. Financial institutions have to report any transactions involving more than $10,000. In 1999, the Legislative Assembly passed legislation allowing for U.S. antidrug patrols to operate in Costa Rican waters.

The press, radio, and television are generally free. The population is 90 percent literate and there are six major privately owned dailies. Television and radio stations are both public and commercial, with at least six private television stations. Libel laws continue to inhibit the press. The assassination of a prominent journalist in the summer of 2001 sparked protests around the country. Freedom of religion is recognized.

Labor can organize freely, but there has been a noticeable reluctance to expand labor rights. Minimum wage and social security laws are often ignored, and fines are insignificant. Often, women workers are sexually harassed, made to work overtime without pay, and fired when they become pregnant. A law criminalizing sex with minors was passed in 1999 in an attempt to crack down on the country's growing sex tourism industry. Violence against women and children is a problem, although the government has shown concrete support for programs and policies to combat it. Indigenous rights are not a priority. The government is making significant efforts to combat human trafficking; Costa Rica is a transit and destination country for trafficked persons.

Cote D'Ivoire

Polity: Presidential-par- **Political Rights:** 6*
liamentary (insurgencies) **Civil Liberties:** 6*
Economy: Capitalist **Status:** Not Free
Population: 16,800,000
PPP: $1,630
Life Expectancy: 45
Religious Groups: Christian (20-30 percent),
Muslim (35-40 percent), Indigenous (25-40 percent)
Ethnic Groups: Akan (42.1 percent), Voltaiques, or Gur (17.6 percent), Northern
Mandes (16.5 percent), Krous (11 percent), Southern Mandes (10 percent), other
(2.8 percent)
Capital: Yamoussoukro (official); Abidjan (de facto)
Ratings Change: Cote d'Ivoire's political rights rating declined from 5 to 6, its civil
liberties rating from 4 to 6, and its status from Partly Free to Not Free, due to an
outbreak of hostilities between government and rebel troops, in which there were
numerous killings of civilians, increased repression of the press, and attacks on foreigners and specific ethnic groups.

Ten-Year Ratings Timeline (Political Rights, Civil Liberties, Status)

1993	1994	1995	1996	1997	1998	1999	2000	2001	2002	2003
6,4PF	6,5NF	6,5NF	6,5NF	6,5NF	6,4NF	6,4NF	6,4PF	6,5PF	5,4PF	6,6NF

Overview: Cote d'Ivoire appeared to emerge from its prolonged political crisis in August 2002 when the country's main political
parties agreed to participate in a government of national
unity. But when the government of President Laurent Gbagbo attempted to demobilize and retire some 700 soldiers in September, unprecedented violence erupted in
the country. By December, much of the nation was engulfed. In what appeared to be
either a coup attempt or mutiny, former military ruler General Robert Guei was killed.
Many soldiers either retreated to the largely Muslim north, or returned from neighboring Burkina Faso, where they had fled during the country's previous periods of
unrest. An insurgent group calling itself the Patriotic Movement of Cote d'Ivoire
emerged in the north. The group called for Gbagbo to step down and for new elections to replace the flawed 2000 polls. The insurgents quickly seized control of more
than half of the country. West African leaders had brokered a shaky ceasefire amid
growing fears that the crisis would affect the entire region. However, fighting erupted
in the west of the country as two more groups declared their intention to oust the
Gbagbo government. The Ivorian Popular Movement for the Great West and the
Movement for Justice and Peace, however, did not appear to be formed from professional troops. Witnesses reported that civilians had joined them, including mercenaries from the troubled border regions of Liberia, Sierra Leone, and Guinea. Six West
African countries agreed to provide 2,000 peacekeeping troops.

Cote d'Ivoire gained independence from France in 1960, and President Felix
Houphouet-Boigny ruled until his death in 1993. Henri Konan Bedie assumed power
and won fraudulent elections in 1995. General Guei seized power in December 1999

and stood for election in 2000. When initial results showed he was losing to Gbagbo, he sacked the electoral commission, detained its officers, and declared himself the winner. Tens of thousands of people took to the streets in a popular uprising that toppled him from power. Clashes followed between supporters of Ouattara's Rally of Republicans (RDR) and Gbagbo's Ivorian Popular Front (FPI). Supported by security forces, Gbagbo refused to call for new polls. The political violence led to a deepening division between the largely Muslim north and mainly Christian south. However, the conflict is not strictly rooted in a north-south, Muslim-Christian divide.

By the end of 2002, the fighting had left at least 400 people dead across the country and more than 250,000 displaced. Human rights violations escalated dramatically, including attacks on the press as well as members of northern ethnic groups, Muslims, and expatriate Africans. Cote d'Ivoire's main opposition leader, Alassane Ouattara, fled into exile in Gabon.

Cote d'Ivoire retains strong political, economic, and military backing from France, which maintains a military garrison near Abidjan, mainly to protect the 20,000 French nationals who live in the country. France evacuated Western foreigners from besieged towns during the year and boosted its military presence to 2,500 soldiers with an expanded mandate to help maintain stability in the country. During the Houphouet-Boigny period, Cote d'Ivoire became an African model for economic growth and political stability. A plunge in the 1990s of the world price of cocoa, Cote d'Ivoire's chief export, and later coffee, its fifth largest export, considerably hurt the economy. Political unrest did further damage. A sharp rise in the price of cocoa was expected to help the economy in 2002 and 2003, but massive instability countered the projected gains.

Political Rights and Civil Liberties:

The people of Cote d'Ivoire have only partially been able to carry out their constitutional right to freely and fairly elect their leaders. In a 1995 election, President Henri Konan Bedie was declared the winner with 95 percent of the vote. The election was neither free nor fair and was boycotted by all of the major opposition parties. Alassane Ouattara, the opposition's most formidable candidate, was barred from the contest. Demonstrations were banned, and the media were intimidated. Voting in the October 2000 presidential election appeared to be carried out fairly, but only five of 19 potential candidates were allowed to contest the vote. Laurent Gbagbo was eventually declared the winner with 59 percent, compared with 33 percent for Robert Guei.

Gbagbo's Ivorian Popular Front (FPI) won 96 seats in the December 2000 legislative elections, while four went to the Democratic Party of Cote d'Ivoire, and five went to the Rally of Republicans (RDR). Twenty-four seats went to smaller parties and independents, and two seats in Ouattara's district went unfilled.

Cote d'Ivoire does not have an independent judiciary. Judges are political appointees without tenure and are highly susceptible to external interference. In many rural areas, traditional courts still prevail, especially in the handling of minor matters and family law. Security forces generally operate with impunity. Prison conditions are harsh.

Respect for human rights deteriorated considerably in 2002. In November the New York-based Human Rights Watch reported that government forces had committed abuses against civilians because of their nationality, ethnicity, religion, or for their support of a particular political party. Raids targeted entire neighborhoods in which homes were razed. In the town of Daloa, men in military uniform reportedly killed dozens of civilians, including Muslims and African foreigners. Human Rights Watch said human rights defenders in Cote d'Ivoire lived in fear and many had gone into hiding. The organization also reported abuses by the Patriotic Movement of Cote d'Ivoire, saying there were reports of unlawful killings and detentions in the north. A mass grave containing more than 100 bodies was discovered in the western village of Monoko-Zohi. Witnesses said men in military uniforms driving government vehicles carried out the killings after accusing civilians of feeding rebel troops.

Press freedom is guaranteed but not always respected in practice. State-owned newspapers and a state-run broadcasting system are usually unreservedly pro-government. Several private radio stations and a cable television service operate, but only the state broadcasting system reaches a national audience. Dozens of independent newspapers are published, many of which are linked to political parties. Press freedom suffered in 2002 with attacks on journalists and publishing houses. A number of local and foreign journalists were assaulted by mobs or security forces, or were detained. A French freelance producer was held without explanation for six days. In September, security forces beat Mamadou Keita, of the opposition newspaper *Le Patriote*. A group of some 50 people ransacked and looted the offices of the private Mayama media group, publisher of three pro-opposition publications. The government jammed the broadcasts of the British Broadcasting Corp., Radio France Internationale, and Africa No. 1.

Freedom from discrimination is guaranteed, but is not respected in practice. Human Rights Watch has accused officials of deliberately encouraging a culture of violent xenophobia in Cote d'Ivoire, whose economy has long attracted workers from neighboring countries. More than one-quarter of the country's population is estimated to be African expatriates. Up to 20,000 Africans returned to their respective countries during the year because of the violence.

Religious freedom is guaranteed but is not respected in practice. The government openly favors Christianity. Muslims have been targeted in the past few years of political unrest and face discrimination. Women suffer widespread discrimination, despite official encouragement for respect for constitutional rights. Equal pay for equal work is offered in the small formal (business) sector, but women have few chances to obtain, or advance in, wage employment. In rural areas that rely on subsistence agriculture, educational and job opportunities for women are even scarcer. Female genital mutilation is still practiced, although it has been a crime since 1998. Violence against women is reportedly common.

Child labor and child trafficking are problems. There were up to 15,000 children from Mali alone estimated to be working on Ivorian plantations in 1999. Cote d'Ivoire is drafting new laws on the issue and has set up a group to fight child trafficking and child labor.

Union formation and membership are legally protected. Notification and conciliation requirements must be met before legal strikes can be conducted. Collective bargaining agreements are often reached with the participation of government negotiators, who influence wage settlements.

⬇ Croatia

Polity: Parliamentary democracy
Economy: Mixed capitalist statist
Population: 4,300,000
PPP: $8,091
Life Expectancy: 74
Religious Groups: Roman Catholic (76.5 percent), Orthodox (11.1 percent), other (11 percent)
Ethnic Groups: Croat (78 percent), Serb (12 percent), Bozniak (1 percent), other (9 percent)
Capital: Zagreb

Political Rights: 2
Civil Liberties: 2
Status: Free

Trend Arrow: Croatia received a downward trend arrow due to the government's refusal to extradite indicted war criminals to the International Criminal Tribunal for the Former Yugoslavia; continuing indications of ethnic bias in the country's judiciary system; and ongoing difficulties in allowing refugees to reclaim their homes and property.

Ten-Year Ratings Timeline (Political Rights, Civil Liberties, Status)

1993	1994	1995	1996	1997	1998	1999	2000	2001	2002	2003
4,4PF	4,4PF	4,4PF	4,4PF	4,4PF	4,4PF	4,4PF	4,4PF	2,3F	2,2F	2,2F

Overview:

In 2002, Croatia faced another year led by a weak coalition government facing a domestic economic crisis, pressure to cooperate more fully with the International Criminal Tribunal for the Former Yugoslavia (ICTY), as well as pressure from the international community to accept tens of thousands of refugees driven from the country in 1995.

In its first multiparty elections in the post-Communist period, Croatia elected Franjo Tudjman, a former Communist-turned-nationalist general, as president in May 1990. Tudjman's Croatian Democratic Union (HDZ), ruled Croatia from 1990 to 1999. As rival nationalisms competed with each other in Croatia in 1990-1991, Croatia's Serb population in the border region known as the Krajina declared their independence from Croatia, even as Croatia itself was declaring its independence from the former Yugoslavia. The result was a de facto partition of the country between 1991 and 1995. In May and August 1995, a majority of the Serb population of Croatia was forcibly expelled or took flight from Krajina during Croatian military offensives to establish control over the disputed areas.

On December 11, 1999, Tudjman died, and in the subsequent extraordinary presidential elections in January 2000, Stjepan Mesic of the Croatian People's Party (HNS) was elected the new president. In legislative elections that also took place in January 2000, two center-left coalitions wrested control of parliament from the HDZ. The leader of the Social Democratic Party (SDP, the former League of Communists of Croatia), Ivica Racan, was named the new prime minister.

In September 2002, the reputation of the Racan government was seriously damaged by its refusal to turn over retired Croatian army chief of staff General Janko Bobetko, who had been indicted for war crimes by the International Criminal Tribunal for the Former Yugoslavia (ICTY).

The issues of dealing with war crimes and cooperating with the ICTY have been painful ones for Croatia in recent years and have repeatedly threatened to destabilize the Croatian government in the post-Tudjman period. In February 2002, five ministers in Racan's government – all of whom were from the coalition's second-largest party, the Croatian Social Liberal Party (HSLS) – resigned from the government over disagreements as to how to cooperate with the ICTY. The Racan government faced further difficulties that summer when the bodies of 18 Serb civilians murdered during the war were discovered 500 kilometers from the site of the massacre. Former Croatian state officials at the highest levels appear to have been implicated in the massacre.

The Racan government's weak political position was made plain in July, when Racan himself tendered his resignation after a majority of representatives from the HSLS, the second-largest party in his ruling five-party coalition, refused to support an agreement he had negotiated with neighboring Slovenia regarding the decommissioning of the Krsko nuclear power station. Racan was able to re-form a new government by the end of the month, but its position remained precarious. Because of such problems, much important legislation, such as the new Constitutional Law on National Minorities (intended, partly, to increase representation of national minorities in parliament), could not be passed through the legislative process in 2002.

Political Rights and Civil Liberties:

Croatian voters can change their government democratically. The constitution guarantees citizens age 18 or older the right to universal and equal suffrage. The presidential and parliamentary elections in 2000 were peaceful, free, and fair, with voter turnout registering more than 60 percent of the electorate in both rounds of voting. In 2000, Croatia's new leaders linked the restoration of civil liberties with reductions in presidential power. Respect for the separation of powers in the Croatian political system, however, still faces some problems, as there have been numerous cases in recent years in which the executive or legislative branch has failed to abide by or implement decisions made by the Constitutional Court.

Croatia's judicial system suffers from numerous problems: a large number of judicial vacancies and a shortage of experienced judges, both of which have led to a huge backlog of cases (estimated at 1.2 million as of May 2002); excessive trial length; and a lack of enforcement of judicial decisions, especially in cases relating to the repossession of property owned by Serbs. The judicial system also faces considerable intimidation in the (always difficult) field of war crimes prosecutions. In the Rijeka-based trial of the Gospic Group, indicted for the murders of several civilians during the war, the presiding judge received death threats in March, while in the Lora case involving the murder of prisoners of war, several witnesses were forced by threats to recant their testimony.

According to international observers, Croatia continues to fail to live up to obligations stemming from accession to the Council of Europe in 1996 to adopt nondiscriminatory laws relating to ethnic minorities. In a status report issued in May, the OSCE found discrimination against ethnic minorities is manifested in a nontransparent and incomplete legal framework for the return and repossession of property by refugees, shortcomings in the legal system, a lack of financial resources, and obstruction by local officials.

Croatia's constitution guarantees freedom of expression and the press. Although Croatia boasts lively media, local outlets (especially in former war zones) are believed to face much greater pressure than more prominent national media. In Croatia's highly charged political atmosphere some degree of self-censorship is still visible. In February 2002, Croatian state television decided to cancel the broadcast of a documentary on the World War II Croatian fascist movement, the Ustasa, which drew parallels with the policies of the Tudjman regime in the 1990s, for fear of political repercussions. Also in February, state prosecutors announced that they were considering charges against a television talk-show host who had aired a program examining corruption in Croatia's judiciary. In March, a court ordered the Split-based newsweekly *Feral Tribune* to pay some 200,000 kuna (approximately U.S.$25,000) to plaintiffs for "mental anguish" caused by articles written in 1993 and 1995. On a better note, however, in February the government passed a new draft law on media, the major objective of which was the regulation of media ownership, reflecting government concerns about the potential dominance of the Croatian media by a few large financial groups or media conglomerates. Croatian government officials in 2002 also acknowledged the need to reform state-owned Croatian Radio and Television, the primary source of information for most citizens.

Respect for freedom of religion, and for freedom of association and assembly has increased in Croatia in the post-Tudjman period, although ethnic minorities enjoy these rights to a significantly lesser degree than ethnic Croatians. The overwhelming majority of Croatians are Roman Catholic. Consequently, the Church has a considerable degree of power and influence, as was evidenced in July 2002 when the Racan government was forced to cancel its plans to nominate Neven Budak, a historian critical of various policies favored by the Church, under severe pressure from the Church's hierarchy. The case re-ignited concerns about an increasing clericalization of polity and society in post-Communist Croatia. The conservative wing of the Roman Catholic hierarchy has also opposed Croatia's cooperation with the ICTY and criticized several domestic trials of individuals accused of war crimes.

▶ Cuba

Polity: One party   **Political Rights:** 7
Economy: Statist   **Civil Liberties:** 7
Population: 11,300,000   **Status:** Not Free
PPP: na
Life Expectancy: 76
Religious Groups: Roman Catholic, Protestant, other
Ethnic Groups: Mulatto (51 percent), white (37 percent),
black (11 percent), Chinese (1 percent)
Capital: Havana
Trend Arrow: Cuba received an upward trend arrow due to the emergence of significant peaceful protest activity by civil society against the Castro dictatorship.

Ten-Year Ratings Timeline (Political Rights, Civil Liberties, Status)

1993	1994	1995	1996	1997	1998	1999	2000	2001	2002	2003
7,7NF	7,7NF	7,7NF	7,7NF	7,7NF	7,7NF	7,7NF	7,7NF	7,7NF	7,7NF	7,7NF

Overview: Despite its almost total lack of access to the media, Cuba's beleaguered dissident movement received several important boosts both internally and abroad. The Varela Project, a referendum initiative seeking broad changes in the four-decades-old socialist system, achieved significant support domestically while its leader, Oswaldo Paya, was showered with international recognition. A June visit by former U.S. president Jimmy Carter also added status and visibility to the protest movement. In October, more than 300 dissident organizations joined together as the Assembly to Promote Civil Society in preparation for a post-Fidel Castro Cuba. Meanwhile the world's longest-lived dictator faced serious popular discontent, particularly because of the failing sugar industry. A former Cuban ambassador to the United Nations who defected in July said that intractable economic problems in his country might produce a "social explosion" against the regime.

Cuba achieved independence from Spain in 1898 as a result of the Spanish-American War. The Republic of Cuba was established in 1902, but was under U.S. tutelage under the Platt Amendment until 1934. In 1959, Castro's July 26th Movement—named after an earlier, failed insurrection—overthrew the dictatorship of Fulgencio Batista, who had ruled for 18 of the previous 25 years.

Since then, Fidel Castro has dominated the political system, transforming the country into a one-party state, with the Cuban Communist Party (PCC) controlling all governmental entities from the national to the local level. Communist structures were institutionalized by the 1976 constitution installed at the first congress of the PCC. The constitution provides for the national assembly, which designates the Council of State. It is that body which in turn appoints the Council of Ministers in consultation with its president, who serves as head of state and chief of government. However, Castro is responsible for every appointment and controls every lever of power in Cuba in his various roles as president of the Council of Ministers, chairman of the Council of State, commander in chief of the Revolutionary Armed Forces (FAR), and first secretary of the PCC.

Since the 1991 collapse of the Soviet Union, and the end of some $5 billion in annual Soviet subsidies, Castro has sought Western foreign investment. Most investment has come from Europe and Latin America. However, a EU study published in 2002 showed that direct foreign investment during the past five years peaked at $488 million in 2000 before falling to $38.9 million in 2001, while the country's foreign debt has risen to $11 billion. The legalization of the U.S. dollar since 1993 has heightened social tensions, as the minority with access to dollars from abroad or through the tourist industry has emerged as a new moneyed class, and the desperation of the majority without has increased.

Under Castro, the cycles of repression have ebbed and flowed depending on the regime's need to keep at bay the social forces set into motion by his severe post-Cold War economic reforms. By mid-June 1998, in the aftermath of the visit of Pope John Paul II five months earlier, the number of dissidents confirmed to be imprisoned dropped nearly 400 percent. In February 1999, the government introduced tough legislation against sedition, with a maximum prison sentence of 20 years. It stipulated penalties for unauthorized contacts with the United States and the import or supply of "subversive" materials, including texts on democracy, by news agencies and journalists.

U.S.-Cuban relations took some unexpected turns in 2000, against a backdrop of unprecedented media coverage of the story of the child shipwreck survivor Elian Gonzalez, who was ordered to be returned to his father in Cuba after a seven-month legal battle involving émigré relatives in Florida. In response to pressure from U.S. farmers and businessmen who pushed for a relaxation of economic sanctions against the island, in October the United States eased the 38-year-old embargo on food and medicine to Cuba.

In June 2001, Castro, who was then 74, collapsed at a long outdoor rally near Havana. The incident centered attention on what might happen once the world's longest-ruling dictator passes from the scene. In November 2001, Hurricane Michelle, the most powerful tropical storm to hit Cuba in a half-century, left a low death toll but a trail of physical destruction, devastating Cuban crops. In the wake of the storm, the first direct food trade was permitted between Cuba and the United States since the latter imposed the embargo in 1962. The renewal of food sales in the wake of Michelle sparked further debate between farmers and others in the United States who want the embargo lifted, and Cuban exile groups and some democracy activists who demand even tougher sanctions.

In May 2002, organizers of the Varela Project submitted more than 11,000 signatures to the National Assembly demanding a referendum be held in which Cubans could vote for fundamental reforms, such as freedom of expression, the right to own private businesses, and electoral reform. After Jimmy Carter mentioned the project on Cuban television the same month, the regime held its own "referendum" in which 8.2 million people supposedly declared the socialist system to be "untouchable."

In October, the EU—long loath to criticize Castro—awarded Paya its prestigious Sakharov human rights prize. While the regime ignored the Varela Project petition, in violation of its own constitution, the new civil society movement was launched. Composed of 321 dissident organizations ranging from human rights groups and independent libraries to labor unions and the independent press, the civil society assembly said it would prepare for a post-Castro transition rather than seek reforms from the regime.

In a move emblematic of the country's worsening economic crisis, in June 2002, the government closed 71 of Cuba's 156 sugar mills, a blow to thousands who were left without work and to a nation whose popular motto used to be: "Without sugar there is no country."

Political Rights and Civil Liberties: Cubans cannot change their government through democratic means. In October 2002, some eight million Cubans voted in tightly controlled municipal elections. Half of those chosen for municipal seats will later be candidates for the one-party National Assembly, with parliamentary elections scheduled for early 2003.

All political and civic organizating outside the PCC is illegal. Political dissent, spoken or written, is a punishable offense, and those so punished frequently receive years of imprisonment for seemingly minor infractions. There has been a slight relaxation of strictures on cultural life; nevertheless, the educational system, the judicial system, labor unions, professional organizations, and all media remain state controlled.

In Cuba the executive branch controls the judiciary. The 1976 constitution concentrates power in the hands of one individual—Castro, president of the Council of State. In practice, the council serves as a de facto judiciary and controls both the courts and the judicial process as a whole. In 1999, the Cuban government showed some willingness to enhance antinarcotics cooperation with the United States.

There are some 320 prisoners of conscience in Cuba, most held in cells with common criminals and many convicted on vague charges such as "disseminating enemy propaganda" or "dangerousness." Members of groups that exist apart from the state are labeled "counterrevolutionary criminals" and are subject to systematic repression, including arrest, beating while in custody, confiscation, and intimidation by uniformed or plainclothes state security agents. Since 1991, the United Nations has voted annually to assign a special investigator on human rights to Cuba, but the Cuban government has refused to cooperate. Cuba also does not allow the International Red Cross and other humanitarian organizations access to its prisons. There are 88 U.S. fugitives from justice in Cuba, including alleged airplane hijackers and murderers of police officers.

The press in Cuba is the object of a targeted campaign of intimidation by the government. Independent journalists, particularly those associated with five small news agencies established outside state control, have been subjected to continued repression, including jail terms at hard labor and assaults while in prison by state security agents. Foreign news agencies must hire local reporters only through government offices, which limits employment opportunities for independent journalists.

Freedom of movement and the right to choose one's residence, education, and job are severely restricted. Attempting to leave the island without permission is a punishable offense.

In 1991, Roman Catholics and other believers were granted permission to join the Communist Party, and the constitutional reference to official atheism was dropped the following year. However, in October 2002, the U.S. State Department issued a report saying that Cuba was one of six countries that engaged in widespread repression of religion. The report said that security agents frequently spy on worshippers; the government continues to block construction of new churches; the number of new foreign priests is limited; and most new denominations are refused recognition. In a positive development, the regime now tolerates the Baha'i faith.

In the post-Soviet era, the rights of Cubans to own private property and to participate in joint ventures with foreigners have been recognized. Non-Cuban businesses have also been allowed. In practice, there are few rights for those who do not belong to the PCC. Party membership is still required for good jobs, serviceable housing, and real access to social services, including medical care and educational opportunities.

About 40 percent of all women work, and they are well represented in the professions. However, violence against women is a problem, as is child prostitution.

Cyprus (Greek)

Polity: Presidential-parliamentary democracy
Economy: Capitalist
Population: 900,000
PPP: $20,824
Life Expectancy: 77
Religious Groups: Greek Orthodox (78 percent), Muslim (18 percent), other (4 percent)
Ethnic Groups: Greek (85 percent), Turkish (12 percent), other (3 percent)
Capital: Nicosia

Political Rights: 1
Civil Liberties: 1
Status: Free

Ten-Year Ratings Timeline (Political Rights, Civil Liberties, Status)

1993	1994	1995	1996	1997	1998	1999	2000	2001	2002	2003
1,1F	1,1F	1,1F	1,1F	1,1F	1,1F	1,1F	1,1F	1,1F	1,1F	1,1F

Overview:

Efforts at resolving Cyprus's decades-old dispute over re-unification of the divided island intensified during much of 2002, ahead of an assessment of the country's European Union (EU) candidacy. However, talks broke down by the autumn and the United Nations intervened directly to revive negotiations. In December Cyprus completed accession negotiations with the EU's Executive Commission, and was invited to join the EU on May 1, 2004. Contenders for presidential elections, scheduled for early 2003, prepared to campaign; one of the candidates faced allegations of facilitating illegal financial transactions for Yugoslavian front companies during the Balkan wars of the 1990s.

Annexed by Britain in 1914, Cyprus gained independence in 1960 after a ten-year guerrilla campaign to demand union with Greece. In July 1974, Greek Cypriot National Guard members, backed by the military junta in power in Greece, staged an unsuccessful coup aimed at unification. Five days later, Turkey invaded, seized control of 37 percent of the island, and expelled 200,000 Greeks from the north. Currently, the entire Turkish Cypriot community resides in the north, and property claims arising from the division and population exchange remain unsettled.

A buffer zone, called the "Green Line," has divided Cyprus since 1974. The capital, Nicosia, is the world's last divided city. The division of Cyprus has been a major point of contention in the long-standing rivalry between Greece and Turkey in the Aegean. Tensions and intermittent violence between the two populations have plagued the island since independence. UN resolutions stipulate that Cyprus is a single country in which the northern third is illegally occupied. In 1982, Turkish-controlled Cyprus made a unilateral declaration of independence that was condemned by the United Nations and that remains unrecognized by every country except Turkey.

Cypriot President Glafcos Clerides met with Turkish Cypriot leader Rauf Denktash in New York and Nicosia throughout the year in an ongoing attempt to reach a comprehensive UN-sponsored settlement of the conflict. Talks broke down just as the EU announced its intention to invite Cyprus to join the Union in 2004. Turkey has threatened to annex the northern part of Cyprus should EU membership occur in the absence of a settlement. Greece in turn has threatened to veto the EU's expansion process if Cypriot membership is delayed.

Attempts by UN Secretary General Kofi Annan in December to secure a peace deal were setback when Mr. Denktash became ill.

Peace in Cyprus remains fragile. Propaganda in schools and in the media has sustained hostility among Cypriot youth. Blatant economic disparity exists between the prosperous south and the stagnating north. Cyprus ranks among the most heavily militarized countries in the world.

A UN war crimes investigator issued a report claiming Cyprus's Popular Bank allowed several Yugoslavian-controlled front companies to operate on the island in violation of UN sanctions. The companies allegedly provided former Yugoslav President Slobodan Milosevic's regime with fuel, raw materials, spare parts, and weapons used during the Bosnia and Kosovo wars in the 1990s. An independent investigation carried out by the *Financial Times* revealed that leading presidential candidate, Tassos Papadopoulos, a prominent Cypriot lawyer and head of the center-right Democratic Party, facilitated the illegal transactions to Yugoslavia.

Papadopoulous, a former member of a guerilla group that fought the British in the 1950s, was vying for the presidency with Yiannakis Omirou, leader of the Kisso, a small socialist party, backed by President Clerides. Presidential elections were expected to take place in February 2003, when President Clerides is scheduled to step down.

Political Rights and Civil Liberties: Greek Cypriots can change their government democratically. Suffrage is universal and compulsory, and elections are free and fair. The 1960 constitution established an ethnically representative system designed to protect the interests of both Greek and Turkish Cypriots.

The independent judiciary operates according to the British tradition, upholding the presumption of innocence and the right to due process. Trial before a judge is standard, although requests for trial by jury are regularly granted.

Freedom of speech is respected, and a vibrant independent press frequently criticizes authorities. Several private television and radio stations in the Greek Cypriot community compete effectively with government-controlled stations.

Workers have the right to strike and to form trade unions without authorization. More than 70 percent of the work-force belongs to independent trade unions.

Czech Republic

Polity: Parliamentary democracy
Economy: Mixed capitalist
Population: 10,300,000
PPP: $13,991
Life Expectancy: 75
Religious Groups: Atheist (39.8 percent), Roman Catholic (39.2 percent), Protestant (4.6 percent), other (16.4 percent)
Ethnic Groups: Czech (81.2 percent), Moravian (13.2 percent), Slovak (3.1 percent), other (2.5 other)
Capital: Prague

Political Rights: 1
Civil Liberties: 2
Status: Free

Ten-Year Ratings Timeline (Political Rights, Civil Liberties, Status)

1993	1994	1995	1996	1997	1998	1999	2000	2001	2002	2003
--	1,2F	1,2F	1,2F	1,2F	1,2F	1,2F	1,2F	1,2F	1,2F	1,2F

Overview:

The year 2002 in the Czech Republic was one of firsts and milestones. During the year, the Czech Republic formerly accepted an invitation to join the European Union by 2004 and hosted the NATO summit in Prague, a first for any former Warsaw Pact nation. In addition, Czech voters returned a ruling party to power for the first time in post-Communist Central and Eastern Europe. However, the year also witnessed an assassination attempt on an investigative journalist and a high-level corruption scandal.

In December 1989, Vaclav Havel and the Civic Forum led anti-Communist opposition forces to topple the Czechoslovak government. The country held its first post-Communist elections in 1990, adopted a new constitution and a charter of freedoms in 1992, and peacefully dissolved Czechoslovakia into separate Czech and Slovak Republics in 1993. Havel became president of the new Czech Republic at its creation in 1993. The Czech Republic became a member of NATO in 1999.

In 1993, Prime Minister Vaclav Klaus and the Civic Democratic Party (ODS) embarked upon an aggressive program of political and economic reform. However, in 1997, growing economic stagnation and a severe currency crisis undermined public confidence in reforms. The Klaus government resigned later that year amid a campaign finance scandal and a deepening recession. Soon after, the center-right ODS brokered a power-sharing agreement with the center-left Czech Social Democratic Party (CSSD). The two parties led a minority government following elections in 1998. Voters in the Czech Republic went to the polls in June to elect members to the 200-

seat Chamber of Deputies. The ruling CSSD won 30.2 percent of the total votes and 70 corresponding mandates. Vaclav Klaus's ODS party gained only 24.5 percent of the vote (58 mandates). The Communist Party of Bohemia and Moravia (KSCM) followed in third place with 18.5 percent (41 mandates). The remnants of the once-popular "Four Party Coalition," now consisting of only the Christian Democrats and the Freedom Union-Democratic Union ("the Coalition"), finished last with 14.3 percent of the vote (31 mandates). No other political formations surmounted the 5 percent threshold. The CSSD formed a majority government in partnership with the Coalition following the election, and CSSD chairman Vlad Spidla became the new prime minister.

Despite a variety of governmental efforts to address problems of crime and corruption in the previous year, a 2002 Interior Ministry report stated that such anti-corruption efforts have been ineffective. Bribery and fraud are present in nearly every level of state administration. The close connection between crime and corruption surfaced in July when Karel Srba, a former Foreign Ministry secretary-general, allegedly contracted individuals to murder Sabina Slonkova, a high-profile investigative journalist. Police moved quickly to arrest Srba and three others before any could harm Slonkova. The Srba affair uncovered allegations of high-level corruption and spawned wider investigations into the Foreign Ministry, the Health Ministry, and the Military Intelligence Service. These investigations prompted the resignation or dismissal of the chief of military intelligence, the Czech ambassador to Kazakhstan, and the Czech defense attaché to India. While some analysts suggest that the case highlights the environment of "mafia capitalism" which has underscored Czech politics since the transition, the Srba affair also demonstrates the Czech government's intention to confront corruption and the willingness of law enforcement to keep journalists free from physical harm.

Nevertheless, Czech journalists must still contend with the threat of politically motivated libel suits. In 2001, then Prime Minister Milos Zeman threatened to sue the weekly newspaper *Respekt* over allegations that his government had failed to fight corruption. When Prime Minister Zeman publicly stated his intention to ensure the newspaper's demise, *Respekt* editor Petr Holub promptly filed a countersuit. In Spring 2002, an appeals court ordered *Respekt* to apologize for statements it printed regarding Miroslav Slouf, a chief adviser to Prime Minister Zeman. Some observers note that such events demonstrate just how uncomfortable Czech politicians are becoming over the increasingly assertive media culture in the country.

The European Commission's 2002 report on the Czech Republic's accession progress applauded some recent steps the government has taken to protect the rights of ethnic minorities. Simultaneously, the commission noted that the ethnic Roma (Gypsy) population continues to suffer from widespread discrimination. Previous efforts to address this issue have not had a fundamental impact on the plight of the Roma. Human Rights Watch identified the Roma situation as the Czech Republic's "most disturbing human rights problem." However, newly elected Prime Minister Spidla's public statements hint that he may depart from the Zeman government's confrontational approach toward ethnic relations.

Political Rights and Civil Liberties: Czech citizens 18 and older can change their government democratically under a system of universal, equal, and direct suffrage. The Czech Republic has a solid record of free and fair elections. Voters elect members of the Chamber of Deputies and the Senate. At the end of 2002, parliament had prepared a constitutional amendment to allow for the country's first direct presidential elections. The president serves as the head of state and appoints judges, the prime minister, and other cabinet members.

The Czech Republic's Charter of Fundamental Rights and Freedoms gives minorities the right to help resolve matters pertaining to their group. The government-sponsored Council for Roma Affairs administers projects to support the Roma community and works to better integrate the Romany minority into mainstream Czech society. Ethnic Roma must still contend with widespread discrimination and racially motivated assaults.

The Czech Republic generally honors freedom of expression, although the charter prohibits threats against individual rights, state and public security, public health, and morality. In 2001, parliament passed a bill designed to limit political influence over Czech Television, the state broadcaster. Under the new law, nongovernmental groups, rather than politicians, will make nominations for membership on Czech television's governing council. A similar law in 2002 applies the same system to Czech Radio.

The government generally respects freedom of religion. However, in 2001, parliament enacted a new religious law over President Vaclav Havel's veto. The law makes it difficult for smaller religious groups to gain official registration status. The law imposes a two-tiered registration system on religious groups. While all religions are free to worship in their own manner, only fully registered groups such as the Roman Catholic Church and Protestant denominations may own community property and receive state aid for clergy salaries, schools, and church maintenance.

Czech citizens may assemble peacefully, form associations, and petition the government. Trade unions and professional associations are free. Judges, prosecutors, and members of the armed forces and police may not strike. In 2001, the International Confederation of Free Trade Unions criticized the Czech Republic for restricting the rights of public sector workers to engage in collective bargaining and, in some professions, to strike.

The Czech Republic's independent judiciary consists of the Supreme Court, a constitutional court, and a supreme administrative court, as well as high, regional, and district courts. The Czech judicial system operates under chronic funding and staff shortages. This leaves the system vulnerable to political and outside influences. Some reports indicate that the courts have been slow to handle cases against former Communist officials.

The charter specifies "fundamental human rights and freedoms," including privacy, property ownership, the sanctity of the home, and choice of residence. It also guarantees the right to education, fair wages, and protection of one's health. Citizens generally enjoy all of these rights, although Roma continue to experience discrimination.

Denmark

Polity: Parliamentary democracy
Economy: Mixed capitalist
Population: 5,400,000
PPP: $27,627
Life Expectancy: 77
Religious Groups: Evangelical Lutheran (95 percent), Muslim (2 percent), other (3 percent)
Ethnic Groups: Scandinavian, Inuit, Faroese, German, Turkish, Iranian, Somali
Capital: Copenhagen

Political Rights: 1
Civil Liberties: 1
Status: Free

Ten-Year Ratings Timeline (Political Rights, Civil Liberties, Status)

1993	1994	1995	1996	1997	1998	1999	2000	2001	2002	2003
1,1F	1,1F	1,1F	1,1F	1,1F	1,1F	1,1F	1,1F	1,1F	1,1F	1,1F

Overview:

Denmark's right-wing minority coalition government, elected November 2001, is composed of the Liberal Party and the Conservative People's Party, headed by Anders Fogh Rasmussen, the Liberal leader. It relies on the extreme-right Danish People's Party to command a majority in parliament. The coalition is expected to remain in office until the parliamentary term expires in 2005. The government is cutting state administration costs to fulfill election promises to raise spending and freeze taxes. It also supports a strict immigration policy. Denmark took over the six-month rotating EU presidency on July 1, with the primary goal of completing the EU's preparations for the Union's enlargement of up to 10 new members in 2004. Human rights organizations noted some erosion in civil liberties and freedom of the press.

Denmark is the oldest monarchy in Europe. Queen Margrethe II, whose reign began in 1972, performs mostly ceremonial functions. The 1953 constitution established a unicameral parliament, or Folketing, in which 135 of the 179 members are elected in 17 mainland districts. Two representatives from each of the semiautonomous regions of the Faeroe Islands and Greenland are also elected. The remaining seats are allocated on a proportional basis to parties receiving more than 2 percent of the vote. An extensive system of local representation includes both regional and local councils.

Danes voted against adopting the euro in a September 2000 referendum, although the krone remains pegged to the euro and monetary policy is aligned with that of the European Central Bank. In voting against the euro, Danes defied the government, main opposition parties, big business, major trade unions, and economists, all of whom support monetary union. Opponents claimed that monetary union would weaken Denmark's welfare system and sovereignty. Others oppose European integration and immigration as a threat to national identity.

The Council of Europe in April 2002 criticized Denmark for discrimination against its Muslim population, immigrants, asylum seekers, and refugees. About 7 percent of the population is of foreign descent. The largest immigrant groups come from Turkey, Pakistan, Iran, and Iraq.

Political Rights and Civil Liberties: Danes can change their government democratically. Representatives are elected to the Folketing at least once every four years in a modified system of proportional representation. In the most recent elections, 87 percent of Danes voted. The semiautonomous territories of Greenland and the Faeroes each have two representatives in the Danish parliament.

Denmark's constitution guarantees freedom of expression. Danish media reflect a wide variety of political opinions and are frequently critical of the government. The state finances radio and television broadcasting, but state-owned television companies have independent editorial boards. Independent radio stations are permitted but tightly regulated.

As of May, it became legal for authorities to retain a person's phone call records, Internet activity and e-mail details for up to one year in order to combat terrorism. The intelligence services and the police may consult these data without prior permission by a judge and can install e-mail interception technology on Internet service providers. The daily newspaper *Morgenavisen Jyllands-Posten* announced in August that one of its journalists had had his telephone tapped and had been ordered by a court to reveal his sources of information among Islamic circles in Denmark.

The judiciary is independent, and citizens enjoy full due process rights. The court system consists of 100 local courts, two high courts, and the 15-member Supreme Court, with judges appointed by the queen on government recommendation.

The rights of racial, ethnic, and religious minorities are widely respected. In the latest elections, a Dane with an immigrant background was elected to parliament for the first time. However, anti-immigrant sentiment has risen, and in 2001 the government proposed strict immigration legislation. In April 2002, the UN High Commissioner for Refugees called on the government to abandon its proposed immigration legislation, which would lengthen the time it takes to receive a permanent residence permit; narrow the definition of a refugee; reserve Denmark the right to return refugees to their home country if the situation there improves; and bar immigrants under age 25 from bringing foreign spouses to Denmark.

Freedom of worship is guaranteed to all. The Evangelical Lutheran Church is the Danish national church, with 95 percent of the population belonging to it. Islam is the country's second-biggest religion. The Evangelical Lutheran faith is taught in public schools, although students are not required to attend religious classes.

As of August 27, the Optional Protocol to the Convention on the Rights of the Child on the involvement of children in armed conflict raised the minimum age for direct participation in hostilities to 18.

In 1989, Denmark became the first country to grant legal recognition to same-sex partnerships. In 2000, homosexuals in registered partnerships gained the right to adopt each other's children.

According to the Swiss-based Inter-Parliamentary Union, Denmark, with 37 percent of parliament members being women, is second in the world only to Sweden in proportional representation of women in legislatures.

Workers are free to organize, bargain collectively, and strike. About 80 percent of the workforce are members of trade unions, and more than 90 percent are covered by collective bargaining agreements, according to the Danish Confederation of Trade Unions.

Djibouti

Polity: Presidential-
parliamentary
(dominant party)
Economy: Capitalist
Population: 700,000
PPP: $2,377
Life Expectancy: 43

Political Rights: 4
Civil Liberties: 5
Status: Partly Free

Religious Groups: Muslim (94 percent), Christian (6 percent)
Ethnic Groups: Somali [Issa] (60 percent), Afar (35 percent), other (5 percent)
Capital: Djibouti

Ten-Year Ratings Timeline (Political Rights, Civil Liberties, Status)

1993	1994	1995	1996	1997	1998	1999	2000	2001	2002	2003
6,6NF	6,6NF	6,6NF	5,6NF	5,6NF	5,6NF	5,6NF	4,6PF	4,5PF	4,5PF	4,5PF

Overview:
President Ismael Omar Guelleh announced in September 2002 that Djibouti was to have a full multiparty system as opposed to a four-party system. A pro-government bloc of four parties under the umbrella Presidential Majority Union (UMP) was to run against an opposition bloc of four parties under the umbrella Union for Democratic Alternative (UAD). The vote was scheduled for January 2003. The country's political opposition is divided and was unable to make a showing in previous elections that were controlled by the government. Guelleh's pledge to further consolidate the country's democratic institutions came at a time of increasing American interest in Djibouti, which is strategically located on the Red Sea. Some 800 U.S. Army and Special Forces troops were stationed in Djibouti by November 2002, and an additional 400 troops were expected. They are there to set up regional headquarters to fight terrorism following the September 11, 2001, terrorist attacks on the United States.

Djibouti was known as the French Territory of the Afar and Issa before gaining independence from France in 1977. President Hassan Gouled Aptidon controlled a one-party system until 1992, when a new constitution adopted by referendum authorized four political parties. In 1993, Aptidon was declared the winner of a fourth six-year term in Djibouti's first contested presidential elections. Both the opposition and international observers considered the poll fraudulent. Aptidon stepped down in 1999 after 22 years in power, opening the way for the country's first free presidential election since independence. Guelleh, who is Aptidon's nephew and a former head of state security, had long been considered the de facto head of government and the president's heir apparent.

Djibouti's people are deeply divided along ethnic and clan lines. The majority Issa (Somali) and minority Afar peoples hold most political power. The government in 2001 followed up a peace agreement it had signed with the radical wing of the Front for the Restoration of Unity and Democracy (FRUD) in 2000 with a more extensive accord. It, like the previous agreement, was aimed at putting an end to the ethnic Afar insurgency that began in 1991. The largest FRUD faction agreed in 1994 to end its insurgency in exchange for inclusion in the government and electoral reforms.

Approximately 2,700 French troops are among 8,000 French residents of Djibouti. French advisors and technicians effectively run much of the country. Although this is slowly changing, President Guelleh favors retaining strong ties with France.

Djibouti has little industry and few natural resources. Services provide most of the national income. Efforts to curb rampant corruption have met with little success.

Political Rights and Civil Liberties: The trappings of representative government and formal administration have had little relevance to the real distribution and exercise of power in Djibouti. Ismael Omar Guelleh, of the ruling Popular Rally for Progress (RPP) party, won the 1999 presidential poll with 74 percent of the vote, compared with 26 percent for Moussa Ahmed Idriss, of the Unified Djiboutian Opposition (ODU). For the first time since elections began in 1992, no group boycotted the vote. Although international observers declared the poll generally fair, the ruling party had the advantage of state resources to conduct its campaign.

The 1997 legislative elections were marginally more credible than the plainly fraudulent 1992 polls, but were also considered unfair. The RPP, which, in coalition with the legalized arm of the FRUD at the time, won all 65 National Assembly seats.

The judiciary is not independent. *Sharia* (Islamic law) prevails in family matters. The former chief of police, General Yacin Yabel Galab, was sentenced to 15 years in prison in 2002 on charges related to an attempted coup in December 2000. Eleven other police, including eight senior officers, received sentences ranging from 3 to 10 years. Galab was chief of police from independence until his dismissal just prior to the coup attempt.

Security forces arrest Djiboutians without proper authority, despite constitutional requirements that arrests may not occur without a decree presented by a judicial magistrate. Prison conditions are harsh, with reports of beatings, torture, and the rape of female inmates. There are complaints of harassment of political opponents and union leaders. Local human rights groups do not operate freely. However, women's groups and other nongovernmental organizations operate without hindrance.

Freedom of assembly and association is nominally protected under the constitution, but the government has little tolerance for political protest.

Despite constitutional protection, freedom of speech is not guaranteed. The government closely controls all electronic media. There is one official newspaper. Independent newspapers, most of which are in the form of newsletters, are generally allowed to circulate freely, but journalists exercise self-censorship. Djibouti and the United States in 2002 agreed to set up radio relay stations in Djibouti to broadcast Arabic radio programs of the Voice of America.

Islam is the official state religion, but freedom of worship is respected, although the government discourages proselytizing.

Despite equality under civil law, women suffer serious discrimination under customary practices in inheritance and other property matters, in divorce, and the right to travel. Female genital mutilation is almost universal, and legislation forbidding mutilation of young girls is not enforced. Women's groups are making efforts to curb the practice.

The economy is largely a rural agricultural one, and the nomadic subsistence economy is small. Workers may join unions and strike, but the government routinely obstructs the free operation of unions.

Dominica

Polity: Parliamentary
democracy
Economy: Capitalist
Population: 100,000
PPP: $5,880
Life Expectancy: 73
Religious Groups: Roman Catholic 77 percent,
Protestant 15 percent, other 8 percent
Ethnic Groups: Mostly black and mulatto, Carib Indian
Capital: Roseau

Political Rights: 1
Civil Liberties: 1
Status: Free

Ten-Year Ratings Timeline (Political Rights, Civil Liberties, Status)

1993	1994	1995	1996	1997	1998	1999	2000	2001	2002	2003
2,1F	2,1F	2,1F	1,1F	1,1F	1,1F	1,1F	1,1F	1,1F	1,1F	1,1F

Overview:

The coalition of the Dominica Labour Party (DLP) and the Dominica Freedom Party (DFP) came to power in the January 30, 2000, elections. The government of Prime Minister Pierre Charles, of the DLP, had a dismal year. The global economic downturn hurt the agriculturally based economy especially hard and contributed to the imposition of an unpopular program of stabilization and adjustment. The austerity measures have led to cabinet resignations and a reshuffling, civil service strikes, and popular protests. Corruption allegations in the police force and the resumption of passport sales have eclipsed the announcement that the Organization of Economic Cooperation and Development and the Financial Action Task Force have removed the island from their lists of uncooperative tax and money laundering havens.

Dominica has been an independent republic within the Commonwealth since 1978. Internally self-governing since 1967, Dominica is a parliamentary democracy headed by a prime minister and the House of Assembly, with 21 members elected to five-year terms. Nine senators are appointed—five by the prime minister and four by the opposition leader. The house elects the president for a five-year term.

Dominica's economy is primarily agricultural, though there have been efforts to build the infrastructure required to promote tourism and high-technology investment. Because of the island's volcanic geology, rugged terrain, and few beaches, most tourist activity is limited to cruise ship visits. Destruction caused by hurricanes, at times devastating, has further strained the banana industry, which has also been affected by changing market forces, especially increasing competition.

Unemployment continues to hover around 20 percent. A major escape valve is the continuing emigration of Dominicans to the United States and the Francophone Caribbean. Dominica's offshore business sector includes several thousand international companies, banks, and Internet gambling companies. Offshore banking interests continue to raise concerns about penetration by international organized crime, particularly Russian organizations. Despite the announcement in January 2000 that the practice will end, Dominica continues to raise money by selling passports and "economic citizenship."

Political Rights and Civil Liberties: Citizens are able to change their government through free and fair elections. In the January 2000 vote, 60,000 people registered to participate. There are no restrictions on political, civic, or labor organizations. There are three major and one minor political parties. Advocacy groups are free to operate and include the Association of Disabled People, the Dominican National Council of Women, and a women's and children's self-help organization.

The press is free and there is no censorship or government interference. There are several private newspapers and political party journals. Though the main radio station is state owned, there is also an independent radio. There is unimpeded access to cable television and regional radio broadcasts, as well as to the Internet. Academic freedom is respected.

Freedom of religion is recognized. While a majority of the population is Roman Catholic, some Protestant churches have been established. In the past, the small Rastafarian community has charged that its religious rights are violated by a policy of cutting off the dreadlocks of prisoners and that Rastafarian women are singled out for drug searches.

There is an independent judiciary, and the rule of law is enhanced by the court's subordination to the inter-island Eastern Caribbean Supreme Court. However, the judicial system is understaffed, which has led to a large backlog of cases. The only prison on Dominica is overcrowded and has sanitation problems. In addition, minors are housed with adults. Prison visits by independent human rights monitors are permitted.

The Commonwealth of Dominica Police Force (CDPF) became responsible for security after the Dominica Defense Force (DDF) was disbanded in 1981. The DDF had been implicated in an attempted coup staged by supporters of former Prime Minister Patrick John, who was convicted in 1986 for his role and given a 12-year prison sentence. He was released by executive order in 1990, became active in the trade union movement, and lost as a DLP candidate in the 1995 election. Occasional instances of excessive use of force by police are among the few human rights complaints heard. In 1997 the commissioner and deputy commissioner of the police were forced to retire as a result of recommendations by a commission of inquiry that investigated allegations of mismanagement, corruption, and police brutality. Under new leadership, the police created the Internal Affairs Department late that year to investigate public complaints against the police and to provide officers with counseling. In 2002 there were allegations of corruption relating to document falsification. Narcotics traffickers use the country as a transshipment point.

Workers have the right to organize, strike, and bargain collectively. Though unions are independent of the government and laws prohibit anti-union discrimination by employers, less than 10 percent of the workforce is unionized.

Inheritance laws do not fully recognize women's rights. When a husband dies without a will, the wife cannot inherit the property, though she may continue to inhabit their home. There are no laws mandating equal pay for equal work for men and women in private sector jobs. Government welfare officials have expressed concern over the growing number of cases of child abuse.

There are 3,000 indigenous Carib Indians, many of whom live on a 3,783-acre reservation on the northeast coast created in 1903 and expanded in 1997. The reservation is governed by the 1978 Carib constitution.

Dominican Republic

Polity: Presidential-parliamentary democracy
Economy: Capitalist-statist
Population: 8,800,000
PPP: $6,033
Life Expectancy: 69
Religious Groups: Roman Catholic (95 percent)
Ethnic Groups: Mixed (73 percent), white (16 percent), black (11 percent)
Capital: Santo Domingo

Political Rights: 2
Civil Liberties: 2
Status: Free

Ten-Year Ratings Timeline (Political Rights, Civil Liberties, Status)

1993	1994	1995	1996	1997	1998	1999	2000	2001	2002	2003
2,3F	3,3PF	4,3PF	4,3PF	3,3PF	3,3PF	2,3F	2,3F	2,2F	2,2F	2,2F

Overview:

The political debate in the Dominican Republic was dominated in 2002 by partisan wrangling over the creation of an electoral board handpicked by the ruling party. The dispute erupted in September when the Senate, which is controlled by the center-left Dominican Revolutionary Party (PRD), appointed seven members to the board, which runs all elections. The move caused opposition parties, which control the Chamber of Deputies, to announce that they were abandoning the lower chamber, paralyzing its work.

After achieving independence from Spain in 1821 and from Haiti in 1844, the Dominican Republic endured recurrent domestic conflict. The assassination of General Rafael Trujillo in 1961 ended 30 years of dictatorship, but a 1963 military coup led to civil war and U.S. intervention. In 1966, under a new constitution, civilian rule was restored with the election of the conservative Joaquin Balaguer. The constitution provides for a president and a congress elected for four-year terms. The congress consists of the 30-member Senate and, as a result of a recent census, a House that in 1998 went from 120 members to 149.

In the May 16, 2000, presidential elections, Hipolito Mejia, a former agriculture minister and a PRD outsider, struck a chord among those who felt left out of the economic prosperity, particularly the 20 percent who live below the poverty level. Mejia won 49.87 percent of the vote, compared with 24.9 percent for ruling party candidate Danilo Medina and 24.6 percent for Balaguer, who was running for his eighth term in office.

In 2002, electrical blackouts and an ailing economy topped the issues of governance confronting Mejia, who also faced problems of increasing street crime. Enron, the failed U.S. corporation, had a stake in a power plant in the Dominican Republic that was in serious financial trouble.

Political Rights and Civil Liberties: Citizens of the Dominican Republic can change their government through elections. At the end of 2001, the Dominican legislature approved constitutional changes allowing presidents to serve consecutive terms, as part of a package of electoral changes that also included reducing from 50 percent to 45 percent the minimum vote required to win presidential elections in the first round. The reforms also established direct election of the president, eliminating an electoral college system in which representative sectors chose the president based on popular votes.

Constitutional guarantees regarding free expression, freedom of religion, and the right to organize political parties and civic groups are generally respected. Civil society organizations in the Dominican Republic are some of the most well organized and effective in Latin America.

The media are mostly private. Newspapers are independent and diverse but subject to government pressure through denial of advertising revenues and the imposition of taxes on imported newsprint. Dozens of radio stations and at least six commercial television stations broadcast. In 1997 the National Commission on Public Events and Radio Broadcasting shut down dozens of programs with religious-magical content.

The judiciary, headed by the Supreme Court, is politicized and riddled with corruption, although significantly less so in recent years. The courts offer little recourse to those without money or influence, although reforms implemented of late show some promise in increasing citizen access to the courts. Prisons, in which 9 out of 10 inmates have not been convicted of a crime, are grossly overcrowded, with poor health and sanitary conditions, and violence is routine. Police salaries are low, and there is a high level of corruption throughout the country's law enforcement institutions.

A major transit country for South American drugs to the United States, the Dominican Republic serves local, Puerto Rican, and Colombian drug smugglers as both a command-and-control center and a transshipment point, mostly for cocaine. The government estimates that some 20 percent of the drugs entering the country remain there as "payment in kind." This phenomenon has contributed to increasing drug abuse and street crime.

Labor unions are well organized. Although legally permitted to strike, they are often subject to government crackdowns. Peasant unions are occasionally targeted by armed groups working for large landowners. Haitian migration to the Dominican Republic has long been a source of tension between the two countries. Violence and discrimination against women is a serious problem, as are trafficking in women and girls, child prostitution, and child abuse. The Dominican Republic is primarily a source country for trafficked women between the ages of 18 and 25, and girls as young as 15.

East Timor

Polity: Presidential-
parliamentary democracy
Economy: Capitalist-statist
Population: 800,000
PPP: na
Life Expectancy: 48

Political Rights: 3*
Civil Liberties: 3
Status: Partly Free

Religious Groups: Roman Catholic (90 percent),
Muslim (4 percent), Protestant (3 percent), other (3 percent)
Ethnic Groups: Autronesian (Malayo-Polynesian), Papuan, small Chinese minority
Capital: Dili
Ratings Change: East Timor's political rights rating improved from 5 to 3 due to the holding of the country's first direct presidential election since it gained independence.

Ten-Year Ratings Timeline (Political Rights, Civil Liberties, Status)

1993	1994	1995	1996	1997	1998	1999	2000	2001	2002	2003
--	--	--	--	--	--	--	6,4PF	6,3PF	5,3PF	3,3PF

Overview:

After becoming the world's newest state in May, East Timor faced the daunting challenge of nation building in a land scarred by neglect and human rights abuses during two centuries of Portuguese rule and 24 years of Indonesian occupation. The country received full independence with the departure of an interim United Nations administration that, in two years, helped rebuild roads and buildings and set up a legislature and other basic democratic institutions. The UN, however, made relatively little progress in getting many basic services up and running, drafting business laws, and sorting out land disputes.

To make matters tougher, the new country is Asia's poorest, 85 to 90 percent of urban adults have no jobs, up to half of East Timorese are illiterate, and small-scale coffee production is virtually the only export industry. Even after revenues from offshore oil and gas production come on stream in 2005, the Southeast Asian country is likely to remain heavily dependent on foreign aid for the foreseeable future. The government of President Xanana Gusmao also faces the divisive question of whether to grant amnesty to past human rights abusers or to pursue justice through the courts.

The Portuguese became the first Europeans to land on Timor Island in the sixteenth century. They retreated to the eastern part of Timor in the eighteenth century following years of fighting for control of the island with the Dutch. After Portugal abruptly abandoned East Timor in early 1975, two armed Timorese groups, the leftist Fretilin and the right-wing Timorese Democratic Union, fought for control of the territory. Indonesia invaded in December 1975 and formally annexed East Timor in 1976.

As Indonesian forces consolidated their hold on the territory, they committed widespread abuses against the local population during counterinsurgency operations against Fretilin's armed wing, the East Timorese National Liberation Army

(Falintil). By 1979, civil conflict and famine had killed up to 200,000 Timorese. For the next two decades, poorly equipped Falintil forces continued to wage a low-grade insurgency from the rugged interior.

East Timor's road to independence began with the 1998 downfall of Indonesia's iron-fisted President Suharto, who had steadfastly rejected even autonomy for the territory. As support for independence mounted in 1999, local militias, armed by the Indonesian military, began attacking pro-independence activists and suspected supporters. Amid the violence, East Timorese voters overwhelmingly approved an August 1999 referendum in favor of independence.

In response, militia fighters and Indonesian forces killed up to 1,000 civilians, drove more than 250,000 others into Indonesia's West Timor, and destroyed up to 80 percent of East Timor's roads and buildings before being ousted in late September by an Australian-led multinational force. UN administrators in 2000 began the arduous task of preparing the fragile territory for independence.

Mindful of the continuing threat posed by militias making their bases in West Timor, the United Nations plans to keep a small contingent of troops in the country until 2004. By then, a small East Timorese defense force is expected to be ready to assume responsibility for national security.

Gusmao, 56, a former resistance commander before being captured and jailed by Indonesian authorities, began running the nation-in-waiting after easily winning a five-year term in presidential elections in April 2002. After the fanfare of independence in May died down, Gusmao's government faced widespread calls to bring to justice pro-Jakarta militia fighters responsible for rights abuses in 1999. For his part, President Gusmao advocated amnesty in the hopes of speeding reconciliation in the young country and encouraging the return from West Timor of tens of thousands of refugees.

The government also faced repeated protests by hundreds of armed men claiming to be former resistance fighters and demanding state welfare benefits as compensation for their roles in the struggle against Indonesian rule. Separately, a protest in December over the arrest of a student turned into a riot that killed at least one person.

Foreign donors, meanwhile, pledged $440 million to East Timor through 2005. Those funds should help the government stay afloat financially until it begins earning income under a 2001 deal with Australia that gives East Timor up to 90 percent of the revenues from Timor Sea oil and gas production. The revenues could be worth $6 billion over 20 years, according to conservative estimates.

Political Rights and Civil Liberties: Having gained their independence, the East Timorese now face the task of building viable democratic institutions, having started largely from scratch after the Indonesian occupation ended. The presidential elections in 2002 and legislative balloting the previous year marked the first time that East Timorese were allowed to choose their own leaders. Fretilin won the most seats in the 2001 legislative vote, which was marred by accusations from smaller parties, not fully substantiated, that Fretilin used intimidation to help secure votes. Fretilin's leader, Mari Alkatiri, is East Timor's prime minister.

The judiciary and other governmental institutions are inexperienced and largely untested, having been built quickly from the ground up by UN administrators and East Timorese leaders. The fledgling civil law court system is poorly funded and heavily backlogged because of a shortage of trained lawyers, prosecutors, and translators, who have to work in four languages (Indonesian, the local Tetum dialect, English, and Portuguese), the Hong Kong-based *Far Eastern Economic Review* reported in August. Like the courts, the prison system is rudimentary, as evidenced in part by an August jailbreak by nearly 200 inmates from Dili's main prison.

In a major step toward bringing to justice suspects in the 1999 violence, a UN tribunal in Dili staffed by local and international judges convicted and jailed several East Timorese for killings that year. The tribunal's work, however, has been hampered by limited resources and Jakarta's reluctance to extradite suspects to East Timor or to allow UN investigators to question suspects in Indonesia.

The key source of news and information in the new country is Radio East Timor, which was set up by UN administrators. However, 5 out of East Timor's 13 districts were not receiving the station as of July because of power shortages, with the cash-strapped central government unable to help, the *Far Eastern Economic Review* reported. Denied voices or roles under the Indonesian occupation, numerous nongovernmental groups are now providing social services and monitoring and promoting human rights. Most are dependent on foreign aid.

Domestic violence against women is a "significant problem" in East Timor, while traditional customs prevent women in some regions and villages from inheriting or owning property, according to the U.S. State Department's global human rights report for 2001, released in March 2002. The report also noted that Protestants, Malay Muslims, and ethnic Chinese businessmen have faced some harassment in mainstream society. Nevertheless, all groups can worship relatively freely in this predominantly Roman Catholic country.

East Timor has several trade unions that represent teachers, nurses, and other professions, but they are inexperienced and poorly funded. With an estimated two-thirds to three-fourths of East Timor's workforce laboring in subsistence agriculture, unions will probably play limited roles for the foreseeable future. Workers seeking higher regular pay or severance pay frequently stage strikes, which at times turn violent.

Agriculture, primarily coffee production, is the backbone of the economy. East Timor has carved out a niche in the high-end, organically certified Arabica coffee market. Coffee production took on even greater importance with the departure of many UN workers at independence, which deflated what had been a booming trade in providing food, lodging, and other goods to well-paid expatriate staff in Dili.

Ecuador

Polity: Presidential-   **Political Rights:** 3
parliamentary democracy   **Civil Liberties:** 3
Economy: Capitalist-statist   **Status:** Partly Free
Population: 13,000,000
PPP: $3,203
Life Expectancy: 71
Religious Groups: Roman Catholic (95 percent), other (5 percent)
Ethnic Groups: Mestizo (65 percent), Indian (25 percent),
white (7 percent), black (3 percent)
Capital: Quito

Ten-Year Ratings Timeline (Political Rights, Civil Liberties, Status)

1993	1994	1995	1996	1997	1998	1999	2000	2001	2002	2003
2,3F	2,3F	2,3F	2,3F	2,4PF	3,3PF	2,3F	2,3F	3,3PF	3,3PF	3,3PF

Overview:

A former coup leader and retired army colonel who pledged to fight corruption and poverty was elected president in November 2002, beating two former presidents who stood as standard-bearers for the country's traditional political parties. Lucio Gutierrez's victory at the head of a leftist coalition in this chronically unstable country was supported by the country's increasingly empowered Indian groups, and constituted the first time Ecuador's chief executive shared the humble background and dark-skinned complexion of the country's majority. Gutierrez, a civil engineer who had never held political office, faced the task of bringing foreign investment to the economically moribund country, and in an early sign of moderation, promised to pay the foreign debt resulting from a 1999 default.

Established in 1830 after achieving independence from Spain in 1822, the Republic of Ecuador has endured many interrupted presidencies and military governments. The last military regime gave way to civilian rule when a new constitution was approved by referendum in 1978. The constitution provides for a president elected for four years, with a runoff between two front-runners if no candidate wins a majority in the first round. The 77-member unicameral congress (National Chamber of Deputies) is composed of 65 members elected on a provincial basis every two years and 12 elected nationally every four years.

Vice President Gustavo Noboa took over as president in January 2000 after demonstrators had forced his predecessor to step down. The protests by indigenous groups, reportedly manipulated by putschist senior army commanders, were joined by significant numbers of mid-level military officers led by Gutierrez. Despite the protestors' acclamation of a three-person "junta" that included Gutierrez, congress met in emergency session in Guayaquil to ratify Noboa, who did not belong to any political party, as the new constitutional president.

Gutierrez, inspired by another coup plotter, Venezuela's Hugo Chavez, won a surprise first-round victory in the October 20, 2002, presidential election and went on to best the banana magnate Alvaro Noboa, a populist, in the November 24 runoff. On a positive note, the appointment of Nina Pacari by Gutierrez as foreign minister marked two firsts in Ecuadoran history: she is the first woman and first Native American to occupy the prestigious foreign policy position.

Political Rights and Civil Liberties: Citizens can change their government through elections, and the 2002 elections were generally considered to be free and fair. In 1998, the national Constituent Assembly decided to retain Ecuador's presidential system. It also mandated that in the year 2002, a presidential candidate would need to win 40 percent of valid votes in first-round balloting and exceed by 10 percent those received by the nearest rival in order to avoid a runoff.

Constitutional guarantees regarding freedom of expression, freedom of religion, and the right to organize political parties are generally respected. The judiciary, generally undermined by the corruption afflicting the entire political system, is headed by a supreme court that, until 1997, was appointed by the legislature and thus subject to political influence. In reforms approved by referendum in May 1997, power to appoint judges was turned over to the Supreme Court, with congress given a final chance to choose that 31-member body on the basis of recommendations made by a special selection commission. In a positive development, in July 2001, a new criminal justice procedural code that fundamentally changes Ecuador's legal system entered into force. The new code empowers prosecutors (*fiscales*) to investigate and prosecute crimes, and alters the role of judges to that of neutral arbiter presiding over oral trials.

Ecuador is a transshipment point for cocaine passing from neighboring Colombia to the United States, as well as a money-laundering haven. Widespread corruption in Ecuador's customs service led the government to privatize it in May 1999. The dollarization of the Ecuadoran economy appears to have had the unintended effect of making the country more attractive for money laundering and other financial criminal activity.

A growing number of incursions from both Colombian guerrilla groups and their paramilitary enemies into Ecuadoran territory added to regional concern (including worries in Panama, Venezuela, Brazil and Peru) about the extent to which the neighboring country's civil war would affect public safety and the survival of democratic institutions. Violent crime has undermined public faith in the police to maintain order. Ecuador has numerous human rights organizations, and despite occasional acts of intimidation, they report on arbitrary arrests and instances of police brutality and military misconduct. Indigenous peoples are the frequent victims of abuse by military officers working in league with large landowners during disputes over land.

The media are mostly private and outspoken. The government controls radio frequencies. Labor unions are well organized and have the right to strike, although the labor code limits public sector strikes. Violence against women, particularly in indigenous areas where victims are reluctant to speak out against other members of their community, is common.

The constitution provides for freedom of religion, and the government generally respects this right in practice. The Government does not require religious groups to be licensed or registered unless they form NGOs that engage in commercial activity. The Government allows missionary activity and religious demonstrations by all religions.

Egypt

Polity: Dominant party (military-influenced)
Economy: Mixed statist
Population: 71,200,000
PPP: $3,635
Life Expectancy: 66
Religious Groups: Muslim (mostly Sunni) 94 percent, Coptic Christian and other (6 percent)
Ethnic Groups: Eastern Hamitic stock [Egyptian, Bedouin, Berber] (99 percent), other (1 percent)
Capital: Cairo

Political Rights: 6
Civil Liberties: 6
Status: Not Free

Ten-Year Ratings Timeline (Political Rights, Civil Liberties, Status)

1993	1994	1995	1996	1997	1998	1999	2000	2001	2002	2003
5,6PF	6,6NF	6,6NF	6,6NF	6,6NF	6,6NF	6,6NF	6,5NF	6,5NF	6,6NF	6,6NF

Overview:

The Egyptian government continued to extensively suppress internal dissent in 2002, drawing broad support from an international community increasingly tolerant of extrajudicial measures to combat terrorism and to silence opposition to the peace process with Israel and the looming war with Iraq. The imprisonment of prominent sociologist Saad Eddin Ibrahim in July evoked unprecedented international criticism, though an appeals court overturned his conviction in December.

Egypt formally gained independence from Great Britain in 1922 and acquired full sovereignty following the end of World War II. After leading a coup that overthrew the monarchy in 1954, Col. Gamel Abdel Nasser established a repressive police state, which he ruled until his death in 1970. The constitution adopted in 1971 under his successor, Anwar al-Sadat, established a strong presidential political system with nominal guarantees for most political and civil rights that were not fully protected in practice. Following the assassination of Sadat in 1981, Hosni Mubarak became president and declared a state of emergency, which he has since renewed every three years (most recently in June 2000). The ruling National Democratic Party (NDP) dominates the tightly controlled political system.

In the early 1990s, Islamic fundamentalist groups launched a violent campaign against police, Coptic Christians, and tourists, prompting the government to jail thousands of suspected dissidents and crack down on political dissent. Although the armed infrastructure of Egyptian Islamist groups was largely eradicated by 1998, the government continued to steadily retract political and civil liberties, while seeking to bolster its religious legitimacy by imposing *Sharia* (Islamic law) in some areas of Egyptian public life, banning books and films considered to be irreverent toward Islam, and declining to adequately investigate attacks by Islamist extremists against Coptic Christians. Mubarak has also distanced himself from Israel, permitted rabidly anti-Jewish and anti-American sentiments to be expressed in educational curricula and the state-run media, and has increasingly adopted inflammatory rhetoric himself.

The government has been unable to address the underlying socioeconomic problems that appear to fuel Islamist militancy, particularly high unemployment among college graduates, which has created a class of "educated poor," and endemic corruption. Since the September 11 attacks on the United State, Egypt's four principal sources of foreign exchange earnings—tourism revenue, oil sales, Suez Canal receipts, and expatriate remittances—have all declined and foreign direct investment has fallen. It has consequently been difficult for the government to achieve its proclaimed goal of generating 800,000 jobs annually.

Economic reforms needed to attract foreign investment have progressed slowly because of fears that austerity measures will increase demands for more representative and accountable government institutions. During his visit to the United States in March 2002, Mubarak sought to persuade the Bush administration to begin free trade negotiations with Egypt. He was told that this would be difficult because of his government's failure to undertake reforms in areas such as intellectual property protection, customs regulations, money laundering, taxation, and privatization.

High-profile efforts by the government to root out corruption resulted in arrests or convictions of several prominent figures in 2002, including former ministers of finance and tourism, the former governor of Giza, a television news director, and the sitting deputy agriculture minister, but critics allege that the anticorruption campaign has been politically motivated.

Critics argue that the government's assault on political and civil rights in recent years has encouraged support for radical extremist groups by eliminating peaceful channels of political expression. Efforts in recent years to neutralize the mainstream Muslim Brotherhood movement have coincided with the growth of small or previously unknown radical Islamist groups, most notably Al-Waad (The Promise), whose members have been arrested for allegedly soliciting donations on behalf of the Palestinian Hamas organization and sending operatives to Chechnya to fight against Russian forces. In April, the authorities arrested dozens of members of Hizb al-Tahrir (The Liberation Party), a fundamentalist group that was crushed in the 1970s but is now enjoying a resurgence.

Since the September 11 attacks, Western governments have been tolerant of the government's crackdown on Islamists. Although European courts had long been unwilling to approve the extradition of expatriate Egyptians on the basis of evidence gathered by Cairo's intelligence services, two key Islamic Jihad figures were deported by Sweden in December 2001. However, the regime's continued efforts to silence the liberal opposition have drawn criticism.

In July 2002, the Supreme State Security Court sentenced the founder and director of the Ibn Khaldun Center for Development Studies, sociologist Saad Eddin Ibrahim, to seven years in prison on charges that included spreading false information that damages Egypt's reputation abroad and receiving foreign funds without authorization (a $250,000 grant from the European Union to raise voter awareness and monitor the 2000 parliamentary elections). The authorities closed the Ibn Khaldun Center and the Hoda Association, an affiliated organization promoting voting rights for women, and arrested Ibrahim and most of his staff in June 2000. Although the initial conviction of Ibrahim and 27 of his colleagues in May 2001 was overturned on procedural grounds, the second trial was also heavily flawed.

On August 15, the White House announced that it was not granting Egypt any additional foreign aid beyond the $2 billion per year stipulated by the Camp David Accords, a decision that media leaks by Bush administration officials indicated was linked to the verdict in Ibrahim's trial. Ibrahim was freed after the judiciary overturned his conviction in December 2002, but at year's end he was still barred from leaving the country for medical treatment.

Political Rights and Civil Liberties: Egyptians cannot change their government democratically. As a result of government restrictions on the licensing of political parties, state control over the audiovisual media, and systemic irregularities in the electoral process, the 454-seat People's Assembly, or lower house of parliament, is dominated by the ruling NDP, as is the upper house, the Consultative Council (Majlis al-Shura), which is two-thirds elected and functions only in an advisory capacity.

There is no competitive process for the election of the Egyptian president; the public is entitled only to confirm in a national referendum the candidate nominated by the People's Assembly for a six-year term. The assembly has limited influence on government policy, and almost all legislation is initiated by the executive. The president directly appoints the prime minister, the cabinet, and the governors of Egypt's 26 provinces.

Political opposition in Egypt remains weak and ineffective. The NDP-controlled Political Parties Committee (PPC) has allowed the legal establishment of only two new political parties in the last 21 years. A ban on religious parties prevents the Muslim Brotherhood and other mainstream Islamists from organizing politically, though they may compete in elections as independents or members of secular parties.

Although a ruling by the Constitutional Court brought parliamentary elections under the supervision of the judiciary for the first time in 2000, the authorities compensated for the lack of vote rigging by arresting hundreds of Brotherhood members in the weeks prior to the election and deploying security forces outside the polls to obstruct voting in pro-opposition districts, sparking clashes that left 10 people dead and dozens injured (including an observer from Amnesty International). Nevertheless, the movement captured 17 seats, becoming the largest parliamentary opposition bloc.

In April 2002, the NDP won around 97 percent of contested seats in municipal elections. During a two-seat parliamentary by-election in the Ramla district of Alexandria in June, which witnessed a fierce electoral campaign between NDP and Brotherhood candidates, security forces blocked voters in pro-Islamist neighborhoods from entering the polls. Many who attempted to push their way past the barricades were later tried on charges of disturbing the peace and attacking government employees (see below).

The Emergency Law restricts many basic rights. Its provisions allow for the arrest without charge and prolonged pretrial detention of suspects, as well as their families and acquaintances. Torture and inadequate food and medical care are pervasive in custody. In November 2002, Amnesty International published a report stating that "everyone taken into detention in Egypt is at risk of torture." The authorities rarely investigate the abuse of detainees (unless they die in custody) or provide compensation to victims or their families.

The Egyptian Organization for Human Rights (EOHR) estimates that there are approximately 13,000 to 16,000 people detained without charge on suspicion of security or political offenses, as well as several thousand who have been convicted and are serving sentences on such charges. An Amnesty International fact-finding delegation that visited the country in the fall of 2002 was denied access to prisoners.

The civilian judiciary is considered to be relatively competent, impartial and independent of the executive branch. However, political and security cases are usually placed under the jurisdiction of either the military courts or the State Security Emergency Courts, both of which answer directly to the president and deny defendants many constitutional protections.

The State Security Emergency Courts are empowered to try defendants charged with violating decrees promulgated under the Emergency Law, as well as ordinary criminal cases that the president places under their jurisdiction. Although judges are usually selected from the civilian judiciary, they are appointed directly by the president. Sentences issued by the state security courts cannot be appealed, except on procedural grounds, and are subject to ratification by the president, who can annul both convictions *and* acquittals.

In September 2002, in a case that appeared to mark an expansion in the government's anti-Islamist campaign from prosecution of hard-core militants to actions against ordinary sympathizers, 101 supporters of the Muslim Brotherhood were brought to trial before a state security court on charges stemming from the June by-election. However, the presiding judge was outraged that the case was brought before the court, and all of the defendants were either acquitted or convicted of minor offenses and released. Afterwards, the judge called on parliament to lift the Emergency Law—an unprecedented rebuke of the government.

Since 1992, civilians charged with terrorism and other security-related offenses have been referred by the president to military courts. Since military judges are appointed by the Ministry of Defense to short, renewable two-year terms, these tribunals are squarely subordinate to the executive branch. Verdicts by military courts are subject to review only by a body of military judges, rather than a court, and to ratification by the president. Moreover, evidence produced by the prosecution in cases before the military courts often consists of little more than the testimony of security officers and informers. Allegations of forced confessions by defendants are routine.

On July 30, 2002, the Supreme Military Court sentenced 16 alleged members of the Muslim Brotherhood to prison terms ranging from three to five years. On September 9, the court handed down sentences ranging from 2 to 15 years in prison for 51 alleged members of Al-Waad. Evidence presented at the trial was thin even by Egyptian standards (prosecutors produced only a baseball bat and an air rifle), and dozens of the accused claimed that they were subjected to electric shock and other forms of torture.

Freedom of the press is limited. The government owns and operates all broadcast media, though it does not block foreign satellite channels, which have few individual subscribers but can be viewed in many public places. Three major daily newspapers are owned in part by the state, and their editors are appointed by the president. Although a number of private papers are published, the government exercises indirect control over them through its monopoly on printing and distribution. Press freedom is heavily restricted by vaguely worded statutes in the Press Law, the Publications Law, the penal code, and libel laws. Direct criticism of the president, his family, or the military can result in the imprisonment of journalists and the closure of publications. Discussion of tensions between Muslims and Christian in Egypt and views regarded as anti-Islamic are also heavily proscribed. However, the government does not significantly restrict or monitor Internet use.

Freedom of assembly and association is heavily restricted. Organizers of public demonstrations, rallies, and protests must receive advance approval from the Interior Ministry. In April 2002, an Egyptian student was killed by security forces during an anti-Israel demonstration. Nongovernmental organizations, particularly human rights groups, are often refused legal registration and, as the continued closure of the Ibn Khaldun center illustrates, those that are allowed to operate have little protection against arbitrary government closures.

On June 3, the People's Assembly approved a new law governing civic associations to replace Law 32 of 1964. The new law, an amended version of legislation rejected by the Constitutional Court in 2000, includes a vaguely worded ban on political activity, prohibits the receipt of foreign funding without explicit government approval, allows the Ministry of Social Affairs to sidestep the judicial process and dissolve NGOs by administrative decree, and closes legal loopholes that allowed human rights groups to avoid NGO restrictions by registering as law firms or civil companies.

The law heavily restricts the formation and activities of labor unions and prohibits strikes. The government-backed Egyptian Trade Union Federation is the only legal labor federation.

Although the law provides for equality of the sexes in most respects, there are exceptions. Unmarried women under the age of 21 are not permitted to obtain passports without permission from their fathers. Women who marry noncitizens may not confer Egyptian citizenship on their children. Marital rape is legal. Job discrimination is evident even in the civil service (for example, there are no female judges in Egypt). The law provides for equal access to education, but the adult literacy rate of women lags behind that of men (34 and 63 percent, respectively).

Islam is the state religion and the government directly controls most mosques, appoints their preachers and other staff, and closely monitors the content of sermons. It is presently implementing a plan to establish control over thousands of small, unauthorized mosques (known as *zawaya*) located in residential buildings. Most Egyptians are Sunni Muslim, but Coptic Christians constitute less than 6 percent of the population and there are small numbers of Jews, Shiite Muslims and Bahais. Although non-Muslims are generally able to worship freely, the government has seized church-owned property and frequently denies permission to build or repair churches. In recent years, Muslim extremists have murdered, kidnapped, raped, and forcibly converted scores of Copts, and burned or vandalized Coptic homes, businesses, and churches; the few perpetrators who have been brought to trial have been acquitted or received light sentences.

El Salvador

Polity: Presidential-par-
liamentary democracy
Economy: Capitalist
Population: 6,600,000
PPP: $4,497
Life Expectancy: 70
Religious Groups: Roman Catholic (83 percent),
other (17 percent)
Ethnic Groups: Mestizo (90 percent), Indian and white (10 percent)
Capital: San Salvador

Political Rights: 2
Civil Liberties: 3
Status: Free

Ten-Year Ratings Timeline (Political Rights, Civil Liberties, Status)

1993	1994	1995	1996	1997	1998	1999	2000	2001	2002	2003
3,3PF	3,3PF	3,3PF	3,3PF	3,3PF	2,3F	2,3F	2,3F	2,3F	2,3F	2,3F

Overview:

The two earthquakes of 2002, the collapse of world coffee prices, and the slowdown of the U.S. economy, where many of the country's exports go, have made governance in El Salvador a challenge one decade after the end of the civil war. High levels of crime, corruption, and incompetence have led to popular distrust of national political leaders, evidenced by the low voter turnout of 39 percent in the 1999 elections. The Alianza Republicana Nacionalista (ARENA) party's candidate, Francisco Flores Perez, was elected with 52 percent of the votes, avoiding a runoff election. By early 2002, control of the Legislative Assembly had also passed to ARENA, which maintained a working majority alliance with the Partido de Conciliacion Nacional (PCN).

The Republic of El Salvador was established in 1859. More than a century of civil strife and military rule followed. The civil war that raged from 1979 to 1991, and left more than 80,000 dead and 500,000 displaced, ended with the Chapultepec Accords. President Flores Perez canceled the 10-year anniversary celebrations set for March 15, 2002, after a boycott was threatened by the Frente Farabundo Marti (FMLN) and declared the accords finished. The 1983 constitution, and subsequent reforms, provide for a president elected for a five-year term and the 84-member, unicameral National Assembly elected for three years.

In 2002 two former generals, Jose Guillermo Garcia and Carlos Eugenio Vides Casanova, were on trial in Florida for torture and extrajudicial killing. After a general amnesty was granted to the armed forces in 1993, legal action for human rights abuses committed during the civil war moved to the United States. A case against the generals, accusing them of bearing ultimate responsibility for the killings of three nuns and a lay worker and for covering up the role of senior officers, had been dismissed by a U.S. appeals court. Former U.S. ambassador Robert White, who served in El Salvador at the time of the murders, had testified that he long believed that there was a cover-up of the killings by both the Salvadoran and the U.S. governments.

**Political Rights
and Civil Liberties:**

Citizens can change their government democratically. The 1999 elections were free and fair, though there were charges that hurricane relief funds were used by ARENA to elect President Francisco Flores Peres, and abstentions reached a new high. There are constitutional guarantees for freedom of expression, freedom of religion, and the right to organize political parties, civic groups, and labor unions. Seven political parties are represented in the assembly, and four more are recognized. There are eight unions and three business organizations, and while public employees are not allowed to have unions, they are represented by professional and employee organizations that engage in collective bargaining. Although the country is overwhelmingly Roman Catholic, evangelical Protestantism has made substantial inroads, leading to friction.

The 1992 peace accords led to a significant reduction in human rights violations; nevertheless, political expression and civil liberties are still circumscribed by sporadic political violence, repressive police measures, a mounting crime wave, and right-wing death squads, including "social cleansing" vigilante groups. The crime wave has also been fed by the deportation of hundreds of Salvadorans with criminal records from the United States; gang violence is pronounced. Random killings, kidnappings, and other crimes—particularly in rural areas—have reinforced the country's reputation as one of the most violent in Latin America. The Office of the Human Rights Ombudsman, who is elected by the National Assembly for a three-year term, was created by the peace accords with an amendment to the constitution defining its role. The office has been accused of corruption and is hampered by staffing problems, including a 17-month period when there was no ombudsman.

The judicial system is ineffectual and corrupt, and a climate of impunity is pervasive. Poor training and a lack of sustained disciplinary action for judges, as well as continued corruption, a lack of professionalism, and a slow system of processing cases, greatly undermine public confidence in the justice system. Violence against women and children is widespread and common. Human trafficking for prostitution is a serious problem, and up to 40 percent of victims are children.

El Salvador is one of the few Latin American countries to formally restrict military involvement in internal security, but the army occasionally joins the police in patrolling San Salvador and some rural districts in crackdowns on gang violence. The National Civilian Police, which incorporated some former FMLN guerrillas into its ranks, has been unable to curb the country's crime while protecting human rights. Complaints of police brutality and corruption are widespread; scores of police have been imprisoned on human rights charges. Prisons are overcrowded, conditions are shameful, and up to three-quarters of the prisoners are waiting to be charged and tried.

The media are privately owned. There are five daily newspapers and 12 television stations. Two cable television systems cover much of the capital, and other cable companies operate in major cities. All carry major local stations and a wide range of international programming. There are approximately 20 small cable television companies across the country, serving limited local areas. There are some 150 licensed radio stations, and broadcasts from neighboring countries are available. A national defense bill approved by the assembly in August of 2002 raised concerns that reporters would have to reveal their sources. Books, magazines, films, and plays are not censored. Academic freedom is respected.

Equatorial Guinea

Polity: Presidential
(military-dominated)
Economy: Capitalist-
statist
Population: 500,000
PPP: $15,073
Life Expectancy: 51

Political Rights: 7*
Civil Liberties: 6
Status: Not Free

Religious Groups: Roman Catholic (predominant) (80 percent)
Ethnic Groups: Bioko [primarily Bubi, some Fernandinos], Rio Muni [primarily
Fang], other
Capital: Malabo
Ratings Change: Equatorial Guinea's political rights rating declined from 6 to 7 after
authorizes conducted an unfair trial of many of the government's political opponents,
jailed them, and then moved up by two months presidential elections that were neither
free nor fair.

Ten-Year Ratings Timeline (Political Rights, Civil Liberties, Status)

1993	1994	1995	1996	1997	1998	1999	2000	2001	2002	2003
7,6NF	7,7NF	7,7NF	7,7NF	7,7NF	7,7NF	7,7NF	7,7NF	7,7NF	6,6NF	7,6NF

Overview:

After initially appearing to be making steps toward improving its records on political and human rights, the government of Equatorial Guinea took several steps back in 2002.
Authorities in March began rounding up members of the political opposition, claiming that a coup plot was underway. By May, 144 people had been detained. International human rights groups condemned the trial that followed in which 68 people
were sentenced to prison terms ranging from 6 to 20 years. Among those convicted
was Placido Miko, the prominent leader of the opposition Convergence for Social
Democracy party, who was sentenced to 14 years. Defendants alleged that their
statements were exacted under torture during incommunicado detention.

The mass arrests appeared to be an effort by the government of President
Teodoro Obiang Nguema Mbasogo to clear the playing field ahead of presidential
elections that were originally scheduled for February 2003. Obiang further consolidated the position of the ruling party by moving the elections up to December 2002.
He won the election with nearly 100 percent of the vote. Four opposition candidates
withdrew from the election at the last minute, citing irregularities and saying there
was no chance of fairness.

Equatorial Guinea achieved independence in 1968 following 190 years of Spanish rule. It has since been one of the world's most tightly closed and repressive
societies. President Obiang seized power in 1979 by deposing and murdering his
uncle, Francisco Macias Nguema. Pressure from donor countries demanding democratic reforms prompted Obiang to proclaim a new "era of pluralism" in January 1992.
Political parties were legalized and multiparty elections announced, but in practice
Obiang and his clique wield all power.

The UN Human Rights Commission terminated the mandate of the special investigator for Equatorial Guinea in April 2002, saying it aimed instead to encourage the government to implement a national human rights action plan.

Equatorial Guinea is the continent's third-largest oil producer and boasts one of the highest figures for per capita gross domestic product in Africa. The oil sector has led to more jobs but the lives of most people have yet to change. U.S. oil companies have invested at least $5 billion in Equatorial Guinea since the mid-1990s. The World Bank resumed cooperation with the country in 2002 after a ten-year break.

Political Rights and Civil Liberties: Equatorial Guinea's citizens are unable to change their government through peaceful, democratic means. The December 2002 election was not credible. The four opposition challengers withdrew from the poll, citing irregularities. The candidates said soldiers, police, and electoral officials were present at polling stations and were opening ballot envelopes after votes were cast. President Teodoro Obiang Nguema Mbasogo was declared the winner of his third 7-year term with 99.5 percent of the vote. The 1996 presidential election was neither free nor fair, and was marred by official intimidation, a near total boycott by the political opposition, and very low voter turnout.

The 1999 parliamentary elections were also marred by intimidation and fraud and were neither free nor fair. Many opposition candidates were arrested or confined to their villages prior to the polls. The ruling Democratic Party of Equatorial Guinea (PDGE) won 75 of 80 seats. Led jointly by the Convergence for Social Democracy and the Popular Union, seven opposition parties claimed massive fraud, demanding an annulment. Those opposition candidates that had won parliamentary seats refused to take them up. Amnesty International said at least 90 opposition party activists were detained for short periods in 1999.

President Obiang wields broad decree-making powers and effectively bars public participation in the policy-making process. Most opposition parties are linked with the ruling party, and several remain officially banned. By moving the presidential election up two months and jailing political opponents, Obiang could be hoping to avoid controversy such as fraud claims that followed previous elections.

The judiciary is not independent, and laws on search and seizure, as well as detention, are routinely ignored by security forces, who act with impunity. Civil cases rarely go to trial. A military tribunal handles cases tied to national security. Unlawful arrests remain commonplace. Prison conditions are extremely harsh. Abuse combined with poor medical care has led to several deaths. There are no effective domestic human rights organizations in the country, and the few international nongovernmental organizations operating in Equatorial Guinea are prohibited from promoting or defending human rights.

The trial of 144 people in 2002 on suspicion of coup plotting received international condemnation as being unfair. London-based Amnesty International said no evidence was presented against any defendant and called on authorities to conduct a new trial within a reasonable time for the 68 people who were sentenced or else to release them. It also demanded an investigation into allegations by the defendants that they were tortured, adding that it had evidence that the torture continued during the trial. Amnesty said the sentences were unfair, heavy, and passed on the sole basis of statements extracted under torture during incommunicado detention. None of the detainees was allowed access to medical treatment, and some were denied food brought by their families.

An opposition political activist, Juan Ondo Nguema, died in detention in July 2002 after he was sentenced to more than six years in jail. International human rights groups blamed his death on injuries resulting from torture during police investigations. Equatorial Guinea accused local political groups and international organizations of "disrespectful judgments" and "acts of open hostility" against the government.

Press freedom is constitutionally guaranteed, but the government restricts those rights in practice. Nearly all print and broadcast media are state run and tightly controlled. The 1992 press law authorizes government censorship of all publications. Mild criticism of infrastructure and public institutions is allowed, but nothing disparaging about the president or security forces is tolerated.

Foreign publications have become more widely available in recent years. The shortwave programs of Radio France Internationale and Radio Exterior (the international shortwave service from Spain) can be heard. A few small independent newspapers publish occasionally but exercise self-censorship, and all journalists must be registered.

Reporters Sans Frontieres said independent journalists covering the trial of opposition figures in May were verbally threatened by presidential guards and police daily. At one point, presidential security guards threatened to bar journalist Rodrigo Angue Nguema and Pedro Nolasco Ndong, president of the Equatorial Guinea Press Association, from entering the court if they continued to "have contact" with the accused. Police also confiscated the equipment of a photographer from the independent newspaper *La Opinion*.

Authorities in May barred the press association from organizing activities it had scheduled to mark World Press Freedom Day. Several journalists, political leaders, and association heads complained in 2002 of increasing difficulties in accessing the Internet. They said illegal wiretapping had increased and that the country's sole Internet service provider allegedly monitored e-mail traffic closely.

About 80 percent of the population is Roman Catholic. Freedom of individual religious practice is generally respected, although President Obiang has warned the clergy against interfering in political affairs. Monopoly political power by the president's Mongomo clan of the majority Fang ethnic group persists. Differences between the Fang and the Bubi are a major source of political tension that often has erupted into violence. Fang vigilante groups have been allowed to abuse Bubi citizens with impunity.

Constitutional and legal protections of equality for women are largely ignored. Traditional practices discriminate against women, and few have educational opportunities or participate in the formal (business) economy or government. Violence against women is reportedly widespread. There is no child rights policy.

Freedom of association and assembly is restricted. Authorization must be obtained for any gathering of ten or more people for purposes the government deems political.

Steps have been made to reform the labor sector. The country's first labor union, the Small Farmers Syndicate, received legal recognition in 2000, and is independent. The government has ratified all International Labor Organization conventions. There are many legal steps required prior to collective bargaining.

Eritrea

Polity: Dominant party   **Political Rights:** 7
Economy: Mixed statist   **Civil Liberties:** 6
Population: 4,500,000   **Status:** Not Free
PPP: $837
Life Expectancy: 56
Religious Groups: Muslim, Coptic Christian,
Roman Catholic, Protestant
Ethnic Groups: Tigrinya (50 percent), Tigre and
Kunama (40 percent), Afar (4 percent), Saho (3 percent), other (3 percent)
Capital: Asmara

Ten-Year Ratings Timeline (Political Rights, Civil Liberties, Status)

1993	1994	1995	1996	1997	1998	1999	2000	2001	2002	2003
--	6,5NF	6,5NF	6,4NF	6,4NF	6,4NF	6,4NF	7,5NF	7,5NF	7,6NF	7,6NF

Overview:
In 2002, the government of President Isaias Afwerki continued its repressive policy of allowing neither opposition nor independent organizations in the political or civil sphere. In April the International Court in The Hague issued a final boundary demarcation of the Ethiopian-Eritrean boundary. Disputes over the border had led to warfare between the two countries. Both sides adopted the common border with reluctance, but also continued to lay claim to the town of Badme.

In 1950, after years of Italian occupation, Eritrea was incorporated into Ethiopia. Eritrea's independence struggle began in 1962 as a nationalist and Marxist guerrilla war against the Ethiopian government of Emperor Haile Selassie. The seizure of power by a Marxist junta in Ethiopia in 1974 removed the ideological basis of the conflict, and by the time Eritrea finally defeated Ethiopia's northern armies in 1991, the Eritrean People's Liberation Front (EPLF) had discarded Marxism. Internationally recognized independence was achieved in May 1993 after a referendum supervised by the United Nations produced a landslide vote for statehood.

War with Ethiopia broke out in 1998. In May 2000, an Ethiopian military offensive succeeded in making significant territorial gains. Eritrea signed a truce with Ethiopia in June 2000 and a peace treaty in December 2000. The agreement provided for a UN-led buffer force to be installed along the Eritrean side of the contested border and further negotiations to determine the final boundary line. The war had dominated the country's political and economic agenda and reflected deeper issues of nationalism and political mobilization by a government that has long used the presence of real or perceived enemies to generate popular support and unity.

In May 2001, a dissident group of 15 senior ruling-party members publicly criticized President Isaias and called for "the rule of law and for justice, through peaceful and legal ways and means." Eleven members of this group were arrested in September 2001, allegedly for treason (three members who were out of the country at the time escaped arrest and one withdrew his support for the group). They remained in jail throughout 2002. The small independent media sector was shut down, and as of September 2002, 18 journalists were imprisoned. Student leaders escaping persecution fled to Ethiopia.

In addition to the war with Ethiopia, since 1993 Eritrea has engaged in hostilities with Sudan and Yemen, and has also had strained relations with Djibouti. Eritrea's proclivity to settle disputes by the force of arms and the continued tight government control over the country's political life have dashed hopes raised by President Isaias's membership in a group of "new African leaders" who promised more open governance and a break with Africa's recent tradition of autocratic rule.

Political Rights and Civil Liberties: Created in February 1994 as a successor to the EPLF, the Popular Front for Democracy and Justice (PFDJ) maintains dominance over the country's political and economic life that is unlikely to change in the near or medium term future. Instead of moving towards creating a framework for a democratic political system, since the end of the war with Ethiopia the PFDJ has taken significant steps backward. The 2001 crackdown against those calling for greater political pluralism has chilled the already tightly controlled political atmosphere. National elections scheduled for December 2001 have been postponed indefinitely.

In 1994, a 50-member constitutional commission was established. In 1997, a new constitution authorizing "conditional" political pluralism with provisions for a multiparty system was adopted. The constitution provides for the election of the president from among the members of the national assembly by a vote of the majority of its members.

In 2000, the National Assembly determined that the first elections would be held in December 2001 and appointed a committee that issued draft regulations governing political parties. These draft regulations remain under consideration, and independent political parties authorized by the constitution do not exist. In theory, polls were supposed to have been held in 1998, but they were postponed indefinitely following the outbreak of hostilities with Ethiopia.

Eritrea's political culture places priority on group interests over those of the individual. This view has been forged in part by years of struggle against outside occupiers and an austere attachment to Marxist principles. Eritrea's aggressive foreign policy has contributed significantly to regional instability and to a sense of victimization among Eritreans, which in turn affords a rationale for continued strong central government control.

The new constitution's guarantees of civil and political liberties are unrealized, as pluralistic media and rights to political organization continue to be absent. A judiciary was formed by decree in 1993 and has yet to adopt positions that are significantly at variance with government perspectives. A low level of training and resources limits the courts' efficiency. Constitutional guarantees are often ignored in cases relating to state security. Arbitrary arrest and detention are problems. The provision of speedy trials is limited by a lack of trained personnel, inadequate funding, and poor infrastructure, and the use of a special court system limits due process.

The government has maintained a hostile attitude towards civil society and has refused international assistance designed to support the development of pluralism in society. The government controls most elements of civil life, either directly or through affiliated organizations.

Government control over all broadcasting and pressures against the independent print media have constrained public debate. The 1996 press law allows only qualified freedom of expression, subject to the official interpretation of "the objective reality of Eritrea." In its September 2001 crackdown, the government banned all privately owned newspapers while claiming that a parliamentary committee would examine conditions under which they would be permitted to re-open. According to Amnesty International, the newspapers were accused of contravening the 1996 Press Law, but their alleged offences were not specified.

In the days following the clampdown, 10 leading journalists were arrested by the police in Asmara. They had protested in writing to the Minister of Information concerning the arrest of members of the Group of 15 and the closure of the newspapers. Other journalists were arrested in 2002; some began a hunger strike in April 2002 and were then transferred from prison to unknown places of detention. This action and the absence of nongovernmental human rights organizations have had a dissuasive effect on the development of other civil society groups.

Official government policy is supportive of free enterprise, and citizens generally have the freedom to choose their employment, establish private businesses, and function relatively free of government harassment. Until recently, at least, government officials have enjoyed a reputation for relative probity.

Women played important roles in the guerilla movement, and the government has worked in favor of improving the status of women. In an effort to encourage broader participation by women in politics, the PFDJ named three women to the party's executive council and 12 women to the central committee in 1997. Women participated in the constitutional commission (filling almost half of the positions on the 50-person committee) and hold senior government positions, including those of minister of justice and minister of labor.

Equal educational opportunity, equal pay for equal work, and penalties for domestic violence have been codified; yet traditional societal discrimination persists against women in the largely rural and agricultural country. In general, religious freedom is observed, although Jehovah's Witnesses face some societal discrimination.

Estonia

Polity: Parliamentary democracy
Economy: Mixed capitalist
Population: 1,400,000
PPP: $10,066
Life Expectancy: 71
Religious Groups: Evangelical Lutheran, Russian Orthodox, Estonian Orthodox, other
Ethnic Groups: Estonian (65 percent), Russian (28 percent), other (7 percent)
Capital: Tallinn

Political Rights: 1
Civil Liberties: 2
Status: Free

Ten-Year Ratings Timeline (Political Rights, Civil Liberties, Status)

1993	1994	1995	1996	1997	1998	1999	2000	2001	2002	2003
3,3PF	3,2F	3,2F	2,2F	1,2F	1,2F	1,2F	1,2F	1,2F	1,2F	1,2F

Overview:

Longtime opposition leader Edgar Savisaar and his left-wing Center Party extended their influence at both the national and local governmental levels during 2002. Municipal elections in October led to Savisaar's reelection as mayor of the capital city, Tallinn, while the resignation of the prime minister in January paved the way for the Center Party to become a partner in the new national ruling coalition. In the foreign policy front, both the European Union (EU) and NATO extended invitations to Estonia for membership in 2004.

After gaining its independence from Russia in 1918, Estonia was occupied and annexed by the U.S.S.R. during World War II. Under Soviet rule, approximately one-tenth of Estonia's population was deported, executed, or forced to flee abroad. Subsequent Russian immigration substantially altered the country's ethnic composition, with ethnic Estonians constituting just over 61 percent of the population in 1989. Estonia regained its independence with the disintegration of the Soviet Union in 1991.

Despite capturing the largest percentage of votes in the March 1999 parliamentary election, the left-wing Center Party was effectively forced into the opposition when the Reform Party, Pro Patria, and the Moderates subsequently formed a center-right majority coalition government with 53 seats. Pro Patria's Mart Laar was named prime minister. Various political forces had expressed reluctance to cooperate with the Center Party and its leader, Edgar Savisaar, who served as Estonia's prime minister from 1990 to 1992.

The last few months of 2001 witnessed several surprising or dramatic political developments, including the September victory of former Soviet Estonian leader Arnold Ruutel to the largely ceremonial post of president. In early December, the Tallinn City Council ruling coalition collapsed when the Reform Party withdrew and formed a new coalition with the opposition Center Party; Savisaar was subsequently elected the capital city's mayor. Prime Minister Laar announced in late December that he would resign in January 2002 because of growing infighting among the national ruling coalition members, particularly after the Reform Party's break with the same coalition partners in Tallinn's City Council.

On January 8, 2002, Prime Minister Laar fulfilled his pledge to step down and was replaced on January 22 by Reform Party leader and former central bank president Siim Kallas. The new national government mirrored that of Tallinn's city government, with the Reform Party and Center Party agreeing to form the ruling coalition. In the October 20 local elections, the Center Party emerged the clear winner in Tallinn, as well as in the largest northwestern cities of Narva and Kohtla-Jarve. The Center and Reform parties signed coalition agreements in Tallinn, of which Savisaar was reelected mayor, and in Tartu, where the Reform Party captured the most seats. Voter turnout was more than 52 percent, higher than for the previous 1996 or 1999 elections.

Estonia achieved two of its long-standing foreign policy goals in 2002, receiving formal invitations in November from NATO and in December from the EU to join both organizations in 2004. On December 18, parliament approved a September 14, 2003, national referendum to vote on Estonia's entering the EU. According to recent public opinion polls, popular support for EU membership is around the 50 percent mark.

Political Rights and Civil Liberties:

Estonians can change their government democratically. However, the country's citizenship law has been criticized for disenfranchising many Russian speakers who arrived in Estonia during the Soviet era and are regarded as immigrants who must apply for citizenship. Although noncitizens may not participate in national elections, they can vote, but not serve as candidates, in local elections. In November 2001, parliament approved the abolition of Estonian-language requirements for candidates to parliament and local councils. Parliament also adopted legislation in late 2001 making Estonian the official working language of both parliament and local councils, although the government may grant local councils the right to use another language if it is the language of the majority of permanent residents in that locality. The 1992 constitution established a 101-member unicameral legislature elected for four-year terms, with a prime minister serving as head of government and a president in the largely ceremonial role of head of state. After the first president was chosen by popular vote in 1992, subsequent presidential elections reverted to parliamentary ballot. According to international observers, the 1995 and 1999 parliamentary elections were free and fair.

The government respects freedom of speech and the press. There are three national television stations, including two in private hands, that broadcast both Estonian- and Russian-language programs. Dozens of independent newspapers and radio stations offer diverse viewpoints.

Religious freedom is respected in law and practice in this predominantly Lutheran country. In April 2002, the government officially registered the statutes of the Estonian Orthodox Church of the Moscow Patriarchate, which is seeking recognition as the legal successor to the pre-World War II Orthodox Church in Estonia. The Estonian Apostolic Orthodox Church, which is under the jurisdiction of Constantinople, was registered in 1993 and became the legal successor to the Orthodox Church, and thus the sole legal heir to the church's postwar property.

The constitution guarantees freedom of assembly, and the government respects this provision in practice. Political parties are allowed to organize freely, although only citizens may be members. Workers have the right to organize freely, to strike, and to bargain collectively, and the main trade unions operate independently of the state.

While the judiciary is independent and generally free from governmental interference, the quality of some court decisions and the heavy workloads of many judges continue to be areas of concern. In March 2002, Judge Merle Parts, who presides over cases involving organized crime, was shot and seriously wounded. There have been reports that some police officers physically or verbally abuse suspects. Despite ongoing improvements in the country's prison system, overcrowding, a lack of financial resources, and inadequately trained staff remain problems.

Of Estonia's population of 1.4 million, more than 1 million are Estonian citizens, of which some 115,000 have been naturalized since 1992. Approximately 170,000 people are noncitizens, with most having obtained permanent or temporary Estonian residence permits. In May 2001, parliament adopted legislation setting out specific requirements of Estonian-language proficiency for private sector employees, such as pilots, rescue workers, and teachers; the law built upon a previous amendment to the language law passed in June 2000 requiring that Estonian be used in areas of the private sector in which it would be in the public interest, such as health or safety.

Although women enjoy the same legal rights as men, they continue to be underrepresented in senior-level business positions and the government.

Ethiopia

Polity: Dominant party
Economy: Mixed statist
Population: 67,700,000
PPP: $668
Life Expectancy: 52
Religious Groups: Muslim (45-50 percent), Ethiopian Orthodox (35-40 percent), other, including animists (10-20 percent)
Ethnic Groups: Oromo (40 percent), Amhara and Tigrean (32 percent), Sidamo (9 percent), other (19 percent)
Capital: Addis Ababa

Political Rights: 5
Civil Liberties: 5
Status: Partly Free

Ten-Year Ratings Timeline (Political Rights, Civil Liberties, Status)

1993	1994	1995	1996	1997	1998	1999	2000	2001	2002	2003
6,4PF	6,5,NF	6,5,NF	4,5PF	4,5PF	4,5PF	4,4PF	5,5PF	5,5PF	5,5PF	5,5PF

Overview:

The past year in Ethiopia was marked by both positive and negative events. In April the International Court in The Hague issued a final boundary demarcation of the Ethiopian-Eritrean boundary. Border disputes had led to warfare between the two countries. Both countries reluctantly agreed to the common border, but they also continued to claim the town of Badme. Ethiopia was also admitted to the joint International

Monetary Fund-World Bank Heavily Indebted Poor Countries (HIPC) initiative, which qualifies the country for debt relief. Internally, however, the year was marked by an upsurge in guerilla activity by the Oromo Liberation Front and heavy-handed government intimidation of regime opponents, especially in the southern Oromo-dominated region.

Ethiopia, with a mixed ethnic makeup reflecting its imperial heritage, is the third most populous country in Africa. The Ethiopian Coptic Church is influential, particularly in the north. In the south there is a large Muslim community, made up mainly of Arabs, Somalis, and Oromos. Christians and Muslims account for approximately 40 percent each of the population, with the remainder largely animists.

Ethiopia's long tradition of imperial rule ended in 1974, when Emperor Haile Selassie was overthrown in a Marxist military coup. Colonel Mengistu Haile Mariam subsequently became the leader of a brutal dictatorship which was overthrown by a coalition of guerilla groups in 1991. These groups were spearheaded by the Ethiopian People's Revolutionary Democratic Front (EPRDF), itself an alliance of five parties.

The EPRDF government instituted a transition period that resulted in the establishment of formal democratic institutions. There are currently more than 60 legally recognized political parties active in Ethiopia, although the political scene continues to be dominated by the EPRDF. Opposition parties claim that their ability to function is seriously impeded by governmental harassment, although observers note that these parties are often reluctant to participate in the political process. In April 2001, students went on strike at the leading institution of higher education, Addis Ababa University, to protest the government's repressive policies and seek an end to police brutality. The strikes and the response by security forces resulted in more than 40 deaths and 200 injuries. Hundreds were arrested, including prominent human rights leaders.

There is a small but growing civil society, which has been subject to some restrictions by the government.

According to Human Rights Watch and the Ethiopian Human Rights Council, in early 2002 five students were killed and dozens arrested as Oromiya state police violently dispersed peaceful marches by high school students protesting regional government educational and land policies. In May, 30 people were reported killed when soldiers fired on 3,000 demonstrators in Awasa, south of the capital. In July, 150 Oromo rebels reportedly were killed and 340 were captured in two battles with the national army near Gambela. The Ethiopian government undertook a violent crackdown on students from Oromiya regional state.

Political Rights and Civil Liberties: Ethiopia is a federation of 11 regions, with a bicameral legislature and an executive prime minister. The EPRDF has been in power since 1991, although six other major parties and numerous smaller ones participate in the political system.

The 1995 constitution has a number of unique features, including decentralization based on ethnicity and the right to secession. The government has devolved some power to regional and local governments and courts. As with many elements of the Ethiopian political system, however, the reality differs from what is constitutionally mandated, in practice seriously limiting the right of the people to select their government. The EPRDF today controls all of the elected regional councils directly or with coalition partners. The government uses divide-and-rule strategies to minimize the influence of larger ethnic groups, selectively harassing opposition parties and impeding their ability to participate in the political process. It is also highly unlikely that any region would, in fact, be allowed to secede.

Executive power is vested in a prime minister, who is selected by the Council of People's Representatives. The first official multiparty elections to the council in 1995 were boycotted by the opposition. As expected, the EPRDF gained a landslide victory against a weak and divided opposition in the 2000 legislative balloting. A handful of opposition candidates were elected, but the parliament subsequently reelected Prime Minister Meles Zenawi to another five-year term.

Opposition parties and some observers criticized the government's conduct of the May 2000 legislative elections. They stated that the polls were subject to governmental interference, that the opposition was denied some access to the media, and that opposition supporters were subjected to harassment and detention. However, the opposition was able to engage in some criticism of the government in the media during the official election campaign, and a series of unprecedented public debates was broadcast over state-run radio and television during the electoral campaign.

Opposition parties also bear some responsibility for limiting in practice the right of Ethiopian people to express their political preferences. Until the 2000 elections, many parties refused to participate openly in the nation's political life. Leaders of one key party, the All Amhara People's Organization (AAPO), made it clear that the party was only taking part because it would lose its legally constituted status if it failed to take part in two consecutive elections. Some parties have supported, either directly or indirectly, armed resistance to the government.

In May 2002 the International Federation of Human Rights charged that "serious human rights violations persist in Ethiopia." Federal and regional government authorities tend to view all forms of protest against their policies as instigated by the rebel Oromo Liberation Front, which is leading a decade-long armed struggle for the autonomy of Oromiya. The state government, the federal police, and the military have a history of repression and abuse, mainly involving Oromo intellectuals and community leaders who are viewed as sympathetic to the OLF. Refugees who have fled to neighboring countries in the past decade have told of the widespread use of torture and extrajudicial killing in the region.

Freedom of association is limited, and civil society organizations often face arbitrary harassment, including suspension and banning. Meetings called by the Addis Ababa Teachers' Association in 2002, for example, were forbidden by the City Administration, which said the association had no legal recognition by the government. In 2001 two leading human rights advocates were arrested on charges of "inciting students" after a meeting to discuss human rights attended by a large number of students from Addis Ababa University. In August 2001 the respected Ethiopian Women Lawyers Association was suspended for three months by the government. The Ministry of Justice stated that the association had been suspended as it was found to be engaged in activities that were "outside its established objectives" after it criticized the government's handling of a woman's abuse case.

A 1992 law guarantees freedom of the press. Televised debates between the prime minister and the academic community on policy directions took place in 2002. However, the law also forbids publishing articles that are defamatory, threaten the safety of the state, agitate for war, or incite ethnic conflict. Journalists also can be jailed for publishing secret court records. Limits on the freedom of the press were clearly reflected in the government's response to the April 2001 unrest, in which journalists were arrested. Broadcast media remain under close scrutiny by the government. Harassment and intimidation of the independent print media have led to significant self-censorship. The press continues to be faced with direct and indirect government intimidation. In 2002, for example, Reporters Sans Frontieres criticized the jailing of three journalists who were imprisoned for "inventing news likely to demoralise the army and make people anxious," libel, and for publishing "immoral and indecent material."

In August 2002 the Committee to Protect Journalists charged that Ethiopia had "a dismal press record," and that the government there "is planning alarming changes to the country's 10-year press laws that would severely restrict the rights of Ethiopia's already beleaguered private press corps."

Women traditionally have few land or property rights and, especially in rural areas, few opportunities for employment beyond agricultural labor. Violence against women and social discrimination are reportedly common despite legal protections. Trade union freedom to bargain and strike has not yet been fully tested. Religious freedom is generally respected. Privatization programs are proceeding, and the government has undertaken a major financial liberalization reform program to attract foreign investment. The judiciary is officially independent, although there are no significant examples of decisions at variance with government policy.

Fiji

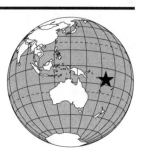

Polity: Parliamentary democracy
Economy: Capitalist
Population: 900,000
PPP: $4,668
Life Expectancy: 67

Political Rights: 4
Civil Liberties: 3
Status: Partly Free

Religious Groups: Christian (52 percent), Hindu (38 percent), Muslim(8 percent), other (2 percent)
Ethnic Groups: Fijian [Melanesian-Polynesian] (51 percent), Indian (44 percent), other (5 percent)
Capital: Suva

Ten-Year Ratings Timeline (Political Rights, Civil Liberties, Status)

1993	1994	1995	1996	1997	1998	1999	2000	2001	2002	2003
4,3PF	4,3PF	4,3PF	4,3PF	4,3PF	4,3PF	4,3PF	2,3F	6,3PF	4,3PF	4,3PF

Overview:

Fijian politics remained sharply polarized in 2002, as agricultural land rights and other divisive issues continued to drive a wedge between the South Pacific country's two main ethnic groups. Talks between the government, dominated by indigenous Fijians, and ethnic Indian leaders over renewing leases held by Indian tenant farmers on land owned by indigenous Fijians broke down in December. Prime Minister Laisenia Qarase's government, meanwhile, defied a court order to give cabinet posts to the main ethnic Indian party — a factor reportedly cited by ethnic Indian leader Mahendra Chaudhry in pulling out of the land talks.

Coming two years after an armed gang of indigenous Fijians ousted Chaudhry after he became Fiji's first ethnic Indian prime minister, the tensions dimmed prospects for a revival of the critical sugar and tourism industries.

The British colonized this isolated archipelago in 1874 and began bringing Indian laborers to work on their sugar plantations five years later. At independence in 1970, the indigenous Fijian and ethnic Indian communities were roughly equal in size.

Following 17 years of rule by the indigenous-Fijian Alliance Party, the 1987 elections brought to power for the first time a government made up largely of ethnic Indians. Backed by indigenous Fijian hard-liners, Sitiveni Rabuka, a senior army officer, seized power in two coups that year. Rabuka and his supporters said that they were concerned with the growing clout of the ethnic Indian community, which already dominated agriculture and business.

Rabuka led an indigenous Fijian party to victory in elections in 1992 and 1994 that were held under a new constitution that ensured indigenous Fijian control of parliament. To help stem a continuing exodus of thousands of skilled ethnic Indians, parliament in 1997 struck these guarantees from the constitution.

The first elections under the amended constitution, in March 1999, brought to power a multiracial coalition government under Chaudhry, head of the Fiji Labor Party (FLP), who became the country's first prime minister of Indian descent. Chaudhry soon angered many indigenous Fijians by pressuring landowners to renew expiring 30-year leases held by ethnic Indian tenant farmers without much of an increase in rents. Many indigenous Fijian landowners, who together own roughly 83 percent of the land, want to put their property to other uses once the leases expire.

This puts them at odds with ethnic Indian tenant farmers, who are the main producers of sugar and other cash crops. The Chaudhry government also awarded a contract for logging on indigenous Fijian land to a British company rather than accepting a more lucrative American bid.

Calling for greater indigenous Fijian rights, an armed gang that included more than 50 rebel soldiers and was led by George Speight, a businessman, seized the parliament building in Suva and held Chaudhry and other officials hostage for 56 days in mid-2000. After defusing the crisis, the military installed Qarase, a banker, to lead an interim government. Speight pleaded guilty to treason charges in 2002.

Qarase led his new Fiji United Party (FUP), a moderate indigenous Fijian group, to victory in elections held in August and September 2001. The FUP won 32 seats, the FLP, 27, and smaller parties and independents, 12. Qarase formed a new government without the FLP despite a constitutional provision requiring that any party receiving more than 10 percent of the parliamentary seats be offered cabinet posts. As 2002 ended, Qarase was continuing to defy court orders earlier in the year to give the FLP cabinet seats.

Despite the collapse of talks late in the year, Qarase vowed to press ahead in 2003 with efforts to replace the current legislation governing agricultural leases with a law that would provide incentives to indigenous Fijians to continue renting out their land for agriculture. Already, some ethnic Indians have been forced off their farms after their leases expired.

The Fiji Cane Growers Association, an industry group, warned that sugar production, an economic mainstay, was falling because of uncertainties over land tenure. Others suggested, however, that the industry's inefficiency was also to blame. To this end, the government said in November that it would begin selling off Fiji's sugar mills in 2003, even though this could lead to large job losses. The government said that privatization is needed in order to sharpen the sugar industry's competitiveness before European Union subsidies are phased out in 2008. Sugar growing accounts for 7 percent of economic output, and around 200,000 people, a quarter of Fiji's population, depend on the industry.

A court martial in November, meanwhile, handed down prison terms to 15 soldiers convicted of trying to stage a mutiny two years earlier. The military, however, appears to be preventing police from investigating and prosecuting soldiers who reportedly beat to death four of the mutineers immediately following the uprising.

Political Rights and Civil Liberties: Fiji returned to elected rule in 2001, although the army's refusal to restore the Chaudhry government to power after the 2000 coup attempt casts doubt on whether a government led by ethnic Indians could survive.

Moreover, the 1997 constitution, while ending the guaranteed parliamentary majority enjoyed by indigenous Fijians, gives them several political advantages. Voting in the 71-seat lower house is still partially along ethnic lines, and indigenous Fijians hold more of the reserved seats than do ethnic Indians. The house has 25 seats open to all races, 23 reserved for indigenous Fijians, 19 for ethnic Indians, 3 for "general electors" (mainly whites and East Asians), and 1 for voters on Rotuma Island.

In addition, the constitution empowers the Great Council of Chiefs, a traditional indigenous Fijian body, to name the largely ceremonial president, who in turn appoints the 32-member Senate. Moreover, it calls for the civil service to reflect the country's ethnic makeup. Successive governments have used this provision to place indigenous Fijians and Rotumans in at least half of public sector jobs at all levels, including in most senior posts.

Press freedom and human rights groups have criticized provisions of a 1998 security law that would allow the government to restrict civil liberties during a state of emergency. The law, the Emergency Powers Act, allows parliament to censor the press, ban public meetings, and authorize searches without warrants and the seizure of private property.

Fiji's judiciary has bolstered its long-standing reputation for independence with several rulings against the government since the 2000 coup attempt. These include the 2002 order to Qarase's government to include the FLP, and a ruling that declared Qarase's previous, interim government to be illegal, forcing it to hold elections. The courts are heavily backlogged, though, so that suspects are often held in custody for long periods before their trials.

Police and soldiers have in past years abused detainees and defendants out on bail and illegally detained suspects, according to the U.S. State Department's global human rights report for 2001, released in March 2002. Prison conditions are "extremely harsh" because of overcrowding and limited food and sanitation, the report added. Human rights groups criticize the government for being slow to punish indigenous Fijians who, during the 2000 crisis, looted and burned many ethnic Indian shops and homes on Fiji's two largest islands, Viti Levu and Vanua Levu.

Fiji's private media vigorously report on alleged official wrongdoing and publish some editorials critical of the government, but journalists generally practice "considerable self-censorship," according to the U.S. State Department Human Rights report. The Qarase government has at times tried to pressure editors and otherwise interfered with the press, the report added. The government owns shares in the *Fiji Post* newspaper and has business links to its main English-language competitor, the *Fiji Sun*, which raises questions about the concentration of media ownership.

Journalists are subject to a strict press law that has never been used but remains on the books. The Press Correction Act authorizes officials to arrest anyone who publishes "malicious" material, or to order a publication to print a "correcting statement" to an allegedly false or distorted article. Past governments, however, did use another law, the Parliamentary Privileges and Powers Act, to bring actions against newspapers over their parliamentary coverage. The journalists ultimately were not punished under the act, which authorizes jail terms of up to two years for breaches of parliamentary privilege.

In another freedom of expression concern, the Qarase government has denied permits for several high-profile political marches and rallies.

Women hold relatively few jobs in government and politics, although they have made significant inroads in the civil service, businesses, and the professions. Credible accounts suggest that 10 percent of Fijian women have been abused in some way, the U.S. State Department report said. Women's groups also are concerned that most rape sentences are lenient, while the practice of *bulubulu* (traditional reconciliation) allows some offenders to apologize to the victim's relatives and avoid felony charges altogether. Modernization, meanwhile, has contributed to an erosion of traditional family and village structures, which is blamed in part for increased child abuse and the growing number of homeless youths in cities.

Fijians of all faiths can generally worship freely. Most indigenous Fijians are Christians, while most ethnic Indians are Hindus.

Fijian trade unions are independent and vigorous, and roughly 55 percent of the workforce is unionized. The country, however, lacks laws on anti-union discrimination in factories. This means that workers in newer industries, such as the garment sector, often are afraid to organize. Newspaper reports and nongovernmental groups allege that some garment factories use bonded or forced labor and make women work excessive hours.

Finland

Polity: Parliamentary democracy
Economy: Mixed capitalist
Population: 5,200,000
PPP: $24,996
Life Expectancy: 78

Political Rights: 1
Civil Liberties: 1
Status: Free

Religious Groups: Evangelical Lutheran (89 percent), Russian Orthodox (1 percent), none (9 percent), other (1 percent)
Ethnic Groups: Finnish (93 percent), Swedish (6 percent), other, including Lapp [Saami] (1 percent)
Capital: Helsinki

Ten-Year Ratings Timeline (Political Rights, Civil Liberties, Status)

1993	1994	1995	1996	1997	1998	1999	2000	2001	2002	2003
1,1F	1,1F	1,1F	1,1F	1,1F	1,1F	1,1F	1,1F	1,1F	1,1F	1,1F

Overview:

Finland adopted the euro and raised the minimum age for engaging in armed conflict. The Green Party withdrew from the governing coalition. Finland came under pressure to accept more asylum seekers and refugees, and Finns continued to debate the merits of joining NATO during the year.

Finnish independence followed eight centuries of foreign domination, first by Sweden (until 1809) and subsequently as a Grand Duchy within the pre-revolutionary Russian Empire. Amendments to Finland's 1919 constitution came into force in 2000. The amendments diminish the president's power and increase the parliament's, giving the latter greater sway over calling elections and the appointing of national representatives to international gatherings, including EU meetings.

In January 2002, Finland adopted the euro as the national currency, the only Nordic EU member to do so.

The Green Party and its solitary minister, Satu Hassi, withdrew from the coalition government that has dominated politics since 1999, in response to parliament's vote on May 24 to approve the construction of a fifth nuclear reactor. Nevertheless, the surviving coalition members—the Social Democratic Party (SDP), the National Coalition Party, the Left Alliance, and the Swedish People's Party—led by the prime minister, Paavo Lipponen of the SDP, looked set to govern until the scheduled general election in March 2003.

In August, Finland deported 88 asylum-seeking Roma; they are now banned from entering Schengen Treaty countries (which consists of all EU member states, except Ireland and the UK, plus Iceland and Norway) and may have their passports confiscated for three years. The goal of the treaty is to eliminate border checks between member states and build a common area of security and justice. Finland had already rejected all 525 asylum requests filed by Roma since the start of 2002; nearly 300 were repatriated before the August expulsion.

Finland accepts fewer asylum seekers than its Nordic neighbors and has come under pressure to increase its intake. In 2001, there were 1,651 people applying for political asylum in Finland, of whom only 37 percent were accepted. Finland also took in 739 refugees through the resettlement program of the UN High Commissioner for Refugees. Over the same period, Sweden received 23,515 asylum applications (55 percent were accepted) and resettled 1,279 refugees. Denmark received 8,385 asylum applications (53 percent were accepted) and resettled 2,020 refugees. Norway received 14,782 asylum applications in 2001 (40 percent were accepted) and resettled 1,480 refugees.

Finland's support of the European security and defence policy and the U.S. fight against terrorism since September 11, 2001, suggests that Finland is no longer a neutral country in the traditional, isolationist sense. Moreover, the government is increasingly positive about NATO membership, but popular opposition remains strong. Finland is part of NATO's Partnership for Peace program.

Political Rights and Civil Liberties: Finns can change their government by democratic means. Finland has a 200-seat unicameral parliament, the Eduskunta; representatives are elected to four-year terms. The president is elected for six-year terms. The Aland Islands, populated mainly by Swedes, have their own provincial parliament; the local Liberal Party won the October 1999 elections. The result was a blow to earlier demands for greater autonomous powers in Aland, as the Liberals do not share either the Conservative Party or the Center Party belief that the current system is inadequate.

Finland has a large variety of newspapers and magazines and has one of the highest rates of Internet users per capita in the world. Newspapers are privately owned, some by political parties or their affiliates; many others are controlled by or support a particular party. A law grants every citizen the right to publish.

The rights of ethnic and religious minorities are protected. The Saamis (Lapps), who make up less than one percent of the population, are guaranteed cultural autonomy by the constitution. Since 1973, the Saami have elected, every four years, representatives to the 20-strong Saami parliament. Since 1991, the Saami have been heard in the Finnish parliament on matters concerning them—the only indigenous people with this right in Finland. Saamis no longer have exclusive right to their traditional livelihoods but may use their own language with authorities.

Both Finnish and Swedish are official languages of the country. Finland has the lowest percentage of foreigners, at 1.8 percent of the total population, of any EU country. Nevertheless, concern has arisen about the increasing number of racist and xenophobic incidents. To facilitate foreigners' absorption, the government revised Finland's Aliens Law and adopted a new law promoting immigrants' integration into Finnish society, both effective from May 1999. Reforms in 2000 allowed for more rapid processing of asylum claims filed by refugees from Poland, Slovakia, the Czech Republic, and Bulgaria. Most asylum seekers come from Russia, Estonia, Ukraine, and Turkey.

Finns enjoy freedom of religion, and both the predominant Lutheran Church and the smaller Russian Orthodox Church are financed through a special tax from which citizens may exempt themselves. The president appoints the archbishop and the bishops of the Lutheran Church.

The constitution provides for an independent judiciary, consisting of the Supreme Court, the supreme administrative court, and the lower courts. The president appoints Supreme Court judges, who in turn appoint the lower court judges.

Finland was rated the "least corrupt country" by Transparency International in 2002.

As of April, the Optional Protocol to the Convention on the Rights of the Child on the involvement of children in armed conflict raised the minimum age for direct participation in hostilities and for compulsory government recruitment to 18.

Finnish workers have the right to organize, bargain collectively, and strike, and most belong to trade unions. The 1.1 million-member Central Organization of Finnish Trade Unions, which is linked to the SDP, dominates the labor movement.

Gender-based equality is guaranteed by law. In 1906, Finland became the first European country to give women full political entitlement, including the right to vote and hold office. Women hold an exceptionally high proportion of parliamentary seats. In February 2000, in the second direct popular vote for president, Finns elected for the first time a woman president, Tarja Halonen, a left-leaning member of the SDP. Women earn about 83 percent of what men earn in the public sector and about 85 percent of what men earn in the private sector, according to Eurostat.

France

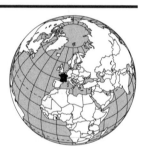

Polity: Presidential-parliamentary democracy
Economy: Mixed capitalist
Population: 59,500,000
PPP: $24,223
Life Expectancy: 79

Political Rights: 1
Civil Liberties: 1*
Status: Free

Religious Groups: Roman Catholic (83-88 percent), Protestant (2 percent), Muslim (5-10 percent), other (less than 10 percent)
Ethnic Groups: Celtic and Latin with Teutonic, Slavic, North African, Indochinese, Basque minorities
Capital: Paris
Ratings Change: France's civil liberties rating improved from 2 to 1 due to changes in the survey methodology.

Ten-Year Ratings Timeline (Political Rights, Civil Liberties, Status)

1993	1994	1995	1996	1997	1998	1999	2000	2001	2002	2003
1,2F	1,2F	1,2F	1,2F	1,2F	1,2F	1,2F	1,2F	1,2F	1,2F	1,1F

Overview:
In the year's polls, Jacques Chirac was reelected president, and his party gained a parliamentary majority. Following the terrorist attacks on September 11, 2001, new security laws, granting police sweeping new search-and-seizure powers, came into effect. Racist, anti-Semitic, and xenophobic behavior increased sharply. Police brutality against minorities remained an issue. Human rights groups voiced concern about the in-

crease in legal proceedings being launched against journalists, claiming such proceedings endanger freedom of the press and freedom of expression.

After World War II, France established a parliamentary Fourth Republic, which was governed by coalitions and ultimately failed because of the Algerian war. The Fifth Republic began in 1958 under Prime Minister (and later President) Charles de Gaulle. Since 1965, the president has been elected by popular vote. In October 2000, a referendum put presidential elections on the same schedule as parliamentary elections, thereby reducing the likelihood of "cohabitation"—having a president and a prime minister from different parties.

The right-of-center president, Jacques Chirac, defeated a far-right veteran, Jean-Marie Le Pen, in the second round of voting on May 5. Mr. Chirac was further rewarded with a huge parliamentary majority at the legislative election on June 16, which ended five years of cohabitation. The prime minister, appointed by the president, is Jean-Pierre Raffarin. The Union for the Presidential Majority (UMP), a federation of the Rally for the Republic (RPR), the Union for French Democracy (UDF), and the Liberal Democrats (DL) parties, won an outright parliamentary majority for the first time in more than 30 years. The government's priorities are to decentralize power; crack down on crime; cut income tax; relax the lois Aubry (a law that limits the workweek to 35 hours); and tackle pension reform.

Now that President Chirac has triumphed over the corruption scandal that dogged him throughout 2001—which involved an alleged slush fund set up to funnel bribes from public works contracts to his RPR party—the French daily *Le Monde* reported that he is working to fire those who he believes helped publicize the scandals. They include the heads of the two main intelligence services, the General Directorate of External Security espionage agency and the Directorate for Territorial Surveillance for Counterespionage.

In January 2002, France adopted the euro as the national currency.

A sharp rise in racist, anti-Semitic, and xenophobic behavior in Western Europe followed the September 11 terrorist attacks on the United States. In France the rise was particularly evident. Between March 29 and April 17, 2002, the police recorded 395 anti-Semitic incidents, 63 percent of which involved anti-Semitic graffiti; between January 1 and April 2, police recorded 34 "serious anti-Semitic actions," for example, attacks on Jewish persons or property, including synagogues and cemeteries.

The European parliament amended in May the 1997 European Community directive on privacy in telecommunications, obliging member states to retain all telecommunications data for one to two years and to provide the relevant authorities unrestricted access to these data in order to assist law enforcement officials in eradicating crime. Human rights groups attacked this move as an assault on privacy and civil liberty.

In July, France and Britain agreed to close the Sangatte Red Cross refugee center, which houses about 1,700 mainly Afghan and Kurdish asylum seekers, by early 2003 with help from the UN High Commissioner for Refugees (UNHCR). Sangatte, located on France's northern coast about a mile from the Channel Tunnel entrance, became a base for constant attempts to cross illegally to England, causing strains in relations between the two countries. By October, five Afghans had voluntarily repatriated to Afghanistan under the Tripartite Agreement signed by France, Afghanistan and the UNHCR.

Political Rights and Civil Liberties: French citizens can change their government democratically by directly electing the president and National Assembly. The constitution grants the president significant emergency powers, including rule by decree under certain circumstances. The president may call referenda and dissolve parliament, but may not veto parliamentary acts or routinely issue decrees. Decentralization has given mayors significant power over housing, transportation, schools, culture, welfare, and law enforcement. The judiciary is independent.

In November 2001, following the terrorist attacks on the United States, parliament adopted new antiterror legislation. Police may search cars with a prosecutor's authorization and other private property without warrants. They have greater access to private telephone conversations and e-mail. Judges can demand that phone and Internet companies save telecommunications data for one to two years.

In December 2001, the Council of the European Union adopted by "written procedure" antiterrorism legislation that requires member states to prevent "the public" from offering "any form of support, active or passive" to terrorists and to check all refugees and asylum seekers for terrorist connections. Human rights groups criticized the legislation because it does not distinguish between conscious or unconscious assistance, treats would-be immigrants as criminals, and was not debated in parliament before being adopted.

In January 2002, *Le Monde* reported that six journalists' phones had been tapped in 2000 and 2001 as part of French National Anti-Terrorist Service investigations into events in Corsica. In February, five journalists and editors of Radio France were charged with making "racist insults" and for "complicity" because of a satirical program about Corsicans broadcast in May 2001 by the affiliated station France Inter. Reporters Without Borders criticized the charges as undermining freedom of expression and contradicting European Court of Human Rights rulings regarding press freedoms.

The Internal Security Guidance and Planning Law was passed in July 2002. The law gives police, with a judge's permission, the power to make remote online searches of Internet service providers and their records of customers' Internet activities and private and professional e-mail traffic. Critics are concerned about Internet-based freedom of expression and individual rights to confidentiality.

In April, journalists were verbally insulted and physically attacked during a demonstration by Jewish organizations that accused the media of "twisting" the news to favor Palestinians over Israelis. In May, several Jewish organizations brought a lawsuit against a journalist and radio host for broadcasting anti-Israeli remarks to listeners. The RSF voiced concern over increasingly common legal actions against the right to free expression.

In December 2001, parliament devolved to Corsica's parliament some legislative autonomy and allowed the island's schools to conduct instruction in the Corsican language.

In January 2002, the case of Pascal Tais, who died in police custody in April 1993, was reopened by the Appeal Court of Bordeaux on the basis of new information alleging police brutality. The Court of Appeal of Versailles, in February, reduced the sentence of two police officers convicted in the death of Aissa Ihich (who died of an asthma attack in 1991 while in police custody) from 10-month suspended prison terms to 8 months, making the officers eligible for amnesty and enabling them to pursue their careers. The National Police directorate, in March, reported that the five officers who were found guilty of torturing Moroccan and Netherlands nationals Ahmed Selmouni and Abdelmajid Madi in 1991 had been transferred to other police services and would not be receiving further disciplinary action.

Despite open suspicion toward Muslims and prohibitions against wearing religious garb or symbols in state schools, religious freedom is protected. Parliament adopted in June 2001 a bill allowing courts to ban groups considered sects.

Transparency International ranked France 25th on its 2002 Corruption Perceptions Index, the lowest evaluation of any EU member state, except Portugal.

Labor rights are respected, and strikes are widely and effectively used to protest government economic policy. Women enjoy equal rights in France but earn only 73 percent of what men earn.

Gabon

Polity: Dominant party
Economy: Capitalist
Population: 1,200,000
PPP: $6,237
Life Expectancy: 50
Religious Groups: Christian (55 -75 percent),
Animist (25-45 percent)
Ethnic Groups: Bantu, other Africans, Europeans
Capital: Libreville

Political Rights: 5
Civil Liberties: 4
Status: Partly Free

Ten-Year Ratings Timeline (Political Rights, Civil Liberties, Status)

1993	1994	1995	1996	1997	1998	1999	2000	2001	2002	2003
4,4PF	5,4PF	5,4PF	5,4PF	5,4PF	5,4PF	5,4PF	5,4PF	5,4PF	5,4PF	5,4PF

Overview:

The coalition cabinet appointed in January is likely to face increasing popular discontent as the true state of Gabon's economy begins to reveal itself. High oil prices have masked falling oil production. However, it is unlikely that Gabon will suffer from widespread popular unrest because the country's civil society is weak, the political opposition lacks cohesion, and President Omar Bongo is adept at the use of patronage. Gabon could draw increasing attention from the United States as Washington looks to alternative sources of oil instead of relying heavily on petroleum from the Persian Gulf states.

Straddling the equator on Central Africa's west coast, Gabon gained independence from France in 1960. Bongo, whom France raised from soldier to president in 1967, completed the consolidation of power begun by his predecessor, Leon Mba, by officially outlawing the opposition. France, which maintains marines in Gabon, has intervened twice to preserve Bongo's regime. In 1990, protests prompted by economic duress forced Bongo to accept a conference that opposition leaders hoped would promote a peaceful democratic transition. However, Bongo retained power in rigged 1993 elections that sparked violent protests, which were repressed by his presidential guard.

Three decades of autocratic and corrupt rule have made Bongo among the world's richest men, while some money has trickled down to rural areas and contributed to education. Oil accounts for 80 percent of the country's exports. State institutions are influenced or controlled by Bongo and a small elite, with strong backing by the Gabonese army and France. Bongo has introduced two new laws to fight corruption, which were approved by the National Assembly.

Political Rights and Civil Liberties: Gabon's citizens have never been able to exercise their constitutional right to change their government democratically, despite a gradual political opening up since 1990. There are numerous political parties, but the ruling Gabonese Democratic Party (PDG) has ruled since President Omar Bongo created it in 1968. Bongo's electoral victory in 1998, with 61 percent of the vote, followed a campaign that made profligate use of state resources and state media. The polling, which was partially boycotted by the opposition, was marked by serious irregularities. The National Election Commission proved neither autonomous nor competent. Legislative elections in 1993 and 1996 were also seriously flawed.

The PDG won parliamentary elections in December 2001. A divided opposition and low voter turnout, as well as government interference in the polls, helped assure the PDG victory. Ruling party candidates won 88 seats compared with 32 for opposition and independent candidates. Some opposition parties boycotted the vote. Following the 1996 local government elections, which gave the opposition several victories, the government transferred key electoral functions to the Interior Ministry, taking them from the electoral commission.

The judiciary suffers from political interference. Rights to legal counsel and a public criminal trial are generally respected. However, judges may deliver summary verdicts, and torture is sometimes used to produce confessions. Prison conditions are marked by beatings and insufficient food, water, and medical care. Arbitrary arrest and long periods of pretrial detention are common.

The rights of assembly and association are constitutionally guaranteed, but permits required for public gatherings are sometimes refused. Freedom to form and join political parties is generally respected, but civil servants may face harassment because of associations. Nongovernmental organizations operate openly, but local human rights groups are weak and not entirely independent.

Press freedom is guaranteed, but sometimes restricted in practice. The state is authorized to criminalize civil libel suits. A government daily and at least 10 private weeklies, which are primarily controlled by opposition parties, are published. At least six private radio and television broadcasters have been licensed and operate, but their viability is tenuous and most of the programming is nonpolitical.

While no legal restrictions on travel exist, harassment on political and ethnic bases has been reported. Discrimination against African immigrants, including harassment by security forces and arbitrary detention, is a problem. Most of Gabon's several thousand indigenous Pygmies live in the forest and are largely independent of the formal government. Religious freedom is constitutionally guaranteed and respected.

Legal protections for women include equal-access laws for education, business, and investment. In addition to owning property and businesses, women constitute more than 50 percent of the salaried workforce in the health and trade sectors, and women hold high-ranking positions in the military and judiciary. Women continue to face legal and cultural discrimination, however, particularly in rural areas, and are reportedly subject to widespread domestic violence.

Gabon has come under scrutiny for the exploitation of thousands of child laborers who are sent from other Central or West African countries to work as domestic servants. The government has cooperated with international organizations to fight child trafficking, but says it lacks sufficient funds and resources to tackle the problem.

The constitution recognizes the right to form unions, and virtually the entire formal private sector workforce is unionized. Collective bargaining is allowed by industry, not by firm.

The Gambia

Polity: Presidential-parliamentary
Economy: Capitalist
Population: 1,500,000
PPP: $1,649
Life Expectancy: 53
Religious Groups: Muslim (90 percent), Christian
(9 percent), indigenous beliefs (1 percent)
Ethnic Groups: Mandinka (42 percent), Fula (18 percent),
Wolof (16 percent), Jola (10 percent), Serahuli (9 percent), other (5 percent)
Capital: Banjul

Political Rights: 4*
Civil Liberties: 4*
Status: Partly Free

Ratings Change: The Gambia's political rights and civil liberties ratings both improved from 5 to 4 due to legislative elections that were more free and fair than previous polls, gradual improvements in the state of civil liberties, and changes in the survey methodology.

Ten-Year Ratings Timeline (Political Rights, Civil Liberties, Status)

1993	1994	1995	1996	1997	1998	1999	2000	2001	2002	2003
1,2F	2,2F	7,6NF	7,6NF	7,6NF	7,6NF	7,5NF	7,5NF	7,5NF	5,5PF	4,4PF

Overview:

The Gambia continued its process of simultaneously moving forward and stepping back in 2002. It held national assembly elections in January that showed signs of improvement over the previous legislative vote, but later the assembly passed a restrictive media bill. President Yahya Jammeh had not signed it into law by year's end. Low turnout marked the January polls, which were boycotted by prominent opposition parties, including the United Democratic Party (UDP). The ruling Alliance for Patriotic Reorientation and Construction (APRC) dominated the elections, following Jammeh's presidential victory in October 2001, although two opposition parties enjoyed minor gains. Neighboring Guinea-Bissau accused The Gambia of complicity in an alleged coup plot in 2002, which The Gambia denied, and the United Nations sent an envoy to help reduce tension between the two countries.

After gaining independence from Britain in 1965, The Gambia functioned as an electoral democracy under President Sir Dawda Jawara and his People's Progressive Party for almost 30 years. A 1981 coup by leftist soldiers was reversed by intervention from Senegal, which borders The Gambia on three sides. The two countries formed the Confederation of Senegambia a year later, but it was dissolved in 1989. Senegal declined to rescue the Jawara government again when Jammeh struck in 1994. The leaders of the 1994 coup denounced the ousted government's alleged corruption, promising transparency, accountability, and early elections. Instead, they quickly imposed draconian decrees curtailing civil and political rights and the free media. A new constitution, adopted by a closely controlled 1996 referendum, allowed Jammeh to transform his military dictatorship to a nominally civilian administration.

The Gambia is a poor, tiny country with few natural resources that depends on exports of peanuts and other commodities.

Political Rights and Civil Liberties: The Gambia's citizens were granted their right to choose or change their government for the first time in several years in 2001, despite sporadic violence preceding the polls. Jammeh repealed the repressive Decree 89, which had prohibited any former ministers from participating in political activity or taking another governmental post until 2024. The opposition was given free airtime on state-controlled radio and television. The Independent Electoral Commission was under some pressure by the ruling party but generally operated freely. Nevertheless, President Yahya Jammeh, of the APRC, defeated opposition leader Ousainou Darboe. Jammeh won 53 percent of the vote compared with 33 percent for Darboe, a human rights lawyer who headed a three-party opposition coalition. Three other candidates won a combined total of 14 percent.

Although observers from the EU and the Commonwealth declared the elections generally free and fair, there were lingering concerns about Jammeh's commitment to democracy when several opposition supporters, human rights workers, and journalists were detained after the polls. Allegations surfaced after the vote that Jammeh's party had brought in members of his ethnic group living in neighboring Senegal and issued them voter cards.

Some international observers described the January 2002 national assembly elections as "generally free and fair," in contrast to the highly flawed 1997 poll. However, the election was boycotted by the main opposition parties, including the UDP, and there were some administrative problems with voter registration. Of the 48 seats in the legislature chosen by popular vote, the ruling APRC won the most seats, 45, and two opposition parties captured a total of 3 seats.

The constitution provides for an independent judiciary. While lower courts are sometimes subject to executive influence, the judiciary in general has demonstrated its independence on several occasions, at times in significant cases. There are a number of judges from Nigeria, Ghana, and other African countries, who tend to operate fairly and vigorously. Local chiefs preside over courts at the village level. The judicial system recognizes customary law, or *Sharia* (Islamic law), primarily in marriage matters.

Although the Jammeh government has made some steps towards political openness, it still has extensive repressive powers. A 1995 decree allows the National Intelligence Agency to cite "state security" in order to "search, arrest, or detain any person, or seize, impound, or search any vessel, equipment, plant, or property without a warrant." In such cases, the right to seek a writ of habeas corpus is suspended. Torture in jails and barracks has been reported. However, conditions in some of the country's prisons have improved.

Civil liberties suffered in 2001 when authorities increased immunity from prosecution for the country's security forces. Parliament passed a law giving amnesty "for any fact, matter or omission of act, or things done or purported to have been done during any unlawful assembly, public disturbance, riotous situation or period of public emergency." The legislation was backdated to April 2000, when security forces had cracked down on demonstrators, killing 16 people. Human rights groups and other nongovernmental organizations generally operate freely in The Gambia, but human rights workers, opposition members, and journalists occasionally face harassment.

Press freedom is guaranteed, but harassment and self-censorship sometimes inhibit free expression of the country's vibrant, independent print media. International press freedom organizations protested the passing in 2002 of a restrictive media bill by the National Assembly. The National Media Commission Bill, which Jammeh had not yet signed into law at the end of 2002, would give government authorities the power to decide who is and is not a journalist, and to deny the right to confidentiality of sources.

Private broadcasters and newspapers in The Gambia struggle with exorbitant licensing fees they are required to pay. State-run Radio Gambia broadcasts only tightly controlled news that is also relayed by private radio stations. A single government-run television station operates. Citizen FM broadcasts in a number of indigenous languages, and it is an important source of independent information for rural Gambians. Authorities have occasionally shut it down.

Freedom of religion is guaranteed, and the government respects this right. Religious and traditional obstacles to the advancement of women are being addressed by both the government and women's organizations. Higher education and wage employment opportunities for women are still far fewer than those for men, especially in rural areas. Sharia provisions regarding family law and inheritance restrict women's rights. Female genital mutilation is widely practiced, but women's groups are working to eliminate the practice.

Gambians, except for civil service employees and members of the security forces, have the right to form unions, strike, and bargain for wages. There are two main labor unions, and about 10 percent of the workforce is unionized.

Georgia

Polity: Presidential-par-
liamentary democracy
Economy: Capitalist-
statist
Population: 4,400,000
PPP: $2,664
Life Expectancy: 73

Political Rights: 4
Civil Liberties: 4
Status: Partly Free

Religious Groups: Georgian Orthodox (65 percent),
Muslim (11 percent), Russian Orthodox (10 percent), other (14 percent)
Ethnic Groups: Georgian (70 percent), Armenian (8 percent),
Russian (6 percent), Azeri (6 percent), Ossetian (3 percent),
Abkhaz (2 percent), other (5 percent)
Capital: Tbilisi

Ten-Year Ratings Timeline (Political Rights, Civil Liberties, Status)

1993	1994	1995	1996	1997	1998	1999	2000	2001	2002	2003
4,5PF	5,5PF	5,5PF	4,5PF	4,4PF	3,4PF	3,4PF	3,4PF	4,4PF	4,4PF	4,4PF

Overview:

Already-tense relations between Georgia and Russia plunged to a new low in 2002 over charges that Georgia was harboring Chechen rebels in its Pankisi Gorge region. After the Russian military conducted several bombing raids on Georgian territory and threatened additional strikes, Tbilisi responded by ordering an anticrime and anti-terrorist operation in Pankisi and extraditing several Chechen rebels to Russia. On the domestic front, local elections held in June saw the long-standing dominance of President Eduard Shevardnadze's former power base, the Citizens' Union of Georgia (CUG), lose ground to several rival parties. A final settlement to the protracted conflicts in the separatist regions of Abkhazia and South Ossetia remained elusive at year's end.

Absorbed by Russia in the early nineteenth century, Georgia gained its independence in 1918. In 1922, it entered the U.S.S.R. as a component of the Transcaucasian Federated Soviet Republic, becoming a separate union republic in 1936. An attempt by the region of South Ossetia in 1990 to declare independence from Georgia and join Russia's North Ossetia sparked a war between rebels and Georgian forces. Although a ceasefire was signed in June 1992, the territory's final political status remains unresolved.

Following a national referendum in April 1991, Georgia declared its independence from the Soviet Union. Nationalist leader and former dissident Zviad Gamsakhurdia was elected president in May. The following year, he was overthrown by opposition forces and replaced with former Georgian Communist Party head and Soviet foreign minister Eduard Shevardnadze. Parliamentary elections held the same year resulted in more than 30 parties and blocs gaining seats, although none secured a clear majority.

In 1993, Georgia experienced the violent secession of the long-simmering Abkhazia region and armed insurrection by Gamsakhurdia loyalists. Although

Shevardnadze blamed Russia for arming and encouraging Abkhazian separatists, he legalized the presence of 19,000 Russian troops in Georgia in exchange for Russian support against Gamsakhurdia, who was defeated and reportedly committed suicide. In early 1994, Georgia and Abkhazia signed an agreement in Moscow that called for a ceasefire, the stationing of Commonwealth of Independent States troops under Russian command along the Abkhazian border, and the return of refugees under UN supervision. Parliamentary elections in November and December 1995 resulted in the Shevardnadze-founded CUG winning the most seats, while a concurrent presidential poll saw Shevardnadze elected with 77 percent of the vote.

The ruling CUG repeated its victory four years later in the October 1999 parliamentary election. Election observers from the OSCE concluded that despite some irregularities, the vote was generally fair. In the April 2000 presidential poll, Shevardnadze easily won a second five-year term with a reported 81 percent of the vote. His closest challenger, former first secretary of the Communist Party Central Committee and leader of the parliament minority Dzhumber Patiashvili, received only 17 percent of the vote. While Shevardnadze's win was widely anticipated, the large margin of his victory led to accusations of electoral fraud. Election monitors noted numerous and serious irregularities, including the stuffing of ballot boxes, the presence of police in polling stations, a lack of transparency in the vote tabulation process, inflated voter turnout figures, and a strong pro-Shevardnadze bias in the state media.

Following the parliamentary elections, various competing factions developed within the CUG, which had dominated Georgian politics for much of the 1990s. Shevardnadze himself faced growing opposition from prominent members, including then-Parliament Speaker Zurab Zhvania and then-Justice Minister Mikhail Saakashvili, who criticized the president's failure to contain widespread corruption throughout the country. While Shevardnadze resigned as CUG chairman in September 2001, Saakashvili left the CUG to form his own party, the National Movement, and a formal party split was ratified in May 2002.

Local elections held on June 2, 2002, saw mixed results in an increasingly fragmented political landscape. Just weeks before the election, a Tbilisi court had ruled that a pro-Shevardnadze faction, and not one led by Zhvania, could compete under the CUG name. In response, Zhvania launched his own party, the United Democrats, shortly after the local polls. The New Rights Party, whose members had split from the CUG in 2000 and included many of the country's most successful businessmen, won a fourth of all available seats nationwide. In Tbilisi, the Labor Party—whose socialist policies appealed to the elderly and disadvantaged—and the National Movement each received some 25 percent of the vote, while the CUG received less than 4 percent of the vote required to gain seats. International election observers noted some irregularities during the poll, including the stuffing of ballot boxes and a failure to provide up-to-date lists of eligible voters, and the official voter turnout figure of around 45 percent was questioned as being too high.

Georgia's already strained relations with Russia grew increasingly tense during the year as Moscow intensified its pressure on Georgia over Chechen rebels alleged to be hiding in its Pankisi Gorge region bordering Russia. Known as a largely lawless area, the Pankisi Gorge has a reputation as a haven for drug smugglers and criminal gangs responsible for numerous kidnappings, as well as a home to several thousand Chechen refugees. Russian military helicopters repeatedly violated Georgian airspace in May and June. Tensions escalated when Russian planes reportedly bombed the Pankisi Gorge in late July and August, killing one person. While the Georgian Foreign Ministry called the bombings acts of military aggression, the chairman of the Russian Duma's international affairs committee insisted that Russia had the right to conduct "targeted retaliatory operations" against "rebel bases outside its borders." Georgia rejected repeated Russian offers to conduct join crackdowns in Pankisi, fearing that a large number of federal troops would exacerbate tensions with its breakaway republics of Abkhazia and South Ossetia. In early August, Georgian authorities apprehended 13 Chechens after they illegally entered the Pankisi Gorge from Russia. However, Georgia refused to extradite them on the grounds that Moscow had not provided evidence that they had committed crimes in Russia.

In an attempt to prevent a Russian armed incursion into Georgia, Tbilisi sent some 1,000 Interior Ministry troops into the Pankisi Gorge in late August to restore law and order and remove any armed separatists in the region. In contrast to Georgian claims a few days later that no rebels had been found, Russia concluded that the operation had been a failure. On September 11, Russian president Vladimir Putin issued an ultimatum that it would order air strikes in the Pankisi Gorge if Tbilisi failed to prevent future cross-border attacks from Chechen separatists. Georgian authorities yielded to Kremlin pressure on October 3 by extraditing to Russia five of the 13 Chechens detained in August. After Russia and Georgia reached an agreement a few days later to prevent Chechen militants from crossing their border, Putin rescinded his ultimatum, but demanded the extradition of the eight remaining Chechens. Although a Georgian court decided in late November to extradite three more Chechens, the Supreme Court at the end of December ordered a reconsideration of the ruling.

In a move that further complicated Tbilisi's relations with Moscow, the United States began sending special forces in April to train and equip the Georgian military in anticrime and antiterrorist operations. Although some senior Russian officials reacted with concern over the increasing U.S. presence in the Caucasus, Washington emphasized that its troops would not participate in combat operations in the Pankisi Gorge or elsewhere in Georgia. Some observers have maintained that Russia's focus on the Pankisi Gorge is part of a broader effort to undermine the authority of Shevardnadze, who has pursued decidedly pro-Western policies, by portraying him as incapable of controlling his country's territory.

Long-standing demands of greater local autonomy continued unresolved throughout the year. A final agreement to the protracted conflict in Abkhazia remains elusive, as leaders in Tbilisi and Sukhumi, the capital of Abkhazia, continued to disagree on key issues, including the territory's final political status. A decade of peace talks between South Ossetia and Georgia have failed to find a solution to the territorial status of the region, which has maintained de facto independence from Tbilisi since 1992. Georgia's military operations in the Pankisi Gorge in 2002 heightened tensions in South Ossetia and Abkhazia; in September, the two territories signed an agreement of mutual military support in the event of Georgian aggression. In the southwestern region of Ajaria, Aslan Abashidze exercises almost complete control over the territory, which has retained considerable autonomy since 1991. In the ethnic Armenian enclave of Javakhetia, residents staged rallies during the year to demand greater autonomy from Tbilisi and to protest the anticipated closure of a Russian military base at Akhalkalaki, which they insist is vital to the local economy.

Political Rights and Civil Liberties: While Georgians can formally elect their government democratically, the most recent presidential election in April 2000 was marred by examples of serious electoral fraud, including inflated voter turnout figures and an unrealistically wide margin of victory for the incumbent, President Eduard Shevardnadze. The 1999 parliamentary vote was deemed to be generally fair, although observers cited numerous irregularities, including the stuffing of ballot boxes and intimidation of precinct election commission members. Widespread fraud was noted in the autonomous republic of Ajaria, while no voting took place in the separatist territories of Abkhazia and South Ossetia, which remained largely outside central governmental control.

While the country's independent press often publishes discerning and critical political analyses, economic difficulties limit the circulation of most newspapers, particularly outside of the capital. Independent newspapers and television stations face harassment by the authorities, and journalists in government-controlled media frequently practice self-censorship. In September, police assaulted the staff and damaged equipment at the Odishi television station in the town of Zugdidi after it had aired a report about violence committed by local law enforcement units.

Although freedom of religion is respected for the country's largely Georgian Orthodox population, members of "nontraditional" religions and foreign missionaries face harassment and intimidation by law enforcement officials and certain Georgian Orthodox Church extremists. According to the 2002 U.S. State Department Report on International Religious Freedom, police have failed to respond to continued attacks by defrocked Georgian Orthodox priest Basili Mkalavishvili against Jehovah's Witnesses and members of other faiths, including Baptists and Seventh-Day Adventists. The attacks have included burning religious material, breaking up religious gatherings, and beating parishioners. In October, the Georgian Orthodox Church and the government signed an agreement giving the church a more privileged status than other religions, although it stopped short of naming it the official church of Georgia.

The authorities generally respect freedom of association. However, on July 10, some dozen assailants attacked personnel and destroyed equipment and furniture at a nongovernmental organization (NGO), the Liberty Institute. Some Liberty Institute staffers and local NGO members maintained that the attack, which Human Rights Watch described as "one of the most vicious assaults on human rights defenders" in the former Soviet Union, was ordered by members of the government.

The judiciary is not fully independent, with courts influenced by pressure from the executive branch. The payment of bribes to judges, whose salaries remain inadequate, is reportedly common, while strong clan-based traditions encourage the granting of personal favors. Police frequently beat prisoners and detainees to extract confessions and fabricate or plant evidence on suspects. Prison inmates suffer from overcrowding and inadequate sanitation, food, and medical care. In early December, Georgian police conducted widespread identity checks throughout the country in which scores of ethnic Chechens, including many officially registered refugees and Georgian citizens, were targeted and detained for several hours or longer.

Ethnic conflicts in Abkhazia and South Ossetia, as well as an influx of thousands of refugees from neighboring Chechnya, have led to a serious refugee problem, with repatriation efforts proceeding slowly.

National and local governments often restrict freedom of assembly, particularly concerning supporters of former President Zviad Gamsakhurdia. The constitution and Law on Trade Unions allow workers to organize and bargain collectively and prohibit anti-union discrimination. Despite the strong legislative framework, unions face some interference in their activities. According to a report by the International Confederation of Free Trade Unions, the Georgian Trade Union Amalgamation has faced harassment and intimidation, and there have been cases of management warning staff not to organize unions. Miners in western Georgia held a number of strikes throughout the year to demand payment of wage arrears.

Although the government initiated a high-profile anticorruption campaign in 2000, corruption remains endemic throughout all levels of Georgian society. The payment of bribes for university admission or during the examination process is reportedly common. In its 2002 Corruption Perceptions Index, Transparency International ranked Georgia 85 out of 102 countries surveyed. The country's economy continued to suffer from problems, including high rates of unemployment, sporadic payment of government pensions, and seasonal energy shortages.

Most women work in low-paying occupations and continue to be underrepresented in parliament and other governmental organs. Social taboos limit the reporting and punishment of rape and spousal abuse, and the trafficking of women abroad for prostitution remains a problem.

Germany

Polity: Parliamentary democracy (federal)
Economy: Mixed capitalist
Population: 82,400,000
PPP: $25,103
Life Expectancy: 78

Political Rights: 1
Civil Liberties: 1*
Status: Free

Religious Groups: Protestant (34 percent), Roman Catholic (34 percent), Muslim (3.7 percent), other (28.3 percent)
Ethnic Groups: German (92 percent), Turkish (2 percent), other (6 percent)
Capital: Berlin
Ratings Change: Germany's civil liberties rating improved from 2 to 1 due to changes in the survey methodology.

Ten-Year Ratings Timeline (Political Rights, Civil Liberties, Status)

1993	1994	1995	1996	1997	1998	1999	2000	2001	2002	2003
1,2F	1,2F	1,2F	1,2F	1,2F	1,2F	1,2F	1,2F	1,2F	1,2F	1,1F

Overview:

Gerhard Schroeder won reelection as chancellor, just after his Social Democratic Party (SPD) and the Greens won a parliamentary majority. As an EU member-state, Germany was obliged to implement telecommunications reforms that severely delimit personal freedoms. Human rights groups continued to be concerned about the rise in anti-

Semitic behavior and the ill-treatment of minorities at the hands of the police. Germany's Constitutional Court rejected a controversial immigration law that would have allowed more foreign skilled workers into the country

Germany was divided into Soviet, U.S., British, and French occupation zones after World War II. Four years later, the Allies helped to establish the democratic Federal Republic of Germany, while the Soviets oversaw the formation of the Communist German Democratic Republic (GDR). The political division of Berlin was reinforced by the 1961 construction of the Berlin Wall. After the collapse of Erich Honecker's hardline GDR regime in 1989 and the destruction of the wall in 1990, citizens voted in the GDR's first free parliamentary election, in which parties supporting rapid reunification prevailed.

In September, the SPD-Green coalition won a narrow parliamentary victory. Then, after vowing not to let Germany participate in a U.S.-led attack on Iraq, Schroeder was re-elected as Germany's chancellor on October 22. Parts of the Schroeder-led 2000 tax reform, the most radical since World War II, had to be postponed to help offset the cost of the ballooning deficit and the devastating August floods that caused 15 billion euros (US$14.7 billion) worth of damage.

The European euro became Germany's national currency in January.

A sharp rise in racist, anti-Semitic, and xenophobic behavior in Western Europe followed the September 11, 2001, terrorist attacks on the U.S. In Germany, synagogues and individual Jews were attacked in Berlin and other cities in 2002. In July, a German court jailed three youths for firebombing an asylum seeker's home in December 2001.

The European Parliament amended the 1997 European Community Directive on privacy in telecommunications in May, obliging member states to retain all telecommunications data for one to two years and to provide the relevant authorities unrestricted access to these data to assist law enforcement officials in eradicating crime. Human rights groups attacked this move as an assault on privacy and civil liberties.

Schroeder's center-left government was dealt a blow in December when Germany's Constitutional Court rejected a controversial immigration law. The legislation would have allowed a controlled number of skilled workers from outside the European Union for the first time in three decades. Conservatives argued that allowing more foreign workers into the country would hurt Germany's four million unemployed workers. The government is expected to revive the bill in 2003. Advocates of the new law argue that it is a necessary response to the declining birth rate in Germany which, economists predict, will lead to shortages of skilled people, particularly in the computer and other high-technology fields.

Political Rights and Civil Liberties: Germans can change their government democratically. The national legislature is a bicameral parliament. The Bundestag (lower house) has 662 members (328 directly elected from individual constituencies; 334 elected through party lists in each state so as to obtain proportional representation). Parties must win at least 5 percent of the national vote, or three constituency seats, to gain representation. The Bundesrat (upper house) consists of members nominated by the 16 state governments. The head of state is the federal president, elected for a maximum of two five-year terms by the Federal Assembly, which consists of members of the Bundestag and representatives of the state legislatures. Each state has an elected legislature and considerable autonomy. The federal government is led by the chancellor elected by the Bundestag on the nomination of the federal president. The judiciary is independent.

The German press and broadcast media are free and independent, offering pluralistic views. However, Nazi propaganda and statements endorsing Nazism are illegal, with violators facing fines or jail terms of up to three years. In December 2000, the Supreme Court ruled that individuals outside Germany who post Nazi propaganda aimed at Internet users inside Germany could be prosecuted under German law. However, it is unlikely that the ruling can be enforced in practice.

Freedom of assembly and association is guaranteed. However, public rallies and marches require official permits, which are routinely denied to right-wing radicals. Individuals are free to form political parties and to receive federal funding if the parties are democratic in nature. In January, the federal government canceled hearings, on procedural grounds, on a petition it had filed at the Federal Constitutional Court in January 2001 to ban the fringe, far-right National Democratic Party (NPD), which advocates pro-German policies, opposes immigration, and has been blamed for inciting violence against foreigners.

The basic law (constitution) guarantees religious freedom. Church and state are separate, although the state collects membership taxes from members of religious communities (public law corporations) and subsidizes affiliated institutions, such as church-run schools and hospitals. Scientologists, who claim 30,000 adherents in Germany, have been at the center of a heated debate over the group's legal status. Major political parties exclude Scientologists from membership, claiming that the group does not constitute a religion, but rather an antidemocratic, for-profit organization. Antiterror measures adopted in November 2001 lifted the constitutional protection of religious organizations—they can now be banned if suspected of inciting violence or undermining democracy.

The Federal Constitutional Court ruled in January 2002 that Muslim butchers could apply for animal-protection-law waivers when slaughtering animals ritually. Without the waiver, animals must be stunned before slaughter. The Jewish community already has a waiver to slaughter animals by kosher procedures.

Under the basic law, descendants of a German mother or father can receive German citizenship, as can former German citizens or their descendants who were deprived of their German nationality by the National Socialist government. To harmonize Germany's citizenship and nationality law with European standards, as of January 2000, under certain conditions, children born in Germany to foreign nationals may receive citizenship, as may adults who have lawfully resided in Germany for eight years and have an adequate command of the German language.

Germany's crime prevention laws, effective December 1994, now target extremist organizations and anti-foreigner violence with new criminal laws, the toughening of existing penalties, and the expediting of criminal prosecution.

Amnesty International voiced concern over unresolved cases of alleged police brutality against minorities. Police brutality allegedly resulted in the death of Stephan Neisius in May 2002. Doviodo Adekou, a Togolese asylum seeker, lost the sight in his right eye in October 2001, and Denis Mwakapi, originally from Kenya, had his arm fractured in December 2001. Police ill-treatment was allegedly responsible for both incidents.

Transparency International ranked Germany 18th on its 2002 Corruption Perceptions Index, ninth among the 15 EU-member states.

Labor, business, and farming groups are free, highly organized, and influential. Trade union federation membership has dropped sharply in recent years, however, as a result of the collapse of industry in the east and layoffs in the west.

Under threat of class-action lawsuits, Germany agreed in 2000 to create a DM10 billion (US$4.6 billion) fund to compensate the 1.5 million Nazi-era slave laborers forced to work for German manufacturers. Industry and government will each contribute one-half the total.

Trafficking in women is a serious problem, according to the International Helsinki Federation of Human Rights. Nearly 90 percent of victims come from Eastern and Central Europe. Laws against trafficking were modified to address the problem more effectively; they currently provide penalties of up to 10 years in prison. In October 2001, parliament approved a law improving the status of prostitutes. The law removed some of the penalties linked to prostitution, as well as giving an estimated 400,000 prostitutes new rights, including entitlement to pensions and health and unemployment insurance. Since August 2001, same-sex partnerships have been legally recognized.

Ghana

Polity: Presidential-parliamentary democracy
Economy: Capitalist-statist
Population: 20,200,000
PPP: $1,964
Life Expectancy: 58
Religious Groups: Indigenous beliefs (21 percent), Muslim (16 percent), Christian (63 percent)
Ethnic Groups: Akan (44 percent), Moshi-Dagomba (16 percent), Ewe (13 percent), Ga (8 percent), other (19 percent)
Capital: Accra

Political Rights: 2
Civil Liberties: 3
Status: Free

Ten-Year Ratings Timeline (Political Rights, Civil Liberties, Status)

1993	1994	1995	1996	1997	1998	1999	2000	2001	2002	2003
5,5PF	5,4PF	5,4PF	4,4PF	3,4PF	3,3PF	3,3PF	3,3PF	2,3F	2,3F	2,3F

Overview:
Ghana's National Reconciliation Commission began meeting in 2002 to investigate human rights abuses committed during the administration of former president Jerry Rawlings. The commission, which is modeled on South Africa's Truth and Reconciliation Commission, was expected to receive hundreds of petitions. The complaints cannot lead to criminal prosecution, but they could lead to compensation. Authorities called Rawlings in for questioning briefly during the year after he publicly urged political opposition to the administration. Also in 2002, the government of President John Kufuor came under criticism for censoring the news media after ethnic violence broke out in the north.

Once a major slaving center and long known as the Gold Coast, the former British possession became black Africa's first colony to achieve independence. After the 1966 overthrow of its charismatic independence leader, Kwame Nkrumah, the country was wracked by a series of military coups for 15 years. Successive military and civilian governments vied with each other in both incompetence and mendacity.

In 1979, Flight Lieutenant Rawlings led a coup against the ruling military junta and, as promised, returned power to a civilian government after a purge of corrupt senior army officers. However, the new civilian administration did not live up to Rawlings's expectations. He seized power again in December 1981 and set up the Provisional National Defense Council (PNDC). The radically socialist, populist, and brutally repressive PNDC junta banned political parties and free expression. Facing a crumbling economy, Rawlings, in the late 1980s, transformed Ghana into an early model for the structural adjustment programs urged by international lenders. A new constitution, adopted in April 1992, legalized political parties, and Rawlings was declared president after elections that were neither free nor fair.

Ghana's economy has suffered in recent years as the result of a fall in the world prices of cocoa and gold, which are among the country's main foreign exchange earners.

Political Rights and Civil Liberties: The December 1996 presidential and parliamentary elections under Ghana's 1992 constitution allowed Ghanaians their first opportunity since independence to choose their representatives in genuine elections. Jerry Rawlings's 5 percent reelection victory, which extended his 16-year rule, was assured by the former ruling party's extensive use of state media and patronage. Opposition disunity also contributed to Rawlings's win.

The 2000 presidential and parliamentary elections were hailed in Africa and abroad as a successful test of Ghana's democracy. The election was the first time in Ghana's history that one democratically elected president was succeeded by another democratically elected leader. The opposition, led by John Kufuor of the National Patriotic Party (NPP), alleged intimidation and other irregularities as the second round of voting in the presidential polls began, but those claims dissipated as the polling proceeded and Kufuor's looming victory became apparent. He won soundly with 57 percent of the vote in the second round of polling, compared with 43 percent for Vice President John Atta Mills.

The opposition also broke the stranglehold of the National Democratic Congress (NDC) on parliament; the NPP won 99 of the 200 seats available, compared with 92 for the NDC, which had previously held 133 seats. Smaller opposition parties and independents won the remainder of seats.

Ghanaian courts have acted with increased autonomy under the 1992 constitution, but are still occasionally subject to executive influence. Traditional courts often handle minor cases according to local customs that fail to meet constitutional standards. Scarce judicial resources compromise the judicial process, leading to long periods of pretrial detention under harsh conditions.

The right to peaceful assembly and association is constitutionally guaranteed, and permits are not required for meetings or demonstrations. Numerous nongovernmental organizations operate openly and freely.

The government has not interfered with the right of workers to associate in labor unions, but civil servants may not join unions. Arbitration is required before strikes are authorized. The Ghana Federation of Labor is intended to serve as an umbrella organization for several other labor unions.

Freedom of expression is constitutionally guaranteed and generally respected. Fulfilling a campaign promise, the Kufuor government in 2001 repealed Ghana's criminal libel law and otherwise eased pressure on the press. The media, however, were required to submit stories on communal violence between the Abudu and Andani clans of the Dagomba ethnic group that broke out in the north in 2002 for approval by government censors. Officials said the measure was needed to stem the violence that claimed some 30 lives and led the government to declare a state of emergency in the area.

Religious freedom is respected, but there is occasional tension between Christians and Muslims and within the Muslim community itself. Communal and ethnic violence occasionally flares in Ghana, usually because of competition for resources or power.

Ghanaian women suffer societal discrimination that is particularly serious in rural areas, where opportunities for education and wage employment are limited, despite women's equal rights under the law. Women's enrollment in universities, however, is increasing. Domestic violence against women is said to be common, but often remains unreported. Legislation in 1998 doubled the prison sentence for rape. Efforts are under way to abolish the tro-kosi system of indefinite servitude to traditional priests in rural areas, and the practice of sending young girls to penal villages in the north after they are accused of practicing witchcraft.

Ghana has been coordinating with regional countries and the International Labor Organization to create a comprehensive plan to address the growing problem of child trafficking and child labor.

Greece

Polity: Parliamentary democracy
Economy: Mixed capitalist
Population: 11,000,000
PPP: $16,501
Life Expectancy: 78
Religious Groups: Greek Orthodox (98 percent), Muslim (1.3 percent), other (0.7 percent)
Ethnic Groups: Greek (98 percent), other, including Macedonian and Turkish (2 percent)
Capital: Athens

Political Rights: 1
Civil Liberties: 2*
Status: Free

Ratings Change: Greece's civil liberties rating improved from 3 to 2 due to the relaxation of laws relating to the now-defunct November 17 urban guerilla group.

Ten-Year Ratings Timeline (Political Rights, Civil Liberties, Status)

1993	1994	1995	1996	1997	1998	1999	2000	2001	2002	2003
1,2F	1,3F	1,3F	1,3F	1,3F	1,3F	1,3F	1,3F	1,3F	1,3F	1,2F

Overview:

The first round of the local elections took place on October 13, 2002. On the basis of those results, the opposition New Democracy party could claim some gains, but the ruling Pan-Hellenic Socialist Movement (PASOK) did a better than expected job of fending off losses, particularly in the wake of success on its domestic terrorism front. In June, a year following the introduction of an antiterrorist law, the Greek police arrested a member of the November 17 urban guerilla group, the first arrest since the group was formed in 1975. The arrest led to the group's unraveling and culminated in the capture in September of Dimitris Koufodinas, a top figure in November 17.

Greece gained independence from the Ottoman Empire in 1830. The ensuing century brought continued struggle between royalist and republican forces. Occupation by the Axis powers in 1941 was followed by a civil war between non-Communist and Communist forces that lasted until 1949. A military junta came to power as the result of a coup in 1967 and ruled until 1973, when naval officers failed to oust the junta and restore the monarchy. The failed 1973 coup led, however, to the formal deposition of the monarch and the proclamation of a republic. The current constitution, adopted in 1975, provides for a parliamentary system with a largely ceremonial president.

Greece continued to improve its relations with Turkey. Building on both countries' signing of the Ottawa Convention in 2001, an agreement that requires signatories to destroy their land mines and prohibits their use and production, the countries elevated their consultation process to the level of "dialogue" in early 2002. The upgrade in diplomatic relations was pursued with the goal of exploring mechanisms for the resolution of the countries' substantive differences. The European Court of Human Rights condemned the Turkish invasion of Cyprus in 1974 as a violation of human rights.

The results of the October elections go some way in silencing some of the government's critics in the short term, but the party still has a long way to go if it is to retain power at the next general election, which is scheduled for late 2003. PASOK garnered some political leverage in the arrests of the November 17 group, which assuaged its losses in the elections. November 17 has admitted to more than 20 killings since its inception. The antiterrorist law, which engendered concerns over infringement of individual rights, gave police broader powers for surveillance and investigation.

Political Rights and Civil Liberties:

Greeks can change their government democratically. The Greek parliament has 300 members, elected for four-year terms by a system of proportional representation. Voting is compulsory for citizens between the ages of 18 and 70. The president is elected for a five-year term by parliament. There are no restrictions on women's participation in government, yet they are underrepresented in Greece's politics, holding only 26 of the 300 seats in the unicameral parliament.

The judiciary is independent. The constitution provides for public trials, and trial court sessions are usually open to the public.

Despite the fact that Greece signed and ratified the Convention for Protection of National Minorities in 1997, it recognizes neither the presence of national minorities nor minority languages. The European Commission against Racism and Intolerance has reported that Roma (Gypsies) living in camps, face extremely harsh living conditions. Systematic abuse against Roma by law enforcement continues, and forced evictions of Roma from these settlements, without alternative housing provided, have frequently been reported. The UN Committee Against Torture has expressed concern about the excessive use of force by law enforcement against ethnic and national minorities and foreigners.

Amnesty International in September 2002 accused Greece of flouting European humanitarian law by employing police brutality and torture in its treatment of detainees, particularly asylum seekers and minorities. In its report, the human rights group referred to 66 cases of alleged human rights violations in Greece, which takes on the European Union presidency in January 2003. It is now calling on the EU to act decisively to combat abuses within its borders. Greece is also a member of NATO.

Greece has a long history of jailing conscientious objectors to military service. In 1997, however, the government passed a new law to allow objectors to perform alternative, civilian service. The measure requires objectors to serve twice as long as military conscripts and was therefore criticized by Amnesty International as "punitive."

Although the constitution guarantees freedom of expression, the government often infringes upon that right. In January 2001 an Aromanian (Vlach) activist was convicted of "disseminating false information" in a leaflet on minority languages. In July 2002 the government enacted Law 3037, which explicitly forbids electronic games from public and private places in an effort to stamp out gambling. People were fined tens of thousands of euros for playing or owning such games; although the law was thrown out two months later, people had already been fined.

Ninety-eight percent of the population belongs nominally to the state-sponsored Greek Orthodox Church. Orthodox bishops have the privilege of granting or denying permission to other faiths to build houses of worship in their jurisdictions.

Greeks enjoy freedom of association, and all workers except military personnel and the police have the right to form and join unions, which are usually linked to political parties. In June, workers in Greece held a general strike to protest the government's plan to slash pension benefits. The country's two main unions, together representing about 800,000 workers, joined in the action, which shut down much of the country.

The U.S. State Department issued its Trafficking in Persons Report in 2001, which stated that Greece had failed to end the problem of human trafficking.

Grenada

Polity: Parliamentary democracy
Economy: Capitalist-statist
Population: 100,000
PPP: $7,580
Life Expectancy: 71

Political Rights: 1
Civil Liberties: 2
Status: Free

Religious Groups: Roman Catholic (53 percent), Anglican (13.8 percent), Protestant and other (33.2 percent)
Ethnic Groups: Black (82 percent), white and South Asian (18 percent)
Capital: St. George's

Ten-Year Ratings Timeline (Political Rights, Civil Liberties, Status)

1993	1994	1995	1996	1997	1998	1999	2000	2001	2002	2003
1,2F	1,2F	1,2F	1,2F	1,2F	1,2F	1,2F	1,2F	1,2F	1,2F	1,2F

Overview:

In November, the government launched a campaign raising popular awareness of constitutional reform for the coming year. In July Prime Minister Keith Mitchell called for national consultation on the increase in crime, often violent and drug related. Following a crackdown on offshore banking, the country was cleared of money laundering practices by the Organization for Economic Cooperation and Development. In October the governement suspended an opposition leader from parliament for a month over an accusation of financial impropriety. A controversial housing of foreign prisoners in Grenada came to a close with the transfer of 11 prisoners back to St. Lucia. After two years on the run in Canada, a prominent journalist, accused of sedition on the basis of statements made during a radio show in 1998, surrendered to authorities. The most serious challenge to Grenada is the apparently unmanageable rise in crime.

Grenada, a member of the Commonwealth, is a parliamentary democracy. The British monarchy is represented by a governor-general. Grenada, which gained independence in 1974, includes the islands of Carriacou and Petite Martinique. The bicameral parliament consists of the 15-seat House of Representatives and the 13-seat Senate, to which the prime minister appoints 10 senators and the opposition leader, 3.

Maurice Bishop's Marxist New Jewel Movement seized power in 1979. In 1983 Bishop was murdered by New Jewel hardliners Bernard Coard and Hudson Austin, who took control of the country in the name of the People's Revolutionary Government (PRG). A joint U.S.-Caribbean military intervention removed the PRG. In 1986 Coard and 18 others were sentenced to death; 2 were pardoned and 17 had their sentences commuted to life imprisonment. The Truth and Reconciliation Commission was formally inaugurated in September 2000. Its mandate was to investigate the period from the mid-1970s to the late 1980s. Since October 2000 the commission has held several weekly sessions, which have not drawn much media or public attention. The commission has the objective of recommending "general amnesty to certain persons who in the opinion of the commission have given truthful information during the hearing of evidence." The commission is expected to review the convictions of the leaders of the former PRG for their roles in the 1983 assassination of former Prime Minister Bishop and his cabinet colleagues.

Political Rights and Civil Liberties:

Citizens are able to change their government through democratic elections. The 1999 elections were considered free and fair; general elections must be held every five years. Constitutional guarantees regarding the right to organize political, labor, or civic groups are respected. There are three major political parties, and few obstacles face those establishing new ones. There has been a decline in turnout, as young people, in particular, appear to have lost confidence in a system riddled with divisive politics and allegations of corruption. After the crushing defeat suffered by Grenada's opposition parties, their role as alternatives in future elections was seriously in doubt.

The independent and prestigious judiciary has authority generally respected by the 782-member Royal Grenada Police Force. There are no military or political courts. In 1991 Grenada rejoined the Organization of Eastern Caribbean States court system, with the right of appeal to the Privy Council in London. Detainees and defendants are guaranteed a range of legal rights that the government respects in practice. There is a substantial backlog of six months to one year for cases involving serious offenses, the result of a lack of judges and facilities. Like many Caribbean island-nations, Grenada has suffered from a rise in violent, drug-related crime, particularly among increasingly disaffected youth. Prison conditions are poor, though they meet minimum international standards and the government allows human rights monitors to visit. Flogging is still legal, but it is rarely used, and then primarily as a punishment for sex crimes and theft cases.

The right to free expression is generally respected. The media, including three weekly newspapers and several other publications, are independent and freely criticize the government. A privately owned corporation, with a minority government share, owns the principal radio and television stations. There are, in addition, five privately owned radio stations, one privately owned television station, and a privately owned cable company. All of the media are independent of the government and regularly report on all political views. There is free access to the Internet. There are no official restrictions on academic freedom.

Numerous independent labor unions include an estimated 20 to 25 percent of the workforce. All unions belong to the Grenada Trades Union Council (GTUC), which is represented in the Senate. A 1993 law gives the government the right to establish tribunals empowered to make "binding and final" rulings when a labor dispute is considered of vital interest to the state. The GTUC claimed the law was an infringement on the right to strike. Workers have the right to organize and to bargain collectively.

Women are represented in the government, though in greater numbers in the ministries than in parliament. No official discrimination takes place, but women generally earn less than men for equal work. Domestic violence against women is common. Police say that most instances of abuse are not reported and others are settled out of court. Child abuse remains a significant issue. Citizens of Grenada generally enjoy the free exercise of religious beliefs. There are no significant minority-related issues.

Guatemala

Polity: Presidential-   **Political Rights:** 4*
parliamentary democracy **Civil Liberties:** 4
Economy: Capitalist-   **Status:** Partly Free
statist
Population: 12,100,000
PPP: $3,821
Life Expectancy: 66
Religious Groups: Roman Catholic, Protestant, indigenous beliefs
Ethnic Groups: Mestizo (55 percent), Indian (43 percent), other (2 percent)
Capital: Guatemala City
Ratings Change: Guatemala's political rights rating declined from 3 to 4 due to the continuing decay of political institutions, the increase of corruption and lawlessness, and the reappearance of death squads.

Ten-Year Ratings Timeline (Political Rights, Civil Liberties, Status)

1993	1994	1995	1996	1997	1998	1999	2000	2001	2002	2003
4,5PF	4,5PF	4,5PF	4,5PF	3,4PF	3,4PF	3,4PF	3,4PF	3,4PF	3,4PF	4,4PF

Overview: Late in the year, the government of President Alfonso Portillo signed an agreement to provide $400 million in compensation to the victims of the nation's 36-year civil war during which more than 200,000 died and over 200 mostly indigenous villages were destroyed. The National Compensation Program is a result of the 1996 UN-brokered peace accords and the ensuing truth commission. A senior military officer was convicted in the murder trial of human rights advocate Myrna Mack in 1990; the acquittal of two other general officers was challenged. While the civil war is over, assassinations, kidnappings, beatings, break-ins, and death threats are still common. Death squads have reappeared and hundreds of street children continue to be murdered or mutilated. President Portillo has admitted that clandestine groups with military ties exist, but claims to be powerless to combat them. Guatemala's governance problems are on the rise as corruption and lawlessness increase with impunity.

The Republic of Guatemala was established in 1839. The nation has endured a history of dictatorships, coups, and guerrilla insurgencies. Civilian rule followed the

1985 elections and a 36-year civil war ended with the signing of a peace agreement in 1996. The peace accords led to the successful demobilization of the Guatemalan National Revolutionary Unity (URNG) guerrillas and their political legalization, the retirement of more than 40 senior military officers on corruption and narcotics charges, and the reduction of the army's strength by one-third. A truth commission mandated by the peace accords began receiving complaints of rights violations committed during the conflict. In a May 1999 referendum voters rejected a package of amendments to the constitution, approved by congress a year earlier, which had been prepared in accordance with the peace plan.

In early 2002 the former guerrillas of the URNG, seriously divided and unable to make electoral gains, offered a blunt assessment of the peace accords: "Genocide is no longer state policy." There is a general consensus that with the failure to implement substantive reforms redressing social and economic inequalities, the peace process is dead. This failure includes the government's inability to end the military's political tutelage and impunity, to fully recognize the rights of the Maya Indians, and to reform taxation to pay for health, educational, and housing programs for the poor.

Political Rights and Civil Liberties: Citizens can change their government through elections. The November 1999 elections were largely free and fair. The 1985 constitution, amended in 1994, provides for a four-year presidential term and prohibits reelection. A unicameral congress consisting of 113 members (increased from 80) is elected for four years. The constitution guarantees religious freedom and the right to organize political parties, civic organizations, and labor unions. Despite increasing freedoms, Guatemala has yet to end a tradition of military dominance. The demobilization, mandated by the peace accords, of the presidential bodyguard and military intelligence, the two units held most accountable for human rights abuses, has not taken place.

The judicial system remains ineffectual for most legal and human rights complaints. In general, it suffers from chronic problems of corruption, intimidation, insufficient personnel, lack of training opportunities, and a lack of transparency and accountability. Drug trafficking is a serious problem, and Guatemala remains a transit point for drugs going to the United States. On similar routes there is also extensive human trafficking, especially of illegal aliens from Asia en route to the United States; women and children are drawn into prostitution both locally and in neighboring countries.

Human rights organizations are the targets of frequent death threats and are victims of frequent acts of violence. In May, Guillermo Ovalle, who worked for an organization set up by Nobel Peace Prize Winner Rigoberta Menchu, was assassinated in Guatemala City. As in other cases, no assailants have been identified or brought to trial. The indigenous population continues to be shut out from the national judicial system. Although indigenous languages are now being used in courtrooms around the country, traditional justice systems are mostly dismissed by Guatemalan authorities. Cursory recruitment efforts have resulted in only a handful of indigenous recruits for the National Civilian Police (PNC).

Guatemala remains one of the most violent countries in Latin America. The closing of military barracks throughout the country—the armed forces were the one Guatemalan institution that had a truly national presence—while the PNC was being created and deployed created a vacuum in which criminal activity escalated. One result was an upsurge of vigilantism and lynchings. Neighborhood patrols—some armed with automatic weapons—have sprung up in an attempt to arrest the spiraling crime wave. Private security guards far outnumber the PNC. President Alfonso Portillo has called out army troops to assist the PNC in patrolling urban areas.

The press and most broadcast media outlets are privately owned; seven dailies are published in the capital, and six are local. There are several radio stations, most of them commercial. Four of the six television stations are commercially operated and are owned by the same financial interest. Reporters Sans Frontieres, a Paris-based organization, noted in June that journalists and human rights activists were targets of intimidation, including death threats. Guatemala has the second-highest rate of illiteracy in the Americas, 32 percent. Eighty percent of the population lives below poverty levels, and infant mortality among the Maya—some 60 percent of the population—is among the highest on the continent. Access to the Internet is not limited. The government does not interfere with academic freedom; however, academics have been targets of death threats.

Workers are frequently denied the right to organize and are subject to mass firings and blacklisting, particularly in export-processing zones, where the majority of workers are women. Existing unions are targets of intimidation, physical attack, and assassination, particularly in rural areas during land disputes. Violence against women and children is widespread and common. Guatemala has the highest rate of child labor in the Americas, with one-third of school-aged children forced to work on farms or in factories.

⬆ Guinea

Polity: Dominant party (military-influenced)
Political Rights: 6
Civil Liberties: 5
Economy: Capitalist
Status: Not Free
Population: 8,400,000
PPP: $1,982
Life Expectancy: 48
Religious Groups: Muslim (85 percent), Christian (8 percent), indigenous beliefs (7 percent)
Ethnic Groups: Peuhl (40 percent), Malinke (30 percent), Soussou (20 percent), other (10 percent)
Capital: Conakry
Trend Arrow: Guinea received an upward trend arrow for an easing of repression of the press and fewer attacks on refugees.

Ten-Year Ratings Timeline (Political Rights, Civil Liberties, Status)

1993	1994	1995	1996	1997	1998	1999	2000	2001	2002	2003
6,5PF	6,5NF	6,5NF	6,5NF	6,5NF	6,5NF	6,5NF	6,5NF	6,5NF	6,5NF	6,5NF

Overview:

Guinea held parliamentary elections in June that had been delayed for two years. The country's most influential opposition parties boycotted the vote, which was marked by low turnout. Although the government of President Lansana Conte created an electoral commission that it said would be independent, the leading Union for Progress party said conditions still did not exist for holding a free and fair vote. The ruling Progress and Unity Party and its allies swept the poll for the National Assembly's 114 seats. Human rights conditions improved slightly in 2002; there were fewer attacks on the press and on refugees from Liberia and Sierra Leone. Many of the Sierra Leonean refugees returned to their country during the year.

Under Ahmed Sekou Toure, Guinea declared independence from France in 1958. Alone among France's many African colonies, it rejected the domination of continued close ties with France. Paris retaliated quickly, removing or destroying all "colonial property" and enforcing an unofficial but devastating economic boycott. Sekou Toure's one-party rule became highly repressive, and Guinea was increasingly impoverished under his Soviet-style economic policies. Lansana Conte seized power in a 1984 coup and was nearly toppled by a 1996 army mutiny. Amid general looting in Conakry, he rallied loyal troops and reestablished his rule.

Guinea's economy has suffered from a world drop in the price of bauxite. The country is the world's second-largest producer of the mineral and is also rich in gold, diamonds, and iron ore.

Political Rights and Civil Liberties:

The Guinean people's constitutional right to freely elect their government is not yet respected in practice. Guinean politics and parties are largely defined along ethnic lines. Lansana Conte was returned to office in a 1998 presidential election that lacked credible opposition, as state patronage and the media strongly backed the incumbent. His reelection to another five-year term, with 54 percent of the vote, was unconvincing, although broad manipulation of the electoral process and opposition disunity probably made more blatant forms of vote rigging unnecessary. Although the polls were an improvement over past elections, hundreds of people were arrested after the vote, including the official third-place finisher, Alpha Conde.

The June 2002 National Assembly elections were not considered fair because of the government's preparations for the vote and the opposition's boycott. The ruling Progress and Unity Party easily won the two-thirds majority required to enact constitutional changes. The EU refused to send observers and financial aid for the vote.

Guinea held a referendum in 2001 on extending presidential terms from five to seven years, allowing for unlimited terms in office, and eliminating presidential age limits. The provisions in the referendum were approved in a flawed vote that was boycotted by members of the opposition and marked by low turnout. Conte's term expires in 2003, but there is little doubt that he will run for president again. The referendum also granted Conte the power to appoint local officials and Supreme Court judges.

While nominally independent, the judicial system remains infected by corruption, nepotism, ethnic bias, and political interference, and lacks resources and training. Minor civil cases are often handled by traditional ethnic-based courts. Arbitrary arrests and detention are common, and persistent maltreatment and torture of detainees is reported. Prison conditions are harsh and sometimes life threatening.

Security forces commit abuses, including torture and extrajudicial execution, with impunity. Vigilantism is a problem.

Several statutes restrict freedom of association and assembly in apparent contravention of constitutional guarantees. The government may ban any gathering that "threatens national unity." Nevertheless, human rights groups and many nongovernmental groups operate openly.

The government has wide powers to bar any communications that insult the president or disturb the peace. All broadcasting outlets, as well as the country's largest and only daily newspaper, are state controlled and offer little coverage of the opposition and scant criticism of government policy. The print media have little impact in rural areas, where incomes are low and illiteracy is high. Several weekly newspapers in Conakry offer sharp criticism of the government despite frequent harassment. A restrictive press law allows the government to censor or shutter publications on broad and ill-defined bases. Defamation and slander are considered criminal offenses.

Constitutionally protected religious rights are respected in practice, although the main body representing the country's Muslims, who constitute 85 percent of the population, is government controlled.

Women have far fewer educational and employment opportunities than men, and many societal customs discriminate against women. Constitutionally protected women's rights are often unrealized. Violence against women is said to be prevalent. Spousal abuse is a criminal offense, but security forces rarely intervene in domestic matters. Female genital mutilation is illegal; women's groups are working to eradicate the practice, but it is still widely carried out.

The constitution provides for the right to form and join unions. However, only a very small formal (business) sector exists. Several labor confederations compete in this small market and have the right to bargain collectively.

Guinea-Bissau

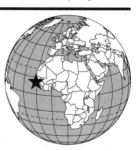

Polity: Presidential-parliamentary democracy
Economy: Mixed statist (transitional)
Population: 1,300,000
PPP: $755
Life Expectancy: 45
Political Rights: 4
Civil Liberties: 5
Status: Partly Free

Religious Groups: Indigenous beliefs (50 percent), Muslim (45 percent), Christian (5 percent)
Ethnic Groups: Balanta (30 percent), Fula (20 percent), Manjaca (14 percent), Mandinga (13 percent), Papel (7 percent), other (16 percent)
Capital: Bissau

Ten-Year Ratings Timeline (Political Rights, Civil Liberties, Status)

1993	1994	1995	1996	1997	1998	1999	2000	2001	2002	2003
6,5PF	6,5PF	3,4PF	3,4PF	3,4PF	3,4PF	3,5PF	3,5PF	4,5PF	4,5PF	4,5PF

Overview:

President Kumba Yala faced mounting criticism of his erratic and increasingly autocratic rule in 2002. The country's Roman Catholic bishops in September called for national reconciliation, citing frequent leadership changes, human rights violations, and the failure to promulgate a new constitution, which parliament approved in 2001, as some of the reasons the country faced a crisis. The political opposition in October called for Yala to resign, accusing him of interfering with the judiciary and encouraging tribalism. Opposition leaders were particularly upset that Yala had appointed the leader of the Supreme Court. Yala's relationship with the army and parliament was increasingly strained in 2002. The president named a new prime minister in November, dissolved parliament, and called for early elections. The polls are scheduled for April 2003. Yala claims there have been three coup attempts or plots against him in as many years, and he stunned regional leaders in May when he accused neighboring Gambia of complicity in an alleged scheme to topple him.

Guinea-Bissau won independence from Portugal in 1973 after a 12-year guerrilla war. The African Party for the Independence of Guinea-Bissau and Cape Verde (PAIGC) held power for the next 13 years. Luis Cabral became president in 1974 and named Joao Bernardo Vieira his prime minister, but Vieira toppled Cabral in 1980. Constitutional revisions in 1991 ended the PAIGC's repressive one-party rule. Vieira won the country's first free and fair presidential election in 1994, but he eventually came to be seen as the leader of a corrupt ruling class.

An army mutiny broke out in 1998 after Vieira sacked General Ansumane Mane, accusing him of smuggling arms to rebels in the southern Casamance region of neighboring Senegal, which for years had complained that Guinea-Bissau was backing the rebels. Encouraged by France, about 3,000 troops from Senegal and Guinea intervened on behalf of Vieira. They were eventually replaced by fewer than 600 unarmed West African peacekeepers, which made Vieira vulnerable to his overthrow in May 1999 by Mane. Legislative and presidential elections were held in November

1999, and populist Yala won the second round of voting. However, fighting broke out in 2000 between military supporters of Yala and those of Mane after Mane declared himself the head of the armed forces. Mane was killed.

The UN Security Council urged Yala to seek national dialogue, to encourage reconciliation and good governance, and to complete the demobilization and reintegration of former combatants. Civil servants had not been paid for five months toward the end of the year, and trade unions were planning walkouts.

The vast majority of Guinea-Bissau's one million citizens survive on subsistence farming. Cashew nuts are a key export. There are hopes for substantial oil reserves offshore.

Political Rights and Civil Liberties: The people of Guinea-Bissau were able to choose their government freely for the first time in 1994, and both direct presidential polls and legislative elections were judged free and fair by international observers. Voting in the 1999 legislative and presidential elections was declared free and fair by international observers despite widespread delays, isolated cases of violence, and other voting irregularities. The January 2000 runoff pitted Kumba Yala, of the Social Renewal Party (PRS), against Malam Bacai Sanha, of PAIGC.

In legislative voting, the opposition PRS obtained 38 of the 102 seats, followed by the Resistance of Guinea with 29 and the PAIGC with 24. The 11 remaining seats went to five of the ten other parties that fielded candidates.

The judiciary has operated independently of the government, but its freedom has been increasingly limited by President Yala. He imposed his choice to head the Supreme Court in 2002, to the protest of opposition leaders, saying the court would soon be able to elect its own officers. Yala dismissed four members of the Supreme Court in 2001, and two of them face charges of misappropriation of funds. Judicial performance is often unpredictable owing to political interference, poor training, and scant resources. Traditional law usually prevails in rural areas. Police routinely ignore privacy rights and protections against search and seizure. Severe mistreatment of detainees is reported.

Freedom of speech and the press is constitutionally guaranteed, but journalists practice self-censorship and face some harassment. There are several private and community radio stations. Few private newspapers publish, and the lack of vibrant, independent media outlets may be more due to financial constraints than to governmental interference. The editor of the independent daily *Correio de Bissau* was detained for two days in June and accused of criticizing President Yala on the private radio station Radio Bombolom. Two private newspapers that had been ordered to stop publishing in 2001 were allowed to resume publishing in 2002.

The right to peaceful assembly and association is guaranteed and usually respected in practice. Nongovernmental organizations and human rights groups operate openly; however, their leaders sometimes face harassment. The London-based human rights group Amnesty International said in February that human rights activists and political opponents in Guinea-Bissau "faced a sustained clampdown" on their activities. The attorney general in April forbid all media from publishing information from the Guinean League of Human Rights. Two of the group's officers faced charges relating to alleged disrespect shown to the attorney general regarding a probe into misappropriation of funds. The head of the opposition Socialist Alliance of Guinea-Bissau, Fernando Gomes, was detained for a week for alleged misappropriation of funds.

Religious freedom is protected and is usually respected in practice. About half of Guinea-Bissau's population is Muslim.

Women face some legal and significant traditional and societal discrimination, despite constitutional protection. They generally do not receive equal pay for equal work and have fewer opportunities for education and jobs in the small formal (business) sector. Domestic violence against women is common, and female genital mutilation is widespread. The government has formed a national committee to discourage the practice.

Eleven labor unions operate, and workers have the right to organize and to strike with prior notice. Most people, however, work in subsistence agriculture. Wages generally are established in bilateral negotiations between workers and employers.

Guyana

Polity: Parliamentary democracy
Political Rights: 2
Civil Liberties: 2
Economy: Mixed statist
Status: Free
Population: 800,000
PPP: $3,963
Life Expectancy: 63
Religious Groups: Christian (50 percent), Hindu (35 percent), Muslim (10 percent), other (5 percent)
Ethnic Groups: East Indian (50 percent), black (36 percent), Amerindian (7 percent), other (7 percent)
Capital: Georgetown

Ten-Year Ratings Timeline (Political Rights, Civil Liberties, Status)

1993	1994	1995	1996	1997	1998	1999	2000	2001	2002	2003
3,3F	2,2F	2,2F	2,2F	2,2F	2,2F	2,2F	2,2F	2,2F	2,2F	2,2F

Overview:

A rising crime rate and a parliamentary impasse dominated Guyana's political scene throughout 2002, with representatives of parliamentary political parties and the Social Partners—a group comprising representatives from the business sector, the labor movement and the government—meeting in November to hammer out a common action plan for citizen security. The effort brought together officials from the ruling People's Progressive Party/Civic (PPP/C) and the main opposition People's National Congress/Reform (PNC/R), as well as three minor parties in parliament. The anticrime initiative came even as the PPP/C and the PNC/R traded bitter words over the issue of payment for opposition members engaged in a boycott of parliament, in effect since March 15. The PNC/R said that unless agreed-upon reforms of the parliamentary system were implemented, it considered participation in National Assembly debates to be meaningless. Independent observers noted that the impasse posed few immediate risks to political stability, given that PNC/R continued to participate in the Public Accounts Committee, which is the only standing committee in the assembly.

Guyana is a member of the Commonwealth. Descendants of indentured workers from India make up about half of the population, while about 36 percent are descended from African slaves. From independence in 1966 until 1992, Guyana was ruled by the autocratic, predominantly Afro-Guyanese, People's National Congress (PNC). The 1980 constitution provides for a strong president and a 65-seat National Assembly, elected every five years. Twelve seats are occupied by elected local officials. The leader of the party winning the plurality of parliamentary seats becomes president for a five-year term. The president appoints the prime minister and cabinet.

The first free and fair elections were held in 1992, and 80 percent of the eligible population voted. The PNC lost to the PPP/C, an alliance of the predominantly Indo-Guyanese People's Progressive Party (PPP) and the Civic Party. PPP leader Cheddi Jagan, having moderated his Marxism since the collapse of communism, became president with 52 percent of the vote. Jagan's work was cut short by his death in March 1997. He was replaced by Samuel Hinds, a member of Civic, the PPP's coalition partner. Hinds called elections for December 15, 1997. Cheddi Jagan's widow, Janet, beat the PNC's Hoyte. Ill health forced Janet Jagan to resign in August 1999, and she was replaced by Finance Minister Bharrat Jagdeo, who promised to heal racial and political divides and to welcome foreign investment.

Jagdeo was reelected on March 19, 2001, after 90 percent of eligible voters turned out to cast their ballots in voting that showed the country's continuing deep divisions along racial lines. Jagdeo's first initiative upon being declared the winner was to make a televised national appeal to his countrymen to begin a process of national healing. In mid-2001, violence erupted in several small towns in protest against crime, poverty, and poor public services. From February to September 2002, nearly a dozen police officers and more than 50 civilians were killed in the crime spiral. In September the PPP/C-dominated parliament passed four anticrime initiatives; however PNC representative who boycotted the legislative session claimed that the measures would not solve Guyana's crime problem, but rather were meant "to arm the regime with the draconian powers of dictatorship." The outbreak of violent crime has exacerbated uneasy relations between the two main races.

Political Rights and Civil Liberties: Citizens can change their government through direct, multiparty elections. The 2001 elections generated a broader consensus about the importance of election reform to the democratic process. Because the constitution lacks explicit guarantees, political rights and civil liberties rest more on government tolerance than on institutional protection. The rights of free expression, freedom of religion, and freedom to organize political parties, civic organizations, and labor unions are generally respected.

The judicial system is independent; however, due process is undermined by the shortages of staff and funds. Prisons are overcrowded and conditions poor. Guyana is the only Caribbean country to have cut all ties to the Privy Council of London, the court of last resort for other former colonies in the region. The Guyana Defence Force and the Guyana Police Force are under civilian control, the latter invested with the authority to make arrests and maintain law and order throughout the country.

Guyana's porous and largely unpatrolled borders have made the country an increasingly attractive transshipment route for South American cocaine, which, together with a small domestic cultivation of marijuana, has caused local consumption of illegal drugs to increase markedly.

Police blame the escapees from a February 2002 jailbreak for much of the current violence. A controversial special police tactical squad, which has been concentrating on apprehending the gang and is said to be behind many of the crimes, has been accused by United States human rights activists and opposition parties of extrajudicial killings. In September 2000 the assembly passed four anticrime initiatives meant to modernize the justice system, including the penalization of terrorist acts and new rules for law enforcement monitoring deportees. The laws included changes in criminal law, crime prevention tactics, incitement of racial hostility, and the use of evidence in court proceedings.

The Guyana Human Rights Association, an autonomous and effective group backed by independent civic and religious groups, has charged the police with frequent recurrence to excessive force, sometimes fatal. Although authorities have taken some steps to investigate extrajudicial killing, and charges against some officers have been brought, abuses are still committed with impunity.

Several independent newspapers operate freely, including the daily *Stabroek News*. Only two radio stations operate; both are government owned. The government owns one television station. Seventeen privately owned television stations freely criticize the government. Labor unions are well organized. In 1995 the government sought to dilute the right to strike among some public sector unions. Companies are not obligated to recognize unions in former state enterprises sold off by the government.

Racial clashes have diminished within the last decade; however, long-standing animosity between Afro- and Indo-Guyanese remains a concern. The Racial Hostility Bill passed in September 2002 increased the penalties for race-based crimes.

There are nine groups or indigenous peoples in Guyana numbering approximately 80,000 people, or 10 percent of the population. Human rights violations against them are widespread and pervasive, particularly concerning the failure of the state to adequately respect indigenous land and resource rights. Indigenous peoples' attempts to seek redress through the courts have been met with unwarranted delays by the judiciary. In 2002, an agreement between the government and Conservation International, establishing southern Guyana as a protected area, was criticized by indigenous groups as "gross disrespect," since the parties did not consult with six Indian communities whose ancestral lands will be encompassed by the accord. Violence against women is common in Guyana.

⬇ Haiti

Polity: Dominant party
Economy: Capitalist-
statist
Population: 7,100,000
PPP: $1,467
Life Expectancy: 49
Religious Groups: Roman Catholic (80 percent),
Protestant (16 percent), other (4 percent)
Ethnic Groups: Black (95 percent), mulatto and white (5 percent)
Capital: Port-au-Prince

Political Rights: 6
Civil Liberties: 6
Status: Not Free

Trend Arrow: Haiti received a downward trend arrow due to violent political warfare involving the former military, Aristide supporters, and others.

Ten-Year Ratings Timeline (Political Rights, Civil Liberties, Status)

1993	1994	1995	1996	1997	1998	1999	2000	2001	2002	2003
7,7NF	7,7NF	5,5PF	5,5PF	4,5PF	4,5PF	4,5PF	4,5PF	6,5NF	6,6NF	6,6NF

Overview:

Haiti is a nation under siege, beset by extreme levels of political and criminal violence, lawlessness, and corruption.

The past year saw no progress in stemming the absolute decline of the political and economic conditions that, for most Haitians, make life extremely difficult. Haiti has the lowest life expectancy and highest infant mortality rates in the Western Hemisphere. Haiti's people are also among the poorest in the Western Hemisphere and have the lowest levels of human development, including a literacy rate of less than 50 percent. Following a mysterious attack on congress in December of 2001 and a subsequent violent retribution, various international efforts, including those of the Organization of American States (OAS), have failed to find a negotiated solution to the political impasse that began after the 2000 parliamentary elections. The opposition Democratic Convergence (DC) has refused to cooperate with President Jean-Bertrand Aristide's efforts to stitch together a coalition that will satisfy the reservations of the United States and the OAS, and that will lead to an end to the sanctions imposed on Haiti. The country has become a dictatorship in all but name, as power has been monopolized by President Aristide and his Lavalas Family (FL) party.

Since gaining independence from France in 1804 following a slave revolt, the Republic of Haiti has endured a history of poverty, violence, instability, and dictatorship. A 1986 military coup ended 29 years of rule by the Duvalier family, and the army ruled for most of the next eight years. Under international pressure, the military permitted the implementation of a French-style constitution in 1987. It provides for a president elected for five years, an elected parliament composed of the 27-member Senate and the 83-member House of Representatives, and a prime minister appointed by the president.

President Aristide was first elected in 1990. Deposed by a military triumvirate after only eight months in office, for having called on his supporters to use force in defending his government, he was sent into exile. While paramilitary thugs terrorized the populace, the regime engaged in blatant narcotics trafficking. The United States and the UN imposed trade and oil embargoes. In September 1994, facing an imminent U.S. invasion, the officers stepped down. U.S. troops took control of the country, and Aristide was reinstated. Aristide dismantled the military before the June 1995 parliamentary elections got under way. International observers questioned the legitimacy of the June election, and Aristide's supporters fell out among themselves. The more militant FL movement remained firmly behind him, while the National Front for Change and Democracy (FNCD), a leftist coalition that had backed him in 1990, claimed fraud and boycotted the runoff elections. The FL won an overwhelming parliamentary majority.

The FL nominated Rene Preval, Aristide's prime minister in 1991, as its presidential candidate in the fall. In the December 17, 1995, election, marred by irregularities and fraud, Preval won about 89 percent of the vote with a turnout of less than one-third of those eligible; he took office February 7, 1996. The UN had planned to withdraw its troops by the end of the month. The new U.S.-trained Haitian National Police (HNP), however, lacked the competence to fill the void. At Preval's urging, the UN extended its stay, but by June cut its presence to 1,300. The final U.S. combat force had withdrawn two months earlier.

In September 1996, Preval purged much of his security force after allegations surfaced that members were involved in the murders of two politicians from the right-wing Mobilization for National Development (MDN) party. Senate elections held in April 1997 were beset by irregularities, and the resultant ongoing election dispute meant that parliament would not approve a new prime minister to replace Rosny Smarth, who resigned in June 1997 following growing criticism of the government's policies. In September, Aristide announced an alliance with other congressional groups to oppose Preval's economic reform plans.

Aristide had been revered as a defender of the powerless and was swept to victory again in November 2000. The elections were boycotted by all major opposition parties and held amidst widespread civil unrest and voter intimidation. Aristide ran on a populist platform of economic reactivation; opponents claimed he was bent on establishing a one-party state. Aristide's nearly 92 percent of the vote in the presidential election was mirrored in contests for nine senate seats—all won by his FL party—giving his new government all but one seat in the upper house. In parliamentary elections, which opponents claimed were rigged, the FL won 80 percent of the seats in the lower house.

Political Rights and Civil Liberties: The 1987 constitution provides citizens with the right to change their government peacefully. Credible charges of irregularities and fraud have beset every election since 1990. The FL has manipulated most legislative and general elections, including the presidential elections of 2000. In practice, the FL controls the presidential, legislative, and judicial branches, while most local and regional elected leaders are members of the FL.

The constitution guarantees a full range of political rights and civil liberties. At a practical level, these rights remain precarious, as the rule of law is tenuous at best and the situation is aggravated by a security vacuum. Political warfare involving the former military, Aristide supporters, and others continues unabated. In 2000 the FL itself appeared to be falling victim to open strife between warring factions.

The judicial system is corrupt, inefficient, and dysfunctional. The legal system is burdened by a large backlog, outdated legal codes, and poor facilities; business is conducted in French, rather than Creole, Haiti's majority language. Prison conditions are harsh, and the ponderous legal system guarantees lengthy pretrial detention periods. International reform efforts ended in 2000 following allegations of corruption involving the U.S. Agency for International Development (USAID), U.S. Justice Department contractors, and others.

The 5,200-member Haitian National Police (HNP) force has been politicized by the PL, is inexperienced, and lacks resources. The HNP has been accused of using excessive force and mistreating detainees, and accusations of corruption are frequent. The HNP is increasingly used against protesters attacking the government. Police brutality is on the rise and there is credible evidence of extrajudicial killing by members of the HNP. Mob violence and armed gangs pose serious threats in urban areas. Former soldiers and others linked to the former military regime, as well as common criminals, are responsible for much of the violence, including political assassinations. Break-ins and armed robberies are commonplace, and many observers tie the growing violence directly to increases in the drug trade and local narcotics consumption. Haitian officials also say that the rise in crime is due to the repatriation of convicted criminals from other countries, particularly the United States. Turf wars between rival drug gangs have resulted in the killing of scores of people, including several policemen. Private security forces that carry out extralegal search and seizure are flourishing.

Freedom of speech and the press are limited, and violence against journalists is common. International observers find that media outlets tend to self-censor in fear of violent retribution. There is a variety of newspapers, including two French-language newspapers, with a combined circulation of less than 20,000 readers. Many newspapers include a page of news in Creole. While opposition to the government can be found in the written press, it is beyond the reach of most, primarily because of illiteracy and cost. There are more than 250 private radio stations, including 40 in the capital. Most stations carry news and talk shows, which many citizens regard as their only opportunity to speak out with some freedom. Television is state run and strongly biased toward the government.

Satellite television is available, though it has minimal impact, as most Haitians cannot afford access to television. The few stations carrying news or opinion broadcasts express a range of views. There is no censorship of books or films, and access to the Internet is free. The official educational system is hostage to patronage and pressure from the PL.

There is freedom of religion. However, labor rights, as with all other legally sanctioned guarantees, are not respected. Unions are too weak to engage in collective bargaining, and their organizing efforts are undermined by the high unemployment rate. There is widespread violence against women and children. Trafficking of both drugs and people is a serious problem.

Honduras

Polity: Presidential-par-
liamentary democracy
Economy: Capitalist-statist
Population: 6,700,000
PPP: $2,453
Life Expectancy: 66
Religious Groups: Roman Catholic (97 percent), Protestant
Ethnic Groups: Mestizo (90 percent), Indian (7 percent),
black (2 percent), white (1 percent)
Capital: Tegucigalpa

Political Rights: 3
Civil Liberties: 3
Status: Partly Free

Ten-Year Ratings Timeline (Political Rights, Civil Liberties, Status)

1993	1994	1995	1996	1997	1998	1999	2000	2001	2002	2003
2,3F	3,3PF	3,3PF	3,3PF	3,3PF	2,3F	2,3F	3,3PF	3,3PF	3,3PF	3,3PF

Overview:

President Ricardo Maduro Joest of the center-left National Party of Honduras (PNH) took office on January 27, 2002, after winning the November elections. He defeated conservative Liberal Party (PL) candidate Rafael Pineda Ponce by 8 percent of the vote. The elections were characterized by international observers as mostly free, fair, and peaceful; they were the sixth held since military rule came to an end. On the eve of the election, however, congressional candidate Angel Pacheco, of the PNH, was gunned down outside his house; the police arrested three employees of the PL, indicating that the crime appeared to be politically motivated. Maduro was elected on a "zero tolerance" pledge aimed at ending crime.

In November, after being shamed by international publicity over the murder of nearly 1,300 children in four years, the government announced the formation of a special security force, in addition to the 6,000 new police officers already put on the streets. Killers have been identified in less than 40 percent of these cases. Impunity and corruption, much of it official, still characterize a country Transparency International has identified as one of the most corrupt in the world.

The Republic of Honduras was established in 1839, eighteen years after independence from Spain. It has endured decades of military rule and an intermittently elected government. The last military regime gave way to elected civilian rule in 1982. The constitution provides for a president and a 130-member, unicameral congress elected for four years.

Official corruption and the lingering power of the military have dominated the political scene since the return to democracy. The aftereffects of Hurricane Mitch, which devastated the country's economy and infrastructure in 1998, continued to be felt. About two-thirds of the country's households live in poverty, and 40 percent of the population lives on less than one dollar a day.

Political Rights and Civil Liberties:

Citizens are able to change their government through regularly scheduled elections. The 2001 contest was considered generally free and fair. Constitutional guarantees regarding free expression, freedom of religion, and the right to form political parties and civic organizations are generally respected, although repressive measures in the face of peaceful protests and mounting crime have limited political rights and civil liberties.

There are constitutional guarantees for freedom of speech and of the press, and the authorities generally respect these rights. There are, however, important exceptions. In 2001 the Inter-American Commission on Human Rights reported that the government had impeded public criticism of government actions. Journalists have admitted to self-censorship when they uncover reports that threaten the political or economic interests of media owners. Newspapers circulate freely, and numerous radio and television stations broadcast freely. There are, however, credible reports of repression against journalists. There is free access to the Internet. Academic freedom is generally honored.

Political Rights and Civil Liberties: The judicial system is weak and open to corruption. Death threats and violent attacks continue against judges who take on human rights cases. Prison conditions are deplorable, and prisoners awaiting trial are housed with convicted inmates; due process is generally not available. There is a generalized lawlessness that has allowed private and vigilante security forces to commit a number of arbitrary and summary executions, including the murder of hundreds of street children. Drug-related corruption is pervasive.

The police are underfunded, ill-trained, understaffed, and highly corrupt. The military controlled the police since 1963, but beginning in 1997 civilian control was reestablished. In the past the military has been used for internal security tasks—suppressing labor unrest, quelling street protests, and combating street crime. Extrajudicial killing, arbitrary detention, and torture by the police still take place. More than 120 youth gangs engage in murder, kidnapping, and robbery, as well as drug trafficking. The need to strengthen and professionalize the poorly equipped civilian police is hampered by a lack of public confidence. At the invitation of the government, the UN Special Rapporteur on Extrajudicial, Arbitrary, and Summary Executions visited Honduras in 2001 and noted evidence of 66 minors killed by police and private security forces from January to June of 2001, and of the government's negligence in investigating or preventing extrajudicial and summary executions.

The military exerts considerable, if waning, influence over the government. A constitutional amendment established a civilian minister of defense in direct control over the armed forces and replaced the armed forces commander in chief with the chief of the joint staff. Congress also passed the Organic Law of the armed forces to solidify civilian control over the military. The Armed Forces made public its budget for the first time in 2001. Most criminal cases against the military remained in military court jurisdiction, and charges were usually dismissed. Since 1999 military personnel have no longer been immune from prosecution in civilian courts. Military officers have been found guilty of drug trafficking, including taking sides in cartel turf wars and protecting drug shipments in transit through Honduras.

Labor unions are well organized and can strike, although labor actions often result in clashes with security forces. Labor leaders and members of religious groups and indigenous-based peasant unions pressing for land rights remain vulnerable to repression and some have been killed. Some 85,000 workers, mostly women, are employed in the low-wage *maquiladora* (export-processing zones). Child labor is a problem in rural areas and in the informal economy. The government of President Carlos Flores Facusse (1997-2001) made efforts to give the concerns of indigenous and black peoples in Honduras a more prominent place in the public agenda.

Hungary

Polity: Parliamentary democracy
Economy: Mixed capitalist
Population: 10,100,000
PPP: $12,416
Life Expectancy: 72

Political Rights: 1
Civil Liberties: 2
Status: Free

Religious Groups: Roman Catholic (67.5 percent), Calvinist (20 percent), Lutheran (5 percent), other (7.5 percent)
Ethnic Groups: Hungarian (90 percent), Roma [Gypsy] (4 percent), German (3 percent), other (3 percent)
Capital: Budapest

Ten-Year Ratings Timeline (Political Rights, Civil Liberties, Status)

1993	1994	1995	1996	1997	1998	1999	2000	2001	2002	2003
2,2F	1,2F	1,2F	1,2F	1,2F	1,2F	1,2F	1,2F	1,2F	1,2F	1,2F

Overview:

In 2002, Hungary welcomed an official invitation to join the EU and began the final legislative measures necessary for accession. The year also witnessed a bitterly fought parliamentary campaign, a series of high-profile Communist-era spy scandals, and ongoing questions over independence of the media.

In the late 1980s, Hungary's economy was in sharp decline. The Hungarian Socialist Worker's Party came under intense pressure to accept reforms. Ultimately, the party congress dissolved itself, and Hungary held its first free, multiparty parliamentary election in 1990. Since that time, government control in Hungary has passed freely and fairly between left- and right-leaning parties. The country has followed an aggressive path of reform and pursued the very popular cause of European integration. Having joined NATO in 1999, Hungary will likely join the EU in 2004.

During 2002, the country witnessed a closely contested parliamentary election. The April elections to the 386-seat unicameral National Assembly were generally free and fair. After two rounds of voting, Prime Minister Viktor Orban's ruling coalition of the Hungarian Civic Party–Hungarian Democratic Forum (Fidesz–MDF) garnered just over 44 percent of the vote (188 mandates) and was unable to retain control of the National Assembly. The Hungarian Socialist Party (MSZP) won 42.8 percent (178 mandates). The Alliance of Free Democrats (SZDSZ) narrowly exceeded the 5 percent threshold (19 mandates). Voters elected one candidate on a joint MSZP-SZDSZ ticket. Following the election, the MSZP formed a majority government in partnership with the SZDSZ. The new Socialist-Liberal government elected Peter Medgyessy as prime minister.

Almost immediately, the new government faced a coalition crisis when reports emerged that Prime Minister Medgyessy had acted as an agent for the Communist Interior Ministry's counterintelligence division (Division III/II). The coalition survived, and the National Assembly soon after introduced legislation to open the Division III/II records of any individual seeking public office. Prime Minister Medgyessy never denied charges that he worked for Division III/II while at the Finance Ministry in the late 1970s and early 1980s. He did, however, allege that opposition forces were attempting to distract his government from investigating corruption in the previous (Orban) government.

While the opposition press first broke the story on Medgyessy's past, the scope of the revelations rapidly widened beyond the prime minister. In the course of a subsequent parliamentary investigation, 10 present and former high-level government officials were alleged to have had connections with Division III/II. Zoltan Pokorni resigned as Fidesz party chairman after revealing that his father had been pressured into acting as a secret police informer. Both a national police commander and a prominent right-wing lawmaker also admitted past links to Division III/II. Despite the political controversy, the spy revelations did not produce a widespread coming-to-terms process with the Communist past, and the Hungarian public was largely uninterested in the entire affair.

Political Rights and Civil Liberties: Citizens age 18 and older enjoy universal suffrage and can change their government democratically. Hungary is a multiparty parliamentary democracy with legislative, executive, and judicial branches of government. Voters elect representatives to the National Assembly under a mixed system of proportional and direct representation. The Hungarian parliament elects both the president and the prime minister.

Post-Communist elections in Hungary have been generally free and fair, although some problems persist. During the heated 2002 parliamentary elections few parties respected campaign spending caps. The OSCE reported complaints that state media coverage frequently favored the ruling Fidesz party and that government-sponsored "voter education" advertisements appeared to mirror Fidesz-sponsored campaign ads. Prior to the election, Fidesz and Lundo Drom, a national Roma (Gypsy) party, concluded a political cooperation agreement. Yet, despite this development, only four Roma candidates were elected to the National Assembly, the same number as in the previous election. Toward the end of 2002, the European Commission reported that Hungary was not meeting its constitutional obligation to ensure direct parliamentary representation of minorities.

The constitution does guarantee national and ethnic minorities the right to form self-governing bodies. All 13 recognized minorities have exercised this right. In 2001, Hungary implemented a legal rights protection network to provide legal aid to the Roma community. The government also created the Roma Coordination Council and appointed special commissioners in the Ministry of Education and Employment and the Ministry Labor to specifically oversee Roma issues. Still, the Roma population continues to face widespread discrimination in employment, education, housing, and health care. In 2001, parliament passed a controversial Status Law granting special health and educational benefits to ethnic Hungarians residing outside the country. The governments of Romania and Slovakia expressed deep concern over the discriminatory nature of the law. In 2002, Hungary agreed to amend the law on the basis of recommendations from the OSCE and the Council of Europe, but had failed to do so by the end of the year.

Hungary largely respects freedom of speech. Independent media thrive in Hungary. However, political controversy continues to trouble state television and radio. A 1996 media law requires both ruling and opposition parties to share appointments to state media oversight boards. Left-leaning opposition parties had previously accused the Fidesz party of stacking the oversight boards with supporters. After losing power in the parliamentary elections, Fidesz leaders accused the new Socialist-Liberal government of attempting to inappropriately influence state television and radio. Both the Medgyessy government and the opposition have pledged to amend the current media law, but neither side possesses the two-thirds parliamentary majority necessary to pass the legislation. Also during the year, editors of a major right-wing opposition newspaper accused the center-left government of exerting pressure on advertisers to cancel their contracts with the publication, thus endangering the paper's financial viability.

The government respects citizens' rights to form associations, strike, and petition public authorities. Trade unions account for less than 30 percent of the workforce. Hungary has some of the most progressive nongovernmental organization tax laws in post-Communist Europe, and the country maintains a robust civil society environment with more than 67,000 registered NGOs and civic groups. The constitution guarantees religious freedom and provides for the separation of church and state. While all religions are generally free to worship in their own manner, the state provides financial support and tax breaks to large or traditional religions such as the Roman Catholic Church. Some critics have charged that these practices effectively discriminate against smaller denominations.

Hungary has a three-tiered independent judiciary and a constitutional court. The constitution guarantees equality before the law, and courts are generally fair, yet limited budgetary resources leave the system vulnerable to outside influence. In its 2002 report, the European Commission found that corruption remains a problem in Hungary. Nevertheless, the commission applauded both the previous and current governments for measures to reform the civil service, introduce stronger penalties for bribery, and implement a long-term anticorruption strategy.

Iceland

Polity: Parliamentary democracy
Economy: Capitalist
Population: 300,000
PPP: $29,581
Life Expectancy: 79
Religious Groups: Evangelical Lutheran (93 percent), Protestant and Roman Catholic (7 percent)
Ethnic Groups: Icelander
Capital: Reykjavik

Political Rights: 1
Civil Liberties: 1
Status: Free

Ten-Year Ratings Timeline (Political Rights, Civil Liberties, Status)

1993	1994	1995	1996	1997	1998	1999	2000	2001	2002	2003
1,1F	1,1F	1,1F	1,1F	1,1F	1,1F	1,1F	1,1F	1,1F	1,1F	1,1F

Overview:

Elected in 1991, Prime Minister David Oddsson, head of the conservative Independence Party, is the longest-serving prime minister in Europe. Under his leadership, the country has enjoyed economic growth, with unemployment at just one percent. The International Whaling Commission (IWC) refused Iceland's bid for membership for the second consecutive year for the country's refusal to sign a commercial whale-hunting ban. Iceland installed facial-imaging scanners in its international airport. American civil liberties groups have criticized such technology. Scientists and government officials explored transforming Iceland's economy into one based entirely on hydrogen power.

Iceland achieved full independence in 1944. Multiparty governments have been in power since then. On August 1, 1996, the former finance minister and former leader of the leftist People's Alliance, Dr. Olafur Ragnar Grimsson, was sworn in as Iceland's fifth president. The current government is composed of a coalition of Prime Minister Oddsson's Independence Party and the liberal Progressive Party.

The standard of living in Iceland ranks among the highest in the world and Icelanders enjoy an extensive social welfare system. With unemployment at only one percent and ecotourism growing, public debt is expected to be dissolved by 2004. Fishing accounts for two-thirds of Iceland's exports and employs one-tenth of its workforce.

While Iceland has strong historical, cultural, and economic ties with Europe, Icelanders are hesitant to join the European Union, primarily because of its Common Fisheries Policy. Icelanders believe the policy would threaten their marine industry. While Prime Minister Oddsson continues to rule out joining the European Union, he has expressed his desire to cultivate a knowledge economy in order to wean the country from dependence on the fishing industry. The left-leaning opposition, consisting of two camps, is divided on the issue of EU membership. The Social Democratic faction of the United Left bloc is in favor of submitting an application to the European Union, and the Green-Left Alliance opposes EU membership. The country already has access to European markets as a member of the European Economic Area (EEA).

Iceland is exploring ways to transform itself into a hydrogen-based economy. The country's abundant hydrothermal and geothermal resources place it in a unique position to phase out the use of fossil fuels in favor of hydrogen, a clean-burning fuel that could power all forms of transport vehicles and eliminate greenhouse gasses. All of Reykjavik is already heated by geothermal power drawn from the ground.

In May, for the second time in two years, Iceland was denied membership in the IWC because of its refusal to sign a commercial hunting ban. Whale hunting is a cultural tradition in Iceland and a lucrative trade. Iceland argues that numbers of endangered whale species have recovered and that a 1986 moratorium on whaling should be lifted. It also argues that the rising whale population consumes fish stocks vital to its economy.

Political Rights and Civil Liberties:

Icelanders can change their government democratically. Iceland's constitution was adopted by referendum in 1944 and vests power in a president (whose functions are mainly ceremonial), a prime minister, a legislature, and a judiciary. The president is directly elected for a four-year term. The unicameral legislature is also elected for four years (subject to dissolution). The prime minister, who performs most executive functions, is appointed by the president but is responsible to the legislature.

The country's judiciary is independent. The law does not provide for trial by jury, but many trials and appeals use panels consisting of several judges. All judges, at all levels, serve for life.

In August, Transparency International ranked Iceland the fourth-least corrupt country in the world in its Corruption Perceptions Index.

The constitution provides for freedom of speech and of the press. A wide range of publications includes both independent and party-affiliated newspapers. An autonomous board of directors oversees the Icelandic State Broadcasting Service, which operates a number of transmitting and relay stations. There are both private and public television stations. Iceland has the highest Internet penetration rate in the world, with more than 80 percent of the population accessing the Internet from home.

Iceland handed over its citizens' genetic data to a private, U.S.-backed, medical research company in 2000, raising some fears over privacy issues. Iceland, the most genetically homogenous nation on earth, went ahead with the plan on the grounds that the data could provide scientists with vital clues into the origin of diseases, thus increasing the chances of discovering cures. While a law was passed requiring doctors to hand over patient information, the law did contain a provision allowing citizens to opt out of providing genetic data. Only 5 percent of Icelanders reportedly decided not to participate in the program.

In the aftermath of the September 11, 2001, terrorist attacks in the United States, Iceland introduced facial-recognition scanners at its airport in Reykjavik. The technology purportedly can identify anyone on a wanted list; its installation was deemed necessary since Iceland serves as a popular transit point between Europe and the United States. The American Civil Liberties Union has criticized facial-recognition technology as unreliable, with the potential to violate the civil liberties of nonsuspects.

In recent years, Iceland has not received a substantial number of refugees or asylum seekers, although it has accepted several dozen refugees from the Balkans.

Legislation adopted in 1996 permits homosexuals to live together in a formal relationship with the same legal rights as in marriage, minus the right to adopt children or to be artificially inseminated.

Virtually everyone in the country holds at least nominal membership in the state-supported Lutheran Church. Freedom of worship is respected, and discrimination on the basis of race, language, social class, or sex is outlawed.

The constitution provides for freedom of association and peaceful assembly. About 76 percent of all eligible workers belong to free trade unions, and all enjoy the right to strike. Disabled persons enjoy extensive rights in employment and education.

Gender-based equality is guaranteed by law. In 2001, the United Nations ranked Iceland second in the world in terms of equal rights between the sexes. In 1995, women held 17 out of the 63 seats in parliament. That number rose to 22, or approximately 35 percent, after the 1999 elections. The Women's Alliance, an Icelandic feminist movement founded in 1983, is registered as a political party and has its own parliamentary faction.

⬇ India

Polity: Parliamentary democracy
Economy: Capitalist-statist
Population: 1,049,500,000
PPP: $2,358
Life Expectancy: 63

Political Rights: 2
Civil Liberties: 3
Status: Free

Religious Groups: Hindu (81.3 percent), Muslim (12 percent), Christian (2.3 percent), other (4.4 percent)
Ethnic Groups: Indo-Aryan (72 percent), Dravidian (25 percent), other (3 percent)
Capital: New Delhi
Trend Arrow: India received a downward trend arrow as a result of ongoing state-sanctioned communal violence in the state of Gujarat and the state's subsequent response.

Ten-Year Ratings Timeline (Political Rights, Civil Liberties, Status)

1993	1994	1995	1996	1997	1998	1999	2000	2001	2002	2003
3,4NF	4,4PF	4,4PF	4,4PF	2,4PF	2,4PF	2,3F	2,3F	2,3F	2,3F	2,3F

Overview:
India's ruling coalition government, headed by the Hindu nationalist Bharatiya Janata Party (BJP), faced a number of challenges in 2002. The BJP suffered further electoral defeats in several key state elections. After part of a train carrying Hindu extremists was torched in Godhra station in February, a frenzy of violence directed at the Muslim minority erupted in the state of Gujarat. The BJP-controlled state government showed an initial unwillingness to contain the unrest, which continued sporadically for several months, and evidence later surfaced that both the state administration and the police force had been complicit in the killing and destruction. The national BJP leadership rejected calls on the part of the opposition, the press, and other non-

governmental actors for accountability, and in December, the BJP won state elections in Gujarat on an anti-minority platform. Analysts expressed concern that the rising majoritarianism expressed by Hindu nationalists threatened India's tradition of vibrant and inclusive democracy. Heightened tensions with neighboring Pakistan over the disputed territory of Kashmir brought the two countries close to war in May and led to increased international concern about the possibility of a nuclear confrontation.

India achieved independence in 1947 with the partition of British India into a predominantly Hindu India, under Prime Minister Jawaharlal Nehru, and a Muslim Pakistan. The centrist, secular Congress Party ruled continuously at the federal level for the first five decades of independence, except for periods of opposition from 1977 through 1980 and from 1989 through 1991.

After winning the 1991 elections, the Congress government responded to a balance-of-payments crisis by initiating gradual reforms of the autarkic, control-bound economy. However, even as the economic crisis receded, the party lost 11 state elections in the mid-1990s. Congress's traditional electoral base of poor, low-caste, and Muslim voters appeared disillusioned with economic liberalization and, in the case of Muslims, the government's failure to prevent communal violence. In December 1992, India experienced some of the worst communal violence since independence after Hindu fundamentalists destroyed a sixteenth-century mosque in the northern town of Ayodhya. The rioting killed some 2,000 people, mainly Muslims. Regional parties made gains in southern India, and low-caste parties and the BJP gained in the northern Hindi-speaking belt.

During 1996 and 1997 a series of minority coalitions—led by both the BJP and a leftist-regional combine—tried unsuccessfully to form a stable government after parliamentary elections held in May 1996. Because of infighting among centrist and leftist parties, the BJP was able to form a government under Atal Behari Vajpayee in 1998. One of the government's first major acts was to carry out a series of underground nuclear tests in May 1998. Holding only a minority of seats, the BJP government faced frequent threats and demands from small but pivotal coalition members. The government fell after a Tamil Nadu-based party defected, but it won reelection in 1999. Final election results gave the BJP-led, 22-party National Democratic Alliance 295 seats (182 for the BJP) against 112 seats for Congress.

The government was shaken in 2001 by a sting operation conducted by an investigative-news Internet site that caught both defense officials and key party leaders taking bribes, which led to the resignation of Defense Minister George Fernandes. While the coalition government survived the loss of one of its partners, its credibility was further weakened by the reinduction of Fernandes into the cabinet prior to the completion of a judicial inquiry into the scandal. The BJP was defeated in five key state elections that year, and in state elections held in February the party suffered further losses, including that of Uttar Pradesh, India's most populous and politically important state. Perhaps as a reaction to its electoral losses, the BJP continued to shift to the ideological right during 2002, with the promotion of hardliner Lal Krishna Advani to the post of deputy prime minister in July as well as the selection of Manohar Joshi of the Hindu extremist Shiv Sena party as speaker of the lower house of parliament in May.

On February 27, at least fifty-eight people were killed when a fire broke out on a train carrying members of a Hindu extremist group, the Vishwa Hindu Parishad (VHP, or World Hindu Council). A Muslim mob was initially blamed for the Godhra fire (although subsequent forensic tests have proved inconclusive), and in the backlash that followed throughout Gujarat, more than 1,000 people were killed and roughly 100,000 were left homeless and dispossessed. Hindu mobs converged on Muslim neighborhoods, looting and destroying homes, businesses, and places of worship. The violence was orchestrated by Hindu nationalist groups such as the VHP, the Rashtriya Swayamsevak Sangh (National Volunteer Service), and the Bajrang Dal, who organized transportation and provisions for the mobs provided printed records of Muslim-owned property, calling for an economic boycott of all Muslims. Evidence that the BJP-headed state government led by Chief Minister Narendra Modi was complicit in the carnage led to calls for Modi's resignation or dismissal, but the party leadership continued to support him. Hoping to capitalize on a wave of Hindu support, Modi dissolved the state assembly in July and asked permission to hold fresh elections immediately, but the Election Commission ruled out holding early elections, citing continuing problems with law and order. In elections held in December in which Modi campaigned on an overtly nationalistic and anti-Muslim platform, the BJP won a landslide reelection victory, gaining control of 126 of the state assembly's 182 seats.

Following an attack on the Indian parliament building in December 2001 by a Pakistan-based militant group, relations between India and Pakistan worsened and remained tense throughout 2002. India accused Pakistan of fostering cross-border terrorism in Kashmir and mobilized hundreds of thousands of troops along their common border. The two countries came close to war in May, prompting a flurry of diplomatic activity on the part of the United States. Pakistan-based militant groups carried out several major attacks during the year, including an attack on the Kaluchak army camp in Kashmir in May and an attack on a Hindu temple in Gujarat in September.

Political Rights and Civil Liberties: Indian citizens can change their government through elections. The 1950 constitution provides for a lower, 543-seat *Lok Sabha* (House of the People), directly elected for a five-year term (plus 2 appointed seats for Indians of European descent), and an upper *Rajya Sabha* (Council of States), whose 245 representatives are either elected by the state legislatures or nominated by the president. Executive power is vested in a prime minister and a cabinet. A new president, nuclear scientist Abdul Kalam, was elected by members of the central and state assemblies in July. Recent elections have generally been free and fair, although violence and irregularities have marred balloting in several electoral districts. In the 1999 national elections, guerrilla attacks in Bihar and northeast India, and interparty clashes in several states, killed some 130 people. The BBC reported that during the state elections in Manipur held in February, 10 people were killed by militants.

Democratic rule continued to be undermined by political infighting, pervasive criminality in politics, decrepit state institutions, and widespread corruption. Transparency International's 2002 Corruption Perceptions Index ranked India in 71st place out of 102 countries. The electoral system depends on a system of "black" money that is obtained though tax evasion and other means. Moreover, criminality is a pervasive feature of political life. In July, the *Asian Times* reported that roughly 10 percent of national and state legislators were facing charges of murder, rape, or armed robbery. A proposed directive issued by the Election Commission that would have required candidates seeking election to declare their financial assets, criminal records, and educational backgrounds, along with their nomination forms was rejected by all major political parties.

India's private press continued to be vigorous although journalists faced a number of constraints. In recent years, the government has occasionally used its power under the Official Secrets Act to censor security-related articles. Intimidation of journalists by a variety of actors increased in 2002. A crime reporter for a Hindi-language daily was assassinated in April, and in October, a television journalist in Manipur was tortured and killed by suspected separatist rebels. In April, police attacked a group of journalists covering a peace demonstration in Gujarat, and an attack on a newspaper in Tamil Nadu in July left several journalists injured. Official harassment of the investigative news Internet portal Tehelka.com and one of its funders continued throughout the year. Radio is both public and private, but the state-owned All India Radio enjoys the dominant position and its news coverage favors the government. Television is no longer a government monopoly, and according to the government press agency, 90 percent of channels are privately owned. In June, the government ended a 50-year ban on foreign ownership of the print media.

Religious freedom continued to be generally respected, but violence against religious minorities remained a problem. In September, the U.S. Commission on International Religious Freedom recommended that India be designated a "country of particular concern" in response to the horrific attacks against Muslims by Hindu mobs in the state of Gujarat, coupled with evidence of state government complicity in the violence and its failure to prosecute those responsible. Attacks on Christian targets, including murders and rapes of clergy and the destruction of property, have dramatically increased since the BJP came to power in 1998, mainly in the predominantly tribal regions of Orissa, Gujarat, Bihar, and Madhya Pradesh. Local media and some members of the *sangh parivar*, a group of Hindu nationalist organizations including the BJP, promote anti-Christian propaganda. In October, legislators in Tamil Nadu overwhelmingly approved a bill banning forced religious conversions. The law had been opposed by Christian, Muslim, and low-caste Hindu groups, who argued that its provisions could be misused.

There are some restrictions on freedom of assembly and association. Section 144 of the criminal procedure code empowers state-level authorities to declare a state of emergency, restrict free assembly, and impose curfews. In recent years, officials have occasionally used Section 144 to prevent demonstrations, and police frequently use excessive force against demonstrators. Human rights groups say that police and hired thugs have occasionally beaten, arbitrarily detained, or otherwise harassed villagers and members of nongovernmental organizations who were protesting forced relocations from the sites of development projects. In July, Amnesty International called for an inquiry into reports of police brutality during an operation to forcibly evict and relocate villagers in Madhya Pradesh. Some minority groups criticized the government's 2001 decision to ban the Students Islamic Movement of India as part of a general crackdown on terrorism while ignoring the activities of right-wing Hindu groups.

Human rights organizations generally operated freely. However, Amnesty International's 2002 annual report noted that the harassment of human rights defenders by state officials and other actors, including beating, shooting, and the use of excessive force by police, remained a concern. An Amnesty International team that was hoping to assess the situation in Gujarat was denied visas by the Indian government in July. A report issued by Human Rights Watch documented numerous cases of police harassment of HIV/AIDS-outreach workers in several states. The work of rights activists could also be hindered by a Home Ministry order issued in July 2001 that requires organizations to obtain clearance before holding conferences or workshops if the subject matter is "political, semi-political, communal or religious in nature or is related to human rights."

Workers regularly exercise their rights to bargain collectively and strike. In April, around 10 million workers held a one-day strike to protest proposed labor-law changes and privatization plans. The Essential Services Maintenance Act enables the government to ban strikes in certain "essential" industries, and limits the right of public servants to strike. The BBC estimated in May that there are up to 100 million child laborers in India. Many work in the informal sector in hazardous conditions, and several million are bonded laborers. Several cases involving the trafficking of child laborers across state lines were reported during 2002.

The judiciary is independent. Judges have exercised unprecedented activism in response to public-interest litigation over official corruption, environmental issues, and other matters. However, during the past two years, courts have initiated several contempt-of-court cases against activists and journalists, raising questions about their misuse of the law to intimidate those who expose the behavior of corrupt judges or who question their verdicts. Corruption is reportedly rife among lower-level judges, and access to justice by the socially and economically marginalized sections of society remains limited. According to the U.S. State Department's human rights report, the court system is severely overloaded, which results in the detention of a large number of unconvicted persons who are awaiting trial.

Police routinely torture suspects to extract confessions and abuse ordinary prisoners, particularly members of the lower castes. Custodial rape of female detainees continues to be a problem. While the National Human Rights Commission (NHRC) monitors custodial deaths (with 1,305 deaths being reported from April 2001 to March 2002) and other abuses, it has few enforcement powers. This is partly because the criminal procedure code requires the central or state governments to approve prosecution of security force members, which is rarely granted. However, in January, a court in Rajasthan sentenced five policemen to life imprisonment for the killing of three people in custody nearly 14 years ago. Nongovernmental organizations alleged that police in Gujarat had been given orders by the state government not to intervene during the communal violence that engulfed the state in March, and that police have also refused to register complaints against those accused of murder, rape, and other crimes, or arrest those known to have played a role in the rioting. Reports by the NHRC, Human Rights Watch, and a number of other groups implicated the state's political leadership, as well as the administrative and police apparatus, in both the initial violence and the official response to it.

Police, army, and paramilitary forces continue to be implicated in "disappearances," extrajudicial killings, rapes, tortures, arbitrary detentions, and destruction of homes, particularly in the context of insurgencies in Kashmir, Andhra Pradesh, Assam, and several other northeastern states. The 1958 Armed Forces (Special Powers) Act grants security forces broad powers to use lethal force and detention in Assam and four nearby states, and provides near immunity from prosecution to security forces acting under it. In August 2001, Indian human rights groups expressed concern over governmental plans to give amnesties to security force personnel facing human rights charges. Security forces continued to detain suspects under the broadly drawn 1980 National Security Act, which authorizes detention without charge for up to one year.

In March, the Prevention of Terrorism Ordinance was passed by a joint session of parliament. In addition to widening the definition of terrorism and banning a number of terrorist organizations, the bill also increases the state's powers of investigation and allows for up to 90 days of preventative detention without charge. Activists are worried that the bill could be used to harass members of certain organizations as well as minority groups. A large number of Muslims suspected of involvement in the Godhra train attack were detained under the provisions of the bill, but were later charged under other legislation.

In India's seven northeastern states, more than 40 mainly tribal-based insurgent groups sporadically attacked security forces and engaged in intertribal and internecine violence. The rebel groups have also been implicated in numerous killings, abductions, and rapes of civilians. The militants ostensibly seek either greater autonomy or complete independence for their ethnic or tribal groups. Police in Andhra Pradesh continue to battle the People's War Group (PWG), a guerilla organization. It is estimated that more than 6,000 people have been killed during its violent 20-year campaign to establish a Communist state in the tribal areas of Andhra Pradesh, Mahrashtra, Orissa, Bihar, and Chhattisgarh. Peace talks between the PWG and the state government broke down in July after the government decided to renew its ban on the group. In a number of states, left-wing guerrillas called Naxalites control some rural areas and kill dozens of police, politicians, landlords, and villagers each year.

The constitution bars discrimination based on caste, and laws set aside quotas in education and government jobs for members of lower castes. However, evidence suggested that members of so-called scheduled castes and scheduled tribes, as well as religious and ethnic minorities, continue to routinely face unofficial discrimination and violence. The worst abuse is faced by the 160 million *dalits*, or untouchables, who are often denied access to land, abused by landlords and police, and forced to work in miserable conditions.

Each year, several thousand women are burned to death, driven to suicide, or otherwise killed, and countless others are harassed, beaten, or deserted by husbands in the context of dowry disputes. Despite the fact that dowry is illegal, convictions in dowry deaths continued to be rare. Rape and other violence against women also continued to be serious problems, with lower-caste and tribal women being particularly vulnerable to attacks. Although the authorities have acknowledged the severity of the issue, local officials continue to ignore complaints, take bribes, and cover up abuses, according to an Amnesty International report issued in May 2001. Muslim women and girls were subjected to horrific sexual violence during the communal violence that engulfed Gujarat in March. Muslim personal status laws as well as traditional Hindu practices discriminate against women in terms of inheritance rights. The increasing use of sex-determination tests during pregnancy has led to a growing imbalance in the male-female birth ratios in a number of states, particularly in the northwest.

Indonesia

Polity: Presidential-
parliamentary democracy
(military-influenced)
Economy: Capitalist-statist
Population: 217,000,000
PPP: $3,043
Life Expectancy: 68

Political Rights: 3
Civil Liberties: 4
Status: Partly Free

Religious Groups: Muslim (88 percent), Protestant (5 percent),
Roman Catholic (3 percent), other (4 percent)
Ethnic Groups: Javanese (45 percent), Sundanese (14 percent), Madurese (8 percent),
Malay (8 percent), other (25 percent)
Capital: Jakarta

Ten-Year Ratings Timeline (Political Rights, Civil Liberties, Status)

1993	1994	1995	1996	1997	1998	1999	2000	2001	2002	2003
6,5PF	7,6NF	7,6NF	7,6NF	7,5NF	7,5NF	6,4PF	4,4PF	3,4PF	3,4PF	3,4PF

Overview:

After four tumultuous years that saw a dictatorship unravel and two presidents ousted by a newly boisterous parliament, Indonesian politics took on more muted tones in 2002, while social problems continued to fester. With Jakarta's political elite jockeying for position in the presidential and legislative elections due in 2004, both President Megawati Sukarnoputri and parliament seemed either unwilling or unable to take bold steps to tackle the many pressing problems faced by the world's fourth most populous country. These include a sluggish economy, widespread graft, and weak political institutions, violent conflicts in several provinces, and the presence of a tiny but growing number of homegrown Islamic militants with possible links to the al-Qaeda terrorism network.

At year's end, however, the government appeared more willing to address at least some of these problems, working out a ceasefire with pro-independence rebels in Aceh province in December and tracking down the suspects in a deadly October terrorist attack on the resort island of Bali.

Indonesia won full independence in 1949 following a four-year, intermittent war against its Dutch colonial rulers. After several parliamentary governments collapsed, the republic's first president, Sukarno, took on authoritarian powers in 1957 under a system that he called "Guided Democracy." Amid continued political turbulence and economic stagnation, the army, led by General Suharto, crushed an apparent coup attempt in 1965 that it blamed on the Communist Party of Indonesia (PKI). In the aftermath, the army reportedly backed the massacre, between 1965 and 1967, of some 500,000 people, mainly PKI members and ethnic Chinese. With the army's support, Suharto rebuffed Sukarno's efforts to stay in power and in 1968 formally became president.

Suharto's autocratic "New Order" regime jailed scores of dissidents, banned most opposition parties and groups, and allowed only three parties to contest elections: the ruling Golkar, the nationalist Indonesian Democratic Party (PDI), and the

Islamic-oriented United Development Party (PPP). In the 1990s, Suharto increasingly concentrated power in himself and family members, who received an outsized share of government contracts.

In part to sustain his power, Suharto's government launched programs that helped lift millions of Indonesians out of poverty. Pundits placed Indonesia in the ranks of the "Asian Tiger" economies as output grew by 7.6 percent per year, on average, between 1987 and 1996. By 1997, however, years of poor investment decisions and profligate borrowing from weakly supervised banks had saddled Indonesian firms with some $80 billion in foreign debt. To stave off a private sector debt default, the government agreed in October 1997 to a $43 billion loan package set up by the International Monetary Fund (IMF) in return for cutting public spending and breaking up business monopolies held by Suharto relatives and cronies.

Suharto made few efforts to meet Indonesia's IMF commitments, while a plunging *rupiah* sent food prices soaring. Suharto resigned in May 1998 following months of unprecedented antigovernment protests and three days of devastating urban riots. Vice President B. J. Habibie, a long-time Suharto loyalist, became president. Having consistently backed Suharto throughout his 32-year rule, the military, then headed by General Wiranto, played a key role in easing him from office.

In Indonesia's first free parliamentary elections in decades, Megawati's Indonesian Democratic Party–Struggle (PDI-P), the successor to the PDI, won 154 of the 462 contested seats; Golkar, 120; PPP, 58; the National Awakening Party, led by Abdurrahman Wahid, then leader of Indonesia's largest Muslim social group, 51; the National Mandate Party, led by Amien Rais, another Muslim leader, 35; and 16 other parties, 44. In addition, 38 seats were reserved for the military and police.

In another break with the Suharto era, in October 1999, Indonesia's national assembly elected Wahid president and Megawati vice president in its first-ever competitive vote. Previously, the body, called the People's Consultative Assembly (MPR), consisting of parliament plus 195 appointed representatives, simply rubber-stamped Suharto's decision to hold another term.

Wahid increased civilian control over Indonesia's powerful armed forces, though he was less successful in jump-starting the economy or in containing the insurgency in Aceh as well as deadly ethnic and sectarian violence in the Moluccas, Kalimantan, and Sulawesi. His relations with the newly forceful parliament grew increasingly bitter in 2000 thanks to the president's repeated criticism of legislative leaders. Megawati, the daughter of the republic's first president, took office as president in July 2001 after the MPR ousted Wahid over his ineffective economic policies and alleged involvement in at least two scandals. The vote highlighted the legislature's growing role as a check on presidential power.

As president, Megawati, 55, has fostered good relations with parliament by bringing into her government all of the major parties. She has also persuaded the IMF to resume lending to Indonesia and pursued corruption cases against senior politicians such as Akbar Tanjung, the parliamentary speaker and Golkar leader. Critics say, however, that her administration has not done enough to crack down on corruption, reform the legal system, strengthen political institutions, and pursue cases against senior military officers for past abuses in East Timor and other areas.

The government may be even more reluctant to carry out reforms as the 2004 elections approach for fear of upsetting potential backers. Already, PDI-P officials reportedly fear that Tanjung's corruption conviction could undermine efforts to forge a secular electoral alliance between the PDI-P, Golkar, and the National Awakening Party. Failure to cobble together an alliance could boost the fortunes of the Islamic parties, which together hold nearly one-fourth of parliament's seats but are riven by internal power struggles and policy differences.

At the same time, some analysts say, a coalition aimed at isolating conservative Islamic parties risks creating a religious opposition bloc and deepening a secular-religious political divide that has arisen since Suharto's ouster. Islamic parties tend to favor preferential economic policies for the majority Malays and partial imposition of Islamic law.

Meanwhile, security concerns have become a leading issue in the wake of the Bali bombing, which killed around 190 people. Western and neighboring Southeast Asian governments expressed concern over the handling of the investigation into both the blast and the small cells of Islamic terrorists supposedly operating in the archipelago.

Some of these concerns may have been alleviated by the police force's diligence in gathering evidence and tracking down suspects in the Bali bombing. However, continuing problems with the military's professionalism and the judiciary's effectiveness could make it harder for the government to address the terrorism threat.

Economists predicted that the Bali bombing could knock off a percentage point from economic growth in 2003. Indonesia's economy has already been hobbled by slowing exports and lower consumer demand. Moreover, investment has declined since 1997 because of concerns, the World Bank says, with security, taxation, the legal system, labor laws, red tape, and customs administration.

Political Rights and Civil Liberties: Indonesians can choose their legislators in free and reasonably fair elections and will be able to elect their president directly for the first time in 2004. Currently, however, the president is chosen by the People's Consultative Assembly (MPR), which consists of the entire 500-member parliament plus 130 regional representatives chosen by provincial legislatures, and 65 members representing various business, labor, and social constituencies. The direct elections are likely to strengthen the already powerful presidency, although parliament has shown that it can check executive authority, most notably by ousting Wahid.

The armed forces, which are being weaned off their long-standing formal role in politics, are due to give up their 38 appointed lower house and MPR seats by 2004. Despite pressure to reform and scale back its involvement in domestic affairs, however, the military continues to have extensive business interests and has increased its grassroots presence. Politicians and analysts told the Hong Kong-based *Far Eastern Economic Review* in September that the military is likely to continue wielding considerable political clout thanks to its "territorial network" of soldiers in every district and village and its burgeoning political and business links with provincial bosses.

While the government's human rights record has improved considerably since Suharto's downfall, the rule of law continues to be weak throughout the archipelago. In Aceh, an oil-rich province of 4.6 million people in northern Sumatra, the army continued to be implicated in extrajudicial killings, disappearances, tortures, rapes, illegal detentions, and other abuses against suspected guerrillas or sympathizers of the pro-independence Free Aceh Movement (GAM), according to the watchdog groups Amnesty International and Human Rights Watch.

Human rights groups also criticized the government in 2002 for largely failing to bring to justice top military officers linked to human rights abuses. A special court in Jakarta, set up to try military and civilian officials implicated in the deaths of some 2,000 East Timorese in 1999, acquitted 10 of the 12 suspects it had tried by year's end. Nine of those acquitted were military or police officers, while both of those convicted of crimes against humanity were civilian East Timorese.

Amnesty International and a local group, the Judicial System Monitoring Program, said in August that the trials to date were "seriously flawed." The trials suffered from procedural flaws and the failure of prosecutors to hand down indictments and argue cases that reflected the widespread and systemic nature of the 1999 violence, the two groups said.

Security forces also enjoy near impunity even in nonconflict areas. Police at times summarily kill alleged common criminals, many of whom were unarmed, according to the U.S. State Department's global human rights report for 2001, released in March 2002. The military and police also often torture criminal suspects, independence supporters in Aceh, and ordinary Indonesians involved in land or labor disputes, Amnesty International said in a 2001 report.

The problem of impunity is linked to the reality that, despite recent reforms, there are "few signs of judicial independence," according to the U.S. State Department report, and government officials "often exert influence over the outcome of cases. While rarely convicting security forces for abuses, courts have recently jailed several peaceful political activists. A court in October, for example, jailed 14 members of a group seeking independence for the southern part of the Moluccan islands chain for between two and five years for raising a banned flag in the provincial capital of Ambon.

In ordinary cases, low judicial salaries lead to widespread corruption, and due process safeguards often are inadequate to ensure fair trials, the U.S. State Department report said; prison conditions are "harsh," and guards routinely mistreat and extort money from inmates.

Besides the military, GAM rebels in Aceh have also committed grave human rights abuses. Divided into some eight factions, GAM forces summarily killed soldiers as well as civilians who allegedly assisted the army, while intimidating and extorting money from ordinary Acehnese, Amnesty International and Human Rights Watch said. GAM rebels have also killed dozens of civic leaders, academics, politicians, and civil servants, according to the U.S. State Department report.

The ceasefire in the 26-year conflict signed in December calls for substantial autonomy for Aceh, elections for a provincial legislature and government by 2004, and a partial army pullback and rebel disarmament. The deal, however, doesn't address the rebels' core demands for independence and provides few details on the mechanism for disarmament.

Sporadic violence along ethnic or sectarian lines continued, meanwhile, in Kalimantan, Sulawesi, and the Moluccas. A February peace deal formally ended a conflict between Christians and Muslims in the Moluccas that killed at least 5,000 people, displaced tens of thousands more, and destroyed many churches and mosques during two years of fierce clashes that abated somewhat in mid-2001. The violence, which flared at times during the year, had been linked in part to disputes over jobs, land, and other economic and political issues.

Meanwhile, some 1,000 people have died since violence between Christians and Muslims broke out in central Sulawesi in late 1998, according to a December report by Human Rights Watch. The report blamed Indonesian authorities for often failing to stop the attacks or to punish perpetrators.

In Kalimantan and other areas, meanwhile, many disputes between ethnic groups are said to be linked to the government's decades-old policy of resettling tens of thousands of Indonesians to remote parts of the archipelago from overcrowded areas such as Java. Conditions for newcomers at some relocation sites are "life threatening," according to the U.S. State Department report. Human rights activists, meanwhile, say that the influx of migrants limits job opportunities for indigenous people and marginalizes their culture. The number of vigilante killings in these areas also remains high. Jakarta announced in 2000 that it would no longer resettle people between islands, only within the same province.

Local human rights groups, such as the Indonesian Legal Aid Foundation, vigorously press Jakarta to investigate abuses. They also aid victims and witnesses. Indonesia's official National Human Rights Commission, though, has become "increasingly ineffective and marginalized," Human Rights Watch said in a July report.

Despite the problems of military impunity and violent conflict in some areas, Indonesia has evolved from a tightly controlled to a politically open society. Most notably, the private press, freed from its Suharto-era shackles, reports aggressively on government policies, corruption, political protests, civil conflicts, and other formerly taboo topics. The Alliance of Indonesian Journalists, however, says that threats from police and civilians lead many journalists to practice self-censorship. Press advocacy groups also criticized a law passed in November that prevents private broadcasters from transmitting their programs on a nationwide basis unless they have local partners. The government said that the bill is needed to ensure that regional news is given sufficient coverage and to create competition in the broadcast industry.

Students, workers, and other Indonesians frequently hold peaceful demonstrations. Security forces, however, break up some protests, at times with deadly force, the U.S State Department report said.

Indonesians of all faiths can generally worship freely, although officials monitor and have outlawed some extremist Islamic groups. In a notable exception to religious freedom, Muslim mobs in the Moluccas have forcibly converted an estimated several thousand Christians, torturing those who refused, according to the U.S. State Department report.

Indonesian women face unofficial discrimination in schooling and employment opportunities and hold relatively few jobs in government and politics, the U.S. State Department report said. Spousal abuse and other forms of violence against women are a continuing concern, although there are no hard figures on the extent of the problem. Anecdotal evidence suggests that among Muslims, female genital mutilation continues to be practiced in some areas, according to the State Department report, which said that the more extreme forms of the practice apparently are becoming less common.

Indonesia is also a source, transit point, and destination for the trafficking of women for prostitution, the report added. One local nongovernmental group estimates that up to 400,000 Indonesian women and children are trafficked each year.

Ethnic Chinese continue to face some harassment and violence, though far less than in the late 1990s, when violent attacks killed hundreds and destroyed many Chinese-owned shops and churches. State universities still limit the enrollment of ethnic Chinese students, the U.S. State Department report said. Ethnic Chinese make up less than 3 percent of the nation's population, but are resented by some Indonesians for holding the lion's share of private wealth. A few ethnic Chinese have amassed huge fortunes in business, though most are ordinary merchants or traders.

Members of Indonesia's tiny indigenous minority tend to have limited say on decisions concerning development projects and the use of natural resources, according to the U.S. State Department report, which added, "When indigenous people clash with those promoting private sector development projects, the developers almost always prevail."

Indonesia's economic woes have contributed to higher infant mortality and school dropout rates and to greater numbers of undernourished children and child laborers, according to recent reports by UNICEF, the International Labor Organization, the government, and local private groups.

Workers can join independent unions, bargain collectively, and, except for civil servants, stage strikes. Employers, however, frequently ignore minimum wage laws and dismiss labor activists. Unions and other nongovernmental groups allege that employers also use plainclothes security forces—often off-duty soldiers and police—or youth gangs to intimidate workers or break strikes. Roughly 10 to 15 percent of Indonesia's 80 million industrial workers are unionized.

Iran

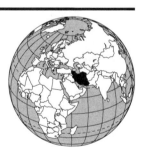

Polity: Presidential-
parliamentary
(clergy-dominated)
Political Rights: 6
Civil Liberties: 6
Status: Not Free
Economy: Capitalist-statist
Population: 65,600,000
PPP: $5,884
Life Expectancy: 69
Religious Groups: Shi'a Muslim (89 percent), Sunni Muslim
(10 percent), other (1 percent)
Ethnic Groups: Persian (51 percent), Azeri (24 percent), Gilaki and Mazandarani (8 percent), Kurd (7 percent), Arab (3 percent), other (7 percent)
Capital: Tehran

Ten-Year Ratings Timeline (Political Rights, Civil Liberties, Status)

1993	1994	1995	1996	1997	1998	1999	2000	2001	2002	2003
6,6NF	6,7NF	6,7NF	6,7NF	6,7NF	6,7NF	6,6NF	6,6NF	6,6NF	6,6NF	6,6NF

Overview:
The Iranian government continued to be divided between reformers on the one hand, who control the presidency, parliament, and most other elected offices, and conserva-

tive hard-liners on the other hand, who dominate the judiciary, security services, and broadcast media. Efforts by reformers to bring about political, social, and economic reforms have ground to a halt, while a drive by conservatives to roll back the expansion of public freedoms has encountered stiff public resistance.

In 1979, Iran witnessed a tumultuous revolution that ousted a hereditary monarchy marked by widespread corruption and brought into power the exiled cleric Ayatollah Ruhollah Khomeini, who presided over the establishment of the modern world's first Islamic republic. The constitution drafted by his disciples amalgamated Western concepts of popular sovereignty and representation with Khomeini's interpretation of the Shi'a concept of *velayat-e faqih* (guardianship of the jurisconsult), which holds that government decisions must be authorized by religious scholars. A president and parliament elected through universal adult suffrage coexisted with the 12-member Council of Guardians, consisting of senior clerics, empowered to approve all presidential and parliamentary candidates and certify that all laws passed by parliament are in accord with *Sharia* (Islamic law).

Khomeini was named supreme leader-for-life and invested with control over the security and intelligence services, armed forces, and judiciary. After Khomeini's death in June 1989, the role of supreme leader passed to Ayatollah Ali Khamenei, a middle-ranking cleric who lacked the religious credentials and popularity of his predecessor. The constitution was changed to consolidate his power and give him final authority on all matters of foreign and domestic policy.

By 1997, dismal economic conditions and a demographic trend toward a younger population had created widespread dissatisfaction. Mohammed Khatami, a former culture minister advocating greater freedoms, extensive political and economic reforms, and improved foreign relations, was elected president with 69 percent of the vote. Reformers made considerable strides over the next few years in expanding freedoms. Dozens of reformist newspapers representing diverse views were allowed to publish, and the authorities relaxed the enforcement of strict Islamic dress codes for women and restrictions on social interaction. Although rogue security operatives acting on behalf of high-ranking clerics murdered several liberal intellectuals, the political tide appeared to be on the side of reformers. Reformists won 80 percent of the seats in the country's first nationwide municipal elections in 1999 and took the overwhelming majority of parliamentary seats the following year.

The 2000 parliamentary elections evidenced a backlash by conservatives that continues to this day. Dozens of reformist newspapers have been shut down, and hundreds of liberal journalists and students, as well as political activists, have been jailed, mostly on charges of defamation and spreading false information about the government. The December 2001 conviction of Hossein Loqmanian on charges of insulting the judiciary marked the first time since the 1979 revolution that a member of parliament was imprisoned. Although Khatami was reelected in June 2001 with 78 percent of the vote, this popular mandate for change has not reduced the virtually absolute power of conservatives. Numerous pieces of legislation intended to introduce further reforms have passed parliament only to be vetoed by the Council of Guardians.

If the reform drive in Iran were merely a struggle for power within the ruling elite, Khatami's lack of real power and failure to institutionalize early gains in the liberalization process would indicate bleak prospects for sweeping change in Iran. However, the elites struggle is largely an institutional response to broad-based demands of society at large. The level of popular hostility to clerical rule in Iran has reached the point where, according to numerous independent press reports, mullahs take off their distinctive robes and headwear when travelling through many areas of the Iranian capital.

Despite Khatami's recurrent pleas to abstain from civil disobedience, popular demonstrations in major cities such as Tehran, Isfahan, Shiraz, and Tabriz have grown in size and intensity. Iran is one of the only countries in the Muslim world where the people are gravitating overwhelmingly away from radical Islamism: sociologists say that less than half of Iranian youth fast or even attend prayers during Ramadan. As a result, a resignation by Khatami could potentially bring the entire system down. Few observers believe that the "rump" clerical regime that remains after his departure would be able to maintain control of the country by force alone.

There appears to be a growing recognition within some sections of the clerical establishment that reform, rather than threatening the Islamic Republic, is the only way to save it. In July 2002, the Imam of Isfahan, Ayatollah Jalaleddin Taheri, resigned from his post and condemned the "crookedness, negligence and weakness" of hard-liners who continue to obstruct change. The defection of Taheri—a contemporary of Khomeini and the highest religious authority in a city regarded as the epicenter of the 1979 revolution—suggests that time may be on Khatami's side.

In September 2002, Khatami introduced two bills that would curb the power of the Council of Guardians to vet electoral candidates and increase presidential oversight of the judiciary. Khatami's aides have said that he will either resign or call a national referendum on the fate of the Islamic Republic if the two bills, both of which were approved by parliament, are rejected by the Council of Guardians. Many believe that Khamenei will not dare take this risk.

However, hard-line elements within the clerical and security establishment appear to have misjudged the depth of popular resentment against the regime and seem intent on provoking tensions, if not outright hostilities, with the United States, in hopes that this will unify ranks within the regime and ensure public quiescence. The involvement of Iranian security agencies in shipping weapons to the Palestinians, harboring al-Qaeda leaders, and covertly funding obstructionist Afghan warlords during the year may have been motivated less by quixotic militancy than by a desire to create conditions ripe for a coup.

Political Rights and Civil Liberties: Iranians cannot change their government democratically. The most powerful governing institutions in Iran, such as the Council of Guardians and the judiciary, are neither elected nor subservient to elected bodies. Moreover, the council vets all national and municipal electoral candidates for strict allegiance to the ruling theocracy and adherence to Islamic principles. Of the 814 candidates who declared their intention to run in the 2001 presidential election, only 10 were approved. The supreme leader is chosen for life by the Assembly of Experts, a clerics-only body whose members are elected to eight-year terms by popular vote from a government-screened list of candidates.

Iranian security forces continued to subject citizens to arbitrary arrest and incommunicado detention in 2002. Suspected dissidents are often held in unofficial, illegal detention centers, such as Prison 59, a facility in Tehran administered by the Intelligence Ministry and the Revolutionary Guards. Hard-line vigilante groups have committed extrajudicial killings in the past with the tacit consent of the security agencies, but Khatami's government was unable to thoroughly investigate and punish those responsible.

During the trial of intelligence officials accused of ordering the 1998 killings of several dissidents, a former intelligence minister was implicated by one of the defendants but never investigated. Recent legislation designed to limit the power of the security agencies was vetoed by the Council of Guardians. In June 2002, the council rejected a bill, passed by parliament, that aimed to limit the use of torture and the admissibility of forced confessions in criminal trials.

The judiciary is not independent. The supreme leader directly appoints the head of the judiciary, who in turn appoints the Supreme Court and other senior judges. Bribery is common. Civil courts provide some procedural safeguards, though judges often serve simultaneously as prosecutors during trials. Political and other sensitive cases are tried before Revolutionary Courts, where detainees are denied access to legal counsel and due process is ignored. The penal code is based on Sharia and provides for flogging, stoning, amputation, or death for a range of social and political offenses.

Freedom of expression is limited. The government directly controls all television and radio broadcasting and has recently begun jamming RFE/RL Persian service broadcasts and selectively enforcing a ban on satellite dishes. Following the reformist sweep of legislative elections in 2000, the outgoing parliament passed amendments to the 1995 Press Law granting extensive procedural and jurisdictional power to the Press Court in prosecuting journalists, editors and publishers for such vaguely-worded offenses as "insulting Islam" or "damaging the foundations of the Islamic Republic." Bills introduced by the current parliament to reverse the amendments and introduce other judicial reforms were rejected by the Guardian Council. Since 2000, over 85 publications have been shut down by the judiciary and dozens of journalists have been arrested, often held incommunicado for extended periods of time and convicted in closed-door trials.

In April 2002, the editor of the regional weekly *Chams-e-Tabriz*, Ali-Hamed Iman, was sentenced to eight months in prison and 74 lashes, while Ahmed Zeid-Abadi, a journalist for the reformist weekly *Hamchahri,* was sentenced to 23 months in prison and a five-year ban on all public activity. In May, a journalist for the weekly *Payam-e-Qom*, Hojat Heydari, was given a four-month suspended sentence and banned from working as a journalist for six months. Siamak Pourzand, a 71-year-old journalist for *Hayat-e-No,* was sentenced to 11 years in prison for "undermining state security" and "having contacts with monarchists and counter-revolutionaries." Mohsen Mirdamadi, a member of parliament and editor of the daily *Nawrooz* who is close to Khatami, was given a six-month prison sentence and banned from holding a "senior position" at any publication for four years. In October, the authorities arrested Yussefi Eshkevari, a theologian and journalist for the monthly *Jamee-e-No,* and enforced a seven-year sentence he had previously received from the religious court for various infractions, such as saying that females are not required by Islam to wear the veil. In early November, reformist scholar Hashem Aghajari was sentenced to death for blasphemy. After thousands of university students demonstrated in his support Ayatollah Khamenei ordered the judiciary to review the sentence.

In 2002, several decrees were issued which explicitly banned media coverage of specific topics. In May, the judiciary announced a ban on publishing articles about Iranian-American relations. In July, a decree banned press coverage of Ayatollah Taheri's resignation. A day later, the reformist daily *Azad* was closed for defying the ban. In September, the managing editor of the Islamic Republic News Agency (IRNA) was summoned for questioning after the IRNA published the results of a public opinion poll showing that 74 percent of Iranians support talks with the United States. The head of the National Institute of Public Opinion was arrested in early October and held incommunicado for over a month for publishing the poll, while the heads of two private research institutes that had conducted the poll were arrested in November.

The government does not censor or monitor the Internet. Periodic closures of cybercafes have been intended mainly to protect the state telecommunications company against competition from inexpensive Internet telephone services. Several newspapers that were banned in 2002, such as *Bonyan* and *Norous*, have continued publishing on the Web.

The 1979 constitution prohibits public demonstrations that "violate the principles of Islam," a vague provision used to justify the heavy-handed dispersal of assemblies and marches. Violent disruptions of demonstration are usually carried out by Ansar-e Hezbollah, a vigilante group linked to hard-line government figures.

The constitution permits the establishment of political parties, professional syndicates, and other civic organizations, provided they do not violate the principles of "freedom, sovereignty and national unity" or question the Islamic basis of the republic. In July 2002, the Revolutionary Court in Tehran outlawed the 44-year-old Iran Freedom Movement and handed down prison sentences of up to 10 years to 33 of its leading members, including such notable political figures as Hashem Sabaghian, the interior minister in Iran's first postrevolutionary cabinet, and former Tehran mayor Mohammed Tavasoli. There are no independent trade unions. The government-controlled Workers' House is the only legal federation, and workers may not strike. Unauthorized labor demonstrations are often forcibly dispersed by police.

Although women enjoy the same political rights as men and currently hold several seats in parliament, a few cabinet positions, and even one of Iran's vice presidencies, they face discrimination in legal and social matters. A woman cannot obtain a passport without the permission of a male relative or her husband and women do not enjoy equal rights under laws governing divorce, child custody disputes, or inheritance. A woman's testimony in court is given only half the weight of a man's. Women must conform to strict dress codes and are segregated from men in most public places. Several pieces of legislation intended to give women equal rights, such as a bill on divorce law that parliament approved in August 2002, have been rejected by the Council of Guardians.

Religious freedom is limited in Iran, which is 89 percent Shi'a Muslim and 10 percent Sunni Muslim. The constitution recognizes Zoroastrians, Jews, and Christians as religious minorities and generally allows them to worship without interference, but they are barred from election to representative bodies (though a set number of parliamentary seats are reserved for them), cannot hold senior government or military positions, and face restrictions in employment, education, and property ownership. In October 2002, Iran granted early release to 3 of the 13 Jews who were convicted in a closed-door trial of spying for Israel in 2000.

Some 300,000 Bahai's, Iran's largest non-Muslim minority, enjoy virtually no rights under the law. They face official discrimination, a complete denial of property rights, a ban on university admission, employment restrictions, and prohibitions on practicing and teaching their faith. Their marriages are not recognized by the government, which leaves women open to charges of prostitution and their children regarded as illegitimate and thus without inheritance rights. Hundreds of Bahai's have been executed since 1979. Recently, prominent Sunni activists have spoken out about discrimination, pointing to the absence of a Sunni mosque in the Iranian capital.

There are few laws that discriminate against ethnic minorities, who are permitted to establish community centers and certain cultural, social, sports, and charitable associations. However, Kurdish demands for more autonomy and a greater voice in the appointment of a regional governor have not been met. Most Kurds are Sunnis and therefore face discrimination on that basis. Advocates protesting for greater cultural autonomy for Azeris have been arrested in recent years.

Iraq

Polity: One party (presidential dictatorship)
Economy: Statist
Population: 23,600,000
PPP: NA
Life Expectancy: 58

Political Rights: 7
Civil Liberties: 7
Status: Not Free

Religious Groups: Muslim (97 percent) [Shi'a (60-65 percent), Sunni (32-37 percent)], Christian or other (3 percent)
Ethnic Groups: Arab (75-80 percent), Kurd (15-20 percent), other (5 percent)
Capital: Baghdad

Ten-Year Ratings Timeline (Political Rights, Civil Liberties, Status)

1993	1994	1995	1996	1997	1998	1999	2000	2001	2002	2003
7,7NF	7,7NF	7,7NF	7,7NF	7,7NF	7,7NF	7,7NF	7,7NF	7,7NF	7,7NF	7,7NF

Overview:

As the United States mobilized military resources and diplomatic support for a possible invasion to oust the government of Iraq, Saddam Hussein took some steps to improve human rights conditions in what many observers regard as the most oppressive state in the world. Public reaction suggested that long-dormant public disaffection with the regime may be as decisive in determining Iraq's future as the military forces poised on the outside.

Iraq was established as a League of Nations mandate in 1921 and gained formal independence in 1932. The British-installed Hashemite monarchy was overthrown by a 1958 military coup and followed by a succession of weak leftist governments for the next decade. In 1968, the pan-Arab Ba'ath (Renaissance) party seized power and has ruled Iraq ever since. In June 1979, the regime's de facto strongman, Vice President Saddam Hussein, formally assumed the presidency.

The ascension of a dictator anxious to establish Iraq as undisputed leader of the Arab world coincided with postrevolutionary chaos in neighboring Iran. Seeing an opportunity to humble a once-powerful enemy, Saddam ordered an invasion of Iran in 1980, setting off a bloody eight-year war. In 1988, Iraq emerged from the war with minor territorial gains, major foreign debt, and catastrophic human and material losses. Unwilling to demobilize what had become the world's third-largest standing army and introduce hundreds of thousands of soldiers into the ranks of the unemployed, Saddam initiated another war two years later with the invasion of Kuwait. Following Iraq's defeat by a 22-nation coalition in 1991, the UN Security Council imposed a strict economic sanctions regime pending the destruction of Iraq's weapons of mass destruction (WMD). While it was originally anticipated that the sanctions would be lifted within a few years, Iraq refused to voluntarily disclose its WMD capabilities for more than a decade and the sanctions remained in place.

Anxious to avert a humanitarian disaster in postwar Iraq, the United Nations offered within months of the ceasefire to permit Baghdad to sell limited amounts of oil, provided that the proceeds be used for food and humanitarian supplies. For more than four years, Saddam refused to accept such proposals, apparently hoping that the suffering of the Iraqi people would move the world to accept the complete and unconditional lifting of the sanctions. After an "oil for food" program was finally implemented in 1996, Saddam exploited the initiative, imposing a clandestine surcharge on oil sales and re-exporting considerable amounts of humanitarian goods in order to earn illicit revenue to finance rearmament.

As a result of Saddam's obstruction of humanitarian assistance to the Iraqi people, a sharp decline in health care services and the use of contaminated water increased the spread and mortality rate of curable diseases in postwar Iraq. According to UNICEF, more than 500,000 Iraqi children under age five died between 1991 and 1998. In 1990, the UN Human Development Index, which ranks countries based on quality of life as measured by indicators such as education, life expectancy, and adjusted real income, ranked Iraq 55 in the world. By 2000, Iraq's ranking had fallen to 126 of 174 countries.

Iraq exploited this humanitarian disaster to rally international opposition to the sanctions and inflame anti-Western sentiment in the Arab world. By 2001, Iraq's neighbors were turning a blind eye to sanctions-violating trade, and according to a September 2002 report by the British government, Iraq's illicit revenue had reached $3 billion per year. These funds were used not only to finance rearmament, but also to secure the loyalty of Sunni tribal elites and the military-security apparatus surrounding Saddam. Flush with illicit revenue, the Iraqi regime became stronger than ever.

In the aftermath of the September 11, 2001, attacks on the United States, U.S. President George W. Bush designated Iraq's WMD a salient threat to American national security and openly committed his administration to engineering Saddam's ouster. In November 2002, after months of intense American diplomacy, the UN Security Council passed a resolution giving Iraq a "final opportunity" to disarm and declaring that false statements, omissions, or noncooperation by Iraq would constitute a "material breach" of the Gulf War ceasefire. The Bush administration made clear its view that the resolution was a sufficient mandate for American military intervention in the event that Iraq failed to cooperate fully with UN weapons inspectors, who returned to the country in late November.

In the face of mounting threats of American military action, the Iraqi regime took some steps in 2002 to improve human rights conditions, as a means of diminishing both domestic and international support for U.S. intervention. In February, Iraq allowed the UN Commission on Human Rights special rapporteur, Andreas Mavrommatis, to enter the country for the first time in 10 years. Exit fees for Iraqis wishing to leave the country were reportedly waived. Following his "reelection" in an October presidential referendum, Saddam issued a sweeping amnesty and released tens of thousands of prisoners.

More surprising than the amnesty was the public reaction that followed: hundreds of women whose husbands or sons had not been released protested outside the Information Ministry. Few observers believe that the Iraqi people will rally around Saddam in the event of an American invasion. In August, former Egyptian Chief Staff Salah Halaby predicted that the Iraqi army will "pounce on Saddam . . . without any hesitation" once a U.S. assault begins. Reports of dissent within the armed forces, mostly unconfirmed, occurred throughout the year. On October 8, the Kuwaiti daily *Al-Qabas* reported that an Iraqi MiG-23 pilot tried to veer off course during a training exercise and bomb a presidential palace, but was shot down. During a visit to Baghdad, Qatari foreign minister Hamad bin Jasem bin Jaber al-Thani offered Saddam and his family political asylum if he would step down (the envoy was quickly expelled from the country). There were also reports that Libya had agreed to accept the Iraqi dictator.

Political Rights and Civil Liberties: Iraqis cannot change their government democratically. Saddam holds supreme power as president and chairman of the nine-member Revolutionary Command Council (RCC), a body with virtually unlimited and unchecked authority. Although the 250-seat National Assembly formally shares legislative responsibilities with the RCC, in practice it ritually endorses RCC decisions with little or no deliberation. Opposition parties are illegal, and all legislative candidates are carefully vetted to ensure their support for the regime. High turnout is typical in elections, as failure to vote may be seen as opposition to the government.

Iraqi citizens live under the constant threat of arbitrary arrest, torture, rape, or summary execution. Tens of thousands of Iraqi citizens have disappeared over the last two decades and thousands are believed to be held in incommunicado detention. The number of political prisoners was estimated to be in the tens of thousands prior to the October 2002 amnesty, and international human rights groups expressed concerns that few political detainees were among those freed. The security forces routinely torture detainees suspected of opposition activity. According to defectors from Iraq's national soccer team, players have been brutally tortured after losing games. There have been credible reports of Iraqi defectors receiving videotapes of their female relatives being raped.

Executions are an integral component of the regime's control over Iraqi society. Military and government officials suspected of disloyalty are routinely executed, as are the relatives of Iraqi defectors. Some mass executions have been carried out to thin the prison population. The Washington-based International Alliance for Justice, an umbrella group of 260 nongovernmental organizations from 120 countries, reported in early 2002 that the Iraqi government had executed 4,000 people since

1998. There were numerous additional reports of executions in 2002. In July, the government itself announced the execution of two people allegedly spying for Iran. According to Iraqi human rights organizations abroad, the regime executed 6 military officers who served at Saddam's presidential retreat at Tharthar and 17 Iraqis from the southern provinces of Muhanna and Najaf in March. In June, 10 people were reportedly executed at Abu Ghareb prison. In October, 6 political prisoners with alleged links to the opposition were put to death.

The judiciary is not independent. Although some safeguards exist in civil cases, those accused of political or economic crimes are usually tried in closed, special security courts, chaired by military officers and Ba'ath-party officials, where no due process protections are recognized. A variety of crimes, including theft, corruption, desertion from the army, and currency speculation, are punishable by amputation, branding, or execution. Doctors have been killed for refusing to carry out punishments or for attempting reconstructive surgery.

Freedom of expression is almost entirely absent in Iraq. All media outlets are either controlled directly by the state or owned by Saddam's loyalists. The Iraqi president's eldest son, Uday Hussein, is head of the Journalists' Union, owner of 11 newspapers, including the daily *Babel*, and director of television and radio stations. Freedom of speech is explicitly restricted by numerous laws, such as RCC Decree Number 840, which prohibits insulting the president or other senior government officials on punishment of death.

Freedom of assembly is restricted to pro-government gatherings, while freedom of association is limited to government-backed political parties and civic groups. Independent trade unions are nonexistent, and the state-backed General Federation of Trade Unions is the only legal labor federation. The law does not recognize the right to collective bargaining and places restrictions on the right to strike.

Islam is the official state religion. While freedom of religion is protected in principle, it is severely restricted in practice. The government appoints all clergy in Iraq and monitors all places of worship. Sunni Arabs, who constitute about 35 percent of the population, dominate political and economic life, although token members of minority communities have been appointed to high-level positions in the government and ruling party. Shi'a Muslims, who are predominantly Arab and constitute around 60 per cent of the population, face severe persecution. Shi'as may not engage in communal Friday prayers, funeral processions, or other religious observances without explicit government approval. Security forces have reportedly arrested thousands of Shi'as, executed an undetermined number of these detainees, and assassinated dozens of Shi'a clerics and religious students in recent years. Government forces in the south have desecrated Shi'a mosques and holy sites, razed homes, and drained the Amara and Hammar marshes in order to flush out Shi'a guerrillas.

The Iraqi regime has long pursued a policy of "Arabization" against ethnic Kurds, Turkomans, and other non-Arab minorities. Thousands of families have been expelled by the central government into northern Iraq, where a Kurdish safe haven has existed under UN protection since 1991.

Iraqi laws grant women equality with men in most respects, but it is difficult to determine the extent to which these rights are respected in practice.

Ireland

Polity: Parliamentary
democracy
Economy: Capitalist
Population: 3,800,000
PPP: $29,866
Life Expectancy: 77
Religious Groups: Roman Catholic (91.6 percent),
Church of Ireland (2.5 percent), other (5.9 percent)
Ethnic Groups: Celtic, English minority
Capital: Dublin

Political Rights: 1
Civil Liberties: 1
Status: Free

Ten-Year Ratings Timeline (Political Rights, Civil Liberties, Status)

1993	1994	1995	1996	1997	1998	1999	2000	2001	2002	2003
1,1F	1,2F	1,2F	1,1F	1,1F	1,1F	1,1F	1,1F	1,1F	1,1F	1,1F

Overview:

Ireland's standing in Europe was boosted when voters accepted a key EU treaty on enlargement in an October referendum, after its standing in Europe was damaged when voters rejected a similar referendum in 2001. Irish voters returned to power in May the Fianna Fail-Progressive Democrats coalition. The euro replaced the Irish Punt in January.

Ireland's struggle for independence dates from its conquest by England in the early Middle Ages. Ruled as a separate kingdom under the British Crown, and as part of the United Kingdom after 1800, Ireland gained some independence in 1921, when Great Britain granted dominion status to southern Ireland's 26 counties. However, six Protestant-majority counties remained within the United Kingdom. The Irish republic initially regarded the partition as provisional, but the 1998 Good Friday Agreement established the "principle of consent," that is, that a united Ireland will not come about without the consent of a majority of people in both jurisdictions. Ireland became a republic in 1948, although the constitution and Anglo-Irish agreement of April 1938 had reduced significantly the role of the United Kingdom. Since 1949, governmental responsibility has alternated between the Fianna Fail and Fine Gael parties.

The Fianna Fail and Progressive Democrats gained, in the May 17 election, a parliamentary majority for their nominally center-right coalition. The prime minister is Bertie Ahern.

Ireland voted "yes" to an October 19 referendum on the EU Nice treaty, clearing the way for 10 new EU members. In January, Ireland adopted the euro as the national currency.

The government published in July its probe of 1980s tax scams but indicated that prosecution against the 190 alleged offenders, including Charles Haughey, the former Fianna Fail prime minister, was unlikely. Although implicated in the tax scams, Ahern managed to hang onto power owing to Ireland's unprecedented economic prosperity—although the double-digit gross domestic product growth fell to 3.9 percent for 2002. Nevertheless, Ireland's skilled workforce, flexible business environment, and favorable corporate tax policies make it an investment haven.

The European Parliament amended the 1997 EC directive on privacy in telecommunications in May to oblige member states to retain all telecommunications data for one to two years and to provide the relevant authorities unrestricted access to these data to assist law enforcement officials in eradicating crime.

Political Rights and Civil Liberties: Irish citizens can change their government democratically. The Irish constitution provides for direct election of the president for a seven-year term and for a bicameral legislature consisting of a directly elected 166-seat Dail (lower house) and an indirectly chosen, 60-seat Seanad (upper house) with power to delay, but not veto, legislation. The cabinet, which is responsible to the Dail, is headed by a prime minister, who is the leader of the majority party or coalition and is appointed by the president for a five-year term on the recommendation of the Dail. Suffrage is universal; citizens over the age of 18 can vote.

Although free expression is constitutionally guaranteed, the five-member Censorship of Publications Board, established under the Censorship of Publications Act of 1946, can halt book publication. The board is widely criticized as an anachronism. Reporters Sans Frontieres ranked Ireland as having the sixth highest press freedom ranking in the world in its Worldwide Press Freedom Index for 2002.

Ireland has an independent judicial system. The president appoints judges on the advice of the government. The Garda Siochana (national police service) is under civilian control. An internal disciplinary body investigates complaints of mistreatment of detainees and prisoners.

The constitution provides for religious freedom; there is no discrimination against nontraditional religious groups. Although Ireland is overwhelmingly Roman Catholic, there is no state religion. Most primary and secondary schools are denominational, and the Catholic Church partially controls their management boards. Although religious instruction is an integral part of the curriculum, parents may exempt their children from such instruction.

The rights of ethnic and racial minorities are generally respected, although increased levels of racial discrimination and violence have accompanied the growing immigration of foreign workers. There are some 25,000 Travellers, a nomadic ethnic group, comparable to the Roma (Gypsies) of continental Europe. Travellers are regularly denied access to premises, goods, facilities, services, and employment. The Employment Equality Act 1998, effective October 1999, prohibits workplace discrimination regarding family status, religious belief, age, race, sexual orientation, disability, or membership in the Travellers' community.

In December 2001, the Council of the European Union adopted by "written procedure" antiterrorist legislation requiring member states to prevent "the public" from offering "any form of support, active or passive" to terrorists and to check all refugees and asylum seekers for terrorist connections. Human rights groups criticized the legislation because it does not distinguish between conscious and subconscious assistance, treats would-be immigrants as criminals, and was not debated in parliament before being adopted.

Ireland tightened its asylum laws in 2000. Critics argue that legitimate asylum seekers do not have enough time to prepare their cases. A corollary policy of dispersing asylum seekers throughout the country was criticized for ostensibly denying fair access to quality legal representation. The police received new powers to detain and deport unsuccessful asylum seekers. Ireland and Bulgaria agreed in January 2002 to facilitate the deportation of failed Bulgarian asylum seekers, illegal immigrants, and non-EU nationals who enter Ireland illegally via Bulgaria. More than 200 Irish police officers raided homes throughout Dublin in July to oust illegal immigrants. Five failed asylum seekers and 34 illegal immigrants were arrested; most were from Eastern Europe and Africa.

Labor unions are free to organize and bargain collectively. Police and military personnel are prohibited from striking, but they may form associations to represent themselves in matters of pay and working conditions.

Transparency International ranked Ireland 23rd on its 2002 Corruption Perceptions Index, better than only France, Portugal, and Italy among EU-member states. Discrimination against women in the workplace is unlawful, but inequalities persist regarding pay and promotions in both the public and private sectors. Abortion is legal only when a woman's life is in danger; an estimated 6,500 women travel to Britain annually to obtain abortions.

Israel

Polity: Parliamentary democracy
Economy: Mixed capitalist
Population: 6,600,000
PPP: $20,131
Life Expectancy: 78

Political Rights: 1
Civil Liberties: 3
Status: Free

Religious Groups: Jewish (80.1 percent), Muslim [mostly Sunni Muslim] (14.6 percent), Christian (2.1 percent), other (3.2 percent)
Ethnic Groups: Jewish (80 percent), non-Jewish [mostly Arab] (20 percent)
Capital: Jerusalem

Ten-Year Ratings Timeline (Political Rights, Civil Liberties, Status)

1993	1994	1995	1996	1997	1998	1999	2000	2001	2002	2003
2,2F	1,3F	1,3F	1,3F	1,3F	1,3F	1,3F	1,2F	1,3F	1,3F	1,3F

Overview:
Palestinian terrorism eroded public security in Israel in 2002, exacerbating an already heightened sense of collective vulnerability. More than 400 Israelis were killed by Palestinian terrorism. Israelis braced for large-scale attacks as authorities thwarted several bombings designed to destroy office buildings or whole city blocks. Prime Minister Ariel Sharon adopted strong tactics, including armored incursions into Palestinian territory, generating intense international and domestic criticism. Rising numbers of reserve army officers, citing moral opposition to government policy, refused to serve in the Occupied Territories. Israel's national unity government collapsed in October, paving the way for new elections early in 2003. A bribery scandal in the Likud party damaged the government's credibility as elections drew near. The Su-

preme Court officially recognized religious conversions conducted under the auspices of the Reform and Conservative movements of Judaism. Approximately one-fifth of the population was estimated to be living below the poverty line.

Israel was formed in 1948 from less than one-fifth of the original British Palestine Mandate. Arab nations rejected a UN partition plan that would also have created a Palestinian state. Immediately following Israel's declaration of independence, its neighbors attacked. While Israel maintained its sovereignty, Jordan seized East Jerusalem and the West Bank, while Egypt took control of Gaza.

In the 1967 Six-Day War, Israel came to occupy the West Bank, Gaza Strip, East Jerusalem, and the Golan Heights, which had been used by Syria to shell towns in northern Israel. Israel annexed East Jerusalem in 1967 and the Golan Heights in 1981. Prime Minister Yitzhak Rabin's Labor-led coalition government secured a breakthrough agreement with the Palestine Liberation Organization (PLO) in 1993. The Declaration of Principles, negotiated secretly between Israeli and Palestinian delegations in Oslo, Norway, provided for a phased Israeli withdrawal from the Israeli-occupied West Bank and Gaza Strip and for limited Palestinian autonomy in those areas. On November 4, 1995, a right-wing Jewish extremist, opposed to the peace process, assassinated Rabin in Tel Aviv.

At Camp David in July 2000, and at Taba, Egypt at the end of the year, Prime Minister Barak and U.S. President Bill Clinton engaged the Palestinian leadership in the most far-reaching negotiations ever. For the first time, Israel discussed compromise solutions on Jerusalem, agreeing to some form of Palestinian sovereignty over East Jerusalem and its Islamic holy sites. Israel also offered over 95 percent of the West Bank and Gaza to the Palestinians. However, the Palestinians effectively rejected the Israeli offers and, following a controversial visit by right-wing Likud party leader Ariel Sharon to the Temple Mount in Jerusalem, initiated an armed uprising in late September 2000. Snap Israeli elections in February 2001 took place against the backdrop of continuing Palestinian violence. Sharon, promising to enhance Israel's security, trounced Barak at the polls.

Sharon assembled a national unity coalition cabinet composed primarily of Likud and Labor party members along with member of several religious, centrist, and right-wing parties. For the first time in Israel's history, an Arab citizen, Salah Tarif, was accorded a full cabinet post.

Israelis experienced a pronounced decline in personal security in 2002. Islamic radicals and other Palestinian militants staged suicide bombings, ambushes, and bus and car bombings. In one suicide bombing in March, 29 people were killed at a Passover Seder in a hotel in the seaside town of Netanya. More than 700 Israelis have been killed since the Palestinian uprising began in September 2000.

Throughout 2002 Israeli police thwarted several major attacks that revealed a new sophistication and determination on the part of terrorists. Early in the year, Israeli intelligence said it had uncovered a plot to blow up the twin Azrieli office towers in Tel Aviv. In May, a rigged tanker truck exploded at a fuel depot in Tel Aviv, nearly causing a massive secondary explosion in a heavily populated area. In September, police stopped a car in northern Israel loaded with 1,300 pounds of explosives.

Israel retaliated for many terrorist attacks throughout the year, employing targeted killings of militants, air strikes, home demolitions, and curfews. The United

States and other nations criticized Israel over the inadvertent deaths of innocent Palestinians. Towards the end of the year, Israel notably restrained itself from responding to suicide bombings in deference to American preparations for possible war against Iraq.

Israeli reprisals for Palestinian terrorist attacks led to sharp divisions within the cabinet; Labor Ministers threatened to resign over what they saw as heavy-handed tactics by the Israeli Defense Forces (IDF) in Palestinian areas. As the Palestinian uprising wore on, a growing number of Israeli troops and reservists refused to report for duty, citing moral opposition to the occupation of Palestinian territory. Approximately 200 reservists signed a petition stating they would no longer serve in the West Bank and Gaza Strip. At the same time, a substantial number of reservists volunteered for duty.

In October, Sharon's coalition collapsed. The Labor party resigned from the government over a dispute concerning state money budgeted for Jewish settlements in the West Bank. Labor wanted the funds—approximately $120 million—to finance social programs. Labor's departure left Sharon without a governing majority in the 120-seat Knesset. National elections were set for the end of January 2003.

As the Likud prepared for national elections, a bribery scandal emerged in December, implicating members of the party's Central Committee. Several members allegedly demanded bribes from Likud candidates in return for votes during the party's primary election. Some candidates with little or no political experience placed higher on the list for Knesset seats than some veteran politicians. Two members of the Central Committee were arrested for fraud.

Tension remained high along Israel's northern border with Lebanon throughout the year. Hezbollah, a radical Shiite Muslim group backed by Iran and Syria and based in southern Lebanon, took delivery of rockets capable of striking Israeli population and industrial centers. The group also attacked Israeli positions patrolling near the Shebba farms area. Hezbollah considers the area "occupied," despite UN confirmation in June 2000 that Israel had withdrawn fully from the "security zone" in southern Lebanon that it occupied for 18 years. Israel held the zone to protect its northern flank from attacks, including repeated Hezbollah rocketing of Israeli towns and farms.

Hezbollah did not cooperate in negotiating the release of three Israeli soldiers kidnapped from Israel's side of the Israel Lebanon border in October 2000. Neither did it release an Israeli businessman kidnapped by Hezbollah in Europe and believed transported to Lebanon.

In September, Lebanon announced its intention to pump the Wazzani Springs, which serve as headwaters for the Jordan River, Israel's primary freshwater source. Israel hinted at possible retaliation.

Peace talks with Syria did not take place during the year. Intensive negotiations broke down in January 2000 over disagreements on final borders around the Golan Heights. Prior to losing the Golan in 1967, Syria had used the territory to shell northern Israeli towns.

In May, Prime Minister Sharon narrowly won passage of a $2.7 billion austerity budget designed to reduce a deficit enlarged by rising defense costs.

The Israeli economy suffered throughout the year from plummeting tourism and the strain of combating Palestinian terrorism. A government report in November revealed that one-fifth of the population, including 531,000 children, was living in poverty.

Political Rights and Civil Liberties: Israeli citizens can change their government democratically. Although Israel has no formal constitution, a series of basic laws has the force of constitutional principles.

Arab residents of East Jerusalem, while not granted automatic citizenship, were issued Israeli identity cards after the 1967 Six-Day War. They were given all rights held by Israeli citizens, except the right to vote in national elections. They do have the right to vote in municipal elections and are eligible to apply for citizenship. Many choose not to seek citizenship out of a sense of solidarity with Palestinians in the West Bank and Gaza Strip. While East Jerusalem's Arab population generally enjoys greater freedoms and social services than other Palestinians, they do not receive a share of municipal services proportionate to their numbers. Arabs in East Jerusalem do have the right to vote in Palestinian elections.

The judiciary is independent, and procedural safeguards are generally respected. Security trials, however, may be closed to the public on limited grounds. The Emergency Powers (Detention) Law of 1979 provides for indefinite administrative detention without trial. The policy stems from emergency laws in place since the creation of Israel. Most administrative detainees are Palestinian, but there are currently two Lebanese detainees being held on national security grounds. They are believed to have direct knowledge of Israeli airman Ron Arad, thought to be held in Lebanon since his plane was shot down in 1986.

Some one million Arab citizens (roughly 19 percent of the population) receive inferior education, housing, and social services relative to the Jewish population. Israeli Arabs are not subject to the military draft, though they may serve voluntarily. Those who do not join the army are not eligible for financial benefits—including scholarships and housing loans—available to Israelis who have served.

Former prime minister Ehud Barak testified before a public inquiry examining the circumstances surrounding the shooting deaths of 13 Arab Israeli citizens in October 2000, after police opened fire on demonstrators protesting in support of the Palestinian uprising. Barak testified that he did not authorize police to use "any means" against the protestors, but the commission suggested Barak had not properly prepared police for rioting and did little to calm the situation. The commission had earlier warned Chief Police Superintendent Shmuel Mermelstein that he could face trial for positioning snipers in the protest areas without proper authority.

Continuing a recent trend, a handful of Israeli Arab citizens were linked to suicide bombings in 2002. Israelis were noticeably alarmed, fearing that Israel's substantial minority might represent a fifth column. In the summer the Interior Ministry proposed taking steps to establish a new policy that revokes citizenship from Arab Israelis charged with involvement in terrorism. The law does not apply to non-Arab Israelis.

Suspicion of Arab Israelis—and Arab citizens' feelings of discrimination—increased in October with the arrest of 11 Arab Israeli soldiers, including a lieutenant colonel, on charges of spying for Hezbollah. The officer allegedly provided intelligence on IDF troop positions on Israel's northern border in exchange for money and drugs.

In July, the cabinet supported a bill submitted by a religious right-wing Knesset member that would allocate state lands exclusively for Jewish residents. Critics called the bill racist and said it would deny non-Jews the right to live in certain parts of Israel. Supporters of the bill argued that it would grant Jews the right to live amongst themselves in secure areas. At the heart of the debate was Israel's perennial challenge of maintaining a state that is simultaneously Jewish and democratic. In response to the highly charged controversy, the cabinet agreed to oppose the bill until a public committee reviewed it and offered its recommendations.

Newspaper and magazine articles on security matters are subject to military censor, though the scope of permissible reporting is wide. Editors may appeal a censorship decision to a three-member tribunal that includes two civilians. Arabic-language publications are censored more frequently than are Hebrew-language ones. Newspapers are privately owned and freely criticize government policy.

In December the interior ministry ordered the closure of the radical Islamic weekly *Sawt al-Haq wa Al-Hurriya*, published by the radical wing of the Islamic Movement in Israel. Israel said the paper was a mouthpiece for Hamas.

Israel's Government Press Office, citing security concerns, did not renew credentials of several Palestinian journalists in 2002. Western news organizations—which rely heavily on Palestinian crews—and press freedom organizations demanded the accreditations be reinstated.

Publishing the praise of violence is prohibited under the Counterterrorism Ordinance. Israeli authorities prohibit expressions of support for groups that call for the destruction of Israel. An Arab Knesset member, Azmi Bishara, stood trial during the year for "voicing solidarity with a terrorist organization" after delivering a speech in Syria in 2001.

In December, the Israeli Election Commission disqualified Bishara and another Arab Knesset member, Ahmed Tibi, for running for reelection over charges that they supported Palestinian violence against Israel. Both had appealed to the Supreme Court and were awaiting a ruling at year's end.

On several occasions during the year, journalists covering events in the West Bank and Gaza Strip came under gunfire by IDF troops. Italian freelance photographer Raffaele Ciriello was shot and killed in Ramallah in March. In some cases the Committee to Protect Journalists and other press freedom groups claimed journalists were deliberately targeted, a charge the Israeli government denied. In July, Israeli military authorities ordered field commanders to protect journalists covering street clashes in the West Bank and Gaza.

The International Press Institute also criticized Israel for not allowing journalists access to some Palestinian towns and villages where the IDF was active. In August, Defense Minister Benjamin Ben-Eliezer apologized to an Israeli journalist shot at by IDF troops while driving in a West Bank military zone. The Israeli Government Press Office also denied press credentials to several Palestinian journalists working for international media organizations. Some Arab journalists traveling to Israel were denied entry visas.

Italy

Polity: Parliamentary democracy
Economy: Capitalist-statist
Population: 58,100,000
PPP: $23,626
Life Expectancy: 80

Political Rights: 1
Civil Liberties: 1*
Status: Free

Religious Groups: Roman Catholic (predominant)
Ethnic Groups: Italian, small minorities of German, French, Slovenian, and Albanian
Capital: Rome
Ratings Change: Italy's civil liberties rating improved from 2 to 1 due to changes in the survey methodology.

Ten-Year Ratings Timeline (Political Rights, Civil Liberties, Status)

1993	1994	1995	1996	1997	1998	1999	2000	2001	2002	2003
1,2F	1,3F	1,2F	1,2F	1,2F	1,2F	1,2F	1,2F	1,2F	1,2F	1,1F

Overview:

Several bills introduced in parliament in 2002 were the focus of opposition protests. The first bill proposed to tackle the potential conflicts of interests of those holding public office, but the government's proposals fell short of eliminating the suspicion that Prime Minister Silvio Berlusconi might be using public office for private gain. Another bill, known as the Cirami law, was also passed, and required trials to be relocated if there is a "legitimate suspicion" that the judge is biased against the defendant. Opponents of the prime minister claimed that this reform was being fast-tracked through parliament, ahead of more pressing issues, in order to bring about the suspension of a trial (in which Berlusconi is accused of bribing judges in the mid-1980s) before a verdict can be reached. A third pending bill deals with broadcasting and the media and includes controversial changes to rules regarding television and press ownership, and the advertising market, areas in which Berlusconi's businesses are dominant.

Modern Italian history dates from the nineteenth-century movement for national unification. Most of Italy had merged into one kingdom by 1870. Italy sided with Germany and Austria-Hungary at the outset of World War I, but switched to side with the Allied powers during the war. From 1922 to 1943, the country was a Fascist dictatorship under Benito Mussolini, who sided with the Axis powers during World War II. A referendum in 1946 replaced the monarchy with a republican constitution, which provides for a president whose role is largely ceremonial. He is elected to a seven-year term by an assembly of members of parliament and delegates from the regional councils. The president chooses the prime minister, who is often, but not always, a member of the largest party in the Chamber of Deputies, the lower house of parliament. Members of the upper house, the Senate, are elected on a regional basis.

Silvio Berlusconi's center-right coalition, Casa delle Liberta, which includes his own Forza Italia, the post-Fascist National Alliance, and the northern-nationalist Northern League, swept to power in national elections held in May 2001. Prime Minister Berlusconi's right-of-center coalition is likely to survive in office beyond 2004. Its potential longevity reflects the unprecedented size of its parliamentary majority and the unchallengeable authority of Berlusconi. The coalition won a comfortable majority of 368 out of 630 seats in the Chamber of Deputies and 177 out of 326 in the Senate, and a strong showing for the Forza Italia gave Berlusconi firm control of his coalition.

Italy's fractious and unstable government has failed during the past several years to implement the reforms necessary to address the country's myriad political problems. (Italy has had over 50 governments since 1945.) Such reforms include overhauling current electoral laws, which engender political instability by allowing dozens of small parties to wield disproportionate influence in parliament, and creating a framework for devolution to neutralize secessionist sentiment among northern Italians.

Italy surprised most skeptics when it joined European Economic and Monetary Union (EMU) in January 1999, after years of high deficits and inflation. Accession followed a program of fiscal austerity, and as a result, the euro replaced the lira as Italy's currency. Italy is experiencing stagnant economic growth, brought on primarily by low growth in its major export markets, including Germany and France. The government's efforts to privatize state assets continues apace, although it has slowed in the past two years because of economic malaise and because many of the most profitable assets have already been sold.

Political Rights and Civil Liberties:

Italians can change their government democratically. Citizens are free to form political organizations, with the exception of the constitutionally forbidden prewar Fascist Party. The postwar constitution, designed to prevent another Mussolini-style dictatorship, sharply restricts the powers of the executive in favor of the legislative and judicial branches of government. The result has been unstable governing coalitions, political deadlock, and heavy reliance on the referendum as a political tool.

The Italian press is free and competitive. Most of approximately 80 daily newspapers are independently owned. The main state-owned television network and the three main channels of Radio Audizioni Italiane (RAI) provide Italians with most of their news. Their boards of directors are parliament appointed. A February 2000 law on political advertising requires broadcasters to give political adversaries equal time, bans paid political ads on national television, and requires public broadcasters to give all parties free television time at certain hours. Private broadcasters must also provide equal time to opposing parties if they choose to run political ads. Fears that the independence of the press could be compromised were raised after Berlusconi's appointment as prime minister, as he has extensive holdings in the media (television and print).

Workers may strike and bargain collectively. Some 40 percent of the workforce is unionized. The law prohibits discrimination by employers against union members and organizers. Over the last decade, relations between employees and employers have generally become less adversarial, although strike action increased in 2001.

In July 2000, the government announced plans to reform Italy's prison system, which officially holds about 7,000 more prisoners than the prisons were designed for. The plans include building new prisons, renovating existing facilities, recruiting new prison officers, and deporting prisoners from outside the EU sentenced to less than three years.

The judiciary is independent but notoriously slow and inefficient. A 1995 law allows for preventive detention as a last resort or in cases where there is convincing evidence of a serious offense, such as illegal activity involving organized crime or related to drugs, arms, or subversion. A maximum of two years is permitted for preliminary investigation. The average waiting period for a trial is about 18 months, but can exceed two years. A decree issued in November 2000 extends the time limit on pretrial incarceration of suspects charged with pedophilia or the prostitution of minors. It will also give judges greater discretion in extending pretrial detention up to a six-year limit. Other provisions include abolishing the plea bargain for suspects facing life imprisonment and increasing surveillance of suspects under house arrest.

Freedom of assembly and association is guaranteed by the constitution, with the exception of organizations that promote racial, ethnic, or religious discrimination. Religious freedom is protected, and the government subsidizes several religions through tax revenues. In March 2000, the government formally recognized Buddhists and Jehovah's Witnesses as official religions for the first time. Official recognition allows religions to establish their own schools and to benefit from a system in which taxpayers can donate a percentage of their income tax payment to the faith of their choice. Observers have raised concern over what appears to be an increase of xenophobia and anti-Semitism, particularly in the north. Public statements made by Umberto Bossi, the leader of the Northern League, against Muslims, homosexuals, and foreigners appear to resonate with Italians who fear that an influx of foreigners threatens national identity.

There are no restrictions on women's participation in government and politics, though few hold elective office. Women currently constitute 9.8 percent of the Chamber of Deputies and 7.7 percent of the Senate. Women enjoy legal equality in marriage, property, and inheritance rights. Foreign women are particular victims of human trafficking. Tens of thousands have been smuggled in to work as prostitutes, primarily by Albanian-organized crime rings. Often, their passports are destroyed, and they are abused in an effort to frighten them into submission. Immigration laws offer special protection to trafficked women, such as automatic six-month legal residency with the possibility of renewal. In addition, an estimated 1,200 women in 48 programs throughout the country have been given assistance in finding alternative employment.

In June the lower house of the Italian parliament passed an immigration law, known as the Bossi-Fini law, that would require non-European citizens to be fingerprinted if they wish to live in Italy. The bill also makes family reunions more difficult — immigrants will only be allowed to bring in their children if they are under the age of 18. The initiative now needs approval of the Senate. Opponents of the legislation claim that such a measure in effect describes such immigrants as criminals; the defenders, led by the northern nationalist Umberto Bossi, say the measure is simply a way to keep track of immigrants. Despite outrage from some circles, the proposed law has widespread popular support.

Italian police frequently harass the Roma (Gypsy) population of Italy. In April 2002 a Rome municipal committee met to discuss plans for dismantling camp Salone, the Roma camp on the southern periphery of Rome, and to create five new camps for

Roma that will be under the "constant surveillance of police." The approximately 1,200 Roma inhabitants of Salone will be either transferred to new sites authorized by the City of Rome or expelled from Italy. Expulsion from home camps is commonplace.

Jamaica

Polity: Parliamentary democracy
Economy: Capitalist
Population: 2,600,000
PPP: $3,639
Life Expectancy: 75
Religious Groups: Protestant (61.3 percent), Roman Catholic (4 percent), other (34.7 percent)
Ethnic Groups: Black (91 percent), other, including white, Chinese, East Indian (9 percent)
Capital: Kingston

Political Rights: 2
Civil Liberties: 3
Status: Free

Ten-Year Ratings Timeline (Political Rights, Civil Liberties, Status)

1993	1994	1995	1996	1997	1998	1999	2000	2001	2002	2003
2,2F	2,3F	2,3F	2,3F	2,3F	2,3F	2,2F	2,2F	2,2F	2,3F	2,3F

Overview:

In 2002, P. J. Patterson became the only prime minister in Jamaican history to be elected to three consecutive terms. His People's National Party (PNP) won 34 of 60 parliamentary seats, and retained the prime minister for an unprecedented fourth term. The opposition Jamaican Labor Party (JLP) took 26 seats. Patterson also became the first premier to swear allegiance to the Jamaican people and constitution, rather than to the Queen of England. The firsts marked by the election, however, did virtually nothing to change the challenges facing the PNP, which in fact lost 15 seats in parliament, including ridding the island of drug kingpins and illegal guns, revving up a flat economy, and rebuilding a slumping tourist industry.

Jamaica, a member of the Commonwealth, achieved independence from Great Britain in 1962. It is a parliamentary democracy, with the British monarchy represented by a governor-general. The bicameral parliament consists of the 60-member House of Representatives elected for five years and the 21-member Senate, with 13 senators appointed by the prime minister and 8 by the leader of the parliamentary opposition. Executive authority is vested in the prime minister, who leads the political party commanding a majority in the house. In August 2002, Patterson helped pass legislation changing the oath of allegiance taken by public officials.

Since independence, power has alternated between the social-democratic PNP and the conservative JLP. In 1992 the PNP elected Patterson to replace Michael Manley as party leader and prime minister. In the 1993 elections, the PNP won 52 parliamentary seats, and the JLP 8. The parties differed little on continuing the structural adjustment begun in the 1980s, but the JLP was hurt by long-standing internal rifts. Irregularities and violence marred the vote. The Patterson government confronted labor unrest and an unrelenting crime wave. Increases in violent crime are largely the work of former politically organized gangs that now operate a lucrative drug trade that is only loosely tied to local party bosses.

In 2000, Patterson promised to stanch Jamaica's "rampant criminality" by introducing new efforts to control guns, creating a new police anti-organized-crime strike force, and reintroducing the death penalty. The get-tough promises came after criticisms from key leaders of the vital tourism industry joined a crescendo of complaints from Jamaicans of all walks of life demanding an end to a more than two-decades-long spiral of mostly drug-related street crime. The fierce crime wave crippled local businesses and created an exodus of middle-class Jamaicans overseas. Gang fighting in West Kingston erupted in May 2001, leaving a toll of 71 dead; and 28 others—including at least three police officers and one soldier—were killed in several days of gunfights as police and soldiers moved into opposition-held communities.

In 2002, a national crime plan, hammered out with the support of the JLP and the country's business community, helped to bring about large cocaine seizures. It included increased training for police, stronger criminal intelligence planning, and greater ties to foreign law enforcement agencies. Patterson vowed to encourage foreign investment and boost tourism by attracting more pleasure boats to the island, constructing 11,000 new hotel rooms in five years, and promoting eco-tourism.

Political Rights and Civil Liberties:

Citizens are able to change their government through elections, although the 56 percent voter turnout was the lowest in years. An observer delegation led by former U.S. president Jimmy Carter said that, despite a crackdown in voter fraud, such activity remained high in areas controlled by politically linked gangs.

Constitutional guarantees regarding the right to free expression, the right to freedom of religion, and the right to organize political parties, civic organizations, and labor unions are generally respected.

The judicial system is headed by the Supreme Court and includes several magistrate's courts and a court of appeals, with final recourse to the Privy Council in London, which is drawn from members of Britain's House of Lords. The justice system is slow and inefficient, particularly in addressing police abuses and the violent conditions in prisons. Despite governmental efforts to improve penal conditions, a mounting backlog of cases and a shortage of court staff at all levels continue to undermine the judicial system.

Jamaica is a main transit point for cocaine being shipped from Colombia through the Caribbean to U.S. markets, and the drug trade is now largely controlled by Colombian organized crime syndicates. Violence is the major cause of death in Jamaica, and the murder rate is one of the highest in the world. Much of the violence is the result of warfare between drug gangs known as "posses." Criminal deportees from the United States and a growing illegal weapons trade are major causes of the violence. Mobs have been responsible for numerous vigilante killings of suspected criminals. Inmates frequently die as a result of prison riots. Jamaican officials complain that the United States was flagrantly applying a double standard by demanding a full effort by Jamaica to help stop the flow of drugs into the United States, but at the same time failing to stem the flow of guns into Jamaica.

Human rights groups report that there are continuing concerns over criminal justice practices in Jamaica, particularly the shooting of suspects by police. Other disputed practices include the imposition of death sentences following trials of questionable fairness; deaths in custody; corporal punishment; alleged ill-treatment by police and prison wardens; appalling detention centers and prisons; and laws punishing consensual sexual acts in private between adult men. A mounting crime rate led the government to take controversial steps toward restoring capital punishment and flogging. Rights groups protested both measures. Critics charge that flogging is unconstitutional because it can be characterized as "inhuman or degrading punishment," which the constitution prohibits.

There are an estimated 1.9 million radios in Jamaica—the highest per capita ratio in the Caribbean—but only 330,000 television sets, and there is generally low newspaper readership. Newspapers are independent and free of government control. Journalists are occasionally intimidated during election campaigns. Broadcast media are largely public but are open to pluralistic points of view. Public opinion polls play a key role in the political process, and election campaigns feature debates on state-run television.

In 1998, a woman was for the first time elected speaker of parliament. Labor unions are politically influential and have the right to strike. The Industrial Disputes Tribunal mediates labor conflicts.

Japan

Polity: Parliamentary democracy
Economy: Capitalist
Population: 127,400,000
PPP: $26,755
Life Expectancy: 81
Religious Groups: Shinto and Buddhist (84 percent), other [including Christian] (16 percent)
Ethnic Groups: Japanese (99 percent), other (1 percent)
Capital: Tokyo

Political Rights: 1
Civil Liberties: 2
Status: Free

Ten-Year Ratings Timeline (Political Rights, Civil Liberties, Status)

1993	1994	1995	1996	1997	1998	1999	2000	2001	2002	2003
1,2F	2,2F	2,2F	1,2F	1,2F	1,2F	1,2F	1,2F	1,2F	1,2F	1,2F

Overview:

Japan faced continued economic malaise after Prime Minister Junichiro Koizumi's efforts to tackle the mountain of bad bank loans that have helped push the world's second-largest economy into recession three times since 1990 were rebuffed by old-guard factions within his own ruling party. Koizumi argued that painful reforms are needed to nurse the economy back to health, but his plans threatened industries that are key ruling-party backers. They also could push up unemployment, already at post-war highs.

Following its defeat in World War II, Japan adopted a U.S.-drafted constitution in 1947 that provided for a parliamentary government, renounced war, and ended the emperor's divine status. Post-war Japanese politics have been dominated by the Liberal Democratic Party (LDP), created in 1955 through a merger of two conservative parties. During the Cold War, the LDP presided over the economy's spectacular growth while fostering close security ties with the United States. Successive governments spent massively on public works projects to benefit the LDP's rural stronghold as well as its corporate backers, who funneled both legal and illegal contributions back to the party. Bureaucrats, meanwhile, imposed costly regulations to protect small businesses, which overwhelmingly supported the LDP.

The LDP's only spell in opposition since its inception came after it lost the 1993 lower house elections. The party's drubbing followed a string of corruption scandals in the late 1980s that brought down Prime Minister Noburu Takeshita and other top LDP politicians. After a fractious reformist government collapsed, the LDP returned to power in 1994 as the head of a three-party coalition.

Successive LDP-led governments in the latter half of the 1990s did little to arrest mounting economic problems stemming from the collapse of Japanese stock market and real estate prices earlier in the decade. The crash left Japanese banks saddled with tens of billions of dollars worth of problem loans and diminished the value of property and other collateral backing the loans.

As the banks' problem loans dragged down the economy by choking off lending and eroding consumer confidence, the government pumped around $1 trillion into the economy in the 1990s. The stimulus packages largely failed to jump-start the economy but helped jack up Japan's huge public debt, now approaching 140 percent of economic output, the highest among rich countries.

Despite the economy's continuing woes and the deep unpopularity of then Prime Minister Yoshiro Mori, the LDP won the most seats in the most recent lower house elections, in June 2000. It formed a coalition government with the New Komeito and New Conservative parties. With 233 seats in the 480-seat house, the LDP easily defeated the main opposition Democratic Party, which took 127 seats behind calls to curb public spending and scale back governmental regulation. Turnout was 62.4 percent.

Koizumi, 60, took office in April 2001 following the resignation of the gaffe-prone Mori. The LDP's conservative factions have opposed Koizumi's reforms because they would cut the public spending and red tape that benefit the party's core constituency of farmers, small businesses, and the construction industry. Construction alone accounts for 10 percent of all jobs in Japan.

Economists, meanwhile, have warned that Koizumi's reforms, if actually carried out, could make matters worse before there is any improvement. They said that cutting government spending and forcing banks to get rid of bad loans could accelerate Japan's vicious economic cycle.

This cycle has seen deflation make banks less willing to lend, healthy firms reluctant to borrow and invest, and consumers tight-fisted with their *yen*. Weak consumer spending erodes corporate profits, which makes it harder for firms to pay off bank loans. Firms respond to weak demand by slashing prices and cutting jobs, while banks curb lending further in response to deadbeat borrowers. Deflation also raises real interest rates, making healthy firms reluctant to take out fresh loans.

Meanwhile, the prospect of even lower prices in the future and the specter of lost jobs make ordinary Japanese even less willing to part with their yen in an economy in which their spending makes up around 60 percent of output. Consumers have also cut spending over fears that they will have to rely on their own retirement savings should the government's swelling public debt and Japan's greying population overwhelm the state pension system. Firms respond to weak demand with more job and price cuts, and the deflationary spiral continues.

LDP conservatives in October blocked plans by chief banking regulator Heizo Takenaka to make banks hold more capital and set aside more money for bad loans. They argued that the moves could cause bankruptcies among banks and tottering borrowers, leading to a credit crunch and heavy job losses at a time when unemployment had already returned to a record high of 5.5 percent. Koizumi has argued that precisely this type of painful reform is needed to stop banks from keeping ailing firms on life support while choking off lending to healthy ones. Analysts say that the current size of the banks' bad loans could be two to four times the official figure of 52 trillion yen (US$426 billion).

Conservatives also watered down Koizumi's efforts to privatize the $2 trillion postal savings system, which he says invests the money inefficiently. The economy grew at a 3.2 percent annual rate in the third quarter compared with the previous quarter. However, the Paris-based Organization for Economic Cooperation and Development predicted late in the year that economic growth would be virtually flat until after the end of 2004.

Signaling disillusionment with mainstream politics, voters elected or nearly elected independents or Communist party members as mayors or governors in several local races early in the year. Koizumi's own political stock rose, however, after he won an admission by North Korea, during a trip to Pyongyang in September, that it had kidnapped 13 Japanese citizens more than two decades ago.

Political Rights and Civil Liberties: Japanese can change their government through elections and enjoy most basic rights. The lower house of parliament has 300 seats that represent single-member districts and 180 seats chosen by proportional representation balloting. The upper house has 152 single-member seats and 100 chosen by proportional representation. Despite recent reforms aimed at curbing the power of the bureaucracy, policy generally is still shaped by senior civil servants rather than elected politicians. The bureaucracy has recently been hit by numerous scandals and operates with little transparency.

Japan's judiciary is independent. Human rights groups say, however, that the criminal process is flawed because defendants often have little access to counsel before their trials. The criminal procedure code allows police and prosecutors to restrict a suspect's access to counsel during investigation and bars attorneys from being present during interrogations, even after indictment. Moreover, rights groups, bar associations, and some prisoners allege that police at times use force to extract confessions from suspects.

Foreign and domestic human rights groups have criticized Japanese prisons for subjecting inmates to severe regimentation that at times includes barring them from talking to each other or even making eye contact. Punishments include forcing inmates to sit motionless for hours at a time, preventing them from washing or exercising, and restraining them with leather handcuffs, the human rights group Amnesty International said in a November statement, which called on the government to set up an independent body to oversee prisons.

Amnesty has also criticized the secrecy surrounding death row and executions in Japan. Officials often notify condemned inmates less than two hours before they are to be executed and do not inform family members until after the execution takes place.

Japan's press is independent, though not always outspoken. The European Union has formally complained about the exclusive access to news sources that major media outlets often enjoy as members of Japan's 800 or more private press clubs. As club members, these media receive information from government ministries, political parties, and private firms that is often unavailable to reporters from foreign or small publications, who are shut out of many clubs. Journalists who belong to the clubs generally do not report aggressively on the conditions of ailing banks or companies and other sensitive financial issues.

Japanese women are frequently tracked by their companies into clerical careers and discriminated against in wages and other areas, according to the U.S. State Department's global human rights report for 2001, released in March 2002. In addition, sexual harassment on the job is widespread, according to recent reports by government agencies and the Japanese Trade Union Confederation. The law bans both sexual discrimination and harassment in the workplace, but authorizes only light sanctions for corporate violators.

Moreover, one in three Japanese women experiences some form of physical abuse at home, a 1998 survey by the prime minister's office found. Women also frequently complain of being groped or otherwise molested on crowded trains. Meanwhile, a relatively small number of women and girls are trafficked into Japan each year for sexual exploitation and forced labor, the U.S. State Department report said. Concern is also growing in society over teenage girls who work as prostitutes or date older men for money and over student-on-student violence and bullying in schools.

Japanese of all faiths worship freely. Buddhism and Shintoism have the most followers. In the wake of the 1995 terrorist attacks in the Tokyo subway by the Aum Shinrikyo cult, parliament amended the Religious Corporation Law to give the government greater oversight over the operations and financial affairs of most religious groups. The law applies only to religious groups that register voluntarily as "religious corporations," but most do register in order to receive tax benefits and other advantages.

Japan's three million Burakumin, who are descendants of feudal-era outcasts, and its tiny, indigenous Ainu minority face unofficial discrimination in housing and employment and social ostracism, the U.S. State Department report said. The government funds programs aimed at promoting Ainu culture and boosting the economic status of Burakumin.

Meanwhile, Japan's 636,000 ethnic Koreans, most of whom were born in Japan, face "deeply entrenched societal discrimination," according to the U.S. State Department report. Koreans and other ethnic minorities born in Japan are considered legal foreign residents but are not automatically Japanese citizens at birth. Instead, those seeking citizenship must apply for naturalization and submit to extensive background checks. Separately, thousands of foreign nationals, many of them asylum seekers or holders of valid visas, are detained each year under harsh conditions in privately run facilities before being deported, Amnesty International said in its May report.

Japanese trade unions are independent and active. The International Labor Organization has criticized laws that prevent soldiers, police, and firefighters from joining unions or staging strikes. Civil servants also cannot strike, and face restrictions on bargaining collectively. Around 22 percent of Japanese workers belong to trade unions. Nongovernmental groups accuse employers of exploiting or discriminating against foreign workers, who often cannot speak Japanese and are unaware of their rights.

China, South Korea, and other regional countries frequently protest passages in Japanese history textbooks that try to justify the country's occupation of other Asian nations before and during World War II and downplay the imperial army's wartime atrocities in occupied lands. These abuses included forcibly using tens of thousands of women as sex slaves. The education ministry, moreover, often censors textbook passages that it considers too critical of Japan's wartime record.

Jordan

Polity: Traditional monar- **Political Rights:** 6*
chy and limited parliament **Civil Liberties:** 5
Economy: Mixed capitalist **Status:** Partly Free
Population: 5,300,000
PPP: $3,966
Life Expectancy: 70
Religious Groups: Sunni Muslim (92 percent),
Christian (6 percent), other (2 percent)
Ethnic Groups: Arab (98 percent), other, including Armenian (2 percent)
Capital: Amman
Ratings Change: Jordan's political rights rating declined from 5 to 6 due to King Abdullah's postponement of elections and his continued rule by decree.

Ten-Year Ratings Timeline (Political Rights, Civil Liberties, Status)

1993	1994	1995	1996	1997	1998	1999	2000	2001	2002	2003
3,3PF	4,4PF	4,4PF	4,4PF	4,4PF	4,4PF	4,5PF	4,4PF	4,4PF	5,5PF	6,5PF

Overview: In the face of continuing domestic opposition to its pro-Western foreign policy, the Jordanian government continued to suspend indefinitely representative political institutions and impose restrictions on civil liberties.

The Hashemite Kingdom of Jordan (known as Transjordan until 1950) was established as a League of Nations mandate under the control of Great Britain in 1921 and granted full independence in 1946. Following the assassination of King Abdullah in 1951, the crown passed briefly to his mentally unstable eldest son, Talal, and then to his grandson, Hussein, in 1953. King Hussein's turbulent 46-year reign witnessed a massive influx of Palestinian refugees (who now comprise a majority of the population), the loss of all territory west of the Jordan River in 1967, and numerous assassination and coup attempts by Palestinian and Arab nationalists. The unlikely survival of Jordan's monarchy during this period was mainly the product of Hussein's remarkable political skills, his firm alliance with the West, and a considerable amount of luck.

Although the 1952 constitution provided for a directly elected parliament, political parties were banned in 1956 and parliament was either suspended entirely or emasculated by government intervention in the electoral process for over three decades. While political and civil liberties remained tightly restricted, Hussein proved adept at co-opting, rather than killing, jailing, or exiling, his political opponents. As a result, Jordan avoided the legacy of brutal repression characteristic of other authoritarian regimes in the Arab world.

As a result of the decline of oil revenues in 1980s, which translated into reduced aid and worker remittances from the Arab gulf countries, Jordan borrowed heavily throughout the decade and was eventually forced to implement economic austerity measures in return for IMF assistance in rescheduling its debt. In April 1989, price increases for fuel and other subsidized commodities provoked widespread rioting that left eight people dead and hundreds detained. Facing mounting internal pressure for greater freedom and representation, the government launched a rapid process of political liberalization. Free elections were held later that year and restrictions on civil liberties were progressively eased. The reform process ground to a halt in the mid-1990s and suffered some reversals.

By the time of Hussein's death in February 1999 and the ascension of his son, Abdullah, the kingdom was again faced with severe economic problems. The "peace dividend" expected to follow from Jordan's 1994 peace treaty with Israel, in the form of improved trade with the West Bank and increased investment from Western Europe, had not matched expectations. Because of rampant government corruption, even this limited economic return did not filter down to the population at large, which suffered from 27 percent unemployment. Faced with a crippling public debt of $11.5 billion, Abdullah launched economic reforms needed to attract international investment during the first two years of his rule and brought Jordan into the World Trade Organization.

The September 2000 outbreak of the "Al-Aqsa Intifada" in the Israeli-occupied West Bank and Gaza had an enormous impact on the country, inflaming anti-Israeli sentiments among Jordanians of Palestinian descent, leftists, and Islamists, who dominate much of civil society. As the violence next door continued unabated, the Professional Associations Council formed an anti-normalization committee to spearhead mass demonstrations demanding the annulment of Jordan's peace treaty with Israel.

The government reacted by suppressing criticism of Jordanian relations with Israel and banning all demonstrations. In January 2001, after the committee issued a blacklist of individuals and businesses with ties to Israel that included the chief of Jordan's Royal Court and other prominent figures, the government arrested seven of its members on charges of "participating in an illegal organization" and "endangering citizens' lives." When an estimated 1,000 Jordanians defied the ban on demonstrations on the anniversary of Israel's founding in May, security forces responded with batons and tear gas. In April, a majority of lower house parliamentary deputies petitioned the government to end the prosecution of anti-normalization activists. Two months later, Abdullah dissolved parliament and postponed general elections scheduled for November, apparently because of concerns that nationalist and Islamist dissidents committed to canceling Jordan's peace treaty with Israel would sweep the polls. The government also replaced elected municipal councils with state-appointed local committees.

The September 11, 2001 attacks on the United States, followed by the American war in Afghanistan and campaign to bring about regime change in Baghdad, helped transform the anti-normalization movement into a broader current of opposition to Jordan's pro-Western foreign policy. Abdullah postponed legislative elections again in August 2002, citing "difficult regional circumstances." Although legislative and municipal elections have been promised for the spring of 2003, most Jordanians recognize that they are not likely to be held until regional tensions subside.

For over a year and a half, King Abdullah has ruled by decree, and issued more than 100 "temporary laws" that are exempt from legislative approval until parliament is reconvened. Many of these laws imposed new restrictions on the freedoms of expression and assembly and weakened due process protections. Others promulgated domestic economic policies, intended to secure loyalty from the ruling political and commercial elites, that would have almost certainly have been rejected by the outgoing parliament.

The crackdown on civil liberties intensified in 2002. In October, the government ordered the closure of the Jordanian Society for Citizens' Rights (JSCR), ostensibly because of irregularities in its annual financial report. In November, the judiciary dissolved the 10-member council of the Engineers Association—the richest and most powerful of the trade unions—and declared the Professional Associations Council to be illegal, a ruling that Prime Minister Ali Abul Ragheb threatened to enforce if it continued to "practice political activities." The government's subsequent release of three members of the PAC's anti-normalization committee who had been in detention for two months was both a gesture of reconciliation and an implied threat.

The crackdown coincided with a public relations campaign, dubbed "Jordan First," designed to discredit the idea that the country's well-being should take a back seat to Palestinian or Iraqi interests. With hundreds of thousands of Palestinian refugees and an estimated 400,000 Iraqis residing in the kingdom, Abdullah fears that widespread opposition to the United States could become a violent challenge to his rule.

Following the killing of a senior American diplomat in Amman on October 28, the government arrested dozens of Islamist militants and deployed thousands of police and soldiers to sensitive locations around the country. The following month, troops backed by tanks and armored personnel carriers clashed with supporters of a renegade Islamic preacher in the town of Maan, leaving up to 10 dead and scores wounded, and arrested 136 suspects.

Political Rights and Civil Liberties: Jordanians cannot change their government democratically. The king holds broad executive powers and may dissolve parliament and dismiss the prime minister or cabinet at his discretion. Parliament may approve, reject, or amend legislation proposed by the cabinet, but is restricted in its ability to initiate legislation. Political parties have been legal since 1992. However, in 1993 the government introduced a single-member-district electoral system, designed to favor traditional elites over party candidates, which resulted in fewer opposition victories in elections that year. The government's refusal to rescind the law prompted boycotts by several opposition groups in 1997. A July 2001 temporary electoral law benefited traditional elites by slightly increasing the proportion of representatives from less-populated areas, but also met two long-standing opposition demands by transferring supervision of elections from the Interior Ministry to the judiciary and stipulating that ballots be counted directly at polling stations, rather than at a center run by the Interior Ministry.

Jordanian citizens enjoy little protection from arbitrary arrest and detention. Under the constitution, suspects may be detained for up to 48 hours without a warrant and up to 10 days without formal charges being filed, but courts routinely grant prosecutors 15-day extensions of this deadline. Even these minimal protections are denied to suspects referred to the State Security Court (SSC), who are often held in lengthy pretrial detention and refused access to legal council until just before trial. Defendants charged with security-related offenses frequently allege the use of torture to extract confessions. Government monitoring of telephone conversations and Internet communication is routine.

The judiciary is subject to executive influence through the Justice Ministry and the Higher Judiciary Council, whose members are appointed by the king. While most trials in civilian courts are open and procedurally sound, proceedings of the SSC are closed to the public. A "temporary" amendment to the State Security Court Law promulgated in 2001 allows the prime minister to refer any case to the SSC and denies the right of appeal to people convicted of misdemeanors (which, in Jordan, can carry short prison sentences).

Freedom of expression is greatly restricted. The state owns all broadcast media and has wide discretionary powers to close publications. An October 2001 temporary amendment to the penal code allows the SSC (rather than the press court) to close publications and imprison individuals for up to three years for publishing information that harms national unity, instigates criminal actions, inspires fanaticism, spreads false rumors, or is "harmful to the state's reputation and dignity." Another temporary law prohibited civil servants from signing petitions that harm the "integrity of the state."

On at least one occasion in 2002, the government pressured newspapers not to run paid advertisements placed by the anti-normalization committee to announce upcoming demonstrations. In January, the editor of the weekly *Al-Majd,* Fahd al-Rimawi, was detained for four days on charges of publishing "false information and rumors which affect the standing of the government." In May, prominent journalist and former member of parliament Toujan al-Faisal was sentenced to 18 months in prison for publishing an article on the Internet claiming that the prime minister's family profited from a temporary law which increased mandatory auto insurance premiums. After a hunger strike drew international attention to her case, King Abdullah commuted her sentence to time served. Hashem al-Khalidi, editor in chief of the weekly *Al-Bilad*, was detained for four days in March for reporting the same allegation. In August, the Interior Ministry shut down the Amman bureau of Qatar's Al-Jazeera satellite TV station and withdrew the credentials of its staff after one of its talk-show guests called Jordan a historic traitor to the Arab cause. During the clashes in Maan, the government issued a statement banning the press from speaking to residents of the town. Jordanian human rights activist Hisham Bustani was detained for two weeks in December after he criticized conditions in an Amman prison in an article for a Lebanese magazine.

Freedom of assembly is heavily restricted. A temporary law on public gatherings introduced in August 2001 bans demonstrations without written consent from the government and allows officials to disperse gatherings if they stray from their stated purpose. An 11-year old Palestinian refugee was killed during an anti-Israeli demonstration in April and around 50 people were injured by police during a similar demonstration the following month. Nongovernmental organizations (NGOs) are routinely licensed in Jordan, and dozens of NGOs address numerous political and social issues. Professional associations have recently come under pressure for their role in the anti-normalization campaign.

Workers have the right to bargain collectively, but must receive government permission in order to strike. More than 30 percent of the workforce is organized into 17 unions. Labor laws do not protect foreign workers. Abuse of mostly South Asian domestic servants is widespread.

Women enjoy equal political rights, but face legal discrimination in matters of inheritance and divorce falling under the jurisdiction of *Sharia* (Islamic law) courts, and in the provision of government pensions and social security benefits. Jordanian law provides for lenient treatment of those convicted of "honor crimes"—the murder or attempted murder of women by relatives for alleged sexual misconduct— mandating a minimum of only six months in prison. Although women constitute only 14 percent of the workforce, the government has made efforts to increase the number of women in the civil service. In December, the government announced plans to guarantee women a quota of seats in parliament

Islam is the state religion. The government appoints all Islamic clergy, pays their salaries, and monitors sermons at mosques, where political activity is banned under Jordanian law. Sunni Muslims constitute 92 percent of the population, but Christians and Jews are officially recognized as religious minorities and allowed to worship freely. Baha'is and Druze are allowed to practice their faiths, but are not officially recognized. Jordanians of Palestinian descent face discrimination in employment by the government and the military and in admission to universities.

↓ Kazakhstan

Polity: Presidential (dominant party)
Economy: Capitalist-statist
Population: 14,800,000
PPP: $5,871
Life Expectancy: 66

Political Rights: 6
Civil Liberties: 5
Status: Not Free

Religious Groups: Muslim (47 percent), Russian Orthodox (44 percent), Protestant (2 percent), other (7 percent)
Ethnic Groups: Kazakh (53 percent), Russian (30 percent), Ukrainian (4 percent), German (2 percent), other (11 percent)
Capital: Astana
Trend Arrow: Kazakhstan received a downward trend arrow due to increasing repression of the political opposition and media outlets, including a new restrictive law on political parties.

Ten-Year Ratings Timeline (Political Rights, Civil Liberties, Status)

1993	1994	1995	1996	1997	1998	1999	2000	2001	2002	2003
5,5NF	6,4NF	6,5NF	6,5NF	6,5NF	6,5NF	6,5NF	6,5NF	6,5NF	6,5NF	6,5NF

Overview:
Domestic challenges to President Nursultan Nazarbayev's authoritarian regime intensified in 2002 with the establishment of a new opposition movement composed of prominent government officials and business leaders. Nazarbayev responded to the threat by increasing the government's campaign against independent media outlets, including the use of physical intimidation and violence against journalists and their organizations. The year also saw the adoption of a new restrictive law on political parties and the convictions of two prominent opposition leaders on politically motivated charges. Meanwhile, the so-called Kazakhgate scandal, in which U.S. oil companies allegedly made secret payments to senior Kazakh officials in exchange for lucrative contracts, continued to attract both domestic and international attention.

This sparsely populated, multiethnic land stretching from the Caspian Sea to the Chinese border was gradually conquered by Russia during the eighteenth and nineteenth centuries. After a brief attempt at independence in 1917 in the wake of the Russian Revolution, Kazakhstan became an autonomous Soviet republic in 1920 and a union republic in 1936.

The former first secretary of the Communist Party, Nazarbayev was elected president on December 1, 1991, just two weeks before Kazakhstan declared independence from the U.S.S.R. The country's first national legislative elections, in March 1994, were invalidated by the Constitutional Court a year later because of numerous irregularities. Nazarbayev subsequently dissolved parliament and called for a referendum on April 29, 1995, in which a reported 95 percent of voters supported the extension of his term until December 2000. An additional referendum in August of that year, which was boycotted by the main opposition parties, approved a new constitution strengthening the powers of the presidency. In December 1995 elections for a new bicameral parliament, Nazarbayev's People's Union of Kazakhstan Unity and its supporters captured most of the seats in the legislature.

In October 1998, parliament approved Nazarbayev's call for presidential elections to be held in January 1999, almost two years before their scheduled date, as well as an amendment to the constitution extending the presidential term of office from five to seven years. The key challenger, former Prime Minister Akezhan Kazhegeldin, was banned from competing on a legal technicality, while two other candidates were known supporters of the incumbent. Nazarbayev was reelected with a reported 80 percent of the vote. The OSCE, which monitored the elections, refused to recognize the results, which it said fell "far short" of being democratic.

In the September and October 1999 parliamentary vote, which was the first multiparty election in Kazakhstan's history, 33 candidates competed for the 16 seats becoming vacant in the 39-seat upper house (Senate), while more than 500 candidates from ten parties vied for the 77 seats of the parliament's lower house (Majlis). As expected, Otan, a newly formed party loyal to Nazarbayev, won the single largest number of seats in the Majlis. Despite some improvement since the controversial presidential ballot in January, the parliamentary poll remained deeply flawed. The OSCE noted obstruction and intimidation of opposition candidates, as well as the lack of an independent election commission. In June 2000, parliament overwhelmingly approved giving Nazarbayev lifetime privileges after the end of his second term in office in 2006, including formal access to key government officials to advise them on policy matters, as well as a permanent place on the Security Council.

Signs of a deepening split within the country's ruling elite became evident following the November 18, 2001, founding of a new political movement, the Democratic Choice of Kazakhstan (DCK). Established by prominent business leaders, some of who held positions in Nazarbayev's administration, the DCK proclaimed its commitment to democratization, rule of law, and anticorruption efforts. However, some observers questioned the sincerity of its stated goals and maintained that the group's primary purpose was to safeguard its members' substantial political and economic interests while countering those of the president's family and close associates. A few days after the group was formed, several senior government officials who were DCK members resigned or were removed from their posts.

Apparently sensing that the DCK posed a growing political threat to his regime, Nazarbayev cracked down increasingly on the group throughout 2002. In January, thousands of people participated in a demonstration organized by the DCK and another prominent opposition group, the United Democratic Party, of which Kazhegeldin was a member. Nazarbayev was reportedly shocked by the large turnout at the rally, which was broadcast live by a local television station. In what critics charged were politically motivated cases, two of the DCK's cofounders—Mukhtar Abliyazov and Galymzhan Zhakiyanov—were subsequently arrested and convicted of abuse of power during their tenure in government.

Criticism of Nazarbayev over "Kazakhgate," a scandal that centered on allegations that the president and other top officials had accepted bribes from U.S. oil conglomerates during the 1990s, continued during the year. On March 13, two prominent opposition parliamentary deputies sent a letter to the prime minister in which they maintained that they had documents proving that Kazakh government funds had been improperly deposited in Swiss bank accounts controlled by Nazarbayev, his family, and his associates. The following month, Prime Minister Imangali Tasmagambetov confirmed the existence of a secret fund of some $1 billion, as well as of foreign bank accounts registered under Nazarbayev's name. However, he insisted that the purpose of the secret fund was to bail out the country during difficult economic times, and that the source of the fund was a 1996 government sale of a share in the Tengiz oil field. Tasmagambetov maintained that the foreign accounts allegedly belonging to Nazarbayev were set up by other people to "compromise" the president, who had ordered the money returned and used for improving the capital, Astana. In response, opposition leaders announced the creation of a fund to monitor the state's oil and gas revenues. In September, a U.S. judge ruled that Nazarbayev may not claim "sovereign immunity" from prosecution in the case, which was under investigation by a U.S. federal grand jury.

Political Rights and Civil Liberties: Citizens of Kazakhstan cannot change their government democratically. The constitution grants the president considerable control over the bicameral legislature, the judiciary, and local governments. President Nursultan Nazarbayev continues to enjoy sweeping executive powers and rules virtually unchallenged. Opposition parties have complained of harassment, surveillance, denial of access to the state-run media, and arbitrary bans on registering candidates.

While the constitution provides for freedom of the press, the government has repeatedly harassed or shut down many independent media outlets. The press is not permitted to criticize the president or his family, and self-censorship on other issues is widespread. The country's criminal code criminalizes "offenses against the honor and dignity of the president." Most newspapers, publishing facilities, and television and radio stations are controlled or otherwise influenced by the government and its supporters, including Nazarbayev's daughter Dariga.

In 2002, the government intensified its crackdown against media outlets critical of the regime, particularly those allied to the opposition political group Democratic Choice of Kazakhstan (DCK). During the year, authorities recalled the broadcasting licenses of a number television stations and suspended the publication of several independent newspapers for alleged technical violations. In March, TAN-TV's broadcasting rights were suspended in a move widely considered to be a politically motivated response to the station's unprecedented live broadcast of a January demonstration by opposition parties, including the DCK. While the station was granted temporary broadcasting rights just days later as a result of international and domestic pressure, its offices were attacked and equipment destroyed in late March.

On May 19, the editor of the independent weekly paper *Delovoye Obozreniye Respublika*, Irina Petrushova, found a decapitated body of a dog hung on an office window with a note saying that this would be the last warning. She later found the dog's head and a similar note near her home. Three days later, the newspaper's office was destroyed by Molotov cocktails. The paper, owned by DCK co-founder Mukhtar Abliyazov, had been reporting on a financial scandal allegedly involving Nazarbayev. Also in May, assailants beat two journalists of the independent paper *SolDat*, which was supported by Nazarbayev's chief political rival, former Prime Minister Akezhan Kazhegeldin. Despite the fact that her body reportedly showed signs of torture, police concluded in July that the daughter of journalist Lira Baysetova had hanged herself. Baysetova had interviewed the Swiss prosecutor-general two months earlier about alleged secret bank accounts linked to Nazarbayev. In August, independent journalist Sergei Duvanov was attacked outside his home by unknown assailants, suffering head injuries. Shortly before he was scheduled in October to travel to the United States to speak about Kazakhstan's human rights situation, Duvanov was arrested for allegedly raping a 14-year-old girl. According to Human Rights Watch, Duvanov's long-standing criticisms of government policy suggested that the case against him was politically motivated. His trial opened on December 24 and continued at year's end.

The constitution guarantees freedom of worship, although the government sometimes harasses certain nontraditional Islamic and Christian groups. Religious organizations must register with the Ministry of Justice to receive legal status, without which they cannot engage in legal transactions, including buying or renting property or hiring employees. Religious organizations that have encountered difficulties during registration include some Protestant sects, as well as certain Muslim and Orthodox Christian groups.

A new law on political parties signed by Nazarbayev on July 15 imposes substantial restrictions on freedom of association. Among the provisions of the law is one that raises from 3,000 to 50,000 the number of members that a party must have to register. Opposition parties and the OSCE criticized the law for leading to the likely closure of most of the country's political parties, including the DCK, which must re-register before January 17, 2003, under the new regulations.

Freedom of assembly is hindered by complicated requirements that restrict the right to hold political gatherings. The government has cited minor infractions of the law to arrest and detain government opponents arbitrarily. In May, police dispersed antigovernment rallies in Almaty and the northeast to protest state crackdowns on the political opposition and independent media. Although workers have the legal right to form and join trade unions, members have been dismissed, transferred to lower-paying jobs, or threatened.

The constitution significantly constrains the independence of the judiciary, which is subservient to the executive branch. Judges are subject to bribery and political bias, and corruption is evident throughout the judicial system. Police frequently abuse detainees during arrest and interrogation. Prisons suffer from severe overcrowding and inadequate food and medical care for inmates. In September, Nazarbayev created the position of human rights ombudsman, naming Bolot Baykadamov, the former secretary of the presidential human rights commission, to the post. Although the ombudsman is charged with monitoring the observance of human rights nationwide, he is not empowered to interfere in the work of the police or judiciary.

While the rights of entrepreneurship and private property are legally protected, bureaucratic hurdles and the control of large segments of the economy by clan elites and government officials loyal to Nazarbayev limit equality of opportunity and fair competition. Kazakhstan abolished the Soviet exit-visa system in 2001. Traditional cultural practices and the country's economic problems limit professional opportunities for women, who are underrepresented in government bodies and in the leadership of major enterprises.

Kenya

Polity: Presidential-par- **Political Rights:** 4*
liamentary democracy   **Civil Liberties:** 4*
Economy: Capitalist   **Status:** Partly Free
Population: 31,100,000
PPP: $1,022
Life Expectancy: 48
Religious Groups: Protestant (45 percent), Roman Catholic
(33 percent), indigenous beliefs (10 percent), Muslim (10 percent), other (2 percent)
Ethnic Groups: Kikuyu (22 percent), Luhya (14 percent), Luo (13 percent), Kalenjin
(12 percent), Kamba (11 percent), Kisii (6 percent), Meru (6 percent), other African
(15 percent), Asian, European, and Arab (1 percent)
Capital: Nairobi
Ratings Change: Kenya's political rights rating improved from 6 to 4, its civil liberties
rating from 5 to 4, and its status from Not Free to Partly Free, due to increased pluralism
reflected by the 2002 national election campaign and the resulting rotation of power,
and to the greater ability of civil society to affect public policy processes.

Ten-Year Ratings Timeline (Political Rights, Civil Liberties, Status)

1993	1994	1995	1996	1997	1998	1999	2000	2001	2002	2003
4,5PF	5,6NF	6,6NF	7,6NF	7,6NF	6,6NF	6,5NF	6,5NF	6,5NF	6,5NF	4,4PF

Overview:

Kenya boiled with political change in 2002 which led to the defeat of longtime President Daniel arap Moi and his party, the Kenyan African National Union (KANU). The run-up to the presidential and parliamentary elections in December reflected the full play of Kenya's free-wheeling political culture. Intense political maneuvering accompanied longtime President Daniel arap Moi's decision not to attempt to change the constitution to permit a third term. Instead, Moi sought to hand-pick Uhuru Kenyatta, son of the country's first president, as his successor; a choice which resulted in considerable criticism from both the opposition and within KANU.

Opposition leader Mwai Kibaki was elected president and his National Rainbow Coalition (NARC) won the majority of seats in parliament. The new leadership's ambitious reform program includes tackling corruption, economic and social issues and undertaking institutional reforms designed to promote democracy.

Britain conquered Kenya in the late eighteenth century in order to open and control a route to the Nile River headwaters in Uganda. In 1963 Kenya achieved its independence. The nationalist leader Jomo Kenyatta was president until his death in 1978, when Moi succeeded him. Moi's ascent to the presidency kept KANU in power, but gradually diminished the power of the previously dominant Kikuyu ethnic group.

In 1992, after a lengthy period as an effectively one-party state and as a result of domestic unrest and pressure from international aid donors, Kenya held multiparty elections. Moi was reelected president in controversial polling. In December 1997 presidential and parliamentary elections took place, and Moi again secured victory over a divided opposition. Moi's reelection was ensured by his massive use of state patronage and the official media to promote his candidacy and by harassment of the divided opposition.

Kenya's economy has been in long-term decline. Most of Kenya's 29 million people are poor and survive through subsistence agriculture. Nepotism and fraud inhibit economic opportunity and discourage greater foreign investment. Kenya was rated 96th out of 102 countries in Transparency International's 2002 Corruption Perceptions Index.

In 2002, as national elections approached and President Moi made clear his preference for Kenyatta to succeed him, other potential successors within KANU and the opposition sought to position themselves for the upcoming polls. KANU dissidents joined with opposition parties to create the NARC and nominate veteran Moi opponent (and former vice president) Mwai Kibaki as their presidential candidate.

Political Rights and Civil Liberties: Until 2002, Kenyans had been limited in their right to choose their leaders in genuinely open and competitive elections. President Daniel arap Moi's election victories were achieved through political repression, media control, and dubious electoral procedures. Physical violence, an often-docile judiciary, police powers, and executive decrees were used against political opponents and in efforts to undermine the wider civil society. Power was heavily concentrated in the executive branch of government. This reality may well be changing with the December 2002 NARC electoral victory, but it remains to be confirmed.

Although NARC is a multi-ethnic movement, Kenya's politics have traditionally been divided along ethnic lines. KANU maintained power through the support of the president's own minority ethnic grouping, the Kalenjin, while combining an alliance of other minority groups and playing two of the largest ethnic groups, the Kikuyu and the Luo, against each other. The country is divided into seven provinces run by provincial commissioners appointed by the president.

The right of citizens to effectively participate in the political life of the country has been limited, but there are now some emerging positive elements. Despite Kenya's history of authoritarian rule, many basic elements necessary for the development of a democratic political system exist. Political parties are active and vocal. Parliament is the setting for much of the nation's political discourse. A varied and energetic civil society plays an important role in public policy debates.

A constitutional review process headed by Dr. Yash Gai, a respected academic, included the participation of a wide range of civic and associational groups. Its report, issued in September 2002, calls for the creation of a senate and an executive prime minister to be elected by parliament; presidential and parliamentary electoral reform; decentralization; and other changes designed to limit the power of the presidency, including giving parliament the power to impeach the president.

During President Moi's rule the press, parliament, and the judiciary did at times highlight examples of government corruption and malfeasance. In 2001, for example, parliament provided evidence of rampant graft and cronyism pervading state-run institutions. A report from the Parliamentary Public Accounts Committee presented numerous credible and detailed examples of government corruption and gross mismanagement. The report was particularly critical of "slow investigation by the police and lack of sanction against the force for disobedience." The parliament had previously published a "list of shame" identifying by name a number of high-ranking government officials who were implicated in corruption. These included Vice President George Saitoti, Trade and Tourism Minister Nicholas Biwott, and nearly a dozen cabinet members. Under governmental pressure the report was subsequently revised and the names deleted.

A 2002 judicial report recommended that prominent current and former Kenyan ministers be investigated for their alleged roles in tribal clashes organized by powerful individuals to force opposition supporters to flee constituencies where KANU faced close election contests. The clashes took place in the run-up to elections in 1992 and 1997 and left thousands dead. The report was submitted to the government in 1999, but only released in October 2002 after a court ordered the government to make its findings public. The judicial report identified by name KANU ministers Nicholas Biwott, Julius Sunkuli and Maalim Mohamed.

Until 2002 the ability of pluralistic forces in society to actually effect public policy remained limited. The security forces regularly violated constitutional guarantees regarding detention, privacy, search, and seizure. Groups such as the Kenyan Human Rights Commission and the National Council of Churches of Kenya publicized abuses and demanded respect for civil and political liberties, but the KANU government's attitude towards civil society was generally hostile and suspicious. Courts were still influenced by the executive and could not be relied on to protect constitutional rights or offer fair trials. Local chiefs still continue to exercise sometimes arbitrary and violent power. Prison conditions are harsh and often life threatening.

Although the press at times adopted independent and probing stances, freedom of expression has been limited by lack of access to the dominant state broadcast media. The country's few private radio and television stations were generally either pro-KANU or carefully apolitical. Journalists have been charged with criminal libel, and independent publications have been subject to harassment in their business operations. President Moi decreed that it was a crime to "insult" him, and sedition laws have been employed in efforts to silence criticism.

Trade unions generally follow government policy on key issues. For example, in 2002 the general secretary of the Central Organization of Trade Unions instructed members not to support calls by opposition parties and civil society groups for demonstrations over constitutional reform. Unions have occasionally defied a 1993 Ministry of Labor decree that forbids all strikes, despite constitutional guarantees to the contrary. A nationwide teachers' strike occurred in 2002 when the 240,000 teachers' umbrella organization demanded that the government implement the remaining part of a deal signed in 1997. In that deal the government promised to raise salaries for teachers by between 150-200 percent. Civil servants and university academic staff may join only government-designated unions. Approximately one-fifth of the country's 1.5 million industrial workforce is unionized.

Ethnically based tension continues. Competing land claims often provide the spark. Approximately 60 people were killed in eastern Kenya in 2001, in one example of ethnic violence based on limited land and livestock resources. In November, tribal clashes sparked by a land dispute in southern Kenya left more than 30 people dead or seriously injured. Pro-KANU elements have at times been accused of instigating ethnic cleansing for political purposes, especially in the Rift Valley area.

In general there is freedom of religion, although uneasy relations between Muslims and those of other faiths at times result in violence. In 2000, rioting between Roman Catholics and Muslims occurred in central Kenya.

The annual population growth rate is 2.4 percent. Approximately three-quarters of the population is confined to 10 percent of the land area, as most of the country is semi-arid or arid. Life expectancy is less than 50 years and the infant mortality rate is 74 per 1,000 live births. Kenya's child mortality rate has been increasing since the early 1990s, mainly as a result of the spread of HIV and AIDS infections.

Women in Kenya continue to face serious obstacles in the exercise of their freedoms. A draft gender equity bill created considerable public controversy, with some Muslims protesting that it was too sweeping in scope. Some evidence suggests that violence against women in increasing. A survey carried out by a women's rights group states that more than 49 women were murdered by their spouses in 1998 alone, a 79 percent increase in cases since 1995. Many of the cases have gone unpunished, despite repeated complaints by women's groups that Kenyan laws remain too lenient in sentencing offenders in cases of violence against women. Women are also seriously underrepresented in Kenya's politics and government.

Kiribati

Polity: Presidential parliamentary democracy
Economy: Capitalist-statist
Population: 100,000
PPP: na
Life Expectancy: 62
Religious Groups: Roman Catholic (52 percent), Protestant (40 percent), other
Ethnic Groups: Micronesian, some Polynesian
Capital: Tarawa

Political Rights: 1
Civil Liberties: 1
Status: Free

Ten-Year Ratings Timeline (Political Rights, Civil Liberties, Status)

1993	1994	1995	1996	1997	1998	1999	2000	2001	2002	2003
1,2F	1,1F	1,1F	1,1F	1,1F	1,1F	1,1F	1,1F	1,1F	1,1F	1,1F

Overview:

The Republic of Kiribati has been a parliamentary democracy since gaining independence from Great Britain in 1979.

It consists of 33 islands of the Gilbert, Line, and Phoenix groups, with a combined land area of 324 square miles, scattered across 1.4 million square miles of the central Pacific Ocean, as well as Banaba Island in the western Pacific. The atoll of Tarawa, now the national capital, was the scene of a bloody battle between U.S. marines and occupying Japanese forces during World War II.

The current president, Teburoro Tito, won a second four-year term in 1998, defeating opposition candidates Harry Tong and Amberoti Nikora. His first election victory, in 1994, followed a constitutional crisis that broke out after police forcibly sacked acting head of state Tekira Tameura, who had taken office following the resignation of President Tetao Teannaki. Tameura had assumed power under a constitutional provision that temporarily vests key executive powers in the chairman of the Public Service Commission (PSC) if the president resigns. The problem was that many claimed that Tameura's tenure as PSC head had expired, and the constitution said nothing about what happens when the PSC chairmanship is vacant.

Tito faces a tough fight for reelection in February 2003. More than half of the lawmakers who supported him were voted out of office in the November 29, 2002, parliamentary elections following a campaign that centered on China's influence in Kiribati. At year's end, the informal Boutokaan Te Koaua (BTK) political faction that opposes Tito had not decided on a candidate to challenge the president. There was speculation that the BTK would dump former presidential candidate Tong as its leader and nominate someone else for the top post. Under Kiribati law, parliament chooses, from within its ranks, three or four presidential candidates, who then square off in a general election.

Should the BTK capture the presidency, it will likely review a 15-year deal that allows China to operate a satellite tracking facility on Tarawa. China's influence became a key issue in the parliamentary elections after Tong tried unsuccessfully to get President Tito to release details of the tracking facility deal and the Chinese ambassador acknowledged making a donation to a government-linked cooperative society. Beijing says that the tracking facility is part of its civilian space program, but some claim it is used to monitor U.S. missile tests in the Pacific. Chinese ambassador Ma Shuxue, meanwhile, defended the donation of roughly US$2,850 to an association linked to President Tito, saying that all of the money was tied to specific projects.

The parliamentary campaign turned particularly bitter after Tito ordered police to seize thousands of Tong's pamphlets because they supposedly violated the law by carrying an emblem of the Kiribati flag.

Political Rights and Civil Liberties: Kiribati's single-chamber parliament, known as the *Maneaba ni Maungatabu*, has 39 members who are directly elected for four-year terms, one lawmaker who represents former Banaba islanders now living in Fiji, and the attorney general, ex officio. The Banaba Island representative is elected from Fiji because the island's residents were forced to move there after phosphate mining under British rule left Banaba Island uninhabitable. The constitution vests executive powers in a president, who is limited to serving three four-year terms.

Kiribati's judiciary is independent, according to the U.S. State Department's global human rights report for 2001, released in March 2002. Litigants may appeal to the Privy Council in London. Village councils on rare occasions have punished wrongdoers by forcibly exiling them from villages, the State Department report said.

The government owns Kiribati's sole radio station and one of its two newspapers. The opposition claimed that it had little access to Radio Kiribati and the government's *Te Uekera* weekly during the 2002 election campaign. Government opponents and others also criticized a 2002 amendment to a press law that allows authorities to close papers if there are complaints against them. The law, the Newspaper Registration Act, also contains restrictions on printing offensive material that are vaguely worded and sets a low standard for allowing officials to censor articles that could incite or encourage crime or disorder.

Kiribati's only private newspaper is owned by Ieremia Tabai, a former president and current opposition member of parliament. Tabai launched the *Kiribati Newstar* after the government blocked his efforts to set up the country's first independent radio station in 1999 by closing the station and fining him for attempting to import broadcasting equipment without a license. In a positive development, Tabai said in December that his station would begin broadcasting in January 2003 after receiving an FM license following a four-year battle to get one. In addition to these formal media, several newsletters and other periodicals are put out by churches.

Women are slowly but steadily entering the workforce in unskilled and semi-skilled jobs, thanks in part to stepped-up government hiring and promotion of female employees. Kiribati's traditional culture of male dominance, however, has made it tough for women to play more active roles in the economy. Throughout the country, spousal abuse and other forms of violence against women, often alcohol-related, are "a significant problem," according to the U.S. State Department report.

Kiribati's trade union sector is small but vigorous. Only about 10 percent of wage earners, however, belong to unions. The largest is the Kiribati Trade Union Congress, with about 2,500 members. Strikes are legal but rare. Overall, around 90 percent of workers are fishermen or subsistence farmers.

Korea, North

Polity: One party
Economy: Statist
Population: 23,200,000
PPP: na
Life Expectancy: 64
Religious Groups: Buddhist, Confucianism, other
Ethnic Groups: Korean
Capital: Pyongyang

Political Rights: 7
Civil Liberties: 7
Status: Not Free

Ten-Year Ratings Timeline (Political Rights, Civil Liberties, Status)

1993	1994	1995	1996	1997	1998	1999	2000	2001	2002	2003
7,7NF	7,7NF	7,7NF	7,7NF	7,7NF	7,7NF	7,7NF	7,7NF	7,7NF	7,7NF	7,7NF

Overview:

North Korea faced further international economic isolation after it confessed to having a nuclear bomb program and took steps in December 2002 to reactivate a mothballed nuclear facility capable of producing weapons-grade plutonium. The moves touched off fresh fears of a nuclear arms race in East Asia and of conflict on the Korean Peninsula.

Pyongyang's brinkmanship was widely viewed as the Stalinist regime's latest attempt to use its long-range missile and nuclear weapons programs as bargaining chips to gain diplomatic recognition and increased aid from the United States. Washington, though, demanded that Pyongyang unilaterally promise to end its uranium-enrichment program before talks could be held on aid and other issues.

Regardless of North Korean leader Kim Jong-il's motives, the crisis will likely make it harder for his impoverished country to gain the international support that it needs to revive its moribund economy. North Korea began lifting some price controls in 2002, but these and other limited free-market reforms will have to be buttressed by foreign aid, advice, and investment in order to have any deep-rooted impact.

The Democratic People's Republic of Korea was established in the northern part of the Korean Peninsula in 1948, three years after the United States occupied the south of the peninsula—and Soviet forces, the north—following Japan's defeat in World War II. At independence, North Korea's uncontested ruler was Kim Il-sung, a former Soviet army officer who claimed to be a guerrilla hero in the struggle against Japanese colonial rule over Korea, which began in 1910. North Korea invaded South Korea in 1950 in an attempt to reunify the peninsula under Communist rule. Drawing in the United States and China, the ensuing three-year conflict killed up to two million people and ended with a ceasefire rather than a peace treaty. Since then, the two Koreas have been on continuous war footing.

Kim Il-sung solidified his power base during the Cold War, purging rivals, throwing thousands of political prisoners into gulags, and fostering a Stalinist-style personality cult promoting him as North Korea's "Dear Leader." The end of the Cold War, however, brought North Korea's command economy to the brink of collapse, as Pyongyang lost crucial Soviet and East Bloc subsidies and preferential trade deals. North Korea's economy shrank an estimated 30 percent between 1991 and 1996, according to UN figures.

With the regime's survival already in doubt, Kim's death in 1994 ushered in even more uncertainty. Under his son and appointed successor, the reclusive Kim Jong-il, Pyongyang has carried out limited economic reforms and made sporadic efforts to improve relations with the United States, Japan, and South Korea in the hopes of gaining increased aid. The moves are widely seen as last-ditch attempts to save the country from economic implosion. Famine killed "an estimated several hundreds of thousands to two million persons" in the 1990s, according to the U.S. State Department's global human rights report for 2001, released in March 2002.

On top of continued food shortages, North Korea is facing an acute health care crisis. Foreign press reports suggest that the state-run health system has all but collapsed, hospitals lack adequate medicine and equipment, and clean water is in short supply because of electricity and chlorine shortages. Some 63 percent of North Korean children are stunted because of chronic undernourishment, according to a 1998 UNICEF survey.

The modest reforms introduced in 2002 could help boost economic output. The government during the year began paying farmers more for their goods and easing price controls on food, housing, and other necessities. It also raised salaries to offset the higher prices. The regime recently has also allowed farmers to set up small markets in the cities, something it has quietly tolerated for decades in the countryside. Prospects appear dim, though, for more far-reaching market reforms, given that the regime fears that loosening its control over the economy will undermine its tight grip on power.

However, the outside help that North Korea needs for the reforms to work seemed further away than ever after Pyongyang touched off the latest crisis over its nuclear bomb program. The crisis began after Washington said in October that Pyongyang had confessed to having a program to produce enriched uranium, a component in nuclear bombs. This violated a 1994 deal under which North Korea pledged to abandon its plutonium nuclear program, including shuttering the plutonium facility at Yongbyon, north of Pyongyang, that it now vows to reopen. In return, the U.S., South Korea, and Japan agreed under the 1994 deal to provide North Korea with two light water nuclear reactors, which, unlike the Yongbyon facility, cannot be used to produce weapons-grade plutonium. They also agreed to provide fuel oil until the new reactors are built.

After North Korea's October admission, the U.S. and its allies decided to suspend the fuel oil shipments. In December, North Korea upped the ante by throwing out international inspectors monitoring the Yongbyon reactor and began delivering fuel rods to the plant.

Political Rights and Civil Liberties: North Korea is one of the most tightly controlled countries in the world. The regime denies North Koreans even the most basic rights, holds tens of thousands of political prisoners, and controls nearly all aspects of social, political, and economic life.

Kim Jong-il, the North Korean leader, and a handful of elites from the Korean Worker's Party (KWP) rule by decree, although little is known about the regime's inner workings. Kim formally is general secretary of the KWP, supreme military commander, and chairman of the National Defense Commission. The latter post officially is the "highest office of state," following the 1998 abolition of the presidency. Vice Marshall Jo Myong-rok, first vice chairman of the National Defense Commission, is believed to be Kim's second-in-command.

North Korea's parliament, known as the Supreme People's Assembly, has little independent power. It meets only a few days each year to rubber-stamp the ruling elite's decisions. In an effort to provide a veneer of democracy, the government occasionally holds show elections for the assembly and provincial, county, and city bodies. All of the candidates belong to either the KWP or one of several small, progovernment "minority parties." The last assembly elections were in 1998.

Defectors and refugees have in recent years reported that the regime regularly executes political prisoners, repatriated defectors, military officers accused of spying or other antigovernment offenses, and other suspected dissidents, according to the U.S. State Department report. Ordinary North Koreans reportedly have been executed merely for criticizing the regime, the report added.

North Korean authorities have also executed some North Koreans who were sent back by Chinese officials after they fled across the border, according to the U.S. State Department report. An estimated 300,000 North Koreans have fled to China in recent years to escape food shortages and other hardships.

North Korea runs a network of jails and prison camps that are notorious for their brutal treatment of inmates. The UN Human Rights Committee in 2001 called on Pyongyang to allow international human rights groups into the country to verify the "many allegations of cruel, inhuman and degrading treatment and conditions and of inadequate medical care in reform institutions, prisons, and prison camps." South Korean media have reported that North Korean officials subject camp inmates to forced labor, beating, torture, and public execution.

Defectors say that the regime holds some 150,000 to 200,000 political prisoners in maximum security camps, while the South Korean government puts the number of political prisoners at 200,000. The number of ordinary prisoners is not known.

The regime has also forcibly relocated "many tens of thousands" of North Koreans to the countryside from Pyongyang, particularly people considered politically unreliable, according to the U.S. State Department report. Officials also continue to restrict travel into Pyongyang, normally granting permission only for governmental business. At the same time, the regime has recently made it easier for North Koreans to travel outside of their home villages.

The state spies extensively on the population, using a network of informers and surprise security checks on homes and even entire communities. Pyongyang also assigns to each North Korean a security rating that partly determines access to education, employment, and health services as well as place of residence. By some foreign estimates, nearly half the population is considered either "wavering" or "hostile," with the rest rated "core."

Religious freedom is virtually nonexistent. The government requires all prayer and religious study to be supervised by the state and severely punishes North Koreans for worshipping independently in underground churches. Officials have killed, beaten, arrested, or detained in prison camps many members of underground churches, foreign religious and human rights groups say.

The regime controls all trade unions and uses them to monitor workers, mobilize them to meet production targets, and provide them with health care, schooling, and welfare services. Strikes, collective bargaining, and other basic organized-labor activities are illegal. Many work sites are dangerous, and the rate of industrial accidents reportedly is high.

In classic totalitarian fashion, officials subject the masses to intensive political and ideological indoctrination through the media, schools, and work and neighborhood associations. Ordinary North Koreans face a steady onslaught of propaganda from radios and televisions that are pretuned to receive only government stations. Foreign visitors and academics say that children receive mandatory military training and indoctrination at their schools. The regime also routinely orchestrates rallies, mass marches, and performances involving thousands of people which glorify the two Kims and the state.

The regime uses a vague guiding philosophy of *juche*, or "I myself," to justify its dictatorship and rabid efforts to root out dissent. Credited to former president Kim Il-sung, juche emphasizes national self-reliance and stresses that the collective will of the people is embodied in a supreme leader. Opposing the leader, therefore, means opposing the national interest. Taking this to the extreme, officials have punished people for offenses as trivial as accidentally defacing photographs of Kim Il-sung or Kim Jong-il, according to the U.S. State Department report.

Few women have reached the top ranks of the ruling KWP or the government. Little is known about how problems such as domestic violence or workplace discrimination may affect North Korean women.

North Korea's economy remains centrally planned even after the recent market reforms. The government prohibits private property, assigns all jobs, and directs and controls nearly all economic activity, with the exception of crops grown in small private gardens. Even the small farmers' markets now allowed in the cities are tightly run. Prior to the economic collapse that began in the early 1990s, the government provided all North Koreans with free food, housing, clothing, and medical care. Today, it barely provides these essentials.

The economy is hobbled not only by rigid state control but also by creaking infrastructure and an inability to borrow on world markets and from the World Bank and other multilateral agencies because of sanctions and a past foreign debt default. Spending on the country's million-man army and other military programs very likely consumes at least one-quarter of economic output, according to the U.S. State Department report.

Korea, South

Polity: Presidential-
parliamentary democracy
Economy: Capitalist-
statist
Population: 48,400,000
PPP: $17,380
Life Expectancy: 76
Religious Groups: Christian (49 percent), Buddhist (47 percent),
Confucianism (3 percent), other (1 percent)
Ethnic Groups: Korean
Capital: Seoul

Political Rights: 2
Civil Liberties: 2
Status: Free

Ten-Year Ratings Timeline (Political Rights, Civil Liberties, Status)

1993	1994	1995	1996	1997	1998	1999	2000	2001	2002	2003
2,3F	2,2F	2,2F	2,2F	2,2F	2,2F	2,2F	2,2F	2,2F	2,2F	2,2F

Overview:

President-elect Roh Moo-hyun takes office in February 2003 with a pro-market, yet populist, economic agenda and a strategy of reaching out to bellicose North Korea, which in 2002 raised tensions in East Asia by threatening to openly restart its nuclear weapons program. The left-leaning Roh's emphasis on defusing the North Korean threat through dialogue rather than containment will likely strain South Korea's critical, decades-old security ties with the United States. The Bush Administration favors a more muscular approach toward Pyongyang, applying economic pressure while holding out the possibility of aid, dialogue, and other rewards for disarmament.

The Republic of Korea was established in 1948, three years after the United States and the Soviet Union divided the Korean Peninsula in the waning days of World War II. During the next four decades, South Korea's mainly military rulers crushed left-wing dissent and kept the country on a virtual war footing in response to the threat from North Korea. They also oversaw state-led industrialization that transformed a poor, agrarian land into the world's 11th-largest economy.

South Korea's democratic transition began in 1987, when military strongman Chun Doo-hwan gave in to widespread student protests and allowed his successor to be chosen in a direct presidential election. In voting that December, Chun's protégé, Roh Tae-woo, defeated the country's best-known dissidents, Kim Young-sam and Kim Dae-jung.

After joining the ruling party in 1990, Kim Young-sam defeated Kim Dae-jung in the 1992 presidential election to become South Korea's first civilian president since 1961. As president, Kim cracked down on corruption, sacked hard-line military officers, and curbed the powers of the domestic security services. His administration also successfully prosecuted former presidents Chun and Roh for corruption and treason.

In 1997, however, South Korea went through its worst financial crisis in decades. Slowing exports, a tumbling currency, and the fallout from years of reckless corporate borrowing brought the nation close to default on $150 billion in private sector debt. Seoul agreed to a $57 billion International Monetary Fund-led bailout in return for pledging to restructure companies and end lifetime job guarantees. Amid public anger over the government's failure to better supervise the country's banks and business conglomerates, Kim Dae-jung in December 1997 became South Korea's first opposition candidate to win a presidential election.

Under Kim's watch, South Korea's economy rebounded to become one of the most robust in Asia. Critics argued, however, that the quick turnaround blunted the administration's zeal for forcing the country's large, family-owned business conglomerates, known as *chaebol*, and other firms to adopt better business practices. Meanwhile, Daewoo Motors and other firms seeking foreign suitors or pressed by foreign creditors laid off thousands of workers. Trade unions charged that workers were being forced to bear the brunt of economic restructuring costs.

Kim also pursued a "sunshine policy" toward North Korea that included making an unprecedented state visit to Pyongyang in 2000 and encouraging South Korean businesses to invest in the North and ordinary citizens to travel there for tourism and family reunions. A former dissident whom military rulers once tried to kill, Kim also freed dozens of political prisoners.

Kim's popularity waned towards the end of his five-year term amid his failure to gain any real concessions from North Korea, a series of corruption scandals, blue-collar anger over layoffs, and the disillusionment that invariably follows high political expectations. The opposition Grand National Party (GNP) won the most seats in the 2000 parliamentary elections, although gains by Kim's Millennium Democratic Party (MDP) prevented the conservative GNP from winning a majority. Under a record-low 57 percent turnout, the GNP won 133 seats, up from 122 in 1996. The MDP won 115, up from 99 in 1996. Smaller parties and independents took the remaining 25 seats. With Kim constitutionally barred from seeking a second term, Roh, 56, won the December 19, 2002, presidential elections as the MDP's candidate even though the party had been battered during the year by corruption scandals involving top bureaucrats and two of Kim's sons. A former human rights lawyer, Roh laced his campaign with anti-American rhetoric and populist promises. He pledged to pursue dialogue with North Korea and not "kowtow" to Washington, and to improve corporate governance and protect local rice farmers.

Roh defeated Lee Hoi Chang, the GNP candidate, by a slim 2.3 percentage points. His MDP now hopes to win control of parliament in elections due in 2004. The GNP gained a majority in the National Assembly in August by winning 11 of 13 by-elections.

North Korea policy will likely take center stage for much of Roh's term. Pyongyang in late 2002 announced that it had reneged on a 1994 deal to scrap its nuclear weapons program. It also threw out UN inspectors monitoring a mothballed nuclear reactor that has the capacity to produce weapons-grade plutonium.

Political Rights and Civil Liberties: South Koreans can change their government through elections and enjoy most basic rights. The 1988 constitution vests executive powers in a directly elected president who is limited to a single five-year term. The National Assembly is directly elected for a four-year term.

South Korea's judiciary "has shown increasing independence," although "several scandals in 1999 involving alleged illegal influence peddling and cronyism have damaged the image of prosecutors and judges," according to the U.S. State Department's global human rights report for 2001, released in March 2002. In a positive development, police abuse of suspects in custody seems to be declining, human rights groups say. Moreover, some police offenders have been punished with dismissal, demotion, or pay cuts. Nevertheless, criminal suspects and prisoners continue to face some ill-treatment by law enforcement officials, according to a December report by the human rights group Amnesty International.

Most of the dozens of political prisoners released by Kim Dae-jung were held under South Korea's broadly drawn National Security Law (NSL). Even while clearing South Korean jails of most long-term political prisoners, however, Kim's administration reportedly used the NSL to arrest more than 990 people, according to the Amnesty International report. Many of the hundreds of arrests were for peaceful activities that allegedly aided or supported North Korea. Many recent NSL detainees have received suspended sentences or short prison terms, although others have been handed long jail terms. At least 39 people were being held under the NSL as of October 2002, the Amnesty report said.

The peaceful activities that brought arrest under the NSL included discussing reunification; traveling to North Korea without official permission; praising the North, its leaders, or its state creed of "self-reliance"; or publishing, possessing, or distributing pro-Pyongyang literature. The government says that it needs to continue using the NSL against suspected dissidents because of the continued threat from North Korea. South Korean jails also hold some 1,600 conscientious objectors who rejected compulsory military service, according to the Amnesty report.

South Korean newspapers are privately owned and report fairly aggressively on governmental policies and alleged official wrongdoing. The government, however, wields indirect influence over the media, in part through vigorous lobbying of reporters and editors, the U.S. State Department report said. In a setback for press freedom, courts have in recent years jailed several journalists under criminal libel laws. Media rights groups say that politicians and businessmen use the libel laws to punish journalists for articles that are critical although factually accurate.

In a controversial move, the government in 2001 fined 23 media companies a record $390 million for tax evasion. Tax authorities also filed related criminal charges against five media executives, including the owners of South Korea's two largest newspapers, *Chosun Ilbo* and *Dong-a Ilbo*. The opposition GNP and some international press freedom groups accused the government of trying to gag the press. Many civic groups and the Brussels-based International Federation of Journalists, however, viewed the cases as ordinary tax-evasion matters.

Women enjoy equal access to education, but face job discrimination in the private sector and are disadvantaged by some government agencies' preferential hiring of military veterans, most of whom are men, according to the U.S. State Department report. Violence and sexual harassment against women continue to be serious problems despite recent legislation and other initiatives to protect women. Women's groups say that rape and sexual harassment generally are not prosecuted and that convicted offenders often receive light sentences.

South Korean labor unions are independent and practice collective bargaining extensively. Under Kim Dae-jung's administration, at least 850 trade unionists were detained for their involvement in strikes or other protests, according to the December Amnesty International report. Some were charged with using violence during confrontations with police, who at times appeared to use excessive force against unarmed protesters; at least 39 of those arrested remained in prison as of October 2002, the report added.

The law prohibits defense and white-collar government workers from forming unions, although the latter can form more limited workplace councils. It also bars strikes in government agencies, state-run enterprises, and defense firms. A 1998 act authorized multiple unions at the company level beginning in 2002, although labor, management, and the government have jointly agreed to postpone implementation until 2006. Around 12 percent of South Korean workers were unionized in 2000, according to official figures. Despite recent government initiatives to improve their situation, some of the more than 300,000 foreign workers in South Korea are, at times, beaten or detained by employers, or have their wages withheld or passports seized, the U.S. State Department report said.

Anecdotal reports suggest that bribery, extortion by officials, and influence peddling continue to be pervasive in politics, business, and daily life. The Berlin-based Transparency International in 2002 ranked South Korea in a four-way tie for fortieth place out of 102 countries it surveyed for corruption, with the top-ranked country, Finland, being the least corrupt.

Because citizenship is based on parentage rather than place of birth, many of South Korea's 20,000 ethnic Chinese residents face difficulty in obtaining citizenship. This makes it hard for them to get government jobs. Ethnic Chinese also face discrimination in mainstream society, according to the U.S. State Department report.

Kuwait

Polity: Traditional
monarchy and limited
parliament
Economy: Capitalist-statist
Population: 2,300,000
PPP: $15,799
Life Expectancy: 76

Political Rights: 4
Civil Liberties: 5
Status: Partly Free

Religious Groups: Muslim (85 percent) [Sunni 70 percent, Shi'a 30 percent], other
(15 percent)
Ethnic Groups: Kuwaiti (45 percent), other Arab (35 percent), South Asian (9 percent),
Iranian (4 percent), other (7 percent)
Capital: Kuwait City

Ten-Year Ratings Timeline (Political Rights, Civil Liberties, Status)

1993	1994	1995	1996	1997	1998	1999	2000	2001	2002	2003
5,5PF	5,5PF	5,5PF	5,5PF	5,5PF	5,5PF	5,5PF	4,5PF	4,5PF	4,5PF	4,5PF

Overview:

A measure of the progress of Kuwait's political reforms over the past decade is the fact that the most contentious political clashes in 2002 took place within the halls of the National Assembly. In April, the education minister narrowly escaped a vote of no confidence by members of parliament who accused him of not fully implementing a law requiring gender segregation in universities. In June, members of parliament endlessly grilled the finance minister over allegations that he squandered public funds.

Kuwait has existed as a political entity since the early eighteenth century, when several families migrated to the area from central Arabia and established a self-governing emirate. Since 1756, all Kuwaiti emirs have come from the al-Sabah family, though there is a long tradition of consultation with leading merchant families and tribes. The emirate gained full independence from Britain in 1961. The country's 1962 constitution assigned broad executive powers to the emir, but also established an elected national assembly. While the assembly functioned as a limited check on the emir's power during the first three decades after independence, its influence was weakened by restrictions on political and civil liberties and the body was suspended from 1976-81 and 1986-92.

Two months after the Iraqi invasion of Kuwait in 1990, the exiled emir, Sheikh Jaber al-Ahmad al-Sabah, met with members of the opposition in Jedda, Saudi Arabia, and agreed to restore the suspended parliament and allow greater freedom once the Iraqis had been driven out. Twelve years later, Kuwait has become the only Arab country in which an elected legislature serves as a powerful check on executive power. What distinguishes the Kuwaiti parliament from its counterparts elsewhere in the Arab world, however, is that it has forced the resignation of cabinet ministers and imposed legislation over the objections of the royal family legislation—such as the law requiring the segregation of universities by gender.

The assembly's assertiveness vis-à-vis the emir is often oversimplified in the Western media as an Islamic backlash. A 1999 decree by the emir granting women the right to vote, for example, was overturned in part because it had been issued when parliament was dissolved—rejection of the bill was seen as an assertion of the assembly's constitutional power. The Islamist position on women's political rights is not uniform. Some support granting women the right to vote, but not to hold office, while some are adamant in their opposition to women's suffrage, others appear willing to accept it if the government yields on other key issues.

Persistent deadlock between the government and the legislature has also slowed the pace of economic reforms. Measures to cut the fiscal deficit, privatize state-run industries, and promote foreign investment have lagged far behind changes in other Persian Gulf countries. The most striking result is that 95 percent of working Kuwaitis continue to draw monthly tax-free salaries from the state, mostly from nominal jobs with few or no responsibilities. In most economic respects, Kuwait has been eclipsed by the United Arab Emirates, where there are no legislative obstacles to economic restructuring. In March 2001, however, lawmakers managed to pass a bill that allows for majority foreign ownership in local companies and a 10-year tax break and customs duties exemptions for investors.

There is a growing consensus, particularly among liberals, that the main reason the government has not been able to further political and economic progress is the emirate's aging leadership. The 76-year-old emir, who returned in January 2002 from a four-month stay in London for medical treatment, is totally incapacitated. Age and illness have also sapped the strength of the 73-year-old crown prince and prime minister, Saad Abdullah al-Sabah, who reportedly cannot recognize his own ministers at times. De facto authority is presently exercised by the 72-year-old deputy prime minister and foreign minister, Sabah al-Ahmad al-Sabah, but infighting within the family is said to have led to the resignation of the cabinet in January 2001. Since there is no set mechanism of succession in Kuwait and Sabah has banned newspapers from discussing the issue, a veil of uncertainty clouds the country's political future. In early 2002, businessmen reportedly formed a committee to press members of the royal family to openly address the issue.

The killing of an American soldier in October 2002 and the wounding of two servicemen the following month, along with anti-American statements from some Islamists interviewed by the Western media, have raised concerns that Islamic radicals opposed to the U.S. military presence in the emirate could threaten stability. However, it is likely that Kuwait's stability and solid ties with the United States are precisely why al-Qaeda launched attacks on Kuwait's soil. Western journalists in the emirate invariably interpret the shocking statements of support for Osama bin Laden they encounter as indications of support for anti-Western terrorism. Above all else, however, these are merely indications of the Kuwaiti people's untrammeled right to make shocking statements—even when foreign reporters are present.

Political Rights and Civil Liberties:

Kuwaitis have only a limited ability to change their government. The emir appoints the prime minister (who, by tradition, is also the crown prince) and cabinet. The elected, 50-member National Assembly can veto the emir's appointment as crown prince, but must then select one of three alternates selected by the emir. It can also impeach, by majority vote, members of the cabinet. While the emir can dissolve parliament, he must call elections within 60 days and cannot dissolve it twice for the same reason.

Political parties are illegal, but the government allows de facto parliamentary blocs and civic groups to be politically active. Legislative elections are relatively free and fair, but suffrage is restricted to males who are 21 years of age or older, do not serve in the armed forces, and were not naturalized within the last twenty years—14.8 percent of the population.

The emir appoints all judges, and the renewal of many judicial appointments is subject to government approval. Sunni and Shi'a Muslims have their own *Sharia* (Islamic law) courts for family law cases. Trials are open and relatively fair, and defendants have the right to appeal verdicts and to be represented by legal counsel, which the courts provide in criminal cases. Suspects may be detained for four days before being brought before an investigating official; arbitrary arrests and detentions are rare. Prison conditions, according to the U.S. State Department, "meet or exceed" international standards.

Freedom of expression is restricted. The broadcast media are government owned, but access to foreign satellite stations is legal and widespread. A variety of independent newspapers exist. Although several laws empower the government to jail or fine journalists for a variety of offenses, indictments have become increasingly rare and convictions virtually nonexistent. Although media outlets openly criticize the government, even on matters of security and foreign policy, direct criticism of the emir is uncommon because of self-censorship. Some Web sites regarded as "immoral" are blocked by Internet service providers.

Freedom of assembly and association is limited. Public gatherings require government approval, and the law requires nongovernmental organizations (NGOs) to obtain licenses from the government. In practice, however, unlicensed associations are free to organize informally. Informal social gatherings, called *diwaniyas,* provide a forum for political discussion. Unions are legal, though only one is permitted per industry or profession, and private sector workers have the right to strike. Roughly 100,000 foreigners who work as domestic servants are not protected under labor laws. Licensed NGOs and labor unions are influenced by government subsidies, which provide up to 90 percent of expenses for the latter.

Women face discrimination in legal and social matters. They are denied the right to vote or run for office; are legally disadvantaged in matters of marriage, divorce, and inheritance; must have the permission of a male relative to obtain a passport; and cannot confer citizenship on their children. Women remain underrepresented in most private and public sector jobs, but the proportion is growing.

Islam is the state religion. Both Sunnis and Shi'as worship freely, though the latter complain of insufficient government funding for mosques and religious training. The Christian community of around 150,000 is allowed to practice without interference. Hindus, Sikhs, Baha'is, and Buddhists can worship privately, but may not construct buildings for public worship. Some 80,000 *bidoon,* or stateless people, are considered illegal residents and denied full citizenship rights. A program initiated in 1999 allows them to apply for citizenship if they can prove that they or their forebears have resided in the country since 1965.

Kyrgyzstan

Polity: Presidential
Economy: Capitalist-statist
Population: 5,000,000
PPP: $2,711
Life Expectancy: 69
Religious Groups: Muslim (75 percent), Russian Orthodox (20 percent), other (5 percent)
Ethnic Groups: Kyrgyz (52 percent), Russian (18 percent), Uzbek (13 percent), Ukrainian (3 percent), other (14 percent)
Capital: Bishkek

Political Rights: 6
Civil Liberties: 5
Status: Not Free

Ten-Year Ratings Timeline (Political Rights, Civil Liberties, Status)

1993	1994	1995	1996	1997	1998	1999	2000	2001	2002	2003
4,2PF	5,3PF	4,3PF	4,4PF	4,4PF	4,4PF	5,5PF	5,5PF	6,5NF	6,5NF	6,5NF

Overview:

The January 2002 arrest of an outspoken parliament member critical of the country's leadership sparked an unprecedented wave of public demonstrations that continued throughout much of the year. Fed by popular discontent over years of economic stagnation and political exclusion, the protestors adopted various demands, including the resignation of President Askar Akayev. The shooting deaths by police of five protestors in March represented the first time that political disputes had turned violent since Kyrgyzstan's independence more than a decade earlier.

Populated by nomadic herders and ruled by tribal leaders for centuries, Kyrgyzstan was conquered by Russia in the mid-1800s and incorporated into the Soviet Union in 1924. The country declared independence from the U.S.S.R. in August 1991. Two months later, Akayev, a respected physicist, was elected president in the country's first direct presidential vote. While Akayev introduced multiparty elections and pursued economic reforms in conjunction with IMF requirements, he faced strong resistance from a Communist-dominated parliament elected in 1990.

In the 1995 parliamentary elections, no single party won a clear majority, with a mix of governing officials, intellectuals, and clan leaders capturing most of the seats in the legislature. Later that year, Akayev was reelected president in early elections with more than 70 percent of the vote. In a February 1996 referendum, 94 percent of voters endorsed constitutional amendments that substantially increased the powers of the presidency.

Opposition parties, including the Democratic Movement of Kyrgyzstan (PDMK), El Bei-Bechora (The People's Party), and Ar-Namys (Dignity), were barred from competing in the February 2000 parliamentary elections over minor technicalities in rulings that were widely regarded as politically motivated. Ar-Namys chairman Felix Kulov, who ran as an independent candidate, lost in the runoff by a suspiciously large margin despite having enjoyed a secure lead in the first round. According to official election results, the Communist Party received the largest percentage of votes, followed by the pro-government Union of Democratic Forces. International election observers, including representatives from the OSCE, noted serious irregularities such as attempts to bribe voters, violations in tabulating the votes, and a state media bias in favor of pro-government parties.

The October 29, 2000, presidential poll was contested by six candidates, including the heavily favored incumbent, who received nearly 75 percent of the vote. Kulov, who was widely regarded as Akayev's main challenger, was denied registration as a candidate for refusing to take a mandatory Kyrgyz language exam, which he charged violated election laws and the constitution. As with the parliamentary elections, international monitors and opposition figures cited widespread irregularities, including the exclusion of candidates for political purposes, the stuffing of ballot boxes, and biased state media coverage.

For the second successive year, Islamic militants engaged in armed incursions in August 2000 in the southern region of Kyrgyzstan. The rebels were members of the Islamic Movement of Uzbekistan, a group seeking the violent overthrow of the secular government of Uzbekistan and its replacement with one based on *Sharia* (Islamic law). After several months of intense battles between the rebels and Uzbek and Kyrgyz troops, the fighting ceased with the onset of winter, with many of the rebels fleeing back to their bases in neighboring Tajikistan.

Following the September 11, 2001, terrorist attacks against the World Trade Center and the Pentagon, Kyrgyzstan offered its support for the U.S.-led war in Afghanistan, including the use of its air bases. For the cash-strapped Kyrgyz economy, U.S. troop deployments promised to be a valuable source of income; Bishkek reportedly received several thousand dollars for each takeoff and landing. At the same time, human rights groups expressed concern that the government would use its increased cooperation with the United States to crack down further on sources of domestic dissent, including independent media outlets and opposition political groups.

Years of simmering frustrations in the economically depressed and politically marginalized south culminated in an unprecedented series of public protests in 2002. The demonstrations were sparked by the January arrest of an outspoken parliament member, Azimbek Beknazarov, on charges of abuse of power allegedly committed in 1995. Critics maintained that Beknazarov had been detained because of his public criticism of a controversial 1999 border agreement ceding land to China.

A few days after his trial began, thousands of pro-Beknazarov demonstrators marched in the southern district of Aksy on March 17 and 18. In the first outbreak of deadly political violence since Kyrgyzstan's independence, five protestors were killed and more than a dozen were wounded when police fired into the crowd. Although the government was quick to blame human rights activists and opposition figures for provoking the confrontation, Beknazarov was released from prison the following day in an apparent effort to quell the protests. However, thousands of his supporters continued to hold rallies, demanding that the charges against him be dismissed and that those responsible for the killings be punished.

After numerous delays, a state commission investigating the clashes released its final report on May 18. While concluding that the violence had been triggered by factors including the illegal use of firearms by law enforcement officials, the report did not address the critical question of who had given the orders to shoot. Under growing domestic and international pressure, Akayev dismissed Prime Minister

Kurmanbek Bakiev, as well as the head of the presidential administration and the interior minister, on May 22; Bakiev subsequently was replaced by Nikolai Tanayev, the first ethnic Russian to hold that post. Two days later, Beknazarov was convicted of abuse of office, given a one-year suspended sentence, and stripped of his seat in parliament.

Tensions continued to mount as protestors staged mass marches in cities in the south, clashing frequently with police. The demonstrators adopted additional demands, including Akayev's resignation and the overturning of a May 8 conviction of Felix Kulov that had resulted in a sentence of 10 years in prison for embezzlement. Kulov was already serving a seven-year prison term, which he had received in January 2001, for abuse of power while national security minister in 1997 and 1998. Most analysts maintained that the cases against him were politically motivated and intended to exclude him from further activities in politics.

The crisis eased somewhat after an appeals court annulled Beknazarov's sentence on June 28, allowing him to retain his seat in parliament. In August, the prosecutor-general's office announced that it was filing charges against several officials in connection with the Aksy shootings. The trial, which opened in late September, concluded on December 28 with the sentencing of four former regional prosecutors and police officials to between two and three years in prison; three other local officials were acquitted. Critics charged that the verdicts were too lenient and maintained that the real responsibility lay with senior government officials, including the former interior minister and the head of the national security service. Many observers believed that Akayev's handling of the fallout from the Aksy shootings—which had prompted criticism from both hard-liners within his government and members of the opposition—had left him increasingly politically isolated by year's end.

Political Rights and Civil Liberties:

Citizens of Kyrgyzstan cannot change their government democratically. International election observers described the 2000 parliamentary and presidential elections as neither free nor fair. The 1996 constitution codifies strong presidential rule and a weak parliament, and the post of prime minister is largely ceremonial. The bicameral legislature is composed of a 45-member upper chamber, which meets only occasionally to approve the budget and confirm presidential appointees, and a 60-seat lower chamber. Although the constitution limits the president to only two terms in office, President Askar Akayev was allowed to run in 2000 after the Constitutional Court ruled that his first term had begun in 1995, rather than in 1991, when he ran effectively unopposed. In September, a new constitutional council began drafting constitutional amendments on the redistribution of power between the executive and legislative branches. The council's members include senior government officials, members of parliament, and leaders of several opposition parties. Discussion on the proposed amendments is scheduled to continue into 2003.

While there is some degree of press freedom in Kyrgyzstan, both state and private media are vulnerable to government pressure, which causes many journalists to practice self-censorship. All media are required to register with the Ministry of Justice. The state printing house has refused at times to print some independent newspapers, including *Res Publica* and *Moya Stolitsa-Novosti*. A controversial resolution adopted in January that severely restricted the activities of independent publishers was canceled in midyear. That resolution had stipulated that only those publishing houses in which the government owned at least a 10 percent stake could operate, and it had required the registration of various publishing activities, including bulletins by nongovernmental organizations (NGOs).

Freedom of religion is generally respected. However, after the events of September 11, 2001, the government increased its efforts to monitor and restrict Islamic groups that it regards as a threat to national security. In order to obtain legal status, all religious organizations must register with the State Commission on Religious Affairs and the Ministry of Justice, a process that is often cumbersome.

Most political parties are weak and poorly organized and centered around a specific leading figure. While some NGOs operate with little or no state interference, others, including the Kyrgyz Committee for Human Rights, have faced harassment by the authorities. In July, Akayev created the post of ombudsman, a position that was filled in November by human rights activist Tursunbai Bakir Uulu.

Freedom of assembly is respected inconsistently. A series of demonstrations throughout 2002 included a March protest in which five people were killed by police. In July, Akayev signed a law on freedom of assembly adopted by parliament the previous month. Critics charged that the law would allow law enforcement officials to ban demonstrations if they determine that the rights of citizens not taking part are being violated. A 1992 law permits the formation of trade unions and protects members from anti-union discrimination, and unions generally are able to conduct their activities without obstruction.

Despite various legislative reforms in the court system, the judiciary is not independent and remains dominated by the executive branch. Corruption among judges is reportedly widespread, and police frequently use violence against suspects during arrest and interrogation. Conditions in the country's prisons, which suffer from overcrowding, food shortages, and a lack of other basic necessities, remain poor.

Personal connections, corruption, organized crime, and widespread poverty limit business competition and equality of opportunity. According to the 2001 U.S. State Department report on human rights, released in March 2002, the government generally respects the right of free travel into and outside the country. However, certain policies complicate internal migration, including a requirement for citizens to have official permission to work and settle in a particular area of the country. In 1999, Kyrgyzstan abolished the Soviet-era exit-visa system.

Many members of the country's sizeable ethnic Uzbek minority have been demanding more political and cultural rights, including greater representation in government and better resources for Uzbek schools. Women are underrepresented in government and politics, and the trafficking of women and girls into forced prostitution abroad is a serious problem. Cultural traditions discourage victims of domestic violence from seeking legal help.

Laos

Polity: One party
Economy: Statist
Population: 5,500,000
PPP: $1,575
Life Expectancy: 54

Political Rights: 7
Civil Liberties: 6
Status: Not Free

Religious Groups: Buddhist (60 percent), animist and other (40 percent)

Ethnic Groups: Lao Loum [lowland] (68 percent), Lao Theung [upland] (22 percent), Lao Soung [highland] including the Hmong (Meo) and the Yao (Mien) (9 percent), ethnic Vietnamese/Chinese (1 percent)

Capital: Vientiane

Ten-Year Ratings Timeline (Political Rights, Civil Liberties, Status)

1993	1994	1995	1996	1997	1998	1999	2000	2001	2002	2003
7,6NF	7,6NF	7,6NF	7,6NF	7,6NF	7,6NF	7,6NF	7,6NF	7,6NF	7,6NF	7,6NF

Overview:

By staging a tightly controlled election in February 2002, the ruling Communist party in Laos signaled that it has few plans to loosen its iron-fisted grip over this impoverished Southeast Asian land after more than a quarter-century in power.

This landlocked, mountainous nation won independence in 1953 following six decades as a French protectorate and occupation by the Japanese during World War II. Backed by Vietnam's Viet Minh rebels, Communist *Pathet Lao* (Land of Lao) guerrillas quickly tried to topple the royalist government in Vientiane. Following several years of political turmoil, Communist, royalist, and so-called neutralist forces in 1960 began waging a three-way civil war.

Amid continued fighting, Laos was drawn into the Vietnam War in 1964, when the United States began bombing North Vietnamese forces operating inside Laos. The Pathet Lao seized power in 1975 shortly after the Communist victory in neighboring Vietnam. The guerrillas set up a one-party Communist state under Prime Minister Kaysone Phomvihane's Lao People's Revolutionary Party (LPRP).

By the mid-1980s, the Laotian economy was a shambles, reeling under a double blow of the LPRP's central planning and the legacy of civil war. In response, the LPRP in 1986 began freeing prices, encouraging foreign investment, and privatizing farms and some state-owned firms. Partially unshackled, the economy grew by 7 percent a year, on average, from 1988 to 1996.

At the same time, the LPRP continued to reject calls for political reforms, jailing two officials in 1990 who called for multiparty elections. Meanwhile, Kaysone's death in 1992 ushered in a new strongman to lead the country. Veteran revolutionary Khamtay Siphandone, now 78, took the reigns of the all-powerful LPRP and later became state president.

At its seventh party congress in 2001, the LPRP added only a few young faces to its Politburo and Central Committee and did not announce any initiatives to boost the nascent private sector. Many diplomats and other observers had expected the party to launch deeper reforms in an effort to sharpen the economy's competitiveness. The LPRP's lack of zest for deeper change, including privatizing the large, creaking state firms that dominate the economy, reflects the aging leadership's concern that reducing the party's control over the economy could undermine its tight grip on power.

Against this backdrop, the February 2002 parliamentary elections provided little suspense. All but one of the 166 candidates for the National Assembly's 109 seats were LPRP members.

In the rugged highlands, several armed Hmong groups have been waging low-grade insurgencies against the government since the Communist takeover. The Hmong are one of the largest of several upland hill tribes. Together with smaller numbers of other ethnic minorities, the hill tribes make up roughly half the population. The politically dominant ethnic Lao Loum make up the remainder.

The economy depends on subsistence agriculture, which accounts for around half of output and provides livelihoods for 80 percent of Laotians. Trade and sales of hydroelectric power to neighboring Thailand are key sources of foreign revenue. The economy, however, has yet to recover from the regional financial crisis that began in 1997. Foreign investors, the majority of whom were Thai, pulled out of Laos in droves and have not returned. In a sign of the economy's fragility, donor aid makes up more than 15 percent of gross domestic product, up from 6.25 percent in the mid-1980s, just before Laos began its tentative market reforms.

Political Rights and Civil Liberties: Laotians cannot change their government through elections and the ruling LPRP sharply restricts most basic rights. The 1991 constitution makes the LPRP the sole legal political party and gives it a leading role at all levels of government. The National Assembly merely rubber-stamps the party's proposals. The LPRP vets all candidates for assembly elections, which are held once every five years.

Both Laotian forces and Hmong rebels reportedly have committed some politically motivated killings and other human rights abuses relating to the Hmong insurgency. The poorly equipped Hmong rebels have little chance of overthrowing the government, and their goals are not clear. The Hmong and other ethnic minorities face some discrimination in mainstream society and have little input in government decisions on how land is used and natural resources are allocated, according to the U.S. State Department's global human rights report for 2001, released in March 2002.

Laos's party-controlled courts provide citizens with little means of addressing government human rights abuses and other grievances. The judiciary "is subject to executive influence, is corrupt, and does not ensure citizens' due process," the U.S. State Department report said, but noted that party and government officials appear to exert less influence over the courts than in the past.

Security forces often illegally detain suspects, and some Laotians have spent more than a decade in jail without trial, according to a June report by the human rights group Amnesty International, adding that prisoners sometimes must bribe jail officials to obtain their freedom, even after a court has ordered their release, are routinely tortured, have limited access to health care, and are provided with meager food rations, the report added.

Laotian jails hold several political prisoners. These include two officials from the pre-1975 government and two who served in the present regime before being jailed in 1990 for advocating multiparty politics, according to a U.S. State Department report. In addition, five students who disappeared after they tried to hold an unprecedented pro-democracy protest in 1999 are serving prison terms, Laotian officials conceded to visiting European members of parliament in June; the officials did not reveal the charges or the lengths of the sentences. As of the end of 2001, the government also was holding an estimated 100 to 200 national security suspects, most of them without trials, the U.S. State Department report said.

The government owns all newspapers and broadcast media, and news coverage parrots the party line. The law subjects journalists who do not file "constructive reports," or who attempt to "obstruct" the LPRP's work, to jail terms of from 5 to 15 years. Freedom of the press, as well as free speech in general, is also restricted by broadly drawn criminal laws that forbid inciting disorder, slandering the state, distorting LPRP or state policies, or disseminating information or opinions that weaken the state.

Laotian authorities monitor e-mail, control all domestic Internet service providers, and block access to some political Web sites, the U.S. State Department report said. The number of Laotian Internet users is not known.

Religious freedom is tightly restricted. Several Laotians are serving jail terms for proselytizing or other peaceful religious activities, according to the U.S. State Department report. Besides those formally tried and jailed, dozens of Christians have recently been detained, some for months, the report said, while others reportedly have been barred from worshipping openly or forced to renounce their beliefs.

Officials also prohibit Laotians from printing non-Buddhist religious texts or distributing them outside their congregations and restrict the import of foreign religious texts and materials; some minority religious groups reportedly are also unable to register new congregations or obtain permission to build new places of worship, the U.S. State Department report added.

In a society where more than half the population is Buddhist, the LPRP controls the Buddhist clergy. It requires monks to study Marxism-Leninism, attend certain party meetings, and weave party and state policies into their Buddhist teachings. Officials have, however, permitted some Buddhist temples to receive support from abroad, expand the training of monks, and emphasize traditional teachings.

Many Laotian women hold important civil service and private sector jobs, though women hold relatively few positions in government and politics, the U.S. State Department report said. The report also stated that Laos is "a source and transit country for trafficking in persons," with rough estimates suggesting that 15,000 to 20,000 Laotian women and girls are trafficked abroad each year for prostitution.

The government recently has scaled back its monitoring of ordinary civilians. The security service, however, still uses a "vast" surveillance network to monitor the personal communications and track the movements of some Laotians, according to the U.S. State Department report. The regime also maintains an informal militia and a sporadically active system of neighborhood and workplace committees that inform on the population, the report added.

Trade unions are state controlled and have little influence. All unions must belong to the official Federation of Lao Trade Unions, and workers lack the right to bargain collectively. Strikes are not expressly prohibited, but they occur rarely. In any case, with subsistence farmers making up around four-fifths of the workforce, few Laotian workers are unionized. Consistent with its policy of neutralizing trade unions, the regime prohibits nongovernmental organizations (NGOs) from having political agendas. However, it permits some professional and socially-oriented NGOs, all of which it controls, to function.

Latvia

Polity: Parliamentary democracy
Economy: Mixed capitalist
Population: 2,300,000
PPP: $7,045
Life Expectancy: 71
Religious Groups: Lutheran, Roman Catholic, Russian Orthodox
Ethnic Groups: Latvian (57 percent), Russian (30 percent), Belarusian (4 percent), Ukrainian (3 percent), Polish (3 percent), other (3 percent)
Capital: Riga

Political Rights: 1
Civil Liberties: 2
Status: Free

Ten-Year Ratings Timeline (Political Rights, Civil Liberties, Status)

1993	1994	1995	1996	1997	1998	1999	2000	2001	2002	2003
3,3PF	3,3PF	3,2F	2,2F	3,2F	1,2F	1,2F	1,2F	1,2F	1,2F	1,2F

Overview:

In the October 2002 parliamentary elections, a new political party led by former central bank chairman, Einars Repse, captured the most seats to lead the country's ninth government since the reestablishment of independence 11 years earlier. Along with three other political parties, Repse's New Era Party formed a center-right coalition government with a majority of seats in parliament. Efforts to privatize one of the country's remaining state-owned industries, the Latvian Shipping Company, finally succeeded in June with the sale of 51 percent of the company. Both the European Union (EU) and NATO extended invitations to Latvia for membership in 2004.

After having been ruled for centuries by Germany, Poland, Sweden, and Russia, Latvia gained its independence in 1918, only to be annexed by the U.S.S.R. during World War II. More than 50 years of Soviet occupation saw a massive influx of Russians and the deportation, execution, and emigration of tens of thousands of ethnic Latvians. In 1991, Latvia regained its independence in the wake of the disintegration of the Soviet Union.

In the October 1998 parliamentary elections, the newly created People's Party, led by former agriculture minister, Adris Skele, received the most votes, although Skele remained unpopular among many political forces for his often authoritarian and abrasive style. After nearly two months of negotiations, parliament finally approved a new 46-seat minority coalition government led by Vilis Kristopans. It consisted of his center-right Latvia's Way, the right-wing nationalist For Fatherland and Freedom/LNNK (FF/LNNK), and the center-left New Party, along with the tacit support of the left-wing Alliance of Social Democrats. The People's Party was excluded from the ruling coalition, which most observers predicted would not survive for long because of the ideological diversity of its members and its minority status in parliament. In June 1999, Latvian-Canadian academic Vaira Vike-Freiberga was elected the country's first female president, succeeding Guntis Ulmanis, who had served as head of state for six years.

After only nine months in office, Prime Minister Kristopans, whose brief term had been plagued by various policy defeats and political crises, stepped down in July 1999, precipitating the collapse of his government. Latvia's Way, the People's Party, and FF/LNNK put aside enough of their differences to agree to form a new 62-seat majority coalition led by Kristopans' political rival, Andris Skele, as prime minister.

Following months of growing strains within the ruling coalition over privatization issues and personality conflicts, the government collapsed and Prime Minister Skele resigned in April 2000. On May 5, Riga mayor Andris Berzins of Latvia's Way was chosen prime minister to lead the new government, which included the previous coalition's three parties.

In parliamentary elections held on October 5, 2002, six parties passed the 5 percent threshold to enter the legislature: the new center-right New Era Party, led by Einars Repse, captured 26 seats; the center-left For Human Rights in a United Latvia, which represents many of the country's Russian-speakers, secured 25 seats; the People's Party won 20 seats; the new center-right Latvia First Party captured 10 seats; the new Union of Greens and Farmers took 12 seats; and FF/LNNK secured 7 seats. Latvia's Way, the longest-serving party in parliament, failed to win enough votes to enter parliament. Repse was named the new prime minister to lead a majority coalition government consisting of the New Era Party, Union of Greens and Farmers, Latvia First Party, and FF/LNNK. Voter turnout was estimated at more than 70 percent.

After several failed attempts to privatize the Latvian Shipping Company (LASCO), 51 percent of the company was successfully sold in June. Latvian investors purchased some 61 percent of the shares, while international investors bought the remaining 39 percent.

Near the end of the year, Latvia achieved two of its long-standing foreign policy objectives when it received formal invitations in November from NATO and in December from the EU to join their organizations in 2004. On December 27, parliament approved a September 120, 2003, national referendum to vote on Latvia's entering the EU.

Political Rights and Civil Liberties: Latvians can change their government democratically. The constitution provides for a unicameral, 100-seat parliament (*Saeima*), whose members are elected for four-year terms by proportional representation, and who in turn select the country's president. According to international observers, the most recent national legislative elections in 2002 were free and fair. Latvia's citizenship laws have been criticized for disenfranchising those who immigrated to Latvia during the Soviet period and who must now apply for citizenship. Moscow continues to accuse Riga of discriminating against the country's 700,000 Russian-speakers, mostly ethnic Russian.

The government respects freedom of speech and the press. Private television and radio stations broadcast programs in both Latvian and Russian, and newspapers publish a wide range of political viewpoints. However, many media outlets routinely report rumors and accusations as fact without benefit of hard evidence.

Freedom of worship is generally respected in this country in which the three largest denominations are Roman Catholic, Lutheran, and Orthodox Russian. An educational law stipulating that secondary-school classes be conducted in Latvian will go into effect in 2004; some 120,000 students attend Russian-language schools throughout Latvia.

Freedom of assembly and association is protected by law, and gatherings occur without governmental interference. Workers have the right to establish trade unions, strike, and engage in collective bargaining. Thousands of health care workers took part in strikes during 2002 to protest low wages and the level of state spending on health services. Latvia has adopted various anticorruption measures, including laws in 2002 to establish a corruption prevention bureau and to prevent conflict of interest among state officials. However, corruption among some government officials remains a recognized problem. Berlin-based Transparency International ranked Latvia 52 out of 102 countries surveyed in its 2002 Corruption Perceptions Index.

While the government generally respects constitutional provisions for an independent judiciary, reform of the courts has been slow and judges continue to be inadequately trained and prone to corruption. Severe backlogs in the court system have led to lengthy delays in reviewing cases and to large numbers of persons being held in pretrial detention. In one prominent case, former chairman of Banka Baltija, Alexander Lavent, who was arrested in connection with the bank's collapse in the mid-1990s, was held in detention for several years before his conviction on fraud charges in December 2001. Lavent filed complaints regarding his lengthy incarceration with the European Court of Human Rights (ECHR), which ruled in November 2002 that both his pre-trial detention period and the court proceedings had been too long. The opinion of the ECHR, which awarded him 15,000 Euros to cover trial expenses in Strasbourg, did not order his release from prison. Lavent's case was pending appeal in Latvia at year's end. Prison facilities remain severely overcrowded and suffer from inadequate sanitary conditions.

Nearly one-fifth of Latvia's residents are noncitizens, who are barred from participating in state and local elections and from holding some civil service jobs. On April 30, 2002, parliament adopted constitutional amendments making Latvian the sole official language in national legislative and local councils. Just nine days later, in a move some critics charged as being largely symbolic, parliament abolished a provision in the country's election law requiring candidates for parliament and local elections to be fluent in Latvian. The change had been proposed by President Vaira Vike-Freiberga in late 2001 and had been mentioned at times as a condition for Latvia's membership to NATO.

Women possess the same legal rights as men, although they frequently face hiring and pay discrimination and are underrepresented in senior-level business and governmental positions.

⬇ Lebanon

Polity: Presidential-
parliamentary (military-
and foreign-influenced,
partly foreign-occupied)
Economy: Mixed statist
Population: 4,300,000
PPP: $4,308
Life Expectancy: 73

Political Rights: 6
Civil Liberties: 5
Status: Not Free

Religious Groups: Muslim [Mostly Shi'a] (70 percent), Christian (30 percent)
Ethnic Groups: Arab (95 percent), Armenian (4 percent), other (1 percent)
Capital: Beirut
Trend Arrow: Lebanon received a downward trend arrow due to the closure of the country's main independent television station, the unprecedented threatening of mainstream opposition figures with investigations for alleged ties to foreign powers, and the invalidation of a June by-election for politically motivated reasons.

Ten-Year Ratings Timeline (Political Rights, Civil Liberties, Status)

1993	1994	1995	1996	1997	1998	1999	2000	2001	2002	2003
5,4PF	6,5PF	6,5PF	6,5NF	6,5NF	6,5NF	6,5NF	6,5NF	6,5NF	6,5NF	6,5NF

Overview:

A series of unprecedented developments in 2002 undermined the state of political and civil liberties in Lebanon. The closure of a major independent television station threatened the country's vibrant independent media, and the ouster of a leading member of the parliamentary opposition dealt a major blow to Lebanon's democratic institutions. The government failed to adequately investigate four major assassinations and political killings during the year, even as it launched investigations against political opponents. The presence of more than 20,000 Syrian troops remains the greatest impediment to freedom in Lebanon and the most salient issue of contention between government and opposition.

For over a thousand years, the rough terrain of Mount Lebanon attracted Christian and heterodox-Muslim minorities fleeing persecution in the predominantly Sunni Muslim Arab world. After centuries of European protection and relative autonomy under Turkish rule, Mount Lebanon and its surrounding areas were established as a French mandate in 1920. After winning its independence in 1943, the new state of Lebanon maintained a precarious democratic system based on the division of parliamentary seats, high political offices, and senior administrative positions among the country's 17 officially recognized sectarian communities. As emigration transformed Lebanon's slight Christian majority into a minority, Muslim leaders demanded amendments to the fixed 6-to-5 ratio of Christian to Muslim parliamentary seats and to exclusive Maronite Christian control of the presidency. In 1975, war erupted between a coalition of Lebanese Muslim and leftist militias aligned with Palestinian guerrilla groups and an array of Christian militias bent on preserving Christian political privileges.

After the first few years of fighting, a loose consensus emerged among Lebanese politicians regarding a new power-sharing arrangement. However, following the entry of Syrian and Israeli troops into Lebanon in 1976 and 1978, the various militias and their foreign backers had little interest in disarming. The civil war lost much of its sectarian character over the next decade, with the bloodiest outbreaks of fighting taking place mainly within the Shi'a, Christian, and Palestinian communities. Outside forces played a more direct role in the fighting. The Syrians battled Israeli forces in 1982, attacked a Palestinian-Islamist coalition in the mid-1980s, and fought the Lebanese army in 1989-90, while the Israelis combated Palestinian and Shi'a groups.

In 1989, the surviving members of Lebanon's 1972 parliament convened in Taif, Saudi Arabia, and agreed to a plan put forward by the Arab League that weakened the presidency, established equality in Christian and Muslim parliamentary representation, and mandated close security cooperation with occupying Syrian troops. After the ouster of General Michel Aoun from east Beirut by Syrian forces in October 1990, a new Syrian-backed government extended its writ throughout most of the country.

Over the next 12 years, Syria consolidated its control over Lebanese state institutions, particularly the presidency, the judiciary, and the security forces. However, in return for tacit Western acceptance of its control of Lebanon, Damascus permitted a degree of political and civil liberties in Lebanon that exceeded those in most other Arab countries. While those who directly criticized the occupation risked arbitrary arrest and imprisonment, criticism of the government was largely tolerated. The motley assortment of militia chiefs, traditional elites, and nouveaux riches who held civilian political positions in postwar Lebanon were persuaded to accept continued Syrian hegemony, primarily through a system of institutionalized corruption fueled by massive deficit spending on reconstruction during the 1990s. By the end of the decade, Lebanon's government debt exceeded its own gross national product and the economy was in deep recession.

As a result of this dismal economic downturn, the May 2000 Israeli withdrawal from south Lebanon, and the death of Syrian president Hafez Assad a month later, a vocal opposition to the Syrian presence began spreading across the political and sectarian spectrum. Mass demonstrations against the occupation grew in size and frequency throughout 2000 and 2001, while traditional Christian political and religious leaders who had previously been silent about the issue began speaking openly. Syria downsized its military presence in 2001, but demands for a complete pullout persisted.

After the September 11, 2001 attacks on the United States, Western pressure to preserve civil liberties subsided, in exchange for Syrian and Lebanese cooperation in the war against al-Qaeda. A number of unprecedented measures were taken to stifle freedoms in 2002. In September, security forces closed Murr Television (MTV), an independent station that had covered government crackdowns against the opposition and given voice to political dissidents. The decision was seen as a move to undermine the growing influence of its prime shareholder, Gabriel Murr, who had won a parliamentary by-election in June. In November, the Constitutional Council invalidated Murr's victory on the grounds that MTV had violated a law prohibiting campaign advertising, handing the seat to a candidate who received just 1,773 of 71,278 votes cast. The resulting public outcry led even pro-Syrian newspapers to condemn the assault on press freedom and democracy.

In the fall of 2002, the government announced that several opposition figures were under investigation for alleged ties to Israel and other foreign powers, and included prominent Christian leaders who had previously enjoyed immunity from government harassment because of their ties to the West, such as former president Amine Gemayel and Dory Chamoun.

Two prominent public figures were assassinated in 2002, reportedly after quarrelling with pro-Syrian politicians. In January, former Christian warlord Elie Hobeika was killed by a car bomb in a high-security Beirut suburb close to key government offices. In May, unknown assailants abducted a prominent student opposition activist, tortured him to death, and left his body in the trunk of his car. These killings, along with the murders of an American missionary and an Iraqi dissident, were eerily reminiscent of the country's 1975 civil war.

In order to preserve economic and political stability in the country, 18 wealthy nations and global financial institutions convened the Paris II conference in November and provided Lebanon with $4.3 billion in financial support to reduce debt servicing and prop up the currency. However, many in the opposition complain that international largesse in the absence of pressure to reform merely prolongs the demise of a corrupt, paralyzed government incapable of solving the country's problems.

Political Rights and Civil Liberties: The Lebanese people have only a limited capacity to choose their own government. The Lebanese president is formally selected every six years by the 128-member parliament. In practice, however, this choice is made after Syrian authorization, known as "the password" in the Lebanese media. Syria and its allies also influence parliamentary and municipal elections more indirectly. The distribution of parliamentary seats is skewed in favor of regions where Syrian forces have been stationed the longest, such as the Beqaa Valley, and electoral districts are blatantly gerrymandered to ensure the election of pro-Syrian politicians. There has also been widespread interference during the elections themselves, with Lebanese security forces often present inside the polls. Prior to the June 2002 by-election in Metn, Interior Minister Elias Murr declared that using voting booth curtains to ensure secrecy was "optional," a remarkably blatant move to facilitate vote buying.

Arbitrary arrests and detentions are commonplace, and security forces have used torture in the past to extract confessions. It is widely known that the Syrian-controlled security agencies monitor the telephones of both cabinet ministers and political dissidents.

The judiciary is strongly influenced by Syrian political pressure, which affects the appointments of key prosecutors and investigating magistrates. The judicial system consists of civilian courts, a military court, and a judicial council. International standards of criminal procedure are not observed in the military court, which consists largely of military officers with no legal training, and cases are often tried in a matter of minutes.

Freedom of expression in Lebanon surpasses that of any other Arab country, but is strictly limited on issues concerning Syria. Lebanon has a long tradition of academic freedom and a vibrant private educational system. There are five independent television stations and more than 30 independent radio stations in Lebanon, though they are owned by prominent political and commercial elites. Dozens of independent print publications reflect a diverse range of views.

In September 1991, the government signed a treaty with its larger neighbor explicitly pledging to "ban all political and media activity that *might* harm" Syria. This treaty, and a variety of subsequent laws drafted to comply with it, allows judges to censor foreign publications and to indict journalists for critical reporting on Syria, the Lebanese military, the security forces, the judiciary, and the presidency. In practice, such laws are mainly used to pressure the media into exercising self-censorship and rarely result in the imprisonment of journalists or the closure of media outlets. However, journalists who persistently violate taboos can be indicted and imprisoned on more serious charges. In March 2002, Antoine Bassil, a journalist for the Saudi-owned, London-based Middle East Broadcasting Corporation (MBC), and Habib Younis, the Beirut bureau chief of *Al-Hayat*, were convicted by a military court of "contacting the Israeli enemy" and sentenced to prison terms, later commuted to 15 months and two-and-a-half years. Permanent closure of licensed media outlets was rare until the closure of Murr Televisions (MTV) in 2002, which generated palpable anxiety among media owners of all political persuasions.

Freedom of association and assembly is restricted. Although political parties are legal, a 1994 ban on the Christian Lebanese Forces (LF) party remains in place. Public demonstrations are not permitted without prior approval from the Interior Ministry, which does not rule according to uniform standards, and security forces routinely beat and arrest those who demonstrate against the Syrian occupation. In late October 2002, a major demonstration organized by the mainstream Christian opposition, Qornet Shehwan Gathering, was canceled after the Interior Ministry declined to issue a license. Clashes between police and student activists occurred periodically throughout the year, particularly after the closure of MTV. Two student demonstrators were wounded in clashes with police on September 8. Eighteen student demonstrators were injured on October 31, and another 16 arrested. In November, on the eve of Lebanon's independence day, 15 students were detained and 4 others hospitalized after security forces dispersed an anti-Syrian demonstration.

All workers except those in government may establish unions, strike, and bargain collectively. However, foreign domestic workers are routinely exploited and physically abused by employers.

Freedom of religion is guaranteed in the Lebanese constitution and protected in practice, though sectarianism is formally enshrined in the political system. Nearly 350,000 Palestinian refugees living in Lebanon are denied citizenship rights and face restrictions on working, building homes, and purchasing property.

Women enjoy most of the same rights as men, but suffer social and some legal discrimination. Women are underrepresented in politics, holding only 2 percent of parliamentary seats, and do not receive equal social security provisions and other benefits. Men convicted of so-called honor crimes against women are seldomly punished severely.

Lesotho

Polity: Parliamentary democracy and traditional chiefs
Economy: Capitalist
Population: 2,200,000
PPP: $2,031
Life Expectancy: 51

Political Rights: 2*
Civil Liberties: 3*
Status: Free

Religious Groups: Christian (80 percent), indigenous beliefs (20 percent)
Ethnic Groups: Sotho (99.7 percent), other, including European and Asian (0.3 percent)
Capital: Maseru
Ratings Change: Lesotho's political rights rating improved from 4 to 2, its civil liberties rating improved from 4 to 3, and its status changed from Partly Free to Free, following the holding of free and fair parliamentary elections which were not marred by violence, and a general improvement in the country's civil liberties.

Ten-Year Ratings Timeline (Political Rights, Civil Liberties, Status)

1993	1994	1995	1996	1997	1998	1999	2000	2001	2002	2003
6,4PF	3,4PF	4,4PF	4,4PF	4,4PF	4,4PF	4,4PF	4,4PF	4,4PF	4,4PF	2,3F

Overview:

Lesotho held long-awaited parliamentary elections in May. International observers declared the vote to be free and fair, but Lesotho's main opposition parties objected to the results, which gave the ruling Lesotho Congress for Democracy (LCD) 77 of 78 constituency seats. The circumstances were similar to the dispute that erupted following the 1998 parliamentary poll, which the 2002 election was organized to replace. This time, however, the objection did not dissolve into violence. The opposition Basotho National Party won 21 of the 40 seats chosen by proportional representation.

Lesotho's status as a British protectorate saved it from incorporation into South Africa. King Moshoeshoe II reigned from independence in 1966 until the installation of his son as King Letsie III in a 1990 military coup. Democratic elections in 1993 did not lead to stability. After violent military infighting, assassinations, and a suspension of constitutional rule in 1994, King Letsie III abdicated to allow his father's reinstatement. He resumed the throne following the accidental death of his father in January 1996.

Troops from South Africa and Botswana were sent to this mountain kingdom at the request of Prime Minster Pakalitha Mosisili, under the mandate of the 14-country Southern Africa Development Community (SADC), in 1998 to quell army-backed violence and a potential overthrow of the government. The violence was touched off by the results of National Assembly elections. Although international observers described the voting as free and fair, the appearance of irregularities and the absence of opposition voices in government prompted demonstrators to reject the results that gave the ruling LCD 79 of 80 National Assembly seats. At least 100 people were reportedly killed before order was restored. An agreement, drafted by the Commonwealth in 1998, allowed the elected, but highly unpopular, government to retain power, but stipulated that new elections be supervised by an independent election commission.

Entirely surrounded by South Africa, Lesotho is highly dependent on its powerful neighbor. Its economy is sustained by remittances from its many citizens who work in South African mines. Retrenchments at the mines, however, has contributed to high unemployment in Lesotho. The kingdom in 2002 was also struggling with hunger following poor harvests.

Political Rights and Civil Liberties: The people of Lesotho are guaranteed the right to change their leaders through free and fair elections. The 2002 legislative election was marked by a turnout of 68 percent. The ruling LCD captured a total of 55 percent of votes cast, winning 77 of 78 constituency seats. The Lesotho People's Congress (LPC) won 1 seat. There are 80 constituency seats, but elections in 2 constituencies failed. The Basotho National Party won 21 of the 40 seats chosen by proportional representation, while the National Independent Party won 5 and the LPC won 4. Smaller parties won the remainder.

The new "mixed member" voting system expanded the number of National Assembly seats by 40, to 120. The additional seats were chosen by proportional representation, while the others continued to be chosen by the first-past-the-post system of awarding seats to whoever gets the most votes. The new system was developed by the electoral commission and the Interim Political Authority, which were set up following the 1998 violence.

The Senate, the upper house of the bicameral legislature, includes royal appointees and Lesotho's 22 principal traditional chiefs, who still wield considerable authority in rural areas. Any elected government's exercise of its constitutional authority remains limited by the autonomy of the military, the royal family, and traditional clan structures.

Courts are nominally independent, but higher courts are especially subject to outside influence. The large case backlog often leads to lengthy delays in trials. Mistreatment of civilians by security forces reportedly continues. Several nongovernmental organizations operate openly. Prison conditions are poor, but not life threatening.

The government generally respects freedom of speech and the press, but journalists have suffered occasional harassment or attack. There are several independent newspapers that routinely criticize the government. There are four private radio stations, and extensive South African radio and television broadcasts reach Lesotho.

Freedom of religion in the predominantly Christian country is generally respected. The constitution bars gender-based discrimination, but customary practice and law still restrict women's rights in several areas, including property rights and inheritance. A woman is considered a legal minor while her husband is alive. Domestic violence is reportedly widespread but is becoming increasingly socially unacceptable. Women's rights organizations have highlighted the importance of women's participation in the democratic process as part of a broader effort to educate women about their rights under customary and common law.

Freedom of assembly is generally respected, and labor rights are constitutionally guaranteed. However, the labor and trade union movement is weak and fragmented. Approximately 10 percent of the country's labor force is unionized. Of the remainder, most are engaged in subsistence agriculture or employment in South African mines. Although collective bargaining rights and the right to strike are recognized by law, they are sometimes denied by government negotiators.

Liberia

Polity: Presidential-parliamentary
Economy: Capitalist
Population: 3,300,000
PPP: na
Life Expectancy: 50
Religious Groups: Indigenous beliefs (40 percent), Christian (40 percent), Muslim (20 percent)
Ethnic Groups: Indigenous tribes (95 percent), other (5 percent)
Capital: Monrovia

Political Rights: 6
Civil Liberties: 6
Status: Not Free

Ten-Year Ratings Timeline (Political Rights, Civil Liberties, Status)

1993	1994	1995	1996	1997	1998	1999	2000	2001	2002	2003
7,6NF	6,6NF	7,6NF	7,6NF	7,6NF	4,5PF	4,5PF	4,5PF	5,6PF	6,6NF	6,6NF

Overview:
Civil liberties suffered dramatically in Liberia in 2002 following the imposition of a state of emergency. The government of President Charles Taylor said it imposed the measure to help counter a rebel incursion by Liberians United for Reconciliation and Democracy (LURD) that reached within 50 miles of the capital, Monrovia, in January. Many Liberians suspected authorities were using the state of emergency as a pretext to crack down on Taylor's opponents. Several journalists, as well as human rights advocates and members of civil society, were arrested during the year. Several political prisoners remained in detention at the end of the year. The state of emergency, which also barred large public gatherings and political rallies, was lifted in September. Exiled opposition leader Ellen Johnson Sirleaf returned to Liberia in November 2002, apparently to prepare for presidential elections scheduled for October 2003. Opposition political parties pledged to rally behind one presidential candidate for the election, but there were no indications at year's end that the polls would be free and fair.

Liberia was settled in 1821 by freed slaves from the United States and became an independent republic in 1847. Americo-Liberians, descendants of the freed slaves, dominated the country until 1980 when army Sergeant Samuel Doe led a bloody coup and murdered President William Tolbert. Doe's regime concentrated power among members of his Kranh ethnic group and suppressed others. Forces led by Charles Taylor, a former government minister, and backed by Gio and Mano ethnic groups that had been subject to severe repression, launched a guerrilla war from neighboring Cote d'Ivoire against the Doe regime on Christmas Eve 1989. In 1990, Nigeria, under the aegis of the Economic Community of West African States (ECOWAS), led an armed intervention force, preventing Taylor from seizing the capital but failing to protect Doe from being captured and tortured to death by a splinter rebel group. The war claimed more than 150,000 lives and forced approximately half of Liberia's population to flee their homes before a 14th peace accord proved successful in 1996.

The United Nations in November 2002 extended sanctions against Liberia for another six months. Although peace was consolidated in neighboring Sierra Leone during the year, the international community still considers Taylor a threat to regional stability. The sanctions, which were initially imposed in May 2001, include an international travel ban on senior Liberian officials and their families, an arms embargo, and a moratorium on diamond exports. International human rights groups have called for a moratorium on timber exports as well. Taylor allegedly has used diamond and timber profits in the past to fund former Revolutionary United Front rebels in Sierra Leone. Tens of thousands of Liberians have been displaced by fighting in the northwest. Unrest in neighboring Côte d'Ivoire in 2002 sent many Liberian refugees fleeing back over the border into Liberia.

Corruption is a major obstacle to economic growth. Diamond smuggling allegedly has provided income for Taylor, although he denies this. Liberia's infrastructure has deteriorated substantially in the past decade.

Political Rights and Civil Liberties: Charles Taylor and his party assumed power after the 1997 elections, which were generally free and fair. The votes for the presidency and the National Assembly, on the basis of proportional representation, were held under provisions of the 1986 constitution. The polls constituted Liberia's most genuine electoral exercise in decades but were conducted in an atmosphere of intimidation. Taylor's victory reflected more of a vote for peace than for a particular personality, as many people believed that the only way to stop the war was to make him president.

The EU in 2001 said considerable changes on the political, legal, and economic fronts were needed to guarantee free and fair elections in 2003. The government hosted a "national conference" in July 2002, but none of the country's main opposition leaders attended; many live in exile.

Liberia's judiciary is subject to executive influence, corruption, and intimidation by security forces. Human rights groups say security forces often ignore summonses to appear in court to explain disappearances, and operate with impunity.

International human rights groups say that civilians have become the main targets in the conflict in the northwest by government troops, their allied militias, and the rebel LURD. Abuses include torture of captives while in incommunicado detention, rape of women and girls, forced labor, forced military recruitment of men and boys, and extrajudicial killing. New York-based Human Rights Watch in April 2002, accused the Liberian government of war crimes and atrocities against civilians. London-based Amnesty International accused security forces of torturing dissidents. Numerous civil society groups, including human rights organizations, operate in the country, but their employees are subject to repeated harassment by security forces. Several human rights activists were detained in 2002. Aloysius Toe, executive director of the Movement for the Defenders of Human Rights, was charged with treason in December. Human rights workers have been allowed access to prisons, where conditions are harsh and torture is used to extract confessions. The government in March 2002 granted clemency to 21 government officials and military officers detained in 1998 and found guilty of high treason. They had been sentenced to 20 years in prison.

Liberia's independent media have survived despite years of war, assaults, and harassment at the cost of extensive self-censorship. Charles Taylor owns KISS-FM, the only countrywide FM radio station. State television and one private station broadcast only irregularly. Some members of the print media have received death threats and are under persistent surveillance. Independent radio stations broadcast religious programming, but the Roman Catholic radio station, Veritas, has had programming on human rights issues. Several independent journalists were detained in 2002. The most prominent, Hassan Bility, was arrested in June and released in December following intervention from the United States. Bility, editor of the independent daily *The Analyst*, was held incommunicado without charge or trial. Authorities contended he led a LURD cell and was a "terrorist involved in an Islamic fundamentalist war." Detained journalists Ansumana Kamara and Mohammad Kamara were described by Taylor as "dissidents" and were to be tried by a military court.

Academic freedom is guaranteed, but student activists can face the same harassment and intimidation as the general population. Security forces stormed the University of Liberia in 2001 and beat several students during a protest.

Societal ethnic discrimination is rife, and the government discriminates against indigenous ethnic groups that opposed Taylor during the civil war, especially the Mandingo and Krahn ethnic groups. Religious freedom is respected in practice, but Muslims have been targeted because many Mandingos follow Islam. Treatment of women varies by ethnic group, religion, and social status. Many women continue to suffer from physical abuse and traditional societal discrimination, despite constitutionally guaranteed equality.

The right to strike, organize, and bargain collectively is permitted by law, but there is little union activity because of the lack of economic activity. Two umbrella unions cover some 60,000 workers, but most of them are unemployed. There is forced labor in rural areas, and child labor is widespread.

Libya

Polity: One party (presidential dictatorship)
Economy: Mixed statist
Population: 5,400,000
PPP: $7,570
Life Expectancy: 75

Political Rights: 7
Civil Liberties: 7
Status: Not Free

Religious Groups: Sunni Muslim (97 percent), other (3 percent)
Ethnic Groups: Arab-Berber (97 percent), other, including Greek, Italian, Egyptian, Pakistani, Turkish, Indian (3 percent)
Capital: Tripoli

Ten-Year Ratings Timeline (Political Rights, Civil Liberties, Status)

1993	1994	1995	1996	1997	1998	1999	2000	2001	2002	2003
7,7NF	7,7NF	7,7NF	7,7NF	7,7NF	7,7NF	7,7NF	7,7NF	7,7NF	7,7NF	7,7NF

Overview:

Libyan leader Colonel Mu'ammar al-Qadhafi continued his campaign for regional and international respectability in 2002. His attempts to position himself as a pan-African leader built upon recent efforts to break Libya out of international isolation, further burnishing his image as a continental gadfly. Libya seemed to cooperate with the United States on the war against terrorism, nevertheless, the United States classified it as a proliferator of weapons of mass destruction. Libya offered a compensation package to the families of the victims of the Pan Am Flight 103 bombing in 1988, but conditioned this offer on the complete removal of international sanctions against the country. At year's end, Libya was slated to chair the UN Commission on Human Rights.

After centuries of Ottoman rule, Libya was conquered by Italy in 1912 and occupied by British and French forces during World War II. In accordance with agreements made by Britain and the United Nations, Libya gained independence under the staunchly pro-Western King Idris I in 1951. Qadhafi seized power in 1969 amid growing anti-Western sentiment toward foreign-controlled oil companies and military bases on Libyan soil.

Qadhafi's open hostility toward the West and his sponsorship of terrorism have earned Libya the status of international pariah. Clashes with regional neighbors, including Chad over the Aozou strip and Egypt over their common border, have led to costly military failures. Suspected Libyan involvement in the 1988 bombing of Pan Am Flight 103 over Lockerbie, Scotland, prompted the United Nations in 1992 to impose sanctions, including embargoes on air traffic and the import of arms and oil-production equipment. The United States has maintained unilateral sanctions against Libya since 1981 because of the latter's sponsorship of terrorism.

With the economy stagnating and the internal infrastructure in disrepair, Qadhafi began taking steps in 1999 to end Libya's international isolation. He surrendered two Libyan nationals suspected in the Lockerbie bombing. He also agreed to pay compensation to the families of 170 people killed in the 1989 bombing of a French airliner over Niger. In addition, he accepted responsibility for the 1984 killing of British police officer Yvonne Fletcher by shots fired from the Libyan Embassy in London, and expelled from Libya the Palestinian terrorist organization headed by Abu Nidal. The United Nations suspended sanctions in 1999, but stopped short of lifting them permanently because Libya has not explicitly renounced terrorism. The United States eased some restrictions to allow American companies to sell food, medicine, and medical equipment to Libya, but maintained its travel ban. Britain restored diplomatic ties with Libya for the first time since 1986; the Libyan embassy in Britain reopened in March 2001. The EU lifted sanctions but maintained an arms embargo.

The two Lockerbie suspects went on trial in May 2000, under Scottish law, in the Netherlands. One, a Libyan intelligence agent named Abdel Basset Ali Mohammed al-Megrahi, was convicted of murder in January 2001 and sentenced to life imprisonment. The other was acquitted for lack of evidence and freed. Following the trial, the Arab League called for a total lifting of UN sanctions; all 22 of its members agreed to disregard them. The United States and Britain reiterated their demand that Libyan authorities renounce terrorism, take responsibility for the attack, and pay compensation to the victims' families. Libya has consistently denied governmental involvement in the attack.

Once a leading advocate of pan-Arab unity, Qadhafi received little Arab support in the wake of Lockerbie and turned instead to promoting a united Africa. In 2001 he worked with Egypt on a peace plan for Sudan and mediated disputes between Sudan and Uganda, and between Eritrea and Djibouti. He also sent troops to the Central African Republic (CAR) to support President Ange Felix Patasse in the wake of a failed coup.

While working to improve his image abroad, Qadhafi has become increasingly isolated at home. Ethnic rivalries among senior junta officials have been reported, while corruption, mismanagement, and unemployment have eroded support for the regime. Disaffected Libyans see little of some $10 billion per year in oil revenue and have yet to reap the benefits of suspended UN sanctions as potential investors from Europe, Asia, and the Middle East stream in seeking oil contracts. Economists stressed the need for deregulation and privatization, and Qadhafi has gradually lifted some state controls on the economy. He has also tried to encourage foreign investment in agriculture and tourism as well as oil. In 2001, as part of an ongoing investigation apparently aimed at cleaning up Libya's image, 47 government and bank officials, including the finance minister, were sent to prison for corruption

Early in 2002, Libyan officials held talks with American counterparts in London over removing Libya from the U.S. State Department's list of countries that sponsor terrorism. While a State Department report published in the spring did indicate that Libya was taking steps "to get out of the terrorism business," Libya was not removed from the official list. Whatever progress Libya has made in this area—including its relative cooperation with the United States in the war against terrorism— was offset later in the year when the United States accused Libya of proliferating weapons of mass destruction.

Expanding its image-rehabilitation drive, the government in May offered a $2.7 billion compensation package to the families of the 270 victims of the Pan Am Flight 103 bombing. However, Libya tied dispensation of the money to a removal of all outstanding sanctions against it and its removal from the U.S. State Department's terrorism-sponsors list.

In October Qadhafi sent troops to protect President Patasse's palace while Libyan jets bombed rebel-held areas of Bangui, the CAR's capital. Analysts speculated Qadhafi's military support was either part of his recent efforts at positioning himself as an African power broker or an attempt to leverage his access to the CAR's mineral resources.

Qadhafi's vision of a unified African state came into clearer focus in July with the formation of the African Union (AU), and Libya's inclusion on the steering committee of the New Partnership for Africa's Development (NEPAD). Libya's inclusion in an economic recovery plan predicated on transparent governance and respect for human rights generated much controversy abroad; most Libyans suffer from rampant corruption, mismanagement, and from severe restrictions on their political and civic freedoms. The union is largely the product of Qadhafi's enthusiasm, and his promises of generous financial aid to many regional leaders have undoubtedly secured their support.

Political Rights and Civil Liberties:

Libyans cannot change their government democratically. Colonel Mu'ammar al-Qadhafi rules by decree, with almost no accountability or transparency. Libya has no formal constitution; a mixture of Islamic belief, nationalism, and socialist theory in Qadhafi's *Green Book* provides principles and structures of governance, but the document lacks legal status. Libya is officially known as a *jamahiriyah*, or state of the masses, conceived as a system of direct government through popular organs at all levels of society. In reality, an elaborate structure of revolutionary committees and people's committees serves as a tool of repression. Real power rests with Qadhafi and a small group of close associates who appoint civil and military officials at every level. In 2000, Qadhafi dissolved 14 ministries, or General People's Committees, and transferred their power to municipal councils, leaving five intact. While some praised this apparent decentralization of power, others speculated that the move was a power grab in response to rifts between Qadhafi and several ministers.

The judiciary is not independent. It includes summary courts for petty offenses, courts of first instance for more serious offenses, courts of appeal, and a supreme court. Revolutionary courts were established in 1980 to try political offenses, but were replaced in 1988 by people's courts after reportedly assuming responsibility for up to 90 percent of prosecutions. Political trials are held in secret, with no due process considerations. According to the U.S. State Department, Libya employs summary judicial techniques to suppress local opposition. Arbitrary arrest and torture are commonplace.

The death penalty applies to a number of political offenses and "economic" crimes, including currency speculation and drug- or alcohol-related crimes. Libya actively abducts and kills political dissidents in exile. The public practice of law is illegal.

In August, the government released from jail several prisoners of conscience affiliated with the banned Islamic Liberation Party. In August 2001, officials released 107 political prisoners, including one who had served 31 years in connection with an attempted coup in 1970. Hundreds of other political prisoners reportedly remain in prison. Some have been in jail for more than ten years without charge or trial. The government does not allow prison visits by human rights monitors.

Earlier in the year, Libya was nominated by the Africa group at the United Nations to chair the UN Commission on Human Rights. The nomination elicited outcry by rights groups, who appealed to the African Union to select a more suitable candidate. After its nomination as chair for the UN Commission on Human Rights, Libya indicated it would invite UN and other human rights monitors to visit Libya. It also declared its intention to review the role of the peoples' courts.

In February, a Libyan court ruled there was no evidence to indicate that seven foreign medical workers were deliberately infecting children with AIDS; Qadhafi had previously accused one Palestinian and six Bulgarian health workers of carrying out a conspiracy to undermine Libya's national security. The matter was referred to a criminal court.

Free media do not exist in Libya. Publication of opinions contrary to government policy is forbidden. The state owns and controls all media and thus controls reporting of domestic and international issues. Satellite television is widely available; access to Western news channels such as CNN is available, but foreign programming is sometimes censored. International publications are censored and sometimes prohibited. Internet access is available via one service provider, which is owned by Col. Qadhafi's son.

Academic freedom is severely restricted. Elementary, middle, and high schools are subject to intensive political indoctrination. In December, the revolutionary committee of the department of politics and economics at Garyounis University in Benghazi reportedly "purified" the department of so-called subversive elements.

Limited public debate occurs within government bodies, but free expression and the right to privacy are not respected. An extensive and pervasive security apparatus exists, including local "Revolutionary Committees" and "Purification Committees" who monitor individual activities and communications.

Independent political parties and civic associations are illegal; only associations affiliated with the regime are tolerated. Political activity considered treasonous is punishable by death. Public assembly must support, and be approved by, the government. Instances of public unrest are rare.

About 97 percent of Libyans are Sunni Muslim. Islamic groups whose beliefs and practices differ from the state-approved teaching of Islam are banned. The government controls most mosques and Islamic institutions. According to the U.S. State Department, small communities of Christians worship openly. The largely Berber and Tuareg minorities face discrimination, and Qadhafi reportedly manipulates, bribes, and incites fighting among tribes in order to maintain power.

Qadhafi's pan-African policy has led to an influx of African immigrants in recent years. Poor domestic economic conditions have contributed to resentment of these immigrants, who are often blamed for increases in crime, drug use, and the incidence of AIDS. In late September 2000, four days of deadly clashes between Libyans and other African nationals erupted as a result of a trivial dispute. Thousands of African immigrants were subsequently moved to military camps, and thousands more were repatriated to Sudan, Ghana, and Nigeria. Security measures were taken, including restrictions on the hiring of foreigners in the private sector. The incident proved an embarrassment to Qadhafi, who blamed "hidden forces" for trying to derail his united-Africa policy.

Women's access to education and employment have improved under the current regime. However, tradition dictates discrimination in family and civil matters. A woman must have her husband's permission to travel abroad.

Arbitrary investment laws, restrictions on foreign ownership of property, state domination of the economy, and continuing corruption are likely to hinder growth for years to come.

Independent trade unions and professional associations do not exist. The only federation is the government-controlled National Trade Unions Federation. There is no collective bargaining, and workers have no legal right to strike.

Liechtenstein

Polity: Principality and parliamentary democracy
Economy: Capitalist-statist
Population: 30,000
PPP: na
Life Expectancy: na
Religious Groups: Roman Catholic (80 percent,) Protestant (7.4 percent,) other (12.6 percent)
Ethnic Groups: Alemannic (88 percent), other, including Italian and Turkish (12 percent)
Capital: Vaduz

Political Rights: 1
Civil Liberties: 1
Status: Free

Ten-Year Ratings Timeline (Political Rights, Civil Liberties, Status)

1993	1994	1995	1996	1997	1998	1999	2000	2001	2002	2003
1,1F	1,1F	1,1F	1,1F	1,1F	1,1F	1,1F	1,1F	1,1F	1,1F	1,1F

Overview:

Liechtenstein faced renewed criticism for its notoriously opaque banking system, despite measurable steps it had taken in 2001 to make the system more transparent. The United States warned the small principality that Islamic militant groups may be using Liechtenstein's banks to fund their operations. The Organization for Economic Cooperation and Development (OECD) threatened sanctions if financial transparency standards were not met.

Liechtenstein was established in its present form in 1719 after being purchased by Austria's Liechtenstein family. Native residents of the state are primarily descendants of the Germanic Alemani tribe, and the local language is a German dialect.

From 1938 until 1997, the principality was governed by a coalition of the Progressive Citizens' Party (FBP) and the Fatherland Union (VU). The FBP was the senior partner for most of this period. Liechtenstein's constitution, adopted in 1921, has been amended several times.

One of the world's most secretive tax havens, Liechtenstein has in recent years faced accusations that it is a money laundering haven, favored by foreign organized-crime syndicates, including drug cartels and international terrorists. In 2000, the Paris-based Financial Action Task Force (FATF), an international anti-money-laundering group attached to the OECD, listed the country as "non-cooperative" for its secrecy laws. The OECD classified Liechtenstein as a "harmful" tax haven.

Approximately $63 billion in client money is managed among 17 local banks in Liechtenstein. The FATF blacklisting led to a marked decrease of capital flow into Liechtenstein's banks.

In June 2001, in a determined effort to burnish its image, Liechtenstein established the Institute for Compliance and Quality Management to teach local bankers and lawyers how to identify illegal banking practices. Liechtenstein also took steps to reveal the identity of banking clients.

In April 2002, however, the OECD threatened to impose sanctions against Liechtenstein after including it on a list of seven states that failed to meet financial transparency and information exchange standards. In October, United States Treasury undersecretary Jimmy Gurule visited Liechtenstein to inform it that Islamic terrorists might be taking advantage of its banking secrecy laws to finance their operations.

On the political front, Prince Hans Adam and the government remained in dispute over the degree of the royal family's powers. The prince, one of the few European monarchs whose powers are not largely ceremonial, promotes constitutional reform. He would like sole authority to appoint judges presiding over illegal banking cases. Some members of parliament claim the prince wants to centralize more authority in his own hands. The prince has threatened to arrange a referendum on constitutional reform, saying he will relocate to Austria should he lose the vote. Such a move would raise the question of how Liechtenstein would be governed.

Prince Hans Adam faced a reprimand by the European Court of Human Rights in 1999 for abusing his subjects' freedom of speech. The court fined the prince for refusing to reappoint a judge he had dismissed for suggesting that the Supreme Court, and not the prince, should have the last word in constitutional matters. The prince, who has ruled the principality since 1989, has ignored the legislature on several occasions, most notably when he had the country join the European Economic Area (EEA) despite deputies' doubts.

Parliamentary elections in February 2001 ushered in a new prime minister. Otmar Hasler, head of the FBP, assumed leadership after his party captured 13 out of 25 seats in the unicameral Landtag (Parliament). Hasler unseated Mario Frick, prime minister since 1997. Frick's VU party captured 11 seats in the latest elections, with the Free List party (FL) taking one seat.

Liechtenstein's economy is closely intertwined with Switzerland's. Its official currency is the Swiss *franc*. To reduce the country's economic dependence on Switzerland, Prince Hans Adam led the principality into membership not only in the EEA but also in the United Nations, the European Free Trade Association, the World Trade Organization, and the General Agreement on Tariffs and Trade.

Political Rights and Civil Liberties:

Liechtensteiners can change their government democratically. The prince exercises legislative powers jointly with the Landtag (parliament). He appoints the prime minister from the Landtag's majority party or coalition, and the deputy chief of the five-member government from the minority. Parties with at least 8 percent of the vote receive representation in the parliament, which is directly elected for four years on the basis of proportional representation. The sovereign possesses power to veto legislation and to dissolve the Landtag. Participation in elections and referendums is compulsory.

The government respects freedom of speech. However, Prince Hans Adam faced a reprimand by the European Court of Human Rights in 1999 for abusing his subjects' freedom of speech. The court fined the prince for refusing to reappoint a judge he had dismissed for suggesting that the Supreme Court, and not the prince, should have the last word in constitutional matters. The prince, who has ruled the principality since 1989, has ignored the legislature on several occasions, most notably when he had the country join the EEA despite deputies' doubts.

Two daily newspapers are published, each representing the interests of one of the two major political parties, as is one weekly newsmagazine. There are two television stations, one owned by the state and one private. While there is only one private radio station, residents regularly receive radio and television broadcasts from neighboring countries.

In 1998 and 1999, Liechtenstein received a high number of asylum seekers who were given temporary protection. The number of asylum seekers reaches almost 2 percent of the total population of Liechtenstein. A strict policy prevents significant numbers of second- and third-generation residents from acquiring citizenship.

Although Roman Catholicism is the state religion, other faiths are practiced freely. Roman Catholic or Protestant religious education is compulsory in all schools, but exemptions are routinely granted.

Liechtensteiners enjoy freedom of association. The principality has one small trade union. Workers have the right to strike, but have not done so in more than 25 years. The prosperous economy includes private and state enterprises. Citizens enjoy a high standard of living.

The independent judiciary, subject to the prince's appointment power, is headed by the Supreme Court and includes civil and criminal courts, as well as an administrative court of appeals and a state court to address questions of constitutionality.

Although only narrowly endorsed by male voters, the enfranchisement of women at the national level was unanimously approved in the legislature in 1984 after defeats in referenda in 1971 and 1973. By 1986, universal adult suffrage at the local level had passed in all 11 communities. In the 1989 general elections, a woman won a Landtag seat for the first time. Three years later, a constitutional amendment guaranteed legal equality. Women occupy approximately 12 percent of Liechtenstein's parliamentary seats.

Lithuania

Polity: Parliamentary democracy
Political Rights: 1
Civil Liberties: 2
Economy: Mixed capitalist **Status:** Free
Population: 3,500,000
PPP: $7,106
Life Expectancy: 73
Religious Groups: Roman Catholic, Lutheran, Russian Orthodox, other
Ethnic Groups: Lithuanian (80 percent), Russian (9 percent), Polish (7 percent), Byelorussian (2 percent), other (2 percent)
Capital: Vilnius

Ten-Year Ratings Timeline (Political Rights, Civil Liberties, Status)

1993	1994	1995	1996	1997	1998	1999	2000	2001	2002	2003
2,3F	1,3F	1,3F	1,2F	1,2F	1,2F	1,2F	1,2F	1,2F	1,2F	1,2F

Overview:
Presidential elections in December 2002 led to the first-round victory of incumbent Valdas Adamkus, who will face a second-round runoff in January 2003. In the domestic energy sector, Russian companies moved to gain control over key Lithuanian energy facilities, while the Lithuanian government agreed to close the second reactor of its Ignalina nuclear power plant in 2009. At the end of the year, the European Union (EU) and NATO both invited Lithuania to join their organizations in 2004.

Lithuania merged with Poland in the sixteenth century and was subsequently absorbed by Russia in the eighteenth century. After gaining its independence at the end of World War I, Lithuania was annexed by the Soviet Union in 1940 under a secret protocol of the 1939 Hitler-Stalin pact. The country regained its independence with the collapse of the U.S.S.R. in 1991.

Following the 1996 parliamentary elections, the Homeland Union/Lithuanian Conservatives (HU/LC) and Christian Democrats formed a center-right coalition government with Gediminas Vagnorius of the HU/LC as prime minister. In January 1998, the Lithuanian-American independent candidate, Valdas Adamkus, was narrowly elected president over former Prosecutor-General Arturas Paulauskas.

Growing tensions between Adamkus and Vagnorius over political, economic, and personal issues eventually led to the resignation of Vagnorius, who was succeeded by Vilnius mayor and HU/LC member Rolandas Paksas on May 18. However, Paksas stepped down just five months later in protest over the controversial sale of part of the state-owned Mazeikiu Nafta oil complex to the U.S. energy firm, Williams International. HU/LC member and parliamentary First Deputy Chairman Andrius Kubilius succeeded Paksas as prime minister in November.

Faced with the public's dissatisfaction over its economic austerity policies, the ruling HU/LC experienced a resounding defeat in the October 2000 parliamentary election. The Social Democratic Coalition, which united four leftist parties, including the Lithuanian Democratic Labor Party (LDDP), the successor to the Communist Party, secured the most votes. The Coalition, led by former Lithuanian Communist leader Algirdas Brazauskas, had campaigned on a platform of greater attention to social issues and increased support for the country's agricultural sector. However, the informal New Policy electoral bloc, composed of the ideologically diverse Liberal Union, New Alliance (Social Liberals), Center Union, and Modern Christian Democratic Union parties, bypassed the Social Democratic Coalition to form a bare-majority centrist government. Paksas was chosen again to be prime minister.

After only eight months in power, the unstable national ruling coalition of right- and left-wing parties collapsed in June 2001 following disagreements over the budget and privatization plans for the country's energy sector. Prime Minister Paksas was replaced in July by Brazauskas, the chairman of the Lithuanian Social Democratic Party (LSDP), which was created in January from the merger of the LDDP and the Social Democratic Party. The more ideologically compatible LSDP and New Alliance (Social Liberals) subsequently formed a new ruling coalition government. Brazauskas dismissed critics' charges that he would slow down economic and social reforms necessary for EU and NATO membership.

In presidential elections held on December 22, 2002, President Adamkus received 35 percent of the vote, not enough for a first-round victory, which requires a candidate to receive more than 50 percent. Adamkus will face Paksas, who was the second-place winner with 20 percent of the vote, in a January 5, 2003, runoff. Voter turnout during the first round was estimated at 53 percent. In concurrent local elections, a coalition of the Liberal Union and Modern Christian Democrats finished first in Vilnius, while the LSDP was the most successful party nationwide.

Russian energy companies moved to gain control over key Lithuanian energy facilities during the year. In September, the Russian oil company, Yukos, obtained a controlling interest in the Mazeikiu Nafta oil complex after Williams International announced that it would sell its 27 percent share in the company to them. One month later, Lithuania's cabinet formally named Russian gas giant Gazprom as the potential buyer of a 34 percent stake of Lietuvos Dujos (Lithuanian Gas).

In June, Lithuania agreed to close the second reactor of its Ignalina nuclear power plant in 2009 with EU financial assistance to pay for the decommissioning costs. The government had already pledged in 1999 to shut down the first reactor by 2005. A commitment to close Ignalina, regarded as one of the world's most dangerous nuclear power facilities, removes a major obstacle to Lithuania's membership in the EU. According to a report by the International Atomic Energy Agency, Lithuania is the world's most nuclear-dependent country, with Ignalina producing over 70 percent of the country's energy needs.

Lithuania achieved two of its long-term foreign policy goals when it received formal invitations in November from NATO and in December from the EU to join in 2004.

Political Rights and Civil Liberties: Lithuanians can change their government democratically. The 1992 constitution established a 141-member parliament (Seimas), in which 71 seats are selected in single-mandate constituencies and 70 seats are chosen by proportional representation, all for four-year terms. The president is directly elected for a five-year term. The 1996 and 2000 national legislative elections and the 1997-1998 presidential vote were conducted freely and fairly. All permanent residents are allowed to run and vote in local government elections.

The government generally respects freedoms of speech and of the press. There is a wide variety of privately owned newspapers, and several independent, as well as state-run, television and radio stations broadcast throughout the country.

Freedom of religion is guaranteed by law and largely enjoyed in practice in this predominantly Roman Catholic country.

Freedom of assembly and association is generally respected. Workers have the right to form and join trade unions, to strike, and to engage in collective bargaining. However, ongoing problems include inadequate or employer-biased legislation, management discrimination against union members, and the court system's lack of expertise in labor-related issues.

While the judiciary is largely independent from the executive branch, there is a severe lack of qualified judges, who consequently suffer from excessive workloads. There have been credible reports of police abuse of suspects and detainees, and overcrowding in prisons and pretrial detention facilities remains a serious problem. A massive outbreak of the HIV virus among inmates was discovered in May 2002 at the Alytus penitentiary; senior prison officials were subsequently dismissed.

To help combat corruption, Lithuania and the United Nations Development Program signed a two-year anti-corruption project in October 2002 that envisages a long-term education program for university students, public opinion polls, and comprehensive studies of corruption.

The rights of the country's ethnic minorities are protected in practice. In 1992, Lithuania extended citizenship to all those born within its borders, and more than 90 percent of nonethnic Lithuanians, mostly Russians and Poles, became citizens. Women are underrepresented in upper-level management positions and earn lower average wages than men.

Luxembourg

Polity: Parliamentary democracy
Economy: Capitalist
Population: 500,000
PPP: $50,061
Life Expectancy: 78
Religious Groups: Roman Catholic (predominant)
Ethnic Groups: Celtic, Portuguese, Italian, others
Capital: Luxembourg

Political Rights: 1
Civil Liberties: 1
Status: Free

Ten-Year Ratings Timeline (Political Rights, Civil Liberties, Status)

1993	1994	1995	1996	1997	1998	1999	2000	2001	2002	2003
1,1F	1,1F	1,1F	1,1F	1,1F	1,1F	1,1F	1,1F	1,1F	1,1F	1,1F

Overview:

Luxembourg further entered the embrace of a unified Europe early in 2002 after it adopted the euro as its official currency. However, it also faced intense criticism for blocking EU efforts to combat money laundering by maintaining its strict banking secrecy laws.

After centuries of domination and occupation by foreign powers, the small, landlocked Grand Duchy of Luxembourg was recognized as an autonomous, neutral state in 1867. After occupation by Germany in both world wars, Luxembourg abandoned its neutrality and became a vocal proponent of European integration. Luxembourg joined NATO in 1949, the Benelux Economic Union (with Belgium and the Netherlands) in 1948, the European Economic Community (later the EU) in 1957, and the European Monetary Union in 1999.

Luxembourg's multiparty electoral system is based on proportional representation. The prime minister and the cabinet exercise executive authority on behalf of the grand duke of Luxembourg. While the grand duke's role is largely ceremonial, he must sign all bills before they became law and he maintains the power to dissolve parliament. The government is appointed by the sovereign, but is responsible to the legislature. Luxembourg's current constitution, adopted in 1868, has been revised several times.

Grand Duke Henri officially opened a session of parliament in October 2001, the first time since 1877 that a member of the royal family has performed this duty. By the close of the year, Grand Duke Henri had received an 88 percent approval rating since his father abdicated his 36-year reign as constitutional monarch and handed over power to his son in September 2000.

In January, a French parliamentary committee criticized Luxembourg for blocking EU efforts to combat money laundering. They recommended the EU take action against Luxembourg to force it to reform its notoriously strong banking secrecy laws.

Political Rights and Civil Liberties:

Luxembourgers can change their government democratically. Voting is compulsory for citizens, and foreigners may register to vote after five years of residence. The prime minister is the leader of the dominant party in the 60-member, unicameral Chamber of Deputies (parliament), for which popular elections are held every five years. The grand duke appoints the 21 members of the Council of State, which serves as an advisory body to the chamber. In the June 1999 parliamentary elections, the Christian Social People's Party (PCS) won 19 seats; the Democratic Party (PD), 15; the Socialist Workers' Party of Luxembourg (POSL), 13; the Committee for Democracy and Pensions (ADR), 7; the Green Alternative (PVA), 5; and the New Left Party (NL), 1.

The constitution provides for freedom of speech and of the press. Print media are privately owned, and all media are free of censorship. The government issues licenses to private radio stations. Radio and television broadcasts from neighboring countries are freely available. In April, the European Court of Human Rights ruled that the conviction and sentencing of Marc Thorne for quoting a newspaper report on corruption was a breach of Article 10 of the European Convention of Human Rights.

Although foreigners constitute one-third of the population, anti-foreigner incidents are infrequent. Luxembourg's population grew 12 percent in the 1990s, and it is expected to nearly double by 2025. EU citizens who reside in Luxembourg enjoy the right to vote and to run in municipal elections; minimum residency requirements are 6 years for voters and 12 years for candidates.

The constitution provides for freedom of religion, and the government respects that right in practice. Roman Catholicism is the predominant religion. There is no state religion, but the state pays the salaries of Roman Catholic, Protestant, Greek and Russian Orthodox, and Jewish clergy, and several local governments subsidize sectarian religious facilities. The Anglican Church and Muslim community applied for financial support, but after four years of government consideration, these religious groups have yet to receive any financial support.

All workers have the right to associate freely and to choose their representatives. Approximately 57 percent of the labor force is unionized. Unions operate free of governmental interference. The two largest labor federations are linked to, but organized independently of, the POSL and PCS. The right to strike is constitutionally guaranteed. The law mandates a maximum workweek of 40 hours for full-time employees.

The independent judiciary is headed by the Supreme Court, whose members are appointed for life by the grand duke. Defendants are presumed innocent. They have the right to public trials and are free to cross-examine witnesses and to present evidence in court.

Women are underrepresented in government and politics. They constitute approximately 16 percent of parliament, holding 10 of the 60 seats. Women constitute 38 percent of the workforce. The law mandates equal pay for equal work and encourages the equal treatment of women. According to the International Confederation of Trade Unions, however, Luxembourg, with the highest per capita income in the EU, has one of the widest gender-pay gaps in the EU. The differences are least in the highest-paid professions and more substantial at lower salary levels. To date, there have been no work-related discrimination lawsuits in the courts.

Macedonia

Polity: Parliamentary democracy
Economy: Mixed statist (transitional)
Population: 2,000,000
PPP: $5,086
Life Expectancy: 73

Political Rights: 3*
Civil Liberties: 3*
Status: Partly Free

Religious Groups: Macedonian Orthodox (67 percent), Muslim (30 percent), other (3 percent)
Ethnic Groups: Macedonian (67 percent), Albanian (23 percent), Turkish (4 percent), Roma (2 percent), Serb (2 percent), other (2 percent)
Capital: Skopje
Ratings Change: Macedonia's political rights and civil liberties ratings both improved from 4 to 3 due to increased stability in the country and the gradual implementation of the 2001 Ohrid Agreement, which led to an end of hostilities between the Macedonian government and ethnic Albanian insurgents.

Ten-Year Ratings Timeline (Political Rights, Civil Liberties, Status)

1993	1994	1995	1996	1997	1998	1999	2000	2001	2002	2003
3,4PF	3,3PF	4,3PF	4,3PF	4,3PF	4,3PF	3,3PF	3,3PF	4,3PF	4,4PF	3,3PF

Overview:

Macedonia managed to pull back from the brink of civil war in 2002. The Macedonian parliament enacted all of the provisions of the Ohrid Agreement of August 2001; the country succeeded in holding parliamentary elections in September; and enough of a sense of normalcy returned to hold a long-awaited census. Nevertheless, relations between the Macedonian majority and the Albanian minority remained extremely tense.

Macedonia, a republic in the former Yugoslavian Communist federation, was recognized as an independent state in 1991. Internally, the country suffers from severe social and political polarization between its two primary ethnic groups—Macedonian Slavs and ethnic Albanians—and from a very weak economy. Externally, for much of the past decade Macedonia has suffered from disputes: over its name, with Greece; the status of the Macedonian language, with Bulgaria; and its northern border, with Yugoslavia. Most of these external disputes have been successfully resolved. The international community has tried in a number of ways to support Macedonia's fragile existence; the most notable example of this came in April, when the EU signed the Stabilization and Association Agreement with Skopje. This agreement is considered to be the first step down the road toward EU accession.

Four sets of multiparty parliamentary elections have been held in the country since 1991, and postindependence governments have always been careful to include Albanian parties in the ruling coalition. Parliamentary elections in 1998 resulted in the first transfer of power from the left-of-center governmental coalition that had ruled Macedonia since independence to a grouping of right-of-center, nationalist-oriented opposition parties.

Macedonian-Albanian relations deteriorated precipitously after the 1999 Kosovo war. By 2000, Albanian guerrillas who had participated in the Kosovo conflict were operating in Macedonia (often using NATO-occupied Kosovo as their base). Early Albanian guerrilla activity concentrated in areas around the Albanian-populated towns of Kumanovo and Tetovo, and involved attacks against Macedonian-government police and military units. Among the guerrillas' political demands were changes to the Macedonian constitution, greater use of the Albanian language in official institutions, and an increase in the number Albanians in the civil services. In August 2001, a meeting that many hoped would provide a political solution to the conflict was held in the town of Ohrid, and an agreement was reached. By this point, however, the conflict was already estimated to have cost the fragile Macedonian economy more than $800 million.

The conflict forced the postponement of parliamentary elections scheduled for January 2002, as well as an extension of the NATO presence in Macedonia, code-named Amber Fox, to October. Tensions remained high throughout the summer, due to a number of violent incidents, including the kidnapping of five Macedonians by Albanian gunmen in western Macedonia in August and the killings of Macedonian police officers in the same region of the country in August and September, raising doubts about whether elections could be held.

Nevertheless, in mid-September the situation had normalized sufficiently for the elections to be held. The elections resulted in a victory for the left-of-center Social Democratic Party of Macedonia (SDSM), led by Branko Crvenkovski, which succeeded in the ouster of the nationalist right-of-center coalition, led by former prime minister Ljubco Georgievski's Internal Macedonian Revolutionary Organization—Democratic Party of Macedonian National Unity (VMRO-DPMNE). The elections, however, were not interpreted as a significant change in the ideological mood of the population, but rather as a vote against the corruption of the incumbents. Governmental corruption has become a recurring theme in post-1991 Macedonian politics. Voter turnout was approximately 70 percent of the electorate.

The wild card in Macedonian politics remains the eventual behavior of the former Albanian rebels, led by Ali Ahmeti, who in June formed a political party, the Democratic Union for Integration (DUI). Ironically, several former guerrilla leaders who are now members of Ahmeti's political organization, and are supposed to enter the Macedonian government, have been banned from entering the United States because of their former activities. The rise of Ahmeti's DUI has eclipsed the older, more established Albanian parties in Macedonia, most particularly Arben Xhaferi's Democratic Party of Albanians (DPA).

Political Rights and Civil Liberties:

By and large, Macedonia's citizens can choose their political representatives in free and fair elections. Macedonia adopted a new parliamentary election law in July that created six election districts with roughly equal numbers of voters in each district. Elections are based on multi-district proportional representation. The new law is intended to simplify voting by eliminating the need for second-round runoff elections, to reduce intercommunal tensions by dividing election results across districts, and to increase minority and small-party representation. At year's end it remained too early to tell whether the law would succeed in these efforts.

Macedonia's September 2002 parliamentary elections were deemed by international organizations to be "largely in accordance with . . . international standards for democratic elections." Although there were numerous complaints about various aspects of the 2002 elections, the fact that Macedonia was able to hold them at all, even if with a small degree of violence, was considered an important success for the country after the violence of 2001.

Macedonia's most important constitutional problem remains satisfying the demands of the Albanian minority for a more privileged status within the country. According to the Ohrid Agreement (the final provisions of which were adopted by the Macedonian parliament in summer 2002), references in the Macedonian constitution to Macedonia as the "land of the Macedonian people" have been eliminated, and the Albanian language has been made an "official" language in municipalities where Albanians comprise at least 20 percent of the population. Additional constitutional reforms include granting more self-government to local municipalities; increasing the number of Albanians in the police force from their current level of about 5 percent of the total force to 25 percent by 2003 (which will be achieved by hiring some 1,000 Albanian police officers); devolving some of the powers of the central government from Skopje to local municipalities; and the granting of an amnesty for Albanian insurgents.

Macedonians are afraid these changes will only prove to be the prelude to either the possible secession of Albanian-populated areas in the country or their annexation by a "Greater Kosovo." These fears are exacerbated by current demographic trends within the country; if current trends continue, Albanians will probably be the majority population in Macedonia by 2015. Indicative of the ethnic divide between Macedonians and Albanians is the general unwillingness of Macedonians to travel into Albanian-populated western areas of the country.

Macedonia has also had difficulties in outlining clear lines of responsibility and authority between different governmental agencies in its post-Communist transition. In May, the EU issued a report criticizing the Macedonian government for failing to delineate the areas of responsibility between the Defense and Interior ministries. In the latter ministry, a specially formed unit known as the "Lions" has been accused of numerous human rights abuses. Even more of a problem in post-1991 Macedonia has been governmental corruption, which outside observers believe has reached proportions unusually high even among post-Communist countries.

The judicial system in Macedonia, apart from suffering from corruption, also has been criticized for not having a representative ethnic balance among its judges and prosecutors and for having a large backlog of cases. Judicial independence has been questioned, as judges are nominated by parliament in less than transparent procedures.

The Macedonian constitution guarantees freedom of religious belief and practice. Sixty-seven percent of the population are Orthodox Christian, and 30 percent are Muslim, while the remaining 3 percent belongs to a variety of different religious groups. A number of religious sites were destroyed or damaged in the fighting in 2001. Another blow to Macedonia's fragile unity occurred in June 2002, when at least one bishop of the unrecognized Macedonian Orthodox Church decided to recognize the canonical authority of the Serbian patriarch.

Although the government does not repress the media per se, many senior positions in state-owned media (from which the majority of the population gets its information) are filled by political appointees rather than by professional journalists. During the 2002 election campaign, state-owned media openly favored the government, and independent media did not uphold rules regulating political advertising and election coverage. Reporters are occasionally subjected to harassment and physical threat. On September 10, the same day that the journalist Ljubco Palevski published an article critical of the "Lions," his car was destroyed by an incendiary device. Also in September, members of the Ministry of the Interior threatened to file criminal charges against journalists who "diminish the reputation of the government." The media in Macedonia, however, are frequently criticized for their lack of professionalism and unwillingness to uphold recognized journalistic standards. Media on both sides of the ethnic divide in Macedonia have frequently been accused of fanning ethnic animosity with sensationalistic stories about atrocities committed by the opposing side.

Women in Macedonia enjoy the same legal rights as men, although lingering patriarchal social attitudes limit women's participation in nontraditional social roles in the economy and in government. Domestic violence and trafficking in women from former Soviet republics remain serious problems. In Muslim areas, many women are effectively disenfranchised because proxy voting by male relatives is common.

Madagascar

Polity: Presidential-parliamentary democracy
Economy: Mixed statist
Population: 16,900,000
PPP: $840
Life Expectancy: 55
Religious Groups: Indigenous beliefs (52 percent),
Christian (41 percent), Muslim (7 percent)
Ethnic Groups: Malay-Indonesian tribes, Arab, African, Indian, French
Capital: Antananarivo

Political Rights: 3*
Civil Liberties: 4
Status: Partly Free

Ratings Change: Madagascar's political rights rating declined from 2 to 3 due to sustained civil unrest and violence resulting from the December 2001 presidential election.

Ten-Year Ratings Timeline (Political Rights, Civil Liberties, Status)

1993	1994	1995	1996	1997	1998	1999	2000	2001	2002	2003
4,4PF	2,4PF	2,4PF	2,4PF	2,4PF	2,4PF	2,4PF	2,4PF	2,4PF	2,4PF	3,4PF

Overview: The year was dominated by fallout from political polarization and unrest. In April the High Constitutional Court declared Marc Ravalomanana the victor of contested December 2001 presidential elections. Official results had previously given Ravalomanana 46 percent of the vote, less than the majority required to avoid a runoff. Subsequent massive demonstrations against President Didier Ratsiraka alleged widespread government fraud, while a runoff was supposed to take place by mid-February 2002. Ravalomanana, however, claimed that he had been denied an outright victory by polling irregularities and refused to take part in a runoff. His position was subsequently endorsed by the High Court, but President Ratsiraka refused to acknowledge the court's ruling.

Unrest and violence occurred between supporters of the two rival candidates during the year, but Ravalomanana succeeded in establishing his authority over the country in stages, with Ratsiraka's supporters holding out the longest in eastern Madagascar, his traditional region of support. Ratsiraka left the country on July 5, and the last of his forces subsequently surrendered. Although most of the country's traditional diplomatic partners, and international bodies such as the United Nations eventually recognized the Ravalomanana government, the African Union had not done so by the end of 2002. The extended crisis had a seriously negative effect on the Malagasy economy.

Parliamentary elections took place on December 15, 2002. Backers of Madagascar's President Marc Ravolamanana won a large majority. Observers from the European Union said the conduct of the poll was "generally positive" despite a few reported "lapses", while the International Francophone Organization said it was "credible and transparent." One provincial governor, a nephew of former president Ratsiraka, resigned, charging that the vote was marred by serious irregularities and nepotism.

Madagascar, the world's fourth-largest island, lies 220 miles off Africa's southeastern coast. After 70 years of French colonial rule and episodes of severe repression, Madagascar gained independence in 1960. A leftist military junta seized power from President Philbert Tsiranana in 1972. A member of the junta, Admiral Ratsiraka, emerged as leader in 1975 and maintained power until his increasingly authoritarian regime bowed to social unrest and nonviolent mass demonstrations in 1991. Under a new 1992 constitution, opposition leader Albert Zafy won the presidency with more than 65 percent of the vote. President Zafy failed to win reelection after being impeached by the Supreme Court in 1996. Ratsiraka won a narrow victory in a December 1996 presidential runoff election that was deemed generally legitimate by international and domestic observers.

Until the 2001-2002 presidential crisis, Madagascar had made some progress in consolidating its democratic institutions, although a weak party system complicated efforts at governance. Legislative elections in May 1998 were viewed as more problematic than preceding polls taken since Madagascar's transition to multiparty politics in 1992. The Council of Christian Churches and several political groups, for example, noted that the elections were marred by fraud and other abuses. AREMA won 63 of 150 parliamentary seats and emerged as the leading force in a coalition government. A new party led by Norbert Ratsirahonana, a former prime minister, fared well in and around the capital of Antananarivo. A decentralization plan was narrowly approved in a 1998 referendum that was boycotted by the country's increasingly fractious opposition. In 2001 the first-ever senate elections, part of a policy to extend democratic governance, finally took place after a long delay.

Race and ethnicity are important factors in Madagascar's politics. Its population, mostly very poor, is divided between highland Merina people of Malay origin and coastal peoples mostly of mixed (Malayo-Polynesian, Arab, and African) descent or of black-African origin.

Political Rights and Civil Liberties: In theory citizens have the right to change their government democratically, although the recent presidential election demonstrates that in practice this right is not yet fully recognized. The president is directly elected by universal adult suffrage. Since 1992, two presidential elections have resulted in the defeat of the incumbent and one president was impeached by parliament.

The legislature is bicameral. The lower chamber, the National Assembly (Antenimieram Pirenena), has 150 members, directly elected for five-year terms. The upper chamber, the Senate, has 90 members—two-thirds of them elected by an electoral college, the remainder nominated by the president—all for six-year terms. Prior to the December 2002 parliamentary election, AREMA was the largest party in the National Assembly; it also had won 49 of the 60 seats in senatorial elections in March 2001. A 1998 constitutional referendum gave the president the power to appoint or dismiss the prime minister (who may come from a party that has a minority of seats in the assembly); formerly the National Assembly had this power.

November 1999 municipal polls resulted in overall success for independents who did not have close identification with a particular party. Elections were held in December 2000 for provincial councils, as the next step in the government's decentralization policy. Approximately 150 parties are registered amid a welter of shifting political alliances. A variety of parties exist and are active, but they suffer from internal divisions and lack of clear ideology and resources.

As has been graphically evidenced by events over the past year, political and civic organizations exercise their right to affect the public policy process. Massive protests against President Didier Ratsiraka's attempts to cling to power highlighted much of this period (as they had 12 years earlier, at the end of Ratsiraka's dictatorship). Less dramatically, in 1999 opposition leaders and the Madagascar Council of Christian Churches undertook a public information campaign to revise the constitution to limit the powers of the president. In 2000, opposition parties not represented in the legislature formed the *Cellule de Crise* (Crisis Cell) to unite against the ruling coalition. In January 2001, demonstrations occurred in the capital with opposition supporters calling for Ratsiraka to step down in favor of Ravalomanana.

With the stated intent of reestablishing a rule of law, President Ravalomanana sought to arrest and prosecute individuals who were involved in acts of "terrorism" or murder during the recent crisis. Most of these people were pro-Ratsiraka and *cotiers* (coastal people). Some observers have claimed that the actual or rumored arrests of key Ratsiraka supporters were designed to intimidate Ravolamana's opponents prior to the December legislative elections. In turn, however, the media and some in the public have denounced this accusation as an attempt to destabilize the new regime by "tribalizing" the arrests.

Overall the judiciary is demonstrating increasing autonomy. A lack of training, resources, and personnel hampers the courts' effectiveness. Case backlogs are prodigious. Most of the 20,000 people held in the country's prisons are pretrial detainees, who suffer extremely harsh conditions. In many rural areas, customary law courts that follow neither due process nor standardized judicial procedure often issue summary and severe punishments.

According to the BBC, since the departure of former President Ratsiraka in July 2002, the media in Madagascar have become less polarized, even though the division of the country into two political camps following the disputed December 2001 presidential elections is still felt in some quarters. Madagascar's 17 million people have access to six daily newspapers and a number of weeklies and monthlies, as well as numerous TV and radio stations. Because of the low literacy rate, the print media are mostly aimed at the French-educated urban elite. Some formerly pro-Ratsiraka radio stations, which used to operate like "hate radios" during the crisis, have switched to more mainstream forms of broadcasting.

Approximately 45 percent of the workforce is female. Malagasy women hold significantly more governmental and managerial positions than women in continental African countries. At the same time, they face societal discrimination and enjoy fewer opportunities than men for higher education and official employment.

The right to free association is respected, and hundreds of nongovernmental organizations, including lawyers' and human rights groups, are active. The government does not interfere with religious rights. More than half of the population adheres to traditional Malagasy religions and coexists with Christians and Muslims. In 1997, the Rally for Madagascar's Muslim Democrats was registered as the country's first Islamic political party.

Workers' rights to join unions and to strike are exercised frequently. Some of the country's labor organizations are affiliated with political groups. More than four-fifths of the labor force is employed in agriculture, fishing, and forestry at subsistence wages. Madagascar ranked 145 out of 173 countries in the U.N. Development Program's 2002 Human Development Index.

Malawi

Polity: Presidential-parliamentary democracy
Economy: Capitalist
Population: 10,900,000
PPP: $615
Life Expectancy: 38
Religious Groups: Protestant (55 percent), Roman Catholic (20 percent), Muslim (20 percent), indigenous beliefs (3 percent), other (2 percent)
Ethnic Groups: Chewa, Nyanja, Lomwe, Ngonde, Tumbuku, Yao, Sena, Tonga, Ngoni, Asian, European
Capital: Lilongwe

Political Rights: 4
Civil Liberties: 4*
Status: Partly Free

Ratings Change: Malawi's civil liberties rating declined from 3 to 4 due to continued attacks on the press and opposition politicians by the ruling party's youth wing, and the president's attempt to ban demonstrations.

Ten-Year Ratings Timeline (Political Rights, Civil Liberties, Status)

1993	1994	1995	1996	1997	1998	1999	2000	2001	2002	2003
6,7NF	6,5NF	2,3F	2,3F	2,3F	2,3F	2,3F	3,3PF	3,3PF	4,3PF	4,4PF

Overview:

Political tension escalated in Malawi in 2002 as President Bakili Muluzi and his supporters attempted to alter the constitution to allow Muluzi to run for a third term in elections scheduled for 2004. The effort failed by only three votes in parliament in July, and the issue is likely to resurface before the next presidential polls. Muluzi in May 2002 banned demonstrations against the third-term issue, but a high court reversed his decree. A group known as the Young Democrats, linked to the ruling United Democratic Front (UDF), continued to wage a campaign of intimidation against the government's opponents and the press. Several foreign donors suspended aid to Malawi in 2002 following revelations that senior government officials and members of parliament allegedly benefited from the sale of strategic grain reserves as the country faced famine. At least three million Malawians faced serious food shortages as the result of floods, drought, and the sale of grain reserves.

President (later President-for-Life) Hastings Kamuzu Banda ruled Malawi for nearly three decades after the country gained independence from Britain in 1963. Banda exercised dictatorial and often eccentric rule through the Malawi Congress Party (MCP) and its paramilitary youth wing, the Malawi Young Pioneers. Facing a domestic economic crisis and strong international pressure, he accepted a referendum approving multiparty rule in 1993. Muluzi won the presidency in an election in

1994 beset by irregularities, but seen as largely free and fair. The army's violent December 1993 dispersal of the Young Pioneers helped clear the way for the polls.

Agriculture in Malawi employs 80 percent of the labor force and the economy is dependent on tobacco. Wealth is concentrated in the hands of a small elite. Foreign donors accused the government of corruption and mismanagement in 2002, in part because of the $38 million sale of the country's strategic grain reserves. President Muluzi sacked the former agriculture minister in connection with the scandal and appointed a commission to investigate the grain sale. By the end of 2002, Denmark, the United States, Great Britain, the EU, and the IMF had suspended development aid, which had totaled more than $70 million.

Political Rights and Civil Liberties:

The citizens of Malawi are guaranteed the right to choose their leaders. Suffrage is universal except for serving members of the military. The opposition appealed the results of the 1994 elections, which were considered Malawi's first generally free and fair multiparty elections. The results of the June 1999 presidential poll went to the courts as well. Three presidential contenders sued the electoral commission, contending that Bakili Muluzi failed to win votes from more than half of the eligible electorate. Muluzi won 51 percent, compared with 44 percent for leading opposition candidate Gwanda Chakuamba, of the MCP and the Alliance for Democracy (MCP-AFORD). The Supreme Court upheld the results of the election. In polls for the national assembly in 1999 the ruling UDF managed to retain a narrow majority.

Violence erupted in opposition strongholds of northern Malawi after the 1999 election results indicated wins for the UDF. Supporters of MCP-AFORD attacked mosques, shops, and homes of suspected UDF supporters. The electoral commission has shown bias in favor of the ruling party in the past, and there have been problems with voter registration.

The judiciary has demonstrated broad independence in its decisions, but due process is not always respected by an overburdened court system that lacks resources and training.

Rights of free expression and free assembly are generally respected. Many human rights organizations and other nongovernmental organizations operate openly and without interference. Police brutality is still said to be common, either while detainees are in custody or when they are just released. Arbitrary arrest and detention are common. Appalling prison conditions lead to many deaths, including suffocation from overcrowding.

The Malawi Human Rights Commission in August 2002 said political violence was on the rise as political divisions deepened ahead of the elections in 2004. The commission said the politicization along the lines of ethnicity and regionalism was encouraging violence and discrimination. Brown Mpinganjira, leader of the opposition pressure group the National Democratic Alliance, was ambushed at a police roadblock in 2002 but escaped. Members of the opposition have blamed the Young Democrats for such attacks. The group is a reminder of the Young Pioneers, who waged their own terror campaign against opponents of the late president, Hastings Kamuzu Banda. An opposition leader, Danga Mughogho, was detained in September 2002 and accused of inciting demonstrations. Judges, lawyers, and journalists have complained of harassment and intimidation as well.

Freedom of speech and of the press is guaranteed. It is generally respected in practice, but there were a number of attacks on the press in 2002, allegedly committed by members of the Young Democrats. The government has used libel and other laws to harass journalists. The government in 2002 banned a debate organized by the Lilongwe Press Club about President Muluzi's attempt to run for a third term. A presidential adviser later assembled a group of at least 1,000 demonstrators in front of the Blantyre Newspaper Limited and allegedly incited the crowd to threaten two journalists who had written articles against a third term for Muluzi. In February 2002, a reporter was abducted from the offices of *The Chronicle,* and an editor and other staff members were assaulted by youths allegedly linked to the ruling party.

Despite occasional restrictions and harassment, a broad spectrum of opinion is presented in Malawi's two-dozen newspapers. The state-owned Malawi Broadcasting Corporation controls television and most radio service, which reach a larger audience than print media does. There are seven private radio stations.

Religious freedom is usually respected, but Muslims were targeted in post-election violence in 1999 in protest against the ruling party. President Muluzi is a Muslim. Malawi is 75 percent Christian and 20 percent Muslim.

Despite constitutional guarantees of equal protection, customary practices maintain de facto discrimination against women in education, employment, and business. Traditional rural structures deny women inheritance and property rights, and violence against women is reportedly routine. However, there has been increased attention to domestic violence and greater effort to improve the rights of widows. Women employees recently won the right to maternity leave.

The right to organize and to strike is legally protected, with notice and mediation requirements for workers in essential services. Unions are active but face harassment and occasional violence during strikes. Collective bargaining is widely practiced.

Malaysia

Polity: Dominant party
Economy: Capitalist
Population: 24,400,000
PPP: $9,068
Life Expectancy: 73
Religious Groups: Muslim, Buddhist, Daoist, Hindu, other
Ethnic Groups: Malay and other indigenous (58 percent), Chinese (27 percent), Indian (8 percent), other (7 percent)
Capital: Kuala Lumpur

Political Rights: 5
Civil Liberties: 5
Status: Partly Free

Ten-Year Ratings Timeline (Political Rights, Civil Liberties, Status)

1993	1994	1995	1996	1997	1998	1999	2000	2001	2002	2003
5,4PF	4,5PF	4,5PF	4,5PF	4,5PF	4,5PF	5,5PF	5,5PF	5,5PF	5,5PF	5,5PF

Overview:

Malaysians were shocked in June 2002 when long-standing prime minister, Mahathir Mohamad, announced his intention to retire from politics in 2003. Deputy Prime Minister Abdullah Badawi was appointed as his successor by the party leadership. Mahathir's retirement signaled a power transition, which has increased infighting in the dominant party, the United Malays National Organization (UMNO), part of a 14-party coalition known as the National Front. This transition is taking place while UMNO is fighting to maintain its superiority over the opposition Islamic Party of Malaysia (PAS). The two parties clashed in July over PAS's attempt to introduce strict *Sharia* (Islamic law) in Terengganu state and continued to disagree over the role of Islam in society and over Malaysia's response to the U.S.-led war on terrorism. The government made liberal use of the harsh Internal Security Act (ISA) throughout the year to constrain the activities of opposition parties as well as suspected Islamic militants. A crackdown on illegal immigrants, in which thousands of workers and their families were rounded up into detention camps and deported, led to rising tensions with neighboring Indonesia and the Philippines as well as to strains in the Malaysian economy.

Malaysia was founded in 1963 through a merger of the former British colony of Malaya with the British colonies of Sarawak, Sabah, and Singapore (Singapore withdrew in 1965). The ruling National Front coalition has won at least a two-thirds majority in all 10 general elections since 1957. The Front consists of 14 mainly race- and ethnic-based parties, led by the conservative, Malay-based UMNO. Since becoming prime minister in 1981, Mahathir, the UMNO leader, has helped transform Malaysia from a sleepy backwater into a high-tech exporter. Arguing that economic development must come before individual liberties, he has also sharply restricted freedom of expression and other basic rights.

Malaysia's economy notched up nearly a decade of growth until 1997, when the regional financial crisis caused growth to slow sharply. As the economy slid into recession in 1998, Mahathir loosened fiscal and monetary policies to stimulate growth. The crisis precipitated a political struggle between Mahathir and Anwar Ibrahim, his deputy prime minister, who disagreed with dimensions of economic policy and launched a challenge to his rule. In September 1998, Mahathir sacked Anwar and had him detained on corruption and sodomy charges. Anwar was later convicted and jailed for abuse of power and covering up corruption, in a trial that international and domestic observers said was politically motivated.

Amnesty International declared Anwar a prisoner of conscience, echoing a widespread belief among Malaysians that Mahathir's real aim in prosecuting Anwar was to sideline him from politics. Mahathir's crude treatment of Anwar contributed to a large swing in the ethnic Malay vote to PAS from UMNO in the November 1999 parliamentary elections. While the National Front kept its two-thirds majority in parliament, UMNO itself lost 20 seats and PAS gained an equal number, overtaking the Chinese-based Democratic Party (DAP) as Malaysia's largest opposition party. The National Justice Party (Keadilan), a new secular party formed by Anwar's wife, Wan Azizah Ismail, won five seats.

Since the election, both Mahathir and PAS have tried to woo ethnic Malay voters with appeals to Malay unity and their competing visions of the proper role of Islam in a modern nation. Mahathir declared Malaysia an "Islamic state" in 2000 to offset PAS's appeal. Long a champion of Muslim Malay interests but within a secular, tolerant society, Mahathir used the terror attacks of September 11, 2001, on the United States to link PAS to Islamic extremism. PAS's condemnation of the U.S. military campaign in Afghanistan also appeared to be aimed at bolstering its support among Malays. It risked, however, alienating moderate Muslims and proved to be too divisive for the DAP, which in October 2001 pulled out of the Alternative Front. Attempts by both parties to use *Sharia* as an issue resurfaced in 2002. In July, the PAS-dominated legislature in the northeastern state of Terengganu approved a bill to introduce Islamic criminal law. However, it has little chance of being implemented because of opposition from the UMNO-dominated federal government. PAS, like UMNO, is undergoing a leadership change—the party president, Fadzil Nor, died after a heart operation in June—and appears to have become more conservative under its new hard-line leader, Abdul Hadi Awang.

In addition to fighting for the Malay heartland, Mahathir has made increasing use of the ISA. Ten opposition activists (most of them senior Keadilan members) were arrested in 2001 for allegedly planning armed anti-government protests, and 12 PAS members or supporters were arrested for allegedly planning an Islamic-based revolt. The government made several further rounds of arrests throughout 2002, although these focused on suspected Islamic militants and members of the Malaysian Mujahideen Group (KMM) rather than members of the political opposition. Close to 120 detainees are currently being held without trial, with around 70 suspected of militant activities.

The government was buoyed by two by-election victories in early 2002 and a by-election in Sabah this fall. The Democratic Party of Sabah (PBS), the leading opposition party in that state, rejoined the National Front and strengthened the government's control of East Malaysia. In September, Mahathir confirmed that he intended to retire completely from politics in 2003. Despite his resignation, Mahathir remains a popular leader.

Political Rights and Civil Liberties: Malaysia's constitution vests executive power in a prime minister and cabinet. The House of Representatives, which has 193 members, is directly elected for a five-year term, while the 70-member Senate serves a six-year term. Over time, the government has concentrated power in the prime minister's hands, while parliament has become less of a forum for real debate, according to the U.S. State Department's report on Malaysia's human rights record in 2001. The report noted, however, that opposition legislators do vigorously question government officials in parliament, although the questions are not often answered.

Malaysians face many hurdles to changing their government through elections as well as restrictions on many basic rights. The government gives itself an overwhelming advantage in elections through its selective allocation of state funds to supporters, use of security laws to restrict the rights to free expression and peaceful assembly, and partisan use of broadcast media. The government tightened its hold on elections through a more restrictive election law and redistricting this year. Opposition parties also allege that the government uses its control of state funds to punish and deter support for the opposition. Despite these obstacles, the opposition PAS in 1999 retained control of Kelantan state and captured oil-rich Terengganu for the first time.

Political news coverage and editorials in Malaysia's main private newspapers strongly support the government line. Most major papers are owned by businessmen and companies close to the ruling National Front. The PAS newspaper has had its ability to publish curtailed. The Printing Presses and Publications Act (PPPA) requires all publishers and printing firms to obtain an annual permit to operate, which can be withdrawn without judicial review. Foreign publications are subject to censorship, and issues containing critical articles are frequently delayed. The Official Secrets Act, the Sedition Act, and the Broadcasting Act also impose wide restrictions on freedom of expression. Government pressure was suspected when more than 40 journalists resigned or were laid off from the *Sun* newspaper after it published a politically sensitive story in January. Mahathir has also increased official pressure on Malaysiakini.com, an online news daily. State-run Radio Television Malaysia and the two private television stations offer flattering coverage of the government and rarely air opposition views. "Sensitive" political issues, including race, language, and religion, are not allowed to be discussed even though they continue to dominate politics. Many journalists practice self-censorship.

Islam is Malaysia's official religion, but Buddhists, Christians, Hindus, Sikhs, and other religious minorities worship freely in this secular country. The government restricts the rights of Muslims to practice teachings other than those of Sunni Islam and monitors the activities of the Shia minority as well as occasionally arresting Shias under the Internal Security Act (ISA). Partly to prevent the opposition PAS from spreading its political message through mosques, authorities keep close tabs on sermons in state-affiliated mosques. In November, the government-controlled state of Kedah announced its intention to install video cameras and recording devices in mosques to deter preachers from delivering political sermons. *Sharia* courts run by each of Malaysia's 13 states have authority among Muslims over family and property matters. Activists allege that women are sometimes subject to discriminatory interpretations of Islamic law in inheritance and divorce matters, according to the U.S. State Department's human rights report. PAS-controlled administrations in Kelantan and Terengganu have imposed some religious-based dress, dietary, and cultural restrictions on Muslims. In September, Kelantan imposed a ban on all performances by women and by rock groups, and a total of 120 women were fined between January and May for not adhering to the state's dress code.

The government places significant restrictions on freedom of assembly. Police have forcibly broken up many of the dozens of antigovernment demonstrations held since Anwar's 1998 jailing and arrested hundreds of protesters, including many opposition leaders. Courts acquitted many of those arrested, but sentenced some to jail terms of from one to three months. Many were accused of violating the 1967 Police Act, which requires permits for all public gatherings except for workers on picket lines. Opposition groups faced a new stumbling block to reaching supporters after the government in July 2001 banned all political rallies, stating they posed a threat to national security. Following the ban, police denied permits for PAS to hold political meetings, broke up several unauthorized gatherings, and used the ISA to arrest at least a dozen PAS members or supporters. At a PAS rally held in the northern state of Kedah in February 2002, police reportedly dispersed crowds with tear gas and arrested 31 people. Lim Kit Siang, the chairman of the opposition DAP, and a number of DAP members were arrested several times during the year for distributing leaflets urging that Malaysia's constitutional status as a secular country remain unchanged.

Malaysia has thousands of active nongovernmental organizations (NGOs), but authorities have refused to register some groups. The 1966 Societies Act requires any NGO with more than six members, including political parties, to register with the government. University students are legally barred from being active without their school's permission in any political party, NGO, or trade union. The Universities and University Colleges Act also bans political rallies and meetings on campuses; the Malaysian government tightened its restrictions on student activities this year, as part of an effort to curb support for the opposition among young voters. Human Rights Watch noted that in October 2001, 61 university lecturers "alleged to be engaged in anti-government activities were warned, transferred, or fired."

Most Malaysian workers can join trade unions, with the exception of police and defense officials and small numbers of "confidential" and "managerial and executive" workers. The law permits a union to represent only workers in single, or similar, trades or industries. Labor laws restrict strikes by allowing the government to refer labor disputes to the Industrial Court and prohibiting strikes while disputes are before that court. In practice, workers rarely strike. Unions, however, bargain collectively in many industries. Less than 10 percent of Malaysian workers are unionized. An immigration law amended in 2002 provides for heavy fines, imprisonment, or caning of illegal workers and those who recruit and employ them. As part of an effort to tighten its borders and curb crime, Malaysia tightened up its policy regarding illegal workers and launched a controversial operation that affected hundreds of thousands of migrants, who are regularly subjected to arbitrary harassment by state officials. In August, allegations of mistreatment and sexual abuse at a detention camp for illegal migrant workers led to complaints from the Philippine government.

Although the impartiality of the judiciary appeared to improve during 2001 under the stewardship of Chief Justice Mohamad Dzaiddin Abdullah, "government action, constitutional amendments, legislation and other factors" continued to undermine its independence, according to the U.S. State Department. Domestic and international human rights groups roundly condemned as politically motivated both former deputy prime minister Anwar Ibrahim's six-year prison sentence in 1999 for abuse of power, and a nine-year sentence in 2000 for sodomy. In July, Malaysia's highest court rejected Anwar's appeal to overturn his 1999 conviction. Meanwhile, Ezam Mohamad Noor, an ally of Anwar's and youth leader of the Keadilan party, was convicted in August under the Official Secrets Act for leaking state secrets and sentenced to two years in prison.

However, the courts did rule against the government several times in 2002. In September, the high court decided that the police had acted wrongly in arresting five opposition activists last year. A court in November ordered the release of Nasharuddin Nasir, a businessman held for more than six months under the ISA on suspicion of belonging to a terrorist organization. He was released the following day but immediately re-arrested. According to the BBC, Mahathir then announced his intention that the courts would be stopped from challenging the police and government over arrests ordered under the ISA.

Malaysia's police have in recent years killed dozens of criminal suspects. Press reports suggest that some of the police killings may have been appropriate under the circumstances. Authorities have prosecuted officers in some death cases. Police also at times torture, beat, or otherwise abuse ordinary prisoners and detainees, according to Amnesty International. Following its first public inquiry, Malaysia's official Human Rights Commission ruled in August 2001 that police used excessive force in breaking up a November 2000 Keadilan rally just outside Kuala Lumpur. The commission, however, lacks enforcement powers and can only recommend governmental action.

The government detains hundreds of suspects each year under the ISA and two other acts that also permit long-term detention without judicial review or formal charges—the 1969 Emergency Ordinance and the 1985 Dangerous Drugs Act. Both the ISA and the Emergency Ordinance allow authorities to detain suspects for up to two years. Enacted in 1960 to mop up the remnants of a Communist insurgency, the ISA has in recent years been used for long-term detention of suspected Communist activists, ordinary criminal suspects, and members of "deviant" Muslim sects. Domestic and international human rights groups have criticized the government's use of the ISA to jail political opponents. At year's end, a number of opposition politicians and activists arrested under the ISA during 2001 remained in jail under two-year detention orders. They included Keadilan deputy leader Tian Chua, and social activist and media columnist Hishamuddin Rais. A pattern of arrests continued throughout 2002, but the focus shifted to alleged Islamic militants, with at least 70 being detained during the year. In May, Human Rights Watch stated that there were 105 ISA detainees being held in Kamunting prison camp.

Despite continued gains, women are still underrepresented in the professions, civil service, and politics. The government has in recent years introduced programs to promote women's equality in education and employment, adopted a law against domestic violence, and created programs to help victims of spousal abuse and rape. Some convicted rapists receive heavy punishments, including caning, but women's groups say many others receive sentences that are too light. In June, the *Asian Times* reported that more than 70 women's groups expressed their concern over the proposed imposition of strict *Sharia* in Terengganu state.

Some ethnic Chinese and Indians as well as many Malays criticized the government's April 2001 decision to extend by 10 years a long-standing policy that aims to boost the economic status of ethnic Malays and indigenous people through favored treatment in many areas. These include property ownership, higher education, civil service jobs, and business affairs. Critics say the system should be based on need rather than race. The government says the quotas have improved racial harmony. They were established in 1970 in response to anti-Chinese riots in 1969 that killed nearly 200 people. Despite some gains in wealth and professional achievement, Malays remain poorer on average than ethnic Chinese. Yet, Chinese and Indians lack the same access to the state and are considered by many as "second class" citizens, and their parties within the National Front lack the clout of earlier years.

Indigenous people in peninsular Malaysia and the Borneo states generally have little input into government and business decisions affecting them. Logging companies continue to encroach on land traditionally held by indigenous groups in the Borneo states. State governments in peninsular Malaysia are moving slowly in carrying out federal orders to transfer individual land titles to many of the roughly 100,000 indigenous people there, according to the U.S. State Department Human Rights report.

Maldives

Polity: Presidential
Economy: Capitalist
Population: 300,000
PPP: $4,485
Life Expectancy: 67
Religious Groups: Sunni Muslim
Ethnic Groups: South Indians, Sinhalese, Arabs
Capital: Male

Political Rights: 6
Civil Liberties: 5
Status: Not Free

Ten-Year Ratings Timeline (Political Rights, Civil Liberties, Status)

1993	1994	1995	1996	1997	1998	1999	2000	2001	2002	2003
6,5NF	6,6NF	6,6NF	6,6NF	6,6NF	6,6NF	6,5NF	6,5NF	6,5NF	6,5NF	6,5NF

Overview:

Early this year, the government entered into a partnership with the Asian Development Bank to help reduce poverty and economic vulnerability. In March, the Maldives was removed by the Organization for Economic Cooperation and Development from its list of uncooperative tax havens. With 80 percent of the country's area being one meter or less above sea level, the government remains concerned that the low-lying islands will be vulnerable if global warming leads to a rise in sea levels.

Consisting of a 500-mile-long string of 26 atolls in the Indian Ocean, the Maldives achieved independence in 1965 after 78 years as a British protectorate. A 1968 referendum set up a republican government, ending 815 years of rule by the ad-Din sultanate.

President Maumoon Abdul Gayoom has ruled since 1978, when he won his first of five 5-year terms under the country's tightly controlled presidential referendum process. Under the 1968 constitution, Maldivians cast straight yes-or-no votes in these referendums on a single candidate chosen by the Majlis (parliament). A 1998 constitutional amendment allowed citizens to declare their candidacies, but not campaign for the presidential nomination. At the most recent presidential referendum on October 16, 1998, Gayoom won the approval of a reported 90.9 percent of participating voters. He faced four minor challengers for the Majlis's nomination.

The most serious threat to Gayoom's survival came in 1988, when Indian commandos crushed a coup attempt by a disgruntled businessman reportedly backed by Sri Lankan mercenaries. In the aftermath, the autocratic Gayoom strengthened the National Security Service and named several relatives to top governmental posts.

Political Rights and Civil Liberties:

Maldivians cannot change their head of government through elections, and they face restrictions on freedom of expression and many other basic rights. The constitution grants the president broad executive powers and allows him to appoint 8 of the Majlis's 48 members (the remainder are directly elected). Nevertheless, in recent years the Majlis has rejected some governmental legislation and has held lively policy debates.

The 1998 presidential referendum took place "in an atmosphere of fear and intimidation," according to Amnesty International. In addition to making arrests prior to the 1999 parliamentary elections, authorities also banned public campaign events, permitting only small meetings on private premises. Political parties are officially discouraged, and candidates for the Majlis run as individuals. Amnesty International reported that in February 2001, 42 people, including academics, intellectuals, businessmen, and three members of parliament, petitioned the Minister for Home Affairs for permission to set up the Maldivian Democratic Party. The president decided against the petition, and several of the signatories were detained throughout the year.

The government has in recent years held several political prisoners. They include Umar Jamaal, one of several candidates arrested in advance of the 1999 Majlis elections. Authorities detained Jamaal and three others in early 2001, presumably because they had supported a bill before parliament on the rights of detainees, Amnesty International said in its report on human rights in the Maldives in 2001.

The law allows authorities to shut newspapers and sanction journalists for articles containing unfounded criticism of the government. Moreover, regulations make editors responsible for the content of material they publish. Four Internet writers were arrested early in the year, and after being held in detention and charged with defamation in May, three were sentenced to life imprisonment. In this environment, journalists practice self-censorship, although less so than in the past, the U.S. State Department Human Rights report said. Today, newspapers such as the daily *Aafathis* criticize government policies, and the state-run television station's news and public affairs programs discuss timely issues and criticize government performance. All broadcast media are government owned and operated.

Freedom of religion is restricted by the government's requirement that all citizens be Sunni Muslims, a legal ban against the practice of other religions, and a constitutional provision making Islam the state religion. In early 2002, four individuals were arrested for distributing Islamist and antigovernment literature, according to the U.S. State Department report on International Religious Freedom. Non-Muslim foreigners are allowed to practice their religion privately. There were no reported restrictions on academic freedom.

The government limits freedom of assembly and association. The government has in recent years imprisoned several dissidents under broadly drawn laws. The penal code bans speech or actions that could "arouse people against the government." A 1968 law prohibits speech considered inimical to Islam, libelous, or a threat to national security.

The Maldives has no known nongovernmental human rights groups. Workers lack the legal rights to form trade unions, stage strikes, or bargain collectively. In practice, no unions exist although some workers have established informal associations that address labor issues. The Maldives has about 27,000 foreign workers out of a total workforce of 70,000 to 75,000 persons. Most workers are in the informal sector, although some work in the country's high-end tourism industry, which provides 70 percent of foreign exchange revenues.

Because President Gayoom can review high court decisions and appoint and dismiss judges, "the judiciary is subject to executive influence," according to the U.S. State Department's report on the Maldives's human rights record in 2001. Civil law is generally used in civil and criminal cases although it is subordinate to *Sharia* (Islamic law). The latter is used in matters not covered by civil law as well as in certain cases such as those involving divorce or adultery. Under Sharia, the testimony of two women is equal to that of one man and men are favored in divorce and inheritance matters.

In a positive move, the government amended the 1990 Prevention of Terrorism Act (PTA) in 1998 to place some limits on police detention of suspects under investigation. Judges, however, can still authorize suspects to be detained without trial, on a monthly basis, if authorities have not started legal proceedings within 22 days of the arrest.

More women are entering the civil service, increasingly receive equal pay to that of men for equal work, and enjoy a 98 percent literacy rate, compared with 96 percent for men. However, traditional norms that oppose letting women lead independent lives outside their homes continue to limit educational and career opportunities for many women. The government has in recent years sponsored programs to help make women aware of their rights. It has also expressed concern about the divorce rate, which according to the United Nations is the highest in the world.

Children's rights are incorporated into law, and government policy provides for equal access to educational and health programs for both male and female children. In October 2002, parliament passed a law raising the age of consent for marriage from 16 to 18, in order to ensure greater protection for children.

Mali

Polity: Presidential-parliamentary democracy
Economy: Mixed statist
Population: 11,300,000
PPP: $797
Life Expectancy: 47
Religious Groups: Muslim (90 percent), indigenous beliefs (9 percent), Christian (1 percent)
Ethnic Groups: Mande (50 percent), Peul (17 percent), Voltaic (12 percent), Tuareg and Moor (10 percent), Songhai (6 percent), other (5 percent)
Capital: Bamako

Political Rights: 2
Civil Liberties: 3
Status: Free

Ten-Year Ratings Timeline (Political Rights, Civil Liberties, Status)

1993	1994	1995	1996	1997	1998	1999	2000	2001	2002	2003
2,3F	2,3F	2,4PF	2,3F	2,2F	3,3F	3,3F	3,3F	2,3F	2,3F	2,3F

Overview:

Former general Amadou Toumani Toure won presidential elections in May 2002, defeating the former ruling party's candidate, Soumaila Cisse. Although many of the other 22 presidential candidates rejected the results after the first round of voting and claimed fraud, international observers said that despite some administrative irregularities the vote was generally free and fair. Toure, who ran as an independent, headed Mali during the transition period to multiparty politics in the early 1990s. He has a strong international profile because he has been active in regional peace and humanitarian efforts as a UN envoy. Shortly after assuming office, he granted civil servants a 30 percent salary increase as complaints mounted over price hikes for food, water, and electricity since March 2002. Legislative elections held in July were marked by low turnout.

After achieving independence from France in 1960, Mali was ruled by military or one-party dictators for more than 30 years. After soldiers killed more than 100 demonstrators demanding a multiparty system in 1991, President Moussa Traore was overthrown by his own military. Traore, and his wife, Mariam, were sentenced to death in January 1999 for embezzlement. Traore had received the death sentence in 1993 as well, for ordering troops to fire on demonstrators in 1991. Sentences for both Traore and his wife have been commuted to life imprisonment. After the 1991 coup, a national conference organized open elections that most observers judged free and fair. Konare and his Alliance for Democracy in Mali (ADEMA) party won the presidency in 1992 and 1997.

Despite steady economic growth, Mali remains desperately poor. About 65 percent of its land is desert or semidesert, and about 80 percent of the labor force is engaged in farming or fishing. Principal exports are cotton, livestock, and gold. Hundreds of thousands of Malians are economic migrants from across Africa and Europe. The Malian economy suffered a blow in 2002 when thousands of Malians returned from neighboring Cote d'Ivoire, where foreign migrants were being targeted during unrest that was sparked by a military rebellion. Mali's cotton profits declined because of increased transportation costs associated with exporting from ports other than those in Cote d'Ivoire.

Political Rights and Civil Liberties: Mali's people first chose their government freely and fairly in presidential and legislative elections in 1992. In 1997, little more than a quarter of registered voters participated as former president Alpha Oumar Konare was overwhelmingly reelected against a weak candidate who alone broke an opposition boycott of the presidential contest. Konare's ADEMA party suffered a split in 2001, adding more competition ahead of the 2002 presidential election. Twenty-four candidates participated. Amadou Toumani Toure, an independent candidate, and Soumaila Cisse, of ADEMA, went to a second round of voting. Toure won with 64 percent, compared with 36 percent for Cisse.

After the first round of voting, the Constitutional Court canceled more than 500,000 ballots cast. Several presidential candidates had petitioned the court to annul the results entirely, alleging fraud and vote rigging. The court cited voting by nonregistered voters and missing election reports as some of the irregularities of the first round. International observers said the polls were well managed and conducted in a spirit of transparency. However, they also noted several logistical and administrative irregularities.

The coalition Hope Party dominated voting for National Assembly elections in July 2002, gaining 66 seats; a coalition led by ADEMA won 51 seats; smaller parties won the remainder.

Since the end of military rule, Mali's domestic political debate has been open and extensive. There are at least 75 political parties. The government holds an annual Democracy and Human Rights Forum in which citizens can air complaints in the presence of the media and international observers.

The judiciary is not independent of the executive, but has shown considerable autonomy in rendering anti-administration decisions, which the government has in turn respected. Reforms are under way. Local chiefs, in consultation with elders, decide the majority of disputes in rural areas. Detainees are not always charged within the 48-hour period set by law. There are often lengthy delays in bringing people to trial.

Mali's human rights record is generally good, although there are reports of police brutality. Prisons are characterized by overcrowding, inadequate medical care, and limited food. The government permits visits by human rights monitors. Independent human rights groups operate openly and freely.

Although libel is still considered a criminal offense and press laws include punitive presumption-of-guilt standards, Mali's media are among Africa's most open. At least 40 independent newspapers operate freely, and more than 100 independent radio stations, including community stations broadcasting in regional languages, broadcast throughout the country. The government controls one television station and many radio stations, but all present diverse views, including those critical of the government.

Mali is predominantly Muslim. However, it is a secular state and minority and religious rights are protected by law. Religious associations must register with the government, but the law is not enforced.

No ethnic group predominates in the government or the security forces, and political parties are not based on ethnicity. There have been long-standing tensions between the marginalized Moor and Tuareg pastoralist groups and more populous nonpastoralist groups, which have been a main cause of political instability and violence, including the Tuareg rebellions of the early 1990s. A 1995 agreement ended the brutal, multi-sided conflicts between Tuareg guerrillas, black ethnic militias, and government troops.

Most formal legal advances in protection of women's rights have not been implemented, especially in rural areas. Societal discrimination against women persists, and social and cultural factors continue to limit their economic and educational opportunities. Legislation gives women property rights, but traditional practices and ignorance prevent many from taking advantage of the laws. Violence against women, including spousal abuse, is tolerated and common. Female genital mutilation remains legal, although the government has conducted educational campaigns against the practice. Numerous groups promote the rights of women and children.

Workers are guaranteed the right to join unions. Nearly all salaried employees are unionized. The right to strike is guaranteed, with some restrictions. Although the constitution prohibits forced labor, thousands of Malian children have been sold into servitude on coffee and cocoa plantations in neighboring Cote d'Ivoire by organized traffickers. Mali now requires children under 18 to carry travel documents, and enacted a law in 2001 that made child trafficking punishable by up to 20 years in prison.

Malta

Polity: Parliamentary democracy
Economy: Mixed capitalist-statist
Population: 400,000
PPP: $17,273
Life Expectancy: 77

Political Rights: 1
Civil Liberties: 1
Status: Free

Religious Groups: Roman Catholic (91 percent), other (9 percent)
Ethnic Groups: Maltese (mixed Arab, Norman, Spanish, Italian, and English)
Capital: Valletta

Ten-Year Ratings Timeline (Political Rights, Civil Liberties, Status)

1993	1994	1995	1996	1997	1998	1999	2000	2001	2002	2003
1,1F	1,1F	1,1F	1,1F	1,1F	1,1F	1,1F	1,1F	1,1F	1,1F	1,1F

Overview:

In December, Malta was one of ten countries invited to join the European Union (EU) in 2004. A national referendum is scheduled to be held in 2003 before Malta can formally accede to the EU, and popular support for accession remains divided. The opposition, the Malta Labor Party (MLP) led by Alfred Sant, continues to oppose EU membership and pledges to disregard the outcome of the referendum.

Since it gained independence in 1964 within the Commonwealth and then became a republic in 1974, Malta has carefully maintained its neutrality, balancing its links with Europe to the north with ties to Arab nations to the south. The strategically located archipelago, of which Malta is the largest island, was occupied by a long succession of foreign powers. From independence in 1964 to 1971, Malta was governed by the Nationalist Party (PN), which pursued its policy of firm alignment with the West. In 1971, however, MLP came to power and implemented its policy of nonalignment and special friendship with leftist governments in Libya and Algeria. The PN returned to power in 1987 and filed an application for membership in the EU in 1991. However, the MLP regained power in 1996 and suspended the application.

Prime Minister Alfred Sant, of the MLP, was ousted from his position in 1998, and the PN once again reclaimed power, with Eddie Fenech Adami as prime minister. Adami promptly revived Malta's EU application after his return to power. In 1999, the PN-dominated parliament installed Guido de Marco as president after he had served 22 years as deputy chairman of the party. The leading political parties, which have alternated in power, have taken conflicting positions as to the direction in which Malta should lean: the currently ruling PN favors closer ties with Europe while the MLP favors strict neutrality. Elections held in March for 22 local councils had a turnout of 72 percent.

In October, the European Commission issued its annual report on EU enlargement. The report praised the Maltese government for achieving "stability of institutions guaranteeing democracy and the rule of law," and added that Malta had "continued to take measures to improve the effectiveness and transparency of its public administration" and to reform its judicial system. However, a scandal that emerged in August, in which two judges were found to have accepted bribes in return for reducing the sentence of a convicted drug trafficker, dented public confidence in the impartiality of the judiciary.

Political Rights and Civil Liberties: Citizens of Malta can change their government democratically. Members of the house of representatives, the country's unicameral legislature, are elected on the basis of proportional representation every five years. Parliament elects the country's president to a five-year term. Although the post is largely ceremonial, the president is charged with formally appointing a prime minister and the cabinet of ministers.

The constitution provides for freedom of the press. Since 1992, the government has sponsored programs to diversify the media. In addition to several Maltese-language newspapers, a few English-language weeklies are published. Malta's two main political parties own television and radio stations, as well as newspapers, which promote their political views. Italian television and radio are also popular. Malta has one of the lowest rates of Internet usage in Europe, with only an estimated four percent of the population having access to the Internet.

The constitution provides for freedom of religion, but also establishes Roman Catholicism as the state religion. The government grants subsidies only to Roman Catholic schools. Students in government schools may opt to decline instruction in Roman Catholicism. Freedom of worship by religious minorities is respected.

Workers have the right to associate freely and to strike. There are more than 35 independent trade unions that represent more than 50 percent of the population. All unions are independent of political parties; however, the largest, the General Workers' Union, is regarded to have informal ties with the MLP.

The judiciary is independent of the executive and legislative branches. The president, on the advice of the prime minister, appoints the chief justice and nine judges. The constitution requires a fair public trial, and defendants have the right to counsel of their choice. Malta abolished the death penalty for all offenses in 1999, replacing it with life imprisonment. Authorities made progress in 2002 in reducing the backlog of pending civil cases, according to the EU accession report.

The Refugee Act of 2000 provides for the granting of refugee or asylum status in accordance with UN principles. In October, Amnesty International criticized the Maltese government for forcibly deporting over 200 Eritrean detainees back to Eritrea after their asylum claims were rejected.

A constitutional amendment banning gender discrimination took effect in 1993. While women constitute a growing portion of the workforce, they are underrepresented in managerial positions and political leadership. There are no women judges, and women make up only about nine percent of the members of parliament. Domestic violence against women remains a problem.

Marshall Islands

Polity: Presidential parliamentary democracy

Political Rights: 1
Civil Liberties: 1
Status: Free

Economy: Capitalist-statist
Population: 100,000
PPP: na
Life Expectancy: 68
Religious Groups: Christian (mostly Protestant)
Ethnic Groups: Micronesian
Capital: Majuro

Ten-Year Ratings Timeline (Political Rights, Civil Liberties, Status)

1993	1994	1995	1996	1997	1998	1999	2000	2001	2002	2003
1,1F	1,1F	1,1F	1,1F	1,1F	1,1F	1,1F	1,1F	1,1F	1,1F	1,1F

Overview:

The Marshall Islands is a small, poor, island-nation consisting of the Ralik and Ratak chains of coral atolls in the central Pacific Ocean. Following decades of Spanish and German colonial rule, the United States wrested the islands from the occupying Japanese during World War II. Beginning in 1947, the United States administered the islands under a UN trusteeship until 1986. That year, the Marshall Islands achieved independence under an accord with the United States that recognizes the country as fully sovereign but leaves Washington in charge of defense and security. The accord, known as the Compact of Free Association, also grants the U.S. government continued use of the Kwajalein Atoll missile test range until 2016.

The current president, Kessai Note, was chosen by parliament in January 2000 after his United Democratic Party (UDP) won general elections in December 1999. The first commoner to hold the post, Note succeeded Imata Kabua, whom opponents accused of misusing government funds and running an administration that lacked openness and accountability. Many also criticized Kabua's proposal to rent remote, uninhabited islands to foreign countries as nuclear waste dumps.

With elections due in 2003, the Note Administration in 2002 negotiated with the United States over three issues that will have a critical impact on the Marshall Islands' future economic development. Following months of bargaining, the two countries agreed on a new Compact of Free Association under which Washington will provide $960 million in aid before the deal expires in 2023.

The Marshall Islands also hired former U.S. attorney general Richard Thornburgh to help it pursue an additional $2 billion in funding from Washington to address cleanup, health care, and compensation related to U.S. nuclear testing on the islands between 1946 and 1958. The money would replenish a trust fund set up by the U.S. Congress in 1986 that has paid out $270 million to the four atolls most affected by the tests: Bikini, Enewetak, Rongelap, and Utrik.

On a third matter, the two countries held talks over a long-term extension of the U.S. lease for the Kwajalein missile test range. Washington currently pays the

Marshall Islands around $13 million annually for use of the range, which plays a key role in field tests of the U.S. anti-missile defense system.

Meanwhile, the Paris-based Organization for Economic Cooperation and Development named the Marshall Islands in April as one of seven countries or territories worldwide that facilitate tax evasion. Separately, however, the multinational Financial Action Task Force removed the Marshall Islands in October from its global list of states that have not cooperated in the fight against money laundering.

Political Rights and Civil Liberties: Marshallese can change their government through elections and enjoy most basic rights. The 1979 constitution vests executive powers in a president, who is chosen by the House of Representatives from among its members. The 33-seat House, known locally as the *Nitijela*, is directly elected for a four-year term. The upper house, the Council of Chiefs, or *Iroji*, consists of 12 traditional leaders who provide advice on customary law. Political parties are legal, although none exist. President Note's UDP is more a loose caucus than a formal party.

The judiciary is independent but has come under scrutiny in recent years. Chief Justice Charles Henry, a U.S. citizen, faces trial in January 2003 on charges of using government funds for unauthorized travel. Three other chief justices either resigned or were fired by the former Kabua administration in the late 1990s. In a positive move, the Note Administration has increased judges' salaries in an effort to attract and retain qualified foreign judges. Because few Marshallese have law degrees, nearly all judges, prosecutors, and public defenders are foreigners.

The chief justice of the High Court acknowledged in 2001 that police at times illegally detain suspects. These cases generally involve suspects who are either not charged or are released within specified periods, often because of police inefficiency, according to the U.S. State Department's global human rights report for 2001, released in March 2002.

The media consists largely of one private weekly newspaper that carries articles in both English and Marshallese and two radio stations: the state broadcaster and a station that offers religious programming along with news from the BBC and other foreign services. In addition, a cable television station carries entertainment, foreign news, and coverage of local events.

Marshallese women historically have enjoyed high social status because inheritance of property and traditional rank is through female bloodlines. However, migration in recent decades to the cities from ancestral lands has undercut the traditional authority of many women, according to the U.S. State Department report. Marshallese women also hold relatively few senior posts in politics and government. Spousal abuse is common, the report said, and often is alcohol related.

Marshallese workers have not formed any trade unions, although they face no legal barriers. The economy depends largely on subsidies from the U.S. under the Compact of Free Association.

Mauritania

Polity: Presidential-parliamentary (military-influenced)
Economy: Capitalist-statist
Population: 2,600,000
PPP: $1,677
Life Expectancy: 53
Religious Groups: Muslim (100 percent)
Ethnic Groups: Mixed Maur/black (40 percent), Maur (30 percent), black (30 percent)
Capital: Nouakchott

Political Rights: 5
Civil Liberties: 5
Status: Partly Free

Ten-Year Ratings Timeline (Political Rights, Civil Liberties, Status)

1993	1994	1995	1996	1997	1998	1999	2000	2001	2002	2003
7,6NF	7,6NF	7,7NF	6,6NF	6,6NF	6,6NF	6,5NF	6,5NF	6,5NF	5,5PF	5,5PF

Overview:

The Mauritanian government ordered a third political party dissolved in January 2002; officials accused the Action for Change party, which campaigned for greater rights for black Mauritanians and discouraged slavery, of being racist and violent. The Union of Democratic Forces was banned in 2000, and the pro-Iraqi Attali party was banned in 1999 following violent demonstrations against Mauritania's establishment of diplomatic ties with Israel. Mauritania is one of three Arab League states, along with Egypt and Jordan, that has diplomatic relations with Israel, despite domestic criticism. Israeli foreign minister Shimon Peres visited Mauritania in October 2002. It was the first visit by an Israeli foreign minister since diplomatic ties were established in 1999. Mauritania in 2002 was suffering from a drought that put thousands of people at risk of going hungry.

After nearly six decades of French colonial rule, Mauritania's borders as an independent state were formalized in 1960. A 1978 military coup ended a civilian one-party state led by Moktaar Ould Daddah. He returned to Mauritania in 2001 after more than 20 years in exile. A 1984 internal purge installed Colonel Maaouya Ould Sid Ahmed Taya as junta chairman. In 1992, Ould Taya won the country's first, and deeply flawed, multiparty election. Ould Taya's Social Democratic Republican Party (PRDS) ruled the country as a de facto one-party state after the main opposition parties boycotted National Assembly elections in 1992 and 1996. The country's narrowly based, authoritarian regime has gradually become liberalized, but most power remains in the hands of the president and a very small elite.

Mauritania's people include the dominant *Beydane* "white Maurs" of Arab extraction and *Haratine* "black Maurs" of African descent. Other, non-Muslim, black Africans inhabiting the country's southern frontiers along the Senegal River valley constitute approximately one-third of the population. For centuries, black Africans were subjugated and taken as slaves by both white and black Maurs. Slavery was outlawed in 1980, but remnants persist.

London-based Amnesty International called on the government in 2002 to take steps to end slavery, which the organization said slavery still existed despite its official abolition 20 years ago. Former slaves are discriminated against, and organizations working to eradicate slavery and improve the rights of former slaves and black Mauritanians have been hindered in their work. Some are denied official recognition.

Mauritania is one of the world's poorest countries. Its vast and mostly arid territory has few resources. Much of the country's wealth is concentrated in the hands of a small elite that controls an economy based on iron ore exports and fishing. The World Bank and IMF in 2002 granted $1.1 billion in debt relief to Mauritania as part of their "heavily indebted poor countries" initiative.

Political Rights and Civil Liberties: In 2001, Mauritanians were, for the first time, permitted to exercise their constitutional right to choose their representatives in relatively open competitive elections. The absence of an independent election commission, state control of broadcasts, harassment of independent print media, and the incumbent's use of state resources to promote his candidacy had devalued Ould Taya's presidential victories in 1992 and 1997.

Mauritania took a step toward political reform in October 2001, when it held municipal and National Assembly elections that included a range of opposition parties. The EU said the polls were smoothly organized and allowed for proper participation in an atmosphere of normalcy and democratic openness. However, the ruling PRDS was the only party to present candidates in every constituency, and the electoral law was modified to ban independent candidates, whose seats mainly went to the PRDS. More than a dozen parties participated in the elections to choose 81 members of the National Assembly. The PRDS won 64 assembly seats, and opposition parties won 17. In the municipal polls, the opposition won 15 percent of available posts, its strongest showing to date.

Mauritania's judicial system is heavily influenced by the government. Many decisions are shaped by *Sharia* (Islamic law), especially in family and civil matters. A judicial reform program is under way. Prison conditions in Mauritania are harsh, but the construction of a new prison has reduced overcrowding and improved treatment. In June 2002, two human rights organizations and a Mauritanian-born Frenchman sued Mauritanian police for alleged torture. The suit said authorities accused the man of links with a banned political opposition group and tortured him after he arrived in Mauritania to visit his family.

Numerous nongovernmental organizations (NGOs) operate, including human rights and antislavery groups. However, a handful of black African activist groups and Islamist parties are banned. The banned *El Hor* (Free Man) movement promotes black rights, while widespread discrimination against blacks continues. Although slavery does not officially exist, a few thousand blacks still live in conditions of servitude. A government campaign against the mainly black southern part of the country in the late 1980s culminated in a massive deportation of blacks to Senegal, and relations between the two countries remain strained.

Freedom of association is restricted. The law requires all recognized political parties and NGOs to apply to the local prefect for permission to hold large meetings or assemblies. Prepublication censorship, arrests of journalists, and seizures and bans of newspapers devalue constitutional guarantees of free expression. The state owns the only two daily newspapers and monopolizes nearly all broadcast media.

Independent publications openly criticize the government, but all publications must be submitted to the Interior Ministry prior to distribution. The constitution forbids dissemination of reports deemed to "attack the principles of Islam or the credibility of the state, harm the general interest, or disturb public order and security."

Mauritania is an Islamic state in which, by statute, all citizens are Sunni Muslims who may not possess other religious texts or enter non-Muslim households. The right to worship in another faith, however, is generally tolerated. Christians and non-Mauritanian Shiite Muslims are permitted to worship privately, and some churches operate openly.

Societal discrimination against women is widespread, but is improving. Under Sharia, a woman's testimony is given only half the weight of a man's. Legal protections regarding property and equality of pay are usually respected only in urban areas among the educated elite. At least one-quarter of women undergo female genital mutilation. The government has intensive media and education campaigns against this practice.

Approximately one-fourth of Mauritania's workers serve in the small formal (business) sector. The constitution provides for freedom of association and the right of citizens to unionize and bargain for wages. All workers except members of the military and police are free to join unions. The right to strike is limited by arbitration.

Mauritius

Polity: Parliamentary democracy
Economy: Capitalist
Population: 1,200,000
PPP: $10,017
Life Expectancy: 72
Political Rights: 1
Civil Liberties: 2
Status: Free

Religious Groups: Hindu (52 percent), Roman Catholic (26 percent), Protestant (2.3 percent), Muslim (16.6 percent), other (3.1 percent)
Ethnic Groups: Indo-Mauritian (68 percent), Creole (27 percent), Sino-Mauritian (3 percent), Franco-Mauritian (2 percent)
Capital: Port Louis

Ten-Year Ratings Timeline (Political Rights, Civil Liberties, Status)

1993	1994	1995	1996	1997	1998	1999	2000	2001	2002	2003
2,2F	1,2F	1,2F	1,2F	1,2F	1,2F	1,2F	1,2F	1,2F	1,2F	1,2F

Overview:
Mauritius enjoyed a relatively tranquil year, although in October, Prime Minister Sir Anerood Jugnauth announced that he would step down on September 30, 2003. Local elections, earlier scheduled for September 2002, were postponed to 2003.

Mauritius, which has no indigenous peoples, was seized and settled as a way station for European trade to the East Indies and India. Its ethnically mixed population is primarily descended from immigrants from the Indian subcontinent who were brought to the island as laborers during its 360 years of Dutch, French, and British colonial administration. Since gaining independence from Britain in 1968, Mauritius has maintained one of the developing world's most successful democracies. In 1992, the island became a republic within the Commonwealth, with a largely ceremonial president as head of state.

In a surprise move, in August 2000 President Cassam Uteem dissolved the National Assembly and called early elections, in large part because of a series of corruption scandals that had led to the resignation of several cabinet ministers. Some 80 percent of eligible voters went to the polls. The previous incumbent had served since 1995. In the elections, the victorious opposition alliance was led by the Socialist Militant Party (MSM). Its leader, the current prime minister, Sir Anerood Jugnauth, had previously served as prime minister from 1982 until 1995, when he was voted out of office.

The MSM is allied with the Mauritian Militant Movement (MMM). The leader of the MMM, Paul Berenger, was subsequently appointed minister of finance and deputy prime minister. He is now slated to become prime minister in September 2003. In 2001 several corruption scandals attracted considerable notice.

Mauritius has achieved a stable democratic and constitutional order, and its focus on political competition rather than violent conflict demonstrates a level of political development enjoyed by few other African states. The political process is used to maintain ethnic balance and economic growth rather than dominance by any single group. In addition, political parties are not divided along the lines of the country's diverse ethnicities and religions.

The country's political stability is underpinned by steady economic growth and improvements in the island's infrastructure and standard of living. Unemployment and crime are rising, but the country's integrated, multinational population has provided a capable and reliable workforce that, along with preferential European and U.S. market access for sugar and garment exports, is attracting foreign investment. Economic development has been achieved, however, at the cost of the country's native forest and fauna, nearly all of which have been destroyed.

Political Rights and Civil Liberties: Citizens have the right to change their government democratically. The head of state is a president, elected by the National Assembly for a five-year term. Executive power resides in the prime minister. The National Assembly is unicameral; it has 62 members that are directly elected by universal adult suffrage and a maximum of 8 (currently 4) members appointed from unsuccessful parliamentary candidates who gained the largest number of votes. The members serve for a five-year term.

Since independence, Mauritius has regularly chosen its representatives in free, fair, and competitive elections. In 2002 the parliament appointed two separate committees to examine recommendations submitted by a constitutional and electoral reform commission. The commission has recommended government funding for political parties. They also suggested that the National Assembly, which is presently comprised of 62 members, be expanded by 30 members chosen proportionately from parties obtaining more than 10 percent of the total votes cast during a general election.

Decentralized structures govern the country's dependent islands. The largest of these is Rodrigues Island, which has its own government, local councils, and two seats in the National Assembly.

The generally independent judiciary is headed by the supreme court. The legal system is an amalgam of French and British traditions. Civil rights are generally well respected, although cases of police brutality have been reported. Freedom of religion is respected. There are no known political prisoners or reports of political or extrajudicial killings.

According to the BBC, the constitution guarantees freedom of expression and of the press. The state-owned Mauritius Broadcasting Corporation (MBC) operates radio and TV services and generally reflects government thinking. A small number of private radio stations have been authorized, but the state-run media enjoy a monopoly in broadcasting local news. Several private daily and weekly publications, however, are often highly critical of both government and opposition politicians and their policies. Four daily newspapers and eight weeklies offer balanced coverage in several languages. They are often critical of both the government and the opposition parties.

Freedom of assembly and association is respected, although police occasionally refuse to issue permits for demonstrations. Numerous nongovernmental organizations operate.

Nine labor federations include 300 unions.

Women constitute approximately 20 percent of the paid labor force and generally occupy a subordinate role in society. The law does not require equal pay for equal work or prohibit sexual harassment in the workplace. Women are underrepresented at the national university. The country is preparing a national gender-action plan with the long-term objective of greater equality. It addresses the integration of gender issues into the mainstream of government and private sector activities, and the enactment of a domestic violence act.

Women are significantly underrepresented in the nation's political life. According to the Southern African Development Community, in 2000 the percentages of women in parliament and in the cabinet (5.9 and 4 percent respectively) were the lowest of the 14 member countries.

Various cultures and traditions flourish in peace, though Mauritian Creoles, descendents of African slaves who make up a third of the population, live in poverty and complain of discrimination. In addition, tensions between the Hindu majority and Muslim minority persist, despite the general respect for constitutional prohibitions against discrimination. These constitute one of the country's few potential political flashpoints.

According to IMF figures, in 2001 Mauritius registered a 5.3 eight percent economic growth rate, and inflation has hovered at around 5 percent. Unemployment has risen to about 9 percent. Just 2.5 percent of the country's labor force is unemployed. Per capita income in Mauritius is $3,710, and is one of the highest in Africa. Adult literacy is 83 percent.

Mexico

Polity: Presidential-parliamentarydemocracy
Economy: Capitalist-statist
Population: 101,700,000
PPP: $9,023
Life Expectancy: 75

Political Rights: 2
Civil Liberties: 2*
Status: Free

Religious Groups: Roman Catholic (89 percent), Protestant (6 percent), other (5 percent)
Ethnic Groups: Mestizo (60 percent), Indian (30 percent), white (9 percent), other (1 percent)
Capital: Mexico City
Ratings Change: Mexico's civil liberties rating improved from 3 to 2 due to improvements in the fight against drug-related corruption and narcotics cartels, including the capture and imprisonment of a number of major narcotics traffickers.

Ten-Year Ratings Timeline (Political Rights, Civil Liberties, Status)

1993	1994	1995	1996	1997	1998	1999	2000	2001	2002	2003
4,3PF	4,4PF	4,4PF	4,4PF	4,3PF	3,4PF	3,4PF	3,4PF	2,3F	2,3F	2,2F

Overview:

Two years after President Vicente Fox bested one of the longest-ruling political regimes in modern history, Mexicans grew impatient with the pace of Fox's ambitious reform agenda and worried about an economic recession. Fox's supporters pointed to a growing string of achievements, such as serious anticorruption initiatives, the opening of secret government files and investigation of past political crimes, and the capture and imprisonment of a number of once-elusive drug kingpins. However, efforts to reform tax and labor laws, and to partially privatize the electricity industry, were stalled in an opposition-controlled congress.

Mexico achieved independence from Spain in 1810 and established itself as a republic in 1822. Seven years after the Revolution of 1910, a new constitution was promulgated under which the United Mexican States became a federal republic consisting of 31 states and a federal district (Mexico City). Each state has elected governors and legislatures. The president is elected to a six-year term and cannot be reelected. A bicameral congress consists of the 128-member Senate elected for six years, with at least one minority senator from each state, and the 500-member Chamber of Deputies elected for three years, 300 directly and 200 through proportional representation. Since its founding in 1929 until 2000, the Institutional Revolutionary Party (PRI) dominated the country by means of its corporatist, authoritarian structure maintained through co-optation, patronage, corruption, and repression. The formal business of government took place mostly in secret and with little legal foundation.

In 1999, the PRI nominated, in first-ever open-party competition, Francisco Labastida, hailed by some as the politician's return to the helm of a party ruled during the three previous administrations by technocrats. In September the National Action Party (PAN) nominated Vicente Fox Quesada, governor of Guanajuato.

Cuauhtemoc Cardenas took leave of the Mexico City mayoralty and announced he would again lead the Democratic Revolutionary Party's (PRD) national ticket. Despite election-eve polls suggesting Fox would lose, on July 2, 2000, he won Mexico's presidency with 42.5 percent of the vote; former interior minister Labastida won 36 percent of the vote; and Cardenas, just 16.6 percent. By nearly becoming the largest party in the lower house of congress, the PAN won enough state governorships to put the long-ruling PRI in danger of becoming a regional party.

Following his election, Fox selected an eclectic cabinet whose new faces signaled an end to the revolving door of bureaucrats in top positions, and included leftist intellectuals, businessmen, and, as attorney general, a serving general—the latter choice bitterly opposed by human rights groups. The business-oriented Fox also announced plans to overhaul Mexico's notoriously corrupt and inefficient law enforcement agencies, breaking the political ties between the police and the presidency, and curbing the armed forces from the expanding internal security role assigned to them under former president Ernesto Zedillo.

According a recent study by the Mexico chapter of Transparency International, some $2.3 billion—approximately 1 percent—of the country's economic production goes to officials in bribes, with the poorest families paying nearly 14 percent of their income in bribes. Public safety concerns, and related problems of corruption and rights violations by Mexico's police and military, headed the list of seemingly intractable difficulties that experts caution are likely to take a generation to solve, in part because of the large volume of existing legislation that needs to be reformed. As Mexico's drug cartels were decapitated, a new breed of crime leaders came to the fore, criminals that experts say are less violent, but also more efficient and even harder to reign in than their predecesors.

Relations with a heavily split congress, the inability to reach a meaningful reform of immigration policy with the United States, and the continued marginalization of Mexico's indigenous peoples, roughly 30 percent of the population, added to concerns about whether Fox could achieve his reform goals. In November 2002 U.S. Secretary of State Colin Powell said lingering concerns about the security of Americans made it highly unlikely that substantial headway would be made toward an immigration overhaul agreement, one of Fox's top priorities. It is estimated that there are more than 4 million illegal Mexican aliens in the United States. On a positive note, former President Luis Echeverria was questioned by a special prosecutor on possible genocide charges stemming from illegal repression in the late 1960s and early 1970s. The move was hailed as one more step in Mexico's effort to come to terms with its authoritarian past. In a similar vein, federal authorities dismantled an extensive network of corrupt federal employees who for years sold classified information to drug traffickers and organized-crime figures.

Political Rights and Civil Liberties: Mexicans can choose their government democratically. In 2001 and 2002, opposition parties made gains in state and municipal contests in elections that were generally considered to be free and fair. In most rural areas, respect for laws by official agencies is still tenuous at best, particularly in towns and villages that receive large influxes of dollars from relatives involved in narcotics trafficking in the United States. Lower courts and law enforcement in general are undermined by widespread bribery, despite some early, significant efforts by the Fox government toward reform. Torture, arbitrary arrest, and abuse of prisoners persist in many areas.

Mexico serves as a transit point for some 66 percent of the cocaine consumed in the United States, as well as being a producer of significant amounts of heroin, marijuana, and methamphetamine. Mexico is a source country for trafficked persons to the U.S., Canada, and Japan, and a transit country for persons from various places, especially Central America and China. Internal trafficking is also a problem.

Constitutional guarantees regarding political and civic organizations are generally respected in the urbanized northern and central parts of the country. Political and civic expression, however, is restricted throughout rural Mexico, in poor urban areas, and in poor southern states. Civil-society participation has grown larger in recent years; human rights, pro-democracy, women's, and environmental groups are active.

Mexico's soaring crime rate and lack of effective law enforcement, characterized by an entrenched culture of bribery and disrespect for the law, are serious barriers to economic development. In Mexico City, approximately 80 percent of crimes go unreported because the notoriously underpaid police are viewed as either inept or in league with the wrongdoers; only about 6 percent of reported crimes are solved. Ten percent of all extortive kidnappings in Mexico are believed to be carried out by former or serving police officers. While Colombia is still the hemispheric leader in kidnappings, those are primarily political in nature; experts say that Mexico may hold the world's record for abductions for money. In early 2001, Fox announced a crusade to clean up Mexico's law enforcement system, urging Mexicans to report common crimes and announcing a citizen program to make the police more accountable by making their files more accessible to the public. In 2002, the center-left mayor of Mexico City announced he was hiring former New York mayor Rudy Giuliani as a security consultant, a move questioned by rights activists familiar with the New York Police Department's record during the 1990s.

During the outbreak of the still-simmering Chiapas rebellion, Mexico's semiautonomous military was responsible for widespread human rights violations. The growing role of the military in internal security—ostensibly to combat domestic terrorism, drug trafficking, and street crime—has contributed to grave human rights problems, particularly in rural areas. Because Mexico has no foreign enemies, the military serves largely as an auxiliary police force, and in places such as the states of Chiapas and Guerrero, army counterinsurgency units, moving through local civilian populations like an occupying force, continue to cause numerous rights violations.

The media, while mostly private, largely depend on the government for advertising revenue. In 2000, Fox pledged to end the PRI practice of buying favorable stories and vowed to respect the media's independence. Despite the improvements, however, violent attacks against journalists, including cases of murder, are common, with reporters investigating police issues, narcotics trafficking, and public corruption at particular risk. Radio and television stations still operate under a law that allows the government to grant broadcast licenses at its discretion, rather than on the basis of professional criteria. In a positive development, in 2002 Mexico enacted its first freedom-of-information law, which expressly prohibits the government from withholding for any reason information about crimes against humanity or gross human rights violations.

In 1992 the constitution was amended to restore the legal status of the Roman

Catholic Church and other religious institutions. Priests and nuns were allowed to vote for the first time in nearly 80 years.

The *maquiladoras* (export-processing zones) have fostered substantial abuses on workers' rights). Most maquiladora workers are young, uneducated women who accept lower pay more readily, with annual labor turnover averaging between 200 and 300 percent. Workers have no medical insurance, holidays, or profit sharing, and female employees are frequently the targets of sexual harassment and abuse. In the period 2000–2002, an estimated 500 maquiladoras closed as many companies sought even lower wage havens in Asia.

Domestic violence and sexual abuse remain serious problems in Mexico, although the Fox government has pledged to fight a problem that some experts say affects 50-70 percent of Mexican women.

Dozens of labor and peasant leaders have been killed in recent years in ongoing land disputes, particularly in the southern states, where Indians constitute close to half the population. Most of Mexico's 10 million Native Americans live in a situation of de facto apartheid, relegated to extreme poverty in rural villages lacking roads, running water, schools, and telephones. Indian groups say a 2001 constitutional reform designed to strengthen their rights fell far short of addressing their concerns.

Micronesia

Polity: Presidential-parliamentary democracy (federal)
Economy: Capitalist
Population: 100,000
PPP: na
Life Expectancy: 66
Religious Groups: Roman Catholic (50 percent), Protestant (47 percent), other (3 percent)
Ethnic Groups: Micronesian , Polynesian
Capital: Palikir

Political Rights: 1
Civil Liberties: 2
Status: Free

Ten-Year Ratings Timeline (Political Rights, Civil Liberties, Status)

1993	1994	1995	1996	1997	1998	1999	2000	2001	2002	2003
1,1F	1,1F	1,1F	1,1F	1,1F	1,2F	1,2F	1,2F	1,2F	1,2F	1,2F

Overview:

The Federated States of Micronesia is a small, poor country consisting of 607 islands of the Caroline archipelago in the northern Pacific Ocean between Guam and Honolulu. Sighted by Portuguese and Spanish explorers in the sixteenth century, the Carolines eventually came under Spanish control and, by the mid-nineteenth century, began attracting growing numbers of missionaries and coconut traders.

Following its defeat in the Spanish-American War, Spain sold most of the Caroline Islands to Germany in 1899. Japan seized the islands in 1914 and ruled them from 1920 under a League of Nations mandate. U.S. and Japanese forces fought bloody battles for control of the Carolines during World War II, with the islands becoming part of the U.S. Trust Territory for the Pacific after the war.

The country's road to independence began in 1978, when four districts of the trust territory—Yap, Chuuk, Kosrae, and Pohnpei—approved a constitution setting up a federal republic. Micronesia achieved full independence in 1986 under an accord with the United States in which Washington agreed to provide around $2 billion in aid through 2001. Under the accord, known as the Compact of Free Association, the United States also maintained responsibility for the country's defense and has the right to set up military bases.

Micronesian voters in August 2002 rejected a proposed constitutional amendment that would have introduced direct elections for president and vice president. Under the current system, Congress chooses the two top officeholders from among its ranks. Thirteen other proposals also failed to garner the 75 percent approval needed to amend the constitution. These included proposals to give the four states control over land and water issues and the right to levy their own value-added and goods and services taxes.

Meanwhile, the government of President Leo Falcam continued to negotiate with Washington over the terms of renewing the Compact of Free Association. Renewing the Compact is critical for Micronesia because U.S. aid is equivalent to about one-third of the country's economic output. A deal on favorable terms will boost Falcam's chances for reelection in balloting due in 2003.

A typhoon that swept across Micronesia in July killed more than 40 people and left up to 2,000 Chuuk Islanders living in emergency shelters.

Political Rights and Civil Liberties: Micronesians can change their government through elections and enjoy most basic rights. The 1979 constitution created a single-house, 14-senator congress. Each of the four states elects one at-large member for a four-year term, with the remaining 10 senators elected from single-seat districts for two-year terms.

The president and vice president are chosen by Congress from among its four at-large members. By informal agreement, these offices are rotated among representatives of the four states. The three smaller states, however, complain about the alleged political dominance of Chuuk state, which has nearly half of the country's population and a proportionate number of congressional seats.

The government does not prevent Micronesians from forming political parties, although none exist. Political support is often based on clan, family or religious ties.

Micronesia's judiciary is independent, according to the U.S. State Department's global human rights report for 2001, released in March 2002. Cultural resistance to dealing with serious crime through the courts has allowed some suspects accused of sexual and other assaults, including murder, to be released indefinitely and to avoid trial, the report said.

The media are free and consist of governmental newsletters, several small private papers, television stations in three of Micronesia's four states, radio stations run by each of the four state governments, and one radio station run by a religious group. Satellite television is increasingly available.

Micronesian women are increasingly active in business and hold some mid-level federal and state posts, but they face "extensive" discrimination in mainstream society, the U.S. State Department report said. Reports of spousal abuse continue to rise, and officials rarely prosecute alleged offenders vigorously, the report said. Victims often decide not to press charges because they are pressured by family, fearful of further assault, or convinced that the police will not take action in what are widely seen as private matters. Cases of physical and sexual assault of women outside of the home are also increasing, the report added.

Micronesians are free to set up civic groups, though they have formed few nongovernmental organizations except for a handful of student and women's groups. Religious freedom is respected in this mainly Christian country.

In a society where most private sector jobs are in small-scale, family-owned businesses, Micronesians have not formed any trade unions, although there are no legal barriers to association. No laws specifically regulate working hours, recognize the right to strike or bargain collectively, or set standards for workplace health and safety. The economy is dependent on U.S. aid, tourism, fishing, and subsistence agriculture.

Moldova

Polity: Parliamentary democracy
Economy: Capitalist-statist
Population: 4,300,000
PPP: $2,109
Life Expectancy: 68

Political Rights: 3*
Civil Liberties: 4
Status: Partly Free

Religious Groups: Eastern Orthodox (98.5 percent), other (1.5 percent)
Ethnic Groups: Moldovan/Romanian (65 percent), Ukrainian (14 percent), Russian (13 percent), other (8 percent)
Capital: Chisinau
Ratings Change: Moldova's political rights rating declined from 2 to 3 due to changes in the survey methodology.

Ten-Year Ratings Timeline (Political Rights, Civil Liberties, Status)

1993	1994	1995	1996	1997	1998	1999	2000	2001	2002	2003
5,5PF	5,5PF	4,4PF	4,4PF	3,4PF	3,4PF	2,4PF	2,4PF	2,4PF	2,4PF	3,4PF

Overview:

In the decade since Moldova declared independence from the Soviet Union, this tiny country has struggled for every success. Moldova maintains one of the highest poverty rates in Europe. Subsistence farming has largely replaced the country's once-notable agricultural capacity; its national territory is divided and partly occupied by Russian troops; its Soviet-era infrastructure continues to decay; and the weight of foreign debt burdens the country's finances. Yet despite all of these substantial problems, the most heated political debates of 2002 centered on the issue of cultural identity.

The Moldavian Soviet Socialist Republic declared independence from the Soviet Union in 1991. Mircea Snegur, chairman of the Communist Supreme Soviet, became the first president of a democratic Republic of Moldova. Snegur's centrist Agrarian Democratic Party (ADP) subsequently won a majority of parliamentary seats in the country's first free and fair popular election in 1994. Two years later, Petru Lucinschi, also a former Communist, defeated Snegur in 1996 presidential elections. While the Party of Moldovan Communists (PCM) won a plurality of votes in the parliamentary elections of 1998, three centrist parties united to form a majority coalition. During this time, Moldova undertook needed economic reforms, drafted a new constitution, and joined NATO's Partnership for Peace program. In the 2001 parliamentary elections, the PCM won a landslide victory on the promise of a return to Soviet-era living standards. PCM leader Vladimir Voronin subsequently became the new president.

Under Voronin, the government reinstated Soviet-style territorial administration, restored the November 7 holiday commemorating the October Revolution, introduced measures to make Russian an official second language, and proposed regulations requiring mandatory Russian-language instruction in schools. These Russification initiatives met fierce resistance from the opposition Christian-Democrat People's Party (CDPP), and sparked a continual series of public protests during the first part of 2002. At times these protests were estimated to have exceeded 100,000 people. In short order, protest leaders began to issue calls for the abdication of the government, and by February the government reversed its previous decision on mandatory Russian-language instruction. The Constitutional Court later voided a draft law that would have made Russian an official state language.

By late April, the CDPP protests drew to a close. The demonstrators had failed to rally greater support to their call for a new government. This failure was partly due to the fact that the CDPP draws its strength from a limited portion of Moldovan society, one that generally identifies with Moldova's Romanian heritage. While focusing largely on the issue of cultural identity, the CDPP has been slow to offer the public a fully viable solution to the country's other pressing concerns, and thus has failed to position itself as a realistic alternative to the Communists. In fact, public support for the PCM actually increased in the wake of the CDPP's four-month political siege of the government.

In retribution, the Communist-controlled government briefly suspended the CDPP and moved to lift the parliamentary immunity of the CDPP chairman and two party deputies in the first step towards criminal prosecution. At this point, the Council of Europe (CE) intervened to negotiate a cessation of the open political hostilities. The CDPP agreed to drop its call for the government's resignation, and the government retracted the threat of prosecution. As part of this agreement, the government also agreed to make good on a variety of CE demands relating to political and civil rights in the country. President Voronin does not want to isolate Moldova from Europe. While the compromise agreement with the CE demonstrates the extent to which his government is open to influence from Euro-Atlantic institutions, it also underscores the delicate nature of Moldova's transitioning democracy and the need for further CE monitoring.

Political Rights and Civil Liberties: Moldova is a parliamentary democracy. Citizens over the age of 18 can change their government under a system of universal, equal, and direct suffrage. In 2000, Moldova ended direct elections of the president and became a full parliamentary democracy. Voters elect members of parliament by proportional representation to four-year terms. Parliament then elects the prime minister and president. Post-Soviet elections in Moldova have generally been free and fair. The self-declared government in Transnistria, however, severely limits the ability of voters in that region to participate in Moldovan elections.

The constitution guarantees freedom of expression and access to public information. At the same time, laws prohibit insults against the state and defamation of senior government officials. These provisions have allowed a multitude of lawsuits against journalists in the decade since independence. In March 2002, nearly 500 journalists and media workers at the state-owned TeleRadio Moldova held demonstrations to protest alleged censorship and demand greater independence of the media. Under an agreement with the Council of Europe (CE), the government subsequently passed legislation transferring state control of TeleRadio Moldova to an independent corporation. Yet questions remain over the editorial independence of this new body, and the CE has expressed concern that TeleRadio Moldova will now derive its sole funding from the state budget.

Moldova's constitution guarantees religious freedom. A 1992 law requires all religious groups to register with the government. Previously, Moldovan authorities had used the law to deny registration to the Bessarabian Orthodox Church on the grounds that the group is a schismatic movement. The Bessarabian Church broke away from the Moldovan Church in 1992 and subordinated itself to the Romanian Orthodox Patriarchate in Bucharest. The Moldovan Church remained subordinate to the Moscow Patriarchate. The Bessarabian Church eventually brought its case before European Court for Human Rights. In 2001, the court found in favor of the Bessarabian Church and refused to hear a subsequent appeal from the government. By late June 2002, the CE threatened to deny Moldova the rotating chair of the CE Ministerial Committee if the country continued to withhold recognition of the Bessarabian Church. Within weeks, parliament altered the registration process for religious organizations and consequently granted the Bessarabian Church official registration.

Moldova's constitution provides for an independent judiciary. It also guarantees equality before the law and the presumption of innocence. There is evidence that some prosecutors, judges, and law enforcement officials accept bribes. The constitution preserves a variety of personal freedoms and entitlements such as the right to choose one's residence, move and travel freely, and have access to education. Moldovan citizens may strike, petition the government, and participate freely in social organizations, political parties, and trade unions. Private organizations must register with the state, and demonstrations require permits from local authorities. Moldovan law allows collective bargaining but prohibits strikes by government employees and essential workers.

Following years of dramatic economic decline, the country remains one of Europe's most impoverished countries. Official unemployment hovers around 30 percent. Amidst this grim economic environment, thousands of Moldovans have elected to sell one of their kidneys to black market dealers in Turkey. Harsh economic conditions have likewise led a substantial number of women into prostitution. Still, there is some good economic news. Moldova became a member of the World Trade Organization in 2001, and strong industrial growth in 2002 has propelled the economy to a second year of recovery.

Monaco

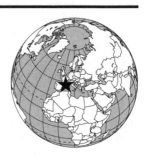

Polity: Principality and parliamentary democracy
Economy: Capitalist-statist
Population: 30,000
PPP: na
Life Expectancy: na
Religious Groups: Roman Catholic (90 percent), other (10 percent)
Ethnic Groups: French (47 percent), Italian (16 percent), Monegasque (16 percent), other (21 percent)
Capital: Monaco

Political Rights: 2
Civil Liberties: 1
Status: Free

Ten-Year Ratings Timeline (Political Rights, Civil Liberties, Status)

1993	1994	1995	1996	1997	1998	1999	2000	2001	2002	2003
--	2,1F	2,1F	2,1F	2,1F	2,1F	2,1F	2,1F	2,1F	2,1F	2,1F

Overview:

In February 2002, Monaco adopted the euro as its official currency, although it is not an official member of the European Community. The authorities remain under pressure to clean up the country's tax and banking systems. In June, a French judge claimed that an investigation into the Italian Mafia in Monaco had been blocked by senior justice officials due to links between those under suspicion and the royal family.

The Principality of Monaco is an independent and sovereign state, although it remains closely associated with neighboring France. In 1997, the royal Grimaldi family celebrated its 700th anniversary of rule over the principality. During the seven centuries of Grimaldi rule, Monaco has been intermittently controlled by various European powers.

It achieved independence from France in 1861. Under a treaty ratified in 1919, France pledged to protect the territorial integrity, sovereignty, and independence of the principality in return for a guarantee that Monegasque policy would conform to French interests. France has promised that in return for reforming its banking practices and tightening the laws on anti-money-laundering, Monaco will be able to re-negotiate the 1919 treaty with France.

For 52 years, Prince Rainier III has been responsible for Monaco's impressive economic growth. Under his direction, the economy has ended its exclusive dependence on gambling revenue. Its main sources of revenue are tourism, financial services, and banking.

Of 32,000 residents, Monaco is home to only 5,000 Monegasques, who alone may participate in the election of the 18-member national council (legislature). The constitution also provides Monegasques with free education, financial assistance in cases of unemployment or illness, and the right to hold elective office. In the elections that took place in February 1998, the National and Democratic Union party won all the seats in the legislature.

Following criticism from France and the international community for not tightening its anti-laundering laws, the Principality of Monaco responded in 2001 by implementing a series of financial reform measures that included doubling the staff of its financial transactions monitoring unit and signing cooperation agreements with several European countries to fight money laundering. However, the OECD announced in April 2002 that Monaco remained on its list of uncooperative tax havens.

Political Rights and Civil Liberties: Citizens of Monaco may change the national council and their municipal councils democratically. Eighteen council members are elected for five years by direct universal suffrage and a system of proportional representation. As head of state, Prince Rainier holds executive authority, formally appoints the four-member cabinet, and proposes all legislation. Legislation proposed by the prince is drafted by the cabinet and voted upon by the national council. The prince holds veto power over the council. The prince also names the prime minister from a list of names proposed by the French government. Political parties operate freely.

Freedom of expression is guaranteed by the constitution; however, denunciations of the royal family are prohibited by the penal code. Two monthly magazines and a weekly governmental journal are published in the principality, and French daily newspapers are widely available. Radio and television are government operated and sell time to commercial sponsors, and all French broadcasts are freely transmitted to the principality. France maintains a financial interest in Radio Monte Carlo, which broadcasts in several languages.

Roman Catholicism is the state religion in Monaco, but adherents of other faiths may practice freely. The government does not, however, permit religious groups that are considered "sects" to operate. There are no reported restrictions on academic freedom.

The constitution provides for freedom of assembly and association. Although outdoor meetings require police authorization, there were no reports that permission was withheld, according to the U.S. State Department's annual Human Rights report.

Workers are free to form unions, but fewer than ten percent of workers are unionized. Trade unions are independent of both the government and political parties. Anti-union discrimination is prohibited. Union members can be fired only with the agreement of a commission that includes two members from the employers' association and two from the labor movement.

Under the 1962 constitution, the prince delegates judicial authority to the courts and tribunals, which adjudicate independently in his name. The judiciary includes a Supreme Tribunal, consisting of seven members appointed by the prince based on nominations by the national council; courts of cassation, appeal, and first instance; and a justice of the peace.

The rights of women are respected, and women are fairly well represented in all professions. Of the 18 members of the national council, 4 are women. The law governing transmission of citizenship provides for equality of treatment between men and women who are Monegasque by birth. Only men, however, may transmit Monegasque citizenship acquired by naturalization to their children; women are denied this right.

Mongolia

Polity: Presidential-par-
liamentary democracy
Economy: Mixed
capitalist (transitional)
Population: 2,400,000
PPP: $1,783
Life Expectancy: 63

Political Rights: 2
Civil Liberties: 2*
Status: Free

Religious Groups: Tibetan Buddhist Lamaism (96 percent),
Muslim and other (4 percent)
Ethnic Groups: Mongol (85 percent), Kazakh (7 percent), other (8 percent)
Capital: Ulaanbaatar
Ratings Change: Mongolia's civil liberties rating improved from 3 to 2 due to continued
improvement in conditions in the country's prisons, including a decline in the abuse
of prisoners.

Ten-Year Ratings Timeline (Political Rights, Civil Liberties, Status)

1993	1994	1995	1996	1997	1998	1999	2000	2001	2002	2003
3,2F	2,3F	2,3F	2,3F	2,3F	2,3F	2,3F	2,3F	2,3F	2,3F	2,2F

Overview:

Mongolia's ruling former Communist party struggled to meet
the high expectations created when it ousted a reformist
government in 2000 behind promises to ease social hard-
ships. The cash-strapped government found it tough to deliver on pledges to create
more jobs and provide better services to Mongolians hard hit by the country's rocky
transition to a market economy.

Once the center of Ghengis Khan's sprawling empire, Mongolia was dominated
for much of the past three centuries by China and Russia. China controlled Mongolia
for two centuries until 1921. A Soviet-backed Marxist revolt led to the creation, in
1924, of a single-party Communist state, the world's second ever, under the Mongolian People's Revolutionary Party (MPRP).

Mongolia's transition from Soviet satellite to democratic republic began in 1990,
when the MPRP responded to pro-democracy protests by legalizing opposition
parties and holding the country's first multiparty elections. Facing an unprepared
and underfunded opposition, the MPRP easily won parliamentary elections that year
and again in 1992.

The dominant political issue in post-Communist Mongolia has been the pace
and extent of economic reform. Market reforms have helped create a fledgling private sector, but have also contributed to soaring unemployment and other social
miseries. MPRP governments in the early 1990s privatized small businesses and
ended collectivized herding, but had difficulty retooling the economy to survive the
loss of Soviet subsidies. Many large firms went bankrupt, throwing thousands out
of work.

The MPRP was swept out of parliamentary power after 72 years in the 1996
elections. The coalition of reformist parties that took office, however, also had difficulty stabilizing the economy. Prescribing shock therapy to speed Mongolia's tran-

sition to a market system, the incoming Democratic Union Coalition (DUC) cut spending, freed prices, slashed pensions, and cut tariffs.

The changes, however, coincided with sharp falls in world prices for two of Mongolia's biggest foreign exchange earners, copper and cashmere. The resulting drop in export revenues gave the government little room to boost social spending at a time when Prime Minister Mendsaihan Enksaikhan's radical policies were helping to send inflation and unemployment soaring.

The MPRP regained power with back-to-back victories in the 1997 election for the mainly ceremonial presidency and the more important 2000 parliamentary vote. Promising to ease social hardships, the MPRP's Natsagiin Bagabandi, a former parliamentary chairman, defeated incumbent Punsalmaagiyn Orchirbat of the DUC in the 1997 presidential election.

Three years later, the MPRP regained control of the government by winning 72 out of 76 seats in the 2000 parliamentary elections. New prime minister Nambariin Enkhbayar, the MPRP chairman, pledged to seek a "third way" between his party's still-powerful Marxist wing and the DUC's rapid-liberalization policies. Many blamed these policies for the doubling of the poverty rate since 1991 and the state welfare system's virtual collapse, though the loss of Soviet subsidies also contributed.

President Bagabandi easily won reelection in 2001. Though he pledged to speed up some reforms, his victory suggested that many Mongolians continue to believe that the former Communists will be more likely than the DUC to rebuild the country's tattered social safety net. Voters told journalists that they were disillusioned with the dismal state of the country's welfare and educational systems, as well as with crime, corruption, and high unemployment.

Additional hardships resulted from the combination of drought and a brutal ice-and-snow phenomenon, known locally as *zud*, that hit Mongolia between summer 1999 and early 2002. This double blow killed off some seven million livestock, wiping out the lifeblood of many herding families. Some 40 percent of Mongolians rely for their livelihoods on the country's 27 million livestock.

As tough economic times continued in 2002, Prime Minister Enkhbayar, 43, faced street protests demanding a more forceful response to poverty and an increase in union members' salaries.

Political Rights and Civil Liberties:

Mongolians can change their government through elections and enjoy most basic rights. The 1992 constitution vested most executive powers in a prime minister and created the 76-seat parliament, known as the Great Hural, which is directly elected for a four-year term. The constitution also vested some governmental powers in a directly elected president, who also serves a four-year term. The president must approve candidates for prime minister and can veto legislation, subject to a two-thirds parliamentary override.

Mongolia's judiciary is independent, but corruption among judges is "a problem," according to the U.S. State Department's global human rights report for 2001, released in March 2002. In a holdover from the country's Communist past, defendants do not enjoy a presumption of innocence.

Despite recent reforms, conditions in jails and pretrial detention centers continue to be life threatening because of insufficient food, heat, and health care, the

U.S. State Department said. Tuberculosis has killed dozens of inmates in recent years. The percentage of prisoners who die each year from tuberculosis continues to drop, however, decreasing by 50 percent to fewer than 50 deaths in 2001, according to the report. Inmates often come to prison already suffering from illnesses because of the long periods many spend in police detention, where conditions are worse.

Police abuse appears to be on the decline, though anecdotal evidence suggests that rural officials occasionally beat suspects and prisoners, according to the U.S. State Department report. Officials have never identified any suspects in the 1998 killing of Sanjaasuren Zorig, the leader of the pro-democracy movement that ended single-party rule. Four years after Zorig's death, this failure continues to raise questions about law enforcement in Mongolia.

Mongolian newspapers and magazines carry a wide range of party and independent views that often are critical of the government, though some outlets practice self-censorship. The press claims that the government pressures news outlets indirectly by frequently filing libel lawsuits and launching tax audits in the wake of critical articles. In a still-controversial move, the government shut down two papers in 2000 for failing to comply with laws on taxes and for their coverage of violence and pornography.

Moreover, the law places the burden of proof on defendants in slander and libel cases, possibly creating a chilling effect on the media. In addition, "lack of access to information and of transparency in government continues to inhibit political dialogue in the media," according to the U.S. State Department report.

The state-owned Radio Mongolia, the major source of news in the vast countryside, is free from political control. It faces competition from at least one private radio station that can reach most of the country and from several small local FM stations. Mongolia also has at least two private television stations, but they have limited reach.

Women make up the majority of university graduates, doctors, and lawyers and have helped set up and manage many of Mongolia's new trading and manufacturing firms. They also run many of Mongolia's most effective nongovernmental organizations, including some that lobby government officials, organize voter-education programs, and promote women's rights and child welfare. However, women hold relatively few senior governmental and judicial posts. Domestic violence continued to be a serious problem, the U.S. State Department report said, although there are no accurate figures on the number of victims each year.

Mongolia's dire economic situation has undermined child welfare. The government lacks the resources to meet many basic health care, social, and educational needs of children. Poverty and alcoholism among parents have led to higher school dropout rates and forced an estimated 3,000 children into the streets and another 58,000 to work regularly, according to NGO estimates.

Mongolians of all faiths worship freely in this mainly Buddhist country. Some religious groups seeking to fulfill mandatory registration requirements, however, have faced demands for bribes and other harassment by local officials, according to the U.S. State Department report.

Mongolian trade unions are independent and active, though the government's slimming down or sale of many state factories has contributed to a sharp drop in union membership, to less than half the workforce. Many laid off state employees now work in small, non-unionized firms or are self-employed. Collective bargaining is legal, but under current economic conditions employers enjoy considerable leverage and often unilaterally set wages and working conditions. The government prohibits strikes in areas it considers essential, including utilities, transportation, and law enforcement. Private land-ownership is not permitted, although the law allows land to be leased for up to 100 years.

Morocco

Polity: Traditional monarchy and limited parliament

Economy: Capitalist-statist

Population: 29,700,000

PPP: $3,546

Life Expectancy: 69

Political Rights: 5
Civil Liberties: 5
Status: Partly Free

Religious Groups: Muslim (98.7 percent), Christian and other (1.3 percent)
Ethnic Groups: Arab and Berber (99 percent), other (1 percent)
Capital: Rabat

Ten-Year Ratings Timeline (Political Rights, Civil Liberties, Status)

1993	1994	1995	1996	1997	1998	1999	2000	2001	2002	2003
6,5PF	5,5PF	5,5PF	5,5PF	5,5PF	5,5PF	5,4PF	5,4PF	5,4PF	5,5PF	5,5PF

Overview:

While Morocco held the freest and fairest elections of its history in 2002, the conspicuous absence of a major Islamist party on the ballot, low voter turnout, and lack of transparency in the formation of a new government underscored how little things have changed politically. Nevertheless, the harsh crackdown on dissent that had continued throughout 2001 was eased.

After 44 years of French rule, Morocco gained independence as a hereditary monarchy headed by King Mohammed V in 1956. After his death five years later, the throne passed to his son, Hassan. Although the constitution provided for multiparty democratic institutions, power remained centralized in the hands of the king, who faced substantial threats to his rule. In 1971 rebellious guards massacred more than 100 people at his birthday party, and the following year Moroccan fighter planes attacked his 727 jet. The withdrawal of Spanish forces from Western Sahara in 1975 provided Hassan with an opportunity to assert his nationalist credentials while distracting the attention of his restless military. Thousands of young Moroccans were imprisoned or sent into exile as the government ruthlessly suppressed serious political dissident. Hundreds disappeared, never to be heard from again. Like many other Arab states, Morocco began a limited process of political liberalization after the 1991 Gulf war.

Hassan died in July 1999, and the throne went to his son, Mohammed, who inherited a country with severe economic and social problems. More than 20 percent of the population was unemployed, nearly half remained illiterate, and a third lived below the poverty line. A huge government debt threatened social spending during the growth of grassroots support for Islamists, who have provided social services to sectors of the population traditionally neglected by the government. A steady outflow of educated Moroccans to Europe sapped the economy of skilled labor and technical expertise.

Upon assuming the throne, King Mohammed VI launched a more extensive program of economic and political liberalization. One of his first acts was to dismiss Driss Basri, the hard-line interior minister whose power was second only to that of Mohammed V for more than 20 years. Thousands of political prisoners were released, families of those who died in captivity were given financial compensation, and ex-iled dissidents were allowed to return. Initiatives were launched to reduce the rampant corruption that had long plagued the civil service. Restrictions on public freedoms were eased. An initiative to advance women's rights was launched in 2000, but dropped after hundreds of thousands of Muslims, including many veiled women, took to the streets in protest.

The new mood of relative tolerance led opposition activists to intensify demands for far-reaching political reform and accountability for past abuses. The young king panicked in December 2000, when thousands of secular and Islamist opposition supporters joined together in nationwide demonstrations to mark the annual UN Human Rights Day. Around 800 people who took part in the protests were arrested in the weeks that followed, though most were released or acquitted in 2001. The independent media came under severe pressure throughout 2001.

Human rights conditions improved in 2002, and the king honored promises to hold free and fair elections in September. A number of measures were taken to fight the rampant corruption that had plagued past elections. A proportional representation system was introduced to prevent tribal leaders from buying votes (voters now vote for political parties, rather than individual candidates). A new single-ballot paper was introduced, displaying logos of the parties to assist the illiterate, in place of color-coded ballots that undermined voting secrecy. Voters' fingers were dipped in permanent ink to prevent repeat voting. However, while the elections were procedurally sound, only 52 percent of registered voters bothered to show up. According to a poll taken on the eve of the elections, 9 out of 10 Moroccans could not identify either the name or basic ideological orientation of any political party.

Interior Minister Driss Jettou was appointed prime minister. The 25-member coalition government he unveiled in December was little different than its predecessor. Indeed, 19 members were carried over from the previous cabinet. The cabinet's size and diffuse ideological composition were widely criticized as an indication that the palace did not want an effective decision-making body. There were widespread complaints that politicians did not consult sufficiently within their respective parties before making decisions.

Another central component of the political reform process—the anticorruption campaign—also stalled in 2002. Following a judicial investigation into the alleged diversion of more than $1 billion from a state bank, Credit Immobilier et Hotelier (CIH), to cronies of the late King Hassan, the Special Court of Justice ordered the arrest of former CIH president Moulay Zine Zahidi and 15 senior CIH executives in October. Zahidi went into hiding and gave an interview with the Casablanca-based *Le Jour-*

nal, claiming that several of the bank's poor decisions regarding well-connected donors (such as its decision to buy back a tourist resort from Morocco's ambassador to the United Nations for $3 million) were ordered by unspecified higher-ups in the Moroccan government. The two reporters who filed the interview were detained and interrogated.

Political reforms have been intended first and foremost to bolster the domestic legitimacy and international standing of King Mohammed VI, not to devolve decision-making power from the palace to the politicians. Concerns that the king's unwillingness to relinquish his grip on power will further inflame Islamist militancy have become widespread among secular liberals, and contributed to a rift within the royal family between King Mohammed and his 38-year old cousin, Prince Moulay Hisham. The latter began openly criticizing the government in 2001, warning of potential political instability and hinting that the principle of primogeniture should not dictate the royal succession in Morocco. Hisham was forced to leave the country in January 2002 after a stream of reports in the pro-government media accused him of conspiring to launch a coup.

Although Morocco is not known for the kind of Islamist violence that wracked neighboring Algeria, the palace moved against radical Islamists following the arrest in May 2002 of three Saudi members of al-Qaeda allegedly plotting to attack NATO warships in the Straits of Gibraltar. Up to 20 Moroccans accused of providing them with financial assistance were reportedly arrested. Over the summer, the authorities launched a crackdown on obscure radical Islamist groups (dubbed "militant Salafists" by the authorities) in low-income districts of Casablanca, Tangiers, and other cities.

Muted public reaction to the crackdown suggests that the militant Islamist current may be neither as popular nor as threatening as some foreign media have claimed. The real threat to the palace is that the stalled reform process and economic stagnation will cause mainstream Islamists and leftists to join together and call for real democracy. Apart from the elections, the only major development in 2002 that gave a clear boost to popular support for the king was his marriage in March to Salma Bennani, an engineer for a mining company. The wedding was said to be the first between a member of the royal family and a commoner in Moroccan history.

Political Rights and Civil Liberties:

Moroccans' right to change their government democratically is limited. The constitution not only grants the king supreme executive power, but accords him religious legitimacy as "commander of the faithful." Since the king appoints the prime minister and selects the cabinet in consultation with the prime minister, the most powerful ministries have always been entrusted to staunch allies of the palace. The king can dissolve the legislature at his discretion and rule by decree during legislative adjournments. He also appoints the governors of Morocco's 16 provinces. Legislative powers are shared by the king and a bicameral legislature, consisting of the directly elected, 325-member Chamber of Representatives (*Majlis al-Nuwwab*) and the Chamber of Advisors (*Majlis al-Mustasharin*), whose members are selected by local assemblies, professional syndicates, trade unions, and other bodies. The government can be dissolved by a vote of no confidence in both houses of parliament. Unlike previous elections, the 2002 parliamentary elections were procedurally free and fair.

Arbitrary arrests, incommunicado detention, and torture continued to be practiced by the security forces, though the number of abuses declined in 2002. The capture of three members of al-Qaeda went unreported in the press for nearly a month as interrogators allegedly tortured the suspects. Several militant Islamists arrested over the summer claimed to have been tortured in custody. On November 8, the French daily *Le Monde* reported that unidentified assailants in Paris attempted to assassinate Hisham Mandari, an exiled member of the late King Hassan's security service who has threatened to expose corruption in the royal family.

The judiciary is subject to corruption, bureaucracy, and governmental interference. Although judicial reform has been identified as a high priority of the government, progress has been slow. Judges have been referred to disciplinary panels for punishment as a result of investigations into alleged corruption and misconduct, and a number have been fired.

Freedom of expression remains restricted. Broadcast media are mostly government controlled and reflect official views, though foreign broadcasting is available via satellite and a large independent print media flourishes. While critical reporting on most topics is tolerated, journalists risk imprisonment for violating taboos on issues such as the monarchy, Islam, and Moroccan claims to Western Sahara. The government periodically confiscates copies of publications that cross these lines. A new media law promulgated in 2002 reduces jail terms stipulated by the 1973 press code, makes it easier to launch a publication, and requires the government to give reasons for confiscations, but the Moroccan Press Union condemned the measure for not eliminating penal sanctions entirely.

The number and severity of punitive actions against journalists and publications declined somewhat in 2002. In January, a journalist for the weekly *Al-Ayyam* was arrested and briefly detained after he visited Islamist prisoners at the central prison of Kenitra. In February, two journalists were given suspended prison sentences on appeal for defaming the Moroccan foreign minister and the authorities seized issues of the French weekly *VSD*, which contained unflattering coverage of the king. In May, the authorities seized 8,000 copies of the quarterly journal *Wijhat Nadhar*, which contained the transcript of a speech by Moulay Hisham. In the weeks prior to the September 2002 elections, the authorities carried out a campaign to close down Islamic bookshops suspected of carrying extremist literature.

Internet access is prohibitively expensive for most Moroccans, but generally unrestricted. Since April 2001, however, the authorities have blocked access to several Islamist Web sites, most notably the Justice and Charity Organization (JCO). Shortly after his appointment in December 2002, the incoming minister of communications, Nabil Benabdallah, pledged not to ban or confiscate any newspaper during his term.

Freedom of association is limited. Organizations must receive approval from the Interior Ministry in order to operate legally. The establishment of several proposed political parties has been blocked in recent years, and membership in two major Islamist groups (the JCO and Al-Jama'a al-Islamiyya) is explicitly prohibited. The Interior Ministry requires permits for public gatherings and has forcibly dispersed demonstrations in the past, but peaceful protests were generally tolerated in 2002. A pro-Palestinian protest in Rabat attracted well over 500,000 participants in April.

Morocco's heavily unionized formal (business) sector includes 17 umbrella federations, some of which are aligned with political parties and all of which are subject to political pressure. Workers may bargain collectively and strike.

Although the Moroccan constitution states that "men and women are equal in rights," this equality is limited to the political sphere. New electoral legislation introduced in 2002 set aside a fixed bloc of 30 parliamentary seats for women. Many women pursue careers in the professions or in government, but they face restrictions in advancement. The personal status code discriminates against women in marriage, divorce, and inheritance matters. Domestic violence is common, and the law is lenient toward men who kill their wives for alleged adultery.

Islam is the official religion, and almost 99 percent of the population is Sunni Muslim. The government closely monitors mosque activities. Christians and Jews can worship freely, though Baha'is are not free to practice their religion. One of the king's top advisors and two army colonels are Jewish.

Some 25 percent of Moroccans speak the Berber language, Tamazight, as their primary language, but Arabic is the only officially recognized language. In 2001, King Mohammed announced the establishment of a royal cultural institute that would work toward integrating Tamazight into public education and ruled that translators must be available at trials of Berbers and expatriates who do not speak Arabic.

Mozambique

Polity: Presidential-parliamentary democracy
Economy: Mixed statist
Population: 19,600,000
PPP: $854
Life Expectancy: 38
Religious Groups: Indigenous beliefs (50 percent), Christian (30 percent), Muslim (20 percent)
Ethnic Groups: Shangaan, Chokwe, Manyika, Sena, Makua (> 99 percent)
Capital: Maputo

Political Rights: 3
Civil Liberties: 4
Status: Partly Free

Ten-Year Ratings Timeline (Political Rights, Civil Liberties, Status)

1993	1994	1995	1996	1997	1998	1999	2000	2001	2002	2003
6,4PF	6,5NF	3,5PF	3,4PF	3,4PF	3,4PF	3,4PF	3,4PF	3,4PF	3,4PF	3,4PF

Overview:

President Joachim Chissano had announced in 2001 that he would not run for president in the next elections, scheduled for 2004. This year Armando Guebeza, a former interior minister and hard-line Marxist, was named secretary general of the ruling Mozambique Liberation Front (FRELIMO) party and its nominee for president in the 2004 elections. The opposition party, the Mozambique National Resistance (RENAMO), led by Alphonse Dhlakama, has resumed its participation in the parliament, although it faces some internal dissension.

In late 2002 the trial of six men arrested for the murder of a leading Mozambican journalist, Carlos Cardoso, began; the murder and subsequent investigation have highlighted the growing corruption in one of Africa's best-performing economies. Cardoso was investigating banking scandals two years ago when he was assassinated. The presiding judge has said he will question a former government minister and President Chissano's son in connection with the case, although he has not yet decided to charge them.

Portuguese traders and settlers arrived in Mozambique in the late fifteenth century, but full-scale colonization did not begin until the seventeenth century. In 1962 FRELIMO was established; it launched a military campaign to drive out the Portuguese. In 1975 Mozambique gained independence. A one-party system was implemented, with FRELIMO as the sole legal party and the party leader, Samora Machel, as president of the republic. Independence was followed by 16 years of civil war against the rebels of RENAMO, which had its origins as a guerrilla movement supported first by Rhodesia (Zimbabwe) and later by South Africa.

In 1986 President Machel was killed in an airplane crash and Chissano became president. In 1989 FRELIMO formally abandoned Marxism-Leninism in favor of democratic socialism and a market economy. In 1992 a ceasefire was signed; it was followed by a full peace agreement. RENAMO recognized the government's legitimacy and agreed to begin operating as the opposition political party.

In 1994 the first multiparty elections were held. The elections attracted a 90 percent turnout and were judged a resounding success by Mozambicans and the international community, despite a last-minute pre-election boycott call by RENAMO, which accused FRELIMO of fraud. In response in large part to pressure from its international sponsors, RENAMO decided to participate in the process. Dhaklama captured 33.7 percent of the presidential vote, against 53.3 percent for the incumbent, Chissano. The parliamentary vote was much closer, as FRELIMO won a narrow, but workable, majority.

The next round of presidential and legislative elections took place in December 1999. Chissano and the ruling FRELIMO were reelected, despite a strong showing by the opposition in both elections. The U.S.-based Carter Center, which observed the elections, determined that there were signs of a maturing political system, although RENAMO complained vociferously of fraud, and resultant political unrest continued throughout much of 2000.

During 2000-2001 a series of major floods seriously affected the Mozambican economy. More than 650 people died and more than 500,000 were forced to flee from their homes. In addition, economic dislocation resulting in part from its post-independence civil war continued.

In December 2000, President Chissano and RENAMO'S Dhlakama began an inconclusive series of meetings which continued sporadically into 2001, raising hopes that the political impasse could be lessened. A key disagreement has been over the appointment of provincial governors, with Dhlakama insisting that RENAMO nominate governors for the six provinces where RENAMO won a majority of votes in the 1999 general elections.

Deep political divisions continue to characterize the country six years after negotiations ended 20 years of anti-colonial and civil wars. FRELIMO maintains its dominance of government institutions. RENAMO, its former guerrilla foe and now primary parliamentary opponent, has continued to complain bitterly of official manipulation of elections and the use of international aid to secure the ruling party's position. Nevertheless, in 2002 RENAMO did participate in parliament.

Abuses by myriad security forces and bandits are endemic. An antigovernment demonstration in November 2000 resulted in the deaths of more than 40 RENAMO supporters; approximately 80 prisoners, mostly RENAMO backers, were suffocated under mysterious circumstances at about the same time. In April 2001, parliament decided to extend the mandate of a commission set up to investigate the killings.

While economic growth has continued with extensive foreign aid, widespread corruption has damaged the government's standing.

Political Rights and Civil Liberties:

Mozambicans are able to select their president and parliament through competitive electoral processes, although this freedom is constrained by the social, political, and economic ravages of years of civil war, in addition to a lack of familiarity with democratic practices. Democratic consolidation remains tenuous, but dialogue and conflict are largely channeled through the country's democratic institutions. The 1999 polls were marred by logistical and administrative difficulties, but were viewed by many Mozambicans and the international community as expressing the will of the people. These national elections were just the second since Mozambique adopted a pluralist multiparty system. In addition, President Joachim Chissano's announcement that he would not run again in 2004 out of respect for the democratic process, both nationally and within FRELIMO, appears to reflect a willingness to accept the principles of democratic practice, including alternance in power.

RENAMO's continued claims of election fraud, however, have resulted in a highly polarized political environment. In protest of alleged fraud, RENAMO deputies repeatedly walked out of parliament or otherwise interrupted its proceedings throughout 2000 and part of 2001. At the peak of the boycott, RENAMO threatened to form a government of its own in the six northern and central provinces where it had won the most votes in the December elections.

A parliamentary ad hoc committee was set up to revise the country's electoral law, and parliament agreed in late 2002 to changes to the electoral law's provisions on settling disputes, on deploying observers, and on naming members to the electoral commission.

Municipal elections are due in 2003, and RENAMO leader Dhlakama has indicated that his party will participate on the basis of the new revised electoral code. A number of procedural changes undertaken in 2001 within the parliament itself, including a strengthening of the committee system, have also resulted in that body's increased effectiveness and impact, although partisan tensions at times impede its work.

In 2002 the Mozambican parliament passed the first reading of a bill to set up the Constitutional Council, a body that will decide whether laws and governmental decisions are in accordance with the country's constitution. Although the Constitutional Council is a body whose powers are set forth in the 1990 constitution, it had never been established, and for the past 12 years its duties have been exercised on a temporary basis by the Supreme Court.

International assistance continues to play an important, but controversial, role in supporting Mozambique's democratization process. For example, more than 80 percent of those eligible were registered to vote in the 1999 elections as part of a $40 million election process largely funded by the European Union and other donors. More controversially, some political campaigns were supported by foreign money. The National Elections Commission was criticized by opposition parties and some independent observers for alleged pro-FRELIMO bias. Parliament is active and is an important player in the political process, although its power is overshadowed by that of the executive branch.

In 2002 Mozambique's attorney general, in his annual report to parliament, admitted that the entire legal system in the country is plagued by corruption; he cited incompetence, corruption, and abuse of power at all levels of the administration of justice, including police, attorneys, judges, lawyers, and prison personnel. Prosecuting attorneys were also blamed for failing to press charges against suspects when there was more than enough evidence to indict them.

Criminal suspects are usually detained for many months before appearing in court without any formal defense, and are tried only in the official language, Portuguese, which many Mozambicans speak very poorly. Mozambique has only 170 judges or magistrates and an estimated 200 defense lawyers for a population of almost 20 million. These problems are compounded by bureaucratic red tape. Bribery of judges by lawyers is alleged to be common practice; judges regularly set bail so low on serious crimes that suspects simply flee justice.

The 1990 constitution provides for press freedom. With the opening up of independent newspapers, the influence of government-run newspapers has fallen. The most important media company to arise is the cooperative Mediacoop, which owns the successful Mediafax (faxed to hundreds of direct subscribers but read very widely), the periodical *Mozambique Interview* and the weekly *Savana*.

The independent media have enjoyed moderate growth, but publications in Maputo have little influence in the largely illiterate rural population. Criminal libel laws are another important deterrent to open expression. The constitution protects media freedom, but the state controls nearly all broadcast media and owns or influences all of the largest newspapers. There are more than a dozen licensed private radio and television stations, which also exercise some degree of self-censorship. The opposition receives inadequate coverage in government-run media, especially radio and television.

Nongovernmental organizations, including the Mozambican Human Rights League, are free to operate openly and issue critical reports. International human rights and humanitarian groups are also allowed to operate in the country. There is no reported interference with free religious practice.

During the period of one-party rule, FRELIMO tightly controlled Mozambique's labor movement. The Organization of Mozambican Workers, the country's major trade confederation, is now nominally independent. The Organization of Free and Independent Unions, a more independent group, was formed in 1994. All workers in nonessential services have the right to strike. The right to bargain collectively is legally protected.

Freedom of assembly is broadly guaranteed, but limited by notification and timing restrictions. Women suffer from both legal and societal discrimination. Domestic violence is reportedly common, despite initiatives by the government and civic groups to reduce it. Despite some economic gains, the country remains among the world's poorest and suffers from one of the world's highest infant mortality rates.

Namibia

Polity: Presidential-
parliamentary democracy
Economy: Capitalist-statist
Population: 1,800,000
PPP: $6,431
Life Expectancy: 43

Political Rights: 2
Civil Liberties: 3
Status: Free

Religious Groups: Christian (90 percent),
indigenous beliefs (10 percent)
Ethnic Groups: Black (87.5 percent), white (6 percent), mixed (6.5 percent)
Capital: Windhoek

Ten-Year Ratings Timeline (Political Rights, Civil Liberties, Status)

1993	1994	1995	1996	1997	1998	1999	2000	2001	2002	2003
2,2F	2,3F	2,3F	2,3F	2,3F	2,3F	2,3F	2,3F	2,3F	2,3F	2,3F

Overview:

Namibia's white farmers became increasingly nervous in 2002 following comments made by President Sam Nujoma about the country's land redistribution program. Nujoma, speaking at the World Development Summit in Johannesburg, South Africa, in September, said that he supported the controversial land seizures being carried out by the government of President Robert Mugabe in neighboring Zimbabwe. There have been increasing calls in Namibia for more rapid land redistribution. Whites, who make up about 6 percent of the population, own just under half of Namibia's arable land. Nujoma, a close ally of Mugabe's, referred to "arrogant white farmers" during a congress of the ruling South West Africa People's Organization (SWAPO) in 2002 when discussing land redistribution. A proposed amendment to the country's land policy of "willing buyer–willing seller" would make it more difficult for foreign nationals to own land in Namibia. Although leaders of the Herero people in 2002 threatened to forcefully repossess farms in Namibia if they did not receive compensation for abuses they suffered during colonialism, the country is not expected to experience the violence that has wracked Zimbabwe. Namibia's cattle farms are of poorer quality, and larger areas are needed to make commercial farms viable.

Namibia was seized by German imperial forces in the late 1800s. Thousands of people were massacred by German troops in efforts to crush all resistance to colonial settlement and administration. The territory became a South African protectorate after German forces were expelled during World War I and was ruled under the apartheid system for 42 years after 1948. After 13 years of violent guerrilla war, Namibia achieved independence in 1990. During a UN-supervised democratic transition, Nujoma was chosen president that year by a freely and fairly elected National Assembly.

SWAPO scored a sweeping victory, and Nujoma was reelected in 1994. Nujoma, the leader of the country's struggle against apartheid, has adopted an increasingly authoritarian governing style. He was easily returned to power with 77 percent of the vote for a third 5-year term in the 1999 elections that also saw SWAPO dominate National Assembly polls. The party had succeeded in passing a bitterly contested constitutional amendment to allow Nujoma to seek a third term. Nujoma in 2001 said he would not seek a fourth term, but there is some pressure within the ruling party for him to run again.

Capital-intensive extractive industries, such as diamond and uranium mining, have drawn significant foreign investment and are the centerpiece of Namibia's economic growth. Most Namibians, however, continue to live as subsistence farmers, and many lack basic services. Insecurity in the northern Kavango region has taken its toll on the country's important tourism industry.

Political Rights and Civil Liberties: Namibia's 1999 elections were judged largely free and fair and allowed Namibians to exercise their constitutional right to choose their representatives for the third time. There were some instances of government harassment of the opposition, as well as unequal access to media coverage and campaign financing. SWAPO retained its two-thirds majority in the 72-member National Assembly in 1999, increasing its number of seats from 53 to 55. The Congress of Democrats and the Turnhalle Alliance each got 7 seats. The United Democratic Front won 2, and the Monitor Action group got 1 seat. The ruling party's main base is among the country's largest ethnic group, the Ovambo, whose prominence within SWAPO has evoked allegations of ethnic discrimination.

The constitution provides for an independent judiciary, and the government respects this. In rural areas, local chiefs use traditional courts that often ignore constitutional procedures. The Supreme Court in June 2002 ruled that the government must provide legal aid for 128 defendants accused of high treason and other crimes in relation to the Caprivi separatist rebellion. Human rights groups in 2002 said eight Caprivi suspects have died in police custody since 1999. Authorities have dismissed allegations of torture.

Respect for human rights in Namibia is good, although allegations of abuses by security forces, including torture and extrajudicial killing, have emerged from the Caprivi Strip, the Kavango region, and the Democratic Republic of Congo. All Namibian troops had withdrawn from Congo by 2002. Fighting in Caprivi flared in October 1998 and in August 1999. Caprivi, a finger of land poking eastwards out of northern Namibia along its borders with Angola and Botswana, differs geographically, politically, and in its ethnic makeup from the rest of Namibia. It was used by South Africa in that country's operations against SWAPO guerrillas. Caprivians accuse the government of neglect in the province, which is among the country's poorest. The National Union for the Total Independence of Angola (UNITA) has been accused of supporting Caprivi insurgents. Human rights groups in 2002 said abuses in the Caprivi region diminished following the truce signed in April between the Angolan government and UNITA. Under a 1999 mutual defense pact, the governments of Angola and Namibia agreed that each could pursue suspected rebels on the other's territory.

The Herero and Damara peoples are among the minority ethnic groups demanding larger government allocations for development in their home areas. Herero leaders in 2002 demanded reparations for abuses they suffered at the hands of German colonists. The Herero were nearly wiped out during colonialism. The government has made efforts to end discrimination of indigenous San (bushmen).

Namibia's constitution guarantees the right to free speech and a free press, and those rights are usually respected in practice. Private radio stations and critical independent newspapers usually operate without official interference, but reporters for state-run media have been subjected to indirect and direct pressure to avoid reporting on controversial topics. There are at least eight private radio stations and one private television station. The state-run Namibia Broadcasting Corporation has regularly presented views critical of the government.

Freedom of assembly is guaranteed, except in situations of national emergency. Freedom of religion is guaranteed and respected in practice. Despite constitutional guarantees, women continue to face serious discrimination in customary law and other traditional societal practices. Violence against women is reportedly widespread, although there is greater attention being focused on the problem. Women are increasingly involved in the political process, but remain underrepresented in government and politics.

Constitutionally guaranteed union rights are respected. Collective bargaining is not practiced widely outside the mining and construction industries. Informal collective bargaining is increasingly common. Essential public sector workers do not have the right to strike. Domestic and farm laborers remain the country's most heavily exploited workers, in part because many are illiterate and do not know their rights.

Nauru

Polity: Presidential-parliamentary democracy
Economy: Mixed capitalist-statist
Population: 10,000
PPP: na
Life Expectancy: 61

Political Rights: 1
Civil Liberties: 2*
Status: Free

Religious Groups: Christian (two-thirds Protestant, one-third Roman Catholic)
Ethnic Groups: Nauruan (58 percent), other Pacific Islander (26 percent), Chinese (8 percent), European (8 percent)
Capital: Yaren
Ratings Change: Nauru's civil liberties rating improved from 3 to 2 due to changes in the survey methodology.

Ten-Year Ratings Timeline (Political Rights, Civil Liberties, Status)

1993	1994	1995	1996	1997	1998	1999	2000	2001	2002	2003
1,2F	1,3F	1,3F	1,3F	1,3F	1,3F	1,3F	1,3F	1,3F	1,3F	1,2F

Overview:
Nauru, a tiny Pacific island nation located 1,600 miles northeast of New Zealand, gained independence from Australia in 1968. The island was a German protectorate from 1888 until the close of World War I, when Australia began administering it under a League of Nations mandate. The Japanese occupied Nauru during World War II, shipping 1,200 Nauruans to Truk Island in the northern Pacific to work as forced laborers. Australian administrators returned to Nauru after the war under a UN mandate. The

island became self-governing in 1966 in preparation for independence two years later.

The ever-shifting coalitions in Nauru's tiny, faction-ridden parliament, which chooses the president, have contributed to chronic political instability. Two veteran politicians—Rene Harris, the current president, and rival Bernard Dowiyogo—have alternated in power over the last several years. Dowiyogo was forced from office in 2001 over allegations that a Russian crime group laundered money through Nauru.

These and other money-laundering allegations led the U.S. government to announce plans in December 2002 to slap sanctions on Nauru, as well as on Ukraine, for the same reason. The U.S. Treasury Department said that it intended to bar U.S. financial institutions from doing business with any institution licensed by Nauru. The potential impact of the measures on Nauru's tiny economy was unclear at year's end.

The move came after the multination Financial Action Task Force called on member states to impose sanctions on Nauru and Ukraine for their failure to set up adequate anti-money laundering frameworks. Separately, the Paris-based Organization for Economic Cooperation and Development lists Nauru as one of seven tax havens worldwide that has refused to meet international norms by adopting tougher oversight.

Nauru established itself as an offshore tax and banking center as part of an effort to find new sources of income to offset the depletion of its once-ample phosphate reserves. Phosphate mining had made the country one of the richest in the world per capita. However, a good part of the royalties have been squandered, and the reserves are likely to become depleted by the middle of the decade.

A trust fund that sets aside a portion of phosphate royalties for future generations has lost millions of dollars through failed investments and financial scams. Moreover, years of government financial mismanagement have saddled Nauru with huge foreign debts relative to its size.

Easing matters somewhat, Australia in 1993 agreed to pay Nauru $70.4 million over 20 years in an out-of-court settlement after Nauru sued its former ruler in the International Court of Justice for additional royalties for mining during the trusteeship period. A century of phosphate mining, much of it during Australian rule, has left more than 80 percent of the eight-square-mile island uninhabitable.

Separately, the government since 2001 has temporarily housed hundreds of mainly Middle Easterners seeking asylum in Australia while their applications are being processed. Australia said in December that the two countries had signed a new deal under which Nauru will take up to 1,500 asylum seekers at a time and Australia will boost aid to the Pacific island nation. Nauru held around 700 asylum seekers in Australian processing centers at year's end.

Political Rights and Civil Liberties: Nauruans can change their government through elections. The 1968 constitution created an 18-seat parliament whose members are directly elected from 14 districts for three-year terms. Parliament elects the president from among its members. The government does not prevent Nauruans from forming political parties, although none exist.

Nauru's judiciary is independent, and defendants generally receive fair trials, according to the U.S. State Department's global human rights report for 2001, released in March 2002. Appeals can be lodged with the High Court of Australia, although this is rarely done. Many cases, in fact, are settled entirely outside the formal legal system through traditional reconciliation. This is done usually by choice, though sometimes under communal—though not governmental—pressure, the State Department report said. Contract workers from Kiribati and Tuvalu, who work mainly in mining, have limited access to this type of communal help and, in the past, have alleged that police rarely act on their formal complaints against Nauru citizens, the report added.

Nauru has no regular print media, but several publications appear on an occasional basis. They include a governmental bulletin and a newsletter, *The Visionary*, which often criticizes the government. The sole radio station is government owned. It regularly broadcasts Radio Australia and BBC news reports. The state-run Nauru TV and a privately owned sports network provide television service.

Citizenship and inheritance are matrilineal, although traditional norms have made it hard for women to pursue higher education, careers, or seats in parliament. Credible reports suggest that some Nauruan women are abused by their husbands, according to the U.S. State Department report.

Nauru has no trade unions and virtually no labor laws, and the government in the past has discouraged efforts to form unions. Foreign workers risk losing their jobs if they leave Nauru without their employer's permission. Moreover, foreign employees who lose their jobs generally must leave Nauru within 60 days. Foreign workers are provided free housing, but in practice this often consists of dilapidated and overcrowded shelters. The government and the state-owned Nauru Phosphate Corporation are the main employers.

Nepal

Polity: Constitutional monarchy (insurgency)
Political Rights: 4*
Civil Liberties: 4
Economy: Capitalist
Status: Partly Free
Population: 23,900,000
PPP: $1,327
Life Expectancy: 58
Religious Groups: Hindu (86.2 percent), Buddhist (7.8 percent), Muslim and other (6 percent)
Ethnic Groups: Brahman, Chetri, Newar, Gurung, Sherpa, Magar, Tamang, Bhotia, Rai, Limbu
Capital: Kathmandu
Ratings Change: Nepal's political rights rating decreased from 3 to 4 due to a protracted political stalemate in which the king, citing the worsening security situation created by the left-wing insurgency, dissolved parliament, postponed national elections, and assumed executive powers.

Ten-Year Ratings Timeline (Political Rights, Civil Liberties, Status)

1993	1994	1995	1996	1997	1998	1999	2000	2001	2002	2003
2,3F	3,4PF	3,4PF	3,4PF	3,4PF	3,4PF	3,4PF	3,4PF	3,4PF	3,4PF	4,4PF

Overview: Nepal faced heightened political instability and a worsening security situation in 2002. Infighting in the ruling Nepali Congress (NC) party led to the dissolution of parliament in May, and in October the king indefinitely postponed elections scheduled for November and assumed executive powers. An escalation in fighting between security forces and Maoist insurgents left more than 4,500 people dead throughout the year and devastated Nepal's infrastructure and economy. The Maoist uprising has affected the majority of Nepal's 75 districts and has claimed more than 7,000 lives since 1996. Both sides have been accused of increased human rights violations in the context of the insurgency.

King Prithvi Narayan Shah unified this Himalayan land in 1769. Following two centuries of palace rule, the left-leaning NC won Nepal's first elections in 1959. King Mahendra abruptly dissolved parliament and banned political parties in 1960, and in 1962 began ruling through a repressive *panchayat* (village council) system. Many parties went underground until early 1990, when the NC and a coalition of Communist parties organized pro-democracy rallies that led King Birendra to re-legalize political parties. An interim government introduced a constitution that vested executive power in the prime minister and cabinet and turned Nepal into a constitutional monarchy.

In Nepal's first multiparty elections in 32 years in 1991, Giraja Prasad Koirala, a veteran dissident, led the NC to victory and formed a government. Riven by intraparty conflicts, the NC was forced in 1994 to call early elections, which it lost to the Communist Party of Nepal (United Marxist-Leninist), or CPN-UML. The Communists, however, failed to win a majority in parliament. Hopes for a more stable government rose after the NC won a majority in elections held in 1999. The campaign centered on the problems of rampant official corruption, stagnant economic growth, and the Maoist insurgency.

In June 2001, Gyanendra ascended the throne after a palace massacre in which the apparently drunk Crown Prince Dipendra shot to death his parents—King Birendra and his queen—and seven other members of the royal family before killing himself. After Sher Bahadur Deuba became prime minister in July, the rebels agreed to a ceasefire, apparently in the belief that Deuba would be more flexible in negotiations than was his predecessor, Koirala, who had been forced to stand down. However, when the rebels broke the ceasefire in late November, King Gyanendra declared a state of emergency and ordered the army to fight the Maoists. The Communist Party of Nepal–Maoist (CPN-M), led by insurgents Baburam Bhattarai and Pushpa Kamal Dahal, said that it wants an end to the constitutional monarchy and the feudal structure that persists in many parts of the country. The government's decision to use the army to fight the Maoists marked a sharp escalation in the conflict. The emergency was extended in February 2002 and again in May, but was allowed to lapse in September.

Political instability heightened in May when the prime minister asked the king to dissolve parliament and called for fresh elections to be held in November. Meanwhile, the ruling NC party split in June. When caretaker Prime Minister Deuba, citing the worsening security situation, asked the king in October to postpone the elections, King Gyanendra dismissed Deuba and assumed executive powers himself. While postponing elections indefinitely, he also installed an interim administration headed by Lokendra Bahadur Chand, a former prime minister and senior leader of a small royalist party. Mainstream political parties termed his decision undemocratic and are worried about a permanent return to an executive monarchy, but were divided on a suitable solution to the political stalemate.

Political Rights and Civil Liberties:

Nepalese can change their government through elections. The 205-seat parliament is directly elected for a five-year term. However, the king can wield emergency powers and suspend many basic freedoms in the event of war, external aggression, armed revolt, or extreme economic depression. Elections are free though not entirely fair; in the 1999 elections, interparty clashes led to several election-related deaths and caused balloting to be postponed in dozens of districts. In August, the government postponed local elections and formed unelected committees to carry out local governmental functions until elections could take place.

Elected governments have made few reforms to Nepal's bloated, inefficient civil service, and ministries operate with little openness or accountability. However, a bill passed in April disqualifies those convicted on corruption charges from contesting political elections for five years, while a new anticorruption law signed by the king in August places the burden of proof on the accused and may lead to a rise in convictions.

Conditions for journalists deteriorated sharply in 2002. The November 2001 emergency regulations restricted press and publication rights as well as free access to information, and journalists were urged by the government not to write articles "sympathetic" to the Maoists. Since the state of emergency was declared, authorities have arrested more than 150 journalists and many remain in detention; a number have reportedly been subjected to harassment and torture. In June, the editor of a pro-Maoist weekly died in police custody, while Maoists abducted and murdered the editor of an independent newspaper in western Nepal in August. Both the constitution and the Press and Publications Act broadly suppress speech and writing that could undermine the monarchy, national security, public order, or interethnic or intercaste relations. While many of Nepal's private publications continue to criticize government policies, self-censorship as a result of official intimidation is a growing concern. The government owns both the influential Radio Nepal, whose political coverage favors the ruling party, as well as Nepal's sole television station.

Although the constitution describes Nepal as a Hindu kingdom, there is a considerable Buddhist minority. The constitution provides for freedom of religion, but proselytizing is prohibited and members of religious minorities occasionally complain of official harassment.

Emergency measures in effect until September 2002 restricted freedom of assembly and movement. The government generally allows political parties and nongovernmental organizations (NGOs) to function freely, although it enforces a constitutional ban on political parties that are formed along religious, caste, ethnic, tribal, or regional lines. Both police and Maoist guerrillas occasionally threaten human rights activists to deter them from investigating rights violations, according to the U.S. State Department's human rights report. The insurgency has forced several NGOs working on agricultural and health projects in western Nepal to curb their activities, the report added.

Nepal's trade unions are independent, but they have notched up few real gains for workers. By law, workers in certain "essential services," such as water supply, cannot stage strikes, and 60 percent of a union's membership must vote in favor of a strike for the strike to be legal. Authorities weakly enforce laws on working hours and health and safety standards, the U.S. State Department report said. Only about

10 percent of workers in the formal (business) sector are unionized. Overall, more than 80 percent of workers are engaged in subsistence agriculture. While export-oriented carpet factories have sharply reduced their use of child workers, smaller carpet factories and several other industries continue to depend on child labor. Illegal bonded labor is common on farms.

The Supreme Court "has demonstrated independence; however, lower level courts remain vulnerable to political pressure, and bribery of judges and court staff is endemic," according to the U.S. State Department's report on Nepal's human rights record in 2001. Because of heavy case backlogs and a slow appeals process, suspects often spend longer in pretrial detention than they would if convicted of the crimes for which they stand accused.

Both the government and the Maoists were accused of increased human rights violations as the insurgency intensified in 2002. According to the Informal Sector Service Centre, violence between the two sides claimed the lives of 4,677 people between November 2001 and October 2002. The Maoists have killed, tortured, or kidnapped civilians, including suspected informers, landowners, local officials, teachers, and members of mainstream political parties. The rebels have also set up "people's courts" in some parts of Nepal that hand down summary justice. Adding to civilian hardship, the guerrillas fund themselves in part through extortion and looting, and ordered several national strikes throughout the year that paralyzed major urban centers. The Maoists reportedly also use forcibly recruited children as soldiers, human shields, and couriers, according to a December 2002 Amnesty International report.

Nepal's poorly equipped police force has been implicated in extrajudicial killings, disappearances, arbitrary arrests and detentions, rapes, and the torture of suspected Maoists and alleged supporters. Domestic human rights groups accuse the government of using tough security laws such as the Public Security Act (PSA) and the newly promulgated Terrorist and Disruptive Activities Ordinance (TADO) to deter civilians from supporting the Maoists. Both laws allow officials to detain suspects for up to six months without filing charges. In March, Amnesty International accused the government of detaining dozens of civilians under TADO, including journalists, teachers, lawyers, and political activists, for their perceived support for the Maoists. As of August 2002, authorities had arrested more than 9,900 suspected Maoists or alleged followers, of whom 1,722 remained in custody, according to Amnesty International. Human rights groups also criticized the government's April offer of bounties for the capture of Maoist leaders.

In ordinary criminal cases, police at times commit extrajudicial killing and cause the disappearance of suspects in custody, the U.S. State Department report said. They also occasionally torture and beat suspects to punish them or to extract confessions, the report added. The government generally has refused to conduct thorough investigations and take serious disciplinary measures against officers accused of brutality. Prison conditions are poor, with overcrowding common and detainees sometimes handcuffed or otherwise fettered. Set up in 2000, the official Human Rights Commission has a mandate to investigate human rights violations but lacks enforcement powers and the resources to pursue cases in court.

Members of the Hindu upper castes largely dominate parliament and the bureaucracy, and low-caste Hindus, ethnic minorities, and Christians face discrimination in the civil service, courts, and governmental offices, the U.S. State Department report said. The government in August 2001 formally banned discrimination against members of the lowest caste and said it would move to end the caste system. Nepalese officials at times extort money from, or otherwise harass, Tibetan asylum seekers who cross the border into Nepal, according to the U.S. State Department report. Some 2,000 to 3,000 Tibetans escape into exile via Nepal each year, with most ending up in India. Nepal also provides asylum to some 97,000 Bhutanese refugees.

Women rarely receive the same educational and employment opportunities as men, and there are relatively few women in government and the civil service. Laws relating to property, divorce, and several other areas discriminate against women. Independent studies and newspaper reports suggest that domestic violence and rape continue to be serious problems. The government has taken few steps to curb violence against women or to assist victims, and authorities generally do not prosecute domestic violence cases. Organized gangs traffic some 5,000 to 7,000 Nepalese girls to work in Indian brothels each year, according to the International Labor Organization. Because the majority of prostitutes who return to Nepal are HIV-positive, nearly all returnees are shunned and are unable to obtain help to rebuild their lives. Women's rights activists welcomed a law legalizing abortion and broadening women's property rights that came into effect in September.

Netherlands

Polity: Parliamentary democracy
Economy: Mixed capitalist
Population: 16,100,000
PPP: $25,657
Life Expectancy: 78
Religious Groups: Roman Catholic (31 percent), Protestant (21 percent), Muslim (4.4 percent), other (43.6 percent)
Ethnic Groups: Dutch (83 percent), other [Turks, Moroccans, Antilleans, Surinamese and Indonesians] (17 percent)
Capital: Amsterdam

Political Rights: 1
Civil Liberties: 1
Status: Free

Ten-Year Ratings Timeline (Political Rights, Civil Liberties, Status)

1993	1994	1995	1996	1997	1998	1999	2000	2001	2002	2003
1,1F	1,1F	1,1F	1,1F	1,1F	1,1F	1,1F	1,1F	1,1F	1,1F	1,1F

Overview:

A coalition of the centrist Christian Democratic Appeal (CDA), the far-right populist Lijst Pim Fortuyn (LPF), and the right-of-center Liberals (VVD), took office on July 22, 2002. However, the coalition collapsed on October 16 because of internal conflict within the LPF. Human rights groups criticized the tightening of asylum procedures, as anti-immigrant feeling developed in the traditionally tolerant Netherlands.

After the Dutch won independence from Spain in the sixteenth century, the House of Orange assumed sovereignty over the United Provinces of the Netherlands. A constitutional monarchy based on representative government emerged in the early 1800s. Today, Queen Beatrix appoints the arbiters of executive authority (the Council of Ministers) and the governor of each province on the recommendation of the majority in parliament.

Following the general election on May 15, a coalition of the centrist CDA, the far-right populist LPF, and the right-of-centre VVD, took office only to collapse on October 16, after internal conflict within the LPF led to the resignation of two of its ministers. A new election will be held on January 22, 2003. Pim Fortuyn, the founder and leader of LPF, was fatally gunned down just nine days before the May general election in an attack blamed on an animal rights activist. Fortuyn had wooed many voters with his slogan "The Netherlands is Full," a call to close Dutch borders.

The Netherlands adopted the euro in January 2002 as the national currency. The European Parliament amended the 1997 European Community directive on privacy in telecommunications in May 2002 to oblige member states to retain all telecommunications data on individual citizens for one to two years and to provide the relevant authorities unrestricted access to these data to assist law enforcement officials in eradicating crime. Human rights groups attacked this move as an assault on privacy and civil liberty.

Political Rights and Civil Liberties:

The Dutch can change their government democratically. The 150-member lower house, or Second Chamber, is elected for a four-year term by universal suffrage. The Second Chamber is empowered to debate bills and pass the approved measures to the upper house (First Chamber) for enactment. The 75 members of the upper house are indirectly elected for a period of four years. Local voting rights are accorded to foreigners after five years in residence. The Netherlands is the only country in the EU without elected mayors. The government appoints mayors from a list of candidates submitted by the municipal council.

The press is free and independent, although journalists practice self-censorship when reporting on the royal family. All Dutch newspapers cooperate in the administration of the independent Netherlands News Agency. Radio and television broadcasters operate autonomously under the supervision and regulation of the state and offer pluralistic views. Free speech is guaranteed, with the exception of promoting racism or incitement to racism. Reporters Sans Frontieres ranked the Netherlands (in a tie with Finland, Iceland, and Norway) as having the greatest press freedom in the world, in its Worldwide Press Freedom Index for 2002.

Freedom of religion is respected. Approximately 31 percent of the population is Roman Catholic; Protestants constitute 21 percent; and Muslims make up 4.4 percent of the population. More than one-third of the population is unaffiliated with any religion. The government provides subsidies to church-affiliated schools based on the number of registered students.

Membership in labor unions is open to all workers, including military, police, and civil service employees. Currently, about 28 percent of the workforce is unionized. The Aliens Employment Act, which took effect in 2000, is intended to further increase the employment opportunities of minority groups and asylum seekers.

As of May 2002, asylum seekers without identity papers were not allowed to request political asylum in the Netherlands—even though about 80 percent of asylum seekers arrive without such documentation. The UN High Commissioner for Refugees said the measure risks lumping legitimate refugees fleeing persecution with illegal immigrants. Because the Foreign Affairs Ministry now regards Afghanistan as safe, the government decided in September that failed Afghan national asylum seekers must return to Afghanistan; an estimated 30,000 Afghans live in the Netherlands.

The judiciary acts independently, though all judicial appointments are made by the crown on the basis of nominations by the parliament. Judges are nominally appointed for life, but retire at age 70. There is no jury system in Dutch courts. In April 2001, the Netherlands became the first country to legalise euthanasia.

Transparency International ranked the Netherlands seventh (tied with Luxembourg) on its 2002 Corruption Perceptions Index, the fourth highest evaluation of any EU member state.

In December 2001, the Council of the European Union adopted by "written procedure" antiterrorism legislation that requires member states to prevent "the public" from offering "any form of support, active or passive" to terrorists and to check all refugees and asylum seekers for terrorist connections. Human rights groups criticized the legislation because it does not distinguish between conscious and subconscious assistance, treats would-be immigrants as criminals, and was not debated in parliament.

Gender-based discrimination is prohibited, and women are well represented in government, education, and other fields. Legislation to better regulate prostitution and to end the 88-year-old ban on brothels went into effect in 2000.

A new marriage law stipulates that same-sex marriages are legal and confers on homosexual couples the same pension, social security, and inheritance rights accorded to married heterosexual couples. Adoption by same-sex couples is also allowed. The law took effect in April 2001.

New Zealand

Polity: Parliamentary democracy
Economy: Capitalist
Population: 3,900,000
PPP: $20,070
Life Expectancy: 78

Political Rights: 1
Civil Liberties: 1
Status: Free

Religious Groups: Anglican (24 percent), Presbyterian (18 percent), Roman Catholic (15 percent), other or none (43 percent)
Ethnic Groups: New Zealand European (74.5 percent), Maori (10 percent), other European (4.5 percent), Pacific Islander (4 percent), Asian and other (7 percent)
Capital: Wellington

Ten-Year Ratings Timeline (Political Rights, Civil Liberties, Status)

1993	1994	1995	1996	1997	1998	1999	2000	2001	2002	2003
1,1F	1,1F	1,1F	1,1F	1,1F	1,1F	1,1F	1,1F	1,1F	1,1F	1,1F

Overview:

After winning reelection in July but failing to gain an outright majority, the Labor Party faced another three years of dependence on minority parties to govern. The results could force Prime Minister Helen Clark's government to shift toward the political center in order to maintain the support of a small party that favors tax cuts and pro-family policies.

New Zealand became self-governing prior to World War II and gained full independence from the United Kingdom in 1947. Since 1935, the main political forces in this parliamentary democracy have been the mildly conservative National Party and the center-left Labor Party. Both parties helped to create one of the world's most progressive welfare states.

Seeking to sharpen New Zealand's economic competitiveness in the face of increasing global competition, the Labor government in 1984 began cutting farm subsidies, trimming tariffs, and privatizing many industries. The harsh effects of these economic changes, and a deep recession, contributed to a National Party landslide at the 1990 elections.

Rather than reverse course, however, Prime Minister Jim Bolger's incoming government pushed the reforms even further by rolling back the welfare state. It slashed welfare payments, ended universal free hospital care, and reworked the labor law to discourage collective bargaining. Bolger led the National Party to reelection victories in 1993 and 1996 before being forced to resign in an intraparty coup.

The Labor Party has been in office since 1999, when it won an election dominated by questions about the National Party's privatization plans and management of state agencies. Like its victory in 1999, Labor's reelection in 2002 left the party with 52 seats in the 120-seat parliament. This means that Labor will have to depend on its allies to form a majority and govern.

Following the election, Labor formed a minority government with the populist Progressive Coalition Party, which had won two seats, and received a pledge of support from the centrist United Future Party (UFP), which had won eight. In return for the UFP's support, Prime Minister Clark, 52, pledged to create a commission on family issues, pass strong crime victims' rights legislation, and introduce transport legislation favored by the UFP. Meanwhile, the main opposition National Party was forced to ponder its future strategy after winning only 27 seats, its worst-ever finish.

In a key post-election move, the government in August named a new central bank chief who favors a somewhat looser monetary policy than his predecessor. The expected policy shift by the new governor, Alan Bollard, could help Clark's government meet its goal of boosting economic growth to 4 percent annually. Prior to Bollard's appointment, experts were predicting that New Zealand's economy would grow by 3 percent a year, on average, for the next three years.

The long-term challenge is to raise productivity enough to make 3-4 percent growth rates sustainable. The Finance Ministry said in the spring that New Zealand's economic growth rate was likely to decline to two percent annually in a decade.

Political Rights and Civil Liberties:

New Zealanders can change their government through elections, and they face few restrictions on basic rights. Parliament is elected under rules that are designed to help smaller parties gain seats. New Zealand's so-called mixed-proportional system combines voting in geographic districts with proportional representation balloting. In addition, six seats are reserved for members of the indigenous Maori minority.

New Zealand's judiciary is independent, and defendants can appeal to the Privy Council in London. Police occasionally abuse suspects, according to the U.S. State Department's global human rights report for 2001, released in March 2002. New Zealand's private newspapers and magazines cover politics tenaciously and offer a range of political views.

While Prime Minister Clark and several other women hold senior government posts, women on the whole are underrepresented in government and politics. They also earned only 85 percent of men's average wages as of the third quarter of 2001. Despite numerous government initiatives aimed at protecting women, violence against women is a "serious and growing" problem, according to the U.S. State Department report. Moreover, 31 percent of women responding to a 2001 survey commissioned by New Zealand's official human rights body reported being victims of sexual harassment.

Members of New Zealand's Maori and smaller Pacific Islander and Asian communities face some discrimination in mainstream society, the U.S. State Department report said. The government's 2000 "Closing the Gaps" report said that Maoris continued to be found in outsized numbers among single-family households, prison inmates and school dropouts, and the ranks of the unemployed and the welfare-dependent. The Maori infant mortality rate is also high. Though they make up just 10 percent of New Zealand's population, Maoris account for more than half of all inmates.

Successive governments have introduced numerous programs to help boost the social and economic status of Maoris and Pacific Islanders. By most accounts, many of these initiatives, such as a policy of bringing more minorities into public sector jobs, have been only marginally successful.

A special tribunal continues to hear Maori tribal claims to land and other resources stemming from the white settlement of New Zealand. The 1840 Treaty of Waitangi, between the Maoris and British, leased Maori land in perpetuity to the white "settlers." Maoris now seek higher "rents" on their land.

Led by the New Zealand Council of Trade Unions, the main labor federation, unions advocate workers' rights forcefully and practice collective bargaining extensively. In a gain for unionized workers, the government in 2000 passed legislation that further promotes collective bargaining. The Employment Relations Act also requires management and workers to bargain in good faith when negotiating employment agreements. However, sympathy strikes, secondary strikes, and walkouts over social or political causes are still illegal. Despite these provisions, the government did not interfere with a brief strike in 2000 expressing solidarity with Fijian trade unionists. Less than 20 percent of New Zealand's wage earners are unionized.

Nicaragua

Polity: Presidential-parliamentary democracy
Economy: Capitalist-statist
Population: 5,400,000
PPP: $2,366
Life Expectancy: 68
Religious Groups: Roman Catholic (85 percent), Protestant and other (15 percent)
Ethnic Groups: Mestizo (69 percent), white (17 percent), black (9 percent), Indian (5 percent)
Capital: Managua

Political Rights: 3
Civil Liberties: 3
Status: Partly Free

Ten-Year Ratings Timeline (Political Rights, Civil Liberties, Status)

1993	1994	1995	1996	1997	1998	1999	2000	2001	2002	2003
4,3PF	4,5PF	4,5PF	4,4PF	3,3PF	3,3PF	2,3PF	3,3PF	3,3PF	3,3PF	3,3PF

Overview:

On January 10, 2002, Enrique Bolanos was sworn in as Nicaragua's third post-Sandinista-era president, with a mandate to tackle widespread and systemic corruption, fraud, and incompetence throughout government. One of the major challenges has become the confrontation with former president Arnoldo Aleman, who, along with family members and cronies, is accused of having stolen $100 million. Aleman, as president of the National Assembly, has immunity from criminal prosecution, and this status is seen by many as an example of the widespread impunity of officials that makes a mockery of justice. Elections have been generally free and fair. However, the process of governing has been clouded by serious concerns over freedom of speech and labor rights, as the government has clamped down on radio stations broadcasting coverage of corrupt government practices and has declared strikes illegal. Further concern is raised by the role Nicaragua plays in the trafficking of weapons—most recently to Colombia's illegal self-defense groups—and of drugs, as well as people. The border tensions with Costa Rica have been defused, while the claim over Colombia's San Andres and Providence archipelago has been rekindled.

The Republic of Nicaragua was established in 1838, seventeen years after independence from Spain. Its history has been marked by internal strife and dictatorship. The authoritarian rule of the Somoza regime was overthrown in 1979 by the Sandinistas. Subsequently, the Sandinista National Liberation Front (FSLN) attempted to establish a Marxist government, which led to a civil war. The United States intervened indirectly, using Argentine military veterans of that country's "dirty war" on behalf on the right-wing irregular army known as the Contras. The FSLN finally conceded in 1987 to a new constitution that provides for a president and the 96-member National Assembly elected every six years.

In 1990, the newspaper publisher Violeta Chamorro easily defeated the incumbent, President Daniel Ortega. Her 14-party National Opposition Union (UNO) won a legislative majority in the National Assembly. In February 1995, after passage of a law ensuring the military's autonomy, Humberto Ortega—Daniel's brother—turned over command of the military to General Joaquin Cuadra. The army was reduced from 90,000 to 15,000 troops, and former Contras were integrated into its ranks; however, the leadership remained essentially the same. The armed forces continued to own a profitable network of businesses and property amassed under the Sandinistas.

Chamorro was forbidden by law to seek a second term. The 1996 elections were held under the auspices of the five-member Supreme Electoral Council, an independent branch of government. During the campaign, Daniel Ortega portrayed himself as a moderate committed to national unity and reconciliation. Arnoldo Aleman ran on a platform that promised economic reforms, the dismantling of the Sandinista-era bureaucracy, the cleaning up of the army, and the return of property confiscated by the Sandinistas to its original owners. He defeated Ortega 51 to 38 percent, avoiding a runoff. President Aleman's first priority was to reform the army and the police. Aleman named a civilian minister of defense, and a new military code was adopted. The size of the National Police was reduced from 16,000 to 6,800. Its leadership, however, is still composed largely of old Sandinista cadres.

In 1999, a governability pact was agreed to by Aleman's right-wing Liberal Constitutionalist Party (PLC) government and the opposition, led by Daniel Ortega. Although the accord ended a 14-year congressional impasse, Nicaragua's smaller parties immediately protested that political power, including greater representation on both the Supreme Court and the Supreme Electoral Council, was being "carved up" between the two historic antagonists.

The reforms guaranteed Aleman a seat in both the Nicaraguan and the Central American parliaments, thus assuring him immunity from prosecution. Throughout his presidency, Aleman was dogged by charges that he enriched himself in office, although he has never faced formal legal proceedings. In the November 4, 2001, elections, ruling Liberal Party candidate Enrique Bolanos, a conservative businessman respected for his personal integrity, defeated Sandinista leader and former president Daniel Ortega, 54 to 45 percent, in a bitterly fought contest in which the two major parties stacked the deck against smaller-party participation.

Political Rights and Civil Liberties: Nicaraguans can change their government democratically. Political and civic activities continue to be conditioned on occasional political violence, corruption, and drug-related crime. The judiciary is independent but continues to be susceptible to political influence and corruption. Large case backlogs, long delays in trials, and lengthy pretrial detention have caused the Supreme Court and National Assembly to initiate comprehensive structural reforms of the judicial system.

The Ministry of Government oversees the National Police, the agency that is formally charged with internal security; in practice, the police share this responsibility with the army in rural areas. Reflecting enhanced civilian control, the conduct of security forces continues to improve, although abuses of human rights still occur. Forced confessions to the police remain a problem, as do cases in which security forces arbitrarily arrest and detain citizens. Prison and police holding-cell conditions are poor.

Violent crime is increasing in Managua and other major Nicaraguan cities, although the country remains relatively tranquil compared to some of its Central American neighbors. With long coastlines on both the Atlantic and Pacific, a high volume of land cargo, and myriad jungle airstrips, Nicaragua is an important transshipment point for drugs making their way to the north from South America. The Pan-American Highway in Nicaragua's southwest region is a primary venue for narcotics traffickers, although smuggling by air is increasing and small aircraft are occasionally commandeered by traffickers for flights to other countries. The growing level of exposure of Nicaraguan society to the drug trade is evidenced by the significant increase in the local use of cocaine.

The print media are varied and partisan, representing hard-line and moderate Sandinista, as well as pro- and anti-government, positions. Before leaving office, the Sandinistas privatized the national radio system, mostly to Sandinista loyalists. There are five television stations, three of which carry news programming with partisan political content. Media outlets covering government corruption have been intimidated and/or closed by the government. There is free access to the Internet. Academic freedom is generally honored.

Like most Latin American countries, Nicaragua nominally recognizes the rights of its indigenous communities in its constitution and laws, but in practice those rights have not been respected. Indigenous peoples, about 5 percent of the population, live in two autonomous regions—the Northern Autonomous Atlantic Region and the Southern Autonomous Atlantic Region. These are primarily Miskito, Sumo, Rama, and Garifuna peoples. In 1998, Indian parties showed significant political strength in the March regional elections, in which 45 autonomous councils were chosen. Indigenous political rights were severely curtailed by legislation enacted in 2000 forcing parties to re-register with an amount of signatures that was nearly impossible to achieve.

In a major development in 2001, the Inter-American Court of Human Rights found that Nicaragua had violated the rights of the Awas Tingni community of eastern Nicaragua. The Aleman government was found to have granted licenses to foreign logging companies for the exploitation of Indian communities' ancestral lands without consulting the original inhabitants. The case was the first time the human rights tribunal ruled on a land dispute between an Indian group and a government.

Labor rights are complicated by the Sandinistas' use of unions as violent instruments to influence government economic policy. By means of the public sector unions, the Sandinistas have managed to gain ownership of more than three dozen privatized state enterprises. The legal rights of non-Sandinista unions are not fully guaranteed. The Ministry of Labor has declared strikes illegal. Citizens have no effective recourse when labor laws are violated either by the government or by violent Sandinista actions. Child labor is also a problem. Violence against women, including rape and domestic abuse, remains a serious problem.

⬇ Niger

Polity: Presidential-
parliamentary
democracy
Economy: Capitalist
Population: 11,600,000
PPP: $746
Life Expectancy: 45

Political Rights: 4
Civil Liberties: 4
Status: Partly Free

Religious Groups: Muslim (80 percent), Indigenous beliefs
and Christian (20 percent)
Ethnic Groups: Hausa (56 percent), Djerma (22 percent), Fula (9 percent), Tuareg (8 percent), Beri Beri (4 percent), other (1 percent)
Capital: Niamey
Trend Arrow: Niger received a downward trend arrow for a crackdown on the opposition, the press, and human rights workers that followed a mutiny in July.

Ten-Year Ratings Timeline (Political Rights, Civil Liberties, Status)

1993	1994	1995	1996	1997	1998	1999	2000	2001	2002	2003
5,4PF	3,4PF	3,5PF	3,5PF	7,5NF	7,5NF	7,5NF	7,5NF	4,4PF	4,4PF	4,4PF

Overview:

The government of President Mamadou Tandja cracked down on the press and others following an army mutiny in August 2002. The mutineers took civilians and members of the military hostage in a siege that lasted for more than a week. The soldiers demanded improved living conditions, payment of overdue allowances, and the dismissal of the army chief of staff. Authorities detained more than 260 soldiers in connection with the uprising. A handful of journalists and a human rights advocate were also detained. They were accused of violating a presidential decree, issued in connection with the mutiny, that banned the dissemination of information the government considered a threat to national defense.

After gaining independence from France in 1960, Niger was governed for 30 years by one-party and military regimes dominated by leaders of Hausa or Djerma ethnicity. After 13 years of direct military rule, Niger was transformed into a nominally civilian, one-party state in 1987 under General Ali Seibou. International pressure and pro-democracy demonstrations led by the Niger Union of Trade Union Workers, an umbrella organization, forced Niger's rulers to accede to the Africa-wide trend towards democratization in 1990. An all-party national conference drafted a new constitution that was adopted in a national referendum in 1992.

Mahamane Ousmane, of the Alliance of Forces for Change, won a five-year term as the country's first democratically elected president in 1993 in elections deemed free and fair. General Ibrahim Bare Mainassara overthrew Ousmane in 1996 and won reportedly fraudulent elections later that year. Mainassara was assassinated in April 1999 by members of the presidential guard. The head of the guard led a transitional government that held a constitutional referendum and elections that year.

Niger is struggling to implement unpopular structural reforms. The economy is based mainly on subsistence farming, small trading, herding, and informal markets. Uranium is the most important export, but world demand has declined.

Political Rights and Civil Liberties: The people of Niger have had two chances, in 1993 and 1999, to change their leaders democratically. The July 1996 presidential election that followed the January 1996 military coup was held under a revised constitution and was not deemed free or fair by independent observers. Polls in 1999 were considered free and fair. Mamadou Tandja won the runoff with 60 percent of the vote.

Parliamentary elections in November 1996 were held in an atmosphere of intense intimidation and were boycotted by most opposition parties. In 1999, Tandja's party, the National Movement for the Development of Society, and its partner, the Democratic and Social Convention, achieved a two-thirds majority in the National Assembly by winning 55 of the 83 seats. The other coalition, the Nigerian Party for Democracy and Socialism and the Rally for Democracy and Progress, won the other 28 seats.

The constitution provides for an independent judiciary, and courts have shown signs of independence. However, the judiciary is occasionally subject to executive interference and other outside influence, is overburdened, and is limited by scant training and resources. Efforts at reform are under way.

Respect for human rights has improved under the government of President Tandja. However, prolonged pretrial detention remains a problem. Prisons are characterized by overcrowding, and poor health and sanitary conditions. The International Committee of the Red Cross and other humanitarian groups have unrestricted access to prisons and detention centers. Human rights and other nongovernmental organizations operate openly and freely in Niger and publish reports that are often highly critical of the government. However, authorities in September 2002 arrested Bagnou Bonkoukou of the Niger Human Rights League for saying in a radio broadcast that the death toll from the August mutiny was higher than government figures stated. Authorities said Bonkoukou violated a presidential decree that banned dissemination of information regarding the mutiny. A court sentenced him to one year in jail.

Constitutional guarantees of freedom of assembly and association are generally respected. Constitutional protections for free expression are guaranteed, but these rights are not always guaranteed in practice. Criminal penalties are exacted for violations such as slander. A government newspaper and at least a dozen private publications circulate. There are several private radio stations, some of which broadcast in local languages. Parliament opened a radio station in 2001 as the Voice of the National Assembly.

The government cracked down on members of the press following the August mutiny. Authorities detained Moussa Kaka, director of the private radio station Saraounia, for 10 hours and Boulama Ligari of the independent Radio Anfani for three days for their coverage of the mutiny. Both were held without charge. Tandja's decree had banned "the propagation of information or allegations likely to be detrimental to the implementation of national defense operations." Media outlets were threatened with suspension or closure if they violated the ban. The decree also stipulated that individuals who disseminated "false information" would be punished. Other journalists were detained earlier in the year for allegedly insulting government officials. The publisher and editor in chief of the satirical weekly *Le Canard Dechainé* was detained in June and sentenced to eight months in prison on libel charges.

Freedom of religion is respected, although, at times, Muslims have not been tolerant of the rights of minority religions to practice their faith. Islam is practiced by 80 percent of the population. The government in 2000 banned six fundamentalist-oriented organizations after rioting by Islamic fundamentalist groups. Discrimination against ethnic minorities persists, despite constitutional protections. The Hausa and Djerma ethnic groups dominate government and business. Tandja is the country's first president who is from neither group. Nomadic peoples, such as the Tuaregs and many Peul, continue to have less access to governmental services. The country's last serious insurgency, led mainly by minority ethnic Tobou, ended with a peace pact in 1999.

Women suffer extensive societal discrimination, especially in rural areas. Family law gives women inferior status in property, inheritance rights, and divorce. In the east, some women among the Hausa and Peul ethnic groups are cloistered and may leave their homes only if escorted by a male and usually only after dark. Domestic violence against women is reportedly widespread. Several women's rights organizations operate in the country. Sexual harassment and female genital mutilation were made illegal in 2001.

Niger's workers have the right to form unions and bargain for wages, although more than 95 percent of the workforce is employed in the nonunionized subsistence agricultural and small trading sectors.

Nigeria

Polity: Presidential-parliament-
ary democracy
Economy: Capitalist
Population: 129,900,000
PPP: $896
Life Expectancy: 52
Religious Groups: Muslim (50 percent),
Christian (40 percent), indigenous beliefs (10 percent)
Ethnic Groups: Hausa and Fulani (29 percent),
Yoruba (21 percent), Ibo (18 percent), other (32 percent)
Capital: Abuja

Political Rights: 4
Civil Liberties: 5
Status: Partly Free

Ten-Year Ratings Timeline (Political Rights, Civil Liberties, Status)

1993	1994	1995	1996	1997	1998	1999	2000	2001	2002	2003
5,4PF	7,5NF	7,6NF	7,7NF	7,6NF	7,6NF	6,4PF	4,3PF	4,4PF	4,5PF	4,5PF

Overview:

Political violence escalated in Nigeria in the run-up to presidential and legislative elections scheduled for 2003, raising fears that the country will struggle to have its first peaceful transfer of power from one civilian government to another. Municipal elections were postponed indefinitely in August 2002, after having been rescheduled from May, ostensibly to allow for further preparations. A voter registration exercise held in September was disastrous. The federal government faced international criticism about harsh sentences handed down by *Sharia* (Islamic law) courts in the north of the country. Intercommunal violence continued in 2002, and clashes between Christians and Muslims in the northern city of Kaduna claimed more than 200 lives in November following controversy over the Miss World Pageant. Security forces continued to commit abuses with impunity, although the government moved to disband a notorious southern vigilante group.

The military ruled Nigeria for all but 10 years since independence from Britain in 1960 until 1999. Its generals and their backers argued that they were the only ones who could keep a lid on simmering tensions between Muslims and Christians, and between the country's 250 ethnic groups. The Hausa-Fulani from northern Nigeria dominated the military and the government from independence until Olusegun Obasanjo, from the south, was elected. The north is largely Muslim while the south is mainly Christian.

Nigeria initially appeared to be emerging from several years of military rule under General Ibrahim Babangida in 1993, when presidential elections were held. Moshood Abiola, a Muslim Yoruba from the south, was widely considered the winner, but the military annulled the results. It continued to rule behind a puppet civilian administration until General Sani Abacha, a principal architect of previous coups, took power himself in November 1993. A predominantly military Provisional Ruling Council (PRC) was appointed, and all democratic structures were dissolved and political parties banned. Abiola was arrested in June 1994 after declaring himself Nigeria's rightful president. He died in detention, after suffering from lack of proper medical care, just five weeks after Abacha himself died suddenly in June 1998.

The departure of the two most significant figures on Nigeria's political landscape opened possibilities for democratic change. General Abdulsalami Abubakar, the army chief of staff, emerged as the consensus choice of the military's PRC as the country's next leader and promised to oversee a transition to real civilian rule in 1999. However, Obasanjo, the People's Democratic Party (PDP) choice, won the presidential poll. A former general who led a military regime in Nigeria from 1976 to 1979, Obasanjo had spent three years in prison under Abacha.

Opinion on Obasanjo in 2002 was divided along ethnic lines. Many northern, Hausa-speaking Muslims, who had shown electoral support for him, believe he has failed to live up to expectations and do not want him to stand for reelection in 2003. On the other hand, many in the southwest who did not support him in 1999 now see opposition against him as an affront to the Yoruba people.

The International Court of Justice at the Hague in 2002 delivered a verdict in favor of Cameroon in its long-running dispute with Nigeria over the oil-rich Bakassi peninsula. Nigeria balked at the ruling and was to meet Cameroonian president Paul Biya to discuss the matter further. Nigeria and Cameroon have clashed militarily over Bakassi in the past, and it is unlikely that Nigeria will let go of the region without some concessions.

The majority of Nigerians are engaged in small-scale agriculture, while most wealth is controlled by a small elite. Nigeria's agricultural and manufacturing sectors deteriorated considerably in the pursuit of oil, which accounts for more than 98 percent of Nigeria's export revenues and almost all foreign investment. Corruption has bled the country of billions of dollars in oil revenue. Economic reform is progressing slowly.

Political Rights and Civil Liberties:

Nigerians exercised the right to change their government for the first time in 16 years in 1999. Although the voting was free, it was not fair in many areas in both the presidential and legislative polls. During the presidential nominating convention, large sums of money were offered by both political camps to delegates to vote against political opponents. International observers witnessed serious irregularities during the presidential election, including the local purchase of false ballots and fraudulent tally sheets. The production of "ghost votes" in some states amounted to as much as 70 or 80 percent of the total reported votes. Olusegun Obasanjo, of the PDP, won the presidency, which carries a four-year term, with 63 percent of the vote compared with 37 percent for Samuel Oluyemi Falae of the Alliance for Democracy (AD). International observers confirmed the results and stated that, despite widespread fraud, Obasanjo's victory reflected the will of most voters.

Members of the bicameral National Assembly are elected for four-year terms to 109 seats in the Senate and 360 in the House of Representatives. Obasanjo's PDP won 59 Senate seats and 206 House seats. The All People's Party won 24 seats in the Senate and 74 in the House, while the AD won 20 Senate seats and 68 House seats.

There were several problems with the September 2002 voter registration exercise. Despite a massive turnout, there was a widespread scarcity of registration materials, which was attributed to the hoarding of forms. There were also numerous cases of double, multiple, and under-age registration. Many people, however, were never able to register at all.

Casting a shadow over the next elections was a wave of political assassinations in 2002. Among those killed were Barnabas Igwe, the chairman of the Onitsha branch of the National Bar Association, and his wife. Igwe was a vocal critic of the Onitsha local government. Human rights groups fear that the violence will escalate as the elections draw nearer.

The judiciary is subject to political influence and is hampered by corruption and inefficiency. Many trials in Islamic courts in several northern states have been characterized by absence of due process. Defendants do not always have legal representation; they are often ill-informed about procedures and about their rights. Lengthy pretrial detention remains a problem. The country's prisons are overcrowded, unhealthful and life threatening. Nevertheless, the government has allowed international nongovernmental organizations to visit detention facilities, and some improvements have been made.

The Human Rights Violations Investigation Commission, which is modeled on South Africa's Truth and Reconciliation Commission, wrapped up its work in 2002 after receiving evidence from more than 2,000 witnesses. The commission heard complaints of alleged abuses spanning from the start of the Biafran war in 1966 through the regime of General Sani Abacha in the 1990s. The commission said some of the victims were eligible for compensation.

Despite efforts to address past abuses, there are continuing reports of violations. Members of the security forces, as well as vigilante groups, committed serious violations in 2002. These included extrajudicial killings, arbitrary detentions, torture, and beatings. A local human rights group, the Center for Law Enforcement Education in Nigeria, reported in October that Nigerian customs had seized more than 2,000 copies of a report, done in collaboration with the Geneva-based World Organization Against Torture, detailing massacres and other abuses by the state. In addition, the group said, three people who contributed to the report had been harassed by the State Security Services.

Vigilante groups were created to fill the gap in the poorly funded police force and to answer the need to address skyrocketing crime. Many of the groups have the support of local officials, which raises fears that vigilantes might be used in the next elections to carry out intimidation campaigns against political opponents as has happened in the past. New York-based Human Rights Watch welcomed the government's efforts in 2002 to crack down on one of the most notorious vigilante groups, the Bakassi Boys, but urged longer-lasting reforms of the police force.

Freedom of speech and expression is guaranteed, and the Obasanjo government respects these rights in practice. Several private radio and television stations broadcast. The government in February 2002 granted television broadcast licenses to five new television companies and 16 private radio stations. Numerous print publications operate largely unhindered. However, criminal defamation laws are still used against journalists. Islamic law imposes severe penalties for alleged press offenses. Foreign journalists have reported efforts by some officials to bribe them with cash.

The freedom of assembly and association is guaranteed and is usually respected in practice. The constitution prohibits ethnic discrimination and requires governmental offices to reflect the country's ethnic diversity. Obasanjo's government is both ethnically and religiously diverse, but societal discrimination is widely practiced, and clashes frequently erupt among the country's 250 ethnic groups. A number of armed youth groups have emerged to defend their ethnic and economic interests. Nigerian human rights groups said in 2002 that inter-communal violence had claimed up to 10,000 lives across the country since 1999.

Ethnic minorities in the Delta region feel particularly discriminated against, mainly in terms of receiving a share of the country's oil wealth. Oil spills and acts of sabotage frequently disrupt petroleum production. The taking of foreign oil workers as hostages continued in 2002, as did clashes between ethnic groups and communities competing for resources. Up to 100 women occupied an oil installation for nine days in 2002. Human Rights Watch said there was still widespread deployment of security forces in the Delta region. Although more money is flowing to the region, ordinary people see few benefits from the funds.

Religious freedom is guaranteed by the constitution, but many sectors of society, including government officials, often discriminate against those of a religion different from their own. Religion-based violence has become increasingly common and often corresponds with regional and ethnic differences, as well as competition for resources. Caning and amputation have been carried out for violations such as adultery and theft. The government pledged in 2002 that it would not allow the sentence of death by stoning, imposed by an Islamic court on a 31-year-old Muslim woman to be carried out. Clashes between Muslims and Christians in the northern city of Kaduna in November 2002 were sparked by an article in *ThisDay* newspaper that said the Prophet Mohammed would have liked to marry a Miss World contestant. The pageant, which was getting under way in the capital, Abuja, was quickly moved to London after violence broke out. Six contestants had already pulled out of the pageant to protest the death by stoning sentence of the 31-year-old Nigerian woman. The journalist who wrote the *ThisDay* article fled the country after her life was threatened. The Obasanjo administration called for the reform of Islamic law in the 12 states that have adopted it. The states so far have refused to do so. By October, three men and two women were facing sentences of death by stoning in the north. In January 2002, for the first time since Sharia was extended to cover criminal cases, a man was sentenced to death and executed.

Nigerian women face societal discrimination, although educational opportunities have eroded a number of barriers over the years. Women play a vital role in the country's informal economy. Marital rape is not considered a crime, and women of some ethnic groups are denied equal rights to inherit property. About 60 percent of Nigerian women are subjected to female genital mutilation. Women's rights have suffered serious setbacks in many northern states governed by Sharia.

Child labor, forced marriages, and the trafficking of women for prostitution remain common, although efforts are under way to combat the practice. Although Nigeria signed the UN Convention on the Rights of the Child in 1991, it has not established a law making the convention's provisions enforceable in its courts.

There are several statutory restrictions on the right of association and on trade unions. Workers, except members of the armed forces and those considered essential employees, may join trade unions. The right to bargain collectively is guaranteed. About 10 percent of the workforce is unionized. Unions held a two-day general strike against increases in fuel prices in January 2002 that shut down most of the country's major cities. A court declared the strike called by the Nigeria Labor Congress (NLC), which groups the country's 29 main trade unions, illegal on the grounds that appropriate legal procedures were not followed. The NLC president was arrested twice in connection with the strike.

Norway

Polity: Parliamentary
democracy
Economy: Mixed capitalist
Population: 4,500,000
PPP: $29,918
Life Expectancy: 79

Political Rights: 1
Civil Liberties: 1
Status: Free

Religious Groups: Evangelical Lutheran (86 percent),
other Protestant and Roman Catholic (3 percent), other (11 percent)
Ethnic Groups: Germanic (Nordic, Alpine, Baltic), Lapp (Saami)
Capital: Oslo

Ten-Year Ratings Timeline (Political Rights, Civil Liberties, Status)

1993	1994	1995	1996	1997	1998	1999	2000	2001	2002	2003
1,1F	1,1F	1,1F	1,1F	1,1F	1,1F	1,1F	1,1F	1,1F	1,1F	1,1F

Overview:
Following Denmark's rule (1450-1814), Norway enjoyed a brief spell of independence during which the Eisvold Convention, Norway's current constitution, was adopted. Subsequently, Norway became part of a Swedish-headed monarchy. Norway gained independence in 1905, when a Danish prince was crowned as Haakon VII. Haakon VII remained head of state in exile during World War II, when the country was occupied by Germany. Haakon's son, Olav V, reigned from 1957 until his death in 1991. He was succeeded by his son, Harald V, who is Norway's current monarch. Since 1905 Norway has functioned as a constitutional monarchy with a multiparty parliamentary structure.

The government is led by a center-right coalition, comprising the Conservative Party, the Christian Democrat Party and the Liberals. Nevertheless, it still does not command a majority in parliament and relies on the far-right Progress Party to legislate.

Norway is not a member of the EU, but it enjoys nearly full access to the EU's single market through membership in the European Economic Area. The Labor government negotiated EU membership in both 1972 and 1994, but the Norwegian electorate rejected it each time by slim margins. The issue of EU membership was pushed further down the agenda in 2002 due to an anti-EU majority in parliament. However, public support for full Norwegian membership stood at 58 percent in 2002, the highest figure since the 1994 referendum.

Norway granted asylum in June to an Iranian who hijacked an airliner to Oslo in 1993. Norwegian law bans the death penalty and prohibits the deportation of persons to a country that might execute them, such as Iran. The Norwegian Pilots' Union and political opposition in parliament criticized the decision.

Political Rights and Civil Liberties: Norwegians can change their government democratically. The parliament (Storting) is directly elected for a four-year term by universal suffrage and proportional representation. It then selects one-quarter of its members to serve as the upper chamber (Lagting), while the remaining members make up the lower chamber (Odelsting). Neither body is subject to dissolution. A vote of no confidence in the Storting results in the resignation of the cabinet, and the leader of the party that holds the most seats is then asked to form a new government.

Since 1989 the approximately 20,000-strong ethnic Saami minority has elected an autonomous, 39-member assembly that functions as an advisory body on issues such as regional control of natural resources and preservation of Saami culture. In 2000, the government granted the Saami assembly its own parliamentary building in Karasjok. In 1999, the Center for Combating Ethnic Discrimination was established by the government to provide legal aid to persons exposed to discrimination on grounds of religion, race, or national or ethnic origin.

In recent years, there have been some instances of xenophobic and nationalist sentiments. The leader of the far-right Progress Party, Carl Hagen, demanded that the number of immigrants granted asylum in Norway be reduced. The estimated net migration rate for 2002 was 2.1 migrants per 1,000 population. The government tightened its asylum policy in 2002. The so-called 15-month rule—which stated that if asylum seekers' applications had not been processed within 15 months, they would be granted asylum automatically—was abolished for those who arrive without identification papers.

Freedom of the press is constitutionally guaranteed, and many newspapers are subsidized by the state in order to promote political pluralism. The majority of newspapers are privately owned and openly partisan. Norway has one of the highest rates of Internet users per capita in the world. Reporters Sans Frontieres ranked Norway (tied with Finland, Iceland, and the Netherlands) as having the greatest press freedom in the world in its Worldwide Press Freedom Index for 2002.

The Church of Norway, the state church, belongs to the Evangelical Lutheran branch of the Christian church. The king is the constitutional head of the Church of Norway, in which about 86 percent of the population holds nominal membership. Other denominations do not have to register with the state unless they seek state support. Muslims, who constitute less than 1 percent, were granted the right to broadcast the *adhan* (calls to prayer) in Oslo in 2000.

The constitution guarantees freedom of peaceful assembly and association and the right to strike. Sixty percent of the workforce belong to unions, which are free from governmental control. The Norwegian Federation of Trade Unions, established 100 years ago, has about 850,000 members and is closely linked to the Labor Party. The independent judiciary system is headed by the Supreme Court and operates at the local and national levels. The king, under advisement from the Ministry of Justice, appoints judges.

Transparency International ranked Norway 12th (tied with Switzerland) on its 2002 Corruption Perceptions Index.

Women's rights are legally protected. In the Storting, women hold 35.8 percent of the seats.

Oman

Polity: Traditional monarchy
Economy: Capitalist-statist
Population: 2,600,000
PPP: $13,356
Life Expectancy: 73

Political Rights: 6
Civil Liberties: 5
Status: Not Free

Religious Groups: Ibadi Muslim (75 percent,) Sunni Muslim, Shi'a Muslim, Hindu (25 percent)
Ethnic Groups: Arab, Baluchi, South Asian, African
Capital: Muscat

Ten-Year Ratings Timeline (Political Rights, Civil Liberties, Status)

1993	1994	1995	1996	1997	1998	1999	2000	2001	2002	2003
6,5PF	6,6NF	6,6NF	6,6NF	6,6NF	6,6NF	6,6NF	6,6NF	6,5NF	6,5NF	6,5NF

Overview:

Oman continues to make steady progress in diversifying its economy and attracting foreign investment, preparing for the day when its modest oil reserves run out. The political reform process took a minor leap forward with the announcement that elections to the Consultative Council next year will be held on the basis of universal suffrage.

Considered to be the oldest independent state in the Arab world, Oman has existed as a sovereign political entity since 1650, when followers of the Ibadi sect of Islam led by Sultan bin Seif expelled the Portuguese from the eastern tip of the Arabian peninsula. The present al-Busaid dynasty came to power in 1749. By the mid-nineteenth century, an Omani commercial empire stretched from trading posts on the Indian subcontinent to east Africa. As a result of British encroachments and the decline of the slave trade, Oman lost its overseas possessions and entered a period of decline and debt.

During the reign of Sultan Said bin Taimur, which began in 1932, Oman remained astonishingly backward, diplomatically isolated (refusing to join either the United Nations or the Arab League), and torn by a Soviet-backed rebellion in the interior. By 1970, when Said was overthrown by his son, Qaboos, there were only about 1,000 automobiles and 10 kilometers of asphalt road in the entire country. Drawing upon modest oil revenues, Sultan Qaboos rapidly modernized Oman's semi-feudal economy, repealed his father's oppressive social restrictions, and ended the country's diplomatic isolation. He regained control of the country's interior in 1975, inaugurating an era of remarkable civil peace, economic prosperity and little political opposition.

In 1991, as authoritarian governments throughout eastern Europe and parts of the third world were falling by the wayside, Qaboos established the Consultative Council (*Majlis al-Shura*), whose members were largely appointed. The 1996 basic charter transformed the council into an 82-member elected body, but it was given no legislative powers and the quasi-electoral system put in place the following year was not binding. The charter also banned discrimination on the basis of sex, ethnicity, religion, and social class, and provided for an independent judiciary, due process protections, and freedom of expression and assembly, but many of these provisions have not been enacted.

While the political reform process has been gradual and half-hearted, economic reform has been pursued with vigor. Oil exports, which account for 80 percent of export earnings and 40 percent of gross domestic product, have preserved stability for the last quarter-century, but Oman's reserves will very likely run out within 20 years. Given the country's high, 3.8 percent annual rate of population growth, developing a diversified economy capable of employing record numbers of new job seekers is imperative. In 1995, Qaboos organized an international conference, called "Economic Vision 2020," that outlined an ambitious program of economic liberalization to attract international investment and develop non-oil sectors of the economy. The government lifted restrictions on majority foreign ownership and reduced the tax burden on foreign investors. In 2000, Oman formalized its full membership in the World Trade Organization as a developing nation. Natural gas, manufacturing, ports, and telecommunications have emerged as fledgling industries, and the government has proposed privatizing water and sanitation, cement, hotels, and airport services and maintenance. In June 2002, the Washington-based Cato Institute ranked Oman first in the Arab world in its annual report on economic freedom.

The government has also introduced measures to "Omanize" the mostly foreign workforce. The government has pledged that all governmental positions will be held by Omanis by 2003 and set target quotas for domestic employment in each sector of the economy. The sultan has encouraged citizens to start their own businesses, offering subsidized loans to cover start-up costs.

In November 2002, the government announced that all Omani citizens over the age of 21 will be allowed to vote in the 2003 Consultative Council elections. In previous elections, only a limited number of citizens selected by tribal leaders were allowed to vote. Moreover, the sultan gave up the right to arbitrarily approve or reject candidates after the elections.

Although the reforms are a step forward for Oman, many in the country and abroad remain worried about the country's political future. While Qaboos is regarded by most as a capable and benevolent leader, he has no sons, which leaves Oman without an heir apparent. As the sultan advances in age, this political question mark may prove to be an impediment in attracting international investment.

Political Rights and Civil Liberties:

Omanis cannot change their government democratically. The sultan has absolute power and rules by decree. There are no formal democratic institutions, and political parties are illegal. Citizens may petition the government indirectly through their local governors to redress grievances or may appeal directly to the sultan during his annual three-week tour of the country.

While police are not required to obtain warrants prior to making arrests and do not always respect legal procedures for pretrial detention, arbitrary arrests and detentions are rare. Security forces have reportedly abused detainees in the past, but the practice was not widespread.

The judiciary is subordinate to the sultan, who appoints all judges and has the final say on all rulings. Magistrate courts handle misdemeanors and criminal cases, while *Sharia* (Islamic law) courts handle personal status cases involving divorce and inheritance. A state security court handles criminal cases as deemed necessary by the government. Security court defendants may not have counsel present and proceedings are not made public. Defendants in national security or serious felony trials may not appeal.

Freedom of expression is very limited. All broadcast media are government owned and offer only official views, though satellite dishes are widely available, which gives citizens access to foreign broadcasts. While there are many privately owned print publications, the government subsidizes their operating costs, discouraging critical reporting on most major domestic issues. Laws prohibit criticism of the sultan and provide for censorship of all domestic and imported publications, though journalists normally practice self-censorship.

All public gatherings must be government approved, though this rule is not strictly enforced. Several pro-Palestinian demonstrations were held peacefully in 2002. All associations must be registered with the government, and independent political groups and human rights organizations do not exist.

There are no labor or trade unions in Oman, and strikes are illegal. The government sets guidelines for private sector wages and employment conditions. Complaints about working conditions can be referred to the Ministry of Social Affairs and Labor, and the government Labor Welfare Board arbitrates disputes.

Islam is the state religion. Most Omanis are Ibadi or Sunni Muslims, but there is a small Shi'a minority, as well as largely foreign Christian and Hindu communities. All are allowed to worship freely, though mosque sermons are monitored by the government for political content.

Women enjoy equal political rights, but suffer from legal and social discrimination.

Sharia courts favor men in inheritance and divorce cases, and a woman must have the permission of a male relative to travel abroad. Although traditional social pressures keep many women from working or taking part in public life, some have come to occupy important positions in commerce, industry, and other sectors. Women hold around 30 percent of civil service positions and enjoy equal educational opportunities. Female genital mutilation is practiced in some rural areas.

↑ Pakistan

Polity: Military
Economy: Capitalist-statist **Political Rights:** 6
Population: 143,500,000 **Civil Liberties:** 5
PPP: $1,928 **Status:** Not Free
Life Expectancy: 63
Religious Groups: Sunni Muslim (77 percent) Muslim
(20 percent), Christian, Hindu, and other (3 percent)
Ethnic Groups: Punjabi, Sindhi, Pashtun, Baloch
Capital: Islamabad
Trend Arrow: Pakistan received an upward trend arrow for holding free, but not entirely
fair, national elections in October 2002.

Ten-Year Ratings Timeline (Political Rights, Civil Liberties, Status)

1993	1994	1995	1996	1997	1998	1999	2000	2001	2002	2003
4,5PF	3,5PF	3,5PF	3,5PF	4,5PF	4,5PF	4,5PF	7,5NF	6,5NF	6,5NF	6,5NF

Overview: General Pervez Musharraf continued to perform a delicate balancing act as ruler of Pakistan. The military regime faced criticism in 2002 from opposition political parties, the press, and civil society, all who favored a return to democratic rule. Attacks on religious minorities and Western targets by a variety of Islamist militant groups, some affiliated to al-Qaeda, also threatened to further destabilize Pakistan. An escalation in tensions with neighboring India led to increased pressure from the international community, and in particular the United States, to modify official policy towards the disputed territory of Kashmir. Nevertheless, Musharraf managed to consolidate his hold on power through a dubious referendum that extended his term as president, as well as a series of constitutional amendments that cemented the future role of the military in governance. Flawed elections held in October led to a reintroduction of the competitive political process and a return to nominal civilian rule by the end of the year. However, the dramatic rise in the influence of Islamist parties, many of whose elected members are openly hostile to religious minorities and to Musharraf's support for the U.S.-led war on terrorism, remains a threat to the prospects for democracy in Pakistan.

Pakistan came into existence as a Muslim homeland with the partition of British India in 1947. Following a nine-month civil war, East Pakistan achieved independence in 1971 as the new state of Bangladesh. Deposing civilian governments at will, the army has ruled Pakistan for 28 of its 55 years of independence. As part of his efforts to consolidate power, the military dictator General Zia ul-Haq amended the constitution in 1985 to allow the president to dismiss elected governments. After Zia's death in 1988, successive presidents cited corruption and abuse of power in sacking elected governments headed by Benazir Bhutto of the Pakistan People's Party (PPP) in 1990 and 1996, and Nawaz Sharif of the Pakistan Muslim League (PML) in 1993.

With Bhutto having been discredited by corruption scandals during her second term, the PML and its allies won the February 1997 elections, although only 35 percent of eligible voters bothered to vote. Over the next 30 months Sharif largely ignored Pakistan's pressing economic and social problems while undermining every institution capable of challenging him. This included repealing the president's constitutional power to dismiss governments, forcing the resignations of the chief justice of the Supreme Court and of an army chief, and cracking down on the press and nongovernmental organizations (NGOs).

Sharif's downfall began in June 1999, when Indian troops bested Pakistani forces that had made incursions into Indian-held Kashmir. Sharif ended the two-month Kargil crisis by ordering a withdrawal, but was blamed by the army for the debacle, and was deposed in October 1999 in a bloodless coup. Army chief Musharraf then appointed himself "chief executive," declared a state of emergency, and issued a Provisional Constitution Order suspending parliament, the provincial assemblies, and the constitution. In December 2000, eighteen of Pakistan's political parties, including archrivals PML and PPP, joined to form the Alliance for the Restoration of Democracy (ARD), an umbrella group calling for an end to military rule. However, Musharraf was able to successfully neutralize Sharif and Bhutto, his primary political opponents, through a combination of court convictions and exile.

While successfully managing to curtail the activities of the political opposition, Musharraf has been less willing to rein in the activities and influence of Islamic fundamentalist groups. In response to growing sectarian violence in 2001, the authorities banned several militant groups and arrested hundreds of alleged fundamentalists. After the attacks of September 11, 2001, on the United States, Musharraf's pledge to support the U.S.-led war on terrorism unleashed opposition from a number of Islamist organizations. Sectarian violence directed at the Shia minority continued in 2002, and there was a dramatic rise in terrorist attacks against both Westerners and Christian targets. Heightened tensions with neighboring India over the disputed territory of Kashmir, which resulted in a massive troop buildup by both sides along their common border in the first half of the year, led to increased international pressure on Musharraf to intensify his crackdown against the militant groups responsible for incursions into Kashmir and suicide attacks within India. However, militant groups continued to operate throughout Pakistan, and the arrest of a number of senior al-Qaeda leaders in 2002 suggested that the group is still using the country as a base.

Musharraf's primary aim throughout the year was to ensure a dominant role for the military after Pakistan made the nominal transition back to democratic rule. Constitutional amendments announced in July and August gave Musharraf (in his role as president) effective control over parliament and restricted the ability of opposition parties to contest the October elections. The regime also openly promoted progovernment political parties, such as the newly formed Pakistan Muslim League Quaid-i-Azam (PML-Q), as a way to counter the PML and PPP. Elections held on October 10 did not produce a clear winner; final results (which include both elected and nonelected seats) gave the PML-Q 118 seats, while the PPP won 81 and the PML won 19. A coalition of five religious parties, the Muttahida Majlis-i-Amal (MMA), performed unexpectedly strongly, winning 60 seats in the national parliament and a majority of seats in the provinces of Baluchistan and the North-West Frontier Province (NWFP). After over a month of wrangling between the three largest parties, the PML-Q was able to muster enough support from independents and deserters from the other main parties to form a government. Musharraf's nominee, Mir Zafrullah Jamali, was elected in November by the National Assembly to head a new coalition government.

Political Rights and Civil Liberties: Pakistan continued to be ruled for most of 2002 by a military government, headed by General Pervez Musharraf, which operated with limited transparency and accountability. The 1973 constitution provides for the lower National Assembly, which is directly elected for a five-year term, and the 87-seat Senate, whose members are appointed by the four provincial assemblies for six-year terms. The constitution also vests executive power in a prime minister, who must be Muslim, and authorizes an electoral college to choose the largely ceremonial president, who also must be Muslim, for a five-year term. In June 2001, Musharraf declared himself president and also dismissed the provincial and national assemblies, which had been suspended shortly after the military coup.

In preparation for the national elections scheduled for October 2002, which were intended to mark the end of a three-year period of military rule, Musharraf further strengthened his hold on power throughout the year. A referendum held in April that was marred by fraud and coercion extended his term as president by five years with an official result of 97.5 percent in his favor. In August, he announced a slew of constitutional amendments that formalized the military's role in governance. The Legal Framework Order (LFO) gave him the right to unilaterally dismiss the national and provincial parliaments, established a National Security Council dominated by military figures that would supervise the work of the civilian cabinet, and restricted freedom of association and the right of individuals to stand for elected office.

Provisions in the LFO limited the right to run as a candidate for election to those persons with a bachelor's degree, which disqualified roughly 96 percent of the Pakistani population. It also disqualified criminal convicts and defaulters on loans and utility bills from running. Other rules restricted political parties in their choice of leadership. Some of these measures were explicitly aimed at preventing Bhutto and Sharif from contesting the elections. Although the government lifted the long-standing ban on political rallies shortly before the elections, significant restrictions remained in place, and the ability of opposition parties to mount effective campaigns was circumscribed. ARD leaders also complained that official favoritism was shown towards pro-government parties prior to the elections. In its statement on the 2002 electoral process, the independent Human Rights Commission of Pakistan (HRCP) noted that governmental machinery had been used openly to pressure, intimidate, and harass opposition candidates. The EU Election Observation Mission expressed concern about the degree of impartiality of the Election Commission, the ability of political parties and candidates to campaign effectively, the partisan misuse of state resources by public authorities, equality of access to the state media, the accuracy of the voters' register, and last-minute alterations in the electoral system. Their preliminary report concluded that there had been "serious flaws" in the electoral process.

Religious minorities have long complained about a system of separate electoral rolls by which they vote for a limited number of candidates from their own communities rather than for general candidates. After they boycotted local elections held in 2001, the government abolished separate electorates in January 2002 (except for the Ahmadi sect). Other electoral reforms provided for the reservation of 60 of the total of 350 seats in parliament to be allotted to women under a system of indirect elections. The residents of Pakistani-administered Kashmir, which includes the Northern Areas as well as Azad (free) Kashmir, have no representation in the national parliament. (A new report on Pakistani-administered Kashmir appears in the Related Territories section).

The constitution and other laws authorize the government to curb freedom of speech on subjects including the constitution, the armed forces, the judiciary, and religion. Blasphemy laws (under which the accused is subject to immediate arrest and if convicted is given a mandatory death sentence) have also been used to suppress the media. Concern was raised that three ordinances adopted in August—the Press Council Ordinance, the Registration Ordinance, and the Defamation Ordinance— would further restrict freedom of expression. Islamic fundamentalists and thugs hired by feudal landlords continued to harass journalists and attack newspaper offices. On several occasions, journalists were also subjected to physical attacks by police and political activists. The kidnap and murder of *Wall Street Journal* reporter Daniel Pearl by Islamic radicals in early 2002 focused international attention on the dangers of reporting in Pakistan. While journalists practice some self-censorship, Pakistan continued to have some of the most outspoken newspapers in South Asia. However, during the year Musharraf appeared to have become less tolerant of criticism. In March, editor Shaheen Sehbai resigned under pressure and left the country after *The News* published a story on the links between Pearl's killers and official intelligence agencies. Sehbai and his family continued to face legal harassment throughout the year. Other prominent editors also complained of receiving threats from intelligence agencies. Nearly all broadcast media are state owned, and coverage favors the government.

Pakistan is an Islamic republic, and there are numerous restrictions on religious freedom. Section 295-C of the penal code mandates the death sentence for defiling the name of the prophet Muhammad. Human rights groups say that instances of Muslims bribing low-ranking police officials to file false blasphemy charges against Ahmadis, Christians, Hindus, and occasionally, other Muslims, have been increasing sharply in recent years. To date, appeals courts have overturned all blasphemy convictions; in August, the Supreme Court overturned the conviction of Ayub Masih, a Christian accused of blasphemy. However, suspects are forced to spend lengthy periods in prison, where they are subject to ill-treatment, and they continue to be targeted by religious extremists even after they are released. According to the U.S. State Department, authorities have charged nearly 200 Ahmadis under the law since its inception. Ahmadis consider themselves to be Muslims, but the constitution classifies them as a non-Muslim minority and the penal code prohibits Ahmadi religious practice. Ahmadis, Christians, and Hindus also face unofficial economic and societal discrimination and are occasionally subjected to violence and harassment. There was a sharp increase in terrorist violence directed at Christian targets in 2002, including armed attacks on churches, missionary schools and hospitals. The U.S. Commission on International Religious Freedom designated Pakistan as a country of particular concern for the first time in 2002, citing the failure of the government to protect religious minorities from sectarian violence as well as discriminatory legislation, which created a climate of "religious intolerance."

After initially permitting some demonstrations, the military government banned all public political meetings, strikes, and rallies in March 2000. Following the ban, authorities forcibly dispersed some protests and arrested activists to prevent other demonstrations. Authorities suppressed rallies planned by the multiparty ARD in April and July, and several ARD leaders were arrested. Some Islamist leaders have been held under house arrest or in preventative detention under the Maintenance of Public Order ordinance, which allows for three months' detention without trial. Laws governing sedition, public order, and terrorism have been used to raid party offices and detain political activists and leaders in Punjab and Sindh for criticizing the army in party meetings. The military regime generally tolerates the work of NGOs. However, in recent years Islamic fundamentalists have issued death threats against prominent human rights defenders and against female NGO activists who work in rural areas.

Despite legislation outlawing bonded labor and canceling enslaving debts, illegal bonded labor continued to be widespread. Trade unions are independent. The law restricts the right to strike, and workers in certain essential industries face restrictions on bargaining collectively and generally cannot hold strikes. Enforcement of labor laws continued to be limited.

The judiciary consists of civil and criminal courts and a special *Sharia* (Islamic law) candidaciescourt for certain offenses. Lower courts remained plagued by corruption; intimidation by local officials, powerful individuals, and Islamic extremists; and heavy backlogs that led to lengthy pretrial detentions. The military regime undermined the Supreme Court's reputation for independence in January 2000, when it ordered all Supreme Court and high court judges to swear under oath to uphold the state of emergency and the Provisional Constitutional Order issued by Musharraf. Authorities removed the chief justice of the Supreme Court and 14 other justices for refusing to take the oath.

The criminal courts include antiterrorism courts that operate with limited due process rights and must conclude trials within seven days. In January 2002, an amendment to the Anti-terrorism Ordinance provided for new courts that would sit in cantonments or jail premises to ensure the security of the accused, witnesses, and judiciary, and that would include one military officer as part of the three-member bench. The November 1999 National Accountability Ordinance vested broad powers of arrest, investigation, and prosecution in a new National Accountability Bureau and established special courts to try corruption cases that operate with limited procedural safeguards. In April 2001, the Supreme Court ordered the government to amend the ordinance to restore the right to bail and reduce pretrial detention to a maximum of 15 days.

The Sharia court enforces the 1979 Hudood Ordinances, which criminalize nonmarital rape, extramarital sex, and several alcohol, gambling, and property offenses. The ordinances provide for Koranic punishments, including death by stoning for adultery, as well as jail terms and fines. In part because of strict evidentiary standards, authorities have never carried out the Koranic punishments. The Federally Administered Tribal Areas (FATA) are under a separate legal system, the Frontier Crimes Regulation, which authorizes tribal elders and leaders to administer justice according to Sharia and tribal custom in proceedings that lack due process rights. Feudal landlords and tribal elders throughout Pakistan continued to adjudicate some disputes and impose punishment in unsanctioned parallel courts called *jirgas*. In June, a woman in Punjab was gang-raped on the orders of a tribal council as punishment for alleged improprieties committed by her brother. A report issued by Amnesty International in August raised concerns that the jirgas abuse a range of human rights, and are particularly discriminatory towards women.

Anecdotal evidence suggested that police continued to routinely engage in crime; used excessive force in ordinary situations; arbitrarily arrested and detained citizens; extorted money from prisoners and their families; accepted money to register cases on false charges; raped female detainees and prisoners; committed extrajudicial killings; and torture detainees, often to extract confessions. Prison conditions continued to be extremely poor. According to the most recent report of the HRCP, the Juvenile Justice System Ordinance of 2000 remains largely unimplemented and thousands of juveniles continue to be jailed alongside adults.

Violence among rival factions of the Karachi-based Muttahida Quami Movement (MQM), which represents Urdu-speaking migrants from India, and between the police and the MQM, killed several thousand people in the 1990s, but has abated in recent years, although harassment of their activists continues. According to a report in the *Asian Times*, intelligence agencies estimate the number of active members of different militant groups to be around 50,000. Sunni and Shia fundamentalist groups continued to engage in tit-for-tat killings, mainly in Punjab and Karachi. In a January 2002 speech, Musharraf said that about 400 people had been killed by sectarian violence in 2001. Attacks on Shia mosques in February and April left dozens of worshippers dead, and Shia professionals in Karachi, including a large number of doctors, were assassinated throughout the year.

A combination of traditional norms and weak law enforcement continued to contribute to rape, domestic violence, and other forms of abuse against women. Women face difficulty in obtaining justice in rape cases because police and judges are reluctant to charge and punish offenders. Although less frequently than in the past, women are still charged under the Hudood Ordinances with adultery or other sexual misconduct arising from rape cases or alleged extramarital affairs. In April, a woman was sentenced to death by stoning for adultery, although her sentence was later overturned on appeal. The threat of being charged with adultery may prevent some women from reporting rape. The HRCP noted in December that at least 461 women had been killed by family members in so-called 'honor killings' in 2002—an increase of 25 percent over the previous year—and, worryingly, that the practice seemed to be spreading to new areas where it had not previously been reported. Usually committed by a male relative of the victim, honor killings punish women who supposedly bring dishonor to the family. Authorities generally do not severely punish the perpetrators of these killings, either because they simply fail to enforce the law or because they can excuse offenders or impose minor sentences under laws reducing punishment for actions supposedly caused by "grave and sudden provocation." Pakistani women face unofficial discrimination in educational and employment opportunities.

Pakistan's underfunded primary-school system continued to offer limited educational opportunities for children. Filling the gap is an extensive network of *madrasans* (Islamic schools), some financed by Islamic groups from Saudi Arabia and Iran, which provide free education and living arrangements for some 700,000 boys. In June, the government attempted to extend some measure of control over this network when it required all madrasans to register with the authorities, as well as provide details of sources of foreign funding and of foreign students and teachers, within six months or face closure. Despite some initiatives, enforcement of child labor laws continue to be inadequate. Both male and female children also continue to be subjected to prostitution, custodial and sexual abuse, and trafficking.

Palau

Polity: Presidential parliamentary democracy
Economy: Capitalist
Population: 20,000
PPP: na
Life Expectancy: 67
Religious Groups: Roman Catholic (49 percent), Protestant, indigenous beliefs (51 percent)
Ethnic Groups: Polynesian, Malayan, Melanesian
Capital: Koror

Political Rights: 1
Civil Liberties: 2
Status: Free

Ten-Year Ratings Timeline (Political Rights, Civil Liberties, Status)

1993	1994	1995	1996	1997	1998	1999	2000	2001	2002	2003
--	--	1,2F	1,2F	1,2F	1,2F	1,2F	1,2F	1,2F	1,2F	1,2F

Overview:

Palau is a small, poor nation consisting of 8 main and more than 250 smaller islands in the Caroline chain, which lies roughly 500 miles southeast of the Philippines. Sighted by Portuguese and Spanish explorers in the sixteenth century, the Carolines eventually came under Spanish control and, by the mid-nineteenth century, began attracting growing numbers of missionaries and coconut traders.

After its defeat in the Spanish-American War, Spain sold most of the Caroline Islands to Germany in 1899. Japan seized the islands in 1914 and ruled them from 1920 under a League of Nations mandate. U.S. and Japanese forces fought bloody battles for control of the Carolines during World War II. The islands became part of the U.S. Trust Territory for the Pacific after the war.

Palau declined to join the Federated States of Micronesia, which was formed in 1979 by four other Caroline Island districts of the U.S. Trust Territory and later became an independent state. Instead, it approved its own constitution and became self-governing in 1981. Palau achieved full independence in 1994 under an accord with the United States in which Washington agreed to provide $442 million in aid over 15 years. Under the accord, known as the Compact of Free Association, the United States also agreed to maintain responsibility for Palau's defense and has the right to set up military bases.

Palau's politics have stabilized since the 1980s, when its first president, Haruo Remelik, was assassinated early in his second term and another president, Lazarus Salii, was found dead in his office of an apparent suicide.

The current president, Tommy E. Remengesau, Jr., took office after winning the November 2000 elections. The Remengesau Administration tightened bank laws in 2001 after Palau was accused by the United States and some European countries of being a money laundering haven. Palau and four other nations joined the International Whaling Commission in 2002, a move that could help push the 47-member body from its present conservationist agenda towards a pro-whaling stance.

Political Rights and Civil Liberties: Citizens of Palau can change their government through elections and enjoy most basic rights. Executive powers are vested in a president, who is directly elected for a four-year term. The Senate has 9 members, each of whom represents the entire country, while the House of Representatives has 16 members, one each from Palau's 16 states. All legislators are directly elected for four-year terms. The Council of Chiefs, consisting of the highest traditional chiefs from each of the 16 states, advises the president on traditional laws and customs. Palau has had political parties in the past, although none currently exist.

Palau's judiciary is independent, according to the U.S. State Department's global human rights report for 2001, released in March 2002. Religious freedom is respected in this mainly Christian society.

Women have traditionally enjoyed high social status in Palau because inheritance of property and traditional rank is through female bloodlines. Women today hold several key traditional leadership posts. Palau's vice president, moreover, is a woman, Sandra Peratozzi. On the whole, however, women hold relatively few senior positions in government and politics. Domestic violence is common, according to the U.S. State Department report, and is often fueled by alcohol and illegal drug abuse.

Palau has no trade unions, although the government does not prevent workers from organizing. The economy is heavily dependent on U.S. aid, and the government employs nearly half of the workforce.

Palau's many foreign workers face some discrimination in housing, education, employment, and access to social services, according to the U.S. State Department report. They are at times targeted in violent and petty crimes, the report added, and allege that officials do not vigorously investigate or prosecute crimes against them.

Foreign workers also face abuse from their employers. Anecdotal reports suggest that employers at times physically abuse foreign workers and pressure them into remaining in jobs by making verbal threats or withholding the workers' passports and return tickets, the U.S. State Department report said. Palauan employers at times also renege on contract terms, withhold pay or benefits, and make foreign laborers work extra hours for no pay, the report added. While officials have taken action in cases brought to their attention, many foreign workers are reluctant to seek assistance for fear of losing their jobs. Foreigners make up nearly 30 percent of Palau's population and 73 percent of the paid workforce, according to the May 2000 census.

Panama

Polity: Presidential-par-
liamentary democracy
Economy: Capitalist-
statist
Population: 2,900,000
PPP: $6,000
Life Expectancy: 74

Political Rights: 1
Civil Liberties: 2
Status: Free

Religious Groups: Roman Catholic (85 percent), Protestant (15 percent)
Ethnic Groups: Mestizo (70 percent), West Indian (14 percent), European (10
percent), Indian (6 percent)
Capital: Panama City

Ten-Year Ratings Timeline (Political Rights, Civil Liberties, Status)

1993	1994	1995	1996	1997	1998	1999	2000	2001	2002	2003
4,3PF	3,3PF	2,3F	2,3F	2,3F	2,3F	2,3F	1,2F	1,2F	1,2F	1,2F

Overview:

Panama's fragile sovereignty has been undermined by the spillover effects of the civil war fought in neighboring Colombia and the trafficking in weapons, drugs, and people that is widespread throughout the region. Emblematic of the use of Panamanian territory for illegal purposes was the discovery of a cache of several thousand weapons and ammunition en route from Nicaragua to Colombia. An agreement was signed with the United States allowing for joint patrols and the arrest of violators. Several polls conducted by the newspaper *La Prensa* early in the year gave failing job ratings to the government, leaving no branch unscathed. Governability is in question as armed violence has increased significantly in Panama in the past several years. Weekend police checkpoints are now commonplace both in Panama City and in crime-ridden Colon, although the country remains relatively safe when compared to many of its regional neighbors. Discrimination against darker-skinned Panamanians, especially those from Colon, is widespread.

Panama was part of Colombia until 1903, when a U.S.-supported revolt resulted in the proclamation of an independent Republic of Panama. A period of weak civilian rule ended with a 1968 military coup that brought General Omar Torrijos to power. After the signing of the 1977 canal treaties with the United States, Torrijos promised democratization. The 1972 constitution had been revised to provide for the direct election of a president and a legislative assembly for five-year terms. After Torrijos's death in 1981, General Manuel Noriega emerged as Panamanian Defense Force (PDF) chief; he subsequently rigged the 1984 election that brought to power the Revolutionary Democratic Party (PRD), then the political arm of the PDF. The Democratic Alliance of Civic Opposition (ADOC) won the 1989 election, but Noriega annulled the vote and declared himself head of state. He was removed during a U.S. military invasion, and ADOC's Guillermo Endara became president.

In May 1999, Mireya Moscoso, the widow of three-time president Arnulfo Arias and herself an unsuccessful presidential candidate in 1994, won 44.8 percent of the vote, more than 7 percent above the amount garnered by her rival, Martin Torrijos, son of General Omar Torrijos, as the head of a PRD-led coalition. In the years following the U.S. handover in 1999, the Panama Canal continued to operate smoothly, although the departure of remaining U.S. troops and the closure of U.S. military bases meant the loss to Panama of some $250 million in revenues.

Repeated incursions into Panamanian territory by Colombian guerrillas continued to spark concerns in the region about the spillover effects of Colombia's civil war. Since being invaded by the United States in 1989, Panama has had no military. It relies on the police to provide both internal security and defense of its borders. Dozens of confrontations between armed Colombian groups and the Panamanian police, who suffered several injuries as a result of the fighting, raised questions about whether the latter are up to the challenge provided by the seasoned Colombians.

Political Rights and Civil Liberties: Panama's citizens can change their government democratically. The 1999 national elections were considered free and fair by international observers. The constitution guarantees freedom of political and civic organization. In early 1999, Panama's largest political parties agreed to ban anonymous campaign contributions in an effort to stem the infiltration of drug money into the political process. The judicial system, headed by a Supreme Court, was revamped in 1990. It remains overworked, however, and its administration is inefficient, politicized, and prone to corruption. An unwieldy criminal code and a surge in cases, many against former soldiers and officials of the military period, complicate the judicial process.

The Panamanian Defense Force (PDF) was dismantled after 1989, and the military was formally abolished in 1994. However, the civilian-run Public Force (the national police) that replaced the PDF, although accountable to civilian authorities through a publicly disclosed budget, is poorly disciplined and corrupt. Like the country's prison guards, officers frequently use "excessive force." The penal system is marked by violent disturbances in decrepit facilities packed with up to eight times their intended capacity. About two-thirds of prisoners face delays of about 18 months in having their cases heard.

Panama's media are a raucous assortment of radio and television stations, daily newspapers, and weekly publications. Restrictive media laws dating back to the regime of General Manuel Noriega remain on the books. The law permits officials to jail without trial anyone who defames the government.

Labor unions are well organized. However, labor rights were diluted in 1995 when President Ernesto Perez Balladares pushed labor code revisions through congress.

There is free access to the Internet. Academic freedom is generally honored.

Since 1993, indigenous groups have protested the encroachment of illegal settlers on Indian lands and delays by the government in formally demarcating the boundaries of those lands. Indian communities do enjoy, however, a large degree of autonomy and self-government. Violence against women and children is widespread and common.

Papua New Guinea

Polity: Parliamentary democracy
Economy: Capitalist
Population: 5,000,000
PPP: $2,280
Life Expectancy: 57

Political Rights: 2
Civil Liberties: 3
Status: Free

Religious Groups: Roman Catholic (22 percent), Lutheran (16 percent), indigenous beliefs and other (62 percent)
Ethnic Groups: Melanesian, Papuan, Negrito, Micronesian, Polynesian
Capital: Port Moresby

Ten-Year Ratings Timeline (Political Rights, Civil Liberties, Status)

1993	1994	1995	1996	1997	1998	1999	2000	2001	2002	2003
2,3F	2,4F	2,4F	2,4F	2,4F	2,4F	2,3F	2,3F	2,3F	2,3F	2,3F

Overview:

Beset by rising crime, economic mismanagement, and staggeringly high unemployment, Papua New Guinea turned for leadership to the man who led the nation to independence in the 1970s. In addition to dealing with crime and the economy, Sir Michael Somare faces the challenge of moving forward a peace process that ended 12 years of secessionist conflict on Bougainville Island.

This South Pacific country, consisting of the eastern part of New Guinea and some 600 smaller islands, achieved independence from Australia in 1975. Heavily dependent on natural resources, the young nation was plunged into crisis in late 1988 after miners and landowners on Bougainville Island began guerrilla attacks against the Australian-owned Panguna copper mine. The rebels demanded compensation and profit sharing from the mine, which provided 40 percent of the country's export revenues. By 1990, the rebels were waging a low-grade, armed struggle for an independent state on Bougainville, located 560 miles northeast of the capital, Port Moresby.

A short-lived ceasefire on Bouganinville collapsed in 1996. The government that brokered the deal was forced to resign in 1997 amid a public outcry over a $27 million state contract with a foreign mercenary outfit to aid the army on Bougainville. In the ensuing parliamentary elections, outgoing prime minister Sir Julius Chan and 54 other lawmakers lost their seats. Many voters complained that official corruption and rising crime were keeping Papua New Guinea impoverished despite its abundance of minerals, forests, fisheries, and other natural resources.

Following two years of scandal-plagued government under Prime Minister Bill Skate, the government of Sir Mekere Morauta that took office in 1999 carried out economic reforms and reached a breakthrough peace deal on Bougainville. Morauta signed an accord in 2001 with Bougainville leader Joseph Kabui that called for the island to gradually receive autonomy ahead of a referendum on independence to take place in 10 to 15 years.

Morauta, a former central bank chief, also restored Papua New Guinea's relations with the International Monetary Fund and sold off some state assets. Amid strong resistance in 2001, however, he was forced to backtrack on plans to revive the economy by speeding up privatization and trimming the size of the army. Dozens of soldiers mutinied for 12 days that March, and students mounted a week-long anti-government rally in June that ended with police shooting dead three protesters. Sir Michael Somare, 66, took the leadership reigns for the third time since independence following an election in 2002 that was marred by some 30 poll-related deaths and other violence and numerous administrative glitches. Poll-related thuggery and problems with the electoral roll dragged out the balloting for weeks after the June 15 start date. Somare formed a seven-party coalition government that controlled more than 40 of parliament's 109 seats.

Somare faces the challenge of keeping the Bougainville peace accord on track by encouraging the rebels to complete an ongoing disarmament process and by setting up an autonomous administration due to take office on the island in 2003. The cash-strapped central government also must deal with a worsening drought and provide relief to the thousands of villagers left homeless over the summer by a volcanic eruption on New Britain Island and a massive earthquake on the north coast. Meanwhile, plans are behind schedule for a $3.75 billion pipeline to transport natural gas from Papua New Guinea's southern highlands to the northeastern Australian state of Queensland. The pipeline is seen as a critical source of future revenues for Papua New Guinea, given that natural resource revenues currently are declining and there is virtually no new exploration. Some 40 percent of working-age Papua New Guineans lack jobs, and the country's annual population growth rate of 3.1 percent is one of the world's highest.

Political Rights and Civil Liberties: Citizens of Papua New Guinea can change their government through elections and enjoy most basic rights. The 1975 constitution vests executive powers in a prime minister and the cabinet. Parliament has 89 members who represent districts within the country's 20 provinces, and 20 who are elected on a province-wide basis. All lawmakers are elected for five-year terms.

Elections are free but are usually marred by some fraud and poll-related violence. The 2002 balloting was particularly violent. Some candidates reportedly used tribal gangs to intimidate voters, kidnap some poll officers, and steal, destroy, or tamper with ballot boxes, according to the London-based *The Economist*.

Since independence, most governments have been made up of unstable coalitions, and no prime minister has served a full term. Although lawmakers are elected in U.S.-style, winner-takes-all constituencies, Papua New Guinea has bucked the trend toward a two-party system that this electoral system tends to produce in other countries. Fifteen parties won at least 2 seats in the 2002 elections, led by Prime Minister Somare's National Alliance Party with 19.

Faced with a severe urban crime problem, Papua New Guinea's ill-equipped and poorly trained police force has committed grave rights abuses. "Criminal suspects, including those not carrying guns and only suspected of non-violent crimes, are frequently shot dead by police, sometimes in disputed circumstances," the human rights group Amnesty International said in 2001. Moreover, some officers have been charged with raping female detainees. Police also often beat suspects while they are being arrested, interrogated, or held in custody awaiting trial, according to the U.S.

State Department's global human rights report for 2001, released in March 2002. The government has prosecuted some officers for abuse.

In the rugged highlands, police have in recent years burned homes to punish communities suspected of harboring criminals or of fighting battles with other tribes. Conflicts between clans tend to be linked to insults, injuries, and disputes over land-ownership and boundaries. Rival tribes in the Southern Highlands Province signed a ceasefire in March to end eight months of fighting in and around the town of Mendi that claimed dozens of lives, Radio New Zealand reported.

Papua New Guinea's judiciary is independent, and defendants receive fair trials, according to the U.S. State Department report. However, the resource-strapped judiciary's high caseload has meant that suspects often spend long periods in detention before their trials, in some cases more than two years. The country's crumbling jails are overcrowded and provide poor basic services to inmates, the U.S. State Department report said.

The government has made few efforts to prosecute soldiers, army-backed paramilitary fighters, and rebel forces accused of summary killing and torture during the Bougainville conflict. By some estimates, at least 20,000 civilians and fighters died during the conflict, mostly as the result of malnutrition and disease.

Papua New Guinea's private press carries hard-hitting reports on alleged official corruption, police abuse and other sensitive matters, though newspapers have low circulation. Radio is a key source of information given the country's low literacy rate and many isolated villages. The state-run National Broadcasting Corporation's two radio networks suffer from inadequate funding and deteriorating equipment. The private NAU-FM network serves Port Moresby and is expanding into other areas, while smaller stations serve other cities. Television reception is limited mainly to Port Moresby and provincial capitals.

Citing concerns of spectator violence, police rarely give approval for demonstrations. Despite limited resources, nongovernmental welfare and advocacy groups are active and outspoken. Among the most prominent is the International and Community Rights Advocacy Forum, which works on human rights and environmental issues.

Women increasingly are in leadership positions in business, the professions, and the civil service, though they continue to hold relatively few senior posts in government and politics. Women also face unofficial discrimination in many areas of daily life, according to the U.S. State Department report. The report also said that gang rape and domestic violence continue to be serious and prevalent problems, and that officials prosecute few cases of violence against women. Most tribal communities view domestic violence as a private matter, while some settle rape cases by having the accused give money or goods to the victim's family. Traditional customs of allowing men to have several wives and of paying a price for brides persist in some highland areas.

Papua New Guinea's trade unions are independent, and workers routinely bargain collectively. The government poorly or selectively enforces laws on minimum wages, working hours, and anti-union discrimination, the U.S. State Department report said. The International Labor Organization has called on the government to repeal labor law provisions allowing the government to strike down wage agreements or arbitration awards that it feels undermine government policy or the national interest. Roughly half of the 250,000 wage-earning workers are unionized.

Papua New Guinea's leaders face the challenge of nation-building in a society where roughly 1,000 tribes speak more than 800 distinct languages, and where extreme social and economic disparities create fault lines between the cities and isolated highlands. Some 85 percent of Papua New Guineans live in remote villages and are subsistence or small-scale farmers.

↓ Paraguay

Polity: Presidential-parliamentary democracy
Economy: Capitalist-statist
Population: 6,000,000
PPP: $4,426
Life Expectancy: 71

Political Rights: 4
Civil Liberties: 3
Status: Partly Free

Religious Groups: Roman Catholic (90 percent), Mennonite and Protestant (10 percent)
Ethnic Groups: Mestizo (95 percent), Indian and white (5 percent)
Capital: Asuncion
Trend Arrow: Paraguay received a downward trend arrow due to the collapse of unelected President Luis Gonzalez Macchi's multiparty coalition and multiple corruption scandals affecting senior members of his government.

Ten-Year Ratings Timeline (Political Rights, Civil Liberties, Status)

1993	1994	1995	1996	1997	1998	1999	2000	2001	2002	2003
3,3PF	3,3PF	4,3PF	4,3PF	4,3PF	4,3PF	4,3PF	4,3PF	4,3PF	4,3PF	4,3PF

Overview:

In December 2002, President Luis Gonzalez Macchi offered to leave office three months early, just a week after lawmakers voted to start impeachment hearings against him. Accused of buying a stolen luxury car and of mishandling millions of dollars in state revenues, Gonzalez Macchi and his Colorado Party struggled unsuccessfully to reverse Paraguay's downward economic spiral in one of Latin America's poorest countries. One out of every three Paraguayans lives below the poverty line, and emigrating to Argentina, the traditional escape of the poor, has become unattractive because of that country's own economic crisis. Paraguay's economy remains heavily based on agriculture and contraband of all sorts, and the country has one of the most unequal distributions of land in the world.

Paraguay achieved independence from Spain in 1811. It has been wracked by a series of crises since civilian rule was restored in 1989 and the 35-year reign of right-wing dictator Alfredo Stroessner was ended. The fragility of the country's democratic institutions has resulted in nearly 15 years of popular uprisings, military mutinies, antigovernment demonstrations, and bitter political rivalries. In July 2002, Gonzalez Macchi was forced to call on the military to help police restore order following protests in the capital, Asuncion. Disillusionment with the entire political system—encompassing the executive, legislative, and judicial branches of government—was evidenced by the low turnout in the 2001 municipal elections, where participation by young people, who constitute nearly three-fourths of the population, was almost nonexistent.

In October 2002, Vice President Julio Cesar Franco, a bitter Gonzalez Macchi critic and a member of the opposition Liberal Radical Authentic Party, resigned in order to run for president in the April 2003 elections. Franco was elected vice president in August 2000, a year after Gonzalez Macchi assumed the presidency. International concern about individuals and organizations with ties to Middle Eastern extremist groups operating in Ciudad del Este and along the tri-border area, where Paraguay, Brazil, and Argentina meet, followed the September 11, 2001 terrorist attacks on the World Trade Center and the Pentagon in the United States.

Political Rights and Civil Liberties: The 1992 constitution provides for a president, a vice president, and a bicameral congress consisting of a 45-member senate and an 80-member chamber of deputies elected for five years. The president is elected by a simple majority, and reelection is prohibited. The constitution bans the active military from engaging in politics.

The constitution also provides for regular elections. Municipal elections held in 2001 were generally free and fair, although electoral participation throughout the country was the lowest since 1989. In a positive development, Colorado Party reformer Enrique Riera won the Asuncion mayoralty, one of the country's most powerful political posts.

The constitution guarantees free political and civic organization and religious expression. However, political rights and civil liberties are undermined by the government's tolerance of threats of intimidation and the use of force, including imprisonment, by its supporters against the opposition.

The judiciary, under the influence of the ruling party and the military, is susceptible to the corruption pervading all public and governmental institutions. Corruption cases languish for years in the courts, and most end without resolution. Allegations include illegal detention by police and torture during incarceration, particularly in rural areas. The presence of law enforcement is scarce throughout Paraguay. Reportedly corrupt police officials remain in key posts and are in a position to give protection to, or compromise law enforcement actions against, narcotics traffickers. Colombian drug traffickers continue to expand operations in Paraguay, and accusations of high official involvement in drug trafficking date back to the 1980s.

The lack of security in border areas, particularly in the tri-border region, has allowed large organized-crime groups to engage in piracy and in the smuggling of weapons, narcotics, and contraband. In the aftermath of the September 11 attacks, attention focused on the serious lack of governmental control over Paraguay's lengthy and undeveloped land borders, extensive river network, and numerous airstrips (both registered and unregistered). The Iguazu triangle, as it is called, given its proximity to Iguazu Falls, is the region extending from the cities of Ciudad del Este in Paraguay, Foz do Iguacu in Brazil, and Puerto Iguazu in Argentina. The region contains more than 100 runways, many clandestine, and the Paraguay-Brazil border has long been a scene of major commercial contraband, including the smuggling of stolen cars. The Islamic extremist organization Hezbollah and other militant organizations are active in the region. A joint intelligence center run by Argentina, Brazil, and

Paraguay monitors the region, and all three countries use their air forces for surveillance and interdiction efforts.

Overcrowding, unsanitary living conditions, and mistreatment are serious problems in Paraguayan prisons. More than 95 percent of the prisoners held are pending trial, many for months or years after arrest. The constitution permits detention without trial until the accused completes the minimum sentence for the alleged crime.

In Paraguay, there is only one state-owned medium, the Radio Nacional, which has a limited listenership. A number of private television and radio stations exist, as do a number of independent newspapers. However, journalists investigating corruption or covering strikes and protests are often the victims of intimidation or violent attack by security forces. Free expression is also threatened by vague, potentially restrictive laws that mandate "responsible" behavior by journalists and media owners.

The Paraguayan constitution provides indigenous people with the right to participate in the economic, social, political, and cultural life of the country; however, the indigenous population, estimated at 75,000 to 100,000, is unassimilated and neglected. Low wages, long work hours, infrequent payment (or nonpayment) of wages, job insecurity, lack of access to social security benefits, and racial discrimination are common.

Peasant and Indian organizations demanding and illegally occupying land often meet with police crackdowns, death threats, detentions, and forced evictions by vigilante groups in the employ of landowners. According to official statistics, 39 percent of Paraguayans speak only Guarani, 49 percent are bilingual, and 12 percent speak only Spanish.

There are numerous trade unions and two major union federations, although they are weak and riddled with corruption. The constitution gives public sector workers the right to organize, bargain collectively, and strike, and nearly all these workers belong to the ruling Colorado Party. A new labor code designed to protect workers' rights was passed in October 1993.

Sexual and domestic abuse of women, which is both widespread and vastly underreported, continues to be a serious problem in Paraguay. Spousal abuse is common.

Peru

Polity: Presidential-parliamentary democracy
Economy: Capitalist-statist
Population: 26,700,000
PPP: $4,799
Life Expectancy: 69
Political Rights: 2*
Civil Liberties: 3
Status: Free

Religious Groups: Roman Catholic (90 percent), other (10 percent)
Ethnic Groups: Amerindian (45 percent), mestizo (mixed Amerindian and white) 37 percent, white (15 percent), other (3 percent)
Capital: Lima
Ratings Change: Peru's political rights rating declined from 1 to 2 due to slippage on government pledges on openness and transparency.

Ten-Year Ratings Timeline (Political Rights, Civil Liberties, Status)

1993	1994	1995	1996	1997	1998	1999	2000	2001	2002	2003
6,5PF	5,5PF	5,4PF	5,4PF	4,3PF	5,4PF	5,4PF	5,4PF	3,3PF	1,3F	2,3F

Overview:

The government of President Alejandro Toledo suffered a serious setback at the polls in November 2002, as voters selected Peru's main opposition party and a group of independents in elections for 25 new regional governments, whose establishment was meant to end Lima's top-down monopoly on political control. The no-confidence vote against Toledo's 16-month-old government was a huge boost for former president Alan Garcia, the once-discredited head of the center-left American Popular Revolutionary Alliance (APRA), and positioned the center-left populist as the early favorite for the 2006 presidential election. Peru has one of Latin America's highest economic growth rates. Nevertheless, Toledo's Peru Possible Party, which won only 1 of the 25 contests, was hampered by voter disillusionment of perceived disarray and cronyism in the government, as well as by cynicism about the government's efforts to spur the economy by selling off state enterprises as part of a free-market reform.

Since independence in 1821, Peru has seen alternating periods of civilian and military rule, with elected civilians holding office since a 12-year dictatorship ended in 1980. However, that same year, the Maoist Shining Path terrorist group launched a guerrilla war that killed 30,000 people over the next two decades. Alberto Fujimori, a university rector and engineer, defeated the novelist Mario Vargas Llosa in the 1990 election. In 1992, Fujimori, backed by the military, suspended the constitution and dissolved congress. The move was popular because of people's disdain for Peru's corrupt, elitist political establishment and fear of the Shining Path.

Fujimori held a state-controlled election for an 80-member constituent assembly to replace the congress. The assembly drafted a constitution that established a unicameral congress more closely under presidential control. The constitution was approved in a state-controlled referendum following the capture of the Shining Path leader, Abimael Guzman. In April 1995, Fujimori was reelected president, besting former UN Secretary-General Javier Perez de Cuellar, who vowed to end Fujimori's "dictatorship." Fujimori crushed his opponent with a vote of about three to one, with a massive public-spending and propaganda campaign that used state resources. The National Intelligence Service, under de facto head Vladimiro Montesinos, a one-time legal counsel to drug kingpins, was employed to spy on and discredit opposition candidates. In August 1996 congress passed a law allowing Fujimori to run for a third term, despite a constitutional provision limiting the president to two terms. The law evaded this restriction by defining Fujimori's current term as his first under the 1993 constitution.

In the April 9, 2000, presidential elections, Fujimori beat Toledo, a U.S.-educated economist who grew up in an Indian shantytown, by 49.9 percent to 40.2 percent. Fujimori, however, came in 20,000 votes short of an outright win, and a runoff election was slated for May 28. Toledo refused to participate in the second round, pointing out that in addition to election-day voting irregularities, he had been routinely assaulted by Fujimori supporters in the earlier campaign, had suffered constant death threats and phone taps, was virtually blacked out from media coverage, and was the target of smear attacks in the press.

In early September 2000 a videotape was released that showed Montesinos bribing an opposition congressman, at the same time that the spy chief was also being linked to the illegal shipment of arms to Colombian guerrillas. Coming after one of the most widely questioned elections the region had seen in decades, the ensuing scandal raised suspicions that Fujimori had secured a parliamentary majority—after having failed to win one outright in the April 9 general elections—by bribing opposition congressmen to change sides. On September 16 a weakened Fujimori agreed to call new elections for 2001 in which he would not run. In late November 2000, Fujimori was removed from office; opposition forces assumed control of congress; and a highly respected opposition leader, Valentin Paniagua, was chosen as interim president of Peru.

Following Fujimori's overthrow, the new opposition-controlled congress began a process of renewing the constitutional tribunal and reforming the constitution, so as to eliminate consecutive reelection and to forestall the rise of another Fujimori. The notorious National Intelligence Service, the key to Montesinos's sinister reach, was abolished. An agreement was also reached to restart a judicial reform program that had been aborted by Fujimori in 1999. At the end of 2000, Fujimori announced he was availing himself of his dual citizenship to remain in Japan. In July 2001, Paniagua announced the appointment of a truth-and-reconciliation commission to investigate two decades of rebel and state-sponsored violence.

Running on the slogan "Toledo Trabajo" (Toledo Means Jobs), the ebullient Toledo bested former president Alan Garcia, a gifted orator whose 1985–1990 administration was wracked by mismanagement, hyperinflation, and guerrilla violence, in runoff elections held June 3, 2001, that were internationally heralded as free and fair. During the campaign, Toledo was accused of using cocaine in a 1998 orgy with five prostitutes and of repeatedly lying about his past. (Toledo claimed he was forced to take the drug after having been kidnapped.) In August 2001, Toledo sacked Peru's top military chiefs and promised to thoroughly restructure the armed forces.

The 2002 reform of Peru's highly centralized political structure gave new regional governments almost a quarter of the national budget and a range of powers long the province of the central government. However, Toledo's standing suffered due to a host of personal incidents, ranging from his having allegedly procured a sweetheart job for his wife at Peru's second-largest bank, and to his long denial, later reversed, of having fathered a child out of wedlock in the 1980s—a stance that led opponents to accuse him of manipulating the judiciary to his advantage. In June, antigovernment riots protesting the selling off of state-owned companies left two people dead and nearly $100 million in damages. In 2002, the Shining Path also made a small comeback, killing 10 people in a car bomb attack outside the U.S. embassy in March and making a limited effort to disrupt the November election. On a positive note, in November authorities captured the head of an army death squad whose arrest could shed light on the still-exiled Fujimori's role in human rights atrocities.

Political Rights and Civil Liberties: Peruvians can change their government through free and fair elections, and the November 2002 elections were held largely without incident. In preparation for the 2001 vote, congress reformed the constitution, replacing a single nationwide district for congressional elections with a system of multiple districts based on the departments (provinces) into which the country is divided for administrative purposes. The move provided fair representation for the almost 50 percent of the population who live outside the four largest cities, and guaranteed them some attention from the state and from political parties, which traditionally have ignored them.

Since Alejandro Toledo assumed office in July 28, 2001, the Justice Ministry has worked to put in to place a broad anticorruption effort. Senior Peruvian officials promised to strip the veil of immunity from corrupt politicians by using independent courts, respect for human rights, and exemplary punishment for those who merit it. Popular perceptions of the justice system—that it is a swamped bureaucracy riddled by political influence and greed—will be hard to change, however. Toledo's own personal behavior meant that transparency promises by his government were jeopardized in the public's opinion. Scant resources have meant that most of Peru's more than 3,000 judges are overworked and underpaid.

Peru's financial woes are the most notable factor contributing to spiraling national crime. The National Statistics Institute estimates that rapid increases in poverty have now placed fully half the population in need, with one-third of the indigent population of 12 million living in extreme poverty. Public safety, particularly in Lima, is threatened by vicious warfare by opposing gangs—some of whom use body armor and high-powered weapons—and violent crime. Police estimate that there are more than 1,000 criminal gangs in the capital alone. Express kidnappings, in which people are held for a short time and forced to withdraw cash from bank accounts or automatic teller machines, are a serious problem in Lima. Conditions remain deplorable in prisons for common criminals.

The press is largely privately owned and is now considered to be free. Radio and television are both privately and publicly owned.

Racism against Peru's large Indian population has been prevalent among the middle and upper classes, although the Fujimori government made some effort to combat it and Toledo's election is considered a watershed. However, the provisions of the 1993 constitution, and subsequent legislation regarding the treatment of native lands, are less explicit about their inalienability and protection from being sold off than were earlier constitutional and statutory laws.

In 1996 the International Labor Organization criticized the labor code for failing to protect workers from anti-union discrimination and for restricting collective bargaining rights. Forced labor, including child labor, is prevalent in the gold-mining region of the Amazon. Violence is perhaps the greatest problem facing women in Peru today, although recently the government has taken some steps to deal with it.

Philippines

Polity: Presidential-par- **Political Rights:** 2
liamentary democracy **Civil Liberties:** 3
(insurgencies) **Status:** Free
Economy: Capitalist-statist
Population: 80,000,000
PPP: $3,971
Life Expectancy: 68
Religious Groups: Roman Catholic (83 percent),
Protestant (9 percent), Muslim (5 percent), Buddhist and other (3 percent)
Ethnic Groups: Christian Malay (91.5 percent), Muslim Malay (4 percent), Chinese
(1.5 percent), other (3 percent)
Capital: Manila

Ten-Year Ratings Timeline (Political Rights, Civil Liberties, Status)

1993	1994	1995	1996	1997	1998	1999	2000	2001	2002	2003
3,3PF	3,4PF	3,4PF	2,4PF	2,3F	2,3F	2,3F	2,3F	2,3F	2,3F	2,3F

Overview:

Islamic militancy and the government's shaky finances topped the Philippines's political agenda in 2002. President Gloria Macapagal-Arroyo tried to reign in a growing budget deficit by cracking down on rampant tax evasion while bringing in U.S. troops to train soldiers battling Muslim rebels in the southern jungles. Despite her crowded agenda however, President Arroyo effectively made herself a lame duck by unexpectedly announcing in December that she would not run in the 2004 presidential elections.

The Philippines won independence in 1946, after having been ruled by the United States for 43 years and occupied by the Japanese during World War II. Once one of Southeast Asia's wealthiest countries, the Philippines has been plagued since the 1960s by insurgencies, economic mismanagement, and widespread corruption.

The country's economic and political development was also set back by Ferdinand Marcos's 14-year dictatorship. Marcos was finally chased out of office in 1986 by massive "People Power" street protests and the defections of key military leaders and units. He was succeeded by Corazon Aquino, who had been cheated out of victory in an election rigged by the strongman's cronies.

Though she came to symbolize the Philippines's return to elected rule, Aquino managed few deep political or economic reforms while facing seven coup attempts.

Her more forceful successor, former army chief Fidel Ramos, ended chronic power shortages, privatized many state firms, and trimmed bureaucratic red tape.

With the popular Ramos constitutionally barred from running for reelection, Vice President Joseph Estrada defeated seven other candidates to win the 1998 presidential election behind pledges to help poor Filipinos. Almost from the outset, the Estrada Administration was dogged by allegations that it was corrupt and that it gave favorable treatment to the business interests of well-connected tycoons. The House of Representatives impeached Estrada in November 2000 on graft, bribery, and other charges. During the resulting trial in the Senate, his supporters blocked prosecutors from unsealing key evidence. This led to massive street protests and a public withdrawal of support by military leaders that forced Estrada to resign in January 2001.

As vice president, Arroyo became president under the constitutional line of succession. She faced the challenges of gaining legitimacy for her unelected administration, meeting the demands of her middle-class and business supporters for more open and accountable governance, and cutting the budget deficit while launching programs to ease poverty among lower-class Filipinos. In the first major test of her administration's popularity, Arroyo's coalition won 8 of 13 contested Senate seats and a majority in the House in the May 2001 legislative elections.

Arroyo's decision in 2002 to temporarily bring in hundreds of U.S. troops to equip and train Filipino soldiers fighting the Abu Sayyaf guerrillas in the southern Mindanao region sparked controversy. Leftists claimed that the U.S. troop presence smacked of American neo-imperialism. Other critics alleged that the Filipino troops had few successes to show for their training. Most of the U.S. forces departed in July after a six-month stint. Washington says that Abu Sayyaf guerrillas are international terrorists on the basis of past links to Osama bin Laden's al-Qaeda terrorism network. Recently, however, Abu Sayyaf's raison d'être seems to be kidnappings for ransom and other extortion.

While trying to wipe out Abu Sayyaf, Arroyo, 54, continued peace talks with another rebel group, the Moro Islamic Liberation Front (MILF), which has been fighting since 1978 for an independent Islamic state in Mindanao. The government and the 15,000-strong MILF signed a ceasefire in 2001, though the rebels' separatist demands stand in the way of a durable peace accord. Separately, Arroyo's government made little progress in reviving stalled talks with Communist rebels, known as the New People's Army, who have been waging a low-grade rural insurgency since 1969.

Arroyo, a U.S.-trained economist, said that her decision not to run in 2004 would avoid worsening the country's political and social rifts and leave her free to deal with the economy. Earlier, she launched the crackdown on tax evasion with several highly publicized arrests of alleged tax dodgers. The Philippines loses an estimated 10 percent of its gross domestic product (GDP), or about $7.6 billion, to tax evasion each year, according to the U.S. investment bank Morgan Stanley. This has contributed to a hefty budget deficit of around 5.4 percent of GDP, which makes it costlier for the government to borrow money while leaving less for education, infrastructure, and other critical needs.

Political Rights and Civil Liberties:

Filipinos enjoy most basic rights and can change their government through elections. Many foreign and domestic observers, however, said that the street protests and military pressure that forced President Joseph Estrada to resign in 2001 amounted to a "soft coup."

Elections continue to be violent, though less so than in the past. Many election-related killings are attributed to local militias linked to politicians. In addition, the New People's Army has claimed responsibility for some poll-related deaths. The military said that 86 people, including 10 candidates, were killed before and during local elections in July 2002. Some 100 people were killed in violence related to the 2001 national elections, according to the U.S. State Department's global human rights report for 2001, released in March 2002.

The 1987 constitution vests executive power in a directly elected president who is limited to a single six-year term. Because she is serving out the remainder of Estrada's term, President Arroyo could have run in the 2004 presidential election. Congress consists of a directly elected, 24-member Senate and a House of Representatives with 201 directly elected members and up to 50 others appointed by the president. Despite recent economic reforms, a few dozen powerful families continue to play an overarching role in politics and hold an outsized share of corporate wealth and land. "Corporate ownership and control in the Philippines is highly concentrated within 40–50 family groups," according to a 2001 World Bank report. In the countryside, meanwhile, the wealthiest 5 percent of Filipinos control nearly 90 percent of the land, the Hong Kong-based *Far Eastern Economic Review* reported in 2001.

Corruption, cronyism, and influence peddling are widely believed to be rife in business and government. The Berlin-based Transparency International ranked the Philippines in a four-way tie for 77th place out of 102 countries in its 2002 corruption survey, with top-ranked Finland being the least corrupt country.

The Philippines's human rights record has improved considerably since the Marcos era, although many problems remain. Police and soldiers recently have committed "a number of" summary killings, including alleged members of organized-crime groups, according to the U.S. State Department report.

The human rights group Amnesty International warned in July that the government's increasingly tough law-and-order stance—including a decision to set up a special police unit that will use military-style tactics to target kidnapping gangs—risked increased human rights abuses if not accompanied by criminal justice reforms. The London-based rights group accused the police of making "widespread" illegal arrests and using torture to extract confessions.

To combat such abuses, the government has expanded human rights training for the police and military. Authorities have also dismissed, and in some cases prosecuted, dozens of police officers accused of rights violations. Local and international human rights groups and the U.S. State Department accuse both soldiers and Islamic militants of politically motivated killing, torture, and other rights violations in Mindanao. The conflict has caused severe hardship for many of the region's 15 million people. Clashes in past years forced hundreds of thousands of villagers to flee their homes.

Moros, Muslims who live in Mindanao, say that they face economic and social discrimination by the country's Roman Catholic majority. Muslim-majority provinces lag behind Christian-majority ones in Mindanao on most development indicators, a 1998 Asian Development Bank survey found.

Critics allege, moreover, that a semiautonomous government that nominally rules several Mindanao provinces has few real powers and has done little to boost local economic development. Composed of former rebels, the Muslim-led government was created under a 1996 peace accord that ended a 24-year insurgency by a separatist group called the Moro National Liberation Front, which is separate from the MILF. Muslims make up around 5 percent of the Philippines's population.

In the countryside, the 9,000-strong New People's Army and smaller Communist groups recently have committed summary killings of "many" local politicians, judges, ordinary villagers, suspected informers, and military and police officers, according to the U.S. State Department report. The guerrillas have also recently kidnapped, tortured, and illegally detained opponents, the report added.

In rural Philippines, businesses and powerful landowning families hire private security teams that operate with near impunity. Dozens of peasants and pro-farmer activists seeking agricultural reforms and better working conditions disappear each year, the *Far Eastern Economic Review* reported in 2001. In urban areas, security also remains a problem in the south and other areas targeted recently by bombs in markets, churches, and bus stations.

The judiciary suffers from corruption, inefficiency, and shortages of judges, according to the U.S. State Department report: "Personal ties undermine the commitment of some government employees to ensuring due process and equal justice, resulting in impunity for wealthy and influential defenders."

The U.S. State Department report also described prison conditions as "harsh," citing overcrowded jails where official corruption is rife and inmates are given inadequate food and have limited access to sanitary facilities. Prisoners are also routinely beaten, according to the Philippines's official human rights commission. Women who are raped or sexually abused in custody by police or prison guards often fear reprisals if they press charges, and those who do make complaints often are pressured into withdrawing them, Amnesty International said in a 2001 report. The Philippines's private press is outspoken and vibrant, although often journalists resort to innuendo rather than investigative reporting. At least two journalists were killed in 2002, bringing to 39 the number of journalists killed in the Philippines as a result of their work since democracy was restored in 1986, according to the New York-based Committee to Protect Journalists.

Government programs to protect women exist, though rape, domestic violence, sexual harassment on the job, and trafficking of Filipino women and girls abroad and at home for forced labor and prostitution continued to be major problems, according to the U.S. State Department report. Prostitution is illegal but widespread; an estimated 500,000 women work as prostitutes in the Philippines, according to a 1998 International Labor Organization (ILO) study.

More Filipino women than men enter high schools and universities. In the job market though, women face some discrimination in the private sector and have a higher unemployment rate than men, the U.S. State Department report said. Women also hold relatively few posts in government and politics.

Recent studies by the government and international agencies suggest that the Philippines has up to 200,000 street children, some 60,000 child prostitutes, and at least 3.7 million working children. The government, UNICEF, the U.S. State Department, and others have accused the New People's Army of using child soldiers.

Members of the Philippines's indigenous minority have limited access to basic services and are sometimes displaced by commercial projects from their ancestral lands, according to the U.S. State Department report. Because they tend to live in mountainous areas favored by guerrillas, indigenous people, who make up around 16 percent of the population, also suffer disproportionately in army counter-insurgency operations, the report added.

Trade unions are independent, though organized labor is hamstrung by strict labor laws. The ILO has criticized labor law provisions that make it hard for state workers to strike, require a union to represent at least 20 percent of workers in a bargaining unit before it can be registered, and penalize workers for strikes deemed illegal because they did not follow proper procedures. Officials have not recently penalized workers for illegal strikes. The ILO has also called on the government to take measures to promote and encourage collective bargaining in the public sector. Making matters tougher, union leaders say, private sector employers often violate minimum-wage standards and dismiss, or threaten to dismiss, union members. Around 11 percent of workers are unionized.

Poland

Polity: Presidential-parliamentary democracy
Economy: Mixed capitalist
Population: 38,600,000
PPP: $9,051
Life Expectancy: 74
Religious Groups: Roman Catholic (95 percent), Eastern Orthodox, Protestant (5 percent)
Ethnic Groups: Polish (98 percent), German (1 percent), Ukrainian and Byelorussian (1 percent)
Capital: Warsaw

Political Rights: 1
Civil Liberties: 2
Status: Free

Ten-Year Ratings Timeline (Political Rights, Civil Liberties, Status)

1993	1994	1995	1996	1997	1998	1999	2000	2001	2002	2003
2,2F	2,2F	2,2FF	1,2F	1,2F	1,2F	1,2F	1,2F	1,2F	1,2F	1,2F

Overview:

At a summit in Copenhagen in December 2002, European leaders issued a formal invitation to Poland to join the EU. This historic milestone provided recognition of the fundamental political and economic gains Poland has made during its post-Communist transition. However, concerns were raised about popular support for joining the EU when populist and far-right parties that oppose membership garnered significant support in local elections. Several events in 2002 also raised questions about the commitment of Prime Minister Leszek Miller's government to the principle of noninterference in the functioning of a free press. The ninth visit by the ailing Pope John Paul II to his Polish homeland since becoming the pontiff was feared to be his last.

From the fourteenth to the eighteenth centuries, Poland and Lithuania maintained a powerful state that Prussia, Austria, and Russia destroyed in three successive partitions. Poland enjoyed a window of independence from 1918 to 1939 but was forced into the Communist sphere at the end of World War II. Polish citizens endured a Soviet-style people's republic from 1952 to 1989, the year Lech Walesa and the Solidarity trade union movement forced the government to accept democratic reforms.

Voters elected Walesa president in 1990, and he presided over five years of economic and political transformation. A former Communist, Aleksander Kwasniewski, defeated Walesa in 1995 and remains in office today. Kwasniewski's Democratic Left Alliance (SLD) controlled the government from 1993 to 1997, when the opposition Solidarity Election Action (AWS) proved victorious in parliamentary elections. The smaller Freedom Union (UW) party joined the AWS in forming a majority government led by Jerzy Buzek as prime minister.

In 2000, voters delivered a solid reelection victory to President Kwasniewski, who pledged to make membership in the EU his top priority. The next year, Polish voters ousted the Buzek's government and handed a parliamentary election victory to a coalition of the SLD and the Labor Union (UP). However, having failed to receive an outright majority, the SLD-UP alliance formed a government with the Polish Peasants Party (PSL). Some observers suggested that a series of corruption scandals involving high-level officials sealed the Buzek government's fate.

In December 2002, the European Commission extended a formal invitation to Poland and nine other nations to join the EU in 2004. During an address to the nation, Prime Minister Leszek Miller declared, "Europe has said yes to us; let us now say yes to Europe." He then called for a national referendum on membership for May 2003.

Although public opinion polls consistently show that a majority of Poles support EU membership, the electoral gains for parties that oppose membership has raised concern both at home and abroad. Local elections in 2002, for example, took on greater significance when the populist Samoobrona (Self-Defense) party and the far-right League of Polish Families together captured 33 percent of the vote. Both groups oppose EU membership. In particular, Andrzej Lepper, the farmer-turned-politician who leads Samoobrona and fears that membership will weaken severely the country's vast agricultural sector, has been likened in style by the Polish press to interwar fascist leaders and been accused of promoting an "anarchist ethos" in the country.

In 2002, Prime Minister Miller stirred concern about his government's commitment to the free press in what the U.S.-based World Press Freedom Committee described as "official attempts to undermine the essential financial independence of Poland's leading free newspapers." First, prosecutors reopened a tax dispute with Presspublica Holding, the Norwegian parent company of the newspaper *Rzeczpospolita*, and brought criminal charges against three of its managers. When the prosecutor's office seized the executives' passports and ordered them to check in regularly with the police, journalists and press freedom advocates denounced the move as injurious to the country's independent media and suggested that the government, which owns a 49 percent stake in *Rzeczpospolita,* was considering a takeover of the company for political gain.

Second, the government submitted a new Broadcast Law to parliament in 2002 that aimed to prohibit private media companies from owning both television and newspaper properties that have a national reach. The draft law appeared to be directed at the daily *Gazeta Wyborcza* and its parent company Agora, which wanted to invest in a private television network. The bill drew ire when reports began to circulate that government ministers and spokespersons had stated publicly that they wanted to punish Agora and *Gazeta Wyborcza* for critical reporting on the government. Although the government softened the law in response to critics, the issue remained unresolved at year's end, when Marek Borowski, the speaker of parliament's lower house, established a special committee to review the law's validity.

At age 82, Pope John Paul II visited his home country in 2002 for the ninth time as pontiff. With nearly three million people estimated in attendance at a Mass near Cracow, the event is believed to have been the largest public gathering ever in Poland. The pope was quoted as saying "unfortunately, this is a farewell meeting," and that it was "entirely in God's hands" whether he would ever return. The pope, who was instrumental in ending communism in Europe, also lamented "the noisy propaganda of liberalism" in Poland and warned of the consequences of "freedom without responsibility."

Political Rights and Civil Liberties: Polish citizens who are age 18 or older can change their government democratically under a system of universal and equal suffrage by secret ballot. Voters elect the president and members of parliament. The president's appointment of the prime minister is subject to confirmation by the Sejm. Elections in Poland are generally free and fair. Women account for 20 percent of Sejm members and 23 percent of Senate members.

In September 2001, voters handed the government of Prime Minister Jerzy Buzek a crushing defeat in parliamentary elections. SLD leader Leszek Miller became Poland's new prime minister. In the Sejm election, a coalition of the center-left SLD and the UP took 41.04 percent of the vote and 216 seats but failed to win an outright majority.

The two parties formed a government with the leftist PSL, which had won 42 seats. Civic Platform (PO), a new centrist party, finished second in the election with 12.68 percent of the vote and 65 seats. The following parties divided the remaining seats: the far-right Samooborona party, 53 seats; the center-right Law and Justice (PIS), 44; the right-wing League of Polish Families (LPR), 38; and the German minority, 2. The AWS and the UW failed to secure a single seat. In the Senate election, the SLD-UP won 75 seats; the bloc Senate 2001, 15; the PSL, 4; the LPR, 2; and Samooborona, 2. Voter turnout was 46 percent.

Incumbent President Aleksander Kwasniewski began his reelection campaign in 2000 with a strong lead in the polls. He easily defeated 11 opponents in the first round of voting with 53.9 percent of the vote. His closest challenger, independent candidate Andrzej Olechowski, received only 17.3 percent. The remaining candidates performed as follows: Marian Krzaklewski (AWS), 15.57 percent; Jaroslaw Kalinowski (PSL), 5.95 percent; and Andrzej Lepper (Samooborona), 3.05 percent. Seven candidates, including Lech Walesa, received less than 2 percent each. After his poor showing, Walesa retired from active political life.

The 1997 constitution guarantees freedom of expression and forbids censorship. However, the country's libel law treats slander as a criminal offense. Journalists, in particular, oppose the growing number of related lawsuits. In 2002, several actions by the Miller government raised concerns about its respect for media independence.

The state respects freedom of religion and does not require religious groups to register. All religious groups enjoy a reduced tax burden. Public schools offer classes in religion and ethics. Ninety-five percent of Poles identify themselves as Roman Catholic. According to polling data released in 2002 by the Warsaw-based Public Opinion Research Center, 56 percent of respondents believe the Catholic Church is too involved in Polish politics; 32 percent believe the Church's involvement is "as it should be." In 2002, Radio Maryja, an ultraconservative radio network that enjoys 6 million listeners per week, came under allegations of tax fraud. The League of Polish Families, which has ties to Radio Maryja, claimed the investigation was politically motivated in response to the party's skepticism of EU membership.

The Institute of National Remembrance confirmed in 2002 that around 1,500 priests had spied for the secret service during the Communist period. In particular, a priest (now deceased) spied on Karol Wojtyla (now Pope John Paul II) when he was the bishop of Cracow. In 2002, the institute also published a report, *Around Jedwabne*, that estimates that Poles participated in the murder of as many as 1,000 Jews at Jedwabne in the 1940s. It had long held that the Nazis were responsible for the killings.

Polish citizens can petition the government, assemble freely, organize professional and other associations, and engage in collective bargaining. Public demonstrations require permits from local authorities. Since the 1980s, when shipyard workers in Gdansk launched a national strike and formed the Solidarity labor union, Poland has had a robust labor movement. Although Solidarity's political strength has waned in recent years, labor groups remain active and influential. In April 2002, for example, Solidarity organized a rally in Warsaw by more than 25,000 workers to protest proposed changes to the country's labor laws. The protesters feared that mass layoffs could result from several liberalizing measures.

Poland has an independent judiciary, but courts are notorious for delays in processing cases. In 2000, the country began a reform process that has sought to increase the independence, efficiency, and professionalism of the judiciary. In its 2002 accession report, the European Commission acknowledged "steady progress" and "improved efficiency" in this process but noted that Poland should continue efforts to increase public access to justice, address public perceptions of corruption within the judiciary, and improve the treatment of detainees by the police. The commission's report also noted that prison conditions continue to deteriorate and that corruption "threatens to undermine the functioning of many public spheres."

The constitution outlines a range of personal rights and freedoms, including the right to privacy, the inviolability of the home, freedom of movement, and choice of residence. The constitution also specifies entitlements such as free education and health care. The rights of minorities in the country are generally protected. In 2002, organizations representing minority interests in the country expressed concern over a question in the census pertaining to ethnicity. Although the interior minister assured minority groups that the question was intended to assist the government in formulating policies designed to protect minorities, groups suggested that individuals feared reporting any ethnicity other than Polish and, as a result, that the census data could prove inaccurate.

In 2002, President Kwasniewski expressed concern that sustained high unemployment (nearly 20 percent) and poverty could pose a threat to Polish democracy. Nevertheless, the country still boasts a competitive market economy in which the private sector makes up 75 percent of gross domestic product and 72 percent of total employment, according to the European Bank for Reconstruction and Development. In 2002, President Kwasniewski promised that in early 2003 he would submit legislation to the Polish parliament on the restitution of private property seized during the Communist period.

Portugal

Polity: Presidential-parliamentary democracy
Economy: Mixed capitalist
Population: 10,400,000
PPP: $17,290
Life Expectancy: 76
Religious Groups: Roman Catholic (94 percent), Protestant (6 percent)
Ethnic Groups: Portuguese, African minority
Capital: Lisbon

Political Rights: 1
Civil Liberties: 1
Status: Free

Ten-Year Ratings Timeline (Political Rights, Civil Liberties, Status)

1993	1994	1995	1996	1997	1998	1999	2000	2001	2002	2003
1,1F	1,1F	1,1F	1,1F	1,1F	1,1F	1,1F	1,1F	1,1F	1,1F	1,1F

Overview:

Prime Minister Antonio Guterres resigned at the end of 2001 after his ruling Socialist Party suffered significant losses in municipal elections. The general election held on March 17, 2002, two years earlier than scheduled, produced a narrow victory for the Social Democratic Party (PSD), Portugal's center-right party, ending six years of Socialist Party government. However, the PSD fell well short of an absolute majority, which forced it to form a governing alliance with the small Popular Party, a populist, right-of-center party. The PSD won 40.1 percent of the vote and 105 seats in the 230-seat parliament, compared with 37.9 percent of the vote and 96 seats for the Socialist Party. The Popular Party took 8.8 percent of the vote and 14 seats.

Formerly a great maritime and colonial empire, Portugal ended its monarchy in a bloodless revolution in 1910. The republic, plagued by chronic instability and violence, ended in a military revolt in 1926. A fascist dictatorship under Antonio Salazar lasted from 1932 to 1968. In 1968, the dying Salazar was replaced by his lieutenant, Marcello Caetano. During what is now termed the "Marcello spring," repression and censorship were relaxed somewhat and a liberal wing developed inside the one-party national assembly. In 1974, Caetano was overthrown in a bloodless coup by the Armed Forces Movement, which opposed the ongoing colonial wars in Mozambique and Angola. A transition to democracy then began with the election of a constitutional assembly that adopted a democratic constitution in 1976. The constitution was revised in 1982 to bring the military under civilian control, curb the president's powers, and abolish an unelected "Revolutionary Council." In 1989, a second revision of the constitution provided for further privatization of nationalized industries and state-owned media.

The election of the Socialist Party's Jorge Sampaio as president in 1996 marked the end of a conservative era in which Portugal benefited economically but failed to satisfy voters' eagerness for social change. The political reversal in 2002 will alter little the country's social policies, though it will press ahead with more economic liberalization. The new government has pledged to reform labor regulations and introduce a new social security law. Employers are reluctant to employ people with permanent job contracts, which have become too difficult and costly to rescind. High levels of job protection also undermine labor mobility, which is partly to blame for the country's low level of productivity.

Political scandal emerged in 2002 as Popular Party leader and defense minister Paulo Portas came under investigation for financial improprieties. Portas has avoided criminal charges, but his continued presence in the cabinet risks undermining the government. Nevertheless, the prime minister has so far supported Portas. Tensions will certainly increase among the coalition parties if the scandal drags on into 2003, and the PSD may well seek to distance itself from the PP.

Political Rights and Civil Liberties: Portuguese can change their government democratically. In direct, competitive elections, voters, including a large number of Portuguese living abroad, select both the president and members of parliament. The president, who also commands the country's armed forces, is elected to a five-year term. The president receives advice from the Council of State, which includes six senior civilian officials, former presidents, five members chosen by the legislature, and five chosen by the president. While the president holds no executive powers, he can delay legislation with a veto or insist on a two-thirds majority to approve some laws. The country's unicameral legislature includes up to 235 deputies. With the exception of fascist organizations, political association is unrestricted. Members of small, extreme-right groups, however, have run candidates for public office without interference. In 1997, the constitution was amended to allow immigrants to vote in presidential elections.

Portugal introduced what was considered the most liberal immigration legislation in the EU in August 2001. Workers who entered the country illegally or on tourist visas are now able to legalize their status. A shortage of 22,000 laborers contributed to the legislation. Workers can stay in Portugal indefinitely by legalizing their status and obtaining either permanent residency or citizenship. They can then move freely to other EU countries. There are an estimated 200,000 foreigners in the country, representing 1.8 percent of the population. Anti-immigrant violence appears rare.

Portuguese courts are autonomous and operate only under the restraints of established law and the constitution. They include a constitutional court, a supreme court of justice, and judicial courts of the first and second instance. Separate administrative courts address administrative and tax disputes. They are generally noted for their adherence to traditional principles of independent jurisprudence, but inefficient bureaucratic organization has created an enormous backlog of cases in the system.

Freedoms of speech and assembly are respected with few exceptions. Although the law forbids insults directed at the government or the armed forces and statements intended to undermine the rule of law, the state has never prosecuted cases under this provision. Human rights organizations have repeatedly criticized Portugal for the occasional beating of prisoners and other detainees. In general, prison conditions are poor.

The print media, which are owned by political parties and private publishers, are free and competitive. Until 1990, all television and radio media, with the exception of the Roman Catholic radio station, were state owned. Although television broadcasting is dominated by the state-owned Radioteleivisao Portuguesa, two independent stations have operated in recent years. Despite the vocal press, in September 2002 a court charged a journalist for declining to reveal his sources related to a drug case, and the police held him in custody for several hours.

Workers have the right to strike and are represented by competing Communist and non-Communist organizations. In recent years, the two principal labor federations, the General Union of Workers and the General Confederation of Portuguese Workers Intersindical, have charged "clandestine" companies with exploiting child labor in the impoverished north.

The status of women has improved with economic modernization. Women account for two-thirds of university graduates. More than 60 percent of women are employed, accounting for 40 percent of Portugal's doctors, judges, and lawyers. Despite these gains, the average pay for women remains 22 percent lower than for men, according to the Ministry of Labor. Women also remain underrepresented in politics and the executive ranks of business. A 1997 constitutional amendment promoting equality in politics has yet to be translated into legislation that would establish minimum quotas. Portugal's constitution provides for freedom of religion, and the government respects this right in practice.

Qatar

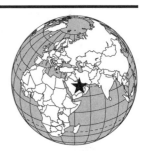

Polity: Traditional monarchy
Economy: Mixed capitalist-statist
Population: 600,000
PPP: $18,789
Life Expectancy: 72

Political Rights: 6
Civil Liberties: 6
Status: Not Free

Religious Groups: Muslim (95 percent), other (5 percent)
Ethnic Groups: Arab (40 percent), Pakistani (18 percent), Indian (18 percent), Iranian (10 percent), other (14 percent)
Capital: Doha

Ten-Year Ratings Timeline (Political Rights, Civil Liberties, Status)

1993	1994	1995	1996	1997	1998	1999	2000	2001	2002	2003
7,6NF	7,6NF	7,6NF	7,6NF	7,6NF	7,6NF	7,6NF	6,6NF	6,6NF	6,6NF	6,6NF

Overview: The gradual expansion of political and civil liberties in this tiny oil-and gas-rich emirate continued in 2002, though the reform process has yet to be institutionalized and appears to be driven primarily by the government's desire to upgrade its military and strategic partnership with the United States. A draft constitution commissioned by the emir four years ago was completed in July, but remained "under review" at the end of the year.

Ruled by the al-Thani family since the mid-1800s, Qatar gained independence in 1971. For nearly a quarter century, Emir Khalifa bin Hamad al-Thani ruled with few checks on his authority, much as his ancestors did under Ottoman and British protection. The al-Thani family had long embraced the Wahhabi interpretation of Sunni Islam founded in neighboring Saudi Arabia and had enforced many of its strict social codes, such as gender segregation. The ruling family also shared with its Saudi counterpart a propensity for corruption, which nearly crippled its economy in the late 1980s.

In 1995, the emir was overthrown by his son, Hamad, who proceeded to launch a progression of economic and social reforms that have thoroughly transformed the emirate. In hopes of establishing Qatar as a regional business and tourist center on par with Dubai, Hamad poured billions of dollars into infrastructure modernization, lifted the prohibition on alcohol, and encouraged Western investment in the tourist sector. Scores of modern hotels, nightclubs, and amusement parks sprang up in Doha, which the guidebook *Lonely Planet* once called the "dullest place on earth."

Hamad broke with the country's tradition of consulting closely with neighboring Gulf of Cooperation Council (GCC) states, several of which he accused of plotting a counter-coup to restore his father to the throne. His $150 million investment in the 1996 creation of Al-Jazeera, an all-news satellite station now watched by more than 30 million viewers in the Arab world, enormously bolstered Qatar's international prestige. To the chagrin of neighboring monarchs, Hamad also expanded the scope of public freedoms in Qatar and lifted some restrictions on women's rights. Press censorship was formally lifted with the dissolution of the Information Ministry in 1995. Four years later, Qatar held elections for a 29-member municipal council, becoming the first GCC state to introduce universal suffrage. However, not one of Qatar's leading families fielded candidates, ensuring that the election would not become an indirect referendum on the new political order.

While Qatar's neighbors declined to offer high-profile diplomatic or military support for the American war in Afghanistan after the September 11, 2001 attacks on the United States and have distanced themselves from the campaign to oust Saddam Hussein, Hamad seized the opportunity to reposition the emirate as the most accommodating strategic American ally in the Persian Gulf region. The U.S. Air Force base at Al-Uneid, 30 miles outside the capital, has been upgraded to accommodate heavy bombers, and the number of American military personnel in Qatar has grown to exceed those in Saudi Arabia. Qatar is expected to serve as the regional headquarters of the U.S. military central command in the event of war with Iraq.

In July 2002, a 38-member committee appointed by the emir presented him with a new draft constitution, still under review, that explicitly provides for political and civil liberties, judicial independence, and the establishment of a consultative council (Majlis al-Shura). Two-thirds of the 45-member chamber are to be directly elected through universal suffrage, while the emir will appoint the remainder. The precise legislative functions of the proposed body are not entirely clear, as the 150-article draft constitution has not yet been published, but they reportedly include approval of legislation and the budget.

Political Rights and Civil Liberties: Qataris cannot change their government democratically. Chosen by law from among the adult male members of the al-Thani family, the emir holds absolute power, though he consults informally with leading members of society on major policy issues. Although the 1970 basic law provided for a partially elected consultative council, no legislative elections have ever been held. An elected municipal council in Doha reports to the minister of municipal affairs, who is not required to heed its advice and may dissolve it at will.

While arbitrary arrests and detentions are prohibited by law, citizens and foreign nationals arrested in security cases have been subjected to prolonged pretrial detention in the past. Detainees generally receive access to legal counsel, and there have been no cases of alleged torture in recent years. The judiciary is not independent, as most judges are foreign nationals whose tenure may be revoked at any time. A separate system of *Sharia* (Islamic law) courts handle most civil cases. Corporal punishment is practiced in accordance with Sharia. Trials are public, though a presiding judge may close proceedings to the public if they are deemed sensitive, and defendants have the right to appeal.

In October 2002, a Qatari court sentenced a Jordanian journalist, Firas Majali, to death on charges of espionage. Majali's family claimed that defense lawyers were not permitted to present a defense of their client, whose conviction appeared timed as retaliation for Jordan's closure of the Amman bureau of Al-Jazeera.

Freedom of expression is limited. State-owned broadcast media generally reflect official views. Independent media outlets encounter little direct governmental interference, but exercise self-censorship on matters concerning the royal family and Qatari foreign relations. Al-Jazeera, which has gained international attention for airing the views of political dissidents from around the Arab world, virtually ignores domestic Qatari politics.

Freedom of association is limited to social, cultural, and professional groups registered with the government. Political parties do not exist, and the government has refused to sanction a number of activist groups concerned with issues such as consumer protection, the environment, and Palestinian rights. Public demonstrations are generally prohibited, though some anti-Israel protests have been tolerated.

Workers may not form independent unions or bargain collectively, though they may belong to joint consultative committees of worker and management representatives that discuss issues such as working conditions and schedules, but not wages. The government's Labor Conciliation Board mediates disputes, and private sector workers may strike if mediation fails. Foreign nationals, who comprise three-quarters of the workforce, are less inclined to assert their rights for fear of losing their residency permits, though strikes by foreign workers in response to employer abuse and nonpayment of wages have become frequent.

Islam is the official religion in Qatar, and the Ministry of Islamic Affairs controls most formal Islamic institutions. The country's small Shiite Muslim minority is allowed to practice openly, but not to organize traditional ceremonies and rituals, such as self-flagellation. While public worship by non-Muslims remains officially prohibited, they are allowed to conduct services privately. In 2000, the government authorized the first-ever construction of three churches to accommodate growing numbers of resident Westerners. Non-Muslims cannot bring suit in Sharia courts, which handle most civil claims.

Women have been granted the same limited political rights as men, but legal discrimination still exists in some areas, such as divorce and inheritance. Women are still prohibited from applying for a driver's license without the permission of a male guardian. The legal system provides for leniency in cases where women are killed or assaulted for violating social norms, though so-called "honor killings" are rare. The government has actively encouraged women to join the workforce. According to official statistics, women hold nearly 40 percent of private sector jobs and 45 percent of governmental jobs, though both figures appear to refer to overall employment, including foreign nationals. In November 2002, the emir announced the appointment of the country's first female cabinet minister.

Romania

Polity: Presidential-parliamentary democracy
Economy: Capitalist-statist
Population: 22,400,000
PPP: $6,423
Life Expectancy: 71

Political Rights: 2
Civil Liberties: 2
Status: Free

Religious Groups: Romanian Orthodox (70 percent), Roman Catholic (6 percent), Protestant (6 percent), other (18 percent)
Ethnic Groups: Romanian (90 percent), Hungarian (7 percent), other, including German and Roma (Gypsy) (3 percent)
Capital: Bucharest

Ten-Year Ratings Timeline (Political Rights, Civil Liberties, Status)

1993	1994	1995	1996	1997	1998	1999	2000	2001	2002	2003
4,4PF	4,4PF	4,3PF	4,3PF	2,3F	2,2F	2,2F	2,2F	2,2F	2,2F	2,2F

Overview:

Throughout the latter half of the Cold War, Romania was ruled by Nicolae Ceaucescu, one of Eastern Europe's most repressive dictators. In the early winter of 1989, however, popular dissatisfaction with the Ceaucescu regime led to his overthrow and execution by disgruntled Communists. A provisional government was formed under Ion Iliescu, a high-ranking Communist and the leader of the National Salvation Front (NSF). The 1992 parliamentary elections saw the NSF split into neo-Communist and reformist factions. In November 1996, Emil Constantinescu of the Democratic Convention of Romania (CDR) defeated Iliescu in the presidential elections. The CDR was prone to considerable instability and lack of unity, however, as was evident in the dismissals of Prime Minister Victor Ciorbea in 1998 and Prime Minister Radu Vasile in 1999.

In the November 2000 parliamentary elections, the Party of Social Democracy (PDSR) won 65 of the 140 seats in the Senate (the upper house of parliament) and

155 of the 327 seats in the Chamber of Deputies (the lower house). A surprising development in these elections, however, was the extent of support for the nationalist Greater Romania Party (PRM) led by Vadim Tudor, which gained 37 seats in the upper house and 84 in the lower house. The remaining seats in parliament were gained by the National Liberal Party (PNL), 13 in the upper and 30 in the lower house); the Democratic Party (PD), 13 and 31, respectively; and the Democratic Alliance of Hungarians in Romania (UDMR), 12 and 27, respectively. Since 2000, Adrian Nastase of the PDSR has served as prime minister.

Public confidence in both governmental institutions and in politicians appeared to suffer considerably in 2002, no doubt influenced by a series of corruption scandals involving leading politicians. Public opinion polls conducted between November 2001 and July 2002 showed that distrust of the government increased 2.5 percent monthly during this period. Pressure from the EU to tackle the problems of official corruption led to the creation of a new anticorruption unit in the Romanian government in 2002.

Throughout 2002, Romania tried to steer a difficult course between satisfying its requirements for eventual EU membership while at the same time maintaining good relations with the United States. In August, Romanian officials angered many Europeans by agreeing to U.S. demands not to turn over American soldiers that could potentially be indicted by the newly formed International Criminal Court (ICC). In November, Romania achieved one of its primary foreign policy goals when it was invited to join NATO.

Political Rights and Civil Liberties: Romanians can change their government democratically. Elections since 1991 have been considered "generally free and fair" by international observers. According to international monitoring groups, the legal framework for elections and laws related to the formation of political parties and the conduct of presidential and parliamentary elections, as well as governmental ordinances, provide an adequate basis for democratic elections. In the second round of Romania's presidential elections in 2000, voter turnout was 57.5 percent.

The judiciary is a separate branch of government, although executive institutions are believed to be exercise undue control over the judicial system. Police on several occasions during the course of the year beat individuals while under arrest, and police treatment of Roma (Gypsies) has been considered exceptionally harsh. Investigations into police brutality have generally been inconclusive.

The 1991 constitution enshrines freedom of expression and the press, and the media are characterized by considerable pluralism and a general absence of direct state interference. There are, however, limits to free expression resulting from provisions prohibiting "defamation of the country and the nation." Under Law No. 40 of the 1996 Romanian penal code, journalists face imprisonment for up to two years for libel and up to five years for disseminating false information that affects Romania's international relations or national security.

Religious freedom is generally respected, although "non-traditional" religious organizations (for instance, Jehova's Witnesses) in Romania sometimes encounter difficulties in registering with the state secretary of religions. Lack of registration denies adherents their right to freely exercise their religious beliefs and prevents them from building places of worship, cemeteries, and so on. In June 2002, the parliament passed a law restituting church property held by the state since the Communist period.

The constitution provides for freedom of assembly, and the government respects this right. Workers have the right to form unions and strike. There are no restrictions on travel within the country, and there are no legal barriers for citizens who want to change their place of residence.

The adoption of the Local Public Administration Act in January 2001 granted minorities the right to use their native tongue in communicating with authorities in areas where they represent at least 20 percent of the population. The act also required signs to be written in minority languages and local government decisions to be announced in those languages. The 1991 constitution provides for additional seats to be allotted to national minorities if they are unable to pass the 5 percent threshold needed to enter parliament. In the 2000 elections, 18 seats were awarded to national minorities on this basis.

Corruption remains a serious problem in Romania. Property rights are secure, though the ability of citizens to start businesses continues to be encumbered by red tape, corruption, and organized crime.

Women have equal rights with men, although gender discrimination is considered widespread. Women are considerably underrepresented in government, as is evident from the fact that only 10.4 percent of the deputies and 5.7 percent of the senators in the current parliament are women. As has become typical of the region as a whole, trafficking in women has become a major problem. Romania is considered both a country of origin for trafficked women and girls and a transit country, as well as a minor destination country. Parliament passed a law in November 2001 outlawing trafficking in human beings, and the country is involved in an extensive education effort to warn people about the dangers of trafficking.

Russia

Polity: Presidential-par-
liamentary democracy
Economy: Capitalist -
statist
Population: 143,500,000
PPP: $8,377
Life Expectancy: 65
Religious Groups: Russian Orthodox, Muslim, other
Ethnic Groups: Russian (82 percent), Tatar (4 percent), Ukrainian (3 percent),
other (11 percent)
Capital: Moscow

Political Rights: 5
Civil Liberties: 5
Status: Partly Free

Ten-Year Ratings Timeline (Political Rights, Civil Liberties, Status)

1993	1994	1995	1996	1997	1998	1999	2000	2001	2002	2003
3,4PF	3,4PF	3,4PF	3,4PF	3,4PF	3,4PF	4,4PF	4,5PF	5,5PF	5,5PF	5,5PF

Overview:
The violence and brutality in Russia's breakaway republic of Chechnya moved from the periphery to the capital when several dozen Chechen militants took more than 750 people hostage in a Moscow theater in October 2002. The crisis intensified President Vladimir Putin's efforts to portray the war in Chechnya as an antiterrorist operation, while hopes of finding a peaceful settlement to the conflict remained elusive at year's end. Throughout 2002, the Kremlin moved to consolidate its authority further by removing Communist deputies from nearly all of their leadership posts in the lower house of parliament (Duma) and putting pressure on independent media outlets that scrutinized or criticized the government. While Putin continued to press ahead with a number of economic and legal reform measures, some other initiatives, such as energy sector restructuring, were delayed during the year. In the foreign policy arena, the creation of a new joint council with NATO and official recognition by the EU and the United States that Russia now has a market economy reinforced Moscow's steadily growing ties with the West. However, U.S.-Russian relations showed signs of strain over the perceived failure of Washington to reciprocate Moscow's support for the U.S.-led antiterrorism campaign in Afghanistan, and to a growing Western military presence in several former Soviet republics.

With the collapse of the Soviet Union in December 1991, the Russian Federation reemerged as a separate, independent state under the leadership of Boris Yeltsin, who had been elected president in June of that year. In 1993, Yeltsin put down an attempted coup by hard-liners in parliament, and a new constitution creating a bicameral national legislature, the Federal Assembly, was approved. The December 1995 parliamentary elections, in which 43 parties competed, saw the victory of Communists and nationalist forces.

In the 1996 presidential elections, Yeltsin, who was openly supported by the country's most influential media and business elites, easily defeated Communist Party leader Gennady Zyuganov. The signing of a peace agreement in August with authorities in the republic of Chechnya put an end to a nearly two-year war with the breakaway territory, in which Russia suffered a humiliating defeat and Chechnya's formal economy and infrastructure were largely destroyed. A final decision on the region's status was officially deferred until 2001.

The August 1998 collapse of the ruble and Russia's financial markets ushered in a new government that signaled a return to greater spending and state control. One year later, Federal Security Service head Vladimir Putin was named the country's new prime minister. Yeltsin, whose term was set to expire in 2000 and who was ineligible to run for a third term, indicated that Putin was his preferred successor in the presidential elections scheduled for June 2000.

The previous conflict with Chechnya was reignited in 1999, after an invasion by Chechen rebels into the neighboring republic of Dagestan in early August and a subsequent string of deadly apartment house bombings in August and September in several Russian cities that the Kremlin blamed on Chechen militants. The Russian government responded by initiating an invasion of the breakaway republic that drove tens of thousands of civilians from their homes and led to accusations of human rights violations committed by both the Russian military and Chechen fighters. However, both the military campaign and Putin enjoyed broad popular support in Russia that was fueled by the media's largely pro-government reporting.

In the December 19, 1999, election for the Duma, the Communist Party captured the most seats, 114. The Unity bloc, a diverse grouping of political figures created by the Kremlin just three months earlier and endorsed by Putin, appealed to voters on the basis of its image as a champion of the restoration of order and tough leadership and gained 73 seats. While the Communists formed the single largest bloc, the results nonetheless were regarded as a victory for pro-government forces. Under a Kremlin-inspired power-sharing deal agreed to the following month, the Communists were given control of one-third of the Duma's committees, as well as the right to choose the legislature's speaker and deputy speaker. The Communists in turn largely supported the pro-government parties backing Putin.

In a surprise end-of-the-year move, Yeltsin announced his resignation on December 31, turning over the reins of power to Putin. Many observers maintained that his sudden departure was linked to the signing of a guarantee of immunity from prosecution for Yeltsin, who recently had been at the center of several corruption scandals, as well as to his worsening health problems. His resignation served to move up the presidential poll by three months, from June to March 2000. In a widely anticipated victory, Putin secured 53 percent of the vote over his closest rival, Communist Party leader Gennady Zyuganov, who received 29 percent. Two months after the election, parliament overwhelmingly approved Finance Minister Mikhail Kasyanov, who had served as Russia's chief foreign debt negotiator, as the new prime minister.

Shortly after taking office in March, Putin moved to consolidate power by limiting the influence of major business leaders over state policy and increasing the central government's authority over the country's far-flung regions. He challenged the long-standing political clout of some of the country's so-called oligarchs, members of the wealthy and powerful business elite—including media owners Vladimir Gusinsky and Boris Berezovsky—through a series of investigations and raids by tax officials that allegedly were part of a new anticorruption campaign. In an effort to rein in the country's often independent-minded 89 governors, Putin pushed through legislation removing them from their positions in the upper house of parliament (Federation Council) and allowing the president to suspend them for breaking federal laws. He also created seven new "super regions" headed by Kremlin appointees, most of whom had backgrounds in the military or security services.

Following the September 11, 2001, attacks on the World Trade Center and the Pentagon, Moscow's support of the U.S.-led antiterrorist campaign was heralded by many as the start of a new era in U.S.-Russian relations. Significantly improved levels of cooperation led to speculation about what concessions the West might be expected to make in return for continued Russian assistance. By mid-November, the United States appeared to have reduced its criticism of the war in Chechnya. It had also moved to accelerate Russia's entry into the World Trade Organization, pledged along with Russia to make deep cuts in nuclear weapons over the next decade, and endorsed a greater voice for Russia in NATO affairs. However, a chill in relations developed late in the year when the United States announced its intention to withdraw from the Anti-Ballistic Missile (ABM) Treaty and Moscow's hopes for a greater voice in NATO went unrealized.

On the domestic front, Putin relied on a largely compliant parliament to hasten the adoption of a series of wide-ranging and often controversial legal and economic reforms with the stated aims of reducing corruption, increasing transparency and efficiency, and boosting foreign investment. Among the various changes were new laws governing labor, taxation, banking, land ownership, pensions, and the judicial system. Some observers cautioned that the reforms were not extensive enough or would face serious obstacles in implementation from the country's entrenched bureaucracy.

In 2002, Putin and the legislature continued to press forward with such reforms as the passage of legislation allowing for the sale of agricultural land and the approval of a bankruptcy act to improve legal protection for debtors. However, other changes—including banking reforms and restructuring of the energy sector to cut costs and attract foreign investment—slowed or were postponed. With parliamentary elections looming in 2003 and presidential elections in 2004, some analysts argued that delays were caused in part by concerns over negative political repercussions associated with the adoption of often unpopular reform measures.

The pattern of increasing concentration of power in the hands of the president and his allies was reinforced when pro-Kremlin legislators in April voted to strip the Communist Party of nearly all of its Duma leadership posts. The decision marked an end to the two-year power-sharing agreement between the Communists and progovernment factions in parliament. According to some observers, the move to reduce the Communists' influence could prove to be a long-term tactical error that will transform them from quasi-allies to a vocal opposition force.

Moscow achieved foreign policy successes with the West by the signing a nuclear arms treaty with Washington and the creation in May of a new joint council with NATO. At the same time, relations with the United States were strained over issues including Russia's extension of economic ties with U.S. adversaries Iraq, Iran, and North Korea, and complaints by some Russian officials that Washington had failed to reciprocate assistance offered by Putin after September 11, 2001. In the economic sphere, the U.S. Commerce Department announced in June that it would recognize Russia as a market economy, easing Russian access to U.S. markets (the

EU made a similar decision a week earlier). However, by year's end, the U.S. Congress had failed to lift the Jackson-Vanik trade restrictions intended to punish countries for their restrictive emigration policies.

Russia sought to reassert its influence in the former Soviet sphere to counter a growing Western presence in the region. In the southern Caucasus nation of Georgia, where the U.S. military was training local troops, Russian planes reportedly conducted bombing raids to dislodge Chechen rebels alleged to be sheltering there. In December, Moscow stationed troops in the Central Asian country of Kyrgyzstan, where the United States had sent military personnel after September 11, 2001. The small Russian exclave of Kaliningrad, which is surrounded by Poland and Lithuania, became the subject of talks with the EU in 2002. Following a series of often tense negotiations, Lithuania and Russia agreed to allow Russian citizens to use alternative travel documents, rather than visas, when visiting Kaliningrad once Poland and Lithuania join the EU in 2004.

Chechnya captured center stage in late October after a group of some 50 Chechen armed rebels took 750 hostages in a Moscow theater and demanded that Russian troops withdraw from the breakaway territory. The standoff ended after three days, when Russian special forces stormed the building in a pre-dawn rescue operation; most of the militants died during the siege. More than 120 hostages were also killed, almost all by a sedative gas used to incapacitate the rebels, which prompted widespread criticism of the authorities' handling of the crisis. Putin responded by reasserting his claim that the war in Chechnya was part of the U.S.-led antiterrorism campaign and vowing to take "appropriate measures" against terrorists in the future.

By year's end, a peaceful settlement to the Chechen conflict remained elusive, as rebel forces engaged in sniper attacks, car bombings, and suicide missions against Russian troops and pro-Moscow Chechens. Human rights groups continued to report cases of torture, extrajudicial executions, and politically motivated disappearance of civilians by Russian troops, which were often committed during so-called mopping-up operations to find separatist fighters.

Political Rights and Civil Liberties: While Russians can change their government democratically, the 2000 presidential vote was marred by irregularities. A highly critical report by *The Moscow Times* following a comprehensive six-month investigation concluded that incumbent President Vladimir Putin would have faced a second-round runoff if not for widespread fraud; the report did concede that Putin would most likely have won in the second round. Among the reasons cited for his victory were biased coverage by large media outlets controlled by the state and by Kremlin supporters. The 1993 constitution established a strong presidency with the power to appoint, pending parliamentary confirmation, and dismiss the prime minister. The bicameral legislature consists of a lower chamber (Duma) and an upper chamber (Federation Council). The 1999 Duma election was regarded as generally free and fair despite some irregularities, including biased media coverage.

Although the constitution provides for freedom of speech and the press, the government and major enterprises with links to the government continued to put pressure on media outlets critical of the Kremlin. According to some analysts, the upcoming 2003 parliamentary and 2004 presidential elections provided the authorities with greater impetus to control the operation and content of print and broadcast media. The financial dependence of many television and radio stations and newspapers on the state or large companies further threatened editorial independence. In 2002, a number of journalists and media groups faced lawsuits based largely on their unfavorable coverage of government policies. In February, the independent newspaper *Novaya Gazeta* lost two separate libel cases. Press-freedom groups maintained that authorities targeted the paper because of its reports on high-profile corruption cases and its criticism of the war in Chechnya.

In January, the country's last private nationwide television channel, TV-6, was closed after a Moscow arbitration court ordered its liquidation. The ruling followed a bankruptcy suit filed by the petroleum giant and TV-6 minority shareholder, LUKoil, against the station for alleged poor financial performance. Exiled businessman Boris Berezovsky, who was one of Putin's most outspoken critics, had been a majority owner of the station. After the state-controlled natural gas company, Gazprom, had effectively taken control of the independent television station NTV in April 2001, many of the station's journalists had joined the staff of TV-6. Press freedom groups criticized the ruling against TV-6 as a move by the state to support loyal businesses in taking over and silencing independent media outlets challenging Russian governmental policy. In March, the federal broadcasting commission awarded the TV-6 broadcasting frequency to a team of former TV-6 journalists, including the station's general director, Yevgeny Kiselyov. The journalists had applied as part of a new media holding company, Media-Socium, which included a group of prominent businessmen and was led by former prime minister and current head of the Russian chamber of commerce, Yevgeny Primakov, and the chief of the Russian Union of Industrialists and Entrepreneurs, Arkady Volsky. The station returned to the airwaves in June under the new name of TVS. Analysts raised doubts that TVS would be fully independent of the government, as both Primakov and Volsky are closely associated with the Kremlin.

The government used draft changes to the media law to censor and shape coverage of the October Moscow theater hostage crisis. Authorities temporarily closed a television station for allegedly promoting terrorism, threatened to shut down the independent Ekho Moskvy radio station for airing a phone interview with a hostage taker, and allowed NTV television to broadcast only some of the statements made by the Chechen rebel leader inside the theater. The amendments, which would limit media coverage of terrorist activities and statements and antiterrorist operations, were hastily passed by both houses of parliament during the next two weeks. On November 25, Putin vetoed the amendments, which critics had argued represented government censorship and would further limit already severely restricted reporting of the war in Chechnya.

Throughout Russia's regions, journalists are coming under increasing attack because of their reporting or affiliation with certain media outlets that scrutinize the authorities; many of the cases are never solved. In the southwestern city of Rostov-on-Don, Natalya Skryl, a business reporter with the newspaper *Nashe Vremya*, was murdered on March 8. Prior to her death, Skryl had been investigating the activities of a number of large companies in the region. Valery Ivanov, the editor of the Togliatti newspaper *Tolyatinskoye Obozreniye*, which was known for publishing reports on organized crime and corruption, was shot dead outside his home in April. A series of violent attacks occurred against journalists in the city of Penza, including the beating of investigative journalist Alexander Kizlov shortly after he published articles in several papers criticizing the city's mayor. In the breakaway republic of Chechnya, the military continued to impose severe restrictions on journalists' access to the war zone, issuing accreditation primarily to those with proven loyalty to the government.

In June 2002, the military branch of the Supreme Court upheld a four-year prison sentence against navy journalist Grigory Pasko, who had been found guilty the previous year on charges of espionage. According to press freedom organizations, the conviction was a politically motivated effort to prevent him from continuing to report on the environmental dangers posed by the Russian navy's nuclear waste dumping practices. The Federal Security Service pursued other cases during the year that it termed examples of espionage, including those against the security and arms control researcher Igor Sutyagin and the physicist Valentin Danilov. Human rights groups contend that cases such as these involve information that has been declassified or is in the public domain.

Freedom of religion is respected unevenly in this primarily Russian Orthodox country. A controversial 1997 law on religion requires churches to prove that they have existed for at least 15 years before being permitted to register. As registration is necessary for a religious group to conduct many of its activities, new, independent congregations consequently are restricted in their functions. Regional authorities often harass nontraditional groups, with the Jehovah's Witnesses and Mormons among the frequent targets. Foreign religious workers continued to be denied visas to return to Russia, while several Roman Catholic priests were deported, barred entry, or refused visa renewals.

The government generally respects freedom of assembly and association. However, a July 2001 law significantly limits the number of political parties in Russia by requiring that parties have at least 10,000 members to be registered, with at least 100 members in each of the country's 89 regions. Critics have charged that the law reduces pluralism by limiting opportunities for smaller, regionally-based parties. In June 2002, parliament adopted legislation that gives the authorities the right to suspend parties or nongovernmental organizations (NGOs) whose members are accused of extremism. Critics argued that the law defines extremism too broadly and gives the government too much power to suppress opposition political activities that may not be genuinely extremist in nature. The NGO sector is composed of thousands of diverse groups, with many of them reliant on funding from foreign sources.

While trade union rights are legally protected, they are limited in practice. Antiunion discrimination and reprisals for strikes are fairly common, and employers often ignore collective bargaining rights. Most unions enjoy limited popular support and are struggling to address evolving economic and labor market conditions. Parliament adopted a new labor code in December 2001 that entered into force in February 2002. The law provides for a 40-hour workweek and seeks to address the problem of wage arrears. However, according to a report issued by the International Confederation of Free Trade Unions, some unions criticized aspects of the new code, including the placement of further limits on the right to strike.

With the long-awaited adoption of a judicial reform package in late 2001 that went into effect in 2002, the government made progress in implementing provisions to ensure due process and fair and timely trials. The changes to Russia's criminal procedure code include establishing jury trials in criminal cases throughout the country by January 2003 (jury trials had been held in only 9 of the nation's 89 regions); transferring the right to issue arrest and search warrants from the prosecutors to the courts; and eliminating trials conducted in absentia. Some critics maintain that the reform measures fail to address other ongoing problems, such as the widespread use of torture and ill-treatment by law enforcement officials to extract confessions, and that the courts will be unable or unwilling to handle their expanded duties. In December, the Duma voted to postpone introducing jury trials in certain parts of the country by up to four years because of financial and technical difficulties. In addition, the judiciary continues to be subject to political interference, corruption, inadequate funding, and a lack of qualified personnel.

While Russia's prison system suffers from overcrowding, inadequate medical attention, and poor sanitary conditions, authorities took steps during the year to reduce the prison population, including introducing alternative sentences to incarceration. Implementation in 2002 of a new criminal procedure code that generally limits pretrial detention to six months has reduced overcrowding in pretrial detention centers (SIZOs). However, conditions for detainees in SIZOs remain extremely harsh, including inadequate food, ventilation, and health care. In 2001, Putin disbanded the presidential pardons commission—which was viewed as a safeguard against the harsh penal system and had resulted in the release of about 60,000 inmates since its inception in 1991—and ordered the creation of commissions in each of the country's 89 regions.

The government places some restrictions on freedom of movement and residence. All adults are legally required to carry internal passports while traveling, documents which are also necessary to obtain many governmental services. Some regional authorities impose residential registration rules that limit the right of citizens to choose their place of residence freely. Police reportedly demand bribes for processing registration applications and during spot checks for registration documents.

Corruption throughout the government and business world is pervasive, with members of the old Soviet elite having used insider information to obtain control of key industrial and business enterprises. Consequently, widespread corruption remains a serious obstacle to the creation of an effective market economy and an impediment to genuine equality of opportunity. According to a report released in May 2002 by the Moscow-based Indem think tank, Russians spend an estimated $37 billion annually on bribes and kickbacks, ranging from small payments to traffic police to large kickbacks by companies to obtain lucrative state contracts. Students are frequently required to pay bribes in order to gain entrance to universities, the report stated. Russia received the lowest possible ranking on the 2002 Transparency International Bribe Payers' Index of 21 leading exporting nations. Legislation to combat money laundering, which entered into force in February 2002, was further toughened in September. As a consequence, the Financial Action Task Force of the Organization for Economic Cooperation and Development, which coordinates international measures against money laundering, removed Russia from its list of noncooperating countries. However, it was unclear when the law's various regulations would be fully operational. Putin's anticorruption efforts have been selectively applied and have often targeted critics or potential political adversaries.

A historic land code that established the legal framework for buying and selling nonagricultural land was adopted in October 2001. In June 2002, parliament passed a law allowing the sale of agricultural land to Russian citizens; such sales had been severely restricted since the 1917 Bolshevik Revolution. The absence of such legislation has been blamed for inhibiting the growth of Russia's economy.

Ethnic minorities, particularly those who appear to be from the Caucasus or Central Asia, are subject to governmental and societal discrimination and harassment. Numerous racially motivated attacks by skinheads and other extremist groups occurred throughout the year. Domestic violence remains a serious problem, while police are often reluctant to intervene in what they regard as internal family matters. Economic hardships throughout the country have led to a rise in the trafficking of women abroad for prostitution. There is credible evidence that women face considerable discrimination in the workplace, including being paid less than their male counterparts for performing the same work.

Rwanda

Polity: Dominant party **Political Rights:** 7
(military-dominated)   **Civil Liberties:** 5*
Economy: Mixed statist **Status:** Not Free
Population: 7,400,000
PPP: $943
Life Expectancy: 39
Religious Groups: Roman Catholic (56.5 percent),
Protestant (26 percent), other (17.5 percent)
Ethnic Groups: Hutu (84 percent), Tutsi (15 percent), Twa [Pygmy] (1 percent)
Capital: Kigali
Ratings Change: Rwanda's civil liberties rating improved from 6 to 5 due to the introduction of the *gacacca* justice system to deal with alleged genocide perpetrators.

Ten-Year Ratings Timeline (Political Rights, Civil Liberties, Status)

1993	1994	1995	1996	1997	1998	1999	2000	2001	2002	2003
6,5NF	6,5NF	7,7NF	7,6NF	7,6NF	7,6NF	7,6NF	7,6NF	7,6NF	7,6NF	7,5NF

Overview: The official transition period under which the Rwandan Patriotic Front (RPF) and its allies have ruled since the 1994 genocide is due to end in July 2003. Carefully controlled discussions about a new constitution continue. The RPF continues to maintain its predominant role in the country's governing structures. The beginning of the use of the traditional justice method of *gacacca* in 2002 posed the prospect of a reduction in the backlog of court cases against alleged perpetrators of genocide.

With the exception of some scattered violence, Rwanda remained peaceful internally. As part of a broad peace agreement, Rwandan troops left the Democratic Republic of Congo. Continued instability in the region, however, including tensions with neighboring Uganda, posed considerable challenges to the country's peaceful development and complicated efforts to improve the exercise of human rights and fundamental freedoms.

Rwanda's ethnic divide is deeply rooted. National boundaries demarcated by Belgian colonists led to often violent competition for power within the fixed borders of a modern state. Traditional and Belgian-abetted Tutsi dominance ended with a Hutu rebellion in 1959 and independence in 1962. Hundreds of thousands of Tutsi were killed or fled the country in recurring violence during the next decades. In 1990, the RPF launched a guerrilla war to force the Hutu regime, led by General Juvenal Habyarimana, to accept power sharing and the return of Tutsi refugees. The Hutus' chauvinist solution for claims to land and power by Rwanda's Tutsi minority, which constituted approximately 15 percent of the pre-genocide population, was to pursue the complete elimination of the Tutsi people.

The 1994 genocide was launched after the suspicious deaths of President Habyarimana and Burundian president Cyprien Ntaryamira in a plane crash in Kigali. The ensuing massacres had been well plotted. Piles of imported machetes were distributed, and death lists were broadcast by radio. A small U.N. force in Rwanda fled as the killings spread and Tutsi rebels advanced. French troops intervened in late 1994, not to halt the genocide, but in a futile effort to preserve a territorial enclave for the crumbling genocidal regime that was so closely linked to the French government.

International relief efforts that eased the suffering among more than two million Hutu refugees along Rwanda's frontiers also allowed retraining and rearming of large numbers of former governmental troops. The UN, which had earlier ignored specific warnings of an impending genocide in 1994, failed to prevent such activities, and the Rwandan army took direct action, overrunning refugee camps in the Democratic Republic of Congo. Nearly three million refugees subsequently returned to Rwanda between 1996 and 1998. Security has improved considerably since 1997, although isolated incidents of killing and "disappearances" continue.

The government, led by the Tutsi-dominated RPF, closely directs the country's political life. In 1999 it extended the transition period after which multiparty national elections could be held for an additional four years, arguing that the move was necessary because the poor security situation in the country did not permit elections to be held. Carefully controlled, nonparty local elections were held in 1999. In 2000 there were a number of important changes in the nation's senior leadership. President Pasteur Bizimungu resigned in March and was replaced by Vice President Paul Kagame, who had already been the de facto leader of the country. A new prime minister, Bernard Makuza, was appointed. The president of the National Assembly fled into exile in the United States and was replaced. The security situation remained generally peaceful, with refugee reintegration continuing to take place. In 2001, nonpartisan municipal elections, a controversial step in the country's political transition, took place.

Political Rights and Civil Liberties: Rwandans have never enjoyed the right to democratically choose their government. Rwanda's current interim basic governance charter is the Fundamental Law, an amalgam of the 1991 constitution, two agreements among various parties and groups, and the RPF's own 1994 declaration of governance. The current, self-appointed government is dominated by the RPF, but also includes several other political parties. The legislature is unicameral. Composed of 70 members, it was appointed in 1994 for a five-year term by the RPF-dominated government. Its mandate was extended by the government in June 1999 for a further four years.

A constitutional drafting process initiated by the government began in 2002. The draft constitution foresees a semi-presidential regime which gives strong powers to the president, who has sole power to appoint the prime minister. Presidential powers would be somewhat limited, however, as the president could not sign international treaties, start or stop war, give a general amnesty or declare a state of emergency without approval from parliament. The president can dissolve parliament, but only once during a five-year term. Only two succeeding presidential terms are allowed. According to the draft constitution, only parties receiving at least 4 percent of the vote in parliamentary elections would be allowed to function. The International Crisis Group (ICG) issued in late 2002 a report on the process stating that "there are multiple restrictions on political and civil liberty and no sign of any guarantee, or even indication, in the outline of the constitutional plan that the political opposition will be able to participate in these elections on an equal footing with the RPF."

Municipal elections, which had been scheduled for October 2000, took place in March 2001, because of legal and administrative delays. Candidates were elected to councils, which in turn chose 106 district town mayors who previously had been appointed by the central government. Political parties were forbidden to campaign; candidates could only present themselves as individuals. About three million voters cast ballots in generally peaceful balloting. Independent observers, including Human Rights Watch and the ICG, were critical of the lack of pluralism permitted. Single candidates appeared on the ballot for almost half the seats.

Political parties closely identified with the 1994 massacres are banned, as are parties based on ethnicity or religion. Several parties participate in government, although they are constrained from campaigning or otherwise engaging in partisan activities. There is some Hutu representation in the government, including Prime Minister Bernard Makuza, who is from the mainly Hutu Republican Democratic Movement (MDR) party. In recent years a number of leading government critics have fled the country. Seth Sendashonga, a former minister of the interior, was assassinated in Nairobi in 1998. Former president Pasteur Bizimungu is under arrest for announcing that he intended to set up an independent political party.

Constitutional and legal safeguards regarding arrest procedures and detention are unevenly applied. The near destruction of Rwanda's legal system and the death or exile of most of the judiciary have dramatically impeded the government's ability to administer postgenocide justice. About 120,000 suspects are incarcerated in jails built for 10,000.

To help address this problem, in 2002 the traditional justice system of *gacaca*, was re-instated. In this system, local notables preside over community trials dealing with the less serious genocide offenses. Some observers have expressed concern about the potential for partiality or for the application of uneven or arbitrary standards.

The International Criminal Tribunal for Rwanda (ICTR) in Arusha, Tanzania, continues its work. The tribunal, similar to that in The Hague dealing with those accused of crimes against humanity and genocide in the former Yugoslavia, is composed of international jurists. Relations between Rwanda and the court in Arusha in northern Tanzania have deteriorated in recent years, with Rwanda accusing the ICTR of incompetence, while the court has accused Rwanda of refusing to cooperate in war crimes investigations on its army. The ICTR has filed a complaint of noncooperation before the UN Security Council, to which Rwanda has responded, but the Security Council has not yet acted on the complaints.

Rwandan media are officially censored and constrained by fear of reprisals. The role of the media in Rwanda has become a contentious test case for media freedom and responsibility. During the genocide, 50 journalists were murdered, while others broadcast incitements to the slaughter. A September 2001 report by Reporters Sans Frontieres, a press watchdog group, concluded that press freedom is not assured in Rwanda. Journalists interviewed admitted that they censor their own writing and that the authorities have made it clear that certain topics cannot be discussed. As a result, Rwandan newspaper coverage is heavily pro-governmental. In 2002 journalists continue to suffer intimidation, arrests, or deportation. The broadcast media are government controlled, although a media bill passed in June 2002 paved the way for the licensing of private radio and TV stations. There are a growing number of newspapers.

Local nongovernmental organizations, such as the Collective Rwandan Leagues and Associations for the Defense of Human Rights, operate openly. International human rights groups and relief organizations are also active. Numerous clerics were among both the victims and perpetrators of the genocide. Religious freedom is generally respected.

There is ongoing de facto discrimination against women in a variety of areas despite legal protection for equal rights. Economic and social dislocation has forced women to take on many new roles, especially in the countryside. Constitutional provisions for labor rights include the right to form trade unions, engage in collective bargaining, and strike. There are 27 registered unions under two umbrella groups. The larger group is the Central Union of Rwandan Workers, which was closely controlled by the previous regime, but which now has relatively greater independence.

St. Kitts and Nevis

Polity: Parliamentary democracy
Economy: Capitalist
Population: 40,000
PPP: $12,510
Life Expectancy: 71
Religious Groups: Anglican, other Protestant, Roman Catholic
Ethnic Groups: Predominantly black, British, Portuguese, and Lebanese
Capital: Basseterre

Political Rights: 1
Civil Liberties: 2
Status: Free

Ten-Year Ratings Timeline (Political Rights, Civil Liberties, Status)

1993	1994	1995	1996	1997	1998	1999	2000	2001	2002	2003
1,1F	1,1F	2,2F	1,2F	1,2F	1,2F	1,2F	1,2F	1,2F	1,2F	1,2F

Overview:

In midyear, the United States and the Paris-based Financial Action Task Force removed the twin-island federation from the list of jurisdictions that were uncooperative in the fight against money laundering and other financial crimes. In late October the government of Prime Minister Denzil Douglas of the St. Kitts Labor Party (SKLP) submitted the Organized Crime (Prevention and Control) Bill along with the Anti-Terrorism Bill of 2002. While the latter will bring the federation in compliance with international agreements, the former is a response to increased crime and lawlessness and provides measures to prevent organized crime, address obstruction of justice, prevent corruption, and establish a Criminals Recovery Fund. Some tension continues to emerge over the role of Nevis in the federation, with sporadic calls for independence being heard. In response, Prime Minister Douglas has indicated an interest in providing greater autonomy for Nevis. The government noted that quality-of-life indicators were steady or showing improvement over the course of the year.

The St. Kitts and Nevis national government is composed of the prime minister, the cabinet, and the bicameral National Assembly. Elected assembly members, eight from St. Kitts and three from Nevis, serve five-year terms. Senators, not to exceed two-thirds of the elected members, are appointed, one by the leader of the parliamentary opposition for every two by the prime minister. Nevis has a local assembly, composed of five elected and three appointed members, and pays for all of its own services except for those involving police and foreign relations. St. Kitts has no similar body. Nevis is accorded the constitutional right to secede if two-thirds of the elected legislators approve and two-thirds of voters endorse, secession through a referendum.

Going into the March 6, 2000, elections, Douglas was able to tout his government's efforts at promoting resort construction in St. Kitts, combating crime, and raising public employees' salaries. The SKLP's critics claimed that the country had accumulated $192 million in debt and had failed to reinvigorate the islands' sugar economy. The SKLP won a stronger parliamentary majority in elections, taking all 8 seats on St. Kitts, out of the 11-member National Assembly. Opposition leader

Kennedy Simmonds's People's Action Movement (PAM), which hoped to oust the SKLP by winning the 3 seats in St. Kitts and forming a coalition with the winners of seats in Nevis, instead lost its only seat on the island to the SKLP, which had previously held 7 seats.

Political Rights and Civil Liberties: Citizens are able to change their government democratically. The 2000 elections were free and fair. Constitutional guarantees regarding free expression, the free exercise of religion, and the right to organize political parties, labor unions, and civic organizations are generally respected. Nevertheless, drugs and money laundering have corrupted the political system.

The judiciary is generally independent. However, in March 1996 when an earlier drug and murder scandal came to trial, the public prosecutors office failed to send a representative to present the case. The charges were dropped, which raised suspicions of a government conspiracy. The highest court is the West Indies Supreme Court in St. Lucia, which includes a court of appeals and a high court. Under certain circumstances there is a right of appeal to the Privy Council in London.

The traditionally strong rule of law has been tested by the increase in drug-related crime and corruption. In 1995, it appeared that the police had become divided along political lines between the two main political parties. In June 1997, despite concerns of its cost to a country of some 40,000 people, parliament passed a bill designed to create a 50-member Special Services Unit, which receives light infantry training, to wage war on heavily armed drug traffickers. The intimidation of witnesses and jurors is a problem. The national prison is overcrowded, and conditions are abysmal. In July 1998, the government hung a convicted murderer, ending a 13-year hiatus in executions and defying pressure from Britain and human rights groups to end the death penalty.

A number of felons deported from the United States under the U.S. Illegal Immigration Reform and Immigrant Responsibility Act of 1996 have helped to make local law enforcement agencies in the region feel overwhelmed. In St. Kitts, in 1998 the druglord Charles "Little Nut" Miller, threatened to kill U.S. students at St. Kitts's Ross University if he were extradited to the United States. A magistrate had twice blocked Miller's extradition, but it was approved by the high court after police stopped and searched his car, finding two firearms, ammunition, and a small amount of marijuana.

Television and radio on St. Kitts are government owned, although managed by a Trinidadian company, and there are some governmental restrictions on opposition access to them. Prime Minister Denzil Douglas has pledged to privatize the St. Kitts media. Each major political party publishes a weekly or fortnightly newspaper. Opposition publications freely criticize the government, and international media are available. There is free access to the Internet. Academic freedom is generally honored.

The main labor union, the St. Kitts Trades and Labour Union, is associated with the ruling SKLP. The right to strike, while not specified by law, is recognized and generally respected in practice. Violence against women is a problem, and there is no domestic legislation prohibiting it. Reports suggest that the country's economic citizenship program, which allows for the purchase of passports through investments ranging from $200,000 to $285,000, has facilitated the illegal immigration of persons from China and other countries into the United States and Canada.

St. Lucia

Polity: Parliamentary democracy
Economy: Capitalist
Population: 200,000
PPP: $5,703
Life Expectancy: 71
Religious Groups: Roman Catholic (90 percent), Protestant (7 percent), Anglican (3 percent)
Ethnic Groups: Black African (90 percent), mulatto (6 percent), East Indian (3 percent), white (1 percent)
Capital: Castries

Political Rights: 1
Civil Liberties: 2
Status: Free

Ten-Year Ratings Timeline (Political Rights, Civil Liberties, Status)

1993	1994	1995	1996	1997	1998	1999	2000	2001	2002	2003
1,2F	1,2F	1,2F	1,2F	1,2F	1,2F	1,2F	1,2F	1,2F	1,2F	1,2F

Overview:

In July, 11 prisoners were transferred to Grenada, which sparked a major crisis for Prime Minister Kenny Anthony of the St. Lucia Labour Party (SLP). The prisoners had been transported after the government declared them to be clear and present threats to the national security. After protests from human rights organizations, the 11 were returned in October. An anonymous letter published in August in several local media outlets underscored the deterioration of the main prison, corruption among personnel, and woeful deficiencies in training, uniforms, and equipment. The appalling conditions of the St. Lucia prison, as well as the delay in completing construction of a new facility, came to light. The midyear resignation of the minister of Planning, Development and Housing, after his admission that he did not hold a doctorate in economics, further tainted the government. In July the government agreed to sign the Inter-American Convention against Corruption. Rising crime, especially violent offenses, and continuing drug trafficking are serious threats to the island's tourism industry.

The SLP swept to victory in the December 3, 2001, general elections, winning 14 of 17 seats in parliament, just short of the 16-1 majority it had achieved in 1997. However, in an election called six months ahead of schedule, constituencies dominated by banana farmers registered their discontent with Anthony's party, reflecting a measure of popular discontent with his efforts to keep the island's ailing banana industry solvent. Anthony was the only party leader to survive the election. Although her United Workers Party (UWP) won the other 3 seats, Morella Joseph— the first woman to lead a party into a general election—lost her seat, and National Alliance leader George Odlum and former UWP prime minister Vaughan Lewis failed in their efforts to be elected.

St. Lucia, a member of the Commonwealth, achieved independence in 1979. The British monarchy is represented by a governor-general. Under the 1979 constitution, a bicameral parliament consists of the 17-member House of Assembly, and an 11-member Senate, elected for five year terms. Six members of the upper body are appointed by the prime minister, three by the leader of the parliamentary opposition, and two in consultation with civic and religious organizations. The island is divided into eight regions, each with its own elected council and administrative services.

Upon taking office, Anthony began to address concerns of an electorate weary of economic distress and reports of official corruption. In 1999, his government faced a series of issues concerning the hotel and airline industries, both vital for the tourism industry. In 2000, Anthony and the SLP gave their approval for regulated casino gambling, brushing aside objections from religious groups and the UWP, focusing even more of their energies on revitalizing the country's tourism trade. In June 2001, Anthony announced a two-month crackdown on crime, including increased police patrols and heavy penalties for gun related crimes, which he said were necessary to combat a wave of murders and armed robberies that he blamed, in part, on a U.S. policy of deporting hardened criminals to the island.

Political Rights and Civil Liberties: Citizens are able to change their government through democratic elections. The 2001 elections were considered free and fair, although less than 50 percent of those eligible actually voted; 60 percent of registered voters turned out in 1997. Constitutional guarantees regarding the right to organize political parties, labor unions, and civic groups are generally respected, as is the free exercise of religion. Civic groups are well organized and politically active, as are labor unions, which represent the majority of wage earners. Nevertheless, legislation passed in 1995 restricts the right to strike.

The judicial system is independent and includes a high court under the West Indies Supreme Court (based in St. Lucia), with ultimate appeal under certain circumstances to the Privy Council in London. In July a treaty replacing the Privy Council with a Caribbean Court of Justice, to be based in Trinidad and Tobago, was approved by St. Lucia; implementation has not yet taken place. The region's governments have voiced concern that the Privy Council prevents the use of the death penalty as a response to high incidences of violent crime. The constitution requires public trials before an independent and impartial court. Traditionally, citizens have enjoyed a high degree of personal security, although there are episodic reports of police misuse of force. In recent years, an escalating crime wave, much of it drug related, violent clashes during banana farmers' strikes, and increased violence in schools created concern among citizens. The island's nineteenth-century prison, built to house a maximum of 101 inmates, houses more than 350. In 2002 the government sought to finish construction of a new $17 million prison facility on the eastern part of the island.

The media carry a wide spectrum of views and are largely independent of the government. There are five privately owned newspapers, two privately held radio stations, and one partially government-funded radio station, as well as two privately owned television stations. There is free access to the Internet. Academic freedom is generally honored.

Though there are no official barriers to their participation, women are underrepresented in politics and the professions. A growing awareness of the seriousness of violence against women has led the government and advocacy groups to take steps to offer better protection for victims of domestic violence.

St. Vincent and the Grenadines

Polity: Parliamentary democracy
Economy: Capitalist
Population: 100,000
PPP: $5,555
Life Expectancy: 72

Political Rights: 2
Civil Liberties: 1
Status: Free

Religious Groups: Anglican (47 percent), Methodist (28 percent), Roman Catholic (13 percent), Hindu, Seventh-Day Adventist, other Protestant (12 percent)
Ethnic Groups: Black (66 percent), other, including mulatto, East Indian, and white (34 percent)
Capital: Kingstown

Ten-Year Ratings Timeline (Political Rights, Civil Liberties, Status)

1993	1994	1995	1996	1997	1998	1999	2000	2001	2002	2003
1,2F	1,1F	2,1F	2,1F	2,1F	2,1F	2,1F	2,1F	2,1F	2,1F	2,1F

Overview:

In June 2002 decision by the Financial Action Task Force kept the island on the list of uncooperative jurisdictions in the fight against money laundering. In the same month the Inter-American Convention against Corruption was signed. In August, Prime Minister Ralph Gonsalves, of the Unity Labour Party (ULP), denied allegations that he used state funds to pay travel costs for family members who accompanied him on a visit to Rome. In October the United Kingdom canceled the country's debt, easing the burden of rebuilding in the wake of tropical storm Lili, which destroyed about 40 percent of the banana acreage and caused extensive damage to infrastructure. The periodic destruction caused by tropical weather has further strained the islands' troubled economy and made efforts of diversification more difficult. Crime continues to discourage tourism, which had begun a slow recovery from the September 11, 2001, attacks in the United States.

In the March 2001 elections, the social-democratic ULP captured 12 of the 15 contested parliamentary seats. The incumbent, conservative New Democrat Party (NDP) won only 3 seats. The election, which had been preceded by serious political unrest and popular mobilization, was monitored by international election observers for the first time in the country's history.

St. Vincent and the Grenadines is a member of the Commonwealth, with the British monarchy represented by a governor-general. St. Vincent achieved independence in 1979, with jurisdiction over the northern Grenadine islets of Bequia, Canouan, Mayreau, Mustique, Prune Island, Petit St. Vincent, and Union Island. The constitution provides for the 15-member unicameral House of Assembly, elected for five years. Six senators are appointed—four by the government and two by the opposition.

Gonsalves, a one-time radical opposition figure, led an initiative in 2001 to save the financially ailing Organization of Eastern Caribbean States by strengthening the organization in order to relieve administrative requirements now carried out by its individual members. After a controversial trip to Libya, Gonsalves was criticized for not revealing publicly that the Arab nation had promised to buy all the bananas that the Caribbean could produce.

Political Rights and Civil Liberties: Citizens can change their government through elections. The March 2001 election was considered free and fair by international observers. The judicial system is independent. The highest court is the West Indies Supreme Court (based in St. Lucia), which includes a court of appeals and a high court. A right of ultimate appeal reports, under certain circumstances, to the Privy Council in London. Murder convictions carry a mandatory death sentence.

Penetration by the hemispheric drug trade is increasingly causing concern. There have been allegations of drug-related corruption within the government and the police force, and of money laundering through St. Vincent banks. The drug trade has also caused an increase in street crime. In 1995 the U.S. government described St. Vincent as becoming a drug-trafficking center and alleged that high-level government officials are involved in narcotics-related corruption. Since then, St. Vincent has taken steps to cooperate with U.S. antidrug trade efforts, such as signing an extradition treaty in 1996 with the United States. In December 1999, a marijuana eradication effort in St. Vincent's northern mountains stirred up controversy after U.S.-trained troops from the Regional Security System (RSS) were accused of brutality and indiscriminate crop destruction in what the Barbados-based RSS claimed was a highly successful exercise. One person, who police said was fleeing from a search scene armed with a shotgun, was killed.

Human rights are generally respected. In 1999 a local human rights organization accused police of using excessive force and illegal searches and seizure, and of improperly informing detainees of their rights in order to extract confessions. The regional human rights organization, Caribbean Rights, estimates that 90 percent of convictions in St. Vincent are based on confessions. The independent St. Vincent Human Rights Association has criticized long judicial delays and the large backlog of cases caused by personnel shortages in the local judiciary. It has also charged that the executive branch of government at times exerts inordinate influence over the courts. Prison conditions remain poor—one prison designed for 75 inmates houses more than 400—and prisons are the targets of allegations of mistreatment. Juvenile offenders are also housed in inadequate conditions.

The press is independent, with two privately owned independent weeklies and several smaller, partisan papers. The opposition has charged one of the weeklies with governmental favoritism. The only television station is privately owned and free from government interference. Satellite dishes and cable are available to those who can afford them. The radio station is government owned, and call-in programs are prohibited. Equal access to radio is mandated during electoral campaigns, but the ruling party takes advantage of state control over programming. There is free access to the Internet. Academic freedom is generally honored.

Constitutional guarantees regarding free expression, freedom of religion, and the right to organize political parties, labor unions, and civic organizations are generally respected. Labor unions are active and permitted to strike. Violence against women, particularly domestic violence, is a major problem.

Samoa

Polity: Parliamentary democracy and traditional chiefs
Economy: Capitalist
Population: 200,000
PPP: na
Life Expectancy: 68

Political Rights: 2
Civil Liberties: 2
Status: Free

Religious Groups: Christian (99.7 percent), other (0.3 percent)
Ethnic Groups: Polynesian (93 percent), Euronesian [European and Polynesian] (7 percent)
Capital: Apia

Ten-Year Ratings Timeline (Political Rights, Civil Liberties, Status)

1993	1994	1995	1996	1997	1998	1999	2000	2001	2002	2003
2,2F	2,2F	2,2F	2,2F	2,2F	2,2F	2,3F	2,2F	2,2F	2,2F	2,2F

Overview:
Located in the South Pacific midway between Hawaii and New Zealand, Samoa consists of two main islands—Upolo (home to nearly three-quarters of the population) and Savai'i—and seven smaller ones. They make up the westernmost islands of the Polynesian island group, which was divided up by colonial powers in 1899. The western islands became a German protectorate, while the eastern islands became a U.S. territory, known today as American Samoa. The westerly Samoan islands came under New Zealand's control in 1920 under a League of Nations mandate, and gained independence in 1962 as Western Samoa, known today simply as Samoa.

Samoan politics have been dominated since 1982 by the centrist Human Rights Protection Party (HRPP), which has won the most seats in six straight elections. Under Prime Minister Tofilau Eti Alesana, who took power after the 1982 elections, economic output per capita expanded and voting rights were extended to all Samoans. Previously, only Samoa's traditional chiefs could vote. The current prime minister, Tuila'epa Sailele Malielegaoi, came to office in 1998 after Tofilau resigned for health reasons.

The HRPP formed the current government after winning 22 of parliament's 49 seats in Samoa's latest elections, on March 2, 2001. After two weeks of intense politicking by all sides to cobble together a parliamentary majority, the HRPP picked up the support of six independents to gain control of the legislature. An independent lawmaker, Asiata Saleimoa Vaai, became the new opposition leader after mounting an unsuccessful bid to form a government. He took over from longtime opposition head Tuiatua Tupua Tamasese Efi of the main opposition Samoa National Development Party (SNDP). The conservative SNDP won 13 seats in the election, while independents took most of the remaining 14 seats.

Corruption allegations have dogged successive HRPP governments. The country's chief auditor implicated half of the cabinet for corrupt practices in 1994. Then-prime minister Tofilau's only real response was to issue a public rebuke to his ministers. Samoa's first assassination since independence, of public works minister Luagalau Levaula Kamu in 1999, allegedly was linked to the minister's anti-corruption efforts.

The economy depends heavily on tourism, foreign aid, agricultural exports, and money sent home by the more than 100,000 Samoans working abroad. Deputy Prime Minister Misa Telefoni said in December that economic output grew by roughly 1 percent in 2002, down from 8 percent in 2001. More than 60 percent of Samoans work in agriculture.

Like several other poor Pacific island countries that turned to offshore finance as a way to raise revenue, Samoa has been threatened with unspecified sanctions by the Paris-based Organization for Economic Cooperation and Development for allegedly acting as a tax haven.

Political Rights and Civil Liberties: Samoans can change their government through elections and enjoy most basic rights. Elections are generally free and fair, although the Supreme Court ordered by-elections in four districts in 2001 in response to allegations of bribery and abuse of the electoral rolls in connection with that year's parliamentary vote.

Samoa's 1960 constitution created a government that combines British-style parliamentary democracy with local customs. The legislature has 49 members—35 elected from single-seat districts and 12 elected from six two-seat districts, all by ethnic Samoans, and 2 who are chosen at large by non-Samoans. All serve five-year terms. Any Samoan over the age of 21 can vote, but only the 25,000 traditional chiefs can run for the Samoan seats. Prior to 1991, only the chiefs, known as *matai*, could vote. Chiefs attain their status by family agreement, and a chief generally must win approval from the high chiefs of the village in order to run for office.

Samoa's highest chief, Malietoa Tanumafili II, is head of state for life, though his successor will be chosen by the legislature for a five-year term. His approval is needed for laws passed by parliament to take effect.

The common law judiciary is independent, and Samoans generally receive fair trials, according to the U.S. State Department's global human rights report for 2001, released in March 2002. Many civil and criminal disputes beyond Apia, the capital, are handled outside of the court system. They are settled by councils of chiefs, called *fonos*, which govern individual villages. Fonos generally punish those found guilty by fining them, or, in rare cases, banishing them from their village, an extremely harsh penalty in this highly traditional society.

Several recent fono punishments have been controversial. The Afega village fono in 2001 banished 10 people, and their families, for giving evidence in a bribery case, although the Supreme Court overturned the order. Also that year, the Falealupo village fono barred a former speaker of parliament, Aeau Peniamina Leavai, and his family from entering their village, reportedly because he ran for parliament without permission.

The 1990 Village Fono Act gave fono decisions legal standing, but allowed some to be appealed to civil courts. However, court rulings overturning banishment orders are often ignored, Agence France-Presse reported in 2001.

The church is highly influential in Samoan society, and fonos have banished or otherwise punished villagers for not following the dominant Christian denomination of their villages, according to the U.S. State Department report. Chiefs generally choose the denomination of their extended families in this mainly Christian society. Fonos justify punishing villagers who refuse to follow this orthodoxy on the grounds of maintaining social harmony. In a ruling that seemed to reign in the power of village chiefs, the Supreme Court in 2000 ordered Saipipi village to take back 32 people who had been banished for following a religion different from that favored by the chiefs. Samoans also face strong societal pressure to provide financial support to church leaders and projects.

Traditional customs afford Samoans little privacy protection in their villages. While the law requires village officials to have permission to enter homes, in practice Samoans at times face strong social pressure to grant such consent, the U.S. State Department report said.

Samoa's press is generally free. In a gain for press freedom, the Supreme Court in 2000 overturned a 1997 ban that prevented state radio and television services from covering the opposition leader. Two English-language newspapers and several Samoan-language papers appear regularly. The government runs the sole domestic television station, although a private satellite cable system serves parts of Apia, and Samoans can easily tune in to television broadcasts from nearby American Samoa. Radio is both public and private.

Women generally play subordinate roles in this conservative society, although the 1,000 or more female chiefs wield considerable influence. Only three women won parliamentary seats in 2001, in part because only chiefs can run for the Samoan seats and only around 5 percent of chiefs are women.

Physical abuse of women in the home is illegal, but is socially tolerated and common, according to the U.S. State Department report. Men who abuse their wives are typically punished, if at all, by village fonos, which generally hand down punishments only if the victims bear physical signs of abuse. Police typically get involved in domestic violence cases only if the victim files a complaint, which social norms discourage, the report said. Like domestic violence victims, many rape victims apparently do not report being assaulted, although the increasing number of reported cases that are reported are treated seriously.

Some 20 percent of Samoan workers belong to one of the country's two trade unions. Both are independent, although their relatively inexperienced leaders generally do not bargain collectively on behalf of union members. The union-like Public Service Association represents state workers and bargains collectively. Several governmental education programs address job safety, although observers say that actual enforcement of workplace safety laws is lax.

San Marino

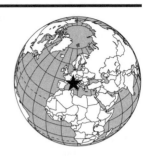

Polity: Parliamentary
democracy
Economy: Capitalist
Population: 30,000
PPP: na
Life Expectancy: 80
Religious Groups: Roman Catholic
Ethnic Groups: Sanmarinese, Italian
Capital: San Marino

Political Rights: 1
Civil Liberties: 1
Status: Free

Ten-Year Ratings Timeline (Political Rights, Civil Liberties, Status)

1993	1994	1995	1996	1997	1998	1999	2000	2001	2002	2003
1,1F	1,1F	1,1F	1,1F	1,1F	1,1F	1,1F	1,1F	1,1F	1,1F	1,1F

Overview:

San Marino adopted the euro as its official currency in January 2002. Following the withdrawal of support from the Socialist Party (PSS), the coalition government led by the Christian Democrats (PDCS) collapsed in June. The Socialists then formed a new coalition government in July with the help of other smaller parties.

Founded in A.D. 301, San Marino is the world's oldest and second-smallest republic. Although the Sanmarinese are ethnically and culturally Italian, they have succeeded in maintaining their independence since the fourth century. The papacy recognized San Marino's independence in 1631. An 1862 customs union with Italy began an enduring relationship of political, economic, and security cooperation.

Despite substantial reliance on Italian assistance ranging from budget subsidies to news media, San Marino maintains its own political institutions and became a member of the United Nations in 1992. Although San Marino has official relations with the European Union (EU) and participates in its security program, it is not a full member of the EU.

The ruling centrist PDCS won 25 of the 60 seats in the Grand and General Council (parliament) in San Marino's June 2001 elections. The two other main political parties, the PSS and the Progressive Democratic Party (PPDS), won 15 and 12 seats, respectively. San Marino has been governed by a long succession of coalition governments, which have dominated its modern multiparty democratic system.

**Political Rights
and Civil Liberties:**

San Marino's citizens can change their government democratically. The country has a long tradition of multiparty politics, with six parties represented in the current council. All citizens having reached the age of 18 have the right to vote. Women were permitted to stand as candidates for seats in the parliament for the first time in 1974. San Marino's constitution, dating from the year 1600, vests legislative power in the Grand and General Council. Its 60 members are directly elected by proportional representation every five years. The secretary of state for foreign affairs has come to assume many of the prerogatives of a prime minister. Directly elected Auxiliary Councils serve as arbiters of local government in each of the country's nine municipalities. A ten-member Congress of State, or cabinet, is elected by the parliament for the duration of the term. Two members of the council are designated for six-month terms as executive captains-regent, one representing the city of San Marino and the other the countryside. In April, Antonio Lazzaro Volpinari (PSS) and Giovanni Francesco Ugolini (PDCS) took office as captains-regent.

There were no press freedom violations reported in San Marino during the year. Newspapers are published by the government, some political parties, and trade unions. Italian newspapers and radio and television broadcasts are freely available. *Radio Titano* is the country's only privately owned radio station.

The law provides for freedom of religion, and the government respects this right in practice. Most Sanmarinese belong to the Roman Catholic Church; however, Catholicism is not the state religion. The Catholic Church does receive direct benefits from the state through income tax revenues if a taxpayer requests that 0.3 percent of his income tax be allocated to the Church.

Workers are free to form and join unions under a 1961 law. Unions may freely form domestic federations or join international labor federations. Union members constitute approximately one-half of the country's workforce. Trade unions are independent of the government and political parties; however, they have close informal ties with the parties, which exercise a strong influence on them. Freedom of association is respected. The right to strike is guaranteed, but no strikes have occurred in the last decade.

The law provides for an independent judiciary, which is based on the Italian legal system. The judicial system delegates some of the authority to Italian magistrates in both criminal and civil cases. A local conciliation judge handles cases of minor importance. Appeals go, in the first instance, to an Italian judge residing in Italy. The final court of review is San Marino's Council of Twelve, a group of judges chosen for six-year terms from among the members of the Grand and General Council.

San Marino has no formal asylum policy. However, it has allowed a small number of refugees to reside and work in the country. Immigrants and refugees are eligible for citizenship only after 30 years' residence. Those born in San Marino remain citizens and are able to vote no matter where they live.

Women enjoy equal rights in the workplace and elsewhere. There have been no reports of discrimination towards women in salary or working conditions. All careers are open to women, including careers in the military and police as well as the highest public offices. As a result of the 2001 elections, women now constitute 16.7 percent of the parliament.

São Tomé and Príncipe

Polity: Presidential-
parliamentary democracy
Economy: Mixed statist
(transitional)
Population: 200,000
PPP: $1,792
Life Expectancy: 65
Religious Groups: Roman Catholic, Evangelical Protestant,
Seventh-Day Adventist
Ethnic Groups: Mestico [Portuguese-African], African minority (Angolan, Mozambican,
immigrants)
Capital: São Tomé

Political Rights: 1
Civil Liberties: 2
Status: Free

Ten-Year Ratings Timeline (Political Rights, Civil Liberties, Status)

1993	1994	1995	1996	1997	1998	1999	2000	2001	2002	2003
2,3F	1,2F	1,2F	1,2F	1,2F	1,2F	1,2F	1,2F	1,2F	1,2F	1,2F

Overview:

After a year adrift, the government of President Fradique de Menezes appeared to be on course by the end of 2002.

De Menezes dissolved the government in 2001 and called for early parliamentary elections after he and the former prime minister disagreed on the government's composition. The elections produced a narrow majority for the opposition Movement for the Liberation of Sao Tome and Principe (MLSTP), which held the majority in the outgoing parliament. It was a blow to De Menezes. The president dissolved the government again in September 2002 after differences emerged in the military over promotions that had been granted. De Menezes appointed a new prime minister, the economist Maria das Neves, who formed a coalition government and is the country's first female prime minister.

Sao Tome and Principe consist of two islands approximately 125 and 275 miles off the coast of Gabon in the Gulf of Guinea. Seized by Portugal in 1522 and 1523, they became a Portuguese Overseas Province in 1951. Portugal granted local autonomy in 1973 and independence in 1975. Upon independence, the MLSTP, formed in 1960 as the Committee for the Liberation of Sao Tome and Principe, took power and functioned as the only legal party until a 1990 referendum established multiparty democracy. In 1991, Miguel dos Anjos Trovoada, an independent candidate backed by the opposition Democratic Convergence Party, became the first democratically elected president.

During 2002, Sao Tome and Principe was in the process of building up its relationship with the United States, which plans to build a sheltering port on the archipelago for the U.S. Navy to patrol waters surrounding the country and protect its oil resources there. The U.S. assistant secretary of state for African affairs, Walter Kansteiner, visited Sao Tome and Principe in October 2002.

Sao Tome and Principe has mostly relied on external assistance to develop its economy. Unemployment is about 45 percent. The government is trying to reduce the country's dependence on cocoa and diversify its economy. Efforts are underway to pursue development of offshore petroleum reserves.

Political Rights and Civil Liberties:

The people of Sao Tome and Principe have the right to change their government freely and fairly. Presidential and legislative elections in 1991 gave the country's citizens their first chance to elect their leader in an open, free, and fair contest. In presidential elections in 2001, Fradique de Menezes, of the Independent Democratic Alliance (ADI), replaced Miguel dos Anjos Trovoada, who had ruled Sao Tome and Principe for 10 years. In the first round of voting, De Menezes won with 56 percent compared with 38 percent for Manuel Pinto da Costa, of the Movement for the Liberation of Sao Tome and Principe (MLSTP).

The MLSTP won 24 seats in parliamentary elections in March 2002. The Democratic Movement of Forces for Change won 23 seats. The remaining 8 seats went to the Ue Kadadji coalition. De Menezes called on parliament to introduce laws against vote buying, which he said was rampant in the March parliamentary election. Nevertheless, international observers had declared the polls to be free and fair.

An independent judiciary, including a supreme court with members designated by, and responsible to, the National Assembly, was established by the 1990 referendum on multiparty rule. It has ruled against both the government and the president, but is occasionally subject to manipulation. The court system is overburdened, understaffed, inadequately funded, and plagued by long delays in hearing cases. Prison conditions are harsh.

Constitutionally protected freedom of expression is respected in practice. One state-run and six independent newspapers and newsletters are published. While the state controls a local press agency and the only radio and television stations, no law forbids independent broadcasting. Opposition parties receive free airtime, and newsletters and pamphlets criticizing the government circulate freely.

Freedom of assembly is respected. Citizens have the constitutional right to gather and demonstrate with advance notice to the government of two days. Freedom of religion is respected within this predominantly Roman Catholic country. The constitution provides for equal rights for men and women, but women encounter significant societal discrimination. Most have fewer opportunites than men for education or formal (business) sector employment. However, several women have been appointed to cabinet positions, including that of prime minister. Domestic violence against women is reportedly common. Although legal recourse is available, many victims are reluctant to bring legal action against their spouses or are ignorant of their rights.

The rights to organize, strike, and bargain collectively are guaranteed and respected. Few unions exist, but independent cooperatives have taken advantage of the government land-distribution program to attract workers. Because of its role as the main employer in the wage sector, the government remains the key interlocutor for labor on all matters, including wages. Working conditions on many of the state-owned cocoa plantations are harsh.

Saudi Arabia

Polity: Traditional monarchy
Economy: Mixed capitalist-statist
Population: 24,000,000
PPP: $11,367
Life Expectancy: 72
Religious Groups: Muslim
Ethnic Groups: Arab (90 percent), Afro-Asian (10 percent)
Capital: Riyadh

Political Rights: 7
Civil Liberties: 7
Status: Not Free

Ten-Year Ratings Timeline (Political Rights, Civil Liberties, Status)

1993	1994	1995	1996	1997	1998	1999	2000	2001	2002	2003
7,7NF	7,7NF	7,7NF	7,7NF	7,7NF	7,7NF	7,7NF	7,7NF	7,7NF	7,7NF	7,7NF

Overview:

Faced with severe economic difficulties and under greater outside scrutiny following the September 11, 2001, attacks on the United States, the Saudi government in 2002 introduced some changes to its oppressive criminal code, introduced minor labor reforms, and ended the clerical establishment's control of female education. However, there does not appear to be a consensus within the royal family in favor of further-reaching reforms.

The origins of the Kingdom of Saudi Arabia date back to a 1744 pact between the ruler of the small central Arabian town of Diriyah, Muhammad ibn Saud, and a puritanical Islamic revolutionary, Muhammad Ibn Abd al-Wahhab. Ibn Saud pledged to purge the land of impurities in return for the latter's endorsement, and together they conquered Riyadh and the central Arabian region of Najd. The Saud family's control of the Najd was later broken by the Ottoman Empire and the rival Rashid family, but was reestablished after Abdelaziz al-Saud recaptured Riyadh in 1902. Over the next three decades, Abdelaziz expanded his domain to encompass most of the Arabian Peninsula, including the holy cities of Mecca and Medina, through a combination of conquest, diplomacy, and strategic polygamous marriages. In 1932, he officially declared the establishment of the Kingdom of Saudi Arabia. Since the death of Abdelaziz in 1953, Saudi kings have been chosen from among his 44 sons on the basis of seniority and consensus within the royal family. King Fahd has held the throne since 1982, though he ceded political authority to Crown Prince Abdullah in 1996 after suffering a stroke.

Throughout the 60-year history of Saudi Arabia, the royal family has ruled without any institutional checks on its authority. Oil revenue facilitated an informal social contract; in return for material prosperity and the provision of free health care, education, and other social services, the population accepted the denial of basic political and civil liberties. The infusion of petrodollars into the country also helped perpetuate enforcement of the fundamentalist Wahhabi interpretation of *Sharia* (Islamic law). The government could afford to maintain an educational system centered around religious indoctrination because the country's material prosperity did not require cultivating an indigenous skilled labor force. Women could be denied the right to drive because most families could afford to import chauffeurs.

Over the last two decades, however, declining oil prices, rampant corruption within the royal family, and gross economic mismanagement have caused a steep decline in the living standards of most Saudis. Per capita income, more than $28,000 in the early 1980s, has today dropped to below $12,000. Unemployment is now estimated at up to 35 percent and is expected to rise in coming years. Growing opposition to the monarchy by religious and liberal dissidents was brutally crushed in the 1990s.

Crown Prince Abdullah has reportedly lobbied within the royal family for relatively sweeping economic and social reforms in recent years (such as permitting employed women over the age of 40 to drive), but few senior princes have been willing to sanction major changes. While other oil-rich states making the transition to market-oriented economies have typically introduced limited political reforms in order to avoid sparking unrest, powerful members of the royal family remain firmly opposed to establishing even powerless representative institutions. Reforms of the legal system and banking sectors—the two most important steps needed to attract international investment and gain membership in the World Trade Organization—have been stalled because greater transparency would undermine royal patronage networks. Most other economic reforms have been insufficient in meeting investors' concerns. Changes in the educational system needed to prepare Saudi students for the job market have been blocked by princes aligned with the religious establishment.

The biggest obstacle to attracting international investment in the years ahead is likely to be uncertainty about political transition in Saudi Arabia. Both Abdullah and Sultan, who is second in line for the throne, are in their seventies, while even the youngest remaining sons of Abdelaziz are in their sixties. As a result, Saudi Arabia is set to experience a rapid series of royal successions in the coming years unless a mechanism for passing power to the next generation of princes can be agreed upon. Speculation that Abdullah will break with tradition after Fahd's death and designate one of his own sons as heir has fueled fears that Sultan may try to seize the throne by force.

Unable to attack decisively the underlying causes of the country's economic malaise, Abdullah has sought to remedy its most politically dangerous symptom—unemployment. In 2002, the government enacted a set of "Saudization" laws that require companies with 20 or more employees to ensure that Saudi citizens constitute at least 30 percent of their workforce (a quota that will gradually increase in future years). In addition to reducing unemployment, the measures should alleviate the government's perennial budget deficits by reducing the estimated $16 billion sent abroad each year by foreign workers in the kingdom. In conjunction with the Saudization initiatives, some reforms were made in the area of workers' rights.

In March 2002, eleven Saudi girls died when a fire broke out at their school and the *mutawwa'in*—baton-wielding religious police—blocked the escape of those who had discarded their veils amid the commotion. The tragedy sparked widespread media criticism of the cleric-controlled General Presidency for Girls Education (GPGE), prompting the government to end the religious establishment's direct control over the education of girls.

Under pressure from the United States to crack down on al-Qaeda activities in the kingdom, the government detained scores of suspects during the year. As of November, around 100 people remained in custody for what the Interior Ministry called "holy-war activities." Although a new criminal procedure code went into effect in May, there was little evidence that it has been observed in practice.

Attacks against Westerners residing in the kingdom continued in 2002. In June, a British bank employee was killed by a bomb placed under his car and an American couple found a similar device beneath their car. In September, a German national was killed by a car bomb. As with most previous cases of attacks on Westerners in recent years, the government blamed the killings on turf wars between Western expatriates engaged in the illegal alcohol trade.

Political Rights and Civil Liberties:

Saudis cannot change their government democratically. The king rules by decree in accordance with the strict Wahhabi interpretation of *Sharia* (Islamic law) and with the consensus of senior princes and religious officials. There are no elections at any level and political parties are illegal.

Saudi citizens enjoy little effective protection from arbitrary arrest, prolonged pretrial detention, or torture at the hands of security forces. Although the new criminal code prohibits torture, protects the right of suspects to obtain legal council, and limits administrative detention to five days, there is little evidence that these statutes have been observed in practice. In July 2002, the son of jailed dissident Said bin Zubeir was taken into custody as he tried to board a plane to Qatar for an interview on Al-Jazeera satellite television, and remains incarcerated, apparently without charge. The younger brother of Virginia-based activist Ali al-Ahmed has been held since September 2001. A Saudi prisoner released in 2002 told Human Rights Watch that he was forced to sign a statement promising not to speak about his experience in police custody.

The judiciary is subject to the influence of the royal family and its associates. The king has broad powers to appoint or dismiss judges, who are generally selected on the basis of their strict adherence to religious principles. Trials are routinely held in secret, and convictions are commonly founded upon little more than signed or videotaped confessions extracted under torture. The legal system, based on Sharia, allows for corporal punishment and death by beheading, both of which are widely practiced. In recent years, about 100 people have been executed annually. In mid-2002, seven foreigners accused of carrying out a series of car bombings were tried and convicted by a secret court on the basis of allegedly coerced confessions.

Freedom of expression is severely restricted by prohibitions on criticism of the government, Islam, and the ruling family. The government owns all domestic broadcast media, closely monitors privately owned (but publicly subsidized) print media, has the authority to remove all editors in chief, routinely censors domestic and foreign publications, and restricts the entry of foreign journalists into the kingdom. Private ownership of satellite dishes is illegal, but is widespread. Internet access is filtered to block Web sites deemed offensive to Islam or a threat to state security.

In March 2002, the Interior Ministry dismissed the editor of the daily *Al-Medina* after the newspaper published a poem about corrupt judges. The author of the poem, Abdel Mohsen Mosallam, was detained without charge for 18 days, banned from publishing in Saudi newspapers, and prohibited from leaving the country.

Public demonstrations pertaining to political issues are completely prohibited. Governmental permission is required to form professional groups and associations, which must be nonpolitical. In April 2002, the authorities dispersed an anti-Israeli demonstration in Skaka and arrested dozens of demonstrators.

Trade unions, collective bargaining, and strikes are prohibited. Foreign workers, who constitute about 60 percent of the kingdom's workforce, are not protected under labor law, and courts generally do not enforce the few legal protections provided to them. Foreign nationals working as domestic servants are frequently abused and often denied legitimate wages, benefits, or compensation. Some steps were taken in 2002 to advance workers' rights. In April, the government issued a new law permitting Saudi workers to establish "labor committees" in companies with 100 or more employees, though the committees are empowered only to issue recommendations. The first such committee was established by Saudi employees of British Aerospace in July. In August, the government announced a multi-stage plan that would require Saudi employers to provide foreign nationals with health insurance by September 2004.

Freedom of religion in Saudi Arabia is virtually nonexistent for those who do not adhere to the Wahhabi interpretation of Sunni Islam. Public expression of non-Islamic religious beliefs is illegal, though private worship is permitted. Shiite Muslims, who constitute 7 to 10 percent of the population, face numerous restrictions on the public practice of their religion and encounter discrimination in all areas of public sector employment. The testimony of Shiite citizens is frequently discounted in the courts. Shiite religious seminaries are not permitted and numerous Shiite clerics have been arrested and sentenced to long prison terms. In January 2002, an Ismaili Shiite tribal leader was arrested six days after he was quoted by the *Wall Street Journal* as saying that "the government is making a mistake against us," and subsequently sentenced to seven years in prison. Two other Ismaili tribal leaders were detained in February.

Women in Saudi Arabia are second-class citizens. In most legal respects, an unmarried adult woman is the ward of her father, a married woman is the ward of her husband, and a widowed woman is the ward of her sons. Women cannot get an identity card, obtain an exit visa, or be admitted to a hospital without the permission of this guardian. Women are segregated from men in public—barred from most workplaces, taught in separate schools, restricted to "family sections" of restaurants and female-only stores, prohibited from driving, unable to travel without a male relative, and required outside the home to wear the *abaya*, a black garment covering the body and most of the face. The religious police (*mutawwa'in*) harass women who violate these social codes. The penalty for female adultery is death by stoning. The testimony of a woman is treated as inferior to that of a man in Saudi courts. Laws governing marriage, divorce, and inheritance discriminate against females. Although women make up half the student population, they may not study engineering, law, or journalism. They account for only about 5 percent of the workforce.

Senegal

Polity: Presidential-par-
liamentary democracy
Economy: Mixed capitalist
Population: 9,900,000
PPP: $1,510
Life Expectancy: 53

Political Rights: 2*
Civil Liberties: 3*
Status: Free

Religious Groups: Muslim (94 percent), Roman Catholic,
Indigenous beliefs (6 percent)
Ethnic Groups: Wolof (43.3 percent), Pular (23.8 percent), Serer (14.7 percent), Jola
(3.7 percent), Mandinka (3 percent), Soninke (1.1 percent), European and Lebanese
(1 percent), other (9.4 percent)
Capital: Dakar
Ratings Change: Senegal's political rights rating improved from 3 to 2, its civil liberties
rating improved from 4 to 3, and its status changed from Partly Free to Free, due to
ongoing efforts at political reform, governmental efforts to end impunity for members
of the security forces, and fewer human rights violations in the Casamance region.

Ten-Year Ratings Timeline (Political Rights, Civil Liberties, Status)

1993	1994	1995	1996	1997	1998	1999	2000	2001	2002	2003
4,3PF	4,5PF	4,5PF	4,5PF	4,4PF	4,4PF	4,4PF	4,4PF	3,4PF	3,4PF	2,3PF

Overview:
There was a shake-up in the government of President
Abdoulaye Wade in 2002 following a maritime disaster that
claimed the lives of nearly 1,200 Senegalese in September.
Although no official reason was announced, the sacking of Prime Minister Mame
Madior Boye was considered a governmental response to the tragedy. Wade also
dismissed the country's naval chief, and a number of other ministers resigned. A
commission of inquiry determined that the delay of the armed forces in rescuing the
passengers of the *MV Le Joola* was to blame for the high death toll. The ferry was
also carrying double its capacity of passengers when it capsized off the coast of
The Gambia. Many of the passengers were from the troubled southern province of
Casamance. Although peace accords between the government and the rebel Movement of the Democratic Forces of Casamance (MFDC) were signed in 2001, little
progress was made in 2002 towards ending the conflict. Human rights abuses, including extrajudicial killing, however, appeared to have abated.

Since independence from France in 1960, Senegal has escaped both military and
harshly authoritarian rule. President Leopold Senghor exercised de facto one-party
rule under the Socialist Party for more than a decade after independence. Most political restrictions were lifted after 1981. Abdou Diouf, of the Socialist Party, succeeded Senghor in 1981 and won large victories in unfair elections in 1988 and 1993.
Wade's victory in the presidential poll in 2000 was judged free and fair by international observers. It was the fifth attempt by Wade to win the presidency.

Senegal's population is mostly engaged in subsistence agriculture. Drought hurt
agricultural production in 2002, bringing increased pressure on the government to
focus on rural needs.

Political Rights and Civil Liberties: The Senegalese have the right to choose their leaders freely. Changes to the 1992 Electoral Code lowered the voting age to 18, introduced secret balloting, and created a nominally fairer electoral framework. The National Observatory of Elections, which was created in 1997, performed credibly in overseeing the 1998 legislative polls and the presidential elections in 2000. The 2000 presidential polls overturned four decades of rule by the Socialist Party as Abdoulaye Wade secured 59.5 percent of the runoff vote, against 41.5 percent for Abdou Diouf.

The people of Senegal adopted a new constitution by an overwhelming majority in January 2001, reducing presidential terms from seven to five years, setting the number of terms to two, and giving women the right to own land for the first time. President Wade dissolved the National Assembly, which had been dominated by the former ruling Socialist Party, and elections were held in April 2001. A coalition led by Wade won 89 of the 120 seats available, followed by the Socialist Party with 10. Smaller parties won the remainder.

Poor pay and lack of tenure protections create conditions for external influence on a judiciary that is, by statute, independent. In high-profile cases, there is often considerable interference from political and economic elites. Uncharged detainees are incarcerated without legal counsel far beyond the lengthy periods already permitted by law. Muslims have the right to choose customary law or civil law for certain civil cases, such as those concerning inheritance and divorce.

Freedom of association and assembly is guaranteed, but authorities have sometimes limited this right in practice. There are credible reports that authorities beat suspects during questioning and pretrial detention, despite constitutional protection against such treatment. Reports of disappearances in connection with the conflict in Casamance occur less often. There have been reports of extrajudicial killings by both government forces and MFDC rebels. Prison conditions are poor. Human rights groups working on local and regional issues are among many nongovernmental organizations that operate freely.

London-based Amnesty International in April 2002 urged Senegal to continue efforts it said the government had recently undertaken to end impunity for the country's security forces. Amnesty said the government has shown signs that it was willing to fight human rights violations and to bring those responsible to justice. As examples, Amnesty said that authorities sacked a police auxiliary who had killed a university student in 2001, ordered the military not to attack civilians in Casamance, and that the government expressed a willingness to extradite former Chadian leader Hissene Habre if a third country could guarantee a fair trial.

Freedom of expression is generally respected, and members of the independent media are often highly critical of the government and political parties. There are 17 independent radio stations, some of which broadcast in rural areas. The government does not carry out formal censorship, but some self-censorship is practiced because of laws against "discrediting the state" and disseminating "false news" that Wade had promised to repeal. International press freedom organizations have said that media rights have become more restricted under Wade. Mamadou Oumar Ndiaye, the publications director of the weekly *Le Temoin*, was sentenced to four months in jail in 2002 for defamation after publishing an article suggesting that the administration of a local Catholic school had misappropriated funds. It is not unusual for journalists to be detained for questioning by authorities and pressured to reveal confidential sources.

Religious freedom in Senegal, which is 94 percent Muslim, is respected. Rivalries between Islamic groups have sometimes erupted into violence. Constitutional rights afforded women are often not honored, especially in the countryside, and women have fewer chances than men for education and formal sector employment. Despite governmental campaigns, spousal abuse and other domestic violence against women are reportedly common. Many elements of Sharia and local customary law, particularly those regarding inheritance and marital relations, discriminate against women. Senegal's first female prime minister was appointed in 2001. Although Senegal banned female genital mutilation in 1999, it is still practiced among some ethnic groups.

Union rights to organize, bargain collectively, and strike are legally protected. Most workers are employed in the informal business and agricultural sectors. Nearly all of the country's small industrialized workforce is unionized, and workers are a potent political force.

Seychelles

Polity: Presidential-par-
liamentary democracy
Economy: Mixed statist
Population: 100,000
PPP: $12,508
Life Expectancy: 70
Religious Groups: Roman Catholic (86.6 percent),
Anglican (6.8 percent), other (6.6 percent)
Ethnic Groups: Seychellois (mixture of Asian, African and European)
Capital: Victoria

Political Rights: 3
Civil Liberties: 3
Status: Partly Free

Ten-Year Ratings Timeline (Political Rights, Civil Liberties, Status)

1993	1994	1995	1996	1997	1998	1999	2000	2001	2002	2003
6,4PF	3,4PF	3,4PF	3,3PF	3,3PF	3,3PF	3,3PF	3,3PF	3,3PF	3,3PF	3,3PF

Overview:

In October 2002 President France Albert Rene dissolved parliament and called for early legislative elections in December. The ruling Seychelles People's Progressive Front (SPPF) won the elections, but the main opposition Seychelles National Party (SNP) made significant inroads, winning 43 percent of the vote.

Seychelles, an archipelago of some 115 islands in the western Indian Ocean, was a French colony until 1810. It was then colonized by Britain until independence in 1976. It has been a member of the Commonwealth since independence. The country functioned as a multiparty democracy for only one year until Rene, then prime minister, seized power by ousting President James Mancham. Mancham and other opposition leaders operated parties and human rights groups in exile after Rene made his SPPF the sole legal party. René and his party continue to control government jobs, contracts, and resources, and René won one-party "show" elections in 1979, 1984, and 1989. By 1992, however, the SPPF had passed a constitutional amendment to legalize opposition parties, and many exiled leaders returned to participate in a constitutional commission and multiparty elections.

Rene won a legitimate electoral mandate in the country's first multiparty elections in 1993. The 1998 polls were accepted as generally legitimate by opposition parties, which had waged a vigorous campaign. The SNP, led by the Reverend Wavel Ramkalawan, emerged as the strongest opposition group by espousing economic liberalization, which René had resisted.

President Rene also heads the country's Defense Ministry and Interior Ministry. Vice President James Michel, who also heads a number of ministries, has assumed a more prominent role in daily governmental affairs and has been viewed as Rene's likely successor. In a recent governmental reshuffle, however, Michel lost the portfolio of economic planning while conserving his other responsibilities as minister of finance, environment, land, and transport.

Rene and his ruling SPPF party's political dominance was shaken in the August 2001 presidential election, when Rene won a narrow victory that engendered widespread opposition complaints of fraud.

Political Rights and Civil Liberties:

The current constitution was drafted in 1993 by an elected constitutional commission. Seychelles had become a one-party state under the regime established following the 1977 military coup, but legislation to allow opposition parties had been passed in December 1991. The present incumbent, France Albert Rene, seized power in June 1977. The president's term of office is five years, with a maximum of three consecutive terms.

The president and the National Assembly are elected by universal adult suffrage for five-year terms. As amended in 1996, the constitution provides for a 34-member national assembly, with 25 members directly elected and 9 allocated on a proportional basis to parties with at least 10 percent of the vote. Other amendments have strengthened presidential powers. Local governments composed of district councils were reconstituted in 1991 after their abolition two decades earlier.

The ability of the people to change their leaders is limited. In presidential and legislative elections in March 1998, the Seychellois people were able to exercise their democratic right to choose their representatives. SPPF control, however, over state resources and most media gave ruling-party candidates significant advantages in the polls. In the 2001 presidential election the opposition increased its vote total from 20 to 45 percent. President Rene's victory, however, was marred by widespread opposition claims that the government had cheated. The SNP subsequently filed a complaint with the Seychelles Constitutional Court, citing irregularities linked to the extension of the incumbent's campaign beyond the official period, posting false information on a number of Web sites, committing acts of intimidation against voters, and the use of votes attributed to deceased or underaged persons whose names were uncovered on the lists of registered voters.

The judiciary includes the Supreme Court, the Constitutional Court, a court of appeals, an industrial court, and magistrates' courts. Judges generally decide cases fairly, but still face interference in cases involving major economic or political actors. There are no Seychellois judges, and the impartiality of the non-Seychellois magistrates can be compromised by the fact that their tenure is subject to contract renewal.

Two private human-rights-related organizations (Friends for a Democratic Society and the Center for Rights and Development) operate in the country along with other nongovernmental organizations. Churches in this predominantly Roman Catholic nation have also been strong voices for human rights and democratization, and generally function without governmental interference. Discrimination against foreign workers has been reported. Security forces have been accused of using excessive force, including torture and arbitrary detention, especially in attempts to curb crime.

Freedom of speech has improved since one-party rule was abolished in 1993, and independent or pro-opposition publications have spoken out despite tough libel laws, although some self-censorship persists. There is one daily government newspaper, *The Nation*, and at least two other newspapers support or are published by the SPPF. Independent newspapers are sharply critical of the government, but governmental dominance and the threat of libel suits restrict media freedom. The opposition weekly *Regar* has been sued repeatedly for libel under broad constitutional restrictions on free expression. High licensing fees have discouraged the development of privately owned broadcast media.

Women are less likely than men to be literate, and they have fewer educational opportunities. While almost all adult females are classified as "economically active," most are engaged in subsistence agriculture. Domestic violence against women is reportedly widespread, but is rarely prosecuted and only lightly punished. Islanders of Creole extraction face de facto discrimination. Nearly all of Seychelles' political and economic life is dominated by people of European and Asian origin. Approximately 34 percent of the total population is under 15 years of age.

The right to strike is formally protected by the 1993 Industrial Relations Act, but is limited by several regulations. The SPPF-associated National Workers' Union no longer monopolizes union activity. Two independent unions are now active. The government does not restrict domestic travel, but may deny passports for reasons of "national interest." Religious freedom is respected.

Sierra Leone

Polity: Presidential-parliamentary democracy (insurgencies)
Economy: Mixed capitalist
Population: 5,600,000
PPP: $490
Life Expectancy: 39

Political Rights: 4
Civil Liberties: 4*
Status: Partly Free

Religious Groups: Muslim (60 percent), indigenous beliefs (30 percent), Christian (10 percent)
Ethnic Groups: Temne (30 percent), Mende (30 percent), other tribes (30 percent), Creole (10 percent)
Capital: Freetown
Ratings Change: Sierra Leone's civil liberties rating improved from 5 to 4 due to increased security in the country.

Ten-Year Ratings Timeline (Political Rights, Civil Liberties, Status)

1993	1994	1995	1996	1997	1998	1999	2000	2001	2002	2003
7,6NF	7,6NF	7,6NF	7,6NF	4,5PF	7,6NF	3,5PF	3,5PF	4,5PF	4,5PF	4,4PF

Overview:

Sierra Leone further consolidated its peace process in 2002 by holding presidential and parliamentary elections that were free and fair. Ahmad Tejan Kabbah, a former UN diplomat, was reelected as president with 70 percent of the vote compared with 22 percent for Ernest Koroma of the All People's Congress (APC). The Revolutionary United Front Party candidate, Alimamy Pallo Bangura, lagged with barely 2 percent of the vote. Kabbah's Sierra Leone People's Party (SLPP) dominated parliamentary elections, winning 83 of 112 available seats, followed by the APC with 27. The party of former junta leader Johnny Paul Karoma won 2 seats. Because of his victory and his party's wins in the parliamentary polls, Kabbah will need to prove that his government is inclusive. Steps were taken in 2002 to get the country's Truth and Reconciliation Commission and the Special Court for Sierra Leone, which is to try people for war crimes, up and running. Respect for human rights improved markedly during the year, although press freedom suffered a slight setback.

Founded by Britain in 1787 as a haven for liberated slaves, Sierra Leone became independent in 1961. The Revolutionary United Front (RUF) launched a guerrilla campaign from neighboring Liberia in 1991 to end 23 years of increasingly corrupt one-party rule by President Joseph Momoh. Power fell into the lap of Captain Valentine Strasser in 1992, when he and other junior officers attempted to confront Momoh about poor pay and working conditions at the front. Momoh fled the country. The Strasser regime hired South African soldiers from the security company Executive Outcomes to help win back key diamond-rich areas. In January 1996, Brigadier Julius Maada-Bio quietly deposed Strasser. Elections proceeded despite military and rebel intimidation, and voters elected Kabbah as president.

The following year, Major Johnny Paul Koroma toppled the Kabbah government, established the Armed Forces Revolutionary Council, and invited the RUF to join the junta. Nigerian-led West African troops, backed by logistical and intelligence support from the British company Sandline, restored President Kabbah to power in February 1998, but the country continued to be racked by war. A peace agreement in July 1999 led to the beginning of disarmament, but the disarmament process stopped in May 2000 with a return to hostilities and the taking of about 500 peacekeepers as hostages. British troops flew in to help, and disarmament resumed in May 2001.

A phased withdrawal of the 17,300-strong UN Mission in Sierra Leone, the world's largest peacekeeping mission, began in October 2002. By December 2004, only 2,000 peacekeepers are expected to remain in Sierra Leone. The more than 300 British soldiers in Sierra Leone began their withdrawal in 2002. More than 45,000 fighters have been disarmed, but their reintegration into civilian life has been slow. The United Nations warned that Liberian President Charles Taylor still supported rebels in Sierra Leone and that delayed resettlement of former combatants could hinder the country's peace process. Sierra Leonean mercenaries reportedly have joined up with a rebel group fighting Taylor or with Taylor's armed forces. Insecurity on Sierra Leone's border with Liberia and Guinea posed a continued threat to lasting peace in 2002. Although Sierra Leone's decade-long war has ended, Kabbah still faces daunting problems, many of which contributed to causing the war. He must adequately address entrenched corruption, a culture of impunity, rampant poverty, and unequal distribution of the country's diamond wealth if Sierra Leone is to have lasting peace.

Sierra Leone has vast resources of diamonds, but smuggling and war have turned it into one of the world's poorest countries. A ban on rough-diamond imports from Sierra Leone does not include diamonds that carry proven certificates of origin from the government. The government earned about $26 million in legal diamond sales in 2001. Sierra Leone also stood to benefit from $950 million in debt relief and $12 million in aid from the IMF in 2002.

Political Rights and Civil Liberties: Presidential and legislative elections in February and March 1996 were imperfect, but considered legitimate. President Ahmad Tejan Kabbah and his SLPP had the advantage of incumbency and state resources for the presidential and parliamentary elections in May 2002, but despite some logistical problems the polls were considered the country's fairest since independence. Eight candidates had vied for the presidency.

The judiciary is active, but corruption and a lack of resources are impediments. Despite these obstacles, it has demonstrated independence, and a number of trials have been free and fair. There are often lengthy pretrial detentions in harsh conditions. A British program, the Law Development Project, has helped Sierra Leone update its legal code and strengthen its judicial system. Eight judges, from Sierra Leone, Canada, Austria, The Gambia, the United Kingdom, and Nigeria were appointed in December 2002 to sit on the Special Court for Sierra Leone. Among those indicted for war crimes include former RUF leader Foday Sankoh. The country's Truth and Reconciliation Commission, modeled on South Africa's truth commission, was also established in 2002. The aim of both the court and the truth commission is to try to help end Sierra Leone's culture of impunity. The United Nations is to send some 170 police officers from member states to train security forces in Sierra Leone. Many have already received training from the United Kingdom.

Sierra Leone once had one of Africa's worst human rights records. Abduction, maiming, rape, forced conscription, and extrajudicial killing were commonplace. By the end of 2002, however, except for areas bordering Guinea and Liberia, virtually all of the countryside was safe for travel because of disarmament and the deployment of peacekeepers, although there were reports that civilians had been abducted and taken into Liberia. Kabbah in March 2002 lifted the state of emergency that had been imposed during the war. A number of national and international nongovernmental organizations and human rights groups operate openly in Freetown.

Freedom of speech and of the press is guaranteed, but the government at times restricts these rights. Criminal libel laws occasionally are used to jail journalists. Several government and private radio and television stations broadcast. The Independent Media Commission has failed to demonstrate independence. It refused to give a broadcast license to an independent radio station in 2002 that planned to broadcast programs by shortwave to Sierra Leone, Liberia, and Guinea. The United Nations sponsors a community radio project that also receives support from the Ministry of Information and the Ministry of Health. Newspapers openly criticize the government and armed factions. Dozens of newspapers are printed in Freetown, but most are of poor quality and often carry sensational or undocumented stories. Editor Paul Kamara, of *For Di People*, was sentenced in November 2002 to nine months in jail, his newspaper was closed, and he was ordered to pay a fine. He was accused of libel and defamation by a judge.

Freedom of religion is guaranteed and respected in practice. The rights of freedom of assembly and association are guaranteed, and these rights are generally respected. Despite constitutionally guaranteed equal rights, women face extensive legal and de facto discrimination as well as limited access to education and formal (business) sector jobs. Married women have fewer property rights than men, especially in rural areas, where customary law prevails. Female genital mutilation is widespread. Abuse of women, including rape, sexual assault, and sexual slavery were rampant during the war.

Workers have the right to join independent trade unions of their choice. About 60 percent of workers in urban areas, including government employees, are unionized. There is a legal framework for collective bargaining.

Singapore

Polity: Dominant party
Economy: Mixed
capitalist
Population: 4,200,000
PPP: $23,356
Life Expectancy: 78
Religious Groups: Buddhist, Muslim, Christian, other
Ethnic Groups: Chinese (77 percent), Malay (14 percent),
Indian (8 percent), other (1 percent)
Capital: Singapore

Political Rights: 5
Civil Liberties: 4*
Status: Partly Free

Ratings Change: Singapore's civil liberties rating improved from 5 to 4 due to modest increases in personal autonomy.

Ten-Year Ratings Timeline (Political Rights, Civil Liberties, Status)

1993	1994	1995	1996	1997	1998	1999	2000	2001	2002	2003
4,5PF	5,5PF	5,5PF	5,5PF	5,5PF	5,5PF	5,5PF	5,5PF	5,5PF	5,5PF	5,4PF

Overview:

Singapore's worst economic recession in more than three decades failed to prevent the ruling People's Action Party (PAP) from once again routing the opposition in parliamentary elections held late last year. In power since independence in 1965, the PAP campaigned on the theme that no other party had the experience and skills to revive the economy. The government remained committed to aggressively fighting terrorism in 2002, with a further round of arrests of suspected al-Qaeda sympathizers taking place in August. It also continued to use the legal process to clamp down on critical opposition politicians.

Located along major shipping routes in Southeast Asia, Singapore became a British colony in 1867. Occupied by the Japanese during World War II, the city-state became self-governing in 1959, entered the Malaysian Federation in 1963, and became fully independent in 1965 under Prime Minister Lee Kuan Yew. Under Lee, the PAP transformed a squalid port city into a technological hub and regional financial center. At the same time, he restricted individual freedoms.

The PAP won every seat in every election from 1968 to 1981, when the Workers' Party's J. B. Jeyaretnam won a seat in a by-election. Lee handed power in 1990 to Goh Chok Tong, who has largely continued Lee's conservative policies and maintained the PAP's dominance in parliament. Although the PAP swept the 1997 elections, the campaign featured a rare airing of diverse views on policy issues. Goh responded by warning that neighborhoods voting against the PAP would be the lowest priority for upgrades of public housing estates, where some 85 percent of Singaporeans live.

During the campaign for the November 2001 parliamentary elections, opposition parties criticized the government for not doing more to help Singaporeans hurt by the economic downturn. Repeating a tactic from the 1997 election campaign, the PAP linked priority for public housing upgrades to support for the ruling party. In the event, the PAP increased its vote share to 75 percent of the popular vote. Its victory was a foregone conclusion because opposition parties contested only 29 of parliament's 84 seats. The leftist Workers' Party and the centrist Singapore People's Party won 1 seat apiece, while the PAP won 82 seats.

Veteran opposition politician Jeyaretnam was barred from contesting the 2001 elections after the court of appeal declared him bankrupt for being a day late in paying an installment on a damages award to PAP politicians who had won a defamation suit. As a bankrupt, Jeyaretnam was thrown out of parliament, barred from practicing law, and prevented from running for office. Two prominent opposition politicians, Chee Soon Juan and Gandhi Ambalam of the Singapore Democratic Party (SDP), refused to pay a fine for holding a rally in May 2002 and were briefly jailed in October. While Ambalam's family paid his fine, Chee opted to serve out a five-week sentence rather than pay the penalty.

Political Rights and Civil Liberties: The government uses civil defamation laws, strict electoral rules, curbs on civil liberties, patronage, and its influence over Singapore's media to undermine the opposition's prospects in elections. Ordinary Singaporeans, meanwhile, are generally free to live, work, and socialize as they choose, but they face some restrictions on their rights to speak openly and enjoy arts and entertainment that are outside the mainstream.

The 1959 constitution vests executive power in a prime minister and stipulates a parliament that is directly elected for a five-year term. Two amendments authorize the government to appoint additional members of parliament to ensure that the opposition has at least three seats. Separately, a 1993 amendment provides for direct presidential elections and gives the president budget-oversight powers and some authority over civil service appointments and internal security matters. The government has used a strict vetting process to prevent any real competition for the office. The current president, S. R. Nathan, a PAP veteran and former ambassador, won the August 1999 election by default after the Presidential Election Commission barred three other candidates on the grounds that they lacked either the requisite competence or integrity.

The PAP runs an efficient, competent, and largely corruption-free government and appears to enjoy genuine popular support. It chalks up its electoral success to its record of having built Singapore into a modern, wealthy society and, it says, the opposition's lack of credible candidates and ideas. Opposition parties, however, say that the playing field is uneven because of the government's control over the press and its use of an array of laws to limit dissent.

Another factor holding back the opposition is its difficulty in fielding viable slates for parliament's multimember districts. Each Group Representation Constituency (GRC) has three to six seats, and each GRC candidate slate must include at least one ethnic minority candidate. The party with a plurality in the district wins all the seats. The current parliament has 15 GRCs and only 9 single-member districts. Moreover, the government requires candidates for all seats to pay a deposit of S$13,000 (US$7,123) that is forfeited if the candidate does not win a certain percentage of votes.

Notwithstanding the difficulty posed by electoral rules, perhaps the most severe constraint on Singapore's opposition is the PAP's filing of civil defamation and other lawsuits against political foes. "The misuse of defamation suits by PAP leaders has contributed to a climate of self-censorship in Singapore," Amnesty International said shortly before the November 2001 election. No PAP leader has ever lost a defamation suit against an opposition figure. In April, the BBC reported that opposition leader Chee Soon Juan was being sued for defamation for comments he made during last year's election campaign.

The media is also subject to governmental influence and restriction. Most journalists work for media outlets that are linked to the government. The privately held Singapore Press Holdings (SPH), which owns all general-circulation newspapers, has close ties to the PAP. By law, the government must approve the owners of key "management shares" in SPH. Government-affiliated agencies operate all domestic broadcast media. Companies with close ties to the government also run Internet service providers and Singapore's cable television service.

Faced with the government's record of suing critics, journalists sometimes refrain from publishing stories about alleged government corruption and nepotism or the supposed compliance of the judiciary. The government has not wielded the harsh Internal Security Act (ISA) against the press in recent years, but its broad provisions leave the press unclear about what may be published. The ISA allows the government to restrict publications that incite violence, might arouse tensions among racial or religious groups, or might threaten national interests, national security, or public order.

Foreign newspapers and magazines are available, although authorities have at times restricted the circulations of *Time*, the *Far Eastern Economic Review*, *The Economist*, and other foreign publications that carried articles the government found offensive. The Newspaper and Printing Presses Act allows authorities to restrict the circulation of any foreign periodical that publishes an article allegedly interfering in domestic politics. Last year this provision was extended to cover foreign broadcast services as well.

The government censors films, television, videos, music, magazines and books, mainly for excessive amounts of sex, violence, and drug references. However, authorities have in recent years loosened some restrictions on the arts. Though the government avidly promotes Internet use for shopping and other daily affairs, 1996 regulations forbid airing of information over the Internet that is against the "public interest" or "national harmony," or that "offends against good taste or decency." In practice, authorities prevent access to some Internet sites, most of them pornographic. Several sites host forums for political chat.

Singaporeans of most faiths can worship freely. Jehovah's Witnesses, however, are banned under the Societies Act from practicing their faith because of their refusal to serve in the military. The government also bans meetings of Jehovah's Witnesses and Unification Church members.

The PAP government prohibits public discussion of sensitive racial and religious issues and closely regulates public speech. Singaporeans must get police permits to hold public talks or make political speeches or else face fines under the Public Entertainment and Meetings Act. Chee Soon Juan of the opposition SDP has served a number of jail terms in recent years for making speeches without the necessary license and refusing to pay the resulting fines. The only place where Singaporeans can make public speeches without a license is Speakers' Corner, which is located in a downtown park. Speakers, however, must register with the police at least 30 days in advance, and their speeches are recorded by the government and kept for six years. Police must approve any public assembly of more than five people. The government has used the 1966 Societies Act to deny registration to groups it considers threats to public order. The act requires most organizations of more than 10 people to be registered and restricts political activity to political parties. Despite this latter restriction, however, the PAP has close ties to seemingly nonpolitical associations such as neighborhood groups. In recent years, authorities have allowed activists to set up several nongovernmental civil society groups. However, Amnesty International reported that in 2001, two such groups that had been critical of the government—the Think Centre and the Open Singapore Centre—were reclassified as political associations. They thus became ineligible for foreign funding and were subjected to other restrictions.

Most unions are affiliated with the National Trade Unions Congress, which acknowledges freely that its interests are closely aligned with those of the PAP. The law prevents uniformed employees from joining unions. Around 15 percent of Singapore's workers are unionized. There have been no strikes since 1986, in part because labor shortages have helped employees secure regular wage increases and have given them a high degree of job mobility.

The president appoints Supreme Court justices on the recommendation of the prime minister with the advice of the chief justice. Chaired by the chief justice, the Legal Services Commission sets the terms of appointment for judges, many of whom have close ties to PAP leaders. It is not clear whether the government pressures judges or simply appoints judges who share its conservative philosophy. In any case, government leaders' use of the courts against political opponents and critics and "consistent awards in favor of government plaintiffs" have "led to a perception that the judiciary reflects the views of the executive in politically sensitive cases," according to the U.S. State Department's report on Singapore's human rights record in 2001.

The government has not used the ISA to hold suspects on political charges since 1989. Historically used mainly against suspected Communist threats, the ISA allows authorities to detain suspects without charge or trial for an unlimited number of two-year periods. A 1989 constitutional amendment prohibits judicial review of the substantive grounds of detentions under the ISA and the constitutionality of the law. In December 2001, the authorities arrested 15 suspected terrorists under the provisions of the ISA (13 of whom remain under arrest), and during another sweep conducted in August, 21 members of the Jemaah Islamiyah group were detained on suspicion of having links with the al-Qaeda terrorist network. The government uses the Criminal Law Act to detain several hundred mainly organized-crime or drug-trafficking suspects each year. Meanwhile, the Misuse of Drugs Act allows authorities to commit without trial suspected drug users to rehabilitation centers for up to three years. In any given year, several thousand people are in mandatory treatment and rehabilitation.

Police reportedly at times abuse detainees, the U.S. State Department report said. It added that courts have jailed several officers convicted of such abuses. Authorities use caning to punish some 30 offenses, including certain immigration violations. The government actively promotes racial harmony and equity in a society where race riots between Malays and the majority Chinese killed scores of people in the late 1960s. Ethnic Malays, however, have not on average achieved the schooling and income levels of ethnic Chinese or Tamils and reportedly face unofficial discrimination in employment. Several governmental programs aim to boost educational achievement among Malay students. In February, three Muslim schoolgirls were suspended from school after they defied a government ban on the wearing of headscarves during lessons. The BBC reported in September that authorities had barred a prominent Malaysian lawyer, representing the families of the girls in a lawsuit challenging the school uniform code, from working in Singapore.

Women enjoy the same legal rights as men in most areas, including civil liberties, employment, commercial activity, and education. They are active in the professions but remain underrepresented in government and politics.

Slovakia

Polity: Parliamentary democracy
Economy: Mixed capitalist
Population: 5,400,000
PPP: $11,243
Life Expectancy: 73

Political Rights: 1
Civil Liberties: 2
Status: Free

Religious Groups: Roman Catholic (60.3 percent), atheist (9.7 percent), Protestant (8.4 percent), other (11.6 percent)
Ethnic Groups: Slovak (86 percent), Hungarian (11 percent), Roma [Gypsy] (2 percent), other, including Czech (1 percent)
Capital: Bratislava

Ten-Year Ratings Timeline (Political Rights, Civil Liberties, Status)

1993	1994	1995	1996	1997	1998	1999	2000	2001	2002	2003
--	3,4PF	2,3F	2,3F	2,4F	2,4F	2,2F	1,2F	1,2F	1,2F	1,2F

Overview:

The year 2002 witnessed several important milestones in Slovakia's post-Communist transition. During the year, Slovakia welcomed an invitation to become a full member of the NATO alliance and celebrated an invitation join the European Union by 2004. In addition, Slovak voters returned to the polls for the third parliamentary election since 1993.

Anti-Communist opposition forces brought about the collapse of the Czechoslovakian government in 1989. The next year the country held its first free elections and began negotiations to divide the country into separate Czech and Slovak Republics. In 1993, a new Slovak constitution took effect and the Czechoslovak union peacefully dissolved.

For the next five years Vladimir Meciar and the Movement for a Democratic Slovakia (HZDS) dominated politics in newly independent Slovakia. During this period, Meciar served three times as prime minister. He battled with then President Michal Kovac over executive and government powers, opposed direct presidential elections, resisted economic liberalization, and disregarded the rule of law and a free press. Reform stagnated under Mecair and Slovakia failed to meet the criteria to open EU accession talks or join NATO.

In the 1998 parliamentary elections, voters signaled a major shift in Slovakia's political environment by rejecting Meciar's rule and electing a broad right-left coalition. The new parliament selected Mikulas Dzurinda as prime minister and pursued policies to increase judicial independence, combat corruption, undertake economic reforms, and actively seek membership in the European Union and NATO. The subsequent four years witnessed a period of general democratic consolidation, yet ideological differences among the ruling coalition hampered the reformist legislative agenda.

In September 2002, Slovak voters again returned to the polls. While Vladimir Meciar's HZDS garnered 19.5 percent (35 mandates) of the vote, his party did not receive enough support to form a new government. Prime Minister Mikulas Dzurinda's Slovak Democratic and Christian Union (SDKU) finished second and succeeded in forming a center-right government in partnership with the Party of the Hungarian Coalition (SMK), the Christian Democratic Movement (KDH), and the Alliance of the New Citizen (ANO). The coalition took control of a majority 78 seats in the 150 seat National Council and President Rudolf Schuster re-appointed Dzurinda as prime minister. Unlike the previous government, the parties which comprise the new ruling coalition share an ideology beyond mere opposition to Mecair's HZDS and have pledged to complete the social and economic reforms left unfinished by the previous government.

In the months following the election, Slovakia accepted two historic invitations further binding the country to Euro-Atlantic institutions. In November, Slovakia accepted an invitation to become a full member of the NATO alliance following ratification of the North Atlantic Treaty. In December, the European Union extended Slovakia an official invitation to join the union by 2004. Both the NATO and EU invitations demonstrate the extent to which Slovakia has successfully undertaken the task of post-Communist reforms in recent years. Nevertheless, this process is still unfinished and will likely continue before full EU accession and NATO membership.

Political Rights and Civil Liberties:

Slovak citizens aged 18 and older can change their government democratically under a system of universal, equal, and direct suffrage. Voters elect the president and members of the 150 seat National Assembly. A 2001 law grants voting privileges to foreigners, allowing permanent residents to vote in elections for municipal and regional governments.

In 2002, 25 parties competed in free and fair parliamentary elections. Only seven parties exceeded the 5 percent representation threshold. Seventy percent of eligible voters participated in the election. Election officials conducted the vote in a transparent and well-organized manner. By law, public television channels provided equal airtime to candidates during the official campaign period. While parties were free to advertise in newspapers, laws prohibited campaign advertising on private television. Slovak nongovernmental organizations (NGOs) were particularly active during the campaign, organizing get-out-the-vote initiatives, publishing voter education materials, and monitoring media coverage. While state and private television generally respected laws regarding objective political reporting, the government broadcast council cited the private TV *Markiza* for overly flattering coverage of the ANO party, led by the station's majority owner Pavol Rusko.

Slovakia's media are largely free but remain vulnerable to criminal libel laws and political interference. In 2001, President Schuster brought legal action against a Slovak journalist for satirizing him in print. In January 2002, the Constitutional Court intervened and suspended controversial sections of the penal code relating to the case. This action effectively negated the legal basis for the president's suit and marked the first time the Constitutional Court had used its expanded judicial powers to negate laws violating basic human rights. Yet other restrictions on criminal liable remain in effect and journalists continue to face the threat of politically motivated lawsuits.

The constitution provides for an independent judiciary and a constitutional court. The European Commission has noted the perception of a high level of corruption in the Slovak courts and expressed concern over of the judiciary's perceived lack of impartiality. During the year, parliament created an 18-member Judicial Council in an attempt to strengthen the courts. The Judicial Council will assign and nominate judges, reduce judicial workloads, streamline court proceedings, and address conflicts of interest. The European Commission applauded these initiatives but highlighted the need for full implementation of the judicial reform process.

The Slovak government respects religious freedom. Registered churches and religious organizations are eligible for tax exemptions and government subsidies. The Roman Catholic Church is the largest denomination in the country and consequently receives a larger share of government subsidies. Slovakia has not banned or impeded any groups from practicing their faith. However, the U.S. Department of State notes the persistence of anti-Semitism among some parts of the population. In 2002, a Jewish cemetery in eastern Slovakia was desecrated for the second time in 5 years. Authorities declined to prosecute the alleged suspects because they were minors.

There are more than ten recognized ethnic minorities in Slovakia. While minorities and ethnic groups have a constitutional right to help resolve issues that concern them, Roma (Gypsy) individuals continue to experience widespread discrimination and inequality in education, housing employment, public services, and the criminal justice system. Roma also face the persistent threat of racially motivated violence. Even though Slovak law criminalizes such acts, reports indicate that law enforcement officials do not always investigate crimes against the Roma. Some police officers have themselves been accused of physically abusing Roma individuals, or pressuring Roma victims not to press charges against their assailants. In response to these problems, the government began a new program to improve Roma education and housing in 2002. The government likewise established an informal advisory board to widen the dialogue with the Roma community. The Interior Ministry approved a new Police Code of Conduct and established a commission to fully investigate racially motivated attacks against the Roma. Nevertheless, there continues to be a recognizable gap between Slovakia's exiting Roma policies and their actual implementation on the ground.

Slovak citizens enjoy a range of personal rights and liberties. The government respects the inviolability of the home, the right to privacy, and the right to move and travel freely. The constitution provides protections for marriage, parenthood, and the family. The government respects the right to assemble peacefully, petition state bodies, associate in clubs, political parties, and trade unions. Judges, prosecutors, firefighters, and members of the armed forces may not strike.

Slovakia has a market economy in which the private (business) sector accounts for approximately 80 percent of gross domestic product and 75 percent of employment. Official unemployment remains high at approximately 20 percent, but the government contends that persons who simultaneously work on the black market and collect unemployment benefits may account for as much as 5 percent of this number.

Slovenia

Polity: Parliamentary democracy
Economy: Mixed capitalist
Population: 2,000,000
PPP: $17,367
Life Expectancy: 76
Religious Groups: Roman Catholic (70.8 percent), other
Ethnic Groups: Slovene (88 percent), Croat (3 percent), Serb (2 percent), Bosniak (1 percent), other (6 percent)
Capital: Ljubljana

Political Rights: 1
Civil Liberties: 1*
Status: Free

Ratings Change: Slovenia's civil liberties rating improved from 2 to 1 due to legislation satisfying European Union membership requirements, including an employment bill banning any form of discrimination, and legislation giving increased rights to foreigners with permanent resident status.

Ten-Year Ratings Timeline (Political Rights, Civil Liberties, Status)

1993	1994	1995	1996	1997	1998	1999	2000	2001	2002	2003
2,2F	1,2F	1,2F	1,2F	1,2F	1,2F	1,2F	1,2F	1,2F	1,2F	1,1F

Overview:

In 2002, Slovenia achieved its two most important foreign policy goals: in October, Slovenia was invited to join the EU, and in November it received an invitation to join NATO, thus becoming the first of the former Yugoslav republics to enter either organization.

The territory now comprising Slovenia was part of the Hapsburg Empire from 1335 to 1918. At the end of World War I, Slovenia became a part of the new Kingdom of Serbs, Croats, and Slovenes, and after World War II it became a constituent republic of the Socialist Federal Republic of Yugoslavia. In 1990 Slovenia held its first postwar multiparty democratic elections, in which the Democratic United Opposition (DEMOS) secured victory. Voters also elected former Communist leader Milan Kucan president. Kucan was reelected president in Slovenia's first post-independence elections in 1992, and again in 1996.

Slovenian society has enjoyed remarkable consensus in the postindependence period in comparison with the other former Yugoslav republics. Popular agreement on the general outlines of what Slovenian foreign and domestic policy should be has focused on entering European and trans-Atlantic organizations, and maintaining a social-democratic model domestically. For most of the postindependence period, Slovenia has been ruled by center-left governments whose most important component has been Janez Drnovsek's Liberal Democratic Party (LDS).

Presidential elections held in Slovenia in November and December were the first in the postindependence period in which one of the most long-lived politicians in Eastern Europe, Milan Kucan, was not running. Kucan, whose political career dated back to the Titoist period, had successfully transformed himself from a Communist functionary in the 1980s, to a nationalist politician at the end of the decade, to a statesman guiding his country toward the EU and NATO in the 1990s.

In the first round of presidential elections, held in November, Drnovsek gained 44.3 percent of the vote, comfortably outdistancing his nearest rival, Slovenian state prosecutor, but political newcomer, Barbara Brezigar of the Social Democratic Party (SDS), who gained 30.7 percent. In the second-round runoff, Brezigar gained surprisingly strong support, winning 43 percent of the vote, although that was not enough to beat Drnovsek's 56 percent.

Political Rights and Civil Liberties: Slovenia is a parliamentary democracy with independent legislative, executive, and judicial branches of government. Government officials respect the separation of powers enshrined in the Slovenian constitution. Institutions function smoothly, and the political opposition to the government plays a constructive, cooperative role in public policy making. Important legislation on civil service reform adopted in June established a framework for a professional, impartial, and accountable civil service.

Voters can change their government under a system of universal, equal, and direct suffrage. They elect the president and members of the 90-seat National Assembly. Parliament chooses the prime minister. The 40-seat National Council, a largely advisory body, represents professional groups and local interests.

The several sets of elections held in Slovenia in 1992, 1996, 2000, and 2002 have been considered free and fair. Seventy-one percent of the electorate turned out to vote in the first round of presidential election in November, and 65 percent for the second round in December.

According to the EU, the Slovenian judiciary enjoys "a high degree of independence." The Slovenian judiciary consists of the Supreme Court, an administrative court, regional and district courts, and an appeals court. There is also a constitutional court. The constitution guarantees individuals due process, equality before the law, and a presumption of innocence until proven guilty. The main problem facing the Slovenian judicial system is the large backlog of cases. As of the end of 2001, the backlog consisted of some 298,000 cases.

According to the Slovenian constitution, Slovenian citizens enjoy all the recognized personal rights and freedoms, including the freedom to travel and to choose their place of residence; the right to privacy; the right to health care and social security; the freedom to work; and the right to own private property. The constitution provides special protection for marriage, the family, and children. It defines specific rights and obligations for parents.

The government respects the constitutional rights of freedom of speech and of the press. Insulting public officials, however, is prohibited by law. Most print media outlets are privately owned and support themselves with advertising revenues. Some electronic media outlets, such as Slovenia Radio-Television (RTV), remain state owned. RTV has three radio stations and two television networks.

The constitution guarantees freedom of conscience and religion. More than 70 percent of the population is Roman Catholic. For the past several years, there have been controversies regarding the continuous refusal of Ljubljana municipal authorities to allow the Muslim community in the capital to build a mosque.

Slovenia's treatment of ethnic minorities is generally considered to be good. Incitement to racial hatred in Slovenia is prohibited under the Criminal Code. Slovenia's constitution entitles Italian and Hungarian ethnic communities to one deputy each in the National Assembly. There have been, however, persistent reports of police harassment of Roma (Gypsies) and of residents from other former Yugoslav republics, the so-called new minorities. International watchdog groups report some governmental and societal discrimination against Serbs, Croats, Bosnians, Kosovo Albanians, and Roma now living in Slovenia.

The government respects the right of individuals to assemble peacefully, to form associations, to participate in public affairs, and to submit petitions. Military and police personnel may not join political parties. Workers enjoy the right to establish and join trade unions, to strike, and to bargain collectively.

Women enjoy the same constitutional rights and freedoms as men under the law. Domestic violence remains a concern, and traditional social norms expect women to do housework even when they are employed outside the home. In recent years, along with the rest of the region, Slovenia has had problems with human trafficking and has become both a transit country and a country of destination for women and girls trafficked from other parts of Eastern Europe for purposes of prostitution.

Solomon Islands

Polity: Parliamentary
democracy
Economy: Capitalist
Population: 500,000
PPP: $1,648
Life Expectancy: 67

Political Rights: 3*
Civil Liberties: 3*
Status: Partly Free

Religious Groups: Anglican (45 percent), Roman
Catholic (18 percent), indigenous beliefs and other (27 percent)
Ethnic Groups: Melanesian (93 percent), Polynesian (4 percent), Micronesian (1.5
percent), other (1.5 percent)
Capital: Honiara
Ratings Change: The Solomon Islands' political rights and civil liberties ratings both
improved from 4 to 3 due to an improvement in the country's security situation.

Ten-Year Ratings Timeline (Political Rights, Civil Liberties, Status)

1993	1994	1995	1996	1997	1998	1999	2000	2001	2002	2003
1,1F	1,2F	1,2F	1,2F	1,2F	1,2F	1,2F	1,2F	4,4PF	4,4PF	3,3PF

Overview:

The Solomon Islands continued to be plagued by lawlessness in some areas two years after a peace deal ended fighting between militias drawn from the South Pacific country's two largest ethnic groups. Many of the land issues said to be at the root of the conflict between the Malaitan and Guadalcanalese militias remain unresolved, while many rebels failed to turn in their weapons by the June 2002 deadline imposed by the peace deal. The instability has dealt a body blow to the nation's economy, as most export industries remain shuttered.

The Solomon Islands is a 900-mile archipelago of more than 27 islands about 1,200 miles northeast of Australia. Britain established a protectorate over the islands between 1893 and 1900 to stop the brutal practice of "blackbirding," or forced recruitment, of laborers to Fiji and Australia. U.S. and Japanese forces fought major land and sea battles in and around the Solomon Islands during World War II before American forces gained control of the territory. After the war, the British colonial rulers returned, and thousands of villagers from the poor, overcrowded island of Malaitae migrated in search of jobs to the more developed island of Guadalcanal. The national capital of Honiara, though located on Guadalcanal, became dominated by Malaitans. The Solomon Islands became self-governing in 1976 and independent two years later.

Since independence, the country's weak party system and the fluidity of its political coalitions have contributed to four changes of government through either parliamentary votes of no confidence or the resignation of the prime minister. Successive governments have largely failed to address long-standing claims by Guadalcanalese that migrants from Malaita and elsewhere have taken their jobs and land.

The recent conflict began in 1998 after armed groups on Guadalcanal began forcing Malaitan settlers out of rural parts of the island. The rebels killed scores of villagers and by 1999 forced some 15,000 to 20,000 Malaitans to flee to Honiara and to other islands. Honiara became a Malaitan enclave, cut off by roadblocks from rural areas controlled by Guadalcanalese militants. Drawing most of their several hundred fighters from impoverished villages along the rugged "Weather Coast" of southern Guadalcanal, the Guadalcanalese militant groups, equipped with stolen police guns, World War II weapons, and other arms, began calling themselves the Isatabu Freedom Movement (IFM).

By 1999, groups of armed Malaitans began fighting the IFM on Guadalcanal, later banding together as the Malaita Eagle Force (MEF). Armed with stolen police weapons, the MEF's several hundred fighters were drawn from displaced Malaitan settlers on Guadalcanal and the ranks of former and serving police officers. Malaitan attacks on rural areas of Guadalcanal forced up to 12,000 Guadalcanalese to flee to remote parts of the island.

Fighting escalated after MEF forces, backed by paramilitary police, seized control of Honiara in June 2000 and overthrew the elected government of Prime Minister Bartholomew Ulufa'alu. The conflict formally ended with an October 2000 peace accord, signed in Townsville, Australia, that called for both sides to surrender their weapons under the supervision of international monitors.

Elections in December 2001 restored a semblance of normalcy to the country. They brought to power a government headed by Sir Allan Kemakeza, who had been dismissed from the previous government over a financial scandal.

The Kemakeza government faces the tasks of restoring law and order to the two main islands and reviving the nation's economy. Having been largely disarmed following the 2000 coup, the police force is slowly being rebuilt with the help of trainers funded by Australia and New Zealand. International monitors overseeing the peace accord said that the June deadline to surrender arms in exchange for amnesty helped take many weapons out of circulation. Local militia leaders, however, continue to effectively control parts of Malaita and Guadalcanal, and former militants are widely believed to still hold several hundred weapons, many of them high-powered. After showing little discipline during the fighting, many ex-militants have turned to outright theft, robbery, extortion, and other crimes since the end of the conflict.

The Solomon Islands' economy is still buckling from the fighting, as many plantations and other export industries that shut down during the conflict remain closed. The loss of tax revenues from these industries has helped put the Kemakeza government in dire financial straits. Visiting Australian Foreign Minister Alexander Downer urged the government in December "to tackle the dire problems of lawlessness, corruption, and economic decline currently facing the country," according to a statement by his office.

Political Rights and Civil Liberties: Solomon Islanders can change their government through elections. Parliament consists of 50 members, drawn from single-seat districts, who are elected to four-year terms.

The country's human rights situation has improved markedly since the height of the conflict in 2000, when police and militants from both sides carried out killings, abductions, tortures, rapes, and other abuses while enriching themselves through looting and extortion. While many of the worst abuses have ended, however, "there were numerous reports of acts of torture and mistreatment attributed to both Malaitan and Guadalcanalese militants, and to members of the police," according to the U.S. State Department's global human rights report for 2001, released in March 2002. Parliament in 2000 passed a blanket amnesty for virtually all crimes committed during the two-year conflict.

The judiciary is independent, although death threats against judges and prosecutors and a lack of resources have left the courts barely functioning at times, the U.S. State Department report said, forcing some suspects to spend long periods in detention while awaiting trial.

Given the country's high illiteracy rate and the remoteness of many islands, most Solomon Islanders get their news from radio. The main broadcaster, the state-run Solomon Islands Broadcasting Corporation, generally offers balanced political coverage. Several private radio stations and newspapers also serve up news and entertainment. Militants at times threaten journalists, according to the U.S. State Department report.

Women are largely relegated to traditional family roles in this male-dominated society and hold relatively few positions of influence in government. Domestic violence against women appears to be common, and the government has done little to address the problem, the U.S. State Department report said. Sexual harassment is also a concern, the report added.

The cash-strapped government lacks sufficient resources to provide for many basic needs of children. Many schools are crumbling, teachers are not paid regularly, and, by some estimates, fewer than 60 percent of school-aged children have access to primary education. Religious freedom is respected in this mainly Christian country.

The National Union of Workers and other smaller trade unions are independent. The country's high unemployment rate, however, means that workers have little leverage to bargain for better pay, benefits, or working conditions. Only 10 to 15 percent of Solomon Islanders have wage or salary jobs, although 60 to 70 percent of these workers are unionized. The majority of Solomon Islanders work to some extent as subsistence farmers or fishermen.

Nongovernmental groups focus mainly on religious outreach or economic development. One of the few exceptions is Civil Society, a private group that criticizes and tries to expose alleged official corruption.

Somalia

Polity: Presidential-par-
liamentary (transitional)
(insurgencies)
Economy: Mixed statist
Population: 7,800,000
PPP: na

Political Rights: 6
Civil Liberties: 7
Status: Not Free

Life Expectancy: 47
Religious Groups: Sunni Muslim (predominant)
Ethnic Groups: Somali (85 percent), other, including Bantu and Arab (15 percent)
Capital: Mogadishu

Ten-Year Ratings Timeline (Political Rights, Civil Liberties, Status)

1993	1994	1995	1996	1997	1998	1999	2000	2001	2002	2003
7,7NF	7,7NF	7,7NF	7,7NF	7,7NF	7,7NF	7,7NF	7,7NF	6,7NF	6,7NF	6,7NF

Overview:

Somalia's Transitional National Government (TNG) and more than 20 rival groups signed a ceasefire in October 2002 in Kenya as a first step toward establishing a federal system of government. However, more than a dozen similar peace agreements have failed, and the latest received support from neither a faction in central Somalia, nor from the self-declared republic of Somaliland in the north. Somalia in 2002 remained racked by violence and lack of security. Somalia's relations with neighboring Ethiopia were strained further in 2002 following persistent reports that Ethiopia was backing Somali factions and making military incursions into Somali territory. Ethiopia denied the claims and countered that Somalia was used as a rear base for terrorist attacks in the Kenyan port city of Mombassa in November 2002.

Somalia, a Horn of Africa nation, gained independence in July 1960 with the union of British Somaliland and territories to the south that had been an Italian colony. Other ethnic Somali-inhabited lands are now part of Djibouti, Ethiopia, and Kenya. General Siad Barre seized power in 1969 and increasingly employed divisive clan politics to maintain power. Civil war, starvation, banditry, brutality, and natural disasters ranging from drought to flood to famine have racked Somalia since the struggle to topple Barre began in the late 1980s. When Barre was deposed in January 1991, power was claimed and contested by heavily armed guerrilla movements and militias based on traditional ethnic and clan loyalties.

Extensive television coverage of famine and civil strife that took approximately 300,000 lives in 1991 and 1992 prompted a U.S.-led international intervention. The armed humanitarian mission in late 1992 quelled clan combat long enough to stop the famine, but ended in urban guerrilla warfare against Somali militias. The last international forces withdrew in March 1995 after the casualty count reached into the thousands. Approximately 100 peacekeepers, including 18 U.S. soldiers, were killed. The $4 billion UN intervention effort had little lasting impact.

The Conference for National Peace and Reconciliation in Somalia adopted a charter in 2000 for a three-year transition and selected a 245-member transitional assembly, which functions as an interim parliament. Minority groups are included, and 25 of the members are women. The breakaway regions of Somaliland and Puntland do not recognize the TNG, nor do several faction leaders. A government security force in Mogadishu has been cobbled together from members of the former administration's military, the police, and militias. U.S. military reconnaissance flights and other surveillance activities were stepped up in Somalia in 2001 as the United States sought to prevent the country from becoming a new base for al-Qaeda. The highest-ranking U.S. delegation in several years visited Somalia in 2002 to discuss the war on terrorism with the TNG and faction leaders. U.S. officials said they believed al-Qaeda had links in Somalia.

Somalia is a poor country where most people survive as pastoralists or subsistence farmers. The country's main exports are livestock and charcoal. The TNG and several faction leaders in November 2002 called on the international community to unfreeze the assets of Somalia's Al-Barakaat telecommunications and money-transfer company to help the country's battered economy. Al-Barakaat was Somalia's largest employer, and hundreds of thousands of Somalis depended on it to receive money transfers from abroad. U.S. authorities froze the assets of Al-Barakaat in 2001 on suspicion that its owners were aiding and abetting terrorism, a charge the owners deny.

Political Rights and Civil Liberties: The elections in 2000 marked the first time Somalis have had an opportunity to choose their government on a somewhat national basis since 1969. Some 3,000 representatives of civic and religious organizations, women's groups, and clans came together as the Inter-Governmental Authority for Development, following Djibouti-hosted peace talks, to elect a parliament in August 2000. The 245 members of the Transitional National Assembly elected the president. More than 20 candidates contested the first round of voting for the presidency. The Inter-Governmental Authority chose the lawyers who drafted the country's new charter.

Somalia's new charter provides for an independent judiciary, although a formal judicial system has ceased to exist. *Sharia* (Islamic law) operating in Mogadishu have been effective in bringing a semblance of law and order to the city. Efforts at judicial reform are proceeding slowly. The *Sharia* courts in Mogadishu are gradually coming under the control of the transitional government. Most of the courts are aligned with various subclans. Prison conditions are harsh in some areas, but improvements are under way.

Human rights abuses, including extrajudicial killing, torture, beating, and arbitrary detention by Somalia's various armed factions remain a problem. Many violations are linked to banditry. Several international aid organizations, women's groups, and local human rights groups operate in the country. Kidnapping, however, is a problem. Two UN workers were kidnapped in 2002 and later released. A Swiss aid worker was killed.

Somalia's charter provides for press freedom. Independent radio and television stations have proliferated. Most of the independent newspapers or newsletters that circulate in Mogadishu are linked to one faction or another. Although journalists face harassment, most receive the protection of the clan behind their publication. The transitional government launched its first radio station, Radio Mogadishu, in 2001. There are three private radio stations and two run by factions.

Somaliland has exercised de facto independence from Somalia since May 1991. A clan conference led to a peace accord among its clan factions in 1997, establishing a presidency and bicameral parliament with proportional clan representation. Somaliland is far more cohesive than the rest of the country, although reports of some human rights abuses persist. Somaliland has sought international recognition as the Republic of Somaliland since 1991. A referendum on independence and a new constitution were approved in May 2001, opening the way for a multiparty system. Fear of potential instability grew in 2002 after leader Mohamed Ibrahim Egal died following surgery. Somaliland's vice president was sworn in as president, but there were concerns that a power struggle would emerge.

Puntland established a regional government in 1998, with a presidency and a single-chamber quasi legislature known as the Council of Elders. Political parties are banned. The traditional elders chose Abdullahi Yusuf as the region's first president for a three-year term. After Jama Ali Jama was elected to replace him in 2001, Abdullahi Yusuf refused to relinquish power, claiming he was fighting terrorism. He seized power in 2002, reportedly with the help of Ethiopian forces.

Although more than 80 percent of Somalis share a common ethnic heritage, religion, and nomadic-influenced culture, discrimination is widespread. Clans exclude one another from participation in social and political life. Minority clans are harassed, intimidated, and abused by armed gunmen.

Somalia is an Islamic state, and religious freedom is not guaranteed. The Sunni majority often view non-Sunni Muslims with suspicion. Members of the small Christian community face societal harassment if they proclaim their religion.

Women's groups were instrumental in galvanizing support for Somalia's peace process. As a result of their participation, women occupy at least 30 seats in parliament. The country's new charter prohibits sexual discrimination, but women experience such discrimination intensely under customary practices and variants of Sharia. Infibulation, the most severe form of female genital mutilation, is routine. UN agencies and nongovernmental organizations are working to raise awareness about health dangers of this practice. Various armed factions have recruited children into their militias.

The charter provides workers with the right to form unions, but civil war and factional fighting led to the dissolution of the single labor confederation, the government-controlled General Federation of Somali Trade Unions. Wages are established largely by ad hoc bartering and the influence of clan affiliation.

South Africa

Polity: Presidential-par-
liamentary democracy
Economy: Capitalist-
statist
Population: 43,600,000
PPP: $9,401
Life Expectancy: 51

Political Rights: 1
Civil Liberties: 2
Status: Free

Religious Groups: Christian (68 percent), Muslim (2 percent), Hindu (1.5 percent), indigenous beliefs and animists (28.5 percent)
Ethnic Groups: Black (75 percent), white (14 percent), mixed (9 percent), Indian (2 percent)
Capital: Pretoria

Ten-Year Ratings Timeline (Political Rights, Civil Liberties, Status)

1993	1994	1995	1996	1997	1998	1999	2000	2001	2002	2003
5,4PF	5,4PF	2,3F	1,2F	1,2F	1,2F	1,2F	1,2F	1,2F	1,2F	1,2F

Overview:

South Africa's remarkable experiment in democratic consolidation continued in 2002. The Constitutional Court issued a groundbreaking ruling on the Treatment Action Campaign, stating that the government would have to provide treatment for women with HIV infections or AIDS. President Thabo Mbeki played a key leadership role in promoting the continent-wide New Economic Partnership for Africa (NEPAD), which places considerable emphasis on improved democracy and governance; the initiative has proven controversial in the early going.

Domestically, heightened protests have taken place regarding governmental social policy and the pace of essential service delivery. Tension within the alliance of the African National Congress (ANC), the Congress of South African Trade Unions (COSATU), and the South African Communist Party (SACP) continued. A five-year ANC policy conference took place in December, staking out a position for the party between the perceived excesses of "neoliberalism" and ultra-leftism."

President Mbeki maintained controversial positions on a number of issues, including his support for authoritarian President Robert Mugabe of Zimbabwe. Mbeki had only muted criticism of Mugabe's reelection, preferring quiet diplomacy to seek resolution of Zimbabwe's ongoing political crisis. Mbeki also spent considerable political capital arguing that AIDS is not necessarily caused by HIV, although he adopted a lower profile on this issue in 2002.

South Africa's apartheid government, which came to power in 1948, reserved political power for the white minority while seeking to balkanize the black, Indian, and mixed-race, or colored, communities. Increasing international ostracism, civil unrest, and the growing strength of the ANC eventually forced the South African government to negotiate with its adversaries. Momentum for change accelerated with the accession to power of Frederick de Klerk and global and regional moves towards greater democratization in the late 1980s. In 1990 De Klerk freed ANC leader Nelson Mandela from 27 years imprisonment, and a negotiation process that resulted in legitimate multiparty elections in 1994 was initiated. These elections brought

Mandela and the ANC to power at the national level. The ANC's electoral primacy was again demonstrated at the second round of national elections in 1999.

In recent years tension has increased between the ruling ANC and various groups, including trade unions, elements of the press, traditional leaders, and the white minority. Key areas of disagreement between the ANC and the COSATU have included the government's approach to dealing with key problems such as the AIDS epidemic and its conservative economic policies. In 2001 the ANC reached a cooperation agreement with the New National Party (NNP), the successor party to the apartheid-era ruling party. The agreement gave the ANC a foothold in the Western Cape, a key province where it previously had had no governing role.

The ANC leadership has focused blame for the country's problems on the former white-supremacist regime. This argument has begun to lose some of its potency with the passage of time and with the growing economic empowerment of a minority of black South Africans.

Serious challenges regarding democratic consolidation, economic and social development, health, and group relations exist. Concerns about rising corruption, as in the case of the Strategic Defense Procurement Package government arms purchase, led to the introduction into parliament of the 2002 Prevention of Corruption bill. The durability of the new democratic structures is uncertain since South Africa remains deeply divided by ethnicity and class. AIDS is rampant throughout the country, which is also plagued by crime levels that have reached endemic proportions.

South Africa's regional relations are highly sensitive and complicated. In addition to Zimbabwe's increasing instability, the specter of famine now haunts the region. Strife in the Great Lakes area, including in the Democratic Republic of Congo, has also impeded economic and political progress. In 2001, long-running negotiations to achieve a possible resolution of Burundi's civil conflict, led by former president Mandela, resulted in the installation of a coalition government. As part of this agreement, South Africa sent troops to Burundi as peacekeepers and continued to act as a mediator.

Political Rights and Civil Liberties: South Africa continues to provide a remarkable, powerful example of a positive democratic transition in an extremely diverse country. Consolidation of South Africa's democratic transition proceeded under the new constitution that took effect in February 1997. The country's independent judiciary continues to function, on balance, very well. Elections at all levels of government have taken place repeatedly. The press, trade unions, and other independent institutions play important roles in articulating a wide variety of interests.

South Africans have the right, in theory and practice, to change their government. Two successful national elections have taken place since 1994. Elections for the 400-seat National Assembly and 90-seat National Council of Provinces are by proportional representation based on party lists. The National Assembly elects the president to serve concurrently with their five-year term. Local and municipal elections were held in 1995, 1996, and early December, 2000.

In general, the electoral process, including extensive civic and voter education, balanced state-media coverage, and reliable balloting and vote counting, has worked properly. An exception is in KwaZulu/Natal, where political violence and credible allegations of vote rigging have devalued the process. Another controversial topic receiving increasing attention is the relationship of traditional leadership to the governing institutions. In particular, the Communal Land Rights bill would reform the administrative structure of local governments.

The South African constitution is one of the most liberal in the world, and includes a sweeping bill of rights. In early 2000 the parliament approved legislation outlawing discrimination on the basis of race, ethnicity, or sex. Parliament has passed more than 500 laws relating to the constitution, revamping the apartheid-era legal system. This legislation is now being implemented: for example, some lower courts have been designated "equality courts," with a particular mandate to review instances of unfair discrimination. In 2000 the cabinet also endorsed a code of ethics requiring the president and national and provincial cabinet ministers to abide by certain standards of behavior regarding potential and real conflicts of interest, and to disclose financial assets and gifts valued above a determined amount.

The now-concluded Truth and Reconciliation Commission sought to heal divisions created by the apartheid regime through a series of open hearings. From 1996 to 1998 the commission received more than 20,000 submissions from victims and nearly 8,000 applications for amnesty from perpetrators. In 1998 the commission released a report on human rights abuses during the apartheid years that largely focused on atrocities committed by the white-minority government, but which also criticized the ANC. The commission's amnesty committee remained in existence until June 2001 to complete the task of assessing thousands of applications for amnesty. A final report has yet to be submitted to parliament. The controversial issue of reparations for victims of apartheid is being actively debated within and between the civil society and government.

The 11-member Constitutional Court, created to enforce the rules of the new democracy, has demonstrated considerable independence. In its Treatment Action Campaign ruling, the court required the government to provide treatment to women with HIV or AIDS. In addition, the court handed down a judgment on the right to vote, validating legislative party switching in local councils. Lower courts generally respect legal provisions regarding arrest and detention, although courts remain understaffed. Efforts to end torture and other abuses by the national police force have been implemented. The constitutionally mandated Human Rights Commission was appointed by parliament to "promote the observance of, respect for, and the protection of fundamental rights."

Freedom of expression is generally respected. A variety of newspapers and magazines publish reporting, analysis, and opinion sharply critical of the government, political parties, and other societal actors. Radio broadcasting has been dramatically liberalized, with scores of small community radio stations now operating. Nevertheless, the state-owned South African Broadcasting Corporation (SABC), although far more independent today than during apartheid, still suffers from self-censorship.

The final version of the Broadcasting Amendment Bill passed by parliament in October 2002 reflects the positive impact of civil society, the media, and parliament on the development of democratic processes. Original draft legislation contained a clause requiring that the SABC report to the minister of communications regarding editorial content. After considerable advocacy and debate, the legislation was revised; the constitutionally mandated Independent Communications Authority of South Africa will ensure that the SABC fulfills its mission of broadcasting in the public interest.

Equal rights for women are guaranteed by the constitution and promoted by the constitutionally mandated Commission on Gender Equality. Laws such as the Maintenance Act and the Domestic Violence Act are designed to protect women in financially inequitable and abusive relationships, as well as in other areas of social inequality. These laws, though a step in the right direction, nevertheless do not provide the infrastructure for their implementation. Discriminatory practices in customary law remain prevalent.

The breakdown of law and order is a serious problem. An estimated four million illegal firearms circulate in South Africa. Nationally, police make arrests in only 45 percent of murder cases and 12 percent of robberies, compared with 70 percent and 30 percent, respectively, in the United States. In recent years South Africa has ranked first in the world in the per capita number of rapes and armed robberies. Tension has also grown between elements of the nation's Muslim minority and the government. A number of self-styled vigilantes, some of them with links to criminals, have been charged with a string of violent actions, especially in the Cape Town area.

In response to this problem and to the September 11 attacks in the United States, the government has drafted a terrorism bill, which is due to be presented to parliament in 2003. Many clauses in the original version alarmed South Africans who remembered the days when groups such as the ANC were persecuted as terrorist organizations and anti-apartheid activists were detained for up to 90 days without trial. A revised text does away with many of the most objectionable clauses, and further amendments are possible as parliament reviews this legislation.

Prison conditions are characterized by overcrowding. The prison system has a capacity of 100,000 but has been holding as many as 170,000 individuals. In 2001 the government announced that spending on the integrated justice system—the police, courts, and correctional services—would increase by 7.2 percent per year to allow for infrastructural improvements and the hiring of 6,000 new police officers. The Jali Commission of Inquiry into corruption in prisons was established in 2002. It has shed light on this volatile issue, and as a result the Special Investigative Unit has been established with powers of prosecution.

Labor rights codified under the 1995 Labor Relations Act (LRA) are respected, and there are more than 250 trade unions. The right to strike can be exercised after reconciliation efforts. The LRA allows employers to hire replacement workers. The ANC government has introduced several labor laws designed to protect the rights of workers, although it has taken other actions that weaken labor union positions in bargaining for job security, wages, and other benefits.

South Africa faces other serious problems. It has one of the fastest-growing AIDS rates in the world. About 4.7 million people in South Africa are believed to be HIV-positive, higher than in any other country. Up to 250,000 deaths from AIDS occur each year, and the health crisis poses an extremely serious political and social problem.

The quality of schooling is extremely uneven. More than three-quarters of South Africa's people are black, but they share less than a third of the country's total income. The white minority retains most economic power. Unemployment stands at about 40 percent among blacks and 4 percent among whites; an estimated 500,000 private sector jobs have been lost since 1994. Attempts to redress these significant economic disparities include initiatives such as the Mining Charter, negotiated in 2002, which requires 25 percent of the mining industry to be black-owned in five years.

Spain

Polity: Parliamentary   **Political Rights:** 1
democracy   **Civil Liberties:** 1*
Economy: Mixed capitalist **Status:** Free
Population: 41,300,000
PPP: $19,472
Life Expectancy: 79
Religious Groups: Roman Catholic (94 percent),
other (6 percent)
Ethnic Groups: Mediterranean and Nordic
Capital: Madrid
Ratings Change: Spain's civil liberties rating improved from 2 to 1 due to changes in
the survey methodology.

Ten-Year Ratings Timeline (Political Rights, Civil Liberties, Status)

1993	1994	1995	1996	1997	1998	1999	2000	2001	2002	2003
1,1F	1,2F	1,2F	1,2F	1,2F	1,2F	1,2F	1,2F	1,2F	1,2F	1,1F

Overview:

The most significant event to affect political rights in 2002 was the passage in June of a law that aims to regulate political parties. The law was directed specifically at Batasuna, the political wing of the Basque paramilitary organization, the Basque Fatherland and Liberty Party (ETA). The new law has triggered further deterioration in the political climate in the Basque Country by uniting moderate and radical Basque nationalists, and has arguably given legitimacy to claims of "political repression" in the region.

The Basque issue has taken center stage in the domestic political drama, but the government of the Partido Popular (PP) is acting with a renewed sense of purpose following a major cabinet reshuffle in June. However, it is unclear whether the shake-up can stem the slow but steady decline in the government's support and the corresponding rise in that of the opposition Spanish Socialist Workers' Party (PSOE). The PP of Prime Minister Jose Maria Aznar still enjoys a narrow lead over the PSOE in most opinion polls, but this could evaporate if the economic outlook fails to improve. The PP's prospects of winning a third term will also be affected by the race to succeed the prime minister, who has committed himself to withdrawing from domestic politics ahead of the next general election, which is due by March 2004.

Economic growth stagnated in 2001 and only a marginal pickup is predicted for 2002 and 2003. Growth in the 2000-01 period was the lowest since 1993. Spain's labor market, which has been made more efficient and responsive to movements in the economy under a number of recent laws, is again experiencing a rise in the unemployment rate, after having fallen to historic lows in the late 1990s.

Spain's Basques were the first group known to have occupied the Iberian Peninsula. However, Spain's current language and laws are based on those of the Romans, who arrived in the second century B.C. In the year 711, the Moors invaded from North Africa, ruling for 700 years. The unification of present-day Spain dates from 1512. After a period of colonial influence and wealth, the country declined as a

European power and was occupied by France in the early 1800s. Subsequent wars and revolts led to Spain's loss of its colonies in the Americas by that century's end. Francisco Franco began a long period of nationalist rule after the victory of his forces in the 1936-1939 civil war. In spite of the country's official neutrality, Franco followed Axis policies during World War II. Even with its closed economy, the country was transformed into a modern industrial nation in the postwar years. After a transitional period upon Franco's death in 1975, the country emerged as a parliamentary democracy. It joined the European Union (EU) in 1986.

The Spanish government began negotiations with the ETA in 1998, establishing a ceasefire and aiming to end a conflict that has claimed approximately 800 lives since 1970. The two sides were emboldened to negotiate after witnessing the positive results of the signing of the Northern Ireland peace accords. By December 1999, however, the ETA had announced an end to the ceasefire, angered by what it perceived as slow progress in the talks. It subsequently stepped up its attacks in both frequency and deadliness. During the violence, marked by car bombings and assassinations, moderate Basque nationalists won regional elections in early 2001.

A bill passed in June that outlawed the ETA's political wing, Batasuna, was approved with the support of the PP, the PSOE, and the moderate Catalan nationalists. The bill also received legal recognition. The law envisages the establishment of a judicial process that would gather evidence relating to any political party accused of supporting or promoting violence. The moderate Basque Nationalist Party (PNV), which controls the regional government, has led street demonstrations alongside Batasuna in protest against the law. Some Basque leaders have been increasingly outspoken for independence as a result. At the same time, the ETA has intensified its campaign of intimidation and violence against local PP and PSOE party members in many Basque municipalities. The Supreme Court had declared in August a temporary three-year suspension of Batasuna under existing legislation, after an investigation concluded that Batasuna is, in fact, an integral part of the ETA. Despite these events, the Basque Country pushed for more independence during 2002 in political moves that call for its eventual and complete independence.

Political Rights and Civil Liberties: Spanish citizens can change their government democratically. Spain has been governed democratically since 1977, after nearly 40 years of dictatorship under Franco and a brief transitional government under Adolfo Suarez. The country is divided into 17 autonomous regions with limited powers, including control over such areas as health, tourism, local police agencies, and instruction in regional languages. The bicameral federal legislature includes the territorially elected Senate and the Congress of Deputies elected on the basis of proportional representation and universal suffrage. Although a law stipulates that women must occupy 25 percent of senior party posts and a feminist party has been officially registered since 1981, female participation in government remains minimal.

The Supreme Tribunal heads the judiciary, which includes territorial, provincial, regional, and municipal courts. The post-Franco constitution and 1996 parliamentary legislation established the right to trial by jury.

Freedom of speech and a free press are guaranteed. The press has been particularly influential in setting the political agenda in recent years, with national daily newspapers such as *El Mundo, ABC*, and *El Pais* covering corruption and other issues. A new conservative daily, *La Razon*, was launched in 1998. In addition to the state-controlled television station, which has been accused of pro-government bias, there are three independent commercial television stations. Members of the press sometimes figure among ETA targets for assassination. There is general agreement that legislation is needed to govern the operation of Web sites since there currently are no laws applicable to e-commerce. A bill pending in the parliament at the end of 2002 is being criticized in some quarters as contrary to free expression on the Internet, and is viewed as favoring large companies given the bill's tax implications. However, the bill is viewed by a number of analysts as applicable to commercial Internet sites, not personal Web sites.

Spain lacks antidiscrimination laws, and ethnic minorities, particularly immigrants, continue to report bias and mistreatment. In particular, North African immigrants report physical abuse and discrimination by authorities and are frequently the subjects of attack by Spanish civilians. After receiving large numbers of illegal immigrants in 2000, which led to severe outbreaks of racial and anti-immigrant violence, Spain faced a continuing influx of illegal immigrants in 2002. Scores of illegal immigrants, mostly North African, arrived by boat throughout the year, many not surviving the short, yet often treacherous, journey. Some estimates are that 3,000 people have drowned over the last five years while trying to reach Spain. The Spanish Interior Ministry estimates that 50,000 legal and illegal workers arrive each year, mainly from North Africa.

In February 2001 the government passed an immigration law allowing for the imposition of heavy fines against those employing illegal immigrants. The law also seeks to stem the flow of immigrants entering Spain illegally, and to crack down on smugglers of immigrants. The Spanish government released figures at the end of 2001, which showed a 16 percent increase in the number of illegal immigrants found on Spanish territory in the first 10 months of 2001, from 15,195 persons in 2000 to 17,692 in 2001. The trend continued but slowed in 2002.

The rights to freedom of association and collective bargaining are constitutionally guaranteed. The country has one of the lowest levels of trade union membership in the EU, and unions have failed to prevent passage of labor laws facilitating dismissals and encouraging short-term contracting.

In 1978, the constitution disestablished Roman Catholicism as the state religion, but directed Spanish authorities to "keep in mind the religious beliefs of Spanish society." Freedom of worship and the separation of church and state are respected in practice. Spain is home to many cultural and linguistic groups, some—such as the Basques—with strong regional identities.

With economic liberalization proceeding apace under the PP government, Spanish citizens are increasingly finding more opportunities for employment as the state recedes from economic life. Citizens have the right to own property and to establish their own businesses.

↑ Sri Lanka

Polity: Presidential-par-
liamentary democracy
Economy: Mixed
capitalist
Population: 18,900,000
PPP: $3,530
Life Expectancy: 72

Political Rights: 3
Civil Liberties: 4
Status: Partly Free

Religious Groups: Buddhist (70 percent), Hindu (15 percent),
Christian (8 percent), Muslim (7 percent)
Ethnic Groups: Sinhalese (74 percent), Tamil (18 percent), other (8 percent)
Capital: Colombo
Trend Arrow: Sri Lanka received an upward trend arrow due to a lasting bilateral ceasefire and continuing peace talks between the government and the Tamil Tiger guerrillas.

Ten-Year Ratings Timeline (Political Rights, Civil Liberties, Status)

1993	1994	1995	1996	1997	1998	1999	2000	2001	2002	2003
4,5PF	4,5PF	4,5PF	4,5PF	3,5PF	3,4PF	3,4PF	3,4PF	3,4PF	3,4PF	3,4PF

Overview:

After winning parliamentary elections held in December 2001 on a pro-peace platform, the United National Front coalition government, led by Prime Minister Ranil Wickremasinghe, negotiated a ceasefire with the Tamil Tiger separatist rebels in February 2002. Talks held in September were judged a success when the Tigers gave up their demand for a separate state, and the two sides continued to negotiate the outlines of a political settlement while addressing issues of disarmament, reconstruction, and the rehabilitation of displaced civilians. The almost complete cessation of armed conflict led to improvements in the human rights climate in the north and east of the country during the year.

Since independence from Britain in 1948, political power in this island nation has alternated between the conservative United National Party (UNP) and the leftist Sri Lanka Freedom Party (SLFP). While the country has made impressive gains in literacy, basic health care, and other social needs, its economic development has been stunted and its social fabric tested by a long-standing civil war that has killed an estimated 64,000 people. The conflict initially pitted several Tamil guerrilla groups against the government, which is dominated by the Sinhalese majority. The war, although triggered by anti-Tamil riots in 1983 that claimed hundreds of lives, came in the context of long-standing Tamil claims of discrimination in education and employment opportunities. By 1986, the Liberation Tigers of Tamil Eelam (LTTE, or Tamil Tigers), which called for an independent Tamil homeland in the Northern and Eastern Provinces, had eliminated most rival Tamil guerrilla groups and was in control of much of the northern Jaffna Peninsula. At the same time, the government was also fighting an insurgency in the south by the leftist People's Liberation Front (JVP). The JVP insurgency, and the brutal methods used by the army to quell it in 1990, killed 60,000 people. As the civil war continued, a LTTE suicide bomber assassinated President Ranasinghe Premadasa in 1993.

In 1994, Chandrika Kumaratunga ended nearly two decades of UNP rule by leading an SLFP-dominated coalition to victory in parliamentary elections and then winning the presidential election. Early in her term, Kumaratunga tried to negotiate a peace agreement with the LTTE. Following a renewal of hostilities by the LTTE, she pursued a military solution while attempting to devolve power to eight semiautonomous regional councils, including one covering the contested north and east, where Tamils would be the majority. Kumaratunga won early presidential elections in 1999, but her coalition failed to win a majority in parliamentary elections held in October 2000. After her government faced a series of no-confidence motions throughout 2001, she dissolved parliament and scheduled snap elections for December. In polling marred by violence and intimidation, the UNP and its allies won 114 out of a possible 225 seats. UNP leader Ranil Wickremasinghe became prime minister, although Kumaratunga remains in office as president. In March, the ruling coalition consolidated its win with a landslide victory in local elections.

In response to a ceasefire offer by the LTTE in December 2001, the new government declared a truce with the rebels, lifted an economic embargo imposed on rebel-held territory, and restarted Norwegian-brokered peace talks. A permanent bilateral ceasefire accord with provisions for international monitoring was signed in February 2002. Shortly before the first round of formal peace talks took place in Thailand in September, the government lifted its ban on the LTTE. In late September, army and rebel representatives met to exchange prisoners of war in another sign of growing confidence in the peace process. Further progress on issues of rehabilitation and military de-escalation was made at negotiations held in October, and by December, the government and Tigers had agreed to share political power in a federal system.

However, progress on ending the civil war has been constrained by growing tensions and political bickering between the president and the UNP-led government. President Kumaratunga made repeated statements throughout the year undermining the peace process, and her power to arbitrarily dismiss parliament casts doubt over the present government's ability to negotiate with the Tigers. In October, the Supreme Court rejected a cabinet proposal that would have stripped the president of her power to dissolve parliament, determining that such legislation would require a two-thirds majority in parliament as well as a national referendum in order to become law.

Political Rights and Civil Liberties: Sri Lankans can change their government through elections based on universal adult suffrage. The 1978 constitution vested strong executive powers in a president who is directly elected for a six-year term and can dissolve parliament. The 225-member parliament is also directly elected for a six-year term, through a mix of single-seat, simple-plurality districts and proportional representation. While elections are generally free, they are marred by irregularities, violence, and intimidation. The independent Center for Monitoring Election Violence recorded 2,734 incidents of election-related violence during the December 2001 parliamentary election campaign, including 47 murders and more than 1,500 assaults, threats, and other abuses.

Although the constitution provides for freedom of expression, the government has restricted this right in practice, particularly with regard to coverage of the civil war. However, authorities lifted censorship of military-related news in June 2001.

The LTTE tightly restricts the media in areas under its control, according to the U.S. State Department's human rights report. In June, an act of parliament removed criminal defamation legislation from the statute books. The government controls the largest newspaper chain, two major television stations, and a radio station; and political coverage in the state-owned media favors the ruling party. While private media criticize governmental policies, journalists practice some self-censorship. Reporters, particularly those who cover human rights issues or police misconduct, continued to face harassment and threats from the police, security forces, government supporters, and the LTTE. In February, a court sentenced two air force officers to prison terms for an attack on a journalist that occurred four years ago. However, the murder of a BBC reporter in October 2000 by unidentified gunmen remains unsolved.

Religious freedom is respected, although the constitution gives special status to Buddhism and there is some discrimination and occasional violence against religious minorities. The LTTE discriminates against Muslims and has attacked Buddhist sites in the past. The U.S. State Department's 2002 Report on International Religious Freedom noted that as part of the ceasefire accord, government security forces had begun the process of vacating Hindu religious properties in the north and east of the country.

Freedom of assembly is generally respected, although both main political parties occasionally disrupt each other's rallies and political events. In July 2001, after students at Jaffna University boycotted classes to protest the arrest of one of their leaders, authorities closed the entire university in a bid to end protests against the security forces. Except in conflict-affected areas, human rights and social welfare nongovernmental organizations generally operate freely.

Trade unions are independent and engage in collective bargaining. Except for civil servants, most workers can hold strikes. However, under the 1989 Essential Services Act, the president can declare a strike in any industry illegal. President Chandrika Kumaratunga has used the act to end several strikes. Employers on tea plantations routinely violate the rights of the mainly Tamil workforce.

While the judiciary is independent, the rule of law is weak. This has allowed security forces to commit abuses with near impunity, often facilitated by sweeping security laws such as the Prevention of Terrorism Act. Successive governments kept all or parts of Sri Lanka under a near continuous state of emergency from 1979 to July 2001. Regulations allowed authorities to hold suspects in preventive detention for up to one year without charge, with a limited right to judicial review.

Human rights groups allege that the security laws contain inadequate safeguards for detainees and facilitate long-standing practices of torture and "disappearances." Despite the cessation of hostilities, some of these regulations remain in place and hundreds of detainees continue to be held without trial, according to a report issued by Human Rights Watch. In November, Amnesty International reiterated its concern about torture "reported both in the context of the armed conflict and in routine police investigations," while a report issued in October by the Hong Kong-based Asian Human Rights Commission alleged that police use of torture was widespread and threatened the rule of law. While there has been little progress in reducing acts of torture, there has been a decline in the number of reported disappearances.

Soldiers, police, and state-organized civilian militias have also committed extrajudicial executions and rapes of LTTE supporters held in custody, as well as of Tamil civilians. A report issued by Amnesty International in January noted a rise in allegations of custodial rape in 2001. However, Amnesty International welcomed a landmark decision by the Supreme Court that granted monetary compensation to a Tamil woman who had been raped by members of the police and security forces in Colombo in June 2001. Although travel restrictions on civilians in the north and east have been lifted as a result of the ceasefire, Tamils continue to face some harassment and other abuses by soldiers and police.

The LTTE directly controls some territory in the northern Vanni jungle and maintains de facto control over many areas in the Eastern Province. The Tigers run a parallel government in the areas under their control, which include their own police and judiciary. The rebels continued to be responsible for summary executions of civilians, disappearances, arbitrary abductions and detentions, torture and the forcible conscription of children. Press reports indicated that the LTTE continued to recruit teenage children in 2002 despite promises to end the practice, while a report issued by the University Teachers for Human Rights group in July alleged that the ceasefire had allowed the Tigers to forcibly conscript children from previously inaccessible government-controlled areas. However, shortly before the first round of peace talks in September, the Tigers released 85 child recruits, according to UNICEF. The Tigers raise money through extortion, kidnapping, theft, and the seizure of Muslim homes, land, and businesses, and have used threats and attacks to close schools, courts, and government agencies in their self-styled Tamil homeland.

The ceasefire negotiated in February held throughout 2002, despite some incidents of violence and complaints of violations on both sides. In July, the 44-member Norwegian-led Sri Lankan Monitoring Mission (SLMM) released information regarding complaints of ceasefire violations received between February and June. Of a total of 380 complaints, 270 were made against the Tigers while 110 were against the government; the Tigers were most frequently accused of kidnapping, abduction, and extortion, while government forces were accused of harassment, occupation of civilian land, and restrictions on movement.

Sporadic violence between the three major ethnic groups remains a concern. Clashes between Hindu and Muslim Tamils that spread across eastern Sri Lanka in June caused 11 deaths and injured more than 50 people. However, in an effort to address continuing tensions between the LTTE and the Muslims, an accord was signed in February between the Tigers and the Sri Lanka Muslim Congress party that explicitly recognized the right of the roughly 65,000 internally displaced Muslim Tamils to return to the north as part of the peace process. In October, the UN High Commissioner for Refugees reported that more than 213,000 people displaced by the civil war (out of a total of roughly 800,000) had returned to their homes in the north and the east.

Women are underrepresented in politics and the civil service. Female employees in the private sector face some sexual harassment as well as discrimination in salary and promotion opportunities. Rape and domestic violence against women remain serious problems, and authorities weakly enforce existing laws.

Sudan

Polity: Presidential-
parliamentary (military-
dominated)
Economy: Capitalist-statist
Population: 32,600,000
PPP: $1,797
Life Expectancy: 56

Political Rights: 7
Civil Liberties: 7
Status: Not Free

Religious Groups: Sunni Muslim (70 percent), indigenous beliefs
(25 percent), Christian (5 percent)
Ethnic Groups: Black (52 percent), Arab (39 percent), Beja (6 percent), other (3 percent)
Capital: Khartoum

Ten-Year Ratings Timeline (Political Rights, Civil Liberties, Status)

1993	1994	1995	1996	1997	1998	1999	2000	2001	2002	2003
7,7NF	7,7NF	7,7NF	7,7NF	7,7NF	7,7NF	7,7NF	7,7NF	7,7NF	7,7NF	7,7NF

Overview:

While there was some progress—including breakthrough agreements—on ending Sudan's long-running civil war, fighting continued in 2002 between the government and rebel groups in the country's south. An international commission confirmed the practice of slavery and religious persecution in Sudan. The United States passed the Sudan Peace Act, officially recognizing Sudan as guilty of genocide. The Sudanese government banned relief and aid organizations access to some war-affected areas of the country. While the government cooperated in the global war against terrorism, it also established camps to train militants for attacks against Israel.

The Sudanese civil war moved into its 20th year, but substantive peace talks and a limited ceasefire agreement provided some hope for a final resolution of the conflict. Peace initiatives have taken on greater urgency since the 1999 inauguration of a Sudanese oil pipeline, which now finances Khartoum's war efforts. The government has intensified fighting around oil-rich civilian areas in an apparent effort to drive out or exterminate their inhabitants.

Africa's largest country has been embroiled in civil wars for 36 of its 46 years as an independent state. It achieved independence in 1956 after nearly 80 years of British rule. The Anyanya movement, representing mainly Christian and animist black Africans in southern Sudan, battled Arab Muslim government forces from 1956 to 1972. The south gained extensive autonomy under a 1972 accord, and for the next decade, an uneasy peace prevailed. In 1983, General Jafar Numeiri, who had toppled an elected government in 1969, restricted southern autonomy and imposed *Sharia* (Islamic law). Opposition led again to civil war, and Numeiri was overthrown in 1985. Civilian rule was restored in 1986 with an election that resulted in a government led by Sadiq al-Mahdi of the moderate Islamic Ummah Party, but war continued. Lieutenant General Omar al-Bashir ousted al-Mahdi in a 1989 coup, and the latter spent seven years either in prison or under house arrest before fleeing to Eritrea. Until 1999, al-Bashir ruled through a military-civilian regime backed by senior Muslim clerics including Hassan al-Turabi, who wielded considerable power as the ruling National Congress (NC) party leader and speaker of the 360-member National Assembly.

Tensions between al-Bashir and al-Turabi climaxed in December 1999; on the eve of a parliamentary vote on a plan by al-Turabi to curb presidential powers, al-Bashir dissolved parliament and declared a state of emergency. He introduced a law allowing the formation of political parties, fired al-Turabi as NC head, replaced the cabinet with his own supporters, and held deeply flawed presidential and parliamentary elections in December 2000, which the NC won overwhelmingly. Al-Turabi formed his own party, the Popular National Congress (PNC), in June 2000, but was prohibited from participating in politics. In January 2001, the Ummah Party refused to join al-Bashir's new government despite the president's invitation, declaring that it refused to support totalitarianism.

Al-Turabi and some 20 of his supporters were arrested in February 2001 after he called for a national uprising against the government and signed a memorandum of understanding in Geneva with the southern-based, rebel Sudanese People's Liberation Army (SPLA). Al-Turabi and four aides were charged with conspiracy to overthrow the government, and al-Turabi was placed under house arrest in May. In September 2002, he was moved to a high-security prison.

The ongoing civil war broadly pits government forces and government-backed, northern Arab Muslims against southern-based, black African animists and Christians. The government also sponsors the Popular Defense Force, a volunteer militant Islamic militia that fights against southern rebels. Some pro-democracy northerners, however, have allied themselves with the SPLA-led southern rebels to form the National Democratic Alliance (NDA), while northern rebels of the Sudan Allied Forces have staged attacks in northeastern Sudan. Some southern groups have signed peace pacts with the government, but there is fighting among rival southern militias. A convoluted mix of historical, religious, ethnic, and cultural tensions makes peace elusive, while competition for economic resources fuels the conflict. Past ceasefire attempts have failed, with Khartoum insisting on an unconditional ceasefire, and the SPLA demanding the establishment of a secular constitution first.

The government regularly bombs civilian as well as military targets. International humanitarian relief efforts are hampered by ceasefire violations and are sometimes deliberately targeted by parties to the conflict. The government has denied access by humanitarian relief workers to rebel-held areas or where large concentrations of internal refugees have gathered.

A peace plan proposed in December 2001 by former U.S. senator John Danforth called for "one country, two systems" in Sudan, with an Islamic government in the north and a secular system in the south.

The international community stepped up its mediation efforts in the civil war in 2002, in part to prevent Sudan from becoming a breeding ground for terror, much as Afghanistan had become prior to September 11, 2001. Peace talks under the auspices of the Intergovernmental Authority on Development (IGAD) focused on southern self-determination, borders, and the application of Sharia in the south.

In January, U.S.-mediated peace talks between the government and rebels took place in Switzerland, leading to a breakthrough agreement affecting the Nuba mountain region, a 30,000-square-mile area in the heart of Sudan. The black Africans native to the Nuba region numbered more than one million in 1985, and have been reduced to some 300,000 today. The government frequently bombed the region and enforced blockades preventing food, fuel, clothing, and medicine from entering. The agreement allowed for humanitarian relief access, which was nonetheless blocked later in the year.

Fighting continued elsewhere throughout the year. While the government agreed to extend the Nuba agreement, and participated in further talks in Machakos, Kenya, rebels reported government-sponsored attacks in several towns and villages. In June, four civilians were reportedly killed during a bombing raid in the town of Malual-Kan as they left a Medecins Sans Frontieres compound to walk to church. The same month, the International Crisis Group (ICG) issued a major report that claimed Khartoum was intensifying its drive southward. The government's capture of oil fields has helped its war effort, enabling it to buy several Russian MIGs used to suppress rebels and bomb civilian areas.

Amid reports of further assaults on villages and fleeing refugees, the government and the SPLA agreed in July on a framework for future talks. The agreement allowed for a referendum in six years for southern self-determination and the preservation of Islamic law in the north. However, a general ceasefire was not reached.

Following the capture by the SPLA of several southern towns, the government suspended the Kenya talks, prompting a further SPLA offensive and a renewed demand from Khartoum for an immediate ceasefire as a precondition for renewed talks. The government continued to bomb southern villages with MIGs and helicopter gunships.

In October, the United States passed the landmark Sudan Peace Act, which recognized Sudan as guilty of genocide. The act authorized direct aid to the south to prepare the population for peace and democratic governance. It also specified sanctions against Khartoum if Sudan is deemed to be hampering humanitarian efforts or not to be negotiating in good faith. In the same month, the Canadian oil company Talisman quit drilling operations in Sudan after enduring years of pressure from human rights organizations. It also sold off its 25 percent stake in Sudan's Greater Nile Petroleum Operating Company.

In November, government and SPLA representatives in Machakos signed a Memorandum of Understanding (MOU) on power sharing. The MOU also extended an earlier understanding on a general ceasefire and unrestricted aid access. Reflecting on the agreement, the ICG said both sides were "closer than they have ever been to ending the twenty-year civil war."

Al-Bashir has begun to lift Sudan out of its international isolation by sidelining al-Turabi, who was seen as the force behind Sudan's efforts to export Islamic extremism. Although new vice president Ali Osman Mohammed Taha, who replaced al-Turabi as Islamic ideologue, maintains a firm commitment to Sudan as an Islamic state and to the government's self-proclaimed *jihad* (holy war) against non-Muslims, al-Bashir has managed to repair relations with several states, including Iran, Eritrea, Saudi Arabia, and even the United States. Following the September 11 terrorist attacks in the United States, al-Bashir issued a statement rejecting violence and offering to cooperate in combating terrorism. In March, Sudanese security reportedly arrested a top operative of Osama bin Laden's al-Qaeda terrorist organization. The Saudi-born bin Laden resided in Sudan for five years in the 1990s before being expelled by the government.

Prior cooperation with the United States in the global war on terrorism may have contributed to the American decision, in September 2001, to abstain from a UN Security Council vote that cleared the way for the lifting of UN sanctions imposed on Sudan in 1996 for its alleged role in an assassination attempt against Egyptian president Hosni Mubarak. Despite its seeming cooperation, the Sudanese military announced in April that it had established training camps throughout the country to prepare volunteers for a jihad against Israel. The United States maintains its own sanctions, citing human rights abuses and Sudan's apparent support for terrorism.

Political Rights and Civil Liberties: Sudanese cannot change their government democratically. December 2000 presidential and parliamentary elections cannot credibly be said to have reflected the will of the people. The major opposition parties, which are believed to have the support of most Sudanese, boycotted in protest of what they called an attempt by a totalitarian regime to impart the appearance of fairness. The EU declined an invitation to monitor the polls to avoid bestowing legitimacy on the outcome. Omar al-Bashir, running against former president Jafar Numeiri and three relative unknowns, won 86 percent of the vote. NC candidates stood uncontested for nearly two-thirds of parliamentary seats. Voting did not take place in some 17 rebel-held constituencies, and government claims of 66 percent voter turnout in some states were denounced as fictitious.

Serious human rights abuses by nearly every faction involved in the civil war have been reported. Secret police operate "ghost houses"—detention and torture centers—in several cities. Government armed forces reportedly routinely raid villages, burn homes, kill men, and abduct women and children to be used as slaves in the north. Relief agencies have liberated thousands of slaves by purchasing them from captors in the north and returning them to the south. International aid workers have been abducted and killed.

In May, the International Eminent Persons Group, a fact-finding mission composed of humanitarian relief workers, human rights lawyers, academics, and former European and American diplomats, confirmed the existence of slavery in Sudan. After conducting extensive research in the country, the group reported a range of human rights abuses, including what under international law is considered slavery. The report also addressed abductions and forced servitude under the SPLA's authority.

While the government has acknowledged forced servitude—especially of black animists and Christians—as a "problem," it continued to use *murahallen* (tribal militias), to pillage Dinka villages and abduct women and children.

Although there has been no organized effort to compile casualty statistics in southern Sudan since 1994, the total number of people killed by war, famine, and disease is believed to exceed two million. More than four million people are internally displaced, and that number is growing as the government fights to clear black Africans from oil fields or potential oil drilling sites.

Distribution of food and medical relief is hampered by fighting and by the government's deliberate blockage of aid shipments. In June, the UN World Food Program complained that a government ban on relief access to the oil-rich region of western Upper Nile in southern Sudan was threatening 350,000 civilians, many of whom had been displaced by fighting. The ban took place during the dry season, exacerbating civilian vulnerability.

Despite the ceasefire reached in the Nuba Mountains region, and a government pledge to allow unfettered humanitarian services access to the area, aid agencies still encountered difficulty delivering food, particularly to SPLA-controlled areas. Prior to the ceasefire, the Sudanese military carried out a policy of "depopulating" the Nuba Mountains. In September, the government suspended all relief flights to areas of active fighting in the south.

The judiciary is not independent. The chief justice of the Supreme Court, who presides over the entire judiciary, is government appointed. Regular courts provide some due process safeguards, but special security and military courts, used to punish political opponents of the government, do not. Criminal law is based on Sharia and provides for flogging, amputation, crucifixion, and execution. Ten southern, predominantly non-Muslim states are officially exempt from Sharia, although criminal law allows for its application in the future if the state assemblies choose to implement it. Arbitrary arrest, detention, and torture are widespread, and security forces act with impunity. Prison conditions do not meet international standards.

In May, the World Organization Against Torture reported that 12 prisoners charged with robbery were hung in Darfour in western Sudan after being sentenced by a Special Court. While the court deals with criminal matters, it is composed of two military judges and one civilian judge. Lawyers were forbidden from appearing before the court. Other prisoners were reportedly awaiting execution.

Press freedom has improved since the government eased restrictions in 1997, but journalists practice self-censorship to avoid harassment, arrest, or closure of their publications. There are reportedly nine daily newspapers and a wide variety of Arabic- and English-language publications. All of these are subject to censorship. Penalties apply to journalists who allegedly harm the nation or economy or violate national security. A 1999 law imposes penalties for "professional errors."

In February, the editor of the English-language daily *Khartoum Monitor* was fined for publishing an article implicating the government in slavery. In July, security officials seized issues of the Arabic daily *Al-Horreya* (Freedom), preventing their publication. No explanation was given for the seizure. In September authorities seized the issues of three papers and arrested one journalist for criticizing the government's withdrawal from peace talks in Kenya. The same month, a Sudanese Sharia court found U.S.-based, Sudanese author Kola Boof guilty of blasphemy. Boof was sentenced to death by beheading should she return to Sudan. Boof wrote a book critical of Sudan's treatment of black women.

Emergency law severely restricts freedom of assembly and association. In February, the College of Technological Science in Khartoum reportedly suspended several students for engaging in human rights activities, including organizing symposiums on women's rights and attending a conference on democracy. In November, the government closed the University of Khartoum indefinitely after students protested attacks on dormitories by pro-government student militias. Several students were injured and arrested. The clashes erupted following student celebrations of the 38th anniversary of protests against Sudan's first military government and against the banning of the University Students Union four years ago, when opposition groups were poised to win campus elections.

Islam is the state religion, and the constitution claims Sharia as the source of its legislation. Seventy percent of Sudanese are Muslim, though most southern Sudanese adhere to traditional indigenous beliefs or Christianity. The overwhelming majority of those displaced or killed by war and famine in Sudan have been non-Muslims, and many starve because of a policy under which food is withheld pending conversion to Islam. Officials have described their campaign against non-Muslims as a *jihad*. Under the 1994 Societies Registration Act, religious groups must register in order to gather legally. Registration is reportedly difficult to obtain. The government denies permission to build churches and destroys Christian schools, centers, and churches. Roman Catholic priests face random detention and interrogation by police.

Women face discrimination in family matters such as marriage, divorce, and inheritance, which are governed by Sharia. Public order police frequently harass women and monitor their dress for adherence to government standards of modesty. Female genital mutilation occurs despite legal prohibition, and rape is reportedly routine in war zones. President al-Bashir announced in January 2001 that Sudan would not ratify the International Convention on Eradication of All Forms of Discrimination Against Women because it "contradicted Sudanese values and traditions." Children are used as soldiers by government and opposition forces in the civil war. The SPLA, which reportedly employs some 13,000 children, promised to demobilize at least 10,000 by the end of 2002.

There are no independent trade unions. The Sudan Workers Trade Unions Federation is the main labor organization, with about 800,000 members. Local union elections are rigged to ensure the election of government-approved candidates. A lack of labor legislation limits the freedom of workers to organize or bargain collectively.

Suriname

Polity: Presidential-parliamentary democracy
Economy: Capitalist-statist
Population: 400,000
PPP: $3,799
Life Expectancy: 71

Political Rights: 1
Civil Liberties: 2
Status: Free

Religious Groups: Hindu (27.4 percent), Muslim (19.6 percent), Roman Catholic (22.8 percent), Protestant (25.2 percent), indigenous beliefs (5 percent)
Ethnic Groups: East Indian (37 percent), Creole (31 percent), Javanese (15 percent), other (17 percent)
Capital: Paramaribo

Ten-Year Ratings Timeline (Political Rights, Civil Liberties, Status)

1993	1994	1995	1996	1997	1998	1999	2000	2001	2002	2003
3,3PF	3,3PF	3,3PF	3,3PF	3,3PF	3,3PF	3,3PF	3,3PF	1,2F	1,2F	1,2F

Overview:

In June 2002, the Surinamese police deported to the United States Carlos Bolas, a member of the Colombian Revolutionary Armed Forces (FARC) guerrillas, to face charges of drug trafficking and murder. U.S. authorities say that Bolas, in addition to providing cocaine to Colombian traffickers in exchange for arms, money, and equipment, also was involved in the murder of three American activists in 2000. In October, authorities from neighboring Guyana complained that Suriname is a major supply route for illegal arms used in a crime wave gripping the Guyanese capital of Georgetown.

The Republic of Suriname achieved independence from the Netherlands in 1975, which had acquired it as a result of the Treaty of Breda with the British in 1667. Five years after independence, a military coup, which brought Desi Bouterse to power as the head of a regime that brutally suppressed civic and political opposition, initiated a decade of military intervention in politics. In 1987, Bouterse permitted elections under the constitution, which provides for the directly elected, 51-seat National Assembly, which serves a five-year term and selects the state president. The New Front for Democracy and Development, a three-party coalition, handily won the 1987 elections. The military-organized National Democratic Party (NDP) won just three seats.

In 1990, the army ousted President Ramsewak Shankar, and Bouterse again took power. International pressure led to new elections in 1991. The New Front, a coalition of mainly East Indian, Creole, and Javanese parties, won a majority, although the NDP increased its share to 12. The National Assembly selected the Front's candidate, Ronald Venetiaan, as president. Bouterse quit the army in 1992 in order to lead the NDP. In the May 25, 2000, national elections, Venetiaan's center-right New Front garnered the majority of 51 National Assembly seats—three times as many as its closest rival.

The May 2001 death of a labor leader, who was to be the star witness in a trial against Bouterse and others accused of 15 political killings, initially appeared to rob the prosecution of key testimony needed to convict the former narcotics-running strongman. However, the government vowed that testimony given by the witness during a preliminary hearing would be submitted in the trial by the judge who questioned him, a move defense lawyers said they would oppose, claiming they will be denied the right to cross-examine the witness. The loss of the lone survivor of the December 8, 1982, massacre of 16 Bouterse opponents came amidst a renewed push by the Dutch to bring the retired army colonel to account for the murders and for his role in the 1982 coup. The once all-powerful dictator had already been tried and convicted by a Dutch court in absentia on charges of having introduced more than two tons of cocaine into the Netherlands between 1989 and 1997.

Political Rights and Civil Liberties: Citizens of Suriname can change their government democratically. Political parties largely reflect the cleavages in Suriname's ethnically complex society. A record of 23 parties competed in the 2000 elections. Civic institutions remain weak. The judiciary is weak, is susceptible to political influence, and suffers from ineffectiveness and a huge backlog of cases. The civilian police abuse detainees, particularly during arrests, guards mistreat prisoners, and the prisons are dangerously overcrowded. The February 2001 release of 100 prisoners from the Paramaribo prison, which authorities said was done to accommodate overcrowded conditions there, created worries about rising crime in what was still one of the safest countries in the Western Hemisphere.

The government generally respects freedom of expression. Radio is both public and private. A number of small commercial radio stations compete with the government-owned radio and television broadcasting system. State-broadcast media generally offer pluralistic viewpoints.

Both indigenous and tribal peoples, the latter called Maroons—the descendants of escaped African slaves who formed autonomous communities in the rain forest in the seventeenth and eighteenth centuries—reside within Suriname's borders. Indigenous people number 12,000 to 15,000 people (approximately 4 percent of the population); Maroons number 40,000 to 50,000. Their rights to their lands and resources, to cultural integrity, and to the autonomous administration of their affairs are not recognized in Surinamese law. Discrimination against indigenous peoples and Maroons is widespread.

Constitutional guarantees of gender equality are not enforced, and the Asian Marriage Act allows parents to arrange marriages for their children without their consent. Human rights organizations function relatively freely. Several organizations specifically address violence against women, reports of the trafficking of Brazilian women for prostitution, and related issues. Despite their central role in agriculture and food production, 60 percent of rural women, particularly those in tribal communities, live below the poverty level.

Workers can join independent trade unions, and the labor movement is active in politics. Collective bargaining is legal and conducted fairly widely. Civil servants have no legal right to strike.

Swaziland

Polity: Traditional monarchy
Economy: Capitalist
Population: 1,100,000
PPP: $4,492
Life Expectancy: 40

Political Rights: 6
Civil Liberties: 5
Status: Not Free

Religious Groups: Zionite [a blend of Christianity and indigenous ancestral worship] (40 percent), Roman Catholic (20 percent), Muslim (10 percent), other (30 percent)
Ethnic Groups: African (97 percent), European (3 percent)
Capital: Mbabane

Ten-Year Ratings Timeline (Political Rights, Civil Liberties, Status)

1993	1994	1995	1996	1997	1998	1999	2000	2001	2002	2003
6,5NF	6,5NF	6,5NF	6,5NF	6,5NF	6,5NF	6,5NF	6,5NF	6,5NF	6,5NF	6,5NF

Overview:
The Constitutional Drafting Committee worked on a draft constitution that was expected to be revealed early in 2003, following five years of work by the Constitutional Review Commission. Party politics are expected to remain banned, and the monarchy is expected to continue to wield absolute power. Although the commission assembled

what it claimed were the views of ordinary Swazis regarding the type of government they want, no record of those submissions has been released, nor has there been an accounting of how many Swazis presented their views or what they said. To counter the draft constitution, Lawyers for Human Rights was drafting its own version of a new constitution in 2002. The group envisions a constitutional monarchy, a multiparty system, and a bill of rights that includes rights for women.

Swaziland, Africa's last remaining absolute monarchy, is the only southern African country without an elected government. King Mswati III is the latest monarch of the Dlamini dynasty, under which the Swazi kingdom expanded and contracted in conflicts with neighboring groups. Britain declared the kingdom a protectorate to prevent Boer expansion in the 1880s and assumed administrative power in 1903. In 1968, Swaziland regained its independence, and an elected parliament was added to the traditional kingship and chieftaincies. Sobhuza II, Mswati's predecessor, who died in 1983, ended the multiparty system in favor of the *tinkhundla* (local council) system in 1973.

In a letter, Father Claudio Avallone, who formerly resided in Swaziland, in 2002 accused King Mswati III of abusing tradition and of failing to alleviate poverty. The letter was authorized by the Roman Catholic archbishop in Swaziland. The Swaziland Democratic Alliance, an umbrella group of labor unions, human rights organizations, and political parties, endorsed the letter. The government in 2002 passed the Internal Security Bill, which upholds a ban on political opposition activity and stipulates that citizens can sue the organizers of protest marches if there is property damage resulting from demonstrations. The government action could have been aimed at stemming protests expected to follow the release of the draft constitution in 2003.

Most Swazis remain engaged in subsistence agriculture. Many Swazi families depend on income from men working in South African mines. AIDS has taken a toll in Swaziland, where an estimated one in three people are infected with HIV. The monarchy provoked anger in 2002 when the king insisted on buying a $45 million jet while one-quarter of Swazis were suffering from food shortages resulting from poor harvests. The government in July 2002 announced that it was establishing formal diplomatic relations with Libya. The move was seen as an effort to seek a possible new source of development aid because the United States conditions aid on democratic reform.

Political Rights and Civil Liberties: Swazis are barred from exercising their right to elect their representatives or to change their government freely. All of Swaziland's citizens are subjects of an absolute monarch, King Mswati III. Royal decrees carry the full force of law. Voting in October 1998 legislative elections was marked by very low turnout and was neither open nor fair. It was based on the Swazi tinkhundla system of closely controlled nominations and voting that seeks to legitimatize the rule of King Mswati III and his Dlamini clan. Security forces arrested and briefly detained labor and other pro-democracy leaders before the elections and after a series of bomb blasts. The 55 elected members of the National Assembly were government approved and were joined by 10 royal appointees. The king also appoints 20 members of the Senate, with the remaining 10 selected by the National Assembly.

A Swazi high court in August acquitted opposition leader Mariko Masuku, of the People's United Democratic Movement. He was detained in late 2001 and charged with sedition.

The dual-system judiciary, which is based on Western and traditional law, is generally independent in most civil cases, although the royal family and the government can influence the courts. Swaziland's judicial system suffered a setback in December 2002, when six South African judges on the country's court of appeals resigned after the prime minister said the government would ignore court judgments that curbed the king's power. The judges had ruled that the king was acting unconstitutionally in ruling by decree and overturning court decisions. The government's relationship with the courts had been strained since the mother of an 18-year-old woman went to court to demand that her daughter be returned after palace aides allegedly abducted her from school to become the king's tenth wife. The government sent authorities, including the police commissioner and army commander, to tell the three judges presiding over the case that they must dismiss the lawsuit or resign.

There are regular reports of police brutality, including torture and beating. Security forces generally operate with impunity. However, prison conditions generally meet Western standards.

Freedom of expression is seriously restricted, especially regarding political issues or matters concerning the royal family. Legislation bans publication of any criticism of the monarchy. Self-censorship is widespread. Broadcast and print media from South Africa are received in the country. There is one independent radio station, but it broadcasts religious programming.

Freedom of religion is respected, although there are no formal constitutional provisions protecting the practice. The government restricts freedom of assembly and association. The Legal Code provides some protection against sexual harassment, but in general Swazi women encounter discrimination in both formal and customary law. Employment regulations requiring equal pay for equal work are obeyed unevenly. Married women are considered minors, requiring spousal permission to enter into almost any form of economic activity, and they are allowed only limited inheritance rights. Violence against women is common despite traditional strictures against it.

The Swaziland Federation of Trade Unions, the country's largest labor organization, has been a leader in demands for democratization. Unions are able to operate independently, and workers in all elements of the economy, including the public sector, can join unions. Wage agreements are often reached by collective bargaining, and 80 percent of the private workforce is unionized.

Sweden

Polity: Parliamentary democracy
Economy: Mixed capitalist
Population: 8,900,000
PPP: $24,277
Life Expectancy: 80

Political Rights: 1
Civil Liberties: 1
Status: Free

Religious Groups: Lutheran (87 percent), Roman Catholic, Eastern Orthodox, other
Ethnic Groups: Swedish (89 percent), Finnish (2 percent), other, including Lapp (Saami) (9 percent)
Capital: Stockholm

Ten-Year Ratings Timeline (Political Rights, Civil Liberties, Status)

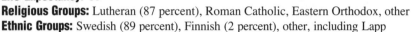

1993	1994	1995	1996	1997	1998	1999	2000	2001	2002	2003
1,1F	1,1F	1,1F	1,1F	1,1F	1,1F	1,1F	1,1F	1,1F	1,1F	1,1F

Overview:
Since 1998, Prime Minister Goran Persson, who was re-elected in September, has led a left-of-center coalition including his Social Democratic Party (SDP), the formerly Communist Left Party, and the Green Party. Sweden's historical position of neutrality was seriously threatened when the government presented a more pragmatic approach to parliament. A date finally was set for a referendum on whether the country should join the European Monetary Union (EMU).

Sweden is a constitutional monarchy and a multiparty parliamentary democracy. After monarchical alliances with Finland, Denmark, and Norway between the eleventh and nineteenth centuries, Sweden emerged as a modern democracy.

Sweden has remained nonaligned and neutral since World War I. However, the government presented to parliament in February a more pragmatic approach to security than the traditional neutrality policy. Although retaining its commitment to remain outside military alliances, the shift in Sweden's policy reflects its EU membership and awareness that intervention in foreign arenas may serve Swedish interests. Discussion regarding NATO membership increased, but most political parties remained opposed to membership. Nevertheless, Sweden is a member of NATO's Partnership for Peace program.

With parliamentary support from the Left and Green parties, the minority SDP government continued in power, following the outcome of the general election on September 15, 2002. On November 29, parliamentary leaders agreed to hold a referendum on Swedish membership in the EMU on September 14, 2003. While the SDP leadership favors joining, the Left and Green parties oppose EMU membership.

The European Parliament amended in May the 1997 European Community Directive on privacy in telecommunications, which obliges member states to retain all telecommunications data on private citizens for one to two years and to provide the relevant authorities unrestricted access to this data to assist law enforcement officials in eradicating crime.

Political Rights and Civil Liberties: Swedes can change their government democratically. The 310-member, unicameral Riksdag (parliament) is elected every four years through universal suffrage. To ensure proportionality for all parties that secure more than 4 percent of the vote, 39 additional representatives are selected from a national pool of candidates.

Citizens abroad are entitled to vote by absentee ballot in national elections, and non-nationals in residence for three years may vote in local elections. The Saami community elects its own local parliament, which has significant powers over education and culture and serves as an advisory body to the government. The role of King Carl XVI Gustaf, who was crowned in 1973, is ceremonial. The prime minister is appointed by the speaker of the house and confirmed by the Riksdag.

The media are independent. Most newspapers and periodicals are privately owned. The government subsidizes daily newspapers regardless of their political affiliation. The ethnic press is entitled to the same subsidies as the Swedish press. The Swedish Broadcasting Corporation and the Swedish Television Company broadcast weekly radio and television programs in several immigrant languages. Reporters Sans Frontieres (RSF) ranked Sweden (tied with Germany and Portugal) seventh in press freedom in the world in its Worldwide Press Freedom Index for 2002. However, RSF condemned the harassment of journalists investigating neo-Nazi activities by members of extreme-right groups.

In December 2001, the Council of the European Union adopted by "written procedure" antiterrorist legislation requiring member states to prevent "the public" from offering "any form of support, active or passive" to terrorists and to check all refugees and asylum seekers for terrorist connections. Human rights groups criticized the legislation because it does not distinguish between conscious or unconscious assistance, treats would-be immigrants as criminals, and was not debated in parliament before being adopted.

Citizens may freely express their ideas and criticize their government. The government is empowered to prevent publication of national security information. A quasi-governmental body censors extremely graphic violence from films, videos, and television programs.

International human rights groups have criticized Sweden for its immigration policies, which have severely limited the number of refugees admitted annually. Stricter asylum criteria were adopted in the 1990s after decades of relatively relaxed rules. Nordic immigrants may become citizens after two years, while others must wait a minimum of five years. Critics charge that the country does not systematically provide asylum seekers with adequate legal counsel or access to an appeals process.

Religious freedom is constitutionally guaranteed. Eighty-seven percent of the population is Lutheran. On January 1, 2000, Sweden separated the Church of Sweden from the state. The move reduced the church's subsidies and redirected the monies to other religious institutions, including those of Catholics, Muslims, and Jews. The growing numbers of non-Lutherans in Sweden prompted the move. There are approximately 200,000 Muslims, 160,000 Roman Catholics, 100,000 Eastern Orthodox, and 16,000 Jews in Sweden.

Freedom of assembly and association is guaranteed, as are the rights to strike and participate in unions. Strong and well-organized trade union federations represent 90 percent of the labor force.

The country's independent judiciary includes the Supreme Court, 6 courts of appeal, 100 district courts, and a parallel system of administrative courts. On the seventh anniversary of the death of Osmo Vallo, 41, a Finn, in police custody, Amnesty International in May reiterated its concern that no one has been held accountable for his ill-treatment. Transparency International ranked Sweden fifth on its 2002 Corruption Perceptions Index, third among EU member states.

Women constitute approximately 45 percent of the labor force, but their wage levels lag behind those of men. Approximately 45 percent of the members of parliament are women, the highest proportion in the world.

Switzerland

Polity: Parliamentary democracy (federal)
Economy: Capitalist
Population: 7,300,000
PPP: $28,769
Life Expectancy: 80
Religious Groups: Roman Catholic (46.1 percent), Protestant (40 percent), other (13.9 percent)
Ethnic Groups: German (65 percent), French (18 percent), Italian (10 percent), Romansch (1 percent), other (6 percent)
Capital: Bern

Political Rights: 1
Civil Liberties: 1
Status: Free

Ten-Year Ratings Timeline (Political Rights, Civil Liberties, Status)

1993	1994	1995	1996	1997	1998	1999	2000	2001	2002	2003
1,1F	1,1F	1,1F	1,1F	1,1F	1,1F	1,1F	1,1F	1,1F	1,1F	1,1F

Overview:
Switzerland became a full member of the United Nations and continued to build a relationship with the EU through bilateral accords, while continuing to reject full EU membership. Nevertheless, criticism of Switzerland's notoriously secret banking system continued. Swiss voters narrowly rejected a proposal to severely tighten the country's asylum application laws.

With the exception of a brief period of centralized power under Napoleonic rule, Switzerland has remained a confederation of local communities as established in the Pact of 1291. Most responsibility for public affairs rests at the local and cantonal levels. The 1815 Congress of Vienna formalized the country's borders and recognized its perpetual neutrality. Switzerland is often cited as a rare example of peaceful coexistence in a multiethnic state. The republic is divided into 20 cantons and 6 half-cantons and includes German, French, Italian, and Romansch communities.

Switzerland has been governed by a four-party coalition—the left-wing Social-Democratic Party (SP), the populist right-wing Swiss People's Party (SVP), the right-wing Radical Democratic Party (FDP), and the center-right Christian Democratic Party (CVP)—since 1999. The composition of the seven-member executive Federal Council (Bundesrat)—in which the SP, the FDP, and the CVP have two seats each and the SVP only one—is a major bone of contention.

Officially neutral and nonaligned, Switzerland became a UN member state on September 10 2002, following a March 3 referendum. The Bilateral Accord I between Switzerland and the EU took effect June 1, 2002; it allows greater freedom of movement between the two areas. Bilateral Accord II negotiations began in late 2002—the main obstacle being Swiss banking secrecy, criticism of which intensified following the terrorist attacks on the United States on September 11, 2001. Switzerland is a member of the European Free Trade Association and NATO's Partnership for Peace program.

In June 2002, victims of the former South African apartheid regime launched legal proceedings against Swiss banks UBS and Credit Suisse. UBS and Credit Suisse were heavily involved in the gold trade at the time, and South Africa was, and remains, a leading gold producer.

Political Rights and Civil Liberties: The Swiss can change their government democratically. Free and fair elections are held at regular intervals. Initiatives and referenda give citizens an additional degree of involvement in the legislative process. The cantonal system allows considerable local autonomy, and localities' linguistic and cultural heritages are zealously preserved.

Switzerland's Federal Assembly (parliament) consists of a 200-seat lower house (the National Council, elected by the Swiss people) and an upper house (the Council of States, elected by the cantons). The parliament appoints the seven-member Federal Council (Bundesrat), which exercises executive authority. The ceremonial office of president rotates annually.

The right to free speech is protected. There are private television and radio stations as well as privately owned publications in each of the most common languages. All are free from governmental interference. Reporters Sans Frontieres ranked Switzerland (tied with Costa Rica) 15th in press freedom in the world in its Worldwide Press Freedom Index for 2002.

Freedoms of assembly, association, and religion are observed. While no single state church exists, many cantons support one or several churches. Unions are independent of the government and political parties, and approximately one-third of the workforce holds union membership.

The judicial system functions primarily at the cantonal level, with the exception of the federal Supreme Court which reviews cantonal court decisions involving federal law. Switzerland's judiciary is independent.

Foreigners constitute 20 percent of the population of Switzerland, which has the strictest naturalization laws in Europe. Immigrants must live in the country for at least 12 years before obtaining citizenship. Towns can hold public votes on whether to grant foreign residents citizenship. The Swiss narrowly rejected a proposal on November 24, 2002, to stop granting asylum to foreigners who arrive overland via any country Switzerland considers a potential safe haven. All of Switzerland's neighbors are considered safe, and with new carrier sanctions, approval would have made it difficult for foreigners to apply for asylum. The country's antiracist law prohibits racist or anti-Semitic speech and actions, and is strictly enforced by the government.

The use of hard drugs has been one of the country's most pernicious social ailments. Government-sanctioned heroin clinics have been operating in Switzerland since the mid-1980s. In 1995, federal laws aimed at dissuading drug traffickers from entering Switzerland authorized pretrial detention of legal residents for as long as nine months.

Refusal to perform military service is a criminal offence. Every male over 18 must be prepared for military service, and many are issued weapons for this purpose. The Optional Protocol to the Convention on the Rights of the Child on the involvement of children in armed conflict raised to 18 the minimum age for direct participation in hostilities and for compulsory government recruitment as of June 2002.

Transparency International ranked Switzerland 12th (tied with Norway) on its 2002 Corruption Perception Index.

Despite a 1996 gender equality law, women still face some barriers to political and social advancement. Only two women serve in the Bundesrat, and women occupy just 23 percent of parliamentary seats. Women were not granted universal suffrage until 1971, and the half-canton Appenzell-Innerrhoden did not relinquish its status as the last bastion of all-male suffrage in Europe until 1990. Until the mid-1980s, women were prohibited from participating in the Bundesrat. The law provides women 10 weeks of maternity leave but no salary guarantee.

Syria

Polity: Dominant party (military dominated)
Political Rights: 7
Civil Liberties: 7
Economy: Mixed statist
Status: Not Free
Population: 17,200,000
PPP: $3,556
Life Expectancy: 70
Religious Groups: Sunni Muslim (74 percent), other
Ethnic Groups: Arab (90 percent), other, including Kurd and Armenian (10 percent)
Capital: Damascus

Ten-Year Ratings Timeline (Political Rights, Civil Liberties, Status)

1993	1994	1995	1996	1997	1998	1999	2000	2001	2002	2003
7,7NF	7,7NF	7,7NF	7,7NF	7,7NF	7,7NF	7,7NF	7,7NF	7,7NF	7,7NF	7,7NF

Overview:

Political and civil liberties in Syria continued to deteriorate in 2002, under the weight of arrests and trials of leading reform advocates. Whether this reversal signifies President Bashar Assad's loss of authority vis-à-vis the regime's "old guard" or the consolidation of his power is the subject of intense debate by outside observers, but it is clear that sweeping reform of the repressive and corrupt political system built by his father is not on the horizon.

Located at the heart of the Fertile Crescent, the Syrian capital of Damascus is the oldest continuously inhabited city in the world and once controlled a vast empire extending from Europe to India. The modern state of Syria is a comparatively recent entity, established by the French after World War I and formally granted independence in 1946. The pan-Arab Baath Party, which seized control of Syria 40 years ago, has long sought to extend its writ beyond Syrian borders.

For all its pan-Arab pretensions, however, the Syrian government has been dominated by Alawites, adherents of an offshoot sect of Islam who constitute just 12 percent of the population, since a 1970 coup brought Gen. Hafez Assad to power. For the next 30 years, the Assad regime managed to maintain control of the majority Sunni Muslim population only by brutally suppressing all dissent. In 1982, government forces stormed the northern town of Hama to crush a rebellion by the Muslim Brotherhood and killed up to 20,000 insurgents and civilians in a matter of days.

In 2000, Assad's son and successor, Bashar, inherited control of a country with one of the most stagnant economies and highest rates of population growth in the region, with skyrocketing unemployment estimated at more than 20 percent anually. In his inaugural speech, the young Syrian leader pledged to eliminate government corruption, revitalize the economy, and establish a "democracy specific to Syria, which takes its roots from its history, and respects its society." After his ascension, Assad permitted a loose network of public figures from all sectors of civil society to organize private gatherings to discuss the country's social, economic, and political problems. Under the guise of conducting an anticorruption campaign, the new president sidelined potential rivals within the regime.

In September, 99 liberal Syrian intellectuals released a statement calling on the government to end the state of emergency imposed by the Baath Party in 1963 and to respect public freedoms. Assad initially responded by releasing more than 600 political prisoners, closing the notorious Mazzeh prison, allowing scores of exiled dissidents to return home, reinstating dissidents who had been fired from state-run media outlets and universities, and instructing the state-run media to give voice to reformers. To the astonishment of outside observers, the government-run daily *Al-Thawra* published an op-ed piece by a prominent economist, Aref Dalilah, stating that one-party rule is "no longer effective." By the end of 2000, a parliamentary opposition bloc had begun to emerge under the leadership of Riad Seif, a maverick member of parliament who repeatedly called for an end to "political and economic monopolies" and restrictions on civil liberties from the floor of Syria's rubber-stamp People's Assembly.

The "Damascus Spring" reached its zenith in January 2001 with the release of a declaration, signed by more than 1,000 intellectuals, calling for comprehensive political reforms, the formation of two independent political parties (without official approval), and the establishment of the country's first privately owned newspaper. The following month, however, the regime abruptly ended its toleration of independent discussion forums and launched an escalating campaign of threat, intimidation, and harassment against the reform movement. By the end of the year, 10 leading reformists who had refused to abide by newly imposed restrictions on public freedoms were behind bars. During 2002, all of the so-called Damascus Ten were sentenced to prison terms, while the security agencies arrested more than a dozen prominent journalists, human rights activists, and political dissidents.

The regime's assault on political and civil liberties elicited little criticism from Western governments. In part, this was in return for Assad's cooperation in the war against al-Qaeda, his support for a key UN Security Council Resolution against Iraq in November, and the reduction in cross-border attacks into Israel by Syrian-backed guerrillas in south Lebanon during the latter half of 2002. It also reflected an assumption by Western observers that the crackdown stemmed from a weakening of Assad's position vis-à-vis the old guard and that outside pressure would benefit hard-liners. However, the crackdown has coincided with major administrative changes in the government and security forces that consolidate Assad's authority. Some dissidents suggest that the president exploited the Damascus Spring to outmaneuver his rivals and then ended it once he had gained full control of the regime.

Economic reform has also fallen by the wayside; dozens of economic reform laws remain unimplemented or have been put into effect half-heartedly, and hopes for a massive influx of foreign investment have faded. The bursting of the Zaytun Dam north of Hama in June, which flooded some 1,200 hectares of arable land and killed 20 people, highlighted both the decay of the once impressive infrastructure and the scope of bureaucratic mismanagement in Syria. The prospect of peace with Israel, which would free up funds for public sector investment and an expansion of social services, remains as distant as ever.

While regional tensions have bought the regime some forbearance domestically, there have been signs of disaffection boiling beneath the surface. In December, 150 Kurdish activists assembled outside the Syrian parliament and staged the country's largest antigovernment protest since the early 1980s. The organizers of the rally were promptly arrested.

Political Rights and Civil Liberties:

The regime of Bashar Assad wields absolute authority in Syria. Under the 1973 constitution, the president is nominated by the ruling Baath Party and approved by a popular referendum. In practice, these referendums are orchestrated by the regime (neither the late Hafez Assad nor his son Bashar ever won by less than a 99 percent margin), as are elections to the 250-member People's Assembly, which holds little independent legislative power. Independent political parties are illegal.

The Emergency Law overrides provisions of the Penal Code that prohibit arbitrary arrest and detention, giving the security agencies virtually unlimited authority to arrest suspects and hold them incommunicado for prolonged periods without charge. Many of the several hundred remaining political prisoners in Syria have never been tried for any offense. The security agencies, which operate independently of the judiciary, routinely extract confessions by torturing suspects and detaining members of their families. Government surveillance of dissidents is widespread.

At least four dissidents who returned from exile in 2002 were arrested shortly after their arrival. Although two were later released, one is still held incommunicado and another, Mohammed Hasan Nassar, died in custody.

While regular criminal and civil courts operate with some independence and generally safeguard defendants' rights, most politically sensitive cases are tried under two exceptional courts established under emergency law: the Supreme State Security Court (SSSC) and the Economic Security Court (ESC). Both courts deny or limit the defendant's right to appeal, limit access to legal counsel, try most cases behind closed doors, and admit as evidence confessions obtained through torture.

According to the U.S. State Department, the SSSC has never ordered a medical examination of any defendant who claimed to have been tortured.

In 2002, two members of parliament, Riad Seif and Maamoun al-Homsi, were sentenced by a criminal court to 5 years in prison, and eight other leading dissidents were sentenced by the SSSC to prison terms ranging from 2 to 10 years (one was later pardoned). Several former government officials, including a former transport minister, were convicted on corruption charges and sentenced by the ESC to prison terms.

Freedom of expression is heavily restricted. The government is allowed considerable discretion in punishing those who express dissent, by vaguely worded articles of the Penal Code and Emergency Law, such as those prohibiting the publication of information that opposes "the goals of the revolution," incites sectarianism, or "prevents authorities from executing their responsibilities." The broadcast media are entirely state-owned. While there are some privately owned newspapers and magazines, a new press law enacted in September 2001 permits the government to arbitrarily deny or revoke publishing licenses for reasons "related to the public interest," and compels privately owned print media outlets to submit all material to government censors on the day of publication. Syrians are permitted to access the Internet only through state-run servers, which block access to a wide range of Web sites. Satellite dishes are illegal, but generally tolerated.

The journalist Aziza Sbayni and her sister, Shirine, were arrested in May 2002 and continue to be held incommunicado awaiting trial before the SSSC on espionage charges. In October, the authorities arrested two journalists who had written articles critical of the government in Lebanese newspapers, Yahia al-Aous and Hayssam Kutaish, along with the latter's brother, Muhammad, and charged them with spying for Israel. In December, police arrested the Damascus bureau chief of the London-based Arabic daily *Al-Hayat*, Ibrahim Humaydi, on charges of "publishing false information." In November, Assad fired the top two officials in charge of state-run broadcast media after they had neglected to edit out portions of a program in which U.S. Ambassador Theodore Kattouf said that Syrian support for terrorist groups hindered its relations with the United States. At least three foreign-media correspondents were expelled during the year.

Freedom of assembly is largely nonexistent. While citizens can ostensibly hold demonstrations with prior permission from the Interior Ministry, in practice only the government, the Baath Party, or groups linked to them organize demonstrations. Freedom of association is restricted. All nongovernmental organizations (NGOs) must register with the government, which generally denies registration to reformist groups. In September 2002, the regime indicted four members of the Syrian Human Rights Association (Association des Droits de l'Homme en Syrie, or ADHS) for illegally establishing a human rights organization, for distributing an illegal publication (the ADHS magazine, *Tayyara*), and on other charges.

All unions must belong to the General Federation of Trade Unions (GFTU). Although ostensibly independent, the GFTU is headed by a member of the ruling Baath Party and is used by the government to control all aspects of union activity in Syria. Although strikes are legal (except in the agricultural sector), they rarely occur.

There is no state religion in Syria, though the constitution requires that the president be a Muslim, and freedom of worship is generally respected. The Alawite minority dominates the officer corps of the military and security forces. Since the eruption of an Islamist rebellion in the late 1970s, the government has tightly monitored mosques and controlled the appointment of Muslim clergy.

The Kurdish minority in Syria faces cultural and linguistic restrictions, and suspected Kurdish activists are routinely dismissed from schools and jobs. Some 200,000 Syrian Kurds are stateless and unable to obtain passports, identity cards, or birth certificates, which in turn prevents them from owning land, obtaining government employment, and voting. The September 2001 press law requires that owners and editors-in-chief of publications be Arabs. Suspected members of the banned Syrian Kurdish Democratic Unity Party (SKDUP) continued to be arrested and jailed in 2002. In March, a suspected member of the party, Hussein Daoud, was sentenced by the SSSC to two years in prison for "involvement in an attempt to sever part of the Syrian territory." At least two Kurds arrested during police raids in April and May remain in detention. In December, SKDUP leaders Hassan Saleh and Marwan Uthman were arrested after organizing a demonstration in front of parliament.

The government has promoted gender equality by appointing women to senior positions in all branches of government and providing equal access to education, but many discriminatory laws remain in force. A husband may request that the Interior Ministry block his wife from traveling abroad, and women are generally barred from leaving the country with their children unless they can prove that the father has granted permission. Syrian law stipulates that an accused rapist can be acquitted if he marries his victim, and it provides for reduced sentences in cases of "honor crimes" committed by men against female relatives for alleged sexual misconduct. Personal status law for Muslim women is governed by *Sharia* (Islamic law) and is discriminatory in marriage, divorce, and inheritance matters. Violence against women is widespread, particularly in rural areas.

Taiwan

Polity: Presidentia-par-
liamentary democracy
Economy: Mixed
capitalist
Population: 22,500,000
PPP: na
Life Expectancy: 75

Political Rights: 2*
Civil Liberties: 2
Status: Free

Religious Groups: Buddhist, Confucian, Taoist (93 percent), Christian
Ethnic Groups: Taiwanese (84 percent), mainland Chinese (14 percent),
aborigine (2 percent)
Capital: Taipei
Ratings Change: Taiwan's political rating declined from 1 to 2 due to changes in the
survey methodology.

Ten-Year Ratings Timeline (Political Rights, Civil Liberties, Status)

1993	1994	1995	1996	1997	1998	1999	2000	2001	2002	2003
3,3PF	4,4P	3,3PF	3,3PF	2,2F	2,2F	2,2F	2,2F	1,2F	1,2F	2,2F

Overview:

With elections looming in 2004, President Chen Shui-bian saw his popularity slide amid a series of policy reversals and criticism that he hasn't done enough to improve economic ties with China. Prospects for closer relations between Taiwan and the mainland appeared dim at year's end, with the two sides unable to agree on a framework for long-awaited talks over improved trade, travel, and communications links. As always, the sticking point is the underlying question of whether Taiwan will eventually be reunited with the mainland or will formally become an independent state.

Located some 100 miles off the southeast coast of China, Taiwan became the home of the Koumintang (KMT), or Nationalist, government-in-exile in 1949, when Communist forces overthrew the Nationalists following two decades of civil war on the mainland. While Taiwan is de facto independent, Beijing considers it to be a renegade province of China and has long threatened to invade if the island formally declares independence.

After four decades of authoritarian KMT rule, Taiwan's democratic transition began in 1987, when the government lifted martial law after 38 years. The KMT's Lee Teng-hui in 1988 became the first native-Taiwanese president. His election broke a stranglehold on politics by mainland refugees, who, along with their descendants, make up 14 percent of Taiwan's population.

In his 12 years in office, Lee oversaw far-reaching political reforms including Taiwan's first multiparty legislative elections in 1991 and direct presidential elections in 1996. Lee also played down the KMT's historic commitment to eventual reunification with China, promoting instead a Taiwanese national identity that undermined Beijing's claim that there is only "one China."

The victory by Chen, of the opposition Democratic Progressive Party (DPP), in the 2000 presidential election signaled that Taiwan would continue promoting an independent identity but also would pursue closer relations with the mainland. With Lee barred by term limits from seeking reelection, Chen and his two rivals all pledged to reverse the outgoing president's policy and seek warmer economic ties across the Taiwan Strait. The main difference between the candidates on mainland policy involved the issue that has polarized Taiwanese politics in recent years: whether Taiwan's long-term goal should be reunification with the mainland or outright independence.

Chen, a former Taipei mayor, downplayed but did not renounce his DPP's core position that Taiwan eventually should be independent. James Soong, a former KMT heavyweight who ran as an independent, seemed to favor outgoing president Lee's policy of gradually moving Taiwan toward formal independence without taking an explicit pro-independence line. Meanwhile, Vice President Lien Chan, who succeeded Lee as KMT leader, tried to return the KMT to its historic policy of supporting eventual reunification with China. With an 82 percent turnout, Chen won 39 percent of the vote, Soong, 37 percent, and Lien, 23 percent.

The DPP followed up on its victory in the presidential election by sweeping the conservative KMT out of parliamentary power, for the first time, in the December 2001 legislative elections. The victory gave Chen a freer hand to pass legislation and suggested that KMT leader Lien's advocacy of eventual reunification resonates little with the island's native-Taiwanese majority. The DPP won 87 of parliament's 225 seats, up from 70 in 1998, while the KMT took 68, down from 123. The new People's First Party, headed by KMT defector Soong, won 46 seats. The Taiwan Solidarity Union, backed by former president Lee, won 13 seats, and two minor parties and independents took the remainder.

Local elections in December 2002 may have breathed new life into the KMT. The party's Ma Ying-jeou, 52, was overwhelmingly reelected as mayor of the capital Taipei. He could be a challenger to Chen in the 2004 elections, although both Soong and Lien may take another shot at the top post. Opinion polls, meanwhile, suggested that Chen's popularity had slumped to 30 to 40 percent late in the year from about 70 percent after his election. Under pressure from farmers and others, he suspended a plan to clean up ailing grassroots financial institutions that would have curbed their commercial operations.

The stalemate in cross-strait relations stems in part from Beijing's continued refusal to negotiate on opening direct links between Taiwan and the mainland unless Taipei concedes that such links are a domestic matter. Such a position would be tantamount to Taiwan's formally conceding that it is not independent.

Eventually, however, Taiwan's recent entry into the World Trade Organization should make it possible for its businessmen to invest directly in China and easier for them to import goods from the mainland. Current restrictions push up costs for the 50,000 Taiwanese businesses operating there. At the same time, closer investment links would accelerate what has been an exodus of Taiwanese factories to the mainland in search of cheaper wages. Analysts say that Taiwan must respond by boosting its high-end manufacturing and services industries.

Political Rights and Civil Liberties:

Taiwanese can change their government through elections and enjoy most basic rights. The constitution vests executive power in a president who is directly elected for a four-year term. The president appoints the prime minister and can dissolve the legislature. The latter is directly elected for a three-year term and can dismiss the prime minister and cabinet in no-confidence votes.

The Chen Administration has taken steps toward cracking down on the vote buying and on links between politicians and organized crime that were widely believed to have flourished under KMT rule. The Justice Department, for example, indicted more than 3,700 persons for vote buying related to the 2001 legislative and local elections.

The sheer number of people indicted, however, suggests that official corruption is still a problem. Two alleged scandals in 2002 further stoked these concerns. The chief shareholder in a development company admitted that she made large loans to several DPP and KMT politicians to win favorable treatment for the company. Meanwhile, police in Kao-hsiung, Taiwan's second-largest city, detained Chu An-hsiung in December for allegedly paying several other city councilors to vote for him as speaker of the municipal body. The Berlin-based Transparency International watchdog group ranked Taiwan in a tie for 29th place out of 102 countries in its annual corruption survey for 2002, with top-ranked Finland being the least corrupt country.

Taiwan's judiciary is independent, the U.S. State Department's annual global human rights report for 2001 said. This marked an improvement from the previous year's report, which had described Taiwan's judiciary as not fully independent. Without directly explaining the upgraded assessment, the report, released in March 2002, cited recent government efforts to eliminate corruption and diminish political influence over the courts. These reforms included the creation of an independent committee to decide judicial appointments and promotions using secret balloting.

Defendants generally receive fair trials, according to the U.S. State Department report, but added however, that police occasionally use force to obtain confessions from suspects and pointed to evidence that such confessions play a role in some convictions.

Taiwanese newspapers report aggressively on corruption and other sensitive issues and carry outspoken editorials and opinion pieces. Laws used by past governments to jail journalists, however, remain on the books. "The most serious threat to press freedom in Taiwan remains the persistence of criminal penalties for libel, defamation, and insult," the New York-based Committee to Protect Journalists said in 2000. Meanwhile, government agents in March raided the Taipei office of the Hong Kong-based *Next* magazine after it published an article alleging that former president Lee's administration used secret government funds to curry influence abroad. In a positive development, the high court in 2000 upheld a lower court ruling that raised the legal barrier for news organizations to be convicted of libel.

Broadcast television stations are subject to some political influence by their owners, the U.S. State Department report said. The government, DPP, KMT, and armed forces are each the largest shareholder in, or are otherwise associated with, one of Taiwan's five islandwide broadcast television stations. The fifth is run by a nonprofit public foundation. Possible party influence over regular television is offset, however, by the availability to more than 80 percent of Taiwanese households of roughly 100 local and international private cable television stations.

The government has refused to license private, islandwide radio stations, though it has in recent years issued more than two dozen licenses for private regional stations. Critics say that many of these stations have limited broadcast ranges and can be heard only in sparsely-populated areas. Moreover, licensing rules require radio station owners to have more capital than actually is required to operate stations. The government says that the $50 million (U.S.$1.45 million) required capitalization is based on actual business costs. It also points out that radio stations serving designated ethnic groups or certain other socially beneficial purposes need put up only $1 million. Though no longer enforced, laws barring Taiwanese from advocating communism or independence from China remain on the books.

Taiwanese women have made impressive gains in recent years in business and the professions, but reportedly continue to face unofficial job discrimination. The government in 2001 passed a law banning gender discrimination in the workplace in response to charges by women's advocates that women are promoted less frequently and receive lower pay than their male counterparts and are sometimes forced to quit jobs because of age, marriage, or pregnancy. Women also hold relatively few senior posts in government and politics, although Annette Lu serves as the country's first-ever female vice president.

Rape and domestic violence are serious problems, according to the U.S. State Department report. Although recent laws allow officials to investigate complaints of domestic violence and to prosecute rape suspects, without the victims' actually pressing charges, cultural norms inhibit many victims from reporting these crimes to the police.

Taiwan's 400,000 aborigines face discrimination in mainstream society and, in general, have little input on major decisions affecting their lands, culture, and traditions, according to the U.S. State Department report. Ethnic Chinese developers often use "connections and corruption" to gain title to aboriginal land, and aborigines say that they are prevented from owning certain ancestral lands under government control, the report added. Moreover, anecdotal evidence suggests that the problem of child prostitution is particularly acute in the aboriginal community. The government tries to curb child prostitution through law enforcement measures such as raiding brothels.

Most Taiwanese workers can legally join trade unions, and roughly 30 percent are unionized. The law, however, restricts the right to strike with provisions that, for example, allow officials to order mediation of labor disputes and ban work stoppages while mediation is in progress. Collective bargaining is not practiced widely. Moreover, teachers, civil servants, and defense industry workers are barred entirely from joining unions or bargaining collectively. Some employers take advantage of illegal foreign workers by deducting money from their wages without their consent and having them work extended hours without overtime pay, the U.S. State Department report said.

Tajikistan

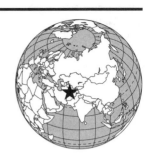

Polity: Presidential   **Political Rights:** 6
Economy: Mixed statist   **Civil Liberties:** 5*
Population: 6,300,000   **Status:** Not Free
PPP: $1,152
Life Expectancy: 68
Religious Groups: Sunni Muslim (85 percent),
Shi'a Muslim (5 percent), other (10 percent)
Ethnic Groups: Tajik (65 percent), Uzbek (25 percent),
Russian (4 percent), other (6 percent)
Capital: Dushanbe
Ratings Change: Tajikistan's civil liberties rating improved from 6 to 5 due to a gradual
strengthening of the rule of law and the renewal of civic life in the aftermath of a civil
war that ended in 1997.

Ten-Year Ratings Timeline (Political Rights, Civil Liberties, Status)

1993	1994	1995	1996	1997	1998	1999	2000	2001	2002	2003
6,6NF	7,7NF	7,7NF	7,7NF	7,7NF	6,6NF	6,6NF	6,6NF	6,6NF	6,6NF	6,5NF

Overview: The geopolitical effects of the September 11, 2001, terrorist attacks on the United States continued to reverberate in Tajikistan's foreign policy throughout 2002. This impoverished and formerly obscure Central Asian country worked to balance its growing strategic ties with the United States with its continued dependence on Russian security, while at the same time enjoying a warming in relations with its more powerful neighbor, Uzbekistan. Five years after the official end of its devastating civil war, Tajikistan continued to face serious economic problems that many analysts regard as a threat to the country's still-fragile stability.

Conquered by Russia in the late 1800s, Tajikistan was made an autonomous region within Uzbekistan in 1924 and a separate socialist republic of the U.S.S.R. in 1929. Tajikistan declared independence from the U.S.S.R. in September 1991, and two months later, former Communist Party leader Rakhman Nabiyev was elected president.

Long-simmering clan-based tensions, combined with various anti-Communist and Islamist movements, soon plunged the country into a five-year civil war for central government control. In September 1992, Communist hard-liners forced the resignation of President Nabiyev, who was replaced in November by leading Communist Party member Emomali Rakhmonov. The following month, Rakhmonov launched attacks that caused tens of thousands to flee into neighboring Afghanistan.

As the fighting continued, Rakhmonov was elected president in November 1994 after most opposition candidates either boycotted or were prevented from competing in the poll. March 1995 parliamentary elections, in which the majority of seats were won by pro-government candidates, were boycotted by the United Tajik Opposition (UTO), a coalition of various secular and Islamic opposition groups that emerged during the war as the main opposition force fighting against Rakhmonov's government.

Following a December 1996 ceasefire, Rakhmonov and UTO leader Said Abdullo

Nuri signed a formal peace agreement in Moscow on June 27, 1997, officially ending the civil war, which had claimed tens of thousands of lives and left several hundred thousand as refugees. The accord called for opposition forces to be merged into the regular army, granted an amnesty for UTO members, provided for the UTO to be allotted 30 percent of senior government posts, and established a 26-member National Reconciliation Commission, with seats evenly divided between the government and the UTO. The commission was charged with implementing the peace agreements, including preparing amendments for a referendum on constitutional changes that would lead to fair parliamentary elections.

During the next two years, the government and the UTO took steps towards implementing the peace accord. In a September 1999 referendum, voters approved a series of constitutional amendments permitting the formation of religion-based political parties. This move paved the way for the legal operation of the Islamic opposition, including the Islamic Renaissance Party (IRP), which constituted the backbone of the UTO. In November, President Rakhmonov was reelected president with a reported 97 percent of the vote in a poll criticized by international election observers for widespread irregularities.

As the final stage in the implementation of the 1997 peace accord, Tajikistan held elections in February 2000 for the 63-seat lower house of parliament. The People's Democratic Party (PDP) of President Rakhmonov received nearly 65 percent of the vote, followed by the Communist Party with 20 percent and the IRP, which was plagued by internal divisions, with 7 percent. Although the participation of six parties and a number of independent candidates in the poll provided some political pluralism, international election observers, including a joint mission by the OSCE and the United Nations, cited serious problems, including the exclusion of certain opposition parties, biased state media coverage, and a lack of transparency in the tabulation of votes. In March elections to the 33-seat upper house of parliament, in which regional assemblies elected 25 members and President Rakhmonov appointed the remaining 8, the PDP obtained the overwhelming majority of seats. After the elections, the National Reconciliation Commission was formally disbanded, and a UN observer mission withdrew in May 2000 after nearly six years in Tajikistan. However, important provisions of the peace accord remained unimplemented, with demobilization of opposition factions incomplete and the government failing to meet the 30 percent quota of senior government posts to be awarded to the UTO.

Following the September 11, 2001, attacks on the World Trade Center and the Pentagon, Tajikistan agreed to open its airspace for humanitarian flights during the U.S.-led war in Afghanistan and announced the arrival of advanced detachments of foreign troops. However, the government denied that it had plans to allow U.S. troops or warplanes to use its territory for military strikes against Afghanistan's then ruling Taliban. Tajikistan's cautious reaction stemmed from fears of possible retaliatory measures by Taliban forces, as well from domestic radical Islamists and others; while the IRP pursues its agenda through established political means, some former UTO members continue to engage in armed opposition against the national government. Tajikistan's participation in the U.S.-backed coalition was further complicated by its dependence on Russia for maintaining its national security, as Tajikistan remains the only Central Asian country in which Moscow has ground forces stationed.

The effects of September 11, 2001, continued to have an impact on Tajikistan's relations with its more powerful neighbors throughout 2002. The government's decision to strengthen ties with the United States as part of its antiterrorism campaign strained relations with Russia, which generally stood opposed to a long-term U.S. presence there. By contrast, its relations with Uzbekistan improved since September 11, as the security threat posed by Islamic radicals, such as the Islamic Movement of Uzbekistan (IMU), appeared to have lessened. In 1999 and 2000, Dushanbe had failed to stop the IMU, which sought the overthrow of the Uzbekistan government, from using Tajikistan as a transit country for armed incursions from Afghanistan into Uzbekistan. Both Tajikistan and Uzbekistan were also eager to improve trade and settle border disputes; in October, the two countries signed an agreement demarcating 86 percent of their shared border. In February, Tajikistan joined NATO's Partnership for Peace program, the last former Soviet republic to do so.

The poor state of Tajikistan's economy, which was devastated by the civil war, continues to be seen as a serious threat to the country's five-year peace. Three years of drought followed by violent rainfalls and swarms of locusts destroyed thousands of acres of crops. Average salaries are less than $10 a month, an estimated 80 percent of the population lives below the poverty line, and the gross domestic product remains less than half the size it was 10 years earlier.

Political Rights and Civil Liberties: Citizens of Tajikistan cannot change their government democratically. The 1994 constitution provides for a strong, directly elected executive who enjoys broad authority to appoint and dismiss officials. Amendments to the constitution adopted in a 1999 referendum further increased the powers of the president by extending his term in office from five to seven years and creating a full-time, bicameral parliament whose members would be appointed directly by the president or elected by indirect vote through local parliaments led by presidential appointees. Neither the country's presidential polls in 1994 and 1999 nor the parliamentary elections of 1995 and 2000 were free and fair.

Despite formal guarantees of freedom of speech and the press, media freedom remains severely curtailed by the government. Independent journalists continue to be threatened by removal of their accreditation, denial of access to state printing facilities, and acts of physical violence. The penal code criminalizes publicly defaming or insulting a person's honor or reputation. Consequently, self-censorship among journalists is widespread. Most newspapers are weeklies and suffer from low advertising revenues and poor circulations. In October, three journalists who were part of a workshop organized by a U.S.-based media training group, Internews, were forcibly conscripted into the Tajik army. Press freedom advocates maintain that the authorities had no right to conscript the journalists, who were from a region outside of the jurisdiction of the city where they were seized. In positive developments, the private broadcaster, TV Service, began providing independent programming in Dushanbe in July, and Asia-Plus became the first private radio station to broadcast in the capital in September. In June, criminal charges against Dodojon Atovulloev, the exiled editor of the independent opposition newspaper *Charogi Ruz*, were dropped. Atovulloev had been arrested in Moscow in July 2001 on charges of sedition and insulting President Emomali Rakhmonov and was threatened with extradition to Tajikistan; international pressure led to his release after six days in custody.

According to the 2002 U.S. State Department Report on International Religious Freedom, the government generally respects religious freedom in this predominantly Muslim country, although it monitors the activities of religious institutions to prevent them from becoming overtly political. Religious communities must register with the State Committee on Religious Affairs. During the year, the authorities reportedly closed a number of unregistered mosques and ordered the removal of some imams for their alleged involvement in politics; by law, religious officials are not allowed to belong to political parties. Members of Hizb-ut-Tahrir, which calls for the establishment of an Islamic caliph throughout the Muslim world, have been subject to arrest and imprisonment for subversion.

The state strictly controls freedom of assembly and association for organizations of a political nature. Nongovernmental and political groups must obtain permits to hold public demonstrations, and organizers of protests have at times faced government reprisals. Although a May 1998 ban on religious-based parties was lifted in September 1999, leading to the registration of the Islamic Renaissance Party (IRP), the government has stopped or limited the activities of certain other political parties. Although citizens have the legal right to form and join trade unions, labor rights are largely ignored in practice.

The judiciary is directly influenced by the executive branch, which most judges depend on for their positions, as well as by some armed paramilitary groups. Many judges are poorly trained and inexperienced, and bribery is reportedly widespread. Police routinely conduct arbitrary arrests of citizens and beat detainees to force them to confess to alleged crimes. In August, in the first such criminal convictions since Tajikistan gained independence, nine senior law enforcement officials were found guilty of using torture to extract confessions from suspects. Prison conditions have been described as life threatening because of overcrowding and unsanitary conditions.

High levels of criminal and political violence, including hostage taking and extortion, continue to affect the personal security of most citizens. Certain regions of the country remain largely under the control of former rebel fighters from the United Tajik Opposition (UTO) who have rejected the terms of the 1997 peace accord. Government and various former opposition groups have engaged in armed skirmishes, and high-level state officials have been targets for assassination. In March, seven former UTO members were found guilty of killing First Deputy Interior Minister Khabib Sanginov in April 2001. They received sentences including 16 to 25 years in prison or the death penalty.

The government imposes some restrictions on the right of its citizens to choose a place of residence and to travel. The process of obtaining an exit visa to travel abroad may take a month or longer and frequently requires the payment of bribes. Checkpoints manned by Interior Ministry troops and customs officials have extorted money from drivers and passengers, limiting their freedom of movement. Corruption, which is reportedly pervasive throughout the government, civil service, and business sectors, restricts equality of opportunity.

Although women are employed throughout the government and the business world, they continue to face traditional societal discrimination. Domestic violence is reportedly common, and there are credible reports of trafficking of women for prostitution. The participation of women in criminal activities, including the drug trade, has increased as a result of the country's widespread poverty.

Tanzania

Polity: Dominant party   **Political Rights:** 4
Economy: Mixed statist   **Civil Liberties:** 3*
Population: 37,200,000   **Status:** Partly Free
PPP: $523
Life Expectancy: 52
Religious Groups: Christian (30 percent), Muslim
(35 percent), indigenous beliefs (35 percent); Zanzibar
(more than 99 percent Muslim)
Ethnic Groups: African (99 percent), other, including Asian, European, and Arab
(1 percent)
Capital: Dar-es-Salaam
Ratings Change: Tanzania's civil liberties rating improved from 4 to 3 due to changes
in the survey methodology.

Ten-Year Ratings Timeline (Political Rights, Civil Liberties, Status)

1993	1994	1995	1996	1997	1998	1999	2000	2001	2002	2003
6,5PF	6,5NF	6,6NF	5,5PF	5,5PF	5,5PF	5,4PF	4,4PF	4,4PF	4,4PF	4,3PF

Overview: Parliament, dominated by the ruling Chama Cha Mapinduzi
(CCM) party, passed restrictive legislation in 2002 regarding anti-terrorism that gives the police and immigration officials sweeping powers to arrest illegal immigrants or anyone suspected to have links with terrorists. It also passed a law governing activities of nongovernmental organizations (NGOs) which could circumscribe civil liberties, including the freedoms of association and expression. As of the end of 2002, however, this law had yet to be implemented.

The parliament of the semi-autonomous region of Zanzibar and Pemba islands has endorsed amendments to its constitution, allowing the Zanzibari president to involve the opposition in the formation of an independent electoral commission. The amendment was passed in what is seen as an important step towards the implementation of a reconciliation agreement signed by the CCM and the rival Civic United Front (CUF) in October 2001 in a bid to end years of turmoil between the two parties.

After Tanzania gained independence from Britain in 1961, the CCM, under President Julius Nyerere, dominated the country's political life. The Zanzibar and Pemba islands were merged with Tanganyika to become the Union of Tanzania after Arab sultans who had long ruled the islands were deposed in a violent revolution in 1964. For much of his presidency, President Nyerere espoused a collectivist economic philosophy known in Swahili as *ujaama*. Although it may have been useful in promoting a sense of community and nationality, this policy resulted in significant economic dislocation and decline, the effects of which continue to be felt. During Nyerere's tenure, Tanzania also played an important role as a "Front Line State" in the international response to white-controlled regimes in southern Africa.

Nyerere retained strong influence after he officially retired in 1985. Although opposition parties were legalized in 1992, the CCM continues to dominate the country's political life. Progress towards democratic consolidation and strong economic growth remain inhibited by high levels of corruption and weak opposition parties.

Although Tanzania has avoided the civil strife that has racked many of its neighbors, and its economy is growing modestly, there are a number of serious issues that, if not addressed, could affect the country's long-term stability. These include relations between the mainland and the Zanzibar archipelago; the presence in Tanzania of 500,000 refugees from Burundi, the Democratic Republic of Congo, and Rwanda; and the need for relief from the country's $8 billion debt.

Tanzania held legislative and presidential elections in October 2000, the second since the reintroduction of multiparty politics. Incumbent president Benjamin Mkapa won reelection with about 70 percent of the vote, and the CCM won an overwhelming victory in the 275-member legislature. The conduct of these elections represented a modest improvement over the preceding polls in 1995.

The elections were marred, however, by fraudulent polls biased in favor of the ruling party in the federated semiautonomous islands of Zanzibar and Pemba. The status of these islands in relation to the mainland has long provoked tension. The opposition CUF and independent observers convincingly demonstrated that the ruling CCM had engaged in fraud to maintain itself in power. Subsequent rioting in Zanzibar in January 2001 resulted in the deaths of more than 40 people. In October the CCM and the CUF announced the agreement designed to resolve the political crisis and allow for more transparent government.

Political Rights and Civil Liberties: The ability of Tanzanians to freely choose their political leaders is not yet firmly entrenched in practice. Although the 2000 national elections avoided the massive logistical and administrative chaos of preceding elections, the CCM continues to enjoy considerable advantages of incumbency that inhibit the realistic prospect of alternation of power. In addition, the 2000 elections in Zanzibar demonstrated that progress towards more legitimate electoral processes is not uniform nationwide. Massive electoral irregularities prompted authorities to annul the vote in almost one-third of constituencies. Ballot papers arrived hours late in some areas, and many people were unable to vote. A claim by the CUF leader that the CCM had manipulated the election to avoid defeat was bolstered by observers from the Commonwealth and the Organization of African Unity. The October 2001 agreement to defuse the Zanzibar crisis represents a positive step, but the accord remains fragile.

The previous legislative and presidential elections, in 1995, had been the most open on mainland Tanzania since independence. The CCM's landslide legislative victory was seriously tainted, however, not only by poor organization but also by fraud and administrative irregularities. In addition, extensive use of state broadcasting and other government resources during the campaign favored the ruling party. The CCM won 80 percent of the 232 directly elected seats in the National Assembly.

The voting in Zanzibar was plainly fraudulent, with the island's high court summarily rejecting opposition demands for fresh polls.

Thirteen opposition parties have formal status. Some of them are active, but they tend to be divided and ineffective. The CUF has sought to establish significant support on the Tanzanian mainland, and its presidential candidate received the second-highest number of votes in the 2000 presidential elections. Another major opposition party, the National Convention for Constitution and Reform (NCCR-Mageuzi), whose leader, Augustine Mrema, was runner-up to President Benjamin Mkapa in the 1995 presidential election, has split. Parties with parliamentary representation receive government subsidies, but they criticize the low level of funding and the formula by which it is allocated.

Tanzania's judiciary has displayed signs of autonomy after decades of subservience to the one-party CCM regime, but it remains subject to considerable political influence. Constitutional protections for the right to free assembly are generally, but not always, respected. Laws allow rallies only by officially registered political parties, which may not be formed on religious, ethnic, or regional bases and cannot oppose the union of Zanzibar and the mainland. Freedom of religion is respected.

Print and electronic media are active, but media impact is largely limited to major urban areas. Private radio and television stations began receiving licenses at the beginning of 1994, but they are not allowed to cover more than 25 percent of the country's territory, according to the 1993 Broadcasting Act. The stated rationale for the limitation is to protect national interests. In Zanzibar the government controls the electronic media.

Arrest and pretrial detention laws are often ignored. The new legislation designed to strengthen the government's ability to deal with terrorist threats has raised civil liberties concerns. Police will not need warrants to detain people suspected of committing certain terrorism-related crimes. Prison conditions are harsh, and police abuses are said to be common. According to government estimates, there are approximately 45,000 inmates in the country's prisons although the prisons' collective capacity is only 21,000. Such overcrowding has caused widespread concern. Questions are raised regarding the safety and health of prisoners, including minors and women, who have been subjected to sexual harassment and human rights abuses.

Many nongovernmental organizations (NGOs) are active, and some have been able to influence the public policy process. The 2002 NGO Act passed by parliament, however, contains many serious flaws, including compulsory NGO registration backed by criminal sanctions, lack of appeals to the courts, and inconsistencies with other related existing legislation. The broad distribution of Tanzania's population among many ethnic groups has largely diffused potential ethnic rivalries that have racked neighboring countries. The refugee influx is currently a big burden for Tanzania, which alone hosts more than 800,000 refugees. It is also estimated that more than 26,000 refugees have been naturalized since 1961.

Women's rights guaranteed by the constitution and other laws are not uniformly protected. Especially in rural areas and in Zanzibar, traditional or Islamic customs discriminatory toward women prevail in family law, and women have fewer educational and economic opportunities. Domestic violence against women is reportedly common and is rarely prosecuted. Human rights groups have sought laws to bar forced marriages, which are most common among Tanzania's coastal peoples. The employment of children as domestic servants is widespread.

Workers do not have the right to organize and join trade unions freely. Essential workers are barred from striking. Other workers' right to strike is restricted by complex notification and mediation requirements. Collective bargaining effectively exists only in the small private (business) sector. Approximately 85 percent of Tanzania's people survive through subsistence agriculture. Economic decline in Zanzibar continues to dim the islands' prospects.

Corruption remains a serious problem, although the government has made some attempts to address it. The government developed a national action plan for the control of corruption. The Prevention of Corruption Bureau recorded an increasing number of reported incidents on corruption from 432 cases in 1998 to 1,461 cases at the end of 2000, although it is not clear whether this represents an increase in corruption or increased reporting and improved detection of corruption. Tanzania ranked 71st out of 102 countries on Transparency International's 2002 Corruption Perceptions Index. Interpol has warned that Tanzania has become a major transit center for drugs from Asia into Europe.

⬇Thailand

Polity: Parliamentary democracy
Economy: Capitalist-statist
Population: 62,600,000
PPP: $6,402
Life Expectancy: 72

Political Rights: 2
Civil Liberties: 3
Status: Free

Religious Groups: Buddhism (95 percent), Muslim (3.8 percent), other (1.2 percent)
Ethnic Groups: Thai (75 percent), Chinese (14 percent), other (11 percent)
Capital: Bangkok
Trend Arrow: Thailand received a downward trend arrow to reflect increasing official intimidation of the independent media, as well as an expansion of executive power over key administrative institutions.

Ten-Year Ratings Timeline (Political Rights, Civil Liberties, Status)

1993	1994	1995	1996	1997	1998	1999	2000	2001	2002	2003
3,4PF	3,5PF	3,5PF	3,4PF	3,3PF	3,3PF	2,3F	2,3F	2,3F	2,3F	2,3F

Overview:

Buoyed by the comfortable parliamentary majority enjoyed by his Thai Rak Thai (Thai Loves Thai, or TRT) party as well as his own considerable financial clout, Prime Minister Thaksin Shinawatra progressively expanded his control over Thailand's major political, administrative, and economic institutions in 2002. Bureaucratic reshuffles elevated Thaksin's political allies and relatives to positions of power, and reformist politicians and activists remain worried that the effectiveness of new anticorruption institutions is being systematically undermined. Relations with neighboring Burma soured in May, leading to the closure of the border for six months. An unexplained surge in violence in Thailand's southern provinces that left a number of policemen dead had abated by the end of the year.

Known as Siam until 1939, Thailand is the only Southeast Asian nation never colonized by a European country. Beginning with a 1932 coup that transformed the kingdom into a constitutional monarchy, the army ruled periodically for the next six decades. The army last seized power in 1991, when it overthrew a hugely corrupt elected government. After soldiers shot dead more than 50 pro-democracy protesters in Bangkok in March 1992, Thailand returned to civilian rule when the country's revered monarch, King Bhumibol Alduyadej, convinced the military to appoint a civilian prime minister.

Thailand's export-led economy registered strong growth in the decade prior to 1997 before being hit by the regional financial crisis. After spending billions of dollars fruitlessly defending the *baht* against speculators, the government floated the currency in July 1997 and agreed to a $17.2 billion bailout led by the IMF. As members of Bangkok's middle class protested against corruption and economic mismanagement, parliament approved a reformist constitution and elected the Democrat Party's Chuan Leekpai, a former prime minister with a clean reputation, to head a coalition government. The new constitution created independent elections and anticorruption bodies and introduced direct Senate elections. Hoping to stabilize the baht, the Chuan government kept interest rates high. The opposition blamed the tight monetary policy for pushing the economy into recession in 1998.

Criticizing the government for supposedly favoring the urban middle class over ordinary Thais, Thaksin, a former deputy prime minister who built his fortune in telecommunications, unseated Chuan in the January 2001 elections. During the campaign, Thaksin pledged to help poorer Thais hurt by the financial crisis by introducing cheap health care, a debt moratorium for farmers, and investment funds for each village. Thaksin's TRT party won 248 out of parliament's 500 seats and then formed a comfortable majority coalition government with three other parties. The TRT won the elections despite a December 2000 ruling by Thailand's new National Counter Corruption Commission (NCCC) that Thaksin had deliberately falsified wealth-disclosure statements as a cabinet minister in 1997. Had the Constitutional Court not cleared him in August 2001, Thaksin could have been banned from holding office for five years. Amid the distraction posed by Thaksin's court case, his government launched populist programs aimed at helping poorer Thais and small-business owners.

Since its election victory, the TRT has absorbed two of its smaller coalition partners, consolidating its hold over parliament. A September military reshuffle placed Thaksin's family members and close aides in positions of power, while an October cabinet reshuffle rewarded TRT supporters and several political allies who are facing impeachment proceedings for corruption or violation of the constitution. Also in October, controversial bureaucratic reform bills were passed into law despite concerns over the constitutionality of some of the articles by the opposition Democrat Party. Meanwhile, the administration has continued to undermine the authority of the NCCC and has failed to reestablish the credibility of the Anti-Money-Laundering Office (AMLO) following the implication of two of its officials in an illegal investigation.

Political Rights and Civil Liberties: Thailand's constitution vests executive power in a prime minister and his cabinet. The House of Representatives has 400 single-member districts and 100 party-list seats, all directly elected for four-year terms. The Senate has 200 members who are directly elected for six-year terms.

Thais can change their government through elections that are marred by fraud, irregularities, and some political killings. As in previous elections, candidates doled out huge sums of money to buy votes in the January 2001 balloting. Politicians handed out to voters at least 20 billion baht ($465 million) during the campaign and on election day, according to Bangkok's Nakhon Ratchsima Rajabhat Institute, which monitors poll fraud. In 62 districts, the Election Commission either disqualified candidates or warned them about graft allegations and ordered a second round of polling. The commission, however, took little or no action on many of the more than 1,000 allegations of fraud. Some critics suggested that Thaksin's party might have pressured commission members to overlook violations.

Observers say that official corruption is widespread and linked to trafficking and other illicit acts. Anecdotal evidence suggests that ordinary Thais often must bribe bureaucrats to receive basic government services and that officials routinely take bribes to ignore many types of crime. Transparency International's 2002 Corruption Perceptions Index ranked Thailand in 64th place out of 102 countries. In a positive development, the AMLO has indicted many small-level money launderers and has ordered police to seize the property and assets of many drug traffickers. The agency has acted under tough laws passed in 1999 that cover crimes ranging from white-collar fraud to prostitution.

Thai newspapers criticize government policies and report allegations of official corruption and human rights abuses, but journalists exercise some self-censorship regarding the monarchy and national security issues. However, media organizations came under increasing pressure from Thaksin's administration in 2002. Editions of the *Far Eastern Economic Review* and *The Economist* were banned early in the year, and in February the government threatened to deport two *Review* journalists on the grounds that they were a threat to national security. In March, after the administration banned its radio programs from being aired on the grounds that they "unreasonably criticized the government," the independent Nation Multimedia Group announced that it was halting all political coverage on its cable news channel pending an end to excessive political interference in its programming. Meanwhile, media organizations accused the government of intimidation after learning that the AMLO had been authorized to investigate the bank accounts of leading journalists and critical publications. The government or armed forces either directly or indirectly own or oversee most radio and broadcast television stations. By law, radio stations must renew their licenses annually. The 1941 Printing Act gives authorities the power to shut down media outlets. Several journalists were jailed throughout the year following the filing of libel suits by politicians.

Thais of all faiths worship freely, with Buddhism having the most followers. The constitution requires the government to "patronize and protect Buddhism and other religions," and the state actively subsidizes the activities of the three largest religious communities, according to the U.S. State Department's Report on International Religious Freedom for 2002.

The rights of peaceful assembly and association are generally respected. Bangkok's middle class and rural farmers frequently and freely hold rallies against governmental policies. Though not used in recent years, laws broadly prohibit verbally defaming the monarchy, inciting public disturbances, threatening national security, or insulting Buddhism. In addition, the constitution allows the government to restrict free expression on national security, public order, and other grounds.

In the workplace, employers often violate the country's poorly enforced labor laws, use child labor, and discriminate against union members and organizers. Unions can bargain collectively, but in practice private sector employers enjoy considerable economic leverage and generally set wages unilaterally. Less than 2 percent of Thai workers are unionized. Strikes are legal in the private sector but not for state enterprise workers. Press reports suggest that more than half of Thai workers, particularly those in rural areas, receive less than the minimum wage. Nongovernmental organizations (NGOs) say that upwards of one million Thai children work on family farms and that 2 to 4 percent of children between the ages of 6 and 14 work in urban jobs.

Though "the judiciary generally is regarded as independent, it is subject to corruption and has a reputation for venality," the U.S. State Department human rights report said. The judiciary also lacks a sufficient number of qualified judges and has huge case backlogs. Nevertheless, defendants generally receive adequate due process rights.

Thailand's poorly trained police frequently are implicated in wrongful killings and rights violations against criminal suspects and detainees. Officers at times kill armed drug traffickers and other criminal suspects while apprehending them. While police occasionally may be justified in using lethal force, at least some of the killings are unwarranted, according to NGOs and the press. In addition, authorities have investigated officers accused of raping or extorting sex from female detainees. Police also use torture to extract confessions or to punish and humiliate suspects, according to a June report issued by Amnesty International. Thai prisons and immigration detention centers are severely overcrowded, and inmates generally lack proper medical care, the report added. In January, hundreds of inmates at a juvenile prison rioted over prison conditions.

Roughly half of the 700,000 to 880,000 members of hill tribes reportedly lack citizenship. This leaves them ineligible to vote, own land, or be covered under labor laws and makes it harder for them to access education and health care. The government in 2000 eased the rules for hill tribe members to be eligible for and obtain citizenship, but it is not yet clear how many so-called highlanders have benefited from the changes. Muslims, who make up around 4 percent of Thailand's population and are concentrated in the five southernmost provinces, face some private sector job discrimination, according to the U.S. State Department human rights report.

Maintaining its long-standing policy of harboring refugees fleeing conflict in neighboring Southeast Asian countries, the government provides in its border areas temporary asylum to more than 120,000 Burmese refugees. Authorities, however, have arrested as illegal aliens some Burmese living outside designated camps. Women make up more than half of university graduates and increasingly are entering the professions, but they continue to face unofficial discrimination in hiring and wages. Women also are underrepresented in politics, government, and senior civil service posts. Domestic violence is a serious problem, although rules of evidence make prosecuting offenders difficult and police do not vigorously enforce relevant laws, according to the U.S. State Department report. The government has taken some positive measures such as deploying teams of female police officers in some station houses to encourage women to report sexual crimes.

Tens of thousands of Thai women and children work as prostitutes, many of them after being trafficked to cities from their villages. Authorities prosecute relatively few traffickers, and many police, soldiers, and local officials are involved in trafficking, the U.S. State Department report said. Some women are forced into prostitution, and in addition, many prostitutes work as bonded laborers in order to pay off loans made to their parents by brothel owners. Thailand has at least 200,000 prostitutes, according to NGO and government estimates.

Togo

Polity: Dominant party (military influenced)
Economy: Mixed statist
Population: 5,300,000
PPP: $1,442
Life Expectancy: 55
Religious Groups: Indigenous beliefs (51 percent), Christian (29 percent), Muslim (20 percent)
Ethnic Groups: Native African (99 percent), European and Syrian-Lebanese (less than 1 percent)
Capital: Lomé

Political Rights: 6*
Civil Liberties: 5
Status: Not Free

Ratings Change: Togo's political rights rating declined from 5 to 6, and its status from Partly Free to Not Free, due to the holding of legislative elections that were neither free nor fair.

Ten-Year Ratings Timeline (Political Rights, Civil Liberties, Status)

1993	1994	1995	1996	1997	1998	1999	2000	2001	2002	2003
6,5NF	7,5NF	6,5NF	6,5NF	6,5NF	6,5NF	6,5NF	5,5PF	5,5PF	5,5PF	6,5NF

Overview:
After numerous delays, Togo held flawed legislative elections in October 2002 that were supposed to be more credible than the 1999 legislative polls, which were boycotted by the opposition over allegations of electoral fraud. Nevertheless, a boycott of the 2002 polls was led by the Union of Forces for Change of veteran opposition leader Gilchrist Olympio. The ruling Rally of the Togolese People won 72 of 81 parliamentary seats. Under a 1999 agreement with the political opposition, the polls were to have been organized and supervised by an independent electoral commission. However, the government changed the electoral framework that had been agreed upon. The National Assembly in December 2002 amended the constitution to allow President Gnasignbe Eyadema, Africa's longest-serving head of state, to run for a third

term in 2003. The National Assembly also passed a restrictive media bill that increased prison sentences for defaming public officials. Eyadema in 2002 resumed his role as regional elder statesman by mediating talks between the government of Cote d'Ivoire and rebels.

Togoland was a German colony for more three decades until France seized it at the outset of World War I. It was held as French territory until its independence in 1960. The country's founding president, Sylvanus Olympio, was murdered in 1963 as Eyadema, then a demobilized sergeant who had served in France's colonial wars, led an army coup to topple the country's democratically elected government. After assuming direct power in 1967, Eyadema suspended the constitution and extended his repressive rule through mock elections and a puppet political party. In 1991, the organizing of free political parties was legalized, and multiparty elections were promised. The transition faltered, however, as soldiers and secret police harassed, attacked, or killed opposition supporters. Eyadema won fraudulent elections in 1993 and 1998.

Eighty percent of Togolese are engaged in subsistence agriculture. Corruption, military spending, and large, inefficient state-owned companies impede economic growth. The government in 2001 created a national anticorruption commission, and several public and private officials were arrested for alleged fraud. Western aid to Togo remained suspended in 2002 because of failure to improve political rights and human rights.

Political Rights and Civil Liberties: The Togolese people cannot choose their representatives freely. In the 1993 presidential election, which the opposition boycotted, President Gnasingbe Eyadema claimed to have won 96 percent of the vote. His June 1998 reelection was blatantly fraudulent, with the government claiming he had won approximately 51 percent of the vote, thereby enabling him to avoid a runoff election against the single opposition candidate. Electoral rolls were suspect, and multiple voter cards were issued. The electoral commission was not independent and was either unable or unwilling to provide adequate logistical support. Hundreds of domestic, EU-trained observers were denied accreditation.

The October 2002 legislative elections were neither free nor fair. Leading opposition parties boycotted the vote to protest preparations for the polls, which they said prevented a free and fair election from taking place. The ruling party won 72 of 81 parliamentary seats. Amendments to the electoral code violated the Lome Framework Agreement of 1999 that the government had signed with the political opposition. The agreement had provided for an independent electoral commission that would have 10 members from the ruling party and 10 from the opposition. The amendments reduced membership by half and stipulated that the commission would reach its decisions by majority and not by consensus. Presidential candidates are also now required to reside in Togo for at least one year prior to presidential elections. The country's main opposition leader, Gilchrist Olympio, lives in exile.

The judiciary is still heavily influenced by the president. Traditional courts handle many minor matters. Courts are understaffed and inadequately funded. Pretrial detentions are lengthy, and prisons are severely overcrowded. Killing, arbitrary arrest, and torture continue. Security forces commit abuses with impunity, and illegal detention is common. Human rights groups are closely monitored and sometimes harassed.

At least 15 private newspapers publish in Lome, but independent journalists are subject to harassment and the perpetual threat of various criminal charges. There are more than a dozen independent newspapers that publish sporadically and some 30 private radio stations, most of which operate as pirates. Most of the independent broadcast media outlets, however, offer little vibrant local news coverage or commentary. The Press and Communication Code of 1998 declares in its first article that the media are free, but restricts press freedom in most of the 108 other articles.

The National Assembly in September 2002 passed an amendment to the media bill that imposes heavy sentences for "defaming or insulting" the president, state institutions, courts, the armed forces, and public administration bodies. The amendment increases the penalty for "insulting the head of state" from the previous penalty of one to six months imprisonment to a jail term of one to five years. Authorities have seized newspaper print runs, harassed and jailed journalists, and shuttered media outlets. The U.S.-based Committee to Protect Journalists said Togo "has one of the most repressive climates for journalists in Africa." A number of journalists were arrested and sentenced to prison terms during 2002.

Constitutionally protected religious freedom is generally respected. Freedom of assembly is allowed, but is often restricted among the government's political opponents. Demonstrations are often banned or violently halted. Ethnic discrimination is rife among the country's 40 ethnic groups. Political and military power is narrowly held by members of a few ethnic groups from northern Togo, especially Eyadema's Kabye ethnic group. Southerners dominate the country's commerce, and violence occasionally flares between the two groups.

Despite constitutional guarantees of equality, women's opportunities for education and employment are limited. A husband may legally bar his wife from working or receive her earnings. Customary law bars women's rights in divorce and denies inheritance rights to widows. Violence against women is common. Female genital mutilation is widely practiced by the country's northern ethnic groups. A 1998 law prohibiting the practice is not enforced. Several organizations promote the rights of women. Child trafficking is a problem.

Togo's constitution includes the right to form and join unions, but essential workers are excluded. Health care workers may not strike. Only 20 percent of the labor force is unionized. Unions have the right to bargain collectively, but this right is restricted.

Tonga

Polity: Traditional monarchy
Economy: Capitalist
Population: 100,000
PPP: na
Life Expectancy: 71

Political Rights: 5
Civil Liberties: 3
Status: Partly Free

Religious Groups: Christian (Free Wesleyan Church claims over 30,000 adherents)
Ethnic Groups: Polynesian
Capital: Nuku'alofa

Ten-Year Ratings Timeline (Political Rights, Civil Liberties, Status)

1993	1994	1995	1996	1997	1998	1999	2000	2001	2002	2003
3,3PF	5,3PF	5,3PF	5,3PF	5,3PF	5,3PF	5,3PF	5,3PF	5,3PF	5,3PF	5,3PF

Overview:

Tonga is a monarchy consisting of 169 islands—only 36 of them inhabited—in the southwest Pacific. Its population is mainly Polynesian, with small Asian and European minorities. Known to European explorers as the Friendly Islands, the archipelago was unified as a kingdom under King George Tupou I in 1845 and became a British protectorate in 1900. Tonga achieved independence in 1970 and is a member of the Commonwealth. King Taufa'ahau Tupou IV has reigned since 1945. The king appointed his son, Prince Lavaka ata 'Ulukalala, as prime minister in 2000.

Since the early 1990s, the government has faced calls from ordinary Tongans, known locally as commoners, to hold direct elections for all of parliament's 30 seats and allow the body to select the cabinet. Currently, the majority of seats are held by nobles, who are chosen by their peers, and cabinet members, who are appointed by the king.

Led by commoner Akilisi Pohiva, Tonga's pro-democracy movement has won a majority of the nine directly elected seats reserved for commoners in four straight general elections since 1993. Most recently, pro-democracy candidates won seven seats in Tonga's March 7, 2002, elections, up from five in 1999. The movement, known as the Human Rights and Democracy Movement (HRDM), generally avoids directly challenging the role and powers of the king.

Tonga depends on tourism, foreign aid, and remittances from Tongans working abroad, worth an estimated $40 million per year, to offset its large trade deficit. Like several other poor Pacific island nations that have turned to offshore finance to raise revenue, Tonga has been accused of facilitating money laundering by the Paris-based Organization for Economic Cooperation and Development. The club of rich nations removed Tonga from its list of "noncooperative" states in 2001 after the government made administrative and legal changes to address the problem. In general, however, the government functions with relatively little transparency, and allegations of official corruption are common.

Political Rights and Civil Liberties:

Tongans cannot change their government through elections. The king wields broad powers that are subject to few democratic checks and balances. The king appoints the prime minister and appoints and heads the policy-making privy council, or cabinet. Commoners make up the vast majority of Tonga's population, but they elect only 9 of parliament's 30 seats. While the nine representatives of the nobles sometimes team up in parliament with the commoner representatives to reject laws proposed by the cabinet, the nobles and the 12 cabinet ministers generally vote as a bloc to pass laws favored by the king. In addition to their political power, the king and Tonga's 33 hereditary nobles also hold a preeminent position in society through substantial landholdings.

Tonga's judiciary is independent, and citizens generally receive fair trials, according to the U.S. State Department's global human rights report for 2001, released in March 2002. The judiciary is based on English common law, and traditionally most senior judges have been foreigners. Law enforcement, however, is subject to some abuses. Police, working with prosecutors, allegedly at times postpone court dates repeatedly and file frivolous charges to intimidate government critics, the State Department report said.

Pro-democracy campaigner Pohiva and others in 2002 criticized the government's practice, first reported in the *Matangi Tonga* magazine, of sentencing several dozen teenage lawbreakers to unsupervised detention on an uninhabited island about one hour from the main island of Tongatapu. The magazine quoted a prison official as saying that the purpose was to separate the children from adult convicts.

Tonga's press carries some criticism of government actions and policies, although the government and private individuals recently have filed several defamation suits against media outlets over their reporting. Two journalists and two pro-democracy activists are facing trial on charges stemming from the publication of a letter claiming that the king had a secret bank account in 1991 containing some $350 million. In a positive development, the Supreme Court in December awarded Pohiva and two journalists nearly $26,000 in damages over their wrongful jailing for 30 days in 1996 on contempt charges.

Tonga's broadcast media are both public and private. The state-run Radio Tonga requires that any on-air references to religion relate to mainstream Christian practices. The policy prevents, for example, Baha'is from discussing on the air the tenets of their faith. Otherwise, religious freedom is generally respected in this predominantly Christian society. The Free Wesleyan Church has the most adherents.

Women generally play subordinate roles in this male-dominated society. They hold relatively few positions of influence in government, although some female commoners are prominent in business. Many Tongan women are abused in their homes, and anecdotal reports suggest that the problem is worsening, according to the U.S. State Department report. Wife beating is generally handled, if at all, within families or by village elders rather than through formal channels. Land inheritance laws discriminate against women, and women cannot own land.

Long-standing tensions between indigenous Tongans and Chinese immigrants apparently have worsened recently, as evidenced by a spate of attacks against Chinese-owned shops.

Tonga has no trade unions, although nurses and teachers have formed "associations" that lobby on some worker's issues but have no formal collective bargaining rights. While labor laws guarantee workers the right to join unions, the government has never set out procedures for forming unions. Most Tongans, in any case, are subsistence farmers.

Trinidad and Tobago

Polity: Parliamentary democracy   **Political Rights:** 3
Civil Liberties: 3
Economy: Capitalist-statist **Status:** Partly Free
Population: 1,300,000
PPP: $8,964
Life Expectancy: 71
Religious Groups: Roman Catholic (29.4 percent), Hindu (23.8 percent), Anglican (10.9 percent), Muslim (5.8 percent), other
Ethnic Groups: Black (40 percent), East Indian (40 percent), mixed (18 percent), other (2 percent)
Capital: Port-of-Spain

Ten-Year Ratings Timeline (Political Rights, Civil Liberties, Status)

1993	1994	1995	1996	1997	1998	1999	2000	2001	2002	2003
1,1F	1,1F	1,2F	1,2F	1,2F	1,2F	1,2F	1,2F	2,2F	3,3PF	3,3PF

Overview: Following street demonstrations, a legal challenge, and a stalemate in the evenly divided legislature, Prime Minister Patrick Manning, of the People's National Movement (PNM), called for elections in October. The polling was generally peaceful and saw the participation of six parties representing more than 100 candidates contesting the 36 open seats. The PNM won 20 seats, while the United National Congress (UNC) had a heavy showing, reinforcing the domination of these two parties. Manning was sworn in for the third time since 1991, as the seventh prime minister of independent Trinidad and Tobago. His cabinet showed few changes and included his wife, Hazel, who again serves as minister of education; nepotism does not seem to be an issue for the electorate. In previous elections there were concerns over the impartiality of the Elections and Boundaries Commission, but no major improprieties surfaced during the recent polls. In October the Inter-American Convention against Terrorism was signed.

Trinidad and Tobago, a member of the Commonwealth, achieved independence in 1962. The 1976 constitution established the two-island nation as a republic, with a president elected by a majority of both houses of parliament, replacing the former governor-general. Executive authority remains vested in the prime minister. The bicameral parliament consists of the 36-member House of Representatives elected for five years and the 31-member Senate, with 25 senators appointed by the prime minister and 6 by the opposition.

In July 1991, Jamaat-al-Muslimeen, a small radical Muslim group, staged a coup attempt in Port-of-Spain. The prime minister and eight cabinet members were held hostage for four days, and 23 people died in bombings at the police headquarters, the state television station, and the parliamentary building. Efforts to heal the wounds of the coup continue to characterize Trinidadian politics. Tensions persist between the black and East Indian communities, each roughly 40 percent of the population, as the latter edged towards numerical, and thus political, advantage. The most recent elections are emblematic of the racial tensions that continue to dominate electoral contests.

In July 2001, Prime Minister Baseo Panday of the UNC lashed out at a Transparency International report that rated Trinidad, for the first time, as a country with high levels of official corruption. The group put Trinidad 31st out of 91 countries in its Corruption Perception index, with a rating of 5.3 out of 10. Panday, who was engaged in a long-running feud with prominent members of the local press, denied that there was corruption in his administration and claimed that Transparency International was repeating "rumors and propaganda that are being spread about my country."

Political Rights and Civil Liberties: Citizens of Trinidad and Tobago can change their government democratically. The judiciary branch is independent, although subject to some political pressure and corruption. As a result of rising crime rates, the court system is severely backlogged, in some cases for up to five years, with an estimated 20,000 criminal cases awaiting trial. Prisons are grossly overcrowded; however, the government does permit visits to them by human rights monitors, who in general operate freely.

In May 1999, the government withdrew as a state party from the American Convention on Human Rights, which prohibits countries from extending the death penalty beyond those crimes for which it was in effect at the time the treaty was ratified. In June 2000, the country withdrew entirely from the International Covenant on Civil and Political Rights. There are more than 100 prisoners on death row.

Street crime is on the rise, with the consumption and trafficking of illegal drugs considered to be largely responsible for the increase in violent crime. The increasing frequency with which illicit drugs are used on the islands has been accompanied by significant growth of the drug trade. Drug corruption extends to the business community, and a significant amount of money is believed to be laundered through front companies. Recently, legislation was approved that provides severe penalties for money laundering and requires that major financial transactions be strictly monitored. The government works closely with U.S. law enforcement agencies to track drug shipments in and out of the country.

Corruption in the police force—often drug-related—is endemic, and law enforcement inefficiency results in the dismissal of some criminal cases. In December 2000, Prime Minister Baseo Panday admitted that, despite governmental efforts to finance reforms, something was "fundamentally wrong" with the police force. The police have won praise, however, for establishing a branch of Crime Stoppers, an international organization that promotes community involvement in preventing and informing on crime through a hotline.

Press outlets are privately owned and vigorous, and thus offer pluralistic views; the broadcast media are both private and public. Prime Minister Panday refused to sign the Inter-American Press Association's Chapultepec Declaration on press freedom until it addressed instances of media dissemination of "lies, half-truths and innuendoes." In April 1999, Information Minister Rupert Griffith reminded the media of the government's power to grant and revoke broadcast licenses and warned that local media operations were being examined "under a microscope." In 2000, a high-court judge ordered Panday to pay newspaper publisher Ken Gordon, an Afro-Trinidadian, $120,000 for defamation, after Panday had called him a "pseudo-racist." There is free access to the Internet. Academic freedom is generally honored.

Violence against women is extensive and remains a low priority for police and prosecutors. However, in a 1999 landmark ruling, the court of appeals overturned a death sentence and reduced the charge from murder to manslaughter in the case of a woman defendant the court said had suffered from battered-wife syndrome. Freedom of association and assembly is respected. Labor unions are well organized, powerful, and politically active, although union membership has declined. Strikes are legal and occur frequently.

Tunisia

Polity: Presidential (dominant party)
Economy: Mixed capitalist
Population: 9,800,000
PPP: $6,363
Life Expectancy: 72
Religious Groups: Muslim (98 percent), other (2 percent)
Ethnic Groups: Arab (98 percent), other (2 percent)
Capital: Tunis

Political Rights: 6
Civil Liberties: 5
Status: Not Free

Ten-Year Ratings Timeline (Political Rights, Civil Liberties, Status)

1993	1994	1995	1996	1997	1998	1999	2000	2001	2002	2003
6,5PF	6,5NF	6,5NF	6,5NF	6,5NF	6,5NF	6,5NF	6,5NF	6,5NF	6,5NF	6,5NF

Overview:

The Tunisian government continued to maintain tight restrictions on political and civil liberties in 2002, while the scope of enforcement expanded with the imprisonment of an activist for Internet activity. A referendum in May changed the constitution to allow President Zine el-Abidine Ben Ali to seek a fourth term.

Tunisia obtained independence in 1956 under the leadership of Habib Bourguiba, a charismatic lawyer who led opposition in the French protectorate. After becoming Tunisia's first president, Bourguiba devoted himself single-mindedly to social liberalization and development. The personal status code he introduced upon assuming office granted women far more extensive rights than they enjoyed anywhere else in Arab world. Eschewing the massive military expenditures and showcase development projects that sidetracked economic progress elsewhere in the region, Bourguiba urged his regional counterparts to make peace with Israel and devoted roughly a third of government spending to education—the cornerstone of long-term prosperity. Political and civil liberties, however, were strictly curtailed.

In 1987, President Ben Ali led a bloodless coup against the aging Bourguiba and promised to open the political system. However, his rule became increasingly autocratic and repressive. Over the last 15 years, the government has jailed hundreds of dissidents for peacefully exercising civil liberties. In particular, Ben Ali has treated Islamists harshly, claiming the need to avoid the kind of unrest seen in neighboring Algeria.

While public freedoms have remained as restricted as ever, Ben Ali has built a strong, diversified, market-oriented economy. Since 1987, the economy has grown at an average rate of 4.5 percent annually and inflation has been cut in half. According to official figures, more than 80 per cent of households now own their own homes.

While the government claims to be moving toward greater political openness, the regime's intolerance of dissent is gradually increasing. Arrests and indictments of dissidents declined in 2002 only because fewer Tunisians are willing to openly criticize the government. In May 2002, a referendum to remove presidential term limits was ostensibly approved by 99.5 percent of voters. As with most electoral outcomes in Tunisia, this margin was largely a reflection of the inhospitable climate of liberties in the country—several opposition activists were arrested after they signed statements opposing the measure. In October, the government barred a delegation of the International Commission of Jurists (ICJ) from entering the country, becoming one of only a handful of regimes worldwide to have obstructed such access in the commission's 50-year history.

While the present state of political and civil liberties in Tunisia leaves much to be desired, the socio-economic foundations for a modern democracy are very strong. The al-Qaeda bombing of a synagogue on the Tunisian resort island of Djerba in April 2002, which killed 19 people, did not lead to the kind of frantic arrest sweeps of suspected Islamists that have occurred in other Middle Eastern countries.

Political Rights and Civil Liberties:

Tunisians cannot change their government democratically. The 1959 constitution provides for a president with broad powers, including the right to select the prime minister and cabinet, to rule by decree during legislative adjournments, and to appoint the governors of Tunisia's 23 provinces. Under Ben Ali, the role of prime minister was reduced from leader of the government to "coordinator" of ministerial activities. Although the president is chosen by popular vote, presidential elections are not even remotely competitive—Ben Ali claimed to have won 99.4 percent of the vote in 1999. Elections for Tunisia's unicameral parliament, the Chamber of Deputies (Majlis al-Nuwwab), are almost as heavily orchestrated, though designed to produce a facade of multiparty democracy. Elections in May 2000 for seats in Tunisia's 257 municipalities were also suspect; the Constitutional Democratic Rally (RCD) party won 94 percent of seats after running unopposed in nearly 75 percent of municipalities. No political party based on religion or region is permitted, and all parties must be licensed.

Although legal reforms introduced in 1999 broadened the state's definition of torture and reduced the permissible length of incommunicado detention, arbitrary arrest, illegal detention, and torture by the security forces have continued unchecked. Frequently, dissidents are harassed and beaten, deprived of their passports, and monitored closely.

The judiciary is subject to political interference by the president and the government. Political dissidents are usually tried in military courts, which issue verdicts that cannot be appealed, often after just minutes of deliberation, and which do not observe international legal standards. There are estimated to be 1,000 political prisoners in captivity, mostly suspected members of the outlawed Islamist group al-Nahda (Renaissance). Many others are in exile.

Freedom of expression is heavily restricted. The government controls domestic broadcasting and is entitled by law to halt circulation of domestic and foreign publications at will. In addition, the government uses newsprint subsidies and control over public advertising revenues to encourage self-censorship. Although amendments to the press code in 2001 reduced the number of offenses punishable by prison terms, the scope of the law remains vague enough to allow for the indictment of journalists whose reporting displeases government officials. Internet use is tightly controlled, and access to opposition Web sites is routinely blocked.

In June 2002, the editor of the dissident online publication *Tunezine* was arrested, tortured into revealing the password of the Web site so that it could be shut down, and sentenced to 28 months in prison for publishing false information and for "unauthorized use of an Internet connection." In August, a journalist for the Islamist weekly *Al-Fajr* was arrested, just 10 weeks after completing an 11-year prison term, because he violated an administrative order banishing him to the south of the country.

Freedom of association is greatly limited. The government has banned a number of opposition groups, most notably al-Nahda and the Tunisian Workers' Communist Party (PCOT). Members of human rights groups have been subjected to harassment and arrests. Permission is required for public gatherings. The size and frequency of demonstrations critical of the government declined precipitously in 2002.

In January 2002, three alleged members of the Islamist group *Ahl al-Sunna wa al-Jama'a* (Followers of the Way of the Prophet and the Islamic Community) were sentenced by a military court to prison terms of 8 to 10 years for belonging to a "terrorist organization operating from abroad." In early February, four members of the PCOT who emerged from hiding were arrested and sentenced to prison terms.

Workers in Tunisia have the right, both by law and in practice, to form unions, bargain collectively, and strike. About 15 percent of the workforce are members of the Tunisian General Federation of Labor (UGTT), and an even larger percentage are covered by union contracts. Although the UGTT and its member unions are independent, they are subject to government pressure by the provision of state subsidies.

Islam is the state religion. While other religious communities may worship freely, Baha'is may not practice publicly. The government controls and subsidizes mosques and pays the salaries of imams (prayer leaders).

Political and social equality for women has advanced more in Tunisia than elsewhere in the Arab world. However, inheritance law still discriminates against women, and female illiteracy is twice as high as male illiteracy. Women constitute 29 percent of the workforce, occupy 21 seats in the national legislature, and hold several secondary cabinet positions.

Turkey

Polity: Presidential-parliamentary democracy
Economy: Capitalist-statist
Population: 67,300,000
PPP: $6,974
Life Expectancy: 69
Religious Groups: Muslim [mostly Sunni] (99.8 percent)
Ethnic Groups: Turkish (80 percent), Kurdish (20 percent)
Capital: Ankara

Political Rights: 3*
Civil Liberties: 4*
Status: Partly Free

Ratings Change: Turkey's political rights rating improved from 4 to 3 due to a new openness in Turkish politics following the freely held November elections that brought to power the hitherto proscribed Islamist party, the Justice and Development Party. Its civil liberties rating improved from 5 to 4 due to progress on an improved human rights framework and a loosening of restrictions on Kurdish culture.

Ten-Year Ratings Timeline (Political Rights, Civil Liberties, Status)

1993	1994	1995	1996	1997	1998	1999	2000	2001	2002	2003
2,4PF	4,4PF	5,5PF	5,5PF	4,5PF	4,5PF	4,5PF	4,5PF	4,5PF	4,5PF	3,4PF

Overview:
The overwhelming election victory on November 3, 2002 of the Justice and Development Party (AK), a moderate Islamic-affiliated group, was the year's most significant event for Turkey. The party dominated the national elections, winning nearly two-thirds of the seats in parliament. The win was momentous since Turkey's secular military has intervened no fewer than four times since 1960 to depose Islamic governments, the last time in 1998. This time it allowed the elections to proceed fairly and the results to hold.

Mustapha Kemal Ataturk, who launched a reform program under which Turkey abandoned much of its Ottoman and Islamic heritage, proclaimed Turkey a republic in 1923. His secular, nationalistic legacy has profoundly influenced Turkish politics ever since, most notably in the post-World War II period. The doctrine of *Kemalism* has been used by the military to justify three coups since 1960. Turkey returned to civilian rule in 1983.

Turkey's relations with many of its neighbors were radically changed by the ending of the Cold War and by the Gulf crisis of 1990–91. Long-running disputes with Greece and the Greek Cypriots have not been resolved, although since mid-1999 Greece and Turkey have been moving towards agreement on bilateral issues. Talks between the Greek and Turkish Cypriot leaders were restarted in January 2002, but little progress had been made by the end of year.

Since being formally declared a candidate for EU membership in 1999, Turkey has outlined a set of economic and political goals that it must meet in order to fulfill membership criteria. On the economic side, Turkey has made considerable progress, lifting obstacles to privatization, attracting foreign investment, and tackling corruption. However, a recent collapse of the financial sector and subsequent currency devaluation and recession have undermined much of the progress. Politically and socially, Turkey is having a tougher time meeting the EU's standards, particularly with regard to issues of civil rights. Some EU members have been highly vocal about Turkey's human rights abuses. In May 2002 a diplomatic row erupted between Turkey and France over the latter country's public criticism of Turkey's lack of press freedom.

Turkey's reluctance to undertake various reforms reflects a struggle within the country between those who advocate membership in the EU as the route to modernity and prosperity, and the entrenched interests of those who champion maintaining the status quo as the way to protect the Turkish founding principles of national unity and secularism. However, in October 2001 the Turkish parliament passed a series of 34 amendments to the constitution, which covered a wide range of issues including freedom of expression and association, gender equality, and the role of the military in the political process.

The complete electoral dominance of the AK in the November 2002 elections meant that the party took 363 of the 550 seats in Turkey's parliament, a fact that was bolstered by the consideration that only one other party surpassed Turkey's 10 percent threshold for parliamentary representation. The AK's Islamic credentials have been played down to assuage the anxiety of the army, which is strongly secular. Nonetheless, the overwhelming win proved that the country had tired of the succession of failed economic policies and tottering coalition governments.

Turkey's chief prosecutor asked the country's highest court on October 23 to ban the AK before the election, particularly its leader, RecepTayyip Erdogan, ostensibly because of a criminal past. Despite this, Erdogan sidestepped the issue and took the premiership. Turkey's secular governments have a long history of cracking down on political parties founded on religion. A predecessor organization, the Virtue Party, was closed down by the Constitutional Court in June 2001 for "activities contrary to the principle of the secular republic." In 1998, the Welfare Party was closed for similar reasons.

With the election euphoria gone, the new administration faces a wrecked economy, and subsequently its room for political and economic maneuvering is narrow. Political instability of recent past governments has done great damage to an already sinking economy, and Turkey's economy may contract by as much 6 percent in 2002. Only strong support from the IMF has staved off catastrophe.

Political Rights and Civil Liberties: Turkish citizens can change their government democratically, though the military wields considerable influence in political matters, especially regarding defense and security. The 1982 constitution provides for a parliament, the Grand National Assembly (currently 550 seats), which is directly elected to a 5-year term. The assembly elects the president to a single 7-year term. The National Security Council (NSC), a military-dominated body, has a policy-setting role. A constitutional amendment passed in October 2001 aims to reduce the military's influence in politics by increasing the number of civilian representatives in the NSC from five to nine (there are five military representatives), as well as emphasizing the "advisory" nature of the body.

The European Commission's 2001 report on Turkey's progress toward EU accession stated that "the constitutional amendments adopted by the Turkish Parliament on October 3, 2001, are a significant step towards strengthening guarantees in the fields of human rights and fundamental freedoms." However, it cautioned that "despite these changes, a number of restrictions on the exercise of fundamental freedoms have remained." By the end of 2002, Turkey had still fallen short of the EU's standards in several respects, notably on the issues of capital punishment and on cultural rights for the Kurds. Its accession therefore has been thrust into limbo.

The conflict between the Turkish military and the Kurdistan Workers' Party (PKK), which has claimed as many as 37,000 lives and has spanned almost two decades, has continued only sporadically since the PKK announced the end of its insurrection in February 2000. (Their leader, Abdullah Ocalan, was captured in 1999 and is currently on death row.) After his capture, Ocalan himself renounced separatism and called for reconciliation, but a few splinter Kurdish elements have vowed to continue fighting for a separate Kurdish state. In 1999, the Kurdish People's Democracy Party (HADEP) won control of 37 local administrations despite attempts by Turkey's chief prosecutor to ban it. However, four southeastern provinces remain under emergency law. Civil governors throughout the region may authorize military operations, expel citizens suspected of Kurdish sympathies, ban demonstrations, and confiscate publications. The Istanbul police arrested three people in January 2002 for allegedly forcing people to submit petitions demanding elective Kurdish courses in school. The government claimed that the outlawed PKK was pressuring activists to assert their Kurdish identity.

According to official figures, 380,000 people were displaced from southeast Turkey during the 16-year conflict between governmental forces and the PKK. Nongovernmental organizations estimate the number of displaced, primarily Kurdish villagers, at over one million. The majority were driven from their homes by government gendarmes in an arbitrary resettlement program. The Turkish government has never acknowledged the human rights violations the security forces inflicted on hundreds of thousands of its citizens.

The judiciary is susceptible to governmental influence through the High Council of Judges and Prosecutors, which names judges and prosecutors to the high courts and controls appointments and promotions of those in lower courts. The council is appointed by the president, and its decisions are not subject to review. Those held for state security court (SSC) offenses, which include political violence, narcotics, organized crime, and some nonviolent political offenses, can legally be detained for up to 4 days without access to family or lawyers. Detentions of up to 10 days continue to be permitted in the southeast. The revised Article 38 of the constitution limits the death penalty to cases of terrorist crimes and during times of war. Although death sentences continue to be imposed, a de facto moratorium on carrying them out has been maintained since 1984.

Prison conditions are abysmal, characterized by widespread torture, sexual abuse, and denial of medical attention to inmates. The parliamentary human rights committee has published nine reports on torture in Turkey since May 2000, based on inspections of police stations and prisons between 1998 and 2000. However, little has been done to stop the practice, and the conviction and sentencing of offending officials is rare. Prison riots occur frequently because of overcrowding and anger over conditions. In December 2000, security forces stormed more than 20 prisons in an effort to end a hunger strike by inmates protesting plans to move them from large, dormitory-based prisons to newly constructed "F-type" prisons, in which prisoners are housed in smaller cells in relative isolation. After dozens died in the ensuing violence and hunger strikes, in July 2001 Justice Minister Hikmet Sami Turk announced that the controversial F-type prisons would no longer be commissioned.

Freedom of expression in Turkey is limited by the criminal code, which forbids insulting state officials and inciting racial or ethnic hatred, and by the Anti-Terror Law, which prohibits separatist propaganda. In December 2000 a state security court banned the publication or broadcast of "statements from illegal organizations or information liable to incite hatred, hostility, or crimes." The military, Kurds, and political Islam are highly sensitive subjects and frequently earn journalists criminal penalties, harassment, detention, or imprisonment. Some 80 journalists had been imprisoned for political activities or for allegedly infringing various laws in 2001, according to the European Commission's annual report. Journalistic harassment continued in 2002 as writers, journalists and newspapers editors were arrested on a number of charges. Three journalists, for instance, were arrested in October 2002 for "insulting the army." Some estimates place the total number of people imprisoned in connection with freedom of expression issues at around 9,000. One of the constitutional amendments passed in October 2001 allows broadcasts to be spoken in Kurdish. However, media outlets that attempted to publish or broadcast in Kurdish were suppressed by authorities in November. In a positive development, President Sezer vetoed new legislation introduced in mid-June 2001 aimed at increasing government vetting of broadcasting, claiming that it would threaten media freedom.

Authorities may restrict freedom of association and assembly on the grounds of maintaining public order, although official authorization will no longer be required for those wishing to stage public rallies. Pro-Kurdish political parties and nongovernmental organizations face severe harassment and restrictions on their activities, particularly in the southeast. In September 2001, police raided the Turkish Human Rights Foundation branch in Diyarbakir and seized computers and confidential medical files concerning the victims of torture. Human rights groups that attempted to document the hunger strikes as well as provide support to the prisoners faced persecution throughout the year. Members of the Human Rights Association were beaten and detained, five of their branches were shut down, and 12 members were charged under the Anti-Terror Law in March 2001. The pro-Kurdish political party HADEP frequently faces difficulties from the authorities.

Islamists continue to face official harassment, although with the resounding victory of the Islamically oriented Justice and Development Party (AK) in November 2002, the practice should decline. According to Human Rights Watch, the ban on women's wearing of the *hijab* (headscarf) was "applied with increasing severity against students and civil servants." Teachers and doctors were dismissed for wearing the headscarf on duty, and new regulations prohibited students from taking the June university examinations while wearing a *hijab*.

More than 99 percent of Turks are Sunni Muslim. Religious freedom is restricted by the limitation of worship to designated sites, constraints on building houses of worship for minority religions, and government crackdowns on political Islam. A 1998 law placed all mosques under government administration, required official authorization for the construction of mosques, and forbade the wearing of uniforms and masks (including *hijab*s) by demonstrators. Christian churches continue to face difficulties, particularly with regard to both ownership of property and their legal status. However, the European Commission reported that there have been some signs of "increased tolerance towards certain non-Muslim religious communities."

Women's legal rights received a boost in November 2001 with the passage of a new law that recognizes men and women as equals and accords women equal property rights in the event of a divorce. Social norms make it difficult to prosecute rape cases, and the penalty for rape may be reduced if a woman was not a virgin prior to her attack. Although the Ministry of Justice banned the practice of "virginity examinations" in 1999, the health minister issued a circular in July 2001 that provides for mandatory exams for female medical students and the expulsion of those proven to be sexually active. The issue of domestic violence against women, as well as legislation that allows for the application of reduced sentences to the perpetrators of such crimes, remains an area of concern.

With the exception of public servants and workers engaged in the protection of life or property, workers may form unions, bargain collectively, and strike. The exception category includes workers in the mining and petroleum industries, sanitation, defense, law enforcement, and education.

Turkmenistan

Polity: Presidential
Economy: Statist
Population: 5,600,000
PPP: $3,956
Life Expectancy: 67
Religious Groups: Muslim (89 percent), Eastern
Orthodox (9 percent), other (2 percent)
Ethnic Groups: Turkmen (77 percent), Uzbek (9 percent),
Russian (7 percent), Kazakh (2 percent), other (5 percent)
Capital: Ashgabat

Political Rights: 7
Civil Liberties: 7
Status: Not Free

Ten-Year Ratings Timeline (Political Rights, Civil Liberties, Status)

1993	1994	1995	1996	1997	1998	1999	2000	2001	2002	2003
7,6NF	7,7NF	7,7NF	7,7NF	7,7NF	7,7NF	7,7NF	7,7NF	7,7NF	7,7NF	7,7NF

Overview:

Cracks in President Saparmurat Niyazov's tightly controlled regime became visible with an apparent attempt on the president's life in November 2002. The secretive nature of the country's authoritarian leadership fueled widespread speculation about who, including Niyazov himself, may have orchestrated the shooting. Several high-level government defections, along with a purge by Niyazov of Turkmenistan's intelligence service, further highlighted growing political tensions and challenges to the government.

The southernmost republic of the former Soviet Union, Turkmenistan was conquered by the Mongols in the thirteenth century and seized by Russia in the late 1800s. Having been incorporated into the U.S.S.R. in 1924, Turkmenistan gained formal independence in 1991 with the dissolution of the Soviet Union.

Niyazov, the former head of the Turkmenistan Communist Party, ran unopposed in elections to the newly created post of president in October 1990. After the adoption of a new constitution in 1992, Niyazov was reelected as the sole candidate for a five-year term with a reported 99.5 percent of the vote. The main opposition group, Agzybirlik, which was formed in 1989 by leading intellectuals, was banned. Niyazov's tenure as president was extended for an additional five years, until 2002, by a 1994 referendum, which exempted him from having to run again in 1997 as originally scheduled. In the December 1994 parliamentary elections, only Niyazov's Democratic Party of Turkmenistan (DPT), the former Communist Party, was permitted to field candidates.

In the December 1999 elections to the National Assembly (Mejlis), every candidate was selected by the government and virtually all were members of the DPT. According to governmental claims, voter turnout was 98.9 percent. The OSCE, citing the lack of provision for nongovernmental parties to participate and the executive branch's control of the nomination of candidates, refused to send even a limited assessment mission. In a further consolidation of Niyazov's extensive powers, parliament unanimously voted in late December to make him president for life. With this decision, Turkmenistan became the first Commonwealth of Independent States (CIS) country to formally abandon presidential elections. However, in February 2001, Niyazov announced that a presidential poll would be held in 2010, although he claimed that he would not run.

After the September 11, 2001, attacks on the World Trade Center and the Pentagon, Niyazov announced that the United States could not use his country for military strikes against the Taliban in Afghanistan, although Turkmenistan would serve as a base for humanitarian aid. Ashgabat cited the country's official political neutrality as a reason for not participating in the U.S.-led campaign. However, Turkmenistan had maintained good relations with the Taliban in recent years in an attempt to secure safe energy-export routes through Afghanistan to destinations including India and China.

Although Niyazov continued to exercise widespread power throughout the country in 2002, cracks in his regime became increasingly visible during the year. In February, former deputy prime minister and head of the central bank, Khudaiberdy Orazov, accused the government of falsifying data to disguise economic troubles and subsequently fled to exile in Russia. In April, another prominent government official, former prime minister Aleksander Dodonov, announced from his exile in Moscow that he was joining the opposition. Apparently fearing the influence and growing independence of the country's powerful security apparatus, Niyazov orchestrated a significant purge of the Committee for National Security (KNB), the successor to the Soviet-era KGB. According to Niyazov, 80 percent of the KNB's senior leadership had been removed for supposed abuse of power and other violations; several were subsequently sentenced to lengthy prison terms. Despite these preemptive efforts, the KNB appears to represent a serious potential challenge to the current regime, with the dismissals further provoking opposition to Niyazov's rule within the current and former ranks of the KNB.

On November 25, Niyazov was the apparent victim of an assassination attempt in which gunmen fired at the president's motorcade in Ashgabat; Niyazov was unhurt in the attack. More than a hundred people—including two chief suspects,

Guvanch Dzhumaev, a prominent Turkmen businessman, and Dzhumaev's business partner, Leonid Komarovsky, a naturalized U.S. citizen—were reportedly detained on suspicion of their involvement in the shootings. According to the government, former foreign minister and opposition leader Boris Shikhmuradov was a key organizer of the attack. Shikhmuradov, who had returned to Turkmenistan from exile in Russia, was arrested on December 25; he made a televised confession on December 29 that critics maintain had been coerced. He was sentenced on December 30 to life in prison after a one-day trial that human rights groups criticized as a Soviet-era-style show-trial.

Alternative theories quickly emerged as to who was responsible for the attack in this highly secretive society. Some speculated that Niyazov himself, out of a high level of concern over the influence of his critics, had planned the shooting as an excuse to increase repression of the opposition. Others argued that the attack was carried out by disgruntled members of the KNB. Regardless of who orchestrated it, the shooting highlighted growing political tensions in Turkmenistan and the internal and external challenges to Niyazov's leadership.

Political Rights and Civil Liberties:

Citizens of Turkmenistan cannot change their government democratically. President Saparmurat Niyazov enjoys virtually absolute power over all branches and levels of the government. He has established an extensive cult of personality, including the erection of monuments to his leadership throughout the country. In 1994, he renamed himself Turkmenbashi, or leader of the Turkmen. In 2002, Niyazov continued to enact often bizarre decrees enhancing his already extensive cult of personality. In August, he ordered the renaming of the days of the week and months of the year, including January (Turkmenbashi), April (his mother's name), and September (*Rukhnama*, after a spiritual guidebook allegedly authored by Niyazov).

The government has undergone a rapid turnover of personnel as Niyazov has dismissed many officials whom he suspects may challenge his authority. Niyazov relies heavily on the Presidential Guard, an elite and powerful group that monitors political developments in the country and carries out operations on Niyazov's personal orders.

The country has two national legislative bodies: the unicameral National Assembly (Mejlis), composed of 50 members elected in single-mandate constituencies for five-year terms, and is the main legislature; and the People's Council (Khalk Maslakhaty), consisting of members of the assembly, 50 directly elected representatives, and various regional and other executive and judicial officials, which meets infrequently to address certain major issues. Neither parliamentary body enjoys independence from the executive. The 1994 and 1999 parliamentary elections were neither free nor fair. Following the November 2002 assassination attempt on Niyazov, the president announced early parliamentary elections for April 2003.

Freedom of speech and the press is severely restricted by the government, which controls all radio and television broadcasts and print media. Reports of dissenting political views are banned, as are even mild forms of criticism of the president. Subscriptions to foreign newspapers are severely restricted. Foreign journalists have few opportunities to visit Turkmenistan and are often limited to certain locations. The state-owned Turkmentelekom is the only authorized Internet provider in the country. In 2002, the government took further steps to limit information coming into the country by ordering the removal of rooftop satellite dishes.

The government restricts freedom of religion through means including strict registration requirements. Only Sunni Muslims and Russian Orthodox Christians have been able to meet the criterion of having at least 500 members to register. Members of religious groups that are not legally registered by the government, including Baptists, Pentecostals, and Baha'is, are frequently harassed or attacked by security forces.

While the constitution guarantees peaceful assembly and association, these rights are restricted in practice. Only one political party, the Niyazov-led Democratic Party of Turkmenistan, has been officially registered. Opposition parties have been banned, and their leading members face harassment and detention or have fled abroad. Two of the leading figures of the opposition-in-exile are Avdy Kuliev, who founded the United Turkmen Opposition in 1992, and former foreign minister Boris Shikhmuradov, who established the National Democratic Movement of Turkmenistan (NDMT) in 2001. In late 2002, Shikhmuradov was imprisoned for his alleged connection with the November assassination attempt against Niyazov. In June, exiled dissidents met in Vienna to discuss the human rights situation in Turkmenistan and to form a coordinating-consultative body of opposition members. However, the opposition continues to be plagued by rivalries and disagreements between different factions. Several small demonstrations were reported in 2002, including one in August at which some 200 women gathered in Ashgabat to protest against the government; they were quickly arrested by police and security personnel.

The government-controlled Colleagues Union is the only central trade union permitted, and there are no legal guarantees for workers to form or join unions or to bargain collectively.

The judicial system is subservient to the president, who appoints and removes judges for five-year terms without legislative review. The authorities frequently deny rights of due process, including public trials and access to defense attorneys. There are no independent lawyers, with the exception of a few retired legal officials, to represent defendants in trials. Police abuse of suspects and prisoners, often to obtain confessions, is reportedly widespread, and prisons are overcrowded and unsanitary. The security services regularly monitor the activities of those expressing criticism of the government.

Freedom of movement is severely restricted, with citizens required to carry internal passports that note the bearer's place of residence and movements into and out of the country. Obtaining passports and exit visas for foreign travel is difficult for most nonofficial travelers and allegedly often requires payment of bribes to governmental officials. Although the government officially ended exit visa requirements for Turkmen in January 2002, unofficial controls remain at Ashgabat airport.

Corruption in the country's educational system is widespread, with personal connections and bribes playing a central role in admittance to higher-level institutions. The *Rukhnama*, a quasi-spiritual guide allegedly authored by Niyazov, is required reading throughout the school system and has largely replaced many other traditional school subjects. Primary- and secondary- school attendance has been reduced from 11 to 9 years, and higher education from 5 to 2 years of study, with 2 years of work.

Both a continuing Soviet-style command economy and widespread corruption diminish equality of opportunity. Profits from the country's extensive energy exports rarely reach the general population, who live in extreme poverty.

Traditional social-religious norms mostly limit professional opportunities for women to the roles of homemaker and mother, and anecdotal reports suggest that domestic violence is common.

Tuvalu

Polity: Parliamentary democracy
Economy: Capitalist
Population: 10,000
PPP: na
Life Expectancy: 67

Political Rights: 1
Civil Liberties: 1
Status: Free

Religious Groups: Church of Tuvalu [Congregationalist] (97 percent), other (3 percent)
Ethnic Groups: Polynesian (96 percent), Micronesian (4 percent)
Capital: Funafuti

Ten-Year Ratings Timeline (Political Rights, Civil Liberties, Status)

1993	1994	1995	1996	1997	1998	1999	2000	2001	2002	2003
1,1F	1,1F	1,1F	1,1F	1,1F	1,1F	1,1F	1,1F	1,1F	1,1F	1,1F

Overview:

Tuvalu is a parliamentary democracy consisting of nine tiny, remote, low-lying atolls spread across 350 miles of the South Pacific north of New Zealand. The population is mainly Polynesian, with a Micronesian minority. Named the Ellice Islands by an American ship captain in 1819, the nine islands were administered by Britain as a protectorate between 1892 and 1914 and then as part of the Gilbert and Ellice Islands colony between 1915 and 1971. During World War II, U.S. forces built an airstrip in the capital of Funafuti that today is used by the handful of commercial flights that serve the country each week. The Ellice Islands gained full independence as Tuvalu in 1978, while the Gilberts today are the independent state of Kiribati. The British monarch, Queen Elizabeth II, is Tuvalu's head of state and is represented by a governor-general, currently Sir Tomasi Puapua.

The current prime minister, Saufatu Sopoaga, is the fourth man to hold Tuvalu's top post in two years. Hailing from Nukufetau island, the former finance minister narrowly defeated Amasone Kilei in a parliamentary leadership vote following the July 25, 2002, general elections. The incumbent, Kolou Telake, failed to win a seat. Telake was in office for barely half a year, having become prime minister in December 2001 after his predecessor, Faimalaga Luka, was ousted in a no-confidence vote. Luka, in turn, had become prime minister only in February of that year after the sudden death in office of Ionatana Ionatana.

The country's history of frequent leadership changes has fueled a debate during the past decade over whether Tuvalu should amend its constitution to allow citizens to directly elect a national leader. Prime Minister Sopoaga said after taking office that a republican government would provide greater political stability. To this end, the new government launched a series of civic education radio programs as a first step towards a possible referendum on leaving the Commonwealth and adopting an elected head of state.

The tropical islands' Elsyian beauty belies the severe lifestyles of many Tuvaluans. Nearly two-thirds are subsistence farmers, and increasing salination of the soil is making this rugged livelihood even harder.

Copra, dried coconut meat, is Tuvalu's only real export, although the country also earns foreign exchange from sales of coins and stamps, money sent home by islanders working abroad, and tuna fishing licenses granted to foreign ships. The country also reaps royalties by leasing its international dialing code and by leasing Tuvalu's Internet domain name—.tv—to a California firm in 2000 for $50 million over 12 years. Some of the money has already been used to pave roads and build schools. The government also gets around 10 percent of its annual budget from a well-run overseas investment trust fund set up by donors in 1987.

Successive governments have warned that the low-slung islands could lose critical underground water tables or even be completely submerged should global warming raise sea levels. Tuvalu several years ago asked Australia to agree to take in its entire population in the event the islands are flooded, but Canberra refused.

Political Rights and Civil Liberties: Citizens of Tuvalu can change their government through elections and enjoy most basic rights. Parliament's 15 members are directly elected for four-year terms. Each of Tuvalu's nine atolls also has a six-person local council that is directly elected for a four-year term. Political parties are legal, although none exist. Instead, politics tends to be based on personal and family ties and on reputation and experience.

Tuvalu's common law judiciary is independent, and citizens generally receive fair trials, according to the U.S. State Department's global human rights report for 2001, released in March 2002.

Tuvalu's media are state owned and provide balanced news coverage. They include Radio Tuvalu, the fortnightly *Tuvalu Echoes* newspaper, and a television station that broadcasts for a few hours each day. Many Tuvaluans also pull in foreign television broadcasts on satellite dishes.

Women increasingly work in health care and education, but in general their job opportunities are limited by both cultural norms and the tiny size of the economy. Religious freedom generally is respected in this mainly Christian society.

Tuvaluans are free to form unions, although organized labor plays a limited role in this largely subsistence economy. The sole trade union is the Tuvalu Seaman's Union, whose roughly 600 members work on foreign merchant ships. Most Tuvaluans who earn regular wages or salaries within the country work for the government, and the fewer than 1,000 nurses, teachers, and civil servants employed by the state have formed associations that are similar to unions. Workers can bargain collectively, although in practice private employers generally set wages unilaterally. Labor disputes generally are resolved through nonconfrontational bargaining in local meeting halls rather than through formal legal procedures.

Uganda

Polity: Dominant party (military-influenced)
Economy: Capitalist-statist
Population: 24,700,000
PPP: $1,208
Life Expectancy: 43

Political Rights: 6
Civil Liberties: 4*
Status: Partly Free

Religious Groups: Roman Catholic (33 percent), Protestant (33 percent), Muslim (16 percent), indigenous beliefs (18 percent)
Ethnic Groups: Baganda (17 percent), Karamojong (12 percent), Basogo (8 percent), Iteso (8 percent), Langi (6 percent), Rwanda (6 percent), other (43 percent)
Capital: Kampala
Rating Change: Uganda's civil liberties rating improved from 5 to 4 due to changes in the survey methodology.

Ten-Year Ratings Timeline (Political Rights, Civil Liberties, Status)

1993	1994	1995	1996	1997	1998	1999	2000	2001	2002	2003
6,5NF	6,5NF	5,5PF	5,4PF	4,4PF	4,4PF	4,4PF	5,5PF	6,5PF	6,5PF	6,4PF

Overview:

President Yoweri Museveni and his National Resistance Movement (NRM) continued in power after comfortably winning presidential and legislative elections in 2001. These elections, however, were held under conditions that called into serious question their legitimacy as a result of the manipulation of the process by the NRM and the existence of current limitations on political party activity.

In 2002, two pieces of legislation affecting political rights and civil liberties were enacted. The Political Organizations Bill restricts the rights of political parties. The Suppression of Terrorism Bill imposes harsh penalties on suspected terrorists and has raised fears that it could be used against political opponents.

Regional tensions stayed high, although Ugandan military forces began to withdraw from the eastern part of the Democratic Republic of Congo. These units had been sent to suppress rebels who had been perpetrating attacks across the border into Uganda. Fighting continued with rebels in northern Uganda.

Uganda has experienced considerable political instability since independence from Britain in 1962. An increasingly authoritarian president, Milton Obote, was overthrown by Idi Amin in 1971. Amin's brutality and buffoonery made world headlines as hundreds of thousands of people were killed. Amin's 1978 invasion of Tanzania finally led to his demise. Tanzanian forces and Ugandan exiles routed Amin's army and prepared for Obote's return to power in the fraudulent 1980 elections. Obote and his backers from northern Uganda savagely repressed his critics, who were primarily from southern Ugandan ethnic groups. Approximately 250,000 people were killed as political opponents were tortured and murdered and soldiers terrorized the countryside. Obote was ousted for a second time in a 1985 army coup. Conditions continued to worsen until the Museveni-led National Resistance Army entered the capital of Kampala in January 1986.

The NRM dominates the nation's political life. The press and civil society remain relatively free and active, however, despite some crackdowns. In addition, the parliament has become increasingly assertive, occasionally rejecting appointments or policy initiatives proposed by the executive branch. Uganda held a referendum in June 2000 on whether to remove a ban on political party activities. The results were mixed. Almost 90 percent of those voting supported continuation of the current de facto single-party system. Opposition parties had called for a boycott, however, and overall voter turnout was just over 50 percent.

Manipulation and exploitation of ethnic divisions pose a serious threat to peace in Uganda. Baganda people in the country's south continue to demand more recognition of their traditional kingdom. Northern ethnic groups complain of governmental neglect; that region, and the west, are subject to continuing guerilla activities.

Political Rights and Civil Liberties: Ugandans do not have the right to select their government through democratic political competition. The country's only open multiparty elections were held in 1961 in preparation for the country's independence from Britain. Since 1986, political parties have been prohibited from functioning, and candidates stand as individuals in elections.

Arguing that majoritarian democracy exacerbates religious and ethnic tensions in Africa, President Yoweri Museveni has substituted an allegedly nonpartisan "Movement" system. In reality, there is little distinction between Museveni's system and a de facto single-party state. The 1995 constitution transformed the administrative restriction on political party activity into a legal ban. Article 269 of the constitution prohibits opening and operating branch offices, holding delegates' conferences, holding rallies, or campaigning for a candidate in an election. Security forces have halted numerous political rallies, some through force, and leading opposition activists have been harassed and, sometimes, subjected to arbitrary arrest. A 1999 report by Human Rights Watch concluded that "Organized political activity has been outlawed in Uganda for the past twelve years, and the NRM government has not hesitated to resort to repressive measures when these legal restrictions on political activity are challenged. Numerous political rallies have been halted, some through force. Political activists who have challenged the NRM's hold on political power are frequently harassed and sometimes arbitrarily arrested."

Reports by human rights groups and donor countries concerning the 2001 presidential election noted that state media and other official resources were mobilized in support of Museveni's successful candidacy, and the ban on formal party activities further hindered the opposition. Most observers believe, however, that Museveni would have won in a multiparty contest and described the actual balloting and vote tabulation processes as largely transparent. The opposition claimed that the elections were rigged and boycotted subsequent parliamentary polls. The elections confirmed the NRM's hold on the legislature, its comfortable majority buttressed by dozens of presidentially nominated special interest representatives.

The Constitutional Review Commission was established by President Museveni in 2001 to examine possible adaptations to the constitution. Issues being discussed include the future of political parties, presidential term limitations, federalism, the size of parliament, and voter and candidate eligibility. Critics suggest that the commission has a pro-NRM bias and does not reflect the broad spectrum of Ugandan public opinion.

In May 2002, parliament passed the Political Organizations Law which permits political party activities only in Kampala and allows just one party conference in a year. It also bars the formation and registration of new parties until 2005, while old political parties are required to register afresh within six months or face dissolution. The law has been severely criticized by the opposition and independent observers as continuing serious limitations on political pluralism and making it difficult for existing political parties to exist and new ones to be formed. The 2002 Suppression of Terrorism Bill defines any act of violence or threat of violence for political, religious, economic or cultural ends as a terrorist act. The unlawful possession of arms is also defined as terrorism. Publishing news that is "likely to promote terrorism" can lead to up to 10 years imprisonment.

Some space is allowed for parliament and civil society to function. Parliament, for example, has occasionally censured government ministers accused of corruption and has forced budgetary amendments. There is no state religion, and freedom of worship is constitutionally protected and respected. Various Christian sects and the country's Muslim minority practice their creeds freely.

With parliamentary approval, the president names a judicial commission that oversees judicial appointments. The judiciary is still influenced by the executive despite increasing autonomy. It is also constrained by inadequate resources and the army's occasional refusal to respect civilian courts. At times, the government liberally applies the charge of treason against nonviolent political dissidents. Local courts are subject to bribery and corruption. Prison conditions are difficult, especially in local jails. More than 500 prisoners die annually as a result of poor diet, sanitation, and medical care. Serious human rights violations by rebel groups and the Uganda People's Defense Forces have been reported.

Nongovernmental organizations (NGOs) currently make a significant contribution to Uganda's social, cultural, and political life. They encourage the expression of different views and, significantly, have been willing to address politically sensitive issues at a time when the Ugandan government continues to restrict ordinary political party activity. The existence and activities of NGOs are, however, subject to stringent legal restrictions. All NGOs in Uganda must be approved and registered by a government-appointed board composed mostly of government officials, including security officials, before they are allowed to operate. In 2001, the government introduced the Non-Governmental Organizations Registration (Amendment) Bill, which would increase state control over NGOs, but that legislation has not progressed because of widespread complaints by NGOs and other observers.

There is some freedom of expression. Independent and print media outlets , including more than two dozen daily and weekly newspapers, are often highly critical of the government and offer a range of opposition views. Buttressed by legislation limiting press freedoms, however, the government at times selectively arrests or harasses journalists. A sedition law remains in force and is applied selectively to journalists and other persons who hold views that are at variance with those of the NRM. In May of 2002, the Suppression of Terrorism Bill came into force, providing a possible death sentence for anyone publishing news "likely to promote terrorism."

Several private radio stations and private television stations report on local political developments. The largest newspapers and broadcasting facilities that reach rural areas remain state owned. Governmental corruption is reported. Opposition positions are also presented, but the coverage is often not balanced. Journalists have asked parliament to enact a freedom-of-information act so that the public is not denied information. A leading independent newspaper, *The Monitor*, was briefly closed in October in a controversy with the government over the veracity of a report regarding the government's fight against guerillas in the northern part of the country.

Women experience discrimination based on traditional law, particularly in rural areas, and are treated unequally under inheritance, divorce, and citizenship statutes. In most areas, women may neither own or inherit property, nor retain custody of their children under local customary law. Domestic violence against women is widespread. Uganda has, by contrast, legislated quotas for women officials in all elected bodies from village councils to the national parliament. Almost 20 percent of Uganda's parliament is female. One-third of local council seats must, by law, go to women.

The National Organization of Trade Unions, the country's largest labor federation, is independent of the government and political parties. An array of essential workers are barred from forming unions. Strikes are permitted only after a lengthy reconciliation process.

Ukraine

Polity: Presidential-parliamentary democracy
Economy: Mixed capitalist (transitional)
Population: 48,200,000
PPP: $3,816
Life Expectancy: 68

Political Rights: 4
Civil Liberties: 4
Status: Partly Free

Religious Groups: Ukrainian Orthodox (Moscow and Kyiv Patriarchates), Ukrainian Catholic, Protestant, Jewish
Ethnic Groups: Ukrainian (73 percent), Russian (22 percent), other (5 percent)
Capital: Kyiv

Ten-Year Ratings Timeline (Political Rights, Civil Liberties, Status)

1993	1994	1995	1996	1997	1998	1999	2000	2001	2002	2003
3,3PF	4,4PF	3,4PF	3,4PF	3,4PF	3,4PF	3,4PF	3,4PF	4,4PF	4,4PF	4,4PF

Overview:

The strong showing of former prime minister Viktor Yushchenko's Our Ukraine bloc in the parliamentary elections of 2002 marked the first postindependence victory for opposition forces other than the Communist Party. Although Yushchenko failed to muster enough support to form a new government, his bloc's win signaled the growing strength of democratic forces in the country and galvanized thousands who took to the streets during the year to demonstrate against President Leonid Kuchma's heavy-handed government. Nevertheless, Ukraine remained characterized in 2002 by pervasive corruption and organized crime, as well as by regular violations of basic political rights and civil liberties. President Kuchma also came under increased scrutiny from Western and other democratic leaders when evidence surfaced that he may have authorized the sale of a powerful radar system to Iraq in violation of a UN embargo. Although the president announced Ukraine's intention to seek membership in NATO, the alliance failed to invite him to its historic summit on enlargement held in Prague in November.

In December 1991, Ukraine ended more than 300 years of Russian ascendancy when voters ratified a declaration of independence and elected Leonid Kravchuk president. In 1994, Communists proved victorious in parliamentary elections, and Leonid Kuchma, a former Soviet director of military production, defeated Kravchuk. Since then, Kuchma has struggled against a Communist-dominated parliament to effect reforms. However, he also has increasingly been the target of domestic and international criticism for his government's failure to respect the basic rights and freedoms of Ukrainian citizens. In particular, the murder in 2000 of independent journalist Heorhiy Gongadze, and the surfacing of evidence that could implicate President Kuchma, sparked continual public demonstrations and calls for Kuchma's dismissal.

Although Ukraine commemorated a decade of post-Soviet independence in 2001, polls that year revealed that more than three-quarters of the country's population believed nothing good had come of it. Less than a quarter of the population considered the country a democracy. When the Communist Party engineered the ouster of the reform-minded prime minister Viktor Yushchenko in 2001, very likely with Kuchma's blessing, thousands of Yushchenko's supporters organized rallies to protest the decision. Yushchenko soon formed an electoral bloc called Our Ukraine and announced his intention to participate in the next parliamentary elections.

According to the OSCE, the parliamentary elections of March 2002 "brought Ukraine closer to meeting international commitments and standards for democratic elections." In particular, the OSCE noted the improved electoral framework contained in Ukraine's new election law (adopted in October 2001) and the orderly, timely, and transparent administration of the election by the Central Election Commission. Still, the election was marked by irregularities, such as the interference of governmental authorities in campaign activities, the monopoly coverage by state media of pro-Kuchma parties, and incidents of campaign-related violence, including the election-eve murder of Mykola Shkribliak, a prominent candidate and deputy governor of the Ivano-Frankivsk Oblast.

Following the election, Viktor Yushchenko accused governmental authorities of falsifying the vote and declared that "democracy is the loser." Although Our Ukraine stripped the Communist Party of its dominant position in parliament, it failed to secure the necessary majority to form a new government and secure top parliamentary leadership posts. Instead, Pro-Kuchma forces led by For a United Ukraine received enough postelection support from the Ukrainian Social Democratic Party–United (SDPUu), the Communists, independent candidates, and even members of Our Ukraine to dominate parliament. Prime Minister Anatoly Kinakh remained in power until November, when Kuchma fired the government allegedly for failing to implement economic reforms.

In the official results of proportional and single-mandate voting, Our Ukraine received 110 seats; followed by For a United Ukraine with 101 seats; the Communist Party with 66 seats; the SDPUu with 24 seats; the Tymoshenko Bloc with 22 seats; and the Socialist Party with 22 seats. Other parties gaining seats were the Democratic Party of Ukraine–Party Democratic Union, 4; the Unity bloc, 3; the Party of National-Economic Development, 1; and the Ukrainian Sea Party, 1. Independent candidates took 93 seats.

Throughout 2002 incidents reinforced the image of pervasive governmental influence on life in Ukraine, particularly with regard to freedom of expression. In September, for example, when thousands of protesters gathered in Kyiv to commemorate the death of Heorhiy Gongadze, television stations were unexpectedly pulled off the air. Government officials defended the move as routine maintenance, but protesters alleged they were blocking coverage of the protest. Also in 2002, Mykola Tomenko, the chair of the parliamentary Committee for the Freedom of Expression, released documents containing directives from the presidential administration to national television channels prescribing acceptable news items and coverage. The instructions, known as *temniki*, apparently are issued weekly, and failure to comply can result in various forms of harassment such as tax audits, canceled licenses, and libel suits.

Political Rights and Civil Liberties: Ukrainian voters can change their government democratically. Citizens aged 18 and older enjoy universal, equal, and direct suffrage. They elect the president and delegates to the Verkhovna Rada, the 450-seat unicameral parliament. Under an election law adopted in 2001, half of parliament is elected in proportional voting and half in single-mandate constituencies. The president appoints the prime minister and other cabinet members.

In the 1999 presidential election, Leonid Kuchma defeated Communist Party leader Petro Symonenko in the second round of voting with 56.21 percent of the vote. Symonenko received only 37.5 percent. Observers declared the election unfair, citing harassment of independent media, biased coverage by state media, intimidation of candidates and their supporters, and illegal campaigning by state officials. The next presidential election will take place in 2004, and President Kuchma has indicated that he will not try to seek a third term. Viktor Medvedchuk, a powerful oligarch and the head of Kuchma's presidential administration, is expected to be a lead candidate in the 2004 election, as is the reform-minded opposition leader Viktor Yushchenko.

The 1996 constitution guarantees freedom of speech and expression, but the government frequently disregards these rights. Under a law that took effect in 2001, libel no longer carries criminal charges. State media reflect a pro-Kuchma bias, while private media typically reflect the views of their owners. Journalists who report on corruption or criticize the government are particularly subject to harassment and violence, and press freedom groups noted numerous cases in 2002. Also in 2002, in response to increased political interference in their work, journalists issued the Manifesto of Ukrainian Journalists against Political Censorship. For example, the chairman of the parliamentary Committee for the Freedom of Expression released documents containing instructions from the presidential administration on appropriate news coverage by national television channels. Like many cases, the murder of investigative journalist Heorhiy Gongadze remained unresolved.

The constitution and the Law on Freedom of Conscience and Religion define religious rights in Ukraine. There are some restrictions on the activities of foreign religious organizations, and all religious groups with more than 10 members must register with the state. In 2002, President Kuchma signed a decree calling for the creation of a commission to explore mechanisms for restoring religious property seized under communism. In April, approximately 50 soccer fans threw stones at Kyiv's main synagogue and shouted anti-Semitic statements as they left a nearby stadium. Ukraine has several thousand nongovernmental organizations and an increasingly vibrant civil society. The constitution guarantees the right to peaceful assembly but requires advance notification to governmental authorities. In 2002, protesters continued to march against President Kuchma's alleged involvement in the murder of journalist Heorhiy Gongadze. In September opposition parties organized the "Rise Up, Ukraine!" campaign to mark the anniversary of Gongadze's death and thousands of protesters gathered around the country to call for the president's resignation. Fifty opposition members of parliament also staged a hunger strike. Authorities allegedly detained some individuals and impounded the cars of others in an effort to limit participation in the demonstrations. Similar protests continued throughout the fall.

The judiciary consists of a supreme court, regional courts, and district courts. There is also a constitutional court. The constitution guarantees equality before the law, but the president, members of parliament, and judges are immune from criminal prosecution unless parliament consents. The judiciary is inefficient and subject to corruption. Although the Constitutional Court is largely free of political interference, other courts lack independence. Judges are often penalized for independent decision making. In 2002, the Council of Europe's Committee for Prevention of Torture issued a report that criticized the Ukrainian police for using methods of interrogation that could be considered torture. These include electric shocks, cigarette burns, asphyxiations, and suspensions by the arms or legs. The report, based on visits to Ukraine between 1998 and 2000, also noted overcrowding, inadequate facilities for washing and cleaning, a lack of adequate food supplies, and extended detention of suspects.

The government generally respects personal autonomy and privacy, and the constitution guarantees individuals the right to own property, to work, and to engage in entrepreneurial activity. However, crime, corruption, and the slow pace of economic reform have effectively limited these rights. In 2001, the Constitutional Court struck down the country's Soviet-era *propiska* system, which had required individuals to register with the Interior Ministry in their place of residence. Opponents of the provision had long argued that the regulation violated freedom of movement. Under a 2001 law, the purchase and sale of land will be allowed beginning in 2005.

United Arab Emirates

Polity: Federation of   **Political Rights:** 6
traditional monarchies   **Civil Liberties:** 5
Economy: Capitalist-   **Status:** Not Free
statist
Population: 3,500,000
PPP: $17,935
Life Expectancy: 74
Religious Groups: Muslim (96 percent) [Shi'a (16 percent)], other
Ethnic Groups: Emirian (19 percent), other Arab and Iranian (23 percent), South Asian
(50 percent), European and East Asian (8 percent)
Capital: Abu Dhabi

Ten-Year Ratings Timeline (Political Rights, Civil Liberties, Status)

1993	1994	1995	1996	1997	1998	1999	2000	2001	2002	2003
6,5NF	7,5NF	6,5NF	6,5NF	6,5NF	6,5NF	6,5NF	6,5NF	6,5NF	6,5NF	6,5NF

Overview:
While the ruling families of the United Arab Emirates (UAE) make little pretense of respecting the political and civil liberties of their subjects, they have managed to minimize the legal capriciousness normally associated with autocratic rule in the Middle East and have built the region's most vibrant, diversified economy. However, revelations that much of the financing for the September 11, 2001, attacks on the Unites States passed through the UAE reinforced the supposition that the country remains a key financial hub of international terrorism. The government enacted stringent anti-money-laundering laws and other regulatory reforms in 2002.

The UAE is a federation of seven emirates, previously known as the Trucial States, established after the British withdrew from the Persian Gulf in 1971. Every five years the rulers of the seven emirates choose one of their own to serve as federal president, but this position has only been held by the ruler of Abu Dhabi, Sheikh Zayed bin Sultan al-Nahayan.

While most of its petroleum-rich neighbors squandered their oil revenue on consumption, over the next three decades the UAE poured petrodollars into developing a diversified modern economy. More remarkable than the country's current per capita income of almost $18,000—more than double that of neighboring Saudi Arabia—is the fact that most of it is *not* derived from the sales of oil or natural gas. Although Abu Dhabi remains the economic powerhouse of the UAE, the emirate of Sharjah has developed into a major manufacturing sector, while Dubai hosts the region's leading free-trade zone and is becoming the largest year-round tourist center in the Persian Gulf region.

This unparalleled economic prosperity has produced an equally unparalleled political stability. Although some radical Islamist figures have challenged the concentration of wealth in the hands of the royal families over the years (and were promptly expelled), their influence remains minimal. The country nevertheless faces significant challenges. With one of the highest rates of population growth in the world, the UAE cannot continue to easily absorb record numbers of citizens entering the job market by expanding the civil service. The country's soaring demand for electricity has made privatization of public utilities a top priority. In 2001, the government launched a major crackdown on corruption, arresting senior officials such as the Dubai customs chief. State newspapers published the full names and photos of the officials in a new "name and shame" policy.

The rise of the UAE as a major financial center has made it a major transshipment point for drug trafficking and terrorism financing. Although the UAE enacted the most region's most stringent anti-money-laundering law in January 2002, there were reports in September that al-Qaeda was shipping gold to the Sudan through Dubai's metal markets. In October, UAE police apprehended a top al-Qaeda operative, Abd al-Rahim al-Nashiri. The UAE's official news agency, which reported the arrest two months later, said he had been planning attacks on "vital economic targets" in the UAE that were likely to inflict "the highest possible casualties among nationals and foreigners."

Political Rights and Civil Liberties:

Citizens of the UAE cannot change their government democratically. The seven dynastic rulers of the emirates collectively constitute the Federal Supreme Council (FSC), which selects the president and vice president every five years and ratifies federal legislation. The president appoints the prime minister and cabinet. The 40-member Federal National Council (Majlis al-Ittihad al-Watani), composed of delegates appointed by the seven rulers, serves as an advisory body but has no legislative authority. There are no elections at any level, and political parties are illegal.

Although the constitution prohibits arbitrary arrest, UAE laws permit incommunicado detention if police believe that communication between a suspect and third parties may compromise an ongoing investigation. Suspects in police custody can be detained without charge indefinitely upon court order and are not entitled to legal counsel until an investigation is completed. Torture and death in police custody are reportedly rare, though governmental claims that the death of a Libyan national under arrest in September 2001 resulted from suicide have been questioned by Amnesty International.

The judiciary is not independent, as most judges are foreign nationals appointed to renewable terms and court rulings are subject to review by the political leadership. The judicial system comprises both *Sharia* (Islamic law) and secular courts. There are no jury trials, but due process protections exist. Sharia allows for corporal punishment for such crimes as adultery, prostitution, and drug or alcohol abuse. Drug trafficking is a capital offense, though executions are rare.

Freedom of expression is protected under the constitution, but strictly limited in practice. Broadcast media are almost entirely state owned and adhere to official guidelines. Journalists and academics exercise self-censorship regarding governmental policy, national security, and religion. Most print publications are privately owned, but receive government subsidies and often publish verbatim articles from the state-run Emirates News Agency. Foreign publications are censored, though satellite dishes are widely owned and provide access to uncensored foreign broadcasting. The state maintains a monopoly on Internet service and blocks access to radical Islamic Web sites.

The government limits freedom of assembly and association. Permits are required for organized public gatherings and are rarely granted, though enforcement varies from emirate to emirate. Informal political discussion forums held in private homes are tolerated. All nongovernmental organizations (NGOs) must be registered by the government. While a number of unregistered groups operate openly, there are no independent human rights groups.

Trade unions, strikes, and collective bargaining are illegal. Foreign nationals, who make up a staggering 98 percent of the private workforce, are subject to abuse and nonpayment of wages by employers. While labor law offers some protection, most abuse goes unreported. In June 2002, the UAE press reported that an Asian worker died and 15 fell ill at a labor camp , where workers lived in sweltering heat without water or electricity for several days because their Dubai-based employer had not paid the utility bills. In September, the government criminalized the hiring of camel jockeys under the age of 15.

Islam is the official religion of the UAE, where 85 percent of citizens are Sunni Muslim and 15 percent are Shiite Muslim. The vast majority of Sunni mosques receive substantial government funding, while all Sunni imams are employees of either federal or local government and do not deviate from approved topics in their sermons. While Shiite mosques operate independently of the government, they also adhere to government guidelines. Non-Muslims, mostly foreign nationals, may practice freely but may not proselytize or distribute religious literature. Although Christian churches and schools are widespread, there are no Buddhist temples and only one Hindu temple in the UAE.

Women are well represented in education, government, and the professions, but face discrimination in job benefits and promotion. There are numerous NGOs that focus on women's issues such as domestic violence. *Sharia* discriminates against women in family matters such as divorce and inheritance, and tradition keeps many women from working. A married woman must have her husband's consent to accept employment or to travel abroad. Polygamy is legal.

United Kingdom

Polity: Parliamentary
democracy
Economy: Mixed
capitalist
Population: 60,200,000
PPP: $23,509
Life Expectancy: 78

Political Rights: 1
Civil Liberties: 1*
Status: Free

Religious Groups: Anglican, Roman Catholic, Muslim, Protestant, other
Ethnic Groups: English (82 percent), Scottish (10 percent), Irish (2 percent), Welsh
(2 percent), other, including Indian and Pakistani (4 percent)
Capital: London
Ratings Change: The United Kingdom's civil liberties rating improved from 2 to 1
due to changes in the survey methodology.

Ten-Year Ratings Timeline (Political Rights, Civil Liberties, Status)

1993	1994	1995	1996	1997	1998	1999	2000	2001	2002	2003
1,2F	1,2F	1,2F	1,2F	1,2F	1,2F	1,2F	1,2F	1,2F	1,2F	1,1F

Overview:

The Good Friday Agreement between the Ulster Unionists and Sinn Fein suffered a serious setback when police found sensitive materials at Sinn Fein houses and offices that prompted the suspension of the 108-member Northern Ireland Assembly. Human rights groups continued to voice concern over the high incidence of racism, anti-Semitism, and the mistreatment of children and the mentally ill. Civil liberties continued to be under siege by the adoption and implementation of antiterrorist legislation.

The United Kingdom of Great Britain and Northern Ireland encompasses the two formerly separate kingdoms of England and Scotland, the ancient principality of Wales, and the six counties of the Irish province of Ulster. The British parliament is bicameral. The House of Commons has 659 members directly elected on a first-past-the-post basis. There is no upper limit on the number of House of Lords members; the chamber includes 26 archbishops and bishops and 92 hereditary peers under the House of Lords Act 1999, and currently there are 692 members. A cabinet of ministers appointed from the majority party exercises executive power on behalf of the mainly ceremonial sovereign. Queen Elizabeth II nominates the party leader with the most support in the House of Commons to form a government.

Prime Minister Tony Blair's centrist "new" Labour Party was reelected in June 2001, achieving the largest majority ever by a governing party entering its second term. Nevertheless, relations with trade unions suffered in 2002 over pay levels and the private finance initiative, whereby private business helps improve public services. The prospect of U.K. participation in a U.S. military action against Iraq exacerbated unease with Blair's autocratic leadership and potential U.K. isolation from other EU states.

Devolution of power to Scotland, Wales, and Northern Ireland took place in 1999, with each territory establishing its own legislature. The 129-member Scottish parliament and the 60-member Welsh assembly exercise control over transportation, health, education, and housing, while foreign, defense, and economic policies remain under London's control. The 108-member Northern Ireland Assembly in Belfast, which arose from the April 1998 Good Friday Agreement between the Ulster Unionists and Sinn Fein, the political wing of the Irish Republican Army, was suspended in October 2002 after police raided Sinn Fein houses and offices and found documents that could be of use to terrorists.

A sharp rise in racist, anti-Semitic, and xenophobic behavior in Western Europe followed the September 11, 2001, terrorist attacks on the United States. In the United Kingdom, 5 attacks on Jews were reported in December 2001; 13 in January 2002; 7 in February; 12 in March; and 48 in April.

The European Parliament amended the 1997 European Commission directive on privacy in telecommunications in May 2002, obliging member states to retain all telecommunications data on individuals for one to two years and to provide the relevant authorities unrestricted access to these data in order to assist law enforcement officials in eradicating crime. Human rights groups attacked this move as an assault on privacy and civil liberty.

Political Rights and Civil Liberties: United Kingdom citizens can change their government democratically. Voters are registered by government survey and include both Northern Irish and Commonwealth citizens resident in Britain. British subjects abroad retain voting rights for 20 years after emigration. Welsh and Scottish legislatures have authority over matters of regional importance. The Scottish parliament has limited power to collect taxes. In 1999, the government abolished hereditary peerage in the House of Lords, but debate on how to make the chamber more representative of the population has delayed further transformations.

Though uncensored and mostly private, the British press is subject to strict libel and obscenity laws. Print media are privately owned and independent, though many of the national daily newspapers are aligned with political parties. The BBC runs about half the electronic media in the country and, although funded by the government, is editorially independent. The Human Rights Act introduced a statutory right to free expression, although the European Convention makes exceptions in the interest of public safety, health, morals, and the reputations and rights of others.

British television owners pay a 112 pound (US$168) licensing fee that helps fund the BBC. In October 2002, a *Sunday Times* journalist refused to pay the fee on the grounds that the 1998 Human Rights Act's definition of freedom of expression overrides the law that enforces collection of the licensing fee.

The Freedom of Information Act of 2000 will come into effect in January 2005, although from November 2002 authorities must publish descriptions of the information they will provide. Rights groups criticized the law for excluding national security, defense, international resolutions, individual or public safety, commercial interests, and law enforcement information. The Scottish parliament passed the Freedom of Information (Scotland) Act in April 2002; it must be in force by the end of 2005.

The Regulation of Investigatory Powers Act of 2000 (RIPA) grants law enforcement agencies access to a wide range of information, primarily Internet based. The legislation has been widely criticized for endangering civil liberties such as freedom of expression, freedom of the press, and the right to privacy.

Governmental policy provides for freedom of religion, and the Human Rights Act prohibits discrimination on the basis of religious affiliation. The Church of England (Anglican) and the Church of Scotland (Presbyterian) are state religions, although their status has come under increasing scrutiny.

As of October 2000, the Human Rights Act of 1998 allows British citizens to take their grievances to British courts rather than seek redress in the European Court of Human Rights. Consequently, British courts are being pressured to bring domestic laws into line with European Convention standards.

Amnesty International expressed concern over the implementation of the Terrorism Act of 2000 and the Anti-terrorism, Crime, and Security Act of 2001 in response to the September 11, 2001, attacks on the United States. These acts call for the detention of non-U.K. nationals for unspecified and unlimited duration; degrading detention conditions; denial of a detainee's right to counsel; and failure to ensure respect for the human rights of UK nationals.

In December 2001, the Council of the European Union adopted by "written procedure" antiterrorist legislation that requires member states to prevent "the public" from offering "any form of support, active or passive" to terrorists and to check all refugees and asylum seekers for terrorist connections. Human rights groups criticized the legislation because it does not distinguish between conscious or unconscious assistance, treats would-be immigrants as criminals, and was not debated in parliament before being adopted.

British workers are free to form and join independent trade unions. The Labour Party introduced a national minimum wage in 1999. Legislation introduced in mid-2000 requires employers to offer part-time workers the same benefits, wages, and employment conditions, such as parental leave and sick pay, as those enjoyed by full-time workers doing equivalent work.

Human rights groups continued to voice concern over the mistreatment of minorities and the mentally ill by police, citing several deaths in police custody.

The Race Relations (Amendment) Act of 2000 strengthens the Race Relations Act of 1976 in Great Britain, making it illegal to discriminate in employment, education, housing, and the provision of goods, services, and facilities. For Northern Ireland, the Race Relations Order 1997 covers the same issues.

The Immigration and Asylum Act of 1999 impedes refugees' abilities to enter the United Kingdom through pre-entry controls, obstacles to appeals, devolution of powers to immigration officers, limited bail hearings, and internment without bail. From April 2002, because of protests about the potential stigma attached to the bearer of vouchers, the proposed voucher system was modified to allow their exchange for cash. Implementation of the bail and internment provisions has been delayed.

Transparency International ranked the United Kingdom 10th on its 2002 Corruption Perceptions Index, the 6th highest evaluation of any EU member state.

Amnesty International voiced concern that the United Kingdom is failing to protect the fundamental human rights of children, citing the deaths of child-soldiers and children being held in young-offender institutions in England and Wales. By November 2002, Britain had still not ratified the Optional Protocol to the Convention on the Rights of the Child regarding involvement of children in armed conflict. The trafficking of children to Britain, particularly from Eastern Europe and West Africa, for child prostitution and labor continues to be a problem.

British women earn on average only 73.7 percent of British men's wages, compared to 76.3 percent in the EU as a whole, according to Eurostat. Some 44.4 percent of women are employed full time. The percentage of women in national parliament is 17.1 percent; in national government, 35.3 percent. The Employment Bill, which received royal assent on July 8, 2002, will increase maternity allowances to the lesser of either 100 pounds (US$150) per week or 90 percent of the employee's average weekly earnings. The bill becomes effective April 2003.

United States of America

Polity: Presidential-parliamentary democracy (federal)
Economy: Capitalist
Population: 287,400,000
PPP: $34,142
Life Expectancy: 77

Political Rights: 1
Civil Liberties: 1
Status: Free

Religious Groups: Protestant (56 percent), Roman Catholic (28 percent), other
Ethnic Groups: White (77 percent), black (13 percent), Asian (4 percent), Native American (2 percent), other (4 percent)
Capital: Washington, D.C.

Ten-Year Ratings Timeline (Political Rights, Civil Liberties, Status)

1993	1994	1995	1996	1997	1998	1999	2000	2001	2002	2003
1,1F	1,1F	1,1F	1,1F	1,1F	1,1F	1,1F	1,1F	1,1F	1,1F	1,1F

Overview:

Political developments in the United States of America were dominated by the country's response to the terrorist attacks of September 11, 2001, in which members of al-Qaeda, a terrorist network, hijacked civilian aircraft and made suicide assaults on the World Trade Center in New York City and the Department of Defense (Pentagon) near Washington, D.C. The reaction of the administration of President George W. Bush was a series of broad-gauged initiatives involving direct war against al-Quaeda and its supporters in Afghanistan; efforts to arrest or kill terror suspects abroad; and plans for a possible war against Iraq. Domestically, President Bush instituted some controversial measures to make it easier for law enforcement authorities and intelligence agencies to monitor American citizens during antiterrorist investigations, including the creation of a new, cabinet-level office, the Department of Homeland Security. National security issues also played a major part in midterm congressional elections, in which President Bush's Republican Party scored modest gains.

Founded in 1776 during a revolution against British colonial rule, the United States began the modern worldwide movement for freedom and self-government. The current system of government began functioning in 1789, following the ratification of the Constitution. Because the founders of the United States distrusted centralized governmental power, they set up a system in which the federal government has three competing centers of power (the executive, legislative, and judicial branches) and left many powers with the state governments and the citizenry.

Immediately after the attacks of September 11, the Bush administration announced an ambitious, global policy of combating terrorists and the governments that support terrorists or give them sanctuary. The initial target was the Taliban, a movement of fundamentalist Muslims who had gained control of Afghanistan and had given protection to al-Quaeda and its leader, Osama Bin Laden. By the end of 2001, the U.S. military, working in concert with the Northern Alliance, an Afghan opposition group, had routed the Taliban and its al-Quaeda allies from that country.

A controversy has emerged from the conflict in Afghanistan over the fate of several hundred fighters—alleged members of al-Quaeda and the Taliban—who were captured by U.S. forces and then imprisoned in the U.S. military base in Guantanamo, Cuba. The United States contends that, as irregular forces, the prisoners do not qualify for status as prisoners of war and do not enjoy the rights guaranteed POWs under international law. Instead, the Bush administration insists on classifying the prisoners as enemy combatants. The refusal to extend POW status to the Guantanamo prisoners has generated a sharp debate among experts on international law and has provoked protests from officials in some foreign governments. In a related move that elicited protests and legal challenges, the government labeled two Americans, citizens detained on charges of involvement with terrorists, as enemy combatants. Concerns have also been raised over the government's plans to establish military tribunals to hear cases brought against foreign terrorists. Critics said that military courts would represent an abandonment of the historic U.S. commitment to a fair trial, and were unnecessary since past experience had demonstrated that civilian courts were capable of dealing effectively with terrorism cases. Thus far, with the exception of the two American citizens classified as enemy combatants, those accused of involvement with terrorist organizations have been dealt with through the normal criminal justice process, although a number of those detained for their possible involvement in terror conspiracies have been denied access to attorneys for all or part of their detention and questioning, a development that has raised particular concern among civil libertarians.

The administration also stirred criticism from civil libertarians and immigrant rights' organizations because of domestic policies instituted as part of the war on terrorism. Immediately after the terror attacks, federal authorities arrested and held in detention some 1,200 individuals for investigation into their possible involvement in terror plots. The overwhelming majority were Muslim men from North Africa, the Middle East, or the Indian subcontinent. Most had overstayed their visas or had other immigration status problems and were eventually deported; by the end of 2002, only a handful of these "special interest detainees" were still in custody. A source of particular discontent was the steadfast refusal of the Justice Department to make public the names of the detainees.

From the very outset, and throughout the post-September 11 period, the country's leading officials, beginning with President Bush, stressed the importance of not placing blame on Muslim-Americans and spoke out against acts of discrimination or hate. Nevertheless, there was a substantial upsurge in criminal acts directed at Muslims and those perceived to be Muslim in the weeks following the terror attacks.

The bulk of hate crimes occurred during the first few months after September 11; according to the federal government and civil liberties organizations, the number of hate crimes against Muslims declined during 2002.

At the same time, the United States has introduced new procedures for visa applications that apply specifically to applicants from the Middle East and other majority-Muslim countries. The new rules have complicated the visa process for male applicants from betwen the ages of 16 and 45.

Civil libertarians were also concerned about certain provisions of the USA PA-TRIOT Act, which was passed in 2001 shortly after the terror attacks. The new law raised a number of issues relating to the right to privacy. It sets a lower standard for law enforcement officials to meet before gaining permission to enter a person's home covertly for the purpose of investigation than was previously in place. Another section makes it easier for the federal government to gain access to an individual's personal records, including e-mails and records of library books checked out. Most of the act's more controversial sections are subject to a "sunset" provision under which they will become invalid in 2005. In another policy shift related to the war on terrorism, the Federal Bureau of Investigation has been given the power to carry out investigations of domestic political, religious, and civic groups. This policy over-turned a prohibition on domestic surveillance instituted in 1976.

The impact of these changes on the civil liberties of the American people is as yet unclear. The federal judiciary, which under the U.S. system holds considerable power in the determination of the constitutionality of laws and policies, has issued several orders limiting the scope of special antiterrorism measures. Cases involving other controversial policies are working their way through the court system.

Another important development was the passage of legislation creating the Department of Homeland Security, a new cabinet-level office that brings together a number of different agencies and functions that relate to domestic security. After a lengthy debate, Congress decided to include the same "whistleblower" protections for employees of the agency that are enjoyed by other federal workers.

Security issues, including the war on terrorism and the prospective war against Iraq, played a major role in the midterm congressional elections, in which the Repub-lican Party demonstrated unexpected strength. While the president's party has his-torically fared poorly in midterm elections, in 2002 the Republicans did well in both the Senate and House races, extending their majority in the House of Representa-tives to 227-206 and winning back control of the Senate from the Democratic Party by a margin of 51-48. (One additional senator, James Jeffords, serves as an indepen-dent but aligns himself with the Democrats.) The election results were something of a surprise, given the decline in the U.S. economy that began prior to September 11 and worsened since the terror attacks. However, most analysts suggest that the election hinged primarily on voter concerns over national security and the possibil-ity of future attacks against U.S. territory or interests, issues that have traditionally benefited the Republicans.

Political Rights and Civil Liberties: The United States has a vibrant and highly competitive political system. In electing a president, the United States uses a unique system that combines the popular vote with ballots cast by an electoral college. The Electoral College apportions votes to each state based on population; the electors then cast all the ballots of a particular state for the candidate who won the popular vote in that state, no matter what the margin; their vote determines the winner of the election. Under this system, it is possible for a candidate to win the presidency even though an opposing candidate may have won a greater number of popular votes nationwide.

The presidential election of 2000 was one of the few elections in which a candidate won a majority of the Electoral College votes while losing the popular vote. Further complicating the election was a bitter and highly partisan controversy over the disposition of the ballots in the state of Florida, a crucial issue that ultimately decided the election's outcome. Both George W. Bush, the Republican nominee, and Al Gore, his Democratic rival, claimed to have won a victory in Florida by razor-thin margins. Much of the controversy revolved around a flawed balloting system that made it difficult to determine which candidate had received the voter's designation on certain ballots. Eventually, the Supreme Court prohibited a recount of the Florida votes, thus effectively declaring Bush the winner. In 2002, Congress passed, and Bush signed, legislation meant to make changes in the election process that will prevent a repetition of the Florida debacle. The midterm elections took place with a minimum of controversy.

Citizens of the United States enjoy a wide range of civil liberties protection through federal legislation and court decisions. In the wake of the terror attacks, however, a major debate has surfaced over a number of the measures adopted through legislation or implemented by the Department of Justice and Department of Defense. The judiciary is expected to play an important role in determining which of the new procedures and laws meet the test of constitutionality.

The press has played an especially important role in the debate over civil liberties in the post-September 11 environment. Many leading newspapers and journals of opinion have published articles and editorials raising questions about the Guantanamo detainees, the secrecy that surrounds certain antiterror policies, and sections of the USA PATRIOT Act that have an impact on the right to privacy. There remains a high degree of academic freedom, as demonstrated by campus activism against the prospect of war with Iraq and a vigorous debate over such varied issues as affirmative action and the Israeli-Palestinian conflict. There have been no restrictions placed on the freedom of assembly, and demonstrations opposing U.S. policies, the war in Afghanistan, and Israeli policies in the occupied territories were held in a number of cities.

The number of hate crimes against Muslims declined in 2002, although a much greater number of religion-based offenses occurred than was the case prior to September 11. Nevertheless, a wide variety of Muslim civic, advocacy, and campus organizations remained active, and many issued statements highly critical of U.S. foreign policy.

The question of the treatment of Muslims somewhat obscured evidence of overall improvement in relations between various racial, religious, and ethnic groups that make up the United States. Unlike many other countries that are host to substantial immigrant populations, the United States has generally encouraged the assimilation of racial and ethnic minorities. Although statistics vary for different groups, there is evidence of growing levels of social integration in the workplace and in schools. Intermarriage among different groups is also on the rise. Although these positive trends are visible among all minority groups, African-Americans continue to suffer from an unequal economic and educational status. Blacks endure higher poverty, joblessness, and school dropout rates than do other groups, and their college enrollment and graduation rates lag behind those of whites and many immigrant groups.

A major source of friction between blacks—and to a lesser degree Latinos—and the institutions of government has been the criminal justice system. Black advocacy organizations complain that incarceration rates for blacks and Latinos are disproportionately high and periodically make allegations about abusive police behavior aimed at minorities. Civil libertarians have advanced a broader critique of the criminal justice system, contending that there are too many Americans (especially minority Americans) in prison, that prison sentences are often excessive, and that too many people are prosecuted for drug offenses. Concern about prison conditions has been prompted by disturbing levels of violence and rape, and reports of inadequate medical attention for prisoners with mental illness. There is also a growing controversy over the death penalty; in 2002, several states announced a moratorium on capital punishment while studies are undertaken on the death penalty's fairness.

Gender equality is guaranteed by law and has been reinforced by court decisions. Although women's income lags somewhat behind that of men, the gap among those with university degrees has narrowed considerably. Women and men in their twenties earn approximately the same, and women have entered such professions as law, medicine, and journalism in substantial numbers, with women enrolling in journalism and law schools at higher rates than men.

The U.S. economy has suffered somewhat since September 11, although there was evidence of economic decline prior to the terror attacks. In recent years, the United States had adopted policies meant to enhance its integration into the global economy to a more substantial degree than has been the case with other advanced capitalist democracies. The United States has a higher degree of inequality of income and wealth than do countries with similar levels of development; on the other hand, the U.S. unemployment rate remains low by world standards, even as it increased to the 6 percent mark at the end of 2002.

Although U.S. law guarantees the right of workers to form trade unions and engage in collective bargaining, the labor movement is relatively weak, representing a little over 13 percent of the workforce and less than 10 percent of private (business) sector employees. Although cultural factors are in part responsible for a three-decades-long decline in organized-labor's strength, unions have also been hampered by strong resistance from employers and labor laws that many believe are geared to the interests of management.

⬇ Uruguay

Polity: Presidential- **Political Rights:** 1
parliamentary democracy **Civil Liberties:** 1
Economy: Capitalist- **Status:** Free
statist
Population: 3,400,000
PPP: $9,035
Life Expectancy: 75
Religious Groups: Roman Catholic (66 percent), Protestant (2 percent), Jewish
(1 percent), other (31 percent)
Ethnic Groups: White (88 percent), mestizo (8 percent), black (4 percent)
Capital: Montevideo
Trend Arrow: Uruguay received a downward trend arrow due to the decision of the
Blanco Party to withdraw from the governing coalition amidst the worst economic
crisis in the country's history, and to growing problems of public safety.

Ten-Year Ratings Timeline (Political Rights, Civil Liberties, Status)

1993	1994	1995	1996	1997	1998	1999	2000	2001	2002	2003
1,2F	2,2F	2,2F	2,2F	1,2F	1,2F	1,2F	1,2F	1,1F	1,1F	1,1F

Overview: In October 2002 the Blanco Party withdrew its members from the cabinet of President Jorge Batlle's coalition government, during the gravest economic crisis in the country's history. The move came just months after Batlle had caused a huge diplomatic flap by calling his neighbors in Argentina "a bunch of thieves" and predicting that his Argentine counterpart, Eduardo Duhalde, might be forced to leave the presidency at any moment. The spillover effect from Argentina's melting economy was blamed for a day of violence in August, when looters ransacked businesses and labor unions staged antigovernment protests that brought much of Montevideo to a standstill.

After gaining independence from Spain, the Oriental Republic of Uruguay was established in 1830. The Colorado Party dominated a relatively democratic political system throughout the 1960s. The 1967 constitution established a bicameral congress consisting of the 99-member Chamber of Deputies and the 31-member Senate, with every member serving a five-year term. The president is also directly elected for a five-year term.

In 1998, the National Party, racked by mutual accusations of corruption, joined the opposition Colorado Party in supporting the latter's presidential nominee, Batlle, a 72-year-old senator and five-time presidential candidate whose father and great-uncle had been respected Colorado Party presidents. Faced with dismal economic prospects and a choice between presidential candidates representing moderate right and an eclectic left, in 1999 Uruguayans gave Batlle 52 percent of the vote. Upon taking office, the new president incorporated several National Party members into his cabinet.

Batlle immediately sought an honest accounting of the human rights situation under a former military regime whose widely acknowledged viciousness had turned Uruguay's reputation as the "Switzerland of Latin America" on its head. Batlle also showed equally firm determination to reduce spending and taxes and to privatize previously sacrosanct state monopolies. In 2001, the crisis-ridden rural sector and an increase in violent crime, in what was still one of Latin America's safest countries, dominated much of the public's attention, as did growing labor unrest. Metropolitan Montevideo, with 1.4 million inhabitants, is Uruguay's only large city and contains most of the highest crime areas.

Political Rights and Civil Liberties: Citizens of Uruguay can change their government democratically. In 1999, for the first time, Uruguayan parties selected a single presidential candidate in open primary elections. Previously, the parties had fielded a number of candidates, and the candidates with the most votes then accumulated the votes cast for the others. Constitutional guarantees regarding free expression, freedom of religion, and the right to form political parties, labor unions, and civic organizations are generally respected.

The judiciary is relatively independent, but has become increasingly inefficient in the face of escalating crime, particularly street violence and organized crime. The court system is severely backlogged, and suspects under arrest often spend more time in jail than they would were they to be convicted and serve the maximum sentence for their crime. Allegations of police mistreatment, particularly of youthful offenders, have increased; however, prosecutions of such acts are also occurring more frequently. Prison conditions do not meet international standards.

Uruguay, long a haven for anonymous foreign bank deposits as a result of its strict banking secrecy laws, has also taken measures to regulate financial activities in order to reduce the potential for money laundering. October 1998 saw the passage of antidrug legislation that made narcotics-related money laundering a crime. The Financial Investigations Unit (FIU) was established in order to present more complete evidence in narcotics-related prosecutions. Upon the request of the Central Bank, financial institutions must provide certain information, and banks (including offshore banks), currency exchange houses, and stockbrokers are required to report transactions of more than $10,000. The FIU also requires all entities under its jurisdiction to report suspicious financial transactions to a financial information analysis unit.

The Transparency Law (Ley Cristal) entered in to force in January 1999. It criminalizes a broad range of potential abuses of power by governmental officeholders, including the laundering of funds related to public corruption cases. It also requires financial disclosure statements to be filed by high-ranking officials. Public officials who know of a drug-related crime or incident and do nothing about it may be charged with a "crime of omission" under the Citizen Security Law. Uruguay ranks near the top of public transparency ratings for Latin America issued annually by Transparency International.

The press is privately owned, and broadcasting is both commercial and public. Numerous daily newspapers publish, many associated with political parties; there are also a number of weeklies. In 1996 a number of publications ceased production because of a governmental suspension of tax exemptions on the import of newsprint. In addition, a June 1996 decree requires governmental authorization to import newsprint.

Civic organizations have proliferated since the return of civilian rule. Numerous women's rights groups focus on violence against women, societal discrimination, and other problems. The small black minority continues to face discrimination. Uruguay's continuing economic crisis has forced thousands of formerly middle-class citizens to join rural migrants in the shantytowns ringing Montevideo.

Workers exercise their right to join unions, bargain collectively, and hold strikes. Unions are well organized and politically powerful. Strikes are sometimes marked by violent clashes and sabotage.

Freedom of religion is a cherished political tenet of democratic Uruguay and is broadly respected.

Uzbekistan

Polity: Presidential (dominant party)
Economy: Mixed statist
Population: 25,400,000
PPP: $2,441
Life Expectancy: 70
Religious Groups: Muslim [mostly Sunni] (88 percent), Eastern Orthodox (9 percent), other (3 percent)
Ethnic Groups: Uzbek (80 percent), Russian (6 percent), Tajik (5 percent), Kazakh (3 percent), other (6 percent)
Capital: Tashkent

Political Rights: 7
Civil Liberties: 6
Status: Not Free

1993	1994	1995	1996	1997	1998	1999	2000	2001	2002	2003
6,6NF	7,7NF	7,7NF	7,7NF	7,6NF	7,6NF	76NF	7,6NF	7,6NF	7,6NF	7,6NF

Overview:

Uzbekistan's continued cooperation with the U.S.-led anti-terrorism campaign in 2002 led to American commitments of increased financial assistance in exchange for promises from President Islam Karimov of political reforms. Although Uzbekistan appeared to have made certain human rights-related concessions—including the abolition of official censorship, the registration of a prominent human rights organization, and the unprecedented conviction of seven law enforcement officials for the deaths of two detainees—there was little evidence at year's end of substantive changes to the Uzbek government's repressive policies. In a move that critics charged would further strengthen Karimov's already sweeping powers, voters officially approved constitutional amendments extending the president's term in office from five to seven years.

Located along the ancient trade route of the famous Silk Road, Uzbekistan was incorporated into Russia by the late 1800s. The Uzbekistan Soviet Socialist Republic was established in 1924, and its eastern region was detached and made a separate Tajik Soviet republic five years later.

On December 29, 1991, the country's independence was endorsed in a popular referendum by more than 98 percent of the electorate. In a parallel vote, Islam Karimov, former Communist Party leader and chairman of the People's Democratic Party (PDP), the successor to the Communist Party, was elected president with a reported 88 percent of the vote over the only independent candidate to challenge him, Erk (Freedom) Party leader Mohammed Solih, who charged election fraud. The largest opposition group, Birlik (Unity), was barred from contesting the election and later refused legal registration as a political party, while the Islamic Renaissance Party (IRP) and other religion-based groups were banned entirely. Only pro-government parties were allowed to compete in elections to the first post-Soviet legislature in December 1994 and January 1995. A February 1995 national referendum to extend Karimov's first five-year term in office until the year 2000 was allegedly approved by 99 percent of the country's voters.

Throughout the 1990s, the government increased its repression of opposition movements, including moderate political and religious groups, often under the pretext of fighting violent Islamist organizations. The growing crackdowns, coupled with widespread poverty, in turn fueled Islamist extremist activities and contributed to the radicalization of some former advocates of peaceful change. The Uzbek government blamed a series of deadly car bombings in Tashkent in February 1999 on the Islamic Movement of Uzbekistan (IMU), which seeks the violent overthrow of Uzbekistan's secular government and its replacement with an Islamic state. The authorities used the attacks, which they described as an assassination attempt on Karimov's life, to justify further arrests and trials of both the religious and secular opposition. As a result, many Uzbeks, including both peaceful Muslims and members of the IMU, fled to neighboring countries. In August, IMU militants attempted to enter Uzbekistan by crossing from Tajikistan into neighboring Kyrgyzstan, where they held several villages hostage until early October.

Of the five parties that competed in December's parliamentary election, which was strongly criticized by international election observers, all supported the president and differed little in their political platforms. The January 2000 presidential poll resulted in an expected victory for Karimov, who defeated his only opponent, Marxist history professor Abdulhasiz Dzhalalov, with 92 percent of the vote. Karimov's former party, the PDP, from which he resigned in 1996, had nominated Dzhalalov, its first secretary, with Karimov's consent. Karimov ran as a candidate of the recently established Fidokorlar Party. Uzbekistan's government refused to register genuinely independent opposition parties or permit their members to stand as candidates.

In August 2000, the IMU engaged in armed clashes with government troops in southeastern Uzbekistan. While Tashkent alleged that the guerillas had entered Uzbek territory from bases in neighboring Tajikistan, that country denied the charge. Uzbekistan also accused Afghanistan's then ruling Taliban of harboring many members of the IMU, which the U.S. government had placed on its list of international terrorist organizations in September for its ties to Osama bin Laden's terrorist network, al-Qaeda, and the Taliban.

After the September 11, 2001, attacks on the Pentagon and the World Trade Center, Uzbekistan became a key strategic ally of the United States in its military operations in Afghanistan. By the end of the year, an estimated 1,500 U.S. troops were reported to be stationed at the Khanabad air base in the south of the country, and President Karimov announced that no deadline had been set for their withdrawal. Tashkent's decision to permit the deployment of U.S. troops on its territory was widely seen as an effort to obtain various concessions from the West, including economic assistance, security guarantees, and reduced criticism of its poor human rights record.

In a sign of the two countries' strengthening ties, the United States and Uzbekistan signed the Declaration on Strategic Partnership and Cooperation Framework on March 12, 2002, in which both countries agreed to cooperate on economic, legal, humanitarian, and nuclear proliferation matters. While Uzbekistan affirmed a commitment to implementing democratic reforms—including establishing a multiparty system, ensuring independence of the media, and improving the judicial system—the United States pledged to provide financial aid to encourage the development of civil society. The United States agreed to triple bilateral aid to $160 million and to guarantee $55 million in credit through the U.S. Export-Import Bank. In July, the U.S. Congress allocated $45 million in aid, contingent upon Uzbekistan's efforts to institute political and legal reforms. Under the law, the U.S. State Department must certify that Tashkent is making progress in meeting the commitments agreed on under the Declaration. According to a Human Rights Watch statement issued in August, Uzbekistan by midyear had failed to make significant improvements in any of the areas outlined in the Declaration.

In a January nationwide referendum that critics charged indicated Karimov's intention to consolidate further his already considerable political power, voters allegedly approved amending the country's constitution to extend the presidential term from five to seven years. Karimov's current term in office would therefore end in 2007, rather than in 2005. In a parallel vote, voters officially supported replacing the country's 250-member single-chamber legislature with a bicameral parliament. According to the Central Election Commission, 91 percent had voted for the term extension and 93 percent for the creation of the bicameral legislature, with voter turnout at 92 percent. Independent observers raised serious doubts about the validity of the referendum, citing the presence of police in polling stations, the confusing design of ballot papers, and the fact that some people had been able to vote on behalf of several other individuals.

Political Rights and Civil Liberties:

Citizens of Uzbekistan cannot change their government democratically. President Islam Karimov and the executive branch dominate the legislature and judiciary, and the government severely represses all political opposition. The primary purpose of the national legislature is to confirm decisions made by the executive branch. The 1994-1995 and 1999 parliamentary elections and the 2000 presidential poll, in which only pro-government candidates could participate, were neither free nor fair.

The state imposes strict limits on freedom of speech and the press, particularly with regard to reports on the government and President Karimov. The country's private broadcast and print media outlets generally avoid political issues, are largely regional in scope, and suffer from administrative and financial constraints. Printing presses are owned by the state, which can grant or deny licenses to media outlets. Self-censorship is widespread, while the few journalists who dare to produce probing or critical reports of the authorities face harassment, physical violence, or closure of their media outlets. In April, the government ordered the surveillance and collection of personal information on opposition party activists and Uzbek journalists employed by Radio Liberty and the BBC.

In a positive development, state-radio reporter Shadi Mardiev was released from prison in January 2002 under a presidential amnesty. Mardiev had been sentenced in 1998 to 11 years in prison for slandering a local government official on a program satirizing the official's alleged corrupt activities. In October, the government no longer required that all Internet service providers (ISPs) route their connections through the government-run ISP, UzPak. Although official censorship was formally abolished in May, the responsibility for censoring material was transferred to newspaper editors, who were warned by the State Press Committee that they would be held personally accountable for what they publish.

The government permits the existence of mainstream religions, including approved Muslim and Jewish communities, as well as the Russian Orthodox Church and some other Christian denominations. However, the activities of other congregations are restricted through legislation that requires all religious groups to register with the state through burdensome registration criteria. In addition, the 1998 Law on Freedom of Conscience and Religious Organizations prohibits proselytizing, the teaching of religious subjects without official permission, and the wearing of religious garments in public by anyone other than clerics. Revisions to the criminal code in May 1998 and May 1999 increased penalties for violating the law and other statutes on religious activities. In November 2002, a Jehovah's Witness, Marat Mudarisov, was given a three-year suspended sentence for disseminating publications inciting national and racial hatred and for undermining the constitution. Mudarisov maintains that the publications were planted on him by security service members, and that he was beaten and threatened with torture.

The government continued to be suspicious and intolerant of followers of Muslim organizations not sanctioned by the state. During the last several years, many of them have been arrested or imprisoned on charges of anti-constitutional activities, often under the pretext of the government's fight against militant Islamists. Authorities have targeted members of the banned Hizb-ut-Tahrir (Islamic Party of Liberation), an international movement calling for the creation of an Islamic caliphate throughout the Muslim world. Suspected members have been forced to give confessions under torture and their family members have been subjected to interrogation, arrest, and extortion. In August, the bodies of two prisoners who had been convicted of involvement with Hizb-ut-Tahrir were returned to their families for burial. According to Human Rights Watch, they had died under suspicious circumstances and their bodies showed apparent signs of torture. Both men had been held at Jaslyk prison, which is notorious for its harsh conditions and ill-treatment of religious prisoners.

Permits for public demonstrations, which must be approved by the government, are not routinely granted, and fear of police persecution makes such rallies uncommon occurrences. In 2002, police detained a number of women who protested against the imprisonment of their male relatives for belonging to illegal Islamic groups.

No genuine political opposition groups function legally or participate in the government. A 1997 law prohibits parties based on ethnic or religious lines and those advocating subversion of the constitutional order. Members of unregistered opposition groups, including Birlik and Erk, are subject to discrimination or have gone into voluntary exile abroad. The Council of the Federation of Trade Unions is dependent on the state, and no genuinely alternative union structures exist.

After years of its having been denied legal status, the authorities in March finally registered the Independent Human Rights Organization of Uzbekistan (NOPCHU), one of the country's principal human rights groups. The decision, which was the first time that the government had formally registered a local human rights organization, came just days before a visit by Karimov to the United States. Two months earlier, police had returned archived records of human rights abuses, along with the passport of NOPCHU director Mikhail Ardzinov, after having held them for more than two years.

Although the registration of NOPCHU was hailed by many observers as a tentatively positive step, other human rights groups, including the Human Rights Society of Uzbekistan (HRSU), continued to be denied registration and to face ongoing harassment by the authorities. Following a protest against human rights abuses that was held outside the Ministry of Justice on August 27, two participants, including HRSU member Elena Urlaeva, were arrested, forcibly detained in a psychiatric hospital, and reportedly given psychiatric drugs. In September, another HRSU member, Yuldash Rasulov, was sentenced in a politically motivated trial to seven years in prison on charges of attempting to overthrow the constitutional order and distributing "extremist" literature.

The judiciary is subservient to the president, who appoints all judges and can remove them from office at any time. Police routinely physically abuse suspects to extract confessions, while arbitrary arrest and detention are common. Law enforcement authorities reportedly often plant narcotics, weapons, or banned religious literature on suspected members of Islamic groups or political opponents to justify their arrests. In the country's first conviction of law enforcement officials on charges of lethal brutality, four policemen were found guilty in January in the beating death of one detainee and the torture of another and were sentenced to 20 years in prison. The verdict followed a visit to Tashkent the previous day of a senior U.S. State Department official, who had expressed dissatisfaction with the lack of democratic reform in Uzbekistan. In a separate case in June, three National Security Service officers received prison sentences of between 5 and 15 years in the death of a suspect alleged to belong to a banned religious group.

Prisons suffer from severe overcrowding and shortages of food and medicine. Following a two-week fact-finding mission, the UN special rapporteur on torture, Theo van Boven, concluded that torture is "systematic" in Uzbekistan's prisons and detention centers. In December, Karimov announced an amnesty for various categories of prisoners in honor of the tenth anniversary of the adoption of the country's constitution. However, the presidential pardon did not apply to those convicted of involvement in extremist organizations or anti-constitutional activities, crimes under which many of the country's estimated 7,000 political prisoners have been sentenced.

Widespread corruption, bureaucratic regulations, and the government's tight control over the economy limit most citizens' equality of opportunity. Duties of up to 90 percent on imported goods that were imposed in mid-2002 led to greater financial hardships for the country's many merchants and shuttle traders and sparked protests in a number of towns and villages. Uzbekistan continues to use Soviet-style residence permits and maintains widespread restrictions on foreign travel. Most people must pay often costly bribes in order to obtain exit visas.

Women's educational and professional prospects are restricted by traditional cultural and religious norms and by ongoing economic difficulties throughout the country. Victims of domestic violence are discouraged from pressing charges against their perpetrators, who rarely face criminal prosecution. According to a Human Rights Watch report, the government is extending its campaign against non-mainstream Muslims to include women. In May, four women charged with membership in the banned group, Hizb-ut-Tahrir, were given suspended sentences of between two and three years.

Vanuatu

Polity: Parliamentary democracy
Economy: Capitalist-statist
Population: 200,000
PPP: $2,802
Life Expectancy: 67

Political Rights: 1
Civil Liberties: 2*
Status: Free

Religious Groups: Presbyterian (36.7 percent), Anglican (15 percent), Roman Catholic (15 percent), indigenous beliefs (7.6 percent), Seventh-Day Adventist (6.2 percent), Church of Christ (3.8 percent), other (15.7 percent)
Ethnic Groups: Melanesian (98 percent), other (2 percent)
Capital: Port Vila
Ratings Change: Vanuatu's civil liberties rating improved from 3 to 2 due to changes in the survey methodology.

1993	1994	1995	1996	1997	1998	1999	2000	2001	2002	2003
2,3F	1,2F	1,3F	1,3F	1,3F	1,3F	1,3F	1,3F	1,3F	1,3F	1,2F

Overview:

Located 1,300 miles northeast of Sydney in the South Pacific, Vanuatu is an archipelago of approximately 80 islands with a mainly Melanesian population. The two largest islands, Espiritu Santo and Malakula, make up nearly one-half the total land area. Known to Europeans as the New Hebrides, the islands were jointly administered by Britain and France from 1906 until 1980, when the country gained independence.

The unique Anglo-French "condominium" colonization divided Vanuatans into English- and French-speaking communities. Prior to independence, English-speaking politicians, such as the late Father Walter Lini and other leaders of his Vanua'aku Party, were the main champions of independence, while French-speaking political leaders tended to favor continued colonial rule. The Francophone Nagriamel movement, led by Jimmy Stevens, led a brief secessionist revolt on Espiritu Santo at independence that was quickly put down.

Lini's left-leaning Vanua'aku Party led the new nation from independence until 1991. That year, a split within the party allowed Maxime Carlot Korman, leader of the francophone Union of Moderate Parties (UMP), to become Vanuatu's first French-speaking prime minister. After the 1995 elections, Carlot was succeeded by Serge

Vohor, who headed a dissident UMP faction. Since then, leadership of the country has changed hands several times through no-confidence votes, as one parliamentary coalition after another collapsed. Many of the rifts between English- and French-speaking politicians mended in the 1990s, as parties increasingly formed coalitions that crossed linguistic lines.

The current prime minister, Edward Natapei, of the Vanua'aku Party, took office in 2001 in a coalition government with the UMP after a parliamentary vote of no confidence ousted Prime Minister Barak Sope, in office since 1999. Natapei retained his post after his Vanua'aku Party formed a new coalition with the UMP following the May 2002 elections. The UMP, led by former prime minister Vohor, won the most seats of any party in the 52-seat parliament, taking 15 compared to the Vanua'aku Party's 14.

No single theme dominated the election campaign, although a key issue was the government's pledge to bring back a program aimed at making public officials more accountable. Widely supported by international aid donors, the Comprehensive Reform Plan (CRP) was introduced by the Vanua'aku Party in the 1990s before being scrapped by then prime minister Sope, who heads the opposition Melanesian Progressive Party. Sope and opposition leader Willy Jimmy, head of the social-democratic National Unity Party, said during the campaign that if elected they would not bring back the CRP.

Sope was jailed in July on fraud charges stemming from his tenure as prime minister, though he was later pardoned on medical grounds by President John Bani. Prime Minister Natapei set up a commission of inquiry in November to examine the president's controversial move. Meanwhile, four senior police officers received two-year suspended jail terms in December for mutiny and other charges in connection with the August arrest of 15 senior officials in response to the appointment of a new police commissioner. The brazen arrests and resulting light sentences raised questions about whether Vanuatu's police force is fully under civilian control.

Some 80 percent of Vanuatans are either subsistence farmers or fishermen. The service sector consists primarily of tourism, the civil service, and offshore banking and makes up the largest share of economic output. Visiting Australian Foreign Minister Alexander Downer in December praised the government for tightening laws to help prevent the country's tax haven status from being used to finance terrorism.

Political Rights and Civil Liberties:

Citizens of Vanuatu can change their government through elections. The nongovernmental Election Observers Group, which monitored the May 2002 polls, called for a review of the electoral law with a view to curbing fraud and bribery.

The 1980 constitution created a directly elected parliament whose 52 members serve four-year terms. The largely ceremonial president is chosen by an electoral college consisting of the parliament and presidents of Vanuatu's regional councils.

Vanuatu's courts "generally are independent of executive interference," according to the U.S. State Department's global human rights report for 2001, released in March 2002. The common law judiciary generally affords citizens fair trials, although the court system is inefficient and lacks enough qualified judges and prosecutors. As a result, criminal defendants often are held for long periods before their trials, and prison conditions for the 30-odd inmates are poor, with the central prison in the capital, Port Vila, "dilapidated and not reliably secured," the report added.

Vanuatu's press is generally free, notwithstanding the government's controversial deportation in 2001 of a leading newspaper publisher, Mark Neil-Jones of the *Trading Post*. Authorities claimed that he had revealed state secrets in his reporting on official corruption. The chief justice overturned the deportation within a week, and Neil-Jones returned to Vanuatu and resumed his work. The government runs a weekly newspaper, two radio stations, and a television station that serves Port Vila. At least three private newspapers compete with the state media.

Women enjoy equal rights under the law, although they generally are limited to traditional family roles in this male-dominated society. Families often are reluctant to educate girls, and social norms discourage women from owning land and encourage them to focus on childbearing.

Violence against women, particularly wife beating, is common, according to the U.S. State Department report. Although courts prosecute some offenders, most cases of violence against women, including rape, go unreported because the victims are unaware of their rights or fear reprisals, the report added. Moreover, police are reluctant to intervene in domestic violence cases because these are widely viewed as private matters. Religious freedom generally is respected in this mainly Christian society.

Vanuatu's five trade unions are independent and are grouped under the umbrella Vanuatu Council of Trade Unions. Only about 1,000 of the country's 25,000 wage or salary earners belong to unions. The workplace safety and health law is inadequate to protect workers engaged in logging, agriculture, construction, and manufacturing, and the labor department lacks sufficient resources to enforce the law effectively as it exists, according to the U.S. State Department report.

Venezuela

Polity: Presidential-parliamentary democracy
Political Rights: 3
Civil Liberties: 4*
Economy: Capitalist-statist
Status: Partly Free
Population: 25,100,000
PPP: $5,794
Life Expectancy: 73
Religious Groups: Roman Catholic (96 percent), Protestant (2 percent), other (2 percent)
Ethnic Groups: Spanish, Italian, Portuguese, Arab, German, African, indigenous people
Capital: Caracas
Ratings Change: Venezuela's civil liberties rating improved from 5 to 4 due to the resiliency of civil society in the face of pressures from the government of President Hugo Chavez.

Ten-Year Ratings Timeline (Political Rights, Civil Liberties, Status)

1993	1994	1995	1996	1997	1998	1999	2000	2001	2002	2003
3,3PF	3,3PF	3,3PF	3,3PF	2,3F	2,3F	2,3F	4,4PF	3,5PF	3,5PF	3,4PF

Overview:

Venezuelan strongman Hugo Chavez successfully escaped his overthrow and imprisonment in a April 2002 coup attempt, and was returned to power as a result of the continued loyalty of key military garrisons around the country and significant sectors of the population. However, throughout the year, the country saw protests by a broad spectrum of civil society and unprecedented discontent in the barracks by officers tired of Chavez's threadbare populism. Chavez, himself the one-time leader of two coup attempts, appeared to remain confident of his own ability to keep order, despite the increasing disorder.

The Republic of Venezuela was established in 1830, nine years after independence from Spain. Long periods of instability and military rule ended with the establishment in 1961 of civilian rule. Under the constitution approved that year, the president and a bicameral congress are elected for five years. The Senate has at least two members from each of the 21 states and the federal district of Caracas. The Chamber of Deputies has 189 seats.

Until 1993, the social-democratic Democratic Action (AD) Party and the Social Christian Party (COPEI) dominated politics. Former president Carlos Andres Perez (1989–1993) of the AD was nearly overthrown by Chavez and other nationalist military officers in two 1992 coup attempts in which dozens were killed. In 1993 Perez was charged with corruption and removed from office by congress. Rafael Caldera, a former president (1969–1974) of COPEI and a populist, was elected president in late 1993 as head of the 16-party National Convergence, which included Communists, other leftists, and right-wing groups. With crime soaring, public corruption unabated, oil wealth drying up, and the country in its worst economic crisis in 50 years, popular disillusionment with politics deepened.

In the 1998 presidential contest, Chavez's antiestablishment, anticorruption populism played well in a country whose political establishment was famous for its interlocking system of privilege and graft and whose elites considered politics their private preserve. Last-minute efforts to find a consensus candidate against Chavez were largely unsuccessful, and the Yale-educated businessman Henrique Salas, the other leading presidential contender, also steered away from association with the old political order. Salas, a respected two-term former state governor, won just 40 percent of the vote, to Chavez's 57 percent. In February 1999, Chavez took control of the world's fifth-largest oil-producing country.

A constituent assembly dominated by Chavez followers drafted a new constitution that would make censorship of the press easier, allow a newly strengthened chief executive the right to dissolve congress, and make it possible for Chavez to retain power until 2013. Congress and the Supreme Court were dismissed after Venezuelans approved the new constitution in a national referendum on December 15, 2000. Despite Chavez's 21-point lead in the presidential contest, the July 2000 election marked a resurgence of political opposition that had been hamstrung in its efforts to contest his stripping of congress and the judiciary of their independence and power. Opposition parties won most of the country's governorships, about half the mayoralties, and a significant share of power in the new congress. In November, Chavez's congressional allies granted him special fast-track powers that allowed him to decree a wide range of laws without parliamentary debate.

By 2001 a dramatic rise in street crime threatened the working class and poor Venezuelans who make up the core of Chavez's constituency, as well as frightening those belonging to the country's beleaguered middle class. The crime wave was centered in Caracas and made even wealthy neighborhoods in the capital city subject to serious public safety threats. Venezuela's continued economic woes and natural disasters, together with weapons and narcotics trafficking, added to the heightened sense of insecurity. A recent study ranked Venezuela as second of the 10 most violent nations in the Americas and Europe; the overwhelmed police proved unable to halt the carnage, which was responsible for one Venezuelan being killed nearly every hour. On December 10, 2001, political opponents and business and labor leaders staged a widely supported national protest strike against Chavez's rule.

The failed coup against Chavez, which the United States was slow to condemn, included a near total shutdown of Venezuela's state-owned oil monopoly, a general strike, a short-lived provisional government, and the slaying of 19 people in an opposition march. Despite Chavez's May announcement of wide-ranging fiscal reforms, political tensions have kept foreign investors wary. In August, charges against four alleged military-coup leaders were dismissed on the grounds of insufficient evidence. In October an estimated one million Venezuelans marched in Caracas demanding that Chavez call either early elections or a referendum on his rule—and threatening a general strike if he did not accede. As the United Nations and the Organization of American States desperately tried to mediate peace talks meant to break the country's political deadlock, the country appeared to move closer to civil war. In November, the government took military control of the 8,000-member Caracas city police, which Chavez claimed had repeatedly repressed pro-government demonstrators. Armed groups operating along Venezuela's western border with Colombia have stepped up their illegal activities, which range from killing and kidnapping to extortion and the smuggling of cocaine. In November a grenade was thrown at the home of the Caracas archbishop, in yet another attack believed to be carried out by government supporters against the Roman Catholic Church.

Political Rights and Civil Liberties: Citizens can change their government democratically, although supporters of President Hugo Chavez appear at times on the verge of mob rule, particularly as constitutional checks and balances have been removed. The July 2000 elections were considered by international observers to be free and fair.

Until Chavez took power, the judicial system was headed by a nominally independent supreme court that was nevertheless highly politicized, undermined by the chronic corruption (including the growing influence of narcotics traffickers) that permeates the entire political system, and unresponsive to charges of rights abuses. An unwieldy new judicial code has hampered some law enforcement efforts, resulting in low rates of conviction and shorter jail terms even for convicted murderers. Police salaries are woefully inadequate.

Widespread arbitrary detention and torture of suspects, as well as dozens of extrajudicial killings by military security forces and the police, have increased as crime continues to soar. By mid-2000, an estimated 500 people had been killed by the police, a sign that, some observers say, is evidence of a growing vigilante mentality among law enforcement personnel. Since the 1992 coup attempts, weakened civilian governments have had less authority over the military and the police, and overall rights abuses are committed with impunity. A separate system of armed forces courts retains jurisdiction over members of the military accused of rights violations and common criminal crimes, and decisions cannot be appealed in civilian court.

Venezuela's 32 prisons, the most violent in the world, hold some 23,000 inmates—fewer than one-third have been convicted of a crime—even though they were designed to hold no more than 14,000. Deadly prison riots are common, and inmate gangs have a striking degree of control over the penal system. Chavez's government has announced an emergency program to modernize the country's prisons, including plans to build five or six new penitentiaries.

The press is mostly privately owned, although the practice of journalism is supervised by an association of broadcasters under government control. Since 1994, the media in general have faced a pattern of intimidation. International media monitors have condemned a constitutional article approved by the Constituent Assembly that would require journalists to publish or broadcast "truthful information," a move that they say opens the door to governmental censorship. In 2001, the Inter-American Press Association accused the government of using the judiciary for its own political purposes and of intimidating the media. Chavez frequently interrupted soap operas, and even a World Series baseball game, to broadcast hours-long diatribes on the government-run television station.

Few Indians hold title to their land, and indigenous communities trying to defend their legal land rights are subject to abuses, including murder, by gold miners and corrupt rural police. In 1999, the Constituent Assembly voted to include a chapter in the new constitution that sets forth the legal rights of indigenous peoples and communities. Chapter VII would guarantee "the right to exist as indigenous peoples and communities with their own social and economic organization, their cultures and traditions, and their language and religion." In the July 2000 national elections, three indigenous candidates were elected to the National Assembly, eight were elected to regional legislative congresses, and four Indians won mayoralties. The lack of effective legal rights, however, has created an unprecedented emigration by Indians to poverty-stricken urban areas.

Labor unions are well organized, but highly politicized and prone to corruption. Chavez supporters have sought to break what they term a "stranglehold" of corrupt labor leaders on the job market, a move labor activists say tramples on the rights of private organizations. The referendum approved in December 2000 allows Chavez to dissolve the Venezuelan Workers Confederation and to organize new state-supervised elections of union representatives, a move that opposition and labor leaders say is the first step towards establishing a government-controlled labor union. The government continued to interfere in union elections, although international observers said they saw no evidence of election fraud. Security forces frequently break up strikes and arrest trade unionists.

Women are more active in politics than in many other Latin American countries and comprise the backbone of Venezuela's sophisticated grassroots network of non-governmental organizations.

Vietnam

Polity: One party   **Political Rights:** 7
Economy: Statist   **Civil Liberties:** 6
Population: 79,700,000   **Status:** Not Free
PPP: $1,996
Life Expectancy: 68
Religious Groups: Buddhist, Hoa Hao, Cao Dai,
Christian, indigenous beliefs, Muslim
Ethnic Groups: Vietnamese (85-90 percent), other, including Chinese, Muong, Thai,
Meo, Khmer, Man, Cham (10-15 percent)
Capital: Hanoi

Ten-Year Ratings Timeline (Political Rights, Civil Liberties, Status)

1993	1994	1995	1996	1997	1998	1999	2000	2001	2002	2003
7,7NF	7,7NF	7,7NF	7,7NF	7,7NF	7,7NF	7,7NF	7,7NF	7,6NF	7,6NF	7,6NF

Overview:
Vietnam held parliamentary elections in 2002 that were as tightly controlled as ever, while authorities cracked down on critics ranging from hill tribesmen to cyber-dissidents. The ruling Communist Party's efforts to solidify its tight grip on power came as it faces protests over corruption and land rights as well as a less-docile workforce empowered by its limited but potent market reforms.

Vietnam won independence from France in 1954, after a century of colonial rule followed by occupation by the Japanese during World War II. At independence, the country was divided into the French-backed Republic of South Vietnam and the Communist-ruled Democratic Republic of Vietnam in the north. Following a decade-long war that killed tens of thousands of soldiers and civilians, North Vietnam defeated the U.S.-backed South in 1975 and reunited the country in 1976.

Victorious on the battlefield, the Communist government proved unable to feed its people. The centralized economy grew at anemic rates, and Vietnam had to import rice. The government responded with reforms in 1986 that dismantled collectivized agriculture and encouraged small-scale private enterprise.

Spurred by the reforms, Vietnam's economy grew by 7.6 percent per year on average, and output doubled, between 1991 and 2000, according to World Bank figures. The Southeast Asian country is now the world's second-biggest rice exporter.

Vietnam's leadership, however, continues to be divided over the pace and depth of privatization and other market reforms. Moderates see deep-rooted reforms as the ticket to modernizing the impoverished country and producing enough jobs to stave off social unrest. Hard-liners, though, fear that loosening the state's control over the economy will undermine the ruling Communist Party of Vietnam's (CPV) tight grip on power. They realize that farmers, who now work for themselves, and other private (business) sector workers cannot be monitored as easily as those who depend on the state for their livelihoods. Moreover, while the government has sold off thousands of small firms, privatization of large companies would very likely throw millions out of work, possibly leading to a backlash against the regime.

The CPV in 2001 signaled its intent to continue carrying out reforms, but in a gradual way, when it tapped as its new party leader a veteran politician who has a reputation for stressing pragmatism over ideology. Nong Duc Manh, now 61, is widely viewed as being capable of forging consensus between the party's conservative old guard and younger, reform-minded cadres. His elevation to the top post came that April at the CPV's ninth party congress, which nominally set out government policy for the next five years. In choosing Manh, a northerner, and then in 2002 re-electing Prime Minister Phan Van Khai and state President Tran Duc Luong, the party also preserved the leadership troika's traditional balance between northern, central, and southern Vietnam.

The May 19, 2002, parliamentary elections, meanwhile, offered little suspense, as all candidates for the 498-seat body had been vetted in advance by the CPV. The number of nonparty legislators elected shrank to 51 from 68.

The elections came as the government faced international criticism over its treatment of ethnic minorities in the mountainous central highlands. The watchdog groups Human Rights Watch and Amnesty International said in January that they had documented beatings and jailings over the past year of dozens of returning hill tribe refugees who had been deported from Cambodia.

The refugees had fled Vietnam in early 2001 to escape a crackdown on members of hill tribes that came after several thousand mainly Christian hill tribesmen held protests in the highlands demanding more religious freedom, greater land rights, and political autonomy for the region. Vietnamese officials have "systematically arrested and repressed those they believe responsible" for the 2001 protests, Amnesty said in a December report. Hill tribesmen, known as Montagnards, routinely complain that their lands are increasingly being converted by lowland Vietnamese into plantations for coffee and other cash crops.

During the year, the regime also intensified its crackdown on pro-democracy activists. Several government critics were arrested, sentenced to long jail terms, placed under house arrest, or otherwise harassed by Vietnamese authorities.

The government, meanwhile, moved slowly in complying with a three-year, $368 million loan package extended by the International Monetary Fund in 2001 to help Vietnam restructure 1,800 state-owned firms, reform its debt-ridden state banks, and free up trade and capital flows. Only 79 of the firms slated for privatization were sold off by the first half of 2002.

Political Rights and Civil Liberties:

Ruled by the CPV as a single-party state, Vietnam is one of the most tightly controlled societies in the world. The regime jails or harasses most dissidents, controls all media, sharply restricts religious freedom, and prevents Vietnamese from setting up independent political, labor, or religious groups. At the same time, authorities recently have tolerated some grassroots protests over nominally nonpolitical issues and loosened their control over the day-to-day lives of ordinary Vietnamese.

Vietnam's 498-member National Assembly generally does not table legislation or pass laws the party opposes. Delegates, however, question state ministers, air grassroots grievances, and debate legal, economic, and social matters. They also criticize officials' performance and governmental corruption and inefficiency. The party-controlled Fatherland Front, however, vets all assembly candidates and allows only CPV members and some independents to run.

In addition to using the National Assembly as an outlet for grassroots complaints, the regime has also tried to address bread-and-butter concerns with a 1998 decree that directs local officials to consult more with ordinary Vietnamese. In many provinces, however, complaints get bogged down in bureaucratic shuffling, the *Far Eastern Economic Review* of Hong Kong reported in 2001.

The leadership increasingly has also allowed farmers and others to hold small protests over local grievances, which most often concern land seizures. Thousands of Vietnamese also try to gain redress each year by writing letters to or personally addressing officials. In addition to land matters, citizens complain about official corruption, economic policy, governmental inefficiency, and opaque bureaucratic procedures. Underscoring these concerns, the Berlin-based Transparency International watchdog group ranked Vietnam in a three-way tie as the 16th most corrupt out of 102 countries covered in its annual survey of corruption for 2002.

Vietnam's judiciary is "subservient to the CPV," with the party closely controlling the courts at all levels and reportedly telling judges how to rule in political cases, according to the U.S. State Department's global human rights report for 2001, released in March 2002. Even in ordinary criminal cases, defendants often lack time to meet with their lawyers and to prepare and present an adequate defense, while defense lawyers are sometimes permitted only to appeal for clemency for their clients, according to Amnesty International. Moreover, many criminal suspects are unable to obtain counsel at all because of Vietnam's shortage of lawyers.

Jails are overcrowded, and inmates lack sufficient food, although prison conditions generally are not life threatening, the U.S. State Department report said. The report noted, however, that guards sometimes badly mistreat prisoners and frequently beat them. Similarly, Amnesty International said in November that it had documented dozens of cases of Vietnamese prisoners who were denied adequate medical care, shackled as a form of punishment, or held in solitary confinement for long periods.

Vietnamese jails hold some political prisoners, including religious dissidents, although there are no accurate figures on the number of prisoners of conscience. Their ranks include Le Chi Quang, a 32-year-old lawyer who received a four-year jail sentence in November after he posted on the Internet articles critical of the government. Another political prisoner, Nguyen Khac Toan, received a 12-year sentence in December, after a trial that lasted less than a day, for allegedly passing information to overseas Vietnamese activist groups and helping farmers draft petitions to the government, according to Amnesty International. The government denies holding any prisoners on political grounds.

In addition to jailing dissidents, officials place restrictions on where some dissidents can work or live, confining some to house arrest, the U.S. State Department report said. They do this under a broad 1997 decree authorizing "administrative probation" for up to two years without trial for Vietnamese whose offenses are deemed to be punishable, without quite warranting "criminal responsibility."

To monitor the population, the regime relies on a household registration system and on block wardens, who use informers to track individual activity. Officials, however, have largely scaled back their surveillance of ordinary Vietnamese, focusing instead mainly on political and religious dissidents, according to the U.S. State Department report.

All media are tightly controlled by the party and government. Officials have punished journalists who overstepped the bounds of permissible reporting by jailing or placing them under house arrest, taking away their press cards, or closing down their newspapers, the *Far Eastern Economic Review* reported in 2001. The media are also kept in check by a 1999 law that requires journalists to pay damages to groups or individuals that are found to be harmed by press articles, even if the reports are true. At least one suit has been filed under this law, although it was withdrawn. In this stifling environment, journalists practice self-censorship on sensitive political and economic matters.

The media, nevertheless, are sometimes permitted to report on high-level governmental corruption and mismanagement. The regime, however, strictly prohibits the media, or ordinary Vietnamese, from promoting democracy, questioning the CPV's leading role, or criticizing individual governmental leaders or the regime's human rights record. These restrictions are backed up by tough national security and anti-defamation provisions in the constitution and criminal code.

The government allows Vietnamese access to the Internet, but blocks some politically sensitive sites and requires service providers and cyber café owners to monitor their customers' use of the Internet. In 2002, the government also ordered all domestic Web sites to obtain licenses. Vietnam has some 150,000 Internet users, according to official figures.

The regime sharply restricts religious freedom by tightly regulating religious organizations and clergy and cracking down on independent religious groups and their leaders. All religious groups must register with the government. They also must get permission to build or remodel places of worship; run religious schools or do charitable work; hold conventions, training seminars, and special celebrations; and train, ordain, promote, or transfer clergy, according to the U.S. State Department report.

As a result of these regulations, religious groups generally have trouble expanding schools, obtaining teaching materials, publishing religious texts, and increasing the number of students training for the clergy, the U.S. State Department report said. Among the hardest hit by the regulations are the Cao Daiists, who are prohibited from ordaining new priests, and Protestants, who are barred from running seminaries and ordaining new clergy; the regulations are enforced most strictly in the northwestern provinces and central highlands, the report added.

Officials also enforce closure orders, in effect since 1975, on Hoa Hao places of worship, according to the U.S. State Department report. Amnesty International said in October that members of the Hoa Hao faith have been jailed over the past year on charges that the London-based rights group believes are linked solely to their religious practices. Hoa Hao followers fought the Communist forces during the Vietnam War.

Both religious groups and most individual clergy must join a party-controlled supervisory body, one of which exists for each religion the state recognizes. These are: Buddhism; Roman Catholicism; Protestantism; Islam; Cao Daism, a synthesis of several religions; and the Hoa Hao faith, a reformist Buddhist church.

Officials frequently jail, arrest, or otherwise harass worshipers who belong to independent religious groups that refuse to join one of the supervisory bodies, according to Amnesty International. For years, the government has tried to undermine the independent Unified Buddhist Church of Vietnam (UBCV). Officials released several prominent UBCV monks in 1998 but continue to harass group members. Buddhists make up three-quarters of Vietnam's population.

Authorities reportedly also subject underground Protestant worshipers in the central highlands and northwestern provinces to "severe abuses," according to the U.S. State Department report, including jailing some congregants and shutting down some churches. Meanwhile, ethnic Hmong converts to Christianity, particularly in the northern provinces of Lao Cai and Lai Chau, have complained since the late 1980s that they are often jailed, harassed, and otherwise pressured to abandon their religious faith by provincial officials, according to Amnesty International and Human Rights Watch.

Vietnamese women are increasingly active in business, but they continue to face unofficial employment and wage discrimination, according to the U.S. State Department report. They also hold relatively few senior positions in government and politics.

Domestic violence against women reportedly is relatively common, and officials do not vigorously enforce relevant laws, the U.S. State Department report said. Despite some governmental initiatives to protect women trafficking of women and girls, both within Vietnam and into China and Cambodia, continues to be a serious and growing problem, the report added. Women are trafficked for both labor and sexual exploitation. Meanwhile, roughly 40,000 Vietnamese children between the ages of 8 and 14 are working illegally full- or part-time, according to official figures.

Vietnam's ethnic minorities face unofficial discrimination in mainstream society, and local officials reportedly sometimes restrict minority access to schooling and jobs, according to the U.S. State Department report. Minorities also generally have little input into development projects that affect them, the *Far Eastern Economic Review* reported in 2001.

In the workplace, the government prohibits independent trade unions and only weakly enforces child labor and other labor laws, the U.S. State Department report said. Despite the ban on free trade unions, hundreds of independent "labor associations" have been permitted to represent many workers at individual firms and in some service occupations. In any case, the vast majority of Vietnamese workers are small-scale farmers in rural areas who are not unionized in any way.

Workers have staged dozens of strikes in recent years, generally against foreign and private companies. The government has tolerated the strikes even though in most cases the workers have not followed a legally mandated conciliation and arbitration process with management. The regime's ban on independent trade unions extends to all private groups, such as human rights organizations, whose agenda touches on politics.

Yemen

Polity: Dominant party (military-influenced) (traditional chiefs)
Economy: Capitalist-statist
Population: 18,600,000
PPP: $893
Life Expectancy: 59

Political Rights: 6
Civil Liberties: 5*
Status: Not Free

Religious Groups: Muslim (including Sunni and Shi'a), other
Ethnic Groups: Predominantly Arab, some Afro-Arab, South Asian
Capital: Sanaa
Ratings Change: Yemen's civil liberties rating improved from 6 to 5 due to changes in the survey methodology.

Ten-Year Ratings Timeline (Political Rights, Civil Liberties, Status)

1993	1994	1995	1996	1997	1998	1999	2000	2001	2002	2003
6,4PF	4,5PF	5,6PF	5,6PF	5,6PF	5,6PF	5,6PF	5,6PF	5,6PF	6,6NF	6,5NF

Overview:

Seeking to maintain stability and stave off the threat of U.S. military intervention, the Yemeni government continued to crack down on suspected al-Qaeda supporters in 2002. In spite of a series of brazen attacks by Islamic militants during the year, the government's campaign of arbitrary arrests and deportations has not been accompanied by increased restriction on freedom of expression or the postponement of parliamentary elections, scheduled for April 2003.

Strategically located at the junction of ancient trading routes, Yemen is one of the oldest centers of civilization in the Middle East. Although unified since the merger of the Yemen Arab Republic (YAR, or North Yemen) and the People's Democratic Republic of Yemen (PDRY) 13 years ago, the northern and southeastern regions of the country have long been geographically and culturally distinct. Since the influx of persecuted Shiites in the seventh and eighth centuries from what is today Iraq and Iran, the tribes of the northern highlands have practiced a distinct form of Shiite Islam known as Zaydism. A succession of Zaydi imams ruled the mountains and coastal plain of northern Yemen until 1962, when military officers launched a coup and established the YAR. The predominantly Sunni Muslim coastal plain and interior of southern Yemen came under British control in the mid-nineteenth century and gained independence in 1967, when British troops withdrew and Marxist rebels seized power.

In 1990, severe economic crises and mounting popular discontent in South Yemen led PDRY president Ali Salim al-Biedh to accept unification with the YAR. The initial transition period, in which Biedh's Yemeni Socialist Party (YSP) shared power with the General People's Congress (GPC) of North Yemeni president Ali Abdullah Saleh, who became head of the new republic, witnessed unprecedented political reforms. Because of the former North Yemen's much larger population, the GPC dominated its rival politically and won an overwhelming victory in the 1993 parliamentary elections. The YSP, which finished third behind the Islamist Islah (Reform) Party, boycotted the new government and tried to reestablish an independent South Yemen the following year. The result was a bloody, 70-day civil war that ended with the exile of Biedh and other YSP leaders.

Yemen's experiment with democracy continued after the war, though the YSP's boycott of national elections allowed the GPC to dominate political life. The GPC-dominated parliament quickly approved constitutional changes that gave the president broad powers and, in return for Islamist support for Saleh during the fighting, declared *Sharia* (Islamic law) to be the unique source of all legislation. Islah was awarded control of several ministries and allowed to run a vast network of government-subsidized religious schools. Saleh, who is from the Sanhan tribe of the Hashid Confederation, appointed his own clansmen to top military commands and secured the support of other tribes through the distribution of state funds and civil service positions, while allowing them to maintain large standing militias, bypass governmental courts in resolving disputes, and hold foreigners hostage for ransom payments. In February 2001, the government won approval in a popular referendum to extend presidential and parliamentary terms, which some observers noted would allow Saleh to retire (assuming he wins in 2006) just as his son turns 40—the minimum age for presidential candidates in Yemen.

The virtual absence of governmental authority outside of major cities and the influx of foreign students to Islamist schools (most notably the American Taliban member John Walker Lindh) facilitated the emergence of armed Islamic groups affiliated with al-Qaeda in Yemen, the ancestral homeland of Osama bin Laden. Unwilling to endanger tribal and Islamist support for his regime, Saleh resisted American pressure to rein in these groups following the October 2000 bombing of the USS Cole in Aden harbor, but relented in the wake of the September 11, 2001, attacks on the United States, when U.S. officials warned that Yemen was a potential target of military action. After 18 Yemeni soldiers died in a botched raid in December 2001, the United States began a crash program to train and equip the security forces.

The crackdown continued in 2002. Although the government said in late May that only 85 people suspected of ties to al-Qaeda were in custody, Islah leader Abdullah al-Ahmar maintained that there were hundreds, and "perhaps thousands," in detention and that some had been turned over to the United States. The government also closed or assumed control over hundreds of *madrasahs* (Islamist schools). In November, the authorities permitted an unmanned U.S. predator aircraft to assassinate a senior al-Qaeda leader and five of his aides. Nevertheless, the year witnessed numerous outbreaks of violence by Islamist radicals. In April, a number of bomb attacks on governmental buildings were carried out by a group calling itself "Sympathizers of al-Qaeda," and unspecified terrorist threats led to the closure of the U.S. embassy for six days. On October 6, suspected al-Qaeda operatives bombed the Limburg, a French oil tanker, off the coast of Mukalla. In December, Islamists assassinated the deputy leader of the YSP, Jarallah Omar, and killed three Americans at a missionary hospital in Jibla.

The government has made little progress in tackling the grinding poverty that fuels Islamic militancy in Yemen. More than a third of the population lives below the poverty line, and unemployment is unofficially estimated at up to 40 percent. The tourism industry virtually collapsed following the September 11 attacks, and the number of ships docking in Aden shrank even further after the Limburg bombing.

Although the government has cut public spending and reduced inflation since it began implementing an IMF-prescribed structural adjustment program in 1995, foreign investment has been negligible outside of the petroleum sector because of widespread corruption and the precarious security situation. Saleh's allies in Islah have opposed family planning programs to combat the country's soaring 3.2 percent population growth rate. Revelations that the government had purchased Scud missiles from North Korea in December prompted Japan to declare that it would reconsider its current level of aid to Yemen.

Political Rights and Civil Liberties: The right of citizens to change their government is limited by the concentration of real political power in the hands of the president and his appointed cabinet. The 301-seat House of Representatives has never exercised its constitutional right to initiate legislation, though it has blocked or revised draft legislation submitted by the government on numerous occasions. The establishment of an appointed 111-member Shura (Consultative) Council in 2001 was seen as diluting the authority of the elected legislature. There are nearly 40 registered political parties representing a diverse ideological spectrum.

Parliamentary and presidential elections are based on universal suffrage, are overseen by an independent electoral commission, and have been deemed relatively free and fair by domestic and international monitors. However, after a leftist boycott of the 1997 parliamentary elections, the GPC gained a commanding majority of 226 seats and Islah won 64 seats. The 1999 presidential election was not competitive, as the main opposition candidate's nomination failed to win the approval of at least 10 percent of parliamentary members, as required by law. Municipal council elections in February 2001 were marred by allegations of vote rigging and widespread election day violence that left at least 40 dead. Provincial governors who wield most local power remain appointed.

Although Yemeni law provides due process safeguards, arbitrary arrests and prolonged incommunicado detention are common. In July 2002, Amnesty International reported that "thousands of people have been subjected to arbitrary arrest and incommunicado detention" since September 11, 2001, including members of Islamic groups, students at religious schools, and anyone who had recently traveled to Afghanistan. It is estimated that between 100 and 200 of these detainees remained imprisoned without trial or access to family or lawyers at the end of 2002. There is credible evidence that the authorities torture and abuse detainees in order to coerce confessions.

Judges are appointed by the executive branch and have been subject to reassignment or removal for issuing rulings against the government. Judicial independence is further hampered by poor training, corruption, and the government's frequent reluctance to carry out sentences. Since 1999, the government has introduced substantial judicial reforms and externally funded training programs, though mainly in commercial and public finance courts. Local tribal leaders frequently adjudicate land disputes and criminal cases in areas under their authority.

Freedom of expression is limited. Broadcast media outlets are government owned and present only official views—particularly significant, given that a slight majority of adults are illiterate. Privately owned print publications give voice to diverse views, but journalists are subject to legal harassment, detention, and prosecution under articles of the Penal Code that impose penalties of up to five years in prison for such vaguely worded offenses as "humiliation of the State" and the publication of "false information" that "threatens public order or the public interest." As a result, journalists exercise self-censorship on issues such as governmental corruption, operations by the security forces, and foreign relations. While the government does not restrict access to the Internet, it remains prohibitively expensive for most Yemenis.

At least three publications were closed in 2002, and around two dozen journalists were reportedly arrested or summoned for questioning (several of them more than once) after writing articles on operations by the security forces, corruption, and other topics. While there were no reports of journalists sentenced to prison terms, four received suspended sentences and several endured lengthy pretrial detention. Amnesty International was still unable to confirm the status of one journalist, Nabil al-Kumaim, two months after his arrest in April.

Although permits are required for public gatherings, they are routinely granted. Several anti-American and anti-Israeli demonstrations drew tens of thousands of people into the streets during the spring, though police forcibly dispersed crowds approaching Western embassies or consulates on two occasions in April, killing one protestor and wounding six. On December 21, police in the southern Yemeni town of Dhaleh arrested eight demonstrators protesting recent appointments by the provincial governor. In late December, parliament postponed consideration of a governmental draft bill that would require organizers to obtain prior approval for demonstrations from the Interior Ministry and permit the ministry to block protests considered detrimental to public order. The government generally respects freedom of association, though members of the YSP claim to experience frequent harassment by the authorities.

Islam is the state religion; Sunni Muslims constitute about 70 percent of the population, while 30 percent are Zaydi Shiites. Followers of other religions may worship freely, but the law prohibits non-Muslims from proselytizing or constructing new places of worship without permits. Yemeni Jews, who number about 500, face restrictions on places of residence and employment. An estimated 200,000 Yemenis of African descent, known as *akhdam* (literally, "servants"), encounter tremendous social discrimination.

Women enjoy equal political rights, but face substantial legal and traditional discrimination. The Penal Code provides for leniency for persons convicted of violent assault or killing women for perceived deviant behavior—so-called honor crimes. The law discriminates against women in matters of marriage and divorce and prohibits a married woman from leaving the home without the consent of her husband. According to government statistics, 73 percent of Yemeni women are illiterate, compared with 32 percent of men. Saleh has aggressively recruited women into most areas of government, appointing the country's first female cabinet minister in April 2001.

Workers may form unions, but the government regularly places its own personnel in influential positions inside unions and syndicates. The Yemeni Confederation of Labor Unions is the sole labor federation. The right to bargain collectively and to strike is limited; collective agreements may be invalidated if judged to "damage the economic interests of the country," and permission to strike must be obtained from the union federation.

Yugoslavia (Serbia and Montenegro)

Polity: Parliamentary   **Political Rights:** 3
democracy   **Civil Liberties:** 2*
Economy: Mixed-statist   **Status:** Free
Population: 10,700,000
PPP: na
Life Expectancy: 72
Religious Groups: Orthodox (65 percent), Muslim (19 percent),
Roman Catholic (4 percent), other (12 percent)
Ethnic Groups: Serb (63 percent), Albanian (17 percent), Montenegrin (5 percent),
Hungarian (3 percent), other (12 percent)
Capital: Belgrade
Ratings Change: Yugoslavia's civil liberties rating improved from 3 to 2, and its status
from Partly Free to Free, due to continued democratization in the post-Milosevic period.
Name Change: On February 5, 2003, the Yugoslav parliament adopted a constitu-
tional charter establishing the state of Serbia and Montenegro. For the purposes of
this report, which covers the events of 2002, references to Yugoslavia and the FRY
have been retained. Unless specifically noted, references to Yugoslavia/FRY do not
pertain to Kosovo.

Ten-Year Ratings Timeline (Political Rights, Civil Liberties, Status)

1993	1994	1995	1996	1997	1998	1999	2000	2001	2002	2003
6,5PF	6,6NF	6,6NF	6,6NF	6,6NF	6,6NF	6,6NF	5,5PF	4,4PF	3,3PF	3,2F

Overview: In 2002, the post-Milosevic reform process in the Federal
Republic of Yugoslavia (FRY) stalled in many respects; as
sharpening disagreements and struggles for power between
rival factions of the country's leadership emerged; continuing difficulties were encountered in agreeing to a new constitutional relationship between Serbia and
Montenegro; and no solution appeared in sight over the final status of Serbia's UN-
administered province of Kosovo.

In April 1992, Serbia and Montenegro jointly proclaimed the formation of the
FRY after the former Socialist Federal Republic of Yugoslavia (SFRY) disintegrated
in 1991. Throughout the 1990s, Slobodan Milosevic's Socialist Party of Serbia (SPS)
ruled the country by virtue of its control over the country's security forces, financial and monetary institutions, and the state-owned media. Nevertheless, Milosevic's
control over the country did slowly wither, as the Serbian opposition won numerous municipal elections in the fall of 1996 resulting in the SPS's losing control of the
main urban areas in the country, and in 1997, an anti-Milosevic coalition of political
forces came to power in Montenegro. In 1999, NATO occupied one of the FRY's
two autonomous provinces, Kosovo, after a 78-day bombing campaign. The final
end for the Milosevic regime came on October 5, 2000, when a botched attempt to
steal the presidential elections resulted in hundreds of thousands of people con-
verging on Belgrade to overthrow the Milosevic regime.

The Democratic Opposition of Serbia (DOS), a coalition of 18 political parties and one independent trade union, took power after October 5. However, the dominant parties (and political leaders) within the DOS for most of the post-Milosevic period have been the Democratic Party of Serbia (DSS) led by Yugoslav federal president Vojislav Kostunica, and the Democratic Party (DS), led by Serbian premier Zoran Djindjic.

The struggle for power between these two men and their respective political philosophies defined much of the political story of 2002. Kostunica, an academician and constitutional lawyer, has consistently emphasized the importance of establishing the rule of law in Serbia and Yugoslavia as a way to prevent the mistakes of the Communist or Milosevic era from ever being repeated. Djindjic, on the other hand, has favored a more radical break with the past and has on occasion been willing to adopt extra-constitutional or extra-legal means to achieve it. Further complicating the relationship between these two politicians has been the fact that while Kostunica is by far the most popular politician in the country, and has enjoyed the greatest moral authority, Djindjic's position holds more de facto power. As a result, struggles between the two men have resulted in a considerable deadlock in the reform process.

The most serious evidence of the disagreement between the Kostunica and Djindjic camps came in May, when Djindjic's faction in the Serbian parliament dismissed 50 legislators from that body, including 21 from Kostunica's DSS. In July, the Federal Constitutional Court ruled that Djindjic's actions had been unconstitutional. In reaction to the federal court's ruling, Djindjic's faction in the DOS responded by stripping all of the DSS representatives of their mandates. The incident brought a conclusive end to any illusion that the coalition that brought down Milosevic still existed and provided an important example of the weakness of the separation of powers in the country.

In June, President Kostunica fired the chief of staff of the Army of Yugoslavia, General Nebojsa Pavkovic, in what was interpreted as an important precedent for establishing civilian control over the military. Pavkovic's dismissal was also believed to be a necessary step for Yugoslavia to improve its chances to join NATO's Partnership for Peace program (Pavkovic had led Yugoslav forces in Kosovo during the confrontation with NATO in 1999). Yugoslavia also adopted a new strategic program in 2002, according to which the overall size of the Yugoslav military was to be reduced to 60,000—65,000 by the end of the year.

Serbia held presidential elections over two rounds in September and October. The two leading candidates emerging from the first round of elections were Kostunica and the federal vice premier, Miroljub Labus, a respected economist and reputed Djindjic favorite. Although Kostunica decisively beat Labus in the second round (by a margin of more than two to one), low voter turnout (just below 45 percent, falling significantly below the 50 percent threshold needed to make the elections valid) in the second round, however, necessitated a third round of elections in December. Apart from the apparent voter apathy exhibited in these elections, another worrisome development for the country was the showing of the leader from the far-right nationalist Serbian Radical Party (SRS), Vojislav Seselj, who came in a strong third in the first round. Moreover, the way the vote split in Serbia's ethnically mixed areas, especially the Sandzak and Vojvodina, between Labus and Seselj, showed that an unhealthy degree of polarization along ethnic lines still exists within the country.

Contributing to citizen apathy is the weak economy. Over the past two years, the government has relied to an excessively large degree on foreign aid. One-third of Serbia's citizens live on less than one dollar a day, and another third survive on less than two dollars a day. The official unemployment rate is 35 percent. Especially hard hit by the poor economy are refugees and displaced persons from the conflicts in Bosnia-Herzegovina, Croatia and Kosovo, believed to number more than 400,000, who constitute the largest displaced persons population (as a percentage of the general population) in Europe.

Another impediment to quicker reform throughout the post-Milosevic period has been Serbia's relationship with Montenegro. In March, the Belgrade Agreement brokered by the EU proposed a new "Union of Serbia and Montenegro" that would preserve some vestiges of a common state but also provide each republic with its own currency, central bank, and separate customs and taxation systems. In July, however, the EU reversed its own previous position (and dealt a setback to Montenegrin aspirations for speedy independence) by insisting on the formation of a federation with stronger economic links. Parliamentary elections in Montenegro in October, however, strengthened Milo Djukanovic's position in parliament, and again raised hopes for the pro-independence position. In November, Djukanovic decided not to run for the Montenegrin presidency and to become the new prime minister, claiming that there was more important work to be done in the parliament than in the president's office. By year's end, the Montenegrin parliament had still failed to ratify the Belgrade Agreement.

Political Rights and Civil Liberties:

Throughout the 1990s, the regime of Slobodan Milosevic used a variety of means to manipulate and falsify election results. For most of the 1990s, opposition parties were routinely denied access to the main electronic media in the country, and the tabulation of votes was extremely suspect.

The DOS victory considerably changed the situation in the FRY with regard to the electoral system. Citizens in both Serbia and Montenegro can now choose their leaders in free and fair elections.

Cultural and ethnic minorities have their own political parties, access to media in their mother tongue, and other types of associations. Nevertheless, the number of individuals from ethnic minorities participating in government does not represent their percentages in the entire population. An important constitutional and political challenge facing the FRY is to satisfy increasing demands from regions with large ethnic minorities, such as Kosovo, Sandzak, and Vojvodina. Similarly, there are frequent complaints of unfair treatment and police harassment by the Roma (Gypsy) community.

According to the FRY constitution, all citizens enjoy freedom of religious belief. Ethnic and religious identities are closely intertwined in the region, however; consequently, increases in interethnic tensions often take on the appearance of religious intolerance. Restitution of church property nationalized by the Communists remains a point of dispute between church and state. In 2002, reports indicate that there was a better police response to crime against religious minorities, and despite some reports of anti-Semitic activity, the Belgrade Municipal Court agreed to try one case involving the publication of an anti-Semitic hate speech.

FRY citizens enjoy freedom of association and assembly. Numerous political parties exist and compete for power in elections. New laws are currently being drafted to codify relations between trade unions and the government. Similarly, on the whole, both foreign and domestic nongovernmental organizations enjoy the freedom to pursue their activities.

During the Milosevic period, the regime enjoyed the support of state-owned media, while independent media outlets were persecuted. Some prominent members of the independent media were assassinated by "unknown" assailants. In the post-Milosevic period, the situation has vastly improved, although journalists are still the targets of occasional harassment, especially outside of large urban areas such as Belgrade or Novi Sad. In July 2002, the Montenegrin parliament passed several changes to its Media Laws that drew criticism from domestic and international watchdog groups. The new regulations require editors to consult political parties about the content and even the headlines of articles, and restrict the number of articles that can be published about parties during the campaign.

Significant legal and judicial reform is under way; however, the judicial system is still plagued by a large backlog of cases, underpaid judges and state prosecutors, and an excess of judges left over from the Milosevic era. There are reports that the system takes an excessively long time in filing formal charges against suspects. In April, the federal parliament adopted the long-awaited Law on Cooperation with the International Criminal Tribunal for the Former Yugoslavia, although some observers criticized several provisions in the law, such as Article 39, which provides for the extradition only of persons indicted prior to passage of the law. There are no legal restrictions on the participation of women in politics; however, they are, in general, vastly underrepresented in higher levels of government. Although women are legally entitled to equal pay for equal work, traditional patriarchal attitudes prevalent throughout the Balkans often limit women's roles in the economy. Domestic violence remains a serious problem, and some towns in southern Serbia have become an important part of the network trafficking women from parts of the former Soviet Union through Kosovo and Albania to Western Europe.

Zambia

Polity: Dominant party
Economy: Mixed statist
Population: 10,000,000
PPP: $780
Life Expectancy: 37
Religious Groups: Christian (50-75 percent),
Muslim and Hindu (24-49 percent), Indigenous
beliefs (1 percent)
Ethnic Groups: African (99 percent), European and other (1 percent)
Capital: Lusaka

Political Rights: 4*
Civil Liberties: 4
Status: Partly Free

Ratings Change: Zambia's political rights rating improved from 5 to 4 due to changes in the survey methodology.

Ten-Year Ratings Timeline (Political Rights, Civil Liberties, Status)

1993	1994	1995	1996	1997	1998	1999	2000	2001	2002	2003
2,3F	3,4PF	3,4PF	3,4PF	5,4PF	5,4PF	5,4PF	5,4PF	5,4PF	5,4PF	4,4PF

Overview:

Zambia's political environment in 2002 was dominated by fallout from presidential and parliamentary elections held at the end of the previous year. Levy Mwanawasa, the candidate of the ruling Movement for Multiparty Democracy (MMD), narrowly won the presidential election against a divided opposition. Mwanawasa's victory with only 29 percent of the vote led to charges of pro-MMD electoral fraud. The ruling MMD enjoys a slim majority in parliament with 80 seats, while opposition parties have 78.

The three main losing candidates have filed a lawsuit to overturn the results, and a judicial decision is expected to take place in 2003. Although widely perceived as former President Frederick Chiluba's handpicked candidate, Mwanawasa has supported wide-ranging inquiries by legal authorities into alleged corruption by Chiluba and his senior associates while they were in power. These resulted in a number of arrests and considerable legal maneuvering on the issue of whether Chiluba himself would be immune from prosecution.

Zambia was ruled by President Kenneth Kaunda and the United National Independence Party (UNIP) from independence from Britain in 1964 until the transition to a multiparty system in 1991. Kaunda's regime grew increasingly repressive and corrupt as it faced security and economic difficulties during the long guerrilla wars against white rule in neighboring Rhodesia (now Zimbabwe) and Portuguese-controlled Mozambique. UNIP's socialist policies, combined with a crash in the price of copper, Zambia's main export, precipitated an economic decline unchecked for two decades.

In the face of domestic unrest and international pressure, Kaunda permitted free elections in 1991. Former labor leader Chiluba and his MMD won convincingly. By contrast, the next national elections, in 1996, lacked legitimacy largely because of a series of repressive measures instituted by the government. Economic liberalization and privatization have earned Zambia substantial external aid, but rampant corruption has distorted the economy and blocked sustainable growth. Chiluba's 2001 attempt, as an incumbent, to amend the constitution to allow himself a third term as president was defeated.

The country is among those suffering most from the AIDS pandemic; it is estimated Zambia will need to care for well over 600,000 AIDS orphans within a few years. The UN-WHO AIDS working group estimated that in 1999 the HIV infection rate among adults in Zambia was about 20 percent, and that 100,000 AIDS-related deaths occurred in that year alone.

High levels of corruption also burden development. Zambia ranked 77 out of 102 countries on Transparency International's 2001 Corruption Perception Index. By mid-2002 the Zambian government had sold off 257 state-owned companies out of 280 enterprises earmarked for privatization since the mid-1990s, but some of these deals, especially in the mining sector, have allegedly involved significant corruption. A public sector reform program also had little effect. New business formation is slowed by the country's weak financial structures.

Political Rights and Civil Liberties: Zambia's president and parliament are elected to serve concurrent five-year terms by universal adult suffrage. The ability of Zambians to change their government democratically, however, is not yet consolidated. While Zambians' constitutional right to change their government freely was honored in the 1991 elections, both the 1996 and 2001 elections won by the ruling MMD were subjects of intense controversy.

The November 1996 presidential and parliamentary polls were neither free nor fair. State resources and state media were mobilized extensively to support President Frederick Chiluba and the ruling MMD. Serious irregularities plagued election preparations. Voter lists were incomplete or otherwise suspect; independent monitors estimated that more than two million people were effectively disenfranchised. Candidate eligibility requirements were changed, which resulted in the exclusion of Kaunda, the most credible opposition candidate. Most opposition parties boycotted the 1996 polls, in which the MMD renewed its parliamentary dominance. International observer groups that did monitor the polls, along with independent domestic monitors and opposition parties, declared the process and the results to be fraudulent.

Prior to the 2001 elections, President Chiluba had supported a move within his party to change the constitution so that he could run for a third term. Dissension within his party, the opposition, and civil society forced him to back off from that plan. Instead, the MMD nominated Mwanawasa. Both domestic and international election monitors cited serious irregularities with the presidential campaign and election. Opposition parties filed complaints with the judicial authorities, which ruled that the inauguration of Mwanawasa as president should go ahead. Mwanawasa began his presidency inauspiciously, having won less than 30 percent of the popular vote amidst numerous allegations of pro-MMD electoral fraud, and with only weak support in parliament.

The judicial system, which has at times been subject to political influence, is under considerable pressure, with several high-level cases pending. In July 2002, for example, in the case brought by three of the losing presidential candidates, Acting Chief Justice Ernest Sakala said there was a clear threat to witnesses. The Supreme Court told President Mwanawasa to stop intimidating witnesses who were to testify to helping him fraudulently engineer his electoral victory.

In July, parliament voted unanimously to lift Chiluba's immunity after President Mwanawasa alleged that Chiluba stole approximately $80 million during his 10 years in office. Chiluba has challenged that decision in the courts. Several Chiluba-era officials have been charged with corruption in recent months as part of a major crackdown on graft ordered by Mwanawasa.

Overall, the court system is severely overburdened. Pretrial detainees are sometimes held for years under harsh conditions before their cases reach trial. The Magistrates and Judges Association identified congestion in prisons and delayed trials as extremely serious problems. Malnourishment and poor health care in Zambia's prisons cause many deaths. Many civil matters are decided by customary courts of variable quality and consistency whose decisions often conflict with both national law and constitutional protections. More than 200 people were on death row in Zambia awaiting execution in 2001, according to Amnesty International. In 1997 eight people were executed, and between 1998 and 2000, at least 97 people were sentenced to death.

The government dominates broadcasting, although an independent radio station, Radio Phoenix, presents nongovernmental views. The Public Order Act, among other statutes, has at times been used to harass and intimidate journalists. Other tools of harassment have included criminal libel suits and defamation suits brought by MMD leaders in response to stories on corruption. For example, in 2001 criminal charges were brought against two Zambian journalists and two political figures on charges of defaming President Frederick Chiluba in an article accusing the president of misappropriating $4 million the government had earmarked for emergency food imports several years ago.

Reporters Sans Frontieres ranked Zambia 81 out of 139 countries in a 2002 study of press freedom.

The independent media supported the 2002 introduction into parliament of the Freedom of Information, Broadcasting, and Independent Broadcasting Authority draft legislation, which aims to facilitate easier access to information held by government and quasi-governmental organs, transform the state-owned and government-controlled Zambia National Broadcasting Corporation (ZNBC) from a government propaganda organ to a public broadcaster, and establish an independent regulator to regulate broadcasting respectively.

Constitutionally protected religious freedom has been respected in practice. Nongovernmental organizations (NGOs) engaged in human rights promotion, such as the Zambian Independent Monitoring Team, the Zambian Civic Education Association, and the Law Association of Zambia, operate openly. In 1999, however, the government drafted a policy that would closely regulate NGOs. The government human rights commission investigated frequent complaints about police brutality and denounced the torture of coup suspects, but has no power to bring charges against alleged perpetrators.

Societal discrimination remains a serious obstacle to women's rights. A 1998 regional human development report noted that Zambia was one of the lowest-performing countries in southern Africa in terms of women's empowerment. Women are denied full economic participation and are discriminated against in rural land allocation. A married woman must have her husband's permission to obtain contraceptives. Discrimination against women is especially prevalent in traditional tribunals that are courts of first instance in most rural areas. Spousal abuse and other violence against women are reportedly common. The Zambian YWCA recorded 903 cases of gender-based violence against women between January and September of 2002.

Zambia's trade unions remain among Africa's strongest, and union rights are constitutionally guaranteed. The Zambia Congress of Trade Unions, an umbrella for Zambia's 19 largest unions, operates democratically without governmental interference. Collective bargaining rights are protected by the 1993 Industrial and Labor Relations Act, and unions negotiate directly with employers. About two-thirds of the country's 300,000 formal (business) sector employees are union members.

↓Zimbabwe

Polity: Dominant party   **Political Rights:** 6
Economy: Capitalist-statist   **Civil Liberties:** 6
Population: 12,300,000   **Status:** Not Free
PPP: $2,635
Life Expectancy: 38
Religious Groups: Christian (25 percent), indigenous
beliefs (24 percent), Muslim and other (51 percent)
Ethnic Groups: Shona (82 percent), Ndebele (14 percent), other (4 percent)
Capital: Harare
Trend Arrow: Zimbabwe received a downward trend arrow due to a significantly reduced political arena caused by governmental repression of political opponents and illegitimate presidential elections.

Ten-Year Ratings Timeline (Political Rights, Civil Liberties, Status)

1993	1994	1995	1996	1997	1998	1999	2000	2001	2002	2003
5,4PF	5,5PF	5,5PF	5,5PF	5,5PF	5,5PF	5,5PF	6,5PF	6,5PF	6,6NF	6,6NF

Overview:

Zimbabwe in 2002 seethed with unrest as its increasingly autocratic president, Robert Mugabe, claimed victory in a deeply flawed 2002 presidential election that failed to meet minimum international standards for legitimacy, although a number of his fellow African leaders refused to condemn the elections. The election pitted him against Morgan Tsvangirai, a popular trade union leader who, along with several other opposition leaders, was arrested a second time for treason, in 2002. Their trial was postponed until 2003.

The government proceeded with its policy of moving white farmers off their land. The country's economy worsened, both because of declining revenues from the agricultural sector and widespread unrest resulting from Mugabe's authoritarian rule.

Aid agencies have warned that up to six million Zimbabweans face severe hunger because of drought and the negative effects of the land-reform policy. In 2002 Zimbabwean armed forces withdrew from the long-running conflict in the Democratic Republic of the Congo (Kinshasa), which had provided commercial and economic benefits for many of Mugabe's elite.

Zimbabwe gained independence in 1980 after a violent guerrilla war against a white-minority regime that had declared unilateral independence from Britain in 1965 in what was then Southern Rhodesia. For a few years Zimbabwe was relatively stable, although from 1983 to 1987, the government suppressed resistance from the country's largest minority group, the Ndebele, to dominance by Mugabe's majority ethnic Shona group. Severe human rights abuses accompanied the struggle, which ended with an accord that brought Ndebele leaders into the government.

In recent years Mugabe has turned against student groups, labor unions, homosexuals, and white landowners. Zimbabwe is now facing its worst crisis since achieving independence in 1980. The grip of the ruling Zimbabwe African National Union-Patriotic Front (ZANU-PF) on parliament has been weakened, but the party remains the predominant power through its control over the security forces and much of the economy. ZANU-PF has dominated Zimbabwe since independence, enacting numerous laws and constitutional amendments to strengthen its hold on power. Despite, or perhaps because of, this, opposition to Mugabe has mushroomed. The opposition Movement for Democratic Change (MDC) has experienced rapid growth under Tsvangirai. Trade unions have been at the forefront of opposition to Mugabe. The small independent media sector and civic groups continue to struggle to promote transparency, but are subject to harassment and intimidation.

Over the past several years the government has taken numerous actions restricting civil liberties and political rights, including legislating severe curbs on press freedom. War veterans and government supporters continued to occupy and disrupt opposition strongholds and white-owned landholdings, with the overt or complicit backing of the government. The independence of the judiciary has come under attack with the pressured resignation and/or replacement of several senior judges. In addition, adverse judicial rulings have repeatedly been ignored by the government. Corruption has been rampant, and living standards have dropped precipitously. In 2002 the government reimposed price controls. Despite a previous price-control scheme, inflation raged at more than 100 percent in 2001. Official government figures predict that the economy will shrink in 2002 by 12 percent, given declines in revenues from agriculture, manufacturing, and tourism. Recent flooding and droughts in the region have also had an adverse impact on the economy, especially on the livelihoods of the rural population. Zimbabwe is currently in arrears to internal and external creditors, which has led to suspension of disbursements and credit lines. This situation has aggravated the foreign-exchange shortage within the country, making key imports such as fuel and electricity in short supply.

Political Rights and Civil Liberties:

Zimbabweans are not yet able to change their government democratically. President Robert Mugabe and ZANU-PF enjoy wide incumbency advantages that reflect their ability and willingness to manipulate the political landscape as needed to ensure continued control. Since 1987, for example, there have been at least 15 amendments to the constitution by ZANU-PF, which have made the constitution less democratic and given the government, and particularly members of the executive, more power. These include the scrapping of the post of prime minister in favor of an executive president in 1987 and the abolition of the upper chamber of parliament, the senate.

The 2000 parliamentary elections, in which 57 members of the opposition MDC were elected out of a total of 150 seats, were deemed by observers to be fundamentally flawed prior to balloting. MDC candidates and supporters faced violence and intimidation, and a constitutional provision empowering President Mugabe and allied traditional leaders to appoint one-fifth of parliament's members helped to ensure ZANU-PF's continued majority in parliament. Voter registration and identification procedures and tabulation of results were judged by independent observers in some constituencies to have been highly irregular. The heavily state-controlled or state-influenced media offered limited coverage of opposition viewpoints, and ZANU-PF used state resources heavily in its campaigning.

Mugabe issued a pardon for thousands of people, most from ZANU-PF, for crimes committed during the election campaign, including individuals guilty of assault, arson, kidnapping, torture, and attempted murder. According to the Zimbabwe Human Rights Forum, more than 18,000 people had their rights violated, and more than 90 percent of the alleged perpetrators were ZANU-PF supporters or government officials.

The 2002 presidential elections proved highly controversial with additional restraints being imposed, such as legislation limiting election observers. Although some African nations backed Mugabe's victory, the poll was condemned as fraudulent by many other countries and international observer missions. The International Crisis Group, for example, concluded that "the strategic use of state-sponsored violence and extra-legal electoral tinkering authorized by President Mugabe effectively thwarted the will of the people."

Freedom of the press has been severely restricted. There are no privately owned radio or television stations in Zimbabwe and just one daily newspaper, which the government routinely condemns. According to the BBC, the state-controlled radio, television, and newspapers are all seen as mouthpieces of the government and cover opposition activities only in a negative light.

The Parliamentary Privileges and Immunities Act has been used to force journalists to reveal their sources regarding reports on corruption before the courts and parliament. The 2002 Access to Information and Protection of Privacy Act (AIPPA) gives the information minister sweeping powers to decide who can work as a journalist in Zimbabwe and created a governmental commission that hands out "licenses" allowing journalists to work in the country. The law bans foreigners from working as journalists if based in Zimbabwe. It also makes it illegal to publish inaccurate information, whether or not a journalist knew the information was false. By the end of 2002, the act had been used to arrest at least a dozen journalists.

Following a recent court challenge to the law by the Independent Journalists Association of Zimbabwe, the Zimbabwean government announced its intention to amend the AIPPA. The proposed amendments cover clarifications of vague terms such as "abuse of journalistic privilege," writing "falsehoods," the powers of the Media Commission set up under the act, and registration of media houses. A new section on "abuse of freedom of expression" has been introduced. Under this section, journalists would no longer be punished for "writing and publishing falsehoods," but only for "intentionally or recklessly falsifying information and for maliciously or fraudulently fabricating information."

Security laws have been widely condemned by human rights and pro-democracy activists as an effort by Mugabe to crush dissent and curb constitutional rights of free expression. Security forces, particularly the Central Intelligence Organization, often ignore basic rights regarding detention, search, and seizure. Judicial rulings have at times been ignored by the government. In addition, the right of free assembly has been circumscribed in recent legislation. President Mugabe has also, on several occasions, invoked the Presidential Powers Act, which enables him to bypass normal governmental review and oversight procedures.

Legislation passed by parliament in the pre-2002 election period includes the Public Order and Security Act, which forbids criticism of the president, limits public assembly, and allows police to impose arbitrary curfews. Several opposition activists have been arrested for alleged subversion under the act since the election. This act provides for jail terms and fines for anyone who "undermines the authority of the president" or "engenders hostility" towards him. Intelligence agencies are included among law enforcement agencies empowered to disperse "illegal" assemblies or arrest participants. Other legislation has disenfranchised thousands of citizens living outside of the country.

Although under increasing pressure by the Mugabe regime, at times the judiciary continues to act independently. A former High Court justice known for his judicial activism, in particular ordering the release of individuals arbitrarily held, was arrested on allegations that he had violated the Prevention of Corruption Act. According to the Lawyers Committee for Human Rights, his record of judicial independence may have been the reason for his arrest and detention.

In 2001 the government forced the resignation and/or replaced five Supreme or High Court judges, including Chief Justice Anthony Gubbay. In the past the courts had repeatedly struck down or disputed government actions, most notably regarding illegal occupation of farms. In early December 2002, however, the reconstituted Supreme Court ruled that the government's land-reform program was legal. Subsequent High Court rulings, however, have determined that many eviction orders were illegal. Some farmers who had been evicted from their properties were granted a temporary reprieve allowing them to return to their properties until the Administrative Court confirmed the confiscation of their farms. In August a judge ruled that the state cannot seize farms that are mortgaged to banks without first informing the financial institutions. The government, however, has refused to enforce court orders that they evict those who had illegally occupied white-owned farms.

According to the BBC, just a few hundred white farmers now remain on their land, out of some 4,000 two years ago. Much of the land has gone to ZANU-PF officials, who often have no farming background, instead of landless black Zimbabweans who were supposed to benefit. Up to two million farm workers and their dependants may also have been displaced by the agrarian reforms.

Donors say that the drastic fall in agricultural production is one of the reasons for Zimbabwe's current food crisis. Six million people—up to half of the population—face starvation this year, aid agencies have warned. Concern about the land reform program was one of the reasons why the IMF suspended financial support for Zimbabwe. The World Food Program has been forced to suspend its operations in some areas, as ZANU-PF youths allegedly denied international emergency food aid to people identified as opposition supporters.

There is an active, although small, nongovernmental organization (NGO) sector. Several groups, including the Catholic Commission for Justice and Peace, the Zimbabwe Human Rights Organization (Zimrights), and the Legal Relief Fund, focus on human rights. The Zimbabwean government plans to impose stringent new controls on charities distributing relief to victims of the current crisis and on the independently owned news media. President Robert Mugabe accused organizations such as the Commission for Justice and Peace of fomenting opposition to his rule and said they would be "dealt with politically."

In 2002, an unprecedented investigation of rights abuses in Zimbabwe by the African Commission on Human and People's Rights reported serious and credible allegations of human rights abuses and, in some cases, evidence of those violations. Amnesty International "strongly condemned a renewed wave of violence and intimidation" in the run-up to September 2002 local council elections.

Prison conditions are harsh. Amnesty International has reported, for example, that prisoners on death row sleep shackled and naked. The report argued that the dreadful conditions and psychological torment endured by death row inmates violates the right to be free from cruel, inhuman, or degrading punishment.

Women enjoy extensive legal protections, but de facto societal discrimination persists. Women have few legal rights outside formal marriage. The Supreme Court issued a ruling relegating African women to the status of "junior males" within the family, declaring that African women who marry under customary law must leave their original families behind and therefore cannot inherit their property. Married women still cannot hold property jointly with their husbands. Especially in rural areas, access to education and employment for women is difficult. Domestic violence against women is common; a 1997 survey by a women's organization found that more than 80 percent of women had been subjected to some form of physical abuse. Zimbabwe has signed international human rights treaties, such as the Women's Convention, but the government has made little effort to enforce, and continues to habitually violate, many human rights standards. Freedom of religion is generally respected, although there have been reports of tensions between mainline Christian churches and practitioners of traditional indigenous religions.

Armenia/Azerbaijan
Nagorno-Karabakh

Polity: Presidential   **Political Rights:** 5
Economy: Mixed statist   **Civil Liberties:** 5*
Population: 150,000   **Status:** Partly Free
Religious Groups: Armenian Apostolic Church (majority)
Ethnic Groups: Armenian (95 percent), other (5 percent)
Ratings Change: Nagorno-Karabakh's civil liberties
rating improved from 6 to 5, and its status from Not Free to Partly Free, due to changes
in the survey methodology.

Ten-Year Ratings Timeline (Political Rights, Civil Liberties, Status)

1993	1994	1995	1996	1997	1998	1999	2000	2001	2002	2003
--	7,7NF	7,7NF	6,6NF	6,6NF	5,6NF	5,6NF	5,6NF	5,6NF	5,6NF	5,5PF

Overview:

Long-standing internationally mediated efforts to find a peaceful settlement to the protracted Nagorno-Karabakh conflict showed few signs of substantive progress in 2002. With the presidents of both Armenia and Azerbaijan facing reelection in 2003, most analysts maintained that neither leader would risk a likely public backlash by agreeing to compromises over the disputed territory's status. In July, the territory's president, Arkady Ghukasian, was overwhelmingly chosen to a second term in office.

The region of Nagorno-Karabakh, whose population is overwhelmingly ethnic Armenian, was transferred from Armenian to Azerbaijani jurisdiction in 1923, and the Nagorno-Karabakh Autonomous Region was subsequently created. In 1930, Moscow permitted Azerbaijan to establish and resettle the border areas between Nagorno-Karabakh and Armenia.

In 1988, Nagorno-Karabakh's Supreme Soviet adopted a resolution calling for union with Armenia. The announcement, as well as February demonstrations in the Armenian capital of Yerevan in support of Nagorno-Karabakh, triggered violent attacks against Armenians in the Azerbaijani city of Sumgait shortly thereafter and in Baku, the capital of Azerbaijan, in January 1990.

Following multiparty elections for a new legislature, Nagorno-Karabakh's parliament adopted a declaration of independence at its inaugural session in January 1992. From 1991 to 1992, Azerbaijan besieged Stepanakert, the territory's capital, and occupied most of Nagorno-Karabakh. A series of counteroffensives in 1993 and 1994 by Karabakh Armenians, assisted by Armenia, resulted in the capture of essentially the entire territory, as well as six Azerbaijani districts surrounding the enclave. By the time a Russian-brokered ceasefire was finally signed in May 1994, the war had resulted in thousands of casualties and nearly one million refugees.

In December 1994, the head of the territory's state defense committee, Robert Kocharian, was selected by parliament for the newly established post of president. Elections to the 33-member parliament were held in April and May 1995, and Kocharian defeated two other candidates in a popular vote for president in November of the following year. In September 1997, Foreign Minister Arkady Ghukasian was elected president with 89 percent of the vote to replace Kocharian, who had been named prime minister of Armenia in March of that year.

In the territory's June 2000 parliamentary vote, 123 candidates representing five parties competed for the national assembly's 33 seats. The ruling Democratic Union Artsakh (ZhAM), which supports Ghukasian, enjoyed a slim victory, winning 13 seats. The Armenian Revolutionary Federation–Dashnaktsutiun won 9 seats, the Armenakan Party captured 1 seat, and formally independent candidates, most of whom support Ghukasian, won 10. International observers described the electoral campaign and voting process as calm and largely transparent, although problems were noted with the accuracy of some voter lists.

In February 2001, former Defense Minister Samvel Babayan was found guilty of organizing a March 2000 assassination attempt against Ghukasian and sentenced to 14 years in prison. His supporters insisted that the arrest was politically motivated, as Babayan had been involved in a power struggle with Ghukasian. However, others welcomed the arrest and conviction of Babayan, who had been accused of corruption and reportedly wielded considerable political and economic power in the territory.

Ghukasian was reelected to a second term as president on August 11, 2002, with 89 percent of the vote. His closest challenger, former parliament Speaker Artur Tovmasian, received just 8 percent. Voter turnout was close to 75 percent. Observers from countries including the United States, United Kingdom, and France reported no serious violations. While a number of domestic and international nongovernmental organizations concluded that the elections marked a further step in Nagorno-Karabakh's democratization, they did voice some criticisms, including the limited access for the opposition to state-controlled media. By contrast, Azerbaijan's Foreign Ministry described the election as a violation of international norms, insisting that a legitimate vote could be held only after a peaceful resolution to the conflict.

Despite continued high-level discussions in the framework of the OSCE Minsk Group—which was established 10 years ago to facilitate dialogue on a political settlement on Nagorno-Karabakh's status—a resolution of the long-standing dispute remained elusive at year's end. While Yerevan has insisted that Nagorno-Karabakh should be left outside Azeri jurisdiction, Baku has maintained that the territory may be granted broad autonomy while remaining a constituent part of Azerbaijan. Azerbaijan also has refused to negotiate with Ghukasian, who has demanded direct representation in the peace process. Few observers expected any major results in 2002 just ahead of presidential elections in Armenia and Azerbaijan in 2003. Both Armenian president Robert Kocharian and Azerbaijani president Heydar Aliyev are seeking reelection and therefore would be unlikely to risk the domestic political consequences of making significant public concessions over the territory before their respective polls.

Political Rights and Civil Liberties: A self-declared republic, Nagorno-Karabakh has enjoyed de facto independence from Azerbaijan since 1994 while retaining close political, economic, and military ties with Armenia. Parliamentary elections in 1995 and 2000 were regarded as generally free and fair, as were the 1996 and 1997 presidential votes. However, the elections were considered invalid by most of the international community, which does not recognize Nagorno-Karabakh's independence. Nagorno-Karabakh's electoral law calls for a single-mandate system to be used in parliamentary elections; lawmakers have rejected the opposition's demands for the inclusion of party-based lists.

The government controls much of the broadcast media, and most journalists practice self-censorship, particularly on subjects dealing with policies related to Azerbaijan and the peace process. Some observers maintain that the government used the attempted murder of President Arkady Ghukasian in 2000 as a pretext to intensify attacks against its critics.

With Christian Armenians constituting more than 95 percent of the territory's population, the Armenian Apostolic Church is the predominant religion. Years of conflict have constrained the religious rights of the few Muslims remaining in the region. Freedom of assembly and association is limited, although political parties and unions are allowed to organize.

The judiciary, which is not independent in practice, is influenced by the executive branch and powerful political and clan forces. Former Defense Minister Samvel Babayan alleged that he had been physically assaulted during his interrogation and detention as a suspect in the failed assassination attempt against President Ghukasian in March 2000. The presiding judge in the case announced that the subsequent guilty verdict against Babayan was based on pretrial testimony in which Babayan confessed to the charges, although he later retracted his admission of guilt, claiming that it had been obtained under duress. With Nagorno-Karabakh still technically at war, the territory remains officially under military law.

The majority of those who fled the war continue to live in squalid conditions in refugee camps in Azerbaijan, while international aid organizations are reducing direct assistance to the refugees. One-fifth of Azerbaijan's territory captured during the war remains occupied by Armenia. Sniper attacks and land mine explosions continue to result in casualties each year.

Nagorno-Karabakh's fragile seven-year peace has failed to bring significant improvement to the economy. Large parts of the territory remain devastated by war. Industrial capacity continues to be limited, with high unemployment forcing many residents to leave for neighboring countries in search of work. Widespread corruption, a lack of substantive economic reforms, and the control of most economic activity by powerful elites limit equality of opportunity for most residents.

↓ China
Hong Kong

Polity: Appointed governor **Political Rights:** 5
and partly-elected legislature **Civil Liberties:** 3
Economy: Capitalist   **Status:** Partly Free
Population: 7,300,000
Religious Groups: Buddhist and Taoist (majority), Protestant (
Catholic (3 percent), Muslim (1 percent), other
Ethnic Groups: Chinese (95 percent), other (5 percent)
Trend Arrow: Hong Kong received a downward trend arrow because the government
introduced plans for new national security laws that could be used to restrict basic rights.

Ten-Year Ratings Timeline (Political Rights, Civil Liberties, Status)

1993	1994	1995	1996	1997	1998	1999	2000	2001	2002	2003
--	--	--	--	--	6,3PF	5,3PF	5,3PF	5,3PF	5,3PF	5,3PF

Overview: The government's decision in 2002 to introduce laws that
would impose heavy penalties for subversion and other
anti-state crimes raised fears that the new powers could be
used to stifle free expression and ban groups that China opposes. The move came
amid continued concern by human rights activists and others that the checks and
balances that underpin liberties in this freewheeling former British colony are being
steadily eroded. Chief Executive Tung Chee-hwa, the territory's top official, added
to these concerns during the year by reducing the policy-making powers of the respected, nonpartisan civil service. The change came as Hong Kong continued to
grapple with high unemployment and a sluggish economy.

Located at the mouth of the Pearl River on the south China coast, Hong Kong
consists of Hong Kong Island and Kowloon Peninsula, both ceded in perpetuity to
Britain by China in the mid-1800s, and the mainland New Territories, which Britain
"leased" for 99 years in 1898.

Hong Kong's transition to Chinese rule began in 1984, when Britain agreed to
return the territory to China in 1997 in return for Beijing's pledge to maintain the
capitalist enclave's legal, political, and economic autonomy for 50 years. London
and Beijing later drafted a mini-constitution for Hong Kong, called the basic law,
that laid the blueprint for introducing direct elections for some Legislative Council
(Legco) seats in 1991 and gradually expanding the number of directly elected seats
over the next 12 years.

Hong Kong's last colonial governor, Christopher Patten, infuriated Beijing with
his attempt to deepen democracy by giving ordinary residents greater say in choosing Legco's indirectly elected seats. After China took control of Hong Kong in 1997,
it retaliated by installing a provisional legislature for ten months that repealed or
tightened several of the territory's civil liberties laws.

As chief executive since the handover, Tung, 65, has seen his popularity wane
as Hong Kong struggles to regain its economic vigor in the wake of the regional financial
crisis that began in 1997. He was chosen by a Beijing-organized committee for the
top job in 1996 after Chinese leaders indicated that he was their preferred choice.

Pro-democracy candidates, however, largely failed to capitalize on Tung's unpopularity at the September 2000 Legco elections. They won only 16 of Legco's 24 directly elected seats and 21 of 60 overall, led by lawyer Martin Lee's opposition Democratic Party, which took 12 seats. The conservative Democratic Alliance won 11 seats.

Tung's move in September 2002 to formally begin enacting laws on subversion, treason, sedition, and secession was widely criticized by students, academics, religious figures, and human rights activists. They argued that Hong Kong lacks democratic checks and balances to ensure that the new laws are not abused. Many warned that the laws could be used to undermine press and academic freedoms, criminalize public advocacy of independence for Tibet or Taiwan, or target groups that Beijing opposes, such as the Falun Gong spiritual movement.

The government noted that the legislation is required by the basic law and targets only actual commission or incitement to commit violence. Legco is expected to pass the laws in 2003.

The security laws are being drafted by a new cabinet of ministers that Tung created in 2002 to shape public policy. The government said that reducing civil servants' policy-making powers would insulate them from political pressure. Critics said the change would increase Tung's power.

Tung, who is publicly supported by Beijing, was reelected to a second five-year term in February by an 800-strong committee of legislators, religious figures, and interest-group representatives. No one challenged Tung for the top spot even though the economy is stagnant and one opinion poll put his support at only 16 percent.

The economy remains weak despite eking out growth of half a percent in the second quarter to snap a nine-month recession. High unemployment and depressed asset prices have made consumers reluctant to spend, and their purchases make up 60 percent of Hong Kong's output.

Unemployment rose to a record high of 7.8 percent before easing later in the year. Property prices, meanwhile, have plummeted to about half their peak in 1997, when the government began easing restrictions on the supply of land for development that had helped to create a speculative property bubble.

In addition to being criticized for weak economic leadership, Tung has been dogged by accusations that his administration is too cozy with business leaders and has taken few steps to make Hong Kong more democratic. Under the basic law, the territory can hold direct elections for the chief executive and all Legco seats after 2007.

Political Rights and Civil Liberties:

Hong Kong residents enjoy most basic rights, but they cannot change their government through elections. The 800-member committee that reelected Tung in 2002 consists of Legco's 60 members; Hong Kong's 36 delegates to China's National People's Congress (NPC); 40 representatives of religious groups; 41 members of an official Chinese consultative body; and 623 people chosen in July 2000 by a narrow electorate of just 180,000 voters.

Those 180,000 voters, representing labor, business, and the professions, also chose 30 of 60 seats in the 2000 Legco elections. Six other Legco seats were chosen by the same 800 people who reelected Tung, leaving only 24 directly elected seats.

Democracy advocates say that it is impossible for Hong Kong to have a true system of checks and balances when the chief executive and more than half of Legco's members are not directly elected.

Moreover, the basic law restricts Legco's law-making powers. It prohibits legislators from introducing bills affecting public spending, Hong Kong's political structure, or governmental operations. Legco members can introduce bills concerning governmental policy, but only with the chief executive's prior approval. And the government has used a very broad definition of "governmental policy" in order to block Legco bills, according to the U.S. State Department's global human rights report for 2001. In order for an individual member's bill to pass, it must have separate majorities among Legco members who are directly elected and those who represent interest groups.

The U.S. State Department and other outside observers say that Hong Kong's judiciary is independent. Local human rights activists generally agree, but many argue that the Tung administration has undermined the territory's rule of law by allegedly granting preferential treatment to well-connected business leaders and by its intervention in a 1999 immigration case. That move resulted in China's NPC interpreting the basic law's provisions on immigration from the mainland in a way that effectively overturned an earlier ruling by Hong Kong's Court of Final Appeal.

Critics say that the NPC's involvement raised doubts over whether any Court of Final Appeal decision is truly final. The basic law requires Hong Kong courts—though not the government—to seek from the NPC an interpretation of the basic law on issues such as immigration that may concern the relationship between Beijing and Hong Kong.

Moreover, many ordinary Hong Kong residents and outside observers have criticized what they see as collusion between the administration and a handful of powerful businessmen. They point, for example, to the government's decision in 2000 to bypass the routine bidding process in awarding a contract to develop the Cyberport industrial park to Richard Li, a son of Li Ka-shing, Hong Kong's wealthiest businessman.

Despite their concerns, even the government's staunchest critics generally acknowledge that ordinary residents enjoy the same basic rights that they had enjoyed before the handover. Many of these rights, however, are now on less solid legal footing. The provisional legislature that served for ten months after the handover watered down Hong Kong's 1991 bill of rights and rolled back some laws on workers' rights. It also amended laws to give officials the power to cite national security concerns in denying registration to nongovernmental organizations (NGOs), de-registering existing groups, and barring public protests.

In practice, Hong Kong NGOs continue to be vibrant and report few problems with the registration process. Thousands of protests, meanwhile, have been staged since the handover, and none have been barred on national security grounds. Some protest organizers, however, say that officials often confine demonstrators to "designated areas" where the rallies receive little public attention. Meanwhile, a court in August convicted and fined 16 Falun Gong practitioners for obstructing pedestrians during a public protest. The judge said religion played no role in his decision.

Hong Kong's hundreds of newspapers and magazines generally are lively but practice some self-censorship when reporting on Chinese politics, powerful local business interests, and calls for Taiwanese or Tibetan independence. The press faces no direct pressure, but some editors and publishers believe that advertising revenues or their business interests in China could suffer if they appear to be too hostile to China or powerful local interests. President Jiang Zemin and other Chinese officials, moreover, have criticized and tried to influence Hong Kong's press.

Raising concerns about protection of privacy, a September 1999 press report said that the government eavesdropped each day on private telephone conversations of more than 100 Hong Kong residents. The law allows the government to use wiretaps and intercept private mail, but only with high-level approval. In practice, the chief executive's office must approve all wiretaps, although the government refuses to say how often Chief Executive Tung actually uses this power. It is not clear whether or how often the colonial government used wiretaps.

Women have equal access to schooling and are entering medicine and other professions in increasingly greater numbers. They continue, however, to face private (business) sector discrimination in landing jobs and getting fair salaries and promotions, the U.S. State Department report said. Women also hold relatively few Legco seats, judgeships, and senior civil service posts.

The government funds programs to curb domestic violence and prosecutes violators, but violence against women remains a problem and sentences generally are lenient, according to the U.S. State Department report. Sexual harassment is also a problem and credible reports also suggest that some residents force their foreign household help to accept less than the minimum wage and poor living conditions, the report added.

Ethnic minorities are well represented in the civil service and many professions. Hong Kong residents of Indian descent and other minorities regularly allege, however, that they face discrimination in renting apartments, landing private sector jobs, getting treated in public hospitals, and competing for public school and university slots, according to the U.S. State Department report. Minorities make up around 5 percent of Hong Kong's population.

Hong Kong's trade unions are independent, but the law restricts some basic labor rights and does not provide for others. Most importantly, the provisional legislature in 1997 repealed laws protecting workers against summary dismissal for union activity and setting out the legal basis for collective bargaining. More than 20 percent of Hong Kong's workers who receive regular wages or salaries are unionized.

Macao

Polity: Appointed governor and partially elected legislature
Economy: Capitalist-statist
Population: 450,000

Political Rights: 6
CivilLiberties: 4
Status: Partly Free

Religious Groups: Buddhist, Taoist, and Confucian (30.7 percent), Roman Catholic (6.7 percent), Protestant (1.7 percent), no affiliation (60.9 percent)
Ethnic Groups: Chinese (95 percent), Macanese [mixed Portuguese and Asian ancestry], Portuguese and other

Ten-Year Ratings Timeline (Political Rights, Civil Liberties, Status)

1993	1994	1995	1996	1997	1998	1999	2000	2001	2002	2003
3,3PF	5,3PF	6,4PF	6,4PF	6,4PF	6,4PF	6,4PF	6,4PF	6,4PF	6,4PF	6,4PF

Overview:

During its 443 years of Portuguese rule, Macao was the first European outpost in the Far East in 1557, the leading gateway for European trade with China until the 1770s, and a hideaway for buccaneers and Chinese criminal gangs until becoming, more recently, a bawdy city of casinos and prostitution. The territory's road to reunification with the mainland began in 1987, when China and Portugal agreed that Beijing would regain control over Macao in 1999 and that the enclave would maintain its legal system and capitalist economy for 50 years.

Macao lacks the vibrant banking, real estate, and trading industries found in Hong Kong, just 40 miles to the east along the south China coast. Its economic fortunes have recently been tied largely to tourism and the casino industry as well as to textile and garment exports. Macao's economy slid into recession in 1995, partly because a surge in gang-related violence, including killings and attacks on several local civil servants and Portuguese officers, hurt tourism, which makes up 40 percent of gross domestic product (GDP). The violence pitted rival triads, or organized-crime groups, in battles for control of loan-sharking, prostitution, and protection rackets. The regional financial crisis that began in 1997 prolonged the recession, which ended in 2000.

Gangland violence tailed off significantly in the lead-up to the handover, which took place in December 1999. China reportedly helped Macao crack down on the triads, and the outgoing Portuguese jailed a major crime boss.

Despite concerns before the handover that China would renege on its pledges to respect Macao's autonomy, there have been few overt signs that Beijing is trying to pressure the administration of Edmund Ho, the territory's appointed top official. Nevertheless, these fears had been heightened by the fact that Macao's press and civic groups are powerless compared with those in Hong Kong. Moreover, under the 1987 Sino-Portuguese deal, Macao's chief executive, like Hong Kong's, is appointed by an elite committee rather than elected directly. Ho, a Canadian-educated banker, was the committee's consensus choice to be the chief executive. The committee's 199 members were themselves appointed by a Beijing-selected committee.

Concerns about Beijing's influence in the territory may have been allayed some-what by the fact that Macao's sole pro-democracy party was the largest single vote-getter in the September 2001 legislative elections, the first since the handover. Led by Ng Kuok-cheong, the Association for a New Democratic Macao party took 2 of the 10 directly elected seats in the 27-member body. Business-backed candidates won 4 seats, and the pro-China camp won another 4. Ten other seats, chosen by special interest groups, were uncontested. Ho appointed the remaining 7 seats. Macao's legislature, in any case, has little influence under a political setup that puts most power in the hands of Chief Executive Ho.

In an expected move, the government in February 2002 broke casino magnate Stanley Ho's 40-year monopoly on Macao's $1.99 billion gaming industry by award-ing him only one of three new licenses to operate casinos in the territory. The other two licenses went to two Las Vegas casino moguls. Analysts say that increased competition should boost an industry that already accounts for an estimated one-third of the territory's $6.2 billion GDP and about half of the government's annual revenues.

Political Rights and Civil Liberties:

Residents of Macao cannot change their government through elections, although they do enjoy many basic rights and freedoms.

Observers question, however, whether the enclave's legal system is robust enough to protect fundamental liberties should they be threatened. The judiciary's development and future independence may be hampered by the need to translate laws and judgments into Chinese from Portuguese, and by a severe shortage of lo-cal bilingual lawyers and magistrates, according to the U.S. State Department's March global human rights report covering 2001. Only about 10 of the 94 lawyers in private practice can read and write Chinese, the report said. Moreover, the chief executive appoints all judges, with recommendations for judicial posts coming from a commis-sion that the chief executive himself names.

Meanwhile, Macao's mini-constitution, the basic law, is "riddled with ambigu-ities," fails to guarantee several basic rights, and grants Beijing vaguely defined emergency powers, Amnesty International said in 1999. In addition, the basic struc-ture of Macao's government contains few democratic checks and balances. Like the Portuguese governors who served in the waning years of colonial rule, Macao's chief executive is appointed and holds broad executive powers. The basic law, mean-while, bars legislators from introducing bills relating to public spending, Macao's political structure, or the operation of its government. Bills relating to governmental policies must receive the chief executive's written approval before they are submitted.

The legislature elected in 2005 will have two additional seats, both of them di-rectly elected. After 2009, the basic law allows the assembly, by a two-thirds vote and subject to the chief executive's approval, to draw up a new mix of directly and indirectly elected seats.

Outside of a handful of opposition politicians like Ng Kuok-cheong, Macao has few outspoken voices for greater political freedom or transparency in governmental and business affairs. Most of the enclave's 10 daily newspapers, including the top-selling *Macao Daily*, are pro-Beijing. None take an independent political line. The press also offers little coverage of people, groups, or activities that challenge Macao's conservative political and business establishment or that call for greater democracy. Meanwhile, human rights groups, such as the Macao Association for the Rights of Laborers and the New Democratic Macao Association, operate freely but generally have little impact on the territory's political life.

Practitioners of the Falun Gong spiritual movement, whose followers on the mainland have been suppressed ruthlessly, routinely perform their exercises in Macao's parks. Police, however, photograph practitioners and at times take them to police stations for checks of their identification documents that last several hours, according to the U.S. State Department report.

Critics say that Macao's dominant labor confederation, the Federation of Trade Unions, is more of a political front for Chinese interests than an advocate for better wages, benefits, and working conditions. Several small private (business) sector unions and two of Macao's four public sector unions are independent. Legislation protecting striking workers from dismissal is inadequate, and government enforcement of labor laws is lax, according to the U.S. State Department report. The report also said that foreign workers often work for less than half the wages paid to Macao residents, live in controlled dormitories, and owe huge sums to the firms that bring them to the enclave. Macao workers, meanwhile, complain that their bargaining power is eroded by the territory's many foreign laborers, who make up around 12 percent of the workforce.

Women are becoming more active in business and increasingly hold senior government posts. They are, however, still underrepresented in politics and the civil service. Traffickers continue to bring women from abroad into Macao for prostitution, although there are no accurate figures on the scale of the problem, the U.S. State Department report said.

Tibet

Polity: One party **Political Rights:** 7
Economy: Statist **Civil Liberties:** 7
Population: 4,590,000* **Status:** Not Free
Religious Groups: Tibetan Buddhist (majority), Muslim, Christian, other
Ethnic Groups: Chinese, Tibetan
*This figure from China's 1990 census includes 2.096 million Tibetans living in the Tibet Autonomous Region (TAR) and 2.494 million Tibetans living in areas of Eastern Tibet which, beginning in 1950, were incorporated into four Chinese provinces.

Ten-Year Ratings Timeline (Political Rights, Civil Liberties, Status)

1993	1994	1995	1996	1997	1998	1999	2000	2001	2002	2003
7,7NF	7,7NF	7,7NF	7,7NF	7,7NF	7,7NF	7,7NF	7,7NF	7,7NF	7,7NF	7,7NF

Overview: China's occupation of Tibet has marginalized a Tibetan national identity that dates back more than 2,000 years.

Beijing's modern-day claim to the region is based solely on Mongolian and Manchurian imperial influence over Tibet in the thirteenth and eighteenth centuries, respectively. China invaded Tibet in late 1949, and in 1951, formally annexed the country. In an apparent effort to undermine Tibetan claims to statehood, Beijing incorporated roughly half of Tibet into four different southwestern Chinese provinces beginning in 1950. As a result, the Tibet Autonomous Region (TAR), which Beijing created in 1965, covers only about half the territory of pre-invasion Tibet.

In what is perhaps the defining event of Beijing's occupation, Chinese troops suppressed a local uprising in 1959 by killing an estimated 87,000 Tibetans in the Lhasa region alone. The massacre forced the Tibetan spiritual and political leader, the fourteenth Dalai Lama, Tenzin Gyatso, to flee to Dharamsala, India, with 80,000 supporters.

The Geneva-based International Commission of Jurists in 1960 called the Chinese occupation genocidal and ruled that between 1911 and 1949, the year China invaded, Tibet had possessed all the attributes of statehood as defined under international law. Mao's Cultural Revolution devastated Tibet, as China jailed thousands of monks and nuns, burned many sacred texts, and destroyed nearly all of Tibet's 6,200 monasteries.

As resistance to Beijing's rule continued, Chinese soldiers forcibly broke up peaceful protests throughout Tibet between 1987 and 1990. Beijing imposed martial law on Lhasa and surrounding areas in March 1989 following three days of antigovernment protests and riots during which police killed at least 50 Tibetans. Officials lifted martial law in May 1990.

Since the 1989 demonstrations, Tibetans have mounted few large-scale protests against Chinese rule in the face of a blanket repression of dissent. In addition to jailing dissidents, officials have stepped up their efforts to control religious affairs and undermine the exiled Dalai Lama's religious and political authority. Foreign observers have reported a slight easing of repression since late 2000, when Beijing tapped the relatively moderate Guo Jinlong to be the region's Communist Party boss. Guo, who served on several party committees in Sichuan Province and the TAR, replaced Chen Kuiyan, the architect of recent crackdowns.

One reason for the change in Tibet's top governmental post may have been Beijing's anger over the escape to India in late 1999 of the teenager recognized by the Dalai Lama, and accepted by Beijing, as the seventeenth Karmapa. The Karmapa is the highest-ranking figure in the Karma Kargyu school of Tibetan Buddhism.

Beijing had interfered in the Karmapa's selection and education as part of an apparent effort to create a generation of more pliant Tibetan leaders. In an even more flagrant case of interference with Tibet's Buddhist hierarchy, China in 1995 detained six-year-old Gedhun Choekyi Nyima and rejected the Dalai Lama's selection of him as the eleventh reincarnation of the Panchen Lama. The Panchen Lama is Tibetan Buddhism's second-highest religious figure. Officials then stage-managed the selection of another six-year-old boy as the Panchen Lama. Since the Panchen Lama identifies the reincarnated Dalai Lama, Beijing potentially can control the identification of the fifteenth Dalai Lama.

China made several goodwill gestures in 2002 that some analysts interpreted as an effort to influence international opinion concerning the situation in Tibet. China hosted visits to Beijing and Lhasa by two of the Dalai Lama's envoys, the first formal contact between Beijing and the Dalai Lama since 1993. Beijing also brought several press and diplomatic delegations to Tibet and released at least six Tibetan political prisoners before the end of their sentences.

One of those released, Jigme Sangpo, 76, was Tibet's longest-serving political prisoner. He was jailed in 1983 for putting up a wall poster calling for Tibetan independence and had his sentence extended for nonviolent protests while behind bars. At year's end it was not clear whether China's moves were solely cosmetic or perhaps also reflected a willingness to open a dialogue with the Dalai Lama on autonomy for Tibet and other issues.

Political Rights and Civil Liberties: Under China's occupation of Tibet, Tibetans enjoy few basic rights, lack the right to determine their political future, and cannot change their government through elections. The Chinese Communist Party (CCP) rules the TAR and neighboring areas that historically were part of Tibet through officials whose ranks include some Tibetans in largely ceremonial posts. While ethnic Tibetans have served as TAR governor, none has ever held the peak post of TAR party secretary. Most of China's policies affecting Tibetans apply both to those living in the TAR and to Tibetans living in parts of pre-invasion Tibet that Beijing has incorporated into China's Gansu, Qinghai, Sichuan, and Yunnan Provinces.

Political dissidents face some of the worst human rights abuses of any Tibetans. Security forces routinely arrest, jail, and torture dissidents to punish nonviolent protest against Chinese rule, according to the U.S. State Department, the London-based Tibet Information Network (TIN) watchdog group, and other sources. Dissidents have been severely punished for distributing leaflets, putting up posters, holding peaceful protests, putting together lists of prisoners, possessing photographs of the Dalai Lama, and displaying Tibetan flags or other symbols of cultural identity.

The CCP-controlled judiciary routinely hands down lengthy jail terms to Tibetans convicted of these and other political offenses. Tibet's jails held 188 known political prisoners as of February 2002, according to TIN. The number of political prisoners has declined in recent years, although the reason for this is not clear. At least 37 Tibetan political prisoners, or about 1 in 50, have died since 1987 as a result of prison abuse, TIN said in 2001.

Throughout Tibet, security forces routinely beat, torture, or otherwise abuse detainees and inmates, according to the U.S. State Department and other sources. "Poor conditions of detention coupled with widespread torture and abuse make life extremely harsh for all those jailed in Tibet," the human rights group Amnesty International said in April. In one of the most notorious cases of abuse in recent years, officials responded to protests at Lhasa's Drapchi Prison in May 1998 by torturing and beating to death nine prisoners, including five nuns and three monks.

Prison officials reportedly at times also sexually abuse female inmates, according to the U.S. State Department's global human rights report covering 2001, released in March 2002. At some jails and detention centers, they also reportedly require inmates to work, often for nominal pay and the possibility of sentence reductions, the report added.

A senior lama and another Tibetan from the Kardze Tibetan Autonomous Prefecture in Sichuan Province were sentenced to death in December following a closed trial in connection with a series of bombings in Sichuan Province that resulted in one fatality. In keeping with Chinese practice, the lama's suspended sentence will likely be commuted. The sentences handed down to the outspoken lama, Tenzin Deleg Rinpoche, 52, and one of his supporters, Lobsang Dondrub, were the first reported instances in many years of Tibetans being sentenced to death on grounds that may be politically motivated.

Chinese officials permit Tibetans to observe some religious practices, but since 1996 they have strengthened their control over monasteries under an intense propaganda campaign that is aimed largely at undermining the Dalai Lama's influence as a spiritual and political leader. Under China's "patriotic education campaign," government-run "work teams" visit monasteries to conduct mandatory sessions on Beijing's version of Tibetan history and other political topics, according to the U.S. State Department report. Officials also require monks to sign a declaration agreeing to denounce the Dalai Lama, reject independence for Tibet, not listen to Voice of America radio broadcasts, and reject the boy the Dalai Lama identified as the eleventh Panchen Lama, the report added.

The intensity of the patriotic education campaign has recently died down somewhat. In past years, though, officials expelled from monasteries hundreds of monks and nuns who refused to comply with these rules.

In addition to trying to force monks and nuns to renounce their beliefs, the government oversees day-to-day affairs in major monasteries and nunneries through state-organized "democratic management committees" that run each establishment. The government also limits the numbers of monks and nuns permitted in major monasteries, although these restrictions are not always enforced. Officials have also restricted the building of new monasteries and nunneries, closed many religious institutions, and demolished several others.

Hundreds of religious figures hold nominal positions in local "people's congresses," although Tibetan members of the CCP and Tibetan governmental workers are banned from most religious practice. Since 1994, governmental workers have also been banned from displaying photographs of the Dalai Lama in state offices.

The government, however, appears to be easing tough restrictions on certain lay religious practices imposed in 2000 that targeted not only party cadres and governmental workers but also students and pensioners. The TAR government that year threatened civil servants with dismissal, schoolchildren with expulsion, and retirees with loss of pensions if they publicly marked the Buddhist Sagadawa festival in Lhasa. Officials also warned Lhasa students that they could be thrown out of their schools if they visited monasteries or temples during the summer holidays.

Beijing's draconian one-child family planning policy is in theory more lenient towards Tibetans and other ethnic minorities. And in keeping with stated policy, officials generally permit urban Tibetans to have two children, while farmers and herders often have three or more children. Officials, however, frequently pressure party cadres and state workers to have only one child, the U.S. State Department report said. Moreover, authorities reportedly are applying a two-child limit to farmers and nomads in several counties, TIN said in 2000.

As one of China's 55 recognized ethnic minority groups, Tibetans also receive some preferential treatment in university admissions and governmental employment.

Tibetans, however, need to learn Mandarin Chinese in order to take advantage of these preferences. Many Tibetans are torn between a desire to learn Chinese in order to compete for school slots and jobs and the realization that increased use of Chinese threatens the survival of the Tibetan language. Chinese has long been the language of instruction in middle schools and reportedly is now being used to teach several subjects in a number of Lhasa primary schools, TIN said 2001.

In the private sector, employers routinely favor Han Chinese for jobs and give them greater pay for the same work, according to the U.S. State Department report and Tibetans also find it more difficult than Han Chinese to get permits and loans to open businesses. As in the rest of China, officials reportedly subject farmers and herders to arbitrary taxes.

Thanks in part to heavy subsidies from Beijing and favorable tax and other economic policies, living standards have improved in recent years for many Tibetans. Han Chinese, however, have been the main beneficiaries of the growing private (business) sector and many other fruits of development. This is seen most starkly in certain areas of Lhasa where Han Chinese run almost all small businesses.

Moreover, the influx of Han Chinese has altered the region's demographic composition, displaced Tibetan businesses, reduced job opportunities for Tibetans, and further marginalized Tibetan cultural identity. Possibly because of these rapid social and economic changes and dislocations, prostitution is a "growing problem" in Tibet, particularly in Lhasa, the U.S. State Department report said. Some 3,000 Tibetans flee to Nepal as refugees each year, according to the UN High Commissioner for Refugees.

In yet another sign of Beijing's tight grip on the region, the government controls all print and broadcast media in Tibet, except for around 20 clandestine publications that appear sporadically, the Paris-based Reporters Without Borders press freedom group said in 2000.

Georgia
Abkhazia

Polity: Presidential   **Political Rights:** 6
Economy: Mixed statist   **Civil Liberties:** 5
Population: 280,000 (est.)   **Status:** Not Free
Religious Groups: Muslim (majority)
Ethnic Groups: Abkhaz (majority)

Ten-Year Ratings Timeline (Political Rights, Civil Liberties, Status)

1993	1994	1995	1996	1997	1998	1999	2000	2001	2002	2003
--	--	--	--	--	6,5NF	6,5NF	6,5NF	6,5NF	6,5NF	6,5NF

Overview: A decade after fighting erupted between Georgian governmental troops and separatist forces in the breakaway republic of Abkhazia, no substantial progress has been made on finding a lasting settlement to the conflict. Abkhaz officials rejected the latest UN proposal to advance peace talks, while the Kodori Gorge region remained a source of tension during much of the year. In March elections to the territory's parliament, deputies loyal to Abkhazia's president won all of the seats in the legislature.

Annexed by Russia in 1864, Abkhazia became an autonomous republic of Soviet Georgia in 1930. The year following the 1991 collapse of the Soviet Union, Abkhazia declared its independence from Tbilisi, igniting a war between Abkhaz secessionists and Georgian troops that lasted nearly 14 months. In September 1993, Abkhaz forces, with covert assistance from Russia, seized control of the city of Sukhumi, ultimately defeating the Georgian army and winning de facto independence for the territory. As a result of the conflict, more than 200,000 residents, mostly ethnic Georgians, fled Abkhazia, while casualty figures were estimated in the thousands. An internationally brokered ceasefire was signed in Moscow in 1994, although a final decision on the territory's status remains unresolved.

In the October 1999 elections for president of Abkhazia, the incumbent, Vladislav Ardzinba, was the only candidate running for office; his inauguration ceremony was held in the capital, Sukhumi, in December. The OSCE, the United Nations, and other international organizations refused to recognize the vote as legitimate. In a concurrent referendum on independence, the results of which were not accepted by any state, a reported 98 percent of voters supported independence for Abkhazia. Georgia denounced the polls as illegal and as an attempt to sabotage peace talks.

A series of violent incidents in late 2001 underscored the precariousness of the region's fragile peace. In October, a group reportedly consisting of Chechen rebels and Georgian partisans clashed with Abkhaz troops following a deadly raid on a village in the Kodori Gorge, a partly Georgian-controlled area located in Abkhazia. The downing of a UN helicopter and the bombing of several Abkhaz villages by aircraft that Georgian authorities alleged had come from Russia intensified the conflict. Tbilisi responded by sending troops to the upper part of the gorge in what it said was an operation to protect ethnic Georgians living there from separatist attacks.

Tensions in Kodori continued in 2002, despite a UN-brokered protocol signed by Russia and Georgia on April 2 that called for the withdrawal of Georgian forces by April 10, and the resumption of joint patrols by Russian peacekeepers and UN observers. On April 12, Russia dispatched a group of soldiers to Kodori in what it called a peacekeeping operation. After protests from Georgian and UN officials, who had not been notified in advance of the troop deployment, Russia withdrew the soldiers the following day. In August, Georgian and Abkhaz forces engaged in a brief exchange of gunfire, although no casualties were reported. During the year, Abkhaz officials insisted that Georgia had not withdrawn all its troops from Kodori, while Georgian authorities countered that the protocol did not require the withdrawal of other military detachments, including border guards.

In the March 2002 parliamentary elections, deputies loyal to Ardzinba won a landslide victory when the two opposition parties—Revival and the People's Party—withdrew most of their candidates in protest over the conduct of the campaign. Officially backed candidates won all 35 seats in the legislature and ran unopposed for 13 of them. Among the problems cited during the elections were that ethnic Georgians displaced by the war were not able to vote, official radio and television promoted pro-government candidates and attacked the opposition, and that the head of the Central Election Commission had disqualified a number of candidates supported by the opposition. As in previous elections in Abkhazia, the international community declared the elections to be illegitimate.

By the end of the year, UN efforts to advance peace negotiations between Tbilisi and Sukhumi remained stalled over the main issue of the region's final political status. In early 2002, the United Nations endorsed a document by then UN special representative for Georgia, Dieter Boden, called "Basic Principles for the Distribution of Competencies between Tbilisi and Sukhumi." Abkhaz authorities refused during the year to begin discussions on the so-called Boden plan, which is intended to be a starting point for talks between Abkhazia and Georgia, because it calls for substantial autonomy for Abkhazia within the Georgian state. While Tbilisi maintains that Abkhazia must remain a constituent part of Georgia, Sukhumi continues to insist on the territory's independence from Georgia, a status that has not been recognized by the international community. Strained relations between Georgia and Russia, which at times has supported the Boden plan, further hurt the peace process; relations worsened during 2002 over Russian accusations that Georgia allowed Chechen rebels to operate in Georgian territory. Some analysts speculated that the sudden dismissal in December of the region's prime minister, Anri Djergenia, and the reported ill health of President Ardzinba could further complicate efforts for future peace talks.

Political Rights and Civil Liberties: Residents of Abkhazia can elect government officials, but the more than 200,000 displaced Georgians who fled the war in the early to mid-1990s could not vote in the October 1999 presidential, March 2001 local, or March 2002 parliamentary elections. International organizations, including the OSCE, as well as the Georgian government, criticized the polls as illegitimate. Although the November 1994 constitution established a presidential-parliamentary system of government, the president exercises almost complete control of the region. The ethnic Georgian Abkhazian Supreme Council has been a government in exile in Tbilisi since being expelled from Abkhazia in 1993.

Several independent newspapers are published in the territory. Electronic media are controlled by the state and generally reflect government positions.

Freedom of religion is respected for Muslims, but Christian Georgians and Armenians face discrimination. President Vladislav Ardzinba issued a decree in 1995 banning Jehovah's Witnesses. Abkhazia's Education Ministry announced in September a rule prohibiting instruction in the Georgian language in the territory's schools, the 2002 U.S. State Department's human rights report for Georgia stated. Local residents in the Gali district, whose population is largely ethnic Georgian, were denied access to education in their mother tongue. Most nongovernmental organizations operating in Abkhazia rely on funding from outside the territory.

Systemic problems in the territory's criminal justice system include the failure to conduct impartial investigations and to bring alleged perpetrators to justice, according to the 2002 U.S. State Department report. Other areas of concern include defendants' limited access to qualified legal counsel, violations of due process, and the length of pretrial detentions. In July, an independent legal aid office in the Gali district began providing free legal advice to the public. A report by the UN secretary-general on the situation in Abkhazia noted a number of cases of abuse of power and arbitrary detention by local law enforcement agencies during two search-and-arrest operations in Gali in November and December.

Personal security in the conflict zone continued to be a serious concern in 2002. The 1994 ceasefire has been tenuous, with abductions, bombings, and killings occurring throughout the year. Since the ceasefire, an unarmed, 108-member UN Observer Mission in Georgia (UNOMIG) has been stationed to monitor the ceasefire and attempt to resolve violations, and a 1,800-strong Commonwealth of Independent States (CIS) peacekeeping force, dominated by Russian troops, has patrolled the region. Despite denials from Moscow, Georgia has accused Russian peacekeepers of supporting the Abkhaz separatists.

Travel and choice of residence are limited by the ongoing conflict. Close to 200,000 ethnic Georgians who fled Abkhazia during the early 1990s are living in western Georgia, most in the Zugdidi district bordering Abkhazia. Most of these internally displaced persons (IDPs) are unable or unwilling to return because of the continued absence of a political agreement on their repatriation and fears for their safety. Hundreds of IDPs held demonstrations during the year, including a blockade of the main bridge over the Inguri River that separates Abkhazia from Georgia proper. The protestors called for the withdrawal of the CIS peacekeeping force and a return to their homes.

Equality of opportunity and normal business activities are limited by widespread corruption, the control by criminal organizations of large segments of the economy, and the continuing effects of the war. Abkhazia's economy is heavily reliant on Russia; the territory uses the Russian ruble as its currency, and many residents earn income by trading citrus fruits across the border in Russia.

India
Kashmir

Polity: Indian-administered **Political Rights:** 5*
Economy: Capitalist-statist **Civil Liberties:** 5*
Population: 9,450,000   **Status:** Partly Free
Religious Groups: Muslim (64.2 percent), Hindu (32.2 percent), Sikh (2.4 percent), Buddhist (1.2 percent)
Ethnic Groups: Kashmiri (majority), Dogra, Ladakhi, other (including Gujjar, Bakerwal, Dard, and Balti)
Ratings Change: Indian-administered Kashmir's political rights rating improved from 6 to 5 due to the holding of relatively fair elections in which the ruling party was removed from power, its civil liberties rating improved from 6 to 5 due to changes to the survey methodology, and its status changed from Not Free to Partly Free.

Ten-Year Ratings Timeline (Political Rights, Civil Liberties, Status)

1993	1994	1995	1996	1997	1998	1999	2000	2001	2002	2003
6,6NF	7,7NF	7,7NF	7,7NF	7,7NF	7,7NF	6,6NF	6,6NF	6,6NF	6,6NF	5,5PF

Overview: Tensions over the disputed territory of Kashmir, where a continuing insurgency has killed at least 35,000 civilians, soldiers, and militants since 1989, remained high throughout 2002. In response to infiltration and attacks by Pakistan-based Islamic militant groups, India amassed troops along its common border with Pakistan and threatened to conduct retaliatory military strikes during the first half of the year. In state elections held in the fall that were judged to be fair but not entirely free, the ruling but unpopular National Conference Party was ejected from power in a surprise result. A new coalition government took office in November amid hopes that elections would pave the way to renewed discussions over the region's status.

After centuries of rule in Kashmir by Afghan, Sikh, and local strongmen, the British seized control of the Himalayan land in 1846 and sold it to the Hindu maharajah of the neighboring principality of Jammu. The maharajah later incorporated Ladakh and other surrounding areas into what became the new princely state of Jammu and Kashmir. At the partition of British India in 1947, Maharajah Hari Singh attempted to preserve Jammu and Kashmir's independence. However, after Pakistani tribesmen invaded, the maharajah agreed to Jammu and Kashmir's accession to India in return for promises of autonomy and eventual self-determination.

Within months of gaining their independence, India and Pakistan went to war in Kashmir. A UN-brokered ceasefire in January 1949 established the present-day boundaries, which gave Pakistan control of roughly one-third of Jammu and Kashmir, including the far northern and western areas. (A separate report on Pakistani-administered Kashmir appears in the Disputed Territories section of the survey). India retained most of the Kashmir Valley along with predominantly Hindu Jammu and Buddhist-majority Ladakh.

Under Article 370 of India's constitution and a 1952 accord, the territory received substantial autonomy. However, New Delhi began annulling the autonomy guarantees in 1953, and in 1957 formally annexed the part of Jammu and Kashmir under its control. Seeking strategic roads and passes, China seized a portion of Kashmir in 1959. India and Pakistan fought a second, inconclusive, war over the territory in 1965. Under the 1972 Simla accord, New Delhi and Islamabad agreed to respect the Line of Control (LOC), which demarcates the Indian- and Pakistani-held parts of Kashmir, and to resolve Kashmir's status through negotiation.

The armed insurgency against Indian rule gathered momentum after 1987, when the pro-India National Conference Party won state elections that were marred by widespread fraud and violence and authorities began arresting members of a new, Muslim-based, opposition coalition. Militant groups with links to political parties assassinated several National Conference politicians and attacked government targets in the Kashmir Valley. The militants included the Jammu and Kashmir Liberation Front (JKLF) and other pro-independence groups consisting largely of indigenous Kashmiris, as well as Pakistani-backed Islamist groups that want to bring Kashmir under Islamabad's control. Muslims make up two-thirds of the state's population but are concentrated in the Kashmir Valley, which is barely one-fifth of the state's area.

As the violence escalated, New Delhi placed Jammu and Kashmir under federal rule in 1990 and attempted to quell the mass uprising by force. By the mid-1990s, the Indian army had greatly weakened the JKLF and had secured most large Kashmir Valley towns and villages. The JKLF abandoned its armed struggle in 1994. The armed insurgency has since been controlled by Pakistani-backed extremist groups, which include in their ranks many non-Kashmiri fighters from elsewhere in the Islamic world. Although opposition parties had joined together to form the All Parties Hurriyat Conference (APHC) in 1993, they boycotted the 1996 state elections and the National Conference was able to form a government under party leader Farooq Abdullah.

In August 2000, Hizbul Mujahideen, the largest armed group in Kashmir, declared a ceasefire and initiated a dialogue with the Indian government, but talks broke down when India refused to include Pakistan in the discussions. The two neighbors had engaged in a two-month limited war in 1999 after Pakistan seized strategic heights on the Indian side of the LOC. An Indo-Pakistani summit held in July 2001 failed to resolve the two countries' long-standing differences over Kashmir. Militants stepped up their attacks in the aftermath of the summit, with an increasing focus on targeting Hindu civilians in the southern districts of the state. Gunmen targeted an army camp in May 2002 and Hindu migrant laborers at a shantytown in July, killing dozens in each attack. In addition, a leading moderate separatist politician, Abdul Ghani Lone, was assassinated in May, possibly by a hard-line militant group.

Seeking legitimacy for the electoral process, New Delhi worked to encourage the participation of all political parties in the fall 2002 state elections, but was unsuccessful in persuading the APHC and Shabir Shah's Jammu and Kashmir Democratic Freedom Party to contest the polls. However, in a surprise result, the National Conference lost 29 of its 57 assembly seats, while the Congress Party and the People's Democratic Party (PDP) made significant gains, winning 16 and 20 seats respectively. On November 2, the two parties formed a coalition government headed by the PDP's Mufti Mohammad Sayeed. The new government promised to address issues of human rights violations, corruption, and economic development, and urged the central government to hold peace talks with Kashmiri militants and separatist political groups.

Political Rights and Civil Liberties:

India has never held a referendum on Kashmiri self-determination as called for in the 1948 UN resolution. The state's residents can nominally change the local administration through elections. However, previous elections have been marred by violence, coercion by security forces, and balloting irregularities. Militants commonly enforce boycotts called by separatist political parties, threaten election officials and candidates, and kill both political activists as well as civilians during the balloting. During the campaign period leading up to the fall elections for the 87-seat state assembly, over 800 people, including more than 75 political activists and candidates, were killed. However, the balloting process itself was carefully monitored by India's Election Commission, and turnout averaged just over 40 percent. Independent observers judged the elections to be fair but not entirely free, largely because of the threat of violence.

Although Jammu and Kashmir was returned to local rule in 1996, many viewed the National Conference government as corrupt, incompetent, and unaccountable to the wishes and needs of Kashmiris. According to a November 2002 report issued by the International Crisis Group, official corruption is "widespread" and corruption cases are seldom prosecuted. Much corrupt behavior and illegal economic activity can be traced directly to political leaders and parties and to militant groups tied to both India and Pakistan, the report added.

The insurgency has forced Kashmiri media to "tread carefully in their reporting," according to the Committee to Protect Journalists. In recent years, militant groups have kidnapped, tortured, killed, or otherwise harassed and threatened numerous journalists, causing some self-censorship. The *New York Times* reported that four journalists were shot and wounded by militants in attacks between April and September. In addition, authorities occasionally beat, detain, or otherwise harass journalists. In May 2001, security forces assaulted 17 journalists as they attempted to cover a funeral procession. Though it is generally not used, under India's 1971 Newspaper Incitements to Offenses Act (in effect only in Jammu and Kashmir) district magistrates can censor publications in certain circumstances. Despite these restrictions, newspapers do report on alleged human rights abuses by security forces. In June, Kashmiri journalist Iftikhar Ali Gilani was arrested, charged under the Official Secrets Act, and detained for more than seven months before the military admitted that the case against him was baseless.

Several human rights activists have been killed since 1989, and only a few individuals and groups continue to do human rights work. Although local and national civil rights groups are permitted to operate, the Indian government has banned some international groups from visiting the state. The APHC, an umbrella group of 23 legal secessionist political parties, is allowed to operate, although its leaders are frequently subjected to preventative arrest and its requests for permits for public gatherings are routinely denied. The Indian government has also denied permission for APHC leaders to travel to Pakistan. Politically motivated strikes, protest marches, and antigovernment demonstrations take place on a regular basis, although some are forcibly broken up by the authorities.

Under heavy pressure from both the government and militants, the judiciary barely functions, according to the U.S. State Department's annual human rights report for 2001. The government frequently disregards judicial orders quashing detentions, while militants routinely threaten judges, witnesses, and the families of defendants.

Many judicial abuses are facilitated by the 1978 Public Safety Act and other broadly drawn laws, which allow authorities to detain persons for up to two years without charge or trial. Amnesty International's 2002 report noted that hundreds of people remain held in preventive detention or on a range of criminal charges despite a court order for a review of all cases. Although detentions under the security laws are nonrenewable, authorities frequently re-arrest suspects on new charges and impose new two-year detentions. The Prevention of Terrorism Act (POTA), which became law in March 2002, gives authorities wide powers of interrogation and detention while expanding the definitions of punishable crimes and prescribing severe punishments for a broad range of criminal acts. Between October 2001 and mid-July 2002, there were 161 people detained under POTA in Jammu and Kashmir, including two high-profile separatist political leaders. However, after the new government was sworn in, a number of political prisoners were released from preventative detention in November.

Two other broadly written laws, the 1990 Armed Forces (Jammu and Kashmir) Special Powers Act and the 1990 Disturbed Areas Act, allow Indian forces to search homes and arrest suspects without a warrant, shoot suspects on sight, and destroy homes or buildings believed to house militants or arms. Moreover, the Special Powers Act requires New Delhi to approve any prosecution of Indian forces. While the state human rights commission investigates some human rights complaints, it cannot directly investigate abuses by the army or other federal security forces. Efforts to bring soldiers to justice for rights violations are rare.

In a continuing cycle of indiscriminate violence, several thousand militants, security force personnel, and civilians are killed each year. Approximately 700,000 security forces, including Indian soldiers, federal paramilitary troops, and the police, carry out arbitrary arrests and detentions, tortures, disappearances, and summary killings of suspected militants and alleged civilian sympathizers. As part of the counterinsurgency effort, the government has recruited former servicemen for Village Defense Committees as well as organizing and arming pro-government militias composed of former militants. Members of these groups act with impunity and have reportedly carried out a wide range of human rights abuses against pro-Pakistani militants as well as civilians.

Armed with increasingly sophisticated and powerful weapons, and relying to a greater degree on the deployment of suicide squads, militant groups continued to kill pro-India politicians, public employees, suspected informers, members of rival factions, soldiers, and civilians. Repeated violence against Kashmiri Hindus throughout the year is part of a pattern since 1990 that has forced hundreds of thousands of Hindus to flee the region. Along the LOC separating the two adversaries, intensified shelling by Indian and Pakistani troops killed numerous civilians during the year, displaced thousands more, and disrupted schools and the local economy. Women continued to be targeted in 2002 by a little-known militant group, the Lashkar-e-Jabbar, which last year issued an ultimatum that all Muslim women wear *burqas,* or head-to-toe veils; members of the group threw acid and sprayed paint at several women who refused to comply with the directive. In December, another militant group active in Rajouri district declared that all girls over the age of 12 should not attend school. Female civilians are also subject to arbitrary harassment and intimidation, including rape, at the hands of both the security forces and militant groups. In April, a 17-year-old girl was gang-raped by members of the Border Security Force in Pahalgam.

Indonesia

West Papua (Irian Jaya)

Polity: Dominant party (military-dominated)
Economy: Capitalist-statist
Population: 1,800,000
Religious Groups: Protestant, Roman Catholic, Sunni Muslim
Ethnic Groups: Indigenous West Papuan (Melanesian), Indonesian groups

Political Rights: 5
Civil Liberties: 4*
Status: Partly Free

Ratings Change: West Papua's civil liberties rating improved from 5 to 4 due to changes in the survey methodology.

Ten-Year Ratings Timeline (Political Rights, Civil Liberties, Status)

1993	1994	1995	1996	1997	1998	1999	2000	2001	2002	2003
7,6NF	7,7NF	7,7NF	7,7NF	7,7NF	7,7NF	7,6NF	6,5PF	5,5PF	5,5PF	5,4PF

Overview:

Located on the western part of the island of New Guinea, West Papua has been dominated by outside powers for nearly two centuries. The Dutch set up the first European outpost in New Guinea in 1828 and formally took control of the island's western part under an 1848 agreement with Britain. That deal paved the way for Britain and Germany to colonize the eastern part, which today is the independent state of Papua New Guinea. The Japanese occupied the Dutch-controlled territory during World War II. The Netherlands ceded its territory to Indonesia in 1963 under a UN agreement calling for Jakarta to hold a referendum on self-determination by 1969.

Seeking an independent homeland, a group of tribesmen calling themselves the Free Papua Movement (OPM) began waging a low-grade insurgency in the mid-1960s. As the violence continued, Jakarta gained UN approval to formally annex West Papua in the summer of 1969 after holding a tightly controlled "Act of Free Choice." The 1,025 traditional leaders who participated voted unanimously against independence. Indonesia in 1973 renamed the land, known locally as West Papua, Irian Jaya.

As the OPM escalated its hit-and-run attacks against the far more powerful Indonesian troops, the army launched a counteroffensive in 1984 that drove hundreds of villagers into neighboring Papua New Guinea. That year, Indonesian forces also killed the prominent Papuan anthropologist Arnold Ap. The army carried out more major anti-OPM offensives in 1989.

While the OPM and other tiny armed groups continue to mount sporadic anti-government attacks, civilian groups have become the main spokesmen for independence ever since Indonesia's democratic transition began in 1998. In an event high on symbolism but short on tangible results, the Papua Presidium Council, a forum for West Papuan leaders seeking peaceful independence, organized a week-long congress in spring 2000. The congress called on Jakarta to recognize a 1961 West

Papuan declaration of independence that took place under Dutch rule and was never recognized internationally.

Jakarta tolerated the holding of the congress, but violence in the town of Wamena later in 2000 increased tensions and pushed the two sides even farther apart. That October, security forces in Wamena killed two people while trying to forcibly lower a pro-independence Morning Star flag. Amid mounting tensions in the town, security forces shot dead 11 more people and local Papuans killed 19 immigrants from other parts of Indonesia.

A court in 2001 sentenced five leading activists to between four and four-and-a-half years in prison for masterminding the Wamena violence. The human rights group Amnesty International said that there is no evidence that the five activists, all of whom are Presidium Council members, were involved.

The independence movement suffered a further blow when the leader of the Presidium Council was killed by unidentified assailants in November 2001. More than a year later, Thueys Eluay's killing was still unsolved. Throughout 2001, moreover, a series of alleged rebel attacks and security force crackdowns caused thousands of villagers to flee their homes, according to the New York-based Human Rights Watch.

Fewer incidents of politically related violence were reported in 2002, although tensions remained high in the province. In August, unidentified gunmen killed two Americans and an Indonesian near the giant Grasberg mine in Tembagapura owned by the local subsidiary of the U.S.-based Freeport McMoRan. The gold and copper mine came under increased scrutiny in the 1990s over environmental concerns and allegations that Indonesian security forces guarding the site committed rights abuses against local Papuans.

Meanwhile, the Presidium Council continued to reject an Indonesian law passed in late 2001 giving West Papua political autonomy and a greater share of local forestry, fishery, and energy revenues.

Political Rights and Civil Liberties: West Papuans enjoy many basic rights previously denied to them under former President Suharto. Discussion and advocacy of independence are no longer illegal, newspapers freely report on West Papua's pro-independence movement and other local political news, and nongovernmental organizations not only provide social services but also monitor and promote human rights. By contrast, during the Suharto era officials banned all expression of support for West Papuan independence, routinely jailed dissidents, and kept a tight lid on the private media and civil society.

Despite these positive changes, serious problems remain. Indonesian forces continue to commit abuses in the province. "Security forces in Papua assaulted, tortured, and killed persons during search operations for members of militant groups," and reportedly assaulted suspects in detention, according to the U.S. State Department's March global human rights report covering 2001, adding that police also killed Papuans while searching for suspects in ordinary crimes. Some detained suspects are either tortured or brutally beaten, Human Rights Watch said in September. Meanwhile, the OPM and other small separatist groups have in recent years killed several soldiers and police while kidnapping foreigners in order to bring attention to their cause.

Since 2001 officials have subjected prominent local human rights organizations, such as the Institute for Human Rights Study and Advocacy and other civic groups, to increased surveillance and harassment. Activists who reported on alleged rights violations, such as the police killings of three students and other abuses in the town of Abepura in December 2000, have been summoned by police for questioning. The killings in Abepura, located near the provincial capital of Jayapura, followed a rebel attack on a police post. Journalists who try to expose abuses by security forces often face intimidation, according to Human Rights Watch.

While the judiciary is more independent than in the past, observers have criticized recent trials of antigovernment activists. The trials of the five Wamena activists in 2001 and of 17 other independence supporters were carried out in "a tense atmosphere of intimidation and secrecy" amid a heavily armed police presence around the courtrooms, according to Amnesty International.

Most Papuans follow either Christian or indigenous beliefs, and all generally enjoy freedom of worship. Traditional norms that put women in a subservient position contribute to unofficial discrimination against women in education and employment.

Indonesian rule has helped modernize West Papua and develop its economy. Most of the benefits, however, have been reaped by foreign investors, the military, and immigrants from other parts of the archipelago, according to the U.S. State Department report and other sources. Papuans also have little control over the territory's abundant natural resources. They say that officials continue to expropriate their ancestral lands and grant mining, logging, and energy contracts without adequate consultation or compensation, while investing little in local development projects.

Critics say that the presence of large numbers of non-Papuans in the territory threatens to marginalize the Papuans' Melanesian culture and makes it harder for them to find work. Local governmental agencies and private mining outfits reportedly tend to fill job openings with immigrants rather than Papuans. Moreover, immigrants dominate small business and reportedly discriminate against indigenous Papuans. The October 2000 killings in Wamena of at least 19 immigrants from other parts of Indonesia were the worst of several incidents in the past few years where Papuans violently attacked or otherwise harassed non-Papuans. Some 170,000 non-Papuans came to West Papua from Indonesia's overcrowded main islands under a largely defunct "transmigration" program that began in the 1970s. Thousands more immigrated on their own.

In addition to having fairly little control over economic affairs, West Papuans lack the right to decide the territory's political future. They had no input in the 1962 New York Agreement between the Netherlands and the United Nations that transferred their land from Dutch to Indonesian control in 1963. Moreover, the 1969 referendum that ratified Indonesian rule was neither free nor fair. The New York Agreement did not specify a procedure for the referendum, but it did call for Indonesia to hold a popular consultation "in accordance with international practice," a standard that Jakarta arguably ignored. The Indonesian military reportedly coerced the traditional leaders into approving Jakarta's rule, with the UN special observer reporting that "the administration exercised at all times a tight political control over the population."

Iraq
Kurdistan

Polity: Dual leadership **Political Rights:** 5
Economy: Capitalist- **Civil Liberties:** 4*
statist **Status:** Partly Free
Population: 4,000,000
Religious Groups: Sunni Muslim (majority)
Ethnic Groups: Kurdish, Assyrian, Armenian, Iraqi Turkoman
Ratings Change: Kurdistan's civil liberties rating improved from 5 to 4 due to changes in the survey methodology.

Ten-Year Ratings Timeline (Political Rights, Civil Liberties, Status)

1993	1994	1995	1996	1997	1998	1999	2000	2001	2002	2003
4,5PF	4,4PF	4,4PF	4,4PF	6,6NF	6,6NF	6,6NF	6,6NF	6,6NF	5,5PF	5,4PF

Overview: In the face of American preparations for war with Iraq in 2002, the Kurdistan Democratic Party (KDP) and the Patriotic Union of Kurdistan (PUK) proclaimed that they had set aside their differences, and the Kurdish National Assembly met for the first time in eight years.

Since the withdrawal of Iraqi military forces and administrative personnel from northern Iraq and the establishment of a U.S.-enforced no fly zone north of the 36th parallel in 1991, most of the three northern provinces of Erbil, Duhok, and Suleimaniyah have been under the control of Massoud Barzani's KDP and Jalal Talabani's PUK. After holding elections in 1992, which produced an evenly divided National Assembly, the KDP and PUK shared power in the nascent Kurdish Regional Government (KRG) for two years. Disputes over power and revenue sparked a three-year civil war from 1994-1997 and the two rival Kurdish groups set up separate administrations, with the KDP controlling the western region from its headquarters in Erbil, and the PUK controlling the southeast from its headquarters in Suleimaniyah.

In spite of this rivalry, northern Iraq experienced rapid development during the 1990s. With their 13 percent share of Iraqi revenue from United Nations-authorized oil exports, and customs duties from Iraqi-Turkish trade, the Kurdish authorities built schools, roads, hospitals, sewage systems, and other development projects. Anxious to win international support for long-term Kurdish self-governance, both the KDP and the PUK allowed a flourishing of political and civil liberties not seen anywhere else in the Arab world.

In 1998, the two sides signed an agreement, known as the Washington Accord, which called for the establishment of an elected government after a transitional period of power sharing, the equitable distribution of revenues from cross-border trade with Turkey, and the elimination of checkpoints to allow for freedom of movement throughout the region. However, implementation of the agreement remained stalled by disputes over revenue and the composition of a joint regional government.

In 2001, the two rival factions took steps to ease restrictions on travel between their respective sectors and resumed dialogue. This reconciliation was facilitated by the emergence of a militant Islamist group linked to al-Qaeda in northeastern Iraq. Initially calling itself Jund al-Islam (Soldiers of Islam) before changing its name to the more moderate-sounding Ansar al-Islam (Supporters of Islam), the group seized two Kurdish villages near the town of Halabja in September 2001, touching off weeks of bloody clashes in which some 150 PUK fighters were killed. The KDP, which had suffered the assassination of a senior official by Islamist terrorists in February, quickly joined the PUK in containing the threat, but the Ansar al-Islam continue to occupy a small enclave of territory near the Iranian border and has reportedly received assistance from the Iraqi government. In 2002, the group carried out several major attacks that left scores of people dead.

The KDP-PUK rapprochement deepened in 2002 as the United States prepared for a possible invasion of Iraq to oust Saddam Hussein. In August, the KDP released a document outlining its vision of a postwar federal system in which a self-governing Kurdish entity would control oil-rich Kirkuk and have its own president, prime minister, and regional assembly. The Turkish government, which has long feared that Kurdish autonomy in Iraq would spawn demands for self-governance from its own restive Kurdish minority, quickly began reinforcing its military presence in northern Iraq and warned that it would respond to any Kurdish attempt to seize Kirkuk with a full-scale invasion. Within days, Barzani and Talabani held their first face-to-face meeting in Iraq in seven years and declared that they had set aside their differences. The Kurdish parliament convened in October for the first time since 1994, ratified the Washington Accord, and set up a committee to prepare for legislative elections in 2003. For the time being, however, there are no plans to form a unified government.

Political Rights and Civil Liberties: Iraqi Kurds cannot change their government democratically, as factional strife has precluded parliamentary elections since 1992. The KDP and the PUK have separate administrations and cabinets for the territories under their control. While municipal elections held by the PUK in February 2000 were generally free and fair, the May 2001 municipal elections in the KDP enclave were marred by Assyrian Christian allegations of vote rigging and intimidation of boycott supporters by Kurdish police.

The KDP and the PUK maintain separate judicial systems in areas under their control, but reliable information about judicial integrity is difficult to obtain. Reportedly, hearings are conducted, adjudicated, and enforced by local officials of the two parties. The two groups also run separate prisons and detention facilities where human rights violations, including denial of due process and torture, have occurred. However, both sides regularly grant access to their prisons to delegations from the International Committee of the Red Cross.

Freedom of expression is generally protected. The KDP and PUK have allowed approximately 200 print publications, two satellite television channels, around 20 local television stations, and scores of radio stations to operate in areas under their control. Most, however, are affiliated with political parties. While few media outlets are, in fact, independent, there is an open climate for discussion of political issues. While 3 journalists were arrested for two weeks by the KDP in 2001, there were no such reports in 2002. Internet access and satellite dishes are available without restriction.

Freedom of association is also protected. Around 30 licensed political parties have been established, representing a broad ideological and sectarian spectrum, though the activities of the Iraqi Turkmen Front and the Iraqi Workers Communist Party have been curtailed in recent years. Scores of human rights groups and other nongovernmental organizations operate freely. Both Kurdish factions have enacted laws protecting workers' rights.

While the Kurdish authorities have been much more tolerant of ethnic and religious minorities than the central government, some Assyrian Christian and Turkmen groups have complained of ethnic cleansing policies by both the KDP and PUK. While most of these claims are highly politicized and unreliable, both Kurdish factions are known to have forced Assyrian and Turkmen schools to fly the Kurdish flag and teach the Kurdish language.

Women face social and legal discrimination in Iraqi Kurdistan. Local women's organizations report widespread "honor killings" of women who deviate from traditional social norms; the PUK has abolished legal provisions legitimizing them. In 2002, the Independent Women's Organization reported that the number of honor killings in PUK territory declined from 75 in 1991 to 15 in 2001. The KDP has not taken similar measures. In areas of Iraqi Kurdistan under the control of Ansar al-Islam, women are reportedly forced to wear veils and barred from employment and education.

Israel
Israeli-Administered Territories

Polity: Military administered
Economy: Capitalist
Population: 3,000,000 (1,200,000: Gaza; 1,800,000 West Bank). In addition, there are approximately 200,000 Israeli settlers in the West Bank and some 6,500 in the Gaza Strip. Approximately 172,000 Jews live in East Jerusalem.

Political Rights: 6
Civil Liberties: 6
Status: Not Free

Religious Groups: Sunni Muslim (majority), Christian, other
Ethnic Groups: Palestinian Arab
Ten-Year Ratings Timeline (Political Rights, Civil Liberties, Status)

1993	1994	1995	1996	1997	1998	1999	2000	2001	2002	2003
--	--	--	--	6,5NF	6,5NF	6,5NF	6,5NF	6,6NF	6,6NF	6,6NF

Overview:
In response to Palestinian terrorism in Israel and against Jewish settlers, Israel re-occupied several areas of the West Bank and Gaza, imposing strict curfews and blockades and besieging and destroying parts of Yasser Arafat's compound in an effort to force the leader of the Palestinian Authority (PA) to clamp down on terrorism. Israel also

staged several reprisal raids and carried out targeted killings in the aftermath of suicide attacks against Israeli civilians. While these were targeted against militants, many civilians were inadvertently killed, leading to widespread international censure of Israel. Israel also destroyed many Palestinian civil and military institutions and homes. Since the outbreak of the Palestinian uprising in September 2000, close to 2,000 Palestinians and more than 700 Israelis have been killed. International human rights groups accused Israel of war crimes.

At the end of the year the United States put forward a "road map" for peace that calls for Palestinian crackdowns on terrorism and subsequent Israeli troop pullbacks. It envisions a Palestinian state by 2005. At the core of the plan is a call for Arafat's removal from power. Peace talks with Syria did not take place during the year. Intensive negotiations between the countries broke down in January 2000 over disagreements on final borders around the Golan Heights.

After Palestinian rejection of a UN partition plan in 1947, Israel declared its independence on the portion of land allotted for Jewish settlement. The fledgling state was jointly attacked by neighboring Arab states in Israel's 1948 War of Independence. While Israel maintained its sovereignty, Jordan seized East Jerusalem and the West Bank, while Egypt took control of Gaza. In the 1967 Six-Day War, Israel came to occupy the West Bank, the Gaza Strip, East Jerusalem, and the Golan Heights, which had been used by Syria to shell towns in northern Israel. Israel annexed East Jerusalem in 1967 and the Golan Heights in 1981.

In what became known as the *intifada*, Palestinians living in the West Bank and Gaza began attacking mainly targets of the Israel Defense Forces (IDF) in 1987 to protest Israeli rule. A series of secret negotiations between Israel and Arafat's Palestine Liberation Organization (PLO) conducted in Oslo, Norway, produced an agreement in September 1993. The Declaration of Principles provided for Israeli troop withdrawals and gradual Palestinian autonomy in the West Bank and Gaza.

Elections for the PA's first Legislative Council and for the head of the council's executive authority were held in January 1996 and were considered to be generally free and fair. Independents won 35 of the 88 council seats, while Arafat's Fatah movement won the remainder. Arafat won the chairmanship of the executive authority with 88 percent of the vote.

Most of Gaza and the West Bank town of Jericho were turned over to the PA in May 1994. Following the assassination of Israeli Prime Minister Yitzhak Rabin in November 1995 by a right-wing Jewish extremist opposed to the peace process, Israel, under the stewardship of Prime Minister Shimon Peres, began redeploying its forces in the West Bank and Gaza. After a wave of Palestinian suicide bombings in early 1996, Peres lost a general election to Likud leader Benjamin Netanyahu, who ruled until 1999. Labor Party leader Ehud Barak was elected prime minister in May of that year and immediately pursued negotiations over the Golan Heights with Syria.

Intensive peace negotiations between Israel and Syria broke down in January 2000 over disagreements on final borders around the Golan Heights. A March summit between U.S. president Bill Clinton and Syrian president Hafez al-Assad, designed to sound out the Syrian leader on his peace terms and jump-start negotiations with Israel, failed to produce any forward momentum. The key sticking point centered on which country should control a strip of shoreline along the eastern edge of the Sea of Galilee, located below the western slopes of the Golan. The sea serves as Israel's primary freshwater source. Israel has agreed in principle to a return of all of the Golan in return for security guarantees. Prior to losing the Golan in 1967, Syria had used the territory to shell northern Israeli towns. With the death of Assad in June 2000, and the ascension to power of his relatively inexperienced son Bashar, the prospect of further talks appeared, at best, remote. Barak then pursued talks with the Palestinians, setting the Oslo peace process on a new course.

Under the provisions of Oslo implemented so far, the Palestinians have had full or partial control of 40 percent of the territory of the West Bank and 98 percent of the territory's Palestinian population. Israel has temporarily reentered and seized some Palestinian lands since the eruption of the second intifada.

At Camp David in July 2000, and at Taba, Egypt, at the end of that year, Prime Minister Barak and U.S. president Bill Clinton engaged the Palestinian leadership in the most far-reaching negotiations ever. For the first time, Israel discussed compromise solutions on Jerusalem, agreeing to some form of Palestinian sovereignty over East Jerusalem and its Islamic holy sites. Israel also offered more than 95 percent of the West Bank and Gaza to the Palestinians. However, the Palestinians effectively rejected the Israeli offers and, following a controversial visit by right-wing Likud leader Ariel Sharon to the Temple Mount in Jerusalem, initiated an armed uprising in late September 2000. Snap Israeli elections in February 2001 took place against the backdrop of continuing Palestinian violence. Sharon, promising to enhance Israel's security, trounced Barak at the polls.

In May 2001, a fact-finding commission headed by former U.S. senator George Mitchell issued a report on the crisis. Apportioning blame for the violence to both sides, the Mitchell Report called for a cessation of violence as an unconditional first step, to be followed by a series of confidence-building measures. These included a total freeze of Israeli settlement activity; a full and sincere effort by the PA in clamping down on terror; the use of nonlethal force by the IDF against Palestinian demonstrators; the prevention by the PA of attacks against Israelis from Palestinian areas; the lifting of border closures by Israel; and the resumption of PA cooperation with Israeli security agencies. The plan was never put into effect.

Violence continued to rage throughout the occupied territories in 2002. In response to successive waves of suicide bombings inside Israel and attacks on Jewish settlers in the West Bank and Gaza, Israeli forces staged several incursions into Palestinian-ruled territory, arresting many suspected militants. After a spate of suicide bombings in Israel in March that killed 80 civilians, the IDF launched Operation Defensive Shield, re-occupying seven of eight major West Bank towns and placing them under 24-hour curfew. Israel in effect re-occupied most areas of the West Bank that had been under complete Palestinian control, known collectively as "Area A." In June, in the wake of a suicide bombing attack on a Jerusalem bus that killed 19 people, Israel announced it would hold Palestinian land for as long as terrorism continued.

The conflict in the territories resembled guerilla warfare as Palestinian tactics became more lethal. Successful attacks were carried out against Israeli tanks in the Gaza Strip, indicating a new sophistication among militants, perhaps garnered from Iranian training, some analysts suggested.

Israel killed several top Palestinian militia figures and radical Islamists suspected of committing or preparing attacks against Israel. Palestinians condemned Israel for the killings—often carried out by helicopter gunships or undercover units—and labeled them "assassinations." Israel also faced international criticism for what it termed "targeted killings." Israel justified the policy on the grounds that its repeated requests to the PA that it detain Palestinians suspected of planning or carrying out attacks had gone unheeded.

Israeli reprisal raids and targeted killings of Palestinian militants sometimes resulted in the deaths of numerous Palestinian civilians. Israel denied the deliberate targeting of civilians, asserting that Palestinian gunmen and other militants were deliberately positioning themselves among civilian populations, thus endangering them.

Israel faced intense international criticism for its handling of the Palestinian uprising. Amnesty International, Human Rights Watch, and the United Nations condemned Israel for using disproportionate lethal force against Palestinian demonstrators. Although the IDF disciplined some soldiers for apparent excessive use of force, Israeli human rights organizations criticized the army for not being more vigilant.

Israel seized thousands of documents they said implicated Arafat and the PA in the sponsorship of terror attacks against Israelis. Israeli forces repeatedly blockaded and bombarded Arafat's Ramallah compound in an attempt to force him to crack down on terrorism.

In April, Palestinian gunmen ambushed IDF troops searching for terror suspects in the West Bank town of Jenin, killing 13 soldiers. Ensuing battles over several days left 56 Palestinians dead, most of who were armed. While some innocent civilians died in the fighting, charges of wholesale Israeli massacre and war crimes were discredited by a UN inquiry. Reports conducted by Human Rights Watch and Amnesty International did criticize the IDF for using Palestinians as human shields during house-to-house searches.

In an attack against Salah Shehadeh, a commander of the radical group Hamas, which rejects peace with Israel, an Israeli F-16 fighter jet dropped a one-ton bomb on a house in Gaza City in July. Shehadeh was killed, but 14 others, including 9 children, also died. The attack incurred international opprobrium; Israel acknowledged that flawed military intelligence had led to the devastating effects of the attack.

Jewish settlements in the West Bank have continued to grow since the signing of the Oslo accords. In 2002, settlers established scores of isolated outposts on land not yet allocated for settlements, a practice deemed illegal by the Israeli government. The government ordered the dismantling of several of those West Bank outposts during the year.

Substantive peace negotiations between the two sides did not take place during the year. In October the United States, in coordination with the EU, Russia, and the United Nations, distributed a draft "road map" plan that envisioned Palestinian statehood by 2005. The multi-stage, performance-based plan was premised on demonstrated Palestinian commitments to ending violence, to be followed by Israeli troop pullbacks and the easing of curfews and travel restrictions on Palestinians. It also called for a freeze of Israeli settlement activity. Progress toward these goals was conditioned on the PA's first implementing sweeping political and economic reforms and establishing an "empowered prime minister" who would ostensibly replace Arafat as lead Palestinian negotiator.

Political Rights and Civil Liberties: Palestinian residents of the West Bank, Gaza, and Jerusalem do not have the right to vote in national elections in Israel. After Israel's annexation of East Jerusalem in 1967, Arab residents there were given the option of obtaining Israeli citizenship. They do have the right to vote in municipal elections. Palestinians in the occupied territories chose their first popularly elected government in 1996. Despite some irregularities, international observers regarded the vote as reasonably reflective of the will of the voters.

Arab residents of East Jerusalem, while not granted automatic citizenship, were issued Israeli identity cards after the 1967 Six-Day War. They were given all rights held by Israeli citizens, except the right to vote in national elections. They do have the right to vote in municipal elections and are eligible to apply for citizenship. Many choose not to seek citizenship out of a sense of solidarity with Palestinians in the West Bank and Gaza Strip. While East Jerusalem's Arab population generally enjoys greater freedoms and social services than other Palestinians, they do not receive a share of municipal services proportionate to their total number. Arabs in East Jerusalem do have the right to vote in Palestinian elections.

Druze and Arabs in the Golan Heights, who were formerly under Syrian rule, possess similar status to Arab residents of East Jerusalem. They cannot vote in Israeli national elections but do have municipal representation.

Palestinians accused by Israel of security offenses in Israeli-controlled areas are tried in Israeli military courts. Security offenses are broadly defined. Some due process protections exist in these courts, though there are limits on the right to counsel, the right to bail, and the right to appeal. Administrative detention is widely used. Most convictions in Israeli military courts are based on confessions, which are often obtained through torture. Confessions are usually spoken in Arabic and translated into Hebrew for official records. Palestinian detainees are seldom able to read Hebrew and thus sign confessions that they cannot read.

Some Palestinian structures built without permits were destroyed during the year. Building permits are difficult for West Bank Palestinians to obtain.

Throughout the Palestinian uprising, Israel has destroyed many homes in the West Bank and Gaza Strip on the grounds that they provided cover for gunmen and bombers. In August Israel's Supreme Court upheld the IDF's right to demolish homes of terror suspects without warning, arguing that prior warning would allow militants to booby-trap houses slated for demolition.

Violence between Palestinians and settlers is not uncommon. Several Jewish settlers in the West Bank and Gaza Strip were ambushed and killed by Palestinian gunmen; some were targeted while traveling in cars or buses; others were attacked while in their homes or schools. In October, following a spate of attacks against settlers, Palestinians fled the village of Khirbat Yanun because of settler intimidation and violence. The villagers eventually returned with promises of IDF protection. Attacks by settlers against Palestinians also took place during the year. Jewish residents of Hebron carried out attacks against Palestinian residents following funerals for slain settlers.

International press freedom groups criticized Israel for barring journalists access to conflict zones in the West Bank. They also called upon the PA to cease harassment of journalists. In March, Italian freelance journalist Raffaele Ciriello was shot and killed by Israeli tank fire during a firefight with Palestinian militants in Ramallah. Other journalists were caught in crossfire while reporting from conflict zones at various times during the year. The Committee to Protect Journalists reported in September that more than 40 journalists had been hit by gunfire since the beginning of the uprising.

All West Bank and Gaza residents must have identification cards in order to obtain entry permits into Israel and Jerusalem. Israel often denies permits to applicants with no explanation. Even senior Palestinian officials are subject to long delays and searches at Israeli checkpoints in the West Bank.

The Israeli army maintained roadblocks throughout the West Bank in order to prevent terrorists from entering Israel. The measure denied Palestinians easy passage from one town to another, making access to jobs, hospitals, and schools extremely difficult. Restrictions of movement between and among Palestinian towns and cities were denounced as collective punishment. Israel exercises overall military control at border crossings between both the West Bank and Jordan and between the Gaza Strip and Egypt.

The intifada has exacted a serious toll on the Palestinian economy. According to the International Labor Organization, unemployment in Palestinian areas was recorded at 43 percent late in the year. Economic output plunged as tens of thousands of Palestinians who normally work in Israel were denied entry into the country for most of the year.

In August, a study released by the U.S. Agency for International Development revealed that 53 percent of women and children in the West Bank and Gaza are malnourished and suffer from anemia.

Labor affairs in the West Bank and Gaza are governed by a combination of Jordanian law and PA decisions pending the enactment of new Palestinian labor codes. Workers may establish and join unions without governmental authorization. Palestinian workers seeking to strike must submit to arbitration by the PA Ministry of Labor. There are no laws in the PA-ruled areas to protect the rights of striking workers. Palestinian workers in Jerusalem are subject to Israeli labor law.

Israel generally recognizes the right to freedom of worship and religion. On several occasions during the renewed intifada, Israel restricted Muslim men under the age of 40 from praying on the Temple Mount compound in Jerusalem's Old City, for fear of violent confrontations. Palestinians have deliberately damaged Jewish shrines and other holy places in the West Bank.

Israel
Palestinain Authority-
Administered Territories

Polity: Military and   **Political Rights:** 5
PLO-administered   **Civil Liberties:** 6
Economy: Capitalist   **Status:** Not Free
Population: 3,000,000 (1,200,000: Gaza; 1,800,000 West
Bank). In addition, there are approximately 200,000 Israeli settlers in
the West Bank and some 6,500 in the Gaza Strip.
Religious Groups: Sunni Muslim (majority), Christian, other
Ethnic Groups: Palestinian Arab

Ten-Year Ratings Timeline (Political Rights, Civil Liberties, Status)

1993	1994	1995	1996	1997	1998	1999	2000	2001	2002	2003
--	--	--	--	5,6NF	5,6NF	5,6NF	5,6NF	5,6NF	5,6NF	5,6NF

Overview:

Palestinians continued their *intifada* (uprising) throughout 2002, leading to Israeli incursions into areas previously ceded to Palestinian control. Israel intermittently re-occupied some West Bank towns and cities, and imposed strict curfews and blockades. Israeli forces besieged and destroyed parts of Yasser Arafat's compound in an effort to force the Palestinian leader to clamp down on terrorism. Israel staged several reprisal raids and carried out targeted killings of militants in the aftermath of suicide attacks against Israeli civilians. Many Palestinian civilians, including children, were inadvertently killed in these operations. As of December 2002, nearly 2,000 Palestinians had been killed since the intifada began in September 2000. Israel also destroyed many Palestinian civil and military institutions and homes.

Facing intense pressure to root out corruption and to fight against terror, Arafat reshuffled his cabinet, but conditioned meaningful political reform on an Israeli troop pullback. Palestinian militants attacked Jewish settlers in the West Bank several times. Prominent Palestinian intellectuals signed a public petition calling for an end to suicide bombing attacks against Israeli civilians. Fissures between the Palestinian Authority (PA) and various radical factions widened during the year, at times culminating in armed confrontations and underscoring Arafat's and the PA's declining credibility. The PA postponed leadership elections indefinitely. International human rights groups accused the Palestinians of war crimes. At the end of the year, the United States put forward a "road map" for peace that calls for Palestinian crackdowns on terrorism and subsequent Israeli troop pullbacks. It envisions a Palestinian state by 2005. At the core of the plan is a call for Arafat's removal from power.

After Palestinian rejection of a UN partition plan in 1947, Israel declared its independence on the portion of land allotted for Jewish settlement. The fledgling state was jointly attacked by neighboring Arab states in Israel's 1948 War of Independence. While Israel maintained its sovereignty, Jordan seized East Jerusalem and the West Bank, while Egypt took control of Gaza. In the 1967 Six-Day War, Israel came to occupy the West Bank, the Gaza Strip, East Jerusalem, and the Golan Heights, which had been used by Syria to shell towns in northern Israel. Israel annexed East Jerusalem in 1967 and the Golan Heights in 1981.

In what became known as the intifada, Palestinians living in the West Bank and Gaza began attacking mainly targets of the Israel Defense Forces (IDF) in 1987 to protest Israeli rule. A series of secret negotiations between Israel and Arafat's Palestine Liberation Organization (PLO) conducted in Oslo, Norway, produced an agreement in September 1993. The Declaration of Principles provided for Israeli troop withdrawals and gradual Palestinian autonomy in the West Bank and Gaza.

Elections for the first PA Legislative Council and for head of the council's executive authority were held in January 1996 and were considered to be generally free and fair. Independents won 35 of the 88 council seats, while Arafat's Fatah movement won the remainder. Arafat won the chairmanship of the executive authority with 88 percent of the vote.

Most of Gaza and the West Bank town of Jericho were turned over to the PA in May 1994. Following the assassination of Israeli Prime Minister Yitzhak Rabin in November 1995 by a right-wing Jewish extremist opposed to the peace process, Israel, under the stewardship of Prime Minister Shimon Peres, began redeploying its forces in the West Bank and Gaza. After a wave of Palestinian suicide bombings in early 1996, Peres lost a general election to Likud leader Benjamin Netanyahu, who ruled until 1999. Labor Party leader Ehud Barak was elected prime minister in May of that year and set the Oslo peace process on a new course. Under the provisions of Oslo implemented so far, the Palestinians have had full or partial control of 40 percent of the territory of the West Bank, and 98 percent of the territory's Palestinian population. Israel has temporarily re-entered and seized some Palestinian lands since the eruption of the second intifada.

At Camp David in July 2000, and at Taba, Egypt, at the end of the year, Prime Minister Barak and U.S. president Bill Clinton engaged the Palestinian leadership in the most far-reaching negotiations ever. For the first time, Israel discussed compromise solutions on Jerusalem, agreeing to some form of Palestinian sovereignty over East Jerusalem and its Islamic holy sites. Israel also offered more than 95 percent of the West Bank and Gaza to the Palestinians. However, the Palestinians effectively rejected the Israeli offers and, following a controversial visit by right-wing Likud leader Ariel Sharon to the Temple Mount in Jerusalem, initiated an armed uprising in late September 2000. Snap Israeli elections in February 2001 took place against the backdrop of continuing Palestinian violence. Sharon, promising to enhance Israel's security, trounced Barak at the polls.

In May 2001, a fact-finding commission headed by former U.S. senator George Mitchell issued a report on the crisis. Apportioning blame for the violence to both sides, the Mitchell Report called for a cessation of violence as an unconditional first step, to be followed by a series of confidence-building measures. These included a total freeze of Israeli settlement activity; a full and sincere effort by the PA in clamping down on terror; the use of nonlethal force by the IDF against Palestinian demonstrators; the prevention by the PA of attacks against Israelis from Palestinian areas; the lifting of border closures by Israel; and the resumption of PA cooperation with Israeli security agencies. The plan was never put into effect.

In January 2002, Arafat's commitment to the original terms of Oslo, specifically the renunciation of violence, appeared called into question by the interception of the *Karine A*, a Palestinian-owned cargo ship. Israeli commandos seized the Gaza-bound freighter in the Red Sea and uncovered 50 tons of Iranian-made weapons, including rockets, mortars, mines, anti-tank missiles, assault rifles, and C-4 plastic explosives, the type commonly used by suicide bombers. Israeli prime minister Ariel Sharon labeled Arafat a "bitter enemy," regarding him as "irrelevant." The United States cited compelling evidence that Arafat knew of the arms shipment, despite his denials. Arafat later fired a top security official connected with the arms transfer.

Violence raged throughout the occupied territories in 2002. In response to successive waves of suicide bombings inside Israel and attacks on Jewish settlers and IDF personnel in the West Bank and Gaza, Israeli forces staged several incursions into Palestinian-ruled territory and arrested many suspected militants. After a spate of suicide bombings in Israel in March that killed 80 civilians, the IDF re-occupied seven of eight major West Bank towns, placing them under 24-hour curfew. In June, in the wake of a suicide bombing attack on a Jerusalem bus that killed 19 people, Israel announced it would hold Palestinian land for as long as terrorism continued.

Radical Islamic groups such as Hamas and Islamic Jihad, and the Al-Aqsa Martyrs Brigade, an offshoot militia of Yasser Arafat's Fatah movement, claimed responsibility for several suicide bombings and ambush attacks against Israelis.

The conflict in the territories resembled guerilla warfare as Palestinian tactics became more lethal. Successful attacks were carried out against Israeli tanks in the Gaza Strip, suggesting a new sophistication among militants, who had perhaps benefited from Iranian training, according to analysts.

Israel killed several top Palestinian militia figures and radical Islamists suspected of committing or preparing attacks against Israel. Palestinians condemned Israel for the killings—often carried out by helicopter gunships or undercover units—and labeled them "assassinations." Israel also faced international criticism for what it termed "targeted killings." Israel justified the policy on the grounds that its repeated requests to the PA that it detain Palestinians suspected of planning or carrying out attacks had gone unheeded.

Israeli reprisal raids and targeted killings of Palestinian militants sometimes resulted in the deaths of numerous Palestinian civilians. Israel denied the deliberate targeting of civilians, asserting that Palestinian gunmen and other militants were deliberately positioning themselves among civilian populations, thus endangering them.

Israel seized thousands of documents the government said implicated Arafat and the PA in sponsoring terror attacks against Israelis. Israeli forces repeatedly blockaded and bombarded Arafat's Ramallah compound in an attempt to force him to crack down on terrorism.

In April, Palestinian gunmen ambushed IDF troops searching for terror suspects in the West Bank town of Jenin, killing 13 soldiers. Ensuing battles over several days left 56 Palestinians dead, most of who were armed. While some innocent civilians died in the fighting, charges of wholesale Israeli massacre and war crimes were discredited by a UN inquiry. Reports conducted by Human Rights Watch and Amnesty International did criticize the IDF for using Palestinians as human shields during house-to-house searches.

By the summer, with the civilian death toll mounting on both sides, prominent

Palestinian intellectuals and political figures signed and published a petition calling for an end to suicide bombings, asserting that they undermined Palestinian aspirations for an independent state. At the same time, U.S. president George W. Bush, after receiving an intelligence report showing Yasser Arafat had authorized a $20,000 payment to a group that had claimed responsibility for the June suicide bombing of a Jerusalem bus, suggested that the Palestinian leader be removed from power.

In October, Human Rights Watch issued a report in which it labeled suicide bombing both a crime against humanity and a war crime. It accused Arafat and the PA's security and judicial services of failing to take a "high degree" of responsibility for the bombings. It also suggested that by not unequivocally condemning suicide operations, Arafat and the PA were complicit in fostering a general climate of incitement of, and tolerance for, deliberate terrorist violence.

The PA continued to face accusations of autocratic leadership, mismanagement, and political corruption. Despite a temporary surge in popularity during Israel's siege of his compound, Arafat faced significant internal—as well as international—pressure to institute widespread political and economic reforms.

In June, Arafat reshuffled his cabinet, appointing Abdel Razak al-Yahya, a known moderate with experience negotiating with Israel, as interior minister. By September, however, the legislature was in full revolt and demanding democratic change and the appointment of a prime minister to manage the day-to-day affairs of state. To ward off a no-confidence motion, Arafat's cabinet resigned en masse. By October, Arafat appointed a new and slightly smaller cabinet, which was largely composed, however, of members of the former cabinet. Palestinians voiced displeasure with the new cabinet, which was made up mostly of outsiders who had returned from exile with Arafat, rather than those who had grown up in the West Bank or Gaza. A close Arafat confidant, Salaam Fayad, replaced al-Yahya.

Factions of Arafat's Fatah organization continued to undermine the PA as they and other militant groups took the lead—at times against Arafat's orders, without his consultation, or perhaps even with his tacit approval—in perpetuating the intifada.

Governmental corruption and popular disaffection with the peace process have benefited Hamas, which operates an extensive social services network. Vocal opposition to Israel and to the Oslo accords has turned Hamas into a growing political alternative to Arafat's Fatah party.

Hamas held talks throughout the year with Arafat's Fatah party on the possible renunciation of the use of suicide bombings, but no formal conclusions were made. The Hamas charter does not recognize Israel's right to exist.

Arafat's refusal or inability to arrest terror suspects underscored his apparent loss of credibility among Israelis. The PA claimed that it was unable to effectively carry out policing and security duties since Israel had destroyed much of its security apparatus. Israel justified its targeting of Palestinian security services on the grounds that they aided and abetted terror.

With the skyrocketing popularity of both Hamas and Islamic Jihad, Arafat's room for maneuverability appeared hampered throughout the year. A poll conducted at the end of September by the Jerusalem Media and Communications Centre, a Palestinian polling institute, found only 26 percent of West Bank and Gaza residents said they trust Arafat. Approximately 64 percent support suicide bombings against Israelis.

Substantive peace negotiations between the two sides did not take place during the year. In October the United States, in coordination with the EU, Russia, and the United Nations, distributed a draft "road map" plan that envisioned Palestinian statehood by 2005. The multi-stage, performance-based plan was premised on demonstrated Palestinian commitments to ending violence, followed by Israeli troop pullbacks and the easing of curfews and travel restrictions on Palestinians. It also called for a freeze of Israeli settlement activity. Progress toward these goals was conditioned on the PA's first implementing sweeping political and economic reforms and establishing an "empowered prime minister" who would ostensibly replace Arafat as lead Palestinian negotiator.

Political Rights and Civil Liberties:

Palestinian residents of the West Bank, Gaza, and Jerusalem chose their first popularly elected government in 1996. Despite some irregularities, international observers regarded the vote as reasonably reflective of the will of the voters. The Legislative Council has complained of being marginalized by the executive authority; though it has debated hundreds of draft laws, few have been signed into law. The Palestinian government indefinitely postponed local elections in May 1998, citing the threat of Israeli interference. After Yasser Arafat, chairman of the executive authority, declared elections would be held early in 2003, on the condition of an Israeli troop pullback, he postponed them indefinitely in December.

Allegations of corruption and abuse of power have become increasingly problematic for Arafat's government. His autocratic tendencies have put him at odds with the Legislative Council. He frequently scuttles the legislative process or refuses to sign council rules into law.

According to Palestinian officials, in May, Arafat signed a basic law detailing and guaranteeing rights and freedoms for Palestinians. The law, akin to a constitution, was passed by the Palestinian Legislative Council in 1997 but was never endorsed by Arafat. Arafat's signing of the law was not officially announced. If the law were actually to be enacted, it would presumably curtail Arafat's own authority.

Palestinian judges lack proper training and experience. Israeli demands for a Palestinian crackdown on terrorism have given rise to state security courts, which lack almost all due process rights. Suspected Islamic militants are rounded up en masse and often held without charge or trial. There are reportedly hundreds of administrative detainees currently in Palestinian jails and detention centers. The same courts are also used to try those suspected of collaborating with Israel or of drug trafficking. Defendants are not granted the right to appeal sentences and are often summarily tried and sentenced to death. Executions often take place immediately after sentencing and are carried out by firing squad.

Armed militias sometimes summarily execute Palestinians accused of collaborating with Israel. These murders generally go unpunished. According to the Palestinian Human Rights Monitoring Group, alleged collaborators are routinely tortured in Palestinian jails and are denied the right to defend themselves in court. This practice is not prohibited under Palestinian law.

The limits of Palestinian justice and the further breakdown of the rule of law were exposed in February, when a mob stormed a West Bank courtroom and murdered three men convicted of killing a Palestinian policeman. Several prisoners were also released from West Bank jails after demonstrators demanded their freedom. In June, Palestinian police in Gaza fired on demonstrators while executing a house arrest warrant on Hamas leader Ahmed Yassin. In July, 21 people were wounded during clashes between police and Hamas supporters in Gaza. The demonstrators were demanding the execution of a detained alleged collaborator with Israel. Two months later, 20 Hamas members killed a PA colonel in Gaza. The colonel had earlier killed two Hamas members during demonstrations in support of al-Qaeda leader Osama bin Laden. Hamas and Palestinian security forces engaged in sporadic firefights during the year.

Amnesty International, Human Rights Watch, and the United Nations criticized Palestinian security forces for not reining in militias whose armed attacks against Israelis further endangered Palestinian civilians.

Violence between Palestinians and settlers is not uncommon. Several Jewish settlers in the West Bank and Gaza Strip were ambushed and killed by Palestinian gunmen; some were targeted while traveling in cars or buses; others were attacked while in their homes or schools. These attacks generally go unpunished by the PA. In October, following a spate of attacks against settlers, Palestinians fled the village of Khirbat Yanun because of settler intimidation and violence. The villagers eventually returned with promises of IDF protection. Attacks by settlers against Palestinians also took place during the year. Jewish residents of Hebron carried out attacks against Palestinian residents following funerals for slain settlers.

Journalists covering the intifada faced harassment by the PA. PA officials reportedly threatened Palestinian journalists who filed stories deemed unfavorable. PA-affiliated militias also warned Israeli journalists to stay out of Palestinian areas. International press freedom groups called on the PA to cease harassment of journalists.

Under a 1995 Palestinian press law, journalists may be fined and jailed and newspapers closed for publishing "secret information" on Palestinian security forces or news that might harm national unity or incite violence. However, another press law, also signed in 1995, stipulates that Palestinian intelligence services do not reserve the right to interrogate, detain, or arrest journalists on the basis of their work. Still, several small media outlets are pressured by authorities to provide favorable coverage of Arafat and the PA. Arbitrary arrests, threats, and the physical abuse of journalists critical of the PA are routine. Official Palestinian radio and television are governmental mouthpieces.

In August, the Palestinian Journalists' Union and the Palestinian Journalists' Syndicate imposed a ban on the use of photographs depicting armed children and masked men. The ban on the images, which were said to serve Israeli interests, was extended to foreign photographers.

Arafat has yet to ratify a 1996 law passed by the Palestinian Legislative Council that guarantees freedom of expression.

The PA requires permits for rallies and demonstrations and prohibits violence and racist sloganeering. Nonetheless, anti-Semitic preaching is a common—and unpunished—feature of daily mosque prayer services and radio and television broadcasts. In the PA, Palestinian and pro-Islamic organizations that oppose Arafat's government have been harassed and detained.

On several occasions during the year, Palestinian demonstrators clashed violently with Palestinian security forces over the PA's detention of militants or people suspected of collaborating with Israel. Some demonstrators died in the clashes. Demonstrators also feared that prisoners would be targeted by Israeli air strikes.

The intifada has exacted a serious toll on the Palestinian economy. According to the International Labor Organization, unemployment in Palestinian areas was recorded at 43 percent late in the year. Economic output plunged as tens of thousands of Palestinians who normally work in Israel were denied entry into the country for most of the year.

In August, a study released by the U.S. Agency for International Development revealed that 53 percent of women and children in the West Bank and Gaza are malnourished and suffer from anemia.

Palestinian women are underrepresented in most professions and encounter discrimination in employment. Under *Sharia* (Islamic law), women are disadvantaged in marriage, divorce, and inheritance matters. Rape, domestic abuse, and "honor killings," in which unmarried women thought not to be virgins are murdered by male relatives, continue. Since societal pressures prevent reporting of such incidents, the exact frequency of attacks is unknown.

Labor affairs in the West Bank and Gaza are governed by a combination of Jordanian law and PA decisions pending the enactment of new Palestinian labor codes. Workers may establish and join unions without governmental authorization. Palestinian workers seeking to strike must submit to arbitration by the PA Ministry of Labor. There are no laws in the PA-ruled areas to protect the rights of striking workers. Palestinian workers in Jerusalem are subject to Israeli labor law.

The PA generally respects freedom of religion, though no law exists protecting religious expression. Some Palestinian Christians have experienced intimidation and harassment by radical Islamic groups and PA officials. Palestinians have deliberately damaged Jewish shrines and other holy places in the West Bank.

Moldova
Transnistria

Polity: Presidential   **Political Rights:** 6
Economy: Statist (transitional) **Civil Liberties:** 6
Population: 700,000   **Status:** Not Free
Religious Groups: Christian Orthodox (94 percent),
Roman Catholic, Protestant, Muslim and other (6 percent)
Ethnic Groups: Moldovan (40 percent) Ukrainian
(28 percent) Russian (23 percent), other (9 percent)

Ten-Year Ratings Timeline (Political Rights, Civil Liberties, Status)

1993	1994	1995	1996	1997	1998	1999	2000	2001	2002	2003
--	--	--	--	6,6NF	6,6NF	6,6NF	6,6NF	6,6NF	6,6NF	6,6NF

Overview:

The Dnestr Moldovan Republic (DMR) is a breakaway region in the eastern part of Moldova. In Moldovan, the region is called Transnistria. During 2002, high-level officials from Moldova, Ukraine, Russia, the DMR, and the OSCE were again unable to reach a multilateral settlement on the political status of this disputed territory. Further complicating a resolution, the Russian Federation failed to honor a 1999 agreement with the OSCE on the withdrawal of weapons and troops from Transnistria.

The Moldovan Soviet Socialist Republic declared independence from the Soviet Union in 1991. At the time, pro-Russian separatists in Transnistria feared that Moldova would join with Romania. They reacted by declaring independence, establishing the DMR, and setting up an authoritarian presidential system. With weapons and other assistance from Russia's 14th Army, the DMR leadership fought a military conflict with Moldova that ended in a 1992 ceasefire. Since that time, the separatist regime has existed as a "ghost state," strong enough to resist absorption by Moldova yet too weak to gain outright international recognition as a sovereign nation.

Representatives of the OSCE, Russia, and Ukraine have attempted to mediate a final settlement between Moldova and the DMR. They also participate in the Joint Control Commission that monitors compliance with the 1992 ceasefire. Despite multiple agreements and memorandums of understanding, the question of DMR's political status remains unsettled.

In 2001, regional observers were optimistic that the election of Moldovan president Vladimir Voronin would lead to improvements in the pace and substance of talks on the status of the DMR. After some initial success, discussions broke down when neither side could agree on the nature of a reunified state. The DMR refused to accept an OSCE plan for a federalized Moldova, insisting instead upon a confederation of two equal states.

Negotiators made little progress during 2002, as all sides remained constant in their positions. In response to Moldova's refusal to recognize the DMR's customs certificates, separatist leader Igor Smirnov imposed a 20 percent tax on all "imports" from Moldova. Moldovan leaders denounced the move as a further obstacle to negotiations and stated that no resolution was possible on the customs issue without a final agreement on the future of Transnistria within the Republic of Moldova. The lingering presence in Transnistria of 2,500 Russian soldiers and a supply of Russian weapons—the second-largest weapons stockpile in Europe—has further complicated a resolution of the dispute. In 1999, Russia agreed to an OSCE initiative for the removal of all Russian weapons and troops by December 2002. As the withdrawal deadline approached, Russia announced that it would not meet its obligation and attempted to refashion the force as "guarantors" of any eventual diplomatic settlement. In response to this development the OSCE extended the deadline by 12 months. However, given the sheer quantity of weapons, and Russia's apparent reluctance to divest itself of this former Soviet military outpost, it seems unlikely that Russian troops will fully complete their withdrawal by the end of 2003.

Political Rights and Civil Liberties: Residents of Transnistria cannot elect their leaders democratically. They are also unable to participate freely in Moldovan elections. While the DMR maintains its own legislative, executive, and judicial branches of government, no country recognizes its sovereignty. The DMR's Supreme Soviet was transformed into a unicameral body with 43 members in 2000.

Parliamentary elections in December 2000 resulted in a victory for separatist leader Igor Smirnov's supporters and the reelection of Grigori Marakusa as chairman of the unicameral Supreme Soviet. Marakusa has held this position continuously since 1990. A local faction of the Communist Party of Moldova is the only group in opposition to Smirnov; however, their influence is limited. There exists no other democratic alternative to the current regime, as all other parties and political formations have ceased to operate in Transnistria.

The DMR government controls most print and electronic media in Transnistria and restricts freedom of speech. Independent newspapers and television stations do exist, but they frequently experience harassment for criticizing the government. Authorities have also confiscated copies of independent newspapers. In 2001, President Smirnov issued a decree on the creation of a state editorial committee to oversee the activity of all print and electronic media. The committee's members include the ministers of security, justice, foreign affairs, and information. Late in 2001, the DMR blocked the local transmission of a report on Russia's RTR television channel about organized crime and illegal-arms trading in the separatist region.

The government restricts most political rights and civil liberties including freedom of association and assembly. Trade unions are holdovers from the Soviet era, and the United Council of Labor Collectives works closely with the government.

Authorities have denied registration to some religious groups and prevented them from distributing literature or leading public meetings. The government also limits the ability of religious groups to rent space for prayer meetings. DMR authorities discriminate again ethnic Moldovans, who constitute 40 percent of the region's population.

The local judiciary is not independent. Politically motivated killings and police harassment have been reported, and political prisoners are frequently denied access to lawyers. Police can detain suspects for up to 30 days. In 2000, the DMR introduced a moratorium on capital punishment. The decision effectively stayed the execution of Ilie Illascu, a member of the Tiraspol Six opposition group that was convicted in 1993 of killing two separatist leaders. In 2001, DMR authorities released Illascu but continued to detain other members of the group. The European Court of Human Rights is investigating their case.

Morocco
Western Sahara

Polity: Appointed governors   **Political Rights:** 7
Economy: Capitalist   **Civil Liberties:** 6
Population: 250,000   **Status:** Not Free
Religious Groups: Sunni Muslim (majority)
Ethnic Groups: Arab, Berber

Ten-Year Ratings Timeline (Political Rights, Civil Liberties, Status)

1993	1994	1995	1996	1997	1998	1999	2000	2001	2002	2003
7,5NF	7,6NF	7,6NF	7,6NF	7,6NF	7,6NF	7,6NF	7,6NF	7,6NF	7,6NF	7,6NF

Overview:

Prospects for a settlement of the dispute in Western Sahara dimmed in 2002, as international consensus on the issue fractured and the Moroccan government declared for the first time that it will not accept a long-awaited UN-sponsored referendum to determine the future of this mineral-rich desert territory. Abuses by Moroccan security forces in the territory declined somewhat during the year.

Western Sahara was a Spanish colony from 1884 until 1975, when Spain withdrew from the territory after two years of bloody conflict with the Polisario Front (Frente Popular para la Liberation del Sagiat al-Hamra Rio de Oro). The following year, Morocco and Mauritania partitioned the territory under a tripartite agreement with Spain, but Polisario declared the establishment of an independent Saharawi Arab Democratic Republic (SADR) and fought to expel foreign forces. Mauritania signed a peace agreement with Polisario in 1979, prompting Morocco to seize Mauritania's section of the territory.

In 1991, the United Nations brokered an agreement between Morocco and Polisario that provided for a ceasefire and the holding of a referendum on independence in January 1992, to be supervised by the newly formed Mission for a Referendum in Western Sahara (MINURSO). However, the referendum was repeatedly postponed after Morocco insisted that the list of eligible voters include an additional 48,000 people who, according to Polisario and most international observers, were Moroccan nationals.

The process remained deadlocked for more than a decade as the Moroccans sought in various ways to undercut domestic and international support for the independence of Western Sahara. The late King Hassan II had offered free housing and salaries to Saharawis who relocated from the territory to Morocco. Since the ascension of King Mohammed VI in 1999, Morocco has released hundreds of Saharawi political prisoners and allowed limited activity by Saharawi human rights groups. The king regularly tours the territory, and his government has financed projects to ease unemployment in the region.

Morocco's bid to win international recognition for its claim to Western Sahara has been boosted by its role in the war on terror. In October 2001, the kingdom signed deals with French and U.S. oil companies allowing for exploration off the coast of Western Sahara. In December, French president Jacques Chirac publicly referred to

Western Sahara as the "southern provinces of Morocco." Since the attacks of September 11, 2001, on the World Trade Center and the Pentagon, the United States has exerted considerable pressure on Algeria to withhold support for Polisario and has been urging members of the UN Security Council to drop their support for a referendum and back an autonomy plan introduced in June 2001 by the UN special envoy to the region, former U.S. secretary of state James Baker. The Baker plan would give the territory autonomy under Moroccan rule for a period of five years and put off final status negotiations. However, intense U.S. lobbying and threats to cut funding to MINURSO during the first half of 2002 won support for the autonomy plan from only five other members of the Security Council (Britain, France, Cameroon, Guinea, and Norway), and the mandate of MINURSO was extended for another six months in July.

A vigorous campaign by Morocco to undercut support for Polisario in Africa, where two dozen governments have officially recognized the SADR, also met with failure in 2002. The king waived $120 million in debt owed to Morocco by African countries and even hinted that he would allow Algeria access to the Atlantic coast to transport oil if it renounced support for the rebel group. However, at the inaugural meeting of the newly formed African Union (AU) in July, African heads of state not only admitted the SADR as a member, but elected SADR president Mohammed Abdelaziz as one of five AU vice presidents.

In a November 2002 speech, King Mohammed for the first time publicly rejected the idea of holding a referendum to allow the Saharawi people to vote on the question of independence, calling the plan "out of date" because of the "growing support of the international community" for Moroccan sovereignty over the region.

Polisario is equally defiant in its rejection of any settlement short of a fair referendum. The group is emboldened not only by the support of African and other developing countries for Saharawi self-determination, but also by recent developments in a small island on the other side of the globe. In May 2002, the people of East Timor formally gained independence after decades of struggle, with no foreign allies and little international interest in their plight. Saharawi nationalists invariably draw the same conclusion from the experience of East Timor—no wait is too long.

Political Rights and Civil Liberties:

Saharawis have never been allowed to elect their own government. The four provinces of Western Sahara have held local elections organized and controlled by the Moroccan government, and pro-Moroccan Saharawis fill the seats reserved for Western Sahara in the Moroccan legislature.

Saharawis are subject to Moroccan law, though many legal protections, such as the maximum limit of 72 hours for incommunicado detention, are not observed in practice. Around 450 Saharawis who disappeared at the hands of Moroccan security prior to the early 1990s remain unaccounted for. Around 170,000 Saharawis have fled the territory and now live in makeshift refugee camps in southwest Algeria.

Although human rights groups report greater freedom from repression in recent years, arbitrary killing, arrest, detention, and torture by Moroccan security forces continued in 2002. In March, security forces reportedly opened fire on civilian cars in the area of Guelta Zemmour, killing one Saharawi civilian and wounding several others. Two leading members of the Western Sahara branch of the Forum for Truth and Justice (FVJSS), Abdessalam Dimaoui and Ahmed Nasiri, were arrested during the summer and reportedly beaten by police in an attempt to force them to sign statements admitting they had instigated violence at an antigovernment protest the previous year. Dimaoui was later acquitted after nearly two months in detention, while Nasiri was sentenced to 18 months in prison. In June, Mohammed Haboub Mouilid (alias Tirsal) was arrested at a checkpoint outside the Saharawi town of Smara and detained for 48 hours after returning from a meeting of the FVJSS in Rabat. Ali Salem Tamek, a member of the FVJSS, was arrested in August and subsequently sentenced to two years in prison for "undermining the internal security of the State." In November, a 35-year-old Saharawi prisoner, Boucetta Mohamed Barka (alias Chaybani) died in prison in Laayoune. According to his family, Chaybani's body showed signs of having been tortured. Several hunger strikes were carried out by Saharawi prisoners during the year.

Torture and other abuses by Polisario forces, including arbitrary killing, have been reported in the past, but most cases have not been verified. Polisario holds 1,362 Moroccan prisoners of war in six centers in Tindouf, Algeria, and in Polisario-controlled areas of Western Sahara. In January 2002, Polisario released 115 Moroccan POWs.

Freedoms of expression, assembly, and association are severely restricted in Western Sahara. Political parties, nongovernmental organizations, and private media are virtually nonexistent, and suspected pro-independence activists and opponents of the government, including former political prisoners, are subject to surveillance and harassment. In May 2002, Moroccan forces forcibly dispersed a crowd of mourners attending a prayer service in memory of the late Polisario representative to the United Kingdom and Ireland, Fadel Ismail, who had died one year earlier. According to Polisario, dozens of Saharawis were arrested, interrogated, and tortured. In September, five members of the Sahara Unemployed Association, which fights discrimination against native Saharawis in the local job market, were sentenced to prison terms of up to one year on charges of disrupting public order.

The overwhelming majority of Sahrawis are Sunni Muslim, and freedom of worship is generally respected by the Moroccan authorities. Restrictions on religious freedom in the Western Sahara are similar to those found in Morocco. There is little verifiable information on the status of women in Western Sahara, though it is known that they are active in Polisario.

Pakistan
Kashmir

Polity: Pakistani-administered **Political Rights:** 7
Economy: Capitalist-statist   **Civil Liberties:** 5
Population: 4,200,000   **Status:** Not Free
Religious Groups: Muslim (99 percent) [Shi'a majority,
Sunni minority], other (1 percent)
Ethnic Groups: Kashmiri, Punjabi, Balti, other (including Gujjar, Ladakhi, and Shina)

Ten-Year Ratings Timeline (Political Rights, Civil Liberties, Status)

1993	1994	1995	1996	1997	1998	1999	2000	2001	2002	2003
--	--	--	--	--	--	--	--	--	--	7,5NF

Overview: Heightened tensions with neighboring India over the disputed territory of Kashmir, which resulted in massive troop
buildups by both sides along their common border in the
first half of 2002, led to increased international pressure on Pakistani leader General
Pervez Musharraf to intensify his crackdown against the Pakistan-based militant
groups responsible for incursions into Kashmir and suicide attacks within India.
Although Musharraf banned the movement of militants from the Pakistani portion
of Kashmir into the Indian-held section of Kashmir in June, hard-line Islamic groups
in Azad Kashmir organized protest rallies denouncing his decision and vowing to
continue their armed insurgency. Meanwhile, pro-independence groups in the Northern Areas continued to agitate for increased political representation.

After centuries of rule by Afghan, Sikh, and local strongmen, the British seized
control of Kashmir in 1846 and sold it to the Hindu maharajah of the neighboring
principality of Jammu. The maharajah later incorporated Ladakh and other surrounding areas into what became the new princely state of Jammu and Kashmir. At the
partition of British India in 1947, Maharajah Hari Singh attempted to preserve Jammu
and Kashmir's independence. However, after Pakistani tribesmen invaded, he agreed
to Jammu and Kashmir's accession to India in return for promises of autonomy and
eventual self-determination.

India and Pakistan went to war over Kashmir within months of gaining their independence. A UN-brokered ceasefire in January 1949 established the present-day
boundaries, which gave Pakistan control of roughly one-third of Jammu and Kashmir, including the far northern and western areas as well as a narrow sliver of land
adjoining Indian-held Kashmir. India retained most of the Kashmir Valley along with
Jammu and Ladakh. (A separate report on Indian-administered Kashmir appears in
the Disputed Territories section of the survey).

Unlike India, Pakistan never formally annexed the portion of Kashmir under its
control. The Karachi Agreement of April 1949 divided Pakistani-administered Kashmir into two distinct entities, Azad (free) Kashmir and the Northern Areas, which
consist of the five districts of Gilgit, Ghizer, Ghanche, Diamer, and Baltistan. Pakistan retained direct administrative control over the Northern Areas, while Azad
Kashmir was given a larger degree of nominal self-government.

For several decades, an informal council administered Azad Kashmir. A legislative assembly was set up in 1970, and an interim constitution in 1974 established a parliamentary system headed by a president and a prime minister. However, the political process in Azad Kashmir has been suspended on several occasions by the military rulers of Pakistan. In 1977, General Zia-ul-Haq dissolved the legislative assembly and banned all political activity until 1985.

Chronic infighting among the state's various political factions has also allowed Islamabad to interfere with ease in the electoral process. In 1991, the prime minister of Azad Kashmir was dismissed, arrested, and imprisoned in Pakistan. In the 1996 state elections, Sultan Mahmud Chaudhary's Azad Kashmir People's Party (AKPP) emerged with a majority of seats. The outgoing Muslim Conference (MC) had boycotted the elections, accusing the AKPP of vote rigging and fraud. In elections held in July 2001 with a 48 percent turnout, the MC swept back into power, winning 30 out of 48 seats. However, General Musharraf installed a serving general as the president of Azad Kashmir later that month, prompting speculation that Islamabad intended to reassert its control over the territory.

The lack of political representation in the Northern Areas has fueled demands for both formal inclusion within the Pakistani state as well as for self-determination. In 1988, Gilgit was racked by unrest after Shias demanded an independent state. The Pakistani army suppressed the revolt with the help of armed Sunni tribesmen from a neighboring province. In May 1999, the Pakistani Supreme Court directed the government to act within six months to give the Northern Areas an elected government with an independent judiciary. After the verdict, the Pakistani government announced a package that provided for an appellate court as well as an expanded and renamed Northern Areas Legislative Council (NALC). Elections to the NALC were held under the military government in 2000. However, financial and legislative powers have yet to be delegated to the NALC, according to a report in the *Dawn* newspaper.

In January 2001, twelve small Kashmiri separatist groups in Azad Kashmir and the Northern Areas announced the formation of the All Parties National Alliance, which committed itself to fighting for an independent Kashmir and demanded that both India and Pakistan release jailed members of the group. While the Pakistani authorities have readily provided support to armed militants fighting in India, they have been less tolerant of groups that espouse Kashmiri self-determination.

Political Rights and Civil Liberties: The political rights of the residents of Pakistani-administered Kashmir remain severely limited. Neither the Northern Areas nor Azad Kashmir has representation in Pakistan's national parliament. The Northern Areas are directly administered by the Pakistani government and have no constitution guaranteeing them fundamental rights, democratic representation, or the separation of powers, according to Amnesty International. Executive authority is vested in the minister for Kashmir affairs, a civil servant appointed by Islamabad. An elected Northern Areas Legislative Council (NALC) serves in an advisory capacity and has no authorization to change laws or spend revenue. In November 1999, the new military government permitted previously scheduled elections to the NALC to take place; candidates who won seats included independents as well as representatives of several political parties. Elections for local governmental posts were held in July 2000.

Azad Kashmir has an interim constitution, an elected unicameral assembly headed by a prime minister, and a president. However, Pakistan exercises considerable control over both the structures of governance and electoral politics. Islamabad's approval is required to pass legislation, and the minister for Kashmir, affairs handles the daily administration of the state. Twelve of the 48 seats in the Azad Kashmir assembly are reserved for Kashmiri "refugees" in Pakistan, whose elections to these seats are the subject of manipulation. In addition, candidates in elections are required to support the accession of Kashmir to Pakistan. According to Human Rights Watch, authorities barred at least 25 candidates from the pro-independence Jammu and Kashmir Liberation Front (JKLF) from contesting the July 2001 elections after they refused to sign a declaration supporting the accession of all of Kashmir to Pakistan. Several hundred JKLF supporters, including its chief, Amanullah Khan, were arrested while protesting against the decision. Fifteen other nationalists who agreed to the "accession" clause competed in the elections, but none won a seat. Azad Kashmir receives a large amount of financial aid from the Pakistani government, but successive administrations have been tainted by corruption and incompetence. A lack of official accountability has been identified as a key factor in the poor socio-economic development of both Azad Kashmir and the Northern Areas.

The Pakistani government uses the constitution and other laws to curb freedom of speech on a variety of subjects, including the status of Kashmir. In recent years, authorities have banned several local newspapers from publishing. In October 2000, the district magistrate revoked the publication license of the independent weekly *K-2* for "promoting anti-Pakistan feelings," a ban that remained in effect until July 2001. In addition to pressure from the authorities, journalists face some harassment from other non-state actors. In June, political party activists attacked the office of the weekly *Naqqara*, a Gilgit-based newspaper, and assaulted the staff. While the Northern Areas have no local broadcast media, a local radio station was inaugurated in AK in September.

Pakistan is an Islamic republic, and there are numerous restrictions on religious freedom. In addition, religious minorities face unofficial economic and societal discrimination and are occasionally subject to violent attack. Shia Muslims, who form the majority of the population in the Northern Areas, include a large number of Ismailis, a group that follows the Aga Khan. Sectarian strife between the majority Shia population and the increasing number of Sunni Muslims (some of who immigrated from Pakistan) continues to be a problem. In June 2001, Sunni organizations protested against the local administration's decision to supply different school textbooks for Shia students. The Aga Khan Rural Support Program, a local development organization, has in recent years been subjected to harassment and violence from extremist Sunni religious leaders.

Freedom of association and assembly is restricted. The constitution of Azad Kashmir forbids individuals and political parties from taking part in activities prejudicial to the ideology of the state's accession to Pakistan. Political parties that advocate Kashmiri independence are allowed to operate, but not to participate in elections. According to Amnesty International, some people who do not support the accession of Azad Kashmir to Pakistan have been dismissed from their jobs and denied access to educational institutions. A number of nationalist political parties have been formed in the Northern Areas that advocate either self-rule or greater political representation within Pakistan. However, their leaders are subject to arbitrary arrest and long jail terms. The Balawaristan National Front estimates that more than 70 individuals are facing sedition or treason cases as a result of their political activities.

In recent years, police have suppressed antigovernment demonstrations, sometimes violently, in both Azad Kashmir and the Northern Areas. These have included rallies by nationalist political organizations as well as student protests. In September, according to the Asian Human Rights Commission, police attacked protestors demonstrating peacefully against the Mangla Dam extension in Mirpur, arresting 13 people and injuring others.

The judiciary of the Northern Areas consists of district courts and a chief court, whose decisions are final. The Northern Areas Council Legal Framework Order of 1994 provides for a court of appeals, but this has not yet been established. The territory continues to be governed by the colonial-era Frontier Crimes Regulations (FCR), under which residents are required to report to local police stations once a month. Law enforcement agencies have reportedly used torture on political activists who have been detained or imprisoned. Azad Kashmir has its own system of local magistrates and high courts, whose heads are appointed by the president of Azad Kashmir. Appeals are adjudicated by the Supreme Court of Pakistan.

Press reports suggest that a number of Islamist militant groups, including members of al-Qaeda, have bases in, and operate from, Pakistani-administered Kashmir with the tacit permission of Pakistani intelligence. Several militant groups that advocate the accession of Kashmir to Pakistan receive weapons and financial aid from the Pakistani government in support of their infiltrations into Indian-administered Kashmir. In January 2002, under pressure from the United States, General Musharraf banned two of the main militant groups, the Lashkar-e-Taiba and the Jaish-e-Mohammad, and the ban was extended to cover Azad Kashmir by the state government. Militants closed some of their training camps in Azad Kashmir in July and temporarily reduced the level of infiltration, but by the fall, it had increased to previous levels.

Shelling between Indian and Pakistani forces around the Line of Control in Kashmir continued to kill or displace numerous civilians throughout the year. The Azad Kashmir government manages relief camps for refugees from Indian-administered Kashmir, which are funded by the Pakistani government.

Russia
Chechnya

Polity: Presidential   **Political Rights:** 7
Economy: Mixed statist   **Civil Liberties:** 7
Population: 500,000 (est.)   **Status:** Not Free
Religious Groups: Muslim (majority), Orthodox
Ethnic Groups: Chechen (majority), Russian (minority)

Ten-Year Ratings Timeline (Political Rights, Civil Liberties, Status)

1993	1994	1995	1996	1997	1998	1999	2000	2001	2002	2003
--	--	--	--	--	--	6,6NF	7,7NF	7,7NF	7,7NF	7,7NF

Overview: Despite some indications of rising support for a political solution to the ongoing war in Chechnya, the brutal conflict continued throughout 2002 with no clear end in sight. Russian forces continued to face daily ambushes and sniper attacks by rebel forces, underscoring the Russian military's tenuous hold over much of the breakaway republic's territory. The fighting struck closer to home for many Russians when Chechen separatists captured 800 people in a Moscow theater in October, a crisis that ended with the deaths of most of the rebels and some 120 of the hostages.

A small Northern Caucasus republic covered by flat plains in the north-central portion and by high mountains in the south, Chechnya has been at war with Russia almost continuously since the late 1700s. In February 1944, the Chechens were deported en masse to Kazakhstan under the pretext of their having collaborated with Germany during World War II. Although rehabilitated by Nikita Khrushchev in 1957 and allowed to return to their homeland, they continued to be politically suspect and were excluded from the region's administration.

Following his election as Chechnya's president in October 1991, former Soviet Air Force Commander Dzhokhar Dudayev proclaimed Chechnya's independence on November 1. Moscow responded by instituting an economic blockade of the republic and engaging in political intimidation of the territory's leadership.

In 1994, Russia began assisting Chechen figures opposed to Dudayev, whose rule was marked by corruption and the rise of powerful clans and criminal gangs. Russian president Boris Yeltsin sent 40,000 troops into Chechnya by mid-December 1994 and attacked the capital city, Grozny, on New Year's Eve. Federal forces intensified the shelling of Grozny and other population centers throughout 1995, with civilians becoming frequent targets. Chechen forces regrouped, making significant gains against ill-trained, undisciplined, and demoralized Russian troops. Russian public opposition to the war increased, fueled by criticism from much of the country's media. In April 1996, Dudayev was killed, reportedly by a Russian missile.

With mounting Russian casualties and no imminent victory for Moscow, a peace deal was signed in August 1996. While calling for the withdrawal of most Russian forces from the breakaway territory, the document postponed a final settlement on the republic's status until 2001. In May 1997, Yeltsin and Chechen president Aslan Maskhadov signed an accord in which Moscow recognized Maskhadov as

Chechnya's legitimate leader. Maskhadov sought to maintain Chechen sovereignty while pressing Moscow to help rebuild the republic, whose formal economy and infrastructure were virtually destroyed. Throughout 1998, a number of former rival field commanders came together as an unruly opposition of often-competing warlords, removing large areas of Chechen territory from Maskhadov's control.

In September 1999, Russian Prime Minister Vladimir Putin launched a second military offensive in Chechnya after incursions into the neighboring republic of Dagestan by a group of Chechen rebels, and a string of deadly apartment bombings in Russia that the Kremlin blamed on Chechen militants. Although Russian troops advanced rapidly over the largely flat terrain in the northern third of the republic, their progress slowed considerably as they neared the heavily defended city of Grozny. In a notable policy shift, Putin in early October effectively withdrew Moscow's recognition of Maskhadov as the republic's main legitimate authority.

Russia's increasingly deliberate and indiscriminate bomb attacks on civilian targets caused some 200,000 people to flee Chechnya, most to the tiny neighboring Russian republic of Ingushetia. After federal troops finally captured the largely destroyed city of Grozny in February 2000, the Russian military turned its offensive against the remaining rebel strongholds in the southern mountainous region. While Russian troops conducted air and artillery raids against towns suspected of harboring large numbers of Chechen fighters—frequently followed by security sweeps in which civilians were beaten, raped or killed—they were subject to almost daily guerilla bomb and sniper attacks by rebel forces. Although the international community issued periodic condemnations of Moscow's operation in Chechnya, the campaign enjoyed broad popular support in Russia that was fueled by the media's now one-sided reporting favoring the official government position.

Following the September 11, 2001, attacks on the United States, Moscow defended its actions in Chechnya as part of the broader war on global terrorism, drawing a connection between Chechen separatists and international terrorist groups associated with Osama Bin Laden's al-Qaeda. Meanwhile, the West softened some of its criticisms of Moscow's conduct in Chechnya in apparent exchange for Russia's support of the U.S.-led operation against the Taliban in Afghanistan.

As the bloody conflict entered its third year, prominent Russian and Chechen figures met in Liechtenstein in August 2002 to discuss a compromise peace plan, an apparent sign of gradual growing support for a political settlement to the protracted conflict. Among the participants were Maskhadov's representative, Akhmed Zakayev; the Russian parliamentary deputy from Chechnya, Aslambek Aslakhanov; the former speaker of Russia's parliament, Ruslan Khasbulatov; and the former Russian security council chief, Ivan Rybkin. The draft plan envisaged giving Chechnya special status within the borders of the Russian Republic.

However, genuine progress toward peace remained elusive, as Chechen rebels continued to engage in guerilla warfare against Russian troops with mine, sniper, and bomb attacks, highlighting Moscow's inability to assert full control over the breakaway republic. In August, rebels reportedly shot down a Russian military helicopter near Grozny, killing more than 100 people on board. In the neighboring republic of Ingushetia, heavy clashes between federal troops and Chechen separatists erupted in September, the first time that such large-scale fighting had occurred in the area since 1994. Moscow stepped up its pressure on neighboring Georgia to crack down on Chechen rebels allegedly hiding in Georgia's lawless Pankisi Gorge region. Russian military airplanes reportedly bombed Georgian territory several times in a stated attempt to flush out Chechen fighters, leading Georgian president Eduard Shevardnadze to order a police operation to cleanse the area of armed rebels and criminals.

In a dramatic development broadcast live on Russian television, a group of some 50 Chechen rebels stormed a Moscow theater on October 23, taking 750 people hostage. More than 120 hostages were killed, most from the effects of a sedative gas that Russian troops used to incapacitate the rebels prior to making a pre-dawn rescue attempt on October 26. Russian authorities reported that 41 of the rebels had been killed.

Following the hostage crisis, Russian officials announced a suspension of a long-planned reduction in the number of federal troops stationed in Chechnya, estimated at 80,000. On October 30, Akhmed Zakayev, who had been attending a world congress of Chechens in Copenhagen, was arrested by Danish police at Moscow's request. Zakayev was accused by Russian authorities of participating in terrorist activities, including the Moscow theater hostage crisis. On December 3, Denmark released him from custody, citing insufficient evidence. Just days later, Zakayev was detained again in London, but was released the next day after British actress Vanessa Redgrave posted his $78,000 bail. He was ordered to return to court in early January 2003. Moscow also asked Qatar to extradite Chechen rebel leader Zelimkhan Yanderbiev.

Political Rights and Civil Liberties:

With the resumption of war in Chechnya in 1999, residents of the republic currently do not have the means to change their government democratically. The 1997 presidential elections were characterized by international observers to have been reasonably free and fair. President Aslan Maskhadov fled the capital city in December 1999, and the parliament elected in 1997 ceased to function. Russia placed Moscow loyalists or Chechens opposed to Maskhadov's central government in various administrative posts throughout the republic.

In June 2000, Putin enacted a decree establishing direct presidential rule over Chechnya, appointing Akhmed Kadyrov, a Muslim cleric and Chechnya's spiritual leader, to head the republic's administration. Kadyrov was denounced by Maskhadov and separatist Chechens as a traitor, while pro-Moscow Chechens objected to his support during the first Chechen war for the republic's independence. On December 12, 2002, Russian president Vladimir Putin signed a decree calling for a public referendum on a constitution in Chechnya and subsequent elections for the republic's president and parliament. Critics of the planned referendum, scheduled to take place in March 2003, insist that it should not be held while fighting continues and that the results are likely to be falsified.

The disruptive effects of the war severely hinder news production and the flow of information to the general public. Russian state-run television and radio resumed broadcasts in Chechnya in March 2001 via a transmitter north of Grozny, although much of the population remains without electricity. The Chechen rebel government operates a Web site with reports about the conflict and other news from its perspective.

The Russian military continued to impose severe restrictions on journalists' access to the Chechen war zone, issuing accreditation primarily to those of proven loyalty to the Russian government. Few foreign reporters are allowed into the breakaway republic. In July 2001, the Russian military announced that journalists covering the war must be accompanied at all times by military officials. In August 2002, Russian soldiers briefly confiscated equipment from ORT television and TV Center crews who were filming fighting between federal troops and rebels near the town of Shalazhi. The journalists were accused by the army of having traveled to the town without a military escort.

Amendments to Russia's media law, which would have placed stricter controls on reporting antiterrorist operations, were vetoed by Putin on November 25. Press freedom advocates had criticized the amendments, which parliament adopted quickly after the Moscow theater crisis, as an attempt to further censor coverage of the war in Chechnya. In April 2002, the U.S.-funded Radio Liberty began airing daily broadcasts from Prague in Chechen and two other North Caucasus languages. Originally scheduled to start broadcasting in February, Radio Liberty's governing body decided to postpone the broadcasts after protests by the Russian government, including threats to revoke Radio Liberty's license in Russia.

Most religious Chechens practice Sufism, a mystical form of Islam characterized by the veneration of local saints and by groups practicing their own rituals. The Wahhabi sect, with roots in Saudi Arabia and characterized by a strict observance of Islam, has been banned. Since the start of the last war in 1994, during which time many of the republic's schools have been damaged or destroyed, education in Chechnya has been sporadic. Most schools have not been renovated and continue to lack such basic amenities as textbooks, electricity, and running water.

Since the resumption of war, the rule of law has become virtually nonexistent. Civilians have been subject to harassment and violence, including torture, rape, and extrajudicial execution, at the hands of Russian soldiers, while senior military authorities have shown general disregard for these abuses. Chechen fighters have targeted Chechens who have cooperated with Russian government officials and work for the pro-Moscow local administration. In November 2002, Putin ordered the creation of a Chechen interior ministry to be in charge of the local police force, a move designed to strengthen the pro-Moscow Chechen administration of Akhmed Kadyrov. Previously, the federal Interior Ministry had been responsible for overseeing Chechen law enforcement activities.

The trial of the first high-ranking Russian officer to be charged with a serious crime against a civilian in Chechnya ended on December 31, 2002, when a military court acquitted Colonel Yuri Budanov on charges of abducting and murdering a young Chechen woman in March 2000. The court ruled that Budanov had been temporarily insane at the time of the killing and ordered him sent to a psychiatric hospital for treatment. The verdict came after nearly two years of procedural delays and repeated psychiatric examinations, including two conducted by the Serbsky Institute, known for its role during the Soviet era of using false psychiatric grounds to condemn political dissidents. The New York-based Human Rights Watch condemned the verdict as "a travesty of justice" and an indication of Russia's resolve to shield its military from accountability for atrocities committed in Chechnya. Human rights groups emphasized that the Budanov case represents only one of many similar crimes committed by Russian soldiers against local civilians.

Prominent Chechen rebel leader Salman Raduyev, who was serving a life sentence in prison for leading a 1996 hostage-taking raid on a hospital in neighboring Dagestan that lead to the deaths of 78 people, died on December 14, 2002. While the Russian Ministry of Justice maintained that he died of natural causes, others, including representatives of the separatist Chechen leadership, insist that he was murdered. The Saudi-born Khattab, an elusive Chechen rebel commander accused of having links to Osama Bin Laden, was reportedly killed in March 2002 by a poisoned letter.

Russian troops continued to engage in so-called mopping-up operations, in which they seal off entire towns and conduct house-to-house searches for suspected rebels. During these security sweeps, soldiers have been accused of beating and torturing civilians, looting, and extorting money. Moreover, thousands of Chechens have gone missing or been found dead after such operations. In a high-level acknowledgment of the extent of these abuses, the commander of federal troops in Chechnya issued new rules in March 2002 for troops conducting sweeps, including being courteous, identifying themselves, and providing a full list of those detained. However, human rights activists have accused federal troops of ignoring these rules, called Order 80. Similarly, under Decree No. 46, which was adopted after notoriously harsh sweeps in mid-2001, officials are supposed to compile comprehensive information on all detainees. However, Human Rights Watch maintains that the decree, meant to prevent forced disappearances or mistreatment of detainees, is not being fully implemented.

More than 100,000 Chechen refugees continue to seek shelter in the neighboring republic of Ingushetia, often living in appalling conditions in tent camps, in abandoned buildings, or in cramped quarters with friends or relatives. Despite assurances from the Russian government that refugees will not be forcibly returned, Human Rights Watch reported that immigration officials were placing enormous pressure on displaced persons to leave in late 2002. In early December, Russian authorities closed a tent camp in neighboring Ingushetia housing some 1,700 Chechen refugees, and announced plans to close the five remaining tent camps sheltering an estimated 20,000 people. Critics charge that Moscow is using the resettlement plans to bolster its argument that it has restored order and stability to Chechnya. However, most refugees fear returning because of ongoing concerns for personal security, as well as the lack of employment and housing opportunities.

In mid-December, the Russian news agency Interfax reported that 4,704 Russian soldiers, officers, and policemen had been killed in Chechnya since 1999. However, the Soldiers' Mothers of Russia group estimates that casualty figures, which are impossible to verify, are more than double the official number provided. Both sides in the conflict routinely inflate enemy losses while downplaying their own casualty figures.

Travel within, into and from the republic is severely restricted. After the resumption of war, the Russian military failed to provide safe exit routes for many civilians out of the conflict zones. Bribes are usually required to pass the numerous military checkpoints.

Widespread corruption and the economic devastation caused by the war severely limit equality of opportunity. Ransoms obtained from kidnapping and the lucrative illegal oil trade provide money for Chechens and members of the Russian military. Much of the republic's infrastructure and housing remains damaged or destroyed after years of war, with reconstruction efforts plagued by chronic funding delays, money shortages, and corruption. The first installments of federal funding earmarked for 2002 were finally released in May. Much of the population ekes out a living selling produce or other goods at local markets. Residents who have found work are employed largely by the local police, the Chechen administration, the oil and construction sectors, or at small enterprises, such as cafés.

While women continue to face discrimination in a traditional male-dominated culture, the war has resulted in many women becoming the primary breadwinners for their families. Russian soldiers reportedly rape Chechen women in areas controlled by federal forces.

Turkey
Cyprus (T)

Polity: Presidential parliamentary democracy (Turkish-occupied)
Political Rights: 2
Civil Liberties: 2
Status: Free
Economy: Mixed capitalist
Population: 180,000
Religious Groups: Muslim (99 percent), Christian and other (1 percent)
Ethnic Groups: Turkish (99 percent), Greek and other (1 percent)

Ten-Year Ratings Timeline (Political Rights, Civil Liberties, Status)

1993	1994	1995	1996	1997	1998	1999	2000	2001	2002	2003
3,3PF	4,2PF	4,2PF	4,2PF	4,2PF	4,2PF	4,2PF	4,2PF	2,2F	2,2F	2,2F

Note: See Cyprus (Greek) under Country Reports.

Overview: In August 2002 the Turkish Cypriot Chamber of Commerce presented a declaration demanding a solution to the Cyprus question: "The Common Vision of the Turkish Cypriot Civil Society." The declaration was supported by 86 civil society organizations that call on the leaders of both the Turkish Cypriots and the Greek Cypriots to find a settlement.

Annexed to Britain in 1914, Cyprus gained independence in 1960 after a 10-year guerrilla campaign seeking Cyprus's union with Greece. In July 1974, Greek Cypriot national guard members, backed by the military junta in power in Greece, staged an unsuccessful coup aimed at unification. Turkey invaded five days later, seized 37 percent of the island, and expelled 200,000 Greek Cypriots from the north. The Turkish Republic of Northern Cyprus declared its independence in 1982, but so far has been recognized only by Turkey, which maintains more than 35,000 troops in the territory and provides an estimated $200 million in annual assistance. The Green Line, a buffer zone controlled by a 1,200-strong UN peacekeeping force, has partitioned Cyprus since 1974. The capital, Lefkosa (Nicosia), remains the world's only divided capital city, and tensions and intermittent violence between the two populations have plagued the island since independence.

Negotiations on the future of the island have stalled over issues of security, territory, property and compensation, and the distribution of power on the island. The Greek Cypriots favor a federation with local autonomy, free movement, and a strong central government. Turkish Cypriots favor a confederation of two independent states, with shared bodies holding very limited powers. Instead of a central assembly, Turkish Cypriots propose a consultative council and joint overseas representation.

The north is far less prosperous than the south. An embargo by the Greek Cypriots significantly hampers the northern economy. Turkish Cypriots' standard of living is roughly a third that of Greek Cypriots, and the north is almost totally reliant on the Cypriot Republic for a free but insufficient power supply that suffers frequent outages, from 12 to 14 hours per day. However, a vibrant black market economy provides for a great deal of unaccounted-for wealth. The Turkish Cypriot area operates on a free-market basis, but a lack of private and governmental investment, shortages of skilled labor, and inflation and the weakness of the Turkish lira (which the Turkish Cypriots use as their currency) continue to plague the economy.

Despite the fact that the economy of Turkish Cyprus would sink if not for trade and support from Turkey, the Turkish Cypriot population is demanding more autonomy from Ankara. In July 2001, some 6,000 people took to the streets, chanting anti-Ankara and anti-Denktash slogans. Turkish Cypriots' increasing disapproval of Rauf Denktash weakens his position in negotiations for a settlement in the divided island.

"The Common Vision of the Turkish Cypriot Civil Society," drawn up in August 2002, builds on the new dialogue started in December 2001 and does not differ greatly from the UN-sponsored talks. However, it does outline a solution that would be acceptable to Turkish Cyprus in particular, including the establishment of a partnership state with a Greek Cypriot state. The partnership state and the constituent states would have shared sovereignty and would have separate functions and responsibilities. Addressing a major fear on the part of the Greek Cypriots that once a solution is achieved Turkish Cypriots would use some pretext to declare their full independence, the declaration also calls for assurances that neither side would leave the partnership state.

Political Rights and Civil Liberties:

Turkish Cypriots can change the government of the Turkish Republic of Northern Cyprus (TRNC) democratically. The presidential-legislative system of government calls for the election of a leader and a national assembly at least every five years. Though Rauf Denktash retains a high degree of control over Cypriot politics, a number of competing parties openly participate, and presidential elections have been considered generally free and fair by outside observers. The local elections held in June 2002 were conducted without incident. Some 1,000 Greek and Maronite residents in the north are disenfranchised in Turkish Cypriot elections, but many vote in Cypriot Republic elections.

The judiciary is independent, and trials generally meet international standards of fairness. Civilians suspected of violating military zones are tried in military courts, which respect due process but have been accused of pro-military bias. Turkish Cypriot police (who are under the control of the Turkish military) sometimes flout due process rights and abuse or intimidate detainees. Detainees are ordinarily held no longer than 24 hours without charge.

Private newspapers and periodicals offer a wide range of views, while at least 11 new private radio and four private television stations broadcast alongside government stations. International broadcasts are available without interference. The small left-wing newspaper *Avrupa* has faced judicial harassment unprecedented in the TRNC for its criticism of Denktash, his policy on the division of the island, and the Turkish military presence in the territory. In May 2000, hearings began before a criminal court on 75 lawsuits against the paper for "instigating hatred against the TRNC and the Turkish army." In August 2002 the Turkish Cypriot Nicosia District Court sentenced two journalists (also from *Avrupa*) to six months' imprisonment and a fine of $30,000 for undermining the authority of Denktash.

Advocates for Greek Cypriots living in the northern city of Karpassia claim that these individuals are denied freedom of movement, free speech, property ownership, and access to Greek media. Outstanding property claims arising from the 1974 division and population exchange remain an obstacle to a final peace and demilitarization settlement on the island. Approximately 85 percent of the land in the north is claimed by its original Greek Cypriot owners. In May 2001, the European Court for Human Rights found Turkey guilty of widespread human rights abuses arising from its 1974 invasion of northern Cyprus.

Turkish Cypriot authorities generally respect freedom of assembly and association, and there are numerous political parties, trade unions, and nongovernmental organizations. About 99 percent of Turkish Cypriots are Sunni Muslim. There is a small Baha'i community, and there are some 650 Greek Orthodox and Maronite residents in the north. All reportedly worship freely. Turkish Cypriots have difficulty traveling to other countries because travel documents issued by the TRNC are recognized only by Turkey. Some restrictions exist on travel to and from the south, but in May 2000 the Turkish Cypriot authorities eliminated the system of fees for crossing the buffer zone. Cypriots from both sides may freely visit religious sites in each other's territory.

Women are underrepresented in government and politics. A 1998 law grants Turkish Cypriot women who marry non-Muslim men a fair distribution of assets in case of divorce. Legal provisions that require equal pay for equal work are not respected in all sectors. Workers may form independent trade unions, bargain collectively, and strike.

United Kingdom
Northern Ireland

Polity: Parliamentary democracy (Protestant/ Catholic power-sharing assembly)
Economy: Mixed capitalist
Population: 1,700,000

Political Rights: 2
Civil Liberties: 2
Status: Free

Religious Groups: Protestant (53.1 percent), Roman Catholic (43.8 percent), other (3.1 percent)
Ethnic Groups: Irish (majority)

Ten-Year Ratings Timeline (Political Rights, Civil Liberties, Status)

1993	1994	1995	1996	1997	1998	1999	2000	2001	2002	2003
3,3PF	5,4PF	4,3PF	4,3PF	4,3PF	3,3PF	3,3PF	3,3PF	2,2F	2,2F	2,2F

Overview:

The peace process suffered a blow in 2002 after police uncovered documents that indicated the Irish Republican Army (IRA) had infiltrated the Northern Ireland Office. The Northern Ireland Assembly was subsequently suspended as of midnight October 14, 2002. Sectarian violence continued.

Northern Ireland comprises 6 of the 9 counties of the Irish province of Ulster. At the insistence of the locally dominant Protestants, these counties remained part of the United Kingdom after the other 26, predominantly Catholic, counties gained independence in 1921. Catholics now constitute a majority in 4 of the 6 counties. This demographic trend has aroused anxiety among Protestants, who are largely descended from seventeenth century Scottish and English settlers. Britain's 1920 Government of Ireland Act established the Northern Irish parliament, which functioned until the British imposed direct rule in 1972.

Disorder resulting from a nonviolent Catholic civil rights movement in the 1960s prompted the deployment of British troops, and these troops remain in the territory today. Amid sectarian violence beginning in the 1970s, divisions grew within the primarily Protestant unionist and Catholic nationalist communities. The numerous political factions include the conservative Ulster Unionist Party, the hard-line Democratic Unionist Party, the interdenominational unionist Alliance Party, the moderate pro-nationalist Social Democratic and Labour Party, and the nationalist Sinn Fein (the political wing of the IRA). Paramilitary groups on both the unionist and the nationalist sides have engaged in terrorism.

Peace negotiations began in June 1996, with British Prime Minister Tony Blair securing an IRA ceasefire and Sinn Fein's participation in July 1997 talks. Blair and Irish prime minister Bertie Ahern kept negotiations on track despite continued violence by paramilitary groups. In April 1998, U.S. Senator George Mitchell, under the direction of President Bill Clinton, presented a plan that became the Good Friday Agreement. The Agreement led to the creation of a 108-member, directly elected Northern Ireland Assembly with full executive and legislative authority. Perhaps most significant, the Agreement recognized the "principle of consent," that is, that a united Ireland is dependent upon the consent of a majority of people in both jurisdictions. Pro-agreement moderates and nationalists dominated the assembly's first elections in June 1998.

Under the Agreement, Sinn Fein was obliged to disarm and renounce violence. A series of negotiation and inspections, however, revealed that Sinn Fein was not meeting its obligations. In response, Britain shut down the Assembly and reasserted control several times from February 2000 to October 2002, the latest suspension occurring as of midnight October 14, 2002, after police raided Sinn Fein houses and offices and found documents of use to IRA terrorists.

Sectarian violence continued, including petrol bombings of homes, shootings and killings. Amnesty International has urged the government and political and community leaders to address these human rights abuses.

The UK and Northern Ireland governments appointed former Canadian Supreme Court judge Peter Cory in May 2002 to investigate allegations of state collusion in six murder cases—those of defense lawyer Patrick Finucane; human rights lawyer Rosemary Nelson; Robert Hamill; Harry Breen and Bob Buchanan (two Royal Ulster Constabulary officers); Lord Justice Maurice and Lady Cecily Gibson; and Billy Wright.

Reporter sans Frontieres expressed concern in September 2002 at the lack of progress in the murder investigation of Irish journalist Martin O'Hagan, who had been investigating armed groups. The Red Hand Defenders, a name used by Protestant paramilitary groups, in particular the Loyalist Volunteer Force, claimed responsibility.

Political Rights and Civil Liberties:

The Good Friday Agreement of April 1998 provides for, among other things, a devolved government, a commitment to human rights, and policing reform in Northern Ireland.

The people of Northern Ireland elected a 108-member legislature in free and fair elections in June 1998. The assembly has full executive and legislative power, though Britain maintains responsibility for defense and security.

The Northern Ireland Human Rights Commission, established by the Northern Ireland Act 1998, advances human rights in Northern Ireland. The Act requires the incorporation of the European Convention on Human Rights into Northern Irish law, so that aggrieved parties may take alleged violations of the convention to Northern Irish courts.

In September 1999, the Independent Commission for Policing in Northern Ireland produced the Patten Report, which made 175 recommendations for change. In response to the report, the name of the police force was changed from the Royal Ulster Constabulary to the more neutral Police Service of Northern Ireland, the symbols used on police badges and uniforms were changed, and the Office of the Police Ombudsman for Northern Ireland was established to provide an independent and impartial police-complaints system.

The Terrorism Act 2000, effective in February of 2001, replaces emergency laws throughout the United Kingdom and extends, for up to five years, most of the emergency provisions already in force in Northern Ireland, including nonjury courts for terrorist offences; a lower standard for the admissibility of confessions than in criminal courts; the interpretation of a suspect's silence as an admission of guilt; the imprisonment of suspected terrorists on the word of a senior police officer; and army and police powers of arrest, entry, search, and seizure without a warrant.

The Independent International Commission on Decommissioning, effective September 24, 1997, was extended by the Northern Ireland Arms Decommissioning (Amendment) Act 2002. By the end of 2002, there were fewer than 13,500 British troops in Northern Ireland, the lowest level since 1970. Routine military patrolling has been halved since the Good Friday Agreement. Since the IRA ceasefire in July 1997, more than 3,000 British troops have been withdrawn and the army has demolished or vacated 48 of the 105 military bases and installations it had occupied, plus two towers.

Antiterror legislation may restrict the right of assembly, association, or freedom of expression, but it is not generally used to do so, and Northern Ireland enjoys a vibrant civil society.

Women are well represented in the workplace and the professions, although domestic violence is a problem. Workers may bargain collectively and strike, and there are at least 33 trade unions in the territory.

United States
Puerto Rico

Polity: Parliamentary with elected governor
Economy: Capitalist
Population: 3,900,000
Religious Groups: Roman Catholic (85 percent), Protestant and other (15 percent)
Ethnic Groups: Spanish origin (80.5 percent), black (8 percent), Amerindian (0.4 percent), Asian (0.2 percent), mixed and other (10.9 percent)

Political Rights: 1
Civil Liberties: 2
Status: Free

Ten-Year Ratings Timeline (Political Rights, Civil Liberties, Status)

1993	1994	1995	1996	1997	1998	1999	2000	2001	2002	2003
1,1F	1,1F	1,2F	1,2F	1,2F	1,2F	1,2F	1,2F	1,2F	1,2F	1,2F

Overview: The year 2002 was marked by continuing controversy over the status of the small island of Vieques. For several years, some leading Puerto Rican political figures, supported by civil rights leaders and political officeholders in the United States, have protested the U.S. Navy's use of the island as a bombing range. A number of protestors were arrested and given jail sentences for participating in demonstrations during naval exercises on the bombing site during 2001; there was also a controversy over a lack of press access to the island. The protest campaign, however, died down after the terrorist attacks on the United States but was reinitiated during the past year. At the end of the year, the United States government announced that it would abandon use of the island for military training during the first half of 2003.

Puerto Rico acquired the status of a commonwealth of the United States following approval by plebiscite in 1952. Under its terms, Puerto Rico exercises approximately the same control over its internal affairs as do the 50 U.S. states. Though U.S. citizens, residents cannot vote in presidential elections and are represented in the U.S. Congress by a delegate to the House of Representatives who can vote in committee but not on the floor. The commonwealth constitution, modeled after that of the U.S., provides for a governor and a bicameral legislature, consisting of a 28-member senate and a 54-member house of representatives, elected for four years. A supreme court heads an independent judiciary, and the legal system is based on U.S. law.

The controversy over Vieques was triggered in 1999, when a Puerto Rican civilian was killed accidentally during a bombing exercise. The incident ignited protests by Puerto Ricans and stimulated a debate over U.S. policy toward Puerto Rico. Puerto Rico's governor, Sila Maria Calderon, a member of the pro-commonwealth Popular Democratic Party (PDP), sided with the protestors and urged a speedy shutdown of the bombing range and a handover of the territory involved to Puerto Rico. Calderon sponsored a referendum in 2001 in which voters opted strongly for the return of Vieques to Puerto Rican control.

Calderon was elected governor in 2000, winning 48.5 percent of the vote against 45.7 percent for her main rival, Carlos Pesquera, of the pro-statehood New Progressive Party (NPP).

The island's relationship with the U.S. remains a fundamental issue. In a nonbinding 1993 referendum, voters narrowly opted to retain commonwealth status. Commonwealth status received 48.4 percent of the vote, statehood 46.3 percent, and independence 4.4 percent. The vote indicated significant gains for statehood, which in the last referendum, in 1967, received only 39 percent of the vote. Voters also opted for the status quo in a 1998 referendum. Although many more voters chose statehood over independence, the percentage who voted for no change in the island's status was greater than it had been in the 1993 referendum. In one of his last acts as president, Bill Clinton created a task force to study whether Puerto Rico should retain its current status, or become a state or an independent country. However, nothing significant has developed from this Clinton initiative. Any vote to change the island's status would have to be approved by the U.S. Congress. As Washington seeks to cut the federal deficit, the benefits the island receives under Section 936 of the Internal Revenue Code will be phased out over the next ten years and the government of Puerto Rico has been lobbying for a replacement.

Calderon was elected on a platform that stressed anticorruption themes while, at the same time, several political figures from her party and the NPP and cabinet members were arrested and faced trials. Among them was a leading NPP representative, Edison Misla Aldarondo, who was arrested and tried for influence peddling; a verdict is expected in early 2003. Another was the Secretary of Educaction during the administration of Gov. Pedro Rosselló, Victor Fajardo, who was tried and convicted on corruption charges, including misappropriation of federal education funds.

Political Rights and Civil Liberties:

As U.S. citizens, Puerto Ricans are guaranteed all civil liberties granted in the United States. The press and broadcast media are well developed, highly varied, and critical. In recent years, the Puerto Rican Journalists' Association and the Overseas Press Club of Puerto Rico have charged successive governments with denying complete access to official information. Renewed efforts to adopt a proposed Freedom of Information Act for the island failed. Press freedom and professional organizations continued to express skepticism about the proposed law, contending that the measure would do more harm than good and urging instead strict adherence to the basic right of freedom of speech and the press.

A protest by statehood supporters, led by NPP President Pesquera, concerning the placement of a U.S. flag in a government agency turned into a riot in which he and other top party officials were arrested, charged and faced trials. Subsequently, the Puerto Rico Justice Department demanded and received the raw footage of the event from several television stations. In addition, the prosecutors and a Special Independent Prosecutor panel summoned the news director of the public television station and some of the reporters and photojournalists who covered the incident as witnesses. The action was seen as a threat to press freedom.

The greatest cause for concern is the steep rise in crime, much of which is drug related. Puerto Rico is one of the Caribbean's main drug transshipment points.

Puerto Rico is predominantly Roman Catholic. Freedom of religion is guaranteed, and a substantial number of Evangelical churches have been established on the island in recent years. Laws have been adopted calling for equal rights for women in education, at the work place, and in other aspects of society. Women's rights' organizations, however, claim that women are still subject to widespread discrimination.

Yugoslavia (Serbia and Montenegro)
Kosovo

Polity: International protectorate
Economy: Mixed-statist (transitional)
Population: 2,000,000

Political Rights: 5*
Civil Liberties: 5*
Status: Partly Free

Religious Groups: Muslim (majority), Serbian Orthodox, Roman Catholic, other
Ethnic Groups: Albanian (90 percent), Serb, Muslim, Montenegrins, and other (10 percent)
Capital: Pristina
Ratings Change: Kosovo's political rights and civil liberties ratings increased from 6 to 5, and its status from Not Free to Partly Free, because the wave of postwar ethnic discrimination and terror has largely subsided.

Ten-Year Ratings Timeline (Political Rights, Civil Liberties, Status)

1993	1994	1995	1996	1997	1998	1999	2000	2001	2002	2003
7,7NF	7,7NF	7,7NF	7,7NF	7,7NF	7,7NF	7,7NF	7,7NF	6,6NF	6,6NF	5,5PF

Overview:

In 2002, there was little noteworthy political progress in the disputed province, which still legally remains a part of the

Federal Republic of Yugoslavia (FRY). Although elections for the provincial assembly were held successfully in October, increasing tensions between the local Albanian political leadership and international officials running the province, along with the lack of a strategy for resolving Kosovo's final status, continued to raise considerable uncertainty over the future of Kosovo's development.

Control over the Yugoslav province of Kosovo has been a source of conflict between Albanians and Serbs in the Balkans for most of the twentieth century. The current round of troubles began in the early 1980s and accelerated after former Serbian strongman Slobodan Milosevic came to power and began to revoke much of Kosovo's autonomy. For most of the 1990s, an uneasy but generally nonviolent status quo was maintained between the Yugoslav government and the Kosovo Albanians, who, under the leadership of Ibrahim Rugova, developed an entire parallel society in Kosovo, replete with quasi-governmental institutions, hospitals, and school systems.

In late 1997, a guerrilla movement called the Kosovo Liberation Army (KLA) began a series of attacks on Serb targets in the province, provoking harsh reprisals from Yugoslav government forces. In March 1999, NATO launched a 78-day air campaign against the FRY to force it to relinquish control over the province.

Under the terms of UN Security Council Resolution (UNSCR) 1244 of June 1999, a NATO-led peacekeeping force (KFOR) assumed responsibility for security in Kosovo. UNSCR 1244 turned Kosovo into a protectorate of the international community, while officially maintaining Yugoslav sovereignty over the province.

Since international forces moved into Kosovo in mid-1999, a campaign of reverse ethnic cleansing has been taking place. More than 250,000 Serbs, Romas (Gypsies), Bosniacs, Croats, Turks, and Jews have been forced to flee the province. Most of the non-Albanian population remaining in Kosovo live in small clusters of villages or in urban ghettoes under round-the-clock KFOR protection. The largest Serb population is concentrated in a triangle-shaped piece of territory north of the Ibar River.

Municipal elections were held in Kosovo on October 25 after a campaign that international observers claimed was "generally free and fair." The election results confirmed the continuing dominance of Rugova's Democratic League of Kosovo (LDK) over former KLA leader Hashim Thaci's Democratic Party of Kosovo (PDK), while Ramush Haradinaj's Alliance for the Future of Kosovo (AAK) made a very strong showing in traditionally sympathetic regions in western Kosovo.

During the year tensions grew between the local Albanian political leadership of the province and international administrators. On May 23, the UN Special Representative for Kosovo, Michael Steiner, immediately declared "null and void" a resolution adopted by the Kosovo Assembly challenging a border agreement between the FRY and Macedonia. Steiner claimed the assembly, which under the terms of UNSCR 1244 has no authority over internal security or Kosovo's relations with the outside world, had no jurisdiction in the matter. The assembly went ahead with the vote despite letters from the UN Security Council and the EU warning it not to proceed with such a vote. A similar effort by the Kosovo Assembly to sign a memorandum of cooperation with Albania a few days later was also immediately struck down by Steiner. By the end of the year, Kosovo Albanian legislators were threatening a unilateral declaration of independence if a proposed agreement between the two remaining Yugoslav republics—Serbia and Montenegro—was ratified; Kosovo Albanian rejection of the agreement was prompted by the stipulation in the draft agreement that should the FRY break up, Serbia would inherit all legal claims to Kosovo in place of Yugoslavia. In a more promising development, however, in November the UN Interim Administration Mission in Kosovo (UNMIK) assumed administrative control over the Serb enclaves north of the Ibar River, thereby unifying the province under international supervision for the first time since the war.

Political Rights and Civil Liberties: According to UNSCR 1244, ultimate authority within Kosovo resides with the UN Special Representative in the province, who is appointed by the UN secretary-general. The Special Representative, who also serves as UNMIK chief, is responsible for implementing civilian aspects of the agreement ending the war. Elections in Kosovo in the post-1999 period, organized by the international community, have been considered "generally free and fair." In the October municipal elections, contested by more than 60 political entities, voter turnout was approximately 54 percent. There was a disproportionately low Serb turnout, however, because of continuing complaints about the lack of freedom of movement to and from polling places.

Freedom of expression is limited because of the overall lack of security in the province. Although a wide variety of print and electronic media operate in Kosovo, journalists report frequent harassment and intimidation. A survey conducted by the OSCE Mission in Kosovo in December 2001 found that 78 percent of the journalists questioned did not feel free to do investigative journalism without fear of threat or reprisal.

The Albanian population in Kosovo on the whole enjoys freedom of belief and religious association. There are, however, frequent attacks on Orthodox churches and other holy sites associated with the Serb population. Since NATO took control of Kosovo, more than 100 churches and other properties belonging to the Serbian Orthodox Church have been destroyed or damaged.

Freedom of movement continues to be a significant problem in Kosovo for ethnic minorities, who face frequent attacks from the majority Albanian population once they leave NATO-protected enclaves. An EU report issued in 2002 noted that because of their poor access to public and private sector employment, income-generation programs, market venues, property rights, vocational education training, and public and social services, minorities are being "economically cleansed" from Kosovo. In September, the coordinator of UNMIK's science and education efforts in Kosovo announced he was leaving his post, saying it was proving impossible to stop discrimination against Serbs and other local ethnic minorities in educational institutions.

Kosovo lacks a functioning criminal justice system. International agencies report that ethnic Albanian judges are unwilling to prosecute cases involving Albanian attacks on non-Albanians, and the physical safety of non-Albanian judges cannot be guaranteed. Criminal suspects who have been arrested according to the Special Representative's power to order executive detentions are frequently released on the orders of local judges.

The lack of a functioning judicial system in Kosovo was apparent in a 2002 case involving several East European women forced into sexual slavery. In September, their Kosovo Albanian pimp was brought to trial, but the proceedings were neither translated into the women's native language nor did the local court provide lawyers for the women. The Albanian judge sentenced the defendant to 3 ½ years (out of a maximum sentence for trafficking of 12 years), but the defendant was released while he appealed his sentence. International officials reported charges of bribery of the judge involved and death threats made against the witnesses to recant their testimony.

Several leading members of the former KLA are under investigation for war crimes by the International Criminal Tribunal for the Former Yugoslavia (ICTY) for actions committed before, during, and after the NATO intervention.

Gender inequality continues to be a serious problem in Kosovo Albanian society. Patriarchal societal attitudes often limit a woman's ability to gain an education or to choose the marriage partner of her choice.

Trafficking is a major problem in Kosovo, which serves as both a point of transit for women trafficked from Eastern to Western Europe and as a point of destination. The presence of a large international military force and of numerous civilian agencies provides a relatively affluent clientele for the white slave trade in the province.

Survey Methodology—2003

INTRODUCTION

The *Freedom in the World* survey provides an annual evaluation of the state of global freedom. The survey, which includes both analytical reports and numerical ratings of countries and select territories, measures freedom by assessing two broad categories: political rights and civil liberties. Political rights enable people to participate freely in the political process. This includes the right to vote and compete for public office and to elect representatives who have a decisive vote on public policies. Civil liberties include the freedom to develop opinions, institutions, and personal autonomy without interference from the state.

Freedom House assigns each country and territory a political rights and civil liberties rating, along with a corresponding status designation of Free, Partly Free, or Not Free. The survey does not rate governments or government performance per se, but rather the real-world rights and freedoms enjoyed by individuals as the result of actions by both state and nongovernmental actors. The survey team does not base its judgment solely on the political conditions in a country or territory (e.g., war, terrorism), but on the effect that these conditions have on freedom.

Freedom House does not maintain a culture-bound view of freedom. The methodology of the survey established basic standards drawn from the Universal Declaration of Human Rights. These standards apply to all countries and territories, irrespective of geographical location, ethnic or religious composition, and level of economic development.

For the purposes of the survey, countries are defined as internationally recognized independent states whose governments reside within their officially claimed borders. In the case of Cyprus, two sets of ratings are provided, as there are two governments on that divided island; however, this does not imply that Freedom House endorses Cypriot division. Freedom House divides territories into two categories: related territories and disputed territories. Related territories consist mostly of colonies, protectorates, and island dependencies of sovereign states that are in some relation of dependency to that state and whose relationship is not currently in serious legal or political dispute. Disputed territories are areas within internationally recognized sovereign states whose status is in serious political or violent dispute and that often are dominated by a minority ethnic group. This group also includes territories whose incorporation into nation-states is not universally recognized. In some cases, the issue of dispute is the desire of the majority of the population of that territory to secede from the sovereign state and either form an independent country or become part of a neighboring state.

HISTORY OF THE SURVEY

Freedom House's first year-end reviews of freedom began in the 1950s as the *Balance Sheet of Freedom*. This modest report provided assessments of political trends and their implications for individual freedom. In 1972, Freedom House launched a new, more comprehensive annual study of freedom called "Freedom in the World." Raymond Gastil, a Harvard-trained specialist in regional studies from the University of Washington at Seattle, developed the survey's methodology, which assigned countries political rights and civil liberties ratings and categorized them as Free, Partly Free, or Not Free. The findings appeared each year in Freedom House's *Freedom at Issue* bimonthly journal (later titled *Freedom Review*). Having served as a consultant to Freedom House, Gastil later moved to New York and became the full-time director of the survey. The survey first appeared in book form in 1978 and continued to be produced by Gastil, with essays by leading scholars on related issues, until 1989, when a larger team of in-house survey analysts was established. Subsequent editions of the survey, including the 2003 edition, have followed essentially the same format.

OVERVIEW OF CURRENT RESEARCH AND RATINGS REVIEW PROCESS

This year's survey covers developments in 192 countries and 18 territories. The research and ratings process involved over 30 analyst/writers and senior-level academic advisors. The seven members of the core research team headquartered in New York, along with nine outside consultant writers, prepared the country and territory reports. To reach its conclusions, the analysts used a broad range of sources of information, including foreign and domestic news reports, nongovernmental organization publications, think tank and academic analyses, individual professional contacts, and visits to the region in preparing their reports.

The country and territory ratings, which were proposed by the writers of each report, were reviewed on a comparative basis in a series of regional discussions involving the analysts and regional academic experts. These reviews were followed by cross-regional assessments in which efforts were made to ensure comparability and consistency in the findings. The ratings were also compared to the previous year's findings and any major numerical shifts or category changes were subjected to more intensive scrutiny. Some of the country essays were also reviewed by the regional academic advisors.

The survey's methodology is reviewed by an advisory committee on methodological issues. This year's committee included Joshua Muravchik, American Enterprise Institute; Larry Diamond, *Journal of Democracy*; Kenneth Bollen, University of North Carolina; Jack Snyder, Columbia University; and Jeane Kirkpatrick, American Enterprise Institute. Over the years, the committee has made a number of modest methodological changes to adapt to evolving ideas about political change and civil liberties. At the same time, the time series data are not revised retroactively and any changes to the methodology are introduced incrementally in order to ensure the comparability of the ratings from year to year.

RATINGS PROCESS
Summary of the ratings process

Each country and territory is awarded from 0 to 4 raw points for each of 10 questions grouped into three subcategories in a political rights checklist, and for each of 15 questions grouped into four subcategories in a civil liberties checklist. The total raw points in each checklist correspond to two final numerical ratings of 1 to 7. These two ratings are then averaged to determine a status category of "Free," "Partly Free," or "Not Free."

(*NOTE: see the full checklists and keys to political rights and civil liberties ratings and status at the end of the methodology essay*)

Steps in the ratings process

Awarding of raw scores—Each question in both the political rights and civil liberties checklists is awarded from 0 to 4 raw points per checklist item, depending on the comparative rights or liberties present. In both checklists, 0 represents the smallest degree and 4 the greatest degree of rights or liberties present as specified in each question. The only exception to the addition of 0 to 4 raw points per checklist item is Additional Discretionary Question B in the Political Rights Checklist, for which 1 to 4 raw points are subtracted depending on the severity of the situation. The highest possible total score for political rights is 40 points, representing a total of up to 4 points for each of 10 questions. The highest possible total score for civil liberties is 60 points, representing a total of up to 4 points for each of 15 questions.

To answer the political rights questions, Freedom House considers to what extent the system offers voters the opportunity to choose freely from among candidates and to what extent the candidates are chosen independently of the state. However, formal electoral procedures are not the only factors that determine the real distribution of power. In many countries, the military retains a significant political role, while in others, the king maintains considerable power over the elected politicians.

In answering the civil liberties questions, Freedom House does not equate constitutional guarantees of human rights with the on-the-ground fulfillment of these rights. For states and territories with small populations, particularly tiny island nations, the absence of trade unions and other forms of association is not necessarily viewed as a negative situation unless the government or other centers of domination are deliberately blocking their establishment or operation.

Calculation of political rights and civil liberties ratings—A country or territory is assigned a numerical rating on a scale of 1 to 7 based on the total number of raw points awarded to the political rights and civil liberties checklist questions. For both checklists, 1 represents the most free and 7 the least free; each 1 to 7 rating corresponds to a range of total raw scores (see Tables 1 and 2).

Assigning of the status of Free, Partly Free, Not Free—Each pair of political rights and civil liberties ratings is averaged to determine an overall status of "Free," "Partly Free," or "Not Free." Those whose ratings average 1-2.5 are considered Free, 3-5.5 Partly Free, and 5.5-7 Not Free (see Table 3). The dividing line between Partly Free and Not Free falls at 5.5. For example, countries that receive a rating of 6 for political rights and 5 for civil liberties, or a 5 for political rights and a 6 for civil liberties, could be either Partly Free or Not Free. The total number of raw points is the definitive factor that determines the final status. Countries and territories with combined raw scores of 0-33 points are Not Free, 34-67 points are Partly Free, and 68-100 are Free.

The designations of Free, Partly Free, and Not Free each cover a broad third of the available raw points. Therefore, countries and territories within any one category, especially those at either end of the category, can have quite different human rights situations. In order to see the distinctions within each category, a country or territory's political rights and civil liberties ratings should be examined. For example, countries at the lowest end of the Free category (2 in political rights and 3 in civil liberties, or 3 in political rights and 2 in civil liberties) differ from those at the upper end of the Free group (1 for both political rights and civil liberties). Also, a designation of Free does not mean that a country enjoys perfect freedom or lacks serious problems, only that it enjoys comparably more freedom than Partly Free or Not Free (or some other Free) countries.

Indications of ratings and/or status changes—Each country or territory's political rights rating, civil liberties rating, and status is included in the statistics section that precedes each country or territory report. A change in a political rights or civil liberties rating since the previous survey edition is indicated with an asterisk next to the rating that has changed. A brief ratings change explanation is included in the statistics section.

Assigning of trend arrows—Upward or downward trend arrows may be assigned to countries and territories. Trend arrows indicate general positive or negative trends since the previous survey that are not necessarily reflected in the raw points and do *not* warrant a ratings change. A country cannot receive both a numerical ratings change and a trend arrow in the same year, nor can it receive trend arrows in the same direction in two successive years. A trend arrow is indicated with an arrow next to the name of the country or territory that appears at the top of each country or territory report.

GENERAL CHARACTERISTICS OF EACH POLITICAL RIGHTS AND CIVIL LIBERTIES RATING
Political Rights

Rating of 1—Countries and territories that receive a rating of 1 for political rights come closest to the ideals suggested by the checklist questions, beginning with free and fair elections. Those who are elected rule, there are competitive parties or other political groupings, and the opposition plays an important role and has actual power. Minority groups have reasonable self-government or can participate in the government through informal consensus.

Rating of 2—Countries and territories rated 2 in political rights are less free than those rated 1. Such factors as political corruption, violence, political discrimination against minorities, and foreign or military influence on politics may be present and weaken the quality of freedom.

Ratings of 3, 4, 5—The same conditions that undermine freedom in countries and territories with a rating of 2 may also weaken political rights in those with a rating of 3, 4, or 5. Other damaging elements can include civil war, heavy military involvement in politics, lingering royal power, unfair elections, and one-party dominance. However, states and territories in these categories may still enjoy some elements of political rights, including the freedom to organize quasi-political groups, reasonably free referenda, or other significant means of popular influence on government.

Rating of 6—Countries and territories with political rights rated 6 have systems ruled by military juntas, one-party dictatorships, religious hierarchies, or autocrats. These regimes may allow only a minimal manifestation of political rights, such as some degree of representation or autonomy for minorities. A few states are traditional monarchies that mitigate their relative lack of political rights through the use of consultation with their subjects, tolerance of political discussion, and acceptance of public petitions.

Rating of 7—For countries and territories with a rating of 7, political rights are absent or virtually nonexistent as a result of the extremely oppressive nature of the regime or severe oppression in combination with civil war. States and territories in this group may also be marked by extreme violence or warlord rule that dominates political power in the absence of an authoritative, functioning central government.

Civil Liberties

Rating of 1—Countries and territories that receive a rating of 1 come closest to the ideals expressed in the civil liberties checklist, including freedom of expression, assembly, association, education, and religion. They are distinguished by an established and generally equitable system of rule of law. Countries and territories with this rating enjoy free economic activity and tend to strive for equality of opportunity.

Rating of 2—States and territories with a rating of 2 have deficiencies in three or four aspects of civil liberties, but are still relatively free.

Ratings of 3, 4, 5—Countries and territories that have received a rating of 3, 4, or 5 range from those that are in at least partial compliance with virtually all checklist standards to those with a combination of high or medium scores for some questions and low or very low scores on other questions. The level of oppression increases at each successive rating level, particularly in the areas of censorship, political terror, and the prevention of free association. There are also many cases in which groups opposed to the state engage in political terror that undermines other freedoms. Therefore, a poor rating for a country is not necessarily a comment on the intentions of the government, but may reflect real restrictions on liberty caused by nongovernmental actors.

Rating of 6—People in countries and territories with a rating of 6 experience severely restricted rights of expression and association, and there are almost always political prisoners and other manifestations of political terror. These countries may be characterized by a few partial rights, such as some religious and social freedoms, some highly restricted private business activity, and relatively free private discussion.

Rating of 7—States and territories with a rating of 7 have virtually no freedom. An overwhelming and justified fear of repression characterizes these societies.

Countries and territories generally have ratings in political rights and civil liberties that are within two ratings numbers of each other. Without a well-developed civil society, it is difficult, if not impossible, to have an atmosphere supportive of political rights. Consequently, there is no country in the survey with a rating of 6 or 7 for civil liberties and, at the same time, a rating of 1 or 2 for political rights.

CHANGES TO THE 2003 SURVEY METHODOLOGY

For the 2003 edition of the survey, several modest changes were made to the methodology. The political rights checklist has been divided into three subcategories: political process, political pluralism and participation, and functioning of government. A question on academic freedom (question A3) was added to the civil liberties checklist. A question on government accountability to the electorate and government openness and transparency (question C3) was added to the political rights checklist. A question on government corruption was moved from the civil liberties to the political rights checklist (question C2). In the civil liberties checklist, the question, "Is the population treated equally under the law?" was separated from question C2 and made a separate question (question C4). In addition, a few questions were reworded slightly or moved within each checklist for the sake of greater clarity.

ELECTORAL DEMOCRACY DESIGNATION

In addition to providing numerical ratings, the survey assigns the designation "electoral democracy" to countries that have met certain minimum standards. Among the basic criteria for designating a country as an electoral democracy are that voters can choose their authoritative leaders freely from among competing groups and individuals not designated by the government; voters have access to information about candidates and their platforms; voters can vote without undue pressure from the authorities; and candidates can campaign free from intimidation. The presence of certain irregularities during the electoral process does not automatically disqualify a country from being designated an electoral democracy.

Freedom House's term "electoral democracy" differs from "liberal democracy" in that the latter also implies the presence of a substantial array of civil liberties. In the survey, all Free countries qualify as both electoral and liberal democracies. By contrast, some Partly Free countries qualify as electoral, but not liberal, democracies.

POLITICAL RIGHTS AND CIVIL LIBERTIES CHECKLIST
Political Rights Checklist
A. Electoral Process

1. Is the head of state and/or head of government or other chief authority elected through free and fair elections?
2. Are the legislative representatives elected through free and fair elections?
3. Are there fair electoral laws, equal campaigning opportunities, fair polling, and honest tabulation of ballots?

B. Political Pluralism and Participation

1. Do the people have the right to organize in different political parties or other competitive political groupings of their choice, and is the system open to the rise and fall of these competing parties or groupings?
2. Is there a significant opposition vote, de facto opposition power, and a realistic possibility for the opposition to increase its support or gain power through elections?
3. Are the people's political choices free from domination by the military, foreign powers, totalitarian parties, religious hierarchies, economic oligarchies, or any other powerful group?
4. Do cultural, ethnic, religious, and other minority groups have reasonable self-determination, self-government, autonomy, or participation through informal consensus in the decision-making process?

C. Functioning of Government

1. Do freely elected representatives determine the policies of the government?
2. Is the government free from pervasive corruption?
3. Is the government accountable to the electorate between elections, and does it operate with openness and transparency?

Additional discretionary Political Rights questions:

A. For traditional monarchies that have no parties or electoral process, does the system provide for consultation with the people, encourage discussion of policy, and allow the right to petition the ruler?
B. Is the government or occupying power deliberately changing the ethnic composition of a country or territory so as to destroy a culture or tip the political balance in favor of another group?

   (*NOTE*: For each political rights and civil liberties checklist question, 0 to 4 points are *added*, depending on the comparative rights and liberties present [0 represents the least, 4 represents the most]. However, for additional discretionary question B only, 1 to 4 points are *subtracted*, as necessary.)

Civil Liberties Checklist
A. Freedom of Expression and Belief

1. Are there free and independent media and other forms of cultural expression? (Note: in cases where the media are state-controlled but offer pluralistic points of view, the survey gives the system credit.)

2. Are there free religious institutions, and is there free private and public religious expression?

3. Is there academic freedom, and is the educational system free of extensive political indoctrination?

4. Is there open and free private discussion?

B. Associational and Organizational Rights

1. Is there freedom of assembly, demonstration, and open public discussion?

2. Is there freedom of political or quasi-political organization? (Note: this includes political parties, civic organizations, ad hoc issue groups, etc.)

3. Are there free trade unions and peasant organizations or equivalents, and is there effective collective bargaining? Are there free professional and other private organizations?

C. Rule of Law

1. Is there an independent judiciary?

2. Does the rule of law prevail in civil and criminal matters? Are police under direct civilian control?

3. Is there protection from police terror, unjustified imprisonment, exile, or torture, whether by groups that support or oppose the system? Is there freedom from war and insurgencies?

4. Is the population treated equally under the law?

D. Personal Autonomy and Individual Rights

1. Is there personal autonomy? Does the state control travel, choice of residence, or choice of employment? Is there freedom from indoctrination and excessive dependency on the state?

2. Do citizens have the right to own property and establish private businesses? Is private business activity unduly influenced by government officials, the security forces, or organized crime?

3. Are there personal social freedoms, including gender equality, choice of marriage partners, and size of family?

4. Is there equality of opportunity and the absence of economic exploitation?

KEY TO RAW SCORES, POLITICAL RIGHTS AND
CIVIL LIBERTIES RATINGS, STATUS

Table 1

Political Rights (PR)	
Total raw scores	PR Rating
36-40	1
30-35	2
24-29	3
18-23	4
12-17	5
6-11	6
0-5	7

Table 2

Civil Liberties (CL)	
Total raw scores	CL Rating
53-60	1
44-52	2
35-43	3
26-34	4
17-25	5
8-16	6
0-7	7

Table 3

Combined Average of the PR and CL Ratings	Country Status
1 to 2.5	Free
3 to 5.5	Partly Free
5.5 to 7	Not Free

Tables and Ratings

Table of Independent Countries

Country	PR	CL	Freedom Rating	Country	PR	CL	Freedom Rating
Afghanistan	6▲	6▲	Not Free	Dominica	1	1	Free
Albania	3	3▲	Partly Free	Dominican Republic	2	2	Free
Algeria	6	5	Not Free	East Timor	3▲	3	Partly Free
Andorra	1	1	Free	Ecuador	3	3	Partly Free
Angola	6	5▲	Not Free	Egypt	6	6	Not Free
Antigua and Barbuda	4	2	Partly Free	El Salvador	2	3	Free
🔽 Argentina	3	3	Partly Free	Equatorial Guinea	7▼	6	Not Free
Armenia	4	4	Partly Free	Eritrea	7	6	Not Free
Australia	1	1	Free	Estonia	1	2	Free
Austria	1	1	Free	Ethiopia	5	5	Partly Free
Azerbaijan	6	5	Partly Free	Fiji	4	3	Partly Free
Bahamas	1	1	Free	Finland	1	1	Free
Bahrain	5▲	5	Partly Free	France	1	1▲	Free
Bangladesh	4▼	4	Partly Free	Gabon	5	4	Partly Free
Barbados	1	1	Free	The Gambia	4▲	4▲	Partly Free
Belarus	6	6	Not Free	Georgia	4	4	Partly Free
Belgium	1	1▲	Free	Germany	1	1▲	Free
Belize	1	2▼	Free	Ghana	2	3	Free
Benin	3	2	Free	Greece	1	2▲	Free
Bhutan	6▲	5▲	Not Free	Grenada	1	2	Free
Bolivia	2▼	3	Free	Guatemala	4▼	4	Partly Free
Bosnia-Herzegovina	4▲	4	Partly Free	🔼 Guinea	6	5	Not Free
Botswana	2	2	Free	Guinea-Bissau	4	5	Partly Free
Brazil	2▲	3	Free	Guyana	2	2	Free
Brunei	6▲	5	Not Free	🔽 Haiti	6	6	Not Free
Bulgaria	1	2▲	Free	Honduras	3	3	Partly Free
🔼 Burkina Faso	4	4	Partly Free	Hungary	1	2	Free
🔼 Burma	7	7	Not Free	Iceland	1	1	Free
Burundi	6	5▲	Not Free	🔽 India	2	3	Free
Cambodia	6	5	Not Free	Indonesia	3	4	Partly Free
🔼 Cameroon	6	6	Not Free	Iran	6	6	Not Free
Canada	1	1	Free	Iraq	7	7	Not Free
Cape Verde	1	2	Free	Ireland	1	1	Free
Central African Republic	5	5	Partly Free	Israel	1	3	Free
				Italy	1	1▲	Free
Chad	6	5	Not Free	Jamaica	2	3	Free
Chile	2	1▲	Free	Japan	1	2	Free
China (P.R.C.)	7	6	Not Free	Jordan	6▼	5	Partly Free
Colombia	4	4	Partly Free	🔽 Kazakhstan	6	5	Not Free
Comoros	5▲	4	Partly Free	Kenya	4▲	4▲	Partly Free
Congo (Brazzaville)	6▼	4	Partly Free	Kiribati	1	1	Free
🔼 Congo (Kinshasa)	6	6	Not Free	Korea, North	7	7	Not Free
Costa Rica	1	2	Free	Korea, South	2	2	Free
Côte d'Ivoire	6▼	6▼	Not Free	Kuwait	4	5	Partly Free
🔽 Croatia	2	2	Free	Kyrgyz Republic	6	5	Not Free
🔼 Cuba	7	7	Not Free	Laos	7	6	Not Free
Cyprus (G)	1	1	Free	Latvia	1	2	Free
Czech Republic	1	2	Free	🔽 Lebanon	6	5	Not Free
Denmark	1	1	Free	Lesotho	2▲	3▲	Free
Djibouti	4	5	Partly Free	Liberia	6	6	Not Free

700

Country	PR	CL	Freedom Rating
Libya	7	7	Not Free
Liechtenstein	1	1	Free
Lithuania	1	2	Free
Luxembourg	1	1	Free
Macedonia	3▲	3▲	Partly Free
Madagascar	3▼	4	Partly Free
Malawi	4	4▼	Partly Free
Malaysia	5	5	Partly Free
Maldives	6	5	Not Free
Mali	2	3	Free
Malta	1	1	Free
Marshall Islands	1	1	Free
Mauritania	5	5	Partly Free
Mauritius	1	2	Free
Mexico	2	2▲	Free
Micronesia	1	2	Free
Moldova	3▼	4	Partly Free
Monaco	2	1	Free
Mongolia	2	2▲	Free
Morocco	5	5	Partly Free
Mozambique	3	4	Partly Free
Namibia	2	3	Free
Nauru	1	2▲	Free
Nepal	4▼	4	Partly Free
Netherlands	1	1	Free
New Zealand	1	1	Free
Nicaragua	3	3	Partly Free
⬇ Niger	4	4	Partly Free
Nigeria	4	5	Partly Free
Norway	1	1	Free
Oman	6	5	Not Free
⬆ Pakistan	6	5	Not Free
Palau	1	2	Free
Panama	1	2	Free
Papua New Guinea	2	3	Free
⬇ Paraguay	4	3	Partly Free
Peru	2▼	3	Free
Philippines	2	3	Free
Poland	1	2	Free
Portugal	1	1	Free
Qatar	6	6	Not Free
Romania	2	2	Free
Russia	5	5	Partly Free
Rwanda	7	5▲	Not Free
St. Kitts and Nevis	1	2	Free
St. Lucia	1	2	Free
St. Vincent and the Grenadines	2	1	Free
Samoa	2	2	Free
San Marino	1	1	Free
Sao Tome and Príncipe	1	2	Free
Saudi Arabia	7	7	Not Free
Senegal	2▲	3▲	Free

Country	PR	CL	Freedom Rating
Seychelles	3	3	Partly Free
Sierra Leone	4	4▲	Partly Free
Singapore	5	4▲	Partly Free
Slovakia	1	2	Free
Slovenia	1	1▲	Free
Solomon Islands	3▲	3▲	Partly Free
Somalia	6	7	Not Free
South Africa	1	2	Free
Spain	1	1▲	Free
⬆ Sri Lanka	3	4	Partly Free
Sudan	7	7	Not Free
Suriname	1	2	Free
Swaziland	6	5	Not Free
Sweden	1	1	Free
Switzerland	1	1	Free
Syria	7	7	Not Free
Taiwan (Rep. of China)	2▼	2	Free
Tajikistan	6	5▲	Not Free
Tanzania	4	3▲	Partly Free
⬇ Thailand	2	3	Free
Togo	6▼	5	Not Free
Tonga	5	3	Partly Free
Trinidad and Tobago	3	3	Partly Free
Tunisia	6	5	Not Free
Turkey	3▲	4▲	Partly Free
Turkmenistan	7	7	Not Free
Tuvalu	1	1	Free
Uganda	6	4▲	Partly Free
Ukraine	4	4	Partly Free
United Arab Emirates	6	5	Not Free
United Kingdom*	1	1▲	Free
United States	1	1	Free
⬇ Uruguay	1	1	Free
Uzbekistan	7	6	Not Free
Vanuatu	1	2▲	Free
Venezuela	3	4▲	Partly Free
Vietnam	7	6	Not Free
Yemen	6	5▲	Not Free
Yugoslavia (Serbia and Montenegro)	3	2▲	Free
Zambia	4▲	4	Partly Free
⬇ Zimbabwe	6	6	Not Free

PR and CL stand for Political Rights and Civil Liberties. 1 represents the most free and 7 the least free category.

⬆⬇ up or down indicates a general trend in freedom.

▲▼ up or down indicates a change in Political Rights or Civil Liberties since the last survey.

The freedom ratings reflect an overall judgment based on survey results. See the essay on survey methodology for more details.

* Excluding Northern Ireland.

Table of Related Territories

Country	PR	CL	Freedom Rating
China			
⬇ Hong Kong	5	3	Partly Free
Macao	6	4	Partly Free
United Kingdom			
Northern Ireland	2	2	Free
United States of America			
Puerto Rico	1	2	Free

Table of Disputed Territories

Country	PR	CL	Freedom Rating
Armenia/Azerbaijan			
Nagorno-Karabakh	5	5▲	Partly Free
China			
Tibet	7	7	Not Free
Georgia			
Abkhazia	6	5	Not Free
India			
Kashmir	5▲	5▲	Partly Free
Indonesia			
West Papua	5	4▲	Partly Free
Iraq			
Kurdistan	5	4▲	Partly Free
Israel			
Israeli-Administered territories	6	6	Not Free
Palestinian Authority-Administered territories	5	6	Not Free
Moldova			
Transnistria	6	6	Not Free
Morocco			
Western Sahara	7	6	Not Free
Pakistan			
Kashmir	7	5	Not Free
Russia			
Chechnya	7	7	Not Free
Turkey			
Cyprus (T)	2	2	Free
Yugoslavia (Serbia & Montenegro)			
Kosovo	5▲	5▲	Partly Free

Table of Social and Economic Indicators

Country	Real GDP Per Capita (PPP$)	Life Expectancy	Country	Real GDP Per Capita (PPP$)	Life Expectancy
Afghanistan	na	45	East Timor	na	48
Albania	$3,506	74	Ecuador	$3,203	71
Algeria	$5,308	70	Egypt	$3,635	66
Andorra	na	na	El Salvador	$4,497	70
Angola	$2,187	45	Equatorial Guinea	$15,073	51
Antigua and Barbuda	$10,541	71	Eritrea	$837	56
Argentina	$12,377	74	Estonia	$10,066	71
Armenia	$2,559	72	Ethiopia	$668	52
Australia	$25,693	80	Fiji	$4,668	67
Austria	$26,765	78	Finland	$24,996	78
Azerbaijan	$2,936	72	France	$24,223	79
Bahamas	$17,012	72	Gabon	$6,237	50
Bahrain	$15,084	74	The Gambia	$1,649	53
Bangladesh	$1,602	59	Georgia	$2,664	73
Barbados	$15,494	73	Germany	$25,103	78
Belarus	$7,544	69	Ghana	$1,964	58
Belgium	$27,178	78	Greece	$16,501	78
Belize	$5,606	72	Grenada	$7,580	71
Benin	$990	54	Guatemala	$3,821	66
Bhutan	$1,412	66	Guinea	$1,982	48
Bolivia	$2,424	63	Guinea-Bissau	$755	45
Bosnia-Herzegovina	na	68	Guyana	$3,963	63
Botswana	$7,184	39	Haiti	$1,467	49
Brazil	$7,625	69	Honduras	$2,453	66
Brunei	$16,779	74	Hungary	$12,416	72
Bulgaria	$5,710	72	Iceland	$29,581	79
Burkina Faso	$976	47	India	$2,358	63
Burma	$1,027	56	Indonesia	$3,043	68
Burundi	$591	41	Iran	$5,884	69
Cambodia	$1,446	56	Iraq	na	58
Cameroon	$1,703	55	Ireland	$29,866	77
Canada	$27,840	79	Israel	$20,131	78
Cape Verde	$4,863	69	Italy	$23,626	80
Central African Rep.	$1,172	44	Jamaica	$3,639	75
Chad	$871	51	Japan	$26,755	81
Chile	$9,417	77	Jordan	$3,966	70
China	$3,976	71	Kazakhstan	$5,871	66
Colombia	$6,248	71	Kenya	$1,022	48
Comoros	$1,588	56	Kiribati	na	62
Congo (Brazzaville)	$825	51	Korea, North	na	64
Congo (Kinshasa)	$765	49	Korea, South	$17,380	76
Costa Rica	$8,650	77	Kuwait	$15,799	76
Cote d'Ivoire	$1,630	45	Kyrgyzstan	$2,711	69
Croatia	$8,091	74	Laos	$1,575	54
Cuba	na	76	Latvia	$7,045	71
Cyprus (Greek)	$20,824	77	Lebanon	$4,308	73
Czech Republic	$13,991	75	Lesotho	$2,031	51
Denmark	$27,627	77	Liberia	na	50
Djibouti	$2,377	43	Libya	$7,570	75
Dominica	$5,880	73	Liechtenstein	na	na
Dominican Republic	$6,033	69	Lithuania	$7,106	73

Table of Social and Economic Indicators

Country	Real GDP Per Capita (PPP$)	Life Expectancy	Country	Real GDP Per Capita (PPP$)	Life Expectancy
Luxembourg	$50,061	78	Slovenia	$17,367	76
Macedonia	$5,086	73	Solomon Islands	$1,648	67
Madagascar	$840	55	Somalia	na	47
Malawi	$615	38	South Africa	$9,401	51
Malaysia	$9,068	73	Spain	$19,472	79
Maldives	$4,485	67	Sri Lanka	$3,530	72
Mali	$797	47	Sudan	$1,797	56
Malta	$17,273	77	Suriname	$3,799	71
Marshall Islands	na	68	Swaziland	$4,492	40
Mauritania	$1,677	53	Sweden	$24,277	80
Mauritius	$10,017	72	Switzerland	$28,769	80
Mexico	$9,023	75	Syria	$3,556	70
Micronesia	na	66	Taiwan	na	75
Moldova	$2,109	68	Tajikistan	$1,152	68
Monaco	na	na	Tanzania	$523	52
Mongolia	$1,783	63	Thailand	$6,402	72
Morocco	$3,546	69	Togo	$1,442	55
Mozambique	$854	38	Tonga	na	71
Namibia	$6,431	43	Trinidad and Tobago	$8,964	71
Nauru	na	61	Tunisia	$6,363	72
Nepal	$1,327	58	Turkey	$6,974	69
Netherlands	$25,657	78	Turkmenistan	$3,956	67
New Zealand	$20,070	78	Tuvalu	na	67
Nicaragua	$2,366	68	Uganda	$1,208	43
Niger	$746	45	Ukraine	$3,816	68
Nigeria	$896	52	United Arab Emirates	$17,935	74
Norway	$29,918	79	United Kingdom	$23,509	78
Oman	$13,356	73	United States	$34,142	77
Pakistan	$1,928	63	Uruguay	$9,035	75
Palau	na	67	Uzbekistan	$2,441	70
Panama	$6,000	74	Vanuatu	$2,802	67
Papua New Guinea	$2,280	57	Venezuela	$5,794	73
Paraguay	$4,426	71	Vietnam	$1,996	68
Peru	$4,799	69	Yemen	$893	59
Philippines	$3,971	68	Yugoslavia (Serbia and Montenegro)		
Poland	$9,051	74		na	72
Portugal	$17,290	76	Zambia	$780	37
Qatar	$18,789	72	Zimbabwe	$2,635	38
Romania	$6,423	71			
Russia	$8,377	65			
Rwanda	$943	39			
St. Kitts and Nevis	$12,510	71			
St. Lucia	$5,703	71			
St. Vincent and Grenadines					
	$5,555	72			
Samoa	na	68			
San Marino	na	80			
Sao Tome and Principe	$1,792	65			
Saudi Arabia	$11,367	72			
Senegal	$1,510	53			
Seychelles	$12,508	70			
Sierra Leone	$490	39			
Singapore	$23,356	78			
Slovakia	$11,243	73			

Combined Average Ratings: Independent Countries

FREE

1.0
Andorra
Australia
Austria
Bahamas
Barbados
Belgium
Canada
Cyprus (G)
Denmark
Dominica
Finland
France
Germany
Iceland
Ireland
Italy
Kiribati
Liechtenstein
Luxembourg
Malta
Marshall Islands
Netherlands
New Zealand
Norway
Portugal
San Marino
Slovenia
Spain
Sweden
Switzerland
Tuvalu
United Kingdom
United States
Uruguay

1.5
Belize
Bulgaria
Cape Verde
Chile
Costa Rica
Czech Republic
Estonia
Greece
Grenada
Hungary
Japan
Latvia
Lithuania
Mauritius
Micronesia
Monaco
Nauru
Palau

Panama
Poland
St. Kitts and Nevis
St. Lucia
St. Vincent and
   Grenadines
Sao Tome and
   Principe
Slovakia
South Africa
Suriname
Vanuatu

2.0
Botswana
Croatia
Dominican Republic
Guyana
Israel
Korea, South
Mexico
Mongolia
Romania
Samoa
Taiwan

2.5
Benin
Bolivia
Brazil
El Salvador
Ghana
India
Jamaica
Lesotho
Mali
Namibia
Papua New Guinea
Peru
Philippines
Senegal
Thailand
Yugoslavia
(Serbia & Montenegro)

PARTLY FREE

3.0
Albania
Antigua and Barbuda
Argentina
East Timor
Ecuador
Honduras
Macedonia
Nicaragua
Seychelles
Solomon Islands
Trinidad and Tobago

3.5
Fiji
Indonesia
Madagascar
Moldova
Mozambique
Paraguay
Sri Lanka
Tanzania
Turkey
Venezuela

4.0
Armenia
Bangladesh
Bosnia-Herzegovina
Burkina Faso
Colombia
The Gambia
Georgia
Guatemala
Kenya
Malawi
Nepal
Niger
Sierra Leone
Tonga
Ukraine
Zambia

4.5
Comoros
Cote d'Ivoire
Djibouti
Gabon
Guinea-Bissau
Kuwait
Nigeria
Singapore

5.0
Bahrain
Central African Rep.
Congo (Brazzaville)
Ethiopia
Malaysia
Mauritania
Morocco
Russia
Uganda

5.5
Azerbaijan
Jordan

NOT FREE

5.5
Algeria

Angola
Bhutan
Brunei
Burundi
Cambodia
Chad
Guinea
Kazakhstan
Kyrgyzstan
Lebanon
Maldives
Oman
Pakistan
Swaziland
Tajikistan
Togo
Tunisia
United Arab
   Emirates
Yemen

6.0
Afghanistan
Belarus
Cameroon
Congo (Kinshasa)
Egypt
Haiti
Iran
Liberia
Qatar
Rwanda
Zimbabwe

6.5
China (PRC)
Equatorial Guinea
Eritrea
Laos
Somalia
Uzbekistan
Vietnam

7.0
Burma
Cuba
Iraq
Korea, North
Libya
Saudi Arabia
Sudan
Syria
Turkmenistan

Combined Average Ratings: Related Territories

FREE
1.5
Puerto Rico (US)

2.0
Northern Ireland (UK)

PARTLY FREE
4.0
Hong Kong (China)

5.0
Macao (China)

Combined Average Ratings: Disputed Territories

FREE Cyprus (Turkey)	Nagorno-Karabakh (Armenia/Azerbaijan)	Transnistria (Moldova)
		6.5
PARTLY FREE **4.5**	**5.5**	Western Sahara (Morocco)
West Papua (Indonesia) Kurdistan (Iraq)	Abkhazia (Georgia) Palestinian Authority- Administered Territories (Israel)	**7.0** Chechnya (Russia) Tibet (China)
NOT FREE **5.0**		
Kashmir (India) Kosovo (Yugoslavia) [Serbia & Montenegro]	**6.0** Israeli-Administered Territories (Israel) Kashmir (Pakistan)	

Electoral Democracies (121)

Albania
Presidential-parliamentary democracy
Andorra
Parliamentary democracy
Argentina
Presidential-parliamentary democracy (federal)
Armenia
Presidential-parliamentary democracy
Australia
Parliamentary democracy (federal)
Austria
Parliamentary democracy (federal)
Bahamas
Parliamentary democracy
Bangladesh
Parliamentary democracy
Barbados
Parliamentary democracy
Belgium
Parliamentary democracy (federal)
Belize
Parliamentary democracy
Benin
Presidential-parliamentary democracy
Bolivia
Presidential-parliamentary democracy
Botswana
Parliamentary democracy and traditional chiefs
Brazil
Presidential-parliamentary democracy (federal)
Bulgaria
Parliamentary democracy
Canada
Parliamentary democracy (federal)
Cape Verde
Presidential-parliamentary democracy
Chile
Presidential-parliamentary democracy
Colombia
Presidential-parliamentary democracy
(insurgencies)
Costa Rica
Presidential-parliamentary democracy
Croatia
Parliamentary democracy
Cyprus
Presidential-parliamentary democracy
Czech Republic
Parliamentary democracy
Denmark
Parliamentary democracy
Dominica
Parliamentary democracy
Dominican Republic
Presidential-parliamentary democracy
East Timor
Presidential-parliamentary democracy
Ecuador
Presidential-parliamentary democracy
El Salvador
Presidential-parliamentary democracy

Estonia
Parliamentary democracy
Fiji
Parliamentary democracy
Finland
Parliamentary democracy
France
Presidential-parliamentary democracy
Georgia
Presidential-parliamentary democracy
Germany
Parliamentary democracy (federal)
Ghana
Presidential-parliamentary democracy
Greece
Parliamentary democracy
Grenada
Parliamentary democracy
Guatemala
Presidential-parliamentary democracy
Guinea-Bissau
Presidential-parliamentary democracy
Guyana
Parliamentary democracy
Honduras
Presidential-parliamentary democracy
Hungary
Parliamentary democracy
Iceland
Parliamentary democracy
India
Parliamentary democracy
Indonesia
Presidential-parliamentary democracy
(military-influenced)
Ireland
Parliamentary democracy
Israel
Parliamentary democracy
Italy
Parliamentary democracy
Jamaica
Parliamentary democracy
Japan
Parliamentary democracy
Kenya
Presidential-parliamentary democracy
Kiribati
Presidential-parliamentary democracy
Korea, South
Presidential-parliamentary democracy
Latvia
Parliamentary democracy
Lesotho
Parliamentary democracy and traditional chiefs
Liechtenstein
Principality and parliamentary democracy
Lithuania
Parliamentary democracy
Luxembourg
Parliamentary democracy

Macedonia
Parliamentary democracy
Madagascar
Presidential-parliamentary democracy
Malawi
Presidential-parliamentary democracy
Mali
Presidential-parliamentary democracy
Malta
Parliamentary democracy
Marshall Islands
Presidential-parliamentary democracy
Mauritius
Parliamentary democracy
Mexico
Presidential-parliamentary democracy
Micronesia
Presidential-parliamentary democracy (federal)
Moldova
Parliamentary democracy
Monaco
Principality and parliamentary democracy
Mongolia
Presidential-parliamentary democracy
Mozambique
Presidential-parliamentary democracy
Namibia
Presidential-parliamentary democracy
Nauru
Presidential-parliamentary democracy
Netherlands
Parliamentary democracy
New Zealand
Parliamentary democracy
Nicaragua
Presidential-parliamentary democracy
Niger
Presidential-parliamentary democracy
Nigeria
Presidential-parliamentary democracy
Norway
Parliamentary democracy
Palau
Presidential-parliamentary democracy
Panama
Presidential-parliamentary democracy
Papua New Guinea
Parliamentary democracy
Paraguay
Presidential-parliamentary democracy
Peru
Presidential-parliamentary democracy
Philippines
Presidential-parliamentary democracy
(insurgencies)
Poland
Presidential-parliamentary democracy
Portugal
Presidential-parliamentary democracy
Romania
Presidential-parliamentary democracy
Russia
Presidential-parliamentary democracy

St. Kitts and Nevis
Parliamentary democracy
St. Lucia
Parliamentary democracy
St. Vincent and the Grenadines
Parliamentary democracy
Samoa
Parliamentary democracy and traditional chiefs
San Marino
Parliamentary democracy
Sao Tome and Principe
Presidential-parliamentary democracy
Senegal
Presidential-parliamentary democracy
Seychelles
Presidential-parliamentary democracy
Sierra Leone
Presidential-parliamentary democracy
(insurgencies)
Slovakia
Parliamentary democracy
Slovenia
Parliamentary democracy
Solomon Islands
Parliamentary democracy
South Africa
Presidential-parliamentary democracy
Spain
Parliamentary democracy
Sri Lanka
Presidential-parliamentary democracy
Suriname
Presidential-parliamentary democracy
Sweden
Parliamentary democracy
Switzerland
Parliamentary democracy (federal)
Taiwan
Presidential-parliamentary democracy
Thailand
Parliamentary democracy
Trinidad and Tobago
Parliamentary democracy
Turkey
Presidential-parliamentary democracy
Tuvalu
Parliamentary democracy
Ukraine
Presidential-parliamentary democracy
United Kingdom
Parliamentary democracy
United States of America
Presidential-parliamentary democracy (federal)
Uruguay
Presidential-parliamentary democracy
Vanuatu
Parliamentary democracy
Venezuela
Presidential-parliamentary democracy
Yugoslavia (Serbia and Montenegro)
Parliamentary democracy

Sources

PUBLICATIONS/BROADCASTS

Africa Confidential
Africa Online
Africa Recovery Magazine
Agence France-Presse
Al-Ahram [Egypt]
AllAfrica.com
ANSA [Italy]
Arabic News
Asia Times
Asia Week
Asian Bulletin
Asian Survey
Asian Wall Street Journal
Associated Press
Assyrian International News Agency
The Atlantic Monthly
Balkan Medja [Bulgaria]
The Baltic Times
The Bangkok Times
British Broadcasting Corporation (BBC)
Business Eastern Europe
Cable News Network (CNN)
Caribbean News Agency (CANA)
Caretas [Peru]
Caribbean Review
The Central Asia-Caucasus Analyst
    (Johns Hopkins University)
Central America Report
Central Europe Review
China Daily
Christian Science Monitor
CIA World Factbook
Clarin [Argentina]
Columbia Journalism Review
Communications Law in Transition
Constitution Finder, University of Richmond
Il Corriere della Sera [Italy]
Covcas Bulletin [France]
Czech News Agency
The Daily Star [Bangladesh]
The Daily Star [Lebanon]
Danas [Yugoslavia]
Dani [Bosnia-Herzegovina]
Dawn [Pakistan]
Dawn News Bulletin (All Burma Students
    Democratic Front)
Deutsche Presse Agentur
East European Constitutional Review
The Economist
The Economist Intelligence Unit reports
eCountries.com
Editor & Publisher
Eesti Paevaleht [Estonia]
EFE Spanish News Agency
El Tiempo [Colombia]
EPOCA [Mexico]
Ethiopian Review
Evenimentul Zilei [Romania]
Far Eastern Economic Review
The Financial Times
El Financiero [Mexico]
EurasiaNet.org
Fedworld.gov [United States]

Free Labour World
The Free Press [Ghana]
The Friday Times [Pakistan]
The Frontier Post [Pakistan]
The Globe & Mail [Canada]
Globus [Croatia]
The Guardian
Gulf News [United Arab Emirates]
Gulf Times [Qatar]
Ha'aretz [Israel]
Hemisphere
The Hindustan Times [India]
Hong Kong Digest
Hornet Online
HuriNet
The Independent [United Kingdom]
Index of Economic Freedom (Heritage Foundation)
Index on Censorship
India Today
Indian Ocean Newsletter
International Crisis Group South Balkans Project Reports
InterPress News Service
The Irish Times
Islamic Republic News Agency [Iran]
ITAR-TASS
The Jerusalem Post
Jordan Times
La Jornada [Mexico]
Journal of Commerce
Journal of Democracy
Kashmir Times [India]
Kathmandu Post
KavkazCenter.org
Kiev Post
Klipsan Press Election Notes
Latin America Political Report
Lettre du Continent
Lexis-Nexis
Los Angeles Times
Mail & Guardian Weekly [South Africa]
Miami Herald
The Middle East
Middle East International
Middle East Quarterly
The Middle East Times
Miist [Ukraine]
Monitor [Uganda]
Monitorul [Romania]
Morocco Press
The Moscow Times
La Nacion [Argentina]
Nacional [Croatia]
The Nation
The National Post [Canada]
New African
The New Republic
New Vision [Uganda]
New York Newsday
The New York Times
The New Yorker
The New Zealand Herald
Nezavisne Novine [Bosnia-Herzegovina]
NIN [Yugoslavia]
North-South Magazine
El Nuevo Herald [Florida]
The Observer [United Kingdom]
Oman Daily Observer
Oslobodjenje [Bosnia-Herzegovina]
The Other Side of Mexico

Outlook [India]
Oxford Analytica
Pacific Islands News Agency
Pagina 12 [Argentina]
Pan African News Agency
The Pioneer [India]
Political Handbook of the World
Politika [Yugoslavia]
The Post [Zambia]
Postimees [Estonia]
Proceso [Mexico]
Radio Australia reports
Radio Free Europe-Radio Liberty reports
Radio New Zealand
Reforma [Mexico]
Reporter [Bosnia-Herzegovina]
La Repubblica
Reuters
The Saigon Times Daily
Semana [Colombia]
Slobodna Bosna [Bosnia-Herzegovina]
Le Soleil [Senegal]
South China Morning Post [Hong Kong]
Sposterihach [Ukraine]
The Standard [Kenya]
The Statesman [India]
The Straits Times [Singapore]
Swiss Press Review
TamilNet.com [Sri Lanka]
Tehelka.com [India]
Tehran Times
The Tico Times [Costa Rica]
Tiempos del Mundo [U.S.]
The Times of Central Asia
The Times of India
The Times of London
Transcaucasus: A Chronology
Transitions Online
Turkish Daily News
Ukrainian Press Agency
Ukrainian Weekly
Uncaptive Minds (Institute for Democracy in Eastern Europe)
United Nations Development Program Early Warning Reports [Romania]
United Nations Development Program Human Development Reports
U.S. News and World Report
U.S. State Department Country Reports on Human Rights Practices
U.S. State Department International Religious Freedom Reports
Voice of America Online
Voice of Bahrain
Vreme [Yugoslavia]
Vuelta [Mexico]
The Wall Street Journal
The Washington Post
The Washington Times
The Week in Germany
West Africa
World Population Data Sheet (Population Reference Bureau)
Xinhua News Agency
Yemen Times

ORGANIZATIONS

AFL-CIO
Africa Policy Information Center

Africa Rights [United Kingdom]
American Anti-Slavery Group
American Institute for Free Labor Development
American Kurdish Information Network
Amnesty International
Andean Commission of Jurists
Anti-Slavery International
Article 19 [United Kingdom]
Association Pour La Fondation Mohsen Hachtroudi
Azerbaijan National Democracy Foundation
Bahrain Freedom Movement
Bangladesh National Women Lawyers Association
British Helsinki Human Rights Group
B'tzelem [Israel]
The Carter Center
Center for Free Speech [Nigeria]
Center for Monitoring Election Violence [Sri Lanka]
Center for Strategic and International Studies
Chadian Association for the Protection of Human Rights
Child Workers in Nepal
Chilean Human Rights Commission
Civic Alliance [Mexico]
Civil Society Development Foundation
Committee of Churches for Emergency Help [Paraguay]
Committee to Protect Journalists
Constitutional Rights Project [Nigeria]
Council of Europe
Croatian Democracy Project
Cuban Committee for Human Rights
Democratic Initiatives [Ukraine]
Digital Freedom Network
EastWest Institute
Election Commission of India
Elections Canada
Emerging Europe Research Group
Equal Access Committee [Ukraine]
Ethnic Federation of Romani [Romania]
European Bank for Reconstruction and Development
European Commission
European Institute for the Media
Fray Bartolome de Las Casas Center for Human Rights [Mexico]
Free Africa Foundation
Free and Democratic Bulgaria Foundation
Free Trade Union Institute
Group for Mutual Support [Guatemala]
Helsinki Committee for Human Rights in Serbia
Honduran Committee for the Defense of Human Rights
Hong Kong Human Rights Monitor
Human Rights Commission [El Salvador]
Human Rights Commission of Pakistan
Human Rights Organization of Bhutan
Human Rights Organization of Nepal
Human Rights Watch
Immigration and Refugee Board of Canada
Indian Law Resource Center
Inform [Sri Lanka]
Institute for Legal Research and Resources [Nepal]
Institute for the Study of Conflict, Ideology and Policy
Institute for War and Peace Reporting [United Kingdom]
Inter-American Commission on Human Rights
Inter-American Press Association
International Campaign for Tibet
International Commission of Jurists

International Confederation of Free Trade Unions
International Crisis Group
International Federation of Journalists
International Foundation for Electoral Systems
International Freedom of Expression Exchange
International Helsinki Federation for Human Rights
International Human Rights Law Group
International League for Human Rights
International Press Institute
International Republican Institute
International Research and Exchange Board
Inter-Parliamentary Union
Iraqi National Congress
Jaan Tonisson Institute [Estonia]
Jamaica Council for Human Rights
Jamestown Foundation
Kashmir Study Group
Kuwait Online
Latvian Center for Human Rights and Ethnic Studies
Lawyers Committee for Human Rights
Lawyers for Human Rights and Legal Aid [Pakistan]
Lithuanian Free Market Institute
Media Institute of South Africa
Mexican Human Rights Academy
National Coalition for Haitian Refugees
National Coordinating Office for Human Rights [Peru]
National Democratic Institute for International Affairs
National Endowment for Democracy
National Human Rights Commission [India]
Network for the Defense of Independent Media
   in Africa
North-South Center [Florida]
Open Society Institute
Operation Lifeline Sudan
Organization for Security and Cooperation in Europe
Organization of American States

Pacific Island Development Program [Hawaii]
Panamanian Committee for Human Rights
Peoples Forum for Human Rights, Bhutan
Permanent Commission on Human Rights
   [Nicaragua]
Physicians for Human Rights
Reporters Sans Frontieres
Royal Institute of International Affairs
Runejel Junam Council of Ethnic Communities
   [Guatemala]
Stratfor
Tibet Information Network
Tibetan Center for Human Rights and Democracy
Transparency International
Tutela Legal [El Salvador]
Ukrainian Center for Independent Political Research
UNICEF
Union of Councils for Soviet Jews
U.N. Integrated Regional Information Networks
U.S. Committee for Refugees
Venezuelan Human Rights Education Action Program
Vicaria de la Solidaridad [Chile]
Vietnam Committee on Human Rights
Voice of Bahrain
Washington Office on Africa
Washington Office on Latin America
West Africa Journalists Association
Women Acting Together for Change [Nepal]
Women's Commission for Refugee Women and
   Children
World Algerian Action Coalition
The World Bank
World Press Freedom Committee
Zambia Independent Monitoring Association

ABOUT FREEDOM HOUSE

Freedom House is a clear voice for democracy and freedom around the world. By supporting democratic change, monitoring freedom, and advocating for democracy and human rights, Freedom House seeks to empower people, to open closed societies, and to assist countries in transition to democratic rule.

Founded more than sixty years ago by Eleanor Roosevelt, Wendell Willkie, and other Americans concerned with the mounting threats to peace and democracy, Freedom House has been a vigorous proponent of democratic values and a steadfast opponent of dictatorship of the far left and the far right. Today, Freedom House is a leading advocate of the world's young democracies, which are coping with the legacies of statism, dictatorship, and political repression.

Freedom House conducts an array of U.S. and overseas research, advocacy, education, and training initiatives that promote human rights, democracy, free market economics, the rule of law, independent media, and U.S. engagement in international affairs. Wherever basic liberties are threatened or democracies are emerging, Freedom House is engaged.

To learn more about Freedom House, visit *www.freedomhouse.org*.